HIGH-INTEREST BOOKS FOR TEENS

SECOND EDITION

HIGH-INTEREST BOOKS FOR TEENS

Joyce Nakamura
Editor

A Guide to Book Reviews and Biographical Sources

Gale Research Company
Book Tower • Detroit, Michigan 48226

Library of Congress Card Catalog Number 81-6889
ISBN 0-8103-1830-X

Computerized photocomposition by
DataServ, Incorporated
Bethesda, Maryland

Printed in the United States

Contents

Introduction

The second edition of *High-Interest Books for Teens (HIBT)* updates and augments the first edition, which was published in 1981, and serves as a guide to 2,000 authors and more than 3,500 titles of fiction and nonfiction that appeal to students in junior and senior high school. This is a tool for librarians, teachers in classrooms and reading laboratories, and others involved in guiding teens known to have learning disabilities or simply undeveloped reading skills. Providing quick access to several levels of information, *HIBT* lists both classic and contemporary books that have been identified as "high interest/low-readability level" materials for young adults. *HIBT* also gives a convenient key to review sources with which each book can be evaluated. Finally, *HIBT* pinpoints sources of information on the author's life that can provide background to spark a student's interest or to help design a booktalk or class assignment.

Features

The Guide to Book Reviews and Biographical Sources, the main section of *High-Interest Books for Teens,* is arranged alphabetically by author. Each entry gives the author's full name (or an identified pseudonym), dates of birth and death (if known), and one or more sources that give further biographical information. A total of 144 sources has been cited. A key to the abbreviations used to designate biographical sources appears on the back endsheets. The complete listing of biographical sources cited, including the abbreviations, appears immediately after this Introduction.

Each author entry also includes one or more book titles, each of which is followed by detailed citations of periodical reviews of that title. A key to the abbreviated periodical sources appears on the front endsheets and immediately following this Introduction.

A Title Index, located at the back of the book, provides access to the main entries in the Guide to Book Reviews and Biographical Sources when the user does not have the author's name.

New Subject Index

An added feature in this edition, the Subject Index enables readers to access titles by topics of interest. This new index, located at the back of the book following the Title Index, covers more than 500 subjects that are of high-interest to teens, such as adventure stories, sports, biography, mystery and detective stories, sexual awareness, and interpersonal relationships.

These subject headings are based on those used by the Library of Congress. Of special usefulness was the Library of Congress's Annotated Card Program (AC), which establishes headings that youthful readers can easily comprehend. This program also utilizes headings found in *Sears List of Subject Headings.* For those titles not classified by the Library of Congress, or those titles for which LC subject headings could not be located in the *National Union Catalog* or other listings consulted, no headings were assigned in *HIBT.* Readers will note that many fiction titles fall in this category.

Subject headings are also cited in the main section of the book, within the author entry, following the periodical review citations.

Criteria

The books included in *HIBT* have been designated in recommended reading lists and in publishers' catalogs as high-interest/low-readability level materials by authorities in the field—librarians, teachers, publishers, book reviewers, and critics. However, any selection of high/low materials for young adults will surely fail to satisfy everyone. Discounting personal preference, such a selection inevitably suffers from the lack of real standards in the field; there are no firm limits to the concept of a "young adult"; and there is no single, universally-accepted measurement of reading difficulty. *HIBT* presents the composite choice of those people who are involved in publishing and evaluating reading materials for teens. The individual teacher or librarian must be the final arbiter of what is most suitable for the young adults in his or her charge.

Further Information Sources

The following information sources, selected from the many consulted in the preparation of this edition of *HIBT,* will be helpful to anyone with a special interest in the high/low field.

Booklist, "High-Low Reading" column, American Library Association, (Chicago, Ill.), 1980—.

Books for You: A Booklist for Senior High School Students, edited by Donald R. Gallo (with a committee of the National Council of Teachers of English), revised edition, NCTE (Urbana, Ill.), 1982.

Easy-to-Read Books for Teenagers, Office of Young Adult Services, New York Public Library (New York City), 1986.

High-Interest/Easy Reading for Junior and Senior High School Students, edited by Hugh Agee (with a committee of the National Council of Teachers of English), 4th edition, NCTE (Urbana, Ill.), 1984.

High-Interest Low-Reading Level Booklist, by the High-Interest/Low-Literacy Level Materials Evaluation Committee, Young Adult Services Division, American Library Association (Chicago, Ill.), 1982, 1983, 1984, 1985, 1986 (also see below).

The High/Low Report, edited by Thetis Powers Reeves, Riverhouse Publications (New York City), 1980-May/June, 1983 (last issue of publication).

Kliatt Young Adult Paperback Book Guide, edited by Doris Hiatt and Claire Rosser (Newton, Mass.), 1980—.

Recommended Books for the Reluctant Young Adult Reader (formerly *High-Interest Low-Reading Level Booklist),* by the Recommended Books for the Reluctant Young Adult Reader Committee (formerly High-Interest/Low-Literacy Level Materials Evalution Committee), Young Adult Services Division, American Library Association (Chicago, Ill.), 1986, 1987.

School Library Journal, edited by Lillian N. Gerhardt (New York City), 1980—.

Sample Entry

Main entries in *HIBT* cite the author's name (or pseudonym) as it was listed in the original book review source. Biographical sources given in *HIBT* can be assumed to list the author under the same name form.

The typical entry in *HIBT* gives the following items of information:

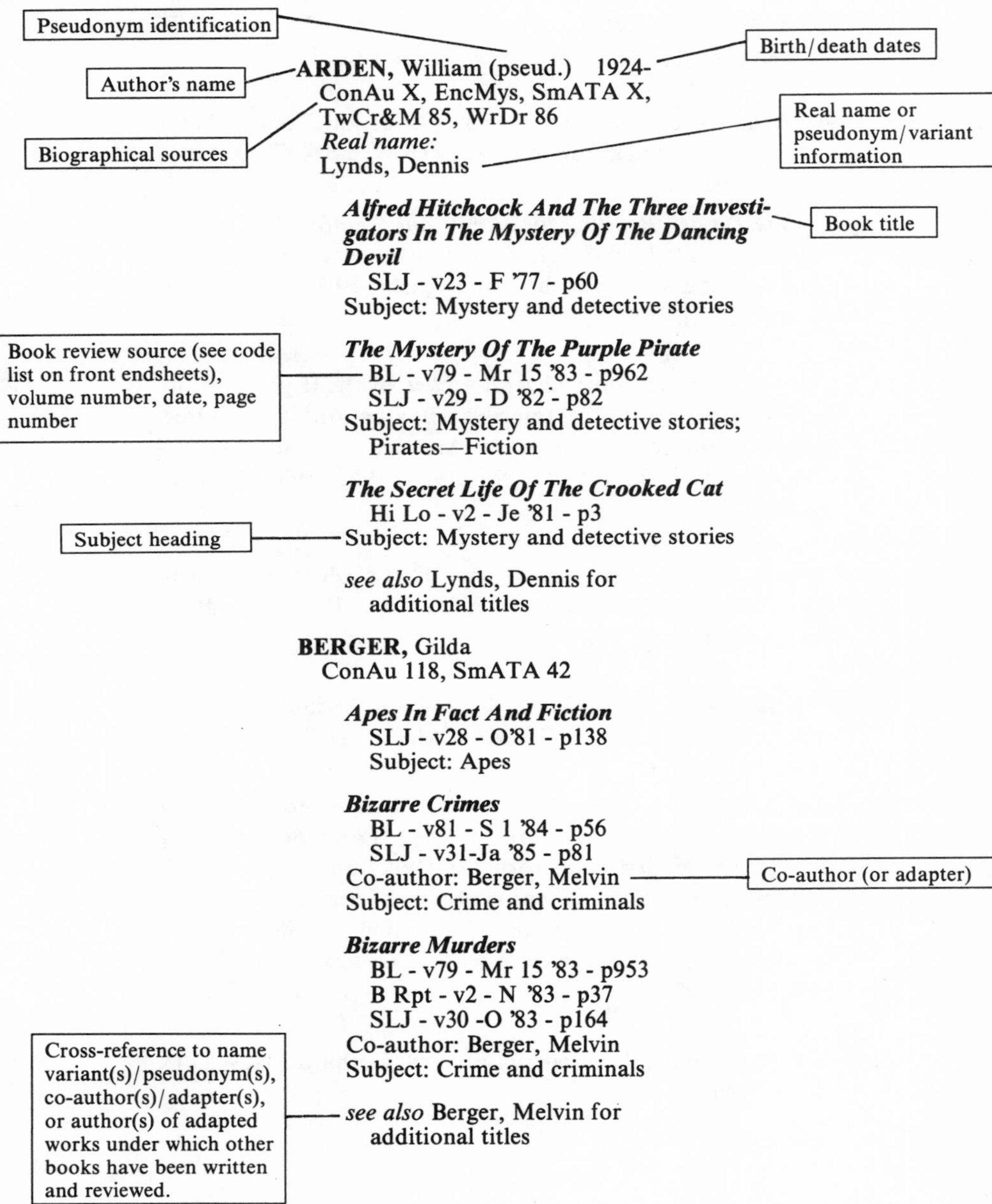

Pseudonym identification
Author's name
Biographical sources
Birth/death dates
Real name or pseudonym/variant information
Book title
Book review source (see code list on front endsheets), volume number, date, page number
Subject heading
Co-author (or adapter)
Cross-reference to name variant(s)/pseudonym(s), co-author(s)/adapter(s), or author(s) of adapted works under which other books have been written and reviewed.
ARDEN, William (pseud.) 1924-
ConAu X, EncMys, SmATA X, TwCr&M 85, WrDr 86
Real name:
Lynds, Dennis
Alfred Hitchcock And The Three Investigators In The Mystery Of The Dancing Devil
SLJ - v23 - F '77 - p60
Subject: Mystery and detective stories
The Mystery Of The Purple Pirate
BL - v79 - Mr 15 '83 - p962
SLJ - v29 - D '82 - p82
Subject: Mystery and detective stories; Pirates—Fiction
The Secret Life Of The Crooked Cat
Hi Lo - v2 - Je '81 - p3
Subject: Mystery and detective stories
see also Lynds, Dennis for additional titles
BERGER, Gilda
ConAu 118, SmATA 42
Apes In Fact And Fiction
SLJ - v28 - O'81 - p138
Subject: Apes
Bizarre Crimes
BL - v81 - S 1 '84 - p56
SLJ - v31-Ja '85 - p81
Co-author: Berger, Melvin
Subject: Crime and criminals
Bizarre Murders
BL - v79 - Mr 15 '83 - p953
B Rpt - v2 - N '83 - p37
SLJ - v30 -O '83 - p164
Co-author: Berger, Melvin
Subject: Crime and criminals
see also Berger, Melvin for additional titles

Entries may lack dates and/or biographical sources when that information was not found in the sources consulted for *HIBT*.

Cross-references are also used in this guide to indicate the following:

1. Variant name forms for the same author

   COMBER, Lillian
   see Beckwith, Lillian

   The cross-reference directs the user to the name under which book reviews have been listed.

2. Co-authorship (or adapter status)

   CLEAVER, Bill
   see Cleaver, Vera (co-author)

   The cross-reference directs the user to the name under which book reviews have been listed.

Suggestions for Future Editions

The editors welcome your comments on this edition as well as your suggestions for additional book titles, information sources, or added features that would be useful in future editions.

Book Review Sources Cited

Anth	American Anthropologist
Art	American Artist
B	AB Bookman's Weekly
BC	American Book Collector
C	American City & County
CSB	Appraisal: Children's Science Books
F	American Forests
HR	American Historical Review
JA	American Journal of Archaeology
L	American Literature
Lead	Adult Leadership
Lib	American Libraries
m	America
nalog	Analog Science Fiction/Science Fact
NQ	American Notes & Queries
RBA	American Reference Books Annual
SBYP	Appraisal: Science Books for Young People
tl	Atlantic Monthly
tl Pro Bk R	Atlantic Provinces Book Review
&B	Books & Bookmen
B	Babbling Bookworm
Ent	Black Enterprise
F	Book Forum
FYC	Books for Your Children
IC	Books in Canada
ks for Keeps	Books for Keeps
ks W	BooksWest
L	Booklist
l Bks B	Black Books Bulletin
l S	Black Scholar
l W	Black World
OT	Books of the Times (NYT)
rit Bk N	British Book News
rit Bk N C	British Book News. Children's Supplement
Rpt	Book Report
S	Best Sellers
W	Book World
an Child Lit	Canadian Children's Literature
ath W	Catholic World
AY	Come-All-Ye
BR	Computer Book Review
BRS	Children's Book Review Service
C	Christian Century
CCB-B	Center for Children's Books. Bulletin
CE	Childhood Education
CF	Canadian Forum
Child Lit	Children's Literature
Choice	Choice
CLW	Catholic Library World
CM	Carleton Miscellany
Comt	Commentary
Comw	Commonweal
CR	Contemporary Review
Cres	Cresset
Cr H	Craft Horizons
Crit	Critic
CSM	Christian Science Monitor
CT	Children Today
Cu H	Current History
Cur R	Curriculum Review
CW	Classical World
Dance	Dancemagazine
Dr	Drama: The Quarterly Theatre Review
Econ	Economist
EJ	English Journal
EL	Educational Leadership
Emerg Lib	Emergency Librarian
Esq	Esquire
Fant R	Fantasy Review
Film Cr	Film Criticism
Fly	Flying
FQ	Film Quarterly
GJ	Geographical Journal
GP	Growing Point
GW	Guardian Weekly
HB	Horn Book Magazine
HE	Human Events
Hi Lo	High/Low Report
HM	Harper's Magazine
Hob	Hobbies
Hort	Horticulture
HR	Hudson Review
HT	History Today
ILN	Illustrated London News
In Rev	In Review: Canadian Books for Young People
Inst	Instructor
Inter BC	Interracial Books for Children Bulletin
JAF	Journal of American Folklore
JAH	Journal of American History

(Continued)

JB	Junior Bookshelf
JGE	Journal of General Education
J Ho E	Journal of Home Economics
JLD	Journal of Learning Disabilities
JLH	Journal of Library History, Philosophy & Comparative Librarianship
JNE	Journal of Negro Education
J Pol	Journal of Politics
J Read	Journal of Reading
Kliatt	Kliatt Young Adult Paperback Book Guide
KR	Kirkus Reviews
LA	Language Arts
LATBR	Los Angeles Times Book Review
Learning	Learning: The Magazine for Creative Teaching
Life	Life
Lis	Listener
LJ	Library Journal
LR	Library Review
LW	Living Wilderness
Mac	Maclean's
M Ed J	Music Educators Journal
MFS	Modern Fiction Studies
MFSF	Magazine of Fantasy and Science Fiction
MN	Museum News
Money	Money
Ms	Ms.
NAR	North American Review
Nat	Nation
Nat R	National Review
NCW	New Catholic World
ND	Negro Digest
N Dir Wom	New Directions for Women
New Age	New Age Journal
New R	New Republic
NH	Natural History
NHB	Negro History Bulletin
NO	National Observer
Notes	Notes (Music Library Association)
NP	National Parks
NS	New Statesman
NW	Newsweek
NY	New Yorker
NYRB	New York Review of Books
NYT	New York Times
NYTBR	New York Times Book Review
NYTBR, pt. 1	New York Times Book Review, pt. 1
NYTBR, pt. 2	New York Times Book Review, pt. 2
Obs	Observer (London)
Par	Parents Magazine

Pet PM	Petersen's Photographic Magazine
PGJ	Personnel and Guidance Journal
Poet	Poetry
P&R	Parks & Recreation
PR	Partisan Review
Prog	Progressive
PS	Prairie Schooner
PT	Psychology Today
Punch	Punch
PW	Publishers Weekly
Quill & Q	Quill & Quire
Rel St	Religious Studies
Rel St Rev	Religious Studies Review
RR	Review for Religious
RSR	Reference Services Review
RT	Reading Teacher
SA	Scientific American
SB	Science Books & Films
Sch Lib	School Librarian
Sci	Science
SE	Social Education
SEP	Saturday Evening Post
SF Chr	Science Fiction Chronicle
SF&FBR	Science Fiction & Fantasy Book Review
S Fict R	Science Fiction Review
S Liv	Southern Living
SLJ	School Library Journal
SMQ	School Media Quarterly
SN	Saturday Night
Spec	Spectator
Spectr	Spectrum
SR	Saturday Review
SR/W	Saturday Review/World
SS	Social Studies
S & T	Sky & Telescope
SWR	Southwest Review
TCR	Teachers College Record
Teacher	Teacher
TES	Times Educational Supplement
Time	Time
TLS	Times Literary Supplement
TN	Top of the News
Trav	Travel Holiday
Trib Bks	Tribune Books (Chicago)
USA T	USA Today
VLS	Village Voice Literary Supplement
VOYA	Voice of Youth Advocates
VQR	Virginia Quarterly Review
VV	Village Voice
WCRB	West Coast Review of Books
WLB	Wilson Library Bulletin
WSJ	Wall Street Journal
Yacht	Yachting
YR	Yale Review

Biographical Sources Cited

Code	*Book Indexed*
AmCath 80	*The American Catholic Who's Who.* Volume 23, 1980-1981. Edited by Joy Anderson. Washington, D.C.: National Catholic News Service, 1979.
AmM&WS	*American Men and Women of Science.* Edited by Jaques Cattell Press. New York: R.R. Bowker Co., 1976-1978, 1979, 1982, 1986.
	AmM&WS 76P — Physical & Biological Sciences, 13th edition, 1976
	AmM&WS 78S — Social & Behavioral Sciences, 13th edition, 1978
	AmM&WS 79P — Physical & Biological Sciences, 14th edition, 1979
	AmM&WS 82P — Physical & Biological Sciences, 15th edition, 1982
	AmM&WS 86P — Physical & Biological Sciences, 16th edition, 1986
AmWomWr	*American Women Writers: A Critical Reference Guide from Colonial Times to the Present.* Four volumes. Edited by Lina Mainiero. New York: Frederick Ungar Publishing Co., 1979-1982.
AmWr	*American Writers: A Collection of Literary Biographies.* New York: Charles Scribner's Sons, 1974, 1979, 1981.
	AmWr — Volumes I-IV. Edited by Leonard Unger, 1974. Originally published as the *University of Minnesota Pamphlets on American Writers.*
	AmWr S1 — Supplement I. Two parts. Edited by Leonard Unger, 1979.
	AmWr S2 — Supplement II. Two parts. Edited by A. Walton Litz, 1981.
AnObit	*The Annual Obituary.* New York: St. Martin's Press, 1981, 1982, 1983.
	AnObit 1980 — *1980*, edited by Roland Turner, 1981.
	AnObit 1981 — *1981*, edited by Janet Podell, 1982.
	AnObit 1982 — *1982*, edited by Janet Podell, 1983.
	Use the "Alphabetical Index of Entrants" at the front of each volume to locate biographies.
AnObit	*The Annual Obituary.* Chicago: St. James Press, 1984, 1985.
	AnObit 1983 — *1983*, edited by Elizabeth Devine, 1984.
	AnObit 1984 — *1984*, edited by Margot Levy, 1985.
	Use the "Alphabetical Index of Entrants" at the front of each volume to locate biographies.
ArtCS	*The Art of the Comic Strip.* By Judith O'Sullivan. College Park, Maryland: University of Maryland, Department of Art, 1971.
	Biographies begin on page 60.

ASpks *The Author Speaks: Selected "PW" Interviews, 1967-1976.* By *Publishers Weekly* editors and contributors. New York: R.R. Bowker Co., 1977.

Au&ICB *Authors and Illustrators of Children's Books: Writings on Their Lives and Works.* By Miriam Hoffman and Eva Samuels. New York: R.R. Bowker Co., 1972.

AuBYP *Authors of Books for Young People.* By Martha E. Ward and Dorothy A. Marquardt. Metuchen, New Jersey: Scarecrow Press, 1971, 1979.

AuBYP	Second edition, 1971
AuBYP SUP	Supplement to the second edition, 1979
AuBYP SUPA	Addendum to the Supplement

AuNews *Authors in the News.* A compilation of news stories and feature articles from American newspapers and magazines covering writers and other members of the communications media. Two volumes. Edited by Barbara Nykoruk. Detroit: Gale Research Co., 1976.

AuNews 1	Volume 1
AuNews 2	Volume 2

Baker 84 *Baker's Biographical Dictionary of Musicians.* Seventh edition. Revised by Nicolas Slonimsky. New York: Macmillan, Schirmer Books, 1984.

BiDFilm *A Biographical Dictionary of Film.* By David Thomson. First edition. New York: William Morrow & Co., 1976.

BioIn *Biography Index.* A cumulative index to biographical material in books and magazines. New York: H.W. Wilson Co., 1949-1984.

BioIn 1	Volume 1: January, 1946-July, 1949; 1949
BioIn 2	Volume 2: August, 1949-August, 1952; 1953
BioIn 3	Volume 3: September, 1952-August, 1955; 1956
BioIn 4	Volume 4: September, 1955-August, 1958; 1960
BioIn 5	Volume 5: September, 1958-August, 1961; 1962
BioIn 6	Volume 6: September, 1961-August, 1964; 1965
BioIn 7	Volume 7: September, 1964-August, 1967; 1968
BioIn 8	Volume 8: September, 1967-August, 1970; 1971
BioIn 9	Volume 9: September, 1970-August, 1973; 1974
BioIn 10	Volume 10: September, 1973-August, 1976; 1977
BioIn 11	Volume 11: September, 1976-August, 1979; 1980
BioIn 12	Volume 12: September, 1979-August, 1982; 1983
BioIn 13	Volume 13: September, 1982-August, 1984; 1984

BioNews *Biography News.* A compilation of news stories and feature articles from American news media covering personalities of national interest in all fields. Edited by Frank E. Bair. Detroit: Gale Research Co., 1974-1975.

BioNews 74	Volume 1, Numbers 1-12, 1974
BioNews 75	Volume 2, Number 1, January-February, 1975

BkP *Books Are by People: Interviews with 104 Authors and Illustrators of Books for Young Children.* By Lee Bennett Hopkins. New York: Citation Press, 1969.

BlkAWP *Black American Writers Past and Present: A Biographical and Bibliographical Dictionary.* Two volumes. By Theressa Gunnels Rush, Carol Fairbanks Myers, and Esther Spring Arata. Metuchen, New Jersey: Scarecrow Press, 1975.

CaW *Canada Writes!* The members' book of the Writers' Union of Canada. Edited by K.A. Hamilton. Toronto: Writers' Union of Canada, 1977.

The "Additional Members" section, indicated in this index by the code *A*, begins on page 387.

ChlLR — *Children's Literature Review.* Excerpts from reviews, criticism, and commentary on books for children and young people. Detroit: Gale Research Co., 1976-1987.

ChlLR 1	Volume 1, 1976
ChlLR 2	Volume 2, 1976
ChlLR 3	Volume 3, 1978
ChlLR 4	Volume 4, 1982
ChlLR 5	Volume 5, 1983
ChlLR 6	Volume 6, 1984
ChlLR 7	Volume 7, 1984
ChlLR 8	Volume 8, 1985
ChlLR 9	Volume 9, 1985
ChlLR 10	Volume 10, 1986
ChlLR 11	Volume 11, 1986
ChlLR 12	Volume 12, 1987

ConAu — *Contemporary Authors.* A bio-bibliographical guide to current writers in fiction, general nonfiction, poetry, journalism, drama, motion pictures, television, and other fields. Detroit: Gale Research Co., 1967-1987.

ConAu 1R	Volumes 1-4, 1st revision, 1967
ConAu 5R	Volumes 5-8, 1st revision, 1969
ConAu 9R	Volumes 9-12, 1st revision, 1974
ConAu 13R	Volumes 13-16, 1st revision, 1975
ConAu 17R	Volumes 17-20, 1st revision, 1976
ConAu 21R	Volumes 21-24, 1st revision, 1977
ConAu 25R	Volumes 25-28, 1st revision, 1977
ConAu 29R	Volumes 29-32, 1st revision, 1978
ConAu 33R	Volumes 33-36, 1st revision, 1978
ConAu 37R	Volumes 37-40, 1st revision, 1979
ConAu 41R	Volumes 41-44, 1st revision, 1979
ConAu 45	Volumes 45-48, 1974
ConAu 49	Volumes 49-52, 1975
ConAu 53	Volumes 53-56, 1975
ConAu 57	Volumes 57-60, 1976
ConAu 61	Volumes 61-64, 1976
ConAu 65	Volumes 65-68, 1977
ConAu 69	Volumes 69-72, 1978
ConAu 73	Volumes 73-76, 1978
ConAu 77	Volumes 77-80, 1979
ConAu 81	Volumes 81-84, 1979
ConAu 85	Volumes 85-88, 1980
ConAu 89	Volumes 89-92, 1980
ConAu 93	Volumes 93-96, 1980
ConAu 97	Volumes 97-100, 1981
ConAu 101	Volume 101, 1981
ConAu 102	Volume 102, 1981
ConAu 103	Volume 103, 1982
ConAu 104	Volume 104, 1982
ConAu 105	Volume 105, 1982
ConAu 106	Volume 106, 1982
ConAu 107	Volume 107, 1983
ConAu 108	Volume 108, 1983
ConAu 109	Volume 109, 1983
ConAu 110	Volume 110, 1984
ConAu 111	Volume 111, 1984
ConAu 112	Volume 112, 1985

ConAu 113	Volume 113, 1985
ConAu 114	Volume 114, 1985
ConAu 115	Volume 115, 1985
ConAu 116	Volume 116, 1986
ConAu 117	Volume 117, 1986
ConAu 118	Volume 118, 1986
ConAu 119	Volume 119, 1987
ConAu 120	Volume 120, 1987

ConAu AS *Contemporary Authors, Autobiography Series.* Detroit: Gale Research Co., 1984-1987.

ConAu 1AS	Volume 1, 1984
ConAu 2AS	Volume 2, 1985
ConAu 3AS	Volume 3, 1986
ConAu 4AS	Volume 4, 1986
ConAu 5AS	Volume 5, 1987

ConAu BS *Contemporary Authors, Bibliographical Series.* Detroit: Gale Research Co., 1986.

ConAu 1BS	Volume 1, 1986
ConAu 2BS	Volume 2, 1986

ConAu NR *Contemporary Authors, New Revision Series.* A bio-bibliographical guide to current writers in fiction, general nonfiction, poetry, journalism, drama, motion pictures, television, and other fields. Detroit: Gale Research Co., 1981-1987.

ConAu 1NR	Volume 1, 1981
ConAu 2NR	Volume 2, 1981
ConAu 3NR	Volume 3, 1981
ConAu 4NR	Volume 4, 1981
ConAu 5NR	Volume 5, 1982
ConAu 6NR	Volume 6, 1982
ConAu 7NR	Volume 7, 1982
ConAu 8NR	Volume 8, 1983
ConAu 9NR	Volume 9, 1983
ConAu 10NR	Volume 10, 1983
ConAu 11NR	Volume 11, 1984
ConAu 12NR	Volume 12, 1984
ConAu 13NR	Volume 13, 1984
ConAu 14NR	Volume 14, 1985
ConAu 15NR	Volume 15, 1985
ConAu 16NR	Volume 16, 1986
ConAu 17NR	Volume 17, 1986
ConAu 18NR	Volume 18, 1986
ConAu 19NR	Volume 19, 1987
ConAu 20NR	Volume 20, 1987
ConAu 21NR	Volume 21, 1987

ConAu P- *Contemporary Authors, Permanent Series.* A bio-bibliographical guide to current authors and their works. Detroit: Gale Research Co., 1975-1978.

ConAu P-1	Volume 1, 1975
ConAu P-2	Volume 2, 1978

ConAu X This code refers to pseudonym entries which appear as cross-references in the cumulative index to *Contemporary Authors.*

ConDr 82 *Contemporary Dramatists.* Third edition. Edited by James Vinson. New York: St. Martin's Press, 1982.

ConDr 82	The "Contemporary Dramatists" section begins on page 9.
ConDr 82A	The "Screen Writers" section begins on page 887.
ConDr 82B	The "Radio Writers" section begins on page 899.
ConDr 82C	The "Television Writers" section begins on page 911.
ConDr 82D	The "Musical Librettists" section begins on page 921.
ConDr 82E	The Appendix begins on page 951.

ConGrA 1 *Contemporary Graphic Artists.* A biographical, bibliographical, and critical guide to current illustrators, animators, cartoonists, designers, and other graphic artists. Volume 1. Edited by Maurice Horn. Detroit: Gale Research Co., 1986.

ConLC *Contemporary Literary Criticism.* Excerpts from criticism of the works of today's novelists, poets, playwrights, short story writers, scriptwriters, and other creative writers. Detroit: Gale Research Co., 1973-1987.

ConLC 1	Volume 1, 1973
ConLC 2	Volume 2, 1974
ConLC 3	Volume 3, 1975
ConLC 4	Volume 4, 1975
ConLC 5	Volume 5, 1976
ConLC 6	Volume 6, 1976
ConLC 7	Volume 7, 1977
ConLC 8	Volume 8, 1978
ConLC 9	Volume 9, 1978
ConLC 10	Volume 10, 1979
ConLC 11	Volume 11, 1979
ConLC 12	Volume 12, 1980
ConLC 13	Volume 13, 1980
ConLC 14	Volume 14, 1980
ConLC 15	Volume 15, 1980
ConLC 16	Volume 16, 1981
ConLC 17	Volume 17, 1981
ConLC 18	Volume 18, 1981
ConLC 19	Volume 19, 1981
ConLC 20	Volume 20, 1982
ConLC 21	Volume 21, 1982
ConLC 22	Volume 22, 1982
ConLC 23	Volume 23, 1983
ConLC 24	Volume 24, 1983
ConLC 25	Volume 25, 1983
ConLC 26	Volume 26, 1983
ConLC 27	Volume 27, 1984
ConLC 28	Volume 28, 1984
ConLC 29	Volume 29, 1984
ConLC 30	Volume 30, 1984
ConLC 31	Volume 31, 1985
ConLC 32	Volume 32, 1985
ConLC 33	Volume 33, 1985
ConLC 34	Volume 34, Yearbook 1984, 1985
ConLC 35	Volume 35, 1985
ConLC 36	Volume 36, 1986
ConLC 37	Volume 37, 1986
ConLC 38	Volume 38, 1986
ConLC 39	Volume 39, 1986
ConLC 40	Volume 40, 1986
ConLC 41	Volume 41, 1987

Use the Table of Contents to locate entries in the Yearbook, Volume 34.

ConNov *Contemporary Novelists.* London: St. James Press; New York: St. Martin's Press, 1976, 1982, 1986.

ConNov 76	Second edition, edited by James Vinson, 1976
ConNov 82	Third edition, edited by James Vinson, 1982
ConNov 86	Fourth edition, edited by James Vinson and D.L. Kirkpatrick, 1986

Biographies in the Appendix, indicated in this index by the code *A*, are located at the back of each volume.

ConPo *Contemporary Poets.* London: St. James Press; New York: St. Martin's Press, 1980, 1985.

ConPo 80	Third edition, edited by James Vinson, 1980.
ConPo 85	Fourth edition, edited by James Vinson and D.L. Kirkpatrick, 1985.

Biographies in the Appendix, indicated in this index by the code *A*, are located at the back of each volume.

ConSFA *Contemporary Science Fiction Authors.* First edition. Compiled and edited by R. Reginald. New York: Arno Press, 1975. Previously published as *Stella Nova: The Contemporary Science Fiction Authors.* Los Angeles: Unicorn & Son, Publishers, 1970.

ConTFT *Contemporary Theatre, Film, and Television.* A biographical guide featuring performers, directors, writers, producers, designers, managers, choreographers, technicians, composers, executives, dancers, and critics in the United States and Great Britain. Detroit: Gale Research Co., 1984-1986. A continuation of *Who's Who in the Theatre.*

ConTFT 1	Volume 1, 1984
ConTFT 2	Volume 2, 1986
ConTFT 3	Volume 3, 1986

Conv *Conversations.* Conversations Series. Detroit: Gale Research Co., 1977-1978.

Conv 1	Volume 1: *Conversations with Writers*, 1977
Conv 2	Volume 2: *Conversations with Jazz Musicians*, 1977
Conv 3	Volume 3: *Conversations with Writers II*, 1978

CurBio *Current Biography Yearbook.* New York: H.W. Wilson Co., 1940-1986.

Number after the source code indicates the year covered by the yearbook. Obituaries, located in the back of some volumes, are indicated in this index by the code *N*.

DcAfL *Dictionary of Afro-Latin American Civilization.* By Benjamin Nunez with the assistance of the African Bibliographic Center. Westport, Connecticut: Greenwood Press, 1980.

DcAmDH *Dictionary of American Diplomatic History.* By John E. Findling. Westport, Connecticut: Greenwood Press, 1980.

DcAmNB *Dictionary of American Negro Biography.* Edited by Rayford W. Logan and Michael R. Winston. New York: W.W. Norton & Co., 1982.

DcIrL *Dictionary of Irish Literature.* Edited by Robert Hogan. Westport, Connecticut: Greenwood Press, 1979. Also published as *The Macmillan Dictionary of Irish Literature.* London: Macmillan Press, 1980.

DcLB *Dictionary of Literary Biography.* Detroit: Gale Research Co., 1978-1987.

DcLB 1	Volume 1: *The American Renaissance in New England.* Edited by Joel Myerson, 1978.
DcLB 2	Volume 2: *American Novelists since World War II.* Edited by Jeffrey Helterman and Richard Layman, 1978.
DcLB 3	Volume 3: *Antebellum Writers in New York and the South.* Edited by Joel Myerson, 1979.
DcLB 4	Volume 4: *American Writers in Paris, 1920-1939.* Edited by Karen Lane Rood, 1980.
DcLB 5	Volume 5: *American Poets since World War II.* Two parts. Edited by Donald J. Greiner, 1980.
DcLB 6	Volume 6: *American Novelists since World War II.* Second series. Edited by James E. Kibler, Jr., 1980.
DcLB 7	Volume 7: *Twentieth-Century American Dramatists.* Two parts. Edited by John MacNicholas, 1981.
DcLB 8	Volume 8: *Twentieth-Century American Science-Fiction Writers.* Two parts, Edited by David Cowart and Thomas L. Wymer, 1981.
DcLB 9	Volume 9: *American Novelists, 1910-1945.* Three parts. Edited by James J. Martine, 1981.
DcLB 10	Volume 10: *Modern British Dramatists, 1900-1945.* Two parts. Edited by Stanley Weintraub, 1982.
DcLB 11	Volume 11: *American Humorists, 1800-1950.* Two parts. Edited by Stanley Trachtenberg, 1982.
DcLB 12	Volume 12: *American Realists and Naturalists.* Edited by Donald Pizer and Earl N. Harbert, 1982.
DcLB 13	Volume 13: *British Dramatists since World War II.* Two parts. Edited by Stanley Weintraub, 1982.
DcLB 14	Volume 14: *British Novelists since 1960.* Two parts. Edited by Jay L. Halio, 1983.
DcLB 15	Volume 15: *British Novelists, 1930-1959.* Two parts. Edited by Bernard Oldsey, 1983.
DcLB 16	Volume 16: *The Beats: Literary Bohemians in Postwar America.* Two parts. Edited by Ann Charters, 1983.
DcLB 17	Volume 17: *Twentieth-Century American Historians.* Edited by Clyde N. Wilson, 1983.
DcLB 18	Volume 18: *Victorian Novelists after 1885.* Edited by Ira B. Nadel and William E. Fredeman, 1983.
DcLB 19	Volume 19: *British Poets, 1880-1914.* Edited by Donald E. Stanford, 1983.
DcLB 20	Volume 20: *British Poets, 1914-1945.* Edited by Donald E. Stanford, 1983.
DcLB 21	Volume 21: *Victorian Novelists before 1885.* Edited by Ira B. Nadel and William E. Fredeman, 1983.
DcLB 22	Volume 22: *American Writers for Children, 1900-1960.* Edited by John Cech, 1983.
DcLB 23	Volume 23: *American Newspaper Journalists, 1873-1900.* Edited by Perry J. Ashley, 1983.
DcLB 24	Volume 24: *American Colonial Writers, 1606- 1734.* Edited by Emory Elliott, 1984.
DcLB 25	Volume 25: *American Newspaper Journalists, 1901-1925.* Edited by Perry J. Ashley, 1984.
DcLB 26	Volume 26: *American Screenwriters.* Edited by Robert E. Morsberger, Stephen O. Lesser, and Randall Clark, 1984.
DcLB 27	Volume 27: *Poets of Great Britain and Ireland, 1945-1960.* Edited by Vincent B. Sherry, Jr., 1984.
DcLB 28	Volume 28: *Twentieth-Century American-Jewish Fiction Writers.* Edited by Daniel Walden, 1984.

DcLB 29	Volume 29: *American Newspaper Journalists, 1926-1950.* Edited by Perry J. Ashley, 1984.
DcLB 30	Volume 30: *American Historians, 1607-1865.* Edited by Clyde N. Wilson, 1984.
DcLB 31	Volume 31: *American Colonial Writers, 1735-1781.* Edited by Emory Elliott, 1984.
DcLB 31A	Volume 31. Appendix I: "Eighteenth-Century Philosophical Background." Use the Table of Contents to locate entries.
DcLB 31B	Volume 31. Appendix II: "Eighteenth-Century Aesthetic Theories." Use the Table of Contents to locate entries.
DcLB 32	Volume 32: *Victorian Poets before 1850.* Edited by William E. Fredeman and Ira B. Nadel, 1984.
DcLB 33	Volume 33: *Afro-American Fiction Writers after 1955.* Edited by Thadious M. Davis and Trudier Harris, 1984.
DcLB 34	Volume 34: *British Novelists, 1890-1929:Traditionalists.* Edited by Thomas F. Staley, 1985.
DcLB 35	Volume 35: *Victorian Poets after 1850.* Edited by William E. Fredeman and Ira B. Nadel, 1985.
DcLB 36	Volume 36: *British Novelists, 1890-1929: Modernists.* Edited by Thomas F. Staley, 1985.
DcLB 37	Volume 37: *American Writers of the Early Republic.* Edited by Emory Elliott, 1985.
DcLB 38	Volume 38: *Afro-American Writers after 1955: Dramatists and Prose Writers.* Edited by Thadious M. Davis and Trudier Harris, 1985.
DcLB 39	Volume 39: *British Novelists, 1600-1800.* Two parts. Edited by Martin C. Battestin, 1985.
DcLB 40	Volume 40: *Poets of Great Britain and Ireland since 1960.* Two parts. Edited by Vincent B. Sherry, Jr., 1985.
DcLB 41	Volume 41: *Afro-American Poets since 1955.* Edited by Trudier Harris and Thadious M. Davis, 1985.
DcLB 42	Volume 42: *American Writers for Children before 1900.* Edited by Glenn E. Estes, 1985.
DcLB 43	Volume 43: *American Newspaper Journalists, 1690-1872.* Edited by Perry J. Ashley, 1985.
DcLB 44	Volume 44: *American Screenwriters.* Second series. Edited by Randall Clark, 1986.
DcLB 45	Volume 45: *American Poets, 1880-1945.* First series. Edited by Peter Quartermain, 1986.
DcLB 47	Volume 47: *American Historians, 1866-1912.* Edited by Clyde N. Wilson, 1986.
DcLB 48	Volume 48: *American Poets, 1880-1945.* Second series. Edited by Peter Quartermain, 1986.
DcLB 50	Volume 50: *Afro-American Writers before the Harlem Renaissance.* Edited by Trudier Harris, 1986.
DcLB 51	Volume 51: *Afro-American Writers from the Harlem Renaissance to 1940.* Edited by Trudier Harris, 1987.
DcLB 51A	Volume 51: Appendix.
DcLB 52	Volume 52: *American Writers for Children since 1960: Fiction.* Edited by Glenn E. Estes, 1986.
DcLB 53	Volume 53: *Canadian Writers since 1960.* First series. Edited by W.H. New, 1986.
DcLB 54	Volume 54: *American Poets, 1880-1945.* Two parts. Third series. Edited by Peter Quartermain, 1987.

DcLB 55 Volume 55: *Victorian Prose Writers before 1867.* Edited by William B. Thesing, 1987.

Volumes 46 and 49 contain no biographies.

DcLB DS *Dictionary of Literary Biography, Documentary Series: An Illustrated Chronicle.* Detroit: Gale Research Co., 1982-1984.

DcLB DS1 Volume 1, edited by Margaret A. Van Antwerp, 1982.
DcLB DS2 Volume 2, edited by Margaret A. Van Antwerp, 1982.
DcLB DS3 Volume 3, edited by Mary Bruccoli, 1983.
DcLB DS4 Volume 4, edited by Margaret A. Van Antwerp and Sally Johns, 1984.

DcLB Y- *Dictionary of Literary Biography Yearbook.* Detroit: Gale Research Co., 1981-1986.

DcLB Y80A Yearbook: 1980. Edited by Karen L. Rood, Jean W. Ross, and Richard Ziegfeld, 1981. The "Updated Entries" section begins on page 3.
DcLB Y80B Yearbook: 1980. The "New Entries" section begins on page 127.
DcLB Y81A Yearbook: 1981. Edited by Karen L. Rood, Jean W. Ross, and Richard Ziegfeld, 1982. The "Updated Entries" section begins on page 21.
DcLB Y81B Yearbook: 1981. The "New Entries" section begins on page 139.
DcLB Y82A Yearbook: 1982. Edited by Richard Ziegfeld, 1983. The "Updated Entries" section begins on page 121.
DcLB Y82B Yearbook: 1982. The "New Entries" section begins on page 203.
DcLB Y83A Yearbook: 1983. Edited by Mary Bruccoli and Jean W. Ross, 1984. The "Updated Entries" section begins on page 155.
DcLB Y83B Yearbook: 1983. The "New Entries" section begins on page 175.
DcLB Y83N Yearbook: 1983. The "Obituaries" section begins on page 103.
DcLB Y84A Yearbook: 1984. Edited by Jean W. Ross, 1985. The "Updated Entry" section begins on page 219.
DcLB Y84B Yearbook: 1984. The "New Entries" section begins on page 225.
DcLB Y84N Yearbook: 1984. The "Obituaries" section begins on page 163.
DcLB Y85A Yearbook: 1985. Edited by Jean W. Ross, 1986. The "Updated Entries" section begins on page 279.
DcLB Y85B Yearbook: 1985. The "New Entries" section begins on page 319.
DcLB Y85N Yearbook: 1985. The "Obituaries" section begins on page 253.

DcLEL *A Dictionary of Literature in the English Language.* Compiled and edited by Robin Myers. Oxford: Pergamon Press, 1970, 1978.

DcLEL *From Chaucer to 1940*, 1970
DcLEL 1940 *From 1940 to 1970*, 1978

DrAP&F 85 *A Directory of American Poets and Fiction Writers.* Names and addresses of 6,020 contemporary poets and fiction writers whose work has been published in the United States. 1985-1986 edition. New York: Poets & Writers, 1985.

Use the Index to locate listings.

DrAS 82 *Directory of American Scholars.* Eighth edition. Four volumes. Edited by Jaques Cattell Press. New York: R.R. Bowker Co., 1982.

DrAS 82H	Volume 1: History
DrAS 82E	Volume 2: English, Speech, & Drama
DrAS 82F	Volume 3: Foreign Languages, Linguistics, & Philology
DrAS 82P	Volume 4: Philosophy, Religion, & Law

DrmM 1 *Dream Makers.* The uncommon people who write science fiction. Interviews by Charles Platt. New York: Berkley Books, 1980.

Use the Table of Contents to locate interviews.

DrmM 2 *Dream Makers Volume II.* The uncommon men & women who write science fiction. Interviews by Charles Platt. New York: Berkley Books, 1983.

Use the Table of Contents to locate interviews.

EncAJ *The Encyclopedia of American Journalism.* By Donald Paneth. New York: Facts on File, 1983.

EncFWF *Encyclopedia of Frontier and Western Fiction.* Edited by Jon Tuska and Vicki Piekarski. New York: McGraw-Hill Book Co., 1983.

EncMys *Encyclopedia of Mystery and Detection.* By Chris Steinbrunner and Otto Penzler. New York: McGraw-Hill Book Co., 1976.

EncO&P *Encyclopedia of Occultism & Parapsychology.* A compendium of information on the occult sciences, magic, demonology, superstitions, spiritism, mysticism, metaphysics, psychical science, and parapsychology, with biographical and bibliographical notes and comprehensive indexes. Edited by Leslie Shepard. Detroit: Gale Research Co., 1978, 1980, 1981, 1984-1985.

EncO&P 78	Main volumes, 1978
EncO&P 78S1	Occultism Update, Issue Number 1, 1978
EncO&P 80	Occultism Update, Issue Number 2, 1980
EncO&P 81	Occultism Update, Issue Numbers 3-4, 1981
EncO&P 2	Second edition, 1984-1985

EncSF *The Encyclopedia of Science Fiction: An Illustrated A to Z.* Edited by Peter Nicholls. London: Granada Publishing Ltd., 1979.

EncTwCJ *Encyclopedia of Twentieth-Century Journalists.* By William H. Taft. Garland Reference Library of the Humanities. New York: Garland Publishing, 1986.

EncWL 2 *Encyclopedia of World Literature in the 20th Century.* Revised edition. Four volumes. Edited by Leonard S. Klein. New York: Frederick Ungar Publishing Co., 1981-1984. Distributed by Gale Research Co., Detroit, Michigan.

EncWT *The Encyclopedia of World Theater.* Translated by Estella Schmid, edited by Martin Esslin. New York: Charles Scribner's Sons, 1977. Based on *Friedrichs Theaterlexikon*, by Karl Groning and Werner Kliess.

FifBJA *Fifth Book of Junior Authors & Illustrators.* Edited by Sally Holmes Holtze. New York: H.W. Wilson Co., 1983.

FifIDA *Fifth International Directory of Anthropologists.* Edited by Sol Tax. Current Anthropology Resource Series. Chicago: University of Chicago Press, 1975.

FourBJA *Fourth Book of Junior Authors & Illustrators.* Edited by Doris De Montreville and Elizabeth D. Crawford. New York: H.W. Wilson Co., 1978.

HalFC 84 *Halliwell's Filmgoer's Companion.* Eighth edition. By Leslie Halliwell. New York: Charles Scribner's Sons, 1984.

HerW 84 *Her Way.* A guide to biographies of women for young people. Second edition. By Mary-Ellen Siegel. Chicago: American Library Association, 1984.

ICPEnP *ICP Encyclopedia of Photography.* New York: Crown Publishers, 1984.

The Appendix, indicated in this index by the code *A*, begins on page 576.

IlBEAAW *The Illustrated Biographical Encyclopedia of Artists of the American West.* By Peggy Samuels and Harold Samuels. Garden City, New York: Doubleday & Co., 1976.

IlrAm 1880 *The Illustrator in America, 1880-1980.* A century of illustration. By Walt Reed and Roger Reed. New York: Madison Square Press (for The Society of Illustrators), 1984. Distributed by Robert Silver Associates, New York, New York.

Use the Index to locate biographies.

IlsBYP *Illustrators of Books for Young People.* Second edition. By Martha E. Ward and Dorothy A. Marquardt. Metuchen, New Jersey: Scarecrow Press, 1975.

IlsCB *Illustrators of Children's Books.* Boston: Horn Book, 1947, 1958, 1968, 1978.

IlsCB 1744 *1744-1945.* Compiled by Bertha E. Mahony, Louise Payson Latimer, and Beulah Folmsbee, 1947. Biographies begin on page 267.

IlsCB 1946 *1946-1956.* Compiled by Ruth Hill Viguers, Marcia Dalphin, and Bertha Mahony Miller, 1958. Biographies begin on page 62.

IlsCB 1957 *1957-1966.* Compiled by Lee Kingman, Joanna Foster, and Ruth Giles Lontoft, 1968. Biographies begin on page 70.

IlsCB 1967 *1967-1976.* Compiled by Lee Kingman, Grace Allen Hogarth, and Harriet Quimby, 1978. Biographies begin on page 93.

InB&W 80 *In Black and White.* A guide to magazine articles, newspaper articles, and books concerning more than 15,000 Black individuals and groups. Third edition. Two volumes. Edited by Mary Mace Spradling. Detroit: Gale Research Co., 1980.

IntAu&W *The International Authors and Writers Who's Who.* Edited by Adrian Gaster. Cambridge, England: International Biographical Centre, 1977, 1982. 1982 edition is combined with *International Who's Who in Poetry* (see below).

IntAu&W 77 Eighth edition, 1977, Biographical Section

IntAu&W 77X The "Pseudonyms of Included Authors" section begins on page 1131.

IntAu&W 82 Ninth edition, 1982, Biographical Section

IntAu&W 82X The "Pseudonyms of Included Authors" section begins on page 719.

IntAu&W 86 Tenth edition, 1986, Biographical Section

IntAu&W 86X The "Pseudonyms of Included Authors" section begins on page 796.

IntDcWB *The International Dictionary of Women's Biography.* Compiled and edited by Jennifer S. Uglow. New York: Continuum Publishing Co., 1982.

IntMPA *International Motion Picture Almanac.* Edited by Richard Gertner. New York: Quigley Publishing Co., 1978, 1979, 1981, 1982, 1984, 1986.

IntMPA 78	1978 edition
IntMPA 79	1979 edition
IntMPA 81	1981 edition
IntMPA 82	1982 edition
IntMPA 84	1984 edition
IntMPA 86	1986 edition

Biographies are found in the "Who's Who in Motion Pictures and Television" section in each volume. The listings are identical to those found in the *International Television Almanac.*

IntWWM 85 *International Who's Who in Music and Musicians' Directory.* 10th edition. Cambridge, England: International Who's Who in Music, 1984. Distributed by Gale Research Co., Detroit, Michigan. Earlier editions published as *Who's Who in Music and Musicians' International Directory.*

IntWWP *International Who's Who in Poetry.* Edited by Ernest Kay. Cambridge, England: International Biographical Centre, 1977, 1982. 1982 edition is combined with *The International Authors and Writers Who's Who* (see above).

IntWWP 77	Fifth edition, 1977, Biographical Section
IntWWP 77A	Addendum begins on page 470.
IntWWP 77X	The "Pseudonyms and Pen Names of Included Authors" section begins on page 702.
IntWWP 82	Sixth edition, 1982. Biographies begin on page 759.
IntWWP 82X	The "Pseudonyms of Included Poets" section begins on page 1035.

JBA 34 *The Junior Book of Authors.* An introduction to the lives of writers and illustrators for younger readers from Lewis Carroll and Louisa Alcott to the present day. First edition. Edited by Stanley J. Kunitz and Howard Haycraft. New York: H.W. Wilson Co., 1934.

JBA 51 *The Junior Book of Authors.* Second edition, revised. Edited by Stanley J. Kunitz and Howard Haycraft. New York: H.W. Wilson Co., 1951.

LesBEnT *Les Brown's Encyclopedia of Television.* By Les Brown. New York: New York Zoetrope, 1982. Previous edition published as *The New York Times Encyclopedia of Television.*

MacBEP *Macmillan Biographical Encyclopedia of Photographic Artists & Innovators.* By Turner Browne and Elaine Partnow. New York: Macmillan Publishing Co.; London: Collier Macmillan Publishers, 1983.

McGEWB *The McGraw-Hill Encyclopedia of World Biography.* An international reference work in 12 volumes, including an index. New York: McGraw-Hill Book Co., 1973.

McGEWD 84 *McGraw-Hill Encyclopedia of World Drama.* Second edition. An international reference work in five volumes. New York: McGraw-Hill Book Co., 1984.

MichAu 80 *Michigan Authors.* Second edition. By the Michigan Association for Media in Education. Ann Arbor: Michigan Association for Media in Education, 1980.

The Addendum, indicated in this index by the code *A*, begins on page 339.

ModBlW *Modern Black Writers.* Compiled and edited by Michael Popkin. A Library of Literary Criticism. New York: Frederick Ungar Publishing Co., 1978.

ModBrL *Modern British Literature.* Five volumes. A Library of Literary Criticism. New York: Frederick Ungar Publishing Co., 1966, 1975, 1985.

ModBrL	Volumes I-III, compiled and edited by Ruth Z. Temple and Martin Tucker, 1966.
ModBrL S1	Volume IV, Supplement, compiled and edited by Martin Tucker and Rita Stein, 1975.
ModBrL S2	Volume V, Second Supplement, compiled and edited by Denis Lane and Rita Stein, 1985.

MorBMP *More Books by More People: Interviews with Sixty-Five Authors of Books for Children.* By Lee Bennett Hopkins. New York: Citation Press, 1974.

MorJA *More Junior Authors.* Edited by Muriel Fuller. New York: H.W. Wilson Co., 1963.

NatCAB *The National Cyclopedia of American Biography.* Volumes 52-63. New York and Clifton, New Jersey: James T. White & Co., 1970-1984.

Number after the source code indicates volume number. Use the Index in each volume to located biographies.

NatPD *National Playwrights Directory.* Edited by Phyllis Johnson Kaye. Waterford, Connecticut: The O'Neill Theater Center, 1977, 1981. Distributed by Gale Research Co., Detroit, Michigan.

NatPD	First edition, 1977
NatPD 81	Second edition, 1981

NegAl 83 *The Negro Almanac: A Reference Work on the Afro-American.* Fourth edition. Compiled and edited by Harry A. Ploski and James Williams. New York: John Wiley & Sons, 1983.

Use the Index to locate biographies.

NewYTBE *The New York Times Biographical Edition: A Compilation of Current Biographical Information of General Interest.* New York: Arno Press, 1970-1973. Continued by *The New York Times Biographical Service* (see below).

NewYTBE 70	Volume 1, Numbers 1-12, 1970
NewYTBE 71	Volume 2, Numbers 1-12, 1971
NewYTBE 72	Volume 3, Numbers 1-12, 1972
NewYTBE 73	Volume 4, Numbers 1-12, 1973

Use the "Annual Index" to locate biographies.

NewYTBS *The New York Times Biographical Service: A Compilation of Current Biographical Information of General Interest.* New York: Arno Press, 1974-1981. A continuation of *The New York Times Biographical Edition* (see above).

NewYTBS 74	Volume 5, Numbers 1-12, 1974
NewYTBS 75	Volume 6, Numbers 1-12, 1975
NewYTBS 76	Volume 7, Numbers 1-12, 1976
NewYTBS 77	Volume 8, Numbers 1-12, 1977
NewYTBS 78	Volume 9, Numbers 1-12, 1978
NewYTBS 79	Volume 10, Numbers 1-12, 1979
NewYTBS 80	Volume 11, Numbers 1-12, 1980
NewYTBS 81	Volume 12, Numbers 1-12, 1981

Use the "Annual Index" to locate biographies.

NewYTBS *The New York Times Biographical Service: A Compilation of Current Biographical Information of General Interest.* Sanford, North Carolina: Microfilming Corp. of America, 1982-1983.

NewYTBS 82	Volume 13, Numbers 1-12, 1982
NewYTBS 83	Volume 14, Numbers 1-12, 1983

Use the "Annual Index" to locate biographies.

NewYTBS *The New York Times Biographical Service: A Compilation of Current Biographical Information of General Interest.* Ann Arbor, Michigan: University Microfilms International, 1984-1986.

NewYTBS 84	Volume 15, Numbers 1-12
NewYTBS 85	Volume 16, Numbers 1-12

Use the "Annual Index" to locate biographies.

NotAW MOD *Notable American Women: The Modern Period.* A biographical dictionary. Edited by Barbara Sicherman and Carol Hurd Green. Cambridge, Massachusetts: Harvard University Press, Belknap Press, 1980.

NotNAT *Notable Names in the American Theatre.* Clifton, New Jersey: James T. White & Co., 1976. First edition published as *The Biographical Encyclopaedia and Who's Who of the American Theatre.*

NotNAT	"Notable Names in the American Theatre" begins on page 489.
NotNAT A	"Biographical Bibliography" begins on page 309.
NotNAT B	"Necrology" begins on page 343.

This book often alphabetizes by titles of address, e.g.: Dr., Mrs., and Sir.

Novels *Novels and Novelists: A Guide to the World of Fiction.* Edited by Martin Seymour-Smith. New York: St. Martin's Press, 1980.

Biographies are located in the "Novelists: An Alphabetical Guide" section which begins on page 87.

ObitOF 79 *Obituaries on File.* Two volumes. Compiled by Felice Levy. New York: Facts on File, 1979.

ObitT *Obituaries from the Times.* Compiled by Frank C. Roberts. Reading, England: Newspaper Archive Developments, 1975, 1978, 1979. Distributed by Meckler Books, Westport, Connecticut.

ObitT 1951	*1951-1960*, 1979
ObitT 1961	*1961-1970*, 1975
ObitT 1971	*1971-1975*, 1978

OxAmL 83 *The Oxford Companion to American Literature.* Fifth edition. By James D. Hart. New York and Oxford: Oxford University Press, 1983.

OxAmT 84 *The Oxford Companion to American Theatre.* By Gerald Bordman. New York: Oxford University Press, 1984.

OxAusL *The Oxford Companion to Australian Literature.* By William H. Wilde, Joy Hooton, and Barry Andrews. Melbourne: Oxford University Press, 1985.

OxCanL *The Oxford Companion to Canadian Literature.* Edited by William Toye. New York: Oxford University Press, 1983.

OxChL *The Oxford Companion to Children's Literature.* By Humphrey Carpenter and Mari Prichard. New York: Oxford University Press, 1984.

OxEng 85 *The Oxford Companion to English Literature.* Fifth edition. Edited by Margaret Drabble. New York: Oxford University Press, 1985.

OxFilm *The Oxford Companion to Film.* Edited by Liz-Anne Bawden. New York and London: Oxford University Press, 1976.

OxFr *The Oxford Companion to French Literature.* Compiled and edited by Sir Paul Harvey and J.E. Heseltine. Oxford: Oxford University Press, Clarendon Press, 1959. Reprinted with corrections, 1966.

OxGer *The Oxford Companion to German Literature.* By Henry Garland and Mary Garland. Oxford: Oxford University Press, Clarendon Press, 1976.

OxMus *The Oxford Companion to Music.* By Percy A. Scholes. 10th edition (corrected). Edited by John Owen Ward. London: Oxford University Press, 1974.

OxThe 83 *The Oxford Companion to the Theatre.* Fourth edition. Edited by Phyllis Hartnoll. New York and Oxford: Oxford University Press, 1983.

PiP *The Pied Pipers: Interviews with the Influential Creators of Children's Literature.* By Justin Wintle and Emma Fisher. New York: Paddington Press, 1974.

Use the Table of Contents to locate biographies.

PlP&P *Plays, Players, and Playwrights: An Illustrated History of the Theatre.* By Marion Geisinger. Updated by Peggy Marks. New York: Hart Publishing Co., 1975.

Use the Index, which begins on page 575, to locate biographies in the main section of the book. A Supplemental Index to the last chapter, "The Theatre of the Seventies," begins on page 797 and is indicated in this index by the code *A*.

Profile 1 *Profiles.* Revised edition. Edited by Irma McDonough. Ottawa: Canadian Library Association, 1975.

Contains articles from *In Review: Canadian Books for Children,* published quarterly by the Ontario Provincial Library Service.

Profile 2 *Profiles 2: Authors and Illustrators, Children's Literature in Canada.* Edited by Irma McDonough. Ottawa: Canadian Library Assocation, 1982.

Contains articles from *In Review: Canadian Books for Children,* published quarterly by the Ontario Provincial Library Service.

RkOn *Rock On: The Illustrated Encyclopedia of Rock n' Roll.* By Norm N. Nite. New York: Thomas Y. Crowell Co., 1974, 1978.

RkOn 74 Volume 1: *The Solid Gold Years,* 1974
RkOn 78 Volume 2: *The Modern Years: 1964-Present,* 1978
RkOn 78A Volume 2: Appendix begins on page 543.

RolSEnR 83 *The Rolling Stone Encyclopedia of Rock & Roll.* Edited by Jon Pareles and Patricia Romanowski. New York: Rolling Stone Press/Summit Books, 1983.

ScF&FL *Science Fiction and Fantasy Literature.* A checklist, 1700-1974, with *Contemporary Science Fiction Authors II.* By R. Reginald. Detroit: Gale Research Co., 1979.

ScF&FL 1 Volume 1: "Author Index" begins on page 3
ScF&FL 1A Volume 1: Addendum begins on page 581
ScF&FL 2 Volume 2: *Contemporary Science Fiction Authors II*

ScFSB *The Science Fiction Source Book.* Edited by David Wingrove. New York: Van Nostrand Reinhold Co., 1984.

Listings are located in the "Science Fiction Writers: A Consumers' Guide" section, which begins on page 87.

SelBAAf *Selected Black American, African, and Caribbean Authors: A Bio-Bibliography.* Compiled by James A. Page and Jae Min Roh. Littleton, Colorado: Libraries Unlimited, 1985.

SelBAAu *Selected Black American Authors: An Illustrated Bio-Bibliography.* Compiled by James A. Page. Boston: G.K. Hall & Co., 1977.

SenS *A Sense of Story: Essays on Contemporary Writers for Children.* By John Rowe Townsend. London: Longman Group, 1971.

SmATA *Something about the Author.* Facts and pictures about authors and illustrators of books for young people. Edited by Anne Commire. Detroit: Gale Research Co., 1971-1987.

SmATA 1	Volume 1, 1971
SmATA 2	Volume 2, 1971
SmATA 3	Volume 3, 1972
SmATA 4	Volume 4, 1973
SmATA 5	Volume 5, 1973
SmATA 6	Volume 6, 1974
SmATA 7	Volume 7, 1975
SmATA 8	Volume 8, 1976
SmATA 9	Volume 9, 1976
SmATA 10	Volume 10, 1976
SmATA 11	Volume 11, 1977
SmATA 12	Volume 12, 1977
SmATA 13	Volume 13, 1978
SmATA 14	Volume 14, 1978
SmATA 15	Volume 15, 1979
SmATA 16	Volume 16, 1979
SmATA 17	Volume 17, 1979
SmATA 18	Volume 18, 1980
SmATA 19	Volume 19, 1980
SmATA 20	Volume 20, 1980
SmATA 20N	Volume 20, Obituary Notices
SmATA 21	Volume 21, 1980
SmATA 21N	Volume 21, Obituary Notices
SmATA 22	Volume 22, 1981
SmATA 22N	Volume 22, Obituary Notices
SmATA 23	Volume 23, 1981
SmATA 23N	Volume 23, Obituary Notices
SmATA 24	Volume 24, 1981
SmATA 24N	Volume 24, Obituary Notices
SmATA 25	Volume 25, 1981
SmATA 25N	Volume 25, Obituary Notices
SmATA 26	Volume 26, 1982
SmATA 26N	Volume 26, Obituary Notices
SmATA 27	Volume 27, 1982
SmATA 27N	Volume 27, Obituary Notices
SmATA 28	Volume 28, 1982
SmATA 28N	Volume 28, Obituary Notices
SmATA 29	Volume 29, 1982
SmATA 29N	Volume 29, Obituary Notices
SmATA 30	Volume 30, 1983
SmATA 30N	Volume 30, Obituary Notices
SmATA 31	Volume 31, 1983

SmATA 31N	Volume 31, Obituary Notices
SmATA 32	Volume 32, 1983
SmATA 32N	Volume 32, Obituary Notices
SmATA 33	Volume 33, 1983
SmATA 33N	Volume 33, Obituary Notices
SmATA 34	Volume 34, 1984
SmATA 34N	Volume 34, Obituary Notices
SmATA 35	Volume 35, 1984
SmATA 35N	Volume 35, Obituary Notices
SmATA 36	Volume 36, 1984
SmATA 36N	Volume 36, Obituary Notices
SmATA 37	Volume 37, 1985
SmATA 37N	Volume 37, Obituary Notices
SmATA 38	Volume 38, 1985
SmATA 38N	Volume 38, Obituary Notices
SmATA 39	Volume 39, 1985
SmATA 39N	Volume 39, Obituary Notices
SmATA 40	Volume 40, 1985
SmATA 40N	Volume 40, Obituary Notices
SmATA 41	Volume 41, 1985
SmATA 41N	Volume 41, Obituary Notices
SmATA 42	Volume 42, 1986
SmATA 42N	Volume 42, Obituary Notices
SmATA 43	Volume 43, 1986
SmATA 43N	Volume 43, Obituary Notices
SmATA 44	Volume 44, 1986
SmATA 44N	Volume 44, Obituary Notices
SmATA 45	Volume 45, 1986
SmATA 45N	Volume 45, Obituary Notices
SmATA 47	Volume 47, 1987
SmATA 47N	Volume 47, Obituary Notices
SmATA 48	Volume 48, 1987
SmATA 48N	Volume 48, Obituary Notices
SmATA 49	Volume 49, 1987
SmATA 49N	Volume 49, Obituary Notices

SmATA AS *Something about the Author, Autobiography Series.* Detroit: Gale Research Co., 1986-1987.

SmATA 1AS	Volume 1, 1986
SmATA 2AS	Volume 2, 1986
SmATA 3AS	Volume 3, 1987
SmATA 4AS	Volume 4, 1987

SmATA X This code refers to pseudonym entries which appear only as cross-references in the cumulative index to *Something about the Author.*

SouST *A Sounding of Storytellers: New and Revised Essays on Contemporary Writers for Children.* By John Rowe Townsend. New York: J.B. Lippincott, 1979.

Str&VC *Story and Verse for Children.* Third edition. By Miriam Blanton Huber. New York: Macmillan Co., 1965.

Biographies begin on page 793.

SupFW *Supernatural Fiction Writers: Fantasy and Horror.* Two volumes. Edited by E.F. Bleiler. New York: Charles Scribner's Sons, 1985.

Use the Index to locate biographies.

ThrBJA *Third Book of Junior Authors.* Edited by Doris De Montreville and Donna Hill. New York: H.W. Wilson Co., 1972.

TwCChW *Twentieth-Century Children's Writers.* Edited by D.L. Kirkpatrick. New York: St. Martin's Press, 1978, 1983.

TwCChW 78	First edition, "Twentieth-Century Children's Writers"
TwCChW 78A	Appendix begins on page 1391.
TwCChW 78B	"Children's Books in Translation" section begins on page 1481.
TwCChW 83	Second edition, "Twentieth-Century Children's Writers"
TwCChW 83A	Appendix begins on page 859.
TwCChW 83B	"Foreign-Language Writers" section begins on page 893.

TwCCr&M *Twentieth-Century Crime and Mystery Writers.* Edited by John M. Reilly. New York: St. Martin's Press, 1980, 1985.

TwCCr&M 80	First edition, "Twentieth-Century Crime and Mystery Writers"
TwCCr&M 80A	"Nineteenth-Century Writers" section begins on page 1525.
TwCCr&M 80B	"Foreign-Language Writers" section begins on page 1537.
TwCCr&M 85	Second edition, "Twentieth-Century Crime and Mystery Writers"
TwCCr&M 85A	"Nineteenth-Century Writers" section begins on page 931.
TwCCr&M 85B	"Foreign-Language Writers" section begins on page 939.

TwCSFW 86 *Twentieth-Century Science-Fiction Writers.* Second edition. Edited by Curtis C. Smith. Twentieth-Century Writers Series. Chicago: St. James Press, 1986.

TwCSFW 86	Twentieth-Century Science-Fiction Writers
TwCSFW 86A	"Foreign-Language Writers" section begins on page 837.
TwCSFW 86B	"Major Fantasy Writers" section begins on page 863.

WebAB *Webster's American Biographies.* Edited by Charles Van Doren. Springfield, Massachusetts: G. & C. Merriam Co., 1974, 1979.

WebAB	1974 edition
WebAB 79	1979 edition

WebE&AL *Webster's New World Companion to English and American Literature.* Edited by Arthur Pollard. New York: World Publishing Co., 1973.

WhAm 1 *Who Was Who in America.* Volume I, 1897-1942. A component volume of *Who's Who in American History.* Chicago: A.N. Marquis Co., 1943.

The Corrigenda, indicated in this index by the code *C*, begin on page x.

WhAm 2 *Who Was Who in America.* Volume II, 1943-1950. A companion biographical reference work to *Who's Who in America.* Chicago: A.N. Marquis Co., 1963.

WhAm 2A	Addendum begins on page 12.
WhAm 2C	Corrigenda begin on page 5.

WhAm 3 *Who Was Who in America.* Volume III, 1951-1960. A component of *Who's Who in American History.* Chicago: Marquis Who's Who, 1966.

The Addendum, indicated in this index by the code *A*, begins on page 952.

WhAm 4 *Who Was Who in America with World Notables.* Volume IV, 1961-1968. A component volume of *Who's Who in American History.* Chicago: Marquis-Who's Who, 1968.

The Addendum, indicated in this index by the code *A*, begins on page 1049.

WhAm 5 *Who Was Who in America with World Notables.* Volume V, 1969-1973. Chicago: Marquis Who's Who, 1973.

WhAm 6 *Who Was Who in America with World Notables.* Volume VI, 1974-1976. Chicago: Marquis Who's Who, 1976.

WhAm 7 *Who Was Who in America with World Notables.* Volume VII, 1977-1981. Chicago: Marquis Who's Who, 1981.

WhAm 8 *Who Was Who in America with World Notables.* Volume VIII, 1982-1985. Chicago: Marquis Who's Who, 1985.

WhAmArt 85 *Who Was Who in American Art.* Compiled from the original thirty-four volumes of *American Art Annual: Who's Who in Art.* Edited by Peter Hastings Falk. Madison, Connecticut: Sound View Press, 1985.

The "European Teachers of American Artists" section, indicated in this index by the code *A*, begins on page xxxiii.

Who *Who's Who.* An annual biographical dictionary. New York: St. Martin's Press; London: Adam & Charles Black, 1982, 1983, 1985.

Who 82	134th Year of Issue, 1982-1983
Who 83	135th Year of Issue, 1983-1984
Who 85	137th Year of Issue, 1985-1986

The Obituary section is indicated in this index by the code *N*.

WhoAm *Who's Who in America.* Chicago: Marquis Who's Who, 1976, 1978, 1980, 1982, 1984, 1986.

WhoAm 76	39th edition, 1976-1977
WhoAm 78	40th edition, 1978-1979
WhoAm 80	41st edition, 1980-1981
WhoAm 82	42nd edition, 1982-1983
WhoAm 84	43rd edition, 1984-1985
WhoAm 86	44th edition, 1986-1987

WhoAmA *Who's Who in American Art.* Edited by Jaques Cattell Press. New York: R.R. Bowker Co., 1978, 1980, 1982, 1984.

WhoAmA 78	1978 edition
WhoAmA 80	1980 edition
WhoAmA 82	1982 edition
WhoAmA 84	1984 edition

The Necrology, indicated in this index by the code *N*, is located at the back of each volume.

WhoAmJ 80 *Who's Who in American Jewry.* Incorporating *The Directory of American Jewish Institutions.* 1980 edition. Los Angeles: Standard Who's Who, 1980.

WhoAmW *Who's Who of American Women.* Chicago: Marquis Who's Who, 1975, 1978, 1979, 1981, 1983, 1984, 1986.

WhoAmW 75	Ninth edition, 1975-1976
WhoAmW 77	10th edition, 1977-1978
WhoAmW 79	11th edition, 1979-1980
WhoAmW 81	12th edition, 1981-1982
WhoAmW 83	13th edition, 1983-1984
WhoAmW 85	14th edition, 1985-1986
WhoAmW 87	15th edition, 1987-1988

WhoArt *Who's Who in Art.* Biographies of leading men and women in the world of art today -- artists, designers, craftsmen, critics, writers, teachers and curators, with an appendix of signatures. 21st edition. Havant, England: Art Trade Press, 1984. Distributed by Gale Research Co., Detroit, Michigan.

The Obituary section, indicated in this index by the code *N*, is located at the back of the volume.

WhoBlA *Who's Who among Black Americans.* Northbrook, Illinois: Who's Who among Black Americans, 1976, 1978, 1981.

WhoBlA 75	First edition, 1975-1976
WhoBlA 77	Second edition, 1977-1978
WhoBLA 80	Third edition, 1980-1981

WhoBlA 85 *Who's Who among Black Americans.* Fourth edition, 1985. Lake Forest, Illinois: Educational Communications, 1985.

WhoCanL 85 *Who's Who in Canadian Literature, 1985-1986.* By Gordon Ripley and Anne Mercer. Toronto: Reference Press, 1985.

WhoChL *The Who's Who of Children's Literature.* Compiled and edited by Brian Doyle. New York: Schocken Books, 1968.

Biographies are found in "The Authors," beginning on page 1, and "The Illustrators," beginning on page 303.

WhoE *Who's Who in the East.* Chicago: Marquis Who's Who, 1975, 1977, 1979, 1981, 1983, 1984.

WhoE 75	15th edition, 1975-1976
WhoE 77	16th edition, 1977-1978
WhoE 79	17th edition, 1979-1980
WhoE 81	18th edition, 1981-1982
WhoE 83	19th edition, 1983-1984
WhoE 85	20th edition, 1985-1986
WhoE 85A	20th edition, Addendum

WhoFtbl 74 *Who's Who in Football.* By Ronald L. Mendell and Timothy B. Phares. New Rochelle, New York: Arlington House, 1974.

WhoGov 77 *Who's Who in Government.* 3rd edition. Chicago: Marquis Who's Who, 1977.

WhoHcky 73 *Who's Who in Hockey.* By Harry C. Kariher. New Rochelle, New York: Arlington House, 1973.

WhoHr&F *Who's Who in Horror and Fantasy Fiction.* By Mike Ashley. London: Elm Tree Books, 1977.

WhoLibI 82 *Who's Who in Library and Information Services.* Edited by Joel M. Lee. Chicago: American Library Association, 1982.

WhoMW *Who's Who in the Midwest.* Chicago: Marquis Who's Who, 1976, 1978, 1980, 1982, 1984, 1985.

WhoMW 76	15th edition, 1976-1977
WhoMW 78	16th edition, 1978-1979

WhoMW 80	17th edition, 1980-1981
WhoMW 82	18th edition, 1982-1983
WhoMW 84	19th edition, 1984-1985
WhoMW 86	20th edition, 1986-1987

WhoProB 73 *Who's Who in Professional Baseball.* By Gene Karst and Martin J. Jones, Jr. New Rochelle, New York: Arlington House, 1973.

WhoS&SW *Who's Who in the South and Southwest.* Chicago: Marquis Who's Who, 1975, 1976, 1978, 1980, 1982, 1984.

WhoS&SW 75	14th edition, 1975-1976
WhoS&SW 76	15th edition, 1976-1977
WhoS&SW 78	16th edition, 1978-1979
WhoS&SW 80	17th edition, 1980-1981
WhoS&SW 82	18th edition, 1982-1983
WhoS&SW 84	19th edition, 1984-1985

WhoSciF *Who's Who in Science Fiction.* By Brian Ash. London: Elm Tree Books, 1976.

WhoSpyF *Who's Who in Spy Fiction.* By Donald McCormick. London: Elm Tree Books, 1977.

WhoThe *Who's Who in the Theatre: A Biographical Record of the Contemporary Stage.* 17th edition. Edited by Ian Herbert. London: Pitman Publishing; Detroit: Gale Research Co., 1981.

The "Obituary" section, indicated in this index by the code *N*, begins on page 743.

WhoTwCL *Who's Who in Twentieth Century Literature.* By Martin Seymour-Smith. New York: Holt, Rinehart & Winston, 1976.

WhoWest *Who's Who in the West.* Chicago: Marquis Who's Who, 1976, 1978, 1980, 1982, 1983.

WhoWest 76	15th edition, 1976-1977
WhoWest 78	16th edition, 1978-1979
WhoWest 80	17th edition, 1980-1981
WhoWest 82	18th edition, 1982-1983
WhoWest 84	19th edition, 1984-1985

WhoWor *Who's Who in the World.* Chicago: Marquis Who's Who, 1978, 1980, 1982, 1984.

WhoWor 78	Fourth edition, 1978-1979
WhoWor 80	Fifth edition, 1980-1981
WhoWor 82	Sixth edition, 1982-1983
WhoWor 84	Seventh edition, 1984-1985

WhoWorJ 78 *Who's Who in World Jewry: A Biographical Dictionary of Outstanding Jews.* Edited by I.J. Carmin Karpman. Tel-Aviv, Israel: Olive Books of Israel, 1978.

WorAl *The World Almanac Book of Who.* Edited by Hana Umlauf Lane. New York: World Almanac Publications, 1980.

Use the "Name Index," which begins on page 326, to locate biographies.

WorAu *World Authors.* Wilson Authors Series. New York: H.W. Wilson Co., 1975, 1980, 1985.

WorAu	1950-1970, edited by John Wakeman, 1975.
WorAu 1970	1970-1975, edited by John Wakeman, 1980.
WorAu 1975	1975-1980, edited by Vineta Colby, 1985.

WorECar *The World Encyclopedia of Cartoons.* Two volumes. Edited by Maurice Horn. Detroit: Gale Research Co. (in association with Chelsea House Publishers, New York), 1980.

The "Notes on the Contributors" section, indicated in this index by the code *A*, begins on page 631.

WrDr *The Writers Directory.* London: St. James Press; New York: St. Martin's Press, 1976, 1979.

WrDr 76	1976-1978 edition
WrDr 80	1980-1982 edition

WrDr 82 *The Writers Directory.* 1982-1984 edition. Detroit: Gale Research Co., 1981.

WrDr *The Writers Directory.* Chicago: St. James Press, 1983, 1986. Distributed by Gale Research Co., Detroit, Michigan.

WrDr 84	1984-1986 edition
WrDr 86	1986-1988 edition

YABC *Yesterday's Authors of Books for Children.* Facts and pictures about authors and illustrators of books for young people, from early times to 1960. Edited by Anne Commire. Detroit: Gale Research Co., 1977-1978.

YABC 1	Volume 1, 1977
YABC 2	Volume 2, 1978

YABC X This code refers to pseudonym entries which appear as cross-references in the cumulative index to *Yesterday's Authors of Books for Children.*

HIGH-INTEREST BOOKS FOR TEENS

A

AARON, Chester 1923-
AuBYP SUP, ConAu 8NR, SmATA 9, TwCChW 83, WrDr 86

Catch Calico!
KR - v47 - Jl 15 '79 - p795
SLJ - v25 - My '79 - p69
Subject: Cats—Fiction; Grandfathers—Fiction; Rabies—Fiction

Duchess
CE - v59 - My '83 - p352
CLW - v55 - N '83 - p186
CSM - v74 - O 8 '82 - pB12
KR - v50 - S 1 '82 - p999
SE - v47 - Ap '83 - p251
Subject: Ranch life—Fiction

Gideon
BL - v78 - Ap 1 '82 - p1014
BL - v81 - O 1 '84 - p213
BS - v42 - Je '82 - p117
CBRS - v10 - Spring '82 - p114
CCB-B - v35 - Je '82 - p181
CLW - v54 - S '82 - p83
CSM - v74 - O 8 '82 - pB12
Inst - v91 - My '82 - p105
KR - v50 - My 1 '82 - p558
PW - v221 - Je 4 '82 - p67
SLJ - v28 - Ap '82 - p78
Subject: Holocaust, Jewish (1939-1945)—Fiction; World War, 1939-1945—Fiction

AASENG, Nathan 1953-
ConAu 106, SmATA 38

Baseball: You Are The Manager
BL - v82 - O 1 '85 - p273
Cur R - v23 - Ap '84 - p57
RT - v40 - O '86 - p52
SLJ - v32 - N '85 - p93
Subject: Baseball

Eric Heiden: Winner In Gold
BL - v77 - Ja 1 '81 - p627
CCB-B - v34 - F '81 - p105
SLJ - v28 - S '81 - p117
Subject: Ice skaters; Olympic Games

Football's Crushing Blockers
BL - v78 - Jl '82 - p1449
SLJ - v28 - My '82 - p88
VOYA - v5 - Ag '82 - p41
Subject: Football

Football's Cunning Coaches
BL - v78 - O 1 '81 - p241
Hi Lo - v3 - My '82 - p5
SLJ - v28 - D '81 - p84
Subject: Football

Hockey: You Are The Coach
SLJ - v30 - D '83 - p86
Subject: Hockey

Little Giants Of Pro Sports
BL - v77 - O 1 '80 - p258
SLJ - v27 - D '80 - p77
Subject: Athletes

Memorable World Series Moments
BL - v79 - O 1 '82 - p250
Subject: Baseball

Pete Rose: Baseball's Charlie Hustle
BL - v77 - Jl 15 '81 - p1451
CCB-B - v34 - Jl '81 - p205
Hi Lo - v3 - My '82 - p5
SLJ - v28 - O '81 - p137
Subject: Baseball—Biography

Superstars Stopped Short
BL - v78 - Jl '82 - p1449
SLJ - v28 - My '82 - p88
Subject: Athletes

Track's Magnificent Milers
BL - v78 - O 1 '81 - p241
Hi Lo - v3 - My '82 - p5
JB - v47 - D '83 - p239
SLJ - v28 - D '81 - p84
Subject: Runners (Sports); Track and field

Winners Never Quit: Athletes Who Beat The Odds
BL - v77 - O 1 '80 - p258
SLJ - v27 - D '80 - p77
Subject: Athletes; Physically handicapped

AASENG, Nathan (continued)

Winning Men Of Tennis
Hi Lo - v3 - My '82 - p5
Subject: Tennis—Biography

Winning Women Of Tennis
BL - v78 - Ap 1 '82 - p1023
SLJ - v28 - Mr '82 - p142
Subject: Tennis—Biography

ABBE, Kathryn M

Twins On Twins
BL - v77 - My 1 '81 - p1175
BW - v15 - Ap 7 '85 - p12
CSM - v73 - Ap 27 '81 - p14
J Read - v25 - Ap '82 - p710
NW - v97 - Mr 2 '81 - p74
NYTBR - v86 - Mr 1 '81 - p8
SLJ - v28 - S '81 - p150
Co-author: Gill, Frances M
Subject: Twins

ABDUL, Raoul 1929-
ConAu 29R, InB&W 80, SelBAAf, SmATA 12, WhoBlA 85, WhoE 81

The Magic Of Black Poetry
BL - v69 - Ja 1 '73 - p447
BL - v69 - My 1 '73 - p837
CCB-B - v26 - Ja '73 - p69
CSM - v64 - N 8 '72 - pB2
LA - v59 - Mr '82 - p283
LJ - v97 - O 15 '72 - p3450
PW - v202 - O 2 '72 - p54
Subject: Blacks—Poetry

ABELS, Harriette Sheffer

Emmy, Beware!
BL - v78 - S 15 '81 - p99
SLJ - v28 - S '81 - p118
Subject: Department stores—Fiction; Mystery and detective stories

First Impression
SLJ - v31 - Ja '85 - p89
Subject: Love—Fiction

Forgotten World
SLJ - v26 - Ap '80 - p102
Subject: Science fiction

Green Invasion
SLJ - v26 - Ap '80 - p102
Subject: Science fiction

The Haunted Motorcycle Shop
BL - v75 - N 15 '78 - p551
SLJ - v25 - Ja '79 - p49
Subject: Ghosts—Fiction

Medical Emergency
SLJ - v26 - Ap '80 - p102
Subject: Diseases—Fiction; Science fiction

Meteor From The Moon
SLJ - v26 - Ap '80 - p102
Subject: Science fiction

Mystery On Mars
SLJ - v26 - Ap '80 - p102
Subject: Science fiction

Planet Of Ice
SLJ - v26 - Ap '80 - p102
Subject: Science fiction

September Storm
BL - v78 - S 15 '81 - p99
SLJ - v28 - S '81 - p118
Subject: Storms—Fiction

Silent Invaders
SLJ - v26 - Ap '80 - p102
Subject: Science fiction

Strangers On NMA-6
SLJ - v26 - Ap '80 - p102
Subject: Science fiction

Unwanted Visitors
SLJ - v26 - Ap '80 - p102
Subject: Science fiction

ABODAHER, David J 1919-
AuBYP SUP, ConAu 10NR, MichAu 80, SmATA 17

Compacts, Subs And Minis
SLJ - v23 - D '76 - p58
Subject: Automobiles

ABRAMS, Kathleen S

Career Prep: Electronics Servicing
Cur R - v23 - Ap '84 - p33
Hi Lo - v3 - Mr '82 - p1
VOYA - v5 - Ag '82 - p41
Subject: Electronics; Vocational guidance

ABRAMS, Lawrence F
SmATA 47

Mysterious Powers Of The Mind
BL - v78 - Je 15 '82 - p1371

ACKINS, Ralph

Energy Machines
ASBYP - v14 - Fall '81 - p29
JB - v45 - D '81 - p245

ACKINS, Ralph (continued)
SLJ - v27 - F '81 - p53
Subject: Machinery; Power resources

ADAMS, Charlotte 1899-
AuBYP SUP, ConAu 107

The Teen-Ager's Menu Cookbook
BL - v66 - Ap 1 '70 - p966
BS - v29 - D 1 '69 - p350
CCB-B - v24 - Jl '70 - p171
KR - v37 - N 1 '69 - p1155
NYTBR, Pt. 2 - N 9 '69 - p42
SR - v53 - My 9 '70 - p69
Subject: Cookery

ADAMSON, Joy 1910-1980
AnObit 1980, BioIn 12, ConAu 93, ConLC 17, CurBio 72, -80N, FourBJA, NewYTBS 80, SmATA 11, -22N

Elsa And Her Cubs
B&B - v11 - D '65 - p12
Inst - v75 - Ap '66 - p108
LJ - v91 - F 15 '66 - p1060
NYTBR - v72 - D 3 '67 - p103
Par - v41 - D '66 - p21
Subject: Lions—Legends and stories

Forever Free
BS - v23 - Ap 15 '63 - p36
Crit - v21 - Je '63 - p80
CSM - Mr 28 '63 - p15
HB - v39 - Ag '63 - p405
HM - v226 - Je '63 - p110
LJ - v88 - Mr 1 '63 - p1022
LJ - v88 - My 15 '63 - p2156
PW - v192 - Ag 21 '67 - p77
TLS - N 30 '62 - p940
Subject: Lions—Legends and stories

Pippa, The Cheetah, And Her Cubs
BL - v67 - F 15 '71 - p492
CLW - v42 - My '71 - p578
Comw - v93 - N 20 '70 - p205
LJ - v96 - Je 15 '71 - p2123
PW - v198 - D 28 '70 - p61
SB - v6 - Mr '71 - p324
Subject: Animals

ADLER, C S 1932-
ConAu 19NR, ConLC 35, DrAP&F 85, SmATA 26

The Cat That Was Left Behind
BL - v78 - N 15 '81 - p436
CBRS - v10 - Winter '82 - p57
CCB-B - v35 - D '81 - p61
CLW - v53 - My '82 - p448
KR - v50 - Ja 1 '82 - p5
SLJ - v28 - N '81 - p85
Subject: Cats—Fiction; Foster home care—Fiction

Down By The River
BS - v41 - Ja '82 - p400
CBRS - v10 - O '81 - p16
CCB-B - v35 - S '81 - p1
KR - v49 - O 1 '81 - p1238
SLJ - v28 - D '81 - p69
VOYA - v4 - F '82 - p28
Subject: Rivers—Fiction

Fly Free
BL - v80 - Ag '84 - p1622
CBRS - v12 - Je '84 - p115
CCB-B - v37 - Je '84 - p179
HB - v60 - Ag '84 - p471
LA - v62 - Mr '85 - p282
SLJ - v31 - O '84 - p153
VOYA - v7 - O '84 - p194
Subject: Birds; Child abuse—Fiction

The Once In Awhile Hero
B Rpt - v2 - N '83 - p37
Inter BC - v15 - #1 '84 p38
NYTBR - v87 - O 10 '82 - p25
Subject: Bullies—Fiction; Schools—Fiction

Roadside Valentine
BS - v43 - F '84 - p430
CBRS - v12 - O '83 - p18
CCB-B - v37 - Ja '84 - p81
Emerg Lib - v12 - My '85 - p48
HB - v59 - D '83 - p714
SLJ - v30 - F '84 - p78
VOYA - v7 - Je '84 - p94
Subject: Valentine's Day—Fiction

Shadows On Little Reef Bay
BL - v80 - Je 1 '84 - p1395
B Rpt - v3 - S '84 - p31
CBRS - v12 - Jl '84 - p139
CCB-B - v37 - Je '84 - p179
Cur R - v24 - My '85 - p5
SLJ - v30 - My '84 - p103
VOYA - v7 - O '84 - p194
Subject: Drug abuse—Fiction; Smuggling—Fiction

Shelter On Blue Barns Road
BL - v77 - My 1 '81 - p1192
BS - v41 - My '81 - p77
CBRS - v9 - F '81 - p55
CCB-B - v35 - S '81 - p1
HB - v57 - Ap '81 - p187

ADLER, C S (continued)
J Read - v25 - O '81 - p88
KR - v49 - My 1 '81 - p569
PW - v219 - Mr 13 '81 - p89
SLJ - v27 - Ja '81 - p66
Subject: Dogs—Fiction; Family problems—Fiction

ADLER, David A 1947-
ConAu 7NR, SmATA 14

Hyperspace!: Facts And Fun From All Over The Universe
ASBYP - v16 - Fall '83 - p10
BL - v81 - O 15 '84 - p314
CLW - v55 - D '83 - p230
PW - v222 - O 22 '82 - p56
SB - v19 - S '83 - p30
Subject: Astronomy

ADLER, Irving 1913-
AuBYP, ConAu 2NR, SmATA 29, ThrBJA

Calendar
BL - v64 - Mr 1 '68 - p777
LJ - v93 - Ja 15 '68 - p287
SB - v3 - Mr '68 - p298
Co-author: Adler, Ruth
Subject: Calendar

Communication
CCB-B - v21 - Ja '68 - p73
KR - v35 - Je 1 '67 - p646
LJ - v92 - Jl '67 - p2646
Co-author: Adler, Ruth
Subject: Communication

Language And Man
BL - v67 - Mr 15 '71 - p618
CCB-B - v25 - O '71 - p21
KR - v38 - D 1 '70 - p1292
SA - v225 - D '71 - p109
Co-author: Adler, Joyce
Subject: Language and languages

Mathematics: Exploring The World Of Numbers And Space
B&B - v11 - Je '66 - p60
Subject: Mathematics

ADLER, Joyce
see Adler, Irving (co-author)

ADLER, Ruth
see Adler, Irving (co-author)

ADLER, William
see David, Jay

ADOFF, Arnold 1935-
AuBYP, AuNews 1, ChlLR 7, ConAu 20NR, FourBJA, MorBMP, SmATA 5, TwCChW 83, WrDr 86

Brothers And Sisters: Modern Stories By Black Americans
BL - v67 - D 15 '70 - p335
Comw - v93 - N 20 '70 - p202
KR - v38 - Ag 1 '70 - p807
LJ - v95 - D 15 '70 - p4359
Subject: American fiction—Black authors; Short stories

Celebrations: A New Anthology Of Black American Poetry
BL - v74 - F 1 '78 - p901
CCB-B - v31 - Mr '78 - p105
Cur R - v17 - Ag '78 - p176
EJ - v67 - Ap '78 - p97
HB - v54 - Ap '78 - p180
SLJ - v24 - Mr '78 - p135
Subject: American poetry (Collections); American poetry—Black authors

I Am The Darker Brother
BL - v65 - Ap 1 '69 - p900
BL - v81 - S 15 '84 - p123
Bl W - v20 - Ag '71 - p95
Comw - v89 - F 21 '69 - p645
CSM - v61 - My 1 '69 - pB7
Poet - v113 - Ja '69 - p265
RR - v86 - Mr '69 - p176
SE - v33 - My '69 - p560
Subject: American poetry—Black authors

It Is The Poem Singing Into Your Eyes
BL - v68 - D 15 '71 - p363
CCB-B - v25 - Ja '72 - p69
CE - v48 - My '72 - p424
CLW - v43 - F '72 - p358
Comw - v95 - N 19 '71 - p191
EJ - v61 - Mr '72 - p436
KR - v39 - O 1 '71 - p1080
LJ - v96 - S 15 '71 - p2923
SR - v54 - Ag 21 '71 - p26
SR - v54 - D 11 '71 - p46
Subject: American poetry—Black authors

Malcolm X
BL - v66 - Jl 1 '70 - p1339
BL - v67 - Ap 1 '71 - p659
BL - v69 - My 1 '73 - p836
CCB-B - v24 - S '70 - p1
Inst - v82 - N '72 - p136
KR - v38 - Ap 15 '70 - p456
LJ - v95 - S 15 '70 - p3044

ADOFF, Arnold (continued)
NYTBR, Pt. 2 - My 24 '70 - p39
PW - v197 - Ap 20 '70 - p62
Teacher - v90 - Mr '73 - p81
TN - v27 - Ja '71 - p208
Subject: Blacks—Biography; Little, Malcolm

My Black Me
BL - v70 - Jl 1 '74 - p1197
BL - v71 - Mr 15 '75 - p765
CCB-B - v28 - O '74 - p21
Choice - v12 - N '75 - p1130
KR - v42 - Ap 15 '74 - p427
LA - v59 - Mr '82 - p283
LJ - v99 - S 15 '74 - p2258
NYTBR - My 5 '74 - p38
PW - v205 - Jl 1 '74 - p82
Subject: American poetry—Black authors; Blacks—Poetry

ADORJAN, Carol 1934-
ConAu 41R, IntAu&W 77, SmATA 10, WhoAmW 87

The Cat Sitter Mystery
BL - v70 - O 15 '73 - p226
JB - v44 - Ag '80 - p171
LJ - v98 - D 15 '73 - p3717
NYTBR - My 20 '73 - p10
Subject: Mystery and detective stories

ADRIAN, Mary (pseud.) 1908-
AuBYP, ConAu X, SmATA X, WhoAmW 75
Real Name:
Jorgensen, Mary Venn

The American Alligator
BW - v2 - F 25 '68 - p16
CSM - v59 - N 2 '67 - pB11
LJ - v93 - F 15 '68 - p857
NYTBR - v72 - N 5 '67 - p52
SB - v3 - D '67 - p241
Subject: Alligators

AHLSTROM, Mark E

The Canada Goose
BL - v80 - Ag '84 - p1622
BL - v81 - Je 15 '85 - p1453
CBRS - v12 - Ag '84 - p149
SB - v20 - Mr '85 - p218
Subject: Geese

The Foxes
BL - v79 - Ag '83 - p1460
SLJ - v30 - S '83 - p114
Subject: Foxes

AIKEN, Conrad 1889-1973
AmWr, BioIn 11, -13, ConAu 4NR, ConLC 1, -3, -5, -10, DcLB 9, -45, OxAmL 83, SmATA 30, WebAB 79

Cats And Bats And Things With Wings: Poems
BL - v62 - Mr 1 '66 - p660
CCB-B - v19 - O '65 - p25
Comw - v83 - N 5 '65 - p156
CSM - v57 - N 4 '65 - pB4
HB - v42 - F '66 - p62
Inst - v75 - Ja '66 - p140
KR - v33 - Ag 1 '65 - p746
LJ - v90 - S 15 '65 - p3776
NYTBR - v70 - O 24 '65 - p34
Subject: Fairy tales; Verses for children

AIKEN, Joan 1924-
BioIn 11, ChlLR 1, ConAu 4NR, ConLC 35, OxChL, SenS, SmATA 30, -1AS, TwCChW 78, TwCCr&M 85, WrDr 86

Night Fall
Am - v125 - D 4 '71 - p490
B&B - v14 - Ag '69 - p48
BL - v67 - Jl 15 '71 - p950
BS - v31 - Jl 15 '71 - p190
BS - v32 - S 1 '72 - p262
CE - v48 - D '71 - p149
Comw - v95 - N 19 '71 - p188
HB - v47 - O '71 - p487
KR - v39 - My 1 '71 - p508
LJ - v96 - My 15 '71 - p1821
PW - v199 - Je 28 '71 - p63
SLJ - v24 - F '78 - p35
Subject: Mystery and detective stories

The Stolen Lake
Brit Bk N C - Autumn '81 - p22
CBRS - v10 - S '81 - p6
GP - v20 - Jl '81 - p3920
HB - v57 - O '81 - p532
LA - v59 - Ap '82 - p373
NS - v102 - D 4 '81 - p20
NYTBR - v87 - F 14 '82 - p28
S Fict R - v12 - Ag '83 - p31
SLJ - v28 - O '81 - p137
TES - Je 5 '81 - p37
TLS - Jl 24 '81 - p839
VOYA - v5 - Ap '82 - p38
Subject: Adventure and adventurers—Fiction

The Whispering Mountain
B&B - v15 - Ag '70 - p54
BL - v66 - Ja 1 '70 - p563

AIKEN, Joan (continued)
CCB-B - v23 - Ap '70 - p123
CE - v46 - Mr '70 - p319
Econ - v237 - D 26 '70 - p38
HB - v46 - F '70 - p39
KR - v37 - N 1 '69 - p1146
LJ - v94 - D 15 '69 - p4610
Obs - D 6 '70 - p23
PW - v196 - D 29 '69 - p67
SR - v53 - Ap 18 '70 - p37
Subject: Fantasy

Winterthing
B&B - v18 - Jl '73 - p140
BL - v69 - Ja 15 '73 - p490
CCB-B - v26 - F '73 - p85
HB - v49 - Ap '73 - p149
KR - v40 - N 15 '72 - p1314
LJ - v97 - D 15 '72 - p4075
NYTBR, pt. 1 - F 11 '73 - p8
Teacher - v92 - D '74 - p14
TLS - Je 15 '73 - p681
TN - v29 - Je '73 - p356
Subject: Plays

AINSWORTH, Norma Ruedi
ConAu 13R, SmATA 9, WhoAmW 75, WhoE 77

Mystery Of The Crying Child
WCRB - v3 - S '77 - p57
Subject: Mystery and detective stories

AKS, Patricia

Change Of Heart
BL - v80 - Ja 1 '84 - p675
VOYA - v7 - Ap '84 - p26
Subject: Love—Fiction; Sports—Fiction

The Searching Heart
Kliatt - v18 - Winter '84 - p4
SLJ - v30 - Mr '84 - p168
Subject: Adoption—Fiction

ALAUX, Michel

Modern Fencing: Foil Epee, Sabre From Initiation To Competition
Kliatt - v15 - Fall '81 - p71
Subject: Fencing

ALBERT, Louise 1928-
ConAu 69

But I'm Ready To Go
BB - v5 - Mr '77 - p4
CCB-B - v30 - F '77 - p85
CLW - v48 - My '77 - p442
Comw - v103 - N 19 '76 - p763
Cur R - v16 - Ag '77 - p206
J Read - v24 - Mr '81 - p522
KR - v44 - S 1 '76 - p980
SLJ - v23 - O '76 - p113
TN - v36 - Winter '80 - p208
Subject: Mentally ill—Fiction

ALDEN, Raymond Macdonald 1873-1924
BioIn 1, WhAm 1

Why The Chimes Rang, And Other Stories
NYTBR - D 2 '45 - p42
Subject: Short stories

ALDERMAN, Clifford Lindsey 1902-
AuBYP, ConAu 3NR, SmATA 3

Annie Oakley And The World Of Her Time
CLW - v51 - My '80 - p459
Subject: Biography; Entertainers

A Cauldron Of Witches
BL - v68 - O 15 '71 - p189
Inst - v82 - My '73 - p78
KR - v39 - Jl 15 '71 - p747
LJ - v96 - O 15 '71 - p3472
NYTBR, Pt. 2 - N 7 '71 - p42
Teacher - v90 - Ap '73 - p90
Subject: Witchcraft

The Devil's Shadow
BS - v30 - O 15 '70 - p300
PW - v198 - S 28 '70 - p82
Subject: Witchcraft

Witchcraft In America
BL - v71 - N 1 '74 - p282
BL - v71 - N 1 '74 - p286
KR - v42 - O 1 '74 - p1068
SE - v39 - Mr '75 - p173
SLJ - v21 - Mr '75 - p103
Subject: Witchcraft

ALDRIDGE, James 1918-
BioIn 10, ConAu 13NR, ConNov 86, CurBio 43, IntAu&W 77, Novels, OxAusL, Who 85, WrDr 86

A Sporting Proposition
BL - v70 - O 15 '73 - p207
BL - v70 - O 15 '73 - p220
BS - v33 - O 1 '73 - p289
BW - v7 - S 23 '73 - p15
CLW - v45 - Mr '74 - p396
EJ - v64 - Ja '75 - p112
KR - v41 - Jl 1 '73 - p697
KR - v41 - Jl 15 '73 - p764

ALDRIDGE, James (continued)
LJ - v98 - Ag '73 - p2330
NYTBR - D 9 '73 - p47
PW - v204 - Jl 23 '73 - p61
Subject: Horses—Fiction

ALEXANDER, Bea

In The Long Run
BL - v80 - F 1 '84 - p809
SLJ - v30 - Ag '84 - p79
VOYA - v7 - Je '84 - p91
Subject: Love—Fiction; Marathon running—Fiction

ALEXANDER, Lloyd 1924-
ChILR 1, -5, ConAu 1NR, ConLC 35, DcLB 52, MorBMP, PiP, SmATA 49, TwCChW 83, WhoAm 86, WrDr 86

The Marvelous Misadventures Of Sebastian
BL - v67 - N 15 '70 - p266
BL - v67 - Ap 1 '71 - p659
BW - v4 - N 8 '70 - p10
BW - v7 - My 13 '73 - p7
CCB-B - v24 - F '71 - p85
CE - v47 - My '71 - p437
CLW - v43 - N '71 - p174
HB - v46 - D '70 - p628
LJ - v95 - N 15 '70 - p4040
LJ - v95 - D 15 '70 - p4324
NYTBR - N 15 '70 - p42
PW - v198 - N 2 '70 - p53
SR - v54 - Ja 23 '71 - p71
Subject: Musicians—Fiction

Time Cat: The Remarkable Journeys Of Jason And Gareth
LJ - v88 - Je 15 '63 - p2548
NS - v66 - N 8 '63 - p668
NYTBR - Ap 14 '63 - p56
PW - v194 - Jl 22 '68 - p65
SR - v46 - My 11 '63 - p49
TLS - N 28 '63 - p980
Subject: Cats—Fiction

ALEXANDER, Marsha

Popularity Plus
SLJ - v33 - D '86 - p111
Subject: Love—Fiction

ALEXANDER, Paul
see Bridges, Laurie (co-author)

ALEXANDER, Rae Pace 1898-1974
ConAu X, SmATA X, WhAm 6, WhoBlA 75

Pseud./variant:
Alexander, Raymond Pace

Young And Black In America
BL - v67 - Ja 15 '71 - p418
BW - v4 - N 8 '70 - p5
CCB-B - v24 - Ap '71 - p117
Inst - v130 - Ap '71 - p135
KR - v38 - S 15 '70 - p1052
LJ - v96 - F 15 '71 - p729
NYRB - v15 - D 17 '70 - p10
NYTBR - D 6 '70 - p58
NYTBR, Pt. 2 - N 8 '70 - p2
NYTBR, Pt. 2 - N 8 '70 - p36
PW - v198 - N 9 '70 - p61
SR - v54 - Mr 20 '71 - p31
TN - v27 - Ap '71 - p305
Subject: Blacks—Biography

ALEXANDER, Sue 1933-
ConAu 19NR, SmATA 12

Finding Your First Job
BL - v77 - O 15 '80 - p322
Hi Lo - v2 - S '80 - p3
Inter BC - v12 - #7 '81 p21
J Read - v24 - Mr '81 - p549
KR - v48 - Jl 1 '80 - p842
SLJ - v27 - Mr '81 - p153
Subject: Vocational guidance

ALFANO, Pete

Super Bowl Superstars: The Most Valuable Players In The NFL's Championship Game
BL - v79 - Ja 1 '83 - p622
B Rpt - v2 - My '83 - p50
Hi Lo - v4 - Mr '83 - p4
SLJ - v29 - D '82 - p85
Subject: Football

ALLAN, Mabel Esther 1915-
AuBYP, ConAu 18NR, OxChL, SmATA 32, TwCChW 83, WrDr 86

The Ballet Family
BS - v26 - Ag 1 '66 - p173
CCB-B - v20 - S '66 - p2
KR - v34 - F 15 '66 - p185
Subject: Ballet dancing

The Horns Of Danger
BL - v78 - S 15 '81 - p100
CBRS - v10 - F '82 - p64
CCB-B - v35 - Ap '82 - p141
SLJ - v28 - D '81 - p83
Subject: Folk dancing—Fiction; Midlands—Fiction; Mystery and detective stories

ALLAN, Mabel Esther (continued)

Mystery Began In Madeira
B&B - v13 - D '67 - p42
KR - v35 - My 1 '67 - p564
LJ - v92 - My 15 '67 - p2039
PW - v194 - O 7 '68 - p54
Subject: Mystery and detective stories

ALLEN, Betty 1896-

Mind Your Manners
BL - v61 - Je 1 '65 - p953
CC - v82 - Je 30 '65 - p838
LJ - v90 - Jl '65 - p3129
Co-author: Briggs, Mitchell Pirie
Subject: Etiquette

ALLEN, Elizabeth 1914-
ConAu X
Pseud./variant:
Thompson, Elizabeth Allen

You Can't Say What You Think
BL - v64 - My 15 '68 - p1085
BS - v28 - Ap 1 '68 - p17
BW - v2 - Ag 11 '68 - p12
CCB-B - v21 - My '68 - p137
KR - v36 - Mr 1 '68 - p268
NYTBR - v73 - N 3 '68 - p10
PW - v193 - Ap 29 '68 - p78
SR - v51 - Ap 20 '68 - p41

ALLEN, Henry Wilson
see Henry, Will

ALLEN, Maury 1932-
ConAu 11NR, SmATA 26

Reggie Jackson: The Three Million Dollar Man
Hi Lo - v2 - O '80 - p6
Subject: Baseball—Biography; Blacks—Biography

Ron Guidry: Louisiana Lightning
CCB-B - v33 - Ja '80 - p86
Hi Lo - v2 - S '80 - p5
SLJ - v26 - D '79 - p102
Subject: Baseball—Biography

ALLISON, Jon

The Pro Basketball Reading Kit
Hi Lo - v2 - S '80 - p5
Subject: Basketball

ALLMAN, Paul

No Pain, No Gain
KR - v54 - D 1 '86 - p1796
Subject: Ethics—Fiction; Football—Fiction

ALMEDINGEN, E M 1898-1971
AuBYP SUP, ConAu X, ConLC 12, OxChL, SmATA 3, ThrBJA, TwCChW 83, WorAu
Pseud./variant:
Almedingen, Martha Edith Von

Katia
BL - v63 - Jl 15 '67 - p1192
CCB-B - v20 - Jl '67 - p165
HB - v43 - Ap '67 - p210
KR - v35 - Ja 15 '67 - p60
LJ - v92 - Je 15 '67 - p2448
NYTBR - v72 - Ag 6 '67 - p27
PW - v191 - Mr 27 '67 - p61
SR - v50 - My 13 '67 - p56
Subject: Russia—Fiction

ALMEDINGEN, Martha Edith Von
see Almedingen, E M

ALTER, Robert Edmond 1925-1965
AuBYP, BioIn 7, ConAu 1NR, SmATA 9

Two Sieges Of The Alamo
BS - v25 - Ag 15 '65 - p214
HB - v42 - F '66 - p64
KR - v33 - Jl 1 '65 - p631
LJ - v90 - S 15 '65 - p3800
Subject: Alamo—Siege, 1836—Fiction

Who Goes Next?
LJ - v91 - N 15 '66 - p5753
Subject: Escapes

ALTMAN, Linda Jacobs

Nobody Wants Annie
BL - v81 - My 1 '85 - p1240
Subject: Schools—Fiction

ALTMAN, Millys N

Racing In Her Blood
BS - v40 - Ag '80 - p191
CCB-B - v34 - S '80 - p1
Hi Lo - v2 - F '81 - p6
J Read - v24 - Mr '81 - p549
SLJ - v26 - Ag '80 - p73
SLJ - v27 - My '81 - p26
Subject: Automobile racing—Fiction

AMES, Lee Judah 1921-
AuBYP, ConAu 18NR, IlsCB 1957, –1967, SmATA 3, WhoAmA 84

Draw 50 Airplanes, Aircraft And Spacecraft
BL - v74 - O 1 '77 - p284
SLJ - v24 - Ja '78 - p84
Subject: Airplanes; Drawing—Technique; Space vehicles

Draw 50 Famous Cartoons
SLJ - v26 - S '79 - p126
Subject: Cartooning

Draw 50 Famous Faces
CCB-B - v32 - D '78 - p58
SLJ - v25 - F '79 - p50
Subject: Drawing—Technique

AMES, Mildred 1919-
ConAu 11NR, FifBJA, SmATA 22

The Dancing Madness
BL - v77 - O 15 '80 - p323
BS - v40 - Ja '81 - p348
CBRS - v9 - D '80 - p26
CCB-B - v34 - N '80 - p45
CLW - v52 - My '81 - p452
HB - v57 - F '81 - p56
J Read - v24 - Ap '81 - p647
KR - v49 - F 1 '81 - p144
NYTBR - v86 - F 1 '81 - p28
PW - v218 - O 31 '80 - p86
SLJ - v27 - O '80 - p152
VOYA - v3 - F '81 - p27
Subject: Brothers and sisters—Fiction; Mothers and daughters—Fiction

AMES, Rose Wyler
see Wyler, Rose

AMON, Aline 1928-
AuBYP SUP, ConAu 8NR, SmATA 9

Reading, Writing, Chattering Chimps
ACSB - v9 - Winter '76 - p5
BB - v3 - N '75 - p3
BL - v72 - N 15 '75 - p448
CCB-B - v29 - F '76 - p90
CLW - v47 - Ap '76 - p409
HB - v51 - D '75 - p604
KR - v43 - O 1 '75 - p1133
SA - v235 - D '76 - p134
SB - v12 - My '76 - p41
SLJ - v22 - S '75 - p94
Subject: Chimpanzees; Communication

ANASTOS, Ernie

'Twixt: Teens Yesterday And Today
SLJ - v30 - F '84 - p79
Co-author: Levin, Jack
Subject: Youth

ANCKARSVARD, Karin 1915-1969
AuBYP, ConAu 9R, –103, SmATA 6, ThrBJA

The Robber Ghost
BL - v57 - Je 15 '61 - p642
CSM - Mr 30 '61 - p7
HB - v37 - Ap '61 - p157
KR - v28 - D 15 '61 - p1031
LJ - v86 - Ap 15 '61 - p1684
NYTBR, Pt. 2 - My 14 '61 - p34
SR - v44 - Je 24 '61 - p20
Subject: Sweden—Fiction

ANDERSON, Alan H, Jr. 1943-
ConAu 69, WrDr 86

The Drifting Continents
BL - v68 - Ja 15 '72 - p428
CCB-B - v25 - F '72 - p85
HB - v48 - Ap '72 - p169
KR - v39 - O 15 '71 - p1133
LJ - v97 - Ja 15 '72 - p286
SB - v8 - My '72 - p38
SR - v55 - Ja 15 '72 - p47
TN - v28 - Je '72 - p433
Subject: Continental drift

ANDERSON, David

The Piano Makers
ASBYP - v16 - Spring '83 - p10
BL - v79 - D 1 '82 - p495
CCB-B - v36 - F '83 - p102
HB - v59 - Ap '83 - p181
Inst - v92 - Mr '83 - p19
Inter BC - v14 - #7 '83 p34
KR - v50 - O 1 '82 - p1107
NYTBR - v88 - Ja 16 '83 - p22
SLJ - v29 - D '82 - p62
Subject: Piano—Construction

ANDERSON, Doug 1919-
BioIn 2, WhoAmA 82

Eye Spy
SLJ - v27 - D '80 - p72
Subject: Puzzles; Visual perception

ANDERSON, Joy 1928-
ConAu 25R, SmATA 1

The Pai-Pai Pig
BL - v64 - N 15 '67 - p384

ANDERSON, Joy (continued)
BW - v1 - N 5 '67 - p45
Comw - v87 - N 10 '67 - p180
KR - v35 - Ag 1 '67 - p875
LJ - v92 - O 15 '67 - p3845
Subject: Short stories

ANDERSON, Lavere 1907-
ConAu 101, SmATA 27, WhoAmW 81, WhoS&SW 80

Allan Pinkerton: First Private Eye
LJ - v97 - S 15 '72 - p2944
Subject: Biography; Detectives

Balto
SLJ - v23 - F '77 - p60
Subject: Alaska—Fiction; Diptheria—Fiction; Sled dogs-Fiction

Mary Mcleod Bethune
Cur R - v16 - D '77 - p363
SLJ - v23 - S '76 - p93
Subject: Biography; Blacks—Biography

ANDERSON, Mary 1939-
AuBYP SUP, BioIn 10, ConAu 16NR, IntAu&W 82

Catch Me, I'm Falling In Love
BL - v82 - S 1 '85 - p52
BS - v45 - N '85 - p319
CBRS - v14 - O '85 - p18
CCB-B - v39 - D '85 - p61
PW - v228 - O 4 '85 - p77
SLJ - v32 - O '85 - p178
VOYA - v9 - Ap '86 - p26
Subject: Family problems—Fiction

Step On A Crack
B&B - v6 - S '78 - p3
BL - v74 - Ap 1 '78 - p1247
CCB-B - v32 - S '78 - p2
CLW - v50 - S '78 - p91
HB - v54 - Je '78 - p282
KR - v46 - F 15 '78 - p182
LA - v56 - Ja '79 - p53
SLJ - v24 - Ap '78 - p90
Subject: Family life—Fiction

ANDES, Eugene

Practical Macrame
LJ - v96 - S 15 '71 - p2760
Subject: Macrame

ANDREWS, Jeanne

All's Fair In Love
Kliatt - v17 - Winter '83 - p4
SLJ - v29 - Ja '83 - p80

ANDREWS, Julie 1935-
AuBYP SUP, BiDFilm, ConAu 37R, CurBio 56, HalFC 84, NewYTBS 82, SmATA 7, WhoAmW 87, WhoThe 81, WrDr 86

Mandy
BL - v68 - Mr 15 '72 - p628
CCB-B - v25 - Je '72 - p154
CSM - v63 - N 11 '71 - pB5
Inst - v81 - F '72 - p139
KR - v39 - O 15 '71 - p1119
LJ - v96 - D 15 '71 - p4183
PW - v200 - D 13 '71 - p42
Teacher - v90 - Ap '73 - p85
Time - v98 - D 27 '71 - p60
TLS - N 3 '72 - p1330
Subject: Orphans—Fiction

ANDREWS, Wendy

Are We There Yet?
CCB-B - v38 - Je '85 - p179
SLJ - v31 - My '85 - p98
VOYA - v8 - Ag '85 - p182
Subject: Texas—Fiction

Vacation Fever!
BL - v80 - Ag '84 - p1608
CBRS - v12 - Ag '84 - p149
CCB-B - v37 - Jl '84 - p199
Kliatt - v19 - Spring '85 - p4
RT - v39 - O '85 - p46
SLJ - v31 - O '84 - p164
VOYA - v7 - O '84 - p194
Subject: Vacations—Fiction

ANEMA, Durlynn

Sharing An Apartment
Hi Lo - v4 - S '82 - p2
VOYA - v6 - Ag '83 - p156
Subject: Dwellings

ANGELL, Judie 1937-
BioIn 13, ConAu 77, SmATA 22

Dear Lola: Or How To Build Your Own Family
BL - v77 - Ja 1 '81 - p622
CBRS - v9 - N '80 - p25
CCB-B - v34 - F '81 - p105
GP - v22 - Ja '84 - p4186
HB - v57 - F '81 - p48
Kliatt - v16 - Spring '82 - p4
KR - v49 - Ja 1 '81 - p5
PW - v218 - N 7 '80 - p61

ANGELL, Judie (continued)
SLJ - v27 - Ja '81 - p56
Subject: Orphans—Fiction; Runaways—Fiction

In Summertime It's Tuffy
BL - v73 - Je 1 '77 - p1492
BW - Ag 14 '77 - pF4
BW - Jl 8 '79 - pE2
CCB-B - v31 - O '77 - p25
Comw - v104 - N 11 '77 - p730
Kliatt - v13 - Fall '79 - p4
KR - v45 - My 1 '77 - p485
NYTBR - O 9 '77 - p28
PW - v211 - My 30 '77 - p45
SLJ - v23 - My '77 - p58
Subject: Camping—Fiction

One-Way To Ansonia
BL - v82 - Ja 1 '86 - p682
BS - v46 - Ap '86 - p38
CBRS - v14 - Ja '86 - p53
CCB-B - v39 - N '85 - p42
EJ - v75 - S '86 - p81
HB - v62 - Mr '86 - p205
LA - v63 - Mr '86 - p301
SLJ - v32 - D '85 - p85
VOYA - v8 - F '86 - p382
Subject: Emigration and immigration—Fiction; Jews—Fiction; Russian Americans—Fiction

Ronnie And Rosey
BB - v6 - My '78 - p3
CCB-B - v31 - Ap '78 - p121
HB - v54 - Ap '78 - p161
KR - v45 - O 15 '77 - p1096
SLJ - v24 - D '77 - p52
TN - v37 - Fall '80 - p56
Subject: Death—Fiction; Friendship—Fiction

Secret Selves
CBRS - v8 - N '79 - p25
CCB-B - v33 - Ja '80 - p86
Emerg Lib - v9 - Ja '82 - p33
HB - v56 - F '80 - p52
KR - v48 - Ja 1 '80 - p8
SLJ - v26 - N '79 - p73
Subject: Self-perception—Fiction

Tina Gogo
Obs - Ag 26 '84 - p19
RT - v32 - Ja '79 - p488
Subject: Foster home care—Fiction; Friendship—Fiction

ANGIER, Bradford
see Dixon, Jeanne (co-author)

ANNIXTER, Jane (pseud.) 1903-
AuBYP, ConAu X, MichAu 80, SmATA 1, WhoAmW 75
Real Name:
Sturtzel, Jane Levington

Ahmeek
KR - v38 - O 13 '70 - p
PW - v198 - S 28 '70 - p80
SR - v53 - S 19 '70 - p35
Co-author: Annixter, Paul
Subject: Beavers

see also Annixter, Paul for additional titles

ANNIXTER, Paul (pseud.) 1894-
BioIn 6, ConAu X, SmATA 1
Real Name:
Sturtzel, Howard A

Swiftwater
BL - v46 - Ja 1 '50 - p160
KR - v17 - N 1 '49 - p613
LJ - v74 - D 1 '49 - p1818
LJ - v75 - Ap 15 '50 - p706
NYTBR - Ja 22 '50 - p26
SR - v33 - F 11 '50 - p36

see also Annixter, Jane (co-author) for additional titles

ANONYMOUS

Go Ask Alice
B&B - v18 - Ja '73 - p99
BL - v68 - Mr 15 '72 - p611
BL - v68 - Ap 1 '72 - p663
BS - v32 - S 1 '72 - p263
CLW - v43 - D '71 - p219
Comw - v95 - N 19 '71 - p190
CSM - v63 - N 11 '71 - pB6
EJ - v62 - Ja '73 - p146
KR - v39 - Jl 15 '71 - p776
LJ - v97 - Mr 15 '72 - p1174
LJ - v97 - My 15 '72 - p1884
NYTBR - S 9 '73 - p8
NYTBR, Pt. 2 - N 5 '72 - p42
PW - v201 - Mr 27 '72 - p80
Teacher - v90 - F '73 - p126
TLS - S 1 '72 - p1012
TN - v28 - Ap '72 - p311
Subject: Drug abuse—Fiction

see also Sparks, Beatrice for additional titles

ANTONOPULOS, Barbara

The Abominable Snowman
Cur R - v17 - Ag '78 - p228
SLJ - v25 - S '78 - p128
Subject: Yeti

APSLER, Alfred 1907-
AuBYP SUP, ConAu 3NR, IntAu&W 77, SmATA 10, WrDr 84

Fighter For Independence: Jawaharlal Nehru
HB - v40 - Ap '64 - p186
LJ - v88 - S 15 '63 - p3360
SR - v47 - Ap 25 '64 - p41
Subject: Biography

ARCHER, Elsie

Let's Face It: The Guide To Good Grooming For Girls Of Color
KR - v36 - Ag 15 '68 - p909
Subject: Beauty (Personal); Etiquette

ARCHER, Jeffrey Howard 1940-
WrDr 86

Shall We Tell The President?
BL - v74 - N 15 '77 - p525
BS - v37 - D '77 - p259
BW - Ag 28 '77 - pF2
KR - v45 - Ag 1 '77 - p796
LJ - v102 - O 15 '77 - p2178
NS - v94 - N 4 '77 - p625
NYT - v127 - O 10 '77 - p33
NYTBR - O 23 '77 - p36
Obs - N 27 '77 - p28
PW - v212 - Ag 8 '77 - p63
PW - v214 - Ag 7 '78 - p81
SLJ - v24 - D '77 - p65
SR - v5 - O 15 '77 - p36
TLS - O 28 '77 - p1258
VV - v22 - O 24 '77 - p105

ARCHIBALD, Joe 1898-1986
AuBYP, ConAu 5NR, –9R, SmATA 3, –X
Pseud./variant:
Archibald, Joseph S

Commander Of The Flying Tigers: Claire Lee Chennault
BL - v62 - Jl 1 '66 - p1042
BS - v26 - Jl 1 '66 - p140
KR - v34 - Ja 15 '66 - p62
LJ - v91 - Ap 15 '66 - p2215
Subject: Biography

Go, Navy, Go
KR - v24 - Ag 1 '56 - p525
NYTBR, Pt. 2 - N 18 '56 - p30

Phantom Blitz
PW - v203 - Ja 22 '73 - p70
Subject: Football—Fiction

Southpaw Speed
KR - v34 - F 15 '66 - p191
LJ - v91 - Jl '66 - p3550

ARDEN, William (pseud.) 1924-
ConAu X, EncMys, SmATA X, TwCCr&M 85, WrDr 86
Real Name:
Lynds, Dennis

Alfred Hitchcock And The Three Investigators In The Mystery Of The Dancing Devil
SLJ - v23 - F '77 - p60
Subject: Mystery and detective stories

The Mystery Of The Purple Pirate
BL - v79 - Mr 15 '83 - p962
SLJ - v29 - D '82 - p82
Subject: Mystery and detective stories; Pirates—Fiction

The Secret Of The Crooked Cat
Hi Lo - v2 - Je '81 - p3
Subject: Mystery and detective stories

see also Lynds, Dennis for additional titles

ARMSTRONG, Fiona

Getting Ready For The World Of Work
Hi Lo - Je '80 - p4
Subject: Applications for positions; Vocational guidance

You And The World Of Work
Hi Lo - Je '80 - p4
Subject: Vocational guidance

ARMSTRONG, Louise
AuBYP SUP, ConAu 117, SmATA 43, WhAmArt 85

Saving The Big-Deal Baby
BS - v40 - O '80 - p263
CBRS - v8 - Jl '80 - p124
CCB-B - v34 - D '80 - p65
Hi Lo - v2 - S '80 - p3
J Read - v24 - Mr '81 - p549
KR - v48 - Jl 1 '80 - p840
SLJ - v27 - S '80 - p66
Subject: Child abuse—Fiction; Parent and child—Fiction

ARMSTRONG, William Howard 1914-
AuNews 1, ChlLR 1, ConAu 9NR, MorBMP, OxChL, SmATA 4, ThrBJA, TwCChW 83, WhoAm 86, WrDr 86

Sounder
A Lib - v1 - Ap '70 - p384
Am - v121 - D 13 '69 - p594
BL - v66 - D 1 '69 - p454
BL - v69 - My 1 '73 - p838
BL - v82 - F 1 '86 - p817
BS - v29 - N 1 '69 - p305
CCB-B - v23 - D '69 - p54
CE - v46 - Mr '70 - p319
CE - v46 - Ap '70 - p368
CLW - v41 - Mr '70 - p477
Comw - v91 - N 21 '69 - p257
Comw - v93 - F 26 '71 - p522
CSM - v61 - N 6 '69 - pB9
HB - v45 - D '69 - p673
Inst - v79 - D '69 - p114
KR - v37 - O 1 '69 - p1063
Lis - v86 - N 11 '71 - p661
LJ - v94 - D 15 '69 - p4580
LJ - v94 - D 15 '69 - p4610
NO - v8 - D 29 '69 - p17
NS - v81 - Je 4 '71 - p778
NYTBR - O 26 '69 - p42
NYTBR - D 7 '69 - p66
NYTBR, Pt. 2 - N 9 '69 - p60
NYTBR, Pt. 2 - F 13 '72 - p14
NYTBR, Pt. 2 - N 5 '72 - p42
Obs - Ap 4 '71 - p36
PW - v196 - N 24 '69 - p42
SLJ - v31 - Ag '85 - p28
SR - v52 - D 20 '69 - p30
Teacher - v90 - Ja '73 - p90
TES - Je 10 '83 - p22
TLS - Jl 2 '71 - p765
TLS - Ap 6 '73 - p381
TN - v26 - Ap '70 - p307
WSJ - v175 - F 18 '70 - p18
Subject: Blacks—Fiction; Poverty—Fiction

ARNOLD, Caroline 1944-
ConAu 107, SmATA 36

The Summer Olympics
BL - v80 - O 1 '83 - p302
Cur R - v23 - Ap '84 - p58
SLJ - v30 - D '83 - p86
Subject: Olympic Games

ARNOV, Boris, Jr. 1926-
AuBYP, ConAu 3NR, SmATA 12

Water
ASBYP - v14 - Winter '81 - p12
CE - v57 - N '80 - p113
HB - v56 - Ag '80 - p440
RT - v34 - D '80 - p352
SB - v16 - N '80 - p91
SLJ - v27 - F '81 - p61
Subject: Water—Experiments

ARQUETTE, Lois S
see Duncan, Lois S

ARRICK, Fran

Steffie Can't Come Out To Play
BL - v75 - D 1 '78 - p606
BS - v38 - Mr '79 - p406
CCB-B - v32 - Mr '79 - p110
EJ - v68 - Mr '79 - p82
Hi Lo - v1 - O '79 - p4
J Read - v25 - My '82 - p777
Kliatt - v14 - Winter '80 - p4
KR - v46 - D 15 '78 - p1361
WLB - v53 - D '78 - p341
Subject: Prostitution—Fiction; Runaways—Fiction

Tunnel Vision
BL - v76 - My 15 '80 - p1355
B Rpt - v1 - Ja '83 - p37
BS - v40 - S '80 - p207
CBRS - v8 - Jl '80 - p124
CCB-B - v34 - S '80 - p1
EJ - v72 - S '83 - p85
KR - v48 - Ag 1 '80 - p983
PW - v217 - Je 20 '80 - p87
SLJ - v26 - Ap '80 - p119
TN - v38 - S '81 - p71
Subject: Suicide—Fiction

ARTHUR, Robert (pseud.) 1909-1969
AuBYP SUP, BioIn 8, ConAu X, HalFC 84, IntMPA 86, SmATA X
Real Name:
Feder, Robert Arthur

Alfred Hitchcock And The Three Investigators In The Mystery Of The Green Ghost
LJ - v90 - N 12 '65 - p5106
Subject: Mystery and detective stories

ARTHUR, Robert (continued)

Alfred Hitchcock And The Three Investigators In The Mystery Of The Talking Skull
Teacher - v96 - O '78 - p177
Subject: Mystery and detective stories

Alfred Hitchcock And The Three Investigators In The Mystery Of The Vanishing Treasure
LJ - v91 - N 15 '66 - p5773
MN - v63 - D '84 - p58
Subject: Mystery and detective stories

Spies And More Spies
BS - v27 - N 1 '67 - p312
LJ - v92 - D 15 '67 - p4619
Subject: Spies—Fiction

ARTHUR, Ruth M 1905-1979
AuBYP SUP, ConAu 4NR, -85, ConLC 12, FifBJA, OxChL, SmATA 26N, -7, TwCChW 83, WrDr 80

A Candle In Her Room
BL - v63 - S 1 '66 - p36
CCB-B - v19 - My '66 - p142
HB - v42 - Ap '66 - p195
KR - v34 - F 1 '66 - p111
LJ - v91 - Ap 15 '66 - p2215
NYTBR - v71 - Ag 7 '66 - p24
Obs - N 27 '66 - p28
PW - v189 - My 2 '66 - p57
Spec - N 11 '66 - p628
TLS - N 24 '66 - p1070

Portrait Of Margarita
BL - v64 - Je 1 '68 - p1137
CLW - v41 - O '69 - p139
KR - v36 - F 1 '68 - p121
LJ - v93 - Ap 15 '68 - p1806
NS - v75 - My 24 '68 - p694
Punch - v255 - Jl 3 '68 - p33
RT - v37 - F '84 - p505
TLS - Je 6 '68 - p579

The Whistling Boy
BL - v65 - Je 15 '69 - p1173
BW - v3 - My 4 '69 - p32
CSM - v61 - Jl 17 '69 - p5
HB - v45 - Je '69 - p310
KR - v37 - Mr 1 '69 - p244
LJ - v94 - Ap 15 '69 - p1789
PW - v195 - My 12 '69 - p58
TLS - O 16 '69 - p1199
Subject: Family life—Fiction

ARUNDEL, Honor 1919-1973
AuBYP SUP, ConAu 41R, ConLC 17, FourBJA, OxChL, SmATA 24N, -4, TwCChW 83

Emma In Love
BL - v68 - Jl 15 '72 - p996
BL - v68 - Jl 15 '72 - p1002
BS - v32 - S 15 '72 - p284
EJ - v61 - D '72 - p1384
KR - v40 - My 15 '72 - p589
LJ - v97 - S 15 '72 - p2958
Obs - D 6 '70 - p27
TLS - D 11 '70 - p1453
Subject: Love—Fiction

A Family Failing
BL - v69 - F 15 '73 - p567
BS - v32 - Ja 15 '73 - p481
CCB-B - v26 - My '73 - p133
LJ - v98 - Ap 15 '73 - p1392
NS - v84 - N 10 '72 - p692
PW - v202 - D 4 '72 - p62
TLS - N 3 '72 - p1324
Subject: Family life—Fiction

ASHE, Arthur 1943-
BioIn 12, -13, ConAu 18NR, CurBio 66, NegAl 83, NewYTBS 85, WhoAm 86, WhoBlA 85, WorAl

Getting Started In Tennis
BL - v74 - Ap 1 '78 - p1263
CCB-B - v31 - Mr '78 - p105
EJ - v67 - Mr '78 - p80
HB - v54 - Ap '78 - p183
SLJ - v24 - F '78 - p53
Co-author: Robinson, Louie
Subject: Tennis

ASHER, Sandy 1942-
ConAu 105, DcLB Y83B, IntAu&W 86, SmATA 36

Summer Begins
BL - v76 - Jl 15 '80 - p1673
BW - v12 - Jl 11 '82 - p12
CBRS - v8 - Spring '80 - p115
CCB-B - v34 - Ja '81 - p86
KR - v48 - S 1 '80 - p1166
PW - v222 - Ag 27 '82 - p358
RT - v34 - Mr '81 - p735
SLJ - v27 - O '80 - p164
Subject: Friendship—Fiction; Mothers and daughters—Fiction; Schools—Fiction

Things Are Seldom What They Seem
BL - v79 - Ap 15 '83 - p1090
BS - v43 - My '83 - p72
CBRS - v11 - Ap '83 - p91

ASHER, Sandy (continued)
CCB-B - v36 - My '83 - p162
JB - v47 - D '83 - p252
Kliatt - v19 - Spring '85 - p4
Sch Lib - v31 - D '83 - p374
SLJ - v30 - S '83 - p130
Subject: Brothers and sisters—Fiction; Child molesting—Fiction; Interpersonal relations—Fiction

ASHFORD, Jeffrey (pseud.) 1926-
AuBYP, ConAu X, EncMys, TwCCr&M 85, WrDr 86
Real Name:
Jeffries, Roderic Graeme

Grand Prix Monaco
KR - v36 - Ag 1 '68 - p822
Subject: Automobile racing

see also Jeffries, Roderic Graeme for additional titles

ASIMOV, Isaac 1920-
ChlLR 12, ConAu 19NR, ConLC 1, -3, -9, -19, -26, ConNov 86, DcLB 8, DrmM 1, SmATA 26, ThrBJA, WhoAm 86, WrDr 86

The Best Mysteries Of Isaac Asimov: The Master's Choice Of His Own Favorites
BL - v82 - Ag '86 - p1664
KR - v54 - Jl 1 '86 - p975
PW - v230 - Jl 11 '86 - p57
Subject: Mystery and detective stories

Earth Invaded
SLJ - v29 - O '82 - p148
VOYA - v5 - D '82 - p37
Subject: Extrasensory perception—Fiction; Science fiction; Short stories

How Did We Find Out About Antarctica?
BOT - v2 - D '79 - p600
BW - v11 - Mr 8 '81 - p12
Kliatt - v15 - Spring '81 - p55
KR - v48 - F 15 '80 - p218
SB - v16 - S '80 - p27
SLJ - v26 - Ap '80 - p102
Subject: Antarctic regions

How Did We Find Out About Atoms?
Kliatt - v17 - Winter '83 - p63
Subject: Atoms

How Did We Find Out About Comets?
BW - v11 - Mr 8 '81 - p12
Kliatt - v15 - Spring '81 - p55
Subject: Comets

How Did We Find Out About Dinosaurs?
Kliatt - v17 - Winter '83 - p63
Subject: Dinosaurs; Fossils

How Did We Find Out About Earthquakes?
BW - v11 - Mr 8 '81 - p12
Kliatt - v15 - Spring '81 - p55
Subject: Earthquakes

How Did We Find Out About Energy?
BW - v11 - Mr 8 '81 - p12
Kliatt - v15 - Spring '81 - p55
Subject: Force and energy

How Did We Find Out About Germs?
BW - v11 - Mr 8 '81 - p12
Kliatt - v15 - Spring '81 - p55
Subject: Microbiology

How Did We Find Out About Life In The Deep Sea?
ASBYP - v15 - Fall '82 - p12
BL - v78 - My 15 '82 - p1253
Cur R - v20 - S '81 - p403
Kliatt - v17 - Winter '83 - p63
SB - v18 - N '82 - p91
Subject: Marine biology; Oceanography

How Did We Find Out About Our Human Roots?
ACSB - v13 - Spring '80 - p8
Kliatt - v17 - Winter '83 - p63
SB - v15 - Mr '80 - p208
SLJ - v26 - F '80 - p51
Subject: Fossils; Man (Prehistoric)

How Did We Find Out About Outer Space?
BW - v11 - Mr 8 '81 - p12
Kliatt - v15 - Spring '81 - p55
Subject: Outer space—Exploration

How Did We Find Out About Solar Power?
ACSB - v15 - Winter '82 - p15
BL - v78 - D 15 '81 - p547
Cur R - v20 - S '81 - p403
HB - v57 - D '81 - p689
Kliatt - v17 - Winter '83 - p63
KR - v49 - D 15 '81 - p1522

ASIMOV, Isaac (continued)
SLJ - v28 - N '81 - p87
Subject: Power resources; Solar energy

How Did We Find Out About Volcanoes?
ACSB - v15 - Winter '82 - p15
Cur R - v20 - S '81 - p403
HB - v57 - D '81 - p688
Kliatt - v17 - Winter '83 - p63
KR - v49 - D 15 '81 - p1522
SLJ - v28 - N '81 - p87
Subject: Volcanoes

The Key Word And Other Mysteries
BL - v74 - Mr 1 '78 - p1098
BW - v0 - Ap 8 '79 - p00L2
CCB-B - v31 - Je '78 - p154
HB - v54 - Je '78 - p272
KR - v46 - Ja 15 '78 - p47
PW - v213 - Ja 2 '78 - p65
SLJ - v24 - My '78 - p83
Subject: Mystery and detective stories

More Words Of Science
CCB-B - v26 - Ja '73 - p70
CLW - v44 - N '72 - p247
KR - v40 - Ap 1 '72 - p410
LJ - v97 - O 15 '72 - p3458
NYTBR - S 10 '72 - p10
SB - v8 - D '72 - p211
WLB - v47 - Ja '73 - p447
Subject: English language; Science

The Roman Empire
CCB-B - v21 - Ja '68 - p73
CW - v61 - F '68 - p220
Subject: Rome—History

The Roman Republic
BL - v63 - O 1 '66 - p164
BS - v26 - Ag 1 '66 - p173
CCB-B - v20 - My '67 - p134
Comw - v85 - N 11 '66 - p178
CSM - v58 - N 3 '66 - pB9
HB - v42 - O '66 - p579
KR - v34 - My 15 '66 - p515
LJ - v91 - Jl '66 - p3541
NYTBR, Pt. 2 - v72 - My 7 '67 - p20
Subject: Rome—History

Tomorrow's Children
BL - v63 - Ap 1 '67 - p843
CCB-B - v20 - Ja '67 - p69
HB - v43 - F '67 - p69
KR - v34 - S 15 '66 - p993
LJ - v91 - D 15 '66 - p6198
NYTBR - v71 - N 6 '66 - p20
SR - v49 - N 12 '66 - p54
Subject: Fantasy; Science fiction

ATKINS, Thomas
see Baxter, John (co-author)

ATKINSON, Linda

Have We Lived Before?
BL - v78 - Ap 15 '82 - p1088
Hi Lo - v3 - Ap '82 - p4
SLJ - v29 - S '82 - p114
WCRB - v8 - Jl '82 - p47
Subject: Reincarnation

Hit And Run
BL - v77 - Je 15 '81 - p1342
CBRS - v9 - Je '81 - p95
Hi Lo - v2 - My '81 - p3
SLJ - v27 - Ag '81 - p62
Subject: Hit-and-run drivers—Fiction; Traffic accidents—Fiction

Incredible Crimes
BL - v77 - Ja 15 '81 - p694
Hi Lo - v2 - My '81 - p6
SLJ - v27 - Ap '81 - p120
VOYA - v5 - Ap '82 - p57
Subject: Crime and criminals

Psychic Stories Strange But True
BL - v76 - O 15 '79 - p347
Hi Lo - v1 - Ja '80 - p3
SLJ - v26 - F '80 - p52
VOYA - v5 - Ap '82 - p57
Subject: Extrasensory perception; Psychical research

Your Legal Rights
BL - v79 - N 15 '82 - p438
B Rpt - v5 - N '86 - p17
CBRS - v11 - Winter '83 - p56
SLJ - v29 - Ja '83 - p81
Subject: Law and legislation

ATWATER, James David 1928-
ConAu 101, WhoAm 86, WhoMW 86

Out From Under: Benito Juarez And Mexico's Struggle For Independence
KR - v37 - Jl 1 '69 - p679
LJ - v94 - N 15 '69 - p4280
Co-author: Ruiz, Ramon E
Subject: Biography; Mexico—History

ATWATER, Montgomery M 1904-
AuBYP, ConAu 73, MorJA, SmATA 15

Snow Rangers Of The Andes
BS - v27 - N 1 '67 - p312
CLW - v39 - My '68 - p665
CSM - v70 - Ja 30 '78 - p15
KR - v35 - Ag 1 '67 - p884
LJ - v92 - D 15 '67 - p4619

AULT, Phil 1914-
AuBYP SUP, BioIn 1, ConAu 18NR, SmATA 23, WhoAm 80

These Are The Great Lakes
LJ - v98 - My 15 '73 - p1687
SB - v9 - My '73 - p64
Subject: Great Lakes Region—History

AUSTIN, R G

The Castle Of No Return
SLJ - v28 - My '82 - p83
VOYA - v5 - Ag '82 - p27
Subject: Fantasy

Curse Of The Sunken Treasure
SLJ - v28 - My '82 - p83
VOYA - v6 - Ap '83 - p35
Subject: Buried treasure—Fiction

Famous And Rich
SLJ - v28 - My '82 - p83
Subject: Money—Fiction

Lost In A Strange Land
SLJ - v28 - My '82 - p83
VOYA - v5 - F '83 - p32
Subject: Fantasy

Vampires, Spies And Alien Beings
SLJ - v28 - My '82 - p83
VOYA - v5 - Je '82 - p38
Subject: Monsters—Fiction

AVI (pseud.) 1937-
ConAu X, FifBJA, SmATA X
Real Name:
Wortis, Avi

Devil's Race
BL - v81 - S 15 '84 - p122
BS - v44 - D '84 - p356
CBRS - v13 - O '84 - p19
CCB-B - v38 - N '84 - p39
EJ - v74 - O '85 - p81
LA - v62 - Mr '85 - p283
PW - v226 - N 16 '84 - p65
SLJ - v31 - O '84 - p164
VOYA - v7 - D '84 - p261
WLB - v59 - Ja '85 - p340
Subject: Devil—Fiction; Ghosts—Fiction

A Place Called Ugly
BL - v77 - Ap 1 '81 - p1095
BS - v41 - Je '81 - p118
CBRS - v9 - Mr '81 - p67
CCB-B - v35 - S '81 - p4
EJ - v70 - N '81 - p94
HB - v57 - Je '81 - p297
J Read - v25 - D '81 - p286
Kliatt - v17 - Spring '83 - p4
KR - v49 - Ap 1 '81 - p436
NYTBR - v86 - Mr 1 '81 - p24
PW - v219 - Ja 30 '81 - p75
SLJ - v27 - Ap '81 - p136
VOYA - v4 - Ag '81 - p23
Subject: Seashore—Fiction; Vacations—Fiction

Sometimes I Think I Hear My Name
BL - v78 - Je 1 '82 - p1308
B Rpt - v1 - Ja '83 - p38
BS - v42 - My '82 - p76
CBRS - v10 - Spring '82 - p115
Inst - v91 - My '82 - p107
Kliatt - v17 - Spring '83 - p5
SLJ - v29 - S '82 - p133
VOYA - v5 - Ag '82 - p27
Subject: Emotional problems—Fiction; Friendship—Fiction; Parent and child—Fiction

Wolf Rider: A Tale Of Terror
BL - v83 - N 15 '86 - p505
CBRS - v15 - O '86 - p20
KR - v54 - O 1 '86 - p1513
PW - v230 - D 26 '86 - p61
SLJ - v33 - D '86 - p111
Subject: Fathers and sons—Fiction; Mystery and detective stories

AWREY, Don 1943-
WhoHcky 73

Power Hockey
BL - v71 - My 15 '75 - p961
Co-author: Hodge, Ken
Subject: Hockey

AXTHELM, Pete 1943-
WhoAm 86

The Kid
BL - v75 - S 1 '78 - p15
BS - v39 - Ap '79 - p16
EJ - v69 - F '80 - p94
KR - v46 - O 1 '78 - p1096
KR - v46 - N 1 '78 - p1198

AXTHELM, Pete (continued)
LJ - v103 - Ag '78 - p1527
NYT - v127 - Je 9 '78 - pC25
SLJ - v25 - O '78 - p164
Subject: Biography; Cauthen, Steve; Jockeys

AYDT, Deborah

I Don't Want To Be Your Shadow
Hi Lo - v3 - Je '82 - p3
Subject: Love—Fiction

AYLESWORTH, Thomas G 1927-
AmM&WS 86P, AuBYP SUP, ChlLR 6, ConAu 10NR, SmATA 4, WhoAm 86, WhoE 77

Monsters From The Movies
BL - v69 - F 15 '73 - p571
KR - v40 - O 15 '72 - p1203
PW - v202 - D 18 '72 - p39
SR - v55 - N 11 '72 - p79
Teacher - v90 - Ap '73 - p90
Subject: Monsters; Motion pictures

Movie Monsters
BB - v3 - O '75 - p3
CLW - v47 - My '76 - p451
Cur R - v16 - Ag '77 - p205
EJ - v65 - My '76 - p91
KR - v43 - S 15 '75 - p1069
SLJ - v22 - Ja '76 - p43
Teacher - v93 - Ap '76 - p125
Subject: Horror films; Monsters

AYLWARD, Jim

You're Dumber In The Summer: And Over 100 Other Things No One Ever Told You
NYTBR - v85 - Ap 27 '80 - p62
Subject: Curiosities and wonders

AYMAR, Brandt 1911-
ConAu 16NR, SmATA 22

Laws And Trials That Created History
BL - v71 - S 1 '74 - p37
Inst - v84 - O '74 - p205
KR - v42 - Je 15 '74 - p639
LJ - v99 - N 15 '74 - p3050
PW - v205 - Je 17 '74 - p69
SE - v39 - Mr '75 - p174
Co-author: Sagarin, Edward
Subject: Trials

B

BACH, Alice 1942-
AuBYP SUP, ConAu 101, FifBJA, SmATA 30

A Father Every Few Years
BB - v5 - Ag '77 - p4
BL - v73 - My 15 '77 - p1416
BS - v37 - Je '77 - p95
CCB-B - v30 - My '77 - p137
J Read - v26 - F '83 - p411
KR - v45 - Ja 15 '77 - p45
PW - v211 - Mr 28 '77 - p79
SLJ - v23 - Ap '77 - p73
Subject: Single-parent family—Fiction

The Meat In The Sandwich
BL - v72 - S 15 '75 - p163
CCB-B - v29 - Ja '76 - p73
Comw - v102 - N 21 '75 - p566
KR - v43 - S 1 '75 - p1002
NYTBR - N 2 '75 - p12
PW - v208 - Ag 11 '75 - p117
SLJ - v22 - D '75 - p68
Subject: Family life—Fiction; Friendship—Fiction; Sports—Fiction

Mollie Make-Believe
BL - v70 - Jl 1 '74 - p1197
BS - v34 - Je 15 '74 - p148
CCB-B - v28 - O '74 - p21
KR - v42 - Ap 15 '74 - p432
LJ - v99 - S 15 '74 - p2282
NYTBR - My 19 '74 - p8
NYTBR - N 3 '74 - p52
Subject: Adolescence—Fiction; Social adjustment—Fiction

They'll Never Make A Movie Starring Me
BS - v33 - Je 15 '73 - p145
KR - v41 - My 15 '73 - p567
PW - v203 - My 7 '73 - p66
Subject: Schools—Fiction

Waiting For Johnny Miracle
B Rpt - v1 - Mr '83 - p23
BS - v40 - Ja '81 - p348
CBRS - v9 - N '80 - p25
CCB-B - v34 - N '80 - p47
EJ - v70 - Ap '81 - p78
HB - v61 - Ja '85 - p86
Inst - v90 - Ja '81 - p24
Inter BC - v12 - #4 '81 p36
J Read - v24 - Ap '81 - p647
KR - v48 - N 15 '80 - p1468
PW - v218 - N 14 '80 - p55
SLJ - v27 - N '80 - p82
WLB - v55 - D '80 - p292
Subject: Cancer—Fiction; Twins—Fiction

BACON, Margaret Hope 1921-
ConAu 25R, SmATA 6

Lamb's Warrior: The Life Of Isaac T. Hopper
BL - v67 - O 1 '70 - p142
BS - v30 - My 1 '70 - p59
KR - v38 - My 1 '70 - p515
LJ - v95 - N 15 '70 - p4040
NYTBR - Ag 9 '70 - p22
Subject: Biography; Slavery

BACON, Martha 1917-1981
AuBYP SUP, ChlLR 3, ConAu 104, -85, SmATA 18, -27N, TwCChW 83

Sophia Scrooby Preserved
BL - v65 - O 1 '68 - p183
BS - v28 - O 1 '68 - p275
CCB-B - v22 - S '68 - p2
HB - v44 - O '68 - p561
KR - v36 - Ag 1 '68 - p822
LJ - v93 - O 15 '68 - p3975
NYTBR - v73 - O 20 '68 - p38
PW - v194 - Ag 12 '68 - p55
SR - v51 - S 21 '68 - p37

BAER, Judy

The Girl Inside
SLJ - v31 - S '84 - p136
Subject: Love—Fiction

BAILEY, John
AuBYP

Prehistoric Man
KR - v36 - Ap 1 '68 - p405
LJ - v93 - O 15 '68 - p3975
Subject: Man (Prehistoric)

BAIN, Geri

The Picture Life Of Bruce Springsteen
BL - v83 - N 15 '86 - p506
Subject: Musicians; Rock musicians

BAIRD, Thomas P 1923-
AuBYP SUP, ConAu 21NR, SmATA 45, WrDr 86

Finding Fever
BL - v79 - D 15 '82 - p561
BS - v42 - N '82 - p324
CBRS - v11 - Winter '83 - p56
CCB-B - v36 - N '82 - p42
Emerg Lib - v14 - S '86 - p21
HB - v59 - F '83 - p50
KR - v50 - S 1 '82 - p1000
SLJ - v29 - D '82 - p82
Subject: Crime and criminals—Fiction; Dogs—Fiction; Interpersonal relations—Fiction

BAKER, A A

Mountain Rescue
BL - v75 - F 15 '79 - p927
Hi Lo - v2 - Ap '81 - p2

BAKER, Betty Lou 1928-
AuBYP, ConAu 2NR, SmATA 5, ThrBJA, TwCChW 83, WhoWest 76, WrDr 86
Pseud./variant:
Venturo, Betty Lou Baker

Dunderhead War
BL - v64 - D 1 '67 - p443
BW - v2 - Ja 14 '68 - p14
CCB-B - v21 - My '68 - p138
CLW - v39 - D '67 - p297
CSM - v59 - N 2 '67 - pB9
HB - v43 - O '67 - p599
KR - v35 - Jl 1 '67 - p744
LJ - v92 - O 15 '67 - p3859
Subject: Mexico—Fiction

Walk The World's Rim
BL - v61 - Je 15 '65 - p995
BS - v25 - My 15 '65 - p96
CCB-B - v18 - Je '65 - p141
CE - v42 - Ja '66 - p314
HB - v41 - Ap '65 - p174
KR - v33 - Ja 15 '65 - p62
LJ - v90 - Mr 15 '65 - p1546
NYTBR - v70 - Jl 11 '65 - p34
Subject: Avavare Indians—Fiction

BAKER, Laura Nelson 1911-
AuBYP, ConAu 5NR, SmATA 3, WrDr 84

Here By The Sea
BS - v28 - O 1 '68 - p275
BW - v2 - N 3 '68 - p26
KR - v36 - Ag 1 '68 - p823
LJ - v93 - N 15 '68 - p4410
NYTBR - Mr 9 '69 - p26

BALDWIN, James 1924-
AmWr S1, ConAu 3NR, –1BS, ConNov 86, DcLB 2, –7, –33, SmATA 9, WhoAm 86, WhoTwCL, WrDr 86

If Beale Street Could Talk
BL - v81 - Jl '85 - p1546
TN - v37 - Fall '80 - p56
Subject: Blacks—Fiction

BALDWIN, Margaret 1948-
ConAu X, SmATA X
Pseud./variant:
Weis, Margaret

The Boys Who Saved The Children
BL - v78 - F 15 '82 - p754
Hi Lo - v3 - F '82 - p5
TN - v41 - Fall '84 - p102
VOYA - v5 - Ag '82 - p41
Subject: Holocaust, Jewish (1939-1945)

Fortune Telling
SLJ - v31 - N '84 - p120
Subject: Fortune telling

Kisses Of Death: A World War II Escape Story
Hi Lo - v4 - My '83 - p3
SLJ - v30 - N '83 - p87
Subject: Escapes; World War, 1939-1945

BALDWIN, Stan 1929-
ConAu 17NR, SmATA 28

Bad Henry: An Authorized Hank Aaron Story
BS - v34 - My 15 '74 - p78
LJ - v99 - My 15 '74 - p1405
NO - v13 - Ag 17 '74 - p14
NYTBR - Je 2 '74 - p7
PW - v205 - Mr 25 '74 - p55
Subject: Baseball—Biography

BALES, Carol Ann 1940-
ConAu 45, SmATA 29

Tales Of The Elders: A Memory Book Of Men And Women Who Came To America As Immigrants, 1900-1930
B&B - v5 - Je '77 - p3
BL - v73 - Jl 15 '77 - p1726
CCB-B - v31 - S '77 - p3
Comw - v104 - N 11 '77 - p733
HB - v53 - O '77 - p543
LA - v54 - O '77 - p811
NYTBR - Jl 3 '77 - p11
PW - v211 - My 2 '77 - p70
SE - v42 - Ap '78 - p319
SLJ - v23 - Ap '77 - p74
Teacher - v96 - D '78 - p22
Subject: Biography; United States—Emigration and immigration

BALL, Charles Elihue 1924-
WhoAm 86

Saddle Up: The Farm Journal Book Of Western Horsemanship
BL - v67 - N 15 '70 - p243
KR - v38 - Mr 15 '70 - p352
LJ - v95 - S 15 '70 - p2931
Subject: Horses

BALLARD, Martin 1929-
ConAu 25R, SmATA 1, TwCChW 83, WrDr 86

The Emir's Son
KR - v35 - O 15 '67 - p1262
LJ - v92 - D 15 '67 - p4608
Spec - v219 - N 3 '67 - p543
TLS - N 30 '67 - p1143

BALMES, Julie
see Balmes, Pat (co-author)

BALMES, Pat

Danger At The Flying Y
BL - v78 - Ag '82 - p1519
Subject: West (U.S.)—Fiction

Danger On The Mountain
SLJ - v31 - Mr '85 - p173
Co-author: Balmes, Vern

Hoop Of Fire
SLJ - v31 - Mr '85 - p173
Co-author: Balmes, Julie

Victory At Icy Bay
SLJ - v31 - Mr '85 - p173
Co-author: Balmes, Vern

BALMES, Vern
see Balmes, Pat (co-author)

BALUKAS, Jean
WhoAm 86

Pocket Billiards
SLJ - v27 - N '80 - p95

BAMMAN, Henry A 1918-
ConAu 7NR, SmATA 12

Flight To The South Pole
Inst - v75 - F '66 - p160
LJ - v90 - D 15 '65 - p5508

Viking Treasure
Inst - v75 - F '66 - p160
LJ - v90 - D 15 '65 - p5508
Co-author: Whitehead, Robert J

BARGAR, Gary W

Life. Is. Not. Fair.
BL - v80 - Je 1 '84 - p1396
CBRS - v12 - My '84 - p107
CCB-B - v37 - My '84 - p160
HB - v60 - Je '84 - p325
Inter BC - v16 - #8 '85 p19
Learning - v13 - N '84 - p71
N Dir Wom - v14 - My '85 - p20
PW - v225 - Je 22 '84 - p100
SLJ - v30 - Ag '84 - p68
Subject: Friendship—Fiction; Prejudices—Fiction; Race relations—Fiction

What Happened To Mr. Forster?
BL - v78 - Ja 1 '82 - p595
CBRS - v10 - Ja '82 - p45
CCB-B - v35 - D '81 - p63
HB - v58 - F '82 - p40
KR - v49 - D 15 '81 - p1518
PW - v220 - S 25 '81 - p88
SLJ - v28 - D '81 - p60
Subject: Homosexuality—Fiction

BARKIN, Carol
ConAu 118, SmATA 42
Pseud./variant:
Hastings, Beverly

Slapdash Decorating
BB - v6 - Mr '78 - p4
BL - v74 - F 1 '78 - p906
KR - v45 - N 1 '77 - p1149
PW - v213 - Ap 10 '78 - p72
SLJ - v24 - Ja '78 - p93
Subject: Handicraft; Interior decoration

BARKIN, Carol (continued)
see also Hastings, Beverly; James, Elizabeth (co-author) for additional titles

BARLETTE, Danielle

I'll Take Manhattan
LATBR - Ag 25 '85 - p9
SLJ - v32 - Ap '86 - p102
VOYA - v8 - F '86 - p391
Subject: Love—Fiction

Lovebound
VOYA - v9 - Ag '86 - p138
Subject: Love—Fiction

BARNESS, Richard 1917-
ConAu 65

Graystone College
LJ - v99 - My 15 '74 - p1471
Subject: Prisoners—Personal narratives

BARNETT, Cynthia

Ben's Gift
BL - v77 - Jl 15 '81 - p1435
J Read - v25 - My '82 - p817

BARNOUW, Victor 1915-
AmM&WS 76P, ConAu 85, FifIDA, SmATA 43

Dream Of The Blue Heron
BS - v26 - D 1 '66 - p337
KR - v34 - S 15 '66 - p982
LJ - v91 - D 15 '66 - p6198

BARON, Virginia Olsen 1931-
AuBYP SUP, ConAu 25R, SmATA 28

Here I Am!
BS - v29 - Ja 1 '70 - p387
CCB-B - v23 - Ap '70 - p124
CT - v10 - My '81 - p10
KR - v37 - N 15 '69 - p1204
LJ - v95 - Je 15 '70 - p2306
NO - v8 - N 24 '69 - p25
NYTBR - D 14 '69 - p34
PW - v196 - D 8 '69 - p47
SR - v53 - Ja 24 '70 - p37
Subject: Poetry

The Seasons Of Time: Tanka Poetry Of Ancient Japan
BL - v64 - Jl 15 '68 - p1285
CLW - v40 - O '68 - p146
KR - v36 - My 1 '68 - p519
LJ - v93 - My 15 '68 - p2118
LJ - v93 - Ag '68 - p2875
NYTBR - v73 - My 5 '68 - p44
PW - v193 - Mr 18 '68 - p54
Subject: Poetry

BARRETT, N S

Trucks
BL - v81 - My 15 '85 - p1329
BL - v82 - Je 15 '86 - p1536
SLJ - v32 - O '85 - p148
Subject: Trucks

BARRETT, William E 1900-1986
AmCath 80, BioIn 3, –4, ConAu 5R, –120, ConSFA, SmATA 49N, WhoAm 76, WhoWor 78

The Lilies Of The Field
BL - v58 - My 1 '62 - p606
KR - v30 - F 1 '62 - p128
LJ - v87 - Ap 1 '62 - p1481
NYTBR - Ap 22 '62 - p23
VOYA - v6 - O '83 - p189
Subject: Friendship—Fiction; Nuns—Fiction

BARTH, Edna 1914-1980
AuBYP SUP, BioIn 12, ConAu 102, –41R, SmATA 24N, –7, WhoAmW 77

Turkeys, Pilgrims, And Indian Corn
BB - v3 - N '75 - p3
BL - v72 - D 15 '75 - p575
KR - v43 - O 15 '75 - p1187
PW - v208 - Ag 25 '75 - p294
SLJ - v22 - N '75 - p68
Subject: Thanksgiving Day

BARTHOLOMEW, Barbara 1941-
ConAu 118, SmATA 42

Anne And Jay
VOYA - v5 - D '82 - p28

Child Of Tomorrow
Emerg Lib - v13 - Mr '86 - p46
GP - v25 - My '86 - p4616
JB - v50 - Ap '86 - p74
SF Chr - v7 - F '86 - p34

The Time Keeper
GP - v25 - My '86 - p4616
JB - v50 - Ap '86 - p74
Sch Lib - v34 - S '86 - p265
SF Chr - v7 - D '85 - p44
SLJ - v32 - D '85 - p97
VOYA - v8 - D '85 - p323

BARTOS-HOEPPNER, Barbara 1923-
ConAu 10NR, FourBJA, IntAu&W 77, SmATA 5, TwCChW 83B

Avalanche Dog
BL - v63 - Jl 1 '67 - p1144
CCB-B - v21 - S '67 - p1
HB - v43 - Ag '67 - p474
KR - v35 - Ap 15 '67 - p505
LJ - v92 - Je 15 '67 - p244B
PW - v191 - Ap 10 '67 - p82
TLS - N 24 '66 - p1091
Subject: Dogs—Fiction

BATES, Betty 1921-
ConAu X, SmATA 19
Pseud./variant:
Bates, Elizabeth

Bugs In Your Ears
CCB-B - v31 - F '78 - p89
KR - v45 - S 15 '77 - p989
PW - v212 - D 26 '77 - p68
SLJ - v24 - F '78 - p54
Subject: Adoption—Fiction; Remarriage—Fiction

It Must've Been The Fish Sticks
BL - v78 - Je 15 '82 - p1366
CBRS - v11 - S '82 - p7
CCB-B - v36 - S '82 - p2
CE - v60 - S '83 - p50
CLW - v54 - S '82 - p83
Kliatt - v18 - Winter '84 - p5
SLJ - v29 - Ja '83 - p70
Subject: Adoption—Fiction; Mothers and sons—Fiction

Love Is Like Peanuts
BS - v40 - Jl '80 - p157
CBRS - v8 - Ap '80 - p86
CCB-B - v33 - My '80 - p166
Kliatt - v15 - Spring '81 - p5
KR - v48 - Ag 1 '80 - p983
RT - v35 - O '81 - p69
SLJ - v26 - My '80 - p73
Subject: Mentally handicapped—Fiction

My Mom, The Money Nut
CCB-B - v33 - N '79 - p41
Subject: Mothers and daughters—Fiction; Schools—Fiction

The Ups And Downs Of Jorie Jenkins
KR - v46 - My 1 '78 - p496
SLJ - v24 - My '78 - p62
Subject: Family life—Fiction

BATSON, Larry 1930-
ConAu 57, SmATA 35, WhoAm 86

Rod Carew
BL - v73 - Je 15 '77 - p1572
BL - v73 - Jl 1 '77 - p1650
SLJ - v23 - My '77 - p80
SLJ - v23 - My '77 - p81
Subject: Baseball—Biography

Walt "Clyde" Frazier
LJ - v99 - D 15 '74 - p3281
Subject: Basketball—Biography

BAUER, Marion Dane 1938-
ConAu 11NR, FifBJA, SmATA 20

Foster Child
BL - v73 - My 1 '77 - p1343
CCB-B - v30 - Je '77 - p153
Comw - v104 - N 11 '77 - p731
Hi Lo - v2 - D '80 - p5
KR - v45 - My 1 '77 - p485
NYTBR - My 1 '77 - p46
PW - v211 - My 2 '77 - p69
RT - v32 - O '78 - p42
SLJ - v23 - Ap '77 - p74
WCRB - v4 - Ja '78 - p66
Subject: Foster home care—Fiction

Shelter From The Wind
BB - v4 - Ja '77 - p4
Comw - v103 - N 19 '76 - p762
HB - v52 - Ag '76 - p394
Kliatt - v12 - Fall '78 - p4
KR - v44 - Ap 1 '76 - p389
NYTBR - Je 6 '76 - p54
PW - v209 - Ap 5 '76 - p101
SLJ - v22 - My '76 - p56
Subject: Oklahoma—Fiction; Runaways—Fiction

Tangled Butterfly
BL - v76 - Mr 15 '80 - p1040
B Rpt - v1 - Mr '83 - p23
BS - v40 - Je '80 - p115
CBRS - v8 - Jl '80 - p124
CCB-B - v33 - Je '80 - p185
J Read - v24 - D '80 - p271
KR - v48 - Ag 1 '80 - p984
PW - v217 - My 9 '80 - p57
SLJ - v26 - My '80 - p73
Subject: Indians of North America—Fiction; Mentally ill—Fiction

BAUMANN, Amy Brown Beeching
see Brown, Alexis

BAUMANN, Hans 1914-
ConAu 3NR, IntAu&W 82, OxChL, SmATA 2, ThrBJA, TwCChW 83B

Lion Gate And Labyrinth
BL - v64 - Mr 1 '68 - p778
BS - v27 - Ja 1 '68 - p391
BW - v2 - Je 23 '68 - p11
CCB-B - v21 - Mr '68 - p105
HB - v43 - D '67 - p761
KR - v35 - N 1 '67 - p1324
LJ - v93 - F 15 '68 - p877
PW - v192 - D 25 '67 - p60
SB - v3 - Mr '68 - p307
SR - v51 - Ap 20 '68 - p41
TLS - N 30 '67 - p1162
Subject: Civilization

BAWDEN, Nina 1925-
AuBYP SUP, ChlLR 2, ConAu X, ConNov 86, FourBJA, OxChL, SmATA X, SouSt, TwCChW 83, WrDr 86
Pseud./variant:
Kark, Nina Mary

Squib
A Lib - v3 - Ap '72 - p419
BL - v68 - N 15 '71 - p290
BL - v68 - Ap 1 '72 - p668
BL - v81 - My 1 '85 - p1261
CCB-B - v25 - Jl '72 - p165
CE - v49 - Ja '73 - p201
Comw - v95 - N 19 '71 - p188
GW - v104 - Je 5 '71 - p19
HB - v47 - O '71 - p482
KR - v39 - Jl 15 '71 - p738
LJ - v96 - D 15 '71 - p4198
NS - v81 - Je 4 '71 - p778
NYRB - v17 - D 2 '71 - p25
PW - v222 - N 12 '82 - p66
RT - v36 - Mr '83 - p716
SLJ - v29 - Ja '83 - p70
TES - Mr 18 '83 - p35
TES - F 24 '84 - p29
TLS - Jl 2 '71 - p775
TN - v28 - Ap '72 - p309

BAXTER, John 1939-
ConAu 29R, EncSF, ScF&FL 1, -2, TwCSFW 86, WrDr 86

The Fire Came By
BL - v73 - O 15 '76 - p312
Choice - v13 - D '76 - p1313
Kliatt - v11 - Fall '77 - p36
KR - v44 - Mr 15 '76 - p352
LJ - v101 - My 15 '76 - p1217
NYTBR - Jl 18 '76 - p4
Obs - D 12 '76 - p26
PW - v209 - Ap 12 '76 - p64
PW - v211 - Mr 7 '77 - p98
SB - v13 - My '77 - p2
WSJ - v187 - Je 22 '76 - p22
WSJ - v188 - D 8 '76 - p24
Co-author: Atkins, Thomas
Subject: Nuclear explosions; Space vehicles

BAYLOR, Byrd 1924-
AuBYP SUP, ChlLR 3, ConAu 81, FourBJA, SmATA 16
Pseud./variant:
Schweitzer, Byrd Baylor

They Put On Masks
A Lib - v6 - Mr '75 - p166
BL - v70 - Je 1 '74 - p1102
BL - v81 - Ap 15 '85 - p1202
CCB-B - v28 - O '74 - p22
CE - v51 - N '74 - p94
KR - v42 - Ap 15 '74 - p428
LJ - v99 - S 15 '74 - p2239
PW - v205 - Ap 22 '74 - p74
RT - v32 - Ja '79 - p444
SLJ - v29 - Ap '83 - p114
Subject: Indians of North America

BAYNER, Rose

Endless Summer
BL - v80 - Je 15 '84 - p1473
VOYA - v7 - O '84 - p200
Subject: Love—Fiction

BEAL, Stephen

Mary Ellen And Ida: Portraits Of Two Women
BL - v81 - Ja 15 '85 - p689
Subject: Grandmothers—Biography

BEAME, Rona 1934-
ConAu 45, SmATA 12

Emergency!
BL - v73 - Je 15 '77 - p1572
BL - v81 - Jl '85 - p1570
CCB-B - v31 - O '77 - p27
KR - v45 - Ap 15 '77 - p429
SB - v14 - My '78 - p40
SLJ - v24 - S '77 - p120
Subject: Hospitals; New York (City)

BEATTY, Patricia Robbins 1922-
AuBYP, BioIn 7, ConAu 3NR, OxChL, SmATA 30, -4AS, ThrBJA, TwCChW 83, WhoAm 86, WrDr 86

By Crumbs, It's Mine
BB - v4 - Ag '76 - p3
BL - v72 - Ap 15 '76 - p1182
BL - v73 - My 15 '77 - p1425
CCB-B - v29 - Jl '76 - p169
CLW - v48 - O '76 - p137
KR - v44 - F 1 '76 - p133
PW - v209 - Ap 26 '76 - p60
SLJ - v22 - Ap '76 - p80
SLJ - v22 - My '76 - p34
Subject: Humorous stories; West (U.S.)—Fiction

Something To Shout About
BL - v73 - D 1 '76 - p534
CCB-B - v30 - F '77 - p86
Comw - v103 - N 19 '76 - p762
HB - v53 - Ap '77 - p157
KR - v44 - S 1 '76 - p973
LA - v54 - Ap '77 - p442
PW - v210 - O 4 '76 - p74
SE - v47 - Ap '83 - p288
SLJ - v23 - N '76 - p52
Subject: Frontier and pioneer life—Fiction; Montana—Fiction

Wait For Me, Watch For Me, Eula Bee
KR - v46 - N 15 '78 - p1246
Subject: Comanche Indians—Fiction; Indians of North America—Fiction; West (U.S.)—Fiction

BECKMAN, Delores
IntAu&W 86

My Own Private Sky
BL - v76 - My 1 '80 - p1287
CBRS - v8 - Mr '80 - p75
CCB-B - v34 - N '80 - p47
CE - v58 - S '81 - p46
KR - v48 - Jl 15 '80 - p909
LA - v58 - F '81 - p185
Ms - v9 - Ag '80 - p92
RT - v34 - Mr '81 - p735
SLJ - v26 - Ag '80 - p60
Subject: Baby sitters—Fiction; Physically handicapped—Fiction; Single-parent family—Fiction

BECKMAN, Gunnel 1910-
ConAu 15NR, ConLC 26, FourBJA, SmATA 6, TwCChW 83B

Admission To The Feast
BL - v69 - Ja 1 '73 - p442
CCB-B - v26 - Ap '73 - p118
EJ - v62 - N '73 - p1187
HB - v48 - O '72 - p474
KR - v40 - S 15 '72 - p1106
LJ - v97 - D 15 '72 - p4075
TLS - O 22 '71 - p1318
Subject: Death—Fiction; Leukemia—Fiction

BECKMAN, Patti

Please Let Me In
Hi Lo - v3 - Ja '82 - p4
SLJ - v28 - Mr '82 - p154

BECKWITH, Lillian (pseud.) 1916-
ConAu X, IntAu&W 82, WrDr 86
Real Name:
Comber, Lillian

The Spuddy
BL - v72 - F 15 '76 - p847
BL - v72 - F 15 '76 - p852
KR - v43 - N 1 '75 - p1248
LJ - v100 - D 1 '75 - p2263
NYTBR - Ja 4 '76 - p22
PW - v208 - D 1 '75 - p60
SLJ - v22 - N '75 - p95

BEDNAR, Jane

Everybody's Dancing In Socks And On Skates
BL - v79 - Ap 1 '83 - p1022
SLJ - v28 - O '81 - p138
Subject: Disco dancing; Roller disco

BEECHCROFT, William
see Hallstead, William Finn, III

BEERY, Mary 1907-
ConAu 5R, WrDr 86

Manners Made Easy
BL - v63 - O 1 '66 - p164
BS - v26 - Ag 1 '66 - p173
LJ - v91 - S 15 '66 - p4346
NYTBR - v72 - Mr 5 '67 - p30
Subject: Etiquette

Young Teens Away From Home
BS - v26 - S 1 '66 - p201
NYTBR - v71 - Je 5 '66 - p42
Subject: Etiquette

BEHRENS, June
AuBYP, ConAu 8NR, SmATA 19, WhoAmW 77

Sally Ride, Astronaut
BL - v82 - S 15 '85 - p142
SLJ - v31 - O '84 - p154
Subject: Astronauts; Biography

BELINA, Tom

Flight To Fear
BL - v74 - Ap 15 '78 - p1329
BL - v75 - O 15 '78 - p357
Subject: Hijacking of aircraft—Fiction

BELLAIRS, John 1938-
ConAu 8NR, FifBJA, IntAu&W 86, SmATA 2, WrDr 86

The Treasure Of Alpheus Winterborn
BW - v16 - Ja 12 '86 - p13
Kliatt - v15 - Winter '81 - p4
NYTBR - v85 - O 12 '80 - p47
PW - v218 - S 26 '80 - p122
Subject: Buried treasure—Fiction

BELTING, Natalia Maree 1915-
AuBYP, ConAu 3NR, DrAS 82H, SmATA 6, ThrBJA

Whirlwind Is A Ghost Dancing
BL - v71 - N 1 '74 - p286
CCB-B - v28 - Mr '75 - p106
Choice - v12 - N '75 - p1130
HB - v50 - D '74 - p688
KR - v42 - S 1 '74 - p945
LJ - v99 - N 15 '74 - p3043
SE - v39 - Mr '75 - p174
SE - v44 - O '80 - p478
Subject: Indian poetry; Poetry

BENARY-ISBERT, Margot 1889-1979
AuBYP, ChlLR 12, ConAu 4NR, ConLC 12, MorJA, SmATA 2, -21N

The Ark
BL - v49 - Mr 15 '53 - p241
CC - v70 - S 2 '53 - p996
Comw - v59 - N 20 '53 - p178
HB - v29 - Ap '53 - p102
HB - v29 - Ap '53 - p124
HB - v62 - N '86 - p756
KR - v21 - Ja 15 '53 - p41
LJ - v78 - My 1 '53 - p819
NY - v29 - N 28 '53 - p194
NYT - Mr 1 '53 - p32
NYTBR - My 6 '56 - p32
SR - v36 - Ap 4 '53 - p64

Rowan Farm
BL - v51 - S 1 '54 - p20
HB - v30 - O '54 - p336
KR - v22 - Je 1 '54 - p341
LJ - v79 - S 15 '54 - p1670
NY - v30 - N 27 '54 - p212
NYTBR - O 10 '54 - p38
SR - v37 - Ag 21 '54 - p35

BENCHLEY, Nathaniel 1915-1981
AnObit 1981, AuBYP SUP, ConAu 105, -12NR, FourBJA, SmATA 25, -28N, TwCChW 83, WorAu, WrDr 82

Gone And Back
BS - v31 - My 15 '71 - p98
BW - v5 - My 9 '71 - p18
CLW - v43 - Ap '72 - p481
KR - v39 - F 15 '71 - p179
LJ - v96 - Ap 15 '71 - p1511
NYTBR - D 5 '71 - p86
NYTBR, Pt. 2 - My 2 '71 - p4
NYTBR, Pt. 2 - N 7 '71 - p28
NYTBR, Pt. 2 - F 13 '72 - p14
NYTBR, Pt. 2 - N 5 '72 - p42
PW - v199 - Mr 22 '71 - p53
Time - v98 - D 27 '71 - p61

BENDICK, Jeanne 1919-
AuBYP, BioIn 2, BkP, ChlLR 5, ConAu 2NR, IlsCB 1946, -1957, MorJA, SmATA 2, -4AS, WhoAmW 87

Electronics For Young People
LJ - v97 - F 15 '72 - p782
Co-author: Lefkowitz, R J
Subject: Electronics

The Emergency Book
BL - v64 - Ja 15 '68 - p590
CCB-B - v21 - F '68 - p90
HB - v44 - F '68 - p78
Inst - v77 - F '68 - p190
KR - v35 - O 1 '67 - p1221
LJ - v92 - D 15 '67 - p4619
PW - v192 - D 11 '67 - p45
SR - v50 - N 11 '67 - p47
Subject: Safety

Filming Works Like This
BL - v67 - Ap 1 '71 - p662
CCB-B - v24 - My '71 - p133
FQ - v24 - Summer '71 - p14
Inst - v81 - Ag '71 - p180
LJ - v96 - O 15 '71 - p3464
NYTBR, Pt. 2 - N 8 '70 - p18

BENDICK, Jeanne (continued)
Co-author: Bendick, Robert
Subject: Amateur motion pictures; Cinematography

The First Book Of Automobiles
BL - v62 - Jl 1 '66 - p1049
BL - v68 - F 1 '72 - p468
LJ - v91 - Jl '66 - p3552
SLJ - v25 - N '78 - p55
Subject: Automobiles

BENDICK, Robert
see Bendick, Jeanne (co-author)

BENJAMIN, Carol Lea

Nobody's Baby Now
BL - v80 - My 15 '84 - p1340
BS - v44 - S '84 - p230
CBRS - v12 - Je '84 - p116
CCB-B - v37 - My '84 - p160
EJ - v73 - N '84 - p99
Inter BC - v16 - #1 '85 p9
NW - v104 - D 3 '84 - p87
NYTBR - v89 - My 13 '84 - p21
SLJ - v31 - S '84 - p125
VOYA - v7 - D '84 - p262
Subject: Grandmothers—Fiction; Weight control—Fiction

BENNETT, Jay 1912-
AuBYP SUP, BioIn 10, ConAu 11NR, ConLC 35, SmATA 41, -4AS, WhoAm 80

The Birthday Murderer: A Mystery
BL - v74 - O 15 '77 - p366
BW - v9 - O 7 '79 - p15
CCB-B - v31 - F '78 - p90
EJ - v68 - Ja '79 - p57
KR - v45 - N 15 '77 - p1205
PW - v212 - Ag 22 '77 - p66
SLJ - v24 - D '77 - p62
Subject: Mystery and detective stories

The Dangling Witness
BS - v34 - N 15 '74 - p377
NYTBR - N 10 '74 - p8
PW - v206 - Ag 12 '74 - p58
Subject: Mystery and detective stories

The Death Ticket
BL - v82 - N 15 '85 - p481
PW - v228 - S 27 '85 - p97
Subject: Mystery and detective stories

Deathman, Do Not Follow Me
BS - v28 - Jl 1 '68 - p154
KR - v36 - Ap 15 '68 - p465
LJ - v93 - Jl '68 - p2736
NYTBR - v73 - Jl 7 '68 - p16
Subject: Mystery and detective stories

The Executioner: A Story Of Revenge
BL - v78 - Ap 1 '82 - p1014
EJ - v71 - S '82 - p88
EJ - v72 - D '83 - p66
Emerg Lib - v10 - N '82 - p33
PW - v221 - Ja 29 '82 - p67
SLJ - v28 - My '82 - p84
VOYA - v5 - Ag '82 - p28
Subject: Mystery and detective stories

The Killing Tree
BL - v69 - N 1 '72 - p238
BL - v69 - N 1 '72 - p242
LJ - v97 - D 15 '72 - p4087
PW - v202 - Ag 14 '72 - p46
Subject: Smuggling—Fiction

The Long Black Coat
KR - v41 - Ap 1 '73 - p395
LJ - v98 - My 15 '73 - p1702
PW - v203 - My 7 '73 - p65
Subject: Mystery and detective stories

The Pigeon
BL - v76 - My 15 '80 - p1356
BS - v40 - Ja '81 - p349
CBRS - v8 - Spring '80 - p115
Emerg Lib - v9 - Ja '82 - p33
HB - v56 - O '80 - p523
KR - v48 - Ag 15 '80 - p1084
PW - v218 - Jl 18 '80 - p62
SLJ - v26 - My '80 - p86
SLJ - v27 - N '80 - p46
Subject: Mystery and detective stories; New York (City)—Fiction; Terrorism—Fiction

Say Hello To The Hit Man
BL - v72 - Ap 1 '76 - p1100
BL - v72 - Ap 1 '76 - p1108
BS - v36 - Ag '76 - p148
KR - v44 - Ap 15 '76 - p481
NYTBR - My 2 '76 - p36
PW - v209 - Mr 8 '76 - p67
SLJ - v22 - My '76 - p77
Subject: Crime and criminals—Fiction

The Skeleton Man
BL - v83 - N 1 '86 - p402

BENNETT, Jay (continued)
CBRS - v15 - O '86 - p20
KR - v54 - O 1 '86 - p1513
SLJ - v33 - O '86 - p185
Subject: Mystery and detective stories

Slowly, Slowly I Raise The Gun
PW - v224 - Jl 1 '83 - p103
SLJ - v30 - D '83 - p84
VOYA - v6 - F '84 - p337
Subject: Crime and criminals—Fiction; Fathers and sons—Fiction; Inheritance and succession—Fiction

BERGAUST, Erik 1925-1978
AuBYP, ConAu 73, –77, SmATA 20, WhAm 7, WhoAm 76

Colonizing Space
KR - v46 - Mr 1 '78 - p249
SLJ - v25 - S '78 - p153
Subject: Space colonies

BERGER, Gilda
ConAu 118, SmATA 42

Apes In Fact And Fiction
SLJ - v28 - O '81 - p138
Subject: Apes

Bizarre Crimes
BL - v81 - S 1 '84 - p56
SLJ - v31 - Ja '85 - p81
Co-author: Berger, Melvin
Subject: Crime and criminals

Bizarre Murders
BL - v79 - Mr 15 '83 - p953
B Rpt - v2 - N '83 - p37
SLJ - v30 - O '83 - p164
Co-author: Berger, Melvin
Subject: Crime and criminals

see also Berger, Melvin for additional titles

BERGER, Maxine
see Mays, Willie (co-author)

BERGER, Melvin 1927-
AuBYP, ConAu 4NR, ConLC 12, FifBJA, SmATA 5, –2AS

Computer Talk
ARBA - v16 - p581
ASBYP - v18 - Spring '85 - p11
BL - v80 - My 1 '84 - p1235
CBR - v2 - Jl '84 - p58
SB - v20 - My '85 - p303
SLJ - v30 - Ag '84 - p69
Subject: Computers

The Funny Side Of Science
KR - v41 - Ap 15 '73 - p458
LJ - v98 - N 15 '73 - p3447
Co-author: Handelsman, J B
Subject: Jokes; Science

The Photo Dictionary Of Football
BL - v77 - O 1 '80 - p258
CE - v57 - Ja '81 - p174
SLJ - v27 - D '80 - p75
Subject: Football

Police Lab
BL - v72 - Ap 1 '76 - p1108
KR - v44 - Ap 15 '76 - p474
SB - v13 - My '77 - p39
SLJ - v22 - F '76 - p43
Subject: Crime and criminals

The Story Of Folk Music
BL - v73 - D 15 '76 - p603
CE - v53 - Mr '77 - p260
KR - v44 - O 1 '76 - p1096
PW - v210 - O 18 '76 - p63
SE - v41 - Ap '77 - p348
SLJ - v23 - N '76 - p54
Subject: Folk music

The Supernatural
BB - v6 - Ap '78 - p4
BL - v74 - Ja 15 '78 - p809
CCB-B - v31 - Je '78 - p154
HB - v54 - Je '78 - p308
KR - v45 - N 15 '77 - p1200
SB - v14 - D '78 - p142
SLJ - v24 - Mr '78 - p135
Subject: Occult sciences; Psychical research

see also Berger, Gilda (co-author) for additional titles

BERGER, Phil 1942-
AuBYP SUP, ConAu 12NR

Championship Teams Of The NFL
BL - v65 - Ap 15 '69 - p959
CSM - v60 - N 7 '68 - pB12
KR - v36 - S 1 '68 - p980
PW - v194 - O 7 '68 - p55
Subject: Football

BERGER, Terry 1933-
ConAu 37R, SmATA 8, WrDr 86

How Does It Feel When Your Parents Get Divorced?
BL - v73 - My 15 '77 - p1423
CLW - v49 - D '77 - p229

BERGER, Terry (continued)
KR - v45 - Mr 1 '77 - p225
SLJ - v24 - N '77 - p53
Subject: Divorce

Stepchild
CCB-B - v34 - S '80 - p2
Cur R - v21 - F '82 - p28
Hi Lo - v2 - S '80 - p4
Inter BC - v12 - #6 '81 p20
SLJ - v27 - S '80 - p56
Subject: Remarriage; Stepparents

BERKE, Sally

Monster At Loch Ness
Cur R - v17 - Ag '78 - p228
SLJ - v25 - S '78 - p128
Subject: Loch Ness monster

BERKOW, Ira 1940-
BioIn 10, ConAu 97, IntAu&W 82, WhoAm 86

Beyond The Dream: Occasional Heroes Of Sports
BL - v72 - D 1 '75 - p487
KR - v43 - Jl 15 '75 - p810
LJ - v100 - S 15 '75 - p1647
PW - v208 - Jl 28 '75 - p117
SLJ - v22 - F '76 - p58
WLB - v50 - Mr '76 - p545

BERLINER, Don 1930-
ConAu 105, -21NR, IntAu&W 86, SmATA 33

Flying-Model Airplanes
BL - v79 - F 15 '83 - p773
SLJ - v29 - Ja '83 - p71
Subject: Airplanes

Helicopters
BL - v80 - Ja 15 '84 - p744
SLJ - v30 - Ap '84 - p121
Subject: Helicopters

Personal Airplanes
BL - v79 - O 15 '82 - p308
PW - v221 - My 28 '82 - p72
SLJ - v29 - F '83 - p72
Subject: Airplanes

BERLONI, William
see Thomas, Allison (co-author)

BERMAN, Connie 1949-
ConAu 93

Leif Garrett
SLJ - v25 - Mr '79 - p135
Subject: Biography; Entertainers

The Shaun Cassidy Scrapbook
Hi Lo - v1 - N '79 - p6
Subject: Biography; Singers

Top Recording Artist And TV Star! Shaun Cassidy
Hi Lo - v1 - N '79 - p6
SLJ - v26 - S '79 - p129
Subject: Actors and actresses; Biography; Singers

BERNA, Paul 1910?-
AuBYP, ConAu 73, OxChL, SmATA 15, ThrBJA, TwCChW 83B

The Clue Of The Black Cat
BL - v62 - O 15 '65 - p218
CCB-B - v19 - N '65 - p42
Comw - v83 - N 5 '65 - p157
CSM - v57 - N 4 '65 - pB12
HB - v41 - D '65 - p631
KR - v33 - S 1 '65 - p910
LJ - v90 - N 15 '65 - p5103
NS - v80 - N 6 '70 - p616
NYTBR - v70 - N 7 '65 - p59
Obs - Ja 10 '71 - p23
Par - v41 - Jl '66 - p98
SLJ - v24 - F '78 - p35

The Mule On The Expressway
BL - v65 - F 15 '69 - p650
HB - v45 - Ap '69 - p168
KR - v36 - S 15 '68 - p1047
Subject: France—Fiction

The Mystery Of Saint-Salgue
CSM - N 5 '64 - p5B
HB - v40 - D '64 - p618
LJ - v89 - S 5 '64 - p3480
NS - v66 - N 8 '63 - p670
NYTBR, Pt. 2 - N 1 '64 - p55
TLS - N 28 '63 - p974
Subject: Mystery and detective stories

BERNHEIM, Evelyne
see Bernheim, Marc (co-author)

BERNHEIM, Marc 1924-
ConAu 21R

African Success Story: The Ivory Coast
BL - v66 - Jl 1 '70 - p1339
BS - v30 - Mr 15 '71 - p548
CCB-B - v24 - S '70 - p3
Comw - v93 - F 26 '71 - p521
HB - v46 - O '70 - p487
SR - v53 - Jl 25 '70 - p29
Co-author: Bernheim, Evelyne
Subject: Ivory Coast

BERNICK, Deborah
see Bershad, Carol (co-author)

BERRY, Barbara J 1937-
ConAu 33R, SmATA 7, WrDr 86

Shannon
BW - v2 - N 3 '68 - p22
KR - v36 - Je 1 '68 - p595
LJ - v93 - N 15 '68 - p4411

BERRY, Erick (pseud.) 1892-1974
AuBYP, ConAu X, IlsCB 1946, JBA 34, –51, SmATA 2, –X
Real Name:
Best, Allena Champlin

When Wagon Trains Rolled To Santa Fe
LJ - v91 - D 15 '66 - p6209
Subject: Overland journeys to the Pacific; Santa Fe Trail

BERRY, James R 1932-
AuBYP SUP, BioIn 7, ConAu 21R

Kids On The Run
B&B - v7 - F '79 - p3
BL - v74 - My 1 '78 - p1420
BS - v38 - D '78 - p270
CCB-B - v32 - S '78 - p3
KR - v46 - Mr 1 '78 - p249
NYTBR - Ap 30 '78 - p53
PW - v213 - My 29 '78 - p52
SE - v43 - Ap '79 - p299
SLJ - v24 - Mr '78 - p136
Subject: Runaways

BERSHAD, Carol

Bodyworks: The Kids' Guide To Food And Physical Fitness
ASBYP - v15 - Spring '82 - p23
BW - v11 - O 25 '81 - p16
Cur R - v21 - My '82 - p212
HB - v57 - O '81 - p560
SLJ - v28 - O '81 - p138
Co-author: Bernick, Deborah
Subject: Health; Nutrition; Physical fitness

BESSER, Marianne

The Cat Book
KR - v35 - S 15 '67 - p1137
LJ - v92 - D 15 '67 - p4608
NYTBR - v72 - N 5 '67 - p6
Obs - N 30 '69 - p35
PW - v192 - S 4 '67 - p57
SB - v3 - D '67 - p246
Subject: Cats

BEST, Allena Champlin
see Berry, Erick

BETANCOURT, Jeanne 1941-
SmATA 43

Am I Normal?
BL - v82 - N 15 '85 - p484
Hi Lo - v4 - My '83 - p4
VOYA - v6 - Ag '83 - p144
WLB - v57 - F '83 - p511
Subject: Puberty; Sex instruction for youth

Between Us
BL - v82 - Ag '86 - p1682
PW - v229 - Ap 25 '86 - p81
SLJ - v33 - O '86 - p186
VOYA - v9 - Ag '86 - p139
Subject: Friendship—Fiction; Remarriage—Fiction

Dear Diary
BL - v82 - N 15 '85 - p484
CCB-B - v36 - Ap '83 - p143
Hi Lo - v4 - My '83 - p4
SLJ - v29 - Ap '83 - p120
VOYA - v6 - Ag '83 - p144
WLB - v57 - F '83 - p511
Subject: Puberty; Sex instruction for youth

Smile!: How To Cope With Braces
BL - v78 - Mr 15 '82 - p954
CCB-B - v36 - D '82 - p61
Inst - v91 - My '82 - p109
PW - v221 - Mr 26 '82 - p74
SB - v18 - N '82 - p94
SLJ - v28 - Ag '82 - p111
VOYA - v5 - O '82 - p53
WCRB - v8 - S '82 - p72
Subject: Health; Orthodontics

BETHANCOURT, T Ernesto (pseud.) 1932-
ChILR 3, ConAu X, FifBJA, SmATA 11
Real Name:
Paisley, Tom

Doris Fein: Legacy Of Terror
BL - v80 - Ap 1 '84 - p1108
CCB-B - v37 - Je '84 - p181
J Read - v28 - O '84 - p83
SLJ - v30 - My '84 - p103
VOYA - v6 - O '83 - p197
VOYA - v7 - O '84 - p195
Subject: Mystery and detective stories

Dr. Doom: Superstar
BL - v75 - O 15 '78 - p366

BETHANCOURT, T Ernesto (continued)
HB - v55 - F '79 - p67
KR - v46 - S 15 '78 - p1020
PW - v214 - Ag 28 '78 - p395
SLJ - v25 - D '78 - p69
Subject: Mystery and detective stories

The Great Computer Dating Caper
BL - v80 - Mr 1 '84 - p963
B Rpt - v3 - My '84 - p31
BS - v44 - My '84 - p78
CBRS - v12 - My '84 - p107
CCB-B - v37 - Ap '84 - p143
Cur R - v24 - Ja '85 - p39
EJ - v74 - D '85 - p54
Inter BC - v15 - #6 '84 p19
J Read - v30 - O '86 - p89
KR - v52 - Mr 1 '84 - pJ20
LATBR - Jl 1 '84 - p6
SLJ - v30 - Ap '84 - p121
VOYA - v7 - O '84 - p195
Subject: Computers—Fiction; Dating (Social customs)—Fiction; Inventions—Fiction

The Me Inside Of Me
BL - v82 - Ja 15 '86 - p751
CBRS - v14 - Ap '86 - p100
CCB-B - v39 - F '86 - p103
SLJ - v32 - Mr '86 - p173
VOYA - v9 - Ag '86 - p139
Subject: Mexican Americans—Fiction; Wealth—Fiction

New York City Too Far From Tampa Blues
BL - v71 - My 15 '75 - p963
CCB-B - v28 - Jl '75 - p174
Inter BC - v14 - #1 '83 p15
KR - v43 - Ap 15 '75 - p464
NYTBR - My 4 '75 - p28
PW - v207 - Ap 28 '75 - p45
SLJ - v22 - S '75 - p117
Subject: Rock music—Fiction

Tune In Yesterday
BL - v74 - My 1 '78 - p1420
BS - v38 - Ag '78 - p153
EJ - v67 - S '78 - p90
HB - v54 - Ag '78 - p400
KR - v46 - Mr 15 '78 - p311
NYTBR - Ap 30 '78 - p44
PW - v213 - Mr 6 '78 - p101
SE - v43 - Ap '79 - p302
SLJ - v24 - My '78 - p73
Subject: Space and time—Fiction

see also Paisley, Tom for additional titles

BETHEL, Dell 1929-
ConAu 29R

Inside Baseball
LJ - v94 - D 15 '69 - p4620
SR - v52 - Je 28 '69 - p1884
Subject: Baseball

BIBBY, Violet 1908-
AuBYP SUP, ConAu 102, SmATA 24, TwCChW 83, WrDr 86

Many Waters Cannot Quench Love
BL - v72 - D 15 '75 - p575
CCB-B - v29 - F '76 - p91
KR - v43 - O 1 '75 - p1136
PW - v208 - S 29 '75 - p50
SLJ - v22 - N '75 - p86
Subject: Great Britain—History—Fiction

BIBER, Yehoash

The Treasure Of The Turkish Pasha
CLW - v41 - O '69 - p139
KR - v36 - Ag 1 '68 - p815
LJ - v94 - F 15 '69 - p880
NYTBR - v73 - N 24 '68 - p42

BIEMILLER, Ruth 1914-
ConAu 37R, WhoAmW 77, WhoE 77

Dance: The Story Of Katherine Dunham
CCB-B - v22 - My '69 - p138
KR - v37 - Mr 1 '69 - p241
LJ - v94 - O 15 '69 - p3827
LJ - v98 - O 15 '73 - p3123
Subject: Biography

BIRCH, Claire

Tight Spot
SLJ - v32 - N '85 - p81
Subject: Mystery and detective stories

BIRO, Balint Stephen
see Biro, Val

BIRO, Val 1921-
ConAu 25R, –X, IlsBYP, IlsCB 1967, OxChL, SmATA 1, TwCChW 83, WhoArt 84, WhoWor 80, WrDr 86
Pseud./variant:
Biro, Balint Stephen

Gumdrop
B&B - v12 - Mr '67 - p60
LJ - v93 - F 15 '68 - p857
RT - v36 - My '83 - p929

BIRO, Val (continued)
Spec - N 11 '66 - p627
TLS - N 24 '66 - p1083
Subject: Automobiles—Fiction

BISHOP, Claire Huchet
AuBYP, BioIn 1, BkP, ConAu 73, JBA 51, OxChL, SmATA 14, TwCChW 83, WrDr 86

Martin De Porres, Hero
Comw - v99 - N 23 '73 - p212
Teacher - v91 - Ja '74 - p107
Subject: Biography; Blacks—Biography

BISHOP, Curtis Kent 1912-1967
AuBYP, ConAu P-1, SmATA 6

Fast Break
BL - v64 - F 15 '68 - p697
KR - v35 - S 1 '67 - p1054
LJ - v92 - D 15 '67 - p4633
Subject: Basketball

Sideline Pass
KR - v33 - Jl 1 '65 - p630
LJ - v90 - O 15 '65 - p4638
Subject: Sports

BLACK, Susan Adams 1953-
ConAu 105, SmATA 40

Crash In The Wilderness
SLJ - v27 - Ja '81 - p57
Subject: Survival

BLACKBURN, Joyce Knight 1920-
ConAu 17R, SmATA 29

Martha Berry
CCB-B - v22 - My '69 - p138
KR - v36 - O 1 '68 - p1116
PW - v194 - O 14 '68 - p65
Subject: Biography

BLACKNALL, Carolyn

Sally Ride: America's First Woman In Space
BL - v81 - F 15 '85 - p841
Inter BC - v16 - #7 '85 p19
SB - v21 - N '85 - p101
SLJ - v31 - Mr '85 - p162
Subject: Astronauts; Biography

BLAIR, Shannon

Call Me Beautiful
BL - v81 - F 1 '85 - p783
Subject: Love—Fiction

Star Struck!
CCB-B - v38 - My '85 - p160
SLJ - v32 - S '85 - p151
VOYA - v8 - O '85 - p264
Subject: Love—Fiction

Wrong Kind Of Boy
CCB-B - v39 - O '85 - p23
SLJ - v32 - S '85 - p151
VOYA - v8 - F '86 - p392
Subject: Love—Fiction

BLAKE, Susan

Summer Breezes
BL - v80 - Je 15 '84 - p1473
SLJ - v31 - S '84 - p137
VOYA - v7 - D '84 - p259
Subject: Love—Fiction; Sailing—Fiction

BLANTON, Catherine 1907-
AuBYP, ConAu 1R

Hold Fast To Your Dreams
BL - v51 - My 15 '55 - p391
CE - v46 - Ap '70 - p368
EJ - v57 - My '68 - p757
KR - v23 - Ja 1 '55 - p4
LJ - v80 - Ap 15 '55 - p1008
NYTBR - Ap 24 '55 - p32

BLASSINGAME, Wyatt 1909-1985
AuBYP, ConAu 3NR, -114, IntAu&W 82, SmATA 34, -41N, WhoHr&F, WrDr 84

The Story Of The United States Flag
Am - v121 - D 13 '69 - p598
Subject: Flags

Thor Heyerdahl: Viking Scientist
SB - v16 - S '80 - p11
Subject: Biography; Explorers

BLAU, Melinda 1943-

Killer Bees
Cur R - v17 - Ag '78 - p228
SLJ - v24 - My '78 - p63
Subject: Brazilian honeybee

Whatever Happened To Amelia Earhart?
CCB-B - v31 - Je '78 - p155
Cur R - v17 - Ag '78 - p228
Subject: Air pilots

BLINN, William
LesBEnT

Brian's Song
BS - v32 - O 1 '72 - p316
Subject: Piccolo, Brian—Drama; Sayers, Gale—Drama

BLIVEN, Bruce, Jr. 1916-
ConAu 7NR, SmATA 2, WhoAm 86, WhoWor 78

The American Revolution
BL - v55 - N 1 '58 - p135
KR - v26 - Jl 15 '58 - p510
NY - v34 - N 22 '58 - p215
NYTBR, Pt. 2 - N 2 '58 - p3
Subject: United States—History—Revolution, 1775-1783

New York
Choice - v18 - Je '81 - p1475
LJ - v106 - Mr 1 '81 - p555
NYTBR - Ja 4 '70 - p12
PW - v196 - D 8 '69 - p49
Co-author: Bliven, Naomi
Subject: New York (City)

BLIVEN, Naomi
see Bliven, Bruce, Jr. (co-author)

BLOUGH, Glenn O 1907-
AuBYP, ConAu P-1, MichAu 80, MorJA, SmATA 1, WhoAm 86

Discovering Insects
LJ - v92 - D 15 '67 - p4609
SA - v217 - D '67 - p146
Subject: Insects

BLUE, Betty A 1922-
ConAu 45

Authentic Mexican Cooking
BW - Mr 5 '78 - pF3
Kliatt - v12 - Spring '78 - p42
PW - v212 - N 21 '77 - p62
Subject: Cookery

BLUE, Rose 1931-
AuBYP SUP, ConAu 14NR, SmATA 5, WhoAmW 85, -87, WhoE 85

Nikki 108
BL - v69 - My 15 '73 - p904
CCB-B - v26 - Je '73 - p150
CE - v50 - N '73 - p97
PW - v203 - Mr 26 '73 - p70
Subject: Drug abuse—Fiction; Social adjustment—Fiction

The Thirteenth Year
BB - v5 - Ag '77 - p3
CCB-B - v31 - O '77 - p27
Cur R - v17 - Ag '78 - p186
SLJ - v23 - Ap '77 - p62
Subject: Bar mitzvah—Fiction; Jews—Fiction

We've Got The Power: Witches Among Us
Hi Lo - v3 - F '82 - p5
SLJ - v28 - Ap '82 - p69
VOYA - v5 - Je '82 - p43
Subject: Witchcraft

BLUE, Zachary

The Petrova Twist
Kliatt - v21 - Spring '87 - p5
Subject: Adventure and adventurers—Fiction

BLUMBERG, Rhoda 1917-
ConAu 9NR, SmATA 35, WhoAmW 83, WhoE 85

Witches
BL - v76 - N 1 '79 - p442
SLJ - v26 - F '80 - p52
Subject: Witchcraft

BLUME, Judy 1938-
ChILR 2, ConAu 13NR, ConLC 12, -30, CurBio 80, DcLB 52, FourBJA, SmATA 31, TwCChW 83, WhoAm 86, WrDr 86

Are You There, God? It's Me, Margaret
BL - v80 - S 1 '83 - p95
B Rpt - v5 - N '86 - p36
CE - v54 - Ja '78 - p125
Choice - v14 - N '77 - p1177
CLW - v52 - Ap '81 - p389
EJ - v69 - S '80 - p86
Emerg Lib - v11 - Ja '84 - p21
GP - v17 - My '78 - p3324
JB - v42 - Ag '78 - p198
KR - v38 - O 1 '70 - p1093
LJ - v95 - D 15 '70 - p4344
NS - v100 - N 14 '80 - p20
NY - v59 - D 5 '83 - p192
NYTBR, Pt. 2 - N 8 '70 - p14
NYTBR, Pt. 2 - N 8 '70 - p36
TES - Ag 4 '78 - p18
Time - v120 - Ag 23 '82 - p65
TLS - Ap 7 '78 - p383
Subject: Adolescence—Fiction

Blubber
BB - v3 - Ap '75 - p4

BLUME, Judy (continued)
BL - v71 - Ja 1 '75 - p459
CCB-B - v28 - My '75 - p142
CE - v51 - Ap '75 - p325
JB - v44 - Ag '80 - p185
KR - v42 - O 1 '74 - p1059
LJ - v99 - N 15 '74 - p3044
NYTBR - N 3 '74 - p42
NYTBR - N 3 '74 - p52
PW - v206 - N 25 '74 - p45
RT - v29 - Ja '76 - p421
Sch Lib - v28 - Je '80 - p147
SLJ - v33 - S '86 - p46
Teacher - v92 - Mr '75 - p112
TES - Ja 18 '80 - p43
Subject: Schools—Fiction

Deenie
BL - v70 - D 15 '73 - p444
CCB-B - v27 - Ap '74 - p123
Choice - v14 - N '77 - p1177
Comw - v99 - N 23 '73 - p215
JB - v45 - Je '81 - p119
J Read - v25 - My '82 - p777
KR - v41 - S 1 '73 - p965
LJ - v99 - My 15 '74 - p1471
NYTBR - N 4 '73 - p46
PT - v8 - S '74 - p132
PW - v204 - O 8 '73 - p97
RT - v31 - Ap '78 - p803
SMQ - v8 - Fall '79 - p27
Teacher - v91 - Ja '74 - p111
Teacher - v92 - F '75 - p116
TES - N 21 '80 - p31
Time - v120 - Ag 23 '82 - p65
Subject: Scoliosis—Fiction

Forever
B&B - My '86 - p20
BL - v72 - O 15 '75 - p291
CCB-B - v29 - Mr '76 - p106
EJ - v65 - Mr '76 - p90
EJ - v66 - Ja '77 - p64
EJ - v67 - My '78 - p90
GP - v15 - S '76 - p2938
HB - v61 - Ja '85 - p86
JB - v41 - F '77 - p49
KR - v43 - O 1 '75 - p1136
NS - v92 - N 5 '76 - p644
NYTBR - D 28 '75 - p20
PW - v208 - Ag 18 '75 - p63
Sch Lib - v32 - S '84 - p209
SLJ - v22 - N '75 - p95
TLS - O 1 '76 - p1238
TN - v37 - Fall '80 - p57
Subject: Sex role—Fiction; Venereal diseases—Fiction

It's Not The End Of The World
BL - v69 - O 1 '72 - p147
Can Child Lit - #25 '82 p30
CCB-B - v26 - O '72 - p23
Choice - v14 - N '77 - p1177
EJ - v61 - S '72 - p936
HB - v48 - O '72 - p466
HB - v61 - Ja '85 - p86
Inst - v82 - N '72 - p125
JB - v44 - F '80 - p26
KR - v40 - Ap 15 '72 - p476
LJ - v97 - O 15 '72 - p3451
NYTBR - S 3 '72 - p8
Teacher - v90 - My '73 - p73
TES - Ja 18 '80 - p43
Subject: Divorce—Fiction

Then Again, Maybe I Won't
BL - v68 - F 1 '72 - p465
CCB-B - v25 - F '72 - p87
Choice - v14 - N '77 - p1177
Comw - v95 - N 19 '71 - p188
JB - v43 - O '79 - p276
KR - v39 - N 1 '71 - p1155
LJ - v97 - Ap 15 '72 - p1612
NYTBR - Ja 16 '72 - p8
NYTBR, Pt. 2 - My 6 '73 - p28
PW - v200 - D 13 '71 - p42
SR - v54 - S 18 '71 - p49
Teacher - v90 - Ap '73 - p90
TES - Ja 18 '80 - p43
TN - v28 - Ap '72 - p309
Subject: Adolescence—Fiction

Tiger Eyes
BL - v78 - S 1 '81 - p36
BW - v11 - S 13 '81 - p9
CBRS - v10 - O '81 - p17
CCB-B - v35 - S '81 - p5
CLW - v53 - S '81 - p91
CSM - v74 - D 14 '81 - pB10
EJ - v70 - N '81 - p95
GP - v21 - Jl '82 - p3924
Inst - v91 - Ja '82 - p145
JB - v46 - O '82 - p194
J Read - v25 - Mr '82 - p614
KR - v50 - Ja 1 '82 - p10
LA - v59 - Ap '82 - p371
Nat - v233 - N 21 '81 - p551
NW - v98 - D 7 '81 - p101
NYTBR - v86 - N 15 '81 - p58
Obs - N 28 '82 - p31
PW - v220 - S 4 '81 - p56
SLJ - v28 - N '81 - p100
VOYA - v4 - O '81 - p30
Subject: Death—Fiction

BLUMENTHAL, Shirley
SmATA 46

Black Cats And Other Superstitions
SLJ - v25 - N '78 - p55
Subject: Superstition

BOATRIGHT, Lori

Out Of Bounds
BL - v79 - N 15 '82 - p442
SLJ - v29 - D '82 - p28
VOYA - v5 - D '82 - p30
Subject: Basketball—Fiction

BOEHM, Bruce

Connecticut Low
CBRS - v9 - Winter '81 - p45
CCB-B - v34 - Mr '81 - p126
SLJ - v27 - Ja '81 - p67
Co-author: Winn, Janet
Subject: Fathers and sons—Fiction; Floods—Fiction; Friendship—Fiction

BOLIAN, Polly 1925-
ConAu 33R, IlsBYP, SmATA 4

Growing Up Slim
BL - v68 - S 15 '71 - p99
Subject: Weight control

BOLOGNESE, Donald Alan 1934-
ConAu 97, FourBJA, IlsBYP, IlsCB 1957, -1967, SmATA 24

Drawing Fashions: Figures, Faces And Techniques
BL - v82 - Je 15 '86 - p1536
B Rpt - v5 - My '86 - p36
SLJ - v32 - Ap '86 - p96
Co-author: Raphael, Elaine
Subject: Fashion drawing

BOLTON, Carole
AuBYP SUP, ConAu 1NR, SmATA 6

The Good-Bye Year
BL - v79 - N 1 '82 - p365
B Rpt - v2 - S '83 - p35
CBRS - v11 - N '82 - p26
SLJ - v29 - N '82 - p95
Subject: Family problems—Fiction; Moving (Household)—Fiction

BOLTON, Evelyn
ConAu X, SmATA X, TwCChW 83, WrDr 86

Pseud./variant:
Bunting, Anne Evelyn

Dream Dancer
SLJ - v22 - S '75 - p97
Subject: Horses—Fiction

Goodbye Charlie
SLJ - v22 - S '75 - p97
Subject: Horses—Fiction

Lady's Girl
SLJ - v22 - S '75 - p97
Subject: Horses—Fiction

Ride When You're Ready
SLJ - v22 - S '75 - p97
Subject: Horses—Fiction; Self-acceptance—Fiction

Stable Of Fear
SLJ - v22 - S '75 - p97
Subject: Fear—Fiction; Horses—Fiction

BOND, Gladys Baker 1912-
ConAu 2NR, SmATA 14, WhoAmW 77, WhoWest 78

A Head On Her Shoulders
HB - v40 - Ag '64 - p373
LJ - v89 - Mr 15 '64 - p1446
NS - v67 - My 15 '64 - p776
PW - v193 - F 12 '68 - p79
TLS - Jl 9 '64 - p602

BONHAM, Frank 1914-
AuBYP, ConAu 4NR, ConLC 12, MorBMP, OxChL, SmATA 49, -3AS, ThrBJA, TwCChW 83, WrDr 86

Chief
BL - v68 - Ja 1 '72 - p390
BL - v68 - Ja 1 '72 - p392
BS - v33 - S 1 '73 - p258
BW - v7 - Ag 26 '73 - p13
CCB-B - v25 - D '71 - p55
CSM - v63 - N 11 '71 - pB1
EJ - v61 - Mr '72 - p435
KR - v39 - Ag 1 '71 - p813
LJ - v96 - N 15 '71 - p3906
PW - v200 - O 18 '71 - p50
SR - v54 - N 13 '71 - p62
Subject: Indians of North America—Fiction

Cool Cat
BL - v67 - Je 1 '71 - p832
CCB-B - v24 - Je '71 - p152
CSM - v63 - My 6 '71 - pB6
KR - v39 - F 15 '71 - p179
LJ - v96 - My 15 '71 - p1810

BONHAM, Frank (continued)
NYTBR - Ag 8 '71 - p8
PW - v199 - Mr 22 '71 - p53
Subject: City and town life—Fiction; Gangs—Fiction

Devilhorn
BL - v74 - Jl 1 '78 - p1676
CCB-B - v32 - O '78 - p23
KR - v46 - Je 15 '78 - p640
Par - v53 - S '78 - p32
PW - v213 - My 1 '78 - p85
SLJ - v25 - S '78 - p130
Subject: Goats—Fiction; Oregon—Fiction

Durango Street
BL - v62 - N 15 '65 - p319
BS - v25 - S 15 '65 - p251
CCB-B - v19 - O '65 - p27
CE - v46 - Ap '70 - p368
CSM - v57 - N 4 '65 - pB11
HB - v41 - O '65 - p505
KR - v33 - Jl 15 '65 - p689
LJ - v90 - N 15 '65 - p5086
NYTBR - v70 - S 5 '65 - p20
SE - v44 - O '80 - p481
Subject: Juvenile delinquency—Fiction

The Forever Formula
BL - v76 - Ja 1 '80 - p663
BS - v39 - F '80 - p407
CCB-B - v33 - Mr '80 - p127
J Read - v24 - O '80 - p85
KR - v48 - Ja 15 '80 - p69
LA - v57 - My '80 - p558
NYTBR - D 30 '79 - p19
SLJ - v26 - N '79 - p74
Subject: Science fiction

The Golden Bees Of Tulami
HB - v51 - Ap '75 - p145
Kliatt - v12 - Winter '78 - p5
KR - v42 - N 1 '74 - p1159
LJ - v99 - D 15 '74 - p3270
NYTBR - N 10 '74 - p10
PW - v206 - S 2 '74 - p69
Subject: City and town life—Fiction

Hey, Big Spender!
BL - v68 - My 15 '72 - p818
CCB-B - v26 - Ap '73 - p119
KR - v40 - F 15 '72 - p201
LJ - v98 - Ja 15 '73 - p266
Subject: Charities—Fiction

The Missing Persons League
BL - v73 - N 1 '76 - p405
CCB-B - v30 - N '76 - p39
KR - v44 - Ag 15 '76 - p909
NYTBR - Ja 9 '77 - p10
PW - v210 - Ag 2 '76 - p113
RT - v31 - O '77 - p20
SLJ - v23 - D '76 - p31
SLJ - v23 - D '76 - p53
Subject: Science fiction

Mystery Of The Fat Cat
BL - v64 - Je 15 '68 - p1183
BW - v2 - O 6 '68 - p20
CCB-B - v22 - O '68 - p23
HB - v44 - Ag '68 - p426
KR - v36 - Ap 1 '68 - p402
LJ - v93 - My 15 '68 - p2110
NYTBR - v73 - Ag 25 '68 - p24
SLJ - v24 - F '78 - p35
SR - v51 - Ag 24 '68 - p43
Subject: Mystery and detective stories

The Mystery Of The Red Tide
BL - v62 - Jl 1 '66 - p1042
CCB-B - v19 - Jl '66 - p174
LJ - v91 - My 15 '66 - p2716
NYTBR - v71 - Je 5 '66 - p42
PW - v189 - Je 6 '66 - p232
Subject: Mystery and detective stories

The Nitty Gritty
BL - v65 - N 1 '68 - p305
BW - v2 - N 3 '68 - p20
EJ - v58 - F '69 - p294
KR - v36 - S 15 '68 - p1056
LJ - v94 - Ja 15 '69 - p292
NYTBR - Ja 19 '69 - p28
Subject: Employment—Fiction

Viva Chicano
BL - v67 - S 15 '70 - p94
CCB-B - v24 - D '70 - p55
EJ - v63 - Ja '74 - p62
KR - v38 - My 15 '70 - p558
LJ - v95 - Jl '70 - p2538
NYTBR, Pt. 2 - My 24 '70 - p20
SR - v53 - Ag 22 '70 - p57
Subject: Juvenile delinquency—Fiction; Latin Americans—Fiction

War Beneath The Sea
NYTBR - O 7 '62 - p36

BONNELL, Dorothy Haworth 1914-
AuBYP SUP, ConAu 3NR

Passport To Freedom
BL - v27 - O 1 '67 - p261
KR - v35 - S 15 '67 - p1142

BONNELL, Dorothy Haworth (continued)
LJ - v92 - O 15 '67 - p3859
Subject: World War, 1939-1945—Fiction

BONTEMPS, Arna Wendell 1902-1973
AuBYP, ChlLR 6, ConAu 4NR, –41R, ConLC 1, –18, DcLB 48, –51, JBA 51, MorBMP, NegAl 83, SmATA 44, Str&VC

Chariot In The Sky
BL - v47 - My 15 '51 - p332
BL - v68 - Ja 15 '72 - p435
BS - v31 - F 15 '72 - p521
HB - v27 - S '51 - p333
KR - v19 - Mr 1 '51 - p129
KR - v39 - O 15 '71 - p1133
LJ - v76 - Je 1 '51 - p970
LJ - v97 - Ap 15 '72 - p1612
Notes - v8 - S '51 - p717
NYTBR - Je 17 '51 - p24
SR - v34 - Jl 21 '51 - p47
Subject: Jubilee singers—Fiction

Famous Negro Athletes
BL - v61 - Mr 15 '65 - p710
CCB-B - v19 - S '65 - p3
LJ - v89 - O 15 '64 - p4202
NYTBR, Pt. 2 - N 1 '64 - p54
Subject: Athletes; Blacks—Biography

Free At Last: The Life Of Frederick Douglas
Am - v125 - O 16 '71 - p295
Choice - v8 - S '71 - p901
KR - v39 - F 15 '71 - p204
LJ - v96 - Ap 15 '71 - p1358
Subject: Blacks—Biography

Golden Slippers: An Anthology Of Negro Poetry For Young Readers
BL - v38 - D 15 '41 - p135
Subject: Blacks—Poetry

BONTRAGER, Frances M

Can You Give First Aid?
BL - v76 - Jl 15 '80 - p1662

BOOKER, Simeon 1918-
BioIn 10, ConAu 9R, InB&W 80, SelBAAf, SelBAAu, WhoBlA 85

Susie King Taylor, Civil War Nurse
BL - v66 - D 15 '69 - p513
CLW - v42 - O '70 - p135
KR - v37 - Jl 15 '69 - p720
LJ - v94 - N 15 '69 - p4292
NYTBR - Je 22 '69 - p22
Subject: Biography

BOONE, Pat 1934-
BioIn 12, –13, ConAu 2NR, CurBio 59, IntMPA 86, RkOn 74, RolSEnR 83, SmATA 7, WhoAm 86, WrDr 86

'Twixt Twelve And Twenty
KR - v26 - O 15 '58 - p814
LJ - v84 - Ja 15 '59 - p255
Subject: Youth

BORISOFF, Norman

Bewitched And Bewildered: A Spooky Love Story
Hi Lo - v4 - Mr '83 - p4
Kliatt - v17 - Winter '83 - p5
SLJ - v29 - D '82 - p70
Subject: Witchcraft—Fiction

Easy Money
BL - v78 - Mr 15 '82 - p950
Hi Lo - v3 - F '82 - p2
Subject: Crime and criminals—Fiction

The Goof-Up
Hi Lo - v1 - N '79 - p4
Subject: Employment—Fiction

BORLAND, Hal 1900-1978
BioIn 6, –8, –11, ConAu 6NR, –77, SmATA 24N, –5, WhAm 7, WhoAm 78, WrDr 86

Penny: The Story Of A Free-Soul Basset Hound
BL - v68 - Jl 15 '72 - p965
BL - v68 - Jl 15 '72 - p997
BS - v32 - Je 15 '72 - p150
HB - v48 - Je '72 - p292
KR - v40 - Mr 15 '72 - p359
PW - v201 - Mr 20 '72 - p67
Subject: Dogs

When The Legends Die
Am - v108 - My 18 '63 - p717
Atl - v212 - Ag '63 - p125
BL - v81 - Jl '85 - p1546
BS - v23 - My 1 '63 - p54
CSM - Ap 25 '63 - p11
EJ - v63 - D '74 - p93
EJ - v73 - N '84 - p56
HM - v227 - S '63 - p115
Inter BC - v15 - #3 '84 p9
LJ - v88 - Ap 15 '63 - p1682
NYTBR - My 19 '63 - p32

BORLAND, Hal (continued)
NYTBR - My 19 '63 - p33
SR - v46 - My 25 '63 - p34
TLS - My 19 '66 - p442
TLS - D 4 '69 - p1384
TLS - Ap 6 '73 - p381

BOSLEY, Judith A

Lady In Pink
BL - v81 - My 1 '85 - p1240

BOSWORTH, J Allan 1925-
AuBYP, SmATA 19

Among Lions
BL - v70 - N 15 '73 - p336
KR - v41 - Jl 1 '73 - p691
LJ - v98 - S 15 '73 - p2661
Subject: Sierra Nevada Mountains—Fiction

A Darkness Of Giants
BL - v69 - O 1 '72 - p138
BL - v69 - O 1 '72 - p147
KR - v40 - Je 15 '72 - p678
LJ - v97 - S 15 '72 - p2944
Subject: Adventure and adventurers

BOTERMANS, Jack

Paper Flight: 48 Models Ready For Take-Off
Kliatt - v19 - Winter '85 - p62
SLJ - v31 - N '84 - p149
VOYA - v7 - F '85 - p342
Subject: Paper airplanes

BOTHWELL, Jean d. 1977
AuBYP, BioIn 1, ConAu 3NR, CurBio 46, JBA 51, SmATA 2

The First Book Of India
BL - v62 - Jl 1 '66 - p1046
BL - v68 - Ap 15 '72 - p727
LJ - v91 - Je 15 '66 - p3255
LJ - v97 - My 15 '72 - p1910
NYTBR - v71 - S 4 '66 - p16
NYTBR - F 27 '72 - p8
SLJ - v25 - N '78 - p56
Subject: India

Mystery Cup
KR - v36 - Ap 1 '68 - p391
LJ - v93 - My 15 '68 - p2127
PW - v193 - My 20 '68 - p62

BOUMA, Hans

An Eye On Israel
Kliatt - v13 - Spring '79 - p60
Subject: Israel—Poetry

BOVA, Ben 1932-
AuBYP, ChlLR 3, ConAu 11NR, ConSFA, DcLB Y81B, FifBJA, SmATA 6, TwCSFW 86, WhoSciF, WrDr 86

Escape!
CSM - v62 - My 7 '70 - pB6
KR - v38 - Ap 1 '70 - p389
NYTBR, Pt. 2 - My 24 '70 - p20

Man Changes The Weather
CCB-B - v27 - Mr '74 - p107
HB - v50 - Ag '74 - p401
KR - v41 - S 15 '73 - p1038
LJ - v99 - Mr 15 '74 - p886
PW - v204 - S 10 '73 - p52
SB - v10 - S '74 - p123
Subject: Air-pollution; Climatology; Weather

Out Of The Sun
Fant R - v7 - Jl '84 - p33
Kliatt - v18 - Spring '84 - p55
KR - v36 - Jl 1 '68 - p697
LATBR - My 13 '84 - p4
LJ - v93 - Jl '68 - p2736
WCRB - v10 - Mr '84 - p43
Subject: Science fiction

The Weather Changes Man
BL - v71 - S 15 '74 - p95
CE - v51 - Mr '75 - p276
KR - v42 - S 1 '74 - p945
PW - v206 - Ag 19 '74 - p84
SB - v10 - Mr '75 - p301
SLJ - v21 - Ap '75 - p49
Subject: Weather

BOWEN, J David 1930-
AuBYP, ConAu 105, SmATA 22

The Island Of Puerto Rico
KR - v36 - My 1 '68 - p520
LJ - v93 - Je 15 '68 - p2544
Subject: Puerto Rico

BOWEN, Robert Sydney 1900-1977
AuBYP, ConAu 73, SmATA 21N

Wipeout
BS - v28 - F 1 '69 - p446
EJ - v58 - My '69 - p778
KR - v36 - N 1 '68 - p1224
LJ - v94 - My 15 '69 - p2126
Subject: Surfing—Fiction

BOWMAN-KRUHM, Mary
see Wirths, Claudine G (co-author)

BOYD, L M

Boyd's Book Of Odd Facts
VOYA - v3 - F '81 - p52
Subject: Curiosities and wonders

BRADBURY, Bianca 1908-
AuBYP, ConAu 5NR, FourBJA, SmATA 3

Dogs And More Dogs
CCB-B - v22 - O '68 - p23
KR - v36 - My 1 '68 - p509
LJ - v93 - Ap 15 '68 - p1794
PW - v193 - My 27 '68 - p58
Subject: Dogs

In Her Father's Footsteps
CCB-B - v29 - Jl '76 - p171
CLW - v48 - O '76 - p137
Cur R - v16 - Ag '77 - p206
KR - v44 - Mr 15 '76 - p320
SLJ - v22 - My '76 - p66
Subject: Veterinarians—Fiction

The Loner
CCB-B - v24 - N '70 - p38
CE - v47 - N '70 - p87
Comw - v93 - N 20 '70 - p201
KR - v38 - My 15 '70 - p551
PW - v197 - Je 15 '70 - p64
SR - v53 - O 24 '70 - p67
Subject: Family life—Fiction

The Loving Year
Hi Lo - v3 - Je '82 - p3
Subject: Love—Fiction

Red Sky At Night
BS - v28 - My 1 '68 - p63
KR - v36 - F 1 '68 - p121
LJ - v93 - Ap 15 '68 - p1807

Where's Jim Now?
SLJ - v25 - O '78 - p152
Subject: Brothers and sisters—Fiction

BRADBURY, Ray 1920-
ConAu 2NR, ConLC 1, -3, -10, -15, ConNov 86, DcLB 2, -8, DrmM 1, SmATA 11, TwCSFW 86, WhoAm 86, WrDr 86

Dandelion Wine
KR - v43 - Ja 15 '75 - p90
Time - v105 - Mr 24 '75 - p78
Subject: Science fiction

BRADFORD, Richard Roark 1932-
ConAu 49, WhoAm 86, WrDr 86

Red Sky At Morning
BS - v34 - D 15 '74 - p428
EJ - v58 - F '69 - p294
Emerg Lib - v9 - Ja '82 - p12
NYTBR - v91 - S 21 '86 - p42
NYTBR, Pt. 2 - F 15 '70 - p22
PW - v195 - My 5 '69 - p55
Subject: Social adjustment—Fiction

BRADLEY, Buff

Where Do I Belong?: A Kids' Guide To Stepfamilies
CBRS - v11 - S '82 - p7
Kliatt - v17 - Winter '83 - p52
SB - v18 - Ja '83 - p149
SLJ - v29 - F '83 - p73
Subject: Divorce; Remarriage; Stepparents

BRADLEY, James J
see Taylor, Dawson (co-author)

BRADLEY, John
see Marshall, Ray (co-author)

BRADY, Mari

Please Remember Me
BL - v74 - N 1 '77 - p440
KR - v45 - Jl 15 '77 - p755
KR - v45 - Ag 15 '77 - p859
LJ - v102 - S 15 '77 - p1839
PW - v212 - Ag 8 '77 - p55
SLJ - v24 - Ja '78 - p99
Subject: Banks, Graham; Cancer—Biography

BRAGDON, Lillian
AuBYP, ConAu 73, SmATA 24

Luther Burbank, Nature's Helper
BL - v55 - Ap 15 '59 - p456
CSM - My 14 '59 - p11
KR - v27 - F 1 '59 - p92
NYTBR - My 24 '59 - p38
Subject: Biography

BRAITHWAITE, Edward 1912-
SelBAAf, WrDr 86

To Sir, With Love
BL - v56 - Mr 1 '60 - p408
KR - v28 - Ja 15 '60 - p70
LJ - v85 - F 15 '60 - p754
NS - v57 - Mr 28 '59 - p454
NY - v36 - Mr 26 '60 - p160

BRAITHWAITE, Edward (continued)
NYTBR - My 1 '60 - p6
SR - v43 - Ap 30 '60 - p18
TLS - Ap 3 '59 - p194
Subject: Teachers—Fiction

BRANCATO, Robin Fidler 1936-
ConAu 11NR, ConLC 35, FifBJA, SmATA 23

Blinded By The Light
BL - v75 - S 15 '78 - p175
B Rpt - v2 - S '83 - p24
BS - v38 - Mr '79 - p406
CCB-B - v32 - F '79 - p94
CLW - v52 - My '81 - p418
EJ - v68 - N '79 - p76
Inter BC - v10 - p17
KR - v46 - N 1 '78 - p1191
NW - v92 - D 18 '78 - p102
PW - v214 - N 13 '78 - p63
PW - v215 - My 21 '79 - p69
SLJ - v25 - O '78 - p152
Subject: Cults—Fiction

Come Alive At 505
BL - v76 - Mr 15 '80 - p1042
CBRS - v8 - Mr '80 - p75
J Read - v24 - N '80 - p173
Kliatt - v15 - Fall '81 - p5
KR - v48 - Mr 15 '80 - p369
NYTBR - v85 - Ap 27 '80 - p65
PW - v217 - Mr 28 '80 - p49
SLJ - v26 - Ag '80 - p74
TN - v38 - Summer '82 - p363
Subject: Disc jockeys—Fiction

Something Left To Lose
Kliatt - v13 - Spring '79 - p5
Subject: Friendship—Fiction

Sweet Bells Jangled Out Of Tune
BL - v78 - Mr 15 '82 - p949
B Rpt - v1 - Ja '83 - p38
BS - v42 - Je '82 - p118
CBRS - v10 - My '82 - p96
CCB-B - v35 - My '82 - p164
EJ - v71 - S '82 - p87
KR - v50 - Mr 15 '82 - p349
PW - v221 - Ja 15 '82 - p99
SLJ - v28 - My '82 - p67
VOYA - v5 - Ag '82 - p28
Subject: Grandmothers—Fiction; Old age—Fiction

Uneasy Money
BL - v83 - Ja 1 '87 - p705
KR - v54 - N 1 '86 - p1651
PW - v230 - N 28 '86 - p78
SLJ - v33 - D '86 - p112
Subject: Fathers and sons—Fiction; Wealth—Fiction

Winning
BB - v6 - My '78 - p3
BL - v74 - S 1 '77 - p30
BL - v74 - S 1 '77 - p36
BS - v37 - D '77 - p261
CCB-B - v31 - My '78 - p138
EJ - v68 - Ja '79 - p58
HB - v54 - Ap '78 - p167
J Read - v24 - Mr '81 - p522
KR - v45 - S 15 '77 - p995
PW - v213 - Ja 2 '78 - p65
SLJ - v24 - O '77 - p120
SMQ - v8 - Fall '79 - p27
TN - v36 - Summer '80 - p364
WLB - v52 - S '77 - p76
Subject: Physically handicapped—Fiction

BRANDON, William 1914-
ConAu 77

The Magic World
ABC - v22 - N '71 - p33
BL - v68 - S 1 '71 - p24
Choice - v8 - O '71 - p1010
CSM - v63 - Jl 8 '71 - p9
EJ - v60 - D '71 - p1263
EJ - v63 - Ja '74 - p70
LJ - v96 - Je 15 '71 - p2088
NYTBR - Ag 29 '71 - p2
Subject: American poetry—Translations; Indian poetry

BRANDRETH, Gyles 1948-
BioIn 9, ConAu 65, IntAu&W 77, SmATA 28, WrDr 86

Biggest Tongue Twister Book In The World
CE - v61 - My '85 - p364
Subject: Tongue twisters

Seeing Is Not Believing
SLJ - v27 - S '80 - p67
Subject: Optical illusions

Writing Secret Codes And Sending Hidden Messages
BL - v81 - Ja 1 '85 - p637
B Rpt - v5 - My '86 - p35
SLJ - v31 - O '84 - p154
Subject: Ciphers; Cryptography

BRANDT, Keith (pseud.)
ConAu X, SmATA X

BRANDT, Keith (continued)
Real Name:
Sabin, Louis

Pete Rose: "Mr. 300"
KR - v45 - Je 1 '77 - p583
SLJ - v24 - S '77 - p122
Subject: Baseball—Biography

see also Sabin, Louis for additional titles

BRANDT, Sue Reading 1916-
ConAu 25R

First Book Of How To Write A Report
KR - v36 - Ag 1 '68 - p821
Subject: Report writing

BRANLEY, Franklyn M 1915-
AmM&WS 86P, AuBYP, BioIn 6, BkP, ConAu 14NR, ConLC 21, MorJA, SmATA 4, WhoAm 80

A Book Of Stars For You
BL - v64 - Mr 1 '68 - p778
HB - v44 - Ap '68 - p203
KR - v35 - O 1 '67 - p1211
LJ - v93 - F 15 '68 - p866
PW - v192 - N 13 '67 - p80
SB - v3 - D '67 - p204
S & T - v35 - F '68 - p114
TN - v24 - Je '68 - p447
Subject: Stars

Feast Or Famine?: The Energy Future
ASBYP - v14 - Spring '81 - p9
BL - v77 - D 15 '80 - p570
BW - v10 - N 9 '80 - p18
CBRS - v9 - D '80 - p27
CCB-B - v34 - F '81 - p107
HB - v56 - D '80 - p668
KR - v49 - Ja 15 '81 - p77
Learning - v13 - S '84 - p146
SB - v16 - My '81 - p273
SLJ - v27 - F '81 - p73
Subject: Energy conservation; Power resources

BRANSCUM, Robbie 1937-
ConAu 8NR, FifBJA, SmATA 23

The Girl
CBRS - v15 - O '86 - p21
PW - v230 - S 26 '86 - p83
SLJ - v33 - O '86 - p187
VOYA - v9 - D '86 - p212
Subject: Friendship—Fiction

The Murder Of Hound Dog Bates
BL - v79 - D 15 '82 - p561
CBRS - v11 - Ja '83 - p47
HB - v58 - D '82 - p647
KR - v50 - Ag 1 '82 - p866
NYT - v132 - N 30 '82 - p23
NYTBR - v87 - O 3 '82 - p30
PW - v222 - N 19 '82 - p77
SLJ - v29 - D '82 - p82
Subject: Aunts—Fiction; Mountain life—Fiction; Mystery and detective stories

Toby Alone
CBRS - v8 - N '79 - p26
CCB-B - v33 - Ja '80 - p89
KR - v47 - N 15 '79 - p1331
LA - v57 - My '80 - p557
NYTBR - Ja 13 '80 - p26
Subject: Arkansas—Fiction; Death—Fiction; Mountain life—Fiction

BRAU, Maria M 1932-

Island In The Crossroads: The History Of Puerto Rico
BL - v65 - My 1 '69 - p1014
Cath W - v209 - Ap '69 - p48
LJ - v94 - Ap 15 '69 - p1790
Subject: Puerto Rico

BRAUN, Thomas 1944-

On Stage: Flip Wilson
SLJ - v23 - S '76 - p110
Subject: Blacks—Biography; Comedians

BRECKLER, Rosemary

Where Are The Twins?
CBRS - v8 - N '79 - p26
Hi Lo - v1 - Ja '80 - p4
SLJ - v26 - O '79 - p158
Subject: Adventure and adventurers—Fiction

BREWTON, John E
see Brewton, Sara Westbrook (co-author)

BREWTON, Sara Westbrook
BkP

America Forever New
BL - v64 - Je 1 '68 - p1138
CLW - v40 - O '68 - p143
HB - v44 - Ag '68 - p433
KR - v36 - Ap 15 '68 - p469
LJ - v93 - Je 15 '68 - p2544

BREWTON, Sara Westbrook (continued)
NYTBR - v73 - My 5 '68 - p44
PW - v193 - Mr 18 '68 - p54
SE - v33 - My '69 - p560
TN - v25 - Ap '69 - p309
Co-author: Brewton, John E
Subject: American poetry; Poetry

Shrieks At Midnight
A Lib - v1 - Ap '70 - p384
BL - v65 - Je 1 '69 - p1122
BW - v3 - My 4 '69 - p24
CE - v46 - Ap '70 - p378
HB - v45 - Ag '69 - p419
Inst - v79 - O '69 - p161
KR - v37 - Ap 1 '69 - p379
LJ - v94 - My 15 '69 - p2097
NYTBR - D 7 '69 - p68
NYTBR, Pt. 2 - My 4 '69 - p47
NYTBR, Pt. 2 - N 6 '69 - p61
PW - v195 - Ap 7 '69 - p56
Co-author: Brewton, John E
Subject: Poetry; Wit and humor

BRIDGES, Laurie (pseud.)
SmATA X
Real Name:
Bruck, Lorraine

Devil Wind
BL - v79 - Mr 1 '83 - p868
PW - v223 - F 11 '83 - p71
SF&FBR - O '83 - p43
SLJ - v29 - Mr '83 - p188
VOYA - v6 - O '83 - p211
WLB - v57 - My '83 - p773
Co-author: Alexander, Paul
Subject: Occult sciences—Fiction

BRIGGS, Mitchell Pirie
see Allen, Betty (co-author)

BRIGGS, Peter 1921-1975
BioIn 10, ConAu 57, –P-2, SmATA 31N, –39

Men In The Sea
BL - v65 - S 15 '68 - p112
KR - v36 - My 1 '68 - p520
LJ - v93 - O 15 '68 - p3976
NYTBR - v73 - Jl 7 '68 - p16
SR - v51 - Ag 24 '68 - p43
Subject: Oceanography; Underwater exploration

Science Ship
CCB-B - v23 - O '69 - p23
CSM - v61 - My 15 '69 - p11
KR - v37 - Ap 1 '69 - p387
LJ - v94 - N 15 '69 - p4293
SB - v5 - My '69 - p36
Subject: Oceanography

BRISCO, Patty (joint pseud.)
ConAu X, IntAu&W 86X, SmATA X, WrDr 86
Real Names:
Matthews, Clayton
Matthews, Patricia

Campus Mystery
BL - v74 - Mr 15 '78 - p1179
Hi Lo - v2 - F '81 - p5
Subject: Mystery and detective stories

Raging Rapids
Hi Lo - v1 - Mr '80 - p4
Teacher - v96 - My '79 - p127
Subject: Grandfathers—Fiction; Runaways—Fiction

BROCK, Virginia
AuBYP SUP

Pinatas
BL - v62 - My 15 '66 - p916
CE - v43 - F '67 - p354
LJ - v91 - Je 15 '66 - p3256
Subject: Pinatas

BROCKWAY, Edith 1914-
ConAu 17R

Land Beyond The Rivers
BS - v26 - My 1 '66 - p56
KR - v34 - F 1 '66 - p116
LJ - v91 - My 15 '66 - p2701

BRODERICK, Dorothy M 1929-
AuBYP, ConAu 13R, SmATA 5

Hank
BL - v63 - Ja 1 '67 - p483
CCB-B - v20 - Ja '67 - p71
Comw - v85 - N 11 '66 - p176
KR - v34 - Jl 1 '66 - p635
LJ - v91 - O 15 '66 - p5244
NYTBR - v71 - O 23 '66 - p34

BRODSKY, Mimi

The House At 12 Rose Street
PW - v195 - F 17 '69 - p160
Subject: City and town life—Fiction; Race relations—Fiction

BROGER, Achim 1944-
IntAu&W 82, SmATA 31

Running In Circles
BB - v6 - Je '78 - p4
BL - v74 - O 15 '77 - p371
CCB-B - v31 - Ja '78 - p75
HB - v54 - F '78 - p51
KR - v45 - Ag 1 '77 - p788
PW - v212 - O 31 '77 - p59
SLJ - v24 - N '77 - p66
Subject: Runaways—Fiction

BROMLEY, Dudley 1948-
ConAu 77

Bad Moon
Hi Lo - v1 - D '79 - p4
SLJ - v26 - D '79 - p98
Subject: Mystery and detective stories

Bedford Fever
CCB-B - v36 - D '82 - p62
Hi Lo - v3 - Ap '82 - p6
Subject: Science fiction

Comet!
Hi Lo - v3 - Ap '82 - p6
Subject: Science fiction

Final Warning
Hi Lo - v3 - Ap '82 - p6
Subject: Science fiction

Fireball
Hi Lo - v3 - Ap '82 - p6
Subject: Science fiction

Lost Valley
Hi Lo - v3 - Ap '82 - p6
Subject: Science fiction

The Seep
Hi Lo - v3 - Ap '82 - p6
Subject: Science fiction

BROOKE, Joshua

Just A Little Inconvenience
Kliatt - v12 - Spring '78 - p5

BROOKINS, Dana 1931-
ConAu 69, SmATA 28

Alone In Wolf Hollow
BL - v74 - Je 1 '78 - p1549
KR - v46 - Je 15 '78 - p636
SLJ - v24 - My '78 - p84
Subject: Mystery and detective stories; Orphans—Fiction

Rico's Cat
BL - v73 - F 15 '77 - p894
CLW - v48 - Ap '77 - p406
KR - v44 - O 1 '76 - p1092
SLJ - v23 - D '76 - p53
Subject: Cats—Fiction

BROOKS, Cathleen

The Secret Everyone Knows
BL - v77 - Jl 1 '81 - p1390
Hi Lo - v4 - S '82 - p2
Subject: Alcohol and youth

BROOKS, Jerome 1931-
BioIn 13, ConAu 2NR, SmATA 23

The Big Dipper Marathon
BL - v75 - Ap 15 '79 - p1286
BS - v39 - Ag '79 - p166
CBRS - v7 - Spring '79 - p116
CCB-B - v33 - S '79 - p2
HB - v55 - Ag '79 - p420
Inter BC - v11 - #7 '80 p20
Kliatt - v16 - Spring '82 - p5
KR - v47 - Jl 1 '79 - p744
SLJ - v25 - Ap '79 - p66
TN - v36 - Summer '80 - p366
Subject: Cousins—Fiction; Physically handicapped—Fiction; Self-acceptance—Fiction

The Testing Of Charlie Hammelman
B Rpt - v1 - Mr '83 - p23
Kliatt - v14 - Winter '80 - p4
SLJ - v28 - Ap '82 - p28

BROOKS, Polly Schoyer 1912-
ConAu 17NR, SmATA 12

When The World Was Rome
BL - v68 - Je 1 '72 - p855
BS - v32 - My 15 '72 - p97
CCB-B - v25 - Je '72 - p151
CE - v49 - Ja '73 - p204
KR - v40 - Ja 15 '72 - p74
LJ - v98 - My 15 '73 - p1687
Subject: Rome—History

BROW, Thea

The Secret Cross Of Lorraine
BL - v77 - Mr 1 '81 - p925
CBRS - v9 - Spring '81 - p105
CCB-B - v34 - Jl '81 - p208
CE - v58 - N '81 - p108
HB - v57 - Je '81 - p299
LA - v58 - O '81 - p846
PW - v219 - Mr 20 '81 - p62
SLJ - v27 - Ap '81 - p121
Subject: France—Fiction; Mystery and detective stories

BROWER, Millicent
ConAu 15NR, SmATA 8

Young Performers
BL - v81 - My 15 '85 - p1329
SLJ - v31 - My '85 - p99
Subject: Actors and actresses

BROWN, Alexis (pseud.) 1922-
ConAu X, SmATA X
Real Name:
Baumann, Amy Brown Beeching

Treasure In Devil's Bay
KR - v33 - Ja 15 '65 - p62
LJ - v90 - Je 15 '65 - p2882

BROWN, Fern G 1918-
ConAu 17NR, SmATA 34

Hard Luck Horse
SLJ - v22 - Mr '76 - p99
Subject: Horses—Fiction

BROWN, Irene Bennett 1932-
ConAu 12NR, SmATA 3

Answer Me, Answer Me
BL - v82 - S 1 '85 - p52
CBRS - v14 - F '86 - p76
CCB-B - v39 - D '85 - p62
SLJ - v32 - O '85 - p180
VOYA - v9 - Ap '86 - p28

BROWN, Jackum

Fair Game
Hi Lo - v1 - My '80 - p3
SLJ - v25 - My '79 - p70
Subject: Juvenile delinquency—Fiction

BROWN, Larry 1947-
WhoFtbl 74

I'll Always Get Up
BL - v70 - Ja 15 '74 - p508
BS - v33 - N 15 '73 - p359
KR - v41 - Ag 1 '73 - p844
LJ - v98 - S 15 '73 - p2566
PW - v204 - Ag 6 '73 - p56
Co-author: Gildea, William
Subject: Brown, Larry; Football—Biography

BROWN, Marion Marsh 1908-
AuBYP, ConAu 3NR, DrAS 82E, IntAu&W 77, SmATA 6

Homeward The Arrow's Flight
BL - v77 - O 15 '80 - p324
CBRS - v9 - S '80 - p6
CCB-B - v34 - N '80 - p48
CE - v57 - Ja '81 - p174
CLW - v52 - My '81 - p452
Inter BC - v13 - #1 '82 p18
SLJ - v28 - S '81 - p133
VOYA - v3 - F '81 - p41
Co-author: Crone, Ruth
Subject: Indians of North America—Biography; Physicians

The Silent Storm
BS - v23 - O 15 '63 - p263
CC - v80 - D 18 '63 - p1586
Comw - v79 - N 15 '63 - p238
LJ - v88 - S 15 '63 - p3346
NYTBR - Ja 26 '64 - p26
Subject: Biography; Keller, Helen; Macy, Anne

BROWN, Roy Frederick 1921-1982
ConAu 117, -65, FourBJA, IntAu&W 82, OxChL, SmATA 39N, TwCChW 83, WrDr 84

The Cage
BL - v74 - N 1 '77 - p467
CCB-B - v31 - My '78 - p139
Comw - v104 - N 11 '77 - p731
EJ - v67 - S '78 - p90
HB - v54 - F '78 - p51
KR - v45 - O 15 '77 - p1103
PW - v212 - Ag 29 '77 - p367
SE - v42 - Ap '78 - p321
SLJ - v24 - N '77 - p66
TLS - Mr 25 '77 - p359
Subject: Behavior—Fiction

The White Sparrow
BL - v71 - Ap 15 '75 - p865
CCB-B - v29 - S '75 - p4
CLW - v47 - D '75 - p234
HB - v51 - Je '75 - p273
KR - v43 - Ap 1 '75 - p371
LR - v24 - Fall '74 - p320
Obs - Ag 4 '74 - p28
SLJ - v21 - My '75 - p53
TLS - S 20 '74 - p1006
Subject: London—Fiction; Survival—Fiction

BROWNMILLER, Susan 1935-
BioIn 10, -12, -13, ConAu 103, CurBio 78, WhoAm 84, WhoAmW 85, WorAl, WrDr 86

Shirley Chisholm
BL - v67 - D 15 '70 - p338
CCB-B - v24 - Je '71 - p152
LJ - v95 - N 15 '70 - p4041
PW - v198 - S 28 '70 - p79

BROWNMILLER, Susan (continued)
RSR - v11 - Spring '83 - p13
Co-author: Mathews, William H
Subject: Blacks—Biography; Legislators

BRUCK, Lorraine
see Bridges, Laurie

BRUNING, Nancy P

The Kids' Book Of Disco
Kliatt - v14 - Winter '80 - p60

BRUNN, Robert

The Initiation
BL - v79 - Ja 15 '83 - p668
Kliatt - v17 - Winter '83 - p16
SLJ - v29 - Ap '83 - p120
VOYA - v6 - Ap '83 - p36
WLB - v57 - My '83 - p773
Subject: Supernatural—Fiction; Vampires—Fiction

BUCHANAN, William (pseud.) 1930-
AuBYP, BioIn 8, ConAu X, WrDr 84
Real Name:
Buck, William Ray

A Shining Season
EJ - v69 - F '80 - p70
EJ - v69 - F '80 - p94
Kliatt - v14 - Winter '80 - p27
KR - v46 - O 15 '78 - p1160
PW - v214 - O 23 '78 - p53
Subject: Baker, John; Cancer—Biography; Runners (Sports)

BUCHENHOLZ, Bruce 1916-

A Way With Animals
BL - v74 - Jl 1 '78 - p1671
Comw - v105 - N 10 '78 - p734
LJ - v103 - Jl '78 - p1422
SLJ - v25 - O '78 - p142
Subject: Animals; Behavior

BUCK, Margaret Waring 1910-
AuBYP, ConAu 5R, IntAu&W 82, SmATA 3, WrDr 86

Where They Go In Winter
BL - v65 - O 15 '68 - p240
CE - v46 - N '69 - p98
HB - v45 - F '69 - p69
KR - v36 - Jl 1 '68 - p693
LJ - v93 - O 15 '68 - p3965
PW - v194 - S 2 '68 - p60
SB - v5 - My '69 - p52
Subject: Animals; Behavior

BUCK, Ray

Pete Rose: "Charlie Hustle"
BL - v80 - O 1 '83 - p302
SLJ - v30 - S '83 - p119
Subject: Baseball—Biography

BUCK, William Ray
see Buchanan, William

BUEHR, Walter 1897-1971
AuBYP, ConAu 3NR, IlsCB 1946, -1957, SmATA 3, ThrBJA

Storm Warning: The Story Of Hurricanes And Tornadoes
BL - v68 - Jl 15 '72 - p1002
CCB-B - v26 - N '72 - p39
KR - v40 - Ap 1 '72 - p403
LJ - v97 - S 15 '72 - p2944
SB - v8 - D '72 - p231
Subject: Hurricanes; Storms; Tornadoes

Volcano
LJ - v87 - Ap 15 '62 - p1692
NYTBR - Ag 19 '62 - p20
Subject: Volcanoes

BULL, Angela 1936-
ConAu 9NR, IntAu&W 82, SmATA 45, TwCChW 83, WrDr 86

Anne Frank
SLJ - v31 - Mr '85 - p162
Subject: Jews—Biography; World War, 1939-1945

BULLA, Clyde Robert 1914-
Au&ICB, AuBYP, BioIn 9, BkP, ConAu 18NR, MorJA, SmATA 41, TwCChW 83, WhoAm 86, WrDr 86

Almost A Hero
B Rpt - v2 - S '83 - p24
CBRS - v10 - F '82 - p65
CCB-B - v35 - Mr '82 - p122
Hi Lo - v3 - My '82 - p4
KR - v50 - F 15 '82 - p207
SLJ - v28 - F '82 - p86
VOYA - v5 - Je '82 - p30

BUNTING, Anne Evelyn
see Bolton, Evelyn; Bunting, Eve

BUNTING, Eve 1928-
AuBYP SUP, ConAu X, FifBJA, SmATA X, TwCChW 83, WhoAm 86, WrDr 86

BUNTING, Eve (continued)
Pseud./variant:
Bunting, Anne Evelyn

The Big Find
Hi Lo - Je '80 - p3
Subject: Crime and criminals—Fiction; Friendship—Fiction

Blacksmith At Blueridge
BL - v74 - O 1 '77 - p283
BL - v74 - O 1 '77 - p285
Cur R - v16 - D '77 - p361
Hi Lo - v2 - F '81 - p6

Day Of The Earthlings
BL - v75 - O 15 '78 - p389
SLJ - v25 - Ja '79 - p51
Subject: Science fiction

Face At The Edge Of The World
BL - v81 - Ag '85 - p1656
B Rpt - v5 - S '86 - p31
BS - v45 - Ja '86 - p397
CBRS - v14 - Winter '86 - p64
EJ - v75 - D '86 - p58
HB - v62 - Ja '86 - p61
SLJ - v32 - D '85 - p98
VOYA - v8 - D '85 - p318
Subject: Blacks—Fiction; Suicide—Fiction

Fifteen
BL - v74 - Je 15 '78 - p1620
SLJ - v25 - S '78 - p130
Subject: Adolescence—Fiction

The Followers
BL - v75 - O 15 '78 - p389
SLJ - v25 - Ja '79 - p51
Subject: Animals—Fiction

For Always
BL - v74 - Je 15 '78 - p1620
SLJ - v25 - S '78 - p130
Subject: Skateboarding—Fiction

Ghost Behind Me
BL - v80 - Jl '84 - p1547
VOYA - v7 - Ag '84 - p143

The Ghosts Of Departure Point
BL - v79 - N 1 '82 - p365
B Rpt - v2 - My '83 - p36
BS - v42 - D '82 - p363
CBRS - v11 - N '82 - p26
CCB-B - v36 - N '82 - p43
Hi Lo - v4 - My '83 - p7
Kliatt - v19 - Winter '85 - p18
KR - v50 - O 1 '82 - p1109
LA - v60 - Mr '83 - p363
RT - v37 - O '83 - p62
SLJ - v29 - Ap '83 - p110
VOYA - v5 - D '82 - p30
Subject: Ghosts—Fiction; Traffic accidents—Fiction

The Giant Squid
BL - v78 - Ap 15 '82 - p1099
Hi Lo - v3 - Je '82 - p5
SB - v18 - S '82 - p33
SLJ - v28 - Ag '82 - p111

The Girl In The Painting
BL - v74 - Je 15 '78 - p1620
BL - v80 - Jl '84 - p1525
SLJ - v25 - S '78 - p130
Subject: Schools—Fiction

The Great White Shark
ASBYP - v16 - Winter '83 - p15
BL - v78 - Je 15 '82 - p1371
Hi Lo - v4 - N '82 - p4
SB - v18 - Mr '83 - p210
SLJ - v29 - N '82 - p78
Subject: Sharks

The Haunting Of Kildoran Abbey
BL - v74 - Jl 1 '78 - p1677
CCB-B - v32 - O '78 - p24
JB - v44 - F '80 - p26
PW - v213 - My 22 '78 - p233
SLJ - v25 - S '78 - p154
WCRB - v4 - N '78 - p59
Subject: Ireland—Fiction

The Haunting Of Safekeep
BL - v81 - Ap 15 '85 - p1179
BS - v45 - N '85 - p319
CBRS - v13 - Jl '85 - p142
CCB-B - v38 - Je '85 - p181
PW - v227 - Je 28 '85 - p75
RT - v39 - O '85 - p98
SLJ - v31 - My '85 - p110
VOYA - v8 - Ag '85 - p183
Subject: Ghosts—Fiction; Mothers and daughters—Fiction

If I Asked You, Would You Stay?
BL - v80 - My 15 '84 - p1340
BS - v44 - S '84 - p231
CBRS - v12 - Je '84 - p116
CCB-B - v37 - Jl '84 - p201
EJ - v74 - F '85 - p100
J Read - v29 - F '86 - p464
SLJ - v31 - S '84 - p126
VOYA - v7 - Ag '84 - p143

The Island Of One
BL - v75 - O 15 '78 - p389
SLJ - v25 - Ja '79 - p51
Subject: Science fiction

Just Like Everyone Else
BL - v74 - Je 15 '78 - p1620

BUNTING, Eve (continued)
SLJ - v25 - S '78 - p130
Subject: Individuality—Fiction

Maggie The Freak
BL - v74 - Je 15 '78 - p1621
BL - v80 - Jl '84 - p1525
SLJ - v25 - S '78 - p130
Subject: Sex role—Fiction; Sports—Fiction

The Mask
BL - v75 - O 15 '78 - p389
CCB-B - v32 - Ja '79 - p74
SLJ - v25 - Ja '79 - p51
Subject: Extrasensory perception—Fiction

The Mirror Planet
BL - v75 - O 15 '78 - p389
SLJ - v25 - Ja '79 - p51
Subject: Science fiction

Nobody Knows But Me
BL - v74 - Je 15 '78 - p1621
SLJ - v25 - S '78 - p130
Subject: Schools—Fiction

Oh, Rick!
BL - v74 - Je 15 '78 - p1621
SLJ - v25 - S '78 - p130
Subject: Weight control—Fiction

One More Flight
Am - v135 - D 11 '76 - p428
B&B - v22 - N '76 - p78
HB - v53 - Ap '77 - p158
JB - v41 - Ap '77 - p85
KR - v44 - Mr 15 '76 - p321
Par - v51 - N '76 - p28
PW - v209 - Ap 26 '76 - p60
SE - v41 - Ap '77 - p348
SLJ - v22 - My '76 - p57
Subject: Birds—Fiction; Emotional problems—Fiction

A Part Of The Dream
BL - v74 - Je 15 '78 - p1621
SLJ - v25 - S '78 - p130
Subject: Divorce—Fiction; Mexico—Fiction; Mothers and daughters—Fiction

The Robot People
BL - v75 - O 15 '78 - p389
SLJ - v25 - Ja '79 - p51
Subject: Robots—Fiction

Someone Is Hiding On Alcatraz Island
HB - v61 - Mr '85 - p177
HB - v62 - Jl '86 - p474
J Read - v28 - My '85 - p759
PW - v226 - O 19 '84 - p47
PW - v229 - Ap 25 '86 - p88
SLJ - v31 - D '84 - p100
TN - v42 - Fall '85 - p95
VOYA - v7 - F '85 - p322
VOYA - v9 - D '86 - p258
Subject: Gangs—Fiction

The Space People
BL - v75 - O 15 '78 - p389
SLJ - v25 - Ja '79 - p51
Subject: Science fiction

Survival Camp!
BL - v74 - Je 15 '78 - p1621
SLJ - v25 - S '78 - p130
Subject: Camping—Fiction; Survival—Fiction

Two Different Girls
BL - v74 - Je 15 '78 - p1621
SLJ - v25 - S '78 - p130
Subject: Schools—Fiction

The Undersea People
BL - v75 - O 15 '78 - p389
SLJ - v25 - Ja '79 - p51
Subject: Science fiction

The Waiting Game
BL - v77 - Je 15 '81 - p1342
BS - v41 - My '81 - p78
CCB-B - v34 - Jl '81 - p208
Hi Lo - v2 - My '81 - p3
J Read - v25 - D '81 - p285
KR - v49 - My 1 '81 - p574
PW - v219 - Ja 30 '81 - p75
SLJ - v27 - My '81 - p86
VOYA - v4 - Je '81 - p27
Subject: Football—Fiction; Friendship—Fiction

BURCH, Robert J 1925-
AuBYP, ConAu 17NR, DcLB 52, MorBMP, OxChL, SmATA 1, ThrBJA, TwCChW 83, WhoAm 86, WrDr 86

Hut School And The Wartime Home-Front Heroes
BL - v70 - My 1 '74 - p998
CCB-B - v28 - S '74 - p2
Comw - v101 - N 22 '74 - p193
HB - v50 - Ag '74 - p374
Inst - v84 - N '74 - p134
J Ho E - v67 - Ja '75 - p58
KR - v42 - Ap 15 '74 - p423
LJ - v99 - N 15 '74 - p3044
NYTBR - My 5 '74 - p40

BURCH, Robert J (continued)
Teacher - v92 - S '74 - p129
Subject: Schools—Fiction; World War, 1939-1945—Fiction

Queenie Peavy
BL - v62 - Je 15 '66 - p998
CCB-B - v19 - Je '66 - p159
HB - v42 - Ag '66 - p433
KR - v34 - Ap 15 '66 - p428
LJ - v91 - Je 15 '66 - p3256
NYTBR - v71 - My 8 '66 - p33
PW - v189 - Je 13 '66 - p128
TCR - v68 - F '67 - p451
Subject: Country life—Fiction; Schools—Fiction

The Whitman Kick
BL - v74 - N 1 '77 - p467
BS - v37 - Mr '78 - p398
CCB-B - v31 - Mr '78 - p107
EJ - v67 - Mr '78 - p80
HB - v54 - Ap '78 - p168
KR - v46 - Ja 1 '78 - p7
Par - v53 - Je '78 - p40
SLJ - v24 - N '77 - p66
Subject: Adolescence—Fiction; Social adjustment—Fiction

BURCHARD, Marshall
AuBYP SUP

Sports Hero: Brooks Robinson
BL - v76 - Ap 1 '80 - p1133
BL - v77 - O 1 '80 - p258
BL - v78 - O 1 '81 - p241
CCB-B - v25 - Mr '72 - p103
Inst - v91 - Ap '82 - p22
KR - v39 - D 1 '71 - p1258
LJ - v97 - My 15 '72 - p1930
SLJ - v26 - Ap '80 - p105
SLJ - v28 - D '81 - p84
Co-author: Burchard, Sue H
Subject: Baseball—Biography

Sports Hero: Joe Morgan
BL - v74 - Je 15 '78 - p1621
BL - v76 - Ap 1 '80 - p1133
BL - v77 - O 1 '80 - p258
CCB-B - v34 - N '80 - p48
Inst - v91 - Ap '82 - p22
KR - v46 - Jl 1 '78 - p690
SLJ - v25 - S '78 - p131
SLJ - v26 - Ap '80 - p105
Subject: Baseball—Biography; Blacks—Biography

Sports Hero: Johnny Bench
BL - v70 - S 1 '73 - p48
BL - v76 - Ap 1 '80 - p1133
BL - v77 - O 1 '80 - p258
CCB-B - v26 - Je '73 - p151
Inst - v91 - Ap '82 - p22
KR - v41 - F 1 '73 - p118
LJ - v98 - My 15 '73 - p1703
SLJ - v26 - Ap '80 - p105
SLJ - v28 - D '81 - p84
Co-author: Burchard, Sue H
Subject: Baseball—Biography

Sports Hero: Kareem Abdul Jabbar
BL - v76 - Ap 1 '80 - p1133
BL - v77 - O 1 '80 - p258
BL - v78 - O 1 '81 - p241
CCB-B - v34 - N '80 - p48
Inst - v91 - Ap '82 - p22
KR - v40 - Jl 15 '72 - p804
LJ - v97 - D 15 '72 - p4089
SLJ - v26 - Ap '80 - p105
SLJ - v28 - D '81 - p84
Co-author: Burchard, Sue H
Subject: Basketball—Biography

see also Burchard, Sue H for additional titles

BURCHARD, Peter Duncan 1921-
AuBYP, ConAu 18NR, IlsCB 1946, -1957, -1967, IntAu&W 86, SmATA 5, ThrBJA, WhoAmA 84

A Quiet Place
BL - v69 - Ja 15 '73 - p488
KR - v40 - N 15 '72 - p1311
LJ - v98 - Ja 15 '73 - p266
NYTBR - N 12 '72 - p14
PW - v202 - D 4 '72 - p62
Subject: Vacations—Fiction

BURCHARD, Sue H 1937-
AuBYP SUP, ConAu 19NR, SmATA 22

Sports Star: Brad Park
BL - v76 - Jl 15 '80 - p1678
BL - v78 - O 1 '81 - p241
BL - v80 - Ap 1 '84 - p1123
CCB-B - v36 - F '83 - p103
Cur R - v20 - N '81 - p471
Cur R - v23 - Ap '84 - p58
Hi Lo - v2 - O '80 - p6
Hi Lo - v3 - S '81 - p7
Inst - v90 - Ja '81 - p116
Kliatt - v17 - Spring '83 - p52
LA - v59 - Mr '82 - p271
RT - v36 - O '82 - p79
RT - v38 - O '84 - p71
SLJ - v26 - Ja '80 - p66
SLJ - v27 - S '80 - p67
SLJ - v27 - Ap '81 - p121
SLJ - v30 - Ja '84 - p73

BURCHARD, Sue H (continued)
SLJ - v30 - Mr '84 - p156
SLJ - v31 - S '84 - p114
Subject: Hockey—Biography

Sports Star: Dorothy Hammill
BL - v76 - Jl 15 '80 - p1678
BL - v78 - O 1 '81 - p241
BL - v80 - Ap 1 '84 - p1123
CCB-B - v36 - F '83 - p103
Cur R - v20 - N '81 - p471
Cur R - v23 - Ap '84 - p58
Hi Lo - v1 - S '79 - p4
Hi Lo - v2 - O '80 - p6
Inst - v90 - Ja '81 - p116
Kliatt - v17 - Spring '83 - p52
LA - v59 - Mr '82 - p271
RT - v36 - O '82 - p79
RT - v38 - O '84 - p71
SLJ - v26 - Ja '80 - p66
SLJ - v27 - S '80 - p67
SLJ - v27 - Ap '81 - p121
SLJ - v30 - Ja '84 - p73
SLJ - v30 - Mr '84 - p156
SLJ - v31 - S '84 - p114
Subject: Biography; Ice skaters

Sports Star: Elvin Hayes
BL - v76 - Jl 15 '80 - p1678
BL - v78 - O 1 '81 - p241
BL - v80 - Ap 1 '84 - p1123
CCB-B - v36 - F '83 - p103
Cur R - v20 - N '81 - p471
Cur R - v23 - Ap '84 - p58
Hi Lo - v2 - O '80 - p6
Hi Lo - v3 - S '81 - p7
Inst - v90 - Ja '81 - p116
Kliatt - v17 - Spring '83 - p52
LA - v59 - Mr '82 - p271
RT - v36 - O '82 - p79
RT - v38 - O '84 - p71
SLJ - v26 - Ja '80 - p66
SLJ - v27 - S '80 - p67
SLJ - v27 - Ap '81 - p121
SLJ - v30 - Ja '84 - p73
SLJ - v30 - Mr '84 - p156
SLJ - v31 - S '84 - p114
Subject: Basketball—Biography; Blacks—Biography

Sports Star: Fernando Valenzuela
BL - v76 - Jl 15 '80 - p1678
BL - v78 - O 1 '81 - p241
BL - v80 - Ap 1 '84 - p1123
CCB-B - v36 - F '83 - p103
Cur R - v20 - N '81 - p471
Cur R - v23 - Ap '84 - p58
Hi Lo - v2 - O '80 - p6
Hi Lo - v3 - S '81 - p7
Inst - v90 - Ja '81 - p116
Kliatt - v17 - Spring '83 - p52
LA - v59 - Mr '82 - p271
RT - v36 - O '82 - p79
RT - v38 - O '84 - p71
SLJ - v26 - Ja '80 - p66
SLJ - v27 - S '80 - p67
SLJ - v27 - Ap '81 - p121
SLJ - v30 - Ja '84 - p73
SLJ - v30 - Mr '84 - p156
SLJ - v31 - S '84 - p114
Subject: Baseball—Biography

Sports Star: Herschel Walker
BL - v76 - Jl 15 '80 - p1678
BL - v78 - O 1 '81 - p241
BL - v80 - Ap 1 '84 - p1123
CCB-B - v36 - F '83 - p103
Cur R - v20 - N '81 - p471
Cur R - v23 - Ap '84 - p58
Hi Lo - v2 - O '80 - p6
Hi Lo - v3 - S '81 - p7
Inst - v90 - Ja '81 - p116
Kliatt - v17 - Spring '83 - p52
LA - v59 - Mr '82 - p271
RT - v36 - O '82 - p79
RT - v38 - O '84 - p71
SLJ - v26 - Ja '80 - p66
SLJ - v27 - S '80 - p67
SLJ - v27 - Ap '81 - p121
SLJ - v30 - Ja '84 - p73
SLJ - v30 - Mr '84 - p156
SLJ - v31 - S '84 - p114
Subject: Blacks—Biography; Football—Biography

Sports Star: John McEnroe
BL - v76 - Jl 15 '80 - p1678
BL - v78 - O 1 '81 - p241
BL - v80 - Ap 1 '84 - p1123
CCB-B - v36 - F '83 - p103
Cur R - v20 - N '81 - p471
Cur R - v23 - Ap '84 - p58
Hi Lo - v2 - O '80 - p6
Hi Lo - v3 - S '81 - p7
Inst - v90 - Ja '81 - p116
Kliatt - v17 - Spring '83 - p52
LA - v59 - Mr '82 - p271
RT - v36 - O '82 - p79
RT - v38 - O '84 - p71
SLJ - v26 - Ja '80 - p66
SLJ - v27 - S '80 - p67
SLJ - v27 - Ap '81 - p121
SLJ - v30 - Ja '84 - p73
SLJ - v30 - Mr '84 - p156
SLJ - v31 - S '84 - p114
Subject: Tennis—Biography

Sports Star: Larry Bird
BL - v76 - Jl 15 '80 - p1678
BL - v78 - O 1 '81 - p241

BURCHARD, Sue H (continued)
BL - v80 - Ap 1 '84 - p1123
CCB-B - v36 - F '83 - p103
Cur R - v20 - N '81 - p471
Cur R - v23 - Ap '84 - p58
Hi Lo - v2 - O '80 - p6
Hi Lo - v3 - S '81 - p7
Inst - v90 - Ja '81 - p116
Kliatt - v17 - Spring '83 - p52
LA - v59 - Mr '82 - p271
RT - v36 - O '82 - p79
RT - v38 - O '84 - p71
SLJ - v26 - Ja '80 - p66
SLJ - v27 - S '80 - p67
SLJ - v27 - Ap '81 - p121
SLJ - v30 - Ja '84 - p73
SLJ - v30 - Mr '84 - p156
SLJ - v31 - S '84 - p114
Subject: Basketball—Biography

Sports Star: Nadia Comaneci
AB - v60 - N 14 '77 - p2819
BL - v74 - Ja 1 '78 - p750
BL - v76 - Jl 15 '80 - p1678
BL - v80 - Ap 1 '84 - p1123
CCB-B - v36 - F '83 - p103
Cur R - v20 - N '81 - p471
Cur R - v23 - Ap '84 - p58
Hi Lo - v2 - O '80 - p6
Hi Lo - v3 - S '81 - p7
Inst - v90 - Ja '81 - p116
KR - v45 - O 15 '77 - p1098
LA - v59 - Mr '82 - p271
RT - v38 - O '84 - p71
SLJ - v24 - D '77 - p64
SLJ - v26 - Ja '80 - p66
SLJ - v27 - S '80 - p67
SLJ - v30 - Ja '84 - p73
SLJ - v30 - Mr '84 - p156
Subject: Biography; Gymnasts

Sports Star: Reggie Jackson
BL - v76 - Jl 15 '80 - p1678
BL - v78 - O 1 '81 - p241
BL - v80 - Ap 1 '84 - p1123
BL - v81 - O 1 '84 - p253
CCB-B - v36 - F '83 - p103
Cur R - v20 - N '81 - p471
Cur R - v23 - Ap '84 - p58
Hi Lo - v2 - O '80 - p6
Inst - v90 - Ja '81 - p116
Kliatt - v17 - Spring '83 - p52
KR - v47 - Jl 15 '79 - p794
LA - v59 - Mr '82 - p271
RT - v36 - O '82 - p79
RT - v38 - O '84 - p71
SLJ - v25 - My '79 - p83
SLJ - v26 - Ja '80 - p66
SLJ - v27 - S '80 - p67
SLJ - v30 - Ja '84 - p73
SLJ - v30 - Mr '84 - p156
SLJ - v31 - S '84 - p114
Subject: Baseball—Biography; Blacks—Biography

Sports Star: Tommy John
BL - v76 - Jl 15 '80 - p1678
BL - v78 - O 1 '81 - p241
BL - v80 - Ap 1 '84 - p1123
CCB-B - v36 - F '83 - p103
Cur R - v20 - N '81 - p471
Cur R - v23 - Ap '84 - p58
Hi Lo - v2 - O '80 - p6
Hi Lo - v3 - S '81 - p7
Inst - v90 - Ja '81 - p116
Kliatt - v17 - Spring '83 - p52
LA - v59 - Mr '82 - p271
RT - v36 - O '82 - p79
RT - v38 - O '84 - p71
SLJ - v26 - Ja '80 - p66
SLJ - v27 - S '80 - p67
SLJ - v27 - Ap '81 - p121
SLJ - v30 - Ja '84 - p73
SLJ - v30 - Mr '84 - p156
SLJ - v31 - S '84 - p114
Subject: Baseball—Biography

Sports Star: Tony Dorsett
BL - v76 - Jl 15 '80 - p1678
BL - v78 - O 1 '81 - p241
BL - v80 - Ap 1 '84 - p1123
CCB-B - v36 - F '83 - p103
Cur R - v20 - N '81 - p471
Cur R - v23 - Ap '84 - p58
Hi Lo - v1 - S '79 - p4
Hi Lo - v2 - O '80 - p6
Inst - v90 - Ja '81 - p116
Kliatt - v17 - Spring '83 - p52
LA - v59 - Mr '82 - p271
RT - v33 - O '79 - p36
RT - v38 - O '84 - p71
SLJ - v25 - D '78 - p70
SLJ - v26 - Ja '80 - p66
SLJ - v27 - S '80 - p67
SLJ - v30 - Ja '84 - p73
SLJ - v30 - Mr '84 - p156
SLJ - v31 - S '84 - p114
Subject: Football—Biography

Sports Star: Wayne Gretzky
BL - v76 - Jl 15 '80 - p1678
BL - v78 - O 1 '81 - p241
BL - v80 - Ap 1 '84 - p1123
CCB-B - v36 - F '83 - p103
Cur R - v20 - N '81 - p471
Cur R - v23 - Ap '84 - p58
Hi Lo - v2 - O '80 - p6
Hi Lo - v3 - S '81 - p7
Inst - v90 - Ja '81 - p116
Kliatt - v17 - Spring '83 - p52

BURCHARD, Sue H (continued)
LA - v59 - Mr '82 - p271
RT - v36 - O '82 - p79
RT - v38 - O '84 - p71
SLJ - v26 - Ja '80 - p66
SLJ - v27 - S '80 - p67
SLJ - v27 - Ap '81 - p121
SLJ - v30 - Ja '84 - p73
SLJ - v30 - Mr '84 - p156
SLJ - v31 - S '84 - p114
Subject: Hockey—Biography

see also Burchard, Marshall (co-author) for additional titles

BURDICK, Eugene
see Lederer, William Julius (co-author)

BURGER, Carl 1888-1967
BioIn 8, ConAu P-2, IlsCB 1957, SmATA 9

All About Cats
BL - v63 - N 15 '66 - p372
CLW - v38 - Ja '67 - p336
CSM - v58 - N 3 '66 - pB11
LJ - v92 - Mr 15 '67 - p1314
Subject: Cats

BURGER, John Robert 1942-
ConAu 81

Children Of The Wild
ACSB - v12 - Fall '79 - p11
BL - v75 - S 1 '78 - p43
CCB-B - v32 - O '78 - p25
SLJ - v24 - My '78 - p73
Co-author: Gardner, Lewis
Subject: Feral children

BURKE, James Lee 1936-
ConAu 13R

To The Bright And Shining Sun
BS - v30 - S 1 '70 - p210
KR - v38 - Je 1 '70 - p617
LJ - v95 - My 15 '70 - p1969
LJ - v95 - Jl '70 - p2514
LJ - v95 - D 15 '70 - p4327
NYTBR - Ag 9 '70 - p33
PW - v197 - Je 1 '70 - p63

BURLESON, Elizabeth

Middl'un
CCB-B - v22 - Mr '69 - p108
KR - v36 - Je 1 '68 - p595

BURNESS, Gordon

How To Watch Wildlife
CLW - v44 - Mr '73 - p509
LJ - v98 - My 15 '73 - p1679
Subject: Wildlife watching

BURNETT, Frances Hodgson 1849-1924
ConAu 108, DcLB 42, DcLEL, IntDcWB, JBA 34, OxChL, TwCChW 83, WhAm 1, WhoChL, YABC 2

A Little Princess
LR - v25 - Spring '75 - p34
NY - v57 - D 7 '81 - p238
Spec - v234 - Ap 12 '75 - p442
Teacher - v93 - N '75 - p118
Subject: London—Fiction; Schools—Fiction

The Secret Garden
B&B - v22 - D '76 - p75
B&B - v22 - Ja '77 - p64
LR - v25 - Fall '76 - p278
NY - v46 - D 5 '70 - p216
NY - v62 - D 1 '86 - p115
NYTBR - My 14 '61 - p793
Obs - D 8 '74 - p25
S Liv - v21 - Ap '86 - p92
Spec - v235 - Jl 26 '75 - p116
TES - O 1 '82 - p31
Subject: Orphans—Fiction; Physically handicapped—Fiction

BURNFORD, Sheila 1918-1984
ChlLR 2, ConAu 1NR, -112, FourBJA, OxChL, Profile 1, SmATA 3, -38N, TwCChW 83, WhoCanL 85

The Incredible Journey
Atl - v207 - Mr '61 - p117
Atl Pro Bk R - v10 - N '83 - p2
B&B - v14 - Ag '69 - p38
BL - v57 - My 1 '61 - p545
BL - v81 - D 15 '84 - p583
CC - v78 - S 13 '61 - p1082
Comw - v74 - My 26 '61 - p234
CSM - Mr 16 '61 - p11
HB - v37 - Je '61 - p253
KR - v28 - D 1 '60 - p1007
LJ - v86 - Ja 1 '61 - p110
NYTBR - Ap 23 '61 - p34
SR - v44 - My 13 '61 - p51
TN - v34 - Winter '78 - p189
Subject: Animals—Fiction

BURTON, Hester 1913-
AuBYP SUP, ChlLR 1, ConAu 10NR, IntAu&W 86, OxChL, SmATA 7, ThrBJA, TwCChW 83, WhoChL, WrDr 86

Castors Away
BL - v23 - Je 15 '63 - p116
HB - v39 - Ag '63 - p388
LJ - v88 - Jl '63 - p2780
NS - v63 - My 18 '62 - p725
NYTBR, Pt. 2 - My 12 '63 - p2
TLS - Je 1 '62 - p398
Subject: Trafalgar (Cape), Battle of, 1805—Fiction

Flood At Reedsmere
BL - v64 - Je 1 '68 - p1138
CCB-B - v21 - Jl '68 - p170
HB - v44 - Je '68 - p322
KR - v36 - F 1 '68 - p122
LJ - v93 - S 15 '68 - p3298
NYTBR - v73 - My 5 '68 - p14
PW - v193 - Je 24 '68 - p68

In Spite Of All Terror
CCB-B - v24 - O '70 - p23
Emerg Lib - v11 - N '83 - p20
HB - v45 - Ag '69 - p414
LJ - v94 - Jl '69 - p2679
LJ - v94 - D 15 '69 - p4380
TLS - O 30 '70 - p1258
TN - v26 - N '69 - p83
Subject: Great Britain—History—Fiction; World War, 1939-1945—Fiction

Time Of Trial
Comw - v80 - My 22 '64 - p270
CSM - My 7 '64 - p8B
HB - v40 - Je '64 - p302
LJ - v89 - Je 15 '64 - p2666
NYTBR, Pt. 2 - My 10 '64 - p8
SR - v47 - Ag 15 '64 - p45
TLS - N 28 '63 - p974

BUSCEMA, John
see Lee, Stan (co-author)

BUSCH, Phyllis S 1909-
ConAu 107, SmATA 30

What About VD?
ACSB - v10 - Winter '77 - p8
BL - v72 - Jl 15 '76 - p1584
BL - v72 - Jl 15 '76 - p1593
BS - v36 - N '76 - p270
CLW - v48 - My '77 - p442
KR - v44 - My 15 '76 - p602
PW - v210 - Jl 12 '76 - p72
SB - v12 - Mr '77 - p214
SLJ - v23 - S '76 - p128
Subject: Venereal diseases

BUSH, Nancy

Bittersweet Sixteen
BL - v80 - F 1 '84 - p809
SLJ - v30 - Ag '84 - p79
VOYA - v7 - Je '84 - p91
Subject: Love—Fiction

BUTLER, Beverly 1932-
AuBYP, ConAu 4NR, SmATA 7

Captive Thunder
BW - v3 - My 4 '69 - p32
CCB-B - v23 - S '69 - p3
KR - v37 - Mr 1 '69 - p245
LJ - v94 - S 15 '69 - p3212
Subject: Prejudices—Fiction

Light A Single Candle
NYTBR - O 14 '62 - p34
Subject: Blind—Fiction

BUTLER, Hal 1913-
AuBYP, ConAu 57, MichAu 80

Sports Heroes Who Wouldn't Quit
BL - v70 - S 1 '73 - p44
KR - v41 - F 15 '73 - p190
LJ - v98 - My 15 '73 - p1706
Subject: Athletes

BUTLER, Marjorie

Man Who Killed A Bear With A Stick
LJ - v93 - F 15 '68 - p866

BUTTERS, Dorothy Gilman
see Gilman, Dorothy

BUTTERWORTH, Ben

Danger In The Mountains
Hi Lo - v2 - N '80 - p4
Co-author: Stockdale, Bill

The Desert Chase
Hi Lo - v2 - N '80 - p4
Co-author: Stockdale, Bill

The Diamond Smugglers
Hi Lo - v2 - N '80 - p4
Co-author: Stockdale, Bill

The Island Of Helos
Hi Lo - v2 - N '80 - p4
Co-author: Stockdale, Bill

Jim And The Dolphin
Hi Lo - v2 - N '80 - p4

BUTTERWORTH, Ben (continued)
Co-author: Stockdale, Bill

Jim And The Sun Goddess
Hi Lo - v2 - N '80 - p4
Co-author: Stockdale, Bill

Jim In Training
Hi Lo - v2 - N '80 - p4
Co-author: Stockdale, Bill

The Missing Aircraft
Hi Lo - v2 - N '80 - p4
Co-author: Stockdale, Bill

Prisoner Of Pedro Cay
Hi Lo - v2 - N '80 - p4
Co-author: Stockdale, Bill

The Shipwreckers
Hi Lo - v2 - N '80 - p4
Co-author: Stockdale, Bill

The Sniper At Zimba
Hi Lo - v2 - N '80 - p4
Co-author: Stockdale, Bill

The Temple Of Mantos
Hi Lo - v2 - N '80 - p4
Co-author: Stockdale, Bill

BUTTERWORTH, W E 1929-
AuBYP SUP, ConAu 18NR, FifBJA, SmATA 5, WhoS&SW 76
Pseud./variant:
Douglas, James M

Air Evac
BS - v27 - F 1 '68 - p429
KR - v35 - Jl 15 '67 - p814
LJ - v93 - Ja 15 '68 - p301

The Air Freight Mystery
BL - v75 - My 15 '79 - p1435
BL - v80 - Ja 15 '84 - p719

Black Gold
BL - v71 - Jl 1 '75 - p1123
BS - v35 - Jl '75 - p94
KR - v43 - Je 1 '75 - p614
SB - v11 - Mr '76 - p182
SLJ - v22 - S '75 - p117
Subject: Petroleum industry and trade

Crazy To Race
KR - v39 - Ap 1 '71 - p380
LJ - v96 - My 15 '71 - p1822
Subject: Automobile racing—Fiction

Dave White And The Electric Wonder Car
BL - v70 - Je 15 '74 - p1149
BS - v34 - Je 15 '74 - p148
KR - v42 - Ap 1 '74 - p370
LJ - v99 - My 15 '74 - p1471
Subject: Automobiles—Fiction

Grand Prix Driver
BL - v66 - Mr 15 '70 - p910
KR - v37 - S 1 '69 - p936
LJ - v94 - D 15 '69 - p4620
LJ - v95 - D 15 '70 - p4377
LJ - v96 - Ja 15 '71 - p282
PW - v196 - N 3 '69 - p49
Subject: Automobile racing—Fiction

Helicopter Pilot
BS - v27 - Ag 1 '67 - p182
KR - v34 - D 15 '66 - p1290
LJ - v92 - Jl '67 - p2658

Hot Wire
BL - v78 - Ag '82 - p1519
Hi Lo - v3 - Je '82 - p4
SLJ - v29 - S '82 - p116
VOYA - v5 - O '82 - p39
Subject: Courage—Fiction; Traffic accidents—Fiction; Trucks—Fiction

The Hotel Mystery
Hi Lo - v2 - N '80 - p5

Leroy And The Old Man
BL - v76 - Jl 1 '80 - p1593
BL - v76 - Jl 1 '80 - p1598
BS - v40 - Ag '80 - p191
CBRS - v8 - Ag '80 - p137
CCB-B - v33 - Jl '80 - p209
EJ - v70 - F '81 - p63
HB - v56 - O '80 - p523
Kliatt - v17 - Winter '83 - p5
SLJ - v27 - N '80 - p83
Subject: Crime and criminals—Fiction; Fishing—Fiction; Grandfathers—Fiction

Moose, The Thing, And Me
BL - v79 - F 15 '83 - p774
CBRS - v11 - F '83 - p68
CCB-B - v36 - F '83 - p103
SLJ - v29 - Ja '83 - p72
Subject: Humorous stories; Schools—Fiction

The Narc
BL - v69 - Mr 15 '73 - p712
CCB-B - v26 - Ap '73 - p121
EJ - v62 - Ap '73 - p647
KR - v40 - O 15 '72 - p1200
LJ - v98 - Ja 15 '73 - p266

BUTTERWORTH, W E (continued)
NYTBR - N 26 '72 - p8
Subject: Drug abuse—Fiction; Police—Fiction

Orders To Vietnam
BL - v64 - Jl 15 '68 - p1285
BS - v28 - Ag 1 '68 - p194
KR - v36 - Je 1 '68 - p604
LJ - v93 - Jl '68 - p2736
Subject: Vietnamese Conflict, 1961-1975—Fiction

The Roper Brothers And Their Magnificent Steam Automobile
KR - v44 - My 1 '76 - p540
SLJ - v23 - S '76 - p111
Subject: Automobiles—Fiction; Brothers and sisters—Fiction

Steve Bellamy
BL - v67 - S 1 '70 - p55
BS - v30 - My 1 '70 - p60
KR - v38 - Ap 15 '70 - p464
LJ - v95 - My 15 '70 - p1939
PW - v197 - Je 15 '70 - p64
Subject: Family life—Fiction; Fishing—Fiction

Stop And Search
BL - v65 - My 15 '69 - p1074
BS - v29 - My 1 '69 - p55
KR - v37 - Ap 15 '69 - p450
PW - v195 - Je 2 '69 - p135
Subject: Vietnamese Conflict, 1961-1975—Fiction

Stop, Thief!
B Rpt - v2 - S '83 - p24

The Tank Driver
BL - v75 - Mr 15 '79 - p1144
Hi Lo - v2 - Ap '81 - p2

Team Racer
KR - v40 - Mr 1 '72 - p266
Subject: Automobile racing—Fiction

Under The Influence
BL - v75 - Je 1 '79 - p1485
KR - v47 - My 15 '79 - p579
SLJ - v25 - Ap '79 - p66
Subject: Friendship—Fiction

Wrecker Driver
Hi Lo - v2 - My '81 - p4

see also Douglas, James M for additional titles

BYARS, Betsy 1928-
ChlLR 1, ConAu 18NR, ConLC 35, DcLB 52, MorBMP, SmATA 46, -1AS, ThrBJA, TwCChW 83, WrDr 86

The Animal, The Vegetable And John D Jones
BL - v78 - Je 1 '82 - p1311
BW - v12 - Ap 11 '82 - p10
CBRS - v10 - Ap '82 - p87
CCB-B - v35 - Je '82 - p183
GP - v21 - Jl '82 - p3932
HB - v58 - Je '82 - p284
Hi Lo - v4 - N '82 - p5
JB - v46 - O '82 - p195
J Read - v26 - O '82 - p88
KR - v50 - Mr 15 '82 - p346
LA - v59 - O '82 - p751
NYTBR - v87 - My 30 '82 - p14
PW - v221 - Ap 30 '82 - p59
Sch Lib - v30 - D '82 - p356
SLJ - v28 - Ap '82 - p67
TES - Je 11 '82 - p39
TES - Ap 27 '84 - p27
TLS - Jl 23 '82 - p794
VOYA - v5 - O '82 - p39
Subject: Beaches—Fiction; Interpersonal relations—Fiction

The Cartoonist
JB - v46 - O '82 - p177
Kliatt - v15 - Spring '81 - p5
TES - N 27 '81 - p23
TN - v38 - Winter '82 - p115
Subject: Family life—Fiction

The Pinballs
BL - v81 - My 1 '85 - p1261
B Rpt - v2 - S '83 - p24
Kliatt - v14 - Winter '80 - p5
Learning - v14 - Mr '86 - p64
NYTBR - v87 - F 28 '82 - p35
RT - v35 - Ap '82 - p793
SLJ - v30 - F '84 - p30
TES - My 2 '80 - p24
Subject: Foster home care—Fiction; Friendship—Fiction

The Summer Of The Swans
BL - v66 - Je 15 '70 - p1276
BL - v67 - Ap 1 '71 - p659
BW - v11 - O 11 '81 - p12
CCB-B - v24 - F '71 - p87
CE - v47 - Mr '71 - p315
CLW - v53 - Ap '82 - p394
Comw - v92 - My 22 '70 - p248
CSM - v62 - My 7 '70 - pB6
Cur R - v19 - Je '80 - p243
HB - v47 - F '71 - p53

BYARS, Betsy (continued)
KR - v38 - Mr 15 '70 - p320
Learning - v14 - Mr '86 - p65
LJ - v95 - Jl '70 - p2538
NYTBR - v86 - Ag 2 '81 - p31
NYTBR, Pt. 2 - N 5 '72 - p42
PW - v197 - My 18 '70 - p38
RT - v37 - F '84 - p505
TES - N 2 '84 - p26
TN - v27 - Ap '71 - p241
VV - v19 - D 16 '74 - p51
Subject: Mentally handicapped—Fiction

BYRON, Amanda

The Warning
BL - v81 - Je 15 '85 - p1448
Fant R - v8 - Ag '85 - p30
SF Chr - v7 - N '85 - p45
SLJ - v32 - N '85 - p94
VOYA - v8 - F '86 - p392
Subject: Love—Fiction; Occult sciences—Fiction

C

CALDER, Ritchie 1906-1982
ConAu 1R, CurBio 63, –86N, WorAu
Pseud./variant:
Ritchie-Calder, Peter

The Evolution Of The Machine
LJ - v94 - F 15 '69 - p882
NYTBR - Je 23 '68 - p3
Subject: Machinery

CALDWELL, Claire

Surf's Up For Laney
VOYA - v7 - D '84 - p258
Subject: Love—Fiction; Surfing—Fiction

CALHOUN, Mary Huiskamp 1926-
AuBYP, BioIn 7, –9, ConAu 5R, SmATA 2, ThrBJA

The Horse Comes First
BL - v70 - My 15 '74 - p1054
CE - v51 - O '74 - p32
HB - v50 - O '74 - p136
KR - v42 - Mr 15 '74 - p297
LJ - v99 - S 15 '74 - p2262
Subject: Horses—Fiction

White Witch Of Kynance
BS - v30 - S 1 '70 - p218
BW - v4 - My 17 '70 - p28
KR - v38 - Jl 1 '70 - p687
LJ - v95 - My 15 '70 - p1951
NYTBR - O 4 '70 - p30
TN - v27 - Je '71 - p431
Subject: Witchcraft—Fiction

CALLAHAN, Dorothy M 1934-
AuBYP, IntAu&W 86

Ruffian
BL - v80 - Ja 1 '84 - p677
SLJ - v30 - F '84 - p66
Subject: Horses

Thoroughbreds
BL - v80 - Ja 1 '84 - p678
SLJ - v30 - F '84 - p66
Subject: Horse racing

CALLAN, Jamie

Just Too Cool
Kliatt - v21 - Spring '87 - p5

CALLEN, Larry 1927-
ConAu X, FifBJA, SmATA 19
Pseud./variant:
Callen, Lawrence Willard Jr.

Sorrow's Song
BL - v75 - Je 1 '79 - p1488
CCB-B - v33 - N '79 - p43
HB - v55 - Ag '79 - p411
KR - v47 - Jl 15 '79 - p792
SLJ - v25 - My '79 - p58
Subject: Physically handicapped—Fiction; Whooping cranes—Fiction

CAMERON, Eleanor 1912-
AuBYP, ChlLR 1, ConAu 2NR, DcLB 52, OxChL, SmATA 25, ThrBJA, TwCChW 83, WhoAm 86, WrDr 86

A Room Made Of Windows
A Lib - v3 - Ap '72 - p419
Am - v125 - D 4 '71 - p488
B&B - v18 - N '72 - p98
BL - v67 - My 15 '71 - p796
BL - v68 - Ap 1 '72 - p668
BS - v31 - My 15 '71 - p98
BW - v5 - My 9 '71 - p5
CCB-B - v24 - Je '71 - p153
CE - v48 - O '71 - p32
CSM - v63 - My 6 '71 - pB6
HB - v47 - Je '71 - p290
LJ - v96 - My 15 '71 - p1780
LJ - v96 - My 15 '71 - p1800
NYT - v121 - D 16 '71 - p67
NYTBR - Ap 25 '71 - p40
NYTBR - D 5 '71 - p86
NYTBR, Pt. 2 - N 7 '71 - p28
PW - v199 - Ap 12 '71 - p83
SR - v54 - Ap 17 '71 - p45
TLS - N 3 '72 - p1319
TN - v28 - N '71 - p73
TN - v28 - Je '72 - p433
Subject: Family life—Fiction

CAMERON, Ian (pseud.) 1924-
ConAu X, ConSFA, IntAu&W 82X, SmATA X, WrDr 86

CAMERON, Ian (continued)
Real Name:
Payne, Donald Gordon

The Lost Ones
BS - v28 - Ap 15 '68 - p25
CLW - v40 - O '68 - p143
HB - v44 - Je '68 - p341
KR - v36 - Ja 15 '68 - p66
LJ - v93 - Mr 15 '68 - p1160
LJ - v93 - Jl '68 - p2739
PW - v193 - Ja 22 '68 - p269
SR - v51 - N 9 '68 - p73

CAMERON, Meg

Savage Spirit
Kliatt - v19 - Fall '85 - p5
SLJ - v32 - Ja '86 - p79
VOYA - v8 - F '86 - p388

CAMPANELLA, Roy 1921-
BioIn 10, -11, -13, CurBio 53, InB&W 80, NegAl 83, WhoAm 78, WhoBlA 85, WhoProB 73, WorAl

It's Good To Be Alive
BL - v56 - N 1 '59 - p152
KR - v27 - S 1 '59 - p678
LJ - v84 - O 1 '59 - p3026
NYTBR - O 25 '59 - p50
NYTBR - F 10 '74 - p25
SR - v42 - N 21 '59 - p46

CAMPBELL, Archie

Diamonds In The Dirt
BL - v75 - O 15 '78 - p357
Subject: Motorcycle racing—Fiction; Mystery and detective stories

CAMPBELL, Gail

Marathon: The World Of The Long-Distance Athlete
Choice - v14 - F '78 - p1679
LJ - v102 - O 1 '77 - p2077
PW - v211 - Mr 21 '77 - p82
SLJ - v24 - My '78 - p90
Subject: Athletes

CAMPBELL, Hope 1925-
ConAu 10NR, SmATA 20, WhoAmW 85, -87

Why Not Join The Giraffes?
BL - v64 - Ap 1 '68 - p920
BW - v2 - My 5 '68 - p26
CCB-B - v22 - S '68 - p3
CSM - v60 - Je 13 '68 - p5
KR - v36 - Ja 15 '68 - p56
LJ - v93 - F 15 '68 - p878
SR - v51 - My 11 '68 - p42

CAMPBELL, Joanna

Love Lost
SLJ - v32 - Ja '86 - p80

Loving
SLJ - v32 - S '85 - p151
Subject: Love—Fiction

Secret Identity
Kliatt - v17 - Winter '83 - p4
SLJ - v29 - Ja '83 - p80
VOYA - v5 - D '82 - p32

The Thoroughbred
BL - v78 - D 1 '81 - p490
Hi Lo - v3 - Ja '82 - p3
Kliatt - v16 - Winter '82 - p6
SLJ - v28 - F '82 - p86
Subject: Adolescence—Fiction; Horses—Fiction

CAPIZZI, Michael 1941-
ConAu 41R

Getting It All Together
CCB-B - v26 - Ap '73 - p121
KR - v40 - O 1 '72 - p1152
LJ - v98 - Ja 15 '73 - p266
PW - v202 - S 25 '72 - p60
Subject: Blacks—Fiction

CAPUTO, Robert

More Than Just Pets: Why People Study Animals
ACSB - v13 - #3 '80 p16
BL - v76 - My 1 '80 - p1288
Hi Lo - v1 - My '80 - p4
Inst - v89 - My '80 - p92
PW - v217 - Mr 14 '80 - p75
SB - v16 - S '80 - p33
SLJ - v27 - F '81 - p55
Subject: Animals; Zoology

CARABATSOS, James

Heroes
Kliatt - v12 - Winter '78 - p5

CARAS, Roger A 1928-
ConAu 5NR, IntAu&W 86, SmATA 12, WhoAm 86, WhoWorJ 78, WrDr 86

The Custer Wolf: Biography Of An American Renegade
B&B - v12 - D '66 - p48

CARAS, Roger A (continued)
BL - v62 - Mr 15 '66 - p686
BS - v27 - S 15 '67 - p238
CLW - v37 - Ap '66 - p554
KR - v33 - D 15 '65 - p1259
KR - v34 - Ja 1 '66 - p16
LJ - v91 - F 1 '66 - p705
LJ - v91 - Ap 15 '66 - p2228
LW - v30 - p33
NP - v40 - Ap '66 - p23
NW - v67 - Mr 14 '66 - p106
NY - v42 - Ap 2 '66 - p174
NYT - v115 - Jl 13 '66 - p45M
NYTBR - v71 - F 27 '66 - p6
Obs - N 30 '69 - p35
PW - v191 - Je 19 '67 - p86
SB - v2 - S '66 - p132
TLS - N 24 '66 - p1091
Subject: Wolves—Fiction

Sarang: The Story Of The Bengal Tiger And Of Two Children In Search Of A Miracle
BS - v28 - N 1 '68 - p313
KR - v36 - Ag 1 '68 - p838
NYTBR, pt. 1 - v73 - N 3 '68 - p54
PW - v194 - Jl 22 '68 - p56

CAREY, Ernestine Gilbreth
see Gilbreth, Frank B, Jr. (co-author)

CAREY, Mary Virginia 1925-
ConAu 17NR, IntAu&W 86, SmATA 44, WhoAmW 87

The Mystery Of Death Trap Mine
SLJ - v23 - Mr '77 - p143
Subject: Mystery and detective stories

The Mystery Of The Blazing Cliffs
BL - v78 - N 15 '81 - p437
SLJ - v28 - D '81 - p81
Subject: Mystery and detective stories

The Mystery Of The Invisible Dog
Hi Lo - v2 - Je '81 - p3
Subject: Mystery and detective stories

The Mystery Of The Magic Circle
Hi Lo - v2 - Je '81 - p3
Subject: Mystery and detective stories; Witchcraft—Fiction

The Mystery Of The Singing Serpent
Hi Lo - v2 - Je '81 - p3
J Read - v25 - D '81 - p284
Subject: Mystery and detective stories; Witchcraft—Fiction

The Mystery Of The Wandering Cave Man
BL - v79 - F 15 '83 - p774
Cur R - v22 - O '83 - p49
SLJ - v29 - D '82 - p82
Subject: Museums—Fiction; Mystery and detective stories

The Secret Of The Haunted Mirror
LJ - v99 - D 15 '74 - p3277
Subject: Mystery and detective stories

CARLISLE, Norman V 1910-

The New American Continent
BL - v69 - Jl 1 '73 - p1020
KR - v41 - Ag 1 '73 - p388
LJ - v99 - Ja 15 '74 - p206
Subject: Continental shelf

Satellites: Servants Of Man
BL - v67 - Je 1 '71 - p833
KR - v39 - Mr 1 '71 - p238
LJ - v96 - My 15 '71 - p1810
SB - v7 - My '71 - p79
Subject: Artificial satellites

CARLSON, Bernice Wells
see Hunt, Kari (co-author)

CARLSON, Dale Bick 1935-
AuBYP SUP, ConAu 3NR, SmATA 1, WhoAmW 87, WhoE 77, WhoWor 84

Baby Needs Shoes
BL - v71 - S 1 '74 - p38
CCB-B - v28 - My '75 - p143
KR - v42 - Jl 15 '74 - p742
LJ - v99 - S 15 '74 - p2285
PW - v206 - Jl 15 '74 - p115
Subject: Gambling—Fiction

The Frog People
BL - v78 - Ag '82 - p1519
CBRS - v10 - Ag '82 - p136
SLJ - v29 - S '82 - p117
Subject: Science fiction

The Plant People
CCB-B - v31 - S '77 - p9
Hi Lo - v1 - S '79 - p4
JB - v42 - Je '78 - p149
JB - v42 - O '78 - p264
NYTBR - O 9 '77 - p28
SLJ - v23 - My '77 - p66
Subject: Science fiction

CARLSON, Dale Bick (continued)

A Wild Heart
BL - v74 - N 15 '77 - p545
Hi Lo - v1 - S '79 - p6
JB - v42 - Ag '78 - p213
Kliatt - v13 - Spring '79 - p5
SLJ - v24 - D '77 - p53
Subject: Family life—Fiction; Social adjustment—Fiction

CARLSON, Diane

You Can't Tell Me What To Do!
Hi Lo - v1 - Ja '80 - p3
Subject: Short stories

CARLSON, Gordon

Get Me Out Of Here!: Real Life Stories Of Teenage Heroism
Hi Lo - v1 - Ja '80 - p3
Subject: Courage; Short stories

CARLSON, Natalie Savage 1906-
Au&ICB, AuBYP, ConAu 3NR, MorBMP, MorJA, OxChL, SmATA 2, -4AS, TwCChW 83, WhoAm 86, WrDr 86

The Half Sisters
Am - v123 - D 5 '70 - p496
B&B - v17 - Ag '72 - p93
BL - v67 - S 1 '70 - p55
BW - v4 - My 17 '70 - p16
CCB-B - v24 - N '70 - p39
CE - v47 - F '71 - p266
CLW - v42 - O '70 - p137
Comw - v93 - N 20 '70 - p200
HB - v46 - Ag '70 - p385
KR - v38 - My 1 '70 - p504
LJ - v95 - Jl '70 - p2531
NYTBR - S 27 '70 - p30
SR - v53 - Jl 25 '70 - p29
TLS - Jl 14 '72 - p805
Subject: Family life—Fiction

CARLSON, Nola

A New Face In The Mirror
CCB-B - v37 - Ja '84 - p84
SLJ - v30 - Mr '84 - p171
Subject: Automobiles—Fiction; Love—Fiction

CARMER, Carl 1893-1976
AuBYP, BioIn 3, -7, -11, ConAu 4NR, OxAmL 83, SmATA 37, Str&VC, WhAm 7, WhoAm 76

The Boy Drummer Of Vincennes
BW - v6 - N 5 '72 - p4
CCB-B - v26 - My '73 - p135
Inst - v82 - N '72 - p131
LJ - v98 - Mr 15 '73 - p992
NYTBR - Ja 28 '73 - p8
PW - v202 - O 30 '72 - p56
SE - v44 - O '80 - p479
Subject: United States—History—Revolution, 1775-1783—Fiction

Flag For The Fort
PW - v193 - Ja 15 '68 - p88
Subject: Flags

CARMICHAEL, Carrie
ConAu X, SmATA 40
Pseud./variant:
Carmichael, Harriet

Bigfoot: Man, Monster, Or Myth
Cur R - v17 - Ag '78 - p228
SLJ - v25 - S '78 - p128
Subject: Sasquatch

Secrets Of The Great Magicians
SLJ - v24 - My '78 - p64
Subject: Magic

CARMICHAEL, Harriet
see Carmichael, Carrie

CARPELAN, Bo 1926-
ConAu 2NR, EncWL 2, IntAu&W 82, IntWWP 82, SmATA 8

Bow Island
HB - v48 - Ap '72 - p143
KR - v39 - N 15 '71 - p1216
LJ - v97 - My 15 '72 - p1911
PW - v200 - S 20 '71 - p48
Subject: Friendship—Fiction

CARR, Harriett H 1899-
AuBYP, ConAu P-1, MichAu 80, MorJA, SmATA 3

The Mystery Of The Aztec Idol
BL - v55 - Jl 15 '59 - p633
HB - v35 - Ag '59 - p287
KR - v27 - F 1 '59 - p89
LJ - v84 - Jl '59 - p2220
NYTBR, Pt. 2 - My 10 '59 - p26
Subject: Mystery and detective stories

CARRICK, Carol 1935-
ConAu 17NR, FourBJA, SmATA 7

Some Friend!
BL - v76 - D 15 '79 - p609
CBRS - v8 - Winter '80 - p64
CCB-B - v33 - Ap '80 - p147
CLW - v51 - My '80 - p459
KR - v48 - F 1 '80 - p125
PW - v216 - D 3 '79 - p51
RT - v34 - O '80 - p103
SLJ - v26 - D '79 - p81
Subject: Friendship—Fiction

CARROLL, Jeffrey 1950-
ConAu 85

Climbing To The Sun
BB - v6 - Ap '78 - p3
BL - v74 - Mr 1 '78 - p1099
Cur R - v17 - Ag '78 - p182
KR - v45 - O 15 '77 - p1103
SLJ - v24 - Ap '78 - p92
Subject: Indians of North America—Fiction; Mountain life—Fiction

CARRUTH, Ella Kaiser
AuBYP SUP

She Wanted To Read: Story Of Mary McLeod Bethune
BL - v62 - My 1 '66 - p874
CCB-B - v19 - Je '66 - p160
LJ - v91 - S 15 '66 - p4328
Subject: Biography

CARSON, John F 1920-
AuBYP, ConAu 13R, MichAu 80, SmATA 1

The Coach Nobody Liked
BL - v56 - Je 15 '60 - p630
CSM - My 12 '60 - p3B
KR - v28 - Ja 15 '60 - p51
LJ - v85 - My 15 '60 - p2047
NYTBR, Pt. 2 - My 8 '60 - p32
PW - v190 - Jl 18 '66 - p79

The Twenty-Third Street Crusaders
Comw - v68 - My 23 '58 - p212
CSM - My 8 '58 - p14
HB - v34 - Ag '58 - p268
KR - v25 - D 1 '57 - p863
LJ - v83 - Ap 15 '58 - p1290

CARSON, Rachel 1907-1964
BioIn 11, -13, ConAu 77, CurBio 64, IntDcWB, McGEWB, NotAW MOD, OxEng 85, SmATA 23, WebAB 79

The Sea Around Us
BL - v55 - Ja 15 '59 - p265
CSM - D 18 '58 - p7
KR - v26 - O 15 '58 - p805
LJ - v84 - Ja 15 '59 - p255
Subject: Ocean

CARTER, Alden R

Wart, Son Of Toad
BL - v82 - N 15 '85 - p481
CBRS - v14 - F '86 - p77
EJ - v75 - O '86 - p84
KR - v53 - N 1 '85 - p1197
SLJ - v32 - F '86 - p93
WLB - v60 - N '85 - p47
Subject: Fathers and sons—Fiction; Schools—Fiction

CASEY, Sara

Cassie And Chris
BL - v80 - Ja 1 '84 - p678
Kliatt - v18 - Winter '84 - p20
SLJ - v30 - F '84 - p80
VOYA - v7 - Je '84 - p92
Subject: Love—Fiction

CATHERALL, Arthur 1906-1980
AuBYP, ConAu 5R, IntAu&W 82, OxChL, SmATA 3, TwCChW 83, WrDr 80

Prisoners In The Snow
BL - v64 - F 15 '68 - p697
CLW - v39 - My '68 - p665
HB - v44 - F '68 - p64
KR - v35 - O 1 '67 - p1204
LJ - v92 - D 15 '67 - p4610
Par - v43 - Jl '68 - p81
Subject: Avalanches—Fiction

Sicilian Mystery
BL - v63 - Jl 15 '67 - p1192
KR - v35 - Mr 1 '67 - p278
LJ - v92 - My 15 '67 - p2039
PW - v191 - Je 12 '67 - p59
Subject: Mystery and detective stories

Ten Fathoms Deep
KR - v35 - N 1 '67 - p1323
LJ - v93 - F 15 '68 - p878
Subject: Mystery and detective stories; Sea stories

CAUDELL, Marian

One Boy Too Many
SLJ - v32 - Ap '86 - p103
Subject: Love—Fiction

CAUFIELD, Don

The Incredible Detectives
CCB-B - v20 - Ja '67 - p71
HB - v42 - D '66 - p708
LJ - v91 - N 15 '66 - p5771
NYTBR - v71 - D 18 '66 - p16
PW - v190 - D 26 '66 - p100
SR - v50 - Ja 28 '67 - p46
Co-author: Caufield, Joan

CAUFIELD, Joan
see Caufield, Don (co-author)

CAVALLARO, Ann

Blimp
BL - v79 - Ap 1 '83 - p1029
CBRS - v11 - Ag '83 - p145
CCB-B - v36 - Ap '83 - p144
KR - v51 - My 1 '83 - p527
SLJ - v29 - Ag '83 - p74
Subject: Weight control—Fiction

CAVANAGH, Helen 1939-
ConAu 104, SmATA 48

Honey
Hi Lo - v3 - Je '82 - p3
Subject: Bees—Fiction

CAVANNA, Betty 1909-
AuBYP, BioIn 2, ConAu 6NR, ConLC 12, CurBio 50, IntAu&W 82, MorJA, SmATA 30, -4AS, TwCChW 83, WrDr 86
Pseud./variant:
Headley, Elizabeth Cavanna

Accent On April
BL - v57 - O 15 '60 - p128
CSM - N 23 '60 - p11
HB - v37 - F '61 - p56
KR - v28 - Jl 15 '60 - p564
LJ - v85 - S 15 '60 - p3229
TN - v37 - Fall '80 - p57
Subject: Family life—Fiction; Schools—Fiction

Almost Like Sisters
BL - v23 - O 15 '63 - p264
CCB-B - v18 - Je '65 - p143
HB - v40 - F '64 - p65
LJ - v88 - N 15 '63 - p4482
Subject: Friendship—Fiction

Angel On Skis
BL - v54 - D 15 '57 - p233
CSM - N 7 '57 - p17
KR - v25 - Jl 15 '57 - p487
LJ - v82 - N 15 '57 - p2977
NYTBR - D 15 '57 - p18
TN - v37 - Fall '80 - p57
Subject: Skis and skiing—Fiction

The Ghost Of Ballyhooly
KR - v39 - Ag 15 '71 - p881
LJ - v96 - D 15 '71 - p4199
Subject: Ireland—Fiction; Mystery and detective stories

Jenny Kimura
BL - v24 - O 15 '64 - p288
BL - v69 - F 15 '73 - p553
CSM - v57 - Ja 21 '65 - p11
HB - v40 - D '64 - p619
LJ - v89 - S 15 '64 - p3487
SR - v47 - N 7 '64 - p54
TLS - My 19 '66 - p442
Subject: Japanese Americans—Fiction

Mystery At Love's Creek
CCB-B - v19 - F '66 - p95
CSM - v57 - N 4 '65 - pB11
HB - v41 - D '65 - p635
KR - v33 - Ag 15 '65 - p834
LJ - v90 - N 15 '65 - p5104
NYTBR - v70 - N 7 '65 - p59
Subject: Love—Fiction; Mystery and detective stories

Mystery In Marrakech
BS - v28 - N 1 '68 - p323
KR - v36 - Ag 1 '68 - p823
PW - v194 - O 7 '68 - p54
Subject: Mystery and detective stories

The Mystery Of The Emerald Buddha
BL - v73 - D 15 '76 - p603
CCB-B - v30 - Ap '77 - p119
KR - v44 - O 1 '76 - p1100
MN - v63 - D '84 - p58
PW - v210 - N 1 '76 - p74
SLJ - v23 - D '76 - p69
Subject: Mystery and detective stories; Thailand—Fiction

Passport To Romance
BL - v52 - S 15 '55 - p38
CSM - N 10 '55 - p5B
HB - v31 - D '55 - p458
KR - v23 - Jl 15 '55 - p497
LJ - v80 - O 15 '55 - p2389
NYT - N 13 '55 - p16

CAVANNA, Betty (continued)
SR - v38 - N 12 '55 - p70
Subject: Love—Fiction

Romance On Trial
BS - v45 - Ap '85 - p39
CCB-B - v38 - Mr '85 - p122
SLJ - v31 - F '85 - p82
VOYA - v8 - Je '85 - p128
Subject: Love—Fiction

Ruffles And Drums
BB - v4 - F '76 - p4
CCB-B - v29 - Ja '76 - p74
Inst - v85 - N '75 - p154
J Read - v20 - O '76 - p80
KR - v43 - Jl 1 '75 - p716
PW - v208 - Jl 28 '75 - p122
SLJ - v22 - O '75 - p96
Subject: United States—History—Revolution, 1775-1783—Fiction

Runaway Voyage
BL - v75 - N 1 '78 - p476
KR - v46 - N 15 '78 - p1252
PW - v214 - O 23 '78 - p61
SLJ - v25 - O '78 - p153
Subject: Voyages to the Pacific coast—Fiction

Stamp Twice For Murder
BL - v78 - O 1 '81 - p233
BS - v41 - F '82 - p439
CBRS - v10 - Ja '82 - p46
CCB-B - v35 - Mr '82 - p123
KR - v49 - D 1 '81 - p1467
PW - v220 - O 16 '81 - p79
SLJ - v28 - D '81 - p83
Subject: France—Fiction; Mystery and detective stories

Storm In Her Heart
BL - v79 - My 15 '83 - p1198
B Rpt - v43 - O '83 - p271
CCB-B - v37 - O '83 - p23
PW - v224 - Jl 8 '83 - p65
SLJ - v30 - S '83 - p130
VOYA - v6 - D '83 - p276
Subject: Schools—Fiction

The Surfer And The City Girl
BL - v77 - Mr 15 '81 - p1024
CCB-B - v34 - Je '81 - p188
Hi Lo - v2 - Je '81 - p4
SLJ - v27 - My '81 - p86
VOYA - v4 - Ag '81 - p24
Subject: Alcohol and youth—Fiction; Grandmothers—Fiction

A Time For Tenderness
NYTBR - O 14 '62 - p34
Subject: Love—Fiction

Touch Of Magic
BL - v58 - S 1 '61 - p34
CSM - My 11 '61 - p4B
HB - v37 - Je '61 - p273
KR - v29 - Mr 1 '61 - p222
LJ - v86 - My 15 '61 - p1991
Subject: United States—History—Revolution, 1775-1783—Fiction

see also Headley, Elizabeth Cavanna for additional titles

CEBULASH, Mel 1937-
ConAu 12NR, IntAu&W 77, SmATA 10, WhoE 75, WrDr 86

Big League Baseball Reading Kit
Hi Lo - v1 - My '80 - p5
Subject: Baseball

The Champion's Jacket
Hi Lo - v1 - F '80 - p4
Subject: Basketball; Friendship—Fiction

The Face That Stopped Time
BL - v80 - Jl '84 - p1525
Subject: Mystery and detective stories

Go All Out
SLJ - v29 - Ag '83 - p74
Subject: Schools—Fiction; Sports—Fiction

Hit The Road
SLJ - v29 - Ag '83 - p74
Subject: Schools—Fiction; Sports—Fiction

Ruth Marini: World Series Star
BL - v81 - Ag '85 - p1661
CCB-B - v39 - S '85 - p3
SLJ - v32 - D '85 - p98
Subject: Baseball—Fiction

Settle A Score
SLJ - v29 - Ag '83 - p74
Subject: Schools—Fiction; Sports—Fiction

The Spring Street Boys Go All Out
Hi Lo - v3 - Je '82 - p5
Subject: Schools—Fiction; Sports—Fiction

The Spring Street Boys Settle A Score
Hi Lo - v3 - F '82 - p1
Subject: Schools—Fiction; Sports—Fiction

CEBULASH, Mel (continued)

The Spring Street Boys Teamup
Hi Lo - v3 - Ja '82 - p2
Subject: Schools—Fiction; Sports—Fiction

Team Up
SLJ - v29 - Ag '83 - p74
Subject: Schools—Fiction; Sports—Fiction

CEDER, Georgiana Dorcas
BioIn 2, ConAu 1R, SmATA 10

Little Thunder
LJ - v91 - Jl '66 - p3533

CHABER, M E (pseud.) 1910-
ConAu X
Real Name:
Crossen, Kendall Foster

The Acid Nightmare
CCB-B - v21 - Jl '68 - p170
KR - v35 - O 15 '67 - p1282
LJ - v92 - N 15 '67 - p4257
NYTBR - v73 - Mr 3 '68 - p30

CHADWICK, Roxane

Don't Shoot
BL - v75 - O 15 '78 - p389
PW - v214 - Jl 24 '78 - p100
SLJ - v25 - F '79 - p39
Subject: Alaska—Fiction; Eskimos—Fiction; Wildlife conservation—Fiction

CHAN, Janis Fisher

Where To Go For Help
Hi Lo - v4 - S '82 - p2
Subject: Assistance in emergencies

CHANDLER, Caroline A 1906-1979
AmCath 80, AmM&WS 78S, AuBYP, BioIn 1, -13, ConAu 17R, -93, SmATA 24, WhAm 7, WhoAm 80

Nursing As A Career
LJ - v96 - My 15 '71 - p1810
SB - v7 - My '71 - p69
Co-author: Kempf, Sharon
Subject: Nursing as a profession

CHANNING, Alissa

Royal Blood
SLJ - v28 - S '81 - p134

CHAPIN, Victor

The Violin And Its Masters
KR - v37 - Ag 1 '69 - p785
LJ - v94 - N 15 '69 - p4293
Subject: Music

CHARUHAS, Mary

Stages In Adult Life
BL - v81 - O 15 '84 - p285
Subject: Conduct of life

CHATTERTON, Louise

Just The Right Age
VOYA - v7 - D '84 - p258
Subject: Love—Fiction

CHETIN, Helen 1922-
ConAu 12NR, SmATA 6

Frances Ann Speaks Out: My Father Raped Me
Ms - v12 - Ap '84 - p75
Subject: Sex role—Fiction

Perihan's Promise, Turkish Relatives, And The Dirty Old Imam
BL - v70 - O 1 '73 - p168
CCB-B - v27 - O '73 - p23
CE - v50 - N '73 - p97
HB - v49 - O '73 - p470
KR - v41 - Je 15 '73 - p641
LJ - v98 - S 15 '73 - p2649
Subject: Turkey—Social life and customs—Fiction

CHICHESTER, Francis 1901-1972
ConAu 37R, -P-1, CurBio 67, NewYTBE 72, WhAm 5

Gypsy Moth Circles The World
Atl - v221 - Mr '68 - p126
B&B - v13 - D '67 - p53
BL - v64 - Ap 15 '68 - p970
BS - v27 - Mr 1 '68 - p458
BW - v2 - F 25 '68 - p1
CLW - v39 - My '68 - p662
Econ - v225 - D 2 '67 - pR9
GJ - v134 - Mr '68 - p135
HM - v236 - Ap '68 - p107
KR - v35 - D 15 '67 - p1499
LJ - v93 - Mr 1 '68 - p1014
LJ - v93 - Mr 15 '68 - p1335
NS - v74 - D 1 '67 - p767
NYTBR - v73 - Mr 10 '68 - p8
PW - v192 - D 25 '67 - p54
SR - v51 - Mr 2 '68 - p27
TLS - D 7 '67 - p1187
WSJ - v171 - Mr 7 '68 - p10

CHICHESTER, Francis (continued)
Yacht - v123 - My '68 - p88
Subject: Voyages around the world

CHIEFARI, Janet

Introducing The Drum And Bugle Corps
BL - v79 - F 15 '83 - p774
Subject: Bands (Music)

CHILDRESS, Alice 1920-
ConAu 3NR, ConDr 82, ConLC 12, -15, DcLB 7, -38, FifBJA, SmATA 48, WhoAm 86, WhoBlA 85, WrDr 86

A Hero Ain't Nothin' But A Sandwich
BL - v70 - N 15 '73 - p333
BL - v70 - N 15 '73 - p336
BL - v81 - D 15 '84 - p583
BW - v7 - N 11 '73 - p3C
BW - v7 - N 11 '73 - p7C
BW - F 10 '74 - p4
CCB-B - v27 - F '74 - p91
Choice - v12 - N '75 - p1132
CLW - v45 - F '74 - p344
CLW - v47 - N '75 - p164
EJ - v64 - Ja '75 - p112
EJ - v64 - D '75 - p79
EJ - v69 - S '80 - p86
JNE - v43 - p398
KR - v41 - Ag 1 '73 - p818
KR - v41 - D 15 '73 - p1355
LJ - v98 - O 15 '73 - p3153
LJ - v98 - D 15 '73 - p3689
NYTBR - N 4 '73 - p36
NYTBR - N 4 '73 - p52
NYTBR - D 2 '73 - p79
NYTBR - O 13 '74 - p46
PW - v204 - Ag 6 '73 - p65
Teacher - v92 - Ja '75 - p110
Subject: Blacks—Social conditions—Fiction; Drug abuse—Fiction

Rainbow Jordan
B Ent - v12 - D '81 - p22
BL - v77 - Je 1 '81 - p1295
Bl Bks B - v7 - #3 '81 p65
CBRS - v10 - Jl '81 - p116
CCB-B - v34 - Je '81 - p188
HB - v57 - Ag '81 - p431
Inter BC - v12 - #7 '81 p24
KR - v49 - Je 15 '81 - p743
LATBR - Jl 25 '82 - p9
NYTBR - v86 - Ap 26 '81 - p52
PW - v219 - My 8 '81 - p254
SLJ - v27 - Ap '81 - p137
VOYA - v4 - Ag '81 - p25
Subject: Foster home care—Fiction

CHITTUM, Ida 1918-
AuBYP SUP, ConAu 14NR, SmATA 7, WrDr 86

Tales Of Terror
BL - v72 - F 1 '76 - p765
PW - v208 - N 24 '75 - p52
SLJ - v22 - Mr '76 - p99
Subject: Short stories; Supernatural—Fiction

CHODES, John 1939-
ConAu 61, IntAu&W 86

Bruce Jenner
BL - v74 - O 15 '77 - p381
SLJ - v24 - D '77 - p65
Co-author: Wohl, Gary
Subject: Athletes; Decathlon

CHRISTESEN, Barbara 1940-
ConAu 107, SmATA 40

The Magic And Meaning Of Voodoo
SLJ - v25 - N '78 - p55
Subject: Voodooism

Myths Of The Orient
SLJ - v25 - S '78 - p105
Subject: China; Folklore

CHRISTGAU, Alice E 1902-
ConAu P-2, SmATA 13

The Laugh Peddler
BW - v2 - My 5 '68 - p20
HB - v44 - Je '68 - p323
KR - v36 - F 15 '68 - p181
LJ - v93 - Ap 15 '68 - p1797
NYTBR - v73 - My 5 '68 - p34

CHRISTIAN, Mary Blount 1933-
ConAu 17NR, IntAu&W 77, SmATA 9, WhoAmW 83, WrDr 86

Deadline For Danger
BL - v79 - My 15 '83 - p1198
CBRS - v11 - Mr '83 - p81
CCB-B - v36 - Mr '83 - p123
Hi Lo - v4 - Mr '83 - p5
SLJ - v29 - Mr '83 - p189
Subject: Honesty—Fiction; Journalism—Fiction

Felina
BL - v75 - My 15 '79 - p1435
Hi Lo - v1 - N '79 - p4
Subject: Social adjustment—Fiction

CHRISTIAN, Mary Blount (continued)

The Firebug Mystery
BL - v78 - My 15 '82 - p1262
SLJ - v28 - My '82 - p83
Subject: Arson—Fiction; Mystery and detective stories

Just Once
BL - v79 - Ap 15 '83 - p1078

Microcomputers
BL - v80 - F 1 '84 - p810
SLJ - v30 - Ap '84 - p110
Subject: Computers

The Mystery Of The Double Double Cross
BL - v79 - D '82 - p496
SLJ - v29 - D '82 - p82
Subject: Hurricanes—Fiction; Kidnapping—Fiction; Mystery and detective stories

CHRISTOPHER, John (pseud.) 1922-
ChlLR 2, ConAu X, ConSFA, FourBJA, OxChL, SenS, SmATA X, TwCChW 83, WhoSciF, WrDr 86
Real Name:
Youd, Samuel

An Empty World
B&B - v23 - Ja '78 - p63
BL - v74 - Je 15 '78 - p1614
BW - Je 11 '78 - pE4
CCB-B - v32 - S '78 - p5
GP - v16 - D '77 - p3225
HB - v54 - Je '78 - p274
JB - v42 - Ap '78 - p99
KR - v46 - Ap 1 '78 - p379
NYTBR - My 14 '78 - p45
Obs - N 27 '77 - p29
SLJ - v24 - My '78 - p64
TES - F 3 '78 - p46
TLS - D 2 '77 - p1415
Subject: Science fiction; Survival—Fiction

The Lotus Caves
BL - v66 - O 15 '69 - p295
Comw - v91 - N 21 '69 - p257
CSM - v61 - N 6 '69 - pB7
Econ - v241 - D 18 '71 - p70
HB - v45 - D '69 - p673
KR - v37 - Jl 1 '69 - p672
LJ - v94 - O 15 '69 - p3827
LR - v22 - p153
NO - v8 - N 3 '69 - p20
NS - v78 - O 31 '69 - p623
Obs - D 7 '69 - p31
PW - v196 - S 8 '69 - p57
Subject: Science fiction

White Mountains
B&B - v12 - Je '67 - p36
BL - v63 - Jl 1 '67 - p1144
CCB-B - v21 - D '67 - p57
CSM - v59 - Ag 3 '67 - p11
EJ - v69 - O '80 - p72
HB - v43 - Je '67 - p351
KR - v35 - F 1 '67 - p136
Lis - v77 - My 18 '67 - p661
LJ - v92 - Je 15 '67 - p2448
NS - v73 - My 26 '67 - p733
NYTBR - v72 - Ag 13 '67 - p26
Spec - v218 - Je 2 '67 - p656
SR - v50 - Je 17 '67 - p36
TES - N 27 '81 - p23
TLS - My 25 '67 - p459
Subject: Science fiction

Wild Jack
BL - v71 - O 1 '74 - p168
CCB-B - v28 - F '75 - p90
CLW - v46 - My '75 - p452
Comw - v101 - N 22 '74 - p194
GP - v13 - Mr '75 - p2569
HB - v50 - Ag '74 - p374
JB - v39 - F '75 - p58
KR - v42 - Ag 1 '74 - p803
KR - v43 - Ja 1 '75 - p5
LJ - v99 - O 15 '74 - p2738
PT - v8 - D '74 - p130
TLS - Ap 4 '75 - p360
Subject: Science fiction

CHRISTOPHER, Matt 1917-
AuBYP, ConAu 5NR, FifBJA, MorBMP, SmATA 2, -47, WrDr 86

The Return Of The Headless Horseman
BL - v78 - Ag '82 - p1521
BL - v83 - D 1 '86 - p585
CBRS - v10 - Ag '82 - p135
SLJ - v28 - Ag '82 - p112
Subject: Ghosts—Fiction; Mystery and detective stories

Shortstop From Tokyo
CCB-B - v24 - Jl '70 - p173
CSM - v62 - My 7 '70 - pB7
KR - v38 - Ap 15 '70 - p451
LJ - v95 - My 15 '70 - p1963
SR - v53 - Je 27 '70 - p38
Subject: Baseball—Fiction

The Team That Couldn't Lose
KR - v35 - Je 15 '67 - p694
LJ - v92 - D 15 '67 - p4632

CHRISTOPHER, Matt (continued)

The Year Mom Won The Pennant
BL - v64 - My 1 '68 - p1040
CCB-B - v21 - My '68 - p139
Inst - v77 - My '68 - p128
KR - v36 - Mr 1 '68 - p260
LJ - v93 - My 15 '68 - p2128
Teacher - v91 - Ap '74 - p89
Subject: Baseball—Fiction

CHUTE, Marchette 1909-
AuBYP, ConAu 5NR, CurBio 50, IntAu&W 82, MorJA, SmATA 1, TwCChW 83, WhoAm 86, WhoAmW 87, WrDr 86

Stories From Shakespeare
Atl - v198 - D '56 - p103
BL - v53 - S 1 '56 - p28
HB - v32 - O '56 - p373
KR - v24 - Je 15 '56 - p407
LJ - v81 - S 15 '56 - p2048
NY - v32 - N 24 '45 - p235
NYTBR - Ag 26 '56 - p28
SR - v39 - N 17 '56 - p67
Subject: Plays

CIUPIK, Larry A

Space Machines
ACSB - v13 - Spring '80 - p49
SB - v15 - My '80 - p280
Co-author: Seevers, James A
Subject: Astronautics; Space vehicles

CLAPP, Patricia 1912-
ConAu 10NR, FifBJA, IntAu&W 82, OxChL, SmATA 4, –4AS, TwCChW 78, –83, WhoE 83, WrDr 86

Constance: A Story Of Early Plymouth
BL - v64 - My 1 '68 - p1041
BS - v28 - My 1 '68 - p63
BW - v2 - My 5 '68 - p26
CCB-B - v21 - Je '68 - p156
CLW - v40 - O '68 - p148
HB - v44 - Je '68 - p328
KR - v35 - D 15 '67 - p1477
NYTBR - v73 - Ag 18 '68 - p34
SR - v51 - My 11 '68 - p42
Subject: Pilgrim fathers—Fiction

Dr. Elizabeth
BL - v70 - Jl 1 '74 - p1198
CCB-B - v28 - O '74 - p25
KR - v42 - Mr 15 '74 - p304
Subject: Biography; Blackwell, Elizabeth; Physicians

I'm Deborah Sampson: A Soldier In The War Of The Revolution
BL - v73 - Jl 1 '77 - p1651
CCB-B - v31 - S '77 - p10
CLW - v49 - D '77 - p234
EJ - v67 - Mr '78 - p81
HB - v53 - Ag '77 - p437
KR - v45 - Mr 15 '77 - p284
LA - v54 - S '77 - p690
SLJ - v24 - N '77 - p68
Teacher - v95 - My '78 - p102
Subject: Gannett, Deborah Sampson—Fiction; United States—History—Revolution, 1775-1783—Fiction

Jane-Emily
BL - v65 - Jl 1 '69 - p1224
CCB-B - v22 - Jl '69 - p172
CLW - v41 - F '70 - p381
Comw - v90 - My 23 '69 - p301
HB - v45 - O '69 - p538
LJ - v94 - Je 15 '69 - p2508
NYTBR - Jl 20 '69 - p22
PW - v195 - My 12 '69 - p58
Subject: Ghosts—Fiction

Witches' Children: A Story Of Salem
BL - v78 - My 15 '82 - p1254
BS - v42 - Ag '82 - p202
CBRS - v10 - Ap '82 - p87
CCB-B - v35 - Mr '82 - p123
HB - v58 - Je '82 - p297
SLJ - v28 - Mr '82 - p156
VOYA - v5 - O '82 - p40
Subject: Witchcraft—Fiction

CLARK, David Allen (pseud.) 1940-
ConAu X, SmATA X
Real Name:
Ernst, John

Jokes, Puns, And Riddles
KR - v36 - Ap 1 '68 - p398
LJ - v93 - Je 15 '68 - p2536
NYTBR - v73 - Je 16 '68 - p24
PW - v193 - Je 17 '68 - p61
Subject: Wit and humor

see also Ernst, John for additional titles

CLARK, James I

Cars
ACSB - v15 - Winter '82 - p39

CLARK, James I (continued)
BL - v77 - Je 15 '81 - p1344
SLJ - v27 - Ag '81 - p63
TES - Mr 12 '82 - p39
Subject: Automobiles

Video Games
BL - v81 - Ag '85 - p1662
SB - v21 - S '85 - p32
Subject: Games; Video games

CLARK, James L 1883-1969
IlBEAAW, NatCAB 55

In The Steps Of The Great American Museum Collector, Carl Ethan Akeley
LJ - v93 - Jl '68 - p2732
SB - v4 - S '68 - p130
Subject: Biography; Zoologists

CLARK, Mary Higgins 1931?-
ConAu 16NR, SmATA 46, WhoAm 86, WhoAmW 87, WrDr 86

A Stranger Is Watching
BL - v74 - Mr 15 '78 - p1164
BS - v37 - Mr '78 - p377
EJ - v68 - D '79 - p80
KR - v45 - D 15 '77 - p1331
LJ - v103 - Mr 1 '78 - p589
Obs - My 7 '78 - p34
Prog - v42 - My '78 - p45
PW - v212 - D 26 '77 - p59
PW - v215 - Ja 15 '79 - p130
Spec - v241 - Ag 19 '78 - p22
WLB - v52 - Je '78 - p801
Subject: Kidnapping—Fiction

CLARK, Mavis Thorpe 1912?-
ConAu 8NR, ConLC 12, FourBJA, OxAusL, SmATA 8, TwCChW 78, –83, WrDr 86

If The Earth Falls In
BL - v72 - Ja 15 '76 - p682
CCB-B - v29 - Ap '76 - p123
HB - v52 - Ap '76 - p161
KR - v43 - N 1 '75 - p1227
SLJ - v22 - F '76 - p50
Subject: Australia—Fiction; Survival—Fiction

CLARKE, Arthur C 1917-
ConAu 2NR, ConLC 1, –4, –13, –18, –35, DrmM 2, FourBJA, OxEng 85, SmATA 13, TwCSFW 86, WhoAm 86, WrDr 86

Dolphin Island
Bks for Keeps - N '86 - p17
NYTBR - Je 9 '63 - p28
PW - v192 - N 27 '67 - p44
TLS - Ap 7 '78 - p377
Subject: Science fiction

Report On Planet Three And Other Speculations
BL - v68 - My 15 '72 - p784
BW - v5 - D 19 '71 - p6
Choice - v9 - My '72 - p388
CSM - v64 - F 10 '72 - p10
CSM - v64 - Jl 12 '72 - p10
KR - v39 - N 1 '71 - p1185
LJ - v96 - D 1 '71 - p4013
LJ - v97 - Ap 15 '72 - p1628
LJ - v98 - Mr 1 '73 - p692
PW - v200 - N 8 '71 - p44
S & T - v43 - Mr '72 - p182
WSJ - v179 - F 9 '72 - p14
Subject: Astronautics; Interplanatary voyages; Outer space—Exploration

CLARKE, John (pseud.) 1907-
BioIn 4, –10, ConAu X, DrAP&F 85, IntAu&W 77X, SmATA 5
Real Name:
Laughlin, Virginia Carli

Black Soldier
CCB-B - v22 - Ja '69 - p75
LJ - v94 - Ap 15 '69 - p1792
Subject: World War, 1939-1945—Fiction

High School Drop Out
CCB-B - v18 - Ap '65 - p115
Subject: Dropouts—Fiction

CLARKE, Mary Stetson 1911-
ConAu 8NR, –21R, SmATA 5, WhoAmW 77, WhoE 85, WrDr 86

The Iron Peacock
BL - v62 - Je 1 '66 - p958
BS - v26 - Je 1 '66 - p99
BS - v26 - Ag 1 '66 - p173
CCB-B - v20 - My '67 - p136
CSM - v58 - Jl 14 '66 - p4
HB - v42 - Je '66 - p315
KR - v34 - Mr 1 '66 - p252
LJ - v91 - N 15 '66 - p5754
NYTBR - v71 - My 8 '66 - p14
Subject: United States—Social life and customs—Fiction

CLARKE, Thomas J

People And Their Religions
BL - v81 - Jl '85 - p1519
Subject: Religions

CLARKSON, Ewan 1929-
ConAu 17NR, SmATA 9, TwCChW 78, WhoWor 78, WrDr 86

Wolves
ASBYP - v14 - Fall '81 - p14
Brit Bk N C - Autumn '80 - p30
JB - v44 - Ag '80 - p187
SB - v17 - S '81 - p33
SLJ - v27 - Ap '81 - p110
Subject: Wolves

CLARY, Jack 1932-
ConAu 57

The Captains
BL - v74 - Jl 1 '78 - p1656
Comw - v105 - N 10 '78 - p735
EJ - v68 - N '79 - p72
KR - v46 - My 1 '78 - p524
LJ - v103 - Jl '78 - p1430
PW - v213 - Je 12 '78 - p76
Subject: Athletes

CLAUS, Marshall 1936-1970
ConAu P-2

Better Gymnastics For Boys
LJ - v95 - D 15 '70 - p4382
Subject: Gymnastics

CLAY, Catherine Lee

Season Of Love
BL - v65 - F 1 '69 - p579
CLW - v41 - O '69 - p139
HB - v45 - F '69 - p58
KR - v36 - Ag 1 '68 - p824
LJ - v93 - O 15 '68 - p3976

CLAY, Patrice
SmATA 47

We Work With Horses
BL - v77 - D 1 '80 - p512
CCB-B - v34 - Ap '81 - p147
Hi Lo - v2 - Ap '81 - p4
SLJ - v27 - Ja '81 - p67
Subject: Horses; Occupations

CLAYPOOL, Jane
ConAu X, SmATA X
Pseud./variant:
Miner, Jane Claypool

How To Get A Good Job
BL - v74 - O 15 '82 - p305
B Rpt - v2 - N '83 - p40
Cur R - v23 - Ap '84 - p32
Hi Lo - v4 - O '82 - p4
SLJ - v29 - Ja '83 - p82
Subject: Job hunting; Vocational guidance

Jasmine Finds Love
BL - v79 - N 15 '82 - p438
CBRS - v11 - Mr '83 - p81
Subject: Chinese Americans—Fiction; Hawaii—Fiction

A Love For Violet
CBRS - v11 - Mr '83 - p81
SLJ - v29 - Ag '83 - p74
Subject: Family life—Fiction; Schools—Fiction

see also Miner, Jane Claypool for additional titles

CLAYTON, Ed 1921-1966

Martin Luther King: The Peaceful Warrior
BL - v82 - S 15 '85 - p142
NYTBR - My 4 '69 - p44
Teacher - v95 - Ja '78 - p45
VOYA - v8 - F '86 - p410
Subject: Biography; Blacks—Biography

CLAYTON, Robert

China
CCB-B - v26 - N '72 - p40
KR - v40 - Ap 1 '72 - p403
NYTBR - My 14 '72 - p8
Spec - v227 - N 13 '71 - p703
TLS - O 22 '71 - p1344
Subject: China

CLEARY, Beverly 1916-
ChlLR 2, -8, ConAu 19NR, DcLB 52, MorBMP, MorJA, SmATA 43, TwCChW 83, WhoAm 86, WrDr 86

Fifteen
Atl - v198 - D '56 - p104
BL - v53 - S 1 '56 - p28
Kliatt - v14 - Fall '80 - p5
KR - v24 - Jl 1 '56 - p442
LJ - v81 - O 15 '56 - p2469
NY - v32 - N 24 '56 - p234
NYT - S 16 '56 - p38
SR - v39 - N 17 '56 - p60
TN - v37 - Fall '80 - p58
Subject: Adolescence—Fiction

The Luckiest Girl
BL - v55 - S 1 '58 - p28
HB - v35 - F '59 - p54
Kliatt - v14 - Fall '80 - p5
KR - v26 - Jl 1 '58 - p463

CLEARY, Beverly (continued)
LJ - v83 - O 15 '58 - p3014
NYT - S 14 '58 - p32
Subject: Adolescence—Fiction

Ramona The Pest
BL - v64 - My 1 '68 - p1041
BW - v2 - S 8 '68 - p24
CCB-B - v21 - Je '68 - p157
CSM - v60 - My 2 '68 - pB7
CSM - v76 - O 5 '84 - pB6
Cur R - v19 - Je '80 - p216
HB - v44 - Ag '68 - p419
KR - v36 - Mr 15 '68 - p335
LJ - v93 - Je 15 '68 - p2536
NYTBR - v73 - My 5 '68 - p32
Par - v57 - Ag '82 - p84
PW - v193 - Ap 15 '68 - p97
RT - v35 - Ap '82 - p793
SE - v33 - My '69 - p555
SR - v51 - My 11 '68 - p38
TLS - Mr 29 '74 - p329
TN - v25 - N '68 - p77
Subject: Adolescence—Fiction

CLEAVER, Bill
see Cleaver, Vera (co-author)

CLEAVER, Vera 1919-
AuBYP, ChILR 6, ConAu 73, DcLB 52, FourBJA, OxChL, SmATA 22, TwCChW 83, WhoAm 86, WrDr 86

Delpha Green And Company
BS - v32 - Ap 15 '72 - p46
CCB-B - v26 - D '72 - p54
EJ - v63 - Mr '74 - p105
GP - v14 - N '75 - p2737
JB - v40 - F '76 - p39
KR - v40 - Mr 15 '72 - p324
LJ - v97 - My 15 '72 - p1911
NYTBR - My 28 '72 - p8
PW - v201 - My 15 '72 - p53
Spec - v235 - D 6 '75 - p733
TLS - D 5 '75 - p1455
Co-author: Cleaver, Bill
Subject: Social adjustment—Fiction

Grover
BL - v66 - My 15 '70 - p1158
CCB-B - v24 - Jl '70 - p174
CE - v47 - D '70 - p159
Comw - v92 - My 22 '70 - p248
HB - v46 - Ap '70 - p158
KR - v38 - F 15 '70 - p172
LJ - v95 - My 15 '70 - p1911
LJ - v95 - My 15 '70 - p1939
LJ - v95 - D 15 '70 - p4325
LJ - v96 - Ja 15 '71 - p286
NS - v81 - Je 4 '71 - p779
NYTBR - Mr 15 '70 - p49
NYTBR, Pt. 2 - N 8 '70 - p38
Par - v60 - Ag '85 - p75
PW - v197 - F 9 '70 - p83
SR - v53 - Mr 21 '70 - p39
TLS - Jl 2 '71 - p767
Co-author: Cleaver, Bill
Subject: Death—Fiction

I Would Rather Be A Turnip
CCB-B - v24 - Je '71 - p154
Choice - v14 - N '77 - p1178
CSM - v63 - My 6 '71 - pB6
GW - v106 - Ap 15 '72 - p24
HB - v47 - Ap '71 - p171
KR - v39 - F 1 '71 - p105
LJ - v96 - Ap 15 '71 - p1500
NYTBR, Pt. 2 - My 2 '71 - p4
Obs - Ap 2 '72 - p28
PW - v199 - Mr 22 '71 - p53
SR - v54 - Ap 17 '71 - p45
Teacher - v95 - O '77 - p168
TLS - Ap 28 '72 - p481
Co-author: Cleaver, Bill
Subject: Prejudices—Fiction

The Mimosa Tree
BL - v67 - D 15 '70 - p340
BW - v4 - N 8 '70 - p22
CCB-B - v24 - Mr '71 - p104
Comw - v93 - N 20 '70 - p202
HB - v46 - O '70 - p477
JB - v42 - F '78 - p35
KR - v38 - Ag 1 '70 - p799
LJ - v96 - Ja 15 '71 - p274
NYTBR, Pt. 2 - N 8 '70 - p10
Obs - S 25 '77 - p25
PW - v198 - S 14 '70 - p70
TES - Ja 6 '78 - p17
Co-author: Cleaver, Bill
Subject: City and town life—Fiction; Social adjustment—Fiction

The Mock Revolt
BL - v68 - D 15 '71 - p365
BW - v5 - N 7 '71 - p13
HB - v47 - O '71 - p488
KR - v39 - Jl 1 '71 - p681
LJ - v96 - O 15 '71 - p3474
NCW - v216 - Mr '73 - p92
NYTBR - Ja 16 '72 - p8
NYTBR, Pt. 2 - N 7 '71 - p47
Spec - v229 - N 11 '72 - p747
Teacher - v90 - My '73 - p73
TLS - N 3 '72 - p1317
Co-author: Cleaver, Bill
Subject: Friendship—Fiction

CLEAVER, Vera (continued)

Where The Lilies Bloom
Am - v121 - D 13 '69 - p595
BL - v66 - D 15 '69 - p513
BW - v11 - My 10 '81 - p14
CCB-B - v23 - D '69 - p56
Comw - v91 - N 21 '69 - p257
CSM - v67 - Ja 22 '75 - p8
Econ - v237 - D 26 '70 - p41
GW - v103 - D 19 '70 - p21
KR - v37 - Ag 15 '69 - p859
Lis - v84 - N 12 '70 - p671
LJ - v94 - D 15 '69 - p4581
LJ - v94 - D 15 '69 - p4602
NO - v8 - D 29 '69 - p17
NS - v81 - Mr 5 '71 - p312
NYTBR - S 28 '69 - p34
NYTBR - D 7 '69 - p68
NYTBR - Ap 14 '74 - p26
NYTBR, Pt. 2 - N 9 '69 - p62
PW - v196 - S 22 '69 - p85
Spec - v225 - D 5 '70 - pR20
SR - v52 - S 13 '69 - p37
TLS - D 11 '70 - p1457
TN - v26 - Ap '70 - p307
Co-author: Cleaver, Bill
Subject: Brothers and sisters—Fiction; Great Smokey Mountains—Fiction

The Whys And Wherefores Of Littabelle Lee
BL - v69 - My 15 '73 - p904
CCB-B - v26 - Jl '73 - p168
CSM - v65 - My 5 '73 - p10
EJ - v63 - Mr '74 - p105
HB - v49 - Ag '73 - p386
KR - v41 - F 1 '73 - p122
NYTBR - Mr 4 '73 - p6
NYTBR - Je 10 '73 - p41
NYTBR - N 4 '73 - p56
NYTBR - D 2 '73 - p79
NYTBR, Pt. 2 - My 6 '73 - p6
Obs - Ap 14 '74 - p31
PT - v7 - Je '73 - p19
PW - v203 - Ap 16 '73 - p54
SE - v41 - O '77 - p531
TLS - Mr 29 '74 - p326
Co-author: Cleaver, Bill
Subject: Ozark Mountains—Fiction

CLEMENS, Virginia Phelps 1941-
ConAu 15NR, SmATA 35

Superanimals And Their Unusual Careers
BL - v76 - F 15 '80 - p833
CCB-B - v33 - Ap '80 - p148
PW - v216 - D 10 '79 - p69
SB - v16 - Ja '81 - p159
Subject: Animals

CLEMENTS, Bruce 1931-
AuBYP SUP, ConAu 5NR, FifBJA, SmATA 27, TwCChW 83, WrDr 86

From Ice Set Free
BL - v68 - Je 15 '72 - p902
BW - v6 - Ag 13 '72 - p6
CCB-B - v25 - Je '72 - p153
EJ - v61 - My '72 - p768
HB - v48 - Ag '72 - p379
KR - v40 - Ap 1 '72 - p412
LJ - v97 - My 15 '72 - p1919
NYTBR, Pt. 2 - N 5 '72 - p3
Subject: Biography; Kiep, Otto

CLIFFORD, Eth
AuBYP SUP, ConAu X, SmATA 3, WhoAmW 87
Pseud./variant:
Rosenberg, Ethel Clifford

The Strange Reincarnations Of Hendrik Verloom
BL - v79 - Ja 15 '83 - p674
CBRS - v11 - F '83 - p68
CCB-B - v36 - F '83 - p104
KR - v50 - O 15 '82 - p1153
Subject: Grandfathers—Fiction; Imposters and imposture—Fiction

see also Rosenberg, Ethel Clifford for additional titles

CLIFTON, Lucille 1936-
ChlLR 5, ConAu 2NR, ConLC 19, DcLB 5, –41, FifBJA, OxChL, SmATA 20, TwCChW 83, WhoAm 86, WrDr 86

Sonora Beautiful
BL - v78 - Ja 15 '82 - p644
CBRS - v10 - Winter '82 - p57
CCB-B - v35 - Mr '82 - p123
Hi Lo - v3 - Ap '82 - p7
KR - v50 - F 15 '82 - p207
VOYA - v5 - Ap '82 - p33
Subject: Beauty (Personal)—Fiction; Family life—Fiction

CLINE, Linda 1941-
ConAu 65, WrDr 84

Weakfoot
KR - v43 - Ap 15 '75 - p452
NYTBR - Mr 30 '75 - p8

CLINE, Linda (continued)
SLJ - v22 - O '75 - p96
Subject: Okefenokee Swamp—Fiction

CLYMER, Eleanor 1906-
AuBYP, ConAu 9NR, FourBJA, IntAu&W 86, SmATA 9, TwCChW 83, WhoAm 86, WrDr 86

The Case Of The Missing Link
A Anth - v65 - Je '63 - p695
HB - v39 - F '63 - p82
LJ - v87 - N 15 '62 - p4266
NH - v72 - D '63 - p13
NYTBR - N 11 '62 - p30
Subject: Man—Origin

Modern American Career Women
BL - v55 - My 15 '59 - p510
KR - v27 - Ja 15 '59 - p44
LJ - v84 - F 15 '59 - p590
Subject: Biography

The Spider, The Cave And The Pottery Bowl
Am - v125 - D 4 '71 - p488
BL - v67 - Je 15 '71 - p870
BL - v69 - O 15 '72 - p177
CCB-B - v24 - Je '71 - p154
CLW - v43 - My '72 - p537
CSM - v63 - Jl 10 '71 - p15
HB - v47 - Ag '71 - p382
KR - v39 - Ap 15 '71 - p431
LJ - v96 - My 15 '71 - p1801
PW - v199 - Mr 8 '71 - p71
Subject: Indians of North America—Fiction

The Trolley Car Family
Atl - v180 - D '47 - p144
BL - v44 - O 1 '47 - p53
KR - v15 - Ag 15 '47 - p427
LJ - v72 - S 15 '47 - p1277
NYTBR - N 16 '47 - p40

CLYNE, Patricia Edwards
AuBYP SUP, SmATA 31

The Corduroy Road
KR - v41 - Ag 1 '73 - p812
LJ - v99 - Ja 15 '74 - p206
PW - v205 - Ja 21 '74 - p85
Subject: United States—History—Revolution, 1775-1783—Fiction

COATES, Belle

Mak
BL - v78 - Ja 15 '82 - p647
CBRS - v10 - F '82 - p65
SLJ - v28 - N '81 - p102
Subject: Indians of North America—Fiction; Orphans—Fiction

COATSWORTH, Elizabeth 1893-1986
ChILR 2, ConAu 4NR, -120, DcLB 22, JBA 51, MorBMP, OxChL, SmATA 2, -49N, TwCChW 83, WrDr 86

The Hand Of Apollo
CCB-B - v19 - F '66 - p96
CE - v43 - O '66 - p103
CW - v59 - Ap '66 - p253
KR - v33 - O 1 '65 - p1046
LJ - v91 - Ja 15 '66 - p424
NYTBR - v71 - Ja 2 '66 - p18

COBB, Vicki 1938-
AuBYP SUP, ChILR 2, ConAu 14NR, FifBJA, SmATA 8, WrDr 86

Science Experiments You Can Eat
HB - v49 - O '73 - p490
KR - v40 - Mr 15 '72 - p327
KR - v40 - D 15 '72 - p1415
LJ - v97 - My 15 '72 - p1920
NY - v48 - D 2 '72 - p191
SA - v227 - D '72 - p119
SB - v8 - S '72 - p126
Subject: Cookery; Science

COEN, Patricia

Beautiful Braids
BL - v80 - My 1 '84 - p1215
Kliatt - v18 - Spring '84 - p67
VOYA - v7 - Ag '84 - p150
Co-author: Maxwell, Joe
Subject: Braids (Hairdressing)

COGGINS, Jack 1911-
AuBYP, ConAu 5R, IntAu&W 77, MorJA, SmATA 2, WhoAm 86, WhoAmA 84, WrDr 86

Prepare To Dive: The Story Of Man Undersea
KR - v39 - N 15 '71 - p1219
LJ - v97 - Jl '72 - p2488
SB - v8 - My '72 - p77
Subject: Diving (Submarine); Submarine boats; Underwater exploration

COHEN, Barbara 1932-
AuBYP SUP, ConAu 19NR, FifBJA, SmATA 10

Benny
BL - v74 - S 1 '77 - p37
CCB-B - v31 - S '77 - p10
CE - v54 - N '77 - p84
KR - v45 - Ap 1 '77 - p350
LA - v54 - O '77 - p808
SE - v42 - Ap '78 - p320
SLJ - v24 - S '77 - p124
Subject: United States—Social life and customs—Fiction

Lovers' Games
J Read - v29 - D '85 - p276
Subject: Love—Fiction

Roses
CE - v61 - Ja '85 - p222
EJ - v73 - N '84 - p99
Emerg Lib - v13 - N '85 - p45
J Read - v28 - Ap '85 - p651
Subject: Girls—Fiction

COHEN, Carl

Earth's Hidden Mysteries
Hi Lo - v1 - Ap '80 - p3

COHEN, Daniel 1936-
AuBYP SUP, ChlLR 3, ConAu 20NR, IntAu&W 82, SmATA 8, -4AS

Bigfoot: America's Number One Monster
BL - v78 - Ag '82 - p1520
Kliatt - v16 - Fall '82 - p68
Subject: Sasquatch

Creatures From UFO's
SLJ - v25 - Mr '79 - p136
Subject: Unidentified flying objects

Famous Curses
BL - v76 - D 15 '79 - p607
Hi Lo - v1 - Ja '80 - p4
Kliatt - v15 - Fall '81 - p73
SLJ - v26 - F '80 - p52
Subject: Blessing and cursing

Frauds, Hoaxes, And Swindles
BL - v75 - My 15 '79 - p1445
Hi Lo - v1 - O '79 - p4
SLJ - v25 - My '79 - p60
Subject: Fraud; Swindlers and swindling

Ghostly Terrors
BL - v78 - N 15 '81 - p436
CCB-B - v35 - Mr '82 - p123
Subject: Ghosts

Great Mistakes
BL - v76 - N 15 '79 - p496
Hi Lo - v1 - F '80 - p3
J Read - v24 - O '80 - p81
SLJ - v26 - Ag '80 - p62
Subject: History—Errors, inventions, etc.

The Greatest Monsters In The World
BL - v72 - F 15 '76 - p858
KR - v43 - Jl 15 '75 - p779
SLJ - v22 - Ja '76 - p44
Subject: Monsters

The Headless Roommate And Other Tales Of Terror
BL - v77 - F 15 '81 - p808
Hi Lo - v3 - My '82 - p5
Kliatt - v16 - Spring '82 - p6
PW - v218 - O 17 '80 - p66
RT - v35 - O '81 - p68
SLJ - v27 - N '80 - p84
Subject: Folklore; Horror stories

Horror In The Movies
Kliatt - v19 - Winter '85 - p67
Subject: Horror films

How To Buy A Car
BL - v79 - O 15 '82 - p305
CCB-B - v36 - N '82 - p44
Hi Lo - v4 - O '82 - p6
SLJ - v29 - N '82 - p97
Subject: Automobiles; Consumer education

How To Test Your ESP
BL - v78 - Ag '82 - p1519
Subject: Extrasensory perception

The Kid's Guide To Home Video
BL - v81 - Mr 15 '85 - p1056
Kliatt - v19 - Winter '85 - p67
Co-author: Cohen, Susan
Subject: Television

The Magic Art Of Foreseeing The Future
BL - v69 - Jl 15 '73 - p1068
Subject: Clairvoyance; Divination

Magicians, Wizards, And Sorcerers
KR - v41 - Ap 15 '73 - p464
LJ - v98 - Jl '73 - p2199
Subject: Magicians

Missing! Stories Of Strange Disappearances
BL - v75 - Je 15 '79 - p1541

COHEN, Daniel (continued)
Hi Lo - v1 - S '79 - p3
KR - v47 - Mr 15 '79 - p330
SLJ - v26 - F '80 - p53
Subject: Curiosities and wonders; Missing persons

Monster Hunting Today
BL - v80 - S 15 '83 - p161
B Rpt - v2 - Mr '84 - p39
SLJ - v30 - F '84 - p67
Subject: Animals (Mythical); Monsters

The Monsters Of Star Trek
Hi Lo - v2 - S '80 - p5
Kliatt - v14 - p14
Kliatt - v14 - Spring '80 - p14
SLJ - v26 - My '80 - p65
Subject: Monsters

Monsters You Never Heard Of
Hi Lo - v1 - My '80 - p6
LA - v57 - N '80 - p899
SLJ - v27 - O '80 - p143
Subject: Animals (Mythical); Monsters

Real Ghosts
BL - v74 - N 15 '77 - p548
KR - v45 - Jl 15 '77 - p729
SLJ - v24 - O '77 - p110
Subject: Ghosts

Real Magic
Hi Lo - v4 - Mr '83 - p3
SLJ - v29 - F '83 - p74
Subject: Magic; Occult sciences

The Restless Dead: Ghostly Tales From Around The World
EJ - v74 - O '85 - p80
Subject: Ghosts—Fiction; Short stories

Science Fiction's Greatest Monsters
BL - v77 - N 15 '80 - p455
CCB-B - v34 - Mr '81 - p129
Hi Lo - v2 - D '80 - p5
Subject: Monsters; Science fiction

Southern Fried Rat And Other Gruesome Tales
BL - v79 - Ag '83 - p1463
CBRS - v11 - Ag '83 - p145
LATBR - v0 - Je 5 '83 - p10
SLJ - v29 - Ag '83 - p63
VOYA - v6 - O '83 - p222
WCRB - v9 - S '83 - p40
Subject: Folklore; Horror stories

Supermonsters
KR - v44 - D 15 '76 - p1308
PW - v211 - Mr 14 '77 - p95
SLJ - v23 - My '77 - p67
Subject: Monsters

Talking With The Animals
BL - v68 - S 15 '71 - p108
BW - v5 - My 9 '71 - p14
Comw - v94 - My 21 '71 - p270
KR - v39 - F 1 '71 - p114
LJ - v97 - Jl '72 - p2482
NYTBR - My 16 '71 - p8
Subject: Animals; Communication

The World Of UFOs
ACSB - v12 - Fall '79 - p14
BL - v74 - Je 1 '78 - p1543
CE - v56 - O '79 - p47
Comw - v105 - N 10 '78 - p735
Cur R - v17 - D '78 - p385
HB - v54 - D '78 - p667
KR - v46 - Je 1 '78 - p600
SLJ - v25 - S '78 - p155
Subject: Unidentified flying objects

The World's Most Famous Ghosts
BL - v74 - Jl 15 '78 - p1738
Hi Lo - v1 - Mr '80 - p5
Hi Lo - v2 - S '80 - p5
NYTBR - Ap 30 '78 - p45
SLJ - v25 - S '78 - p132
TN - v36 - Winter '80 - p199
Subject: Ghosts

Young Ghosts
BL - v75 - Ja 15 '79 - p808
CCB-B - v32 - Ap '79 - p132
SLJ - v25 - O '78 - p143
Subject: Ghosts

COHEN, Joel H
AuBYP SUP

Jim Palmer: Great Comeback Competitor
KR - v46 - F 1 '78 - p112
SLJ - v24 - My '78 - p86
Subject: Baseball—Biography

Steve Garvey: Storybook Star
SLJ - v24 - D '77 - p63
Subject: Baseball—Biography

COHEN, Peter Zachary 1931-
ConAu 12NR, IntAu&W 82, SmATA 4, WhoAm 86, WhoMW 84, WrDr 86

Bee
BL - v71 - Ap 1 '75 - p815
CE - v52 - Ja '76 - p153
HB - v51 - Je '75 - p267
KR - v43 - Mr 15 '75 - p306

COHEN, Peter Zachary (continued)
LA - v52 - N '75 - p1165
SLJ - v21 - Ap '75 - p50
Subject: Horses—Fiction

Foal Creek
CLW - v44 - Mr '73 - p510
EJ - v62 - Ja '73 - p145
HB - v49 - Ap '73 - p141
KR - v40 - Ag 1 '72 - p864
LJ - v98 - Ja 15 '73 - p259

COHEN, Randy

Easy Answers To Hard Questions
Kliatt - v14 - Winter '80 - p70

COHEN, Robert C 1930-
AuBYP SUP, ConAu 57, SmATA 8

The Color Of Man
BL - v65 - S 1 '68 - p61
BL - v65 - Ap 1 '69 - p900
BS - v28 - My 1 '68 - p63
BW - v2 - My 5 '68 - p30
CCB-B - v21 - Jl '68 - p171
Comw - v88 - My 24 '68 - p308
Comw - v89 - F 21 '69 - p645
Cres - v33 - D '69 - p23
CSM - v61 - My 1 '69 - pB7
EJ - v58 - F '69 - p291
HB - v45 - Ag '69 - p420
Inst - v78 - O '68 - p158
KR - v36 - Ap 1 '68 - p406
LJ - v93 - Je 15 '68 - p2545
NYTBR - v73 - My 5 '68 - p5
SB - v11 - My '75 - p5
SE - v33 - My '69 - p562
SR - v51 - My 11 '68 - p41
Subject: Color of man

COHEN, Susan
see Cohen, Daniel (co-author)

COLBY, Carroll Burleigh 1904-1977
AuBYP, ConAu 6NR, IntAu&W 77, MorJA, SmATA 35, WhAm 7, WhoAm 78

The Weirdest People In The World
Inst - v82 - My '73 - p75
PW - v203 - F 12 '73 - p68
Subject: Ghosts—Fiction

COLE, Brenda

Don't Fence Me In
BL - v81 - F 1 '85 - p783
Subject: Love—Fiction

COLE, Sheila R 1939-
ConAu 4NR, SmATA 24, WrDr 86

Working Kids On Working
BL - v77 - Ja 15 '81 - p697
CCB-B - v34 - O '80 - p29
HB - v57 - Ap '81 - p202
Inter BC - v13 - #4 '82 p26
J Read - v24 - Ap '81 - p647
VOYA - v3 - F '81 - p42
Subject: Employment

COLEMAN, Joseph

Space Wars: And Six More Stories Of Time And Space
BL - v77 - Mr 15 '81 - p1024
Subject: Science fiction

COLES, Robert Martin 1929-
AmM&WS 86P, AuBYP SUP, BioIn 10, -11, -13, ConAu 3NR, CurBio 69, SmATA 23, WhoAm 86, WrDr 86

Dead End School
BL - v64 - My 15 '68 - p1092
BL - v69 - My 1 '73 - p837
BW - v2 - S 8 '68 - p24
CLW - v41 - Ja '70 - p321
Comw - v88 - My 24 '68 - p304
Comw - v89 - F 21 '69 - p645
CSM - v60 - My 2 '68 - pB1
HB - v44 - Je '68 - p323
KR - v36 - Ap 15 '68 - p458
LJ - v93 - My 15 '68 - p2112
NYTBR - v73 - My 5 '68 - p32
SR - v51 - My 11 '68 - p39
Subject: Schools—Fiction

The Grass Pipe
BS - v29 - My 1 '69 - p56
BW - v3 - My 4 '69 - p28
CCB-B - v23 - My '70 - p141
CLW - v41 - My '70 - p575
Comw - v90 - My 23 '69 - p300
CSM - v61 - My 1 '69 - pB7
KR - v37 - Ap 15 '69 - p451
LJ - v94 - Jl '69 - p2680
NYTBR, Pt. 2 - My 4 '69 - p10
PW - v195 - My 12 '69 - p58
SR - v52 - My 10 '69 - p59
Subject: Drug abuse—Fiction

COLLIER, Christopher
see Collier, James Lincoln (co-author)

COLLIER, James Lincoln 1928-
AuBYP SUP, BioIn 7, ChILR 3, ConAu 4NR, ConLC 30, FifBJA, SmATA 8

The Bloody Country
Am - v135 - D 11 '76 - p430
BB - v4 - D '76 - p4
BL - v72 - Je 1 '76 - p1403
BW - My 2 '76 - pL3
CCB-B - v30 - D '76 - p55
CE - v53 - O '76 - p33
Comw - v103 - N 19 '76 - p759
HB - v52 - Je '76 - p293
KR - v44 - F 15 '76 - p204
LA - v54 - Ja '77 - p83
NO - v15 - Ag 21 '76 - p16
NYTBR - My 2 '76 - p26
PW - v209 - My 10 '76 - p84
SLJ - v22 - My '76 - p67
Teacher - v94 - N '76 - p134
Co-author: Collier, Christopher
Subject: Frontier and pioneer life—Fiction; Pennsylvania—Fiction

Jump Ship To Freedom
BL - v78 - O 1 '81 - p233
BS - v41 - Mr '82 - p475
CBRS - v10 - O '81 - p17
CCB-B - v35 - O '81 - p26
CSM - v73 - O 13 '81 - pB10
HB - v58 - F '82 - p50
KR - v50 - F 1 '82 - p139
LA - v59 - My '82 - p485
NYTBR - v87 - F 14 '82 - p28
PW - v220 - N 13 '81 - p88
SLJ - v28 - O '81 - p140
VOYA - v5 - Je '82 - p32
Co-author: Collier, Christopher
Subject: Blacks—Fiction; Slavery—Fiction

Rich And Famous: The Further Adventures Of George Stable
BL - v72 - N 15 '75 - p451
BS - v35 - D '75 - p299
CCB-B - v29 - F '76 - p93
HB - v52 - F '76 - p48
KR - v43 - S 1 '75 - p997
SLJ - v22 - N '75 - p72
Subject: New York (City)—Fiction

The Teddy Bear Habit, Or How I Became A Winner
KR - v34 - N 15 '66 - p1183
LJ - v92 - Ap 15 '67 - p1746
NYTBR - v72 - Mr 12 '67 - p28
PW - v191 - My 22 '67 - p64
SR - v50 - My 13 '67 - p57

COLLIGAN, Douglas

Amazing Real Life Coincidences
BL - v77 - Ja 15 '81 - p684
Kliatt - v15 - Winter '81 - p57
SLJ - v27 - Ap '81 - p123
VOYA - v4 - Je '81 - p42

COLLINS, Jim

The Bermuda Triangle
Cur R - v17 - Ag '78 - p228
SLJ - v25 - S '78 - p128
Subject: Bermuda triangle

The Strange Story Of Uri Geller
Cur R - v17 - Ag '78 - p228
SLJ - v25 - N '78 - p55
Subject: Biography; Psychical research

Unidentified Flying Objects
Cur R - v17 - Ag '78 - p228
SLJ - v25 - Ap '78 - p128
Subject: Unidentified flying objects

COLLINS, Ruth Philpott 1890-1975
BioIn 10, ConAu 4NR, -53, SmATA 30N

The Flying Cow
CC - v80 - D 18 '63 - p1585
CSM - N 14 '63 - p4B
HB - v40 - F '64 - p58
LJ - v88 - D 15 '63 - p4851
NYTBR, Pt. 2 - N 10 '63 - p46

COLLINS, Tom

Steven Spielberg: Creator Of E.T.
BL - v80 - Ap 1 '84 - p1113
CCB-B - v37 - Jl '84 - p202
SLJ - v30 - My '84 - p78
Subject: Biography; Motion pictures

COLMAN, Hila
AuBYP, ConAu 7NR, MorBMP, SmATA 1, ThrBJA

Accident
BL - v77 - O 15 '80 - p320
CBRS - v9 - N '80 - p26
CCB-B - v34 - Ap '81 - p148
KR - v49 - Ja 1 '81 - p11
RT - v35 - O '81 - p68
SLJ - v27 - Ja '81 - p68
VOYA - v3 - F '81 - p28
Subject: Friendship—Fiction; Physically handicapped—Fiction

COLMAN, Hila (continued)

After The Wedding
CCB-B - v29 - F '76 - p93
EJ - v66 - Ja '77 - p64
KR - v43 - S 1 '75 - p1004
PW - v208 - S 29 '75 - p50
SLJ - v22 - S '75 - p118
Subject: Divorce—Fiction; Marriage—Fiction

The Amazing Miss Laura
BB - v4 - Ja '77 - p3
CCB-B - v30 - Ja '77 - p73
KR - v44 - Jl 15 '76 - p799
NO - v15 - D 25 '76 - p15
SLJ - v23 - N '76 - p67
Subject: Old age—Fiction

Claudia, Where Are You?
Atl - v224 - D '69 - p150
BS - v29 - O 1 '69 - p254
CCB-B - v23 - N '69 - p41
CSM - v61 - N 6 '69 - pB9
EJ - v58 - N '69 - p1257
Inst - v79 - D '69 - p114
KR - v37 - Ag 15 '69 - p859
LJ - v95 - Mr 15 '70 - p1200
NYTBR, Pt. 2 - N 9 '69 - p48
PW - v196 - S 22 '69 - p85
SR - v52 - N 8 '77 - p71
Subject: Family life—Fiction

Daughter Of Discontent
CCB-B - v25 - N '71 - p39
CSM - v63 - N 11 '71 - pB1
KR - v39 - Ag 1 '71 - p814
LJ - v96 - D 15 '71 - p4188
PW - v200 - Ag 16 '71 - p57
Subject: Family life—Fiction; Politics—Fiction

Don't Tell Me That You Love Me
BL - v79 - Jl '83 - p1399
Kliatt - v17 - Fall '83 - p8
SLJ - v30 - F '84 - p80
VOYA - v6 - D '83 - p278
Subject: Fathers and daughters—Fiction; Marriage—Fiction

Ellie's Inheritance
BL - v76 - N 15 '79 - p493
BS - v39 - Mr '80 - p464
CBRS - v8 - N '79 - p26
CCB-B - v33 - Mr '80 - p130
HB - v56 - F '80 - p59
KR - v47 - N 15 '79 - p1331
SLJ - v26 - D '79 - p90
Subject: Depression, 1929—Fiction; Jews—Fiction; New York (City)—Fiction

The Girl From Puerto Rico
NYTBR - F 25 '62 - p36
Subject: New York (City)—Fiction; Puerto Ricans—Fiction

Girl Meets Boy
BL - v78 - N 15 '82 - p437
Kliatt - v17 - Winter '83 - p5
VOYA - v5 - F '83 - p34
Subject: Feminism—Fiction; Love—Fiction

The Happenings At North End School
BS - v30 - O 15 '70 - p297
EJ - v60 - Mr '71 - p405
KR - v38 - Ag 1 '70 - p804
LJ - v95 - D 15 '70 - p4360
NYTBR - Ap 25 '71 - p40
Subject: Teachers—Fiction

Just The Two Of Us
CCB-B - v38 - N '84 - p43
SLJ - v31 - Ja '85 - p82
VOYA - v7 - D '84 - p262
Subject: Fathers and daughters—Fiction

Mixed-Marriage Daughter
BS - v28 - O 1 '68 - p276
HB - v49 - Ap '73 - p173
Inst - v78 - N '68 - p154
KR - v36 - S 1 '68 - p986
LJ - v94 - Ja 15 '69 - p308
LJ - v95 - F 15 '70 - p741
NYTBR - Mr 9 '69 - p26
Subject: Discrimination—Fiction; Jews—Fiction

Nobody Has To Be A Kid Forever
BL - v72 - F 15 '76 - p853
CCB-B - v29 - My '76 - p140
EJ - v66 - N '77 - p81
KR - v44 - F 1 '76 - p138
LA - v54 - F '77 - p210
PW - v209 - Ja 19 '76 - p102
SLJ - v22 - Ap '76 - p72
Teacher - v95 - O '77 - p168
Subject: Family life—Fiction

Nobody Told Me What I Need To Know
CBRS - v13 - D '84 - p41
CCB-B - v38 - N '84 - p43
CLW - v56 - D '84 - p234
EJ - v74 - D '85 - p54
SLJ - v31 - Ja '85 - p83
VOYA - v7 - F '85 - p324
Subject: Family life—Fiction

Sometimes I Don't Love My Mother
BL - v74 - O 1 '77 - p279

COLMAN, Hila (continued)
BL - v74 - O 1 '77 - p286
CCB-B - v31 - D '77 - p58
Inst - v87 - N '77 - p160
KR - v45 - Ag 1 '77 - p788
PW - v212 - Ag 8 '77 - p69
SLJ - v24 - O '77 - p122
Subject: Death—Fiction; Mothers and daughters—Fiction

Tell Me No Lies
Cur R - v18 - F '79 - p29
LA - v56 - Ja '79 - p53
RT - v32 - Ja '79 - p487
Subject: Parent and child—Fiction

Triangle Of Love
SLJ - v32 - N '85 - p95
VOYA - v8 - Ag '85 - p183
Subject: Love—Fiction

What's The Matter With The Dobsons?
BL - v77 - O 15 '80 - p324
CBRS - v9 - O '80 - p17
CCB-B - v34 - Mr '81 - p129
Hi Lo - v2 - Ja '81 - p5
J Read - v24 - Ap '81 - p647
KR - v48 - N 1 '80 - p1398
RT - v35 - O '81 - p71
SLJ - v27 - N '80 - p84
Subject: Family problems—Fiction; Fathers and daughters—Fiction

COLUMBU, Franco

Coming On Strong
Kliatt - v12 - Fall '78 - p59
KR - v46 - Ja 1 '78 - p31
LJ - v103 - Mr 1 '78 - p580
Subject: Weightlifters

COLVER, Alice Ross 1892-
AuBYP, BioIn 2, ConAu 69

Vicky Barnes, Junior Hospital Volunteer
BS - v26 - D 1 '66 - p338

COLWELL, Robert 1931-
ConAu 33R

Introduction To Backpacking
BL - v67 - F 15 '71 - p466
CC - v87 - D 16 '70 - p1517
LJ - v95 - D 1 '70 - p4191
LJ - v95 - D 15 '70 - p4382
Subject: Backpacking

COMBER, Lillian
see Beckwith, Lillian

COMPTON, Grant

What Does A Coast Guardsman Do?
BL - v65 - My 1 '69 - p1014
SB - v4 - Mr '69 - p264
Subject: United States Coast Guard

COMPTON, Margaret (pseud.) 1852-1903
Real Name:
Harrison, Amelia Williams

American Indian Fairy Tales
BL - v67 - My 1 '71 - p752
KR - v39 - Ja 15 '71 - p53
LJ - v96 - My 15 '71 - p1801
PW - v199 - My 3 '71 - p57
Subject: Folklore; Indians of North America—Fiction

CONE, Molly Lamken 1918-
AuBYP, ConAu 16NR, IntAu&W 77, SmATA 28, ThrBJA, WrDr 86

Call Me Moose
BB - v6 - S '78 - p4
BL - v74 - Je 15 '78 - p1614
CCB-B - v32 - S '78 - p6
HB - v54 - Je '78 - p275
KR - v46 - My 15 '78 - p547
LA - v55 - O '78 - p862
SLJ - v24 - My '78 - p65
Subject: Family life—Fiction; Individuality—Fiction

Paul David Silverman Is A Father
CBRS - v11 - Jl '83 - p135
CCB-B - v37 - S '83 - p3
SLJ - v29 - Ag '83 - p74
VOYA - v6 - O '83 - p198
Subject: Marriage—Fiction; Pregnancy—Fiction

CONFORD, Ellen 1942-
AuBYP SUP, BioIn 10, ChILR 10, ConAu 13NR, FifBJA, SmATA 6, TwCChW 83, WrDr 86

Anything For A Friend
BL - v78 - Jl '82 - p1452
Subject: Moving (Household)—Fiction; Schools—Fiction

Hail, Hail Camp Timberwood
BL - v75 - O 1 '78 - p291
CCB-B - v32 - F '79 - p97
KR - v46 - D 1 '78 - p1306
RT - v33 - O '79 - p95
SLJ - v25 - S '78 - p133
Subject: Camping—Fiction

CONFORD, Ellen (continued)

Seven Days To A Brand-New Me
BL - v77 - Mr 1 '81 - p926
CBRS - v9 - Je '81 - p95
CCB-B - v34 - My '81 - p168
HB - v57 - Ap '81 - p195
KR - v49 - Ap 15 '81 - p507
PW - v219 - Ja 16 '81 - p77
SLJ - v27 - Mr '81 - p155
VOYA - v4 - Ap '81 - p32
WLB - v55 - Mr '81 - p530
Subject: Schools—Fiction

Strictly For Laughs
BL - v82 - O 15 '85 - p334
CBRS - v14 - D '85 - p43
CCB-B - v39 - Ja '86 - p83
KR - v53 - S 15 '85 - p989
SLJ - v32 - D '85 - p98
VOYA - v9 - Ap '86 - p28
Subject: Comedians—Fiction; Radio broadcasting—Fiction

We Interrupt This Semester For An Important Bulletin
BL - v76 - S 15 '79 - p117
CBRS - v8 - D '79 - p36
CCB-B - v33 - Ap '80 - p148
HB - v56 - F '80 - p59
Kliatt - v15 - Fall '81 - p6
KR - v48 - F 15 '80 - p221
RT - v34 - O '80 - p54
SLJ - v26 - S '79 - p154
WLB - v54 - Mr '80 - p456
Subject: Journalism—Fiction; Reporters and reporting—Fiction

Why Me?
BL - v82 - O 15 '85 - p334
B Rpt - v5 - My '86 - p29
CBRS - v14 - Mr '86 - p90
CCB-B - v39 - O '85 - p24
HB - v62 - Ja '86 - p56
Inter BC - v17 - #2 '86 p15
SLJ - v32 - N '85 - p95
VOYA - v8 - F '86 - p383
Subject: Interpersonal relations—Fiction

CONKLIN, Barbara

First, Last, And Always
SLJ - v32 - Ja '86 - p79
Subject: Love—Fiction

P.S. I Love You
CBRS - v10 - Ja '82 - p46
SLJ - v28 - Ag '82 - p124
VOYA - v4 - D '81 - p28

Summer Dreams
BL - v79 - My 15 '83 - p1196
SLJ - v30 - N '83 - p88
VOYA - v6 - O '83 - p210
Subject: Blind—Fiction; Love—Fiction

The Summer Jenny Fell In Love
BL - v79 - S 1 '82 - p36
SLJ - v29 - O '82 - p158
Subject: Friendship—Fiction; Love—Fiction

CONKLIN, Mike
see Zolna, Ed (co-author)

CONLON, Jean
see Lawson, Donna (co-author)

CONLY, Robert Leslie
***see* O'Brien, Robert C**

CONNELL, Abby

Jed And Jessie
BL - v80 - Ja 1 '84 - p678
Kliatt - v18 - Winter '84 - p20
SLJ - v30 - F '84 - p80
Subject: Love—Fiction

CONNOR, James, III
AuBYP SUP

I, Dwayne Kleber
KR - v38 - Ag 15 '70 - p884
LJ - v96 - Je 15 '71 - p2136
NYTBR - N 22 '70 - p38
Subject: City and town life—Fiction

CONRAD, Dick

Tony Dorsett: From Heisman To Superbowl In One Year
SLJ - v25 - My '79 - p86
Subject: Football—Biography

Walter Payton: The Running Machine
SLJ - v25 - My '79 - p86
Subject: Blacks—Biography; Football—Biography

CONRAD, Pam 1947-
SmATA 49

Holding Me Here
BL - v82 - Mr 15 '86 - p1080
B Rpt - v5 - N '86 - p26
BS - v46 - Ag '86 - p196
CBRS - v14 - Je '86 - p123

CONRAD, Pam (continued)
CCB-B - v40 - S '86 - p4
HB - v62 - Jl '86 - p453
Learning - v15 - N '86 - p102
PW - v229 - Je 27 '86 - p95
SLJ - v32 - Mr '86 - p174
VOYA - v9 - Je '86 - p77
Subject: Divorce—Fiction; Family problems—Fiction; Wife abuse—Fiction

CONSIDINE, Tim

The Photographic Dictionary Of Soccer
ARBA - v11 - p321
BW - Jl 15 '79 - pH2
Subject: Soccer

CONWAY, Caron A

Sometimes Nightmares Are Real
BL - v83 - Ap 15 '87 - p1277

COOK, Chris
see **McWhirter, Norris (co-author)**

COOK, David 1940-
ConNov 86, WrDr 86

A Closer Look At Apes
GP - v15 - Ja '77 - p3053
JB - v40 - Ag '76 - p197
SA - v235 - D '76 - p134
SB - v13 - My '77 - p43
SLJ - v23 - Ap '77 - p63
TLS - Jl 16 '76 - p887
Co-author: Hughes, Jill
Subject: Apes

COOK, Fred J 1911-
AuBYP, BioIn 4, –5, ConAu 3NR, EncAJ, EncTwCJ, SmATA 2, WhoAm 86

City Cop
BL - v75 - Je 15 '79 - p1533
CBRS - v7 - Ag '79 - p136
CCB-B - v32 - Jl '79 - p187
Hi Lo - v1 - S '79 - p5
NYTBR - Mr 25 '79 - p33
SLJ - v25 - Ap '79 - p67
VOYA - v4 - O '81 - p58
Subject: Acha, Carlos; New York (City); Police

Dawn Over Saratoga: The Turning Point Of The Revolutionary War
BL - v70 - S 15 '73 - p110
BS - v33 - Je 15 '73 - p145
KR - v41 - My 1 '73 - p523
LJ - v98 - N 15 '73 - p3462
NYTBR - Ag 5 '73 - p8
Subject: United States—History—Revolution, 1775-1783

COOK, Joseph Jay 1924-
AuBYP, ConAu 2NR, SmATA 8

Better Surfing For Boys
CCB-B - v21 - Je '68 - p157
LJ - v92 - D 15 '67 - p4634
Co-author: Romeika, William L
Subject: Surfing

Famous Firsts In Tennis
CCB-B - v31 - Je '78 - p156
KR - v46 - Ja 15 '78 - p50
SLJ - v24 - My '78 - p86
Subject: Tennis

COOK, Olive Rambo 1892-
AuBYP, ConAu 13R

Serilda's Star
BL - v56 - Mr 15 '60 - p456
HB - v36 - F '60 - p34
KR - v27 - Jl 1 '59 - p443
LJ - v85 - Mr 15 '60 - p1301
Subject: Horses—Fiction

COOKE, David C 1917-
AuBYP, ConAu 2NR, SmATA 2

Famous U.S. Navy Fighter Planes
KR - v40 - Je 1 '72 - p628
LJ - v98 - F 15 '73 - p642
Subject: Airplanes; United States Navy

How Automobiles Are Made
LJ - v98 - Mr 15 '73 - p1001
Subject: Automobiles

COOKE, Sarah Fabyan
see Palfrey, Sarah

COOKSON, Catherine McMullen 1906-
BioIn 8, –9, –10, ConAu 9NR, Novels, SmATA 9, Who 85, WrDr 86

Our John Willie
BL - v71 - D 15 '74 - p405
PW - v208 - Ag 18 '75 - p70
Subject: Brothers and sisters—Fiction; Orphans—Fiction

COOLEN, Norma
see Tuck, Jay Nelson (co-author)

COOMBS, Charles Ira 1914-
AuBYP, ConAu 19NR, SmATA 43

Auto Racing
BL - v68 - Ja 1 '72 - p393
KR - v39 - Ag 15 '71 - p884
LJ - v96 - D 15 '71 - p4203
Subject: Automobile racing

Be A Winner In Soccer
BL - v74 - S 1 '77 - p37
BW - v10 - N 9 '80 - p8
Comw - v104 - N 11 '77 - p734
KR - v45 - Mr 1 '77 - p228
SLJ - v23 - My '77 - p80
Subject: Soccer

Be A Winner In Track And Field
BL - v72 - My 1 '76 - p1262
KR - v44 - Ap 1 '76 - p396
SLJ - v22 - My '76 - p80
Subject: Track and field

Deep-Sea World: The Story Of Oceanography
BL - v62 - My 1 '66 - p874
BS - v26 - Ap 1 '66 - p17
Inst - v75 - Je '66 - p139
KR - v34 - F 1 '66 - p114
LJ - v91 - O 15 '66 - p5224
NYTBR - v71 - Je 12 '66 - p22
PW - v189 - My 30 '66 - p88
SB - v2 - My '66 - p27
Subject: Oceanography

Drag Racing
BL - v67 - N 1 '70 - p226
LJ - v95 - D 15 '70 - p4378
Subject: Drag racing

Rocket Pioneer
SB - v1 - Mr '66 - p237
Subject: Goddard, Robert Hutchings—Fiction

Skylab
HB - v48 - Ag '72 - p391
KR - v40 - F 15 '72 - p196
SA - v227 - D '72 - p116
SB - v8 - D '72 - p264
Subject: Astronautics; Space stations

COOMBS, Orde M
BlkAWP, ConAu 73, SelBAAu, WhoBlA 77

Do You See My Love For You Growing?
Am - v128 - Ja 20 '73 - p42
Bl W - v22 - F '73 - p51
BW - v6 - O 1 '72 - p15
KR - v40 - Jl 1 '72 - p761
LJ - v97 - N 15 '72 - p3821
LJ - v98 - F 15 '73 - p557
PW - v202 - Jl 10 '72 - p45
Subject: Blacks—Addresses, essays, lectures

COONEY, Caroline B 1947-
ConAu 97, SmATA 48

An April Love Story
Hi Lo - v3 - Ja '82 - p6
VOYA - v4 - F '82 - p29
Subject: Love—Fiction

Don't Blame The Music
BL - v82 - Ag '86 - p1682
B Rpt - v5 - N '86 - p27
CBRS - v14 - Jl '86 - p145
CCB-B - v39 - Jl '86 - p205
PW - v229 - Je 27 '86 - p94
SLJ - v32 - Ag '86 - p99
VOYA - v9 - D '86 - p214
WLB - v60 - Ap '86 - p49
Subject: Family problems—Fiction; Schools—Fiction; Sisters—Fiction

Holly In Love
BL - v80 - F 1 '84 - p809
SLJ - v30 - My '84 - p87
VOYA - v7 - Ag '84 - p146
Subject: Love—Fiction

COONEY, Linda A

Deadly Design
BL - v81 - My 15 '85 - p1325
Kliatt - v19 - Spring '85 - p8
SLJ - v32 - S '85 - p150
VOYA - v8 - F '86 - p391
Subject: Mystery and detective stories

Fatal Secrets
BL - v82 - S 15 '85 - p124
Kliatt - v19 - Fall '85 - p6
SLJ - v32 - Ja '86 - p80

COONTZ, Otto 1946-
ConAu 105, SmATA 33

Mystery Madness
BL - v78 - Jl '82 - p1442
KR - v50 - Ap 15 '82 - p489
SLJ - v28 - My '82 - p83
Subject: Mystery and detective stories

The Night Walkers
BL - v79 - D 15 '82 - p562
CBRS - v11 - F '83 - p69

COONTZ, Otto (continued)
CCB-B - v36 - Mr '83 - p123
Kliatt - v18 - Winter '84 - p6
KR - v50 - O 15 '82 - p1157
NYTBR - v88 - F 27 '83 - p37
SLJ - v30 - D '83 - p72
Subject: Horror stories

COOPER, Paulette 1944-
ConAu 37R, IntAu&W 77, WhoAmW 87, WrDr 86

Growing Up Puerto Rican
Choice - v10 - Jl '73 - p858
LJ - v97 - Ag '72 - p2626
NO - v11 - Ag 19 '72 - p19
PW - v201 - Je 12 '72 - p60
PW - v203 - My 28 '73 - p42
Subject: Puerto Ricans

COPPARD, Audrey 1931-
ConAu 29R

Who Has Poisoned The Sea?
B&B - v15 - My '70 - p38
KR - v38 - Mr 15 '70 - p321
LJ - v95 - Je 15 '70 - p2307
NYTBR - Ag 23 '70 - p20
PW - v197 - My 18 '70 - p39
SR - v53 - My 9 '70 - p69
Subject: Science fiction

CORBETT, Scott 1913-
AuBYP, ChILR 1, ConAu 1NR, FourBJA, IntAu&W 82, SmATA 42, -2AS, TwCChW 83, WhoAm 84, WrDr 86

The Baseball Bargain
BL - v66 - My 15 '70 - p1158
CCB-B - v23 - Ap '70 - p126
Comw - v92 - My 22 '70 - p247
KR - v38 - Mr 1 '70 - p242
LJ - v95 - My 15 '70 - p1963
SR - v53 - Je 27 '70 - p38
Subject: Baseball—Fiction

Diamonds Are Trouble
KR - v35 - O 1 '67 - p1217
LJ - v92 - N 15 '67 - p4257
NYTBR - v72 - N 5 '67 - p44
Subject: Mystery and detective stories

The Donkey Planet
CCB-B - v33 - N '79 - p44
Subject: Donkeys—Fiction; Science fiction

The Home Run Trick
CCB-B - v27 - S '73 - p5
HB - v49 - Je '73 - p270
Inst - v82 - My '73 - p74
KR - v41 - Mr 1 '73 - p254
LJ - v98 - My 15 '73 - p1703
NYTBR - Jl 15 '73 - p10
Subject: Baseball—Fiction

Jokes To Read In The Dark
BL - v77 - S 1 '80 - p43
CLW - v52 - F '81 - p309
NYTBR - v85 - Ap 27 '80 - p62
PW - v218 - Jl 4 '80 - p90
RT - v35 - O '81 - p69
SLJ - v27 - N '80 - p59
Subject: Jokes; Riddles

What About The Wankel Engine?
BL - v71 - Ja 15 '75 - p506
CCB-B - v28 - My '75 - p144
KR - v42 - N 15 '74 - p1203
SB - v11 - My '75 - p27
SLJ - v21 - Mr '75 - p93
Subject: Engines

What Makes A Plane Fly?
BL - v64 - Ja 15 '68 - p591
CCB-B - v21 - Mr '68 - p107
HB - v44 - Ap '68 - p203
LJ - v93 - Ap 15 '68 - p1797
NYTBR - v73 - My 5 '68 - p52
SB - v3 - Mr '68 - p339
SR - v51 - Mr 16 '68 - p39
Subject: Aerodynamics

CORCORAN, Barbara 1911-
AuBYP SUP, ConAu 11NR, -2AS, ConLC 17, DcLB 52, FifBJA, IntAu&W 86, SmATA 3, WhoAm 86, WrDr 86
Pseud./variant:
Dixon, Paige

A Dance To Still Music
Am - v131 - D 7 '74 - p374
BB - v3 - Ap '75 - p4
BL - v71 - S 1 '74 - p39
CCB-B - v28 - Ja '75 - p75
CE - v51 - F '75 - p215
Choice - v14 - N '77 - p1178
CLW - v46 - Ap '75 - p404
CLW - v47 - Ap '76 - p397
HB - v50 - O '74 - p136
Inter BC - v11 - #1 '80 p23
KR - v42 - Jl 15 '74 - p742
KR - v43 - Ja 1 '75 - p5
LA - v52 - S '75 - p857
LJ - v99 - S 15 '74 - p2287
NYTBR - N 17 '74 - p8
PW - v206 - Ag 26 '74 - p306

CORCORAN, Barbara (continued)
Teacher - v92 - D '74 - p78
Subject: Deaf—Fiction

The Faraway Island
BB - v5 - Ag '77 - p2
BL - v73 - Ap 1 '77 - p1165
CCB-B - v31 - O '77 - p31
CLW - v49 - N '77 - p188
Cur R - v17 - My '78 - p127
HB - v53 - Ag '77 - p438
KR - v45 - F 1 '77 - p97
SLJ - v23 - My '77 - p60
Subject: Grandmothers—Fiction; Nantucket (Mass.)—Fiction

Hey, That's My Soul You're Stomping On
BL - v74 - Ap 1 '78 - p1247
CCB-B - v31 - Je '78 - p156
EJ - v67 - S '78 - p90
HB - v54 - Je '78 - p282
KR - v46 - Mr 1 '78 - p247
Subject: Divorce—Fiction; Family problems—Fiction; Old age—Fiction

Make No Sound
BL - v74 - O 15 '77 - p373
CLW - v49 - Mr '78 - p356
KR - v45 - Jl 15 '77 - p727
SLJ - v24 - S '77 - p125
Subject: Hawaii—Fiction

Making It
BL - v77 - Ap 1 '81 - p1083
CCB-B - v34 - F '81 - p109
HB - v57 - Ap '81 - p195
KR - v49 - Ag 15 '81 - p1010
SLJ - v27 - Ap '81 - p138
VOYA - v3 - F '81 - p28
Subject: Brothers and sisters—Fiction

Me And You And A Dog Named Blue
BL - v75 - Mr 15 '79 - p1153
HB - v55 - Je '79 - p300
KR - v47 - Mr 15 '79 - p331
SLJ - v25 - Mr '79 - p136
Subject: Baseball—Fiction; Fathers and daughters—Fiction; Friendship—Fiction

Rising Damp
BL - v76 - Ap 1 '80 - p1124
CCB-B - v34 - S '80 - p5
CLW - v52 - D '80 - p237
KR - v48 - Je 15 '80 - p783
SLJ - v26 - Ap '80 - p121
Subject: Friendship—Fiction; Ireland—Fiction

Sam
BL - v64 - Ja 1 '68 - p542
BW - v1 - O 22 '67 - p14
CCB-B - v21 - N '67 - p39
CLW - v39 - D '67 - p291
CSM - v59 - N 2 '67 - pB11
KR - v35 - Jl 15 '67 - p815
LJ - v92 - N 15 '67 - p4258
NYTBR - v72 - N 5 '67 - p68
SR - v50 - N 11 '67 - p48
Subject: Montana—Fiction; Schools—Fiction

The Shadowed Path
Kliatt - v19 - Spring '85 - p8
SLJ - v32 - S '85 - p151
VOYA - v8 - F '86 - p391
Subject: Hawaii—Fiction

Strike!
BL - v79 - Ap 1 '83 - p1031
B Rpt - v2 - N '83 - p32
CBRS - v12 - S '83 - p7
CCB-B - v36 - Ap '83 - p146
Inter BC - v15 - #5 '84 p17
KR - v51 - My 1 '83 - p527
SLJ - v29 - My '83 - p80
VOYA - v6 - O '83 - p199
Subject: Strikes and lockouts—Fiction

When Darkness Falls
BL - v82 - Ja 15 '86 - p751
SLJ - v32 - Ap '86 - p103
Subject: Love—Fiction; Mystery and detective stories

The Woman In Your Life
CBRS - v13 - Winter '85 - p60
CCB-B - v38 - D '84 - p63
PW - v226 - N 2 '84 - p78
SLJ - v31 - F '85 - p82
Subject: Prisoners—Fiction

see also Dixon, Paige for additional titles

CORDELL, Alexander (pseud.) 1914-
ConAu X, DcLEL 1940, SmATA 7, TwCChW 83, WrDr 86
Real Name:
Graber, Alexander

Witches' Sabbath
BL - v67 - Ja 1 '71 - p371
CCB-B - v24 - Jl '71 - p168
Comw - v93 - N 20 '70 - p202
KR - v38 - N 1 '70 - p1200

CORDELL, Alexander (continued)
NS - v80 - N 6 '70 - p610
PW - v198 - N 30 '70 - p41
TLS - Jl 2 '70 - p710
TLS - Ap 6 '73 - p382
TN - v27 - Je '71 - p431
Subject: Ireland—Fiction

CORET, Harriette

In And Out Of Windows
BL - v79 - Ja 15 '83 - p660
Hi Lo - v4 - N '82 - p6
VOYA - v6 - D '83 - p278

CORN, Frederick Lynn

Basketball's Magnificent Bird: The Larry Bird Story
BL - v79 - Ja 1 '83 - p622
B Rpt - v2 - My '83 - p50
SLJ - v29 - D '82 - p85
Subject: Basketball—Biography

CORNELL, Jean Gay 1920-
ConAu 1NR, SmATA 23, WhoAmW 77

Louis Armstrong: Ambassador Satchmo
JLD - v11 - Ap '78 - p44
Subject: Blacks—Biography; Musicians

Mahalia Jackson: Queen Of Gospel Song
PW - v205 - My 13 '74 - p58
SLJ - v21 - Ja '75 - p43
Subject: Blacks—Biography; Singers

Ralph Bunche: Champion Of Peace
SLJ - v22 - My '76 - p58
Subject: Blacks—Biography; United Nations—Biography

CORRIGAN, Barbara 1922-
ConAu 57, SmATA 8

Of Course You Can Sew!
BL - v67 - Mr 15 '71 - p618
CE - v48 - O '71 - p29
HB - v47 - Je '71 - p298
Inst - v130 - Je '71 - p74
LJ - v96 - Ap 15 '71 - p1502
PW - v200 - Jl 5 '71 - p50
Subject: Dressmaking; Sewing

COUPER, Heather

Comets And Meteors
BFYC - v20 - Autumn '85 - p27
GP - v24 - Ja '86 - p4566
SLJ - v32 - F '86 - p84
Subject: Comets; Meteors

COURTNEY, Dale
see Goldsmith, Howard

COVILLE, Bruce 1950-
ConAu 97, SmATA 32

Spirits And Spells
BL - v80 - Ja 1 '84 - p676
SLJ - v30 - Mr '84 - p171
VOYA - v7 - Ap '84 - p29
Subject: Horror stories; Supernatural—Fiction

COVINGTON, John P
AuBYP SUP

Motorcycle Racer
LJ - v98 - D 15 '73 - p3723
Subject: Motorcycle racing—Fiction

COWAN, Dale

Campfire Nights
BL - v80 - F 1 '84 - p809
SLJ - v30 - Ap '84 - p122
VOYA - v7 - Ag '84 - p145
Subject: Camping—Fiction; Love—Fiction

COWEN, Eve (pseud.)
ConAu X, SmATA X
Real Name:
Werner, Herma

Catch The Sun
BL - v78 - O 15 '81 - p297
Hi Lo - v3 - Mr '82 - p2
SLJ - v28 - S '81 - p122
Subject: Running—Fiction

High Escape
BL - v78 - O 15 '81 - p297
Hi Lo - v3 - Mr '82 - p2
SLJ - v28 - S '81 - p122
Subject: Skis and skiing—Fiction

Race To Win
Hi Lo - v3 - F '82 - p1
SLJ - v28 - S '81 - p122
Subject: Sports—Fiction

see also Werner, Herma for additional titles

COX, William R 1901-
AuBYP, ConAu 6NR, EncFWF, SmATA 46, TwCCr&M 85, WhoAm 86, WrDr 86

Battery Mates
BL - v74 - Je 1 '78 - p1550
CCB-B - v31 - Jl '78 - p173
KR - v46 - F 1 '78 - p107
SLJ - v24 - My '78 - p87
Subject: Baseball—Fiction

Big League Sandlotters
CLW - v43 - N '71 - p174
KR - v39 - Ja 15 '71 - p56
LJ - v96 - My 15 '71 - p1823
SR - v54 - Jl 17 '71 - p36
Subject: Baseball—Fiction

Rookie In The Backcourt
BS - v29 - F 1 '70 - p422
CSM - v62 - My 7 '70 - pB7
KR - v37 - D 15 '69 - p1322
LJ - v95 - My 15 '70 - p1964
Subject: Basketball—Fiction

Third And Goal
BS - v31 - O 15 '71 - p334
LJ - v96 - D 15 '71 - p4201
Subject: Football—Fiction; Prejudices—Fiction

Trouble At Second Base
LJ - v91 - Jl '66 - p3550
NYTBR - v71 - My 8 '66 - p47
Subject: Baseball—Fiction

CRAIG, Margaret 1911-1964
BioIn 7, ConAu 1R, MorJA, SmATA 9

Trish
BL - v47 - Mr 15 '51 - p258
KR - v19 - Ja 1 '51 - p3
LJ - v76 - Mr 15 '51 - p530
NYTBR - Mr 11 '51 - p26
SR - v34 - My 12 '51 - p57

CRAMER, Kathryn
see Terzian, James P (co-author)

CRANE, Caroline 1930-
AuBYP SUP, ConAu 19NR, SmATA 11, WhoE 85, WrDr 86

A Girl Like Tracy
BS - v26 - My 1 '66 - p57
CCB-B - v19 - Je '66 - p161
LJ - v91 - My 15 '66 - p2702

Wedding Song
BS - v27 - O 1 '67 - p262
CLW - v39 - D '67 - p291
CSM - v59 - N 2 '67 - pB11
KR - v35 - Jl 15 '67 - p816
LJ - v92 - O 15 '67 - p3861

CRANE, M A
see Wartski, Maureen Crane

CRARY, Margaret 1906-
AuBYP, ConAu 5R, SmATA 9

Mexican Whirlwind
KR - v37 - Ap 15 '69 - p451
LJ - v94 - My 15 '69 - p2098
Subject: Basketball—Fiction; Student (Foreign)—Fiction

CRAVEN, Margaret 1901-1980
BioIn 10, –12, ConAu 103, ConLC 17, WhAm 7, WhoAm 80, WrDr 82

I Heard The Owl Call My Name
Am - v130 - My 4 '74 - p349
BL - v70 - F 1 '74 - p569
BL - v71 - Mr 15 '75 - p747
BS - v33 - F 1 '74 - p475
CC - v92 - My 14 '75 - p501
CLW - v47 - N '75 - p167
CSM - v66 - Ja 30 '74 - p00F5
LJ - v99 - F 15 '74 - p503
LJ - v99 - Mr 15 '74 - p908
LJ - v99 - My 15 '74 - p1452
NS - v88 - Ag 2 '74 - p163
NS - v88 - N 8 '74 - p666
NYTBR - v0 - F 3 '74 - p28
Rel St - v204 - D 3 '73 - p35
SLJ - v26 - Ag '80 - p44
Time - v10 - Ja 28 '74 - p73
TLS - v0 - D 6 '74 - p1375
TN - v31 - Ap '75 - p331

CRAWFORD, Alice Owen

Please Say Yes
BL - v80 - Je 15 '84 - p1473
SLJ - v31 - S '84 - p138
VOYA - v7 - O '84 - p202
Subject: Basketball—Fiction; Love—Fiction

CRAWFORD, Charles P 1945-
ConAu 45, SmATA 28

Letter Perfect
NYTBR - Jl 22 '79 - p27
Subject: Friendship—Fiction; Schools—Fiction; Teachers—Fiction

CRAWFORD, Charles P (continued)

Three-Legged Race
BS - v34 - D 15 '74 - p430
Comw - v101 - N 22 '74 - p194
EJ - v64 - Ap '75 - p90
KR - v42 - Ag 1 '74 - p809
LJ - v99 - O 15 '74 - p2745
PW - v206 - N 25 '74 - p46
Subject: Friendship—Fiction

CRAYDER, Dorothy 1906-
AuBYP SUP, ConAu 33R, SmATA 7

She, The Adventuress
BL - v69 - Je 1 '73 - p946
CCB-B - v26 - Jl '73 - p169
HB - v49 - O '73 - p465
KR - v41 - F 15 '73 - p186
LJ - v98 - My 15 '73 - p1680
Obs - D 7 '75 - p32
Teacher - v91 - D '73 - p73
TES - D 14 '79 - p21
TN - v30 - Ja '74 - p205
Subject: Adventure and adventurers—Fiction; Voyages and travels—Fiction

CROCKER, Chris

Cyndi Lauper
B Rpt - v4 - Mr '86 - p35
SLJ - v32 - S '85 - p131
Subject: Biography; Rock musicians; Singers

CROFUT, William 1934-
ConAu 25R, SmATA 23

Troubadour: A Different Battlefield
BL - v65 - S 1 '68 - p28
KR - v36 - F 15 '68 - p222
KR - v36 - Mr 1 '68 - p281
LJ - v93 - Ap 1 '68 - p1473
PW - v193 - F 19 '68 - p90
TN - v25 - N '68 - p80
Subject: Musicians; Voyages and travels

CROMIE, William J 1930-
AuBYP SUP, ConAu 13R, SmATA 4, WhoMW 84

Living World Of The Sea
BL - v63 - D 1 '66 - p395
CC - v83 - S 14 '66 - p1116
Choice - v4 - Ap '67 - p181
CLW - v38 - D '66 - p271
HB - v43 - F '67 - p95
KR - v34 - Jl 1 '66 - p669
KR - v34 - Jl 15 '66 - p702
LJ - v91 - D 1 '66 - p5986
NH - v76 - F '67 - p68
SB - v2 - Mr '67 - p289
Subject: Marine fauna

CRONE, Ruth
see Brown, Marion Marsh (co-author)

CROSBY, Alexander L 1906-1980
AuBYP, BioIn 12, ConAu 29R, -93, MorBMP, NewYTBS 80, SmATA 2, -23N

One Day For Peace
CCB-B - v25 - N '71 - p40
Comw - v94 - My 21 '71 - p268
KR - v39 - Ap 15 '71 - p431
LJ - v96 - Jl '71 - p2369
Subject: Vietnamese Conflict, 1961-1975—Fiction

CROSHER, G R 1911-
ConAu 69, SmATA 14

Pacemaker Story Books
Inst - v76 - N '66 - p188

CROSSEN, Kendall Foster
see Chaber, M E

CUNNINGHAM, Chet 1928-
ConAu 19NR, IntAu&W 86, SmATA 23, WrDr 86

Apprentice To A Rip-Off
Hi Lo - v1 - S '79 - p4
Subject: Employment—Fiction

Locked Storeroom Mystery
BL - v75 - Mr 15 '79 - p1145
Hi Lo - v1 - N '79 - p4
Subject: Mystery and detective stories

Narc One Going Down
BL - v74 - O 15 '77 - p370
Cur R - v16 - D '77 - p361
Hi Lo - v2 - F '81 - p6
Subject: Drug abuse—Fiction

CUNNINGHAM, Julia Woolfolk 1916-
AuBYP, ConAu 19NR, ConLC 12, MorBMP, SmATA 26, -2AS, ThrBJA, TwCChW 83, WhoAm 86, WrDr 86

Dorp Dead
BW - v11 - My 10 '81 - p14
CCB-B - v19 - O '65 - p30
LJ - v90 - Ap 15 '65 - p2018

CUNNINGHAM, Julia Woolfolk (continued)
NYTBR - v70 - Ap 25 '65 - p26
SR - v48 - Je 19 '65 - p40
Subject: Orphans—Fiction

Macaroon
CSM - v71 - Ap 9 '79 - pB10
Teacher - v96 - My '79 - p124
Subject: Fantasy; Raccoons—Fiction

Onion Journey
BW - v1 - D 10 '67 - p20
CCB-B - v21 - D '67 - p57
Comw - v87 - N 10 '67 - p176
HB - v43 - D '67 - p738
KR - v35 - O 1 '67 - p1206
NYTBR - v72 - D 3 '67 - p68

CURRY, Jane Louise 1932-
AuBYP, ConAu 7NR, FourBJA, IntAu&W 82, SmATA 1, TwCChW 83, WhoAm 84, WhoAmW 83, WrDr 86

The Ice Ghosts Mystery
B&B - v18 - Je '73 - p133
BL - v69 - N 15 '72 - p299
CSM - v64 - N 8 '72 - pB4
HB - v48 - O '72 - p467
KR - v40 - Ag 1 '72 - p859
LJ - v97 - D 15 '72 - p4086
NYTBR - N 26 '72 - p8
TLS - Ap 6 '73 - p383
Subject: Mystery and detective stories

CURTIS, Bruce
see Haney, Lynn (co-author)

CURTIS, Edward S 1868-1952
BioIn 10, -11, -12, -13, ICPEnP, MacBEP, ObitOF 79, WhAm 4, WhAmArt 85

The Girl Who Married A Ghost: And Other Tales From The North American Indian
CAY - v5 - Summer '84 - p3
Sch Lib - v28 - Mr '80 - p35
SE - v44 - O '80 - p478
Subject: Indians of North America—Fiction

CURTIS, Robert H
AuBYP SUP

On ESP
CCB-B - v29 - O '75 - p25
KR - v43 - My 1 '75 - p515
SB - v11 - Mr '76 - p207
SLJ - v22 - Ja '76 - p52
Subject: Extrasensory perception

Questions And Answers About Alcoholism
J Read - v21 - F '78 - p472
KR - v44 - O 15 '76 - p1147
SLJ - v23 - Ja '77 - p100
Subject: Alcohol and youth

CUTHBERTSON, Tom 1945-
ConAu 45

Anybody's Bike Book
A Lib - v4 - F '73 - p99
BL - v68 - N 1 '71 - p244
BL - v72 - D 15 '75 - p560
BW - v6 - Ja 2 '72 - p6
Kliatt - v14 - Winter '80 - p69
LJ - v96 - D 15 '71 - p4101
Money - v3 - N '74 - p114
NYTBR - Je 4 '72 - p8
Subject: Bicyles and bicyling

Anybody's Skateboard Book
Kliatt - v11 - Winter '77 - p35
LJ - v101 - S 15 '76 - p1874
WLB - v51 - N '76 - p209
Subject: Skateboarding

Bike Tripping
A Lib - v4 - F '73 - p98
BL - v72 - D 15 '75 - p560
BW - v6 - Je 11 '72 - p1
KR - v40 - Mr 15 '72 - p391
LJ - v97 - My 15 '72 - p1823
LJ - v97 - O 15 '72 - p3474
NYTBR - Je 4 '72 - p8
NYTBR - Je 2 '74 - p12
Subject: Bicyles and bicyling

CUTTING, Edith

A Quilt For Bermuda
BL - v74 - My 15 '78 - p1487
Cur R - v17 - My '78 - p87
Subject: Schools—Fiction

CUYLER, Margery Stuyvesant 1948-
ConAu 117, SmATA 39, WhoAmW 77, WhoLibI 82
Pseud./variant:
Wallace, Daisy

The Trouble With Soap
BL - v78 - Mr 1 '82 - p857
CBRS - v10 - Ap '82 - p88
CCB-B - v35 - Jl '82 - p204
HB - v58 - Ap '82 - p162
KR - v50 - Ap 1 '82 - p417

CUYLER, Margery Stuyvesant
(continued)
NYTBR - v87 - Je 13 '82 - p27
PW - v221 - My 28 '82 - p72
PW - v228 - S 6 '85 - p66
SLJ - v28 - Ap '82 - p68
Subject: Behavior—Fiction; Friendship—Fiction; Schools—Fiction

D

DAHL, Roald 1916-
ChlLR 1, –7, ConAu 6NR, ConLC 1, –6, –18, MorBMP, PiP, SmATA 26, ThrBJA, TwCChW 83, WrDr 86

Charlie And The Great Glass Elevator
B&B - v18 - Jl '73 - p140
CCB-B - v27 - S '73 - p5
HB - v49 - Ap '73 - p142
Kliatt - v12 - p6
KR - v40 - Jl 15 '72 - p802
Lis - v90 - N 8 '73 - p642
LJ - v97 - D 15 '72 - p4070
NYRB - v19 - D 14 '72 - p41
NYTBR - S 17 '72 - p8
NYTBR - N 4 '73 - p54
NYTBR - D 18 '77 - p35
PW - v202 - S 4 '72 - p51
Sch Lib - v29 - Je '81 - p113
SR - v1 - Mr 10 '73 - p67
TLS - Je 15 '73 - p683
Subject: Fantasy

The Wonderful Story Of Henry Sugar And Six More
B&B - v6 - F '78 - p4
BS - v37 - Ja '78 - p334
BW - N 13 '77 - pE1
BW - D 11 '77 - pE4
HB - v54 - F '78 - p52
JB - v42 - Ap '78 - p100
KR - v45 - N 1 '77 - p1148
NS - v94 - N 4 '77 - p626
Obs - D 11 '77 - p31
PW - v212 - O 31 '77 - p59
Spec - v239 - D 10 '77 - p24
TES - N 18 '77 - p35
Subject: Short stories

DAHNSEN, Alan

Bicycles
BL - v75 - D 15 '78 - p693
Subject: Bicyles and bicyling

DALTON, Stephen

Split Second: The World Of High Speed Photography
SA - v253 - D '85 - p43
Subject: Photography

DALY, Maureen 1921-
AuBYP, ConAu X, ConLC 17, CurBio 46, MorJA, SmATA 2, –1AS, TwCChW 83, WhoAmW 77, WrDr 86
Pseud./variant:
McGivern, Maureen Daly

Acts Of Love
BL - v83 - S 1 '86 - p52
CBRS - v15 - N '86 - p31
CCB-B - v39 - Jl '86 - p206
KR - v54 - Ag 1 '86 - p1206
Par - v61 - N '86 - p75
PW - v230 - S 26 '86 - p87
SLJ - v33 - O '86 - p189
VOYA - v9 - D '86 - p214
Subject: Family problems—Fiction; Interpersonal relations—Fiction

Seventeenth Summer
EJ - v74 - S '85 - p85
NYTBR - My 3 '42 - p7
NYTBR, Pt. 2 - F 16 '69 - p22
NYTBR, Pt. 2 - My 4 '69 - p38
NYTBR, Pt. 2 - F 13 '72 - p14
Subject: Love—Fiction

D'AMATO, Janet Potter 1925-
AuBYP SUP, ConAu 18NR, SmATA 9

Who's A Horn? What's An Antler?: Crafts Of Bone And Horn
BL - v79 - O 15 '82 - p310
SLJ - v29 - Mr '83 - p190
Subject: Handicraft

DANA, Barbara 1940-
ConAu 8NR, SmATA 22

Crazy Eights
BB - v7 - Je '79 - p4
BL - v75 - S 1 '78 - p36
BS - v38 - F '79 - p371

DANA, Barbara (continued)
CCB-B - v32 - Ja '79 - p77
Kliatt - v15 - Spring '81 - p6
KR - v46 - S 15 '78 - p1020
PW - v214 - Ag 28 '78 - p394
SLJ - v25 - O '78 - p153
TN - v37 - Spring '81 - p292
Subject: Identity—Fiction; Reformatories—Fiction

DANIEL, Colin (pseud.) 1938-
ConAu X
Real Name:
Windsor, Patricia

Demon Tree
Fant R - v7 - Ap '84 - p41
Subject: Supernatural—Fiction

see also Windsor, Patricia for additional titles

DANIELS, Kim

Your Changing Emotions
BL - v82 - Ja 15 '86 - p747
Kliatt - v20 - Winter '86 - p41
Subject: Emotions

DANIELS, Patricia
see Melville, Herman (author of adapted works)

DANZIGER, Paula 1944-
ConAu 115, ConLC 21, FifBJA, SmATA 36

Can You Sue Your Parents For Malpractice?
BL - v75 - My 1 '79 - p1361
BL - v75 - Jl 15 '79 - p1634
CBRS - v7 - Ap '79 - p87
CCB-B - v32 - Je '79 - p172
EJ - v69 - My '80 - p91
J Read - v23 - F '80 - p473
KR - v47 - Je 1 '79 - p641
NY - v55 - D 3 '79 - p196
NYTBR - Je 17 '79 - p25
RT - v33 - N '79 - p217
SLJ - v25 - Ap '79 - p67
Subject: Family life—Fiction; Individuality—Fiction

The Cat Ate My Gymsuit
BFYC - v21 - Autumn '86 - p16
BL - v81 - D 15 '84 - p583
CCB-B - v28 - Ja '75 - p76
J Read - v19 - Ja '76 - p333
J Read - v22 - N '78 - p126
KR - v42 - N 15 '74 - p1206
LJ - v99 - N 15 '74 - p3052
NYTBR - Ja 5 '75 - p8
NYTBR - v85 - N 16 '80 - p47
PW - v206 - O 7 '74 - p62
Subject: Schools—Fiction; Teachers—Fiction

The Divorce Express
BL - v79 - S 15 '82 - p112
CCB-B - v36 - S '82 - p6
CLW - v56 - O '84 - p127
GP - v25 - S '86 - p4670
HB - v58 - O '82 - p516
KR - v50 - S 1 '82 - p1000
SLJ - v29 - O '82 - p158
Subject: Divorce—Fiction; Parent and child—Fiction

It's An Aardvark-Eat-Turtle World
BL - v82 - Je 15 '86 - p1536
Can Child Lit - #4 '86 p69
CCB-B - v38 - Je '85 - p182
EJ - v74 - S '85 - p86
Inter BC - v16 - #8 '85 p18
LATBR - S 15 '85 - p6
PW - v229 - Je 27 '86 - p98
RT - v40 - O '86 - p54
SLJ - v31 - Ap '85 - p96
VOYA - v8 - Je '85 - p129
Subject: Divorce—Fiction; Family life—Fiction

The Pistachio Prescription
BL - v74 - Ap 15 '78 - p1347
BS - v38 - Ag '78 - p154
CCB-B - v31 - My '78 - p140
EJ - v67 - S '78 - p90
KR - v46 - Ap 1 '78 - p379
PW - v213 - My 8 '78 - p75
SLJ - v24 - My '78 - p75
Subject: Family life—Fiction; Schools—Fiction

There's A Bat In Bunk Five
BL - v77 - D 15 '80 - p571
CBRS - v9 - N '80 - p26
CCB-B - v34 - D '80 - p68
EJ - v70 - S '81 - p76
Hi Lo - v2 - Mr '81 - p4
Kliatt - v16 - Spring '82 - p8
KR - v49 - Ja 1 '81 - p12
LATBR - Jl 25 '82 - p9
NYTBR - v85 - N 23 '80 - p36
RT - v35 - O '81 - p71
SLJ - v27 - Ja '81 - p68
TN - v38 - Fall '81 - p71
VOYA - v4 - Ap '81 - p34
WLB - v55 - D '80 - p292
Subject: Camping—Fiction

This Place Has No Atmosphere
BL - v83 - O 15 '86 - p347

DANZIGER, Paula (continued)
CBRS - v15 - N '86 - p31
KR - v54 - S 1 '86 - p1368
PW - v230 - O 31 '86 - p70
SLJ - v33 - N '86 - p99
Subject: Moon—Fiction; Moving (Household)—Fiction; Science fiction

DARLING, David J
SmATA 44

Diana: The People's Princess
BL - v81 - Ap 15 '85 - p1190
SLJ - v31 - Ag '85 - p63
Subject: Biography; Princesses

DAVID, Andrew

Famous Criminal Trials
BL - v76 - Ja 1 '80 - p666
SLJ - v26 - Ap '80 - p107
Subject: Trials (Murder)

DAVID, Jay (pseud.) 1929-
ConAu X
Real Name:
Adler, William

Growing Up Black
BL - v65 - Ja 1 '69 - p479
BS - v28 - N 1 '68 - p323
Choice - v6 - S '69 - p862
CLW - v40 - Ap '69 - p521
EJ - v60 - My '71 - p662
KR - v36 - Jl 15 '68 - p791
LJ - v93 - Ag '68 - p2842
LJ - v94 - Ja 15 '69 - p319
PW - v194 - Jl 8 '68 - p163
PW - v196 - Ag 11 '69 - p44
SR - v52 - Mr 22 '69 - p63
WSJ - v172 - O 18 '68 - p16
Subject: Blacks—Biography; Blacks—Collected works

DAVIDSON, Margaret 1936-
AuBYP SUP, BioIn 10, ConAu 17NR, SmATA 5

The Golda Meir Story
BL - v72 - Je 15 '76 - p1466
BL - v73 - Ap 1 '77 - p1174
BL - v82 - S 15 '85 - p142
BS - v36 - O '76 - p239
CCB-B - v34 - Je '81 - p190
HB - v52 - O '76 - p509
KR - v44 - My 1 '76 - p537
LA - v59 - Mr '82 - p271
PW - v209 - Ap 5 '76 - p101
SE - v41 - Ap '77 - p351
SLJ - v23 - S '76 - p113
Subject: Biography; Statesmen

Seven True Horse Stories
ACSB - v13 - Spring '80 - p24
Hi Lo - v1 - F '80 - p3
PW - v216 - S 10 '79 - p74
SLJ - v26 - Ja '80 - p68
Subject: Horses

DAVIDSON, Mary S

A Superstar Called Sweetpea
CBRS - v9 - D '80 - p27
CCB-B - v34 - N '80 - p50
Kliatt - v16 - Fall '82 - p6
KR - v48 - D 15 '80 - p1572
SLJ - v27 - N '80 - p85
TN - v38 - Summer '82 - p364
VOYA - v3 - F '81 - p28
Subject: Charleston (S.C.)—Fiction

DAVIES, L P 1914-
ConAu 21R, ConSFA, TwCSFW 86, WrDr 86

Genesis Two
KR - v38 - Je 15 '70 - p659
KR - v38 - Jl 15 '70 - p753
LJ - v95 - Je 15 '70 - p2279
LJ - v95 - N 15 '70 - p4065
MFSF - v40 - Mr '71 - p16
PW - v197 - Je 15 '70 - p59

DAVIES, Peter 1937-
ConAu 53, Profile 1

Fly Away Paul
BS - v34 - O 15 '74 - p329
KR - v42 - S 1 '74 - p949
LJ - v99 - O 15 '74 - p2745
NYTBR - N 24 '74 - p8
PT - v8 - Ja '75 - p17
PW - v206 - Ag 5 '74 - p58
SLJ - v27 - S '80 - p43
Subject: Runaways—Fiction

DAVIS, Burke 1913-
AuBYP, BioIn 3, -4, -5, -7, ConAu 4NR, IntAu&W 86X, SmATA 4, WhoAm 82, WrDr 86

Black Heroes Of The American Revolution
BL - v72 - Jl 15 '76 - p1594
CCB-B - v29 - Jl '76 - p172
CE - v53 - O '76 - p37
Comw - v103 - N 19 '76 - p758
Cur R - v17 - Ag '78 - p173
KR - v44 - Ap 15 '76 - p475
SE - v41 - Ap '77 - p346

DAVIS, Burke (continued)
SLJ - v23 - S '76 - p114
Subject: Blacks—Biography; United States—History—Revolution, 1775-1783

DAVIS, Charles
BioIn 9

On My Own
LJ - v96 - Ap 15 '71 - p1514
Co-author: Simon, R E
Subject: Public relations as a profession

DAVIS, Clive E 1914-
AuBYP, ConAu 17R

Book Of Air Force Airplanes And Helicopters
BL - v64 - Mr 15 '68 - p867
SB - v4 - S '68 - p147
Subject: Airplanes

DAVIS, Daniel Sheldon 1936-
ConAu 45, IntAu&W 77, SmATA 12, WhoE 77

Marcus Garvey
SE - v37 - D '73 - p785
SS - v65 - Mr '74 - p139
Subject: Blacks—Biography

DAVIS, Leslie

Something Out There
BL - v82 - N 1 '85 - p397
SLJ - v32 - Ja '86 - p79
VOYA - v8 - F '86 - p391
Subject: Love—Fiction; Mystery and detective stories

DAY, Beth 1924-
AuBYP SUP, ConAu 18NR, IntAu&W 86, SmATA 33, WhoAmW 77

Life On A Lost Continent: A Natural History Of New Zealand
BL - v68 - D 15 '71 - p366
CCB-B - v25 - F '72 - p89
KR - v39 - O 1 '71 - p1074
LJ - v97 - F 15 '72 - p783
SB - v8 - My '72 - p83
SR - v55 - Ja 15 '72 - p47
Subject: Natural history; New Zealand

DAY, Nancy Raines

Help Yourself To Health
BL - v76 - Jl 15 '80 - p1662
Hi Lo - v1 - My '80 - p4
Subject: Health

DAY, Veronique

Landslide!
CCB-B - v18 - Je '65 - p145
PW - v190 - Ag 29 '66 - p351

DEAN, Karen Strickler 1923-
SmATA 49

Between Dances: Maggie Adams' Eighteenth Summer
Kliatt - v16 - Fall '82 - p6
SLJ - v29 - S '82 - p136
VOYA - v5 - Ag '82 - p29
Subject: Ballet dancing—Fiction; Marriage—Fiction

Maggie Adams, Dancer
CCB-B - v34 - O '80 - p30
Kliatt - v16 - Fall '82 - p6
SLJ - v27 - O '80 - p164
Subject: Ballet dancing—Fiction; Dancers—Fiction

Stay On Your Toes, Maggie Adams!
B Rpt - v5 - N '86 - p35
PW - v229 - Ap 25 '86 - p84
SLJ - v33 - D '86 - p114
VOYA - v9 - Ag '86 - p141
Subject: Ballet dancing—Fiction; Love—Fiction

DEANE, Shirley 1920-
ConAu 2NR, IntAu&W 77, WrDr 80

Vendetta
TLS - Ap 3 '69 - p360
Subject: Adventure and adventurers—Fiction; Corsica—Fiction

DEARMOND, Dale
WhoAmA 78

Dale DeArmond: A First Book Collection Of Her Prints
Kliatt - v14 - Spring '80 - p48
LJ - v105 - Ja 1 '80 - p94
Subject: Artists

DEARY, Terry 1946-
ConAu 110, SmATA 41

Calamity Kate
Brit Bk N C - Spring '80 - p14
Subject: Mystery and detective stories

The Custard Kid
CBRS - v11 - N '82 - p25
JB - v42 - O '78 - p254
SLJ - v29 - Ja '83 - p74
Subject: Robbers and outlaws—Fiction; West (U.S.)—Fiction

DECKER, Sunny

An Empty Spoon
BL - v65 - Jl 15 '69 - p1244
BS - v29 - My 1 '69 - p52
BW - v4 - F 22 '70 - p13
CLW - v41 - My '70 - p576
EJ - v60 - Ap '71 - p518
JGE - v22 - Jl '70 - p149
KR - v37 - F 1 '69 - p146
KR - v37 - Mr 1 '69 - p253
LJ - v94 - Ap 15 '69 - p1612
LJ - v94 - Jl '69 - p2687
LJ - v94 - D 15 '69 - p4584
PW - v195 - F 17 '69 - p153
PW - v196 - N 24 '69 - p44
SR - v52 - O 18 '69 - p57
TN - v26 - N '69 - p85
TN - v27 - Je '71 - p424
Subject: Blacks—Education; Teachers

DEE, M M

The Mystery Of Room 105
Hi Lo - v3 - F '82 - p2
Subject: Mystery and detective stories

The Mystery Of The Frightened Aunt
BL - v78 - F 15 '82 - p754
Hi Lo - v3 - F '82 - p2
Subject: Mystery and detective stories

Mystery On The Night Shift
BL - v75 - F 15 '79 - p927
Hi Lo - v2 - Ap '81 - p2
Subject: Mystery and detective stories

DEEGAN, Paul Joseph 1937-
ConAu 102, SmATA 48

Almost A Champion
SLJ - v22 - S '75 - p100
Subject: Basketball—Fiction

Close But Not Quite
SLJ - v22 - S '75 - p100
Subject: Basketball—Fiction

Dan Moves Up
SLJ - v22 - S '75 - p100
Subject: Basketball—Fiction

The Important Decision
SLJ - v22 - S '75 - p100
Subject: Basketball—Fiction

The Team Manager
SLJ - v22 - S '75 - p100
Subject: Basketball—Fiction

The Tournaments
CLW - v48 - F '77 - p280
SLJ - v22 - S '75 - p100
Subject: Basketball—Fiction

DEGENS, T
FifBJA

Friends
CBRS - v9 - Spring '81 - p106
CCB-B - v34 - Jl '81 - p210
EJ - v70 - S '81 - p75
KR - v49 - Ag 1 '81 - p934
NYTBR - v86 - S 20 '81 - p32
PW - v219 - Mr 27 '81 - p51
SLJ - v27 - My '81 - p63
VOYA - v3 - F '81 - p29
Subject: Family problems—Fiction; Friendship—Fiction

Transport 7-41-R
BL - v71 - S 1 '74 - p39
BL - v71 - Mr 15 '75 - p765
BL - v73 - Mr 15 '77 - p1100
BS - v34 - Ja 15 '75 - p474
BW - N 10 '74 - p8
CCB-B - v28 - Mr '75 - p109
CE - v51 - F '75 - p215
Choice - v12 - N '75 - p1132
CLW - v47 - D '75 - p208
EJ - v64 - Ap '75 - p90
EJ - v65 - Ja '76 - p97
HB - v50 - O '74 - p140
KR - v42 - Ag 1 '74 - p809
KR - v43 - Ja 1 '75 - p9
LA - v53 - My '76 - p521
LJ - v99 - O 15 '74 - p2745
LJ - v99 - D 15 '74 - p3246
NYTBR - F 9 '75 - p8

DEGENS, T (continued)
PW - v206 - N 11 '74 - p49
Subject: Refugees—Fiction; World War, 1939-1945—Fiction

The Visit
KR - v50 - O 1 '82 - p1109
SLJ - v29 - O '82 - p159
Subject: Aunts—Fiction; Germany—History—1933-1945—Fiction; World War, 1939-1945—Fiction

DEJONG, Meindert 1906-
ChlLR 1, ConAu 13R, DcLB 52, MorBMP, MorJA, OxChL, SmATA 2, TwCChW 83, WhAm 8, WrDr 86

Hurry Home, Candy
BL - v50 - D 15 '53 - p172
Comw - v59 - N 20 '53 - p180
HB - v29 - D '53 - p456
KR - v21 - Ag 1 '53 - p483
LJ - v79 - Ja 1 '54 - p72
SR - v36 - N 14 '53 - p76
Subject: Animals—Fiction

DEKAY, James T 1930-
ConAu 10NR

The Natural Superiority Of The Left-Hander
Kliatt - v14 - Winter '80 - p70
NYTBR - O 14 '79 - p56
Subject: Wit and humor; Left- and right-handedness

DELANO, Hugh 1933-
ConAu 65, SmATA 20

Eddie
CCB-B - v30 - N '76 - p41
KR - v44 - F 15 '76 - p225
LJ - v101 - Ap 15 '76 - p1040
PW - v209 - Mr 1 '76 - p94
Subject: Giacomin, Eddie; Hockey—Biography

DELEAR, Frank J 1914-
AuBYP SUP, ConAu 9NR, WhoE 75, WrDr 86

The New World Of Helicopters
BL - v63 - My 15 '67 - p991
CCB-B - v20 - Jl '67 - p168
CSM - v59 - S 21 '67 - p11
KR - v35 - Ja 15 '67 - p65
LJ - v92 - S 15 '67 - p3196
SB - v3 - S '67 - p160
Subject: Helicopters

DELREY, Lester 1915-
AuBYP, ConAu 17NR, ConSFA, DcLB 8, SmATA 22, ThrBJA, TwCSFW 86, WhoAm 86, WhoSciF, WrDr 86

Marooned On Mars
BL - v48 - Jl 15 '52 - p384
KR - v20 - Ap 1 '52 - p228
LJ - v77 - Je 15 '52 - p1081
NYT - Je 22 '52 - p15
Subject: Science fiction

Nerves
BW - Je 27 '76 - pG4
MFSF - v41 - S '71 - p45
Subject: Atomic power plants—Fiction; Science fiction

DELTON, Jina

Two Blocks Down
BL - v77 - Ap 1 '81 - p1084
BS - v41 - Je '81 - p119
CBRS - v9 - Ap '81 - p77
CCB-B - v34 - Je '81 - p191
KR - v49 - Ag 1 '81 - p938
PW - v219 - Ja 23 '81 - p124
SLJ - v27 - Ap '81 - p138
VOYA - v4 - Je '81 - p28
Subject: Emotional problems—Fiction; Friendship—Fiction

DEMAS, Vida 1927-
ConAu 49, SmATA 9

First Person, Singular
BL - v71 - Mr 15 '75 - p747
KR - v41 - O 15 '73 - p1179
KR - v41 - N 15 '73 - p1278
LJ - v99 - Ja 1 '74 - p65
LJ - v99 - Ja 15 '74 - p225
LJ - v99 - My 15 '74 - p1452
LJ - v99 - D 15 '74 - p3248
TN - v31 - Ap '75 - p331
Subject: Social adjustment—Fiction

DENAN, Jay

The Glory Ride
BL - v76 - Jl 1 '80 - p1612
Hi Lo - v2 - D '80 - p5
SLJ - v26 - Ap '80 - p108
Subject: Automobile racing

DENGLER, Marianna

Catch The Passing Breeze
BL - v74 - N 1 '77 - p474
KR - v45 - Ag 15 '77 - p849

DENGLER, Marianna (continued)
SLJ - v24 - S '77 - p126
WCRB - v4 - Ja '78 - p67
Subject: Sailing—Fiction

A Certain Kind Of Courage
BL - v79 - My 15 '83 - p1196
SLJ - v30 - O '83 - p166
Subject: Schools—Fiction

DENNY, Norman George 1901-1982
AuBYP SUP, ConAu 107, SmATA 43

The Bayeux Tapestry: The Story Of The Norman Conquest, 1066
Am - v115 - N 5 '66 - p556
Atl - v218 - D '66 - p152
B&B - v12 - D '66 - p75
BL - v63 - O 15 '66 - p264
BL - v81 - O 15 '84 - p305
CCB-B - v20 - Ja '67 - p72
CLW - v38 - Ja '67 - p339
CSM - v58 - N 3 '66 - pB9
HB - v42 - O '66 - p581
KR - v34 - Jl 1 '66 - p627
LJ - v91 - S 15 '66 - p4329
Nat R - v18 - D 13 '66 - p1285
NYRB - v7 - D 15 '66 - p29
NYTBR - v71 - O 23 '66 - p34
PW - v190 - S 26 '66 - p133
SR - v49 - D 10 '66 - p57
TLS - Je 9 '66 - p519
Co-author: Filmer-Sankey, Josephine
Subject: Bayeux tapestry

DENZEL, Justin F 1917-
ConAu 4NR, SmATA 46

Genius With A Scalpel: Harvey Cushing
BL - v67 - Ap 15 '71 - p696
BS - v31 - My 15 '71 - p98
KR - v39 - F 1 '71 - p115
LJ - v96 - O 15 '71 - p3474
SB - v7 - My '71 - p69
Subject: Biography; Physicians

DENZER, Ann Wiseman
see Wiseman, Ann Sayre

DEROSIER, John

Chuck Foreman
BL - v73 - Je 15 '77 - p1572
SLJ - v23 - My '77 - p81
Subject: Football—Biography

DEROSSI, Claude J 1942-
ConAu 53

Computers: Tools For Today
LJ - v98 - Mr 15 '73 - p1001
Subject: Computers

DEVANEY, John 1926-
AuBYP SUP, ConAu 7NR, IntAu&W 86, SmATA 12

Baseball's Youngest Big Leaguers
BS - v28 - Mr 1 '69 - p490
CCB-B - v23 - S '69 - p6
CSM - v61 - My 1 '69 - pB10
LJ - v95 - My 15 '70 - p1964
SR - v52 - Je 28 '69 - p38
Subject: Baseball—Biography

The Bobby Orr Story
BL - v70 - N 1 '73 - p285
BL - v70 - N 1 '73 - p290
Inst - v83 - N '73 - p125
KR - v41 - S 15 '73 - p1042
LJ - v98 - D 15 '73 - p3722
Subject: Hockey—Biography

Tiny: The Story Of Nate Archibald
BL - v74 - Ja 1 '78 - p750
Comw - v104 - N 11 '77 - p734
KR - v45 - S 1 '77 - p939
SLJ - v24 - D '77 - p63
Subject: Basketball—Biography

DEWEESE, Gene 1934-
ScFSB, SmATA X, TwCSFW 86, WrDr 86
Pseud./variant:
DeWeese, Thomas Eugene

Black Suits From Outer Space
BL - v82 - N 15 '85 - p492
CBRS - v14 - D '85 - p44
S Fict R - v15 - F '86 - p9
SLJ - v32 - F '86 - p84
VOYA - v9 - Ap '86 - p39
Subject: Extraterrestrial beings—Fiction; Science fiction

Nightmares From Space
BL - v78 - S 15 '81 - p99
CBRS - v10 - N '81 - p27
Hi Lo - v3 - Ja '82 - p2
SLJ - v29 - S '82 - p119
Subject: Science fiction

Major Corby And The Unidentified Flapping Object
BL - v75 - Ap 15 '79 - p1300
CBRS - v7 - My '79 - p97
Hi Lo - v1 - N '79 - p5

DEWEESE, Gene (continued)
SLJ - v25 - Mr '79 - p138
Subject: Humorous stories; Unidentified flying objects—Fiction

DEXLER, Paul R

Vans: The Personality Vehicles
BL - v74 - F 15 '78 - p1000
Inst - v87 - My '78 - p116
SLJ - v24 - F '78 - p56
Subject: Vans

DI FRANCO, Anthony 1945-
ConAu 118, DrAP&F 85, SmATA 42

Pope John Paul II: Bringing Love To A Troubled World
BL - v80 - N 1 '83 - p406
SLJ - v30 - N '83 - p76
Subject: Biography; Popes

DIAMOND, Donna 1950-
ConAu 115, FifBJA, IlsCB 1967, SmATA 35

Swan Lake
BL - v76 - My 1 '80 - p1289
CBRS - v8 - My '80 - p98
Inst - v89 - My '80 - p91
KR - v48 - Ag 15 '80 - p1082
LA - v57 - N '80 - p896
NYTBR - v85 - My 11 '80 - p24
PW - v217 - F 29 '80 - p135
SLJ - v26 - My '80 - p66
WLB - v55 - O '80 - p133
Subject: Ballets—Stories, plots, etc.; Fairy tales

DICKMEYER, Lowell

Teamwork
SLJ - v30 - My '84 - p105
Co-author: Humphreys, Martha
Subject: Sports

Track Is For Me
SLJ - v26 - D '79 - p101
Subject: Track and field

see also Humphreys, Martha for additional titles

DICKS, Terrance

The Case Of The Blackmail Boys
CE - v58 - Ja '82 - p180
Subject: Mystery and detective stories

The Case Of The Cinema Swindle
BL - v77 - F 15 '81 - p808
CCB-B - v34 - Jl '81 - p210
RT - v35 - N '81 - p237
Subject: Mystery and detective stories

The Case Of The Cop Catchers
Brit Bk N C - Autumn '81 - p21
SLJ - v28 - My '82 - p83
Subject: Mystery and detective stories

The Case Of The Crooked Kids
CE - v58 - Ja '82 - p180
Subject: Mystery and detective stories

The Case Of The Ghost Grabbers
BL - v77 - F 15 '81 - p808
CLW - v53 - D '81 - p230
RT - v35 - N '81 - p237
Subject: Mystery and detective stories

The Case Of The Missing Masterpiece
CBRS - v8 - N '79 - p27
KR - v48 - Mr 1 '80 - p287
SLJ - v26 - D '79 - p98
SLJ - v27 - N '80 - p47
Subject: Mystery and detective stories

DIETZ, Lew 1907-
AuBYP, ConAu 3NR, SmATA 11, WrDr 84

Jeff White: Young Trapper
HB - v27 - My '51 - p186
Kliatt - v14 - Fall '80 - p5
KR - v18 - D 1 '50 - p693
LJ - v76 - Mr 15 '51 - p530
NYT - F 4 '51 - p26
SR - v34 - My 12 '51 - p53

Jeff White: Young Woodsman
Kliatt - v14 - Fall '80 - p5
LJ - v74 - S 15 '49 - p1334
NYT - N 13 '49 - p33
SR - v32 - N 12 '49 - p32

DIGGINS, Julia E
AuBYP

String, Straightedge, And Shadow: The Story Of Geometry
CCB-B - v18 - Jl '65 - p159
Comw - v82 - My 28 '65 - p332
HB - v41 - Ag '65 - p404
LJ - v90 - My 15 '65 - p2416
SA - v213 - D '65 - p114
Subject: Mathematics

D'IGNAZIO, Fred 1949-
ConAu 110, SmATA 39,
WhoS&SW 84

Chip Mitchell: The Case Of The Stolen Computer Brains
Cur R - v24 - Ja '85 - p38
Subject: Computers—Fiction;
Mystery and detective stories

DINES, Glen 1925-
AuBYP, ConAu 9R, IlsCB 1946,
–1957, –1967, SmATA 7

Sun, Sand, And Steel: Costumes And Equipment Of The Spanish-Mexican Southwest
BL - v69 - F 1 '73 - p527
KR - v40 - F 15 '72 - p204
LJ - v97 - O 15 '72 - p3452
Subject: Costume

DINNEEN, Betty 1929-
ConAu 8NR

The Family Howl
BL - v78 - O 1 '81 - p234
CCB-B - v35 - Mr '82 - p126
SLJ - v28 - F '82 - p74
Subject: Jackals; Zoology

DIXON, Jeanne 1936-
ConAu 105, SmATA 31

The Ghost Of Spirit River
CLW - v41 - O '69 - p139
KR - v36 - Ag 1 '68 - p817
LJ - v93 - O 15 '68 - p3968
Co-author: Angier, Bradford

DIXON, Pahl

Hot Skateboarding
BW - Ap 10 '77 - pE10
Kliatt - v11 - Spring '77 - p41
LJ - v102 - My 15 '77 - p1203
Co-author: Dixon, Peter
Subject: Skateboarding

DIXON, Paige (pseud.) 1911-
AuBYP SUP, ConAu X, DrAP&F 85,
IntAu&W 86X, WrDr 86
Real Name:
Corcoran, Barbara

The Search For Charlie
BB - v4 - My '76 - p4
BL - v72 - Mr 15 '76 - p1040
CSM - v68 - My 12 '76 - p28
J Read - v21 - O '77 - p86
KR - v44 - F 1 '76 - p139
PW - v209 - My 10 '76 - p84
SLJ - v22 - My '76 - p77
Subject: Kidnapping—Fiction;
Montana—Fiction

Summer Of The White Goat
BL - v74 - S 15 '77 - p192
CCB-B - v31 - O '77 - p31
CLW - v49 - N '77 - p188
KR - v45 - Mr 1 '77 - p223
LA - v55 - Ja '78 - p49
SLJ - v24 - N '77 - p55
Subject: Glacier National Park—
Fiction

Walk My Way
BL - v76 - My 1 '80 - p1289
CLW - v52 - D '80 - p237
KR - v48 - Je 1 '80 - p716
SLJ - v26 - Ag '80 - p62

see also Corcoran, Barbara for additional titles

DIXON, Peter
see Dixon, Pahl (co-author)

DIZENZO, Patricia

Phoebe
BL - v67 - F 15 '71 - p489
CCB-B - v24 - D '70 - p57
EJ - v60 - F '71 - p278
KR - v38 - Ag 15 '70 - p885
LJ - v96 - Ja 15 '71 - p274
NYTBR, Pt. 2 - N 8 '70 - p8
NYTBR, Pt. 2 - N 7 '71 - p47
PW - v197 - Je 8 '70 - p180
TN - v30 - Ja '74 - p196
Subject: Unwed mothers—Fiction

Why Me?
BL - v72 - Ap 1 '76 - p1101
BL - v72 - Ap 1 '76 - p1112
EJ - v66 - Ja '77 - p64
NYTBR - Ap 4 '76 - p16
PW - v209 - Ap 26 '76 - p60
SLJ - v22 - Mr '76 - p112

DOBLER, Lavinia G 1910-
ConAu 2NR, MorBMP, SmATA 6,
WhoAmW 77

Pioneers And Patriots: The Lives Of Six Negroes Of The Revolutionary Era
CCB-B - v19 - Ja '66 - p81
JNE - v35 - Summer '66 - p266

DOBLER, Lavinia G (continued)
Co-author: Toppin, Edgar Allan
Subject: Blacks—Biography; United States—History—Revolution, 1775-1783

DOBRIN, Arnold 1928-
AuBYP SUP, BioIn 7, ConAu 25R, IlsCB 1957, -1967, SmATA 4, WhoAmA 80

The New Life - La Vida Neuva: The Mexican-Americans Today
BL - v68 - Je 15 '72 - p894
KR - v39 - Jl 1 '71 - p685
Subject: Mexican Americans

DODSON, Susan 1941-
ConAu 97, SmATA 40

The Creep
BL - v75 - Je 1 '79 - p1490
CCB-B - v32 - Jl '79 - p189
EJ - v68 - N '79 - p75
KR - v47 - My 1 '79 - p522
PW - v215 - Mr 19 '79 - p94
SLJ - v25 - F '79 - p62
SLJ - v27 - N '80 - p47
WCRB - v5 - My '79 - p38
Subject: Child molesting—Fiction; Crime and criminals—Fiction

DOHERTY, C H 1913-
BioIn 10, ConAu 9R, SmATA 6

Roads: From Footpaths To Thruways
LJ - v98 - My 15 '73 - p1680
Subject: Roads—History

DOLAN, Edward Francis, Jr. 1924-
AuBYP SUP, ConAu 33R, SmATA 45

Archie Griffin
CE - v54 - F '78 - p198
SLJ - v24 - D '77 - p64
Co-author: Lyttle, Richard Bard
Subject: Football—Biography

The Bermuda Triangle And Other Mysteries Of Nature
BL - v76 - Ap 15 '80 - p1196
Hi Lo - v2 - N '80 - p3
Subject: Bermuda triangle; Unidentified flying objects

Bobby Clarke
BL - v74 - O 1 '77 - p302
KR - v46 - Ja 1 '78 - p5
SLJ - v24 - D '77 - p64
Co-author: Lyttle, Richard Bard
Subject: Hockey—Biography

Fred Lynn: The Hero From Boston
BL - v74 - Jl 15 '78 - p1729
Co-author: Lyttle, Richard Bard
Subject: Baseball—Biography

Janet Guthrie: First Woman Driver At Indianapolis
B&B - v7 - Ap '79 - p2
BB - v7 - Ap '79 - p2
BL - v74 - Jl 15 '78 - p1729
CCB-B - v32 - O '78 - p27
Hi Lo - v1 - O '79 - p6
J Read - v22 - Mr '79 - p565
SEP - v24 - My '78 - p86
Co-author: Lyttle, Richard Bard
Subject: Automoblie racing drivers

Jimmy Young: Heavyweight Challenger
BL - v75 - Ap 15 '79 - p1301
Hi Lo - v1 - S '79 - p3
SLJ - v25 - My '79 - p88
TN - v36 - Winter '80 - p200
Co-author: Lyttle, Richard Bard
Subject: Blacks—Biography; Boxing—Biography

Kyle Rote, Jr., American-Born Soccer Star
Hi Lo - v1 - N '79 - p5
LA - v56 - N '79 - p933
SLJ - v25 - My '79 - p85
Co-author: Lyttle, Richard Bard
Subject: Soccer—Biography

Martina Navratilova
BL - v74 - Ja 15 '78 - p808
CCB-B - v31 - Mr '78 - p109
KR - v45 - D 1 '77 - p1272
SLJ - v24 - D '77 - p64
Co-author: Lyttle, Richard Bard
Subject: Tennis—Biography

Scott May: Basketball Champion
BL - v74 - Jl 15 '78 - p1730
SLJ - v24 - My '78 - p86
Co-author: Lyttle, Richard Bard
Subject: Basketball—Biography

see also Lyttle, Richard Bard for additional titles

DONOVAN, John 1928-
ChlLR 3, ConAu 97, ConLC 35, FifBJA, OxChL, SmATA 29, TwCChW 83, WrDr 86

Family
BL - v72 - Ap 1 '76 - p1112

DONOVAN, John (continued)
BS - v36 - Ag '76 - p149
CCB-B - v29 - Jl '76 - p173
Comw - v103 - N 19 '76 - p763
EJ - v65 - O '76 - p87
Emerg Lib - v11 - Ja '84 - p21
HB - v52 - Ag '76 - p404
KR - v44 - Ap 1 '76 - p405
LA - v54 - My '77 - p582
NYTBR - My 16 '76 - p14
PW - v209 - Ap 26 '76 - p60
SE - v41 - Ap '77 - p350
SLJ - v23 - S '76 - p131
Subject: Apes—Fiction; Laboratory animals—Fiction

I'll Get There. It Better Be Worth The Trip
Atl - v224 - D '69 - p150
BL - v65 - Je 15 '69 - p1174
BS - v29 - Je 1 '69 - p100
BW - v3 - My 4 '69 - p5
CCB-B - v22 - Je '69 - p156
CLW - v40 - My '69 - p589
CLW - v41 - Ap '70 - p534
Comw - v90 - My 23 '69 - p300
HB - v45 - Ag '69 - p415
KR - v37 - Ap 1 '69 - p385
Lis - v83 - Ap 16 '70 - p519
LJ - v94 - My 15 '69 - p2072
LJ - v94 - My 15 '69 - p2111
LJ - v94 - D 15 '69 - p4581
NYTBR - D 7 '69 - p68
NYTBR, Pt. 2 - My 4 '69 - p8
NYTBR, Pt. 2 - N 9 '69 - p60
NYTBR, Pt. 2 - N 7 '71 - p46
PW - v195 - Mr 17 '69 - p57
PW - v199 - F 8 '71 - p82
SR - v52 - My 10 '69 - p59
SR - v52 - Jl 19 '69 - p42
TLS - Jl 2 '70 - p712
TN - v26 - Ja '70 - p207
Subject: Death—Fiction; Social adjustment—Fiction

Remove Protective Coating A Little At A Time
BL - v70 - D 15 '73 - p440
BS - v33 - O 15 '73 - p333
BW - v7 - N 11 '73 - p6C
CCB-B - v27 - D '73 - p62
HB - v50 - F '74 - p54
KR - v41 - Jl 15 '73 - p759
LJ - v99 - My 15 '74 - p1481
NYTBR - N 4 '73 - p34
NYTBR - N 4 '73 - p52
PW - v204 - Jl 16 '73 - p111
TN - v30 - N '73 - p81
Subject: Family life—Fiction; Friendship—Fiction

Wild In The World
BL - v68 - N 1 '71 - p240
BS - v31 - Ag 15 '71 - p234
BW - v5 - N 7 '71 - p8
CCB-B - v25 - N '71 - p40
CSM - v63 - N 11 '71 - pB6
EJ - v61 - Ja '72 - p138
HB - v48 - F '72 - p56
KR - v39 - Jl 1 '71 - p682
LJ - v96 - O 15 '71 - p3475
LJ - v96 - D 15 '71 - p4158
NYTBR - S 12 '71 - p8
NYTBR - D 5 '71 - p86
NYTBR - My 12 '74 - p39
NYTBR, Pt. 2 - N 7 '71 - p28
PW - v200 - Ag 2 '71 - p64
SR - v54 - S 18 '71 - p49

DONOVAN, Pete

Carol Johnston: The One-Armed Gymnast
CCB-B - v36 - F '83 - p106
SLJ - v29 - Mr '83 - p160
Subject: Biography; Gymnasts; Physically handicapped

DORIAN, Edith 1900-
ConAu P-1, SmATA 5, WhoAmW 77

No Moon On Graveyard Head
BL - v50 - D 1 '53 - p148
HB - v29 - D '53 - p461
KR - v21 - S 1 '53 - p588
LJ - v79 - Ja 1 '54 - p76
NYTBR, Pt. 2 - N 15 '53 - p10

DOTY, Jean Slaughter 1929-
AuBYP SUP, ConAu 2NR, SmATA 28

Winter Pony
CCB-B - v29 - O '75 - p25
CLW - v47 - D '75 - p234
KR - v43 - Mr 1 '75 - p238
LA - v53 - My '76 - p516
RT - v29 - F '76 - p511
SLJ - v21 - My '75 - p54
SR - v2 - My 31 '75 - p34
Subject: Ponies—Fiction

DOTY, Roy 1922-
ConAu 8NR, IlsBYP, SmATA 28, WorECar

Pinocchio Was Nosey
SLJ - v24 - F '78 - p46
Subject: Jokes; Riddles

DOUGLAS, James M (pseud.) 1929-
ConAu X, SmATA 5

DOUGLAS, James M (continued)
Real Name:
Butterworth, W E

Hunger For Racing
BL - v64 - Mr 1 '68 - p773
LJ - v92 - D 15 '67 - p4633

see also Butterworth, W E for additional titles

DOUTY, Esther Morris 1911-1978
AuBYP SUP, ConAu 3NR, SmATA 23N, -8

The Brave Balloonists: America's First Airmen
Inst - v84 - My '75 - p100
Subject: Aeronautics; Balloon ascensions

DOWDELL, Dorothy Karns 1910-
ConAu 20NR, SmATA 12, WhoAmW 77

The Japanese Helped Build America
BL - v67 - S 15 '70 - p105
BL - v69 - F 15 '73 - p553
KR - v38 - Ap 1 '70 - p385
LJ - v95 - O 15 '70 - p3626
Co-author: Dowdell, Joseph
Subject: Japanese Americans

DOWDELL, Joseph
see Dowdell, Dorothy Karns (co-author)

DOWLATSHAHI, Ali

Persian Designs And Motifs For Artists And Craftsmen
Hob - v85 - Ag '80 - p107
Kliatt - v14 - Spring '80 - p48
Subject: Design (Decorative)—Iran

DOYLE, Arthur Conan 1859-1930
ConAu 104, DcLB 18, JBA 34, OxChL, PlP&P, SmATA 24, TwCSFW 86, WhoChL, WhoTwCL

The Adventures Of Sherlock Holmes
B&B - v22 - F '77 - p52
BL - v73 - S 1 '76 - p18
CR - v226 - Ja '75 - p45
GP - v13 - Ja '75 - p2565
MFS - v23 - Summer '77 - p297
WLB - v50 - Ja '76 - p367
Subject: Mystery and detective stories

The Boys' Sherlock Holmes
BL - v58 - S 15 '61 - p74
KR - v29 - Je 15 '61 - p501
LJ - v86 - Jl '61 - p2540
NYTBR, Pt. 2 - N 12 '61 - p62
Subject: Mystery and detective stories; Short stories

The Hound Of The Baskervilles
B&B - v19 - Jl '74 - p111
BL - v65 - Ja 15 '69 - p538
CR - v224 - Ap '74 - p213
LATBR - Jl 7 '85 - p9
Lis - v91 - Ja 10 '74 - p53
MFS - v23 - p297
NS - v87 - My 24 '74 - p743
NYT - v125 - D 1 '75 - p29
NYTBR - My 3 '02 - p298
Obs - Ja 20 '74 - p26
SLJ - v23 - My '77 - p85
Spec - v232 - F 9 '74 - p172
TLS - F 1 '74 - p113
WLB - v50 - Ja '76 - p367
WLB - v52 - O '77 - p140
Subject: Mystery and detective stories

DRAGONWAGON, Crescent 1952-
BioIn 13, ConAu 12NR, DrAP&F 85, IntAu&W 86, SmATA 41

To Take A Dare
BS - v42 - Je '82 - p118
CBRS - v10 - My '82 - p97
CCB-B - v35 - Ap '82 - p145
EJ - v71 - S '82 - p88
J Read - v26 - D '82 - p277
NYTBR - v87 - Ap 25 '82 - p49
PW - v221 - Mr 19 '82 - p71
SLJ - v28 - My '82 - p68
VOYA - v5 - Ag '82 - p38
Co-author: Zindel, Paul

see also Zindel, Paul for additional titles

DRIMMER, Frederick

The Elephant Man
BL - v82 - Ja 15 '86 - p756
BW - v15 - N 10 '85 - p21
CBRS - v14 - Mr '86 - p91
CCB-B - v39 - D '85 - p66
Inter BC - v17 - #3 '86 p33
SE - v50 - Ap '86 - p298
SLJ - v32 - F '86 - p94
VOYA - v9 - Ap '86 - p29
Subject: Biography; Physically handicapped

DRISKO, Carol F 1929-

The Unfinished March: The History Of The Negro In The United States, Reconstruction To World War I
BL - v63 - Jl 1 '67 - p1146
HB - v43 - Ag '67 - p488
KR - v35 - Ja 1 '67 - p11
LJ - v92 - Ap 15 '67 - p1733
NYTBR - v72 - N 5 '67 - p65
NYTBR, Pt. 2 - v72 - My 7 '67 - p5
Co-author: Toppin, Edgar Allan
Subject: Blacks—History

DROTNING, Phillip T 1920-
ConAu 25R

Up From The Ghetto
BL - v66 - Je 15 '70 - p1258
BS - v30 - F 1 '71 - p482
Choice - v7 - O '70 - p1096
LJ - v95 - F 15 '70 - p677
NHB - v34 - D '71 - p191
NYTBR, Pt. 2 - F 21 '71 - p2
PW - v197 - Ja 19 '70 - p74
SR - v53 - My 9 '70 - p70
Co-author: South, Wesley W
Subject: Blacks—Biography

DRUCKER, Malka 1945-
ConAu 14NR, SmATA 39

The George Foster Story
KR - v47 - Je 1 '79 - p640
PW - v215 - My 21 '79 - p69
SLJ - v25 - My '79 - p83
SLJ - v27 - S '80 - p69
Co-author: Foster, George
Subject: Baseball—Biography; Blacks—Biography

Tom Seaver: Portrait Of A Pitcher
BL - v74 - Jl 1 '78 - p1683
BS - v38 - Je '78 - p77
KR - v46 - Je 1 '78 - p601
NYTBR - Ap 30 '78 - p49
PW - v213 - F 6 '78 - p102
SLJ - v25 - S '78 - p135
Co-author: Seaver, Tom
Subject: Baseball—Biography

DRYDEN, Pamela (pseud.)
SmATA X, WrDr 86
Real Name:
Johnston, Norma

Mask For My Heart
Kliatt - v17 - Spring '83 - p6
VOYA - v6 - Je '83 - p96

see also Johnston, Norma for additional titles

DU BOIS, Shirley Graham
see Graham, Shirley Lola

DUE, Linnea A

High And Outside
BL - v76 - Jl 15 '80 - p1670
BS - v40 - S '80 - p208
KR - v48 - My 15 '80 - p663
LJ - v105 - Jl '80 - p1538
PW - v217 - My 16 '80 - p200
SLJ - v27 - O '80 - p166
SLJ - v29 - D '82 - p28

DUGDALE, Vera

Album Of North American Animals
BL - v63 - Mr 15 '67 - p794
BL - v64 - Ja 15 '68 - p592
CCB-B - v21 - S '67 - p4
CSM - v58 - N 3 '66 - pB11
CSM - v60 - N 30 '67 - pB5
KR - v34 - S 15 '66 - p992
KR - v35 - O 15 '67 - p1277
LJ - v91 - N 15 '66 - p5747
NYTBR - v71 - N 6 '66 - p54
PW - v192 - N 13 '67 - p79
SB - v3 - My '67 - p62
SR - v50 - My 20 '67 - p56
Subject: Animals

Album Of North American Birds
CCB-B - v22 - S '68 - p5
LJ - v93 - F 15 '68 - p866
SB - v3 - Mr '68 - p322
Subject: Birds

DUJARDIN, Rosamond 1902-1963
AuBYP SUP, BioIn 2, -3, -6, ConAu 1R, -103, CurBio 53, MorJA, SmATA 2, WhAm 4

Double Feature
KR - v21 - Ag 1 '53 - p489
LJ - v79 - Ja 1 '54 - p76
NYTBR, Pt. 2 - N 15 '53 - p8

DUKORE, Jesse

Never Love A Cowboy
SLJ - v29 - Ap '83 - p122

DUNBAR, Robert Everett 1926-
ConAu 15NR, SmATA 32, WhoE 81

Into Jupiter's World
BL - v77 - Je 15 '81 - p1342
CBRS - v9 - Spring '81 - p106

DUNBAR, Robert Everett (continued)
Cur R - v22 - O '83 - p51
Hi Lo - v2 - Je '81 - p3
SLJ - v27 - Ag '81 - p74
Subject: Science fiction

DUNCAN, Fred B

Deepwater Family
BL - v66 - D 15 '69 - p508
CCB-B - v23 - Ja '70 - p78
CLW - v41 - My '70 - p590
KR - v37 - Ap 15 '69 - p460
LJ - v94 - Jl '69 - p2675
SR - v52 - S 13 '69 - p37
Yacht - v126 - N '69 - p88
Subject: Seafaring life

DUNCAN, Lois S 1934-
AuBYP, ConAu 2NR, ConLC 26, FifBJA, IntAu&W 82, SmATA 36, -2AS, TwCChW 83, WrDr 86
Pseud./variant:
Arquette, Lois S

A Gift Of Magic
PW - v220 - S 25 '81 - p92
Subject: Extrasensory perception—Fiction

I Know What You Did Last Summer
BL - v70 - Ja 1 '74 - p483
CCB-B - v27 - F '74 - p93
J Read - v22 - N '78 - p127
KR - v41 - S 1 '73 - p972
LJ - v99 - Ap 15 '74 - p1226
PW - v204 - O 29 '73 - p36
PW - v227 - Ap 19 '85 - p82
TLS - Mr 26 '82 - p343
Subject: Mystery and detective stories

Killing Mr. Griffin
BL - v74 - Mr 1 '78 - p1092
BS - v38 - Ag '78 - p154
CCB-B - v32 - O '78 - p27
GP - v19 - N '80 - p3781
HB - v54 - Ag '78 - p400
JB - v44 - D '80 - p304
Kliatt - v14 - Winter '80 - p6
KR - v46 - My 1 '78 - p500
NYTBR - Ap 30 '78 - p54
Obs - N 30 '80 - p36
PW - v213 - F 20 '78 - p127
PW - v216 - Ag 27 '79 - p385
SLJ - v24 - My '78 - p86
SLJ - v27 - N '80 - p47
TES - S 26 '80 - p24
Subject: Mystery and detective stories

Locked In Time
EJ - v75 - D '86 - p61
JB - v50 - Ap '86 - p76
Punch - v290 - Ap 16 '86 - p52
PW - v227 - My 31 '85 - p57
Sch Lib - v34 - S '86 - p266
SLJ - v32 - N '85 - p96
TES - Jl 25 '86 - p21
TLS - My 9 '86 - p514
VOYA - v8 - O '85 - p257
Subject: Mystery and detective stories

Peggy
BL - v67 - F 1 '71 - p446
CLW - v43 - O '71 - p116
HB - v46 - D '70 - p622
KR - v38 - S 15 '70 - p1047
Subject: United States—History—Revolution, 1775-1783—Fiction

Ransom
CCB-B - v20 - Mr '67 - p107
KR - v34 - F 1 '66 - p111
LJ - v91 - S 15 '66 - p4349
NYTBR - v71 - Je 5 '66 - p42
PW - v226 - O 12 '84 - p51

Summer Of Fear
BL - v73 - S 15 '76 - p136
BL - v73 - S 15 '76 - p173
BS - v36 - D '76 - p286
Comw - v103 - N 19 '76 - p763
HB - v53 - Ap '77 - p167
Inst - v86 - N '76 - p146
JB - v45 - Ag '81 - p157
Kliatt - v12 - Winter '78 - p6
KR - v44 - Je 15 '76 - p691
NYTBR - Mr 6 '77 - p29
PW - v209 - Je 7 '76 - p75
Sch Lib - v29 - S '81 - p252
SLJ - v23 - D '76 - p69
TES - Ap 10 '81 - p24
TLS - Mr 27 '81 - p339
WCRB - v3 - S '77 - p58
Subject: New Mexico—Fiction; Witchcraft—Fiction

DUNLOP, Agnes Mary Robinson
see Kyle, Elisabeth

DUNNAHOO, Terry 1927-
ConAu 14NR, IntAu&W 86, SmATA 7, WhoAm 86

This Is Espie Sanchez
CCB-B - v30 - F '77 - p89

DUNNAHOO, Terry (continued)
CLW - v48 - Mr '77 - p358
HB - v53 - F '77 - p55
KR - v44 - Ag 15 '76 - p906
SLJ - v23 - D '76 - p68
Subject: Mexican Americans—Fiction; Police—Fiction

Who Cares About Espie Sanchez?
BL - v72 - Ja 1 '76 - p624
CCB-B - v29 - F '76 - p94
KR - v43 - O 15 '75 - p1183
SLJ - v22 - F '76 - p51
SLJ - v30 - F '84 - p30
Subject: Mexican Americans—Fiction; Police—Fiction

Who Needs Espie Sanchez?
BL - v74 - S 15 '77 - p192
CCB-B - v31 - My '78 - p140
KR - v45 - Ag 15 '77 - p849
SLJ - v24 - N '77 - p55
Subject: Alcohol and youth—Fiction; Mexican Americans—Fiction

DUNNING, Stephen 1924-
AuBYP SUP, ConAu 25R

Reflections On A Gift Of Watermelon Pickle And Other Modern Verse
A Lib - v5 - Je '74 - p297
BL - v63 - Ap 1 '67 - p856
BL - v64 - Ja 15 '68 - p597
CCB-B - v21 - Mr '68 - p107
CE - v43 - Mr '67 - p412
CLW - v39 - F '68 - p441
EJ - v56 - Ap '67 - p635
EL - v24 - Ja '67 - p358
HB - v44 - F '68 - p73
KR - v35 - N 1 '67 - p1326
LJ - v92 - N 15 '67 - p4259
NY - v43 - D 16 '67 - p188
NYTBR - v72 - D 10 '67 - p38
NYTBR, Pt. 2 - v73 - F 25 '68 - p20
Par - v43 - Ag '68 - p76
PW - v192 - N 13 '67 - p79
RR - v86 - Mr '69 - p176
SR - v51 - Ja 27 '68 - p35
Subject: American poetry

DUPRAU, Jeanne

Golden God
BL - v79 - Ap 15 '83 - p1078
Hi Lo - v3 - My '82 - p3
Subject: Archaeology—Fiction

DURANT, John 1902-
AuBYP, ConAu 5NR, SmATA 27, WhoAm 82

The Heavyweight Champions
BL - v70 - Ja 15 '74 - p509
EJ - v64 - F '75 - p104
LJ - v97 - My 15 '72 - p1931
WLB - v46 - Ap '72 - p706
Subject: Boxing—Biography

DURHAM, Mae
ConAu 57
Pseud./variant:
Roger, Mae Durham

Tit For Tat And Other Latvian Folk Tales
BL - v63 - My 15 '67 - p991
CCB-B - v20 - Jl '67 - p168
HB - v43 - Ag '67 - p461
Inst - v77 - Ag '67 - p207
KR - v35 - F 15 '67 - p203
LJ - v92 - My 15 '67 - p2020
NYTBR, Pt. 2 - v72 - My 7 '67 - p44
PW - v191 - Ap 10 '67 - p82
SR - v50 - My 13 '67 - p54
Subject: Folklore

DURHAM, Philip 1912-1977
ConAu 7NR

The Adventures Of The Negro Cowboys
CCB-B - v19 - Ja '66 - p81
JAH - v52 - D '65 - p640
LJ - v91 - Mr 15 '66 - p1716
PW - v195 - F 24 '69 - p69
SR - v49 - Ag 20 '66 - p37
Subject: Blacks—Biography; Cowboys

DURISH, Jack

Dream Pirate
BL - v79 - Ap 15 '83 - p1078
Hi Lo - v3 - My '82 - p3
Co-author: Street, Nicki
Subject: Mystery and detective stories

see also Street, Nicki for additional titles

DURSO, Joseph

Amazing: The Miracle Of The Mets
BL - v67 - S 1 '70 - p23
BW - v4 - Jl 12 '70 - p13
CSM - v62 - Je 25 '70 - p13

DURSO, Joseph (continued)
KR - v38 - F 1 '70 - p144
KR - v38 - Mr 1 '70 - p257
LJ - v95 - My 15 '70 - p1858
NYT - v119 - Ap 29 '70 - p39
NYTBR - Ap 26 '70 - p14
PW - v197 - F 2 '70 - p85
SR - v53 - My 9 '70 - p68
SR - v53 - Je 27 '70 - p38
Subject: Baseball; New York (City)

DWYER-JOYCE, Alice 1913-
ConAu 53, WrDr 86

The Master Of Jethart
KR - v44 - O 15 '76 - p1150

DYER, Mike

Getting Into Pro Baseball
SLJ - v25 - My '79 - p86
Subject: Baseball; Vocational guidance

DYER, T A

A Way Of His Own
BL - v78 - S 1 '81 - p44
CBRS - v9 - Spring '81 - p107
HB - v57 - Ag '81 - p421
KR - v49 - Ag 1 '81 - p939
LA - v59 - Ap '82 - p370
RT - v35 - Mr '82 - p752
SLJ - v27 - Ap '81 - p126
Subject: Physically handicapped—Fiction; Survival—Fiction

DYGARD, Thomas J 1931-
ConAu 15NR, SmATA 24, WhoAm 86, WhoMW 84

Halfback Tough
BL - v82 - Ap 1 '86 - p1135
B Rpt - v5 - S '86 - p31
CCB-B - v39 - Jl '86 - p207
HB - v62 - S '86 - p596
KR - v54 - Jl 1 '86 - p1021
SLJ - v33 - O '86 - p189
VOYA - v9 - Je '86 - p77
Subject: Conduct of life—Fiction; Football—Fiction; Schools—Fiction

Outside Shooter
BL - v75 - F 1 '79 - p859
CCB-B - v33 - O '79 - p26
KR - v47 - F 15 '79 - p199
SLJ - v25 - My '79 - p84
Subject: Basketball—Fiction

Point Spread
BL - v76 - F 1 '80 - p764
BL - v48 - Mr 15 '80 - p370
CCB-B - v33 - My '80 - p170
NYTBR - v85 - Ap 27 '80 - p56
SLJ - v27 - Ja '81 - p68
Subject: Football—Fiction; Gambling—Fiction

Quarterback Walk-On
BL - v78 - F 15 '82 - p754
BS - v42 - Je '82 - p119
CSM - v74 - O 8 '82 - pB12
EJ - v72 - D '83 - p67
J Read - v26 - O '82 - p88
NYTBR - v87 - Ap 25 '82 - p49
SLJ - v28 - My '82 - p86
VOYA - v5 - Ag '82 - p29
Subject: Football—Fiction

Rebound Caper
BL - v79 - Mr 15 '83 - p957
CE - v60 - N '83 - p137
J Read - v27 - D '83 - p281
KR - v51 - Mr 1 '83 - p249
SLJ - v29 - My '83 - p96
VOYA - v6 - Ag '83 - p145
Subject: Basketball—Fiction; Schools—Fiction

Soccer Duel
BL - v77 - Jl 1 '81 - p1392
CCB-B - v34 - Jl '81 - p211
J Read - v25 - F '82 - p487
KR - v49 - O 15 '81 - p1300
LA - v58 - O '81 - p847
SLJ - v28 - S '81 - p123
VOYA - v4 - O '81 - p32
Subject: Soccer—Fiction

Winning Kicker
BB - v6 - N '78 - p2
BL - v74 - F 1 '78 - p901
BL - v74 - F 1 '78 - p906
KR - v46 - F 1 '78 - p110
NYTBR - Ap 23 '78 - p32
SLJ - v24 - My '78 - p87
Subject: Football—Fiction

E

EAST, Ben

Danger In The Air
SLJ - v26 - Ap '80 - p108
Adapter: Nentl, Jerolyn Ann
Subject: Storms; Wilderness survival

Desperate Search
BL - v77 - Ap 15 '81 - p1142
SLJ - v26 - Ap '80 - p108
Adapter: Nentl, Jerolyn Ann
Subject: Rescue work; Wilderness survival

Forty Days Lost
BL - v77 - O 15 '80 - p309
SLJ - v26 - Ap '80 - p108
Adapter: Nentl, Jerolyn Ann
Subject: Wilderness survival

Found Alive
CCB-B - v33 - My '80 - p170
SLJ - v26 - Ap '80 - p108
Adapter: Nentl, Jerolyn Ann
Subject: Wilderness survival

Frozen Terror
Hi Lo - v2 - Ap '81 - p4
SLJ - v26 - Ap '80 - p108
Adapter: Nentl, Jerolyn Ann
Subject: Michigan, Lake; Wilderness survival

Grizzly!
SLJ - v26 - Ap '80 - p108
Adapter: Nentl, Jerolyn Ann
Subject: Bears—Fiction

Mistaken Journey
SLJ - v26 - Ap '80 - p108
Adapter: Nentl, Jerolyn Ann
Subject: Wilderness survival

Trapped In Devil's Hole
BL - v77 - O 15 '80 - p309
SLJ - v26 - Ap '80 - p108
Adapter: Nentl, Jerolyn Ann
Subject: Wilderness survival

see also Nentl, Jerolyn Ann for additional titles

EATON, Jeanette 1886-1968
AuBYP SUP, BioIn 8, –13, ConAu 73, JBA 34, –51, SmATA 24, Str&VC

Trumpeter's Tale: The Story Of Young Louis Armstrong
BL - v51 - Mr 15 '55 - p302
HB - v31 - Je '55 - p195
KR - v23 - F 1 '55 - p87
LJ - v80 - Ap 15 '55 - p1009
NYTBR - F 27 '55 - p32
SR - v38 - Je 18 '55 - p45
Subject: Blacks—Biography; Musicians

ECKERT, Allan W 1931-
AuBYP SUP, ConAu 14NR, ConLC 17, FourBJA, SmATA 29, WhoAm 86

The Crossbreed
BL - v64 - My 15 '68 - p1081
KR - v35 - D 15 '67 - p1503
LJ - v93 - F 1 '68 - p571
LJ - v93 - F 15 '68 - p893
NYTBR - v73 - Mr 3 '68 - p40
PW - v192 - D 11 '67 - p40
TN - v24 - Je '68 - p449

The King Snake
BL - v65 - O 15 '68 - p246
BS - v28 - Ag 1 '68 - p195
BW - v2 - N 3 '68 - p34
HB - v44 - O '68 - p578
KR - v36 - Jl 1 '68 - p697
LJ - v93 - N 15 '68 - p4402
SB - v4 - S '68 - p134
Subject: Snakes

EDELSON, Edward 1932-
AuBYP SUP, ConAu 13NR, WhoAm 78, WhoE 85

Great Monsters Of The Movies
HB - v49 - Je '73 - p279
Inst - v82 - My '73 - p69
KR - v41 - Je 1 '73 - p602
LJ - v98 - O 15 '73 - p3144
PT - v8 - F '75 - p21
Subject: Horror films

EDMONDS, Ivy Gordon 1917-
AuBYP SUP, ConAu 13NR, SmATA 8

Drag Racing For Beginners
BL - v69 - Mr 1 '73 - p646
Subject: Drag racing

Hot Rodding For Beginners
BL - v67 - Ap 1 '71 - p656
LJ - v96 - My 15 '71 - p1822
Subject: Automobile racing

Jet And Rocket Engines
BL - v70 - O 15 '73 - p229
KR - v41 - Je 15 '73 - p649
LJ - v98 - O 15 '73 - p3153
Subject: Rocket engines

Motorcycle Racing For Beginners
BL - v74 - O 15 '77 - p367
EJ - v67 - Mr '78 - p80
KR - v45 - D 15 '77 - p1325
SLJ - v24 - N '77 - p69
Subject: Motorcycle racing

EDWARDS, Audrey Marie 1947-
ConAu 81, InB&W 80, SmATA 31, WhoAmW 87

Muhammad Ali, The People's Champ
BL - v74 - Ja 1 '78 - p750
EJ - v67 - Ap '78 - p90
KR - v45 - Ag 15 '77 - p857
NYTBR - Ap 30 '78 - p56
PW - v212 - N 7 '77 - p83
SLJ - v24 - D '77 - p63
Co-author: Wohl, Gary
Subject: Blacks—Biography; Boxing—Biography

The Picture Life Of Muhammad Ali
Cur R - v15 - D '76 - p315
SLJ - v23 - D '76 - p72
Teacher - v96 - O '78 - p174
Co-author: Wohl, Gary
Subject: Blacks—Biography; Boxing—Biography

The Picture Life Of Stevie Wonder
BL - v73 - Ap 15 '77 - p1265
Cur R - v15 - D '76 - p315
SLJ - v23 - D '76 - p72
Teacher - v96 - O '78 - p174
Co-author: Wohl, Gary
Subject: Blacks—Biography; Musicians

EDWARDS, Cecile Pepin 1916-
AuBYP, BioIn 7, ConAu 5R, SmATA 25

Roger Williams, Defender Of Freedom
BL - v54 - O 15 '57 - p110
CSM - N 7 '57 - p12
KR - v25 - Je 1 '57 - p384
LJ - v82 - S 15 '57 - p2910
NYTBR, Pt. 2 - N 17 '57 - p40
Subject: Biography

EDWARDS, Frank

Stranger Than Science
Kliatt - v18 - Winter '84 - p82
Subject: Curiosities and wonders

EDWARDS, Page, Jr. 1941-
WrDr 86

Scarface Joe
BL - v81 - O 1 '84 - p245
CBRS - v13 - S '84 - p8
CCB-B - v37 - Jl '84 - p204
KR - v52 - S 1 '84 - pJ79
SLJ - v31 - O '84 - p166
Subject: Mines and mineral resources—Fiction

EDWARDS, Phil

You Should Have Been Here An Hour Ago
CCB-B - v21 - N '67 - p40
KR - v35 - Ap 1 '67 - p458
LJ - v92 - S 15 '67 - p3212
NYTBR, pt. 1 - v72 - F 26 '67 - p41
Punch - v252 - My 10 '67 - p697
PW - v190 - D 26 '66 - p94
PW - v191 - Ap 10 '67 - p79
SR - v50 - F 25 '67 - p58
SR - v50 - Ag 19 '67 - p35
TLS - Je 29 '67 - p583
TN - v24 - Ja '68 - p225
Co-author: Ottum, Bob
Subject: Surfing

EIMERL, Sarel Henry 1925-
ConAu 21R

Hitler Over Europe
BL - v68 - Je 15 '72 - p908
BS - v32 - Ap 15 '72 - p46
KR - v40 - Ja 15 '72 - p75
LJ - v97 - My 15 '72 - p1921
Subject: Biography; World War, 1939-1945

EISEMAN, Alberta 1925-
AuBYP SUP, ConAu 77, SmATA 15

Manana Is Now: The Spanish-Speaking In The United States
BL - v69 - Jl 15 '73 - p1072
CCB-B - v27 - S '73 - p6
Inter BC - v14 - #1 '83 p16
KR - v41 - Ap 1 '73 - p399
LJ - v98 - My 15 '73 - p1654
LJ - v98 - My 15 '73 - p1687
RR - v33 - Ja '74 - p224
Subject: Spanish Americans

EISENBERG, Lisa

Break-In
BL - v83 - O 15 '86 - p328

Falling Star
BL - v76 - Mr 15 '80 - p1045
Hi Lo - v1 - Mr '80 - p3
Kliatt - v14 - Spring '80 - p6
SLJ - v27 - D '80 - p72
Subject: Mystery and detective stories

Fast Food King
BL - v76 - Mr 15 '80 - p1045
Hi Lo - v1 - Mr '80 - p3
Kliatt - v14 - Spring '80 - p6
SLJ - v27 - D '80 - p72
Subject: Australia—Fiction; Mystery and detective stories

Golden Idol
BL - v76 - My 15 '80 - p1358
Hi Lo - v1 - Mr '80 - p3
Kliatt - v14 - Spring '80 - p6
SLJ - v27 - D '80 - p72
Subject: Mystery and detective stories

Hit Man
BL - v83 - O 15 '86 - p328

House Of Laughs
BL - v76 - Ap 15 '80 - p1196
B Rpt - v2 - S '83 - p24
CSM - v73 - D 1 '80 - pB11
Hi Lo - v1 - Mr '80 - p3
Kliatt - v14 - Spring '80 - p6
SLJ - v27 - D '80 - p72
Subject: Mystery and detective stories

Kidnapped
BL - v83 - O 15 '86 - p328

Killer Music
Hi Lo - v1 - Mr '80 - p3
Kliatt - v14 - Spring '80 - p6
SLJ - v27 - D '80 - p72
Subject: Mystery and detective stories

Man In The Cage
BL - v79 - Ap 15 '83 - p1078
Hi Lo - v3 - My '82 - p3
Subject: Mystery and detective stories; Robbers and outlaws—Fiction

On The Run
BL - v83 - O 15 '86 - p328

The Pay Off Game
BL - v83 - O 15 '86 - p328

Tiger Rose
BL - v78 - Ap 15 '82 - p1073
Hi Lo - v1 - Mr '80 - p3
Kliatt - v14 - Spring '80 - p6
SLJ - v27 - D '80 - p73
Subject: Mystery and detective stories

ELBERT, Virginie Fowler 1912-
AuBYP SUP, ConAu 8NR

Grow A Plant Pet
SLJ - v24 - N '77 - p69
Subject: House plants

ELDER, Lauren

And I Alone Survived
BL - v74 - Jl 15 '78 - p1726
BS - v38 - Ag '78 - p159
HB - v55 - O '78 - p546
KR - v46 - F 15 '78 - p215
LJ - v103 - Je 1 '78 - p1166
PW - v213 - F 27 '78 - p149
SLJ - v25 - S '78 - p171
Co-author: Streshinsky, Shirley
Subject: Aeronautics; Survival

ELFMAN, Blossom 1925-
ConAu 17NR, SmATA 8

The Girls Of Huntington House
BL - v69 - Ja 1 '73 - p423
BS - v32 - S 15 '72 - p269
BS - v33 - F 1 '74 - p496
EJ - v62 - D '73 - p1299
J Read - v22 - N '78 - p127
KR - v40 - Je 1 '72 - p650
KR - v40 - Je 15 '72 - p684
LJ - v97 - S 1 '72 - p2720
LJ - v97 - N 15 '72 - p3819
PW - v201 - Je 5 '72 - p138
TN - v29 - Ap '73 - p255

ELFMAN, Blossom (continued)
TN - v30 - Ja '74 - p199
Subject: Teachers—Fiction; Unwed mothers—Fiction

A House For Jonnie O
BL - v73 - N 1 '76 - p401
CLW - v49 - D '77 - p198
KR - v44 - N 1 '76 - p1182
KR - v44 - N 15 '76 - p1231
NYTBR - Ja 30 '77 - p24
PW - v210 - N 1 '76 - p65
SLJ - v23 - F '77 - p75
SLJ - v23 - My '77 - p37
WCRB - v3 - My '77 - p31
Subject: Unwed mothers—Fiction

Sister Act
BW - v10 - F 24 '80 - p13
EJ - v68 - N '79 - p76
EJ - v68 - D '79 - p78
Kliatt - v14 - Winter '80 - p6

ELGIN, Kathleen 1923-
ConAu 25R, IlsBYP, IlsCB 1946, -1957, IntAu&W 77, SmATA 39, WhoAmW 77

The Human Body: The Heart
BL - v65 - O 15 '68 - p247
CCB-B - v22 - O '68 - p25
KR - v36 - Je 15 '68 - p646
LJ - v93 - O 15 '68 - p3968
Spec - v226 - My 29 '71 - p756
Subject: Heart

ELISOFON, Eliot
see Newman, Marvin (co-author)

ELLEN, Jaye

The Trouble With Charlie
BL - v79 - Mr 1 '83 - p904
Kliatt - v17 - Winter '83 - p6
SLJ - v29 - F '83 - p88
VOYA - v5 - F '83 - p35
Subject: Schools—Fiction

ELLERBY, Leona

King Tut's Game Board
CBRS - v8 - Ap '80 - p87
LA - v57 - S '80 - p652
SLJ - v26 - Ag '80 - p76
Subject: Atlantis—Fiction; Egypt—Fiction

ELLIS, Carol

A Kiss For Good Luck
SLJ - v31 - S '84 - p137
Subject: Love—Fiction

Small Town Summer
BL - v78 - My 15 '82 - p1235
Kliatt - v16 - Spring '82 - p8
VOYA - v5 - O '82 - p40
Subject: Adolescence—Fiction

ELLIS, Jim 1893-1978
BioIn 9, -11

Run For Your Life
LJ - v96 - Ap 15 '71 - p1514
Subject: Occupations; Social work as a profession

ELLIS, Melvin Richard 1912-1984
ConAu 113, -13R, SmATA 39N, -7

No Man For Murder
Am - v129 - D 1 '73 - p430
BL - v70 - N 15 '73 - p338
BS - v33 - Ag 15 '73 - p232
BW - v7 - S 16 '73 - p10
CCB-B - v27 - Mr '74 - p109
Comw - v99 - N 23 '73 - p216
HB - v50 - F '74 - p55
KR - v41 - Je 1 '73 - p607
LJ - v98 - D 15 '73 - p3719
PW - v204 - Ag 6 '73 - p65
Subject: Mystery and detective stories

Sad Song Of The Coyote
LJ - v92 - N 15 '67 - p4257
NYTBR - v72 - Mr 26 '67 - p22

The Wild Horse Killers
BB - v4 - My '76 - p4
BL - v72 - Mr 1 '76 - p974
BS - v36 - O '76 - p239
BW - Ap 11 '76 - p4
CSM - v68 - My 12 '76 - p28
Kliatt - v15 - Fall '81 - p9
KR - v44 - F 1 '76 - p134
LA - v54 - Ja '77 - p85
PW - v209 - Ja 26 '76 - p287
SLJ - v22 - Ap '76 - p85
Subject: Horses—Fiction; Mustang—Fiction

ELLISON, Elsie C

Fun With Lines And Curves
BL - v69 - Je 15 '73 - p984
BL - v69 - Je 15 '73 - p988
KR - v40 - N 1 '72 - p1242
LJ - v98 - My 15 '73 - p1681

ELLISON, Elsie C (continued)
SB - v8 - Mr '73 - p312
Subject: Drawing—Technique; Handicraft

ELMORE, Patricia 1933-
ConAu 114, DrAP&F 85, SmATA 38

Susannah And The Blue House Mystery
BL - v77 - N 15 '80 - p458
CBRS - v8 - Ag '80 - p137
CCB-B - v34 - Mr '81 - p131
CE - v58 - S '81 - p48
KR - v49 - F 15 '81 - p212
SLJ - v27 - D '80 - p73
Subject: Inheritance and succession—Fiction; Mystery and detective stories

EMERSON, Mark

Looking At You
BL - v81 - F 1 '85 - p783
VOYA - v8 - Ap '85 - p44
Subject: Love—Fiction

EMERT, Phyllis R

Guide Dogs
RT - v39 - My '86 - p987
SLJ - v32 - Ag '86 - p91
Subject: Dogs

Hearing Ear Dogs
RT - v39 - My '86 - p987
SLJ - v32 - Ag '86 - p91
Subject: Dogs

Jane Frederick: Pentathlon Champion
BL - v78 - F 1 '82 - p710
Subject: Track and field

Law Enforcement Dogs
RT - v39 - My '86 - p987
SLJ - v32 - Ag '86 - p91
Subject: Dogs

Military Dogs
BL - v82 - Je 15 '86 - p1536
RT - v39 - My '86 - p987
SLJ - v32 - Ag '86 - p91
Subject: Dogs

Search And Rescue Dogs
RT - v39 - My '86 - p987
SLJ - v32 - Ag '86 - p91
Subject: Dogs

Sled Dogs
RT - v39 - My '86 - p987
SLJ - v32 - Ag '86 - p91
Subject: Dogs

EMERY, Anne 1907-
AuBYP, BioIn 2, -3, ConAu 2NR, CurBio 52, MorJA, SmATA 33

A Dream To Touch
BL - v55 - S 1 '58 - p26
KR - v26 - Ap 1 '58 - p286
LJ - v83 - Jl '58 - p2075
Subject: Love—Fiction

First Love Farewell
BL - v55 - Ja 15 '59 - p262
KR - v26 - Ag 1 '58 - p550
LJ - v83 - O 15 '58 - p3015
Subject: Love—Fiction

First Orchid For Pat
CSM - N 7 '57 - p17
KR - v25 - Ag 1 '57 - p534
LJ - v82 - O 15 '57 - p2706
Subject: Love—Fiction

Sorority Girl
BL - v48 - Mr 15 '52 - p234
CSM - My 15 '52 - p9
HB - v28 - Je '52 - p178
KR - v20 - Ja 15 '52 - p32
NYTBR - Mr 30 '52 - p30
Subject: Schools—Fiction

EMMENS, Carol Ann 1944-
ConAu 106, SmATA 39

Stunt Work And Stunt People
BL - v78 - My 15 '82 - p1236
Hi Lo - v4 - O '82 - p6
SLJ - v29 - N '82 - p99
VOYA - v5 - F '83 - p49
Subject: Stunt men and women

EMRICH, Duncan 1908-197?
AuBYP SUPA, BioIn 4, ConAu 9NR, CurBio 55, SmATA 11

The Nonsense Book Of Riddles, Rhymes, Tongue Twisters, Puzzles And Jokes From American Folklore
BL - v67 - Ap 1 '71 - p659
CCB-B - v24 - Je '71 - p156
JAF - v84 - Jl '71 - p357
TN - v27 - Ja '71 - p208
Subject: Riddles

ENDERLE, Judith 1941-
ConAu 106, SmATA 38

Secrets
BL - v81 - F 1 '85 - p783

ENDERLE, Judith (continued)
SLJ - v31 - S '84 - p137
Subject: Love—Fiction

S.W.A.K.: Sealed With A Kiss
BL - v79 - My 15 '83 - p1196
Subject: Love—Fiction; Schools—Fiction

ENGDAHL, Sylvia Louise 1933-
AuBYP SUP, ChlLR 2, ConAu 14NR, FourBJA, IntAu&W 77, ScFSB, SmATA 4, TwCChW 83, TwCSFW 86, WrDr 86

Enchantress From The Stars
CLW - v54 - Ap '83 - p369
TLS - S 20 '74 - p1006
TN - v34 - Spring '78 - p265
Subject: Science fiction

ENGEL, Beth Bland

Big Words
BL - v79 - Mr 1 '83 - p904
CBRS - v11 - F '83 - p69
CCB-B - v36 - Mr '83 - p125
J Read - v27 - D '83 - p280
KR - v50 - N 15 '82 - p1240
SLJ - v29 - F '83 - p88
Subject: Race relations—Fiction

ENGEL, Lyle Kenyon 1915-
ConAu 120, -85, EncSF, WhoAm 86

Road Racing In America
BL - v67 - Je 1 '71 - p813
Subject: Automobile racing

ENGLE, Eloise 1923-
ConAu 2NR, IntAu&W 86X, SmATA 9, WhoAmW 81, WrDr 86
Pseud./variant:
Paananen, Eloise K

Medic
BS - v27 - Jl 1 '67 - p144
KR - v35 - Ap 1 '67 - p459
PW - v191 - Ap 3 '67 - p52
Subject: Medicine

ENGLEBARDT, Stanley L
IntAu&W 82

How To Get In Shape For Sports
BL - v73 - N 15 '76 - p472
KR - v44 - O 1 '76 - p1098
SLJ - v23 - D '76 - p72
Subject: Exercise; Physical fitness; Sports

ENGLISH, Diane
see Zizmor, Jonathan (co-author)

EPSTEIN, Beryl Williams
see Epstein, Sam (co-author)

EPSTEIN, Sam 1909-
AuBYP, BioIn 13, ConAu 18NR, MorJA, SmATA 31, WhoWorJ 78

Baseball: Hall Of Fame, Stories Of Champions
LJ - v90 - Ap 15 '65 - p2019
Co-author: Epstein, Beryl Williams
Subject: Baseball—Biography

George Washington Carver: Negro Scientist
JNE - v38 - Fall '69 - p420
Co-author: Epstein, Beryl Williams
Subject: Biography; Blacks—Biography

Harriet Tubman: Guide To Freedom
BL - v65 - F 1 '69 - p586
CLW - v41 - O '69 - p138
LJ - v94 - F 15 '69 - p871
Teacher - v93 - Ap '76 - p120
Co-author: Epstein, Beryl Williams
Subject: Blacks—Biography

Jackie Robinson: Baseball's Gallant Fighter
SLJ - v21 - Ap '75 - p52
Co-author: Epstein, Beryl Williams
Subject: Baseball—Biography

Winston Churchill
Inst - v81 - Ap '72 - p144
LJ - v97 - Jl '72 - p2483
Co-author: Epstein, Beryl Williams
Subject: Biography

Young Paul Revere's Boston
CCB-B - v20 - Ap '67 - p119
CE - v44 - S '67 - p54
LJ - v92 - Ja 15 '67 - p334
Co-author: Epstein, Beryl Williams
Subject: Biography; Boston—Social life and customs

ERDOES, Richard 1912-
BioIn 1, -3, ConAu 77, IlsBYP, IlsCB 1957, SmATA 33

The Sun Dance People: The Plains Indians, Their Past And Present
BL - v69 - O 1 '72 - p147
BW - v6 - Jl 16 '72 - p7
CCB-B - v26 - S '72 - p5
KR - v40 - Ap 15 '72 - p488
LJ - v97 - O 15 '72 - p3459
NYTBR - Ag 13 '72 - p8

ERDOES, Richard (continued)
PW - v202 - Jl 31 '72 - p71
Subject: Indians of North America

ERLICH, Lillian 1910-
AuBYP, ConAu 5NR, SmATA 10

Modern American Career Women
BL - v55 - My 15 '59 - p510
KR - v27 - Ja 15 '59 - p44
LJ - v84 - F 15 '59 - p590
Subject: Biography

ERNST, John
ConAu 45, SmATA 39
Pseud./variant:
Clark, David Allan

Jesse James
Kliatt - v15 - Winter '81 - p23
Subject: Biography; Crime and criminals

see also Clark, David Allan for additional titles

ERSKINE, H Keith

Know What's Happening
Hi Lo - v2 - S '80 - p6
Co-author: Gilber, E S

ERSKINE, Helen

Kate Herself
Hi Lo - v3 - Ja '82 - p4
SLJ - v28 - Mr '82 - p154
VOYA - v4 - F '82 - p30

ESHERICK, Joseph
see Schell, Orville (co-author)

ETHRIDGE, Kenneth E

Toothpick
BL - v82 - N 15 '85 - p481
CBRS - v14 - Ja '86 - p54
CCB-B - v39 - F '86 - p106
KR - v53 - O 1 '85 - p1087
SLJ - v32 - D '85 - p99
VOYA - v9 - Ap '86 - p30
Subject: Friendship—Fiction; Schools—Fiction; Terminally ill—Fiction

ETS, Marie Hall 1893?-
Au&ICB, BkP, ConAu 4NR, DcLB 22, JBA 51, OxChL, SmATA 2, TwCChW 83, WhAmArt 85, WrDr 86

Bad Boy, Good Boy
BL - v64 - Mr 1 '68 - p783
BW - v1 - N 5 '67 - p47
CCB-B - v21 - F '68 - p93
KR - v35 - S 15 '67 - p1130
LJ - v92 - N 15 '67 - p4242
NYTBR - v72 - N 5 '67 - p63
SR - v50 - N 11 '67 - p42

ETTER, Lester Frederick 1904-
ConAu 25R

Bull Pen Hero
BS - v26 - Ag 1 '66 - p174
KR - v34 - My 15 '66 - p512
LJ - v91 - Jl '66 - p3550

The Game Of Hockey
SLJ - v24 - D '77 - p64
Subject: Hockey

Hockey's Masked Men: Three Great Goalies
SLJ - v23 - Ja '77 - p90
Subject: Hockey—Biography

EVANS, Harold 1928-
ConAu 41R, WhoAm 86, WhoWor 78, WrDr 86

We Learned To Ski
BW - Ag 31 '75 - p2
ILN - v272 - N '84 - p97
KR - v43 - Ag 1 '75 - p908
NYTBR - N 9 '75 - p4
PW - v208 - Ag 4 '75 - p53
VV - v20 - S 15 '75 - p50
Subject: Skis and skiing

EVANS, Jessica

Blind Sunday
Emerg Lib - v9 - N '81 - p32

EVANS, Larry 1939-

How To Draw Monsters
A Art - v42 - Je '78 - p16
Subject: Animals (Mythical); Drawing—Technique; Monsters

EVARTS, Hal G, Jr. 1915-
AuBYP SUP, ConAu 2NR, EncFWF, SmATA 6, WhoWest 84, WrDr 86

The Pegleg Mystery
BS - v31 - Mr 15 '72 - p566
CLW - v44 - O '72 - p193
EJ - v61 - S '72 - p938
HB - v48 - Je '72 - p274
KR - v40 - F 15 '72 - p201
LJ - v97 - My 15 '72 - p1929
Subject: Mystery and detective stories

EVARTS, Hal G, Jr. (continued)

Smuggler's Road
BL - v64 - Je 15 '68 - p1184
BS - v28 - My 1 '68 - p64
BW - v2 - My 5 '68 - p24
HB - v44 - Ag '68 - p427
KR - v36 - F 1 '68 - p122
LJ - v93 - Ap 15 '68 - p1809
NYTBR - v73 - Je 16 '68 - p24

EVERS, Alf

Deer Jackers
Comw - v83 - N 5 '65 - p158
Inst - v75 - N '65 - p94
KR - v33 - Jl 1 '65 - p630
LJ - v90 - N 15 '65 - p5103

EVSLIN, Bernard 1922-
AuBYP SUP, ConAu 9NR, SmATA 45

Heroes, Gods And Monsters Of The Greek Myths
CC - v84 - D 13 '67 - p1601
LJ - v93 - Ja 15 '68 - p303
NYTBR - v73 - Ja 21 '68 - p26
Subject: Mythology (Greek)

EWEN, David 1907-1985
AuBYP, BioIn 10, ConAu 1R, –2NR, –118, OxAmT 84, SmATA 4, –47N, WhoAm 84, WrDr 86

Famous Conductors
BL - v62 - Je 1 '66 - p952
BS - v26 - S 1 '66 - p201
LJ - v92 - Ja 15 '67 - p342
Subject: Conductors (Music)

EWY, Donna

Teen Pregnancy: The Challenges We Faced, The Choices We Made
Kliatt - v19 - Fall '85 - p42
Kliatt - v20 - Winter '86 - p41
SLJ - v31 - My '85 - p100
VOYA - v8 - Je '85 - p145
Co-author: Ewy, Rodger
Subject: Pregnancy

EWY, Rodger
see Ewy, Donna (co-author)

EYERLY, Jeannette 1908-
AmCath 80, AuBYP SUP, ConAu 19NR, FifBJA, SmATA 4, WhoAm 86, WhoAmW 77

Escape From Nowhere
BW - v3 - My 4 '69 - p32
CCB-B - v23 - S '69 - p6
Comw - v90 - My 23 '69 - p300
HB - v45 - Ap '69 - p195
KR - v37 - F 15 '69 - p184
LJ - v94 - Ap 15 '69 - p1794
NYTBR - Je 8 '69 - p44
NYTBR, Pt. 2 - My 4 '69 - p10
NYTBR, Pt. 2 - N 9 '69 - p60
PW - v195 - My 12 '69 - p58
Subject: Drug abuse—Fiction

The Girl Inside
CCB-B - v22 - O '68 - p25
EJ - v58 - My '69 - p778
HB - v44 - Ag '68 - p428
KR - v36 - Mr 1 '68 - p271
LJ - v93 - Ap 15 '68 - p1810
NYTBR - v73 - Ap 21 '68 - p34

A Girl Like Me
Am - v115 - N 5 '66 - p554
BL - v63 - D 15 '66 - p446
CCB-B - v20 - Ja '67 - p73
Comw - v85 - N 11 '66 - p176
CSM - v58 - N 3 '66 - pB1
EJ - v56 - F '67 - p316
KR - v34 - Ag 15 '66 - p841
LJ - v91 - S 15 '66 - p4349
NYTBR - v71 - N 6 '66 - p16
Subject: Unwed mothers—Fiction

If I Loved You Wednesday
BL - v77 - O 1 '80 - p205
BS - v40 - Ja '81 - p352
CBRS - v9 - N '80 - p27
CCB-B - v34 - D '80 - p70
J Read - v24 - Ap '81 - p647
KR - v49 - Ja 15 '81 - p79
SLJ - v27 - O '80 - p154
Subject: Love—Fiction

The Phaedra Complex
BL - v68 - N 15 '71 - p286
CCB-B - v25 - F '72 - p90
CSM - v63 - N 11 '71 - pB1
EJ - v61 - Ap '72 - p603
KR - v39 - Jl 1 '71 - p682
LJ - v96 - O 15 '71 - p3475
SR - v54 - N 13 '71 - p62

Radigan Cares
BS - v30 - N 15 '70 - p361
CCB-B - v24 - D '70 - p58
EJ - v60 - My '71 - p667

EYERLY, Jeannette (continued)
KR - v38 - Jl 15 '70 - p748
LJ - v96 - Ja 15 '71 - p275
Subject: Politics—Fiction

EZZELL, Marilyn 1937-
ConAu 109, SmATA 42

The Phantom Of Featherford Falls
MN - v63 - D '84 - p60
SLJ - v29 - My '83 - p94
VOYA - v6 - Je '83 - p96

F

FABER, Doris 1924-
AuBYP, ConAu 8NR, SmATA 3

Clarence Darrow: Defender Of The People
CC - v82 - Je 30 '65 - p838
CCB-B - v18 - Je '65 - p146
KR - v33 - Ja 15 '65 - p61
LJ - v90 - My 15 '65 - p2404
NYTBR - v70 - Jl 25 '65 - p20
Subject: Biography

Enrico Fermi: Atomic Pioneer
KR - v34 - Ja 15 '66 - p62
LJ - v91 - F 15 '66 - p1062
SB - v1 - Mr '66 - p208
Subject: Biography

Horace Greeley: The People's Editor
CSM - My 7 '64 - p9B
LJ - v89 - Mr 15 '64 - p1449
NYTBR - Mr 22 '64 - p22
Subject: Biography

Lucretia Mott
BL - v68 - F 15 '72 - p506
CCB-B - v25 - Ja '72 - p73
LJ - v96 - D 15 '71 - p4197
NHB - v34 - D '71 - p191
Subject: Abolitionists; Biography

Robert Frost: America's Poet
AL - v36 - Ja '65 - p551
Am - v111 - N 21 '64 - p672
CSM - N 5 '64 - p8B
LJ - v89 - D 15 '64 - p5006
NYRB - v3 - D 3 '64 - p13
Subject: Biography

FAIR, Ronald L 1932-
BlkAWP, ConAu 69, SelBAAu, WhoBlA 77

Hog Butcher
BL - v63 - N 1 '66 - p300
BS - v26 - S 15 '66 - p207
CC - v83 - Ag 31 '66 - p1057
CLW - v38 - N '66 - p209
KR - v34 - Je 15 '66 - p602
KR - v34 - Jl 1 '66 - p636
LJ - v91 - Ag '66 - p3764
NW - v68 - S 5 '66 - p90
PW - v189 - Je 20 '66 - p77
SR - v49 - S 3 '66 - p36

We Can't Breathe
BL - v68 - N 15 '71 - p272
Choice - v9 - Jl '72 - p644
CSM - v64 - D 30 '71 - p6
EJ - v62 - D '73 - p1300
EJ - v63 - Ja '74 - p65
KR - v39 - O 15 '71 - p1139
LJ - v96 - D 1 '71 - p4029
Nat - v214 - F 21 '72 - p253
NY - v47 - F 5 '72 - p103
NYTBR - F 6 '72 - p6
PW - v200 - O 18 '71 - p42
SR - v55 - F 19 '72 - p74
TN - v29 - Ap '73 - p257
YR - v61 - Summer '72 - p599

FALES, E D, Jr. 1906-

The Book Of Expert Driving
KR - v38 - S 15 '70 - p1068
KR - v38 - O 15 '70 - p1173
LJ - v95 - S 1 '70 - p2819
SLJ - v26 - D '79 - p106
Subject: Automobiles

FALL, Thomas (pseud.) 1917-
AuBYP, ConAu X, FourBJA, SmATA X
Real Name:
Snow, Donald Clifford

Canalboat To Freedom
BL - v63 - O 1 '66 - p187
CCB-B - v20 - N '66 - p40
CE - v44 - S '67 - p48
HB - v42 - O '66 - p568
KR - v34 - My 15 '66 - p513
LJ - v91 - Jl '66 - p3534
NYTBR - v71 - Ag 14 '66 - p24

Dandy's Mountain
BL - v64 - O 1 '67 - p200
BW - v1 - S 24 '67 - p22
CCB-B - v21 - O '67 - p26
HB - v43 - Ag '67 - p469
KR - v35 - My 1 '67 - p560
LJ - v92 - O 15 '67 - p3862
SR - v50 - Jl 22 '67 - p43

FANBURG, Walter H 1936-

How To Be A Winner
KR - v430 - F 1 '75 - p153
LJ - v100 - Ja '75 - p1336
Subject: Weight control

FARLEY, Walter 1920-
AuBYP, ConAu 8NR, ConLC 17, DcLB 22, JBA 51, MorBMP, OxChL, SmATA 43, TwCChW 83, WhoAm 86

The Black Stallion
GP - v17 - N '78 - p3406
Teacher - v95 - My '78 - p109
TES - Jl 11 '80 - p28
Subject: Horses—Fiction

FAUST, S R

Loaded And Rollin'
BL - v72 - Jl 15 '76 - p1560
Subject: Motor-truck drivers

FEAGLES, Anita MacRae 1926-
AuBYP, ConAu 4NR, FourBJA, SmATA 9

Emergency Room
LJ - v98 - Mr 15 '73 - p1020
Subject: Hospitals; Medical emergencies

Me, Cassie
BL - v65 - S 1 '68 - p53
BS - v28 - Jl 1 '68 - p154
BW - v2 - My 5 '68 - p26
CCB-B - v21 - Jl '68 - p173
KR - v36 - Ap 15 '68 - p465
LJ - v93 - Je 15 '68 - p2546
NYTBR - v73 - My 5 '68 - p8
PW - v193 - My 6 '68 - p45
SR - v51 - Jl 20 '68 - p31

Sophia Scarlotti And Ceecee
BL - v75 - Mr 1 '79 - p1048
CBRS - v7 - Ag '79 - p136
CCB-B - v32 - Jl '79 - p190
KR - v47 - Ap 1 '79 - p391
SLJ - v25 - Mr '79 - p147
Subject: Identity—Fiction

The Year The Dreams Came Back
BL - v73 - S 15 '76 - p173
CLW - v48 - My '77 - p443
HB - v52 - O '76 - p503
KR - v44 - Jl 1 '76 - p738
LA - v54 - Ap '77 - p443
PW - v210 - D 27 '76 - p60
SLJ - v23 - S '76 - p132
Subject: Fathers and daughters—Fiction

FECHER, Constance 1911-
AuBYP SUP, ConAu X, IntAu&W 77X, SmATA 7, WrDr 86
Pseud./variant:
Heaven, Constance

The Last Elizabethan: A Portrait Of Sir Walter Raleigh
BL - v68 - My 1 '72 - p765
BL - v68 - Ag 15 '72 - p769
BS - v32 - Ag 15 '72 - p243
BW - v6 - Ag 13 '72 - p6
HB - v48 - Je '72 - p281
KR - v40 - Ja 15 '72 - p75
LJ - v98 - Mr 15 '73 - p1101
NY - v48 - D 2 '72 - p211
PW - v201 - Ap 10 '72 - p59
Subject: Biography

FEDDER, Ruth 1907-
ConAu 2NR

A Girl Grows Up
BL - v63 - Je 15 '67 - p1096
BS - v27 - My 1 '67 - p64
KR - v35 - Mr 15 '67 - p353
Subject: Adolescence

FEDER, Robert Arthur
see Arthur, Robert

FEELINGS, Thomas 1933-
BioIn 8, -9, BkP, ConAu 49, IlsBYP, IlsCB 1967, SelBAAu, SmATA 8, ThrBJA, WhoBlA 85

Black Pilgrimage
BL - v68 - Je 15 '72 - p903
BL - v69 - My 1 '73 - p837
Bl W - v22 - N '72 - p91
BW - v6 - My 7 '72 - p13
CCB-B - v26 - S '72 - p6
HB - v48 - Ag '72 - p380
HB - v61 - Mr '85 - p212
HB - v61 - My '85 - p337
KR - v40 - Ap 15 '72 - p489
LJ - v98 - Ja 15 '73 - p267
NYTBR, Pt. 2 - My 7 '72 - p30
SR - v55 - My 20 '72 - p82
Subject: Artists; Blacks—Biography

FEINGLASS, Sanford J.
see Lappin, Myra A (co-author)

FELSEN, Henry Gregor 1916-
AuBYP, ConAu 1NR, ConLC 17, JBA 51, SmATA 1, –2AS

Hot Rod
BL - v47 - S 15 '50 - p44
KR - v18 - Je 1 '50 - p305
LJ - v75 - N 1 '50 - p1913
NYTBR - Jl 30 '50 - p16
Subject: Automobiles—Fiction

Street Rod
KR - v21 - My 15 '53 - p307
LJ - v78 - Ag '53 - p1339
NYTBR - S 6 '53 - p13
Subject: Automobiles—Fiction

To My Son, The Teen-Age Driver
BL - v24 - Ap 15 '64 - p41
CLW - v41 - My '70 - p576
LJ - v89 - Ap 1 '64 - p1603
Par - v40 - Jl '65 - p14
Subject: Automobiles

FELSER, Larry

Baseball's Ten Greatest Pitchers
Inst - v89 - Ja '80 - p112
Kliatt - v13 - Fall '79 - p64
SLJ - v26 - D '79 - p102
Subject: Baseball—Biography

FELTON, Harold W 1902-
AuBYP, ConAu 1NR, MorJA, SmATA 1

James Weldon Johnson
BL - v67 - Jl 1 '71 - p907
CCB-B - v24 - Jl '71 - p169
Comw - v97 - F 23 '73 - p473
LJ - v96 - N 15 '71 - p3900
NYTBR, Pt. 2 - My 2 '71 - p43
PW - v199 - My 10 '71 - p43
Subject: Blacks—Biography

Mumbet: The Story Of Elizabeth Freeman
BL - v66 - Jl 15 '70 - p1407
CCB-B - v24 - S '70 - p7
CSM - v62 - My 7 '70 - pB1
HB - v46 - Ag '70 - p399
KR - v38 - My 1 '70 - p509
PW - v197 - Mr 30 '70 - p65
SR - v53 - Je 27 '70 - p39
Subject: Biography

Nat Love, Negro Cowboy
LJ - v95 - D 15 '70 - p4382
Subject: Blacks—Biography; Cowboys

FENDERSON, Lewis H 19071-1983
ConAu 106, –111, SmATA 47

Thurgood Marshall: Fighter For Justice
BL - v66 - Ja 1 '70 - p564
CLW - v41 - My '70 - p590
KR - v37 - My 1 '69 - p509
LJ - v95 - Mr 15 '70 - p1194
NYTBR, Pt. 2 - My 4 '69 - p16
Subject: Biography

FENNER, Phyllis Reid 1899-1982
AuBYP, BioIn 3, –12, ConAu 2NR, –106, SmATA 1, –29N, WhoAmW 77

Lift Line: Stories Of Downhill And Cross-Country Skiing
CSM - v68 - N 3 '76 - p20
KR - v44 - Jl 15 '76 - p799
SLJ - v23 - D '76 - p71
Subject: Short stories; Skis and skiing—Fiction

FENNER, Sal

Sea Machines
ASBYP - v14 - Fall '81 - p29
SB - v17 - S '81 - p34
Subject: Ships

FENTEN, Barbara
see Fenten, D X (co-author)

FENTEN, D X 1932-
AuBYP SUP, ConAu 5NR, SmATA 4, WhoE 77, WrDr 86

Behind The Circus Scene
Hi Lo - v4 - Mr '83 - p4
SLJ - v27 - Ja '81 - p59
Co-author: Fenten, Barbara
Subject: Circus

Behind The Newspaper Scene
Hi Lo - v4 - Mr '83 - p4
SLJ - v27 - Ja '81 - p59
Co-author: Fenten, Barbara
Subject: Newspapers

Behind The Radio Scene
Hi Lo - v4 - Mr '83 - p4
SLJ - v27 - Ja '81 - p59
Co-author: Fenten, Barbara
Subject: Radio broadcasting

Behind The Sports Scene
Hi Lo - v4 - Mr '83 - p4
SLJ - v27 - D '80 - p75
Co-author: Fenten, Barbara
Subject: Baseball

FENTEN, D X (continued)

Behind The Television Scene
Hi Lo - v4 - Mr '83 - p4
SLJ - v27 - Ja '81 - p60
Co-author: Fenten, Barbara
Subject: Television

FENTON, Edward B 1917-
AuBYP, ConAu 13NR, SmATA 7, ThrBJA, TwCChW 78, –83, WrDr 86

A Matter Of Miracles
Am - v117 - N 4 '67 - p518
BL - v64 - O 15 '67 - p273
BW - v1 - S 10 '67 - p36
CCB-B - v21 - D '67 - p58
CE - v44 - Ap '68 - p501
HB - v43 - O '67 - p592
KR - v35 - Je 1 '67 - p645
LJ - v92 - S 15 '67 - p3185
NYTBR - v72 - Ag 6 '67 - p26
NYTBR - v72 - N 5 '67 - p66
PW - v192 - N 27 '67 - p43

FERRIGNO, Lou

The Incredible Lou Ferrigno
BL - v79 - S 1 '82 - p20
LJ - v107 - Ag '82 - p1476
SLJ - v29 - S '82 - p151
Co-author: Hall, Douglas K
Subject: Biography; Deaf; Weightlifters

FICHTER, George Siebert 1922-
AuBYP SUP, BioIn 2, ConAu 7NR, IntAu&W 86, SmATA 7, WhoS&SW 76, WrDr 86
Pseud./variant:
Warner, Matt

Birds Of North America
ARBA - v15 - p657
ASBYP - v16 - Winter '83 - p58
BL - v79 - O 15 '82 - p311
SLJ - v29 - N '82 - p82
Subject: Birds

Reptiles And Amphibians Of North America
ARBA - v15 - p670
ASBYP - v16 - Winter '83 - p58
BL - v79 - O 15 '82 - p311
SLJ - v29 - N '82 - p82
Subject: Amphibians; Reptiles

Rocks And Minerals
ASBYP - v16 - Winter '83 - p58
BL - v79 - O 15 '82 - p311
SLJ - v29 - N '82 - p82
Subject: Minerology; Petrology

Wildflowers Of North America
ARBA - v15 - p646
ASBYP - v16 - Winter '83 - p58
BL - v79 - O 15 '82 - p311
Inst - v92 - Ap '83 - p20
SLJ - v29 - N '82 - p82
Subject: Wildflowers

FIELDS, Terri

Hearts Don't Lie
SLJ - v32 - Ap '86 - p103
Subject: Love—Fiction

FIFE, Dale 1910-
AuBYP SUP, ConAu 19NR, FourBJA, SmATA 18

Destination Unknown
BL - v78 - F 1 '82 - p706
CBRS - v10 - Ja '82 - p47
HB - v58 - F '82 - p41
SLJ - v28 - N '81 - p90
Subject: Sea stories

North Of Danger
BL - v74 - Ap 15 '78 - p1348
HB - v54 - Ag '78 - p394
KR - v46 - Je 15 '78 - p636
NYTBR - Ap 30 '78 - p32
SLJ - v24 - My '78 - p66
Teacher - v96 - O '78 - p167
Subject: World War, 1939-1945—Fiction

FILICHIA, Peter

Everything But Tuesdays And Sundays
Kliatt - v18 - Fall '84 - p8
VOYA - v7 - F '85 - p325

A Matter Of Finding The Right Girl
BL - v81 - Ap 15 '85 - p1177
SLJ - v32 - S '85 - p144
VOYA - v8 - Je '85 - p130
WLB - v59 - Mr '85 - p485
Subject: Love—Fiction

FILMER-SANKEY, Josephine
see Denny, Norman George (co-author)

FILSON, Brent

The Puma
BL - v75 - My 15 '79 - p1435
CE - v56 - Ja '80 - p169
Hi Lo - v1 - S '79 - p2

FILSON, Brent (continued)
SLJ - v25 - My '79 - p88
Subject: Fathers and sons—Fiction; Wrestling—Fiction

Smoke Jumpers
KR - v46 - F 1 '78 - p110
NYTBR - Ap 30 '78 - p45
SLJ - v24 - F '78 - p56
Subject: California—Fiction; Firefighters—Fiction

FINKEL, George 1909-1975
ConAu P-2, SmATA 8, TwCChW 83

Watch Fires To The North
BL - v64 - Je 1 '68 - p1133
BS - v28 - My 1 '68 - p64
CCB-B - v22 - O '68 - p26
CLW - v39 - F '68 - p468
CSM - v60 - My 2 '68 - pB8
KR - v35 - S 1 '67 - p1055
KR - v36 - Mr 15 '68 - p343
LJ - v93 - Je 15 '68 - p2546
NYTBR - v73 - Ap 14 '68 - p20
SR - v51 - Jl 20 '68 - p31

FINLAYSON, Ann 1925-
ConAu 29R, SmATA 8

Decathlon Men: Greatest Athletes In The World
LJ - v92 - My 15 '67 - p2040
Subject: Decathlon

Redcoat In Boston
BS - v31 - Jl 15 '71 - p191
LJ - v96 - O 15 '71 - p3475
PW - v199 - My 10 '71 - p43
Subject: United States—History—Revolution, 1775-1783—Fiction

FINNEY, Jack 1911-
ConSFA, EncSF, ScF&FL 1, ScFSB, TwCSFW 86, WhoSciF, WrDr 86

Time And Again
BL - v67 - S 1 '70 - p36
BL - v67 - S 15 '70 - p95
BL - v67 - Ap 1 '71 - p654
BL - v81 - Jl '85 - p1546
BS - v30 - Jl 15 '70 - p151
BW - v4 - Je 28 '70 - p6
HB - v46 - O '70 - p502
KR - v38 - Mr 1 '70 - p272
KR - v38 - Ap 15 '70 - p473
Lis - v103 - Ap 3 '80 - p450
LJ - v95 - O 1 '70 - p3304
LJ - v95 - O 15 '70 - p3649
NO - v9 - S 28 '70 - p21
NYT - v119 - Jl 25 '70 - p21
NYTBR - Ag 2 '70 - p24
Obs - Je 15 '80 - p28
PW - v197 - Mr 9 '70 - p81
PW - v199 - My 31 '71 - p136
SR - v54 - O 23 '71 - p86
SR - v54 - N 27 '71 - p48
Time - v96 - Jl 20 '70 - p76
TN - v27 - Ap '71 - p308

FIORE, Evelyn L 1918-

Mystery At Lane's End
CCB-B - v22 - Jl '69 - p174
CSM - v61 - Je 26 '69 - p7
KR - v375 - Mr 1 '69 - p246
LJ - v94 - My 15 '69 - p2124
PW - v195 - Ap 7 '69 - p56
Subject: Mystery and detective stories

FIRST, Julia

Amy
KR - v43 - S 1 '75 - p998
SLJ - v22 - N '75 - p76
Subject: Schools—Fiction

FISCHLER, Stanley I
ConAu 116, SmATA 36

Getting Into Pro Soccer
BL - v75 - Jl 1 '79 - p1583
SLJ - v26 - F '80 - p54
Co-author: Friedman, Richard
Subject: Soccer; Vocational guidance

FISHER, Aileen 1906-
AuBYP, BioIn 13, BkP, ConAu 17NR, MorJA, SmATA 1, -25, TwCChW 83, WhoAmW 83, WrDr 86

Jeanne D'Arc
BL - v66 - My 1 '70 - p1098
CCB-B - v24 - O '70 - p24
Comw - v92 - My 22 '70 - p245
HB - v46 - Je '70 - p304
KR - v38 - F 1 '70 - p106
LJ - v95 - My 15 '70 - p1941
NYTBR, Pt. 2 - My 24 '70 - p30
PW - v197 - Mr 2 '70 - p82
SR - v53 - Je 27 '70 - p39
Subject: Biography

FISHER, Leonard Everett 1924-
BioIn 12, ConAu 2NR, IntAu&W 86, MorBMP, SmATA 34, –1AS, ThrBJA, WhoAm 86, WrDr 86

Across The Sea From Galway
BL - v72 - F 15 '76 - p854
KR - v43 - Ag 1 '75 - p848
PW - v208 - S 22 '75 - p132
SLJ - v22 - Ja '76 - p52
Subject: Ireland—Fiction; Irish Americans—Fiction

The Unions
BL - v78 - Je 1 '82 - p1311
CCB-B - v35 - Jl '82 - p205
CE - v59 - N '82 - p138
PW - v221 - Je 11 '82 - p62
SLJ - v29 - Ja '83 - p74
Subject: Labor unions

FISHER, Lois I 1948-
ConAu 113, SmATA 38

I Can't Forget You
SLJ - v30 - My '84 - p88
VOYA - v7 - Je '84 - p92

FISK, Nicholas 1923-
ConAu 11NR, ConSFA, IlsBYP, OxChL, ScFSB, SmATA 25, TwCChW 83, TwCSFW 86, WrDr 86

Escape From Splatterbang
CCB-B - v33 - Ja '80 - p94
Subject: Science fiction

Space Hostages
KR - v37 - F 15 '69 - p184
LJ - v94 - Jl '69 - p2675
Punch - v253 - D 6 '67 - p875
TES - Mr 10 '78 - p52
TES - Je 8 '84 - p46
TLS - N 30 '67 - p1160
Subject: Science fiction

FITZHARDINGE, Joan Margaret
see Phipson, Joan

FITZHUGH, Louise 1928-1974
BioIn 10, ChlLR 1, ConAu 53, –P-2, DcLB 52, OxChL, SmATA 24N, –45, ThrBJA, TwCChW 83

Sport
BL - v75 - My 15 '79 - p1438
BS - v39 - N '79 - p289
BW - My 13 '79 - pK2
CBRS - v7 - Je '79 - p107
CCB-B - v32 - Jl '79 - p191
CE - v56 - Ja '80 - p169
CLW - v51 - D '79 - p233
HB - v55 - Ag '79 - p413
KR - v47 - Jl 15 '79 - p793
LA - v57 - Ja '80 - p85
LJ - v57 - Ja '80 - p85
NY - v55 - D 3 '79 - p212
NYTBR - Je 3 '79 - p44
PW - v215 - Je 25 '79 - p123
RT - v33 - Ja '80 - p482
SLJ - v25 - My '79 - p61
WCRB - v5 - S '79 - p83
Subject: Divorce—Fiction; New York (City)—Fiction; Remarriage—Fiction

FLACK, Naomi John
see Sellers, Naomi

FLEISCHER, Leonore
see Thomas, Allison

FLEISCHMAN, Albert Sidney
see Fleischman, Sid

FLEISCHMAN, H Samuel

Gang Girl
CCB-B - v21 - S '67 - p5
EJ - v57 - My '68 - p759
Subject: Juvenile delinquency—Fiction

FLEISCHMAN, Paul 1952-
ConAu 113, FifBJA, SmATA 39

Path Of The Pale Horse
BL - v79 - Ap 1 '83 - p1032
BW - v13 - My 8 '83 - p15
CCB-B - v36 - My '83 - p165
CLW - v56 - O '84 - p139
EJ - v73 - Ja '84 - p88
HB - v59 - Ap '83 - p170
KR - v51 - Ap 1 '83 - p375
LA - v60 - S '83 - p771
LA - v61 - Ap '84 - p421
NYTBR - v88 - My 15 '83 - p26
PW - v223 - Ap 8 '83 - p58
SLJ - v30 - S '83 - p133
VOYA - v6 - O '83 - p200
Subject: Yellow fever—Fiction

FLEISCHMAN, Sid 1920-
ChlLR 1, ConAu 5NR, OxChL, SmATA 8, ThrBJA, TwCChW 78, –83, WrDr 86
Pseud./variant:
Fleischman, Albert Sidney

Chancy And The Grand Rascal
Am - v115 - N 5 '66 - p553

FLEISCHMAN, Sid (continued)
BL - v63 - S 15 '66 - p119
CCB-B - v20 - N '66 - p41
CE - v44 - S '67 - p50
CSM - v58 - N 3 '66 - pB6
HB - v42 - O '66 - p569
KR - v34 - Jl 1 '66 - p625
LJ - v91 - O 15 '66 - p5226
NYTBR - v71 - N 6 '66 - p40
NYTBR - v71 - D 4 '66 - p66
PW - v190 - Ag 15 '66 - p64
SR - v49 - D 10 '66 - p57
TLS - N 30 '67 - p1145
TN - v23 - Ap '67 - p291

The Ghost In The Noonday Sun
Am - v113 - N 20 '65 - p640
BL - v62 - S 1 '65 - p54
CCB-B - v19 - N '65 - p43
HB - v41 - O '65 - p490
KR - v33 - Mr 1 '65 - p245
KR - v33 - My 1 '65 - p472
LJ - v90 - S 15 '65 - p3790
NYTBR - v70 - O 24 '65 - p34
Obs - N 27 '66 - p28
TLS - N 24 '66 - p1069

FLEISCHMANN, Harriet 1904-
ConAu P-2

The Great Enchantment
BS - v27 - Ap 1 '67 - p16
KR - v35 - Ja 1 '67 - p13
LJ - v92 - Je 15 '67 - p2458

FLEMMING, Lois

Ten Psalms
Hi Lo - v2 - O '80 - p4

FLETCHER, Alan Mark 1928-
AuBYP SUP, ConAu 73, WrDr 86

Unusual Aquarium Fishes
BL - v64 - Jl 1 '68 - p1234
CE - v45 - Ap '69 - p468
LJ - v93 - Je 15 '68 - p2538
SB - v4 - S '68 - p134
Subject: Aquarium fishes

FLORENTZ, Christopher

So Wild A Dream
BL - v74 - F 15 '78 - p997
Subject: United States—History—Revolution, 1775-1783—Fiction

FLYNN, Charlotte

Dangerous Beat
BL - v81 - Ag '85 - p1656
SLJ - v32 - S '85 - p150
VOYA - v8 - F '86 - p391
Subject: Love—Fiction; Mystery and detective stories

FLYNN, James J 1911-1977
AuBYP SUP, BioIn 11, ConAu 21R

Negroes Of Achievement In Modern America
Bl W - v20 - Ja '71 - p97
BS - v30 - Ag 1 '70 - p179
KR - v38 - Je 15 '70 - p646
Subject: Blacks—Biography

FOLCH-RIBAS, Jacques 1928-
ConAu 69

Northlight, Lovelight
KR - v44 - Ag 15 '76 - p917
NYTBR - D 26 '76 - p15
PW - v210 - Ag 9 '76 - p67
SLJ - v23 - Ap '77 - p81

FOLEY, June 1944-
ConAu 109, SmATA 44

Falling In Love Is No Snap
BL - v83 - S 15 '86 - p120
CBRS - v15 - N '86 - p31
SLJ - v33 - D '86 - p102
VOYA - v9 - D '86 - p215
Subject: New York (City)—Fiction; Parent and child—Fiction; Single-parent family—Fiction

Love By Any Other Name
BL - v79 - Mr 15 '83 - p966
BS - v43 - My '83 - p73
CBRS - v11 - Ap '83 - p93
CCB-B - v36 - My '83 - p166
CLW - v55 - D '83 - p239
EJ - v72 - O '83 - p85
J Read - v27 - F '84 - p467
Kliatt - v17 - Fall '83 - p8
SLJ - v30 - S '83 - p134
VOYA - v6 - O '83 - p200
Subject: Schools—Fiction

FOLSOM, Franklin Brewster 1907-
AuBYP, ConAu 1R, IntAu&W 82, SmATA 5, WhoAm 86, WrDr 86

The Life And Legend Of George McJunkin
ABC - v25 - Jl '75 - p9
BL - v70 - F 15 '74 - p656
KR - v41 - Jl 1 '73 - p694
LJ - v99 - Ja 15 '74 - p217

FOLSOM, Franklin Brewster (continued)
PW - v204 - D 3 '73 - p40
Subject: Blacks—Biography; Cowboys

FORBES, Esther 1891-1967
BioIn 12, ConAu P-1, ConLC 12, DcLB 22, DcLEL, MorJA, NotAW MOD, OxChL, SmATA 2, TwCChW 83

Johnny Tremain
BL - v40 - D 15 '43 - p150
BW - v11 - My 10 '81 - p14
CSM - N 18 '43 - p10
HB - v19 - N '43 - p413
Inst - v78 - N '68 - p156
LJ - v68 - N 15 '43 - p965
Nat - v157 - N 20 '43 - p592
NY - v19 - D 4 '43 - p124
NYTBR - N 14 '43 - p5
NYTBR, Pt. 2 - F 13 '72 - p14
PW - v194 - Jl 22 '68 - p65
SR - v26 - N 13 '43 - p44
Subject: United States—History—Revolution, 1775-1783—Fiction

FORESTER, C S 1899-1966
ConAu 73, SmATA 13, WebE&AL, WhoChL

Last Nine Days Of The Bismarck
BL - v55 - Ap 15 '59 - p448
CSM - Ap 23 '59 - p5
HB - v35 - Ja '59 - p229
KR - v27 - Ja 15 '59 - p75
LJ - v84 - Mr 1 '59 - p754
NY - v35 - Ap 4 '59 - p169
NYTBR - Ap 5 '59 - p14
SR - v42 - My 2 '59 - p38
Time - v73 - Mr 23 '59 - p96
TLS - My 1 '59 - p260
Subject: World War, 1939-1945

FORMAN, James Douglas 1932-
ConAu 19NR, SmATA 8, ThrBJA

Ceremony Of Innocence
BL - v67 - D 15 '70 - p336
BL - v67 - D 15 '70 - p341
CCB-B - v24 - Ja '71 - p73
EJ - v60 - My '71 - p668
EJ - v69 - O '80 - p16
Inter BC - v13 - #6 '82 p19
KR - v38 - Ag 1 '70 - p805
LJ - v95 - N 15 '70 - p4053
LJ - v95 - D 15 '70 - p4325
NYTBR - Ja 10 '71 - p26
SR - v53 - N 14 '70 - p39

Horses Of Anger
BL - v64 - S 1 '67 - p54
BS - v27 - My 1 '67 - p64
CCB-B - v21 - My '68 - p140
HB - v43 - Je '67 - p352
KR - v35 - Mr 1 '67 - p278
LJ - v92 - My 15 '67 - p2027
NYTBR, Pt. 2 - v72 - My 7 '67 - p2
TN - v24 - N '67 - p99
Subject: Germany—History—1933-1945—Fiction

My Enemy, My Brother
BL - v66 - S 1 '69 - p44
BS - v29 - Jl 1 '69 - p149
BW - v3 - My 4 '69 - p3
CCB-B - v22 - Jl '69 - p174
HB - v45 - Je '69 - p328
J Pol - v94 - My 15 '69 - p2112
KR - v37 - Ap 15 '69 - p452
LJ - v95 - F 15 '70 - p742
NYTBR - My 25 '69 - p32
PW - v195 - My 19 '69 - p70
SR - v52 - Je 28 '69 - p39
Subject: Israel—Fiction

People Of The Dream
BL - v68 - Jl 15 '72 - p997
BL - v68 - Jl 15 '72 - p1004
BW - v6 - Jl 16 '72 - p7
CE - v49 - F '73 - p257
KR - v40 - My 15 '72 - p589
LJ - v97 - N 15 '72 - p3813
NYTBR, Pt. 2 - N 5 '72 - p14
Subject: Nez Perce Indians—Wars, 1877—Fiction

Ring The Judas Bell
BL - v61 - Je 15 '65 - p993
BS - v25 - Ap 15 '65 - p51
CCB-B - v18 - Jl '65 - p160
CLW - v36 - Ap '65 - p573
Comw - v82 - My 28 '65 - p329
CSM - v57 - My 6 '65 - p6B
HB - v41 - Je '65 - p284
Inter BC - v13 - #6 '82 p20
KR - v33 - Ja 1 '65 - p11
LJ - v90 - Mr 15 '65 - p1558
NYTBR - v70 - Ap 4 '65 - p22
SR - v48 - Je 19 '65 - p41

The Traitors
BS - v28 - N 1 '68 - p324
KR - v36 - S 15 '68 - p1058
NYTBR - v73 - N 3 '68 - p18

FORREST, Rose Ann

Welcome To Paradise
SLJ - v28 - S '81 - p134

FORSHAY-LUNSFORD, Cin 1965-
ConAu 119

Walk Through Cold Fire
Bks for Keeps - Ja '86 - p18
EJ - v75 - D '86 - p59
PW - v230 - Ag 22 '86 - p103
SLJ - v32 - D '85 - p43
WLB - v60 - S '85 - p63
Subject: Mystery and detective stories

FORSYTH, Elizabeth Held
see Hyde, Margaret Oldroyd (co-author)

FORSYTH, Frederick 1938-
BioIn 12, ConAu 85, ConLC 2, -5, -36, ConNov 86, CurBio 86, TwCCr&M 85, WhoWor 84, WrDr 86

The Shepherd
BL - v73 - D 15 '76 - p586
BL - v73 - D 15 '76 - p606
CCB-B - v30 - D '76 - p56
Fly - v99 - D '76 - p115
KR - v44 - Ag 1 '76 - p874
LJ - v101 - N 15 '76 - p2393
NS - v90 - N 28 '75 - p686
NYTBR - O 16 '77 - p55
Punch - v269 - O 29 '75 - p788
PW - v210 - Ag 2 '76 - p108
PW - v212 - Ag 22 '77 - p64
SLJ - v23 - F '77 - p75
TLS - D 19 '75 - p1508

FORTMAN, Jan

Creatures Of Mystery
Cur R - v17 - Ag '78 - p228
SLJ - v24 - My '78 - p63
Teacher - v96 - S '79 - p183
Subject: Animals; Insectivorous plants

Houdini And Other Masters Of Magic
SLJ - v24 - My '78 - p64
Subject: Magicians

FORTUNATO, Pat

When We Were Young: An Album Of Stars
CCB-B - v33 - Mr '80 - p132
Hi Lo - v1 - F '80 - p3
SLJ - v26 - F '80 - p54
Subject: Biography

FORTUNE, J J

Revenge In The Silent Tomb
SLJ - v30 - My '84 - p88
VOYA - v7 - Je '84 - p94
Subject: Space and time—Fiction

Trapped In The U.S.S.R.
VOYA - v8 - Je '85 - p127

FOSTER, Alan Dean 1946-
ConAu 53, EncSF, ScF&FL 1, -2, ScFSB, TwCSFW 86, WrDr 86

Splinter Of The Mind's Eye
BL - v74 - My 1 '78 - p1412
EJ - v68 - D '79 - p77
KR - v46 - F 1 '78 - p136
PW - v213 - F 6 '78 - p92
Subject: Science fiction

FOSTER, George
see Drucker, Malka (co-author)

FOSTER, Stephanie

Love Times Two
SLJ - v31 - S '84 - p139
VOYA - v7 - D '84 - p259
Subject: Love—Fiction; Twins—Fiction

Rhythm Of Love
BL - v80 - Je 15 '84 - p1473
SLJ - v31 - S '84 - p137
VOYA - v7 - O '84 - p202
Subject: Love—Fiction; Rock music—Fiction

FOX, Mary Virginia 1919-
AuBYP, ConAu 12NR, SmATA 44

Jane Fonda: Something To Fight For
KR - v48 - Jl 15 '80 - p912
SLJ - v26 - Ja '80 - p69
Subject: Actors and actresses; Biography

Jane Goodall: Living Chimp Style
BL - v78 - F 15 '82 - p756
BL - v82 - S 15 '85 - p143
CCB-B - v35 - F '82 - p106
SLJ - v28 - My '82 - p61
Subject: Biography; Chimpanzees; Zoologists

Janet Guthrie: Foot To The Floor
BL - v78 - S 15 '81 - p104
BL - v82 - S 15 '85 - p143
SLJ - v28 - F '82 - p75
Subject: Automoblie racing drivers; Biography

FOX, Mary Virginia (continued)

Justice Sandra Day O'Connor
BL - v79 - Ap 1 '83 - p1033
SLJ - v29 - Ag '83 - p65
VOYA - v6 - Je '83 - p102
Subject: Biography; United States—Supreme Court

Lady For The Defense: A Biography Of Belva Lockwood
B&B - v3 - Ag '75 - p4
Comw - v102 - N 21 '75 - p566
HB - v51 - Ag '75 - p391
KR - v43 - Ap 15 '75 - p461
PW - v207 - F 24 '75 - p116
SLJ - v22 - S '75 - p102
Subject: Biography

FOX, Paula 1923-
ChILR 1, ConAu 20NR, ConLC 2, DcLB 52, FourBJA, OxChL, SenS, SmATA 17, TwCChW 83, WhoAmW 87

Blowfish Live In The Sea
BL - v67 - F 15 '71 - p492
BS - v30 - F 15 '71 - p506
CCB-B - v24 - Mr '71 - p106
CSM - v63 - My 6 '71 - pB6
HB - v46 - D '70 - p623
HB - v53 - O '77 - p517
KR - v38 - N 1 '70 - p1200
LJ - v96 - Ja 15 '71 - p275
NYRB - v18 - Ap 20 '72 - p13
NYTBR, Pt. 2 - N 8 '70 - p12
Obs - Ap 2 '72 - p28
PW - v198 - N 30 '70 - p41
Spec - v228 - Ap 22 '72 - p625
SR - v54 - Ja 23 '71 - p71
Teacher - v92 - My '75 - p93
TLS - Ap 28 '72 - p477
Subject: Fathers and sons—Fiction

How Many Miles To Babylon?
Atl - v220 - D '67 - p136
BL - v69 - My 1 '73 - p837
BL - v77 - S 15 '80 - p114
BW - v1 - O 8 '67 - p24
CCB-B - v21 - D '67 - p59
HB - v43 - O '67 - p593
KR - v35 - Jl 15 '67 - p807
LJ - v92 - D 15 '67 - p4612
NYTBR - v72 - S 3 '67 - p24
NYTBR - v72 - S 24 '67 - p34
NYTBR - v72 - N 5 '67 - p66
NYTBR, Pt. 2 - N 8 '70 - p30
NYTBR, Pt. 2 - F 13 '72 - p12
Obs - Ag 4 '68 - p22
Obs - Ja 14 '73 - p30
Punch - v255 - Jl 3 '68 - p33
PW - v198 - Jl 13 '70 - p166
SR - v50 - N 11 '67 - p46
TLS - Je 6 '68 - p583
TN - v24 - Ap '68 - p323

A Place Apart
BL - v77 - O 15 '80 - p325
B Rpt - v1 - Mr '83 - p24
BW - v12 - F 14 '82 - p12
GP - v20 - Ja '82 - p4010
JB - v45 - O '81 - p209
KR - v48 - S 15 '80 - p1235
NS - v102 - D 4 '81 - p20
NYTBR - v85 - N 9 '80 - p55
PW - v218 - N 28 '80 - p50
SLJ - v27 - O '80 - p155
TES - Je 5 '81 - p39

Portrait Of Ivan
A Lib - v1 - Ap '70 - p385
BL - v66 - F 1 '70 - p670
BW - v4 - Mr 29 '70 - p12
CCB-B - v23 - F '70 - p96
GW - v103 - D 19 '70 - p21
HB - v46 - Ap '70 - p159
KR - v37 - O 15 '69 - p1112
LJ - v94 - D 15 '69 - p4581
LJ - v94 - D 15 '69 - p4604
NYTBR - D 7 '69 - p68
NYTBR, Pt. 2 - N 9 '69 - p34
NYTBR, Pt. 2 - N 9 '69 - p60
PW - v196 - N 24 '69 - p42
SR - v52 - D 20 '69 - p30
Teacher - v91 - My '74 - p84
TLS - D 11 '70 - p1451
Subject: Fathers and sons—Fiction

The Slave Dancer
B&B - v23 - N '77 - p82
BL - v70 - Ja 1 '74 - p484
BL - v70 - Mr 15 '74 - p827
BL - v81 - D 15 '84 - p583
BW - F 10 '74 - p4
CCB-B - v27 - Ja '74 - p77
CE - v50 - Ap '74 - p335
CLW - v47 - N '75 - p165
EJ - v66 - O '77 - p58
EJ - v69 - S '80 - p87
Emerg Lib - v11 - Ja '84 - p21
HB - v49 - D '73 - p596
HB - v53 - O '77 - p515
KR - v41 - O 1 '73 - p1095
KR - v41 - D 15 '73 - p1350
Lis - v92 - N 7 '74 - p613
LJ - v98 - D 15 '73 - p3689
LJ - v98 - D 15 '73 - p3711
NS - v88 - N 8 '74 - p666
NYTBR - Ja 20 '74 - p8
Obs - D 8 '74 - p30

FOX, Paula (continued)
Obs - Je 26 '77 - p29
PW - v204 - D 10 '73 - p36
Teacher - v91 - My '74 - p79
TES - Je 10 '83 - p22
TES - Jl 15 '83 - p18
TLS - D 6 '74 - p1375
TN - v30 - Ap '74 - p243
VV - v19 - D 16 '74 - p52
Subject: Slave trade—Fiction

FRANCHERE, Ruth 1906-
ConAu 73, FourBJA, SmATA 18

Cesar Chavez
BL - v67 - N 1 '70 - p226
BL - v68 - Je 15 '72 - p894
BL - v70 - O 15 '73 - p225
CC - v87 - D 16 '70 - p1516
CCB-B - v24 - F '71 - p90
Comw - v93 - N 20 '70 - p203
Inst - v80 - O '70 - p142
KR - v38 - Ag 15 '70 - p879
LJ - v96 - Mr 15 '71 - p1132
NYTBR, Pt. 2 - N 8 '70 - p46
RT - v36 - D '82 - p277
Teacher - v91 - S '73 - p154
Subject: Biography

Hannah Herself
HB - v40 - Ap '64 - p181
LJ - v89 - Mr 15 '64 - p1459
NYTBR - Ag 2 '64 - p20
SE - v47 - Ap '83 - p288

Jack London: The Pursuit Of A Dream
CSM - N 15 '62 - p6B
HB - v38 - D '62 - p613
LJ - v87 - D 15 '62 - p4623
NYTBR - D 9 '62 - p36
Subject: Biography

The Travels Of Colin O'Dae
BL - v63 - Ja 1 '67 - p488
CCB-B - v20 - Ap '67 - p120
CE - v44 - N '67 - p188
KR - v34 - O 1 '66 - p1052
LJ - v92 - Ja 15 '67 - p334
NYTBR - v72 - Ja 8 '67 - p30
SR - v50 - F 18 '67 - p42

Willa: The Story Of Willa Cather's Growing Up
Atl - v202 - D '58 - p100
BL - v55 - S 15 '58 - p52
HB - v34 - D '58 - p480
KR - v26 - Ag 15 '58 - p611
LJ - v83 - O 15 '58 - p3007
NYTBR - O 12 '58 - p29
SR - v41 - N 1 '58 - p59
Subject: Cather, Willa Sibert—Fiction

FRANCIS, Dorothy Brenner 1926-
ConAu 9NR, SmATA 10, WhoAmW 75, WrDr 86

Blink Of The Mind
Kliatt - v17 - Winter '83 - p18
SLJ - v29 - Ap '83 - p120
VOYA - v6 - Ap '83 - p37
WLB - v57 - My '83 - p773
Subject: Science fiction

Captain Morgana Mason
BL - v78 - Jl '82 - p1443
CBRS - v10 - Jl '82 - p127
SLJ - v29 - S '82 - p120
Subject: Fishing—Fiction; Grandfathers—Fiction

The Flint Hills Foal
BB - v5 - Ap '77 - p2
RT - v31 - Ap '78 - p841
SLJ - v23 - Ja '77 - p91
Subject: Horses

Kiss Me, Kit!
BL - v80 - Je 15 '84 - p1474
VOYA - v7 - O '84 - p200
Subject: Fishing—Fiction; Love—Fiction

The Magic Circle
BL - v81 - F 1 '85 - p783
VOYA - v8 - Je '85 - p123
Subject: Ghosts—Fiction; Love—Fiction

Mystery Of The Forgotten Map
KR - v36 - Je 1 '68 - p596

New Boy In Town
B&B - My '83 - p31
Hi Lo - v3 - Ja '82 - p4
SLJ - v28 - Mr '82 - p154
VOYA - v4 - F '82 - p30

FRANK, Anne 1929-1945?
BioIn 8, –10, –12, –13, ConAu 113, HerW 84, IntDcWB, SmATA 42, WorAl

Anne Frank: Diary Of A Young Girl
Atl - v190 - S '52 - p70
BL - v48 - Je 1 '52 - p318
BL - v82 - Ja 1 '86 - p679
Cath W - v175 - Ag '52 - p395
Comw - v56 - Je 27 '52 - p297
CSM - Jl 3 '52 - p13
EJ - v73 - Ja '84 - p85

FRANK, Anne (continued)
HB - v28 - Ag '52 - p248
HB - v28 - D '52 - p425
LJ - v77 - My 15 '52 - p889
NS - v43 - My 17 '52 - p592
NY - v28 - Je 21 '52 - p106
Spec - v188 - My 30 '52 - p726
SR - v35 - Jl 19 '52 - p20
Time - v59 - Je 16 '52 - p102
Subject: Netherlands—German occupation, 1940-1945; World War, 1939-1945

FRANKLIN, Joe

Classics Of The Silent Screen
LJ - v85 - F 15 '60 - p774
NYTBR - F 21 '60 - p7
Subject: Actors and actresses; Motion pictures

FREDERICK, Lee (pseud.) 1934-
ConAu X
Real Name:
Nussbaum, Albert F

Crash Dive
BL - v74 - Ja 15 '78 - p808
BL - v75 - O 15 '78 - p357
Subject: World War, 1939-1945—Fiction

see also Nussbaum, Albert F for additional titles

FREEDMAN, Benedict 1919-
BioIn 1, -3, ConAu 69, CurBio 47, SmATA 27, WhoAm 76

Mrs. Mike
BL - v43 - Mr 1 '47 - p205
Cath W - v165 - Jl '47 - p380
Comw - v45 - Mr 28 '47 - p596
CSM - F 28 '47 - p16
HB - v24 - Ja '48 - p69
KR - v15 - Ja 1 '47 - p5
LJ - v72 - F 15 '47 - p319
NY - v23 - Mr 1 '47 - p92
NYT - Mr 2 '47 - p5
SR - v30 - Mr 8 '47 - p31
WLB - v43 - Ap '47 - p68
Co-author: Freedman, Nancy
Subject: Flannigan, Katherine Mary—Fiction

FREEDMAN, Florence B 1908-

Two Tickets To Freedom
BL - v68 - Ja 15 '72 - p433
CCB-B - v26 - S '72 - p7
CSM - v63 - N 11 '71 - pB6
KR - v39 - O 1 '71 - p1075
LJ - v97 - Ap 15 '72 - p1604
PW - v200 - N 15 '71 - p72
Subject: Blacks—Biography

FREEDMAN, Nancy
see Freedman, Benedict (co-author)

FREEMAN, Mae Blacker 1907-
ConAu 73, MorJA, SmATA 25

Finding Out About The Past
CE - v44 - My '68 - p562
CLW - v39 - F '68 - p435
CSM - v60 - My 2 '68 - pB6
LJ - v93 - Ja 15 '68 - p290
SB - v4 - S '68 - p114
Subject: Archaeology

When Air Moves
CCB-B - v22 - S '68 - p7
KR - v36 - My 15 '68 - p551
LJ - v93 - S 15 '68 - p3301
SB - v4 - S '68 - p148
SR - v51 - Jl 20 '68 - p31
Subject: Aerodynamics

FREIDEL, Frank
see Sullivan, Wilson (co-author)

FREMON, David

Secrets Of The Super Athletes: Basketball
BL - v79 - O 15 '82 - p302
B Rpt - v1 - Mr '83 - p53
SLJ - v29 - D '82 - p85
Subject: Basketball

FRENCH, Dorothy Kayser 1926-
AuBYP, ConAu 3NR, IntAu&W 86, SmATA 5, WhoAmW 77

I Don't Belong Here
BL - v76 - Jl 15 '80 - p1673
CCB-B - v34 - S '80 - p7
Hi Lo - v2 - S '80 - p4
SLJ - v26 - Ap '80 - p124
Subject: Grandmothers—Fiction; Old age—Fiction

Out Of The Rough
BL - v78 - O 15 '81 - p289
J Read - v25 - My '82 - p817

Pioneer Saddle Mystery
SLJ - v22 - Mr '76 - p102
Subject: Mystery and detective stories; Physically handicapped—Fiction

FRENCH, Michael 1944-
ConAu 89, SmATA 49

The Throwing Season
BL - v76 - Je 1 '80 - p1418
CBRS - v8 - My '80 - p98
CCB-B - v33 - Je '80 - p189
EJ - v70 - F '81 - p62
Emerg Lib - v14 - S '86 - p22
Inter BC - v12 - #3 '81 p20
KR - v48 - My 15 '80 - p650
NYTBR - v85 - Ap 27 '80 - p56
NYTBR - v88 - D 25 '83 - p19
SLJ - v27 - N '80 - p85
VOYA - v7 - Ap '84 - p54
Subject: Bribery—Fiction; Indians of North America—Fiction; Track and field—Fiction

FRESE, Dolores Warwick
see Warwick, Dolores

FRICK, Constance H 1913-
BioIn 3, ConAu X, IntAu&W 77X, SmATA 6
Pseud./variant:
Irwin, Constance Frick

The Comeback Guy
BS - v25 - N 1 '65 - p310
CSM - My 11 '61 - p5B
HB - v37 - Ag '61 - p346
KR - v29 - Ja 1 '61 - p16
LJ - v86 - Ap 15 '61 - p1694
NYTBR, Pt. 2 - My 14 '61 - p34
Subject: Schools—Fiction

Five Against The Odds
BL - v52 - D 1 '55 - p149
KR - v23 - Je 1 '55 - p362
LJ - v80 - O 15 '55 - p2390
NYT - N 13 '55 - p20
SR - v38 - N 12 '55 - p68

FRIEDMAN, Ina Rosen 1926-
AuBYP SUP, ConAu 53, SmATA 49

Black Cop: A Biography Of Tilmon O'Bryant
BL - v70 - Jl 15 '74 - p1253
CCB-B - v28 - O '74 - p27
KR - v42 - Ap 15 '74 - p435
LJ - v99 - S 15 '74 - p2290
PW - v205 - F 18 '74 - p74
Subject: Blacks—Biography; Police

FRIEDMAN, Richard
see Fischler, Stanley I (co-author)

FRIES, Chloe

The Full Of The Moon
Hi Lo - Je '80 - p3
Subject: Fathers and sons—Fiction; Fishing—Fiction

No Place To Hide
Hi Lo - v1 - Mr '80 - p4
Subject: Brothers and sisters—Fiction; Earthquakes—Fiction

FRIIS-BAASTAD, Babbis 1921-1970
AuBYP SUP, ConAu 17R, ConLC 12, SmATA 7, ThrBJA

Don't Take Teddy
CCB-B - v20 - Jl '67 - p169
KR - v35 - F 1 '67 - p137
LJ - v92 - My 15 '67 - p2020
NYTBR - v72 - My 21 '67 - p30
SR - v50 - Ap 22 '67 - p100

Kristy's Courage
KR - v33 - Jl 15 '65 - p678
LJ - v90 - N 15 '65 - p5076
NYTBR - v70 - D 12 '65 - p26

FRITZ, Jean 1915-
ChILR 2, ConAu 16NR, DcLB 52, MorBMP, OxChL, SmATA 29, –2AS, ThrBJA, TwCChW 83, WrDr 86

Brady
B&B - v16 - Ag '71 - pR12
BL - v57 - Ja 15 '61 - p300
HB - v36 - D '60 - p512
KR - v28 - Ag 15 '60 - p682
LJ - v85 - S 15 '60 - p3215
Obs - Ap 10 '66 - p20
Obs - Jl 25 '71 - p23
Spec - Je 3 '66 - p706
TLS - My 19 '66 - p434
Subject: Underground railroad—Fiction

Early Thunder
BL - v64 - D 1 '67 - p446
BS - v27 - O 1 '67 - p263
BW - v1 - O 1 '67 - p24
Can Child Lit - #23 '81 p58
CCB-B - v21 - F '68 - p93
CLW - v39 - F '68 - p438
Comw - v87 - N 10 '67 - p180
HB - v43 - D '67 - p757
Inst - v77 - F '68 - p190
KR - v35 - O 1 '67 - p1218
LJ - v92 - N 15 '67 - p4260
NS - v77 - My 16 '69 - p700
NYTBR - v72 - O 22 '67 - p62
SR - v50 - N 11 '67 - p48

FRITZ, Jean (continued)
TLS - Ap 3 '69 - p350
TN - v24 - Ja '68 - p223
Subject: Salem (Mass.)—History—Fiction

What's The Big Idea, Ben Franklin?
BL - v73 - S 15 '76 - p174
BL - v82 - S 15 '85 - p143
BW - D 5 '76 - pH5
CCB-B - v30 - S '76 - p10
CE - v53 - Ja '77 - p152
Comw - v103 - N 19 '76 - p758
Cur R - v16 - D '77 - p363
HB - v52 - O '76 - p507
Inst - v96 - Ag '86 - p80
KR - v44 - Je 1 '76 - p636
LATBR - Jl 25 '82 - p9
LJ - v54 - F '77 - p211
NYTBR - Jl 4 '76 - p16
NYTBR - N 14 '76 - p52
PW - v209 - Je 7 '76 - p74
RT - v31 - O '77 - p18
SB - v13 - My '77 - p39
SE - v41 - Ap '77 - p347
SLJ - v23 - S '76 - p99
Teacher - v94 - N '76 - p134
Subject: Biography; Statesmen

Why Don't You Get A Horse, Sam Adams?
BB - v3 - Ap '75 - p3
BL - v71 - D 15 '74 - p423
BL - v71 - Mr 15 '75 - p766
BW - v12 - F 14 '82 - p12
CCB-B - v28 - Ap '75 - p129
CE - v52 - O '75 - p36
Choice - v12 - N '75 - p1132
Comw - v102 - N 21 '75 - p570
HB - v51 - F '75 - p57
KR - v43 - Ja 1 '75 - p20
LATBR - Jl 25 '82 - p9
LJ - v99 - D 15 '74 - p3262
NYTBR - N 3 '75 - p26
NYTBR - N 3 '75 - p55
Teacher - v92 - Ap '75 - p108
Subject: Biography; United States—History—Revolution, 1775-1783

FROLOV, Vadim 1913-
AuBYP SUP, TwCChW 83B

What It's All About
BW - v2 - N 3 '68 - p30
J Read - v25 - F '82 - p459
KR - v36 - Ag 1 '68 - p824
NYTBR - v73 - N 3 '68 - p2
PW - v194 - S 2 '68 - p58
SR - v51 - N 9 '68 - p71

FROMAN, Robert Winslow 1917-
AuBYP, ConAu 1NR, FourBJA, SmATA 8

Seeing Things
B&B - v22 - Je '77 - p72
CCB-B - v28 - S '74 - p7
EJ - v64 - F '75 - p102
KR - v42 - Mr 1 '74 - p248
LJ - v99 - S 15 '74 - p2245
NYTBR - My 5 '74 - p38
SLJ - v25 - N '78 - p30
WLB - v48 - My '74 - p718
Subject: American poetry

FROST, Betty

Voyage Of The Vagabond
BL - v78 - Je 15 '82 - p1365
Subject: Adventure and adventurers—Fiction

FUJA, Abayomi
AuBYP SUP

Fourteen Hundred Cowries And Other African Tales
BL - v68 - S 1 '71 - p56
CCB-B - v25 - N '71 - p42
CE - v48 - Ap '72 - p377
HB - v47 - Ag '71 - p379
KR - v39 - Ap 1 '71 - p372
LJ - v96 - D 15 '71 - p4158
LJ - v96 - D 15 '71 - p4184
Subject: Folklore

FULLER, Elizabeth

My Search For The Ghost Of Flight 401
BL - v75 - Ap 1 '79 - p1212
Kliatt - v13 - Spring '79 - p33
Subject: Aeronautics; Ghosts; Spiritualism

FURNISS, Cathy
see Lipman, Michel (co-author)

FUTCHER, Jane

Crush
HB - v57 - D '81 - p668
Kliatt - v18 - Spring '84 - p8
PW - v220 - D 11 '81 - p62
SLJ - v28 - D '81 - p70
VOYA - v4 - D '81 - p29
Subject: Schools—Fiction

G

GAEDDERT, Lou Ann 1931-
BkP, ConAu 13NR, SmATA 20

Just Like Sisters
BL - v78 - D 15 '81 - p548
CBRS - v10 - F '82 - p66
HB - v58 - F '82 - p41
KR - v50 - F 1 '82 - p135
PW - v220 - D 11 '81 - p62
SLJ - v28 - O '81 - p141
Subject: Cousins—Fiction; Divorce—Fiction

GAINES, Ernest J 1933-
AuBYP SUP, BlkAWP, ConAu 6NR, ConLC 3, -11, -18, ConNov 86, DcLB 2, -33, -Y80A, ModBlW

The Autobiography Of Miss Jane Pitman
A Lib - v2 - S '71 - p897
BL - v67 - Jl 15 '71 - p930
BL - v68 - Ap 1 '72 - p664
Bl W - v20 - O '71 - p88
BS - v31 - N 1 '71 - p354
BS - v32 - Jl 1 '72 - p180
Comw - v95 - Ja 21 '72 - p380
CSM - v63 - Je 3 '71 - p9
CSM - v64 - N 26 '71 - pB3
EJ - v63 - Ja '74 - p65
KR - v39 - F 15 '71 - p190
Life - v70 - Ap 30 '71 - p18
Lis - v89 - F 8 '73 - p189
LJ - v96 - Mr 1 '71 - p860
LJ - v96 - Ap 15 '71 - p1536
LJ - v96 - D 15 '71 - p4161
Nat - v212 - Ap 5 '71 - p436
NS - v85 - F 9 '73 - p205
NW - v77 - My 3 '71 - p103
NYTBR - My 23 '71 - p6
NYTBR - D 5 '71 - p82
Obs - F 4 '73 - p36
PW - v199 - Mr 8 '71 - p64
SR - v54 - My 1 '71 - p40
SR - v54 - N 27 '71 - p46
Time - v97 - My 10 '71 - pK13
TLS - Mr 16 '73 - p303
TN - v28 - Ap '72 - p312
Subject: Civil rights; Slavery—Fiction

GAINES, M C

Picture Stories From The Bible: The New Testament In Full-Color Comic-Strip Form
SLJ - v27 - S '80 - p58
SLJ - v27 - F '81 - p56
Subject: Bible

GALAN, Fernando Javier

One Summer
BL - v80 - Jl '84 - p1525

GALBRAITH, Catherine Atwater

India: Now And Through Time
BL - v68 - Ap 1 '72 - p671
BS - v31 - D 15 '71 - p433
HB - v48 - Ap '72 - p158
LA - v58 - Mr '81 - p342
LJ - v97 - F 15 '72 - p784
NYTBR - F 27 '72 - p8
SLJ - v27 - Ja '81 - p69
Co-author: Mehta, Rama
Subject: India

GALLAGHER, I J

The Case Of The Ancient Astronauts
Cur R - v17 - Ag '78 - p227
SLJ - v25 - S '78 - p128
Subject: Civilization; Interplanatary voyages; Man (Prehistoric)

GALLANT, Roy A 1924-
AuBYP, ConAu 4NR, ConLC 17, FifBJA, SmATA 4, WhoE 85, WrDr 86

Exploring The Universe
CSM - v60 - N 7 '68 - p89
KR - v36 - Je 15 '68 - p653
LJ - v93 - O 15 '68 - p3970
SB - v4 - S '68 - p98
Subject: Astronomy

Man Must Speak: The Story Of Language And How We Use It
BL - v66 - Je 15 '70 - p1272
BS - v29 - N 1 '69 - p306
KR - v37 - N 1 '69 - p1158

GALLANT, Roy A (continued)
LJ - v95 - Jl '70 - p2539
Subject: Language and languages

Man's Reach For The Stars
BL - v68 - O 1 '71 - p159
BS - v31 - D 15 '71 - p433
CLW - v43 - My '72 - p536
KR - v39 - Ag 1 '71 - p818
LJ - v96 - S 15 '71 - p2928
SB - v7 - Mr '72 - p328
Subject: Astronautics; Outer space—Exploration

GALLO, Donald R

Sixteen: Short Stories By Outstanding Young Adult Writers
BL - v81 - S 1 '84 - p60
CBRS - v13 - O '84 - p19
CCB-B - v38 - F '85 - p106
Cur R - v25 - S '85 - p60
Kliatt - v20 - Winter '86 - p29
KR - v52 - S 1 '84 - pJ79
SLJ - v31 - O '84 - p166
VOYA - v7 - F '85 - p332
VOYA - v8 - D '85 - p344
WLB - v59 - Ja '85 - p340
Subject: Short stories

GARCIA, Ann O'Neal

Spirit On The Wall
BL - v78 - Je 1 '82 - p1312
BS - v42 - Je '82 - p119
CBRS - v10 - Je '82 - p106
CLW - v54 - Mr '83 - p334
Inst - v91 - My '82 - p107
J Read - v26 - Ja '83 - p375
PW - v221 - F 12 '82 - p98
RT - v36 - O '82 - p117
SLJ - v28 - Mr '82 - p147
VOYA - v5 - O '82 - p42
Subject: Cave dwellers—Fiction; Grandmothers—Fiction; Physically handicapped—Fiction

GARDAM, Jane 1928-
AuBYP SUP, ChlLR 12, ConAu 18NR, DcLB 14, FifBJA, OxChL, SmATA 39, TwCChW 83, WrDr 86

The Summer After The Funeral
B&B - v19 - Ja '74 - p93
BL - v70 - F 1 '74 - p592
CCB-B - v27 - Ap '74 - p128
Comw - v99 - N 23 '73 - p216
Emerg Lib - v12 - S '84 - p44
HB - v50 - F '74 - p55
ILN - v265 - My '77 - p87
KR - v41 - N 1 '73 - p1211
KR - v41 - D 15 '73 - p1356
Lis - v90 - N 8 '73 - p641
LJ - v98 - O 15 '73 - p3154
NO - v12 - D 29 '73 - p15
NS - v86 - N 9 '73 - p699
NYTBR - F 17 '74 - p8
Obs - Mr 6 '77 - p22
Spec - v231 - D 22 '73 - p822
TES - D 23 '83 - p23
TLS - N 23 '73 - p1429
Subject: England—Fiction

GARDEN, Nancy 1938-
AuBYP SUP, ConAu 13NR, DrAP&F 85, FifBJA, SmATA 12, WrDr 86

The Loners
BL - v69 - F 1 '73 - p524
CCB-B - v26 - Ap '73 - p123
KR - v40 - N 1 '72 - p1245
LJ - v98 - Mr 15 '73 - p1012
NYTBR, Pt. 2 - N 5 '72 - p2
Subject: Drug abuse—Fiction

Vampires
KR - v41 - Mr 1 '73 - p261
LJ - v98 - Jl '73 - p2199
Teacher - v90 - My '73 - p78
Subject: Vampires

Werewolves
KR - v41 - Ap 1 '73 - p400
LJ - v98 - Jl '73 - p2199
Teacher - v90 - My '73 - p78
Subject: Werewolves

GARDNER, Lewis
see Burger, John Robert (co-author)

GARDNER, Martin 1914-
AuBYP SUP, BioIn 6, -10, -12, -13, ConAu 73, SmATA 16

Codes, Ciphers, And Secret Writing
BL - v69 - F 15 '73 - p572
CCB-B - v26 - F '73 - p89
Inst - v83 - My '74 - p97
Kliatt - v19 - Fall '85 - p66
KR - v40 - N 15 '72 - p1316
LJ - v98 - My 15 '73 - p1681
Par - v48 - Ap '73 - p67
PW - v203 - Ja 15 '73 - p65
SB - v9 - My '73 - p62
Subject: Ciphers

GARDNER, Richard Alan 1931-
AuBYP SUP, ConAu 33R, SmATA 13, WhoE 77, WhoWor 78, WrDr 86

The Boys And Girls Book About Stepfamilies
CE - v60 - My '84 - p308
Kliatt - v16 - Spring '82 - p46
Subject: Stepparents

GARDNER, Sandra

Six Who Dared
BL - v78 - Ja 15 '82 - p644
CCB-B - v35 - My '82 - p168
Hi Lo - v3 - Mr '82 - p1
SLJ - v29 - S '82 - p121
Subject: Adventure and adventurers; Stunt men and women

GARFIELD, Leon 1921-
ConAu 17R, ConLC 12, FourBJA, OxChL, PiP, SenS, SmATA 32, TwCChW 83, WhoChL, WrDr 86

Smith
B&B - v12 - Je '67 - p36
B&B - v13 - Ag '68 - p49
BL - v64 - F 1 '68 - p637
BS - v27 - N 1 '67 - p313
BW - v1 - N 5 '67 - p43
CCB-B - v21 - My '68 - p141
Comw - v87 - N 10 '67 - p181
EJ - v72 - S '83 - p71
HB - v43 - D '67 - p758
KR - v35 - Jl 1 '67 - p746
Lis - v77 - My 18 '67 - p660
LJ - v92 - N 15 '67 - p4250
LR - v21 - Summer '67 - p93
NS - v73 - My 26 '67 - p732
NYTBR - v72 - N 26 '67 - p62
PW - v192 - O 23 '67 - p52
Spec - v218 - Je 2 '67 - p654
SR - v51 - F 24 '68 - p51
TLS - My 25 '67 - p446
Subject: London—Fiction

GARLITS, Don

King Of The Dragsters: The Story Of Big Daddy Garlits
KR - v35 - Ag 1 '67 - p923
LJ - v93 - F 15 '68 - p896
Co-author: Yates, Brock
Subject: Drag racing

GARRATY, John A 1920-
BioIn 10, ConAu 2NR, DcLB 17, DrAS 82H, SmATA 23, WhoAm 80

Theodore Roosevelt: The Strenuous Life
BL - v64 - S 15 '67 - p130
BS - v27 - Ag 1 '67 - p183
CCB-B - v21 - D '67 - p54
CLW - v39 - Ja '68 - p373
KR - v35 - Je 1 '67 - p652
LJ - v92 - N 15 '67 - p4260
NYTBR - v72 - Jl 16 '67 - p20
PW - v191 - Je 5 '67 - p176
Subject: Biography

GARRIGUE, Sheila 1931-
AuBYP SUP, ConAu 69, SmATA 21

Between Friends
BB - v6 - N '78 - p4
BL - v74 - Je 15 '78 - p1616
CCB-B - v32 - O '78 - p28
CLW - v50 - S '78 - p92
Cur R - v17 - O '78 - p272
Inst - v88 - N '78 - p140
KR - v46 - Je 15 '78 - p636
NYTBR - Ap 30 '78 - p28
Par - v53 - O '78 - p40
PW - v213 - My 22 '78 - p233
SLJ - v24 - My '78 - p66
Teacher - v96 - O '78 - p162
Subject: Friendship—Fiction; Moving (Household)—Fiction

GARRISON, Webb B 1919-
ConAu 18NR, SmATA 25

What's In A Word?
BL - v62 - D 1 '65 - p344
LJ - v90 - N 15 '65 - p4979
SR - v49 - Mr 19 '66 - p35
Subject: English language

Why You Say It
BL - v52 - O 1 '55 - p49
KR - v23 - Ag 1 '55 - p568
Subject: English language

GASKIN, Carol

The Forbidden Towers
SLJ - v32 - S '85 - p153
Subject: Fantasy; Plot-your-own-stories

The Magician's Ring
SLJ - v32 - S '85 - p153
Subject: Fantasy; Plot-your-own-stories

GASKIN, Carol (continued)

Master Of Mazes
SLJ - v32 - S '85 - p153
Subject: Fantasy; Plot-your-own-stories

The War Of The Wizards
SLJ - v32 - S '85 - p153
Subject: Fantasy; Magic—Fiction; Plot-your-own-stories

GATES, Doris 1901-
Au&ICB, AuBYP, BioIn 1, ConAu 1NR, DcLB 22, JBA 51, SmATA 34, -1AS, TwCChW 83, WrDr 86

Blue Willow
BL - v37 - N 15 '40 - p122
CSM - N 11 '40 - p9
HB - v16 - N '40 - p430
HB - v16 - N '40 - p437
LJ - v65 - N 15 '40 - p983
Nat - v151 - N 9 '40 - p455
New R - v103 - D 16 '40 - p844
NY - v16 - D 7 '40 - p128
NYT - Ja 5 '41 - p10
Subject: Migrant labor—Fiction

GATHJE, Curtis

The Disco Kid
BL - v76 - O 15 '79 - p347
CBRS - v8 - D '79 - p37
Hi Lo - v1 - D '79 - p4
SLJ - v26 - N '79 - p77
VOYA - v4 - Ag '81 - p47
Subject: Disco dancing—Fiction

GAUCH, Patricia Lee 1934-
ConAu 9NR, FifBJA, SmATA 26

Fridays
BL - v76 - N 15 '79 - p501
CBRS - v8 - N '79 - p27
HB - v56 - F '80 - p60
KR - v47 - D 1 '79 - p1379
NYTBR - F 17 '80 - p24
SLJ - v26 - Ja '80 - p78
Subject: Friendship—Fiction

GAULT, Clare 1925-
ConAu 97, SmATA 36

Pele: The King Of Soccer
Cur R - v15 - D '76 - p315
Co-author: Gault, Frank
Subject: Soccer—Biography

GAULT, Frank
see Gault, Clare (co-author)

GAULT, William Campbell 1910-
AuBYP, BioIn 5, ConAu 16NR, EncMys, SmATA 8, TwCCr&M 85, WrDr 86

Backfield Challenge
BL - v64 - O 1 '67 - p176
CCB-B - v21 - S '67 - p5
KR - v35 - Ap 15 '67 - p505
LJ - v92 - My 15 '67 - p2042
SR - v50 - Jl 22 '67 - p43

The Big Stick
BL - v72 - N 1 '75 - p366
KR - v43 - Ag 1 '75 - p856
SLJ - v22 - D '75 - p69
Subject: Hockey—Fiction

The Checkered Flag
BS - v24 - My 15 '64 - p87
HB - v40 - Ag '64 - p380
LJ - v89 - My 15 '64 - p2228
Subject: Automobile racing—Fiction

Dirt Track Summer
BL - v57 - Ap 15 '61 - p523
CSM - My 11 '61 - p5B
KR - v28 - D 15 '60 - p1034
NYTBR, Pt. 2 - My 14 '61 - p34
Subject: Automobile racing—Fiction

Drag Strip
BL - v56 - Ja 1 '60 - p271
CSM - N 5 '60 - p3B
KR - v27 - Ag 1 '59 - p553
LJ - v85 - Ja 15 '60 - p358
NYTBR, Pt. 2 - N 1 '59 - p28
Subject: Automobile racing—Fiction

The Long Green
BL - v62 - O 1 '65 - p144
BS - v25 - Ap 15 '65 - p51
KR - v33 - Ja 15 '65 - p65
LJ - v90 - Mr 15 '65 - p1559

Quarterback Gamble
BL - v67 - Ja 1 '71 - p372
CLW - v43 - O '71 - p116
KR - v38 - Jl 15 '70 - p748
LJ - v95 - D 15 '70 - p4380
LJ - v96 - Ja 15 '71 - p284
Subject: Football—Fiction

Speedway Challenge
BL - v53 - O 15 '56 - p96
KR - v24 - S 1 '56 - p634
NYTBR - S 16 '56 - p38

GAULT, William Campbell (continued)
SR - v39 - N 17 '56 - p70
Subject: Automobile racing—Fiction

Thin Ice
BL - v75 - N 1 '78 - p478
KR - v46 - S 1 '78 - p953
Subject: Hockey—Fiction

Thunder Road
BL - v49 - O 15 '52 - p72
HB - v28 - D '52 - p426
KR - v20 - S 15 '52 - p606
LJ - v77 - O 1 '52 - p1668
NYTBR - S 28 '52 - p38
SR - v35 - N 15 '52 - p62
Subject: Automobile racing—Fiction

GEE, Maurine H
AuBYP SUP

Firestorm
KR - v35 - D 15 '67 - p1471
Obs - My 19 '68 - p1309

GELFAND, M Howard

Paul Mccartney
BL - v81 - Je 15 '85 - p1453
Subject: Musicians; Rock musicians

GELMAN, Jan

Summer In The Sun
Kliatt - v17 - Spring '83 - p6
VOYA - v6 - O '83 - p210
Subject: Summer resorts—Fiction

GELMAN, Steve 1934-
AuBYP SUP, ConAu 16NR, SmATA 3

Young Olympic Champions
BL - v70 - O 1 '73 - p170
KR - v41 - Ap 15 '73 - p459
Subject: Athletes; Olympic Games

GEMME, Leila Boyle 1942-
ConAu 81

Ten-Speed Taylor
BL - v75 - O 15 '78 - p390
RT - v32 - My '79 - p975
SLJ - v25 - D '78 - p71
Subject: Bicyles and bicyling—Fiction

GENNARO, Joseph
see Grillone, Lisa (co-author)

GEORGE, Jean Craighead 1919-
ChlLR 1, ConAu 5R, ConLC 35, DcLB 52, MorBMP, MorJA, OxChL, SmATA 2, TwCChW 83, WrDr 86

Julie Of The Wolves
BFYC - v20 - Spring '85 - p4
BL - v69 - F 1 '73 - p529
BS - v33 - Ap 15 '73 - p45
BS - v7 - My 13 '73 - p6
BW - v11 - My 10 '81 - p14
CCB-B - v26 - Mr '73 - p105
CE - v49 - Mr '73 - p317
Cur R - v22 - F '83 - p83
HB - v49 - F '73 - p54
KR - v40 - N 15 '72 - p1312
KR - v40 - D 15 '72 - p1418
LA - v60 - Ap '83 - p438
LJ - v98 - Ja 15 '73 - p267
NYTBR - Ja 21 '73 - p8
PW - v203 - F 12 '73 - p66
SE - v44 - O '80 - p479
SLJ - v31 - Ag '85 - p28
Teacher - v90 - My '73 - p43
Subject: Eskimos—Fiction; Survival—Fiction; Wolves—Fiction

River Rats, Inc.
BB - v7 - Ja '80 - p3
BL - v75 - Mr 15 '79 - p1156
HB - v55 - Ap '79 - p193
Kliatt - v17 - Spring '83 - p8
KR - v47 - Jl 1 '79 - p740
PW - v215 - F 12 '79 - p127
SLJ - v25 - Mr '79 - p139
Subject: Feral children—Fiction; Survival—Fiction

Who Really Killed Cock Robin?
BL - v68 - D 15 '71 - p366
BW - v5 - N 7 '71 - p14
CCB-B - v25 - Ja '72 - p74
CE - v48 - My '72 - p421
CSM - v64 - D 30 '71 - p6
HB - v47 - D '71 - p610
KR - v39 - S 1 '71 - p945
LJ - v96 - D 15 '71 - p4184
SB - v8 - My '72 - p49
SR - v55 - F 19 '72 - p80
TN - v28 - Ap '72 - p309
Subject: Ecology—Fiction

GERBER, Dan 1940-
ConAu 33R

Indy
BL - v73 - Jl 1 '77 - p1626
KR - v45 - Mr 1 '77 - p258
LJ - v102 - Mr 15 '77 - p724

GERBER, Dan (continued)
SLJ - v24 - Mr '78 - p106
Subject: Automobile racing

GERBER, Merrill Joan

Please Don't Kiss Me Now
BL - v77 - My 1 '81 - p1191
BS - v41 - Ag '81 - p197
CBRS - v9 - Ap '81 - p77
CCB-B - v34 - My '81 - p170
Kliatt - v16 - Fall '82 - p10
KR - v49 - S 1 '81 - p1086
SLJ - v27 - My '81 - p73
Subject: Divorce—Fiction; Mothers and daughters—Fiction; Single-parent family—Fiction

GERGEN, Joe

World Series Heroes And Goats: The Men Who Made History In America's October Classic
BL - v79 - Ja 1 '83 - p622
SLJ - v29 - D '82 - p85
Subject: Baseball

GERINGER, Laura 1948-
BioIn 13, ConAu 107, SmATA 29

Seven True Bear Stories
Hi Lo - v1 - F '80 - p3
LA - v56 - N '79 - p930
PW - v215 - Ap 30 '79 - p114
SLJ - v25 - Ap '79 - p42
SR - v6 - My 26 '79 - p63
Subject: Bears

GERSH, Marvin J

The Handbook Of Adolescence
BL - v68 - D 15 '71 - p345
KR - v39 - Je 1 '71 - p595
LJ - v96 - N 15 '71 - p3917
Subject: Adolescence; Health

GERSON, Corinne 1927-
ConAu 93, DrAP&F 85, SmATA 37

Passing Through
BL - v75 - O 1 '78 - p284
EJ - v68 - N '79 - p76
EJ - v68 - D '79 - p78
Emerg Lib - v9 - N '81 - p32
Inter BC - v13 - #4 '82 p15
SLJ - v25 - O '78 - p154
TN - v36 - Summer '80 - p366
TN - v42 - Summer '86 - p380
Subject: Friendship—Fiction; Physically handicapped—Fiction; Suicide—Fiction

GIBSON, Walter B 1897-1985
BioIn 7, ConAu 110, -118, EncMys, TwCCr&M 85, WrDr 86

Master Magicians: Their Lives And Most Famous Tricks
BL - v63 - N 1 '66 - p308
KR - v34 - Je 1 '66 - p542
LJ - v91 - S 15 '66 - p4350
Subject: Magicians

GIFF, Patricia Reilly 1935-
ConAu 18NR, FifBJA, SmATA 33

Suspect
BL - v78 - Ag '82 - p1520
CBRS - v10 - Ag '82 - p138
Hi Lo - v4 - O '82 - p8
SLJ - v29 - D '82 - p82
Subject: Crime and criminals—Fiction

GILBER, E S
see Erskine, H Keith (co-author)

GILBERT, Miriam 1919-
ConAu X, IntAu&W 77X, SmATA X, WhoAmW 77, WrDr 82
Pseud./variant:
Presberg, Miriam Goldstein

Glory Be! The Career Of A Young Hair Stylist
KR - v35 - Ap 1 '67 - p423
Subject: Occupations—Fiction

Shy Girl: The Story Of Eleanor Roosevelt
SE - v48 - N '84 - p543
Subject: Biography

GILBERT, Sara Dulaney 1943-
AuBYP SUP, ConAu 6NR, SmATA 11

Fat Free
BB - v3 - Ag '75 - p4
BL - v71 - Mr 1 '75 - p690
BL - v82 - S 1 '85 - p74
CCB-B - v29 - O '75 - p27
CLW - v47 - N '75 - p187
Comw - v102 - N 21 '75 - p571
KR - v43 - F 1 '75 - p129
NYTBR - My 4 '75 - p25
PW - v207 - My 26 '75 - p60
Subject: Weight control

Feeling Good: A Book About You And Your Body
BL - v75 - D 1 '78 - p613
KR - v46 - S 1 '78 - p954

GILBERT, Sara Dulaney (continued)
SLJ - v25 - S '78 - p157
WCRB - v4 - N '78 - p60
Subject: Adolescence; Health

How To Live With A Single Parent
BL - v78 - F 15 '82 - p753
BS - v42 - Ag '82 - p202
CBRS - v10 - Ap '82 - p88
CCB-B - v35 - My '82 - p168
CLW - v54 - D '82 - p224
Kliatt - v16 - Fall '82 - p38
SB - v18 - Mr '83 - p212
SLJ - v28 - My '82 - p69
VOYA - v5 - O '82 - p54
VOYA - v9 - D '86 - p205
Subject: Single-parent family

Ready, Set, Go: How To Find A Career That's Right For You
BL - v76 - N 15 '79 - p493
EJ - v69 - My '80 - p75
KR - v47 - D 1 '79 - p1381
SB - v16 - N '80 - p66
SLJ - v26 - F '80 - p66
Subject: Vocational guidance

Trouble At Home
BL - v77 - My 1 '81 - p1190
CBRS - v9 - Je '81 - p96
CCB-B - v34 - My '81 - p171
J Read - v25 - Ja '82 - p390
KR - v49 - Ap 15 '81 - p509
SLJ - v27 - Ag '81 - p74
VOYA - v4 - D '81 - p42
Subject: Family problems

GILBRETH, Frank B, Jr. 1911-
BioIn 2, ConAu 9R, ConLC 17, CurBio 49, SmATA 2, WhoAm 86

Cheaper By The Dozen
NYTBR - Ja 9 '49 - p18
Co-author: Carey, Ernestine Gilbreth
Subject: Gilbreth, Frank Bunker; Gilbreth, Lillian Evelyn

GILDEA, William
see Brown, Larry (co-author)

GILFOND, Henry
ConAu 9NR, NatPD 81, SmATA 2

Genealogy: How To Find Your Roots
BL - v74 - Ap 15 '78 - p1348
BL - v82 - F 15 '86 - p876
SLJ - v25 - S '78 - p157
Subject: Genealogy

GILL, Derek L T 1919-
ConAu 19NR, SmATA 9

Tom Sullivan's Adventures In Darkness
BL - v73 - My 1 '77 - p1351
CCB-B - v30 - Je '77 - p157
Kliatt - v12 - Winter '78 - p22
KR - v44 - N 15 '76 - p1227
SLJ - v23 - F '77 - p71
Subject: Biography; Blind; Musicians

GILL, Frances M
see Abbe, Kathryn M (co-author)

GILLIANTI, Simone

Rick Springfield
BL - v81 - N 1 '84 - p367
SLJ - v31 - F '85 - p84
Subject: Actors and actresses; Musicians

GILLIS, Ruby

Get Where You're Going
Hi Lo - v2 - S '80 - p6

GILMAN, Dorothy 1923-
BioIn 7, -12, ConAu X, SmATA 5, TwCCr&M 85, WhoAm 86, WorAl, WrDr 86
Pseud./variant:
Butters, Dorothy Gilman

The Elusive Mrs. Polifax
BL - v68 - D 15 '71 - p353
BS - v31 - O 15 '71 - p314
KR - v39 - Jl 15 '71 - p771
LJ - v96 - S 1 '71 - p2674
NYT - v121 - Ja 1 '72 - p17
NYTBR - D 12 '71 - p39
PW - v200 - Jl 5 '71 - p49
Subject: Mystery and detective stories

GILSON, Jamie Marie 1933-
ConAu 111, SmATA 37, WhoAmW 87

Can't Catch Me, I'm The Gingerbread Man
BL - v77 - My 1 '81 - p1196
BL - v82 - S 1 '85 - p74
CBRS - v9 - Je '81 - p96
CCB-B - v34 - My '81 - p171
CE - v58 - Mr '82 - p257
Kliatt - v17 - Winter '83 - p8
KR - v49 - Jl 15 '81 - p872
LA - v58 - S '81 - p700

GILSON, Jamie Marie (continued)
PW - v222 - D 3 '82 - p60
SLJ - v28 - S '81 - p124
Subject: Baking—Fiction; Family life—Fiction

Dial Leroi Rupert, DJ
BL - v75 - Je 1 '79 - p1491
CBRS - v7 - Ag '79 - p137
KR - v47 - Je 15 '79 - p686
SLJ - v26 - S '79 - p138
Subject: Disc jockeys—Fiction; Musicians—Fiction

Do Bananas Chew Gum?
BL - v77 - N 1 '80 - p404
CCB-B - v34 - Mr '81 - p133
Inter BC - v13 - #4 '82 p8
KR - v48 - D 15 '80 - p1570
SLJ - v26 - Ag '80 - p64
SLJ - v32 - Ja '86 - p30
VOYA - v4 - Ap '81 - p34
Subject: Reading disability—Fiction

GIOFFRE, Marisa

Starstruck
BL - v82 - Mr 1 '86 - p1018
VOYA - v8 - F '86 - p384
Subject: Mothers and daughters—Fiction; Occupations—Fiction

GIPSON, Frederick B 1908-1973
AuBYP, BioIn 12, ConAu 3NR, -45, CurBio 57, EncFWF, SmATA 2, -24N, ThrBJA, TwCChW 83

Old Yeller
BL - v52 - Je 15 '56 - p421
BL - v53 - S 1 '56 - p21
CSM - Jl 12 '56 - p7
HB - v32 - O '56 - p371
KR - v24 - My 1 '56 - p320
LJ - v81 - Jl '56 - p1699
NY - v32 - Jl 14 '56 - p93
NYTBR - Jl 15 '56 - p5
SR - v39 - Jl 21 '56 - p17
SR - v39 - N 17 '56 - p70
Time - v68 - Jl 23 '56 - p88

Savage Sam
NYTBR - F 25 '62 - p37

GIRION, Barbara 1937-
ConAu 15NR, SmATA 26

In The Middle Of A Rainbow
BL - v79 - Je 15 '83 - p1333
EJ - v73 - D '84 - p66
J Read - v27 - D '83 - p281
J Read - v29 - D '85 - p276
SLJ - v30 - O '83 - p167
VOYA - v6 - D '83 - p279
Subject: Love—Fiction

A Tangle Of Roots
BL - v75 - My 1 '79 - p1356
B Rpt - v1 - Mr '83 - p24
CCB-B - v33 - N '79 - p47
CSM - v71 - Jl 9 '79 - pB6
EJ - v68 - N '79 - p76
EJ - v69 - N '80 - p88
Kliatt - v15 - Fall '81 - p10
KR - v47 - Ap 1 '79 - p392
SLJ - v25 - My '79 - p71
Subject: Death—Fiction; Fathers and daughters—Fiction

GLASER, Dianne 1937-
ConAu 77, SmATA 31

The Diary Of Trilby Frost
BB - v4 - N '76 - p2
BL - v72 - My 1 '76 - p1264
HB - v52 - Ag '76 - p404
KR - v44 - My 1 '76 - p541
PW - v209 - Je 28 '76 - p99
SE - v41 - Ap '77 - p350
SLJ - v23 - S '76 - p133
TN - v37 - Fall '80 - p59
Subject: Death—Fiction

GLASNER, Lynne
see Thypin, Marilyn (co-author)

GLASS, Frankcina

Marvin And Tige
BL - v74 - D 1 '77 - p601
BS - v37 - Ja '78 - p302
CSM - v70 - Ja 23 '78 - p11
KR - v45 - Ag 15 '77 - p869
LJ - v102 - O 15 '77 - p2181
PW - v212 - Ag 29 '77 - p354
SLJ - v24 - F '78 - p69
WCRB - v4 - Ja '78 - p30
WLB - v52 - Ja '78 - p430
Subject: Loneliness—Fiction; Love—Fiction

GLASSMAN, Carl

Dangerous Lives
BL - v76 - Je 15 '80 - p1520
SLJ - v27 - F '81 - p74

GLENDINNING, Richard 1917-
ConAu 21R, SmATA 24, WhoS&SW 76

Circus Days Under The Big Top
LJ - v95 - D 15 '70 - p4371
Subject: Circus

GLENN, Mel 1943-
SmATA 45

Class Dismissed II
KR - v54 - O 1 '86 - p1522
Subject: American poetry; High schools—Poetry

One Order To Go
BL - v81 - O 1 '84 - p211
CBRS - v13 - Ja '85 - p51
J Read - v28 - My '85 - p759
SLJ - v31 - D '84 - p89
Subject: Fathers and sons—Fiction

GLICKMAN, William G

Winners On The Tennis Court
BL - v74 - Ap 15 '78 - p1357
Subject: Tennis—Biography

GLOECKNER, Carolyn

Fernando Valenzuela
BL - v81 - Jl '85 - p1562
Subject: Baseball—Biography

Sugar Ray Leonard
BL - v81 - Jl '85 - p1562
Subject: Blacks—Biography; Boxing—Biography

GLUBOK, Shirley 1933-
AuBYP, ChlLR 1, ConAu 4NR, MorBMP, SmATA 6, ThrBJA, WhoAmW 77, WrDr 86

Art And Archaeology
BL - v62 - Jl 15 '66 - p1086
CCB-B - v20 - S '66 - p9
CSM - v58 - N 3 '66 - pB5
KR - v34 - My 1 '66 - p476
LJ - v91 - Je 15 '66 - p3258
NYTBR - v71 - My 8 '66 - p34
PW - v189 - My 30 '66 - p89
SB - v2 - D '66 - p198
SR - v49 - My 14 '66 - p42
Subject: Archaeology

The Art Of Ancient Peru
BL - v63 - D 1 '66 - p416
BL - v82 - D 1 '85 - p582
CCB-B - v20 - Ja '67 - p73
CLW - v38 - Ja '67 - p336
HB - v43 - F '67 - p87
LJ - v91 - D 15 '66 - p6191
NH - v76 - N '67 - p29
NYT - v116 - F 2 '67 - p26
SR - v49 - N 12 '66 - p50
Subject: Art; Indians of South America

The Art Of Colonial America
BL - v67 - N 15 '70 - p268
CE - v47 - F '71 - p266
CLW - v42 - D '70 - p257
Comw - v93 - N 20 '70 - p206
HB - v47 - Je '71 - p299
KR - v38 - Jl 15 '70 - p745
LJ - v95 - O 15 '70 - p3626
NYTBR, Pt. 2 - N 8 '70 - p3
PW - v198 - O 19 '70 - p53
Subject: Art

The Art Of The New American Nation
BL - v68 - Jl 1 '72 - p942
CCB-B - v26 - N '72 - p42
HB - v48 - Ag '72 - p386
KR - v40 - My 1 '72 - p538
NYTBR - Jl 2 '72 - p8
PW - v201 - My 15 '72 - p54
Subject: Art

The Art Of The Spanish In The United States And Puerto Rico
BL - v69 - Ja 1 '73 - p448
BL - v69 - Ja 15 '73 - p479
CC - v89 - N 29 '72 - p1218
CCB-B - v26 - Mr '73 - p106
CE - v49 - Ap '73 - p378
HB - v49 - F '73 - p64
Inst - v82 - N '72 - p132
KR - v40 - O 1 '72 - p1147
LJ - v98 - Mr 15 '73 - p1002
PW - v203 - Ja 15 '73 - p65
Subject: Art

GODFREY, Martyn

The Beast
Emerg Lib - v13 - N '85 - p45
Subject: Monsters—Fiction

Fire! Fire!
Emerg Lib - v14 - S '86 - p51
Quill & Q - v52 - F '86 - p21
Subject: Firefighters—Fiction; Sex role—Fiction

Ice Hawk
Emerg Lib - v14 - S '86 - p51
Quill & Q - v52 - F '86 - p21
Subject: Hockey—Fiction; Schools—Fiction

GODFREY, Martyn (continued)

Spin Out
Emerg Lib - v13 - N '85 - p45
Subject: Prisoners—Fiction

GOFFSTEIN, M B 1940-
AuBYP SUP, ChlLR 3, ConAu 21R, FourBJA, IlsCB 1967, SmATA 8, WhoAmW 77

Daisy Summerfield's Style
BS - v35 - D '75 - p300
BW - F 11 '79 - pF2
CCB-B - v29 - F '76 - p96
HB - v52 - F '76 - p56
J Read - v20 - O '76 - p80
KR - v438 - O 1 '75 - p1137
PW - v208 - S 8 '75 - p60
SLJ - v22 - N '75 - p89
Subject: Artists—Fiction

The Underside Of The Leaf
BL - v69 - S 15 '72 - p86
BW - v6 - My 7 '72 - p15
CCB-B - v26 - O '72 - p25
EJ - v61 - D '72 - p1385
KR - v40 - Ap 15 '72 - p485
KR - v40 - D 15 '72 - p1419
LJ - v97 - N 15 '72 - p3813
NYTBR - My 28 '72 - p8
PW - v201 - My 15 '72 - p53
Subject: Adolescence—Fiction

GOGOLAK, Peter 1942-
WhoFtbl 74

Kicking The Football Soccer Style
BW - v6 - D 3 '72 - p10
LJ - v98 - Ja 15 '73 - p179
LJ - v98 - My 15 '73 - p1704
Subject: Football; Soccer

GOHMAN, Fred 1918-
ConAu 5R

Spider Webb Mysteries
LJ - v94 - My 15 '69 - p2124
Subject: Mystery and detective stories

GOLD, Sharlya
BioIn 11, ConAu 8NR, SmATA 9

Amelia Quackenbush
Am - v129 - D 1 '73 - p429
BL - v70 - Ja 1 '74 - p488
CSM - v66 - My 1 '74 - pF4
KR - v41 - N 1 '73 - p1200
LJ - v99 - Ja 15 '74 - p209

Time To Take Sides
BB - v5 - My '77 - p4
CLW - v48 - Mr '77 - p358
Inst - v86 - N '76 - p146
KR - v44 - O 1 '76 - p1093
SLJ - v23 - Ja '77 - p92
Subject: Schools—Fiction; Strikes and lockouts—Fiction

GOLDBERGER, Judith M

The Looking Glass Factor
CCB-B - v33 - F '80 - p108
HB - v56 - F '80 - p54
KR - v48 - F 15 '80 - p216
NYTBR - D 30 '79 - p19
SLJ - v26 - D '79 - p84
Subject: Science fiction

GOLDMAN, Katie

In The Wings
BL - v79 - D 15 '82 - p563
BS - v42 - Ja '83 - p405
CBRS - v11 - N '82 - p28
CCB-B - v36 - S '82 - p9
KR - v50 - O 15 '82 - p1157
SLJ - v29 - N '82 - p99
VOYA - v6 - O '83 - p201
WLB - v57 - Ja '83 - p419
Subject: Divorce—Fiction; Schools—Fiction; Theater—Fiction

GOLDREICH, Gloria
DrAP&F 85

Lori
BL - v75 - My 15 '79 - p1432
EJ - v68 - N '79 - p77
KR - v47 - My 1 '79 - p522
SLJ - v25 - My '79 - p72
Subject: Israel—Fiction

GOLDSMITH, Howard 1943-
ConAu 21NR, SmATA 24, WhoAm 86
Pseud./variant:
Courtney, Dale
Smith, Ward

Invasion: 2200 A.D.
CBRS - v8 - D '79 - p37
Hi Lo - v1 - N '79 - p5
J Read - v23 - Ap '80 - p662
SLJ - v26 - N '79 - p77
Subject: Science fiction

GOLDSTON, Robert C 1927-
AuBYP SUP, ConAu 17R, FourBJA, SmATA 6, WhAm 8, WhoAm 82

Pearl Harbor
BS - v32 - D 15 '72 - p445
LJ - v98 - My 15 '73 - p1688
Subject: Japan; Pearl Harbor, Attack on, 1941

GOLDWATER, Daniel 1922-
WhoAm 76

Bridges And How They Are Built
BL - v62 - Ja 15 '66 - p486
CCB-B - v19 - Ap '66 - p129
Comw - v83 - N 5 '65 - p161
HB - v41 - D '65 - p646
KR - v33 - Ag 15 '65 - p825
LJ - v90 - N 15 '65 - p5090
NYTBR - v70 - N 28 '65 - p46
SB - v2 - My '66 - p56
Subject: Bridges

GONZALEZ, Gloria 1940-
ConAu 65, NatPD, SmATA 23

The Glad Man
CCB-B - v29 - Je '76 - p156
Kliatt - v13 - Fall '79 - p7
KR - v43 - S 15 '75 - p1066
PW - v208 - Ag 25 '75 - p293
SLJ - v22 - O '75 - p98
Subject: Friendship—Fiction

GOODMAN, Burton

Spotlight On Literature
BL - v78 - Ja 15 '82 - p636
Cur R - v19 - N '80 - p446
Hi Lo - v2 - O '80 - p3

GOODMAN, Linda 1933?-
BioIn 11, -12, WhoAm 82, WhoWor 84

Linda Goodman's Sun Signs
BW - v5 - Je 27 '71 - p9
JLH - v199 - My 17 '71 - p64
KR - v36 - Jl 15 '68 - p794
LJ - v94 - Ja 1 '69 - p89
PW - v194 - Ag 5 '68 - p49
Subject: Astrology; Horoscopes

GOODWIN, Harold L 1914-
ConAu 2NR, SmATA 13, WhoE 77, WhoGov 77, WhoS&SW 75

All About Rockets And Space Flight
LJ - v95 - D 15 '70 - p4383
SB - v6 - S '70 - p165
Subject: Astronautics; Space flight

GORDON, Ethel Edison 1915-
ConAu 53, WrDr 86

Where Does The Summer Go?
BW - v1 - O 22 '67 - p14
CCB-B - v21 - Ja '68 - p78
CSM - v59 - N 2 '67 - pB11
KR - v35 - Je 1 '67 - p648
LJ - v92 - O 15 '67 - p3863
SR - v50 - Ag 19 '67 - p35

GORDON, Gordon 1912-
AuBYP SUP, BioIn 7, -8, ConAu 7NR, EncMys, WrDr 86

Undercover Cat Prowls Again
BS - v26 - O 15 '66 - p264
HB - v43 - F '67 - p93
KR - v34 - Jl 15 '66 - p718
LJ - v91 - O 15 '66 - p5264
LJ - v91 - D 1 '66 - p6005
NYTBR - v71 - O 16 '66 - p54
Punch - v252 - Je 14 '67 - p889
SR - v49 - D 31 '66 - p28
Co-author: Gordon, Mildred D

GORDON, Mildred D
see Gordon, Gordon (co-author)

GORDON, Sol 1923-
AmM&WS 78S, AuBYP SUP, BioIn 11, ConAu 4NR, ConLC 26, IntAu&W 77, SmATA 11, WhoE 83

Facts About Sex For Today's Youth
BL - v70 - O 15 '73 - p221
BL - v70 - O 15 '73 - p232
KR - v41 - Ap 15 '73 - p467
LJ - v98 - S 15 '73 - p2664
Ms - v12 - Jl '83 - p43
Subject: Sex instruction for youth

Facts About VD For Today's Youth
BL - v70 - O 15 '73 - p221
Inst - v83 - N '73 - p126
KR - v41 - Ag 15 '73 - p890
LJ - v98 - N 15 '73 - p3464
WLB - v54 - Ja '80 - p327
Subject: Venereal diseases

Signs Of Our Times 3
Hi Lo - v2 - S '80 - p6

GORDY, Berry, Sr.
WhoAm 86

Movin' Up: Pop Gordy Tells His Story
BL - v76 - D 15 '79 - p612
Bl S - v11 - My '80 - p86
BW - v10 - Ja 13 '80 - p10
CBRS - v8 - Winter '80 - p67
CCB-B - v33 - Mr '80 - p133
Inter BC - v13 - #1 '82 p18
KR - v48 - F 1 '80 - p138
SLJ - v26 - D '79 - p84
Subject: Blacks—Biography

GORENSTEIN, Shirley 1928-
ConAu 73, WhoAm 86, WhoAmW 81

Introduction To Archaeology
A Anth - v68 - Ag '66 - p1080
BL - v62 - F 15 '66 - p564
CE - v43 - O '66 - p103
Choice - v3 - My '66 - p246
LJ - v91 - Ja 15 '66 - p252
LJ - v91 - F 15 '66 - p1084
NH - v75 - N '66 - p24
NYRB - v6 - F 17 '66 - p20
SA - v215 - D '66 - p144
SB - v1 - Mr '66 - p216
Sci - v151 - Mr 11 '66 - p1210
Subject: Archaeology

GORHAM, Charles 1911-1975
BioIn 10, ConAu 6NR, SmATA 36

The Lion Of Judah: Haile Selassie I, Emperor Of Ethiopia
Am - v115 - Jl 2 '66 - p16
BL - v62 - Je 1 '66 - p959
BS - v26 - Ap 1 '66 - p18
CCB-B - v20 - S '66 - p10
KR - v34 - Ja 15 '66 - p66
LJ - v91 - My 15 '66 - p2706
NYTBR - v71 - Ap 17 '66 - p30
NYTBR - v71 - D 4 '66 - p66
SR - v49 - My 14 '66 - p42
Subject: Biography

GORODETZKY, Charles W 1937-
AmM&WS 86P, AuBYP SUP, WhoAm 86, WhoS&SW 78

What You Should Know About Drugs
BL - v67 - D 15 '70 - p341
BL - v67 - Ap 1 '71 - p660
CCB-B - v24 - F '71 - p91
CE - v48 - O '71 - p29
CLW - v42 - My '71 - p578
Comw - v93 - N 20 '70 - p205
HB - v47 - Ap '71 - p181
KR - v38 - O 15 '70 - p1154
LJ - v95 - D 15 '70 - p4350
NYTBR - F 7 '71 - p33
NYTBR, Pt. 2 - N 8 '70 - p36
PW - v198 - N 16 '70 - p77
SB - v6 - D '70 - p251
TN - v27 - Ap '71 - p305
Co-author: Gorodetzky, Charles W
Subject: Drug abuse

GORODETZKY, Charles W
see Gorodetzky, Charles W (co-author)

GOUDGE, Eileen

Afraid To Love
BL - v81 - F 1 '85 - p784
SLJ - v31 - Ap '85 - p102
Subject: Love—Fiction

Before It's Too Late
CCB-B - v38 - My '85 - p165
SLJ - v31 - Ap '85 - p102
VOYA - v8 - Je '85 - p125
Subject: Love—Fiction

Don't Say Good-Bye
SLJ - v32 - Ap '86 - p104
VOYA - v9 - Ag '86 - p156
Subject: Friendship—Fiction

Forbidden Kisses
SLJ - v32 - Ja '86 - p81
VOYA - v8 - F '86 - p391
Subject: Love—Fiction

Gone With The Wish
BL - v83 - O 1 '86 - p221
Subject: Computers—Fiction; Love—Fiction

Hands Off, He's Mine
SLJ - v32 - S '85 - p151
VOYA - v8 - F '86 - p391
Subject: Love—Fiction

Kiss And Make Up
SLJ - v32 - Ap '86 - p103
Subject: Love—Fiction

Looking For Love
SLJ - v33 - S '86 - p150
Subject: Love—Fiction

Night After Night
VOYA - v9 - D '86 - p229
Subject: Love—Fiction

Presenting Superhunk
SLJ - v32 - Ja '86 - p81
Subject: Love—Fiction

GOUDGE, Eileen (continued)

Smart Enough To Know
BL - v81 - F 1 '85 - p784
SLJ - v31 - Ja '85 - p90
Subject: Love—Fiction

Sweet Talk
VOYA - v9 - D '86 - p229
Subject: Love—Fiction

Too Hot To Handle
SLJ - v32 - S '85 - p151
VOYA - v8 - O '85 - p264
Subject: Love—Fiction

Too Much Too Soon
BL - v81 - F 1 '85 - p784
Kliatt - v18 - Fall '84 - p19
SLJ - v31 - S '84 - p139
Subject: Love—Fiction

A Touch Of Ginger
SLJ - v32 - Ja '86 - p81

Treat Me Right
VOYA - v9 - D '86 - p229
Subject: Love—Fiction

Winner All The Way
BL - v81 - F 1 '85 - p784
SLJ - v31 - Ja '85 - p90
Subject: Love—Fiction

GRABER, Alexander
see Cordell, Alexander

GRABLE, Ron
see Olney, Ross Robert (co-author)

GRAFF, Stewart 1908-
AuBYP, ConAu 49, SmATA 9

The Story Of World War II
BL - v74 - My 15 '78 - p1492
Comw - v105 - N 10 '78 - p734
KR - v46 - Ja 15 '78 - p49
SLJ - v24 - Mr '78 - p128
Subject: World War, 1939-1945

GRAHAM, Leslie

Rx For Love
BL - v80 - Je 15 '84 - p1474
VOYA - v7 - Je '84 - p91
Subject: Cancer—Fiction; Love—Fiction

GRAHAM, Lorenz Bell 1902-
AuBYP SUP, ChlLR 10, ConAu 9R, InB&W 80, MorBMP, SelBAAf, SmATA 2, ThrBJA, TwCChW 83, WrDr 86

North Town
Kliatt - v12 - Winter '78 - p7
Subject: Race relations—Fiction

Whose Town?
BL - v65 - Jl 1 '69 - p1226
BW - v3 - My 4 '69 - p3
CCB-B - v22 - Je '69 - p158
HB - v45 - Ag '69 - p416
KR - v37 - Ap 15 '69 - p452
LJ - v94 - Je 15 '69 - p2509
SR - v52 - My 10 '69 - p59
Subject: Race relations—Fiction

GRAHAM, Robin Lee 1949-
BioIn 8, -9, -10, -13, ConAu 49, SmATA 7

The Boy Who Sailed Around The World Alone
CCB-B - v27 - Je '74 - p156
CSM - v65 - N 7 '73 - pB7
CSM - v67 - Je 10 '75 - p16
LJ - v99 - S 15 '74 - p2268
PW - v205 - Ja 28 '74 - p301
Subject: Voyages around the world

Dove
B&B - v18 - Mr '73 - p83
BL - v69 - O 1 '72 - p126
BL - v69 - O 1 '72 - p138
BS - v32 - Je 1 '72 - p111
BS - v33 - Ag 1 '73 - p215
BW - v6 - Je 18 '72 - p5
BW - v7 - Je 24 '73 - p13
EJ - v62 - D '73 - p1298
KR - v40 - Ap 1 '72 - p445
LJ - v97 - Ag '72 - p2596
LJ - v97 - D 15 '72 - p4058
LJ - v97 - D 15 '72 - p4095
PW - v201 - My 1 '72 - p44
TN - v29 - Ap '73 - p257
Yacht - v133 - F '73 - p92
Subject: Voyages around the world

GRAHAM, Shirley Lola 1907?-1977
AmM&WS 86P, ConAu X, CurBio 77N, MorJA, SelBAAu, SmATA X, WhoAmW 87, WhoBlA 77

GRAHAM, Shirley Lola (continued)
Pseud./variant:
Du Bois, Shirley Graham

The Story Of Phillis Wheatley, Poetess Of The American Revolution
BL - v46 - O 15 '49 - p69
KR - v17 - Ag 15 '49 - p432
LJ - v74 - O 15 '49 - p1549
LJ - v74 - D 15 '49 - p1920
NYTBR - N 13 '49 - p30
SR - v32 - N 12 '49 - p38
Subject: Biography

GRANT, C L

The Hour Of The Oxrun Dead
BL - v74 - O 15 '77 - p355
KR - v45 - Ag 1 '77 - p801

GRAVES, Charles P 1911-1972
AuBYP, BioIn 9, ConAu 4NR, SmATA 4

John F. Kennedy
RR - v86 - Mr '69 - p172
Subject: Biography

GRAY, Elizabeth Janet 1902-
AuBYP, ConAu X, CurBio 43, JBA 34, -51, OxChL, SmATA 6, TwCChW 83, WrDr 86
Pseud./variant:
Vining, Elizabeth Gray

Adam Of The Road
BL - v38 - My 1 '42 - p334
CSM - Je 29 '42 - p10
HB - v18 - My '42 - p178
Inst - v82 - My '73 - p78
LJ - v67 - My 15 '42 - p476
LJ - v67 - O 15 '42 - p890
NY - v18 - My 23 '42 - p75
NYTBR - My 17 '42 - p8
SR - v25 - D 5 '42 - p60

GREAVES, Griselda

The Burning Thorn: An Anthology Of Poetry
BL - v68 - Mr 15 '72 - p612
CCB-B - v25 - F '72 - p91
KR - v39 - S 15 '71 - p1026
LJ - v96 - D 15 '71 - p4189
SR - v55 - Ja 15 '72 - p47
TLS - Jl 2 '71 - p773
Subject: Poetry

GREBEL, Rosemary

Caring For Your Car
Hi Lo - v4 - S '82 - p2
Co-author: Pogrund, Phyllis
Subject: Automobiles

GREEN, Carl R

Ghost Of Frankenstein
RT - v39 - O '85 - p98
SLJ - v32 - S '85 - p132
Co-author: Sanford, William R
Subject: Horror stories

The Mole People
RT - v39 - O '85 - p98
SLJ - v32 - O '85 - p172
Co-author: Sanford, William R
Subject: Horror stories; Monsters—Fiction

The Rattlesnake
BL - v80 - Ag '84 - p1622
BL - v81 - Je 15 '85 - p1452
CBRS - v12 - Ag '84 - p149
SB - v20 - Mr '85 - p219
Co-author: Sanford, William R
Subject: Rattlesnakes

Black Friday
SLJ - v32 - S '85 - p132
Co-author: Sanford, William R
Subject: Horror stories; Monsters—Fiction

Dracula's Daughter
SLJ - v32 - S '85 - p132
Co-author: Sanford, William R
Subject: Horror stories; Vampires—Fiction

Tarantula
SLJ - v32 - O '85 - p172
Co-author: Sanford, William R
Subject: Horror stories

The Raven
SLJ - v32 - O '85 - p172
Co-author: Sanford, William R
Subject: Horror stories

Werewolf Of London
CCB-B - v38 - Je '85 - p184
RT - v39 - O '85 - p99
SLJ - v32 - O '85 - p172
Co-author: Sanford, William R
Subject: Horror stories; Werewolves—Fiction

GREEN, Gerald 1922-
ASpks, WhoAm 86, WorAu, WrDr 86

Girl
BL - v74 - N 15 '77 - p527
KR - v45 - Ag 15 '77 - p870
LJ - v102 - N 15 '77 - p2367
PW - v212 - Ag 22 '77 - p60
Subject: Dogs—Fiction

GREEN, Iris

Anything For A Friend
Hi Lo - v2 - N '80 - p5

Second Chance
BL - v75 - Ap 15 '79 - p1290
Hi Lo - v1 - D '79 - p5
Subject: Love—Fiction

GREEN, Janet

Us: Inside A Teenage Gang
Cur R - v23 - F '84 - p60
SLJ - v29 - O '82 - p160
Subject: England—Fiction; Gangs—Fiction

GREEN, Sheila Ellen
see Greenwald, Sheila

GREENE, Bette 1934-
AuBYP SUP, ChlLR 2, ConAu 4NR, ConLC 30, FifBJA, OxChL, SmATA 8, TwCChW 83, WhoAm 86, WrDr 86

The Summer Of My German Soldier
BL - v70 - N 15 '73 - p334
BL - v70 - N 15 '73 - p339
BL - v70 - Mr 15 '74 - p827
BL - v81 - D 15 '84 - p583
BS - v33 - D 15 '73 - p428
BS - v34 - D 15 '74 - p428
CCB-B - v27 - F '74 - p94
Child Lit - v9 - p203
Choice - v12 - N '75 - p1132
CLW - v47 - N '75 - p166
CSM - v77 - My 31 '85 - p19
EJ - v64 - O '75 - p92
EJ - v66 - O '77 - p58
EJ - v69 - O '80 - p16
EJ - v72 - D '83 - p37
Emerg Lib - v11 - N '83 - p21
Emerg Lib - v11 - Ja '84 - p21
GP - v13 - Ja '75 - p2557
HB - v50 - F '74 - p56
Inter BC - v13 - #6 '82 p19
JB - v39 - F '75 - p62
J Read - v22 - N '78 - p126
KR - v41 - O 15 '73 - p1170
LJ - v98 - O 15 '73 - p3154
NYTBR - N 4 '73 - p29
NYTBR - N 4 '73 - p52
NYTBR - D 2 '73 - p79
NYTBR - N 10 '74 - p44
Obs - D 8 '74 - p30
PW - v204 - Ag 27 '73 - p280
SE - v47 - Ap '83 - p289
SLJ - v33 - N '86 - p30
TES - D 9 '77 - p21
Subject: Love—Fiction; World War, 1939-1945—Fiction

GREENE, Constance C 1924-
AuBYP SUP, ConAu 8NR, FourBJA, SmATA 11, TwCChW 83, WrDr 86

Beat The Turtle Drum
BL - v73 - N 15 '76 - p472
BW - N 7 '76 - pG8
CCB-B - v30 - Ap '77 - p124
Choice - v14 - N '77 - p1178
Comw - v103 - N 19 '76 - p762
HB - v52 - D '76 - p624
KR - v44 - Ag 1 '76 - p845
LA - v54 - Ap '77 - p441
NYTBR - N 14 '76 - p52
NYTBR - N 21 '76 - p62
NYTBR - Ja 27 '80 - p35
Par - v60 - Ag '85 - p75
PW - v210 - Ag 9 '76 - p78
RT - v31 - O '77 - p15
SLJ - v23 - F '77 - p64
SLJ - v25 - D '78 - p33
Teacher - v94 - My '77 - p109
Subject: Brothers and sisters—Fiction; Death—Fiction

Getting Nowhere
Emerg Lib - v14 - S '86 - p22
Subject: Family life—Fiction; Parent and child—Fiction; Remarriage—Fiction

GREENE, Shep

The Boy Who Drank Too Much
BL - v75 - My 1 '79 - p1356
CBRS - v7 - Je '79 - p107
CCB-B - v33 - S '79 - p9
HB - v55 - Ap '79 - p198
Hi Lo - v1 - S '79 - p3
KR - v47 - Je 1 '79 - p641
PW - v215 - My 21 '79 - p69
SLJ - v25 - My '79 - p84
WLB - v54 - N '79 - p184
Subject: Alcohol and youth—Fiction

GREENE, Yvonne

Cover Girl
BL - v78 - Mr 15 '82 - p950
Hi Lo - v3 - Je '82 - p3
Kliatt - v16 - Spring '82 - p10
VOYA - v5 - Je '82 - p32
Subject: Models and modeling—Fiction

Little Sister
BL - v78 - N 1 '81 - p378
Hi Lo - v3 - Ja '82 - p3
SLJ - v28 - O '81 - p142
VOYA - v4 - F '82 - p32
Subject: Brothers and sisters—Fiction

GREENFELD, Howard
AuBYP SUP, BioIn 10, ConAu 19NR, SmATA 19

Pablo Picasso
BL - v67 - Jl 1 '71 - p905
BW - v5 - My 9 '71 - p12
CCB-B - v25 - Mr '72 - p107
Choice - v8 - Je '71 - p540
LJ - v97 - F 15 '72 - p784
PW - v200 - Jl 5 '71 - p50
TN - v28 - Ja '72 - p203
Subject: Biography

GREENFIELD, Eloise 1929-
BioIn 12, ChlLR 4, ConAu 19NR, FifBJA, InB&W 80, SelBAAf, SmATA 19, TwCChW 83, WhoBlA 85, WrDr 86

Alesia
BL - v78 - F 1 '82 - p706
CBRS - v10 - F '82 - p66
CCB-B - v35 - Ja '82 - p85
CLW - v53 - Ap '82 - p401
Hi Lo - v3 - F '82 - p6
Inter BC - v13 - #4 '82 p7
SLJ - v28 - Mr '82 - p157
Co-author: Revis, Alesia
Subject: Physically handicapped

GREENWALD, Sheila 1934-
ConAu X, FifBJA, IlsBYP, IlsCB 1957, SmATA 8
Pseud./variant:
Green, Sheila Ellen

The Atrocious Two
BL - v74 - Jl 1 '78 - p1678
CCB-B - v32 - S '78 - p9
KR - v46 - Mr 15 '78 - p305
SLJ - v24 - My '78 - p84
Subject: Behavior—Fiction; Mystery and detective stories

Blissful Joy And The SATs: A Multiple-Choice Romance
BL - v78 - Mr 15 '82 - p950
BW - v12 - Ag 8 '82 - p6
CBRS - v10 - Ag '82 - p138
CCB-B - v35 - Ap '82 - p148
HB - v58 - Ag '82 - p412
J Read - v26 - D '82 - p277
KR - v50 - Ap 15 '82 - p494
PW - v221 - Mr 19 '82 - p71
SLJ - v28 - Ap '82 - p82
VOYA - v5 - Je '82 - p33
WLB - v57 - Ja '83 - p419
Subject: Friendship—Fiction

GREENYA, John

One Punch Away
Hi Lo - v1 - My '80 - p3
Subject: Blacks—Fiction; Boxing—Fiction

GREGORY, Diana 1933-
ConAu 97, SmATA 49

Two's A Crowd
Kliatt - v19 - Fall '85 - p8
SLJ - v32 - S '85 - p152
VOYA - v8 - F '86 - p392
Subject: Love—Fiction

GREY, Elizabeth (pseud.) 1917-
AuBYP, ConAu X
Real Name:
Hogg, Elizabeth

Friend Within The Gates: The Story Of Nurse Edith Cavell
BL - v57 - Jl 15 '61 - p699
CSM - My 11 '61 - p7B
HB - v37 - D '61 - p568
LJ - v86 - Je 15 '61 - p2364
NYTBR - Ag 6 '61 - p20
SR - v44 - My 13 '61 - p52
TLS - N 25 '60 - pR26
Subject: Biography

GRIESE, Bob 1945-
WhoAm 78, WhoFtbl 74

Offensive Football
BW - v6 - D 3 '72 - p10
LJ - v98 - Ja 15 '73 - p179
LJ - v98 - My 15 '73 - p1704
Nat R - v24 - Jl 21 '72 - p801
Co-author: Sayers, Gale
Subject: Football

GRILLONE, Lisa

Small Worlds Close Up
BL - v80 - O 15 '83 - p369
BL - v81 - Jl '85 - p1566
CE - v56 - N '79 - p114
CSM - v74 - O 8 '82 - pB6
GP - v19 - My '80 - p3687
JB - v44 - Ag '80 - p176
Lis - v104 - N 6 '80 - p626
TES - Ja 2 '81 - p14
TLS - Mr 28 '80 - p363
Co-author: Gennaro, Joseph
Subject: Microscope and microscopy

GRIMES, Frances Hurley

Sunny Side Up
BL - v80 - F 1 '84 - p809
SLJ - v31 - S '84 - p136
VOYA - v7 - Je '84 - p91
Subject: Love—Fiction

GRINNELL, George Bird 1849-1938
BioIn 4, -9, -12, JBA 34, -51, OxAmL 83, SmATA 16, Str&VC, WebAB 79, WhAm 1

The Punishment Of The Stingy And Other Indian Stories
Kliatt - v17 - Winter '83 - p31
Subject: Indians of North America—Fiction

GRIPE, Maria 1923-
AuBYP SUP, ChlLR 5, ConAu 17NR, IntAu&W 82, OxChL, SmATA 2, ThrBJA, TwCChW 83B

Pappa Pellerin's Daughter
B&B - v11 - Je '66 - p66
BS - v26 - Ag 1 '66 - p174
CCB-B - v20 - S '66 - p11
KR - v34 - My 1 '66 - p479
LJ - v91 - O 15 '66 - p5229
NYTBR - v71 - S 18 '66 - p30
Obs - Ap 10 '66 - p20
Punch - v250 - Ap 20 '66 - p594
PW - v189 - Je 13 '66 - p128
Spec - Je 3 '66 - p706
SR - v49 - Je 25 '66 - p61
TLS - My 19 '66 - p430

GROHSKOPF, Bernice 1921-
AuBYP SUP, ConAu 3NR, DrAP&F 85, IntAu&W 82, SmATA 7, WrDr 86

End Of Summer
BL - v78 - Je 1 '82 - p1307
BS - v42 - O '82 - p286
CCB-B - v35 - My '82 - p170
PW - v221 - Ap 23 '82 - p93
SLJ - v29 - Ja '83 - p84
Subject: Friendship—Fiction

GRUBER, Ruth
BioIn 1, -2, ConAu 12NR, WhoWorJ 78

Felisa Rincon De Gautier: The Mayor Of San Juan
BL - v69 - My 15 '73 - p907
CCB-B - v26 - Ap '73 - p124
Inter BC - v14 - #1 '83 p16
KR - v40 - N 1 '72 - p1249
NYTBR - D 17 '72 - p8
SE - v48 - N '84 - p556
Subject: Puerto Ricans

GRUBER, Terry Deroy

Cat High: The Yearbook
BW - v14 - Jl 15 '84 - p8
Kliatt - v18 - Spring '84 - p67

GUESS, Edward Preston
see Preston, Edward

GUEST, Elissa Haden

Over The Moon
BL - v82 - Je 15 '86 - p1532
B Rpt - v5 - S '86 - p32
CBRS - v14 - Ag '86 - p153
CCB-B - v39 - Mr '86 - p128
HB - v62 - Jl '86 - p454
PW - v229 - Ap 25 '86 - p81
SLJ - v32 - My '86 - p104
Subject: Sisters—Fiction

GUGLIOTTA, Bobette 1918-
ConAu 14NR, SmATA 7

Nolle Smith: Cowboy, Engineer, Statesman
BL - v68 - Ap 1 '72 - p672
LJ - v97 - Jl '72 - p2489
Subject: Blacks—Biography; Statesmen

GUILCHER, Jean Michel

A Fern Is Born
BL - v68 - Mr 1 '72 - p563
CCB-B - v25 - F '72 - p92
CLW - v43 - Ap '72 - p479
Inst - v81 - Je '72 - p66
SR - v55 - Ja 15 '72 - p47
TLS - Jl 14 '72 - p815

GUILCHER, Jean Michel (continued)
Co-author: Noailles, R H
Subject: Ferns

GULLEY, Judie

Rodeo Summer
BL - v81 - Ja 15 '85 - p717
BS - v45 - Jl '85 - p154
SLJ - v31 - D '84 - p90
SLJ - v32 - Ag '86 - p37
Subject: Horses—Fiction; Rodeos—Fiction

GUNNING, Thomas G

Amazing Escapes
B Rpt - v3 - S '84 - p40
CCB-B - v37 - Jl '84 - p204
RT - v38 - D '84 - p338
SLJ - v31 - O '84 - p157
VOYA - v7 - O '84 - p211
Subject: Adventure and adventurers; Escapes; Survival

Unexplained Mysteries
CCB-B - v36 - Jl '83 - p210
SLJ - v29 - Ag '83 - p65
VOYA - v6 - D '83 - p286
Subject: Curiosities and wonders

GUNTHER, John 1901-1970
AuBYP, ConAu 9R, -25R, CurBio 70, EncAJ, NewYTBE 70, ObitT 1961, OxAmL 83, SmATA 2, WebAB 79

Death Be Not Proud
BL - v45 - Mr 1 '49 - p224
Comw - v49 - F 18 '49 - p475
EJ - v62 - N '73 - p1189
EJ - v73 - N '84 - p67
HB - v25 - My '49 - p241
J Read - v22 - N '78 - p126
KR - v16 - Jl 15 '48 - p350
LJ - v74 - F 1 '49 - p197
Ms - v13 - Je '85 - p84
NS - v37 - Je 18 '49 - p654
NY - v25 - F 26 '49 - p98
NYTBR - F 6 '49 - p6
SLJ - v30 - Ja '84 - p42
Spec - v182 - My 20 '49 - p700
SR - v32 - Mr 5 '49 - p27
Time - v53 - F 7 '49 - p92
TLS - My 27 '49 - p348
Subject: Death; Gunther, John

GUTH, Deborah
see Schwartz, Anita K (co-author)

GUTMAN, Bill
AuBYP SUP, SmATA 43

Baseball Belters: Jackson, Schmidt, Parker, Brett
BL - v77 - Je 15 '81 - p1339
SLJ - v28 - D '81 - p71
VOYA - v4 - Ag '81 - p36
Subject: Baseball—Biography

Dr. J
BL - v74 - O 15 '77 - p381
SLJ - v24 - D '77 - p65
Subject: Basketball—Biography; Irving, Julius

Great Baseball Stories
BL - v74 - Jl 1 '78 - p1683
BS - v38 - O '78 - p230
SLJ - v24 - My '78 - p88
Subject: Baseball; Baseball—Fiction

Mark Fidrych
BL - v74 - O 15 '77 - p381
SLJ - v24 - D '77 - p65
Subject: Baseball—Biography

Modern Baseball Superstars
Comw - v99 - N 23 '73 - p220
KR - v41 - N 1 '73 - p1210
LJ - v99 - Ap 15 '74 - p1219
Subject: Baseball—Biography

Modern Football Superstars
SLJ - v21 - Ap '75 - p52
Subject: Football—Biography

Modern Hockey Superstars
CCB-B - v30 - Ap '77 - p124
Inst - v86 - My '77 - p121
SLJ - v23 - D '76 - p71
Subject: Hockey—Biography

Modern Soccer Superstars
CCB-B - v33 - Je '80 - p190
Hi Lo - v1 - Ap '80 - p3
SLJ - v26 - My '80 - p88
Subject: Soccer—Biography

Modern Women Superstars
BL - v74 - Ja 15 '78 - p809
BL - v74 - Ja 15 '78 - p817
CCB-B - v31 - Je '78 - p160
SLJ - v24 - Mr '78 - p128
Subject: Athletes

More Modern Baseball Superstars
SLJ - v25 - My '79 - p83
Subject: Baseball—Biography

More Modern Women Superstars
BL - v76 - N 15 '79 - p496
SLJ - v26 - D '79 - p101
Subject: Athletes

GUTMAN, Bill (continued)

"My Father, The Coach" And Other Sports Stories
KR - v44 - Ap 1 '76 - p406
SLJ - v22 - My '76 - p80
Subject: Short stories; Sports—Fiction

The Picture Life Of Reggie Jackson
Teacher - v96 - My '79 - p124
Subject: Baseball—Biography

Women Who Work With Animals
BL - v79 - O 1 '82 - p245
CCB-B - v35 - Jl '82 - p207
Hi Lo - v4 - O '82 - p6
SLJ - v29 - N '82 - p84
VOYA - v5 - D '82 - p42
Subject: Animals; Occupations

GUTTMACHER, Alan F 1898-1974
ConAu 6NR, CurBio 65, NewYTBS 74, WhAm 6

Understanding Sex
BL - v67 - N 15 '70 - p244
BL - v67 - N 15 '70 - p263
KR - v38 - My 1 '70 - p537
KR - v38 - My 15 '70 - p571
LJ - v95 - N 15 '70 - p4068
NS - v81 - Je 4 '71 - p783
Subject: Sex instruction for youth

GUY, Anne Welsh
ConAu 5R

Steinmetz: Wizard Of Light
KR - v33 - O 1 '65 - p1048
LJ - v90 - D 15 '65 - p5515
NYTBR - v71 - Ja 16 '66 - p36
SB - v1 - Mr '66 - p206
Subject: Biography

GUY, Rosa 1928-
BioIn 12, BlkAWP, ConAu 14NR, ConLC 26, DcLB 33, FifBJA, OxChL, SmATA 14, TwCChW 83, WrDr 86

The Disappearance
BL - v76 - O 1 '79 - p228
BOT - v2 - D '79 - p601
BW - v9 - N 11 '79 - p21
CBRS - v8 - Ja '80 - p46
CSM - v71 - O 15 '79 - pB4
HM - v259 - D '79 - p77
Inst - v89 - N '79 - p59
KR - v47 - D 1 '79 - p1380
NYTBR - N 25 '79 - p22
NYTBR - D 2 '79 - p40
PW - v216 - Ag 6 '79 - p92
Sch Lib - v28 - S '80 - p289
SLJ - v26 - N '79 - p88
SLJ - v27 - N '80 - p47
TES - Je 6 '80 - p27
TES - Mr 1 '85 - p29
TLS - Jl 18 '80 - p807
WLB - v54 - O '79 - p122
Subject: Foster home care—Fiction; Mystery and detective stories

Edith Jackson
BL - v74 - Ap 15 '78 - p1339
CSM - v70 - O 23 '78 - pB13
EJ - v69 - S '80 - p87
HB - v55 - O '78 - p524
Kliatt - v16 - Winter '82 - p8
KR - v46 - My 1 '78 - p501
Lis - v102 - N 8 '79 - p643
NYTBR - Jl 2 '78 - p11
PW - v213 - My 29 '78 - p52
SLJ - v24 - Ap '78 - p93
TES - Jl 15 '83 - p18
TES - Mr 1 '85 - p29
TLS - D 14 '79 - p124
WLB - v52 - Ap '78 - p639
Subject: Blacks—Social conditions—Fiction; Family problems—Fiction

New Guys Around The Block
CLW - v55 - D '83 - p239
CLW - v55 - Ap '84 - p409
EJ - v72 - O '83 - p86
GP - v22 - Jl '83 - p4099
JB - v48 - F '84 - p32
J Read - v27 - D '83 - p281
Punch - v285 - Ag 17 '83 - p51
TES - Jl 15 '83 - p18
VOYA - v6 - O '83 - p202
Subject: Blacks—Fiction; Mystery and detective stories

H

HAAS, Ben 1926-1977
BioIn 11, ConAu 8NR, EncFWF, WrDr 80

The Troubled Summer
BS - v26 - Ja 1 '67 - p368
CCB-B - v20 - F '67 - p89
CLW - v38 - F '67 - p395
KR - v34 - O 1 '66 - p1058
LJ - v91 - D 15 '66 - p6201
NYTBR - v72 - Ja 22 '67 - p26
PW - v193 - Je 10 '68 - p63

HABER, Louis 1910-
ConAu 29R, SmATA 12, WhoE 75

Black Pioneers Of Science And Invention
BL - v67 - S 15 '70 - p107
CCB-B - v24 - Ja '71 - p74
Comw - v93 - F 26 '71 - p521
KR - v38 - My 15 '70 - p563
LJ - v95 - D 15 '70 - p4363
SB - v6 - S '70 - p97
Subject: Blacks—Biography

HADDAD, Carolyn

The Last Ride
BL - v81 - O 1 '84 - p211
BS - v44 - Ja '85 - p398
CBRS - v13 - Winter '85 - p61
CCB-B - v38 - Ja '85 - p85
SLJ - v31 - Ja '85 - p85
Subject: Death—Fiction; Traffic accidents—Fiction

HAGERMAN, Paul Stirling

It's An Odd World
Par - v52 - N '77 - p112
SLJ - v24 - Mr '78 - p128
Subject: Curiosities and wonders

HAGGARD, Elizabeth

Nobody Waved Good-Bye
NYTBR, Pt. 2 - N 7 '71 - p47
Subject: Runaways—Fiction

HAHN, Christine

Amusement Park Machines
ACSB - v13 - Spring '80 - p49
Subject: Amusement rides

HAHN, James 1947-
ConAu 17NR, SmATA 9

Ali! The Sports Career Of Muhammad Ali
BL - v78 - Ap 1 '82 - p1023
SLJ - v28 - F '82 - p76
Co-author: Hahn, Lynn
Subject: Blacks—Biography; Boxing—Biography

Babe! The Sports Career Of George Ruth
BL - v78 - Ap 1 '82 - p1023
SLJ - v28 - F '82 - p76
Co-author: Hahn, Lynn
Subject: Baseball—Biography

Brown! The Sports Career Of James Brown
BL - v78 - Ap 1 '82 - p1023
SLJ - v28 - F '82 - p76
Co-author: Hahn, Lynn
Subject: Blacks—Biography; Football—Biography

Casey! The Sports Career Of Charles Stengel
BL - v78 - S 15 '81 - p113
SLJ - v28 - O '81 - p142
Co-author: Hahn, Lynn
Subject: Baseball—Biography

Chris! The Sports Career Of Chris Evert Lloyd
BL - v78 - Ap 1 '82 - p1023
SLJ - v28 - F '82 - p76
Co-author: Hahn, Lynn
Subject: Tennis—Biography

Henry! The Sports Career Of Henry Aaron
BL - v78 - S 15 '81 - p113
Hi Lo - v3 - S '81 - p6
SLJ - v28 - O '81 - p142

HAHN, James (continued)
Co-author: Hahn, Lynn
Subject: Baseball—Biography; Blacks—Biography

Killy! The Sports Career Of Jean-Claude Killy
BL - v78 - Ap 1 '82 - p1024
SLJ - v28 - F '82 - p76
Co-author: Hahn, Lynn
Subject: Skis and skiing—Biography

King! The Sports Career Of Billie Jean King
BL - v78 - Ap 1 '82 - p1024
CCB-B - v35 - Mr '82 - p129
SLJ - v28 - F '82 - p76
Co-author: Hahn, Lynn
Subject: Tennis—Biography

Pele! The Sports Career Of Edson Do Nascimento
BL - v78 - S 15 '81 - p113
Hi Lo - v3 - S '81 - p6
SLJ - v28 - O '81 - p142
Co-author: Hahn, Lynn
Subject: Soccer—Biography

Sayers! The Sports Career Of Gale Sayers
BL - v78 - Ap 1 '82 - p1024
CCB-B - v35 - My '82 - p171
SLJ - v28 - F '82 - p76
Co-author: Hahn, Lynn
Subject: Blacks—Biography; Football—Biography

Tark! The Sports Career Of Francis Tarkenton
BL - v78 - S 15 '81 - p113
Hi Lo - v3 - S '81 - p6
SLJ - v28 - O '81 - p142
Co-author: Hahn, Lynn
Subject: Football—Biography

Thorpe! The Sports Career Of James Thorpe
BL - v78 - S 15 '81 - p113
Hi Lo - v3 - S '81 - p6
SLJ - v28 - O '81 - p142
Co-author: Hahn, Lynn
Subject: Athletes; Indians of North America—Biography

Wilt! The Sports Career Of Wilton Chamberlain
BL - v78 - S 15 '81 - p113
Hi Lo - v3 - S '81 - p6
SLJ - v28 - O '81 - p142
Co-author: Hahn, Lynn
Subject: Basketball—Biography; Blacks—Biography

Zaharias! The Sports Career Of Mildred Zaharias
BL - v78 - S 15 '81 - p113
Hi Lo - v3 - S '81 - p6
SLJ - v28 - O '81 - p142
Co-author: Hahn, Lynn
Subject: Athletes; Golfers

HAHN, Lynn
see Hahn, James (co-author)

HAHN, Mary Downing 1937-
SmATA 44

The Time Of The Witch
BL - v79 - O 15 '82 - p311
B Rpt - v2 - S '83 - p36
CBRS - v11 - Ja '83 - p49
HB - v59 - F '83 - p44
SLJ - v29 - N '82 - p84
Subject: Family problems—Fiction; Wishes—Fiction; Witchcraft—Fiction

HALACY, Daniel Stephen, Jr. 1919-
AuBYP, ConAu 9NR, FifBJA, SmATA 36

Dive From The Sky!
KR - v35 - S 15 '67 - p1144

Now Or Never
BL - v68 - Mr 15 '72 - p629
BS - v31 - F 15 '72 - p522
CCB-B - v25 - Ap '72 - p123
KR - v39 - N 1 '71 - p1165
LJ - v97 - F 15 '72 - p784
NYTBR - Ja 9 '72 - p8
NYTBR, Pt. 2 - N 7 '71 - p28
SB - v8 - My '72 - p49
Subject: Pollution

The Shipbuilders: From Clipper Ships To Submarines To Hovercraft
BL - v63 - S 15 '66 - p119
BS - v26 - Jl 1 '66 - p142
NYTBR - v71 - My 8 '66 - p24
Subject: Ships

HALDEMAN, Joe 1943-
BioIn 12, ConAu 6NR, DcLB 8, DrmM 2, ScFSB, TwCSFW 86, WhoAm 86, WrDr 86

War Year
NYTBR - v90 - F 10 '85 - p40
Subject: Vietnamese Conflict, 1961-1975—Fiction

HALL, Douglas K
see Ferrigno, Lou (co-author)

HALL, Lynn 1937-
AuBYP SUP, ConAu 9NR, FifBJA, SmATA 47, -4AS, TwCChW 83, WrDr 86

Captain
SLJ - v23 - F '77 - p64
Subject: Ponies—Fiction

Careers For Dog Lovers
BB - v6 - N '78 - p2
BL - v74 - My 15 '78 - p1485
EJ - v67 - O '78 - p79
KR - v46 - F 1 '78 - p113
SLJ - v24 - Mr '78 - p129
WCRB - v4 - Jl '78 - p46
Subject: Vocational guidance

Danger Dog
BL - v83 - D 15 '86 - p647
SLJ - v33 - D '86 - p117
VOYA - v9 - D '86 - p217
Subject: Dogs—Fiction; Responsibility—Fiction

Denison's Daughter
BL - v80 - S 15 '83 - p170
BS - v43 - D '83 - p345
CBRS - v12 - Ja '84 - p52
CCB-B - v37 - D '83 - p68
HB - v59 - O '83 - p581
SLJ - v30 - N '83 - p92
VOYA - v7 - Ap '84 - p30
Subject: Fathers and daughters—Fiction

Flowers Of Anger
BB - v5 - Mr '77 - p3
BL - v73 - Ja 15 '77 - p718
CCB-B - v30 - Ap '77 - p125
Kliatt - v12 - Fall '78 - p9
PW - v210 - D 6 '76 - p63
Subject: Friendship—Fiction; Horses—Fiction

The Horse Trader
BL - v77 - Ap 1 '81 - p1099
HB - v57 - Ag '81 - p422
J Read - v25 - D '81 - p285
KR - v49 - Ap 15 '81 - p507
LA - v58 - O '81 - p846
PW - v219 - Mr 20 '81 - p62
SLJ - v27 - Ap '81 - p139
VOYA - v4 - O '81 - p33
Subject: Horses—Fiction

If Winter Comes
BL - v82 - Je 1 '86 - p1454
CCB-B - v39 - Jl '86 - p209
CCB-B - v40 - S '86 - p7
PW - v229 - Je 27 '86 - p95
SLJ - v33 - S '86 - p144
VOYA - v9 - Ag '86 - p144
Subject: Conduct of life—Fiction; Interpersonal relations—Fiction; Nuclear warfare—Fiction

Just One Friend
BL - v82 - S 15 '85 - p124
CCB-B - v39 - O '85 - p27
HB - v62 - Mr '86 - p207
SLJ - v32 - D '85 - p88
SLJ - v32 - Ja '86 - p31
SLJ - v32 - Ap '86 - p32
VOYA - v9 - Ap '86 - p31
WLB - v60 - F '86 - p47
Subject: Friendship—Fiction; Learning disabilities—Fiction

The Leaving
BL - v77 - O 1 '80 - p206
CCB-B - v34 - Ap '81 - p151
EJ - v70 - S '81 - p77
SLJ - v27 - D '80 - p63
VOYA - v3 - F '81 - p30
Subject: Family problems—Fiction; Farm life—Fiction

The Secret Of Stonehouse
BL - v65 - Ja 1 '69 - p496

Shadows
BL - v74 - D 15 '77 - p684
SLJ - v24 - Ap '78 - p84
Subject: Death—Fiction; Dogs—Fiction

The Siege Of Silent Henry
BL - v69 - Ja 15 '73 - p493
CCB-B - v26 - F '73 - p91
KR - v40 - D 1 '72 - p1358
LJ - v98 - My 15 '73 - p1688
NYTBR, Pt. 2 - N 5 '72 - p2
Subject: Friendship—Fiction

The Solitary
BL - v83 - N 15 '86 - p502
PW - v230 - N 28 '86 - p77
Subject: Arkansas—Fiction; Family problems—Fiction; Self-reliance—Fiction

HALL, Lynn (continued)

Sticks And Stones
BL - v68 - Jl 1 '72 - p939
CCB-B - v26 - O '72 - p25
Choice - v14 - N '77 - p1178
EJ - v62 - Mr '73 - p481
EJ - v62 - D '73 - p1300
LJ - v97 - N 15 '72 - p3813
NYTBR - My 28 '72 - p8
NYTBR, Pt. 2 - N 5 '72 - p26
PW - v201 - F 14 '72 - p69
TN - v29 - Ap '73 - p257
TN - v30 - Ja '74 - p203
Subject: Prejudices—Fiction

Stray
CCB-B - v28 - F '75 - p94
KR - v42 - Ap 15 '74 - p424
LJ - v99 - S 15 '74 - p2269
NYTBR - My 4 '75 - p23
PW - v205 - Je 17 '74 - p69
Subject: Dogs—Fiction; Friendship—Fiction

HALLIBURTON, Warren J 1924-
ConAu 33R, SelBAAf, SelBAAu, SmATA 19

Harlem
LJ - v99 - O 15 '74 - p2746
PW - v205 - Je 3 '74 - p160
Co-author: Kaiser, Ernest
Subject: New York (City)

see also Katz, William Loren (co-author) for additional titles

HALLMAN, Ruth 1929-
ConAu 15NR, SmATA 43

Breakaway
BL - v77 - Mr 15 '81 - p1024
CBRS - v9 - My '81 - p87
Hi Lo - v2 - Je '81 - p4
Inter BC - v13 - #4 '82 p15
Kliatt - v17 - Fall '83 - p10
SLJ - v27 - Ap '81 - p139
Subject: Deaf—Fiction; Physically handicapped—Fiction; Runaways—Fiction

Gimme Something, Mister!
Hi Lo - v1 - S '79 - p5
SLJ - v25 - Ap '79 - p56
Subject: New Orleans—Fiction; Robbers and outlaws—Fiction; Voodooism—Fiction

I Gotta Be Free
BL - v74 - N 15 '77 - p545
Cur R - v16 - D '77 - p360
KR - v46 - Ja 1 '78 - p8
SLJ - v24 - D '77 - p62
Subject: Hitchhiking—Fiction; Runaways—Fiction

Midnight Wheels
BL - v76 - D 15 '79 - p607
CSM - v73 - D 1 '80 - pB11
Hi Lo - v1 - D '79 - p5
SLJ - v26 - S '79 - p138
Subject: Automobiles—Fiction; Mystery and detective stories; Sex role—Fiction

Panic Five
BL - v82 - My 15 '86 - p1389
SLJ - v32 - My '86 - p104
Subject: Self-confidence—Fiction; Survival—Fiction; United States Navy—Fiction

Rescue Chopper
BL - v77 - O 15 '80 - p322
Kliatt - v16 - Winter '82 - p9
SLJ - v27 - N '80 - p75
VOYA - v5 - Je '82 - p53
Subject: Rescue work—Fiction

Secrets Of A Silent Stranger
BL - v73 - S 15 '76 - p182
Cur R - v16 - D '77 - p360
KR - v44 - Jl 15 '76 - p794
SLJ - v23 - D '76 - p68
Subject: World War, 1939-1945—Fiction

Tough Is Not Enough
BL - v79 - Ap 1 '83 - p1022
CBRS - v10 - Mr '82 - p77
Hi Lo - v3 - Mr '82 - p7
VOYA - v5 - Je '82 - p33
Subject: Camping—Fiction; Mountain life—Fiction

HALLSTEAD, William Finn, III 1924-
AuBYP SUP, ConAu 21NR, SmATA 11, WhoE 77
Pseud./variant:
Beechcroft, William

Conqueror Of The Clouds
BL - v76 - Jl 15 '80 - p1670
BS - v40 - S '80 - p208

HALVORSON, Marilyn

Cowboys Don't Cry
BIC - v13 - Ag '84 - p32
BL - v82 - S 1 '85 - p63
BS - v45 - Jl '85 - p154
CBRS - v13 - My '85 - p110

HALVORSON, Marilyn (continued)
CCB-B - v38 - Je '85 - p184
Emerg Lib - v12 - N '84 - p45
Emerg Lib - v14 - S '86 - p22
HB - v61 - My '85 - p316
Mac - v97 - D 10 '84 - p63
Quill & Q - v50 - Ap '84 - p14
SLJ - v32 - S '85 - p144
VOYA - v8 - Je '85 - p130
Subject: Death—Fiction; Fathers and sons—Fiction; Moving (Household)—Fiction

HAMILTON, Dorothy 1906-1983
ConAu 110, –33R, SmATA 12, –35N

Amanda Fair
Kliatt - v15 - Spring '81 - p8
SLJ - v28 - F '82 - p76
Subject: Divorce—Fiction; Shoplifting—Fiction; Sisters—Fiction

HAMILTON, Virginia 1936-
ChlLR 11, ConAu 20NR, ConLC 26, DcLB 33, –52, MorBMP, OxChL, SmATA 4, TwCChW 83, WrDr 86

The House Of Dies Drear
BL - v65 - N 1 '68 - p311
BL - v65 - Ap 1 '69 - p900
Bl W - v20 - Ag '71 - p94
BW - v2 - N 3 '68 - p12
Comw - v91 - F 27 '70 - p584
HB - v44 - O '68 - p563
Inst - v78 - F '69 - p180
KR - v36 - Ag 1 '68 - p818
Learning - v13 - Ap '85 - p28
NYTBR - v73 - O 13 '68 - p26
NYTBR - My 21 '78 - p51
NYTBR, Pt. 2 - N 8 '70 - p30
NYTBR, Pt. 2 - F 13 '72 - p12
PW - v194 - S 30 '68 - p61
SE - v33 - My '69 - p555
SLJ - v24 - F '78 - p35
SR - v51 - N 9 '68 - p69
Teacher - v86 - Ap '69 - p184
TN - v25 - Ap '69 - p310

The Planet Of Junior Brown
A Lib - v3 - Ap '72 - p420
BL - v68 - D 1 '71 - p333
BL - v68 - Ap 1 '72 - p669
BL - v69 - My 1 '73 - p838
Bl W - v21 - Mr '72 - p70
B Rpt - v1 - Mr '83 - p24
CCB-B - v25 - D '71 - p57
CE - v48 - Ja '72 - p206
Comw - v95 - N 19 '71 - p188
CSM - v63 - N 11 '71 - pB5
CSM - v64 - My 2 '72 - p4
EJ - v63 - Ja '74 - p65
EJ - v67 - My '78 - p88
Emerg Lib - v11 - Ja '84 - p21
HB - v48 - F '72 - p81
KR - v39 - S 1 '71 - p954
LJ - v96 - S 15 '71 - p2928
LJ - v96 - D 15 '71 - p4159
NYRB - v18 - Ap 20 '72 - p13
NYTBR - Ag 24 '71 - p8
NYTBR - Mr 10 '74 - p35
NYTBR - My 21 '78 - p51
PW - v200 - Ag 23 '71 - p81
SR - v54 - N 13 '71 - p61
TN - v28 - Ap '72 - p309

HAMORI, Laszlo 1911-
ConAu 9R

Adventure In Bangkok
BS - v26 - Je 1 '66 - p100
HB - v42 - Ag '66 - p438
KR - v34 - Mr 1 '66 - p248
LJ - v91 - My 15 '66 - p2706
NYTBR - v71 - Je 5 '66 - p42
TLS - N 24 '66 - p1069

Dangerous Journey
BL - v58 - My 1 '62 - p614
CC - v79 - Je 20 '62 - p781
CSM - My 10 '62 - p6B
HB - v38 - Je '62 - p280
KR - v30 - F 1 '62 - p112
LJ - v87 - Je 15 '62 - p2431
NYTBR - Ag 12 '62 - p26
NYTBR - v71 - Je 5 '66 - p43
Subject: Refugees—Fiction

HAMRE, Leif 1914-
ConAu 4NR, FourBJA, IntAu&W 82, SmATA 5, TwCChW 83B, WrDr 86

Leap Into Danger
BL - v56 - D 15 '59 - p245
HB - v36 - F '60 - p41
LJ - v85 - Mr 15 '60 - p1310
LJ - v91 - O 15 '66 - p5272

HANDELSMAN, J B
see Berger, Melvin (co-author)

HANEY, Lynn 1941-
ConAu 1NR, SmATA 23

I Am A Dancer
BL - v77 - My 1 '81 - p1197
BW - v11 - Je 14 '81 - p11
CBRS - v9 - My '81 - p87
CCB-B - v35 - S '81 - p9
Kliatt - v15 - Spring '81 - p50

HANEY, Lynn (continued)
NYTBR - v86 - Ap 26 '81 - p69
PW - v219 - Mr 20 '81 - p62
SLJ - v27 - Ap '81 - p127
Co-author: Curtis, Bruce
Subject: Ballet dancing; Dancers

HANLON, Stuart
see Meyer, Jerome Sydney (co-author)

HANNAHS, Herbert

People Are My Profession
LJ - v96 - Ap 15 '71 - p1514
Co-author: Stein, R Conrad
Subject: Occupations; Social work as a profession

see also Stein, R Conrad for additional titles

HANO, Arnold 1922-
AuBYP, ConAu 5NR, SmATA 12, WhoWest 82

Muhammad Ali: The Champion
BL - v74 - O 1 '77 - p303
KR - v45 - My 15 '77 - p544
NYTBR - Ap 30 '78 - p56
SLJ - v24 - S '77 - p144
Subject: Boxing—Biography

HANSEN, Caryl 1929-
ConAu 108, SmATA 39

I Think I'm Having A Baby
BL - v78 - Je 1 '82 - p1307
CCB-B - v36 - S '82 - p10
Kliatt - v16 - Fall '82 - p11
SLJ - v29 - S '82 - p138
VOYA - v5 - Ag '82 - p31
Subject: Sexual ethics—Fiction

One For The Road
BL - v81 - N 1 '84 - p363
SLJ - v31 - S '84 - p138
VOYA - v8 - Je '85 - p124
Subject: Love—Fiction

HANSEN, Joyce 1942-
ConAu 105, SmATA 46

Home Boy
BL - v79 - O 15 '82 - p304
BS - v42 - F '83 - p445
CBRS - v11 - F '83 - p70
CCB-B - v36 - Ja '83 - p89
Inter BC - v15 - #4 '84 p10
KR - v50 - N 1 '82 - p1195
PW - v222 - N 26 '82 - p60
SLJ - v29 - N '82 - p100
VOYA - v5 - F '83 - p36
Subject: New York (City)—Fiction

HARDIN, Gail

The Road From West Virginia
LJ - v97 - Mr 15 '72 - p1175
Co-author: Stein, R Conrad
Subject: Manual labor

see also Stein, R Conrad for additional titles

HARDWICK, Mollie
ConAu 2NR, IntAu&W 82, Novels, Who 85, WrDr 86

The Merrymaid
BL - v81 - Je 1 '85 - p1370
KR - v53 - My 1 '85 - p383
LJ - v110 - Je 1 '85 - p143
PW - v227 - My 17 '85 - p97
SLJ - v32 - N '85 - p105

HARKER, Ronald 1909-
ConAu 77

Digging Up The Bible Lands
BL - v70 - S 1 '73 - p46
CCB-B - v27 - O '73 - p31
HB - v49 - O '73 - p477
KR - v41 - Ap 1 '73 - p401
LJ - v98 - My 15 '73 - p1581
LJ - v98 - My 15 '73 - p1655
LJ - v98 - My 15 '73 - p1689
NY - v49 - D 3 '73 - p219
Obs - Jl 16 '72 - p31
PW - v203 - Ap 2 '73 - p65
SB - v9 - Mr '74 - p321
TLS - Jl 14 '72 - p810
Subject: Archaeology

HARKINS, Philip 1912-
AuBYP, ConAu 29R, MorJA, SmATA 6

Young Skin Diver
BL - v53 - S 15 '56 - p51
HB - v32 - O '56 - p361
KR - v24 - Je 1 '56 - p358
NYTBR - S 9 '56 - p34
SR - v39 - N 17 '56 - p71

HARMON, Lyn 1930-
ConAu 21R

Clyde's Clam Farm
LJ - v91 - Mr 15 '66 - p1700

HARPER, Elaine

Christmas Date
BL - v81 - F 1 '85 - p784
Subject: Dating (Social customs)—Fiction; Love—Fiction

Short Stop For Romance
BL - v80 - F 1 '84 - p809
Subject: Baseball—Fiction; Love—Fiction

Turkey Trot
BL - v81 - F 1 '85 - p784
SLJ - v31 - Ap '85 - p102
VOYA - v8 - Je '85 - p123
Subject: Love—Fiction

HARRELL, Janice

Heavens To Bitsy
BL - v80 - Je 15 '84 - p1474
VOYA - v7 - Je '84 - p91
Subject: Love—Fiction

Killebrew's Daughter
SLJ - v31 - Ap '85 - p102
VOYA - v8 - Je '85 - p124
Subject: Love—Fiction

One Special Summer
BL - v80 - Je 15 '84 - p1474
SLJ - v31 - Ja '85 - p90
VOYA - v7 - Ag '84 - p146
Subject: Love—Fiction

Secrets In The Garden
BL - v81 - Je 1 '85 - p1392

HARRIES, Joan 1922-
ConAu 107, IntAu&W 86X, SmATA 39
Pseud./variant:
Katsarakis, Joan Harris

They Triumphed Over Their Handicaps
BL - v77 - Je 15 '81 - p1342
Hi Lo - v2 - Ap '81 - p5
SB - v17 - Mr '82 - p212
SLJ - v27 - Ag '81 - p75
Subject: Physically handicapped

HARRINGTON, Lyn 1911-
AuBYP, BioIn 10, CaW, ConAu 5R, Profile 1, SmATA 5

China And The Chinese
BL - v63 - Mr 15 '67 - p795
BS - v26 - Ja 1 '67 - p371
CCB-B - v20 - Mr '67 - p108
LJ - v92 - Ja 15 '67 - p343
NH - v76 - N '67 - p29
NYTBR, Pt. 2 - v72 - My 7 '67 - p4
SR - v50 - Ap 22 '67 - p100
Subject: China

HARRIS, Christie 1907-
ConAu 6NR, ConLC 12, FourBJA, OxCanL, OxChL, Profile 1, SmATA 6, TwCChW 83, WhoCanL 85, WrDr 86

Confessions Of A Toe-Hanger
BL - v64 - S 1 '67 - p54
CCB-B - v20 - Jl '67 - p170
CLW - v39 - D '67 - p292
CSM - v59 - My 4 '67 - pB10
HB - v43 - Ap '67 - p213
KR - v35 - F 1 '67 - p144
LJ - v92 - Ap 15 '67 - p1748
TN - v24 - N '67 - p99

Let X Be Excitement
CCB-B - v22 - Jl '69 - p176
CLW - v41 - O '69 - p133
KR - v37 - F 15 '69 - p185
LJ - v94 - S 15 '69 - p3218
PW - v195 - My 12 '69 - p58
SR - v52 - My 10 '69 - p60
Subject: Occupations—Fiction

You Have To Draw The Line Somewhere
BS - v23 - Mr 15 '64 - p442
CSM - My 7 '64 - p5B
HB - v40 - Je '64 - p290
LJ - v89 - Ap 15 '64 - p1870
NYTBR - Ag 16 '64 - p18

HARRIS, Jacqueline
see Hayden, Robert Carter (co-author)

HARRIS, Janet 1932-1979
AuBYP SUP, BioIn 12, ConAu 33R, –93, SmATA 23N, –4

The Long Freedom Road: The Civil Rights Story
CCB-B - v21 - S '67 - p7
Lis - v79 - My 16 '68 - p643
TLS - Je 6 '68 - p596
Subject: Blacks—Civil rights

HARRIS, Lavinia (pseud.)
ConAu X, SmATA X, WrDr 86
Real Name:
Johnston, Norma

The Great Rip-Off
BL - v81 - Ja 15 '85 - p708

HARRIS, Lavinia (continued)
SLJ - v31 - Ap '85 - p97
Subject: Computers—Fiction

see also Johnston, Norma for additional titles

HARRIS, Leon A, Jr. 1926-
AuBYP, ConAu 3NR, SmATA 4, WhoAm 86, WhoAmA 84, WhoS&SW 84

Behind The Scenes In A Car Factory
KR - v40 - Mr 1 '72 - p261
LJ - v98 - Mr 15 '73 - p1003
Subject: Automobiles

Behind The Scenes In A Department Store
KR - v40 - Mr 1 '72 - p262
LJ - v98 - Mr 15 '73 - p1003
Subject: Department stores

Behind The Scenes Of Television Programs
KR - v40 - Mr 1 '72 - p262
LJ - v98 - Mr 15 '73 - p1003
Subject: Television programs

The Russian Ballet School
AB - v46 - N 23 '70 - p1570
BL - v67 - N 1 '70 - p227
BW - v4 - N 8 '70 - p25
CCB-B - v24 - Mr '71 - p107
Comw - v93 - N 20 '70 - p206
CSM - v63 - Ja 30 '71 - p13
Dance - v45 - Ja '71 - p80
Dance - v46 - Jl '72 - p90
HB - v47 - Je '71 - p299
KR - v38 - Jl 1 '70 - p683
LJ - v95 - S 15 '70 - p3048
LJ - v98 - O 15 '73 - p3123
SR - v53 - O 24 '70 - p67
Subject: Ballet dancing

HARRIS, Marilyn 1931-
ConAu X, SmATA X, WrDr 86
Pseud./variant:
Springer, Marilyn Harris

The Runaway's Diary
BL - v68 - F 1 '72 - p463
BS - v31 - N 15 '71 - p386
CCB-B - v26 - S '72 - p8
KR - v39 - O 15 '71 - p1131
LJ - v97 - Mr 15 '72 - p1178
Teacher - v91 - Ap '74 - p89
Subject: Runaways—Fiction

HARRIS, Mark Jonathan 1941-
ConAu 104, SmATA 32

The Last Run
BL - v78 - Ja 15 '82 - p648
CBRS - v10 - O '81 - p18
CCB-B - v35 - Ja '82 - p86
CLW - v53 - Ap '82 - p401
KR - v50 - F 15 '82 - p208
SLJ - v28 - N '81 - p104
Subject: Grandfathers—Fiction; Horses—Fiction; Mustang—Fiction

HARRIS, Robie H

Before You Were Three: How You Began To Walk, Talk, Explore And Have Feelings
BL - v81 - Mr 1 '85 - p991
Co-author: Levy, Elizabeth

see also Levy, Elizabeth for additional titles

HARRISON, Amelia Williams
see Compton, Margaret

HARRISON, Harry Max 1925-
AuBYP SUP, BioIn 11, ConAu 1R, –21NR, ConSFA, DrmM 2, ScFSB, SmATA 4, TwCSFW 86, WhoSciF, WrDr 86

The Men From P.I.G. And R.O.B.O.T.
BL - v74 - Mr 15 '78 - p1187
CCB-B - v31 - My '78 - p142
HB - v54 - Ag '78 - p395
JB - v39 - F '75 - p63
KR - v46 - Mr 15 '78 - p311
NYTBR - Ap 16 '78 - p26
Obs - F 23 '75 - p28
Obs - Jl 23 '78 - p21
SLJ - v24 - My '78 - p68
Spec - v233 - D 21 '74 - p797
TES - S 22 '78 - p23
TLS - Ap 4 '75 - p360
WLB - v52 - Ap '78 - p639
Subject: Science fiction

The Stainless Steel Rat Saves The World
B&B - v19 - N '73 - p129
BL - v69 - Mr 1 '73 - p620
KR - v40 - O 15 '72 - p1216
LJ - v98 - Jl '73 - p2205
PW - v202 - O 30 '72 - p50

HART, Bruce 1938-
BioIn 12, ConAu 107, SmATA 39

Breaking Up Is Hard To Do
Kliatt - v21 - Spring '87 - p10
Co-author: Hart, Carole

Waiting Games
SLJ - v28 - Ja '82 - p87
VOYA - v4 - F '82 - p32
Co-author: Hart, Carole

HART, Carole
see Hart, Bruce (co-author)

HART, Carolyn 1936-
ConAu 13R

Dangerous Summer
BS - v28 - My 1 '68 - p64
LJ - v93 - My 15 '68 - p2128

HART, Nicole

Lead On Love
BL - v80 - Je 15 '84 - p1474
SLJ - v31 - S '84 - p138
VOYA - v7 - Je '84 - p91
Subject: Love—Fiction

HARTER, Walter

The Phantom Hand And Other American Hauntings
KR - v44 - My 15 '76 - p596
SLJ - v23 - N '76 - p58
Subject: Ghosts

HASEGAWA, Sam

Stevie Wonder
SLJ - v22 - S '75 - p95
Subject: Blacks—Biography; Musicians

HASKINS, James 1941-
AuBYP SUP, BioIn 11, ChlLR 3, ConAu 33R, InB&W 80, NegAl 83, SelBAAf, SelBAAu, SmATA 9, -4AS, WrDr 80

Always Movin' On
BL - v73 - Ja 1 '77 - p666
BS - v36 - Ja '77 - p323
Cur R - v17 - Ag '78 - p173
SLJ - v23 - N '76 - p69
Subject: Blacks—Biography; Hughes, Langston

Babe Ruth And Hank Aaron: The Home Run Kings
BL - v71 - D 15 '74 - p425
KR - v42 - O 1 '74 - p1063
LJ - v99 - D 15 '74 - p3278
Subject: Baseball—Biography

Barbara Jordan: Speaking Out
BL - v74 - D 1 '77 - p607
BS - v38 - Ap '78 - p18
CCB-B - v31 - F '78 - p95
Cur R - v17 - Ag '78 - p176
EJ - v67 - Ap '78 - p91
KR - v45 - D 1 '77 - p1273
SLJ - v24 - Ja '78 - p94
Subject: Blacks—Biography; Legislators

Dr. J: A Biography Of Julius Erving
BL - v72 - N 15 '75 - p453
KR - v43 - Jl 1 '75 - p715
SLJ - v22 - D '75 - p68
Subject: Basketball—Biography

From Lew Alcindor To Kareem Abdul-Jabbar
BL - v74 - Jl 1 '78 - p1683
CCB-B - v26 - Ja '73 - p76
CSM - v64 - N 8 '72 - pB5
EJ - v62 - My '73 - p825
KR - v40 - Jl 15 '72 - p805
KR - v46 - Jl 15 '78 - p752
LJ - v97 - D 15 '72 - p4089
SLJ - v25 - S '78 - p138
Subject: Basketball—Biography

The Life And Death Of Martin Luther King, Jr.
BL - v74 - O 1 '77 - p294
BW - S 11 '77 - pE6
CCB-B - v31 - Ja '78 - p78
CE - v55 - N '78 - p106
EJ - v66 - N '77 - p80
EJ - v67 - Mr '78 - p93
HB - v53 - O '77 - p553
KR - v45 - Je 1 '77 - p583
PW - v211 - Je 13 '77 - p107
SE - v42 - Ap '78 - p318
SLJ - v24 - O '77 - p112
Subject: Blacks—Biography; Blacks—Civil rights

The Story Of Stevie Wonder
BL - v73 - S 1 '76 - p38
CCB-B - v30 - Ap '77 - p125
CLW - v48 - Ap '77 - p405
J Read - v27 - Mr '84 - p521
Kliatt - v13 - Fall '79 - p30
KR - v44 - My 15 '76 - p604
RT - v31 - O '77 - p22
SLJ - v23 - Ja '77 - p92
SLJ - v26 - Ag '80 - p39
Subject: Blacks—Biography; Musicians

HASKINS, James (continued)

Street Gangs, Yesterday And Today
BL - v71 - N 1 '74 - p284
BS - v34 - O 15 '74 - p330
BW - N 10 '74 - p8
CCB-B - v28 - Ja '75 - p78
CE - v51 - Ap '75 - p329
LJ - v99 - N 15 '74 - p3054
PW - v206 - Ag 12 '74 - p59
Subject: Gangs—History

HASSLER, Jon Francis 1933-
ConAu 21NR, -73, SmATA 19

Four Miles To Pinecone
CCB-B - v31 - O '77 - p33
HB - v53 - O '77 - p531
NYTBR - My 15 '77 - p40
PW - v211 - Je 13 '77 - p108
SLJ - v24 - S '77 - p144
Subject: Crime and criminals—Fiction; Friendship—Fiction

HASTINGS, Beverly (joint pseud.)
ConAu X
Real Names:
Barkin, Carol
James, Elizabeth

Watcher In The Dark
BL - v82 - Je 15 '86 - p1533
PW - v229 - My 30 '86 - p70
SLJ - v33 - O '86 - p190
Subject: Mystery and detective stories

see also Barkin, Carol; James, Elizabeth for additional titles

HASZARD, Patricia Moyes
see Moyes, Patricia

HAUGAARD, Erik Christian 1923-
AuBYP, BioIn 12, ChlLR 11, ConAu 3NR, IntAu&W 82, SmATA 4, ThrBJA, TwCChW 83, WrDr 86

Orphans Of The Wind
BL - v63 - O 15 '66 - p265
HB - v42 - Ag '66 - p438
KR - v34 - My 1 '66 - p479
Lis - v78 - N 16 '67 - p643
LJ - v91 - Je 15 '66 - p3266
Nat R - v18 - D 13 '66 - p1285
NYTBR - v71 - Jl 31 '66 - p18
Obs - N 26 '67 - p28
PW - v189 - Je 20 '66 - p77
SR - v49 - S 17 '66 - p46
TLS - N 30 '67 - p1159

A Slave's Tale
BL - v62 - S 15 '65 - p96
CCB-B - v19 - Ap '66 - p131
Comw - v82 - My 28 '65 - p329
HB - v41 - Ag '65 - p395
KR - v33 - Ap 15 '65 - p436
LJ - v90 - Je 15 '65 - p2894
NYTBR - v70 - Ag 22 '65 - p18
Obs - D 4 '66 - p28
Punch - v251 - N 16 '66 - p754
Spec - N 11 '66 - p625
TLS - N 24 '66 - p1079
Subject: Norsemen—Fiction

HAUTZIG, Deborah 1956-
ConAu 89, FifBJA, SmATA 31

Hey, Dollface
BL - v75 - S 1 '78 - p38
CCB-B - v32 - O '78 - p30
Kliatt - v14 - Fall '80 - p7
KR - v46 - Ag 1 '78 - p811
PW - v214 - Ag 21 '78 - p60
PW - v218 - O 24 '80 - p50
Subject: Friendship—Fiction

Second Star To The Right
CBRS - v9 - Ag '81 - p127
CCB-B - v35 - S '81 - p9
EJ - v75 - Ja '86 - p86
J Read - v25 - F '82 - p487
Kliatt - v16 - Fall '82 - p11
KR - v49 - S 1 '81 - p1086
LA - v59 - Ap '82 - p370
NYTBR - v87 - Ja 17 '82 - p30
PW - v220 - Jl 31 '81 - p58
Sch Lib - v30 - Je '82 - p154
SLJ - v27 - Ag '81 - p75
VOYA - v4 - D '81 - p30
Subject: Anorexia nervosa—Fiction; Emotional problems—Fiction

HAUTZIG, Esther 1930-
AuBYP, BioIn 8, ConAu 20NR, HerW 84, IntAu&W 82, MorBMP, OxChL, SmATA 4, ThrBJA, WrDr 86

The Endless Steppe: Growing Up In Siberia
BL - v64 - My 1 '68 - p1043
BS - v28 - My 1 '68 - p64
BW - v2 - My 5 '68 - p5
CCB-B - v21 - My '68 - p142
Comw - v88 - My 24 '68 - p302
Emerg Lib - v11 - N '83 - p21
HB - v44 - Je '68 - p311
KR - v36 - Mr 15 '68 - p343
LJ - v93 - O 15 '68 - p3982
NYTBR - v73 - My 5 '68 - p2

HAUTZIG, Esther (continued)
PW - v193 - Mr 25 '68 - p49
RT - v33 - Ap '80 - p810
Sch Lib - v33 - S '85 - p206
SR - v51 - My 11 '68 - p42
TN - v25 - N '68 - p78
Subject: Siberia—Description and travel

HAWKINS, Robert

On The Air: Radio Broadcasting
BL - v81 - F 1 '85 - p787
SLJ - v31 - N '84 - p131
Subject: Radio broadcasting; Vocational guidance

HAYDEN, Karen

The Look Of Love
Hi Lo - v3 - Mr '82 - p7

HAYDEN, Naura 1942-
ConAu 73

The Hip, High-Prote, Low-Cal, Easy-Does-It Cookbook
B Rpt - v4 - Mr '86 - p41
BS - v32 - N 1 '72 - p364
Subject: Weight control

HAYDEN, Robert Carter 1937-
ConAu 69, SelBAAf, SelBAAu, SmATA 47, WrDr 86

Eight Black American Inventors
BL - v68 - Je 1 '72 - p857
BL - v68 - Je 1 '72 - p860
HB - v61 - Mr '85 - p212
LJ - v98 - F 15 '73 - p654
Subject: Blacks—Biography

Nine Black American Doctors
CLW - v48 - Mr '77 - p357
SB - v13 - S '77 - p86
SE - v41 - Ap '77 - p347
Co-author: Harris, Jacqueline
Subject: Blacks—Biography; Physicians

Seven Black American Scientists
BL - v68 - S 1 '71 - p58
HB - v61 - Mr '85 - p212
LJ - v96 - N 15 '71 - p3910
SB - v7 - My '71 - p17
Subject: Blacks—Biography

HAYES, William D 1913-
AuBYP, ConAu 5R, SmATA 8

Project: Scoop
KR - v34 - Ag 1 '66 - p751
LJ - v91 - S 15 '66 - p4334

HAYMAN, LeRoy 1916-
AuBYP SUP, ConAu 85

O Captain: The Death Of Abraham Lincoln
KR - v35 - D 1 '67 - p1428
LJ - v93 - My 15 '68 - p2120
PW - v193 - My 13 '68 - p59
Subject: Biography

HAYNES, Mary

Wordchanger
BL - v80 - O 1 '83 - p294
B Rpt - v2 - Mr '84 - p33
CCB-B - v37 - O '83 - p29
CE - v60 - My '84 - p362
Fant R - v7 - Ag '84 - p47
HB - v59 - O '83 - p573
J Read - v27 - Ap '84 - p662
Kliatt - v19 - Fall '85 - p22
SLJ - v30 - S '83 - p134
VOYA - v7 - Ap '84 - p30
Subject: Books and reading—Fiction; Physics—Fiction

HEAD, Ann 1915-
ConAu X
Pseud./variant:
Morse, Anne Christensen

Mr. And Mrs. Bo Jo Jones
TN - v24 - N '67 - p101
TN - v24 - Ap '68 - p326
Subject: Marriage—Fiction

see also Morse, Charles (co-author) for additional titles

HEADLEY, Elizabeth Cavanna 1909-
AuBYP, BioIn 2, ConAu X, CurBio 50, MorJA, SmATA 1, -X, TwCChW 83, WrDr 80
Pseud./variant:
Cavanna, Betty

Diane's New Love
BL - v51 - Je 15 '55 - p434
KR - v23 - Mr 1 '55 - p175
LJ - v80 - Je 15 '55 - p1512
NYT - My 15 '55 - p28
Subject: Adolescence—Fiction

see also Cavanna, Betty for additional titles

HEALEY, Larry
ConAu 101, SmATA 44

Angry Mountain
BL - v79 - Mr 1 '83 - p870
B Rpt - v2 - N '83 - p34
BS - v43 - Jl '83 - p154
SLJ - v29 - Ap '83 - p123
Subject: Alaska—Fiction; Volcanoes—Fiction

The Hoard Of The Himalayas
BL - v78 - S 15 '81 - p98
BS - v41 - O '81 - p277
CBRS - v10 - O '81 - p18
CSM - v74 - D 14 '81 - pB10
SLJ - v28 - D '81 - p85
Subject: Adventure and adventurers—Fiction; Mountaineering—Fiction; Mystery and detective stories

The Town Is On Fire
BL - v76 - F 15 '80 - p829
CBRS - v8 - N '79 - p27
SLJ - v26 - D '79 - p99
SLJ - v27 - N '80 - p47
Subject: Mystery and detective stories; Pennsylvania—Fiction

HEATH, Charles

The A-Team
VOYA - v7 - O '84 - p199

HEAVEN, Constance
see Fecher, Constance

HEAVILIN, Jay
AuBYP SUP

Fast Ball Pitcher
CCB-B - v19 - S '65 - p9

HECK, Bessie Holland 1911-
ConAu 5R, SmATA 26

Golden Arrow
CCB-B - v35 - O '81 - p30
SLJ - v28 - N '81 - p104
Subject: Farm life—Fiction; Horses—Fiction; Motorcycles—Fiction

HECK, Joseph

Dinosaur Riddles
PW - v222 - D 24 '82 - p65
TES - D 23 '83 - p23
Subject: Jokes; Riddles

HEHL, Eileen

Playing Games
VOYA - v9 - D '86 - p231
Subject: Love—Fiction

HEIDE, Florence Parry 1919-
AuBYP SUP, ConAu 19NR, FourBJA, SmATA 32, TwCChW 83, WrDr 86

Black Magic At Brillstone
BL - v78 - O 15 '81 - p315
SLJ - v28 - Ja '82 - p77
Co-author: Heide, Roxanne
Subject: Mystery and detective stories

Body In The Brillstone Garage
SLJ - v26 - My '80 - p86
SLJ - v27 - N '80 - p47
Co-author: Heide, Roxanne
Subject: Mystery and detective stories

Face At The Brillstone Window
BL - v75 - My 15 '79 - p1445
CCB-B - v32 - Je '79 - p176
SLJ - v25 - My '79 - p81
Co-author: Heide, Roxanne
Subject: Mystery and detective stories

Mystery Of The Forgotten Island
BL - v76 - Je 15 '80 - p1540
SLJ - v27 - S '80 - p72
Co-author: Heide, Roxanne
Subject: Mystery and detective stories

Mystery Of The Midnight Message
BL - v74 - F 15 '78 - p1013
CCB-B - v31 - Ap '78 - p128
SLJ - v24 - Ap '78 - p84
Subject: Mystery and detective stories

Time Bomb At Brillstone
BL - v79 - Ja 15 '83 - p681
Hi Lo - v4 - Mr '83 - p5
SLJ - v29 - Mr '83 - p176
Co-author: Heide, Roxanne
Subject: Mystery and detective stories

The Wendy Puzzle
BS - v42 - Ja '83 - p406
Inst - v92 - N '82 - p151
KR - v50 - O 15 '82 - p1154
PW - v222 - O 8 '82 - p63
SLJ - v29 - N '82 - p85
VOYA - v6 - Je '83 - p96

HEIDE, Florence Parry (continued)

When The Sad One Comes To Stay
CCB-B - v29 - Mr '76 - p111
HB - v52 - Ap '76 - p155
Kliatt - v11 - Winter '77 - p4
KR - v43 - Ag 15 '75 - p917
NYTBR - N 16 '75 - p52
PW - v208 - Ag 25 '75 - p293
SLJ - v22 - O '75 - p99
Subject: Friendship—Fiction

HEIDE, Roxanne
see Heide, Florence Parry (co-author)

HEINLEIN, Robert A 1907-
ConAu 20NR, ConLC 1, -3, -8, -26, CurBio 55, DcLB 8, MorJA, OxChL, SmATA 9, TwCChW 83, TwCSFW 86, WrDr 86

Rocket Ship Galileo
Atl - v180 - D '47 - p148
BL - v44 - D 15 '47 - p155
KR - v15 - N 1 '47 - p602
LJ - v73 - Ja 1 '48 - p49
NY - v23 - D 6 '47 - p156
NYTBR - F 22 '48 - p31

HELFMAN, Elizabeth S 1911-
AuBYP, ConAu 5NR, SmATA 3, WhoE 83, WrDr 86

Our Fragile Earth
BL - v69 - Mr 15 '73 - p715
KR - v40 - O 15 '72 - p1196
LJ - v98 - My 15 '73 - p1682
SB - v9 - My '73 - p64
Subject: Agriculture; Soil conservation

HELLER, Doris

Little Big Top
Hi Lo - v1 - D '79 - p4

HELLMAN, Harold 1927-
AuBYP SUP, ConAu 10NR, IntAu&W 82, SmATA 4, WrDr 80

The Lever And The Pulley
CCB-B - v26 - O '72 - p27
HB - v49 - F '73 - p73
LJ - v97 - Ap 15 '72 - p1605
SB - v8 - My '72 - p29
Subject: Levers; Pulleys

HEMPHILL, Paul 1936?-
AuBYP SUP, AuNews 2, BioIn 9, -10, ConAu 49, WrDr 86

The Nashville Sound
AB - v45 - Je 1 '70 - p1880
Atl - v225 - Je '70 - p128
KR - v38 - Mr 1 '70 - p294
KR - v38 - Ap 15 '70 - p474
LJ - v95 - Jl '70 - p2547
LJ - v95 - O 15 '70 - p3474
New R - v162 - Je 27 '70 - p21
NYRB - v17 - N 4 '71 - p33
NYT - v119 - Ap 27 '70 - p31
NYTBR - Jl 19 '70 - p7
PW - v197 - F 23 '70 - p155
SR - v53 - Je 27 '70 - p57
TN - v27 - N '70 - p93
Subject: Country musicians

HENDERSON, Zenna 1917-1983
BioIn 12, ConAu 1NR, ConSFA, DcLB 8, ScFSB, SmATA 5, TwCSFW 86, WhoSciF, WrDr 86

Holding Wonder
BL - v68 - O 1 '71 - p133
BL - v68 - Ap 1 '72 - p664
KR - v39 - Mr 1 '71 - p258
KR - v39 - Ap 1 '71 - p385
LJ - v96 - My 15 '71 - p1730
LJ - v96 - My 15 '71 - p1830
PW - v199 - Mr 8 '71 - p66
TN - v28 - Ap '72 - p312

HENKEL, Stephen C 1933-
ConAu 37R, WhoE 75, WrDr 86

Bikes: A How-To-Do-It Guide To Selection, Care, Repair, Maintenance, Decoration, Etc.
A Lib - v4 - F '73 - p98
BL - v68 - Jl 15 '72 - p998
BL - v68 - Jl 15 '72 - p1004
CE - v49 - D '72 - p148
Choice - v10 - O '73 - p1240
KR - v40 - My 15 '72 - p594
LJ - v98 - F 15 '73 - p654
NYTBR - Je 4 '72 - p8
PW - v202 - O 16 '72 - p51
SA - v227 - D '72 - p117
SB - v8 - Mr '73 - p350
Subject: Bicyles and bicyling

HENRY, Marguerite 1902-
Au&ICB, ChlLR 4, ConAu 9NR, CurBio 47, DcLB 22, JBA 51, OxChL, SmATA 11, TwCChW 83, WrDr 86

Album Of Dogs
CLW - v42 - Ap '71 - p523
LJ - v96 - Ja 15 '71 - p268
PW - v198 - D 28 '70 - p61
SB - v7 - My '71 - p82
Subject: Dogs

Mustang, Wild Spirit Of The West
BL - v63 - F 1 '67 - p582
CCB-B - v20 - Ja '67 - p74
CE - v44 - S '67 - p54
CLW - v39 - N '67 - p241
KR - v34 - N 1 '66 - p1140
LJ - v92 - My 15 '67 - p2021
NYTBR - v72 - Ja 15 '67 - p28
PW - v190 - N 21 '66 - p76
SR - v49 - N 12 '66 - p51
TN - v23 - Ap '67 - p291
Subject: Mustang

HENRY, Will (pseud.) 1912-
AuBYP SUP, BioIn 13, EncFWF, WrDr 86
Real Name:
Allen, Henry Wilson

Maheo's Children
BS - v28 - Ap 1 '68 - p18
LJ - v93 - Je 15 '68 - p2547
Subject: Cheyenne Indians—Wars, 1964—Fiction

HENTOFF, Nat 1925-
AuBYP, ChlLR 1, ConAu 5NR, ConLC 26, CurBio 86, SmATA 42, ThrBJA, TwCChW 83, WhoAm 86, WrDr 86

I'm Really Dragged, But Nothing Gets Me Down
BS - v28 - O 1 '68 - p277
CCB-B - v22 - Ja '69 - p78
EJ - v58 - My '69 - p776
KR - v36 - S 15 '68 - p1059
LJ - v93 - N 15 '68 - p4414
LJ - v96 - Ja 15 '71 - p282
NYTBR - v73 - N 3 '68 - p2
NYTBR, Pt. 2 - F 15 '70 - p22
PW - v194 - S 2 '68 - p59
PW - v196 - S 29 '69 - p60
SR - v51 - S 7 '68 - p34
SR - v51 - N 9 '68 - p71
Time - v92 - O 11 '68 - pE8

Jazz Country
BL - v61 - Jl 1 '65 - p1025
BS - v25 - My 15 '65 - p98
CCB-B - v18 - Je '65 - p150
Comw - v82 - My 28 '65 - p330
CSM - v57 - Je 24 '65 - p7
HB - v41 - O '65 - p517
KR - v33 - Mr 1 '65 - p252
LJ - v90 - My 15 '65 - p2418
LJ - v96 - Ja 15 '71 - p282
NYTBR - v70 - My 9 '65 - p3
NYTBR - v72 - N 5 '67 - p54
NYTBR, Pt. 2 - v73 - F 25 '68 - p20
Obs - Ag 7 '66 - p21
PW - v192 - Jl 10 '67 - p188
Spec - Je 3 '66 - p705
SR - v50 - Ja 28 '67 - p45
TLS - My 19 '66 - p442
TN - v38 - Summer '82 - p364
Subject: Jazz music—Fiction; Professions—Fiction

Journey Into Jazz
AB - v43 - Ja 27 '69 - p280
BW - v3 - Mr 30 '69 - p16
CSM - v60 - N 7 '68 - pB4
KR - v36 - O 15 '68 - p1157
LJ - v94 - Ja 15 '69 - p300
PW - v194 - S 2 '68 - p59
RR - v86 - Mr '69 - p174
SR - v51 - N 9 '68 - p67
Subject: Jazz music—Fiction

This School Is Driving Me Crazy
BL - v72 - O 15 '75 - p302
CCB-B - v29 - Ja '76 - p78
Inst - v85 - My '76 - p124
JB - v42 - Je '78 - p155
Kliatt - v12 - Fall '78 - p9
KR - v43 - N 15 '75 - p1296
NO - v15 - F 28 '76 - p21
Obs - D 11 '77 - p31
PW - v209 - Ja 5 '76 - p65
SLJ - v22 - F '76 - p53
TES - Ja 20 '78 - p23
TLS - Ap 7 '78 - p382
Subject: Fathers and sons—Fiction; Schools—Fiction

HERBERT, Frank 1920-1986
ConAu 5NR, -118, ConLC 12, -23, -35, DcLB 8, SmATA 37, -47N, TwCSFW 86, WrDr 86

Under Pressure
Bks W - v1 - Je '77 - p17
MFSF - v53 - Jl '77 - p103
NYTBR - S 8 '74 - p40
Subject: Science fiction

HERMAN, Charlotte 1937-
ConAu 15NR, SmATA 20

What Happened To Heather Hopkowitz?
BL - v78 - N 1 '81 - p388
CBRS - v10 - N '81 - p28
CCB-B - v35 - F '82 - p108
HB - v58 - F '82 - p52
PW - v221 - Ja 8 '82 - p83
SLJ - v28 - D '81 - p64
Subject: Jews—Fiction

HERMANN, Charles F

Read For The Job
Hi Lo - v2 - S '80 - p6

HERRIOT, James (pseud.) 1916-
BioIn 11, -12, ConAu X, ConLC 12, IntAu&W 77, SmATA X, Who 85, WhoWor 84, WorAu 1975, WrDr 86
Real Name:
Wight, James Alfred

All Creatures Great And Small
Atl - v234 - Ag '74 - p91
BL - v69 - Ja 15 '73 - p464
BL - v69 - F 15 '73 - p569
BL - v82 - Ja 1 '86 - p679
BS - v32 - D 1 '72 - p410
BW - v6 - D 24 '72 - p10
CC - v92 - Ap 30 '75 - p449
CC - v92 - My 14 '75 - p500
EJ - v62 - D '73 - p1298
KR - v40 - Ag 15 '72 - p995
LJ - v97 - Ag '72 - p2575
LJ - v98 - My 15 '73 - p1657
LJ - v98 - My 15 '73 - p1713
NYT - v122 - D 14 '72 - p45
NYTBR - F 18 '73 - p10
PW - v202 - Ag 14 '72 - p42
Time - v101 - F 19 '73 - p88
Subject: Veterinarians

HERZ, Peggy 1936-
ConAu 37R

TV Time '79
CLW - v53 - D '81 - p228
Inst - v88 - My '79 - p114

HESSELBERG, Erik
AuBYP SUP

Kon-Tiki And I
BL - v67 - O 15 '70 - p198
CCB-B - v24 - N '70 - p43
NYTBR - S 13 '70 - p42
NYTBR, Pt. 2 - N 8 '70 - p38
PW - v198 - Jl 20 '70 - p70
Subject: Kon-Tiki

HEST, Amy

Maybe Next Year....
BL - v79 - S 1 '82 - p43
CBRS - v11 - F '83 - p70
CCB-B - v36 - F '83 - p109
HB - v58 - D '82 - p649
Kliatt - v19 - Fall '85 - p10
PW - v222 - N 5 '82 - p70
SLJ - v29 - N '82 - p86
Subject: Ballet dancing—Fiction

HEUMAN, William 1912-1971
AuBYP, ConAu 7NR, SmATA 21, WrDr 86

Famous American Indians
BL - v69 - S 15 '72 - p100
NYTBR, Pt. 2 - N 5 '72 - p22
Subject: Indians of North America—Biography

Gridiron Stranger
KR - v38 - F 1 '70 - p111
LJ - v95 - My 15 '70 - p1965
Subject: Football—Fiction

Horace Higby And The Field Goal Formula
Am - v113 - N 20 '65 - p642
CSM - v57 - N 4 '65 - pB9
KR - v33 - My 15 '65 - p501
LJ - v90 - O 15 '65 - p4636

Horace Higby, Coxswain Of The Crew
LJ - v96 - D 15 '71 - p4204
Subject: Boats and boating—Fiction

HEYERDAHL, Thor 1914-
ConAu 5NR, ConLC 26, CurBio 47, -72, IntAu&W 82, SmATA 2, WhoAm 86, WhoWor 84, WorAl, WrDr 86

Kon-Tiki
Atl - v186 - O '50 - p80
BL - v47 - S 1 '50 - p2
BW - v14 - D 9 '84 - p10
CC - v67 - S 27 '50 - p1138
CSM - S 7 '50 - p18
HB - v26 - N '50 - p502
HM - v269 - Ag '84 - p65
KR - v18 - Ag 15 '50 - p492
LJ - v75 - O 1 '50 - p1664
NS - v39 - Ap 1 '50 - p380
NY - v26 - S 16 '50 - p117

HEYERDAHL, Thor (continued)
NYTBR - S 3 '50 - p1
Spec - v184 - Mr 31 '50 - p434
SR - v33 - S 23 '50 - p12
Time - v56 - S 18 '50 - p112
TLS - Ap 7 '50 - p216
Subject: Kon-Tiki

HEYLAR, Jane Penelope Josephine
see Poole, Josephine

HIBBERT, Christopher 1924-
ConAu 2NR, IntAu&W 86, SmATA 4, Who 85, WhoWor 80, WorAu 1975, WrDr 86

The Search For King Arthur
B&B - v15 - My '70 - p40
BL - v66 - My 1 '70 - p1100
BS - v29 - Mr 1 '70 - p454
BW - v4 - My 17 '70 - p26
CCB-B - v24 - Jl '70 - p180
CSM - v62 - My 2 '70 - p17
LJ - v95 - Jl '70 - p2540
NS - v79 - My 15 '70 - p706
NYTBR - Mr 15 '70 - p49
Obs - Jl 26 '70 - p24
PW - v197 - Ja 26 '70 - p278
Spec - v224 - My 9 '70 - p622
SR - v53 - My 9 '70 - p70
TLS - Ap 16 '70 - p424
Co-author: Thomas, Charles
Subject: Great Britain—History

HIBBERT, Eleanor Burford
see Holt, Victoria

HIGDON, Hal 1931-
AuBYP SUP, BioIn 12, ConAu 3NR, IntAu&W 86, SmATA 4, WhoMW 84, WrDr 86

The Electronic Olympics
BL - v68 - Ap 1 '72 - p660
BL - v68 - Ap 1 '72 - p675
CCB-B - v25 - F '72 - p92
KR - v39 - N 1 '71 - p1155
LJ - v96 - D 15 '71 - p4200
SR - v55 - Ap 22 '72 - p86
Subject: Humorous stories; Sports—Fiction

HILDICK, E W 1925-
AuBYP, ConAu 25R, OxChL, ScFSB, SmATA 2, TwCChW 83, WhoChL, WrDr 86

The Active-Enzyme Lemon-Freshened Junior High School Witch
BL - v75 - O 1 '78 - p305
CCB-B - v26 - Je '73 - p155
KR - v41 - F 15 '73 - p187
LJ - v98 - N 15 '73 - p3452
PW - v203 - Mr 5 '73 - p83
Subject: Witchcraft—Fiction

Manhattan Is Missing
B&B - v18 - Ja '73 - p123
BL - v65 - Ap 1 '69 - p894
BS - v28 - Mr 1 '69 - p490
BW - v3 - My 4 '69 - p30
CCB-B - v22 - Ap '69 - p127
HB - v45 - Je '69 - p306
KR - v37 - Ja 15 '69 - p54
Lis - v88 - N 9 '72 - p644
LJ - v94 - My 15 '69 - p2073
LJ - v94 - My 15 '69 - p2100
LJ - v94 - D 15 '69 - p4582
PW - v195 - F 3 '69 - p65
PW - v198 - Ag 3 '70 - p62
SLJ - v24 - F '78 - p35
Spec - v229 - N 11 '72 - p750
SR - v52 - Mr 22 '69 - p63
TLS - D 8 '72 - p1490
Subject: Cats—Fiction; Mystery and detective stories

The Top-Flight Fully-Automated Junior High School Girl Detective
CCB-B - v31 - D '77 - p60
HB - v53 - D '77 - p663
KR - v45 - Ag 1 '77 - p785
SLJ - v23 - My '77 - p78
Subject: Credit cards—Fiction; Mystery and detective stories

HILL, Douglas Arthur 1935-
BioIn 11, ConAu 4NR, ConSFA, MacBEP, ScFSB, SmATA 39, WhoCanL 85, WrDr 86

Galactic Warlord
BL - v76 - Ap 1 '80 - p1116
BS - v40 - My '80 - p78
GP - v18 - N '79 - p3614
HB - v56 - Je '80 - p306
JB - v44 - F '80 - p27
SLJ - v26 - Ap '80 - p125
Subject: Science fiction

HILL, Elizabeth Starr 1925-
AuBYP SUP, ConAu 17R, IntAu&W 77, SmATA 24, WrDr 86

Master Mike And The Miracle Maid
KR - v35 - O 1 '67 - p1219
LJ - v92 - N 15 '67 - p4257

HILLARY, Louise

A Yak For Christmas
BL - v66 - S 1 '69 - p29
GJ - v135 - Je '69 - p260
LJ - v94 - Ap 15 '69 - p1631
NYTBR - Je 8 '69 - p12
PW - v195 - F 3 '69 - p64
SR - v52 - S 13 '69 - p37
Subject: Himalaya mountains

HILLER, Doris (pseud.) 1934-
ConAu X
Real Name:
Nussbaum, Albert F

Black Beach
BL - v74 - Ja 15 '78 - p809
BL - v75 - O 15 '78 - p357
Subject: Buried treasure—Fiction; Hawaii—Fiction

Little Big Top
SLJ - v26 - D '79 - p98
Subject: Circus—Fiction

see also Nussbaum, Albert F for additional titles

HILLER, Douglas

Better Than New
BL - v79 - Ap 15 '83 - p1078
Hi Lo - v3 - Ap '82 - p7

HILTON, Suzanne 1922-
AuBYP SUP, ConAu 12NR, SmATA 4, WrDr 86

How Do They Get Rid Of It?
AF - v77 - Ag '71 - p54
Am - v123 - D 5 '70 - p498
BL - v66 - Jl 1 '70 - p1341
BS - v30 - Je 1 '70 - p105
Comw - v92 - My 22 '70 - p253
KR - v38 - Mr 15 '70 - p332
LJ - v95 - S 15 '70 - p3062
SB - v6 - My '70 - p60
Subject: Pollution

The Way It Was—1876
BL - v71 - Je 15 '75 - p1070
CCB-B - v29 - N '75 - p46
CLW - v47 - D '75 - p234
HB - v51 - O '75 - p482
KR - v43 - Je 1 '75 - p608
NYTBR - Ag 17 '75 - p8
NYTBR - N 16 '75 - p55
PW - v207 - My 19 '75 - p176
SE - v44 - O '80 - p479
SLJ - v21 - My '75 - p64
SLJ - v22 - D '75 - p31
SLJ - v32 - Ag '86 - p92
Subject: United States—Social life and customs

HINTON, Nigel 1941-
ConAu 85

Collision Course
BL - v74 - S 15 '77 - p194
BS - v37 - O '77 - p203
EJ - v67 - F '78 - p79
GP - v15 - Ap '77 - p3086
JB - v41 - Ag '77 - p235
KR - v45 - My 15 '77 - p543
NYTBR - O 9 '77 - p28
Obs - N 28 '76 - p31
SLJ - v24 - S '77 - p144
TES - My 2 '80 - p24
TES - Jl 1 '83 - p27
TLS - D 10 '76 - p1544
Subject: Hit-and-run drivers—Fiction

HINTON, S E 1950-
AuBYP SUP, ChlLR 3, ConAu 81, ConLC 30, FourBJA, OxChL, SmATA 19, TwCChW 83, WhoAm 86, WrDr 86

The Outsiders
Atl - v220 - D '67 - p136
BL - v64 - O 1 '67 - p176
BS - v27 - Jl 1 '67 - p144
CCB-B - v20 - Jl '67 - p171
CLW - v39 - D '67 - p292
EJ - v58 - F '69 - p295
EJ - v67 - My '78 - p88
HB - v43 - Ag '67 - p475
Hi Lo - v2 - Ja '81 - p4
J Read - v22 - N '78 - p126
KR - v35 - Ap 15 '67 - p506
LJ - v92 - My 15 '67 - p2028
Nat - v242 - Mr 8 '86 - p276
NYTBR, Pt. 2 - v72 - My 7 '67 - p10
NYTBR, Pt. 2 - F 16 '69 - p22
NYTBR, Pt. 2 - My 4 '69 - p6
PW - v191 - My 22 '67 - p64
SR - v50 - My 13 '67 - p59
SR - v51 - Ja 27 '68 - p34
TLS - O 30 '70 - p1258

HINTON, S E (continued)
WLB - v60 - S '85 - p63
Subject: Juvenile delinquency—Fiction

Rumble Fish
BL - v72 - S 1 '75 - p41
B Rpt - v2 - S '83 - p24
BS - v35 - F '76 - p362
CCB-B - v29 - D '75 - p63
EJ - v65 - My '76 - p91
GP - v15 - My '76 - p2891
HB - v51 - D '75 - p601
Inst - v85 - N '75 - p155
JB - v40 - Ag '76 - p229
J Read - v22 - N '78 - p127
KR - v43 - O 15 '75 - p1193
Nat - v242 - Mr 8 '86 - p276
NS - v91 - My 21 '76 - p690
NYT - v125 - D 20 '75 - p25
NYTBR - D 14 '75 - p8
Obs - N 28 '76 - p31
PW - v208 - Jl 28 '75 - p122
SLJ - v22 - O '75 - p106
SLJ - v22 - D '75 - p31
TLS - Ap 2 '76 - p388
TN - v32 - Ap '76 - p284
Subject: Brothers and sisters—Fiction; City and town life—Fiction; Social problems—Fiction

Tex
BL - v76 - O 15 '79 - p353
BS - v39 - Mr '80 - p465
CBRS - v8 - O '79 - p17
CCB-B - v33 - D '79 - p71
EJ - v70 - Ap '81 - p76
GP - v19 - My '80 - p3686
HB - v55 - D '79 - p668
Hi Lo - v2 - Ja '81 - p4
JB - v44 - D '80 - p307
J Read - v24 - O '80 - p83
KR - v48 - Ja 1 '80 - p9
Nat - v242 - Mr 8 '86 - p276
NYTBR - D 16 '79 - p23
Sch Lib - v28 - Je '80 - p177
SLJ - v26 - N '79 - p88
TLS - Mr 28 '80 - p356
WLB - v54 - O '79 - p122
Subject: Brothers and sisters—Fiction; Self-reliance—Fiction

That Was Then, This Is Now
BL - v67 - Jl 15 '71 - p951
BL - v68 - Ap 1 '72 - p664
BL - v82 - F 1 '86 - p817
BS - v31 - Ag 15 '71 - p235
BW - v5 - My 9 '71 - p5
CCB-B - v25 - S '71 - p8
EJ - v67 - My '78 - p88
HB - v47 - Ag '71 - p388
Hi Lo - v2 - Ja '81 - p4
J Read - v22 - N '78 - p126
KR - v39 - Ap 15 '71 - p442
LJ - v96 - Je 15 '71 - p2138
Nat - v242 - Mr 8 '86 - p276
NYTBR - Ag 8 '71 - p8
Obs - N 28 '71 - p35
PW - v199 - My 31 '71 - p135
SLJ - v29 - N '82 - p35
SR - v54 - Je 19 '71 - p27
TLS - O 22 '71 - p1318
TN - v28 - Ap '72 - p312
Subject: Friendship—Fiction; Social problems—Fiction

HINTZE, Naomi A 1909-
BioIn 8, ConAu 1NR, WrDr 86

The Stone Carnation
BL - v68 - S 15 '71 - p83
KR - v39 - Ja 1 '71 - p20
LJ - v96 - Mr 1 '71 - p865
NYTBR - Mr 7 '71 - p42
PW - v199 - Ja 18 '71 - p48
Subject: Ghosts—Fiction

HINZ, Bob

Philadelphia Phillies
SLJ - v29 - Mr '83 - p170
Subject: Baseball

HIRSCH, S Carl 1913-
AuBYP SUP, ConAu 2NR, IntAu&W 77, SmATA 2, ThrBJA, WrDr 86

Four Score...And More: The Life Span Of Man
Comw - v82 - My 28 '65 - p332
HB - v41 - Je '65 - p295
KR - v33 - Mr 15 '65 - p324
LJ - v90 - F 15 '65 - p970
SA - v213 - D '65 - p115
Subject: Longevity

The Living Community: A Venture Into Ecology
BL - v62 - Je 15 '66 - p1000
BS - v26 - My 1 '66 - p58
CCB-B - v19 - Je '66 - p164
KR - v34 - Mr 15 '66 - p310
NH - v75 - N '66 - p62
SB - v2 - S '66 - p124
Subject: Ecology

HIRSHBERG, Al 1909-1973
AuBYP, BioIn 9, ConAu 4NR, SmATA 38, WhAm 6

The Greatest American Leaguers
BS - v30 - Ap 1 '70 - p18
CCB-B - v24 - S '70 - p9
KR - v38 - F 1 '70 - p107
LJ - v95 - My 15 '70 - p1964
SR - v53 - Je 27 '70 - p38
Subject: Baseball—Biography

Henry Aaron: Quiet Superstar
KR - v37 - Je 15 '69 - p633
LJ - v94 - D 15 '69 - p4620
Subject: Baseball—Biography

see also Piersall, James (co-author) for additional titles

HITCHCOCK, Alfred 1899-1980
BiDFilm, ConAu 97, ConLC 16, ConTFT 1, CurBio 60, -80N, EncMys, HalFC 84, NewYTBS 80, OxFilm, SmATA 27

Alfred Hitchcock's Sinister Spies
BS - v26 - O 1 '66 - p250
LJ - v91 - N 15 '66 - p5775
NYTBR - v71 - N 6 '66 - p58
PW - v190 - N 7 '66 - p66
SR - v49 - O 29 '66 - p43
Subject: Spies—Fiction

HOARD, Edison 1934?-
BioIn 9

Curse Not The Darkness
LJ - v96 - Ap 15 '71 - p1514
Co-author: Reuben, Michael
Subject: Blacks—Biography

HOBSON, Burton Harold 1933-
ConAu 2NR, SmATA 28, WhoAm 86

Coins You Can Collect
Hob - v75 - N '70 - p141
LJ - v92 - Jl '67 - p2655
Subject: Numismatics

HOCHMAN, Stan

Mike Schmidt: Baseball's King Of Swing
BL - v80 - Ja 15 '84 - p754
B Rpt - v3 - My '84 - p54
SLJ - v30 - D '83 - p87
Subject: Baseball—Biography

HODGE, Ken
see Awrey, Don (co-author)

HODGES, C Walter 1909-
AuBYP, ConAu 5NR, IlsCB 1946, -1957, OxChL, SmATA 2, ThrBJA, TwCChW 83, WhoChL, WrDr 86

The Overland Launch
B&B - v17 - My '72 - pR14
BL - v66 - Jl 15 '70 - p1407
BL - v67 - Ap 1 '71 - p660
BS - v30 - Jl 1 '70 - p145
CCB-B - v24 - O '70 - p26
HB - v46 - Ag '70 - p393
KR - v38 - Je 1 '70 - p604
LJ - v95 - O 15 '70 - p3638
NS - v78 - O 31 '69 - p623
Obs - N 30 '69 - p35
PW - v197 - Je 1 '70 - p68
Spec - v223 - N 1 '69 - p598
SR - v53 - Ag 22 '70 - p53
TLS - D 4 '69 - p1400
Subject: Life saving—England

HOFF, Syd 1912-
AuBYP, ConAu 4NR, ConGrA 1, IlsCB 1957, -1967, SmATA 9, -4AS, ThrBJA, TwCChW 83, WorECar, WrDr 86

Irving And Me
BL - v64 - N 1 '67 - p334
BS - v27 - S 1 '67 - p223
CCB-B - v21 - O '67 - p28
Choice - v14 - N '77 - p1178
CSM - v59 - N 2 '67 - pB10
HB - v43 - O '67 - p594
KR - v35 - Je 1 '67 - p649
LJ - v92 - S 15 '67 - p3186
LJ - v95 - F 15 '70 - p742
NYTBR - v72 - O 8 '67 - p38
NYTBR - v72 - N 5 '67 - p64
SR - v50 - S 16 '67 - p49

HOFFMAN, Anne Byrne

Echoes From The Schoolyard
BL - v74 - F 15 '78 - p970
LJ - v103 - F 1 '78 - p380
Pet PM - v7 - D '78 - p107
Subject: Basketball

HOFFMAN, Elizabeth P

This House Is Haunted!
SLJ - v25 - N '78 - p55
Subject: Ghosts

Visions Of The Future: Palm Reading
SLJ - v25 - N '78 - p55
Subject: Divination; Palmistry

HOFFMAN, Jeffrey

Corvette: America's Supercar
BL - v80 - Ag '84 - p1610
BL - v81 - Je 15 '85 - p1452
SLJ - v31 - S '84 - p118
VOYA - v8 - Ap '85 - p64
Subject: Automobiles

HOFSINDE, Robert 1902-1973
AuBYP, BioIn 7, -10, ConAu 73, IlsCB 1946, SmATA 21, ThrBJA

Indian Warriors And Their Weapons
BL - v61 - Je 1 '65 - p958
LJ - v90 - Ap 15 '65 - p2041
NYTBR - v70 - My 30 '65 - p20
Subject: Indian warfare

HOGAN, Elizabeth

The Curse Of King Tut And Other Mystery Stories
Hi Lo - v1 - Mr '80 - p5
Subject: Mystery and detective stories; Short stories

HOGBEN, Lancelot 1895-1975
BioIn 1, -2, -5, -10, -11, -12, -13, ConAu 61, CurBio 41, WhAm 6

The Wonderful World Of Mathematics
BS - v28 - Ja 1 '69 - p424
HB - v45 - F '69 - p75
KR - v36 - N 1 '68 - p1236
LJ - v94 - My 15 '69 - p2113
SB - v5 - My '69 - p18
TLS - O 3 '68 - p1127
Subject: Civilization; Mathematics

HOGG, Elizabeth
see Grey, Elizabeth

HOKE, Helen L 1903-
AuBYP, BioIn 8, ConAu 73, SmATA 15

More Jokes, Jokes, Jokes
CC - v82 - Jl 21 '65 - p918
LJ - v90 - S 15 '65 - p3805
Subject: Wit and humor

HOLDEN, Raymond P 1894-1972
AuBYP, BioIn 9, ConAu 4NR, NewYTBE 72

All About Famous Scientific Expeditions
NYTBR - O 19 '58 - p60
Subject: Scientific expeditions

Wildlife Mysteries
KR - v40 - O 1 '72 - p1157
LJ - v98 - F 15 '73 - p644
SB - v9 - My '73 - p44
Subject: Animals; Zoology

HOLLAND, Isabelle 1920-
AuBYP SUP, ConAu 10NR, ConLC 21, FifBJA, IntAu&W 86, OxChL, SmATA 8, TwCChW 83, WrDr 86

Amanda's Choice
BW - v4 - My 17 '70 - p16
CCB-B - v24 - S '70 - p9
CSM - v62 - My 7 '70 - pB6
HB - v46 - Je '70 - p297
KR - v38 - F 15 '70 - p173
LJ - v96 - Mr 15 '71 - p1116
NYTBR - My 3 '70 - p23
PW - v197 - My 18 '70 - p38
SR - v53 - My 9 '70 - p69
Subject: Emotional problems—Fiction; Family life—Fiction

Heads You Win, Tails I Lose
A Lib - v5 - My '74 - p235
BL - v70 - O 15 '73 - p234
BS - v33 - S 15 '73 - p280
CCB-B - v27 - Ja '74 - p80
EJ - v63 - My '74 - p91
HB - v50 - F '74 - p56
KR - v41 - Jl 15 '73 - p759
LJ - v98 - O 15 '73 - p3155
NO - v12 - D 29 '73 - p15
NYTBR - N 25 '73 - p10
PW - v204 - S 17 '73 - p57
TN - v30 - N '73 - p81
Subject: Family problems—Fiction

Hitchhike
CCB-B - v31 - Ja '78 - p79
EJ - v67 - F '78 - p99
HB - v53 - D '77 - p668
Kliatt - v14 - Winter '80 - p8
KR - v45 - Ag 1 '77 - p789
NYTBR - O 30 '77 - p34
PW - v212 - S 12 '77 - p133
SLJ - v24 - S '77 - p145
Subject: Fathers and daughters—Fiction; Hitchhiking—Fiction

HOLLAND, Isabelle (continued)

Jennie Kissed Me
BL - v81 - Ag '85 - p1656
Subject: Love—Fiction

The Man Without A Face
BL - v68 - My 15 '72 - p816
BS - v32 - Ap 15 '72 - p46
BW - v6 - Ag 6 '72 - p2
CCB-B - v25 - Jl '72 - p170
Comw - v97 - N 17 '72 - p157
HB - v48 - Ag '72 - p375
KR - v40 - Ja 15 '72 - p73
LJ - v97 - Jl '72 - p2489
Nat R - v24 - Jl 7 '72 - p754
NYTBR - Ap 9 '72 - p8
NYTBR, Pt. 2 - N 5 '72 - p26
PW - v201 - Ap 17 '72 - p59
TN - v29 - Ap '73 - p257
Subject: Family problems—Fiction; Friendship—Fiction

Perdita
BL - v79 - Ap 15 '83 - p1084
BW - v13 - My 8 '83 - p18
CBRS - v12 - S '83 - p8
CCB-B - v37 - O '83 - p30
HB - v59 - O '83 - p582
HB - v61 - Ja '85 - p74
Kliatt - v18 - Fall '84 - p12
KR - v51 - Je 15 '83 - p663
PW - v223 - Je 10 '83 - p64
SLJ - v30 - O '83 - p168
Subject: Amnesia—Fiction; Horses—Fiction; Mystery and detective stories

HOLLANDER, Phyllis 1928-
AuBYP SUP, ConAu 18NR, SmATA 39

American Women In Sports
KR - v40 - Mr 15 '72 - p329
LJ - v97 - My 15 '72 - p1932
NYTBR, Pt. 2 - My 7 '72 - p24
SE - v37 - D '73 - p788
Subject: Athletes

Touchdown!
BL - v79 - Ja 1 '83 - p622
B Rpt - v1 - Mr '83 - p54
SLJ - v29 - D '82 - p85
Co-author: Hollander, Zander
Subject: Football

Winners Under 21
BL - v78 - Jl '82 - p1450
B Rpt - v1 - Mr '83 - p54
VOYA - v5 - Ag '82 - p49
Co-author: Hollander, Zander
Subject: Athletes

see also Hollander, Zander for additional titles

HOLLANDER, Zander 1923-
AuBYP SUP, ConAu 18NR

The Baseball Book
ARBA - v14 - p306
BL - v78 - Jl '82 - p1450
B Rpt - v2 - My '83 - p51
SLJ - v29 - D '82 - p85
VOYA - v5 - O '82 - p52
Subject: Baseball

Roller Hockey
BL - v72 - N 1 '75 - p366
Comw - v102 - N 21 '75 - p571
LJ - v100 - O 15 '75 - p1944
SLJ - v22 - D '75 - p70
Subject: Roller-skate hockey

Strange But True Football Stories
CLW - v39 - F '68 - p438
LJ - v92 - D 15 '67 - p4633
Subject: Football

see also Hollander, Phyllis (co-author) for additional titles

HOLM, Anne S 1922-
ConAu 17R, FourBJA, OxChL, SmATA 1, TwCChW 83B

North To Freedom
BL - v62 - S 1 '65 - p56
BS - v25 - Je 15 '65 - p145
CCB-B - v19 - S '65 - p10
EJ - v72 - Ja '83 - p26
HB - v41 - Ag '65 - p380
KR - v33 - Mr 1 '65 - p243
LJ - v90 - My 15 '65 - p2420
NYTBR - v70 - Jl 4 '65 - p12
SLJ - v28 - N '81 - p39
SR - v48 - My 15 '65 - p46
TCR - v68 - F '67 - p451

HOLMAN, Felice 1919-
AuBYP, ConAu 18NR, FourBJA, IntAu&W 82, OxChL, SmATA 7, TwCChW 83, WhoAmW 83, WrDr 86

Slake's Limbo
BL - v80 - S 1 '83 - p95
B Rpt - v1 - Mr '83 - p24
Emerg Lib - v11 - Ja '84 - p21
HB - v62 - S '86 - p616
Hi Lo - v2 - D '80 - p6
JB - v44 - D '80 - p307

HOLMAN, Felice (continued)
Obs - Ag 24 '80 - p27
Obs - Jl 21 '85 - p22
TES - D 26 '80 - p17
Subject: Subways—Fiction

HOLMES, Anita

Pierced And Pretty: The Complete Guide To Ear Piercing, Pierced Earrings, And How To Create Your Own
Kliatt - v19 - Winter '85 - p77
NYTBR - v90 - F 24 '85 - p30
SLJ - v31 - F '85 - p75
VOYA - v7 - F '85 - p345
Subject: Earrings

HOLMES, Burnham 1909-

Basic Training
KR - v47 - Jl 1 '79 - p746
SLJ - v25 - Ap '79 - p68
Subject: Military education; United States Army

Nefertiti: The Mystery Queen
Cur R - v17 - Ag '78 - p228
SLJ - v25 - N '78 - p64
Subject: Egypt; Kings, queens, rulers, etc.

HOLMES, Marjorie Rose 1910-
AuBYP, AuNews 1, BioIn 10, ConAu 5NR, IntAu&W 86, SmATA 43, WhoAm 86, WhoAmW 77, WrDr 86

Saturday Night
Kliatt - v16 - Fall '82 - p12
KR - v27 - F 1 '59 - p96
LJ - v84 - Ap 15 '59 - p1338
NYTBR - My 24 '59 - p38
SLJ - v29 - S '82 - p122
VOYA - v5 - O '82 - p43

HOLT, Victoria (pseud.) 1906-
BioIn 11, ConAu X, EncMys, IntAu&W 77X, Novels, SmATA 2, TwCCr&M 85, WhoAm 86, WorAu, WrDr 86
Real Name:
Hibbert, Eleanor Burford

Menfreya In The Morning
B&B - v11 - Je '66 - p45
BS - v26 - My 15 '66 - p72
HB - v42 - O '66 - p588
KR - v34 - Ja 15 '66 - p80
LJ - v91 - Mr 15 '66 - p1444
NYTBR - v71 - Ap 17 '66 - p37
PW - v189 - Ja 17 '66 - p129
PW - v191 - Mr 20 '67 - p62
Time - v87 - My 13 '66 - p114

HOLZ, Loretta 1943-
ConAu 65, SmATA 17

The How-To Book Of International Dolls: A Comprehensive Guide To Making, Costuming And Collecting Dolls
Hob - v85 - Ag '80 - p122
Kliatt - v14 - Spring '80 - p52
LJ - v105 - Ap 1 '80 - p848
Subject: Dollmaking

HONIG, Donald 1931-
ConAu 9NR, DrAP&F 85, IntAu&W 77, SmATA 18

Dynamite
KR - v39 - Je 1 '71 - p593
LJ - v96 - Jl '71 - p2369
PW - v200 - Jl 26 '71 - p52

Fury On Skates
BL - v71 - D 15 '74 - p425
CSM - v67 - F 5 '75 - p8
KR - v42 - S 1 '74 - p950
LJ - v99 - D 15 '74 - p3280
Subject: Hockey—Fiction

Going The Distance
BL - v72 - Jl 15 '76 - p1601
BS - v36 - O '76 - p239
JB - v41 - Ap '77 - p112
SLJ - v22 - My '76 - p80
Subject: Swimming

Johnny Lee
CCB-B - v25 - S '71 - p8
CLW - v42 - My '71 - p581
Comw - v94 - My 21 '71 - p268
KR - v39 - Mr 1 '71 - p236
LJ - v96 - My 15 '71 - p1823
SR - v54 - Jl 17 '71 - p36
Subject: Baseball—Fiction; Prejudices—Fiction

Winter Always Comes
BL - v73 - Je 1 '77 - p1490
BL - v73 - Je 1 '77 - p1498
BS - v37 - Ag '77 - p142
CCB-B - v31 - S '77 - p16
KR - v45 - Ap 1 '77 - p351
NYTBR - My 1 '77 - p41
SLJ - v23 - My '77 - p79
Subject: Baseball—Fiction

HOOBLER, Dorothy
ConAu 11NR, SmATA 28

Photographing History: The Career Of Matthew Brady
B&B - v6 - O '78 - p4
BL - v74 - Ja 15 '78 - p806
CE - v55 - O '78 - p42
KR - v45 - O 1 '77 - p1055
PW - v212 - S 19 '77 - p146
SLJ - v24 - F '78 - p65
Co-author: Hoobler, Thomas
Subject: Photographers

HOOBLER, Thomas
see Hoobler, Dorothy (co-author)

HOOKER, Ruth 1920-
AuBYP SUP, ConAu 69, SmATA 21

The Kidnapping Of Anna
SLJ - v26 - D '79 - p98
Co-author: Smith, Carole
Subject: Kidnapping—Fiction; Mystery and detective stories

HOOPER, Meredith 1939-
ConAu 106, IntAu&W 77, SmATA 28, WrDr 86

Everyday Inventions
BL - v73 - S 15 '76 - p137
BL - v73 - S 15 '76 - p175
LJ - v101 - O 15 '76 - p2186
LJ - v102 - Mr 1 '77 - p553
Obs - Mr 23 '75 - p27
Obs - Jl 18 '76 - p20
PW - v210 - Jl 19 '76 - p133
TLS - D 8 '72 - p1500
TLS - D 6 '74 - p1385
Subject: Inventions

HOOVER, H M 1935-
ConAu 105, FifBJA, IntAu&W 86X, ScF&FL 1, ScFSB, SmATA 44, TwCSFW 86, WrDr 86

The Bell Tree
BL - v79 - O 15 '82 - p312
BS - v42 - D '82 - p365
BW - v13 - Ja 9 '83 - p11
CBRS - v11 - Winter '83 - p57
CCB-B - v36 - Ja '83 - p90
HB - v58 - D '82 - p658
J Read - v26 - D '82 - p277
LA - v60 - Mr '83 - p363
SLJ - v29 - N '82 - p100
VOYA - v5 - F '83 - p44
Subject: Science fiction

The Lost Star
BL - v75 - Ap 15 '79 - p1295
CBRS - v7 - Ap '79 - p88
CCB-B - v32 - Mr '79 - p119
CE - v56 - Ja '80 - p169
CLW - v51 - N '79 - p183
GP - v19 - Ja '81 - p3816
HB - v55 - Ap '79 - p199
JB - v45 - Ap '81 - p82
Kliatt - v14 - Fall '80 - p14
KR - v47 - Je 1 '79 - p642
LA - v57 - F '80 - p190
SLJ - v25 - Mr '79 - p148
TLS - N 20 '81 - p1361
Subject: Science fiction

The Rains Of Eridan
BL - v74 - N 1 '77 - p477
BS - v37 - D '77 - p265
CCB-B - v31 - F '78 - p96
CE - v54 - Ap '78 - p306
EJ - v67 - S '78 - p90
HB - v54 - Ap '78 - p169
KR - v45 - Ag 15 '77 - p855
SLJ - v24 - N '77 - p57
TN - v39 - Fall '82 - p71
Subject: Science fiction

Return To Earth
BL - v76 - My 1 '80 - p1292
CBRS - v8 - Spring '80 - p117
CCB-B - v33 - My '80 - p173
EJ - v69 - My '80 - p91
HB - v56 - Je '80 - p306
Inst - v89 - My '80 - p92
JB - v45 - O '81 - p211
Kliatt - v15 - Fall '81 - p22
LA - v58 - Ja '81 - p84
Obs - N 29 '81 - p27
Sch Lib - v30 - Mr '82 - p51
SLJ - v26 - Mr '80 - p141
TES - Je 5 '81 - p41
TLS - N 20 '81 - p1361
Subject: Science fiction

This Time Of Darkness
BL - v77 - N 15 '80 - p459
CCB-B - v34 - Ap '81 - p152
GP - v21 - S '82 - p3953
HB - v56 - D '80 - p641
Inst - v90 - N '80 - p158
KR - v48 - D 15 '80 - p1573
S Fict R - v10 - N '81 - p59
SLJ - v27 - O '80 - p147
TLS - Jl 23 '82 - p791
VOYA - v4 - Ap '81 - p40
Subject: Science fiction

HOPKINS, Lee Bennett 1938-
AuBYP SUP, BioIn 13, ConAu 25R, FifBJA, IntAu&W 82, SmATA 3, -4AS, WhoBlA 80, WhoE 75, WrDr 86

A-Haunting We Will Go
BL - v73 - My 1 '77 - p1343
CCB-B - v30 - Jl '77 - p175
Cur R - v17 - My '78 - p127
SLJ - v23 - My '77 - p78
Subject: Ghosts—Fiction; Short stories

Monsters, Ghoulies And Creepy Creatures: Fantastic Stories And Poems
BL - v74 - Mr 1 '78 - p1110
CCB-B - v31 - Jl '78 - p178
Cur R - v17 - My '78 - p127
Subject: Ghouls and ogres—Fiction; Monsters—Fiction; Short stories

Wonder Wheels
BL - v75 - Mr 15 '79 - p1145
BS - v39 - Ag '79 - p168
CBRS - v7 - Ap '79 - p89
CCB-B - v32 - Je '79 - p177
Hi Lo - v1 - Mr '80 - p3
KR - v47 - Ap 1 '79 - p392
NYTBR - Ap 8 '79 - p32
SLJ - v25 - My '79 - p86
Subject: Roller skating—Fiction

HOPMAN, Harry

Better Tennis For Boys And Girls
BL - v68 - Je 15 '72 - p903
KR - v40 - Mr 15 '72 - p339
LJ - v97 - My 15 '72 - p1932
Subject: Tennis

HOPPE, Joanne 1932-
ConAu 81, SmATA 42

April Spell
EJ - v68 - N '79 - p75
Subject: Spiritualism—Fiction; Supernatural—Fiction

HOPPER, Nancy J 1937-
ConAu 115, SmATA 38

Lies
BL - v80 - Je 1 '84 - p1392
CBRS - v12 - Spring '84 - p128
CCB-B - v37 - Ap '84 - p148
HB - v60 - Ag '84 - p476
SLJ - v31 - S '84 - p119
Subject: Schools—Fiction

Rivals
B Rpt - v5 - My '86 - p31
BS - v46 - Ap '86 - p39
CBRS - v14 - F '86 - p78
CCB-B - v39 - Mr '86 - p129
SLJ - v32 - D '85 - p101
VOYA - v9 - Je '86 - p79
Subject: Cousins—Fiction

HORN, Daniel
see Terry, Luther L (co-author)

HORNER, Dave 1934-
ConAu 17R, SmATA 12

Better Scuba Diving For Boys
Am - v115 - N 5 '66 - p556
BL - v63 - F 1 '67 - p582
LJ - v92 - Ja 15 '67 - p351
Subject: Diving

HOUSEHOLD, Geoffrey 1900-
AuBYP SUP, ConAu 77, ConLC 11, ConNov 86, OxEng 85, SmATA 14, TwCCr&M 85, WhoChL, WhoSpyF, WrDr 86

Escape Into Daylight
Am - v135 - D 11 '76 - p429
BL - v73 - D 15 '76 - p608
BS - v36 - Ja '77 - p324
CCB-B - v30 - F '77 - p91
CSM - v68 - N 3 '76 - p20
GP - v14 - Ap '76 - p2844
JB - v40 - Ag '76 - p230
Kliatt - v12 - p8
KR - v44 - S 1 '76 - p974
SLJ - v23 - D '76 - p68
Spec - v236 - Ap 10 '76 - p25
Teacher - v95 - My '78 - p109
TLS - Ap 2 '76 - p388
Subject: Kidnapping—Fiction

HOUSER, Norman W
AuBYP SUP

Drugs: Facts On Their Use And Abuse
BL - v66 - N 1 '69 - p347
BL - v66 - N 15 '69 - p366
BS - v29 - S 1 '69 - p211
CC - v86 - D 10 '69 - p1585
CLW - v41 - O '69 - p134
CLW - v41 - My '70 - p577
HB - v45 - D '69 - p687
KR - v37 - Je 15 '69 - p636
LJ - v94 - O 15 '69 - p3845
NYTBR - S 21 '69 - p30
NYTBR, Pt. 2 - N 9 '69 - p60
SB - v5 - D '69 - p267

HOUSER, Norman W (continued)
Co-author: Richmond, Julius Benjamin
Subject: Drug abuse

HOUSH, Barbara

Brashki: A Gypsy Fantasy
BS - v40 - My '80 - p49
LJ - v104 - D 1 '79 - p2588

HOUSTON, James 1921-
ChlLR 3, ConAu 65, FourBJA, IlsCB 1967, OxCanL, OxChL, Profile 2, SmATA 13, TwCChW 83, WrDr 86

Frozen Fire: A Tale Of Courage
B&B - v6 - Ap '78 - p4
BL - v74 - F 15 '78 - p1009
BS - v37 - Ja '78 - p335
CCB-B - v31 - Mr '78 - p113
CE - v54 - Mr '78 - p258
Cur R - v17 - Ag '78 - p184
GP - v19 - My '80 - p3698
HB - v54 - F '78 - p47
KR - v45 - N 15 '77 - p1197
LA - v55 - Mr '78 - p367
RT - v32 - O '78 - p43
SE - v42 - Ap '78 - p321
SLJ - v24 - N '77 - p57
Subject: Arctic regions—Fiction; Survival—Fiction

HOWARD, Don

Moving Dirt
BL - v75 - Ap 15 '79 - p1290
Hi Lo - v2 - Ap '81 - p2

HOWARD, Elizabeth 1907-
AuBYP, CurBio 51, IntAu&W 82X, MichAu 80, MorJA, SmATA X
Pseud./variant:
Mizner, Elizabeth Howard

Out Of Step With The Dancers
BB - v6 - Ag '78 - p4
BL - v74 - Ap 1 '78 - p1255
CCB-B - v32 - S '78 - p10
KR - v46 - My 1 '78 - p501
SLJ - v24 - Ap '78 - p94
Subject: Shakers—Fiction

HOWARD, Sam

Communications Machines
ASBYP - v14 - Fall '81 - p29
JB - v45 - O '81 - p197
SB - v17 - S '81 - p34
SLJ - v27 - F '81 - p53
Subject: Communication

HOWE, Fanny

Taking Care
BL - v82 - Ja 1 '86 - p677
Kliatt - v20 - Winter '86 - p12
KR - v53 - O 15 '85 - p1140
SLJ - v32 - Mr '86 - p176

Yeah, But
BL - v79 - Ja 15 '83 - p677
Kliatt - v16 - Fall '82 - p12
PW - v222 - Jl 9 '82 - p49
SLJ - v29 - O '82 - p161
VOYA - v6 - Ap '83 - p37
Subject: City and town life—Fiction; Friendship—Fiction; Interpersonal relations—Fiction

HOWE, Janet Rogers 1901-

The Mystery Of The Marmalade Cat
CSM - v61 - My 1 '69 - pB6
KR - v37 - F 1 '69 - p100
LJ - v94 - My 15 '69 - p2122
Subject: Mystery and detective stories

HOYT, Edwin P 1923-
AuBYP, BioIn 2, ConAu 1NR, SmATA 28

Andrew Johnson
BS - v25 - My 15 '65 - p98
CSM - v57 - My 6 '65 - p8B
KR - v33 - Ja 15 '65 - p65
LJ - v90 - F 15 '65 - p970
NYTBR - v70 - My 9 '65 - p20
Subject: Biography

Deadly Craft: Fire Ships To PT Boats
BL - v64 - Jl 1 '68 - p1234
BS - v28 - My 1 '68 - p65
KR - v36 - Ap 1 '68 - p399
LJ - v93 - My 15 '68 - p2122
Subject: Warships

HOYT, Mary Finch 1924?-
AuBYP, BioIn 11, ConAu 107, WhoAm 86, WhoAmW 81

American Women Of The Space Age
BL - v62 - Jl 15 '66 - p1087
Inst - v75 - Je '66 - p139
KR - v34 - F 15 '66 - p189
LJ - v91 - Ap 15 '66 - p2226
NYTBR - v71 - Je 12 '66 - p22

HOYT, Mary Finch (continued)
SB - v2 - My '66 - p59
Subject: Astronautics

HUFFMAN, Suanne

Get What You Pay For
Hi Lo - v2 - S '80 - p6

HUGHES, Jill
see Cook, David (co-author)

HUGHES, Langston 1902-1967
AmWr S1, AuBYP, ConAu 1NR, ConLC 1, -5, -10, -15, -35, CurBio 40, -67, DcAmNB, DcLB 4, -7, -48, -51, FourBJA, McGEWD 84, ModBlW, SmATA 33

The Book Of Negro Humor
Bl W - v20 - F '71 - p68
LJ - v91 - F 15 '66 - p947
Subject: Wit and humor

HUGHES, Monica 1925-
ChlLR 9, ConAu 77, OxCanL, OxChL, Profile 2, SmATA 15, TwCChW 83, TwCSFW 86, WhoCanL 85, WrDr 86

Hunter In The Dark
BIC - v11 - Je '82 - p32
CCB-B - v36 - Jl '83 - p211
Emerg Lib - v12 - S '84 - p44
Emerg Lib - v12 - N '84 - p20
Emerg Lib - v14 - S '86 - p22
GP - v25 - Jl '86 - p4647
HB - v59 - Je '83 - p313
In Rev - v16 - Ap '82 - p50
JB - v50 - Ag '86 - p156
KR - v51 - F 15 '83 - p187
Mac - v95 - Je 28 '82 - p56
Quill & Q - v48 - Ap '82 - p32
SE - v48 - My '84 - p379
SLJ - v29 - My '83 - p82
SLJ - v30 - Mr '84 - p125
TES - My 16 '86 - p27
VOYA - v6 - O '83 - p203
Subject: Hunting—Fiction; Leukemia—Fiction; Self-reliance—Fiction

HUGHES, Walter Llewellyn
see Walters, Hugh

HUGO, Victor Marie 1802-1885
BioIn 13, EncMys, EncO&P 78, EncWT, McGEWB, NotNAT A, OxFr, OxMus, OxThe 83, SmATA 47

Hunchback Of Notre Dame
BL - v79 - Ap 1 '83 - p1022
Adapter: Stewart, Diana
Subject: France—Fiction

HULL, Jessie Redding

The Other Side Of Yellow
BL - v77 - Jl 15 '81 - p1435
Hi Lo - v2 - Je '81 - p5

Stanley's Secret Trip
SLJ - v28 - Mr '82 - p158
Subject: Life on other planets—Fiction; Space flight—Fiction

Take Care Of Millie
BL - v76 - Jl 15 '80 - p1662
Hi Lo - v2 - O '80 - p4

HULSE, Jerry

Jody
BL - v73 - Ja 1 '77 - p644
BS - v36 - F '77 - p357
Kliatt - v12 - Spring '78 - p21
KR - v44 - Ag 1 '76 - p881
LJ - v101 - N 15 '76 - p2364
PW - v210 - Ag 2 '76 - p107
PW - v212 - O 17 '77 - p82
WLB - v51 - Mr '77 - p606
Subject: Biography

HUMPHREYS, Martha

Side By Side
SLJ - v31 - Ja '85 - p89
Subject: Love—Fiction

see also Dickmeyer, Lowell (co-author) for additional titles

HUNT, Irene 1907-
AuBYP, ChlLR 1, ConAu 8NR, DcLB 52, MorBMP, OxChL, SmATA 2, ThrBJA, TwCChW 83, WrDr 86

Across Five Aprils
Am - v110 - Je 20 '64 - p850
BS - v24 - Je 15 '64 - p129
CSM - Je 11 '64 - p9
CSM - v76 - O 5 '84 - pB7
HB - v40 - Je '64 - p291
LJ - v89 - Ap 15 '64 - p1871
NYTBR, Pt. 2 - My 10 '64 - p8
Obs - N 7 '65 - p26

HUNT, Irene (continued)
Par - v40 - Ap '65 - p32
Par - v40 - N '65 - p153
Spec - N 12 '65 - p632
TLS - D 9 '65 - p1147
Subject: United States—History—Civil War, 1861-1865—Fiction

The Lottery Rose
BL - v72 - My 1 '76 - p1265
BS - v36 - Ag '76 - p149
CCB-B - v29 - Jl '76 - p176
CE - v53 - Ja '77 - p147
CLW - v48 - O '76 - p138
Comw - v103 - N 19 '76 - p762
KR - v44 - Ap 15 '76 - p470
LA - v54 - Ja '77 - p84
NYTBR - My 16 '76 - p16
PW - v209 - Mr 22 '76 - p46
PW - v218 - S 26 '80 - p122
SLJ - v22 - Ap '76 - p74
Subject: Child abuse—Fiction

No Promises In The Wind
BL - v66 - Je 15 '70 - p1279
BW - v4 - My 17 '70 - p24
CCB-B - v24 - S '70 - p11
CE - v47 - O '70 - p29
CSM - v62 - My 7 '70 - pB6
EJ - v70 - D '81 - p58
HB - v46 - Je '70 - p301
KR - v38 - Mr 15 '70 - p329
LJ - v95 - Mr 15 '70 - p1202
NYTBR - Ap 5 '70 - p26
PW - v197 - Mr 16 '70 - p56
SE - v47 - Ap '83 - p289
SR - v53 - My 9 '70 - p69
TN - v27 - Ja '71 - p209
Subject: Depression, 1929—Fiction; Family life—Fiction

Up A Road Slowly
BL - v63 - Ja 1 '67 - p490
CCB-B - v20 - Ja '67 - p75
CE - v44 - O '67 - p117
HB - v43 - F '67 - p72
KR - v34 - N 15 '66 - p1188
LJ - v92 - F 15 '67 - p894
NYTBR - v71 - N 6 '66 - p8
Obs - D 3 '67 - p26
Obs - Mr 21 '71 - p31
PW - v190 - D 12 '66 - p56
PW - v194 - S 2 '68 - p63
SR - v49 - D 10 '66 - p57
TLS - N 30 '67 - p1141
TN - v23 - Ap '67 - p232

William
BL - v73 - Je 15 '77 - p1576
CCB-B - v31 - S '77 - p17
CLW - v49 - O '77 - p142
HB - v53 - O '77 - p540
KR - v45 - Je 1 '77 - p580
SLJ - v23 - Ap '77 - p77
Subject: Family problems—Fiction

HUNT, Kari 1920-
AuBYP, ConAu 41R, WhoAmA 82

Masks And Mask Makers
BL - v57 - Je 1 '61 - p613
HB - v37 - Ag '61 - p356
KR - v29 - F 1 '61 - p106
LJ - v86 - Ap 15 '61 - p1688
NYTBR - Je 11 '61 - p34
Co-author: Carlson, Bernice Wells
Subject: Masks

HUNTER, Evan 1926-
AuBYP, ConAu 5NR, ConLC 11, -31, CurBio 56, DcLB Y82B, DcLEL 1940, SmATA 25, TwCCr&M 85, TwCSFW 86

Me And Mr. Stenner
B&B - v22 - Ag '77 - p54
BL - v73 - S 15 '76 - p175
CCB-B - v30 - F '77 - p91
CE - v60 - My '84 - p308
JB - v41 - Je '77 - p179
Kliatt - v12 - Fall '78 - p10
KR - v44 - Jl 15 '76 - p795
LA - v54 - Ap '77 - p442
PW - v210 - O 4 '76 - p74
SE - v41 - Ap '77 - p348
SLJ - v23 - O '76 - p117
Teacher - v96 - O '78 - p177
TLS - Mr 25 '77 - p359
Subject: Divorce—Fiction; Remarriage—Fiction; Stepfathers—Fiction

HUNTER, Hilda
see Smaridge, Norah Antoinette (co-author)

HUNTER, Kristin Eggleston 1931-
ChILR 3, ConAu 13NR, ConLC 35, ConNov 86, DcLB 33, FourBJA, OxChL, SmATA 12, TwCChW 83, WrDr 86

Guests In The Promised Land
BL - v69 - Je 1 '73 - p947
Bl W - v23 - S '74 - p91
BS - v33 - Ap 15 '73 - p45
CCB-B - v26 - Je '73 - p156
CE - v50 - O '73 - p29
Choice - v14 - N '77 - p1178
Comw - v99 - N 23 '73 - p216

HUNTER, Kristin Eggleston (continued)
HB - v49 - Ag '73 - p386
KR - v41 - My 15 '73 - p567
LJ - v98 - S 15 '73 - p2651
NO - v12 - Ag 11 '73 - p21
PW - v203 - My 28 '73 - p40
Teacher - v92 - S '74 - p130
Teacher - v94 - O '76 - p151
Subject: Blacks—Social conditions—Fiction

The Soul Brothers And Sister Lou
BL - v65 - N 1 '68 - p312
BL - v65 - Ap 1 '69 - p901
BL - v69 - My 1 '73 - p838
BS - v28 - O 1 '68 - p277
BW - v2 - N 3 '68 - p20
CE - v46 - Ap '70 - p368
Choice - v14 - N '77 - p1178
Comw - v91 - F 27 '70 - p585
EJ - v64 - D '75 - p80
EL - v31 - Ap '74 - p593
HB - v45 - Ap '69 - p177
KR - v36 - Jl 15 '68 - p765
LJ - v93 - N 15 '68 - p4419
NS - v81 - Mr 5 '71 - p312
NYTBR - Ja 26 '69 - p26
NYTBR, Pt. 2 - F 15 '70 - p22
PW - v194 - S 30 '68 - p61
PW - v196 - S 29 '69 - p60
SE - v33 - My '69 - p558
SR - v51 - O 19 '68 - p37
TN - v38 - Summer '82 - p364
Subject: Blacks—Social conditions—Fiction

HUNTER, Mollie 1922-
AuBYP, BioIn 11, -12, ConAu X, ConLC 21, OxChL, SmATA 2, ThrBJA, TwCChW 83, WrDr 86
Pseud./variant:
McIlwraith, Maureen Mollie Hunter McVeigh

The Spanish Letters
BL - v63 - Je 1 '67 - p1048
BS - v27 - Ag 1 '67 - p183
CCB-B - v21 - S '67 - p9
HB - v43 - Ag '67 - p471
KR - v35 - F 15 '67 - p208
LJ - v92 - S 15 '67 - p3199
LR - v20 - Spring '65 - p45
PW - v191 - My 22 '67 - p64
SR - v50 - My 13 '67 - p57
Subject: Great Britain—History—Fiction

see also McIlwraith, Maureen Mollie Hunter McVeigh for additional titles

HUNTSBERRY, William E 1916-
ConAu 2NR, DrAS 82E, SmATA 5

The Big Hang-Up
Am - v123 - D 5 '70 - p497
BS - v30 - My 1 '70 - p61
CCB-B - v24 - D '70 - p60
Comw - v92 - My 22 '70 - p248
KR - v38 - F 15 '70 - p178
Subject: Traffic accidents—Fiction

The Big Wheels
Am - v117 - N 4 '67 - p518
BL - v64 - Ap 15 '68 - p983
BS - v27 - O 1 '67 - p263
BW - v1 - N 19 '67 - p24
CCB-B - v21 - D '67 - p60
CSM - v59 - N 2 '67 - pB12
HB - v43 - O '67 - p601
KR - v35 - Jl 15 '67 - p816
LJ - v93 - F 15 '68 - p882
NYTBR - v72 - O 8 '67 - p38
SR - v50 - N 11 '67 - p50

HURMENCE, Belinda

A Girl Called Boy
BL - v78 - Jl '82 - p1445
CBRS - v10 - Spring '82 - p117
CCB-B - v36 - S '82 - p12
CE - v59 - N '82 - p133
HB - v58 - Ag '82 - p404
KR - v50 - Ap 15 '82 - p490
LA - v60 - Ap '83 - p506
RT - v36 - N '82 - p242
SLJ - v28 - My '82 - p63
Subject: Slavery—Fiction; Space and time—Fiction

HUSS, Barbara
see Lubowe, Irwin Irville (co-author)

HUTCHINS, Ross E 1906-1983
AuBYP, ConAu 5NR, SmATA 4, ThrBJA, WhAm 8, WhoAm 80

The Last Trumpeters
BL - v81 - D 1 '84 - p529
CCB-B - v21 - Mr '68 - p111
CSM - v59 - N 2 '67 - pB11
KR - v35 - Jl 1 '67 - p743
Obs - O 15 '67 - p28
PW - v192 - Ag 14 '67 - p50
SB - v3 - Mr '68 - p322
TLS - N 2 '67 - p1030
Subject: Trumpeter swan

HYDE, Margaret Oldroyd 1917-
AuBYP, ConAu 1NR, ConLC 21,
SmATA 42, ThrBJA

Exploring Earth And Space
KR - v35 - Ag 15 '67 - p978
LJ - v92 - D 15 '67 - p4623
LJ - v96 - Ja 15 '71 - p276
SB - v6 - Mr '71 - p285
Subject: Geophysics

Flight Today And Tomorrow
BL - v67 - Mr 15 '71 - p623
LJ - v96 - My 15 '71 - p1827
SB - v7 - My '71 - p78
Subject: Aeronautics

Know Your Feelings
ACSB - v8 - Fall '75 - p17
Co-author: Forsyth, Elizabeth Held
Subject: Emotions

My Friend Wants To Run Away
CBRS - v8 - D '79 - p38
SB - v15 - My '80 - p274
SLJ - v27 - O '80 - p156
Subject: Runaways

VD: The Silent Epidemic
BL - v70 - O 15 '73 - p222
CCB-B - v27 - S '73 - p10
LJ - v98 - My 15 '73 - p1655
LJ - v98 - My 15 '73 - p1690
SB - v9 - Mr '74 - p312
SLJ - v30 - S '83 - p45
Subject: Venereal diseases

HYDE, Shelley
see Reed, Kit

HYNDMAN, Jane Andrews Lee
see Wyndham, Lee

I

IBBITSON, John

The Wimp
Emerg Lib - v14 - S '86 - p51
Quill & Q - v52 - F '86 - p21
Subject: Elections—Fiction; Schools—Fiction

IGMANSON, Dale
see Stone, A Harris (co-author)

ILOWITE, Sheldon A 1931-
ConAu 106, SmATA 27

Fury On Ice: A Canadian-American Hockey Story
CLW - v42 - My '71 - p581
Inst - v130 - Ap '71 - p132
LJ - v95 - D 15 '70 - p4381
Subject: Hockey—Fiction

IRELAND, Karin

Kitty O'Neil: Daredevil Woman
Cur R - v20 - N '81 - p471
Hi Lo - v2 - Ap '81 - p5
Subject: Deaf; Physically handicapped; Stunt men and women

IRWIN, Constance Frick
see Frick, Constance H

ISH-KISHOR, Sulamith 1897?-1977
AuBYP, BioIn 11, ConAu 73, FifBJA, SmATA 17, TwCChW 83

Our Eddie
A Lib - v1 - Ap '70 - p385
BL - v65 - My 15 '69 - p1076
BS - v29 - F 1 '70 - p423
BW - v3 - My 4 '69 - p36
CCB-B - v23 - O '69 - p25
CSM - v61 - My 1 '69 - pB6
HB - v45 - Ag '69 - p417
Inst - v79 - Ag '69 - p191
KR - v37 - Mr 15 '69 - p315
LJ - v94 - My 15 '69 - p2114
NYTBR - Jl 20 '69 - p22
PW - v195 - Je 9 '69 - p63
SR - v52 - My 10 '69 - p60
Subject: Family life—Fiction; Jews—Fiction

ISHMOLE, Jack 1924-
ConAu 49

Walk In The Sky
BS - v32 - My 15 '72 - p98
KR - v40 - F 1 '72 - p143
LJ - v98 - Mr 15 '73 - p1013
NYTBR, Pt. 2 - N 5 '72 - p7
SE - v37 - D '73 - p790
Subject: Mohawk Indians—Fiction

IZENBERG, Jerry
AuBYP SUP

Great Latin Sports Figures: Proud People
BL - v73 - S 1 '76 - p38
Comw - v103 - N 19 '76 - p764
KR - v44 - My 15 '76 - p596
Subject: Athletes

J

JABLONSKI, Edward 1922-
AuBYP, ConAu 18NR, WhoAm 86, WhoE 77

Warriors With Wings: The Story Of The Lafayette Escadrille
BL - v63 - D 15 '66 - p448
BS - v26 - O 1 '66 - p250
KR - v34 - Je 15 '66 - p579
LJ - v91 - N 15 '66 - p5760
NYTBR - v71 - O 16 '66 - p38
Subject: France—History

JACKER, Corinne 1933-
AuBYP, ConAu 17R, NatPD, WhoAm 86, WhoAmW 87, WrDr 86

The Biological Revolution: A Background Book On Making A New World
BL - v68 - F 15 '72 - p502
BL - v68 - F 15 '72 - p506
CCB-B - v25 - F '72 - p92
KR - v39 - N 15 '71 - p1220
SB - v8 - My '72 - p44
SR - v55 - Ja 15 '72 - p47
Subject: Biology

JACKSON, Anita

'57 T-Bird
BL - v75 - Jl 15 '79 - p1610
Hi Lo - v2 - O '80 - p5
Kliatt - v13 - Winter '79 - p16

The Actor
BL - v75 - Jl 15 '79 - p1610
Hi Lo - v2 - O '80 - p5
Kliatt - v13 - Winter '79 - p16

A Deadly Game
BL - v75 - Jl 15 '79 - p1610
B Rpt - v2 - S '83 - p24
Hi Lo - v2 - O '80 - p5
Kliatt - v13 - Winter '79 - p16

Dreams
BL - v75 - Jl 15 '79 - p1610
Hi Lo - v2 - O '80 - p5
Kliatt - v13 - Winter '79 - p16

The Ear
BL - v75 - Jl 15 '79 - p1610
Hi Lo - v1 - Mr '80 - p2
Hi Lo - v2 - O '80 - p5
Kliatt - v13 - Winter '79 - p16
TN - v36 - Winter '80 - p198
Subject: Ghosts—Fiction

Homecoming
BL - v75 - Jl 15 '79 - p1610
Hi Lo - v2 - O '80 - p5
Kliatt - v13 - Winter '79 - p16

No Rent To Pay
BL - v75 - Jl 15 '79 - p1610
Hi Lo - v2 - O '80 - p5
Kliatt - v13 - Winter '79 - p16

ZB-4
BL - v75 - Jl 15 '79 - p1610
Hi Lo - v2 - O '80 - p5
Kliatt - v13 - Winter '79 - p16
Subject: Science fiction

JACKSON, Caary Paul 1902-
AuBYP, ConAu 6NR, MichAu 80, SmATA 6

No Talent Letterman
KR - v34 - F 15 '66 - p186
LJ - v91 - Jl '66 - p3551
PW - v190 - O 3 '66 - p84
Co-author: Jackson, Orpha B

JACKSON, Jesse 1908-1983
AuBYP, ConAu 109, -25R, ConLC 12, InB&W 80, SelBAAf, SmATA 29, -48N, TwCChW 83, WrDr 84

Make A Joyful Noise Unto The Lord!: The Life Of Mahalia Jackson
BL - v82 - S 15 '85 - p143
CCB-B - v28 - N '74 - p44
HB - v50 - D '74 - p700
SLJ - v21 - Ja '75 - p43
Subject: Biography; Singers

Tessie
BL - v65 - S 15 '68 - p122
BS - v28 - Jl 1 '68 - p154
BW - v2 - My 5 '68 - p34
CCB-B - v22 - S '68 - p9
Comw - v88 - My 24 '68 - p306

JACKSON, Jesse (continued)
CSM - v60 - Je 13 '68 - p5
HB - v44 - Ag '68 - p430
KR - v36 - My 1 '68 - p518
LJ - v93 - O 15 '68 - p3983
NYTBR - v73 - My 26 '68 - p30
SR - v51 - Je 15 '68 - p33
Subject: Schools—Fiction

JACKSON, Orpha B
see Jackson, Caary Paul (co-author)

JACKSON, Robert Blake 1926-
AuBYP, ConAu 5R, -6NR, SmATA 8

Behind The Wheel
KR - v39 - My 15 '71 - p556
LJ - v96 - My 15 '71 - p1822
Subject: Automoblie racing drivers

Earl The Pearl: The Story Of Baltimore's Earl Monroe
KR - v37 - D 1 '69 - p1262
LJ - v95 - My 15 '70 - p1965
Subject: Basketball—Biography

Fighter Pilots Of World War I
BL - v74 - F 1 '78 - p903
BS - v37 - F '78 - p358
LR - v26 - p264
Subject: Air pilots; European War, 1914-1918

Fighter Pilots Of World War II
BL - v73 - My 1 '77 - p1339
LJ - v90 - O 15 '65 - p4636
LJ - v101 - D 1 '76 - p2485
Subject: Air pilots; World War, 1939-1945

Fisk Of Fenway Park: New England's Favorite Catcher
BL - v72 - Jl 15 '76 - p1596
KR - v44 - My 15 '76 - p597
SLJ - v23 - S '76 - p118
Subject: Baseball—Biography

Grand Prix At The Glen
BL - v62 - D 1 '65 - p363
KR - v33 - S 1 '65 - p913
LJ - v90 - O 15 '65 - p4636
Subject: Automobile racing

Here Comes Bobby Orr
BL - v68 - Ap 1 '72 - p676
KR - v39 - N 1 '71 - p1161
LJ - v96 - D 15 '71 - p4202
Subject: Hockey—Biography

Road Race Round The World: New York To Paris, 1908
SLJ - v24 - S '77 - p130
Subject: Automobile racing

Sports Cars
BL - v69 - My 1 '73 - p863
LJ - v98 - My 15 '73 - p1705
Subject: Automobiles

Stock Car Racing: Grand National Competition
BL - v64 - Ap 15 '68 - p995
KR - v36 - Ja 15 '68 - p60
LJ - v93 - My 15 '68 - p2130
Subject: Automobile racing

Supermex: The Lee Trevino Story
KR - v41 - My 15 '73 - p563
LJ - v98 - D 15 '73 - p3724
PW - v203 - My 14 '73 - p47
Subject: Golfers

JACKSON, Shirley 1919-1965
ConAu 4NR, ConLC 11, ConNov 76, -82A, DcLB 6, DcLEL 1940, OxAmL 83, SmATA 2, SupFW, TwCCr&M 80

The Witchcraft Of Salem Village
Kliatt - v11 - Winter '77 - p27
NYTBR - N 25 '56 - p56
Subject: Witchcraft

JACOBS, David 1939-
WhoAm 86

Beethoven
BL - v66 - Je 1 '70 - p1214
BS - v30 - Ap 1 '70 - p18
CCB-B - v24 - Jl '70 - p180
CSM - v62 - My 7 '70 - pB7
KR - v38 - F 1 '70 - p115
LJ - v96 - Jl '71 - p2373
PW - v197 - Mr 30 '70 - p65
SR - v53 - My 9 '70 - p70
TLS - O 30 '70 - p1268
Subject: Biography

JACOBS, Emma Atkins

A Chance To Belong
BL - v50 - D 1 '53 - p151
KR - v21 - Ag 1 '53 - p489
LJ - v78 - N 1 '53 - p1943
RT - v33 - Mr '80 - p688
SR - v36 - N 14 '53 - p68

JACOBS, Karen Folger 1940-
AmM&WS 78S

Girl Sports
Inter BC - v12 - #1 '81 p13
LJ - v103 - My 15 '78 - p1075
SLJ - v24 - My '78 - p86
WLB - v52 - Ap '78 - p639
Subject: Sports—Biography

The Story Of A Young Gymnast Tracee Talavera
Inter BC - v12 - #3 '81 p17
SLJ - v27 - D '80 - p76
Subject: Gymnasts

JACOBS, Linda C 1943-
SmATA 21

Barbara Jordan: Keeping Faith
SLJ - v26 - S '79 - p140
Subject: Blacks—Biography; Legislators

A Candle, A Feather, A Wooden Spoon
Hi Lo - v4 - F '83 - p2
Subject: Jews—Fiction

Checkmate Julie
Hi Lo - v4 - F '83 - p2
Subject: Chess—Fiction

Everyone's Watching Tammy
Hi Lo - v4 - F '83 - p2
Subject: Friendship—Fiction

Henry Winkler: Born Actor
SLJ - v251 - N '78 - p64
Subject: Actors and actresses

Jane Pauley: A Heartland Style
SLJ - v25 - N '78 - p64
Subject: Biography; Television

Will The Real Jeannie Murphy Please Stand Up
Hi Lo - v4 - F '83 - p2
Subject: Friendship—Fiction

JACOBS, Lou, Jr. 1921-
AuBYP SUP, ConAu 9NR, IntAu&W 77, SmATA 2, WhoWest 78

Jumbo Jets
BL - v66 - Mr 1 '70 - p847
CCB-B - v24 - S '70 - p12
SB - v6 - My '70 - p63
Subject: Airplanes

JACOBSON, Ethel
ConAu 37R, WrDr 84

The Cats Of Sea-Cliff Castle
LJ - v97 - S 15 '72 - p2936
PW - v201 - My 22 '72 - p51
Subject: Cats

JAGENDORF, Moritz 1888-1981
AnObit 1981, ConAu 5R, -102, MorJA, SmATA 2, -24N, WrDr 82

The First Book Of Puppets
BL - v49 - F 1 '53 - p192
KR - v20 - O 1 '52 - p659
LJ - v78 - F 1 '53 - p226
WLB - v49 - Mr '53 - p87
Subject: Puppets and puppet plays

JAMES, Charles L 1934-
ConAu 29R, SelBAAu

From The Roots: Short Stories By Black Americans
Bl W - v19 - S '70 - p97
Subject: American fiction—Black authors

JAMES, Elizabeth 1942-
SmATA 45
Pseud./variant:
Hastings, Beverly

How To Write A Term Paper
BL - v77 - S 15 '80 - p109
CBRS - v9 - S '80 - p8
CCB-B - v34 - O '80 - p34
J Read - v24 - Ap '81 - p647
KR - v48 - O 1 '80 - p1303
Co-author: Barkin, Carol
Subject: Report writing; Research

A Place Of Your Own
Hi Lo - v3 - Mr '82 - p6
KR - v50 - Ja 15 '82 - p72
SLJ - v28 - Ap '82 - p82
VOYA - v5 - Ap '82 - p45
Co-author: Barkin, Carol
Subject: Apartments; Interior decoration

see also Barkin, Carol; Hastings, Beverly for additional titles

JAMES, Stuart

The Firefighters
Hi Lo - v2 - N '80 - p5

JAMES, T G H

The Archaeology Of Ancient Egypt
BL - v70 - S 1 '73 - p46
CCB-B - v27 - O '73 - p31
CLW - v45 - N '73 - p185
HB - v49 - O '73 - p478
KR - v41 - Ap 1 '73 - p401
LJ - v98 - My 15 '73 - p1581
LJ - v98 - My 15 '73 - p1655
LJ - v98 - My 15 '73 - p1689
NY - v49 - D 3 '73 - p219
Obs - Jl 16 '72 - p31
PW - v203 - Ap 2 '73 - p65
SLJ - v25 - S '78 - p43
TLS - Jl 14 '72 - p810
Subject: Archaeology; Egypt

JAMESON, Jon

The Picture Life Of O. J. Simpson
Comw - v104 - N 11 '77 - p734
SLJ - v23 - My '77 - p80
Subject: Football—Biography

JANE, Mary C 1909-
AuBYP, ConAu 4NR, SmATA 6

Mystery On Nine-Mile Marsh
KR - v35 - Jl 1 '67 - p740
LJ - v92 - N 15 '67 - p4269
PW - v193 - Ja 8 '68 - p67
Subject: Mystery and detective stories

JANECZKO, Paul

The Crystal Image: A Poetry Anthology
Kliatt - v11 - Fall '77 - p15
Subject: American poetry (Collections)

JARUNKOVA, Klara

Don't Cry For Me
BL - v65 - O 15 '68 - p234
BS - v28 - Ag 1 '68 - p195
CCB-B - v22 - O '68 - p30
EJ - v58 - F '69 - p295
LJ - v93 - My 15 '68 - p2123
NYTBR - v73 - S 22 '68 - p28
RT - v33 - Mr '80 - p688

JASPERSOHN, William

Motorcycle
BL - v81 - F 1 '85 - p787
J Read - v29 - O '85 - p82
KR - v52 - N 1 '84 - pJ101
SLJ - v31 - F '85 - p85
Subject: Motorcycles

JEFFERIS, David

Trail Bikes
BL - v80 - Je 15 '84 - p1483
BL - v82 - Je 15 '86 - p1537
GP - v23 - My '84 - p4267
JB - v48 - Je '84 - p128
SLJ - v31 - S '84 - p119
Subject: Motorcycle racing

JEFFRIES, Roderic Graeme 1926-
AuBYP, ConAu 9NR, EncMys, SmATA 4, TwCCr&M 85, WrDr 86
Pseud./variant:
Ashford, Jeffrey

Patrol Car
BL - v63 - Jl 15 '67 - p1193
CCB-B - v21 - S '67 - p10
HB - v43 - Je '67 - p354
KR - v35 - F 1 '67 - p138
LJ - v92 - My 15 '67 - p2039
PW - v191 - Je 12 '67 - p59

Trapped
BL - v83 - D 15 '86 - p655
CCB-B - v25 - Ap '72 - p124
HB - v48 - Je '72 - p269
KR - v40 - F 1 '72 - p136
LJ - v97 - Je 15 '72 - p2243
Subject: Adventure and adventurers—Fiction; England—Fiction

see also Ashford, Jeffrey for additional titles

JOFFO, Joseph

A Bag Of Marbles
BL - v71 - N 1 '74 - p264
CSM - v66 - O 2 '74 - p13
GP - v14 - Jl '75 - p2676
KR - v42 - Ag 1 '74 - p851
KR - v42 - Ag 15 '74 - p886
LJ - v99 - Ag '74 - p1937
NO - v13 - N 2 '74 - p23
PW - v206 - Ag 5 '74 - p57

JOHNS, Janetta

The Truth About Me And Bobby V.
BL - v80 - S 15 '83 - p171
Kliatt - v17 - Fall '83 - p13
SLJ - v30 - Ap '84 - p125
VOYA - v6 - D '83 - p281
Subject: Schools—Fiction

JOHNSON, Annabel 1921-
AuBYP, BioIn 4, ConAu 9R, SmATA 2, ThrBJA, TwCChW 83, WrDr 80

The Burning Glass
BL - v63 - D 1 '66 - p418
BS - v26 - N 1 '66 - p294
CCB-B - v20 - D '66 - p60
CLW - v38 - Ja '67 - p340
CSM - v58 - N 3 '66 - pB11
HB - v42 - D '66 - p719
KR - v34 - S 1 '66 - p913
LJ - v91 - N 15 '66 - p5760
Co-author: Johnson, Edgar Raymond
Subject: West (U.S.)—Fiction

Count Me Gone
BL - v64 - Jl 15 '68 - p1281
BW - v2 - O 13 '68 - p14
CCB-B - v21 - Jl '68 - p176
CSM - v60 - Je 13 '68 - p5
HB - v44 - Ag '68 - p431
LJ - v93 - O 15 '68 - p3983
NYTBR - v73 - My 5 '68 - p8
Co-author: Johnson, Edgar Raymond

A Golden Touch
BS - v23 - Ap 15 '63 - p41
Comw - v78 - My 24 '63 - p257
CSM - My 9 '63 - p5B
HB - v39 - Ap '63 - p177
LJ - v88 - Je 15 '63 - p2561
NYTBR - O 25 '64 - p36
NYTBR, Pt. 2 - My 12 '63 - p26
Co-author: Johnson, Edgar Raymond

The Grizzly
Am - v111 - N 21 '64 - p667
Comw - v81 - N 6 '64 - p206
CSM - N 5 '64 - p5B
HB - v40 - D '64 - p616
LJ - v89 - D 15 '64 - p5018
NYTBR - O 25 '64 - p36
Par - v40 - O '65 - p108
Co-author: Johnson, Edgar Raymond

JOHNSON, Corinne Benson
AuBYP SUP

Love And Sex And Growing Up
BL - v81 - Mr 1 '85 - p991
Ms - v9 - Je '81 - p70
SLJ - v24 - Mr '78 - p130
Co-author: Johnson, Eric Warner
Subject: Sex instruction for youth

see also Johnson, Eric Warner for additional titles

JOHNSON, Edgar Raymond
see Johnson, Annabel (co-author)

JOHNSON, Eric Warner 1918-
AuBYP SUP, ConAu 4NR, SmATA 8, WhoE 77, WrDr 86

Love And Sex In Plain Language
BL - v81 - Mr 1 '85 - p991
BL - v82 - N 1 '85 - p392
BL - v82 - N 15 '85 - p485
WLB - v60 - O '85 - p51
Subject: Sex instruction for youth

Sex: Telling It Straight
BL - v67 - D 1 '70 - p303
Comw - v93 - N 20 '70 - p205
KR - v38 - N 15 '70 - p1257
NYTBR, Pt. 2 - N 7 '71 - p47
Par - v46 - F '71 - p42
SB - v6 - Mr '71 - p331
SB - v15 - My '80 - p274
Subject: Sex instruction for youth

see also Johnson, Corinne Benson (co-author) for additional titles

JOHNSON, Gerald W 1890-1980
AuBYP, ConAu 85, -97, DcLB 29, EncTwCJ, NewYTBS 80, OxAmL 83, SmATA 19, -28N, ThrBJA

Franklin D. Roosevelt: Portrait Of A Great Man
BL - v63 - Jl 15 '67 - p1194
BS - v27 - Jl 1 '67 - p145
CCB-B - v20 - Jl '67 - p171
CE - v44 - Ja '68 - p324
EJ - v56 - N '67 - p1221
Inst - v76 - Je '67 - p142
KR - v35 - Mr 15 '67 - p346
LJ - v92 - S 15 '67 - p3200
NY - v43 - D 16 '67 - p182
NYTBR - v72 - N 5 '67 - p65
NYTBR, Pt. 2 - v72 - My 7 '67 - p36
PW - v191 - Ap 10 '67 - p82
SR - v50 - My 13 '67 - p56
Subject: Biography

JOHNSON, Martha P

Mystery At Winter Lodge
BL - v78 - Mr 15 '82 - p965
SLJ - v28 - Mr '82 - p158
Subject: Mystery and detective stories

JOHNSON, Maud 1918?-1985
SmATA 46N

Christy's Love
SLJ - v31 - Ja '85 - p90
Subject: Love—Fiction

JOHNSON, Pat

Horse Talk
Am - v117 - N 4 '67 - p520
CSM - v60 - N 30 '67 - pB5
LJ - v93 - Ja 15 '68 - p292
PW - v192 - O 16 '67 - p58
Subject: Horses

JOHNSTON, Johanna 1914?-1982
AuBYP, BioIn 13, ConAu 7NR, -108, FourBJA, SmATA 12, -33N

Kings, Lovers & Fools
Kliatt - v15 - Fall '81 - p29
SLJ - v28 - F '82 - p88
Subject: Kings, queens, rulers, etc.

Paul Cuffee: America's First Black Captain
BL - v67 - Mr 1 '71 - p560
KR - v38 - N 15 '70 - p1251
LJ - v96 - Je 15 '71 - p2131
Subject: Biography

Together In America: The Story Of Two Races And One Nation
BL - v62 - S 1 '65 - p56
BS - v25 - Ap 15 '65 - p52
CC - v82 - Je 30 '65 - p838
CCB-B - v18 - Ap '65 - p119
CLW - v36 - My '65 - p639
Comw - v82 - My 28 '65 - p331
KR - v33 - F 1 '65 - p113
LJ - v90 - F 15 '65 - p972
Subject: Blacks—History

JOHNSTON, Norma
ConAu 105, FifBJA, SmATA 29, WrDr 86
Pseud./variant:
Dryden, Pamela
Harris, Lavinia

The Sanctuary Tree
Kliatt - v16 - Spring '82 - p12
VOYA - v6 - Ag '83 - p158
Subject: Family life—Fiction

see also Dryden, Pamela; Harris, Lavinia for additional titles

JONES, Adrienne 1915-
ConAu 33R, FifBJA, SmATA 7, WhoAmW 77, WrDr 86

Another Place, Another Spring
BL - v68 - Ap 15 '72 - p717
BL - v68 - Ap 15 '72 - p724
CLW - v43 - Ap '72 - p470
CLW - v43 - Ap '72 - p481
HB - v48 - F '72 - p57
KR - v39 - N 1 '71 - p1164
LJ - v96 - D 15 '71 - p4190
PW - v200 - N 22 '71 - p41
Subject: Russia—Fiction

JONES, Claire
WhoAmA 78

Pollution: The Noise We Hear
B&B - v18 - Jl '73 - p141
Subject: Noise pollution

Sailboat Racing
BL - v77 - Mr 15 '81 - p1028
SLJ - v27 - My '81 - p88
Subject: Sailing

JONES, Cordelia

A Cat Called Camouflage
Am - v125 - D 4 '71 - p488
BL - v68 - Ja 15 '72 - p433
BS - v31 - O 15 '71 - p335
CE - v49 - O '72 - p28
EJ - v61 - Mr '72 - p433
KR - v39 - S 15 '71 - p1013
LJ - v96 - D 15 '71 - p4184
PW - v200 - S 6 '71 - p51
SR - v54 - O 16 '71 - p57
Subject: Divorce—Fiction

JONES, Diana Wynne 1934-
ConAu 4NR, ConLC 26, FifBJA, IntAu&W 77, OxChL, SmATA 9, TwCChW 83, WrDr 86

Dogsbody
BL - v80 - Ap 15 '84 - p1200
Subject: Fantasy

The Homeward Bounders
BL - v78 - S 15 '81 - p98
CBRS - v9 - Ag '81 - p127
CCB-B - v35 - S '81 - p12
CE - v59 - S '82 - p56
GP - v20 - My '81 - p3880
HB - v57 - O '81 - p542
JB - v45 - O '81 - p212
KR - v49 - S 15 '81 - p1164
Sch Lib - v29 - S '81 - p254
SLJ - v28 - S '81 - p137

JONES, Diana Wynne (continued)
TES - Je 5 '81 - p37
TES - F 24 '84 - p29
TLS - Mr 27 '81 - p339
Subject: Space and time—Fiction

JONES, Hettie 1934-
AuBYP SUP, ConAu 81, DrAP&F 85, SmATA 42

Big Star Fallin' Mama: Five Black Women In Music
BL - v70 - Mr 1 '74 - p741
Bl W - v24 - Jl '75 - p62
BS - v34 - Ap 15 '74 - p53
CCB-B - v27 - My '74 - p145
Inst - v83 - N '73 - p125
KR - v41 - O 15 '73 - p1173
KR - v41 - D 15 '73 - p1359
LJ - v99 - My 15 '74 - p1483
NYTBR - D 30 '73 - p10
PW - v205 - Ja 28 '74 - p301
Subject: Blacks—Biography; Musicians

JONES, McClure
ConAu 112, SmATA 34

Lucky Sun Signs For Teens
BL - v81 - O 15 '84 - p296
Subject: Astrology; Horoscopes

JONES, Rebecca C 1947-
ConAu 106, SmATA 33

Angie And Me
BL - v78 - O 15 '81 - p306
BL - v81 - Jl '85 - p1570
BS - v41 - Mr '82 - p475
CBRS - v10 - D '81 - p39
CCB-B - v35 - D '81 - p70
CLW - v53 - My '82 - p448
HB - v58 - Ap '82 - p164
Inter BC - v14 - #6 '83 p17
KR - v50 - Ja 15 '82 - p68
PW - v220 - Jl 31 '81 - p59
SLJ - v28 - N '81 - p92
Subject: Hospitals—Fiction; Physically handicapped—Fiction; Rheumatoid arthritis—Fiction

JONES, Ron

The Acorn People
Bks W - v1 - Ap '77 - p38
BL - v73 - My 1 '77 - p1331
CE - v57 - Mr '81 - p208
Inter BC - v13 - #4 '82 p7
Subject: Physically handicapped

JONES, Weyman B 1928-
AuBYP, ConAu 17R, FourBJA, SmATA 4, WhoE 83

Computer
BL - v66 - My 1 '70 - p1092
BS - v30 - Ap 1 '70 - p18
KR - v37 - D 1 '69 - p1271
LJ - v95 - Ap 15 '70 - p1651
SB - v6 - My '70 - p18
Subject: Computers

Edge Of Two Worlds
BL - v64 - Jl 15 '68 - p1286
BL - v81 - Ap 15 '85 - p1203
BW - v2 - S 29 '68 - p18
KR - v36 - Ap 15 '68 - p466
LJ - v93 - Ap 15 '68 - p1812
NYTBR - v73 - My 5 '68 - p32
PW - v193 - Ap 29 '68 - p78
SR - v51 - N 9 '68 - p68

JORDAN, Ben

Sky Jumpers: A Novel About Free Fall Parachuting
KR - v33 - Mr 1 '65 - p249
LJ - v90 - Jl '65 - p3133

JORDAN, Hope Dahle 1905-
ConAu 13NR, SmATA 15

The Fortune Cake
BL - v68 - Jl 1 '72 - p942
HB - v48 - O '72 - p467
KR - v40 - Ja 15 '72 - p68
LJ - v97 - Ap 15 '72 - p1606
Subject: Mystery and detective stories

Haunted Summer
CCB-B - v21 - S '67 - p10
HB - v43 - Ag '67 - p475
KR - v35 - My 15 '67 - p608
LJ - v92 - S 15 '67 - p3200
NYTBR - v72 - N 5 '67 - p64
NYTBR, Pt. 2 - v72 - My 7 '67 - p12
TN - v24 - N '67 - p99
Subject: Traffic accidents—Fiction

JORDAN, June 1936-
ChlLR 10, ConAu 33R, ConLC 5, -11, -23, ConPo 85, DcLB 38, FourBJA, OxChL, SmATA 4, TwCChW 83, WrDr 86

Dry Victories
BL - v69 - Ja 1 '73 - p449
CCB-B - v26 - Ap '73 - p125
EJ - v63 - Ja '74 - p67

JORDAN, June (continued)
KR - v40 - Jl 15 '72 - p809
KR - v40 - D 15 '72 - p1424
LJ - v97 - N 15 '72 - p3806
NYTBR, pt. 1 - F 11 '73 - p8
SE - v37 - D '73 - p785
Teacher - v93 - Ap '76 - p122
Subject: Civil rights

His Own Where
BL - v68 - Ja 1 '72 - p391
BL - v68 - Ja 1 '72 - p394
BL - v68 - Ap 1 '72 - p664
CCB-B - v25 - D '71 - p58
Comw - v95 - N 19 '71 - p188
CSM - v63 - N 11 '71 - pB6
CSM - v64 - F 24 '72 - p7
EJ - v63 - Ja '74 - p65
EJ - v67 - My '78 - p88
HB - v47 - D '71 - p620
KR - v39 - S 15 '71 - p1021
LJ - v96 - D 15 '71 - p4159
LJ - v96 - D 15 '71 - p4190
NYRB - v18 - Ap 20 '72 - p13
NYT - v121 - D 16 '71 - p67
NYTBR, Pt. 2 - N 7 '71 - p6
NYTBR, Pt. 2 - N 7 '71 - p28
NYTBR, Pt. 2 - My 6 '73 - p28
PW - v200 - O 18 '71 - p50
TN - v28 - Ap '72 - p312
Subject: Family life—Fiction; Social adjustment—Fiction

Soulscript
BL - v67 - O 15 '70 - p165
BL - v67 - Ap 1 '71 - p654
Bl W - v20 - Ja '71 - p95
KR - v38 - Ap 1 '70 - p425
KR - v38 - My 1 '70 - p519
LJ - v95 - Jl '70 - p2540
PW - v197 - My 18 '70 - p36
TN - v27 - Ap '71 - p309
VQR - v47 - Winter '71 - pR20
Subject: American poetry—Black authors

JORGENSEN, Mary Venn
see Adrian, Mary

JOYCE, Donald P

Studying For A Driver's License
Hi Lo - v2 - My '81 - p5
Subject: Automobiles

JOYCE, Rosemary

Anything To Win!
PW - v230 - Ag 22 '86 - p101
Subject: Love—Fiction

JULESBERG, Elizabeth Rider Montgomery
see Montgomery, Elizabeth Rider

K

KAATZ, Evelyn

Motorcycle Road Racer
KR - v45 - D 1 '77 - p1268
SLJ - v24 - F '78 - p59
Subject: Motorcycle racing—Fiction

KADESCH, Robert R 1922-
AmM&WS 86P, AuBYP SUP, ConAu 57, SmATA 31, WhoAm 80

Math Menagerie
BL - v67 - F 15 '71 - p490
BL - v67 - Ap 1 '71 - p660
BS - v30 - Ja 15 '71 - p452
CCB-B - v24 - Jl '71 - p173
Comw - v93 - N 20 '70 - p205
KR - v38 - O 15 '70 - p1169
LJ - v96 - Ja 15 '71 - p277
NY - v46 - D 5 '70 - p208
SB - v6 - Mr '71 - p293
Subject: Mathematics

KAHN, Albert E 1912-1979
ConAu 118

Days With Ulanova: An Intimate Portrait Of The Legendary Russian Ballerina
BW - v9 - S 9 '79 - p13
Dance - v54 - Je '80 - p117
Kliatt - v14 - Winter '80 - p61
NYTBR - N 11 '79 - p43
Subject: Biography; Dancers

KAHN, Ely Jacques 1916-
BioIn 2, –4, –11, ConAu 65, WhoAm 86, WhoAmJ 80

A Building Goes Up
BL - v65 - Je 15 '69 - p1176
CCB-B - v22 - Je '69 - p160
KR - v37 - Mr 15 '69 - p310
LJ - v95 - My 15 '70 - p1944
SB - v5 - My '69 - p84
SR - v52 - My 10 '69 - p59
Subject: Architecture

KAHN, Joan 1914-
AuBYP SUP, BioIn 3, –8, ConAu 77, SmATA 48, WhoAm 84

Some Things Fierce And Fatal
BL - v68 - N 1 '71 - p242
BS - v31 - N 15 '71 - p386
BW - v5 - N 7 '71 - p11
CCB-B - v25 - D '71 - p58
CE - v49 - N '72 - p85
CLW - v43 - F '72 - p361
KR - v39 - Ag 15 '71 - p886
LJ - v96 - D 15 '71 - p4200
NY - v47 - D 4 '71 - p199
NYTBR, pt. 1 - F 13 '72 - p8
PW - v200 - O 18 '71 - p51
TLS - Ap 28 '72 - p484
WLB - v57 - My '83 - p773
Subject: Mystery and detective stories

KAISER, Ernest
see Halliburton, Warren J (co-author)

KALB, Jonah 1926-
AuBYP SUP, ConAu 4NR, SmATA 23

The Easy Ice Skating Book
HB - v58 - F '82 - p66
SLJ - v28 - D '81 - p85
Co-author: Kalb, Laura
Subject: Ice skating

KALB, Laura
see Kalb, Jonah (co-author)

KAMM, Herbert 1917-
ConAu 69, WhoAm 86, WhoMW 84

The Junior Illustrated Encyclopedia Of Sports
SLJ - v22 - N '75 - p92
Subject: Sports

KANTOR, MacKinlay 1904-1977
ASpks, AuBYP, ConAu 61, -73, ConLC 7, ConNov 76, DcLB 9, DcLEL, EncFWF, OxAmL 83

The Daughter Of Bugle Ann
KR - v21 - Ja 15 '53 - p54
LJ - v78 - Ap 15 '53 - p729
LJ - v78 - Je 15 '53 - p1164
NYT - Ap 19 '53 - p4
Subject: Dogs—Fiction

The Voice Of Bugle Ann
BL - v32 - S '35 - p15
CSM - Ag 27 '35 - p13
Cu H - v43 - O '35 - pR12
LJ - v60 - N 1 '35 - p828
NAR - v240 - D '35 - p550
Nat - v141 - S 4 '35 - p279
New R - v84 - O 23 '35 - p312
NYT - Ag 25 '35 - p7
SR - v12 - Ag 31 '35 - p4
TLS - D 7 '35 - p841
Subject: Dogs—Fiction

KAPLAN, Janice

First Ride
Kliatt - v16 - Spring '82 - p12
SLJ - v29 - Mr '83 - p193
VOYA - v5 - Ag '82 - p32
Subject: Rodeos—Fiction

If You Believe In Me
BL - v80 - Ag '84 - p1609
VOYA - v7 - F '85 - p327
Subject: Love—Fiction

KAPLOW, Robert

Two In The City
CLW - v51 - D '79 - p234
J Read - v23 - D '79 - p279
Subject: New York (City)—Fiction

KARK, Nina Mary
see Bawden, Nina

KASSEM, Lou

Dance Of Death
BL - v80 - My 15 '84 - p1339
SLJ - v30 - Ag '84 - p84
VOYA - v7 - Ag '84 - p147
Subject: Ghosts—Fiction

Listen For Rachel
BL - v83 - N 15 '86 - p512
CSM - v79 - D 5 '86 - pB4
KR - v54 - S 1 '86 - p1374
PW - v230 - Ag 22 '86 - p101
Subject: Mountain life—Fiction; Tennessee—Fiction; United States—History—Civil War, 1861-1865—Fiction

KASTNER, Erich 1899-1974
ChlLR 4, CurBio 64, -74, ObitT 1971, OxChL, SmATA 14, ThrBJA, TwCChW 83B, WhoChL, WorAu

Lisa And Lottie
BL - v65 - Jl 1 '69 - p1229
CCB-B - v24 - Jl '70 - p181
KR - v37 - Ap 15 '69 - p443
LJ - v94 - S 15 '69 - p3206
Subject: Family life—Fiction

KATSARAKIS, Joan Harris
see Harries, Joan

KATZ, Bobbi 1933-
ConAu 16NR, SmATA 12, WrDr 86

Volleyball Jinx
BL - v74 - F 15 '78 - p1013
CCB-B - v31 - My '78 - p143
SLJ - v24 - Ap '78 - p86
Subject: Superstition—Fiction; Volleyball—Fiction

KATZ, Susan

Kristy And Jimmy
SLJ - v25 - Mr '79 - p140
Subject: Biography; Entertainers

KATZ, William Loren 1927-
AuBYP SUP, ConAu 9NR, IntAu&W 77, SmATA 13, WhoAm 86, WrDr 86

A History Of Black Americans
SS - v65 - O '74 - p231
Co-author: Halliburton, Warren J
Subject: Blacks—History

see also Halliburton, Warren J for additional titles

KAUFMAN, Bel
ConAu 13R, WhoAm 86, WhoAmW 87, WrDr 86

Up The Down Staircase
Am - v112 - F 6 '65 - p198
Am - v112 - My 8 '65 - p677
BL - v61 - Ja 1 '65 - p424
BS - v24 - F 1 '65 - p416
CC - v82 - Ja 27 '65 - p113

KAUFMAN, Bel (continued)
Choice - v2 - Mr '65 - p22
Comw - v82 - My 14 '65 - p260
Cres - v28 - S '65 - p24
CSM - Mr 6 '65 - p9
LJ - v90 - Ja 1 '65 - p135
Nat R - v17 - Je 1 '65 - p476
NYRB - v6 - Jl 7 '66 - p20
NYT - v114 - F 9 '65 - p39M
NYTBR - v70 - F 14 '65 - p42
PW - v191 - Mr 27 '67 - p62
SE - v30 - F '66 - p143
SR - v48 - Mr 20 '65 - p71
TCR - v66 - My '65 - p777
TCR - v66 - My '65 - p778
Time - v85 - F 12 '65 - p96
Subject: Schools—Fiction

KAULA, Edna Mason 1906-
AuBYP, ConAu 5R, SmATA 13

African Village Folktales
KR - v36 - Je 1 '68 - p599
LJ - v93 - Jl '68 - p2734
NYTBR - v73 - My 5 '68 - p30
PW - v193 - Je 3 '68 - p129
Subject: Folklore

KAVALER, Lucy 1930-
AuBYP, ConAu 7NR, SmATA 23

Freezing Point: Cold As A Matter Of Life And Death
BL - v67 - Ja 1 '71 - p350
BL - v67 - Ja 1 '71 - p654
BS - v30 - O 15 '70 - p286
BW - v4 - Ag 30 '70 - p3
KR - v38 - Ap 1 '70 - p426
KR - v38 - Ap 15 '70 - p475
KR - v38 - Jl 1 '70 - p726
LJ - v95 - Je 1 '70 - p2170
LJ - v96 - Mr 1 '71 - p788
NYTBR - S 27 '70 - p10
PW - v198 - Jl 20 '70 - p61
SA - v224 - Je '71 - p132
SB - v6 - D '70 - p221
TN - v27 - Ap '71 - p309
WSJ - v176 - S 28 '70 - p14
Subject: Cryobiology

KAY, Eleanor

Nurses And What They Do
BL - v64 - My 1 '68 - p1045
KR - v36 - F 15 '68 - p194
Obs - My 19 '68 - p1322
SB - v4 - My '68 - p53
Subject: Nursing as a profession

KAYE, Annene

Van Halen
B Rpt - v4 - Mr '86 - p35
SLJ - v32 - S '85 - p131
Subject: Musicians; Rock musicians

KAYE, Marilyn

Max In Love
CCB-B - v39 - My '86 - p169
SLJ - v33 - S '86 - p144
Subject: Love—Fiction; Rock music—Fiction

Max On Earth
BL - v82 - Je 15 '86 - p1533
CCB-B - v39 - My '86 - p169
SLJ - v33 - S '86 - p144
Subject: Science fiction

KEEFE, John E 1942-
ConAu 107

Aim For A Job In Appliance Service
BL - v66 - S 1 '69 - p46
Subject: Vocational guidance

KELLER, Mollie

Marie Curie
ASBYP - v16 - Spring '83 - p28
BL - v79 - D 15 '82 - p565
CBRS - v11 - Ja '83 - p50
SB - v18 - My '83 - p270
SE - v47 - Ap '83 - p245
SLJ - v29 - N '82 - p101
Subject: Biography; Chemists

KELLER, Roseanne

Five Dog Night And Other Tales
BL - v76 - Ap 15 '80 - p1184
Hi Lo - v1 - D '79 - p3
Subject: Alaska—Fiction; Short stories

Two For The Road
Hi Lo - v1 - D '79 - p3
Subject: Short stories

When A Baby Is New
Hi Lo - v2 - My '81 - p4

KELLEY, Leo P 1928-
ConAu 107, ConSFA, EncSF, ScF&FL 1, –2, ScFSB, SmATA 32, TwCSFW 86, WrDr 86

Backward In Time
BL - v76 - Ja 15 '80 - p715
Hi Lo - v1 - Ja '80 - p5

KELLEY, Leo P (continued)
SLJ - v27 - F '81 - p67
Subject: Science fiction; Space and time—Fiction

Dead Moon
BL - v75 - Jl 15 '79 - p1632
Hi Lo - v2 - O '80 - p4
SLJ - v27 - F '81 - p67
Subject: Science fiction

Death Sentence
BL - v76 - Ja 15 '80 - p715
Hi Lo - v1 - Ja '80 - p5
SLJ - v27 - F '81 - p67
Subject: Science fiction

Earth Two
BL - v76 - Ja 15 '80 - p715
Hi Lo - v1 - Ja '80 - p5
SLJ - v27 - F '81 - p67
Subject: Old age—Fiction; Science fiction

Good-Bye To Earth
BL - v75 - Jl 15 '79 - p1632
CCB-B - v34 - Mr '81 - p135
Hi Lo - v2 - O '80 - p4
SLJ - v27 - F '81 - p67
Subject: Outer space—Fiction

Johnny Tall Dog
BL - v79 - Ap 15 '83 - p1078
Hi Lo - v3 - Ap '82 - p7

King Of The Stars
BL - v75 - Jl 15 '79 - p1632
Hi Lo - v2 - O '80 - p4
SLJ - v27 - F '81 - p67
Subject: Science fiction

Night Of Fire And Blood
Hi Lo - v1 - O '79 - p3
SLJ - v26 - D '79 - p82
Subject: Witchcraft—Fiction

On The Red World
BL - v75 - Jl 15 '79 - p1632
Hi Lo - v2 - O '80 - p4
SLJ - v27 - F '81 - p67
Subject: Science fiction

Prison Satellite
BL - v76 - Ja 15 '80 - p715
CSM - v73 - D 1 '80 - pB11
Hi Lo - v1 - Ja '80 - p5
SLJ - v27 - F '81 - p67
Subject: Science fiction

Star Gold
BL - v76 - Ap 15 '80 - p1184
Hi Lo - v1 - O '79 - p3
SLJ - v26 - D '79 - p82
Subject: Science fiction

Sunworld
Hi Lo - v1 - Ja '80 - p5
SLJ - v27 - F '81 - p67
Subject: Science fiction

Vacation In Space
BL - v75 - Jl 15 '79 - p1632
Hi Lo - v2 - O '80 - p4
SLJ - v27 - F '81 - p67
Subject: Science fiction

Where No Sun Shines
BL - v75 - Jl 15 '79 - p1633
Hi Lo - v2 - O '80 - p4
SLJ - v27 - F '81 - p67
Subject: Science fiction

Worlds Apart
BL - v76 - Ja 15 '80 - p715
Hi Lo - v1 - Ja '80 - p5
SLJ - v27 - F '81 - p67
Subject: Science fiction; Space and time—Fiction

KEMPF, Sharon
see Chandler, Caroline A (co-author)

KENDAL, Wallis 1937-
ConAu 107, Profile 1

Just Gin
KR - v41 - Ap 1 '73 - p384
LJ - v98 - S 15 '73 - p2665
Subject: Social adjustment—Fiction

KENDALL, Lace (pseud.) 1916-
ConAu X, SmATA 3, ThrBJA, WhoAm 78, WrDr 86
Real Name:
Stoutenburg, Adrien Pearl

Houdini: Master Of Escape
BL - v57 - Ap 1 '61 - p500
KR - v28 - Jl 1 '60 - p509
LJ - v85 - D 15 '60 - p4567
Subject: Biography

Masters Of Magic
BL - v63 - O 1 '66 - p188
BS - v26 - My 1 '66 - p58
KR - v34 - Ja 1 '66 - p12
LJ - v91 - My 15 '66 - p2708
Subject: Magicians

see also Stoutenburg, Adrien Pearl for additional titles

KENEALY, James P 1927-
ConAu 93, SmATA 29
Better Camping For Boys
BL - v70 - Mr 15 '74 - p821
CCB-B - v27 - Je '74 - p159
CLW - v45 - My '74 - p503
KR - v42 - Ja 15 '74 - p57
LJ - v99 - Ap 15 '74 - p1220
NYTBR - My 5 '74 - p44
Subject: Camping

KENNA, Gail Wilson
Along The Gold Rush Trail
BL - v79 - Ap 15 '83 - p1078

KENNEDY, Kim
In-Between Love
BL - v80 - Je 15 '84 - p1474
SLJ - v31 - S '84 - p137
VOYA - v7 - O '84 - p202
Subject: Love—Fiction; Theater—Fiction

KENNEDY, M L
Here To Stay
SLJ - v31 - Ja '85 - p90

KENNEDY, Richard 1932-
ConAu 7NR, FifBJA, SmATA 22, TwCChW 83, WrDr 86
The Boxcar At The Center Of The Universe
BL - v78 - Je 1 '82 - p1307
BS - v42 - Ag '82 - p203
CBRS - v10 - Ap '82 - p88
CCB-B - v36 - D '82 - p70
J Read - v26 - N '82 - p184
KR - v50 - Ap 15 '82 - p496
LA - v59 - N '82 - p867
NYTBR - v87 - Ag 5 '82 - p22
PW - v221 - My 28 '82 - p72
SLJ - v28 - Ag '82 - p126
VOYA - v5 - Ag '82 - p33
Subject: Arabs—Fiction; Fantasy; Tramps—Fiction

KENT, Deborah 1948-
ConAu 103, SmATA 47
Belonging
CLW - v50 - O '78 - p109
Kliatt - v14 - Spring '80 - p6
TN - v36 - Summer '80 - p367
Subject: Blind—Fiction; Individuality—Fiction; Physically handicapped—Fiction

KERR, M E (pseud.) 1932?-
ConAu X, ConLC 12, -35, FourBJA, OxChL, SmATA X, -1AS, TwCChW 83, WrDr 86
Real Name:
Meaker, Marijane

Dinky Hocker Shoots Smack
BL - v69 - D 1 '72 - p351
BL - v69 - D 1 '72 - p357
BS - v32 - O 15 '72 - p339
BS - v33 - N 1 '73 - p355
CCB-B - v26 - D '72 - p59
Econ - v249 - D 29 '73 - p59
EJ - v62 - D '73 - p1298
EJ - v63 - My '74 - p91
HB - v49 - F '73 - p56
J Read - v26 - O '82 - p65
KR - v40 - O 1 '72 - p1152
KR - v40 - D 15 '72 - p1420
LJ - v97 - D 15 '72 - p4056
LJ - v97 - D 15 '72 - p4079
NS - v86 - N 9 '73 - p700
NY - v48 - D 2 '72 - p190
NYTBR, pt. 1 - F 11 '73 - p8
PW - v203 - Ja 1 '73 - p57
Spec - v231 - O 20 '73 - pR10
Teacher - v90 - Mr '73 - p80
TES - N 1 '85 - p26
TLS - N 23 '73 - p1433
TN - v29 - Ap '73 - p253
TN - v30 - Ja '74 - p203

Gentlehands
BL - v74 - Mr 15 '78 - p1175
BS - v38 - S '78 - p180
BW - Jl 9 '78 - pE4
CCB-B - v31 - Ap '78 - p129
Comw - v105 - N 10 '78 - p733
EJ - v67 - S '78 - p90
EJ - v68 - D '79 - p78
HB - v54 - Je '78 - p284
J Read - v22 - N '78 - p183
KR - v46 - F 15 '78 - p183
NYTBR - Ap 30 '78 - p30
PW - v213 - Ja 9 '78 - p81
SLJ - v24 - Mr '78 - p138
SLJ - v24 - My '78 - p36
TN - v37 - Fall '80 - p60
Subject: Grandfathers—Fiction; War criminals—Germany—Fiction

If I Love You, Am I Trapped Forever?
B&B - My '86 - p20
BL - v69 - Je 15 '73 - p984
BS - v33 - My 15 '73 - p98
CCB-B - v26 - Je '73 - p157
CSM - v65 - My 5 '73 - p10
EJ - v66 - O '77 - p57
HB - v49 - Je '73 - p276
KR - v41 - F 1 '73 - p123
LJ - v98 - Ap 15 '73 - p1395

KERR, M E (continued)
NYTBR - S 16 '73 - p8
NYTBR - N 4 '73 - p52
NYTBR - My 12 '74 - p39
PT - v7 - D '73 - p126
PW - v203 - F 12 '73 - p68
TN - v37 - Fall '80 - p60

I'll Love You When You're More Like Me
BB - v5 - Ja '78 - p3
BL - v74 - S 1 '77 - p32
BL - v74 - S 1 '77 - p42
BS - v37 - D '77 - p294
CCB-B - v31 - S '77 - p18
EJ - v67 - F '78 - p99
HB - v53 - D '77 - p668
Kliatt - v13 - Spring '79 - p9
KR - v45 - Jl 1 '77 - p673
NYTBR - N 13 '77 - p50
PW - v211 - Je 27 '77 - p111
SLJ - v24 - O '77 - p124
TN - v37 - Fall '80 - p60
WCRB - v3 - N '77 - p48
Subject: Parent and child—Fiction

Love Is A Missing Person
BB - v3 - O '75 - p4
BL - v72 - S 1 '75 - p34
BS - v35 - D '75 - p299
CCB-B - v29 - N '75 - p48
EJ - v65 - Mr '76 - p90
EJ - v68 - O '79 - p102
J Read - v20 - O '76 - p79
Kliatt - v11 - Spring '77 - p6
KR - v43 - Jl 1 '75 - p717
NYTBR - O 19 '75 - p10
PW - v207 - Je 30 '75 - p58
SLJ - v22 - N '75 - p92
Subject: Love—Fiction

Night Kites
BL - v82 - Ap 1 '86 - p1135
BS - v46 - Ag '86 - p198
BW - v16 - My 11 '86 - p17
CBRS - v14 - My '86 - p113
CCB-B - v39 - My '86 - p169
EJ - v75 - O '86 - p83
HB - v62 - S '86 - p597
J Read - v30 - O '86 - p81
KR - v54 - Jl 1 '86 - p1022
NYTBR - v91 - Ap 13 '86 - p30
PW - v229 - My 30 '86 - p68
SLJ - v32 - My '86 - p104
SLJ - v33 - S '86 - p47
VOYA - v9 - Je '86 - p80
WLB - v60 - Ap '86 - p49
Subject: AIDS (Disease)—Fiction; Brothers and sisters—Fiction; Family problems—Fiction

What I Really Think Of You
BL - v78 - Ap 15 '82 - p1086
BS - v42 - Ag '82 - p203
BW - v12 - Jl 11 '82 - p11
CBRS - v10 - My '82 - p98
CCB-B - v35 - Je '82 - p190
KR - v50 - Mr 15 '82 - p349
NYTBR - v87 - S 12 '82 - p49
NYTBR - v88 - Je 5 '83 - p39
PW - v221 - F 12 '82 - p98
SLJ - v28 - My '82 - p71
VOYA - v5 - F '83 - p37
Subject: Religions—Fiction

KESTER, Ellen Skinner

The Climbing Rope
SLJ - v25 - Ja '79 - p51
Subject: Camping—Fiction; Christian life—Fiction

KETCHAM, Hank 1920-
ArtCS, BioIn 3, -4, -5, -11, ConAu X, CurBio 56, EncAJ, SmATA X, WhoAmA 84
Pseud./variant:
Ketcham, Henry King

I Wanna Go Home!
BS - v25 - F 15 '66 - p433
KR - v33 - S 15 '65 - p1024
LJ - v90 - D 1 '65 - p5277
Trav - v125 - F '66 - p61
Subject: Voyages and travels

KETTELKAMP, Larry Dale 1933-
AuBYP, ConAu 29R, ConLC 12, IlsCB 1957, -1967, IntAu&W 77, SmATA 2, -3AS, ThrBJA, WrDr 86

Mischievous Ghosts
BL - v77 - F 15 '81 - p810
HB - v57 - F '81 - p68
KR - v48 - N 1 '80 - p1397
RT - v34 - My '81 - p967
SLJ - v27 - Mr '81 - p146
Subject: Poltergeists

KEVLES, Bettyann 1938-
ConAu 11NR, SmATA 23

Listening In
Hi Lo - v2 - Je '81 - p4

KEY, Alexander 1904-1979
AuBYP, BioIn 12, ConAu 6NR, IntAu&W 77, ScFSB, SmATA 23N, -8, TwCSFW 86, WrDr 80

Escape To Witch Mountain
BL - v64 - Ap 15 '68 - p996

KEY, Alexander (continued)
BW - v2 - S 29 '68 - p18
CSM - v60 - My 2 '68 - pB8
KR - v36 - Mr 15 '68 - p344
PW - v193 - My 13 '68 - p58
Teacher - v92 - My '75 - p92
Subject: Fantasy

The Golden Enemy
BW - v3 - My 4 '69 - p20
KR - v37 - Mr 15 '69 - p316
LJ - v94 - Ap 15 '69 - p1782
Subject: Science fiction

KHERDIAN, David 1931-
ConAu 21R, –2AS, ConLC 6, –9, DrAP&F 85, FifBJA, IntAu&W 77, SmATA 16, WhoAm 86, WrDr 86

It Started With Old Man Bean
BL - v76 - Ja 1 '80 - p668
CBRS - v8 - F '80 - p58
CCB-B - v34 - S '80 - p13
KR - v48 - Mr 15 '80 - p365
NYTBR - v85 - Ap 27 '80 - p63
SLJ - v26 - Ja '80 - p79
Subject: Camping—Fiction

KIDD, Ronald 1948-
ConAu 116, SmATA 42

Dunker
BS - v42 - Ag '82 - p204
CBRS - v10 - Je '82 - p107
SLJ - v28 - My '82 - p86
VOYA - v5 - O '82 - p43
Subject: Advertising—Fiction; Basketball—Fiction

Sizzle And Splat
BL - v80 - N 15 '83 - p498
CBRS - v12 - Mr '84 - p84
CCB-B - v37 - Mr '84 - p130
KR - v51 - N 1 '83 - pJ204
SLJ - v30 - D '83 - p85
Subject: Mystery and detective stories; Orchestra—Fiction

Who Is Felix The Great?
BL - v79 - Ag '83 - p1465
BS - v43 - Je '83 - p110
CBRS - v11 - Mr '83 - p82
CCB-B - v36 - Jl '83 - p212
HB - v59 - Ap '83 - p171
KR - v51 - Ja 1 '83 - p7
SLJ - v30 - S '83 - p136
Subject: Baseball—Fiction; Mothers and sons—Fiction; Single-parent family—Fiction

KILEY, Denise

Biggest Machines
ASBYP - v14 - Fall '81 - p29
SB - v17 - S '81 - p34
Subject: Machinery

KILLENS, John Oliver 1916-
ConAu 77, –2AS, ConLC 10, ConNov 76, –82, –86, DcLB 33, ModBlW, NegAl 83, SelBAAf, WhoBlA 85, WrDr 86

Great Gittin' Up Morning: A Biography Of Denmark Vesey
BL - v68 - Je 1 '72 - p862
BL - v69 - My 1 '73 - p838
BS - v31 - Mr 15 '72 - p566
CCB-B - v26 - Mr '73 - p108
CSM - v64 - My 4 '72 - pB5
KR - v40 - Ja 1 '72 - p11
LJ - v97 - S 15 '72 - p2962
NYRB - v18 - Ap 20 '72 - p39
NYTBR - Ap 30 '72 - p8
PW - v201 - Ap 10 '72 - p58

KILLIEN, Christi

Putting On An Act
BL - v82 - Ag '86 - p1689
CBRS - v15 - S '86 - p9
CCB-B - v40 - S '86 - p10
KR - v54 - Je 1 '86 - p865
PW - v229 - Ap 25 '86 - p82
SLJ - v32 - Ag '86 - p101
VOYA - v9 - Ag '86 - p145
Subject: Interpersonal relations—Fiction

KILLILEA, Marie 1913-
ConAu 5R, SmATA 2

Karen
A Lead - v17 - F '69 - p366
BL - v49 - O 1 '52 - p44
KR - v20 - Ag 1 '52 - p484
LJ - v77 - S 15 '52 - p1499
NYTBR - S 28 '52 - p10
SR - v35 - S 20 '52 - p15
VOYA - v5 - Ap '82 - p58
Subject: Biography; Cerebral palsy

KINGMAN, Lee 1919-
AuBYP, BioIn 1, ConAu 5R, ConLC 17, MorJA, SmATA 1, –3AS, TwCChW 83, WrDr 86

Break A Leg, Betsy Maybe!
BL - v73 - N 15 '76 - p466
BL - v73 - N 15 '76 - p474
CCB-B - v30 - My '77 - p144

KINGMAN, Lee (continued)
EJ - v69 - Ja '80 - p78
HB - v53 - F '77 - p56
KR - v44 - O 1 '76 - p1101
SLJ - v23 - O '76 - p118
Subject: Schools—Fiction; Theater—Fiction

Head Over Wheels
EJ - v68 - N '79 - p76
EJ - v68 - D '79 - p78
Emerg Lib - v9 - N '81 - p32
Inter BC - v12 - #7 '81 p19
JB - v44 - F '80 - p29
Kliatt - v15 - Spring '81 - p9
RSR - v11 - Fall '83 - p27
Sch Lib - v28 - Je '80 - p181
SLJ - v25 - O '78 - p156
TN - v36 - Summer '80 - p364
Subject: Family problems—Fiction; Physically handicapped—Fiction; Twins—Fiction

The Peter Pan Bag
BL - v67 - S 15 '70 - p96
CCB-B - v24 - O '70 - p29
Comw - v92 - My 22 '70 - p250
CSM - v62 - My 7 '70 - pB6
HB - v46 - Ag '70 - p394
KR - v38 - Ap 15 '70 - p465
LJ - v96 - Ap 15 '71 - p1516
NYTBR - Jl 12 '70 - p26
NYTBR, Pt. 2 - N 7 '71 - p47
SR - v53 - Je 27 '70 - p56
Subject: Hippies—Fiction

KINGSBURY, Dawn

South Of The Border
BL - v80 - Je 15 '84 - p1474
VOYA - v7 - Je '84 - p91
Subject: Love—Fiction; Pen pals—Fiction

KINNEY, Cle
see Kinney, Jean (co-author)

KINNEY, Jean 1912-
AuBYP SUP, ConAu 9R, SmATA 12

21 Kinds Of American Folk Art And How To Make Each One
BL - v69 - O 1 '72 - p149
CLW - v44 - N '72 - p248
HB - v48 - Ag '72 - p387
NYTBR - Jl 2 '72 - p8
NYTBR, Pt. 2 - N 5 '72 - p28
Co-author: Kinney, Cle
Subject: Folk art; Handicraft

KINNICK, B J

Voices Of Man/I Have A Dream
EJ - v58 - Ja '69 - p145
Co-author: Perry, Jesse

Voices Of Man/Let Us Be Men
EJ - v58 - Ja '69 - p145
Co-author: Perry, Jesse

KINTER, Judith

Cross-Country Caper
BL - v78 - Mr 15 '82 - p965
SLJ - v28 - Mr '82 - p158
Subject: Drug abuse—Fiction; Running—Fiction

KJELGAARD, Jim 1910-1959
ConAu X, JBA 51, OxChL, SmATA 17, –X, TwCChW 83
Pseud./variant:
Kjelgaard, James Arthur

Big Red
BL - v42 - D 15 '45 - p132
GP - v19 - N '80 - p3775
Kliatt - v11 - Winter '77 - p5
KR - v13 - O 1 '45 - p437
LJ - v71 - Ja 1 '46 - p58
NYTBR - N 11 '45 - p26
Subject: Dogs—Fiction

Dave And His Dog, Mulligan
BS - v26 - Ag 1 '66 - p175
LJ - v91 - Jl '66 - p3543
Subject: Dogs—Fiction

Hidden Trail
HB - v38 - Ag '62 - p377
LJ - v87 - My 15 '62 - p2034
NYTBR - Ap 29 '62 - p42

Outlaw Red
BL - v50 - N 15 '53 - p125
KR - v21 - S 1 '53 - p587
LJ - v78 - N 15 '53 - p2046
NYTBR - D 20 '53 - p16
Subject: Animals—Fiction

KLAGSBRUN, Francine Lifton
ConAu 21R, SmATA 36, WhoAmW 81

Psychiatry
LJ - v95 - My 15 '70 - p1954
Subject: Psychiatry

KLASS, Sheila Solomon 1927-
ConAu 13NR, DrAP&F 85, SmATA 45, WhoAmW 83, WrDr 86

The Bennington Stitch
BL - v82 - S 15 '85 - p125
BS - v45 - Ja '86 - p398
CBRS - v14 - Ap '86 - p101
CCB-B - v39 - Ja '86 - p89
NYTBR - v90 - O 27 '85 - p37
PW - v228 - Jl 26 '85 - p167
PW - v230 - N 28 '86 - p80
SLJ - v32 - O '85 - p182
VOYA - v9 - Ap '86 - p31
Subject: Mothers and daughters—Fiction

KLEIN, Aaron
see Pearce, W E (co-author)

KLEIN, Dave 1940-
ConAu 89

On The Way Up: What It's Like To Be In The Minor Leagues
BL - v74 - O 1 '77 - p303
KR - v45 - S 1 '77 - p940
SLJ - v24 - D '77 - p63
Subject: Baseball

Pro Basketball's Big Men
KR - v41 - S 15 '73 - p1042
LJ - v98 - D 15 '73 - p3721
Subject: Basketball—Biography

KLEIN, H Arthur
AuBYP, ConAu 13R, SmATA 8

Surf's Up!: An Anthology Of Surfing
BL - v63 - D 1 '66 - p414
CE - v43 - F '67 - p355
LJ - v92 - Ja 15 '67 - p352
SA - v215 - D '66 - p148
Co-author: Klein, Mina Cooper
Subject: Surfing

KLEIN, Mina Cooper
see Klein, H Arthur (co-author)

KLEIN, Norma 1938-
ChlLR 2, ConAu 15NR, ConLC 30, FifBJA, OxChL, SmATA 7, -1AS, TwCChW 83, WhoAm 86, WrDr 86

Breaking Up
BL - v77 - S 15 '80 - p110
BS - v40 - N '80 - p301
CBRS - v9 - D '80 - p29
CCB-B - v34 - N '80 - p56
Emerg Lib - v9 - Ja '82 - p33
Inter BC - v12 - #3 '81 p19
J Read - v24 - Ap '81 - p647
KR - v49 - Ja 1 '81 - p12
SLJ - v27 - O '80 - p156
TES - Jl 11 '86 - p25
VOYA - v4 - Je '81 - p28
WLB - v55 - D '80 - p293
Subject: Divorce—Fiction; Lesbians—Fiction; Remarriage—Fiction

The Cheerleader
BL - v82 - O 1 '85 - p263
B Rpt - v4 - Mr '86 - p30
BS - v45 - Ja '86 - p398
BW - v15 - N 10 '85 - p17
CBRS - v14 - N '85 - p31
CCB-B - v39 - S '85 - p11
Par - v60 - N '85 - p66
SLJ - v32 - N '85 - p98
VOYA - v9 - Ap '86 - p31
Subject: Cheerleading—Fiction; Schools—Fiction; Sex role—Fiction

It's Not What You Expect
BL - v70 - S 15 '73 - p122
BS - v33 - My 15 '73 - p98
BS - v34 - Je 1 '74 - p127
BW - v7 - My 13 '73 - p7
CCB-B - v26 - Jl '73 - p172
Choice - v14 - N '77 - p1178
KR - v41 - F 15 '73 - p194
NYTBR - Je 3 '73 - p8
PW - v203 - Mr 5 '73 - p82
TES - S 26 '86 - p31
TN - v30 - Ja '74 - p199
Subject: Family life—Fiction; Youth—Fiction

Mom, The Wolf Man And Me
BL - v69 - Ja 1 '73 - p449
CCB-B - v26 - F '73 - p93
Comw - v97 - N 17 '72 - p158
Emerg Lib - v11 - Ja '84 - p21
HB - v49 - F '73 - p56
KR - v40 - S 1 '72 - p1027
LJ - v97 - D 15 '72 - p4057
LJ - v97 - D 15 '72 - p4072
NW - v83 - Mr 4 '74 - p83
NYTBR - S 24 '72 - p8
NYTBR - F 10 '74 - p30
NYTBR, Pt. 2 - N 5 '72 - p28
PW - v202 - N 13 '72 - p46
Teacher - v90 - Ja '73 - p92
TN - v30 - Ja '74 - p203
Subject: Illegitimacy—Fiction; Unwed mothers—Fiction

Sunshine
BL - v71 - O 15 '74 - p238

KLEIN, Norma (continued)
CLW - v49 - O '77 - p109
EJ - v65 - Ja '76 - p98
EJ - v65 - My '76 - p91
Hi Lo - v4 - Mr '83 - p5
KR - v43 - S 15 '75 - p1083
LJ - v99 - S 15 '74 - p2176
LJ - v99 - N 15 '74 - p3061
PW - v206 - Ag 12 '74 - p58
Subject: Cancer—Fiction

Taking Sides
BL - v70 - Jl 15 '74 - p1254
CCB-B - v28 - N '74 - p46
KR - v42 - Jl 1 '74 - p688
LJ - v99 - O 15 '74 - p2747
NYTBR - S 29 '74 - p8
PW - v205 - Jl 22 '74 - p70
Subject: Divorce—Fiction

KLEINER, Art

Robots
ACSB - v15 - Winter '82 - p39
BL - v77 - Je 15 '81 - p1344
SLJ - v27 - Ag '81 - p63
TES - Mr 12 '82 - p39
Subject: Robots

KLEVIN, Jill Ross 1935-
ConAu 111, IntAu&W 86, SmATA 39

The Summer Of The Sky-Blue Bikini
Hi Lo - v3 - Ja '82 - p5
Subject: Love—Fiction

KLUGER, Ruth

The Secret Ship
BL - v77 - Ap 15 '81 - p1142
Hi Lo - v1 - S '79 - p3
J Read - v22 - F '79 - p477
Co-author: Mann, Peggy
Subject: World War, 1939-1945

see also Mann, Peggy for additional titles

KNAPP, Ron
ConAu 103, SmATA 34

Tutankhamun And The Mysteries Of Ancient Egypt
Hi Lo - v1 - D '79 - p6
SB - v16 - S '80 - p36
SLJ - v26 - F '80 - p57
Subject: Egypt; Kings, queens, rulers, etc.

KNIGHT, Damon 1922-
BioIn 11, ConAu 17NR, DcLB 8, DrmM 1, SmATA 9, TwCSFW 86, WhoSciF, WorAu, WrDr 82

A Pocketful Of Stars
KR - v39 - Ag 1 '71 - p836
LJ - v96 - S 1 '71 - p2673
PW - v200 - Ag 23 '71 - p76
TLS - O 13 '72 - p1235
Subject: Science fiction

Toward Infinity
KR - v36 - S 1 '68 - p991
Subject: Science fiction

KNIGHT, David C 1925-
AuBYP, ConAu 73, SmATA 14

Harnessing The Sun: The Story Of Solar Energy
ACSB - v10 - Winter '77 - p27
BL - v72 - Je 1 '76 - p1407
KR - v44 - My 15 '76 - p605
SB - v12 - D '76 - p133
SLJ - v23 - S '76 - p134
Subject: Solar energy

Poltergeists
BL - v69 - Mr 1 '73 - p649
CE - v50 - O '73 - p32
KR - v40 - O 15 '72 - p1207
SR - v55 - N 11 '72 - p78
Subject: Ghosts; Poltergeists

The Spy Who Never Was And Other True Spy Stories
BL - v75 - D 15 '78 - p681
Hi Lo - v2 - D '80 - p2
Par - v54 - Ap '79 - p24
SLJ - v25 - D '78 - p54
Subject: Spies

KNIGHT, Eric 1897-1943
AuBYP, CurBio 42, -43, FourBJA, HalFC 84, OxChL, SmATA 18, TwCChW 83, WhoChL, WorAl

Lassie Come-Home
BL - v68 - F 1 '72 - p468
BL - v74 - Jl 15 '78 - p1734
BL - v81 - Ap 1 '85 - p1127
BL - v82 - F 1 '86 - p817
GP - v19 - Mr '81 - p3851
LJ - v97 - Ap 15 '72 - p1606
NYTBR, Pt. 2 - F 13 '72 - p12
Par - v60 - Je '85 - p164
PW - v200 - N 22 '71 - p41
Teacher - v90 - F '73 - p125
Subject: Dogs—Fiction

KNIGHT, Frank 1905-
ConAu 73, SmATA X, TwCChW 83, WhoChL, WrDr 86

KNIGHT, Frank (continued)
Pseud./variant:
Knight, Francis Edgar

Ships: From Noah's Ark To Nuclear Submarine
BL - v67 - Je 1 '71 - p834
KR - v39 - Ja 15 '71 - p62
LJ - v96 - My 15 '71 - p1805
Subject: Ships

Stories Of Famous Explorers By Land
LJ - v92 - Ja 15 '67 - p336
Subject: Explorers

KNIGHTLEY, Phillip 1929-
ConAu 25R, WrDr 86

Lawrence Of Arabia
B&B - v21 - Jl '76 - p40
BB - v5 - Je '77 - p3
BS - v37 - Jl '77 - p126
CE - v54 - Ja '78 - p142
GP - v14 - Ap '76 - p2836
KR - v44 - S 15 '76 - p1041
LJ - v94 - D 15 '69 - p4520
SLJ - v23 - D '76 - p55
Subject: European War, 1914-1918; Soldiers

KNOTT, Bill 1927-
AuBYP SUP, ConAu 5R, SmATA 3, WrDr 86

The Secret Of The Old Brownstone
LJ - v94 - My 15 '69 - p2122
PW - v195 - Ap 7 '69 - p56
Subject: Mystery and detective stories; Urban renewel—Fiction

KNUDSEN, James 1950-
ConAu 111, SmATA 42

Just Friends
BL - v78 - Ag '82 - p1518
PW - v222 - O 29 '82 - p45
SLJ - v29 - D '82 - p72
Subject: Friendship—Fiction

KNUDSON, R R 1932-
ConAu 33R, SmATA 7, WrDr 86
Pseud./variant:
Knudson, Rozanne Ruth

Fox Running
BL - v72 - S 15 '75 - p166
BS - v36 - Ap '76 - p30
CCB-B - v29 - My '76 - p147
HB - v52 - F '76 - p56
KR - v43 - N 1 '75 - p1239
SLJ - v22 - D '75 - p69
Subject: Indians of North America—Fiction; Running—Fiction

You Are The Rain
KR - v42 - Mr 15 '74 - p308
LJ - v99 - O 15 '74 - p2747
PW - v205 - Ja 21 '74 - p85
Subject: Camping—Fiction; Survival—Fiction

Zanballer
BL - v69 - Ap 1 '73 - p764
CCB-B - v26 - Ap '73 - p127
EJ - v62 - Ap '73 - p649
EJ - v64 - S '75 - p80
KR - v40 - O 15 '72 - p1201
LJ - v97 - D 15 '72 - p4089
SLJ - v24 - My '78 - p39
Subject: Football—Fiction

KNUDSON, Richard L 1930-
ConAu 20NR, DrAS 82E, SmATA 34

Land Speed Record Breakers
BL - v77 - Mr 15 '81 - p1028
SLJ - v27 - My '81 - p88
Subject: Automobile racing

Model Cars
BL - v77 - Mr 15 '81 - p1028
SLJ - v27 - Ag '81 - p68
Subject: Automobiles

Rallying
BL - v77 - Mr 15 '81 - p1028
SLJ - v27 - My '81 - p88
Subject: Automobiles

Restoring Yesterday's Cars
SLJ - v30 - Ap '84 - p121
Subject: Automobiles

KOCH, Charlotte
see Raymond, Charles

KOCH, Raymond
see Raymond, Charles

KOLLER, William D

I Am The Greatest: And Other True Stories Of Sports Greats
BL - v77 - Mr 15 '81 - p1024
Subject: Sports—Biography

KOMAROFF, Katherine

Sky Gods: The Sun And Moon In Art And Myth
BL - v71 - S 1 '74 - p43

KOMAROFF, Katherine (continued)
CSM - v67 - F 5 '75 - p8
KR - v42 - D 15 '74 - p1308
Subject: Moon in art; Sun lore

KOMROFF, Manuel 1890-1974
AuBYP, BioIn 10, ConAu 4NR, DcLB 4, NewYTBS 74, OxAmL 83, SmATA 2, -20N, WhAm 6, WrDr 76

Napoleon
B&B - v18 - Je '73 - p133
BL - v51 - D 15 '54 - p180
HB - v30 - O '54 - p341
KR - v22 - Jl 1 '54 - p397
LJ - v79 - N 15 '54 - p2257
NY - v30 - N 27 '54 - p221
Subject: Biography

True Adventures Of Spies
KR - v22 - Ja 15 '54 - p36
LJ - v79 - S 15 '54 - p1672
NYTBR - Je 27 '54 - p18
Subject: Spies

KONIGSBURG, E L 1930-
Au&ICB, ChILR 1, ConAu 17NR, DcLB 52, MorBMP, OxChL, SmATA 48, ThrBJA, TwCChW 83, WrDr 86

About The B'nai Bagels
BL - v65 - Je 15 '69 - p1176
CCB-B - v23 - S '69 - p12
CE - v46 - F '70 - p263
CLW - v41 - D '69 - p262
CLW - v41 - Ja '70 - p318
CLW - v43 - F '72 - p330
CLW - v48 - F '77 - p281
Comw - v90 - My 23 '69 - p297
Comw - v91 - N 21 '69 - p256
HB - v45 - Je '69 - p307
HB - v49 - Ap '73 - p173
KR - v37 - F 15 '69 - p179
LJ - v94 - Mr 15 '69 - p1329
LJ - v95 - F 15 '70 - p742
NCW - v216 - Mr '73 - p93
NO - v8 - S 1 '69 - p17
NYTBR - Mr 30 '69 - p28
NYTBR - Je 8 '69 - p44
NYTBR, Pt. 2 - N 9 '69 - p61
PW - v195 - Mr 31 '69 - p57
RR - v28 - Jl '69 - p700
SLJ - v24 - My '78 - p39
SR - v52 - Mr 22 '69 - p63
Subject: Baseball—Fiction; Family life—Fiction; Jews—Fiction

From The Mixed-Up Files Of Mrs. Basil E. Frankweiler
Am - v117 - N 4 '67 - p516
B&B - v14 - Jl '69 - p36
BL - v64 - O 1 '67 - p199
BW - v1 - N 5 '67 - p20
CCB-B - v21 - Mr '68 - p112
CLW - v39 - Ja '68 - p371
CLW - v39 - F '68 - p438
CSM - v59 - N 2 '67 - pB10
Emerg Lib - v11 - Ja '84 - p21
GP - v22 - N '83 - p4177
HB - v43 - O '67 - p595
KR - v35 - Jl 1 '67 - p740
Lis - v82 - N 6 '69 - p638
LJ - v92 - O 15 '67 - p3851
MN - v63 - D '84 - p62
NYTBR - v72 - N 5 '67 - p44
NYTBR, Pt. 2 - N 5 '72 - p42
Obs - Ap 6 '69 - p26
Obs - Je 2 '74 - p29
Par - v43 - Je '68 - p68
PW - v192 - Ag 7 '67 - p54
Spec - v222 - My 16 '69 - p657
SR - v50 - O 21 '67 - p43
Teacher - v90 - Ja '73 - p90
TLS - Ap 3 '69 - p355
TN - v24 - Ja '68 - p223

A Proud Taste For Scarlet And Miniver
Am - v129 - D 1 '73 - p431
BL - v70 - N 1 '73 - p287
BL - v70 - N 1 '73 - p292
BL - v70 - Mr 15 '74 - p827
CCB-B - v27 - S '73 - p10
Choice - v12 - N '75 - p1133
Comw - v99 - N 23 '73 - p216
CSM - v66 - My 1 '74 - pF1
GP - v14 - My '75 - p2652
HB - v49 - O '73 - p466
JB - v39 - Ap '75 - p119
Kliatt - v11 - Spring '77 - p6
KR - v41 - Jl 1 '73 - p685
LJ - v98 - O 15 '73 - p3147
NYTBR - O 14 '73 - p8
NYTBR - N 4 '73 - p52
PW - v204 - Ag 6 '73 - p65
Teacher - v91 - N '73 - p130
TLS - Ap 4 '75 - p370
TN - v40 - Fall '83 - p79
Subject: Eleanor of Aquitaine—Fiction; Great Britain—History

The Second Mrs. Giaconda
BB - v3 - O '75 - p2
BL - v72 - S 1 '75 - p42
BS - v35 - N '75 - p259
CCB-B - v29 - Ja '76 - p80
HB - v51 - O '75 - p470

KONIGSBURG, E L (continued)
JB - v41 - F '77 - p39
J Read - v20 - O '76 - p80
KR - v43 - Jl 1 '75 - p718
LA - v53 - F '76 - p202
NYTBR - O 5 '75 - p8
PW - v208 - D 1 '75 - p66
SLJ - v22 - S '75 - p121
Teacher - v93 - Ap '76 - p117
TLS - O 1 '76 - p1249
Subject: Leonardo da Vinci—Fiction

KOOB, Theodora 1918-
AuBYP, ConAu 5R, SmATA 23

The Deep Search
BS - v29 - Ap 1 '69 - p21
CCB-B - v23 - S '69 - p12
KR - v37 - F 15 '69 - p185
LJ - v94 - N 15 '69 - p4298
Subject: Family life—Fiction; Mentally handicapped—Fiction

This Side Of Victory
BS - v27 - D 1 '67 - p362
KR - v35 - Ag 15 '67 - p967
LJ - v92 - S 15 '67 - p3200

KOTZWINKLE, William 1938-
ChlLR 6, ConAu 3NR, ConLC 5, -35, ScFSB, SmATA 24, TwCSFW 86, WhoAm 86, WrDr 86

The Leopard's Tooth
BB - v4 - Ag '76 - p4
CCB-B - v30 - S '76 - p12
Kliatt - v17 - Spring '83 - p16
KR - v44 - Ap 1 '76 - p390
SLJ - v22 - My '76 - p60
Subject: Supernatural—Fiction

KOUFAX, Sandy 1935-
ConAu 89, CurBio 64, WhoAm 76, WhoProB 73
Pseud./variant:
Koufax, Sanford

Koufax
BL - v63 - O 1 '66 - p148
BS - v26 - O 1 '66 - p251
CLW - v38 - N '66 - p209
Comt - v42 - N '66 - p87
LJ - v91 - O 1 '66 - p4691
LJ - v91 - D 15 '66 - p6220
Nat - v204 - Ja 30 '67 - p149
NYTBR - v71 - S 18 '66 - p46
Subject: Baseball—Biography

KOUFAX, Sanford
see Koufax, Sandy

KOVALIK, Nada
see Kovalik, Vladimir (co-author)

KOVALIK, Vladimir 1928-
ConAu 25R

The Ocean World
Am - v115 - Jl 2 '66 - p15
BL - v62 - Jl 15 '66 - p1083
BS - v26 - Jl 1 '66 - p142
KR - v34 - Ap 1 '66 - p379
LJ - v91 - My 15 '66 - p2718
NH - v75 - N '66 - p76
NYTBR - v71 - My 8 '66 - p16
PW - v189 - My 30 '66 - p89
SB - v2 - S '66 - p117
SR - v49 - Je 25 '66 - p61
Co-author: Kovalik, Nada
Subject: Marine resources; Ocean; Oceanography as a profession

KOWET, Don 1937-
AuBYP SUP, ConAu 10NR

Vida Blue: Coming Up Again
LJ - v99 - D 15 '74 - p3279
Subject: Baseball—Biography

KRAFT, Betsy Harvey

Oil And Natural Gas
ASBYP - v16 - Fall '83 - p34
BL - v79 - F 15 '83 - p778
Cur R - v22 - O '83 - p76
SB - v18 - My '83 - p269
SLJ - v29 - F '83 - p77
Subject: Gas; Petroleum

KRAKOWSKI, Lili 1930-
ConAu 85

Starting Out: The Guide I Wish I'd Had When I Left Home
BL - v70 - F 15 '74 - p616
BL - v70 - F 15 '74 - p650
KR - v41 - Ag 15 '73 - p938
LJ - v98 - O 1 '73 - p2859
LJ - v98 - D 15 '73 - p3728
RSR - v2 - Ja '74 - p32
Subject: Finance (Personal)

KRASKE, Robert
ConAu 116, SmATA 36

Harry Houdini
Teacher - v91 - S '73 - p143
Subject: Biography; Magicians

KRASKE, Robert (continued)

The Twelve Million Dollar Note
KR - v45 - O 1 '77 - p1056
SA - v239 - D '78 - p34
SLJ - v24 - S '77 - p131
Subject: Ocean bottles

KREMENTZ, Jill 1940-
AuNews 1, -2, ChlLR 5, ConAu 41R, FifBJA, ICPEnP A, MacBEP, NewYTBS 82, SmATA 17, WhoAmW 87

How It Feels To Be Adopted
BL - v79 - F 1 '83 - p724
BW - v13 - Ja 9 '83 - p10
CBRS - v11 - F '83 - p71
CCB-B - v36 - F '83 - p111
JB - v48 - O '84 - p217
J Read - v26 - Ap '83 - p653
KR - v50 - N 15 '82 - p1239
LATBR - D 5 '82 - p10
LJ - v108 - Ja 1 '83 - p60
Ms - v12 - D '83 - p70
Par - v60 - Mr '85 - p48
PW - v222 - N 5 '82 - p70
Sch Lib - v33 - S '85 - p276
SLJ - v29 - D '82 - p65
TES - Ja 11 '85 - p21
VOYA - v6 - Ap '83 - p50
Subject: Adoption

How It Feels When A Parent Dies
BL - v78 - S 1 '81 - p48
BOT - v4 - S '81 - p403
BS - v41 - Ag '81 - p197
CBRS - v10 - Jl '81 - p117
CLW - v53 - D '81 - p231
Cur R - v21 - F '82 - p31
HB - v57 - O '81 - p553
JB - v47 - Je '83 - p127
J Read - v25 - Ja '82 - p390
KR - v49 - Ag 1 '81 - p937
NYTBR - v86 - Jl 19 '81 - p8
PW - v219 - Ap 17 '81 - p63
SLJ - v28 - S '81 - p127
SLJ - v30 - Ja '84 - p42
TES - Je 17 '83 - p28
VOYA - v5 - Je '82 - p45
Subject: Death; Parent and child

KRESSE, Bill

An Introduction To Cartooning
Kliatt - v18 - Fall '84 - p64
Subject: Cartooning

KROLL, Francis Lynde 1904-1973
ConAu P-1, SmATA 10

Top Hand
KR - v33 - F 1 '65 - p112

KROLL, Steven 1941-
AuBYP SUP, BioIn 12, ConAu 9NR, FifBJA, SmATA 19

Breaking Camp
BS - v46 - Je '86 - p116
CBRS - v14 - F '86 - p79
CCB-B - v39 - Mr '86 - p131
KR - v53 - D 1 '85 - p1329
SLJ - v32 - Ja '86 - p74
Subject: Camping—Fiction

KROPP, Paul
ConAu 112, SmATA 38, WhoCanL 85

Amy's Wish
Emerg Lib - v13 - N '85 - p45
Subject: Friendship—Fiction; Leukemia—Fiction

Baby, Baby
BL - v79 - Je 15 '83 - p1334
BL - v81 - Je 15 '85 - p1453
Can Child Lit - #37 '85 p59
Quill & Q - v48 - O '82 - p13
Subject: Pregnancy—Fiction; Unwed mothers—Fiction

Burn Out
BIC - v9 - Mr '80 - p23
BL - v78 - Mr 15 '82 - p951
Hi Lo - v2 - N '80 - p4
Subject: Arson—Fiction; Fires—Fiction; Mystery and detective stories

Dead On
BL - v78 - Ap 15 '82 - p1099
Hi Lo - v4 - S '82 - p4
Subject: Family life—Fiction; Supernatural—Fiction

Dirt Bike
BL - v78 - Ap 15 '82 - p1088
Hi Lo - v4 - S '82 - p4
Subject: Alcohol and youth—Fiction; Motorcycle racing—Fiction

Dope Deal
BIC - v9 - Mr '80 - p23
BL - v78 - Ap 15 '82 - p1088
B Rpt - v2 - S '83 - p23
Hi Lo - v4 - S '82 - p4

KROPP, Paul (continued)
Quill & Q - v46 - O '80 - p6
Subject: Drug abuse—Fiction

Fair Play
BL - v78 - Mr 15 '82 - p951
Hi Lo - v4 - S '82 - p4
Subject: Prejudices—Fiction; Race relations—Fiction

Gang War
Can Child Lit - #37 '85 p59
Quill & Q - v48 - O '82 - p13
Subject: Gangs—Fiction

Hot Cars
BIC - v9 - Mr '80 - p23
BL - v78 - Mr 15 '82 - p951
Hi Lo - v2 - N '80 - p4
Subject: Crime and criminals—Fiction

Micro Man
Emerg Lib - v13 - N '85 - p45
Subject: Computers—Fiction; Mystery and detective stories; Schools—Fiction

No Way
BL - v78 - Ap 15 '82 - p1088
Hi Lo - v4 - S '82 - p4
Quill & Q - v46 - O '80 - p6
Subject: Family problems—Fiction; Shoplifting—Fiction

Runaway
BIC - v9 - Mr '80 - p23
BL - v78 - Mr 15 '82 - p951
Hi Lo - v4 - S '82 - p4
Quill & Q - v46 - O '80 - p6
Subject: Alcohol and youth—Fiction; Child abuse—Fiction; Runaways—Fiction

Snow Ghost
BL - v79 - Je 15 '83 - p1334
Can Child Lit - #37 '85 p59
Quill & Q - v48 - O '82 - p13
Subject: Ghosts—Fiction; Survival—Fiction

Take Off
BIC - v14 - D '85 - p15
Quill & Q - v52 - F '86 - p21
Subject: Child abuse—Fiction; Family problems—Fiction; Runaways—Fiction

Wild One
BL - v79 - Je 15 '83 - p1334
Can Child Lit - #37 '85 p59
Quill & Q - v48 - O '82 - p13
Subject: Horses—Fiction

KUGELMASS, J Alvin 1910-1972
AuBYP, BioIn 9, ConAu 4NR, WhoAm 76

Ralph J. Bunche: Fighter For Peace
NYTBR - N 16 '52 - p20
Subject: Biography

KURLAND, Michael 1938-
ConAu 61, ConSFA, EncSF, ScF&FL 1, -2, ScFSB, SmATA 48, TwCSFW 86, WrDr 86

The Princes Of Earth
BL - v74 - Ap 1 '78 - p1249
KR - v46 - F 15 '78 - p205
SLJ - v25 - N '78 - p76
Subject: Science fiction

KUSAN, Ivan 1933-
AuBYP, ConAu 6NR

Mystery Of Green Hill
CSM - My 10 '62 - p6B
HB - v38 - Ap '62 - p173
KR - v30 - Ja 1 '62 - p13
LJ - v87 - Je 15 '62 - p2420
NYTBR, Pt. 2 - My 13 '62 - p31
RT - v33 - F '80 - p564

KWOLEK, Constance 1933-
ConAu X, WrDr 82
Pseud./variant:
Porcari, Constance Kwolek

Loner
CCB-B - v24 - Mr '71 - p108
KR - v38 - Jl 1 '70 - p689
LJ - v95 - O 15 '70 - p3638
Subject: Hippies—Fiction; Youth—Fiction

KYLE, Elisabeth (pseud.) d. 1982
AuBYP, ConAu X, IntAu&W 77, MorJA, SmATA 3, TwCChW 83, Who 82, WhoChL, WrDr 82
Real Name:
Dunlop, Agnes Mary Robinson

Girl With A Pen, Charlotte Bronte
BS - v24 - Ap 15 '64 - p42
CSM - My 7 '64 - p6B
HB - v40 - Ap '64 - p186
LJ - v89 - My 15 '64 - p2230
NYTBR, Pt. 2 - My 10 '64 - p10
SR - v47 - My 16 '64 - p91
Subject: Biography

KYTE, Kathy S 1946-
SmATA 44

The Kid's Complete Guide To Money
BL - v81 - Ap 1 '85 - p1120
BL - v82 - Mr 15 '86 - p1090
Cur R - v25 - S '85 - p93
SLJ - v31 - N '84 - p132
WCRB - v11 - Ja '85 - p59
Subject: Consumer education; Finance (Personal)

L

LADD, Veronica (pseud.)
ConAu X, IntAu&W 86X, SmATA X
Real Name:
Miner, Jane Claypool

Flowers For Lisa
Hi Lo - v3 - Ja '82 - p4
SLJ - v28 - Mr '82 - p154
VOYA - v4 - F '82 - p35

see also Miner, Jane Claypool for additional titles

LAGUMINA, Salvatore J 1928-
ConAu 77, DrAS 82H

An Album Of The Italian-American
BL - v69 - My 1 '73 - p859
LJ - v98 - My 15 '73 - p1690
Subject: Italian Americans

LAIKEN, Deirdre S 1948-
ConAu 104, SmATA 48

Listen To Me, I'm Angry
BL - v76 - Ap 1 '80 - p1117
CCB-B - v33 - Jl '80 - p217
J Read - v24 - D '80 - p272
KR - v48 - Je 1 '80 - p719
SB - v16 - Ja '81 - p152
SLJ - v26 - Ap '80 - p125
Co-author: Schneider, Alan J
Subject: Anger; Psychology

The Sweet Dreams Love Book
BL - v79 - Ap 15 '83 - p1082
SLJ - v29 - My '83 - p82
VOYA - v6 - Ag '83 - p153
Co-author: Schneider, Alan J

LAKLAN, Carli (pseud.) 1907-
AuBYP SUP, ConAu 1NR, IntAu&W 77, SmATA 5
Real Name:
Laughlin, Virginia Carli

Migrant Girl
BL - v68 - Je 15 '72 - p895
CCB-B - v24 - Jl '71 - p173
EJ - v60 - My '71 - p667
KR - v38 - Ag 15 '70 - p886
LJ - v95 - N 15 '70 - p4055
NYTBR, Pt. 2 - N 8 '70 - p2
Subject: Migrant labor—Fiction

Nurse In Training
CCB-B - v19 - S '65 - p12
Subject: Nursing—Fiction

Ski Bum
LJ - v98 - D 15 '73 - p3720
Subject: Skis and skiing—Fiction

LAMBERT, Eloise

Our Names: Where They Came From And What They Mean
BL - v57 - F 1 '61 - p329
CSM - F 2 '61 - p7
KR - v28 - Ag 15 '60 - p689
LJ - v85 - D 15 '60 - p4576
NYTBR - Ap 9 '61 - p34
SR - v43 - D 17 '60 - p35
Co-author: Pei, Mario
Subject: Names (Personal)

L'AMOUR, Louis 1908-
AuNews 1, -2, ConAu 1R, WhoAm 86, WhoWor 78, WrDr 86

The Proving Trail
Esq - v91 - Mr 13 '79 - p22
Kliatt - v13 - Spring '79 - p9

LAMPEL, Rusia

That Summer With Ora
BL - v64 - Ap 1 '68 - p931
CCB-B - v21 - F '68 - p96
CSM - v60 - My 2 '68 - pB11
KR - v35 - D 1 '67 - p1425
LJ - v93 - F 15 '68 - p883
Subject: Israel—Fiction

LAMPMAN, Evelyn Sibley 1907-1980
AuBYP, ConAu 101, -11NR, MorJA, NewYTBS 80, SmATA 4, -23N, TwCChW 83, WhoAmW 77, WrDr 80

Once Upon The Little Big Horn
EJ - v60 - D '71 - p1260
KR - v39 - Je 1 '71 - p591

LAMPMAN, Evelyn Sibley (continued)
LJ - v96 - S 15 '71 - p2918
NYTBR - Jl 11 '71 - p8
NYTBR, Pt. 2 - N 7 '71 - p30
Subject: Little Big Horn, Battle of the, 1876

The Year Of Small Shadow
BL - v68 - O 1 '71 - p152
BL - v69 - O 15 '72 - p177
BW - v5 - N 7 '71 - p13
CCB-B - v25 - D '71 - p59
CE - v48 - F '72 - p258
Comw - v97 - F 23 '73 - p474
EJ - v61 - F '72 - p304
HB - v47 - D '71 - p611
KR - v39 - Je 15 '71 - p642
LJ - v96 - S 15 '71 - p2918
PW - v200 - Ag 2 '71 - p64
Subject: Indians of North America—Fiction; Prejudices—Fiction

LAND, Charles

Calling Earth
Hi Lo - v1 - Mr '80 - p4
Subject: Science fiction

LANDAU, Elaine 1948-
AuBYP SUP, ConAu 5NR, IntAu&W 77, SmATA 10, WhoAmW 81

Death: Everyone's Heritage
CCB-B - v30 - D '76 - p59
SB - v13 - D '77 - p127
Subject: Death

Yoga For You
BL - v74 - Ja 15 '78 - p807
KR - v45 - D 1 '77 - p1274
SLJ - v24 - Ja '78 - p95
Subject: Yoga

LANE, Rose Wilder 1886?-1968
AuBYP SUP, BioIn 8, -10, ConAu 102, EncFWF, NotAW MOD, SmATA 29, WhAm 5

Let The Hurricane Roar
BL - v29 - Mr '33 - p206
CSM - Mr 4 '33 - p8
New R - v75 - Ag 2 '33 - p324
NYTBR - F 26 '33 - p7
SLJ - v27 - N '80 - p39
SR - v9 - Mr 4 '33 - p465
TLS - O 5 '33 - p662

Young Pioneers
BL - v72 - Je 1 '76 - p1387
BL - v72 - Je 1 '76 - p1407
JB - v44 - Ap '80 - p85
TES - N 23 '79 - p34

LANGE, Suzanne 1945-
ConAu 29R, SmATA 5

The Year: Life On An Israeli Kibbutz
CCB-B - v24 - Ja '71 - p76
EJ - v60 - S '71 - p827
LJ - v95 - N 15 '70 - p4056

LANGER, Richard W

The Joy Of Camping
BL - v70 - O 15 '73 - p202
KR - v41 - Ap 1 '73 - p449
LJ - v98 - Je 15 '73 - p1932
NYTBR - Jl 14 '74 - p12
Subject: Camping

LANGTON, Jane 1922-
AuBYP, BioIn 13, ConAu 18NR, FifBJA, IntAu&W 86, OxChL, SmATA 3, TwCChW 83, TwCCr&M 85, WrDr 86

The Boyhood Of Grace Jones
BL - v69 - F 1 '73 - p529
BW - v6 - N 5 '72 - p5
CCB-B - v27 - O '73 - p30
CE - v49 - Mr '73 - p320
CSM - v66 - D 5 '73 - pB12
CSM - v67 - Je 10 '75 - p16
HB - v49 - F '73 - p49
KR - v40 - N 15 '72 - p1306
Teacher - v93 - N '75 - p117
TN - v29 - Je '73 - p357

LANTZ, Francess Lin 1952-
IntAu&W 86

Good Rockin' Tonight
BL - v79 - N 1 '82 - p371
SLJ - v29 - F '83 - p90
VOYA - v6 - Ap '83 - p38
Subject: Rock music—Fiction

A Love Song For Becky
BL - v79 - Mr 15 '83 - p958
CCB-B - v36 - Mr '83 - p128
SLJ - v29 - Ap '83 - p125
Subject: Love—Fiction

Rock 'n' Roll Romance
BL - v80 - Je 15 '84 - p1474
SLJ - v31 - S '84 - p138
Subject: Love—Fiction; Rock music—Fiction

LAPPIN, Myra A

Need A Doctor?
Hi Lo - v4 - S '82 - p2
VOYA - v6 - Ag '83 - p156
Co-author: Feinglass, Sanford J.
Subject: Health; Medicine; Physicians

LARIMER, Tamela

Buck
PW - v230 - N 28 '86 - p77
Subject: Adolescence—Fiction

LARRANAGA, Robert O 1940-
ConAu 49

Famous Crimefighters
BL - v77 - O 15 '80 - p310
LJ - v96 - F 15 '71 - p741
Subject: Crime and criminals

Pirates And Buccaneers
BL - v77 - O 15 '80 - p310
LJ - v96 - F 15 '71 - p741
Subject: Pirates

LARRICK, Nancy 1910-
AuBYP, ConAu 1R, IntAu&W 86, MorBMP, SmATA 4, WhoAmW 77, WrDr 86

Bring Me All Of Your Dreams
BL - v76 - My 15 '80 - p1361
CE - v57 - Ja '81 - p174
KR - v48 - Ag 1 '80 - p981
LA - v58 - Ap '81 - p478
NYTBR - v85 - Ap 27 '80 - p61
PW - v217 - F 22 '80 - p109
SLJ - v26 - Ag '80 - p66
Subject: Dreams—Poetry; Poetry

On City Streets
BL - v65 - Ja 1 '69 - p491
BL - v65 - Ja 1 '69 - p497
CCB-B - v22 - F '69 - p97
CE - v45 - My '69 - p532
EJ - v58 - F '69 - p292
HB - v45 - Ap '69 - p181
NYTBR, Pt. 2 - F 15 '70 - p22
Teacher - v93 - F '76 - p29
Subject: Poetry

LARSON, Randy

Backpacking
Hi Lo - v2 - My '81 - p5
Subject: Backpacking; Camping

LASKY, Kathryn
ChlLR 11, ConAu 11NR, SmATA 13

Prank
BL - v80 - My 1 '84 - p1250
BS - v44 - S '84 - p234
CBRS - v12 - Je '84 - p117
CCB-B - v37 - My '84 - p168
Inter BC - v16 - #1 '85 p7
J Read - v29 - F '86 - p464
NW - v104 - D 3 '84 - p88
SLJ - v31 - O '84 - p168
VOYA - v7 - F '85 - p328
Subject: Brothers and sisters—Fiction; Vandalism—Fiction

LATHAM, Frank B 1910-
AuBYP SUP, ConAu 49, SmATA 6

FDR And The Supreme Court Fight 1937: A President Tries To Reorganize The Federal Judiciary
BL - v68 - Je 15 '72 - p909
BS - v32 - Ap 15 '72 - p45
Subject: United States—Supreme Court

LATHAM, Jean Lee 1902-
AuBYP, AuNews 1, ConAu 7NR, ConLC 12, MorBMP, MorJA, OxChL, SmATA 2, TwCChW 83, WrDr 86

Elizabeth Blackwell: Pioneer Woman Doctor
BL - v72 - D 15 '75 - p579
Inst - v85 - My '76 - p113
SB - v12 - My '76 - p43
SLJ - v22 - F '76 - p40
Subject: Physicians

LAUBER, Patricia 1924-
AuBYP, ConAu 6NR, SmATA 33, ThrBJA

Look-It-Up Book Of Mammals
CLW - v39 - F '68 - p436
CSM - v59 - N 2 '67 - pB11
Inst - v77 - Ja '68 - p152
KR - v35 - S 1 '67 - p1051
Obs - My 19 '68 - p1312
PW - v192 - N 13 '67 - p79
SB - v3 - My '68 - p325
Subject: Mammals

Look-It-Up Book Of Stars And Planets
CSM - v59 - N 2 '67 - pB8
PW - v192 - N 13 '67 - p80
Subject: Astronomy

LAUGHLIN, Virginia Carli
see Clarke, John; Laklan, Carli

LAW, Carol R

Dave's Double Mystery
Hi Lo - v3 - F '82 - p3

LAWICK-GOODALL, Jane Van
ASpks, ConAu 45, CurBio 67
Pseud./variant:
Van Lawick-Goodall, Jane

In The Shadow Of Man
BL - v68 - Ja 1 '72 - p374
BL - v68 - Ja 1 '72 - p391
BL - v68 - Ap 1 '72 - p664
BS - v31 - N 15 '71 - p376
BS - v32 - F 1 '73 - p503
BS - v34 - Jl 1 '74 - p179
BW - v5 - O 17 '71 - p6
Choice - v8 - Ja '72 - p1471
CSM - v63 - O 13 '71 - p9
Econ - v241 - O 30 '71 - p61
EJ - v64 - O '75 - p90
HB - v47 - D '71 - p629
KR - v39 - Ag 15 '71 - p914
Lis - v86 - N 25 '71 - p728
LJ - v96 - D 1 '71 - p4023
LJ - v97 - Mr 1 '72 - p831
Nat - v214 - Ja 17 '72 - p89
NS - v82 - D 3 '71 - p790
NW - v78 - N 15 '71 - p122A
NYT - v121 - N 26 '71 - p34
NYTBR - D 3 '72 - p6
Obs - O 24 '71 - p36
PW - v200 - Ag 9 '71 - p45
PW - v202 - O 2 '72 - p56
SA - v225 - D '71 - p106
SB - v7 - Mr '72 - p318
Time - v98 - N 8 '71 - p104
TLS - N 19 '71 - p1440
TN - v28 - Ap '72 - p313
Subject: Chimpanzees

LAWLESS, Joann A

Mysteries Of The Mind
Cur R - v17 - Ag '78 - p228
SLJ - v25 - S '78 - p128
Subject: Psychical research

Strange Stories Of Life
SLJ - v24 - My '78 - p63
Subject: Curiosities and wonders

LAWRENCE, Amy

Color It Love
BL - v79 - Je 15 '83 - p1340
SLJ - v30 - O '83 - p170
Subject: Camping; Love—Fiction

LAWRENCE, Mildred 1907-
AuBYP, BioIn 3, ConAu 5NR, CurBio 53, MichAu 80, MorJA, SmATA 3, TwCChW 78, WhoAmW 75

Along Comes Spring
BL - v55 - N 1 '58 - p132
HB - v34 - O '58 - p398
LJ - v83 - S 15 '58 - p2509

Good Morning, My Heart
BL - v54 - O 15 '57 - p108
CSM - O 10 '57 - p11
KR - v25 - Ag 1 '58 - p531
LJ - v82 - O 15 '57 - p2707
NYT - S 22 '57 - p36

Inside The Gate
BW - v2 - N 3 '68 - p26
CCB-B - v23 - S '69 - p12
CSM - v60 - N 7 '68 - pB11
EJ - v58 - F '69 - p294
HB - v44 - O '68 - p564
KR - v36 - Je 15 '68 - p649

The Questing Heart
BL - v56 - O 1 '59 - p85
CSM - N 5 '59 - p6B
HB - v36 - F '60 - p41
KR - v27 - Ag 1 '59 - p554
LJ - v84 - N 15 '59 - p3640

Walk A Rocky Road
EJ - v61 - Mr '72 - p434
KR - v39 - S 15 '71 - p1022
LJ - v96 - D 15 '71 - p4191
Subject: Appalachian mountains—Fiction

LAWSON, Donald Elmer 1917-
AuBYP, ConAu 1R, SmATA 9, WhoAm 86, WhoMW 84

Geraldine Ferraro
BL - v81 - Jl '85 - p1556
B Rpt - v5 - My '86 - p36
SLJ - v32 - S '85 - p146
Subject: Biography; Legislators; Vice-presidential candidates

The United States In The Civil War
BL - v74 - N 15 '77 - p552
KR - v45 - Jl 1 '77 - p670
SLJ - v24 - O '77 - p125
Subject: United States—History—Civil War, 1861-1865

LAWSON, Donald Elmer (continued)

The United States In The Spanish-American War
BL - v73 - S 15 '76 - p178
Inst - v86 - N '76 - p157
KR - v44 - My 1 '76 - p538
SLJ - v22 - Ap '76 - p90

LAWSON, Donna 1937-
ConAu 41R

Beauty Is No Big Deal: The Common Sense Beauty Book
KR - v39 - Ap 1 '71 - p414
KR - v39 - My 1 '71 - p520
LJ - v96 - Je 1 '71 - p1978
LJ - v96 - D 15 '71 - p4209
Co-author: Conlon, Jean
Subject: Beauty (Personal)

LAWSON, Robert 1892-1957
Au&ICB, AuBYP, ChlLR 2, DcLB 22, IlsBYP, IlsCB 1946, JBA 51, OxChL, TwCChW 83, WhAmArt 85

Mr. Revere And I
CSM - v66 - Ja 9 '74 - pF4
Teacher - v91 - Mr '74 - p110
Teacher - v92 - Ap '75 - p112
Subject: Horses—Fiction; Revere, Paul—Fiction

LAYCOCK, George 1921-
AuBYP, ConAu 19NR, SmATA 5, WhoMW 76

Air Pollution
KR - v40 - Mr 15 '72 - p330
LJ - v98 - Mr 15 '73 - p1005
LJ - v98 - My 1 '73 - p1441
NYTBR, Pt. 2 - My 7 '72 - p8
SB - v8 - S '72 - p171
Subject: Air-pollution

King Gator
BS - v28 - My 1 '68 - p65
LJ - v93 - Ap 15 '68 - p1800
PW - v193 - Ap 15 '68 - p98

Water Pollution
CCB-B - v26 - Mr '73 - p108
KR - v40 - Ap 15 '72 - p482
LJ - v97 - O 15 '72 - p3453
LJ - v98 - My 1 '73 - p1441
NYTBR, Pt. 2 - My 7 '72 - p8
Subject: Water

LAYMON, Carl

Your Secret Admirer
SLJ - v27 - D '80 - p63
VOYA - v4 - Je '81 - p30

LAYMON, Richard

The Cellar
PW - v216 - N 5 '79 - p66

Dawson's City
BL - v81 - Je 15 '85 - p1453

The Intruder
J Read - v30 - D '86 - p209

The Night Creature
BL - v83 - Ap 15 '87 - p1278

LAZARUS, Keo Felker 1913-
AuBYP SUP, ConAu 41R, IntAu&W 82, SmATA 21, WrDr 86

The Gismo
CCB-B - v24 - My '71 - p139
KR - v38 - Ag 15 '70 - p875
LJ - v96 - F 15 '71 - p724
Subject: Science fiction

Rattlesnake Run
BL - v64 - Jl 15 '68 - p1286
BW - v2 - My 5 '68 - p22
KR - v36 - Ja 15 '68 - p57
LJ - v93 - Ap 15 '68 - p1800

LEACH, Christopher

Free, Alone And Going
BL - v69 - My 1 '73 - p859
KR - v41 - F 15 '73 - p194
LJ - v98 - S 15 '73 - p2666
PW - v203 - Mr 26 '73 - p71
Subject: Runaways—Fiction

Rosalinda
B&B - v23 - Je '78 - p72
BL - v74 - Je 1 '78 - p1552
CCB-B - v32 - S '78 - p12
CR - v233 - O '78 - p216
EJ - v67 - N '78 - p83
GP - v17 - S '78 - p3387
LA - v55 - S '78 - p740
SLJ - v25 - S '78 - p142
TES - Je 16 '78 - p46
TLS - Jl 7 '78 - p765
Subject: England—Fiction; Ghosts—Fiction

LEACH, Maria 1892-1977
AuBYP, BioIn 11, ConAu 53, –69, FourBJA, SmATA 39

Noodles, Nitwits, And Numskulls
LA - v55 - N '78 - p962
NYTBR - Ja 13 '80 - p33
Subject: Wit and humor

Whistle In The Graveyard
BL - v71 - S 1 '74 - p44
CCB-B - v28 - Ja '75 - p81
HB - v50 - D '74 - p689
KR - v42 - Je 1 '74 - p584
LJ - v99 - S 15 '74 - p2273
NYTBR - Jl 28 '74 - p8
Subject: Folklore; Ghosts—Fiction

LECKIE, Robert 1920-
AuBYP, ConAu 13R

Helmet For My Pillow
BS - v32 - Ag 15 '72 - p244
Subject: World War, 1939-1945

LEDER, Jane M

Cassettes & Records
BL - v80 - F 1 '84 - p810
SLJ - v30 - Ap '84 - p110
Subject: Phono tapes

Champ Cars
BL - v80 - F 1 '84 - p810
SLJ - v30 - Mr '84 - p161
Subject: Automobile racing

Marcus Allen
BL - v81 - Jl '85 - p1562
Subject: Blacks—Biography; Football—Biography

Martina Navratilova
BL - v81 - Jl '85 - p1562
Subject: Tennis—Biography

Moses Malone
BL - v81 - Jl '85 - p1562
Subject: Basketball—Biography

Stunt Dogs
RT - v39 - My '86 - p953
RT - v39 - My '86 - p987
SLJ - v32 - Ag '86 - p91
Subject: Dogs

Video Games
BL - v80 - F 1 '84 - p810
SLJ - v30 - Ap '84 - p110
Subject: Games; Video games

Walter Payton
CCB-B - v40 - F '87 - p112
Subject: Blacks—Biography; Football—Biography

Wayne Gretzky
BL - v81 - Jl '85 - p1562
Subject: Hockey—Biography

LEDERER, William Julius 1912-
BioIn 2, –5, ConAu 5NR, WhoAm 86, WhoSpyF, WorAl, WorAu

The Ugly American
BL - v55 - O 15 '58 - p99
Choice - v24 - Ja '87 - p730
CSM - N 26 '58 - p15
KR - v26 - Ag 15 '58 - p615
LJ - v83 - O 15 '58 - p2842
Nat - v187 - O 4 '58 - p199
NYT - O 5 '58 - p5
NYTBR - O 5 '58 - p5
NYTBR - v90 - Mr 24 '85 - p40
SR - v41 - O 4 '58 - p32
Time - v72 - O 6 '58 - p92
Co-author: Burdick, Eugene

LEE, Betsy
ConAu 106, SmATA 37

Mother Teresa: Caring For All God's Children
KR - v49 - Jl 1 '81 - p803
PW - v219 - Ap 24 '81 - p75
SLJ - v28 - F '82 - p68
Subject: Biography; Nuns

LEE, C Y 1917-
ConAu 9R, NatPD, WorAu

The Land Of The Golden Mountain
BL - v64 - O 1 '67 - p169
BS - v27 - Jl 1 '67 - p138
HB - v43 - O '67 - p601
KR - v35 - Ap 1 '67 - p439
KR - v35 - Je 1 '67 - p655
LJ - v92 - S 15 '67 - p3201

LEE, Essie E 1920-
ConAu 4NR

Alcohol—Proof Of What?
ACSB - v10 - Winter '77 - p28
BL - v72 - My 15 '76 - p1330
BL - v72 - My 15 '76 - p1337
BS - v36 - Ag '76 - p151
Cur R - v16 - Ag '77 - p176
KR - v44 - Mr 15 '76 - p334
SB - v12 - D '76 - p129
Subject: Alcohol and youth

LEE; H Alton 1942-
ConAu 81

Seven Feet Four And Growing
BL - v74 - F 15 '78 - p997
Inter BC - v13 - #4 '82 p13
SLJ - v25 - S '78 - p142
Subject: Basketball—Fiction; Veterinarians—Fiction

LEE, Mildred 1908-
AuBYP SUP, BioIn 11, ConAu X, SmATA 6, ThrBJA, TwCChW 83, WrDr 86
Pseud./variant:
Scudder, Mildred Lee

Fog
BL - v69 - D 1 '72 - p351
BS - v6 - N 5 '72 - p8
BS - v32 - N 15 '72 - p395
CCB-B - v26 - D '72 - p59
CE - v49 - Mr '73 - p320
HB - v49 - F '73 - p57
KR - v40 - O 15 '72 - p1202
KR - v40 - D 15 '72 - p1420
LJ - v97 - N 15 '72 - p3814
LJ - v97 - D 15 '72 - p4057
NO - v11 - N 18 '72 - p28
NYTBR - D 3 '72 - p80
NYTBR, Pt. 2 - N 5 '72 - p2
PW - v202 - S 4 '72 - p51
Teacher - v90 - F '73 - p126
TN - v29 - Ap '73 - p257
Subject: Social adjustment—Fiction

The Skating Rink
Am - v121 - D 13 '69 - p595
BL - v65 - Je 1 '69 - p1120
BW - v3 - My 4 '69 - p5
CCB-B - v23 - N '69 - p48
EJ - v69 - D '80 - p56
HB - v45 - Ap '69 - p178
KR - v37 - F 15 '69 - p185
LJ - v94 - Ap 15 '69 - p1798
LJ - v94 - My 15 '69 - p2073
NYTBR - Je 29 '69 - p26
NYTBR, Pt. 2 - N 9 '69 - p60
PW - v195 - My 12 '69 - p57
SR - v52 - My 10 '69 - p60
Subject: Emotional problems—Fiction; Roller skating—Fiction

Sycamore Year
B&B - v3 - F '75 - p4
BL - v71 - O 1 '74 - p173
BW - D 15 '74 - p6
CCB-B - v28 - F '75 - p95
HB - v51 - F '75 - p55
KR - v42 - Jl 1 '74 - p688
LJ - v99 - S 15 '74 - p2293
NYTBR - Ja 26 '75 - p8
Subject: Friendship—Fiction; Unwed mothers—Fiction

LEE, Robert C 1931-
AuBYP SUP, ConAu 10NR, SmATA 20

Summer Of The Green Star
BL - v77 - Ap 1 '81 - p1085
CBRS - v9 - Spring '81 - p107
CE - v58 - Ja '82 - p182
J Read - v25 - Mr '82 - p614
SLJ - v27 - Ag '81 - p76
VOYA - v4 - O '81 - p43
Subject: Science fiction

LEE, Stan 1922-
BioIn 9, -11, ConAu 111, ConLC 17, WhoAm 86

How To Draw Comics The Marvel Way
BL - v74 - Ap 15 '78 - p1311
Co-author: Buscema, John
Subject: Comic books, strips, etc.; Drawing—Technique

LEECH, Jay
see Spencer, Zane (co-author)

LEEN, Nina
BioIn 4, ICPEnP A

Snakes
BB - v6 - Ag '78 - p2
BL - v74 - My 15 '78 - p1495
CCB-B - v32 - O '78 - p32
CE - v56 - N '79 - p115
Comw - v105 - N 10 '78 - p734
EJ - v67 - O '78 - p80
HB - v55 - O '78 - p541
KR - v46 - My 1 '78 - p499
NYTBR - Ap 30 '78 - p47
PW - v213 - Mr 27 '78 - p72
SLJ - v24 - My '78 - p69
Subject: Snakes

LEETE, Harley M 1918-

The Best Of Bicycling
CM - v13 - Spring '73 - p175
KR - v38 - Ag 1 '70 - p848
LJ - v96 - F 15 '71 - p651
NYTBR - Je 4 '72 - p8
Subject: Bicyles and bicyling

LEFKOWITZ, R J
see Bendick, Jeanne (co-author)

LEFKOWITZ, William

Government At Work: From City Hall To State Capitol
Hi Lo - v4 - My '83 - p4
Co-author: Urlich, R
Subject: United States—Politics and government

It's Our Government: Congress, The President, And The Courts
Hi Lo - v4 - My '83 - p4
Co-author: Uhlich, R
Subject: United States—Politics and government

see also Urlich, R for additional titles

LEGUIN, Ursula Kroeber 1929-
ChlLR 3, ConAu 9NR, ConLC 8, -13, -22, ConNov 86, DcLB 8, -52, FourBJA, SmATA 4, TwCChW 83, WrDr 86

Very Far Away From Anywhere Else
BB - v5 - Mr '77 - p4
BL - v73 - S 15 '76 - p138
BL - v73 - S 15 '76 - p178
B Rpt - v1 - Mr '83 - p24
BW - O 10 '76 - pE6
CCB-B - v30 - Ja '77 - p77
CE - v53 - F '77 - p213
CLW - v49 - D '77 - p199
Comw - v103 - N 19 '76 - p763
CSM - v68 - N 3 '76 - p20
EJ - v66 - S '77 - p84
EJ - v67 - My '78 - p89
HB - v53 - F '77 - p57
J Read - v25 - My '82 - p777
KR - v44 - Jl 1 '76 - p739
LA - v54 - Ap '77 - p442
NO - v15 - D 25 '76 - p15
NYTBR - N 14 '76 - p29
NYTBR - Mr 5 '78 - p41
SLJ - v23 - O '76 - p118
TN - v37 - Fall '80 - p61
Subject: Friendship—Fiction

LEHRMAN, Steve
see Shapiro, Neal (co-author)

LEISER, Harry W

The Secret Of Bitter Creek
BL - v78 - Mr 15 '82 - p951
Hi Lo - v3 - F '82 - p3
Subject: West (U.S.)—Fiction

LEMBECK, Ruth

Teenage Jobs
BL - v67 - Je 1 '71 - p831
LJ - v96 - My 15 '71 - p1834
Subject: Employment

L'ENGLE, Madeleine 1918-
ChlLR 1, ConAu 21NR, ConLC 12, DcLB 52, MorBMP, MorJA, OxChL, PiP, SmATA 27, TwCChW 83, WrDr 86

The Journey With Jonah
BL - v64 - D 15 '67 - p502
BS - v27 - O 1 '67 - p263
BW - v1 - N 5 '67 - p34
CCB-B - v21 - D '67 - p62
CLW - v39 - D '67 - p298
CSM - v59 - N 2 '67 - pB7
EJ - v57 - My '68 - p752
HB - v44 - Ap '68 - p184
KR - v35 - Ag 15 '67 - p975
LJ - v93 - Ja 15 '68 - p307
NYTBR - v73 - Ja 21 '68 - p28
SR - v50 - N 11 '67 - p48
Subject: Plays

A Wind In The Door
BL - v69 - Je 1 '73 - p944
BL - v69 - Je 1 '73 - p948
BS - v33 - My 15 '73 - p98
CCB-B - v27 - S '73 - p12
CE - v50 - O '73 - p30
Comw - v99 - N 23 '73 - p215
HB - v49 - Ag '73 - p379
Inst - v83 - Ag '73 - p74
KR - v41 - Ap 15 '73 - p463
LJ - v98 - My 15 '73 - p1655
LJ - v98 - My 15 '73 - p1691
NYTBR - Jl 8 '73 - p8
PW - v203 - Ap 16 '73 - p54
Teacher - v91 - D '73 - p73
TLS - Ap 4 '75 - p360
TN - v30 - N '73 - p81
TN - v34 - Spring '78 - p265
Subject: Science fiction

The Young Unicorns
B&B - v15 - N '69 - p41
BS - v28 - Jl 1 '68 - p154
BW - v2 - My 5 '68 - p5
CCB-B - v21 - Je '68 - p161
CSM - v60 - Je 13 '68 - p5
EJ - v58 - F '69 - p296
HB - v44 - Je '68 - p329
KR - v36 - My 15 '68 - p555
NYTBR - v73 - My 26 '68 - p30
Obs - Ag 24 '69 - p20
PW - v193 - Ap 15 '68 - p97

L'ENGLE, Madeleine (continued)
SR - v51 - My 11 '68 - p42
TLS - O 16 '69 - p1190

LENSKI, Lois 1893-1974
Au&ICB, ConAu 53, DcLB 22, IlsCB 1967, JBA 51, NatCAB 63, OxChL, SmATA 26, TwCChW 83, WhoAmA 82N

Deer Valley Girl
KR - v36 - F 15 '68 - p183
Obs - My 19 '68 - p1312
Subject: Country life—Fiction; Vermont—Fiction

LENT, Henry B 1901-1973
AuBYP, BioIn 1, ConAu 73, JBA 34, -51, SmATA 17, Str&VC

The Look Of Cars: Yesterday, Today, Tomorrow
KR - v34 - Ap 15 '66 - p433
LJ - v91 - Jl '66 - p3552
PW - v189 - My 30 '66 - p89
Subject: Automobiles

LENZ, Jeanne R

Do You Really Love Me?
BL - v80 - O 15 '83 - p338
Kliatt - v18 - Winter '84 - p14
SLJ - v30 - F '84 - p82

LEONARD, Constance 1923-
ConAu 49, IntAu&W 86, SmATA 42, WrDr 86

The Marina Mystery
BL - v77 - Ap 1 '81 - p1085
CCB-B - v35 - N '81 - p49
J Read - v25 - D '81 - p284
SLJ - v27 - My '81 - p86
Subject: Sailing—Fiction

Stowaway
BL - v79 - Ap 15 '83 - p1095
B Rpt - v2 - S '83 - p38
BS - v43 - Je '83 - p111
CBRS - v11 - Jl '83 - p139
SLJ - v29 - My '83 - p94
Subject: Mystery and detective stories

Strange Waters
BL - v82 - F 1 '86 - p804
SLJ - v32 - N '85 - p98
VOYA - v9 - Ap '86 - p32
Subject: Greece—Fiction; Mystery and detective stories

LERNER, Carol 1927-
ConAu 102, SmATA 33

Pitcher Plants
ASBYP - v16 - Fall '83 - p38
BL - v79 - My 15 '83 - p1218
CCB-B - v36 - Ap '83 - p154
CE - v60 - S '83 - p56
HB - v59 - Je '83 - p333
KR - v51 - Ja 15 '83 - p67
SB - v19 - S '83 - p32
SLJ - v29 - Ap '83 - p115
Subject: Insectivorous plants

LEROE, Ellen

Confessions Of A Teenage TV Addict
BL - v80 - F 1 '84 - p809
CBRS - v12 - S '83 - p9
CCB-B - v37 - D '83 - p72
SLJ - v30 - Mr '84 - p172
Subject: Soap operas—Fiction; Television—Fiction

Enter Laughing
BL - v80 - F 1 '84 - p809
VOYA - v7 - O '84 - p200
Subject: Love—Fiction

Give And Take
BL - v81 - F 1 '85 - p784
Subject: Love—Fiction

Have A Heart
BL - v83 - N 1 '86 - p403
Subject: Schools—Fiction

LESKOWITZ, Irving
see Stone, A Harris (co-author)

LESLIE, Clare Walker

Notes From A Naturalist's Sketchbook
Hort - v60 - F '82 - p68
Kliatt - v16 - Winter '82 - p61
NYTBR - v86 - D 6 '81 - p91
Subject: Natural history

LESLIE-MELVILLE, Betty 1929-
ConAu 81

Raising Daisy Rothschild
BL - v74 - Ja 1 '78 - p742
GW - v119 - D 10 '78 - p22
Kliatt - v13 - Spring '79 - p55
KR - v45 - Ag 1 '77 - p831
LJ - v103 - Ja 15 '78 - p180
NYTBR - N 13 '77 - p18
NYTBR - F 11 '79 - p37
PW - v212 - S 5 '77 - p64

LESLIE-MELVILLE, Betty (continued)
Co-author: Leslie-Melville, Jock
Subject: Animals—Fiction

LESLIE-MELVILLE, Jock
see Leslie-Melville, Betty (co-author)

LESTER, Julius 1939-
Au&ICB, AuBYP, ChILR 2, ConAu 8NR, FourBJA, SelBAAf, SmATA 12, TwCChW 83, WhoAm 86, WrDr 86

Long Journey Home
BL - v69 - O 15 '72 - p190
BL - v69 - My 1 '73 - p838
BW - v6 - S 3 '72 - p9
CCB-B - v26 - O '72 - p28
CSM - v64 - Ag 2 '72 - p11
EJ - v63 - Ja '74 - p66
HB - v49 - Ap '73 - p146
HT - v23 - D '73 - p885
JNE - v43 - Summer '74 - p395
KR - v40 - Je 1 '72 - p629
KR - v40 - D 15 '72 - p1420
LJ - v97 - Jl '72 - p2490
LJ - v97 - D 15 '72 - p4057
NYRB - v18 - Ap 20 '72 - p39
NYTBR - Je 4 '72 - p28
NYTBR - Jl 23 '72 - p8
NYTBR, Pt. 2 - N 5 '72 - p26
Obs - Jl 22 '79 - p37
PW - v201 - Je 5 '72 - p140
SE - v44 - O '80 - p480
TLS - S 28 '73 - p1118
TN - v29 - Je '73 - p357
Subject: Blacks—Fiction

This Strange New Feeling
BL - v80 - Ag '84 - p1621
Kliatt - v20 - Winter '86 - p48
SE - v47 - Ap '83 - p243
VOYA - v5 - O '82 - p44
Subject: Love—Fiction; Short stories; Slavery—Fiction

To Be A Slave
BL - v65 - F 15 '69 - p648
BL - v65 - Ap 1 '69 - p901
BL - v69 - My 1 '73 - p838
BL - v81 - Jl '85 - p1567
BW - v3 - Mr 16 '69 - p12
CCB-B - v22 - Ap '69 - p129
CE - v46 - F '70 - p267
CE - v46 - Ap '70 - p368
CLW - v41 - D '69 - p262
CSM - v61 - My 1 '69 - pB7
Econ - v237 - D 26 '70 - p40
EJ - v63 - Ja '74 - p67
HB - v45 - F '69 - p65
KR - v36 - N 1 '68 - p1233
ND - v18 - Je '69 - p51
NYRB - v18 - Ap 20 '72 - p39
NYTBR - v73 - N 3 '68 - p7
NYTBR, Pt. 2 - N 8 '70 - p30
NYTBR, Pt. 2 - F 13 '72 - p14
Obs - N 29 '70 - p31
PW - v197 - Ja 19 '70 - p83
SE - v33 - Je 5 '95 - p63
SLJ - v30 - Ja '84 - p42
Spec - v231 - O 20 '73 - pR21
SR - v52 - Mr 22 '69 - p63
Teacher - v86 - My '69 - p129
Teacher - v93 - Ap '76 - p121
TLS - D 11 '70 - p1456
Subject: Slavery

LETCHWORTH, Beverly J

Pax And The Mutt
SLJ - v28 - Mr '82 - p158
Subject: Birthdays—Fiction; Dogs—Fiction; Poverty—Fiction

LEVIN, Jack
see Anastos, Ernie (co-author)

LEVIN, Jane Whitbread
ConAu 106

Star Of Danger
BL - v63 - Ja 15 '67 - p538
CCB-B - v20 - Ja '67 - p75
Comw - v85 - N 11 '66 - p176
CSM - v58 - N 3 '66 - pB11
KR - v34 - Jl 15 '66 - p691
LJ - v92 - Ja 15 '67 - p344
NYTBR - v72 - Ja 8 '67 - p30
Subject: World War, 1939-1945

LEVINE, Betty 1933-
AuBYP SUP, ConAu 93, WhoAmW 77

The Great Burgerland Disaster
BL - v77 - Mr 1 '81 - p965
CBRS - v9 - Je '81 - p98
CCB-B - v34 - My '81 - p174
CSM - v73 - My 11 '81 - pB5
HB - v57 - Je '81 - p303
KR - v49 - My 1 '81 - p575
SLJ - v27 - Ap '81 - p141
Subject: Divorce—Fiction

LEVINE, Joseph
see Pine, Tillie S (co-author)

LEVINGER, Elma Ehrlich 1887-1958
AuBYP, BioIn 4, WhAm 3

Albert Einstein
BL - v45 - Ap 1 '49 - p264
BOT - v17 - F 15 '49 - p87
CSM - My 26 '49 - p12
HB - v25 - My '49 - p218
LJ - v74 - Ap 15 '49 - p669
NY - v25 - D 3 '49 - p186
NYTBR - My 29 '49 - p14
SR - v32 - Ag 13 '49 - p35
Subject: Biography

LEVINSON, Nancy Smiler 1938-
ConAu 107, SmATA 33

Second Chances
SLJ - v32 - Ja '86 - p81

Silent Fear
BL - v79 - Ap 1 '83 - p1022
SLJ - v28 - Mr '82 - p158
Subject: Child abuse—Fiction; Foster home care—Fiction

World Of Her Own
BL - v78 - Ja 15 '82 - p644
CBRS - v10 - Winter '82 - p58
Cur R - v21 - F '82 - p35
VOYA - v4 - F '82 - p35
Subject: Physically handicapped—Fiction

LEVITIN, Sonia 1934-
AuBYP SUP, ConAu 14NR, ConLC 17, FifBJA, SmATA 4, -2AS

The Mark Of Conte
BB - v4 - Jl '76 - p3
BL - v72 - Ap 15 '76 - p1186
BL - v73 - My 15 '77 - p1426
B Rpt - v1 - Mr '83 - p25
BS - v36 - Ag '76 - p151
BW - D 12 '76 - pH4
CCB-B - v29 - Jl '76 - p177
HB - v52 - Je '76 - p289
J Read - v21 - O '77 - p86
KR - v44 - Mr 15 '76 - p331
LJ - v53 - S '76 - p700
SLJ - v22 - Ap '76 - p90
Subject: Schools—Fiction

The No-Return Trail
BL - v74 - Je 15 '78 - p1618
BS - v38 - O '78 - p230
KR - v46 - Je 1 '78 - p600
SLJ - v24 - Ap '78 - p94
Subject: Overland journeys to the Pacific—Fiction

LEVOY, Myron
AuBYP SUP, ConAu 18NR, FifBJA, SmATA 49

A Shadow Like A Leopard
BL - v77 - Ap 1 '81 - p1085
BS - v41 - Je '81 - p119
CBRS - v9 - Mr '81 - p68
CCB-B - v34 - My '81 - p175
HB - v57 - Je '81 - p310
Inter BC - v13 - #2 '82 p34
Inter BC - v14 - #1 '83 p15
J Read - v25 - O '81 - p88
Kliatt - v17 - Winter '83 - p11
KR - v49 - Je 15 '81 - p745
SLJ - v27 - Mr '81 - p158
VOYA - v4 - Je '81 - p30
WLB - v55 - My '81 - p691
Subject: Artists—Fiction; Friendship—Fiction; Gangs—Fiction

The Witch Of Fourth Street And Other Stories
BL - v68 - Je 1 '72 - p862
BW - v6 - My 7 '72 - p4
CCB-B - v26 - Ja '73 - p78
HB - v48 - Ag '72 - p372
KR - v40 - F 1 '72 - p136
LJ - v97 - My 15 '72 - p1915
NYTBR - Je 18 '72 - p8
PW - v201 - Ap 3 '72 - p72
Teacher - v92 - Ap '75 - p112
TLS - D 8 '72 - p1491
VV - v19 - D 16 '74 - p51
Subject: New York (City)—Fiction; Short stories

LEVY, Elizabeth 1942-
AuBYP SUP, ConAu 15NR, FifBJA, IntAu&W 82, SmATA 31

The Case Of The Counterfeit Racehorse
BL - v77 - Mr 1 '81 - p965
Hi Lo - v2 - My '81 - p3
Kliatt - v15 - Winter '81 - p7
NS - v104 - D 3 '82 - p24
PW - v219 - Mr 27 '81 - p52
SLJ - v27 - Ag '81 - p68
VOYA - v4 - Je '81 - p35
Subject: Mystery and detective stories

The Case Of The Fired-Up Gang
SLJ - v28 - S '81 - p138
Subject: Gangs—Fiction

The Case Of The Frightened Rock Star
CCB-B - v34 - Ja '81 - p97

LEVY, Elizabeth (continued)
Hi Lo - v2 - My '81 - p3
SLJ - v27 - D '80 - p73
VOYA - v4 - Je '81 - p35
Subject: Mystery and detective stories

The Case Of The Wild River Ride
BL - v78 - Mr 1 '82 - p898
SLJ - v28 - D '81 - p82
Subject: Mystery and detective stories

The Dani Trap
BL - v81 - S 1 '84 - p58
CBRS - v13 - N '84 - p31
CCB-B - v38 - N '84 - p49
KR - v52 - N 1 '84 - pJ105
SLJ - v31 - D '84 - p101
Subject: Alcohol and youth—Fiction; Mystery and detective stories; Police—Fiction

see also Harris, Robie H (co-author) for additional titles

LEWIS, Alfred 1912-1968
AuBYP, ConAu 111, SmATA 32

The New World Of Computers
KR - v33 - Ja 15 '65 - p64
LJ - v90 - F 15 '65 - p974
Subject: Computers

LEWIS, Carrie

Call Of The Wild
BL - v81 - F 1 '85 - p784
SLJ - v31 - S '84 - p137
Subject: Love—Fiction

LEWIS, Claude Aubrey 1934-
ConAu 9R, EncTwCJ, WhoAm 82

Benjamin Banneker: The Man Who Saved Washington
BL - v67 - S 1 '70 - p58
CCB-B - v24 - O '70 - p30
KR - v38 - Ap 1 '70 - p392
LJ - v96 - Mr 15 '71 - p1134
NHB - v34 - Mr '71 - p70
Subject: Biography

LEWIS, Richard 1935-
AuBYP, BkP, ConAu 5NR, DrAP&F 85, SmATA 3

Miracles: Poems By Children Of The English-Speaking World
BL - v63 - D 1 '66 - p400
CCB-B - v20 - Mr '67 - p111
CE - v44 - My '68 - p561
Choice - v4 - S '67 - p730
CSM - v59 - N 23 '66 - p15
HB - v42 - D '66 - p726
HR - v20 - Spring '67 - p137
Inst - v77 - Ag '67 - p208
KR - v34 - Jl 15 '66 - p744
LJ - v91 - O 1 '66 - p4671
NYRB - v7 - O 20 '66 - p25
NYTBR - v71 - N 6 '66 - p1
PW - v190 - Jl 18 '66 - p76
PW - v190 - N 28 '66 - p61
SR - v50 - F 18 '67 - p42
Time - v89 - Ja 6 '67 - p101
TLS - N 30 '67 - p1132
Subject: English poetry

Out Of The Earth I Sing: Poetry And Songs Of Primitive Peoples Of The World
BL - v64 - Ap 1 '68 - p931
BW - v1 - N 5 '67 - p26
BW - v2 - My 5 '68 - p5
CCB-B - v21 - Jl '68 - p176
HB - v44 - Ap '68 - p187
Inst - v77 - Je '68 - p142
KR - v36 - Ja 1 '68 - p11
LJ - v93 - F 15 '68 - p883
Subject: English poetry; Poetry

LEWITON, Mina 1904-1970
AuBYP, BioIn 8, ConAu 29R, –P-2, MorJA, SmATA 2

Especially Humphrey
CLW - v39 - F '68 - p439
LJ - v93 - Ja 15 '68 - p293
Subject: Dogs—Fiction

LEXAU, Joan M
see Seth, Marie

LIBBY, Bill 1927-1984
AuBYP SUP, ConAu 10NR, SmATA 5, WrDr 84

Baseball's Greatest Sluggers
Inst - v82 - My '73 - p69
KR - v41 - Ap 1 '73 - p395
LJ - v98 - My 15 '73 - p1703
LJ - v98 - D 15 '73 - p3721
Subject: Baseball—Biography

Joe Louis: The Brown Bomber
BL - v77 - O 1 '80 - p259
BS - v41 - Ap '81 - p39
J Read - v24 - Ap '81 - p647
PW - v218 - D 19 '80 - p51
SLJ - v27 - D '80 - p77

LIBBY, Bill (continued)
VOYA - v3 - F '81 - p44
Subject: Blacks—Biography; Boxing—Biography

The Reggie Jackson Story
KR - v47 - Jl 15 '79 - p800
SLJ - v25 - My '79 - p83
SLJ - v26 - O '79 - p160
Subject: Baseball—Biography; Blacks—Biography

Rocky
BS - v31 - My 15 '71 - p99
KR - v39 - F 15 '71 - p183
LJ - v96 - My 15 '71 - p1825
Subject: Biography; Boxing—Biography

LIBERATORE, Karen

The Horror Of Montauk Cave
B Rpt - v2 - S '83 - p25
Subject: Caves—Fiction; Horror stories

LICHTMAN, Gail

Alcohol: Facts For Decisions
BL - v72 - My 1 '76 - p1247

LIEBERMAN, Mark 1942-
ConAu 29R

The Dope Book: All About Drugs
BL - v68 - N 1 '71 - p242
Inst - v81 - N '71 - p133
KR - v39 - Ap 1 '71 - p383
LJ - v96 - Je 15 '71 - p2139
LJ - v96 - Jl '71 - p2291
NYTBR, Pt. 2 - My 2 '71 - p32
NYTBR, Pt. 2 - N 7 '71 - p28
SB - v7 - D '71 - p256
Subject: Drug abuse

LIEBERS, Arthur 1913-
ConAu 3NR, SmATA 12, WrDr 84

You Can Be A Carpenter
BL - v70 - N 1 '73 - p293
CCB-B - v27 - Ap '74 - p131
CLW - v45 - N '73 - p190
KR - v41 - My 15 '73 - p570
LJ - v99 - F 15 '74 - p581
Subject: Vocational guidance

You Can Be A Mechanic
BL - v72 - S 1 '75 - p43
KR - v43 - Je 1 '75 - p617
SLJ - v22 - S '75 - p107
Subject: Vocational guidance

You Can Be A Plumber
BL - v70 - Jl 1 '74 - p1201
KR - v42 - Ap 1 '74 - p376
LJ - v99 - O 15 '74 - p2747
Subject: Vocational guidance

You Can Be A Professional Driver
BL - v73 - S 1 '76 - p40
KR - v44 - My 1 '76 - p548
SLJ - v23 - S '76 - p120
Subject: Vocational guidance

LIGHTBODY, Donna M

Hooks And Loops
BL - v72 - N 15 '75 - p455
SLJ - v22 - Ja '76 - p54
Subject: Crocheting

LINDBLOM, Steven 1946-
ConAu 106, SmATA 42

The Fantastic Bicycles Book
HB - v55 - D '79 - p679
SA - v243 - D '80 - p48
SLJ - v26 - Mr '80 - p142
Subject: Bicyles and bicyling

LINDGREN, Astrid 1907-
Au&ICB, AuBYP, BioIn 13, ChlLR 1, ConAu 13R, MorJA, OxChL, SmATA 38, TwCChW 83B, WhoAmW 77

Rasmus And The Vagabond
BL - v56 - Je 1 '60 - p608
Comw - v72 - My 27 '60 - p233
CSM - My 12 '60 - p3B
HB - v36 - Ap '60 - p133
KR - v28 - F 1 '60 - p90
LJ - v85 - My 15 '60 - p2040
NYTBR, Pt. 2 - My 8 '60 - p18
PW - v193 - My 20 '68 - p63
SR - v43 - N 12 '60 - p94
TLS - D 1 '61 - pR18

LINDSAY, Jeanne Warren

Pregnant Too Soon
Cur R - v20 - Ja '81 - p89
J Ho E - v73 - Summer '81 - p58
Kliatt - v14 - Spring '80 - p30
PGJ - v61 - N '82 - p180
WLB - v58 - S '83 - p53
Subject: Adolescent mothers; Adoption; Pregnancy

Teens Parenting
BL - v77 - Je 15 '81 - p1339
BL - v82 - N 15 '85 - p485
Kliatt - v15 - Fall '81 - p46

LINDSAY, Jeanne Warren (continued)
SB - v17 - Mr '82 - p208
SLJ - v28 - O '81 - p151
VOYA - v4 - O '81 - p49
WCRB - v8 - F '82 - p46
WLB - v58 - S '83 - p53
Subject: Adolescent parents

LINEHAM, Don

Soft Touch: A Sport That Lets You Touch Life
LJ - v101 - N 15 '76 - p2391
WLB - v51 - Mr '77 - p606
Subject: Basketball

LINGARD, Joan 1932-
AuBYP SUP, ConAu 18NR, FifBJA, IntAu&W 86, OxChL, SmATA 8, TwCChW 83, WrDr 86

Into Exile
BL - v70 - Ja 1 '74 - p489
BS - v33 - N 15 '73 - p382
CCB-B - v27 - Mr '74 - p113
Comw - v99 - N 23 '73 - p216
LJ - v99 - F 15 '74 - p581
Spec - v231 - O 20 '73 - pR10
TLS - S 28 '73 - p1118
Subject: London—Fiction

LINN, Ed 1922-
ConAu 97, WhoAm 78

Koufax
BS - v26 - O 1 '66 - p251
CLW - v38 - N '66 - p87
Comt - v42 - N '66 - p87
LJ - v91 - O 1 '66 - p4691
LJ - v91 - D 15 '66 - p6220
Nat - v204 - Ja 30 '67 - p149
NO - v5-7 - N '66 - p23
NYTBR - S 18 '66 - p46
Subject: Baseball—Biography

LIPMAN, David 1931-
AuBYP SUP, ConAu 21R, IntAu&W 86, SmATA 21, WhoAm 86, WhoMW 86, WrDr 86

Jim Hart: Underrated Quarterback
BL - v73 - Je 1 '77 - p1499
KR - v45 - Mr 15 '77 - p293
SLJ - v23 - My '77 - p80
Co-author: Lipman, Marilyn
Subject: Football—Biography

LIPMAN, Marilyn
see Lipman, David (co-author)

LIPMAN, Michel

You Are The Boss!
Cur R - v23 - Ap '84 - p33
Co-author: Furniss, Cathy

You Are The Judge Book 1
Cur R - v21 - My '82 - p191
J Read - v25 - My '82 - p813
Co-author: Furniss, Cathy

LIPSYTE, Robert 1938-
AuBYP SUP, BioIn 13, ConAu 8NR, ConLC 21, FifBJA, SmATA 5

The Contender
BL - v64 - D 15 '67 - p497
BW - v1 - N 5 '67 - p38
CCB-B - v21 - My '68 - p145
CE - v46 - Ap '70 - p368
Comw - v87 - N 10 '67 - p181
CSM - v59 - N 2 '67 - pB13
EJ - v59 - Ap '70 - p591
HB - v43 - D '67 - p759
J Read - v22 - N '78 - p128
KR - v35 - S 15 '67 - p1146
LJ - v92 - N 15 '67 - p4262
NYTBR - v72 - N 5 '67 - p64
NYTBR - v72 - N 12 '67 - p42
SR - v51 - Mr 16 '68 - p39
TN - v24 - Ap '68 - p323
TN - v39 - Winter '83 - p199
Subject: Boxing—Fiction

One Fat Summer
BL - v80 - O 15 '83 - p353
EJ - v69 - D '80 - p56
TN - v39 - Winter '83 - p200
Subject: Weight control—Fiction

The Summerboy
BL - v79 - S 1 '82 - p36
CCB-B - v36 - S '82 - p15
Kliatt - v18 - Fall '84 - p14
KR - v50 - S 1 '82 - p1001
Nat - v236 - Mr 12 '83 - p312
PW - v222 - N 5 '82 - p70
SLJ - v29 - Ja '83 - p85
TN - v39 - Winter '83 - p201
VOYA - v5 - F '83 - p38
Subject: Summer employment—Fiction

LISKER, Tom

Tall Tales: American Myths
SLJ - v25 - S '78 - p142
Subject: Folklore

Terror In The Tropics: The Army Ants
Cur R - v17 - Ag '78 - p228

LISKER, Tom (continued)
SLJ - v24 - My '78 - p63
Teacher - v96 - Mr '79 - p119
Subject: Ants

LISS, Howard 1922-
AuBYP, ConAu 16NR, SmATA 4

Bobby Orr: Lightning On Ice
SLJ - v22 - D '75 - p69
Subject: Hockey—Biography

Football Talk For Beginners
BL - v66 - Je 15 '70 - p1280
CCB-B - v24 - O '70 - p30
KR - v38 - Mr 1 '70 - p247
LJ - v95 - My 15 '70 - p1965
PW - v197 - Je 15 '70 - p66
Subject: Football

The Front 4: Let's Meet At The Quarterback
BL - v68 - Ap 15 '72 - p718
BL - v68 - Ap 15 '72 - p725
CCB-B - v25 - Mr '72 - p111
LJ - v96 - D '71 - p4200
Subject: Football

Hockey's Greatest All-Stars
KR - v40 - Ag 1 '72 - p862
LJ - v98 - My 15 '73 - p1705
Subject: Hockey—Biography

More Strange But True Baseball Stories
KR - v40 - Ap 15 '72 - p482
LJ - v97 - My 15 '72 - p1930
NY - v48 - D 2 '72 - p190
Subject: Baseball

Picture Story Of Dave Winfield
BL - v79 - O 1 '82 - p251
SLJ - v29 - D '82 - p86
Subject: Baseball—Biography; Blacks—Biography

Triple Crown Winners
LJ - v94 - D 15 '69 - p4620
PW - v196 - N 3 '69 - p49
SR - v53 - Je 27 '70 - p38
Subject: Baseball—Biography

LISTON, Robert A 1927-
AuBYP, ConAu 12NR, SmATA 5

Our Career In Civil Service
BL - v62 - Je 15 '66 - p997
Subject: Occupations

Your Career In Civil Service
BS - v26 - Jl 1 '66 - p141
LJ - v91 - My 15 '66 - p2710
Subject: Vocational guidance

LITSKY, Frank

Winners In Gymnastics
BL - v74 - Ap 15 '78 - p1357
JB - v43 - F '79 - p36
SLJ - v24 - My '78 - p87
Subject: Gymnasts

The Winter Olympics
BL - v76 - O 1 '79 - p283
CCB-B - v33 - Ja '80 - p99
SLJ - v26 - D '79 - p101
Subject: Athletes; Olympic Games

LITTERICK, Ian

Computers And You
CBRS - v12 - Ag '84 - p152
SLJ - v31 - O '84 - p159
Co-author: Smithers, Chris
Subject: Computers

LITTKE, Lael J 1929-
ConAu 15NR

Cave-In!
BL - v78 - S 15 '81 - p99
SLJ - v28 - S '81 - p118
Subject: Caves—Fiction; Rescue work—Fiction

Tell Me When I Can Go
BL - v75 - F 15 '79 - p927
Hi Lo - v1 - O '79 - p4
Subject: Family life—Fiction

LITTLE, Jean 1932-
AuBYP, CaW, ChlLR 4, ConAu 21R, FourBJA, OxCanL, Profile 1, SmATA 2, TwCChW 83, WrDr 86

Kate
BL - v68 - N 15 '71 - p292
BW - v5 - N 7 '71 - p14
Can Child Lit - #33 '84 p42
CCB-B - v25 - D '71 - p59
CLW - v43 - F '72 - p361
CSM - v63 - N 11 '71 - pB5
EJ - v61 - Mr '72 - p434
HB - v48 - F '72 - p49
KR - v39 - O 1 '71 - p1070
LJ - v96 - D 15 '71 - p4185
NYTBR - Ja 16 '72 - p8
PW - v200 - O 18 '71 - p50
SR - v54 - O 16 '71 - p57
Subject: Friendship—Fiction; Jews—Fiction

Look Through My Window
BL - v67 - S 15 '70 - p108
CCB-B - v24 - Ja '71 - p76
HB - v46 - D '70 - p620

LITTLE, Jean (continued)
KR - v38 - Je 1 '70 - p599
PW - v197 - Je 29 '70 - p104
Spec - v47 - Mr '71 - p43
SR - v53 - O 24 '70 - p67
Subject: Family life—Fiction; Friendship—Fiction

LIVINGSTON, Myra Cohn 1926-
AuBYP SUP, ChlLR 7, ConAu 1NR, FourBJA, IntWWP 82, SmATA 5, -1AS, TwCChW 83, WhoAmW 87, WrDr 86

The Malibu And Other Poems
CCB-B - v26 - Ja '73 - p79
CSM - v64 - N 8 '72 - pB2
Inst - v82 - N '72 - p128
KR - v40 - Jl 1 '72 - p726
LJ - v97 - O 15 '72 - p3453
NYTBR, Pt. 2 - N 5 '72 - p32
RT - v36 - Ja '83 - p381
Subject: American poetry

LIVINGSTON, Peter
AuBYP SUP

On Astrology
KR - v43 - Mr 15 '75 - p313
SLJ - v21 - My '75 - p57
Subject: Astrology

LLOYD-JONES, Buster
IntAu&W 77

Animals Came In One By One
BL - v63 - Ap 1 '67 - p824
CCB-B - v20 - My '67 - p142
KR - v34 - D 1 '66 - p1264
LJ - v92 - Mr 15 '67 - p1170
LJ - v92 - Mr 15 '67 - p1336
Punch - v251 - O 12 '66 - p567
PW - v190 - N 28 '66 - p57
SR - v50 - My 13 '67 - p58
Subject: Veterinarians

LOCKWOOD, Charles A 1890-1968
ConAu 1R, NatCAB 53, WhAm 4

Down To The Sea In Subs: My Life In The U.S. Navy
BL - v63 - Ap 15 '67 - p882
KR - v34 - D 15 '66 - p1332
LJ - v92 - Mr 1 '67 - p1007
PW - v190 - N 28 '66 - p57
TN - v24 - N '67 - p102
Yacht - v121 - Je '67 - p102
Subject: United States Navy

LOGAN, Les

The Game
BL - v79 - F 15 '83 - p772
SF&FBR - O '83 - p43
SLJ - v29 - Mr '83 - p188
VOYA - v6 - Ag '83 - p146
WLB - v57 - My '83 - p773
Subject: Exorcism—Fiction

LOGAN, Rayford Wittingham
see Sterling, Philip (co-author)

LOMASK, Milton Nachman 1909-
AuBYP, ConAu 1NR, SmATA 20, WhoAm 86

This Slender Reed: A Life Of James K. Polk
BS - v26 - N 1 '66 - p295
CLW - v38 - N '66 - p213
Comw - v85 - N 11 '66 - p176
HB - v43 - F '67 - p88
KR - v34 - Jl 1 '66 - p632
LJ - v91 - O 15 '66 - p5252
Subject: Biography

LONDON, Jack 1876-1916
AmWr, ConAu X, DcLB 8, -12, DcLEL, JBA 34, OxAmL 83, OxChL, SmATA 18, Str&VC, TwCSFW 86
Pseud./variant:
London, John Griffith

The Call Of The Wild
B&B - v22 - Je '77 - p68
BB - v6 - My '78 - p4
BL - v65 - F 1 '69 - p597
BW - v11 - N 8 '81 - p14
LA - v55 - S '78 - p742
SLJ - v24 - F '78 - p72
TLS - Mr 14 '68 - p263
Subject: Dogs—Fiction; Sea stories

LONG, Judy 1953-
ConAu 65, SmATA 20

Volunteer Spring
BW - Ap 11 '76 - p4
CCB-B - v30 - N '76 - p45
PW - v209 - Mr 15 '76 - p58
SLJ - v22 - My '76 - p71
Teacher - v95 - O '77 - p171
TN - v36 - Winter '80 - p208
Subject: Mentally handicapped—Fiction

LONGMAN, Harold S 1919-
ConAu 25R, SmATA 5

Would You Put Your Money In A Sand Bank?: Fun With Words
BL - v64 - Je 15 '68 - p1187
CSM - v60 - My 2 '68 - pB4
Inst - v78 - Ag '68 - p192
LJ - v93 - Je 15 '68 - p2540
LJ - v98 - O 15 '73 - p3163
NYTBR - Ap 13 '69 - p30
RT - v32 - N '78 - p148
TN - v25 - N '68 - p78
Subject: Games

LORD, Beman 1924-
AuBYP, ConAu 33R, FourBJA, SmATA 5

Guards For Matt
Inst - v78 - Ap '69 - p148
NYTBR - N 12 '61 - p46

Look At Cars
BL - v67 - Mr 15 '71 - p623
LJ - v96 - F 15 '71 - p744
Subject: Automobiles

Mystery Guest At Left End
CCB-B - v18 - Jl '65 - p165
NYTBR - N 1 '64 - p46

Quarterback's Aim
BL - v57 - F 1 '61 - p330
HB - v36 - O '60 - p402
KR - v28 - Ag 1 '60 - p621
LJ - v85 - S 15 '60 - p3224
NYTBR - D 11 '60 - p44
SR - v43 - D 17 '60 - p35
Subject: Football—Fiction

Rough Ice
NYTBR - N 10 '63 - p49

Shot-Put Challenge
KR - v37 - My 1 '69 - p505
LJ - v94 - D 15 '69 - p4620
PW - v195 - Ap 21 '69 - p66
Subject: Track and field—Fiction

Shrimp's Soccer Goal
CCB-B - v24 - Mr '71 - p109
KR - v38 - S 15 '70 - p1038
LJ - v95 - D 15 '70 - p4381
SR - v53 - N 14 '70 - p35
Subject: Soccer—Fiction

The Trouble With Francis
BL - v55 - O 1 '58 - p80
LJ - v84 - Ja 15 '59 - p244
NYTBR - Ja 18 '59 - p28
SR - v42 - Ja 24 '59 - p37

LORD, Walter 1917-
BioIn 5, -9, ConAu 5NR, CurBio 72, IntAu&W 86, SmATA 3, WhoAm 86, WorAu, WrDr 86

A Night To Remember
BL - v73 - Ap 1 '77 - p1139
BL - v73 - Ap 1 '77 - p1170
BL - v82 - Ja 1 '86 - p680
NYTBR - F 5 '78 - p41
SLJ - v23 - Mr '77 - p158
Spec - v237 - N 20 '76 - p20
TLS - N 26 '76 - p1472
VV - v21 - D 13 '76 - p77
Yacht - v141 - My '77 - p122
Subject: Ships; Titanic (Steamship)

LORIMER, L T

Secrets
CBRS - v10 - Winter '82 - p58
CCB-B - v35 - N '81 - p49
CLW - v53 - Mr '82 - p356
KR - v49 - D 15 '81 - p1524
SLJ - v28 - N '81 - p108
VOYA - v4 - D '81 - p32
Subject: Adultery—Fiction; Fathers and daughters—Fiction

LOVE, Sandra 1940-
ConAu 11NR, SmATA 26

Dive For The Sun
B Rpt - v2 - My '83 - p37
CCB-B - v36 - Ja '83 - p92
SLJ - v29 - O '82 - p162
Subject: Buried treasure—Fiction; Shipwrecks—Fiction; Space and time—Fiction

Melissa's Medley
BL - v74 - Ap 15 '78 - p1352
CCB-B - v32 - S '78 - p13
SLJ - v24 - My '78 - p87
Subject: Swimming—Fiction

LOWELL, Anne Hunter

Getting In
KR - v54 - Mr 1 '86 - p391
SLJ - v33 - S '86 - p149
VOYA - v9 - D '86 - p230
Subject: Greek letter societies—Fiction; Love—Fiction

LOWRY, Lois 1937-
AuBYP SUP, ChILR 6, ConAu 13NR, DcLB 52, FifBJA, SmATA 23, -3AS

Find A Stranger, Say Goodbye
B&B - v6 - S '78 - p2
BL - v74 - Ap 15 '78 - p1341
BW - v10 - F 3 '80 - p13
CCB-B - v32 - O '78 - p33
Comw - v105 - N 10 '78 - p733
EJ - v68 - D '79 - p78
EJ - v69 - F '80 - p70
GP - v19 - S '80 - p3758
HB - v54 - Je '78 - p285
JB - v44 - Ag '80 - p194
Kliatt - v14 - Winter '80 - p11
KR - v46 - Mr 1 '78 - p248
PW - v213 - My 15 '78 - p104
Sch Lib - v29 - Mr '81 - p54
SLJ - v24 - My '78 - p77
TES - Je 6 '80 - p27
TES - My 15 '81 - p29
TLS - Mr 28 '80 - p356
TN - v37 - Fall '80 - p61
Subject: Adoption—Fiction; Mothers and daughters—Fiction

LUBOWE, Irwin Irville 1905-
ConAu 53

A Teen-Age Guide To Healthy Skin And Hair
BL - v62 - Je 12 '65 - p24
BL - v69 - F 1 '73 - p525
KR - v33 - O 1 '65 - p1052
LJ - v91 - Ja 15 '66 - p437
Par - v41 - D '66 - p10
Co-author: Huss, Barbara
Subject: Health

LUGER, H C

Chasing Trouble
BL - v72 - Ap 15 '76 - p1187
CCB-B - v30 - O '76 - p27
KR - v44 - Ap 1 '76 - p406
NYTBR - Je 6 '76 - p54
SLJ - v23 - O '76 - p118
Subject: Ecology—Fiction; Gophers—Fiction; Youth—Fiction

The Elephant Tree
BL - v74 - My 15 '78 - p1496
Hi Lo - v4 - My '83 - p6
Kliatt - v16 - Spring '82 - p13
KR - v46 - Je 1 '78 - p600
NYTBR - Ap 30 '78 - p45
SLJ - v24 - My '78 - p78
Subject: Deserts—Fiction; Survival—Fiction

Lauren
CBRS - v8 - D '79 - p38
HB - v55 - D '79 - p670
Kliatt - v15 - Fall '81 - p12
KR - v48 - Ja 15 '80 - p70
SLJ - v26 - D '79 - p91
WLB - v54 - N '79 - p184
Subject: Unwed mothers—Fiction

LUIS, Earlene W 1929-
ConAu 61, SmATA 11

Wheels For Ginny's Chariot
Am - v115 - Jl 2 '66 - p14
BL - v63 - S 15 '66 - p120
BS - v26 - Ja 5 '66 - p58
CCB-B - v20 - S '66 - p14
LJ - v91 - Je 15 '66 - p3268
Co-author: Millar, Barbara
Subject: Physically handicapped—Fiction

LUNDGREN, Hal

Mary Lou Retton: Gold Medal Gymnast
BL - v82 - O 1 '85 - p273
SLJ - v32 - Mr '86 - p156
Subject: Gymnasts

LYLE, Katie Letcher 1938-
ConAu 49, DrAP&F 85, SmATA 8

Dark But Full Of Diamonds
BL - v78 - D 15 '81 - p546
BW - v12 - Mr 14 '82 - p7
CBRS - v10 - D '81 - p39
CCB-B - v35 - My '82 - p175
EJ - v71 - Ap '82 - p82
KR - v49 - D 15 '81 - p1524
NYTBR - v86 - N 15 '81 - p56
PW - v223 - Mr 11 '83 - p87
SLJ - v28 - N '81 - p108
Subject: Fathers and sons—Fiction; Remarriage—Fiction

Fair Day, And Another Step Begun
A Lib - v5 - Jl '74 - p360
BL - v70 - Ap 1 '74 - p870
BS - v34 - Ap 15 '74 - p54
CCB-B - v28 - S '74 - p12
KR - v42 - Ap 15 '74 - p433
LJ - v99 - S 15 '74 - p2294
NY - v50 - D 2 '74 - p182
NYTBR - My 19 '74 - p8
NYTBR - N 3 '74 - p52
PW - v205 - Mr 4 '74 - p76

LYLE, Katie Letcher (continued)
VQR - v50 - Fall '74 - pR120
Subject: Pregnancy—Fiction

Finders Weepers
B Rpt - v2 - My '83 - p38
CBRS - v11 - Ja '83 - p50
CCB-B - v36 - D '82 - p72
Kliatt - v19 - Fall '85 - p12
SLJ - v29 - F '83 - p90
Subject: Blue Ridge Mountains—Fiction; Buried treasure—Fiction; Grandmothers—Fiction

I Will Go Barefoot All Summer For You
A Lib - v5 - Jl '74 - p360
BL - v69 - Je 15 '73 - p990
BW - v7 - My 13 '73 - p7
KR - v41 - F 1 '73 - p124
LJ - v98 - My 15 '73 - p1682
NYTBR - Ap 29 '73 - p8
PW - v203 - My 7 '73 - p66
Teacher - v92 - S '74 - p130

LYNDS, Dennis 1924-
ConAu 6NR, DrAP&F 85, EncMys, IntAu&W 86, SmATA 47, TwCCr&M 85, WrDr 86
Pseud./variant:
Arden, William

The Mystery Of The Dead Man's Riddle
LJ - v99 - D 15 '74 - p3277
Subject: Mystery and detective stories

The Mystery Of The Deadly Double
SLJ - v25 - D '78 - p68
Subject: Mystery and detective stories

see also Arden, William for additional titles

LYNN, Elizabeth A 1946-
ConAu 81, ScFSB, TwCSFW 86

The Silver Horse
Fant R - v8 - F '85 - p34
KR - v52 - Jl 15 '84 - p660
SF Chr - v6 - Ja '85 - p33
Subject: Fantasy; Lost and found possessions—Fiction; Toys—Fiction

LYON, Elinor 1921-
ConAu 25R, IntAu&W 77X, SmATA 6, WrDr 86
Pseud./variant:
Wright, Elinor Bruce

Cathie Runs Wild
CCB-B - v22 - F '69 - p98
LJ - v93 - Jl '68 - p2734

Rider's Rock
BL - v65 - Ja 15 '69 - p547
LJ - v93 - My 15 '68 - p2127
PW - v194 - O 7 '68 - p54

LYON, Nancy

The Mystery Of Stonehenge
CCB-B - v31 - My '78 - p145
Cur R - v17 - Ag '78 - p227
SLJ - v25 - N '78 - p64
Subject: Stonehenge

Totems And Tribes
SLJ - v25 - N '78 - p64
Subject: Indians of North America

LYTTLE, Richard Bard 1927-
AuBYP SUP, ConAu 13NR, SmATA 23

Getting Into Pro Basketball
SLJ - v25 - My '79 - p86
Subject: Basketball; Vocational guidance

Nazi Hunting
Cur R - v21 - D '82 - p569
Hi Lo - v4 - O '82 - p4
SLJ - v29 - O '82 - p162
Subject: Holocaust, Jewish (1939-1945); War criminals—Germany

see also Dolan, Edward F, Jr. (co-author) for additional titles

M

MACAULAY, David Alexander 1946-
AuBYP SUP, BioIn 12, -13, ChlLR 3, ConAu 5NR, FifBJA, IlsCB 1967, SmATA 46, WhoAmA 84, WrDr 84

Baaa
B Rpt - v4 - Mr '86 - p49
CBRS - v14 - Mr '86 - p86
NYTBR - v90 - D 1 '85 - p38
SF Chr - v7 - Mr '86 - p36
S Fict R - v15 - F '86 - p39
SLJ - v32 - O '85 - p183
Subject: Allegories; Civilization—Fiction; Sheep—Fiction

MACCRACKEN, Mary 1926-
ConAu 49, WrDr 86

Lovey: A Very Special Child
BL - v73 - O 1 '76 - p223
BS - v36 - D '76 - p295
HB - v53 - F '77 - p82
KR - v44 - Jl 1 '76 - p775
LJ - v101 - S 1 '76 - p1782
NYTBR - O 17 '76 - p8
NYTBR - O 23 '77 - p51
PW - v210 - Jl 12 '76 - p67
PW - v212 - S 5 '77 - p71
SLJ - v23 - Ja '77 - p108
Subject: Child psychotherapy; Mentally ill

MACDONALD, Shelagh 1937-
BioIn 13, ConAu 97, SmATA 25, WrDr 84

Five From Me, Five From You
BL - v77 - Jl 1 '81 - p1395
SLJ - v28 - S '81 - p138
TLS - v0 - S 20 '74 - p1005

MACDONALD, Zillah 1885-
AuBYP, ConAu P-1, SmATA 11, WhoAmW 77

Marcia, Private Secretary
CSM - Jl 14 '49 - p7
KR - v17 - F 15 '49 - p86
LJ - v74 - Ap 15 '49 - p669
NYTBR - Mr 13 '49 - p24

MACHOL, Libby 1916-
ConAu 21R

Giana
BL - v64 - F 15 '68 - p682
CCB-B - v21 - Ja '68 - p79
KR - v35 - Ag 15 '67 - p1013
LJ - v92 - O 1 '67 - p3414
LJ - v93 - Ap 15 '68 - p1824
NYTBR - v72 - D 10 '67 - p26
SR - v50 - D 16 '67 - p36
Subject: American field service

MACK, John 1935-
BioIn 9

Nobody Promised Me
LJ - v96 - Ap 15 '71 - p1514
Subject: Blacks—Civil rights; Library science as a profession

MACKELLAR, William 1914-
AuBYP, ConAu 13NR, SmATA 4

Score!: A Baker's Dozen Sports Stories
KR - v35 - S 1 '67 - p1057
LJ - v92 - D 15 '67 - p4634
Subject: Sports—Fiction

MACLEOD, Charlotte 1922-
ConAu 18NR, SmATA 28, TwCCr&M 85, WrDr 86

The Fat Lady's Ghost
LJ - v93 - S 15 '68 - p3319

MACPHERSON, Margaret 1908-
AuBYP, ConAu 49, FourBJA, SmATA 9, -4AS, TwCChW 83, WrDr 86

The Rough Road
BL - v62 - Jl 15 '66 - p1088
CCB-B - v20 - Mr '67 - p112
CSM - v58 - Je 30 '66 - p11
HB - v42 - Je '66 - p316
KR - v33 - D 15 '65 - p1230
LJ - v91 - Mr 15 '66 - p1720
Punch - v249 - D 15 '65 - p897
PW - v189 - F 14 '66 - p144

MACPHERSON, Margaret (continued)
TLS - D 9 '65 - p1134
Subject: Scotland—Fiction

MADDEN, Betsy

The All-America Coeds
CCB-B - v24 - Je '71 - p159
KR - v39 - My 1 '71 - p501
LJ - v96 - My 15 '71 - p1823
Subject: Basketball—Fiction

MADDOCK, Reginald 1912-
AuBYP SUP, ConAu 81, SmATA 15, TwCChW 78, WrDr 80

The Pit
B&B - v11 - Je '66 - p67
BL - v64 - Ap 1 '68 - p932
BS - v28 - Ap 1 '68 - p18
BW - v2 - My 5 '68 - p5
CCB-B - v21 - Mr '68 - p113
CSM - v60 - My 9 '68 - p15
HB - v44 - Je '68 - p330
KR - v36 - F 1 '68 - p123
NS - v71 - My 20 '66 - p742
SR - v51 - F 24 '68 - p51
TLS - My 19 '66 - p439
Subject: England—Fiction

MADISON, Arnold 1937-
AuBYP SUP, ConAu 9NR, SmATA 6

Great Unsolved Cases
BL - v75 - O 15 '78 - p370
Hi Lo - v1 - O '79 - p5
Hi Lo - v1 - Mr '80 - p2
Kliatt - v14 - Fall '80 - p43
TES - Ja 11 '80 - p26
TN - v36 - Winter '80 - p198
Subject: Aeronautics; Crime and criminals

Lost Treasures Of America
BB - v6 - Je '78 - p3
BL - v74 - Ja 15 '78 - p813
SE - v42 - Ap '78 - p318
SLJ - v25 - S '78 - p161
Subject: Buried treasure

MADISON, Winifred
ConAu 37R, SmATA 5

Dance With Me
Hi Lo - v3 - Ja '82 - p5
VOYA - v4 - D '81 - p33
Subject: Dancing—Fiction

Homecoming Queen
BL - v80 - F 1 '84 - p810
VOYA - v7 - Je '84 - p93
Subject: Love—Fiction

Max's Wonderful Delicatessen
BS - v32 - D 15 '72 - p446
KR - v40 - O 15 '72 - p1202
LJ - v98 - Ap 15 '73 - p1396
NO - v11 - N 18 '72 - p28
PW - v202 - O 16 '72 - p50
Subject: Sculptors—Fiction

Suzy Who?
Hi Lo - v3 - Ja '82 - p6
SLJ - v26 - Ja '80 - p73
Subject: Love—Fiction

MAGNUSSON, Magnus 1929-
ConAu 105, IntAu&W 82, Who 85, WhoWor 84, WrDr 86

Introducing Archaeology
BL - v70 - S 1 '73 - p47
CCB-B - v27 - O '73 - p31
CLW - v45 - N '73 - p185
HB - v49 - Ag '73 - p391
KR - v41 - Ap 1 '73 - p401
LJ - v98 - My 15 '73 - p1581
LJ - v98 - My 15 '73 - p1655
LJ - v98 - My 15 '73 - p1689
LR - v23 - Fall '72 - p300
NY - v49 - D 3 '73 - p219
Obs - Jl 16 '72 - p31
PW - v203 - Ap 2 '73 - p65
SB - v9 - Mr '74 - p321
TLS - Jl 14 '72 - p810
Subject: Archaeology

MAHONY, Elizabeth Winthrop
see Winthrop, Elizabeth

MAJOR, Kevin 1949-
ChlLR 11, ConAu 21NR, -97, ConLC 26, OxCanL, Profile 2, SmATA 32, TwCChW 83, WhoAm 86, WhoCanL 85, WrDr 86

Hold Fast
Atl Pro Bk R - v10 - N '83 - p2
Atl Pro Bk R - v10 - N '83 - p18
BIC - v8 - Ap '79 - p3
CCB-B - v33 - Je '80 - p196
CSM - v76 - O 5 '84 - pB9
Emerg Lib - v9 - Ja '82 - p33
HB - v60 - F '84 - p99
J Read - v24 - N '80 - p174
KR - v48 - My 15 '80 - p651
Quill & Q - v48 - Je '82 - p5
SLJ - v26 - My '80 - p78
SLJ - v27 - S '80 - p43

MAJOR, Kevin (continued)
SN - v93 - O '78 - p14
Subject: Runaways—Fiction

MAKRIS, Kathryn

One Of The Guys
VOYA - v7 - O '84 - p201
Subject: Love—Fiction

Only A Dream Away
BL - v80 - F 1 '84 - p810
SLJ - v30 - Ap '84 - p126
Subject: Love—Fiction

MALEK, Doreen Owens

Season Of Mist
BL - v81 - F 1 '85 - p784
Subject: Ghosts—Fiction; Love—Fiction

That Certain Boy
BL - v80 - F 1 '84 - p810
SLJ - v30 - Ap '84 - p121
VOYA - v7 - Je '84 - p92
Subject: Love—Fiction

MALIN, Amita

Carlotta's House
BL - v79 - Ja 15 '83 - p660

MALMGREN, Dallin

The Whole Nine Yards
BL - v82 - Jl '86 - p1605
B Rpt - v5 - S '86 - p34
CBRS - v14 - Jl '86 - p147
PW - v229 - My 30 '86 - p68
SLJ - v32 - Ag '86 - p103
VOYA - v9 - Je '86 - p80
WLB - v60 - Ap '86 - p49

MALONE, Lucy

Handle With Care
BL - v80 - Je 15 '84 - p1474
SLJ - v31 - Ja '85 - p90
VOYA - v7 - D '84 - p259
Subject: Love—Fiction

MALONE, Robert

Rocketship: An Incredible Journey Through Science Fiction And Science Fact
Kliatt - v12 - Winter '78 - p13
SLJ - v24 - Mr '78 - p146
S & T - v54 - D '77 - p519
Subject: Astronautics

MANES, Stephen 1949-
ConAu 97, DrAP&F 85, SmATA 42

Pseud./variant:
Stephensen, A M

Be A Perfect Person In Just Three Days!
BL - v78 - Jl '82 - p1446
CBRS - v10 - Jl '82 - p124
New Age - v8 - D '82 - p68
PW - v221 - Ap 23 '82 - p93
SLJ - v29 - N '82 - p88
Subject: Behavior—Fiction; Humorous stories

see also Stephensen, A M for additional titles

MANGAN, Doreen

How To Be A Super Camp Counselor
SLJ - v26 - F '80 - p68
Subject: Camp counselors; Vocational guidance

MANGURIAN, David 1938-
BioIn 12, ConAu 10NR, SmATA 14

Children Of The Incas
BL - v81 - Jl '85 - p1567
BL - v82 - D 1 '85 - p582
CCB-B - v33 - Mr '80 - p137
HB - v56 - F '80 - p74
TN - v41 - Fall '84 - p97
Subject: Indians of South America

MANN, Peggy
BioIn 3, ConAu 10NR, DrAP&F 85, IntAu&W 82, SmATA 6, WrDr 86

The Drop-In
BL - v75 - Je 15 '79 - p1533
BL - v80 - Ja 15 '84 - p719
Hi Lo - v1 - S '79 - p2
Subject: High school dropouts—Fiction

Luis Munoz Marin: The Man Who Remade Puerto Rico
BL - v73 - N 1 '76 - p410
Inter BC - v14 - #1 '83 p16
KR - v44 - Jl 1 '76 - p741
SE - v41 - Ap '77 - p350
SLJ - v23 - O '76 - p109
Subject: Puerto Ricans

There Are Two Kinds Of Terrible
Am - v137 - D 3 '77 - p406
BL - v73 - F 1 '77 - p836
BS - v37 - O '77 - p203
CCB-B - v31 - S '77 - p21
KR - v45 - Je 15 '77 - p626
PW - v211 - My 2 '77 - p60

MANN, Peggy (continued)
RT - v31 - Ap '78 - p840
RT - v34 - O '80 - p54
SLJ - v23 - Ja '77 - p94
Teacher - v95 - My '78 - p103
Subject: Death—Fiction; Fathers and sons—Fiction; Mothers and sons—Fiction

see also Kluger, Ruth (co-author) for additional titles

MANNING-SANDERS, Ruth 1895-
AuBYP SUP, ConAu 73, OxChL, SmATA 15, ThrBJA, TwCChW 83, WrDr 86

A Book Of Witches
BL - v63 - O 15 '66 - p267
CCB-B - v20 - D '66 - p60
CSM - v67 - Je 10 '75 - p17
HB - v42 - O '66 - p564
LJ - v91 - S 15 '66 - p4339
NYTBR - v72 - Ja 15 '67 - p28
PW - v190 - O 3 '66 - p84
Spec - N 12 '65 - p631
SR - v49 - N 12 '66 - p50
Subject: Witchcraft—Fiction

MANNIX, Daniel 1911-
AuBYP SUP, BioIn 1, -2

The Outcasts
BL - v62 - O 1 '65 - p162
CCB-B - v18 - Jl '65 - p166
HB - v41 - Ag '65 - p387
Inst - v75 - N '65 - p94
KR - v33 - Ja 15 '65 - p58
LJ - v90 - Mr 15 '65 - p1550
NYTBR - v70 - Je 13 '65 - p24
Subject: Skunks—Fiction

MANTLE, Mickey 1931-
BioNews 74, ConAu 89, CurBio 53, NewYTBS 74, WhoAm 86, WhoProB 73

The Education Of A Baseball Player
BL - v64 - Ja 1 '68 - p526
BS - v27 - O 15 '67 - p268
KR - v35 - Jl 1 '67 - p784
KR - v35 - Ag 15 '67 - p980
LJ - v92 - Ag '67 - p2800
LJ - v92 - O 15 '67 - p3876
NYTBR - v72 - O 1 '67 - p8
NYTBR - v72 - D 3 '67 - p64
PW - v192 - Jl 10 '67 - p179
PW - v195 - F 24 '69 - p68
Subject: Baseball

MARA, Barney
see Roth, Arthur J

MARAVEL, Gailanne

Lights, Camera, Love
BL - v80 - F 1 '84 - p810
Kliatt - v18 - Winter '84 - p16
SLJ - v30 - Mr '84 - p173
Subject: Love—Fiction; Soap operas—Fiction

Too Young For Love
BL - v79 - Mr 15 '83 - p971
SLJ - v29 - Ag '83 - p78
VOYA - v6 - Ap '83 - p38
Subject: Adolescence—Fiction

MARCEAU, Adrienne

Serenade
B&B - My '83 - p31
Hi Lo - v3 - Ja '82 - p4
SLJ - v28 - Mr '82 - p154
VOYA - v4 - F '82 - p35

MARIOTTI, Mario

Hanimals
Kliatt - v18 - Spring '84 - p68
Subject: Games

Humands
Kliatt - v18 - Spring '84 - p68
Par - v59 - N '84 - p64
Subject: Games

MARLOW, Curtis

Break Dancing
Emerg Lib - v12 - Ja '85 - p45
Subject: Dancing

MARR, John S 1940-
ConAu 81, SmATA 48

A Breath Of Air And A Breath Of Smoke
CCB-B - v25 - Jl '72 - p173
CLW - v43 - My '72 - p536
LJ - v97 - Jl '72 - p2485
SB - v8 - S '72 - p160
Spec - v226 - My 29 '71 - p1260
Subject: Smoking

MARRIOTT, Alice 1910-
AuBYP, BioIn 2, -8, ConAu 57, CurBio 50, SmATA 31

The Black Stone Knife
PW - v193 - Ja 8 '68 - p69
Subject: Indians of North America—Fiction

MARSHALL, Andrea

Handle With Care
BL - v81 - F 1 '85 - p784
SLJ - v31 - Ja '85 - p89
Subject: Love—Fiction

Written In The Stars
BL - v80 - Je 15 '84 - p1474
VOYA - v7 - O '84 - p201
Subject: Love—Fiction

MARSHALL, Anthony D 1924-
ConAu 29R, SmATA 18, WhoAm 78, WhoGov 77

Africa's Living Arts
LJ - v95 - Jl '70 - p2541
Subject: Art

MARSHALL, Ray

Watch It Work! The Car
TES - v0 - N 16 '84 - p26
Co-author: Bradley, John
Subject: Automobiles

MARSTON, Elsa

The Cliffs Of Cairo
B Rpt - v1 - Ja '83 - p40
Kliatt - v16 - Fall '82 - p13
Subject: Egypt—Fiction; Mystery and detective stories

MARSTON, Hope Irvin 1935-
ConAu 101, SmATA 31

Machines On The Farm
BL - v79 - N 15 '82 - p447
NYTBR - v87 - N 14 '82 - p63
SLJ - v29 - D '82 - p66
Subject: Agriculture; Machinery

MARTIN, Albert (pseud.) 1934-
ConAu X
Real Name:
Nussbaum, Albert F

Secret Spy
BL - v75 - Jl 15 '79 - p1622
Hi Lo - v1 - D '79 - p4
SLJ - v26 - D '79 - p98
Subject: Spies—Fiction

see also Nussbaum, Albert F for additional titles

MARTIN, Ann M 1955-
ConAu 111, SmATA 44

Just You And Me
BL - v80 - F 1 '84 - p810
SLJ - v30 - My '84 - p87
VOYA - v6 - F '84 - p336
VOYA - v7 - Je '84 - p93
Subject: Love—Fiction

Missing Since Monday
BL - v83 - D 15 '86 - p650
KR - v54 - O 1 '86 - p1519
PW - v230 - N 28 '86 - p76
SLJ - v33 - N '86 - p105
Subject: Kidnapping—Fiction

MARTIN, Joseph Plumb 1760-1850
BioIn 7, –10, –11

Yankee Doodle Boy
BL - v61 - F '65 - p526
CE - v42 - O '65 - p116
HB - v41 - F '65 - p65
LJ - v89 - D 15 '64 - p5019
NYTBR, Pt. 2 - N 1 '64 - p56
Subject: United States—History—Revolution, 1775-1783

MARTIN, Mollie

Atlanta Braves
SLJ - v29 - Mr '83 - p170
Subject: Baseball

MARTIN, Susan

Duran Duran
BL - v81 - N 1 '84 - p367
SLJ - v31 - F '85 - p84
Subject: Bands (Music); Musicians; Rock musicians

MARTINELLI, Pat

Public Enemy: And Other True Stories From The Files Of The Fbi
BL - v77 - Mr 15 '81 - p1024
Subject: Crime and criminals

MARX, Robert F 1936-
AuBYP, BioIn 11, ConAu 6NR, SmATA 24, WrDr 86

They Dared The Deep: A History Of Diving
BL - v64 - O 1 '67 - p178
BS - v27 - Jl 1 '67 - p145
KR - v35 - My 15 '67 - p612
LJ - v93 - F 15 '68 - p884
NYTBR - v72 - Ag 6 '67 - p26
Subject: Diving (Submarine)

MARZOLLO, Jean 1942-
BioIn 13, ConAu 15NR, SmATA 29

Halfway Down Paddy Lane
EJ - v72 - Ja '83 - p78
J Read - v25 - Mr '82 - p613
VOYA - v4 - D '81 - p33
Subject: Irish Americans—Fiction; Space and time—Fiction; United States—Social life and customs—Fiction

MASIN, Herman L 1913-

How To Star In Basketball
BL - v63 - Mr 15 '67 - p796
LJ - v92 - Ja 15 '67 - p351
Teacher - v92 - Mr '75 - p41
Subject: Basketball

How To Star In Football
BL - v63 - Mr 15 '67 - p796
LJ - v92 - Ja 15 '67 - p352
Teacher - v92 - Mr '75 - p41
Subject: Football

MASON, Herbert Molloy, Jr. 1927-
ConAu 6NR, WrDr 86

Secrets Of The Supernatural
BL - v72 - N 1 '75 - p359
BS - v35 - Ja '76 - p325
KR - v43 - D 1 '75 - p1341
SLJ - v22 - Ja '76 - p55
Subject: Supernatural

MASON, Steve

Johnny's Song: Poetry Of A Vietnam Veteran
LATBR - My 25 '86 - p8
SLJ - v33 - O '86 - p195
VOYA - v9 - Ag '86 - p177
Subject: Poetry

MASSIE, Diane Redfield 1930-
AuBYP, ConAu 81, IlsCB 1957, -1967, SmATA 16

Cockle Stew And Other Rhymes
KR - v35 - Ag 15 '67 - p956
LJ - v92 - N 15 '67 - p4245
NYTBR - v72 - N 5 '67 - p61
Subject: Fairy tales; Verses for children

MATHER, Melissa

One Summer In Between
BL - v63 - Je 15 '67 - p1088
BS - v27 - Ap 1 '67 - p17
HB - v43 - D '67 - p770
KR - v35 - Ja 15 '67 - p80
LJ - v92 - F 15 '67 - p795
LJ - v92 - My 15 '67 - p2048
NYTBR - v72 - Mr 19 '67 - p46
PW - v190 - N 7 '66 - p62
PW - v193 - Mr 4 '68 - p66
SR - v50 - Ap 22 '67 - p101
TN - v24 - N '67 - p102
TN - v24 - Ap '68 - p327

MATHEWS, William H
see Brownmiller, Susan (co-author)

MATHIS, Sharon Bell 1937-
ChlLR 3, ConAu 41R, DcLB 33, FourBJA, OxChL, SelBAAf, SmATA 7, -3AS, TwCChW 83, WrDr 86

Listen For The Fig Tree
BL - v70 - My 15 '74 - p1052
BL - v70 - My 15 '74 - p1057
BL - v71 - Mr 15 '75 - p748
BS - v34 - Jl 15 '74 - p202
CCB-B - v27 - Jl '74 - p182
Choice - v14 - N '77 - p1178
Comw - v101 - N 22 '74 - p192
EJ - v64 - D '75 - p80
HB - v50 - Je '74 - p287
J Read - v25 - My '82 - p778
KR - v42 - F 1 '74 - p121
LJ - v99 - Mr 15 '74 - p904
NYTBR - Ap 7 '74 - p8
PW - v205 - Ja 21 '74 - p85
SLJ - v29 - N '82 - p34
Subject: Blacks—Social conditions—Fiction; Blind—Fiction; Family problems—Fiction

Teacup Full Of Roses
BL - v69 - O 1 '72 - p139
BL - v69 - O 1 '72 - p150
Bl W - v22 - Ag '73 - p86
BW - v6 - Ag 6 '72 - p2
CCB-B - v26 - O '72 - p29
CE - v49 - My '73 - p422
Choice - v14 - N '77 - p1178
EJ - v62 - D '73 - p1300
EJ - v63 - Ja '74 - p66
EJ - v63 - F '74 - p92
EJ - v64 - D '75 - p80
HB - v49 - F '73 - p58
Inter BC - v15 - #4 '84 p10
KR - v40 - Je 1 '72 - p629
LJ - v97 - N 15 '72 - p3814
NHB - v36 - Mr '73 - p69
NYTBR - Je 4 '72 - p28
NYTBR - S 10 '72 - p8
NYTBR, Pt. 2 - N 5 '72 - p28

MATHIS, Sharon Bell (continued)
PW - v202 - Jl 17 '72 - p122
SE - v37 - D '73 - p787
SLJ - v28 - Ap '82 - p28
Teacher - v91 - F '74 - p98
TN - v29 - Ap '73 - p257
Subject: Blacks—Fiction; Family life—Fiction

MATTHEWS, Clayton
see Brisco, Patty

MATTHEWS, Gordon

Prince
B Rpt - v4 - Mr '86 - p35
SLJ - v32 - S '85 - p131
Subject: Musicians; Rock musicians

MATTHEWS, Patricia
see Brisco, Patty

MATTHEWS, William H, III 1919-
AmM&WS 86P, AuBYP SUP, ConAu 9R, SmATA 45, WhoS&SW 78

Introducing The Earth
BL - v69 - O 15 '72 - p192
KR - v40 - Je 1 '72 - p633
LJ - v97 - O 15 '72 - p3462
Subject: Geology

Wonders Of Fossils
BL - v64 - Jl 15 '68 - p1287
Comw - v88 - My 24 '68 - p308
KR - v36 - Mr 15 '68 - p349
LJ - v93 - My 15 '68 - p2114
SB - v4 - My '68 - p34
Subject: Paleontology

MAXWELL, Edith 1923-
AuBYP SUP, ConAu 49, SmATA 7, WhoAmW 77

Just Dial A Number
BS - v31 - Ap 15 '71 - p47
KR - v38 - D 15 '70 - p1348
LJ - v96 - My 15 '71 - p1815
NYTBR - Ap 18 '71 - p40
PW - v199 - F 8 '71 - p81

MAXWELL, Joe
see Coen, Patricia (co-author)

MAY, John

Curious Facts
Obs - D 2 '84 - p24
TLS - D 21 '84 - p1481
Subject: Curiosities and wonders

MAY, Julian 1931-
AuBYP, ConAu 6NR, ScFSB, SmATA 11, TwCSFW 86

Pseud./variant:
Thorne, Ian

The Cincinnati Bengals
SLJ - v28 - O '81 - p145
Subject: Football

Hank Aaron Clinches The Pennant
CCB-B - v26 - O '72 - p29
Subject: Baseball—Biography

The New York Jets
BL - v79 - Ap 1 '83 - p1023
Subject: Football

see also Thorne, Ian for additional titles

MAYER, Ann M 1938-
ConAu 57, SmATA 14

Who's Out There? UFO Encounters
Hi Lo - v1 - Ja '80 - p3
SLJ - v26 - Ja '80 - p73
Subject: Unidentified flying objects

MAYERSON, Charlotte Leon
ConAu 13R, SmATA 36

Two Blocks Apart: Juan Gonzales And Peter Quinn
BL - v62 - S 1 '65 - p14
CC - v82 - Jl 7 '65 - p871
Crit - v24 - O '65 - p86
EJ - v56 - N '67 - p1215
HB - v41 - D '65 - p650
HM - v231 - S '65 - p141
KR - v33 - My 1 '65 - p494
KR - v33 - Je 1 '65 - p536
LJ - v90 - Jl '65 - p3064
LJ - v90 - S 15 '65 - p3818
NYTBR, Pt. 2 - v72 - F 26 '67 - p32
PW - v190 - S 26 '66 - p135
Subject: New York (City)

MAYS, Willie

"Play Ball!"
BL - v77 - Ja 1 '81 - p627
Kliatt - v15 - Winter '81 - p55
PW - v218 - S 26 '80 - p122
SLJ - v27 - D '80 - p75
VOYA - v4 - Ap '81 - p46
Co-author: Berger, Maxine
Subject: Baseball

MAZER, Harry 1925-
ConAu 97, FifBJA, SmATA 31

Guy Lenny
Kliatt - v11 - Fall '77 - p7

MAZER, Harry (continued)
KR - v39 - O 15 '71 - p1121
LJ - v96 - O 15 '71 - p3478
Teacher - v90 - F '73 - p125
Subject: Divorce—Fiction

The Last Mission
BB - v7 - Ja '80 - p3
BOT - v2 - D '79 - p601
CBRS - v8 - O '79 - p18
KR - v48 - Ja 1 '80 - p10
NYTBR - N 25 '79 - p22
NYTBR - D 2 '79 - p41
PW - v216 - D 10 '79 - p70
SE - v47 - Ap '83 - p289
SLJ - v26 - N '79 - p91
VOYA - v5 - F '83 - p20
WLB - v54 - O '79 - p123
Subject: Jews—Fiction; Prisoners—Fiction; World War, 1939-1945—Fiction

Snow Bound
BL - v70 - S 15 '73 - p123
J Read - v22 - N '78 - p128
KR - v41 - Ap 1 '73 - p384
LJ - v98 - Jl '73 - p2202
NYTBR - Ag 12 '73 - p8
PW - v203 - Mr 26 '73 - p70
VOYA - v5 - F '83 - p19
Subject: Survival—Fiction

The War On Villa Street
BL - v75 - N 15 '78 - p547
CBRS - v7 - F '79 - p69
CCB-B - v32 - Ja '79 - p84
J Read - v25 - My '82 - p778
Kliatt - v14 - Winter '80 - p12
KR - v46 - D 1 '78 - p1311
PW - v214 - D 25 '78 - p60
SLJ - v25 - D '78 - p62
TN - v36 - Winter '80 - p209
WLB - v53 - Ja '79 - p380
Subject: Fathers and sons—Fiction; Running—Fiction

When The Phone Rang
BL - v82 - Je 15 '86 - p1536
BS - v45 - Ja '86 - p399
CBRS - v14 - N '85 - p32
CCB-B - v39 - D '85 - p73
EJ - v75 - D '86 - p60
PW - v228 - N 1 '85 - p65
PW - v230 - D 12 '86 - p58
SLJ - v32 - N '85 - p100
VOYA - v8 - D '85 - p321
WLB - v60 - F '86 - p47
Subject: Death—Fiction; Family problems—Fiction

see also Mazer, Norma Fox (co-author) for additional titles

MAZER, Norma Fox 1931-
ConAu 12NR, ConLC 26, DrAP&F 85, FifBJA, SmATA 24, -1AS, WhoAmW 87

Dear Bill, Remember Me?
NYTBR - F 26 '78 - p41
SLJ - v29 - Ap '83 - p122
Subject: Adolescence—Fiction; Short stories

A Figure Of Speech
BL - v70 - Ja 15 '74 - p544
BS - v33 - N 15 '73 - p382
Can Child Lit - #25 '82 p30
CCB-B - v27 - Ja '74 - p82
CE - v54 - Ja '78 - p124
Choice - v14 - N '77 - p1178
HB - v50 - Ap '74 - p152
KR - v41 - S 15 '73 - p1043
Learning - v14 - Mr '86 - p65
LJ - v99 - F 15 '74 - p582
NYTBR - Mr 17 '74 - p8
PW - v204 - S 17 '73 - p57
Subject: Grandfathers—Fiction; Old age—Fiction

Mrs. Fish, Ape, And Me, The Dump Queen
BL - v76 - Je 15 '80 - p1533
BW - v14 - N 11 '84 - p21
CBRS - v8 - Mr '80 - p78
Inter BC - v12 - #7 '81 p17
KR - v48 - Je 15 '80 - p779
PW - v217 - Ap 4 '80 - p75
PW - v221 - Ja 29 '82 - p67
PW - v227 - Ja 4 '85 - p70
SLJ - v26 - Ap '80 - p114
Subject: Friendship—Fiction; Schools—Fiction; Uncles—Fiction

The Solid Gold Kid
BB - v6 - Je '78 - p3
BL - v73 - Je 1 '77 - p1499
BS - v37 - O '77 - p204
BW - Jl 10 '77 - pH10
CCB-B - v30 - Jl '77 - p178
EJ - v67 - F '78 - p79
HB - v53 - Ag '77 - p451
KR - v45 - Ap 1 '77 - p360
PW - v211 - Mr 28 '77 - p78
RT - v32 - O '78 - p44
SLJ - v24 - S '77 - p147
Co-author: Mazer, Harry
Subject: Kidnapping—Fiction

MAZER, Norma Fox (continued)

Taking Terri Mueller
BL - v78 - D 1 '81 - p500
BS - v43 - Je '83 - p112
BW - v13 - Ap 10 '83 - p10
CBRS - v11 - Spring '83 - p125
Cur R - v22 - F '83 - p59
HB - v59 - Ap '83 - p172
Kliatt - v16 - Winter '82 - p13
VOYA - v5 - Ap '82 - p36
Subject: Divorce—Fiction; Kidnapping—Fiction

Up In Seth's Room
BL - v76 - N 1 '79 - p440
CBRS - v8 - D '79 - p39
J Read - v24 - O '80 - p86
KR - v47 - D 1 '79 - p1380
NYTBR - Ja 20 '80 - p30
PW - v216 - S 10 '79 - p74
SLJ - v26 - Ja '80 - p80
WLB - v54 - O '79 - p123
Subject: Family life—Fiction; Social adjustment—Fiction

see also Mazer, Harry for additional titles

MCAULIFFE, Jim

Three Mile House
BL - v75 - O 15 '78 - p357
Subject: Mystery and detective stories

MCCAGUE, James 1909-1977
ConAu 2NR

Tecumseh
CE - v47 - D '70 - p160
LJ - v95 - N 15 '70 - p4062
Subject: Biography; Indians of North America—Biography

MCCALL, Joseph R
see **McCall, Virginia Nielsen** (co-author)

MCCALL, Virginia Nielsen 1909-
AuBYP SUP, ConAu 17NR, SmATA 13, WhoAmW 75
Pseud./variant:
Nielsen, Virginia

Your Career In Parks And Recreation
BL - v67 - S 15 '70 - p97
BS - v30 - My 1 '70 - p62
Choice - v7 - S '70 - p822
LJ - v96 - F 15 '71 - p744
Co-author: McCall, Joseph R
Subject: Vocational guidance

see also Nielsen, Virginia for additional titles

MCCALLUM, John Dennis 1924-
ConAu 53, IntAu&W 77

Getting Into Pro Football
BL - v75 - Jl 1 '79 - p1583
SLJ - v25 - My '79 - p86
Subject: Football; Vocational guidance

MCCANNON, Dindga 1947-
ConAu 114, SmATA 41

Peaches
BL - v71 - Ja 15 '75 - p508
BW - N 10 '74 - p5
KR - v42 - N 1 '74 - p1151
SLJ - v21 - Ja '75 - p55
Subject: New York (City)—Fiction

MCCARTHY, Pat

True Ghost Stories: Tales Of The Supernatural Based On Actual Reports
Hi Lo - v1 - Ap '80 - p3
Subject: Ghosts; Short stories

MCCONNELL, James Douglas R
see Rutherford, Douglas

MCCRACKIN, Mark

A Winning Position
BL - v78 - Ag '82 - p1520
Hi Lo - v3 - My '82 - p4
Kliatt - v16 - Spring '82 - p13
PW - v221 - Mr 26 '82 - p75
SLJ - v28 - My '82 - p86
VOYA - v5 - Ag '82 - p34
Subject: Automobile racing—Fiction

MCDONALD, Gerald 1905-1970
BioIn 1, -6, -8, -9, ConAu P-1, SmATA 3

A Way Of Knowing: A Collection Of Poems For Boys
BL - v55 - Jl 15 '59 - p634
HB - v35 - Ag '59 - p302
KR - v27 - Mr 15 '59 - p227
LJ - v84 - My 15 '59 - p1705
NYTBR - S 13 '59 - p58

MCDONALD, Gerald (continued)
SR - v42 - Jl 18 '59 - p38
Subject: American poetry; English poetry

MCDONNELL, Virginia B 1917-
AuBYP SUP, ConAu 8NR, WhoAmW 85, WhoE 85, WhoWor 84

Trouble At Mercy Hospital
CCB-B - v22 - Ja '69 - p82
LJ - v94 - F 15 '69 - p875
Subject: Nursing—Fiction

MCFALL, Karen

Pat King's Family
BL - v74 - Jl 15 '78 - p1722
Subject: Family life—Fiction

MCFARLAND, Kenton Dean 1920-
AuBYP SUP, ConAu 61, SmATA 11

Airplanes: How They Work
BL - v63 - O 15 '66 - p266
Subject: Aeronautics

MCFARLAND, Kevin

More Incredible!
Kliatt - v13 - Winter '79 - p63
Subject: Curiosities and wonders

MCGILL, Joyce

Lovetalk
BL - v81 - F 1 '85 - p784
SLJ - v31 - Ap '85 - p102
Subject: Love—Fiction

MCGIVERN, Maureen Daly
see Daly, Maureen

MCGONAGLE, Bob

Careers In Sports
BL - v72 - N 1 '75 - p370
CLW - v47 - Ap '76 - p408
SLJ - v22 - D '75 - p68
Co-author: McGonagle, Marquita
Subject: Sports; Vocational guidance

MCGONAGLE, Marquita
see **McGonagle, Bob (co-author)**

MCGRATH, Judith

Pretty Girl: A Guide To Looking Good, Naturally
BL - v78 - D 15 '81 - p550
CCB-B - v35 - My '82 - p175
CE - v59 - S '82 - p62
PW - v221 - Ja 29 '82 - p67
SLJ - v28 - Ap '82 - p72
Subject: Beauty (Personal); Health

MCGRAVIE, Anne V

All The Way Back
BL - v79 - Ja 15 '83 - p660
Subject: Amputees—Biography; Physically handicapped; Veterans (Disabled)—U.S.—Biography

MCGRAW, Barbara

Those Who Dared: Adventure Stories From The Bible
BL - v79 - Ja 15 '83 - p660
Subject: Bible

MCGRAW, Eloise Jarvis 1915-
AuBYP, BioIn 6, ConAu 19NR, CurBio 55, IntAu&W 82, MorJA, SmATA 1, TwCChW 83, WrDr 86

Greensleeves
BW - v2 - N 3 '68 - p26
CSM - v60 - N 7 '68 - pB11
KR - v36 - S 15 '68 - p1060
LJ - v93 - O 15 '68 - p3984

MCHARGUE, Georgess 1941-
AuBYP SUP, ChlLR 2, ConAu 25R, FifBJA, SmATA 4

Little Victories, Big Defeats: War As The Ultimate Pollution
EJ - v68 - F '79 - p94
Subject: Short stories; War—Fiction

Meet The Vampire
BL - v76 - N 1 '79 - p450
Kliatt - v17 - Spring '83 - p54
RT - v34 - O '80 - p50
SLJ - v26 - Ap '80 - p113
TLS - v0 - N 21 '80 - p1330
Subject: Vampires

Meet The Werewolf
BL - v72 - Ap 15 '76 - p1191
CLW - v48 - D '76 - p234
HB - v52 - Ag '76 - p421
Kliatt - v17 - Spring '83 - p54
KR - v44 - Ap 15 '76 - p478
LA - v54 - Ja '77 - p81
SLJ - v23 - S '76 - p122
Teacher - v94 - O '76 - p148
Subject: Werewolves

Mummies
BL - v69 - Mr 15 '73 - p698

MCHARGUE, Georgess (continued)
CE - v50 - O '73 - p34
HB - v49 - Ap '73 - p152
KR - v40 - O 1 '72 - p1158
LJ - v98 - My 15 '73 - p1683
PW - v202 - D 18 '72 - p40
Teacher - v90 - Ap '73 - p90
TN - v29 - Je '73 - p357
Subject: Mummies

MCHUGH, John

Filling Out Job Application Forms
Hi Lo - v4 - F '83 - p4
Subject: Applications for positions

Finding A Job
BL - v78 - My 15 '82 - p1236
Hi Lo - v4 - F '83 - p4
Subject: Vocational guidance

Getting Ready To Work
Hi Lo - v4 - F '83 - p4
Subject: Job hunting; Vocational guidance

Interviewing For Jobs
Hi Lo - v4 - F '83 - p4
Subject: Employment

Keeping And Changing Jobs
Hi Lo - v4 - F '83 - p4
Subject: Job security; Work

Starting A New Job
BL - v78 - F 15 '82 - p754
Hi Lo - v4 - F '83 - p4
Subject: Vocational guidance; Work

MCILWRAITH, Maureen Mollie Hunter McVeigh 1922-
BioIn 11, -12, ConAu 29R, IntAu&W 77, SmATA 2, ThrBJA, WrDr 80
Pseud./variant:
Hunter, Mollie

The Walking Stones: A Story Of Suspense
Am - v123 - D 5 '70 - p496
BL - v67 - N 1 '70 - p228
BW - v4 - N 8 '70 - p8
CCB-B - v24 - Je '71 - p157
CSM - v62 - N 12 '70 - pB7
HB - v47 - F '71 - p51
KR - v38 - Ag 1 '70 - p800
LJ - v95 - D 15 '70 - p4375
NYTBR, Pt. 2 - N 8 '70 - p24
TN - v27 - Ap '71 - p305
Subject: Magic—Fiction; Scotland—Fiction

see also Hunter, Mollie for additional titles

MCKAY, Robert W 1921-
AuBYP SUP, ConAu 10NR, SmATA 15

Canary Red
BL - v65 - O 15 '68 - p234
BS - v28 - S 1 '68 - p227
KR - v36 - Je 15 '68 - p649
LJ - v93 - O 15 '68 - p3984

Dave's Song
BL - v66 - Ap 1 '70 - p968
CCB-B - v24 - O '70 - p30
EJ - v59 - My '70 - p735
KR - v37 - N 15 '69 - p1203
SR - v53 - My 9 '70 - p69
Subject: Family life—Fiction; Poultry breeding—Fiction

The Running Back
BL - v76 - N 15 '79 - p494
KR - v48 - F 1 '80 - p134
SLJ - v26 - D '79 - p100
Subject: Football—Fiction

The Troublemaker
BL - v68 - My 1 '72 - p766
BS - v31 - F 15 '72 - p523
EJ - v61 - My '72 - p769
LJ - v97 - My 15 '72 - p1923
Subject: Strikes and lockouts—Fiction

MCKENNA, Rose Anne

A Change Of Heart
BL - v81 - F 1 '84 - p810
Subject: Love—Fiction

MCKILLIP, Patricia A 1948-
AuBYP SUP, ConAu 18NR, FifBJA, ScFSB, SmATA 30

The Throme Of The Erril Of Sherill
CCB-B - v27 - Ja '74 - p82
Kliatt - v18 - Spring '84 - p20
KR - v41 - Jl 1 '73 - p686
LJ - v98 - S 15 '73 - p2654
PW - v204 - Ag 27 '73 - p282
Subject: Fantasy

MCKIMMEY, James 1923-
ConAu 85

Buckaroo
Hi Lo - v2 - N '80 - p5

MCKOWN, Robin 1907-
AuBYP, ConAu 1R, SmATA 6, ThrBJA, WhoE 75

Patriot Of The Underground
CCB-B - v19 - D '65 - p65
NYTBR - Je 7 '64 - p28
Subject: World War, 1939-1945

MCLENIGHAN, Valjean 1947-
ConAu 108, SmATA 46

Diana: Alone Against The Sea
SLJ - v27 - Ja '81 - p57
Subject: Nyad, Diana; Swimmers

MCLOONE-BASTA, Margo

The Kids' Book Of Lists
CCB-B - v34 - Ap '81 - p156
Hi Lo - v2 - My '81 - p6
SLJ - v27 - Mr '81 - p148
Co-author: Siegel, Alice
Subject: Curiosities and wonders

MCMILLAN, Brett
see **McMillan, Bruce (co-author)**

MCMILLAN, Bruce 1947-
BioIn 13, ConAu 73, SmATA 22

Making Sneakers
CCB-B - v33 - Je '80 - p195
Film Cr - v48 - Je 15 '80 - p781
SLJ - v27 - S '80 - p61
Subject: Rubber industry and trade; Shoes

Puniddles
CCB-B - v35 - Jl '82 - p211
Hi Lo - v78 - Ap 1 '82 - p1020
LATBR - v0 - S 26 '82 - p6
Co-author: McMillan, Brett
Subject: Rebuses

MCMULLEN, David

Atlantis: The Missing Continent
Cur R - v17 - Ag '78 - p228
SLJ - v25 - S '78 - p128
Subject: Atlantis

Mystery In Peru: The Lines Of Nazca
Cur R - v17 - Ag '78 - p227
SLJ - v25 - N '78 - p64
Subject: Balloon ascensions; Indians of South America

MCNALLY, Raymond T

A Clutch Of Vampires
Choice - v11 - O '74 - p1119
KR - v42 - Ap 1 '74 - p405
PW - v205 - Ap 1 '74 - p54
Subject: Monsters

MCNAMARA, John

Model Behavior
CBRS - v14 - N '85 - p32
CCB-B - v39 - N '85 - p52
Subject: Interpersonal relations—Fiction; Models and modeling—Fiction

MCNEAR, Robert

The Marathon Race Mystery
SLJ - v32 - S '85 - p153
Subject: Mystery and detective stories; Plot-your-own-stories

MCPHEE, Richard B 1934-
ConAu 111, SmATA 41

Rounds With A Country Vet
BL - v74 - F 15 '78 - p1009
CCB-B - v31 - Je '78 - p164
Comw - v105 - N 10 '78 - p734
Inst - v87 - My '78 - p115
KR - v46 - Ja 15 '78 - p51
PW - v213 - Ja 2 '78 - p65
SLJ - v24 - Mr '78 - p131
SR - v5 - My 27 '78 - p58
Subject: Veterinarians

MCVEY, R Parker

The Missing Rock Star Caper
SLJ - v32 - S '85 - p153
Subject: Mystery and detective stories; Plot-your-own-stories

Mystery At The Ball Game
SLJ - v32 - S '85 - p153
Subject: Kidnapping—Fiction; Mystery and detective stories; Plot-your-own-stories

MCWHIRTER, Norris 1925-
BioIn 8, –12, ConAu 13R, IntAu&W 86, SmATA 37, Who 85, WhoWor 84, WorAl

Guinness Book Of Amazing Achievements
EJ - v65 - My '76 - p91
Inst - v85 - My '76 - p112
SLJ - v22 - Mr '76 - p105

MCWHIRTER, Norris (continued)
Co-author: McWhirter, Ross
Subject: Curiosities and wonders

Guinness Book Of Astounding Feats And Events
Inst - v85 - My '76 - p112
SLJ - v22 - Mr '76 - p105
Co-author: McWhirter, Ross
Subject: Curiosities and wonders

Guinness Book Of Phenomenal Happenings
BL - v72 - My 1 '76 - p1268
SLJ - v23 - S '76 - p122
Co-author: McWhirter, Ross
Subject: Curiosities and wonders

Guinness Book Of Sports Records: Winners And Champions
ARBA - v12 - p327
ARBA - v14 - p8303
BL - v77 - N 1 '80 - p386
BL - v77 - Je 1 '81 - p1312
LATBR - Ag 22 '82 - p8
SLJ - v28 - My '82 - p20
Co-author: Cook, Chris
Subject: Curiosities and wonders

Guinness Book Of Young Recordbreakers
BL - v72 - My 1 '76 - p1268
SLJ - v23 - D '76 - p72
Co-author: McWhirter, Ross
Subject: Curiosities and wonders

MCWHIRTER, Ross
see **McWhirter, Norris (co-author)**

MEADER, Stephen W 1892-1977
AuBYP, ConAu 5R, JBA 34, –51, OxChL, SmATA 1, TwCChW 78, –83, WhAm 7, WrDr 80

Lonesome End
BS - v28 - N 1 '68 - p325
CSM - v60 - N 7 '68 - pB12
KR - v36 - O 1 '68 - p1121
PW - v194 - O 7 '68 - p55

River Of The Wolves
BL - v45 - N 1 '48 - p92
Comw - v49 - D 3 '48 - p214
CSM - Ja 27 '49 - p7
HB - v25 - Ja '49 - p41
KR - v16 - O 1 '48 - p530
LJ - v73 - D 1 '48 - p1747
NY - v24 - D 11 '48 - p132
NYTBR - Ja 30 '49 - p28
SR - v31 - N 13 '48 - p32

MEADOWCROFT, Enid LaMonte 1898-1966
AuBYP, BioIn 1, –2, –7, ConAu X, CurBio 49, JBA 51, SmATA 3
Pseud./variant:
Wright, Enid Meadowcroft

By Secret Railway
BL - v45 - N 1 '48 - p92
CSM - O 28 '48 - p11
KR - v16 - Ag 15 '48 - p400
NY - v24 - D 11 '48 - p131
NYTBR - N 14 '48 - p58
SR - v31 - N 13 '48 - p28
Subject: Underground railroad—Fiction

Scarab For Luck
Comw - v80 - My 22 '64 - p268
HB - v40 - Ap '64 - p179
LJ - v89 - Mr 15 '64 - p1452
NYTBR - Ag 2 '64 - p20

When Nantucket Men Went Whaling
LJ - v92 - Ja 15 '67 - p336
Subject: Whaling

MEAKER, Marijane
see Kerr, M E

MEANS, Florence Crannell 1891-1980
AuBYP, ConAu 1R, –103, IntAu&W 82, JBA 51, OxChL, SmATA 1, –25N, TwCChW 83, WhAm 7

Candle In The Mist
NYTBR - Ja 24 '32 - p19

Shuttered Windows
BL - v35 - S 15 '38 - p31
Comw - v29 - D 2 '38 - p157
HB - v14 - S '38 - p290
LJ - v63 - O 15 '38 - p799
LJ - v63 - N 1 '38 - p825
NYTBR - Ag 28 '38 - p10

MEBANE, Robert C

Adventures With Atoms And Molecules
ASBYP - v19 - Summer '86 - p48
BL - v82 - N 15 '85 - p498
B Rpt - v5 - My '86 - p47
CBRS - v14 - N '85 - p32
SB - v21 - Ja '86 - p139
SLJ - v32 - N '85 - p88
VOYA - v8 - F '86 - p402
VOYA - v9 - Je '86 - p95
Co-author: Rybolt, Thomas R
Subject: Science

MEDEARIS, Mary 1915-
ConAu 69, SmATA 5

Big Doc's Girl
BS - v45 - Jl '85 - p158
NYTBR - S 13 '42 - p7

MEEK, Jacklyn **O'Hanlon**
see **O'Hanlon, Jacklyn**

MEHTA, Rama
see Galbraith, Catherine Atwater (co-author)

MEIGS, Cornelia 1884-1973
AuBYP, ConAu 9R, -45, JBA 51, OxChL, SmATA 6, TwCChW 83, WhAm 7

Invincible Louisa: The Story Of The Author Of Little Women
BS - v28 - O 1 '68 - p274
BW - v2 - N 3 '68 - p1
CSM - v75 - My 13 '83 - pB7
NYTBR - v73 - S 29 '68 - p46
PW - v194 - S 2 '68 - p29
SE - v48 - N '84 - p563
Subject: Biography

MELTZER, Milton 1915-
AuBYP SUP, ConAu 13R, ConLC 26, DrAS 82H, MorBMP, SmATA 1, -1AS, ThrBJA, WhoAm 86

Langston Hughes
AL - v41 - Mr '69 - p142
BL - v65 - Ja 1 '69 - p498
BL - v65 - Ap 1 '69 - p901
BS - v28 - Ja 1 '69 - p423
BW - v3 - F 2 '69 - p12
Cres - v33 - D '69 - p23
CSM - v61 - My 1 '69 - pB7
EJ - v58 - My '69 - p783
HB - v45 - Ap '69 - p183
Inst - v79 - Ag '69 - p191
LJ - v94 - Ja 15 '69 - p313
SE - v33 - My '69 - p562
Subject: Biography

Underground Man
BL - v69 - Ja 1 '73 - p446
CCB-B - v27 - S '73 - p14
CE - v49 - Ap '73 - p374
KR - v40 - N 15 '72 - p1313
LJ - v98 - Ap 15 '73 - p1397
NYTBR - Mr 18 '73 - p12
SE - v37 - D '73 - p786
Teacher - v92 - Ap '75 - p113
TN - v29 - Ap '73 - p253
Subject: Slavery—Fiction; Underground railroad—Fiction

MELVILLE, Herman 1819-1891
AmWr, BioIn 11, -12, -13, DcLB 3, DcLEL, OxAmL 83, OxChL, OxEng 85, WorAl

Moby Dick
Nat - v233 - D 26 '81 - p711
Adapter: Daniels, Patricia
Subject: Sea stories; Whaling—Fiction

MENASHE, Abraham

The Face Of Prayer
B Rpt - v2 - N '83 - p47
CC - v100 - Mr 9 '83 - p227
Choice - v21 - S '83 - p84
Kliatt - v17 - Spring '83 - p30
New Age - v8 - Ap '83 - p62
PW - v223 - Ja 7 '83 - p65
Rel St Rev - v9 - Jl '83 - p245
Subject: Prayer

MENDONCA, Susan 1950-
ConAu 102, SmATA 45

Tough Choices
BS - v40 - N '80 - p303
CBRS - v8 - Spring '80 - p119
CCB-B - v33 - My '80 - p179
HB - v56 - Ag '80 - p415
Kliatt - v17 - Spring '83 - p10
KR - v48 - S 15 '80 - p1236
SLJ - v27 - S '80 - p85
Subject: Divorce—Fiction

MENNINGER, William C 1899-1966
BioIn 1, -3, -4, -5, -7, ConAu 25R, CurBio 66, WhAm 4

How To Be A Successful Teenager
LJ - v92 - F 15 '67 - p896
NYTBR - v72 - Mr 5 '67 - p30
Subject: Adolescence

MERCER, Charles Edward 1917-
AuBYP SUP, ConAu 1R, SmATA 16, WhoAm 86

Miracle At Midway
KR - v46 - Ja 1 '78 - p9
PW - v212 - O 31 '77 - p59
SLJ - v24 - F '78 - p66
Subject: World War, 1939-1945

MERGENDAHL, T E, Jr.

What Does A Photographer Do?
LJ - v90 - Ap 15 '65 - p2023
Co-author: Ramsdell, Sheldon
Subject: Occupations; Photography

MERIWETHER, Louise 1923-
BlkAWP, ConAu 77, DcLB 33, DrAP&F 85, SelBAAf, SelBAAu, SmATA 31, WhoBlA 85

Daddy Was A Number Runner
A Lib - v1 - D '70 - p1088
B&B - Je '86 - p31
BL - v67 - Ap 1 '71 - p654
Bl W - v19 - My '70 - p51
Bl W - v19 - Jl '70 - p85
BW - v5 - Je 20 '71 - p11
EJ - v60 - My '71 - p657
EJ - v63 - Ja '74 - p66
EJ - v64 - D '75 - p80
Emerg Lib - v9 - Ja '82 - p16
KR - v38 - Ja 1 '70 - p22
KR - v38 - F 1 '70 - p119
LJ - v95 - F 15 '70 - p685
LJ - v95 - S 15 '70 - p3080
LJ - v95 - D 15 '70 - p4328
NS - v83 - Ja 7 '72 - p23
NY - v46 - Jl 11 '70 - p77
NYTBR - Je 28 '70 - p31
NYTBR - D 6 '70 - p100
NYTBR - v41 - D 21 '86 - p24
Obs - Ja 9 '72 - p31
PW - v197 - Ja 19 '70 - p78
PW - v199 - My 3 '71 - p58
SR - v53 - My 23 '70 - p51
SR - v54 - Jl 24 '71 - p42
TLS - Ja 21 '72 - p57
TN - v27 - Ap '71 - p309
Subject: Family problems—Fiction

MERRIAM, Eve 1916-
AuBYP, BioIn 12, -13, ConAu 5R, ConTFT 1, OxChL, SmATA 40, ThrBJA, TwCChW 83, WhoAm 86, WrDr 86

Out Loud
CCB-B - v27 - O '73 - p32
HB - v49 - O '73 - p475
KR - v41 - Ap 15 '73 - p460
LJ - v98 - S 15 '73 - p2642
PW - v203 - Je 25 '73 - p74
RT - v36 - Ja '83 - p381
Subject: American poetry

MERTZ, Barbara Gross
see Peters, Elizabeth

MEYER, Carolyn 1935-
AuBYP SUP, ConAu 2NR, FifBJA, SmATA 9

C. C. Poindexter
BL - v75 - S 1 '78 - p40
KR - v46 - O 15 '78 - p1142
SLJ - v25 - O '78 - p157
WLB - v53 - O '78 - p180
Subject: Family life—Fiction; Social adjustment—Fiction

The Luck Of Texas McCoy
BL - v81 - S 1 '84 - p59
CCB-B - v38 - O '84 - p32
EJ - v74 - S '85 - p85
SLJ - v31 - F '85 - p86
Subject: Motion pictures—Fiction; Ranch life—Fiction; Western films—Fiction

MEYER, Jerome Sydney 1895-1975
AuBYP, BioIn 10, ConAu 4NR, SmATA 25N, -3

Fun With The New Math
BL - v62 - Jl 15 '66 - p1070
CCB-B - v20 - D '66 - p60
HB - v42 - D '66 - p732
LJ - v91 - S 15 '66 - p4340
NYTBR - v71 - Mr 6 '66 - p46
SB - v2 - D '66 - p176
Co-author: Hanlon, Stuart
Subject: Mathematics

Great Accidents In Science That Changed The World
LJ - v93 - F 15 '68 - p885
SB - v3 - Mr '68 - p325
Subject: Science

MEYER, Miriam Weiss

The Blind Guards Of Easter Island
Cur R - v17 - Ag '78 - p227
SLJ - v25 - N '78 - p64
Subject: Man (Prehistoric)

MEYERS, James

Incredible Animals
BS - v36 - Je '76 - p103
Subject: Animals

MEYERS, Susan 1942-
AuBYP SUP, BioIn 12, ConAu 13NR, SmATA 19, WrDr 86

Pearson: A Harbor Seal Pup
BL - v77 - Ap 15 '81 - p1156
CCB-B - v34 - My '81 - p176
CE - v58 - N '81 - p113

MEYERS, Susan (continued)
HB - v57 - Je '81 - p319
KR - v49 - Mr 1 '81 - p286
SB - v17 - N '81 - p95
SLJ - v27 - Ag '81 - p69
Subject: Animals

MICHENER, James A 1907-
ConAu 5R, -21NR, ConLC 11, ConNov 86, Conv 3, CurBio 75, WhoAm 86, WrDr 86

The Bridges At Toko-Ri
Atl - v192 - S '53 - p78
BL - v50 - S 1 '53 - p13
Comw - v58 - Jl 31 '53 - p426
CSM - Jl 9 '53 - p7
HB - v29 - D '53 - p469
KR - v21 - Jl 1 '53 - p395
LJ - v78 - Jl '53 - p1232
New R - v129 - Ag 17 '53 - p20
NY - v29 - Ag 1 '53 - p59
NYTBR - Jl 12 '53 - p5
SR - v36 - Jl 11 '53 - p22
Time - v62 - Jl 13 '53 - p102
Subject: Korean War, 1950—Fiction

MIKLOWITZ, Gloria D 1927-
AuBYP SUP, ConAu 10NR, IntAu&W 82, SmATA 4, WhoAmW 81, WrDr 86

After The Bomb
BL - v81 - Je 15 '85 - p1448
CBRS - v13 - Ag '85 - p133
CCB-B - v38 - Je '85 - p191
Fant R - v9 - My '86 - p30
PW - v227 - Je 14 '85 - p73
SLJ - v32 - S '85 - p147
VOYA - v8 - Ag '85 - p187
Subject: Atomic bomb—Fiction; Survival—Fiction

Carrie Loves Superman
BL - v80 - O 15 '83 - p361
SLJ - v30 - D '83 - p76
VOYA - v6 - F '84 - p340

Close To The Edge
BL - v79 - Ap 15 '83 - p1089
B Rpt - v2 - N '83 - p34
BS - v43 - Je '83 - p113
CBRS - v11 - Spring '83 - p126
CCB-B - v36 - My '83 - p172
EJ - v73 - Ja '84 - p88
EJ - v73 - D '84 - p65
Kliatt - v19 - Winter '85 - p12
KR - v51 - Mr 15 '83 - p310
PW - v223 - Mr 25 '83 - p51
SLJ - v29 - My '83 - p83
VOYA - v6 - O '83 - p206
WCRB - v9 - My '83 - p56
Subject: Conduct of life—Fiction; Family life—Fiction

The Day The Senior Class Got Married
BL - v80 - O 1 '83 - p234
BS - v43 - F '84 - p431
CBRS - v12 - N '83 - p31
CCB-B - v37 - N '83 - p54
SLJ - v30 - O '83 - p171
VOYA - v6 - D '83 - p279
Subject: Family problems—Fiction; Marriage—Fiction; Schools—Fiction

Did You Hear What Happened To Andrea?
BL - v75 - Jl 1 '79 - p1576
BS - v39 - D '79 - p354
CBRS - v8 - S '79 - p9
CCB-B - v33 - D '79 - p75
EJ - v72 - S '83 - p84
Hi Lo - v1 - Mr '80 - p4
Inter BC - v11 - #5 '80 p16
J Read - v23 - Ap '80 - p662
KR - v47 - S 1 '79 - p1005
PW - v215 - Je 11 '79 - p103
SLJ - v26 - S '79 - p159
WLB - v54 - N '79 - p184
Subject: Rape—Fiction

Dr. Martin Luther King, Jr.
BL - v74 - Je 15 '78 - p1621
Subject: Blacks—Biography; Civil rights

Love Story, Take Three
BL - v82 - Je 15 '86 - p1542
B Rpt - v5 - S '86 - p34
CBRS - v14 - Spring '86 - p136
CCB-B - v39 - Je '86 - p191
SLJ - v32 - My '86 - p106
VOYA - v9 - Je '86 - p81
Subject: Actors and actresses—Fiction; Mothers and daughters—Fiction; Self-assertion—Fiction

Paramedic Emergency!
BL - v74 - O 1 '77 - p283
BL - v74 - O 1 '77 - p299
Cur R - v16 - D '77 - p361
Hi Lo - v2 - Mr '81 - p5
Subject: Allied health personnel—Fiction

Steve Cauthen
BL - v75 - Mr 15 '79 - p1162

MIKLOWITZ, Gloria D (continued)
Hi Lo - v1 - N '79 - p6
SLJ - v26 - O '79 - p152
Subject: Jockeys

The War Between The Classes
BL - v81 - Ap 15 '85 - p1179
BS - v45 - Jl '85 - p153
CBRS - v13 - Je '85 - p121
EJ - v75 - D '86 - p60
HB - v61 - Jl '85 - p455
Inter BC - v17 - #3 '86 p33
J Read - v29 - Ap '86 - p689
New Age - v2 - D '85 - p68
SLJ - v31 - Ag '85 - p79
VOYA - v8 - Je '85 - p133
Subject: Japanese Americans—Fiction; Prejudices—Fiction

MILES, Betty 1928-
AuBYP, ConAu 20NR, FifBJA, SmATA 8, WrDr 86

All It Takes Is Practice
BL - v73 - Ja 1 '77 - p667
BW - Je 10 '79 - pE2
CCB-B - v30 - F '77 - p95
HB - v53 - F '77 - p54
Inter BC - v15 - #6 '84 p14
KR - v44 - O 15 '76 - p1138
RT - v31 - My '78 - p915
SE - v41 - Ap '77 - p350
SLJ - v23 - D '76 - p70
Subject: Friendship—Fiction; Race relations—Fiction

Looking On
BL - v74 - My 1 '78 - p1436
CCB-B - v32 - S '78 - p14
HB - v54 - Je '78 - p278
KR - v46 - My 15 '78 - p552
PW - v213 - My 29 '78 - p52
SLJ - v24 - Mr '78 - p139
TN - v37 - Fall '80 - p61
VOYA - v9 - Ag '86 - p147
Subject: Identity—Fiction

MILGROM, Harry 1912-
AmM&WS 76P, AuBYP SUP, ConAu 3NR, SmATA 25, WhoE 77

ABC Of Ecology
CCB-B - v26 - O '72 - p30
Emerg Lib - v11 - N '83 - p37
KR - v40 - F 15 '72 - p198
LJ - v98 - F 15 '73 - p638
SB - v8 - S '72 - p139
Subject: Pollution

MILLAR, Barbara
see Luis, Earlene W (co-author)

MILLARD, Adele

Cats In Fact And Legend
ACSB - v10 - Spring '77 - p38
Brit Bk N C - Autumn '81 - p3
Obs - F 1 '81 - p29
Subject: Cats; Cats—Fiction

MILLER, Christopher Ransom

Stroke Of Luck
Hi Lo - v3 - Mr '82 - p2
SLJ - v28 - S '81 - p122
Subject: Sports—Fiction

MILLER, Marilyn

The Bridge At Selma
BL - v82 - N 1 '85 - p412
B Rpt - v4 - Ja '86 - p42
CCB-B - v39 - S '85 - p14
SLJ - v32 - D '85 - p92
VOYA - v8 - O '85 - p278
Subject: Blacks—Civil rights; Civil rights; Riots

MILLER, Melba 1909-

The Black Is Beautiful Beauty Book
CCB-B - v28 - Je '75 - p164
KR - v43 - Mr 15 '75 - p319
SLJ - v21 - My '75 - p66
Subject: Beauty (Personal); Health

MILLER, Nancy Gridley

Managing Your Money
CSM - v73 - D 1 '80 - pB11
Subject: Finance (Personal)

MILLER, Sandra Peden
see Miller, Sandy

MILLER, Sandy 1948-
ConAu X, SmATA 41
Pseud./variant:
Miller, Sandra Peden

Chase The Sun
BL - v80 - S 1 '83 - p75
Kliatt - v17 - Fall '83 - p17
SLJ - v30 - N '83 - p95
VOYA - v6 - O '83 - p206
Subject: Pilots and pilotage—Fiction

Smart Girl
SLJ - v29 - Mr '83 - p193
Subject: Girls—Fiction

MILLER, Sandy (continued)

Two Loves For Jenny
BL - v78 - My 15 '82 - p1236
VOYA - v5 - O '82 - p44
Subject: Adolescence—Fiction; Musicians—Fiction

MILLER, W Wesley

Dirt Bike Adventure
BL - v78 - My 15 '82 - p1237
Subject: Deserts—Fiction; Motorcycle racing—Fiction; Snakes—Fiction

MILLS, Claudia 1954-
ConAu 109, IntAu&W 86, SmATA 44

Luisa's American Dream
BL - v77 - Jl 1 '81 - p1392
BS - v41 - Ag '81 - p199
CBRS - v9 - Spring '81 - p108
CCB-B - v34 - Jl '81 - p215
KR - v49 - Ag 1 '81 - p940
SLJ - v28 - S '81 - p139
TN - v38 - Fall '81 - p85
VOYA - v4 - D '81 - p33
Subject: Cuban Americans—Fiction

MILLS, Donia Whiteley

A Long Way Home From Troy
BL - v68 - F 15 '72 - p503
BL - v68 - F 15 '72 - p507
LJ - v97 - F 15 '72 - p786
Subject: Youth—Fiction

MILTON, Hilary 1920-
ConAu 21NR, SmATA 23

Mayday! Mayday!
BL - v75 - Je 15 '79 - p1537
CBRS - v7 - Je '79 - p108
CCB-B - v33 - S '79 - p12
NYTBR - Je 3 '79 - p44
SLJ - v25 - My '79 - p74
Subject: Survival—Fiction

Shutterbugs And Car Thieves
SLJ - v28 - D '81 - p82
Subject: Crime and criminals—Fiction

Tornado!
BL - v79 - Jl '83 - p1403
CCB-B - v37 - O '83 - p34
SLJ - v29 - Mr '83 - p195
Subject: Floods—Fiction; Tornadoes—Fiction

MINAHAN, John 1933-
ConAu 45, WhoAm 86

Jeremy
BW - v7 - D 16 '73 - p6
J Read - v22 - N '78 - p128
Subject: Love—Fiction

MINER, Jane Claypool 1933-
ConAu 106, SmATA 38
Pseud./variant:
Claypool, Jane
Ladd, Veronica

Alcohol And Teens
ASBYP - v18 - Winter '85 - p27
SLJ - v31 - N '84 - p135
VOYA - v7 - F '85 - p348
Subject: Alcohol and youth

Career Prep: Working In A Hospital
B Rpt - v2 - Mr '84 - p45
Hi Lo - v4 - My '83 - p3
SB - v19 - Ja '84 - p153
SLJ - v30 - S '83 - p126
Subject: Vocational guidance

Choices
Hi Lo - v2 - Je '81 - p4

A Day At A Time: Dealing With An Alcoholic
Hi Lo - v4 - Ja '83 - p3
SLJ - v29 - Mr '83 - p195
Subject: Alcohol and youth—Fiction; Family problems—Fiction

Dreams Can Come True
Hi Lo - v3 - Ja '82 - p6
SLJ - v28 - S '81 - p139
VOYA - v4 - Ag '81 - p27
Subject: Weight control—Fiction

A Man's Pride: Losing A Father
Hi Lo - v4 - Ja '83 - p3
SLJ - v29 - Mr '83 - p195
Subject: Single-parent family—Fiction; Work—Fiction

Miracle Of Time: Adopting A Sister
Hi Lo - v4 - Ja '83 - p3
SLJ - v29 - Mr '83 - p195
Subject: Brothers and sisters—Fiction; Family problems—Fiction; Orphans—Fiction

Mountain Fear: When A Brother Dies
Hi Lo - v4 - Ja '83 - p3

MINER, Jane Claypool (continued)
SLJ - v29 - Mr '83 - p195
Subject: Brothers and sisters—Fiction; Death—Fiction; Twins—Fiction

Navajo Victory: Being A Native American
Hi Lo - v4 - Ja '83 - p3
SLJ - v29 - Mr '83 - p195
Subject: Indians of North America—Fiction; Prejudices—Fiction

New Beginning: An Athlete Is Paralyzed
Hi Lo - v4 - Ja '83 - p3
SLJ - v29 - Mr '83 - p195
Subject: Football—Fiction; Physically handicapped—Fiction

No Place To Go
BL - v78 - F 15 '82 - p754
Hi Lo - v3 - F '82 - p3
Subject: Alcohol and youth—Fiction; Schools—Fiction

She's My Sister: Having A Retarded Sister
CLW - v54 - Ap '83 - p383
Hi Lo - v4 - Ja '83 - p3
SLJ - v29 - Mr '83 - p195
Subject: Mentally handicapped—Fiction; Sisters—Fiction

Split Decision: Facing Divorce
Hi Lo - v4 - Ja '83 - p3
SLJ - v29 - Mr '83 - p195
Subject: Divorce—Fiction

This Day Is Mine: Living With Leukemia
Hi Lo - v4 - Ja '83 - p3
SLJ - v29 - Mr '83 - p195
Subject: Hospitals—Fiction; Leukemia—Fiction; Sick—Fiction

The Tough Guy: Black In A White World
CLW - v54 - Ap '83 - p383
Hi Lo - v4 - Ja '83 - p3
SLJ - v29 - Mr '83 - p195
Subject: Race relations—Fiction; Schools—Fiction

see also Claypool, Jane; Ladd, Veronica for additional titles

MINTONYE, Grace
see Seidelman, James E (co-author)

MIZNER, Elizabeth Howard
see Howard, Elizabeth

MOERI, Louise 1924-
BioIn 13, ConAu 9NR, FifBJA, SmATA 24

Save Queen Of Sheba
BL - v77 - My 15 '81 - p1255
CBRS - v9 - Je '81 - p98
CCB-B - v35 - S '81 - p13
CE - v58 - My '82 - p326
HB - v57 - O '81 - p536
Kliatt - v16 - Fall '82 - p14
KR - v49 - S 15 '81 - p1160
LA - v59 - Ja '82 - p56
PW - v219 - My 1 '81 - p67
SLJ - v27 - My '81 - p67
Subject: Survival—Fiction; West (U.S.)—Fiction

MOHN, Peter B 1934-
ConAu 106, SmATA 28

Bicycle Touring
SLJ - v22 - My '76 - p61
Subject: Bicyles and bicyling

The Golden Knights
BL - v74 - D 15 '77 - p684
SLJ - v25 - S '78 - p144
Subject: Parachuting; Skydiving; United States Army

Hot Air Ballooning
SLJ - v22 - My '76 - p61
Subject: Balloon ascensions; Hot air balloons

MOHR, Nicholasa 1935-
AuBYP SUP, BioIn 11, ConAu 1NR, -49, ConLC 12, FifBJA, IntAu&W 77, SmATA 8

El Bronx Remembered
Inter BC - v14 - #1 '83 p15
Subject: Puerto Ricans—Fiction; New York (City)—Fiction

Nilda
BL - v70 - Ja 15 '74 - p544
BL - v70 - F 1 '74 - p593
BW - F 10 '74 - p4
CCB-B - v27 - Mr '74 - p115
Choice - v12 - N '75 - p1133
Comw - v99 - N 23 '73 - p216
EJ - v71 - N '82 - p61
HB - v50 - Ap '74 - p153
Inter BC - v14 - #1 '83 p15
KR - v41 - O 1 '73 - p1097
KR - v41 - D 15 '73 - p1350
LJ - v98 - D 15 '73 - p3690

MOHR, Nicholasa (continued)
LJ - v98 - D 15 '73 - p3713
NW - v83 - Mr 4 '74 - p83
NYTBR - N 4 '73 - p27
NYTBR - N 4 '73 - p52
NYTBR - D 2 '73 - p79
NYTBR - N 10 '74 - p43
PW - v204 - Ag 27 '73 - p280
Teacher - v96 - Ja '79 - p64
Subject: Puerto Ricans—Fiction

MOLLOY, Anne S 1907-
AuBYP, ConAu 13R, SmATA 32

Girl From Two Miles High
BL - v64 - F 1 '68 - p640
CCB-B - v21 - F '68 - p97
KR - v35 - Jl 15 '67 - p808
LJ - v92 - O 15 '67 - p3866
SR - v50 - O 21 '67 - p43
Subject: Maine—Fiction

MONJO, F N 1924-1978
AuBYP SUP, BioIn 11, -12, ChlLR 2, ConAu 81, FifBJA, OxChL, SmATA 16, TwCChW 83, WrDr 80

Grand Papa And Ellen Aroon
BB - v3 - Ap '75 - p2
CCB-B - v28 - My '75 - p151
KR - v43 - Ja 1 '75 - p23
NY - v50 - D 2 '74 - p198
PW - v206 - O 21 '74 - p51
Teacher - v94 - O '76 - p146
Subject: Jefferson, Thomas—Fiction

MONTGOMERY, Elizabeth Rider 1902-1985
AuBYP, BioIn 3, ConAu 3NR, -X, CurBio 52, IntAu&W 82, SmATA 34, -41N, WhoAmW 81
Pseud./variant:
Julesberg, Elizabeth Rider Montgomery

Duke Ellington
CCB-B - v25 - Jl '72 - p174
JLD - v11 - Ap '78 - p44
LJ - v97 - S 15 '72 - p2952
Subject: Biography; Musicians

Walt Disney
BL - v68 - Ap 1 '72 - p676
JLD - v11 - Ap '78 - p44
LJ - v97 - Jl '72 - p2485
Subject: Biography; Motion pictures

Will Rogers: Cowboy Philosopher
JLD - v11 - Ap '78 - p44
Subject: Biography

MONTGOMERY, Herb

On The Run
WLB - v51 - F '77 - p491
Co-author: Montgomery, Mary

MONTGOMERY, Mary
see Montgomery, Herb (co-author)

MONTGOMERY, Raymond A
SmATA 39

Abominable Snowman
SLJ - v29 - F '83 - p80
VOYA - v5 - Ag '82 - p34

Space And Beyond
BW - v10 - Ja 20 '80 - p13
Hi Lo - v3 - Mr '82 - p4
SLJ - v26 - My '80 - p71

MONTGOMERY, Robert

Rabbit Ears
BL - v81 - Ag '85 - p1657
Kliatt - v19 - Fall '85 - p14
VOYA - v8 - D '85 - p321
Subject: Baseball—Fiction

MONTGOMERY, Rutherford George 1894-
AuBYP, ConAu 9R, MorJA, OxChL, SmATA 3, TwCChW 83, WhoAm 78, WrDr 86

Kildee House
Atl - v184 - D '49 - p103
BL - v46 - O 15 '49 - p70
CSM - N 17 '49 - p10
KR - v17 - S 1 '49 - p470
LJ - v74 - O 15 '49 - p1540
LJ - v74 - N 15 '49 - p1761
NYT - N 13 '49 - p28
Subject: Animals—Fiction

MOON, Sheila 1910-
AuBYP SUP, ConAu 25R, SmATA 5

Knee-Deep In Thunder
BL - v64 - D 15 '67 - p503
BW - v1 - O 1 '67 - p24
CCB-B - v21 - F '68 - p98
CLW - v39 - D '67 - p293
HB - v43 - O '67 - p589
KR - v35 - Ag 15 '67 - p968
LJ - v92 - O 15 '67 - p3853
NYTBR - v72 - O 22 '67 - p62

MOON, Sheila (continued)
TN - v24 - Ap '68 - p324

MOONEY, Thomas J

One Cool Sister And Other Modern Stories
Hi Lo - v1 - Ap '80 - p4
Subject: Girls—Fiction; Short stories

MOORE, Emily

Just My Luck
BL - v79 - Mr 1 '83 - p908
CBRS - v11 - Mr '83 - p83
CCB-B - v36 - Mr '83 - p130
CLW - v56 - O '84 - p141
HB - v59 - F '83 - p47
Inter BC - v15 - #4 '84 p16
KR - v50 - N 15 '82 - p1235
SLJ - v29 - Ja '83 - p77
Subject: Friendship—Fiction

Something To Count On
BL - v76 - Jl 1 '80 - p1609
BS - v40 - O '80 - p264
CBRS - v8 - Ap '80 - p89
CCB-B - v33 - Jl '80 - p220
HB - v56 - Je '80 - p301
Inter BC - v13 - #1 '82 p17
KR - v48 - Jl 1 '80 - p837
LA - v58 - F '81 - p186
PW - v217 - Ap 11 '80 - p77
RT - v34 - Mr '81 - p735
SLJ - v27 - O '80 - p149
Subject: Divorce—Fiction; Schools—Fiction

MOORE, Patrick 1923-
AuBYP, ConAu 8NR, DcLEL 1940, FourBJA, IntAu&W 82, ScFSB, SmATA 49, TwCSFW 86, WhoSciF, WrDr 86

Seeing Stars
BL - v68 - Ap 1 '72 - p676
KR - v39 - N 1 '71 - p1161
LJ - v97 - My 15 '72 - p1915
Subject: Astronomy; Stars

MOOSER, Stephen 1941-
BioIn 13, ConAu 15NR, SmATA 28

Into The Unknown
BL - v76 - Jl 1 '80 - p1609
BS - v40 - S '80 - p210
RT - v35 - O '81 - p69
SLJ - v26 - Mr '80 - p135
Subject: Curiosities and wonders

MORAN, Lyn

The Young Gymnasts
SLJ - v25 - My '79 - p88
Subject: Gymnasts

MORAY, Ann

The Rising Of The Lark
Am - v110 - Mr 28 '64 - p452
Crit - v22 - Je '64 - p74
HB - v40 - Je '64 - p306
LJ - v89 - F 1 '64 - p656
NYTBR - F 2 '64 - p34
SR - v47 - Mr 14 '64 - p30

MOREY, Walter Nelson 1907-
AuBYP, ConAu 29R, OxChL, SmATA 3, ThrBJA, TwCChW 83, WhoAm 82, WrDr 84

Canyon Winter
BL - v69 - F 1 '73 - p530
KR - v40 - N 1 '72 - p1246
LJ - v98 - Ja 15 '73 - p262
Obs - Ag 4 '74 - p28
RT - v34 - Ap '81 - p795
TLS - S 20 '74 - p1010
Subject: Rocky Mountains—Fiction

Gentle Ben
BFYC - v20 - Spring '85 - p4
Brit Bk N C - Je '86 - p37
Obs - D 6 '70 - p27
Subject: Alaska—Fiction; Bears—Fiction

The Lemon Meringue Dog
HB - v56 - Ag '80 - p410
RT - v35 - O '81 - p69
SLJ - v27 - D '80 - p74
Subject: Crime and criminals—Fiction; Police dogs—Fiction

Sandy And The Rock Star
BL - v75 - Jl 1 '79 - p1581
CLW - v51 - D '79 - p234
HB - v55 - Ag '79 - p416
J Read - v23 - F '80 - p472
KR - v47 - Jl 1 '79 - p745
LA - v57 - My '80 - p557
NYTBR - Je 3 '79 - p44
PW - v215 - Mr 19 '79 - p94
RT - v34 - O '80 - p51
SLJ - v26 - S '79 - p145
SLJ - v31 - S '84 - p48
Subject: Hunting—Fiction; Islands—Fiction

Scrub Dog Of Alaska
BL - v68 - Ja 1 '72 - p394

MOREY, Walter Nelson (continued)
CCB-B - v25 - My '72 - p143
GP - v13 - Ap '75 - p2601
HB - v48 - F '72 - p50
JB - v39 - Ap '75 - p125
KR - v39 - O 15 '71 - p1132
LJ - v96 - N 15 '71 - p3902
PW - v200 - Ag 16 '71 - p57

Year Of The Black Pony
BB - v4 - N '76 - p2
BL - v72 - Jl 1 '76 - p1528
BW - Ap 11 '76 - p4
CCB-B - v29 - Jl '76 - p179
CLW - v48 - O '76 - p138
HB - v52 - Ag '76 - p399
JB - v42 - Je '78 - p158
KR - v44 - Mr 1 '76 - p257
LA - v54 - Ja '77 - p83
SLJ - v22 - Ap '76 - p77
Subject: Family life—Fiction; Frontier and pioneer life—Fiction; Horses—Fiction

MORGAN, Barbara Ellen 1944-
WhoMW 78

Journey For Tobiyah
CCB-B - v20 - N '66 - p46
CE - v43 - My '67 - p537
HB - v42 - D '66 - p720
Inst - v76 - N '66 - p51
KR - v34 - S 1 '66 - p909
LJ - v91 - D 15 '66 - p6195

MORGAN, Joe 1943-
BioIn 10, -11, WhoAm 86, WhoBlA 85, WhoProB 73

Baseball My Way
BL - v73 - N 15 '76 - p468
BL - v73 - N 15 '76 - p476
CLW - v48 - Mr '77 - p358
SLJ - v23 - D '76 - p70
Subject: Baseball

MORIN, Relman 1907-1973
ConAu 4NR, CurBio 58, EncTwCJ, NewYTBE 73, WhAm 6

Dwight D. Eisenhower: A Gauge Of Greatness
BL - v66 - N 15 '69 - p381
Choice - v6 - O '69 - p1106
LJ - v94 - S 15 '69 - p3045
Subject: Biography

MORRIS, Jeannie

Brian Piccolo: A Short Season
BL - v68 - Ap 1 '72 - p644
BW - v6 - Jl 16 '72 - p10
KR - v39 - S 1 '71 - p990
LJ - v96 - O 15 '71 - p3342
NYTBR - N 21 '71 - p34
NYTBR - D 5 '71 - p44
PW - v201 - My 29 '72 - p34
SR - v54 - D 11 '71 - p46
WLB - v46 - Ap '72 - p704
Subject: Football—Biography

MORRIS, Rosamund
ScF&FL 1

Masterpieces Of Horror
Kliatt - v17 - Fall '83 - p30
NYTBR - v71 - Jl 24 '66 - p29
Subject: Horror stories

Masterpieces Of Mystery And Detection
NYTBR - v71 - Jl 24 '66 - p29
Subject: Mystery and detective stories

Masterpieces Of Suspense
Kliatt - v17 - Fall '83 - p30
NYTBR - v71 - Jl 24 '66 - p29
Subject: Mystery and detective stories

MORRIS, Terry 1914-
ConAu 9R, WhoAmW 77, WhoE 77

Shalom, Golda
BL - v68 - F 15 '72 - p503
BS - v31 - O 15 '71 - p335
KR - v39 - Jl 1 '71 - p723
LJ - v97 - Jl '72 - p2490
PW - v200 - N 15 '71 - p73
SE - v39 - Mr '75 - p145
Subject: Biography

MORRIS, Winifred

The Jell-O Syndrome
BL - v82 - Ap 15 '86 - p1203
PW - v229 - My 30 '86 - p70
SLJ - v32 - Ap '86 - p99
Trib Bks - D 28 '86 - p2
VOYA - v9 - Ag '86 - p147
Subject: Girls—Fiction

MORRIS, Wright 1910-
ConAu 9R, -21NR, ConLC 7, ConNov 86, DcLB Y81B, WhoTwCL, WrDr 86

In Orbit
Atl - v219 - Ap '67 - p144
BS - v26 - F 15 '67 - p409
BW - v2 - Je 23 '68 - p13

MORRIS, Wright (continued)
Comw - v86 - Ap 7 '67 - p98
HM - v234 - Mr '67 - p139
KR - v34 - D 15 '66 - p1298
LJ - v92 - F 1 '67 - p196
NO - v6 - Mr 20 '67 - p21
NYRB - v8 - My 4 '67 - p35
NYT - v116 - F 23 '67 - p37M
NYTBR - v72 - F 5 '67 - p44
PR - v35 - Winter '68 - p141
PW - v190 - D 12 '67 - p48
PW - v193 - My 13 '68 - p61
SR - v50 - F 18 '67 - p29
SR - v50 - D 30 '67 - p19
Time - v89 - F 17 '67 - p104

MORRISON, Lillian 1917-
BioIn 9, BkP, ConAu 7NR,
SmATA 3, WhoLibI 82

Best Wishes, Amen
BL - v71 - F 1 '75 - p572
CCB-B - v28 - Ap '75 - p135
CE - v61 - My '85 - p364
HB - v51 - F '75 - p63
KR - v42 - D 1 '74 - p1257
NY - v51 - D 1 '75 - p185
PW - v206 - N 11 '74 - p49
SLJ - v21 - Mr '75 - p100
Teacher - v92 - Ap '75 - p32
Subject: Autographs; Poetry

The Sidewalk Racer And Other Poems Of Sports And Motion
BW - N 13 '77 - pE4
CCB-B - v31 - D '77 - p64
CE - v54 - N '77 - p90
EJ - v67 - F '78 - p99
HB - v53 - O '77 - p548
KR - v45 - Je 1 '77 - p584
LA - v54 - N '77 - p951
NYTBR - N 13 '77 - p47
PW - v211 - My 23 '77 - p246
RT - v36 - Ja '83 - p381
SLJ - v24 - S '77 - p133
Subject: American poetry; Poetry

Sprints And Distances: Sports In Poetry
BL - v62 - Ja 15 '66 - p482
CCB-B - v20 - S '66 - p15
CE - v42 - My '66 - p564
HB - v41 - D '65 - p641
KR - v33 - S 1 '65 - p916
LJ - v90 - O 15 '65 - p4636
NYTBR - v70 - N 7 '65 - p6
Poet - v108 - Ag '66 - p343
SR - v48 - N 13 '65 - p62
Subject: Poetry

Touch Blue
NYTBR - Jl 6 '58 - p13
Subject: Folklore

MORRISON, Susan Dudley
ConAu 119

Balls
BL - v80 - F 1 '84 - p810
SLJ - v30 - Mr '84 - p161
Subject: Balls (Sporting goods)

Shoes For Sport
BL - v80 - F 1 '84 - p810
SLJ - v30 - Mr '84 - p161
Subject: Shoes

MORSE, Anne Christensen
see Head, Ann; Morse, Charles (co-author)

MORSE, Charles

Jackson Five
RT - v29 - Ja '76 - p415
SLJ - v22 - S '75 - p95
Co-author: Morse, Ann Christensen
Subject: Blacks—Biography; Musicians

Roberta Flack
CCB-B - v28 - Jl '75 - p181
SLJ - v22 - S '75 - p95
Co-author: Morse, Ann Christensen
Subject: Blacks—Biography; Singers

MORSE, Evangeline 1914-

Brown Rabbit: Her Story
BW - v1 - O 8 '67 - p24
CCB-B - v21 - O '67 - p30
HB - v43 - D '67 - p754
KR - v35 - Mr 15 '67 - p342
LJ - v93 - Ja 15 '68 - p293
NYTBR - v72 - Ag 13 '67 - p26

MORTON, Jane

Running Scared
CLW - v51 - N '79 - p183
J Read - v23 - F '80 - p472
SLJ - v25 - My '79 - p65
Subject: Juvenile delinquency—Fiction; Social adjustment—Fiction

MOSKIN, Marietta D 1928-
ConAu 13NR, SmATA 23

A Paper Dragon
KR - v36 - Ja 1 '68 - p13

MOSKIN, Marietta D (continued)
LJ - v93 - My 15 '68 - p2124

MOTT, Michael 1930-
ConAu 7NR, ConLC 15, DcLEL 1940, IntAu&W 86

Master Entrick: An Adventure, 1754-1756
Am - v115 - N 5 '66 - p553
BS - v26 - D 1 '66 - p340
HB - v43 - F '67 - p73
KR - v34 - S 1 '66 - p906
LJ - v91 - N 15 '66 - p5762
TLS - D 9 '65 - p1147

MOWAT, Farley 1921-
AuBYP, ConAu 4NR, ConLC 26, CurBio 86, OxChL, Profile 2, SmATA 3, ThrBJA, TwCChW 83, WrDr 86

The Curse Of The Viking Grave
CCB-B - v20 - D '66 - p61
CLW - v39 - O '67 - p157
KR - v34 - Jl 1 '66 - p635
LJ - v92 - Ja 15 '67 - p346
SLJ - v27 - S '80 - p43
SR - v49 - N 12 '66 - p53

MOYES, Patricia 1923-
ConAu X, EncMys, Novels, TwCCr&M 85, WrDr 86
Pseud./variant:
Haszard, Patricia Moyes

Helter-Skelter
BL - v64 - My 1 '68 - p1031
BS - v28 - Ap 1 '68 - p18
CSM - v60 - My 2 '68 - pB9
KR - v36 - F 15 '68 - p191
LJ - v93 - Ap 15 '68 - p1813
NYTBR - v73 - Ap 7 '68 - p26
SE - v33 - My '69 - p558
SLJ - v24 - F '78 - p35
SR - v51 - Jl 20 '68 - p31
TLS - Ap 3 '69 - p354

MUESER, Annie

Cobra In The Tub: And Eight More Stories Of Mystery And Suspense
BL - v77 - Mr 15 '81 - p1025
Co-author: Otfinoski, Steve
Subject: Mystery and detective stories

see also Otfinoski, Steve for additional titles

MUESNER, Anne Marie

The Picture Story Of Steve Cauthen
Hi Lo - v2 - N '80 - p4
Subject: Biography; Jockeys

MULLIGAN, Kevin

Kid Brother
BL - v78 - My 1 '82 - p1153
CBRS - v10 - Je '82 - p109
CCB-B - v35 - Je '82 - p193
KR - v50 - Ap 1 '82 - p423
SLJ - v28 - Ag '82 - p128
Subject: Brothers and sisters—Fiction

MULLIN, Penn

Earthquake!
SLJ - v31 - Mr '85 - p173

Search And Rescue
BL - v78 - Ag '82 - p1520
Subject: Fear—Fiction; Lost children—Fiction; Rescue work—Fiction

Terror At Sundown
SLJ - v31 - Mr '85 - p173

MUNN, Vella

Rodeo Riders
Hi Lo - v3 - Je '82 - p5
Subject: Cowboys; Rodeos

MUNSHOWER, Suzanne 1945-
ConAu 97

John Travolta
Kliatt - v12 - Fall '78 - p30
SLJ - v26 - S '79 - p129
Subject: Actors and actresses; Biography

MUNSTERHJELM, Erik 1905-
ConAu 49

A Dog Named Wolf
Teacher - v91 - F '74 - p97
Subject: Dogs—Fiction

MURPHY, Barbara Beasley 1933-
BioIn 10, ConAu 20NR, DrAP&F 85, SmATA 5

Ace Hits Rock Bottom
BL - v82 - S 1 '85 - p53
CCB-B - v39 - Ja '86 - p93
SLJ - v32 - N '85 - p100
VOYA - v8 - D '85 - p321

MURPHY, Barbara Beasley (continued)
Co-author: Wolkoff, Judie
Subject: Actors and actresses—Fiction; Arson—Fiction; Gangs—Fiction

Ace Hits The Big Time
BL - v78 - D 1 '81 - p491
BS - v41 - F '82 - p442
CBRS - v10 - Ja '82 - p49
CCB-B - v35 - D '81 - p74
HB - v58 - F '82 - p53
J Read - v25 - My '82 - p813
Kliatt - v17 - Spring '83 - p4
KR - v50 - F 15 '82 - p209
SLJ - v28 - D '81 - p72
VOYA - v4 - F '82 - p36
Co-author: Wolkoff, Judie
Subject: Gangs—Fiction; New York (City)—Fiction

Home Free
KR - v38 - F 1 '70 - p104
LJ - v95 - Je 15 '70 - p2309
SR - v53 - Ap 18 '70 - p37
Subject: Race relations—Fiction

No Place To Run
B&B - v6 - Je '78 - p3
BL - v74 - D 15 '77 - p157
BL - v74 - D 15 '77 - p197
CCB-B - v31 - D '77 - p64
EJ - v67 - F '78 - p79
HB - v53 - D '77 - p669
KR - v45 - Je 15 '77 - p628
PW - v212 - S 5 '77 - p73
SLJ - v24 - N '77 - p74
Subject: City and town life—Fiction; Crime and criminals—Fiction

MURPHY, Jim 1947-
ConAu 111, SmATA 37

Death Run
BL - v78 - My 1 '82 - p1153
BS - v42 - Ag '82 - p205
CBRS - v10 - Spring '82 - p118
HB - v58 - Ag '82 - p415
J Read - v26 - Ja '83 - p375
KR - v50 - Ap 15 '82 - p496
PW - v221 - Je 18 '82 - p75
SLJ - v28 - My '82 - p85
VOYA - v5 - O '82 - p45
Subject: Death—Fiction; Mystery and detective stories; Police—Fiction

MURPHY, Shirley Rousseau 1928-
ConAu 13NR, SmATA 36, WhoAmW 79, WrDr 86

Caves Of Fire And Ice
BL - v77 - D 15 '80 - p575
CLW - v52 - My '81 - p453
SLJ - v27 - Mr '81 - p158
Subject: Fantasy

The Sand Ponies
CCB-B - v21 - Ja '68 - p80
KR - v35 - S 1 '67 - p1049
LJ - v92 - D 15 '67 - p4615

MURRAY, Michele 1933-1974
AuBYP SUP, BioIn 10, -13, ConAu 49, NewYTBS 74, ObitOF 79, SmATA 7

The Crystal Nights
BL - v69 - Je 1 '73 - p944
BS - v33 - Je 15 '73 - p146
BW - v7 - My 13 '73 - p3
BW - v7 - N 11 '73 - p3C
BW - My 4 '75 - p4
CCB-B - v27 - S '73 - p15
CE - v50 - Ja '74 - p166
Comw - v99 - N 23 '73 - p216
EJ - v69 - O '80 - p17
KR - v41 - Ap 1 '73 - p397
KR - v41 - D 15 '73 - p1356
LJ - v98 - My 15 '73 - p1655
LJ - v98 - My 15 '73 - p1691
LJ - v98 - D 15 '73 - p3691
NO - v12 - D 29 '73 - p15
NYTBR - S 16 '73 - p8
PW - v203 - My 7 '73 - p65
TN - v30 - Je '74 - p434

MUSICK, Phil

The Tony Dorsett Story
BL - v74 - Ap 1 '78 - p1264
EJ - v67 - Ap '78 - p91
KR - v46 - Ja 1 '78 - p39
LJ - v103 - Ap 1 '78 - p771
SLJ - v24 - My '78 - p87
Subject: Football—Biography

MYERS, Walter Dean 1937-
AuBYP SUP, BlkAWP, ChlLR 4, ConAu 20NR, ConLC 35, DcLB 33, FifBJA, SelBAAf, SmATA 41, -2AS

Adventure In Granada
BL - v82 - Ap 15 '86 - p1226
PW - v228 - N 15 '85 - p57

MYERS, Walter Dean (continued)
SLJ - v32 - Ap '86 - p91
Subject: Adventure and adventurers—Fiction; Mystery and detective stories; Spain—Fiction

Brainstorm
CCB-B - v31 - Ap '78 - p132
Hi Lo - v1 - N '79 - p4
JB - v43 - F '79 - p58
SLJ - v24 - N '77 - p60
Subject: Science fiction

The Hidden Shrine
BL - v82 - Ap 15 '86 - p1226
SLJ - v32 - F '86 - p98
Subject: Adventure and adventurers—Fiction; Hong Kong—Fiction; Mystery and detective stories

Hoops
BL - v78 - S 15 '81 - p98
BS - v41 - F '82 - p442
CBRS - v10 - N '81 - p29
CCB-B - v35 - D '81 - p74
CLW - v53 - My '82 - p449
J Read - v25 - My '82 - p813
Kliatt - v17 - Fall '83 - p17
SLJ - v28 - D '81 - p86
VOYA - v5 - Ap '82 - p36
Subject: Basketball—Fiction

The Legend Of Tarik
BL - v77 - Jl 15 '81 - p1449
CBRS - v10 - S '81 - p8
CCB-B - v35 - N '81 - p52
HB - v57 - Ag '81 - p434
Kliatt - v17 - Spring '83 - p16
NYTBR - v86 - Jl 12 '81 - p30
SLJ - v27 - My '81 - p76
VOYA - v4 - O '81 - p36
Subject: Adventure and adventurers—Fiction

Motown And Didi
BL - v81 - O 1 '84 - p211
CBRS - v13 - O '84 - p20
CCB-B - v38 - Ja '85 - p90
HB - v61 - Mr '85 - p186
Inter BC - v16 - #8 '85 p19
J Read - v28 - Ap '85 - p651
PW - v226 - O 26 '84 - p105
SLJ - v31 - Mr '85 - p180
VOYA - v7 - F '85 - p329
Subject: Blacks—Fiction; New York (City)—Fiction

The Outside Shot
BL - v81 - O 15 '84 - p300
BS - v44 - F '85 - p439
CBRS - v13 - D '84 - p43
CCB-B - v38 - Ja '85 - p91
EJ - v74 - Ja '85 - p95
SLJ - v31 - N '84 - p135
VOYA - v7 - F '85 - p329
Subject: Basketball—Fiction; Blacks—Fiction; Universities and colleges—Fiction

Tales Of A Dead King
BL - v80 - Ja 1 '84 - p683
B Rpt - v3 - My '84 - p34
CBRS - v12 - F '84 - p75
CCB-B - v37 - Ja '84 - p93
KR - v51 - N 1 '83 - pJ205
PW - v224 - D 2 '83 - p86
SLJ - v30 - D '83 - p83
Subject: Archaeology—Fiction; Egypt—Fiction; Mystery and detective stories

Won't Know Till I Get There
BL - v78 - Je 1 '82 - p1315
CBRS - v10 - Spring '82 - p118
CCB-B - v35 - Je '82 - p193
HB - v58 - Ag '82 - p415
KR - v50 - My 1 '82 - p558
NYTBR - v87 - Je 13 '82 - p26
PW - v221 - Je 4 '82 - p67
RT - v36 - N '82 - p242
SLJ - v28 - My '82 - p72
VOYA - v5 - D '82 - p34
Subject: Foster home care—Fiction; Old age—Fiction

The Young Landlords
BL - v76 - D 1 '79 - p560
Bl S - v12 - Mr '81 - p85
CBRS - v8 - Ja '80 - p48
CCB-B - v33 - N '79 - p52
EJ - v69 - My '80 - p91
Inter BC - v12 - #1 '81 p15
KR - v48 - Ja 15 '80 - p70
NYTBR - Ja 6 '80 - p20
NYTBR - v85 - N 9 '80 - p41
Subject: Landlord and tenant—Fiction; New York (City)—Fiction

MYRUS, Donald 1927-
AuBYP, ConAu 4NR, SmATA 23

Ballads, Blues, And The Big Beat
BS - v26 - D 1 '66 - p341
CCB-B - v20 - D '66 - p61
CLW - v38 - Mr '67 - p484
Comw - v85 - N 11 '66 - p181
CSM - v58 - N 3 '66 - pB8
HB - v42 - D '66 - p725

MYRUS, Donald (continued)
KR - v34 - S 15 '66 - p990
NYTBR - v71 - N 6 '66 - p28
Subject: Folk music; Music

N

NADEN, C J

High Gear
BL - v76 - Jl 1 '80 - p1612
Hi Lo - v2 - D '80 - p5
SLJ - v26 - Ap '80 - p108
Subject: Motorcycles

Rough Rider
BL - v76 - Jl 1 '80 - p1612
Hi Lo - v2 - D '80 - p5
SLJ - v26 - Ap '80 - p108
Subject: Motorcycle racing

NAGEL, Shirley 1922-
ConAu 93

Escape From The Tower Of London
Hi Lo - v1 - F '80 - p4
Teacher - v96 - My '79 - p127
Subject: England—Fiction; London—Fiction

Tree Boy
BW - v0 - Ag 13 '78 - p00E4
BW - v0 - D 3 '78 - p00E4
KR - v46 - Ag 1 '78 - p810
PW - v214 - Jl 31 '78 - p99
SB - v15 - S '79 - p106
SE - v43 - Ap '79 - p299
SLJ - v25 - D '78 - p55
Subject: Forests; Trees

NAMIOKA, Lensey 1929-
ConAu 11NR, SmATA 27

The Samurai And The Long-Nosed Devils
BL - v73 - N 15 '76 - p468
BL - v73 - N 15 '76 - p476
CCB-B - v30 - Ja '77 - p78
Kliatt - v13 - Spring '79 - p12
KR - v44 - Ag 1 '76 - p848
Subject: Japan—Fiction; Samurai—Fiction

NANCE, John

Lobo Of The Tasaday
BL - v78 - Jl '82 - p1447
BL - v81 - Jl '85 - p1567
BW - v12 - Ag 8 '82 - p6
CCB-B - v35 - Je '82 - p193
HB - v58 - Ag '82 - p424
Inst - v92 - S '82 - p20
KR - v50 - Ap 15 '82 - p493
SE - v47 - Ap '83 - p244
SLJ - v29 - S '82 - p124
Subject: Man (Primitive); Philippines—Native races

NATHAN, Dorothy d. 1966
BioIn 7, ConAu 81, SmATA 15

The Shy One
CCB-B - v21 - S '67 - p14
KR - v34 - S 15 '66 - p979
LJ - v91 - O 15 '66 - p5234
NYTBR - v72 - Ja 22 '67 - p26
PW - v190 - O 17 '66 - p63

NAYLOR, Phyllis Reynolds 1933-
AuBYP SUP, BioIn 11, ConAu 21R, DrAP&F 85, FifBJA, IntAu&W 82, SmATA 12, WhoAmW 87, WrDr 86

The Keeper
BL - v82 - Ap 1 '86 - p1144
BS - v46 - Jl '86 - p159
BW - v16 - Mr 9 '86 - p10
CCB-B - v39 - My '86 - p175
HB - v62 - S '86 - p598
KR - v54 - Mr 1 '86 - p392
SLJ - v32 - My '86 - p107
Subject: Fathers—Fiction; Mentally ill—Fiction

No Easy Circle
BS - v33 - S 1 '73 - p257
LJ - v97 - S 15 '72 - p2965
NYTBR - S 3 '72 - p8

NEAL, Harry Edward 1906-
AuBYP, ConAu 2NR, IntAu&W 86, SmATA 5, WhoAm 86, WrDr 86

Communication: From Stone Age To Space Age
CCB-B - v27 - Jl '74 - p182
LJ - v99 - Ap 15 '74 - p1231
SB - v10 - D '74 - p206
Subject: Communication

NEAL, Harry Edward (continued)

The Mystery Of Time
BL - v63 - S 1 '66 - p57
KR - v34 - F 15 '66 - p192
LJ - v91 - My 15 '66 - p2711
NYTBR - v71 - Ag 21 '66 - p20
SB - v2 - S '66 - p104
Subject: Clocks and watches; Time

NEFF, Fred

Running Is For Me
BL - v76 - Jl 1 '80 - p1613
JB - v46 - F '82 - p28
SLJ - v27 - D '80 - p77
Subject: Running

NEIGOFF, Mike 1920-
ConAu 2NR, SmATA 13

Runner-Up
BL - v72 - S 15 '75 - p171
SLJ - v22 - D '75 - p70
Subject: Track and field—Fiction

Ski Run
LJ - v98 - My 15 '73 - p1706
Subject: Skis and skiing—Fiction

NEIMARK, Paul
see Owens, Jesse (co-author)

NELSON, Cordner 1918-
ConAu 29R, IntAu&W 86, SmATA 29, WhoWest 82, WrDr 86

The Miler
BS - v29 - D 1 '69 - p354
KR - v37 - S 15 '69 - p1009
LJ - v94 - D 15 '69 - p4621
Subject: Track and field—Fiction

NELSON, Marg 1899-
AuBYP, ConAu 1R

Mystery At Land's End
BL - v57 - Jl 15 '61 - p704
KR - v29 - Ja 15 '61 - p61
LJ - v86 - Ap 15 '61 - p1697
SR - v44 - Je 24 '61 - p20
Subject: Mystery and detective stories

NELSON, O Terry

Girl Who Owned A City
CCB-B - v29 - Ja '76 - p83
Kliatt - v12 - Winter '78 - p10
KR - v43 - Je 1 '75 - p605
SLJ - v22 - D '75 - p54
Subject: Science fiction; Survival—Fiction

NENTL, Jerolyn Ann

The Beaver
SLJ - v30 - O '83 - p160
Subject: Beavers

Big Rigs
BL - v80 - F 1 '84 - p811
SLJ - v30 - Mr '84 - p161
Subject: Tractor trailers

Draft Horses
BL - v80 - Ja 1 '84 - p678
SLJ - v30 - F '84 - p66
Subject: Horses

Pleasure Horses
BL - v80 - Ja 1 '84 - p678
SLJ - v30 - F '84 - p66
Subject: Horses

see also East, Ben (author of adapted works) for additional titles

NESS, Evaline 1911-
ChILR 6, ConAu 5NR, -120, IlsCB 1967, OxChL, SmATA 26, -49N, -1AS, TwCChW 83, WrDr 86

Amelia Mixed The Mustard And Other Poems
Am - v133 - D 6 '75 - p406
BL - v71 - My 15 '75 - p966
CCB-B - v28 - Jl '75 - p182
CLW - v47 - My '76 - p452
Cur R - v16 - F '77 - p47
HB - v51 - Ag '75 - p394
KR - v43 - Ap 1 '75 - p368
NYTBR - My 4 '75 - p24
PW - v207 - Ap 28 '75 - p44
SLJ - v21 - My '75 - p49
SR - v2 - My 31 '75 - p36
Teacher - v93 - F '76 - p29
Teacher - v94 - N '76 - p137
Subject: Poetry

NESTOR, William P 1947-
SmATA 49

Into Winter: Discovering A Season
BL - v82 - F 15 '86 - p876
Subject: Winter

NEUFELD, John 1938-
AuBYP, ConAu 11NR, ConLC 17, SmATA 6, -3AS

Edgar Allan
BL - v65 - F 1 '69 - p594
BL - v65 - Ap 1 '69 - p901
BS - v28 - Ja 1 '69 - p423
CCB-B - v22 - My '69 - p147
EJ - v58 - My '69 - p778
HB - v45 - Ap '69 - p172
KR - v36 - N 1 '68 - p1226
NYTBR - v73 - N 3 '68 - p33
NYTBR, Pt. 2 - F 13 '72 - p12
RT - v31 - My '78 - p915
SE - v33 - My '69 - p558
SR - v52 - Ja 18 '69 - p41
Teacher - v86 - Ap '69 - p184
TN - v38 - Winter '82 - p154
Subject: Adoption—Fiction

Lisa, Bright And Dark
BS - v29 - Ja 1 '70 - p389
CCB-B - v23 - F '70 - p103
KR - v37 - O 15 '69 - p1124
LJ - v95 - F 15 '70 - p790
NYTBR - N 16 '69 - p52
NYTBR, Pt. 2 - N 9 '69 - p60
SMQ - v8 - Fall '79 - p27
Subject: Mental illness—Fiction

Sunday Father
J Read - v25 - My '82 - p778
NYTBR - Ja 30 '77 - p24
PW - v210 - N 22 '76 - p50
WLB - v51 - Ap '77 - p674
Subject: Divorce—Fiction

Touching
EJ - v59 - D '70 - p1303
KR - v38 - O 15 '70 - p1163
LJ - v95 - N 15 '70 - p4057
NYTBR - N 29 '70 - p38

NEVILLE, Emily Cheney 1919-
AmWomWr, ConAu 3NR, ConLC 12, MorBMP, OxChL, SmATA 1, -2AS, ThrBJA, TwCChW 83, WrDr 86

It's Like This, Cat
CSM - My 9 '63 - p3B
LJ - v88 - Jl '63 - p2782
LJ - v96 - Ja 15 '71 - p283
NYTBR, Pt. 2 - My 12 '63 - p2
SR - v46 - Jl 20 '63 - p34
TCR - v68 - O '66 - p90
TCR - v68 - F '67 - p450
TLS - Ap 16 '70 - p416

NEWBY, P H 1918-
BioIn 3, -4, -10, ConAu 5R, ConLC 13, ConNov 86, CurBio 53, DcLB 15, ModBrL S2, WrDr 86

The Spirit Of Jem
CSM - v59 - Ag 3 '67 - p11
KR - v35 - My 1 '67 - p566
Lis - v78 - N 16 '67 - p643
LJ - v92 - D 15 '67 - p4625
NYTBR - v72 - S 10 '67 - p38
NYTBR - v72 - N 5 '67 - p64
Obs - D 3 '67 - p26
SR - v50 - N 11 '67 - p50
TLS - N 30 '67 - p1145
TLS - D 4 '69 - p1384
Subject: Adventure and adventurers—Fiction

NEWELL, Hope 1896-1965
AuBYP, BioIn 13, ConAu 73, MorJA, SmATA 24

A Cap For Mary Ellis
CE - v46 - Ap '70 - p368
NYTBR - Ja 24 '54 - p22
Subject: Nursing—Fiction

NEWLON, Clarke 1905?-1982
AuBYP SUP, ConAu 10NR, SmATA 6, -33N

Famous Mexican-Americans
BL - v69 - S 1 '72 - p42
BS - v32 - My 15 '72 - p98
CCB-B - v25 - Je '72 - p160
KR - v40 - Ja 1 '72 - p13
LJ - v98 - F 15 '73 - p656
SE - v37 - D '73 - p789
SR - v55 - My 20 '72 - p82
Subject: Mexican Americans

NEWMAN, Marvin

Africa's Animals
NYTBR - v72 - D 3 '67 - p12
SB - v3 - D '67 - p235
Co-author: Elisofon, Eliot
Subject: Zoology

NEWMAN, Matthew

Dwight Gooden
CCB-B - v40 - F '87 - p115
Subject: Baseball—Biography; Blacks—Biography

Watch/Guard Dogs
BL - v82 - Je 15 '86 - p1536
RT - v39 - My '86 - p987

NEWMAN, Matthew (continued)
SLJ - v32 - Ag '86 - p91
Subject: Dogs

NEWMAN, Robert Howard 1909-
AuBYP, ConAu 19NR, ScF&FL 1, -2, SmATA 4, TwCChW 83, WrDr 86

Night Spell
Am - v137 - D 3 '77 - p406
BB - v5 - Je '77 - p3
BL - v73 - Ap 15 '77 - p1268
HB - v53 - Ag '77 - p443
KR - v45 - Ap 15 '77 - p427
SLJ - v23 - My '77 - p78
Subject: Parapsychology—Fiction

The Twelve Labors Of Hercules
KR - v40 - My 15 '72 - p585
NYTBR - Ag 27 '72 - p24
Subject: Hercules—Fiction

NEWMAN, Shirlee P 1924-
AuBYP SUP, ConAu 5R, SmATA 10, WhoAmW 77

Marian Anderson: Lady From Philadelphia
BL - v63 - S 1 '66 - p57
BS - v26 - Je 1 '66 - p102
Inst - v76 - Ag '66 - p217
KR - v34 - F 1 '66 - p115
LJ - v91 - Jl '66 - p3545
NYTBR - v71 - Jl 10 '66 - p38
PW - v189 - My 16 '66 - p80
SR - v49 - My 14 '66 - p42
Subject: Biography

NEWTON, Suzanne 1936-
AuBYP SUP, BioIn 10, ConAu 14NR, ConLC 35, DrAP&F 85, IntAu&W 77, SmATA 5, WrDr 86

M. V. Sexton Speaking
BL - v78 - S 15 '81 - p98
CBRS - v10 - Winter '82 - p59
CCB-B - v35 - Ja '82 - p92
HB - v57 - D '81 - p670
J Read - v25 - Mr '82 - p613
KR - v49 - D 15 '81 - p1524
SLJ - v28 - D '81 - p72
Subject: Bakers and bakeries—Fiction; Identity—Fiction; Orphans—Fiction

NICHOLS, Ruth 1948-
AuBYP SUP, BioIn 10, -12, ConAu 16NR, FourBJA, OxChL, Profile 1, SmATA 15, TwCChW 83, WrDr 86

A Walk Out Of The World
Atl Pro Bk R - v10 - N '83 - p2
Can Child Lit - #15 '80 p29
CSM - v76 - O 5 '84 - pB8
Emerg Lib - v13 - My '86 - p44
Subject: Fantasy

NICKEL, Helmut

Warriors And Worthies: Arms And Armours Through The Ages
A Lib - v1 - Ap '70 - p386
BL - v66 - Ja 15 '70 - p622
CCB-B - v24 - S '70 - p16
HB - v46 - Ap '70 - p176
LJ - v95 - My 15 '70 - p1912
LJ - v95 - My 15 '70 - p1946
SR - v53 - My 9 '70 - p69
Subject: Arms and armor

NIELSEN, Virginia 1909-
ConAu X, SmATA X
Pseud./variant:
McCall, Virginia Nielsen

Keoni, My Brother
BL - v62 - Mr 15 '66 - p701
CCB-B - v19 - Ap '66 - p135
HB - v42 - F '66 - p65

see also McCall, Virginia Nielsen for additional titles

NIXON, Joan Lowery 1927-
AuBYP SUP, BioIn 13, ConAu 7NR, FifBJA, SmATA 44

Days Of Fear
BL - v79 - Ag '83 - p1458
CBRS - v11 - Ag '83 - p149
SLJ - v30 - S '83 - p138
VOYA - v7 - Ap '84 - p34
Subject: Crime and criminals—Fiction

A Deadly Game Of Magic
BL - v80 - O 1 '83 - p234
BS - v43 - Ja '84 - p389
SLJ - v30 - D '83 - p86
VOYA - v7 - Je '84 - p96
Subject: Magic—Fiction; Mystery and detective stories

The Ghosts Of Now
BL - v81 - S 1 '84 - p59
B Rpt - v5 - N '86 - p36

NIXON, Joan Lowery (continued)
CBRS - v13 - S '84 - p9
EJ - v74 - D '85 - p57
PW - v226 - O 5 '84 - p91
PW - v230 - Jl 25 '86 - p196
VOYA - v8 - Ap '85 - p50
Subject: Mystery and detective stories

The Kidnapping Of Christina Lattimore
BL - v75 - Mr 15 '79 - p1143
BW - My 13 '79 - pK3
Cur R - v19 - Ap '80 - p159
EJ - v68 - N '79 - p74
Kliatt - v14 - Fall '80 - p9
KR - v47 - My 15 '79 - p580
NYTBR - My 13 '79 - p27
PW - v215 - F 12 '79 - p127
SLJ - v27 - N '80 - p47
Subject: Kidnapping—Fiction; Mystery and detective stories

The Other Side Of Dark
BL - v83 - S 15 '86 - p121
CBRS - v15 - S '86 - p10
CCB-B - v40 - O '86 - p33
HB - v62 - N '86 - p748
KR - v54 - Ag 1 '86 - p1208
PW - v230 - N 28 '86 - p77
SLJ - v33 - S '86 - p145
VOYA - v9 - D '86 - p221
Subject: Mystery and detective stories

NOAILLES, R H
see Guilcher, Jean Michel (co-author)

NOBILE, Jeanette

Portrait Of Love
BL - v79 - Jl '83 - p1398
SLJ - v30 - O '83 - p172
Subject: Love—Fiction

NOBLE, Iris 1922-1986
AuBYP, ConAu 2NR, –120, SmATA 49N, –5

Cameras And Courage: Margaret Bourke-White
BL - v70 - S 1 '73 - p52
BS - v33 - Je 15 '73 - p146
KR - v41 - F 15 '73 - p199
LJ - v98 - Jl '73 - p2203
NYTBR - Jl 15 '73 - p8
PW - v203 - Je 4 '73 - p90
Subject: Biography; Photographers

NOLAN, William Francis 1928-
ConAu 1NR, ConSFA, DcLB 8, EncMys, SmATA 28, TwCSFW 86, WhoAm 82, WhoSciF, WrDr 86

Carnival Of Speed: True Adventures In Motor Racing
KR - v41 - F 15 '73 - p199
LJ - v98 - My 15 '73 - p1705
Subject: Automobile racing

NORBACK, Craig
see Norback, Peter (co-author)

NORBACK, Peter

Great Songs Of Madison Avenue
Choice - v14 - Mr '77 - p55
CSM - v68 - O 29 '76 - p26
Co-author: Norback, Craig

NORRIS, Gunilla B 1939-
AuBYP SUP, ConAu 93, SmATA 20

The Good Morrow
BL - v65 - Jl 15 '69 - p1276
BW - v3 - My 4 '69 - p10
CCB-B - v23 - N '69 - p50
Comw - v91 - N 21 '69 - p254
CSM - v61 - My 1 '69 - pB4
HB - v45 - Ap '69 - p172
KR - v37 - F 15 '69 - p179
LJ - v94 - My 15 '69 - p2105
NYTBR - Je 8 '69 - p42
PW - v195 - My 5 '69 - p52
RR - v28 - Jl '69 - p700
Subject: Camping—Fiction; Friendship—Fiction

NORRIS, Marianna
AuBYP SUP

Father And Son For Freedom
BL - v64 - My 1 '68 - p1048
KR - v36 - Ja 15 '68 - p61
LJ - v93 - F 15 '68 - p885
Subject: Munoz Marin, Luis; Munoz Rivera, Luis; Puerto Ricans

NORTH, Sterling 1906-1974
AuBYP, ConAu 5R, –53, CurBio 43, NewYTBS 74, SmATA 26N, –45, ThrBJA, TwCChW 83, WhAm 6

Raccoons Are The Brightest People
BL - v63 - S 15 '66 - p88
BS - v26 - Ag 15 '66 - p186
CLW - v38 - N '66 - p210
CSM - v58 - S 8 '66 - p13
KR - v34 - Je 1 '66 - p566

NORTH, Sterling (continued)
KR - v34 - Je 15 '66 - p581
LJ - v91 - Jl '66 - p3457
LJ - v91 - O 15 '66 - p5270
Nat R - v18 - N 15 '66 - p1182
NH - v76 - N '67 - p85
NYT - v115 - S 10 '66 - p27
NYTBR, Pt. 2 - F 16 '69 - p22
PW - v189 - My 23 '66 - p81
PW - v192 - Jl 3 '67 - p62
PW - v194 - Jl 8 '68 - p166
SB - v2 - Mr '67 - p298
SR - v50 - S 30 '67 - p47
Subject: Raccoons—Fiction

Rascal: A Memoir Of A Better Era
Atl - v212 - D '63 - p154
BS - v23 - S 1 '63 - p190
CC - v80 - Ag 7 '63 - p983
CSM - Ag 8 '63 - p11
HM - v227 - S '63 - p118
LJ - v88 - S 1 '63 - p3096
LJ - v88 - S 15 '63 - p3374
NYTBR - Ag 25 '63 - p24
NYTBR - v90 - Ja 20 '85 - p27
Subject: Raccoons—Fiction

NORTON, Alice Mary
see Norton, Andre

NORTON, Andre (pseud.) 1912-
ConAu X, ConLC 12, CurBio 57, DcLB 8, -52, MorJA, OxChL, SmATA X, TwCChW 83, WhoAm 86, WrDr 86
Real Name:
Norton, Alice Mary

Catseye
Analog - v100 - D '80 - p159
KR - v29 - Jl 15 '61 - p614
TLS - N 23 '62 - p914

Exiles Of The Stars
B&B - v17 - Je '72 - p72
BL - v67 - Je 15 '71 - p868
CCB-B - v24 - Jl '71 - p175
HB - v47 - Ag '71 - p389
KR - v39 - Mr 1 '71 - p243
LJ - v96 - Je 15 '71 - p2140
NS - v83 - Je 2 '72 - p759
Spec - v228 - Ap 22 '72 - p626
TLS - Ap 28 '72 - p480
Subject: Science fiction

Fur Magic
CSM - v61 - My 1 '69 - pB5
HB - v45 - Ap '69 - p172
LJ - v94 - F 15 '69 - p877
NS - v78 - O 31 '69 - p623
Obs - D 7 '69 - p31
TLS - Je 26 '69 - p689
Subject: Fantasy; Indians of North America—Fiction

The Opal-Eyed Fan
BL - v74 - O 15 '77 - p368
BS - v37 - F '78 - p342
KR - v45 - S 15 '77 - p1008
LJ - v102 - D 15 '77 - p2513
PW - v212 - O 3 '77 - p93

NUGENT, Jean

Prince Charles: England's Future King
BL - v78 - Ag '82 - p1527
Hi Lo - v4 - F '83 - p3
Subject: Princes

NURNBERG, Maxwell 1897-1984
ConAu 2NR, -5R, -114, NewYTBS 84, SmATA 27, -41N

Wonders In Words
BL - v65 - F 1 '69 - p595
CE - v46 - My '70 - p434
LJ - v94 - Mr 15 '69 - p1330
NYTBR - Ap 13 '69 - p30
Subject: English language

NUSSBAUM, Albert F 1934-
ConAu 85
Pseud./variant:
Frederick, Lee
Hiller, Doris
Martin, Albert
Oreshnik, A F

Gypsy
BL - v74 - Ja 15 '78 - p809
BL - v75 - O 15 '78 - p357
Subject: Motorcycle racing—Fiction

see also Frederick, Lee; Hiller, Doris; Martin, Albert; Oreshnik, A F for additional titles

NYE, Peter

The Storm
CBRS - v11 - F '83 - p71
Hi Lo - v4 - O '82 - p8
SLJ - v29 - Ja '83 - p86

O

OAKES, Vanya 1909-1983
AuBYP, ConAu 111, –33R, SmATA 6, –37N, WhoWest 76
Pseud./variant:
Oakes, Virginia Armstrong

Willy Wong: American
BL - v47 - My 1 '51 - p316
HB - v27 - Jl '51 - p248
LJ - v76 - Ap 15 '51 - p713
NYT - Ap 15 '51 - p18

OAKES, Virginia Armstrong
see Oakes, Vanya

OATES, Jean

Maintaining Your Car
BL - v78 - O 15 '81 - p289
Hi Lo - v2 - My '81 - p5
Subject: Automobiles

O'BRIEN, Jack 1898-1938
MorJA, WhoAm 86
Pseud./variant:
O'Brien, John Sherman

Return Of Silver Chief
LJ - v69 - F 1 '44 - p120
NYTBR - Mr 19 '44 - p27
Subject: Dogs—Fiction

O'BRIEN, Robert C 1918?-1973
AuBYP SUP, ChlLR 2, ConAu X, FourBJA, OxChL, ScFSB, SmATA 23, –X, TwCChW 78, –83

Z For Zachariah
Am - v133 - D 6 '75 - p403
BB - v3 - My '75 - p4
BL - v71 - Mr 1 '75 - p687
BL - v73 - Mr 15 '77 - p1101
BS - v35 - My '75 - p50
CCB-B - v29 - N '75 - p51
CLW - v47 - N '75 - p188
EJ - v67 - D '78 - p83
GP - v13 - Mr '75 - p2570
HB - v51 - Je '75 - p276
JB - v39 - Je '75 - p201
Kliatt - v11 - Spring '77 - p7
KR - v43 - Ja 15 '75 - p85
KR - v43 - F 15 '75 - p189
LJ - v100 - Ap 1 '75 - p694
NYT - v125 - D 20 '75 - p25
NYTBR - Mr 2 '75 - p8
NYTBR - Je 1 '75 - p29
NYTBR - N 16 '75 - p55
NYTBR - My 29 '77 - p23
Obs - Mr 30 '75 - p24
Obs - Jl 23 '78 - p21
PW - v207 - Ja 20 '75 - p77
PW - v207 - Ja 27 '75 - p278
SLJ - v21 - Mr '75 - p109
SLJ - v22 - D '75 - p32
Spec - v234 - Ap 12 '75 - p444
TLS - Ap 4 '75 - p360
TN - v32 - Ap '76 - p285
TN - v34 - Spring '78 - p265

O'CONNOR, Dick 1930-
ConAu 97

Foul Play
Hi Lo - v3 - F '82 - p1
SLJ - v28 - S '81 - p122
Subject: Sports—Fiction

Rick Barry: Basketball Ace
BL - v73 - Jl 1 '77 - p1654
KR - v45 - Mr 15 '77 - p293
SLJ - v23 - My '77 - p80
Subject: Basketball—Biography

O'CONNOR, Karen 1938-
SmATA 34
Pseud./variant:
Sweeney, Karen O'Connor

Sally Ride And The New Astronauts: Scientists In Space
ASBYP - v17 - Winter '84 - p40
BL - v79 - Je 1 '83 - p1278
B Rpt - v2 - Ja '84 - p41
CCB-B - v36 - Jl '83 - p215
CE - v60 - N '83 - p141
N Dir Wom - v13 - Jl '84 - p11
RT - v37 - D '83 - p309
SB - v19 - Ja '84 - p160
SLJ - v29 - Ag '83 - p70
Subject: Astronauts; Space flight

O'CONNOR, Karen (continued)
see also Sweeney, Karen O'Connor for additional titles

O'CONNOR, Patrick (pseud.) 1915-1983
AuBYP, BioIn 9, ConAu X, EncMys, IntAu&W 82X, SmATA 2, –X, TwCChW 83, WrDr 86
Real Name:
Wibberley, Leonard

The Black Tiger
NYTBR - S 16 '56 - p38

Black Tiger At Lemans
BL - v54 - My 15 '58 - p539
KR - v26 - Mr 15 '58 - p230
LJ - v83 - My 15 '58 - p1610

A Car Called Camellia
BL - v67 - O 1 '70 - p142
KR - v38 - My 15 '70 - p559
LJ - v95 - D 15 '70 - p4377
PW - v197 - Je 15 '70 - p65
Subject: Automobile racing—Fiction

Mexican Road Race
BL - v53 - Jl 1 '57 - p562
KR - v25 - Ap 15 '57 - p309
LJ - v82 - S 15 '57 - p2199
SR - v40 - N 16 '57 - p90

see also Wibberley, Leonard for additional titles

O'DELL, Scott 1903?-
ChlLR 1, ConAu 12NR, ConLC 30, DcLB 52, IntAu&W 86, MorJA, SmATA 12, TwCChW 83, WhoAm 86, WrDr 86

Black Pearl
B&B - v17 - D '71 - pR16
BL - v64 - D 1 '67 - p450
BS - v27 - F 1 '68 - p431
BW - v1 - N 5 '67 - p30
CCB-B - v21 - D '67 - p64
CE - v45 - F '69 - p338
HB - v43 - O '67 - p603
KR - v35 - S 1 '67 - p1058
LJ - v92 - D 15 '67 - p4625
NYTBR - v72 - N 5 '67 - p20
NYTBR, Pt. 2 - N 5 '72 - p42
Obs - Ag 4 '68 - p22
Par - v43 - Je '68 - p68
PW - v192 - O 23 '67 - p52
SR - v50 - O 21 '67 - p43
TLS - Je 6 '68 - p588
TN - v24 - Ap '68 - p324
Subject: Pearl diving and divers—Fiction

Child Of Fire
BL - v71 - S 15 '74 - p93
BS - v34 - O 15 '74 - p330
BW - N 10 '74 - p6
CCB-B - v28 - D '74 - p66
Choice - v12 - N '75 - p1133
Choice - v14 - N '77 - p1178
CLW - v46 - My '75 - p453
CLW - v47 - N '75 - p166
Comw - v101 - N 22 '74 - p194
HB - v50 - D '74 - p695
KR - v42 - Ag 1 '74 - p810
KR - v43 - Ja 1 '75 - p11
LJ - v99 - S 15 '74 - p2295
LJ - v99 - D 15 '74 - p3247
NYTBR - N 3 '74 - p23
NYTBR - N 3 '74 - p52
NYTBR - D 1 '74 - p76
NYTBR - Mr 12 '78 - p45
PT - v8 - N '74 - p26
PW - v205 - Jl 22 '74 - p70
Subject: Mexican Americans—Fiction

Island Of The Blue Dolphins
BL - v56 - Ap 1 '60 - p489
HB - v36 - Ap '60 - p137
LJ - v85 - Ap 15 '60 - p1702
NYTBR - Mr 27 '60 - p40
NYTBR, Pt. 2 - N 7 '71 - p46
NYTBR, Pt. 2 - F 13 '72 - p14
Obs - Ap 10 '66 - p18
Spec - Je 3 '66 - p706
SR - v43 - My 7 '60 - p42
TLS - My 19 '66 - p442

Kathleen, Please Come Home
BB - v6 - N '78 - p2
BL - v74 - My 15 '78 - p1486
CCB-B - v32 - S '78 - p15
KR - v46 - Mr 15 '78 - p311
NYTBR - Ap 30 '78 - p53
PW - v213 - My 22 '78 - p233
SLJ - v24 - My '78 - p78
Subject: Runaways—Fiction

The King's Fifth
Atl - v218 - D '66 - p154
B&B - v13 - D '67 - p43
BL - v63 - D 15 '66 - p452
CCB-B - v20 - Ja '67 - p78
CLW - v39 - N '67 - p241
Comw - v85 - N 11 '66 - p175
CSM - v58 - N 3 '66 - pB12
HB - v42 - D '66 - p721
Inst - v83 - My '74 - p97

O'DELL, Scott (continued)
KR - v34 - S 1 '66 - p913
LJ - v92 - F 15 '67 - p897
NYTBR - v72 - Ja 15 '67 - p28
Obs - N 26 '67 - p28
PW - v190 - O 10 '66 - p74
SR - v49 - N 12 '66 - p53
TLS - N 30 '67 - p1138
TN - v23 - Ap '67 - p292

Sarah Bishop
BL - v76 - My 1 '80 - p1297
BOT - v4 - F '81 - p79
CBRS - v8 - Je '80 - p109
CCB-B - v33 - Je '80 - p198
HB - v56 - Ap '80 - p174
Kliatt - v16 - Spring '82 - p14
NY - v56 - D 1 '80 - p222
NYTBR - v85 - Ap 4 '80 - p26
NYTBR - v87 - Ja 3 '82 - p19
PW - v217 - Mr 21 '80 - p69
PW - v211 - Ja 1 '82 - p51
SLJ - v26 - My '80 - p79
Subject: Survival—Fiction; United States—History—Revolution, 1775-1783—Fiction

Sing Down The Moon
BL - v67 - N 1 '70 - p230
BL - v67 - Ap 1 '71 - p660
BL - v69 - O 15 '72 - p178
BW - v4 - N 8 '70 - p23
CCB-B - v24 - Ja '71 - p78
CLW - v42 - F '71 - p383
CLW - v49 - D '77 - p212
Comw - v93 - N 20 '70 - p202
HB - v46 - D '70 - p623
HT - v22 - D '72 - p891
KR - v38 - O 15 '70 - p1149
LJ - v95 - N 15 '70 - p4046
NS - v84 - N 10 '72 - p694
NYTBR - O 18 '70 - p34
NYTBR, Pt. 2 - N 8 '70 - p38
NYTBR, Pt. 2 - My 6 '73 - p28
Obs - D 3 '72 - p38
PW - v198 - S 28 '70 - p79
SR - v53 - N 14 '70 - p38
TLS - N 3 '72 - p1320
Subject: Navajo Indians—Fiction

The Spanish Smile
BL - v79 - O 1 '82 - p199
B Rpt - v1 - Ja '83 - p41
BS - v42 - D '82 - p366
BW - v13 - Ja 9 '83 - p11
CBRS - v11 - Ja '83 - p51
CCB-B - v36 - Ja '83 - p94
KR - v50 - O 15 '82 - p1158
LA - v60 - Mr '83 - p362
PW - v222 - O 22 '82 - p55
SLJ - v29 - O '82 - p163
VOYA - v6 - Ap '83 - p40
Subject: Fathers and daughters—Fiction; Islands—Fiction

Zia
BB - v4 - My '76 - p4
BL - v72 - Ap 15 '76 - p1188
BW - My 2 '76 - pL2
CCB-B - v29 - Jl '76 - p180
CE - v53 - O '76 - p34
EJ - v65 - O '76 - p88
HB - v52 - Je '76 - p291
JB - v41 - O '77 - p304
J Read - v20 - My '77 - p732
Kliatt - v12 - Fall '78 - p13
KR - v44 - Mr 15 '76 - p324
LA - v53 - S '76 - p701
NO - v15 - Ag 21 '76 - p17
NYTBR - My 2 '76 - p38
Obs - Je 12 '77 - p25
Obs - Je 26 '77 - p29
PW - v209 - Ap 5 '76 - p101
SLJ - v22 - My '76 - p62
TLS - Jl 15 '77 - p860
Subject: Indians of North America—Fiction

O'DONOGHUE, Bryan 1921-
ConAu 77

Wild Animal Rescue!
KR - v39 - Je 1 '71 - p589
LJ - v96 - S 15 '71 - p2920
PW - v199 - Je 21 '71 - p71
SB - v7 - D '71 - p264
Subject: Wildlife conservation

OGAN, George F
see Ogan, Margaret E Nettles (co-author)

OGAN, Margaret E Nettles 1923-1979
AuBYP SUP, ConAu 4NR, SmATA 13

Acuna Brutes
KR - v41 - S 15 '73 - p1043
LJ - v98 - My 15 '73 - p1706
Co-author: Ogan, George F
Subject: Motorcycle racing—Fiction

Desert Road Racer
KR - v38 - S 15 '70 - p1050
LJ - v95 - D 15 '70 - p4378
Co-author: Ogan, George F
Subject: Automobile racing—Fiction

OGAN, Margaret E Nettles (continued)

Grand National Racer
Cur R - v16 - D '77 - p360
KR - v45 - F 15 '77 - p169
SLJ - v24 - S '77 - p148
SLJ - v24 - Mr '78 - p107
Co-author: Ogan, George F
Subject: Automobile racing—Fiction

Green Thirteen
BL - v74 - Je 15 '78 - p1613
Hi Lo - v1 - S '79 - p5
NYTBR - Ap 30 '78 - p45
SLJ - v24 - F '78 - p66
Co-author: Ogan, George F
Subject: Automobile racing—Fiction

OGILVIE, Elisabeth 1917-
AuBYP, BioIn 5, ConAu 103, -19NR, CurBio 51, SmATA 40, WhoAmW 77, WrDr 86

Beautiful Girl
Hi Lo - v3 - Je '82 - p2
SLJ - v26 - Ag '80 - p78

The Pigeon Pair
BL - v64 - S 1 '67 - p66
BS - v27 - My 1 '67 - p66
HB - v43 - Je '67 - p354
KR - v35 - F 15 '67 - p209
LJ - v92 - My 15 '67 - p2031
NYTBR, Pt. 2 - v72 - My 7 '67 - p8

Too Young To Know
BL - v79 - N 15 '82 - p437
Kliatt - v17 - Winter '83 - p12
Subject: Scotland—Fiction

O'HANLON, Jacklyn 1933-
ConAu X
Pseud./variant:
Meek, Jacklyn O'Hanlon

Fair Game
BS - v37 - Ag '77 - p141
CCB-B - v31 - D '77 - p65
EJ - v66 - N '77 - p81
KR - v45 - Mr 15 '77 - p291
NYTBR - My 1 '77 - p46
PW - v211 - My 23 '77 - p247
SLJ - v23 - My '77 - p70
Subject: Alcohol and youth—Fiction; Family problems—Fiction; Sexual harassment—Fiction

OJIGBO, A Okion

Young And Black In Africa
BL - v68 - Mr 1 '72 - p566
CCB-B - v25 - Je '72 - p161
KR - v39 - O 1 '71 - p1084
LJ - v96 - D 15 '71 - p4192
NYTBR, Pt. 2 - N 7 '71 - p45
SE - v37 - O '73 - p561
Subject: Africa

OKIMOTO, Jean Davies 1942-
ConAu 16NR, SmATA 34

It's Just Too Much
BL - v77 - S 1 '80 - p46
CBRS - v9 - D '80 - p29
CCB-B - v34 - Ja '81 - p99
Kliatt - v16 - Spring '82 - p14
SLJ - v27 - N '80 - p78
Subject: Family life—Fiction; Remarriage—Fiction

My Mother Is Not Married To My Father
Kliatt - v15 - Fall '81 - p14
RSR - v10 - Winter '82 - p39
RT - v36 - Ap '83 - p802
Subject: Divorce—Fiction

Who Did It, Jenny Lake?
BL - v80 - O 15 '83 - p362
CBRS - v12 - Mr '84 - p86
CCB-B - v37 - Ja '84 - p93
Kliatt - v19 - Spring '85 - p14
KR - v51 - N 1 '83 - pJ206
VOYA - v6 - F '84 - p340
Subject: Friendship—Fiction; Hawaii—Fiction; Mystery and detective stories

OLEKSY, Walter 1930-
ConAu 17NR, SmATA 33
Pseud./variant:
Olesky, Walter

Nature Gone Wild!
Hi Lo - v4 - Ja '83 - p4
SB - v19 - S '83 - p31
SLJ - v29 - Mr '83 - p182
VOYA - v6 - Ap '83 - p50
Subject: Disasters; Natural disasters

The Pirates Of Deadman's Cay
BL - v79 - N 15 '82 - p439
Hi Lo - v4 - My '83 - p6
SLJ - v29 - F '83 - p91
Subject: Pirates—Fiction

UFO: Teen Sightings
BL - v80 - Ag '84 - p1610

OLEKSY, Walter (continued)
SLJ - v31 - N '84 - p127
Subject: Unidentified flying objects

Up From Nowhere
SLJ - v29 - F '83 - p91
VOYA - v5 - D '82 - p34

OLESKY, Walter
see Oleksy, Walter

OLIVER, Carl R

Plane Talk: Aviators' And Astronauts' Own Stories
BL - v77 - D 1 '80 - p510
HB - v56 - D '80 - p656
SLJ - v27 - Ja '81 - p72
Subject: Air pilots; Astronauts

OLNEY, Ross Robert 1929-
AuBYP, ConAu 7NR, IntAu&W 82, SmATA 13, WhoWest 78, WrDr 86

A. J. Foyt: The Only Four Time Winner
Hi Lo - v1 - S '79 - p4
Subject: Automoblie racing drivers

The Amazing Yo-Yo
SLJ - v27 - Mr '81 - p149
Subject: Games

Auto Racing's Young Lions
KR - v45 - Je 1 '77 - p585
SLJ - v24 - S '77 - p134
Subject: Automoblie racing drivers

How To Understand Auto Racing
BL - v76 - Ja 15 '80 - p721
Subject: Automobile racing

Janet Guthrie: First Woman At Indy
BL - v75 - Jl 1 '79 - p1584
Hi Lo - v1 - O '79 - p6
SLJ - v25 - Mr '79 - p143
Subject: Automoblie racing drivers

Modern Auto Racing Superstars
SE - v44 - Mr '80 - p248
Subject: Automoblie racing drivers

Modern Drag Racing Superstars
BL - v77 - Je 15 '81 - p1342
SLJ - v27 - My '81 - p87
Subject: Automoblie racing drivers; Drag racing

Modern Motorcycle Superstars
Hi Lo - v1 - Ap '80 - p3
SLJ - v26 - My '80 - p88
Subject: Motorcycle racing

Modern Speed Record Superstars
BL - v79 - S 15 '82 - p106
CLW - v55 - N '83 - p188
SLJ - v29 - F '83 - p81
Subject: Athletes

Out To Launch
ACSB - v13 - Mr '80 - p51
BL - v76 - Ja 15 '80 - p721
HB - v56 - Ap '80 - p193
SLJ - v26 - Mr '80 - p142
Subject: Aeronautics

The Racing Bugs
BL - v71 - F 15 '75 - p613
SLJ - v21 - Mr '75 - p100
Co-author: Grable, Ron
Subject: Automobile racing

Super Champions Of Auto Racing
BL - v80 - Jl '84 - p1554
SLJ - v30 - My '84 - p105
VOYA - v7 - O '84 - p212
Subject: Automoblie racing drivers

Super Champions Of Ice Hockey
BL - v79 - Ja 15 '83 - p682
Subject: Hockey

OLSEN, Gene

The Bucket Of Thunderbolts
BL - v56 - F 15 '60 - p356
KR - v27 - Jl 15 '59 - p497
LJ - v85 - F 15 '60 - p854
NYTBR, Pt. 2 - N 1 '59 - p28

OLSEN, Tillie 1913-
ConAu 1R, ConLC 13, ConNov 76, -86, WhoAm 86, WorAu 1970, WrDr 86

Tell Me A Riddle
Am - v136 - Ja 29 '77 - p81
BF - v6 - #2 '82 p222
Choice - v15 - Jl '78 - p656
Crit - v38 - Ag '79 - p6
GW - v123 - D 21 '80 - p22
Ms - v3 - S '74 - p26
Nat - v214 - Ap 10 '72 - p472
New R - v173 - D 6 '75 - p29
NS - v100 - O 31 '80 - p23
Obs - Mr 1 '81 - p32
TLS - N 14 '80 - p1294
Subject: Short stories

ONEAL, Elizabeth
see Oneal, Zibby

ONEAL, Zibby 1934-
ConAu X, ConLC 30, SmATA X

ONEAL, Zibby (continued)
Pseud./variant:
Oneal, Elizabeth

The Language Of Goldfish
CE - v57 - My '81 - p300
EJ - v70 - Ap '81 - p77
LA - v57 - O '80 - p792
NYTBR - v85 - Ap 27 '80 - p52
NYTBR - v86 - Ap 26 '81 - p43
SLJ - v26 - F '80 - p70
Subject: Goldfish

O'NEILL, Mary 1908-
AuBYP, ConAu 5R, SmATA 2, ThrBJA

Take A Number
BW - S 15 '68 - p24
CSM - v60 - N 7 '68 - p84
Inst - v78 - N '68 - p154
LJ - v93 - O 15 '68 - p3958
NYTBR - v73 - S 8 '68 - p
PW - v194 - Jl 15 '68 - p57
Subject: Fairy tales; Verses for children

OPPENHEIMER, Joan Letson 1925-
ConAu 17NR, IntAu&W 82, SmATA 28

Gardine Vs. Hanover
BL - v78 - Ap 15 '82 - p1097
CBRS - v10 - My '82 - p98
CCB-B - v36 - S '82 - p18
CLW - v54 - O '82 - p134
CSM - v74 - My 14 '82 - pB8
J Read - v26 - Ap '83 - p653
KR - v50 - Mr 15 '82 - p350
SLJ - v28 - Ag '82 - p119
Subject: Brothers and sisters—Fiction; Family life—Fiction; Remarriage—Fiction

The Missing Sunrise
BL - v80 - Mr 1 '84 - p965
SLJ - v30 - Ap '84 - p125
Subject: Friendship—Fiction

The Voices Of Julie
Kliatt - v14 - Winter '80 - p12

Which Mother Is Mine?
BL - v76 - Jl 1 '80 - p1601
Subject: Foster home care—Fiction; Parent and child—Fiction

Working On It
BL - v76 - My 1 '80 - p1269
KR - v48 - Ag 15 '80 - p1085
PW - v218 - Jl 18 '80 - p62
SLJ - v27 - Ja '81 - p63
Subject: Identity—Fiction; Schools—Fiction

O'REGAN, Susan K

Neil Diamond
SLJ - v23 - S '76 - p114
Subject: Biography; Musicians

ORESHNIK, A F (pseud.) 1934-
ConAu X
Real Name:
Nussbaum, Albert F

The Demeter Star
BL - v74 - D 15 '77 - p679
BL - v75 - O 15 '78 - p357
Subject: Buried treasure—Fiction; Skin diving—Fiction

see also Nussbaum, Albert F; Street, Nicki (co-author) for additional titles

ORGEL, Doris 1929-
AuBYP, AuNews 1, ConAu 2NR, -45, FourBJA, SmATA 7, TwCChW 78, -83, WrDr 86

A Certain Magic
BB - v5 - Mr '77 - p3
Subject: Jews—Fiction

ORR, Frank 1936-

The Story Of Hockey
CCB-B - v25 - Jl '72 - p175
LJ - v96 - D 15 '71 - p4202
Subject: Hockey

ORTIZ, Victoria 1942-
ConAu 107

Sojourner Truth, A Self-Made Woman
CE - v51 - N '74 - p96
Choice - v12 - N '75 - p1133
Subject: Abolitionists; Blacks—Biography

OSBURN, Jesse

Nightshade
VOYA - v8 - Je '85 - p124

OSTER, Maggie

The Illustrated Bird
BL - v75 - D 1 '78 - p603
Hob - v84 - Jl '79 - p123

OSTER, Maggie (continued)
Kliatt - v13 - Spring '79 - p55
Subject: Art; Birds

OSTRANDER, Sheila

Psychic Experiences: E.S.P. Investigated
CCB-B - v31 - Jl '78 - p182
SLJ - v24 - Ap '78 - p96
Co-author: Schroeder, Lynn
Subject: Psychical research

OTFINOSKI, Steven

The Monster That Wouldn't Die And Other Strange But True Stories
Hi Lo - v1 - Ap '80 - p3
Subject: Supernatural

Sky Ride And Other Exciting Stories
Hi Lo - v1 - D '79 - p4
Subject: Short stories

Village Of Vampires
SLJ - v26 - D '79 - p82
Subject: Monsters—Fiction

The Zombie Maker: Stories Of Amazing Adventures
Hi Lo - v1 - Mr '80 - p5
Subject: Short stories; Supernatural—Fiction

see also Mueser, Annie (co-author) for additional titles

OTTUM, Bob
see Edwards, Phil (co-author)

OWEN, Evan 1918-1984
ConAu 109, SmATA 38

On Your Own
Hi Lo - v1 - My '80 - p3
SLJ - v25 - My '79 - p65
Subject: Schools—Fiction; Track and field—Fiction

OWENS, Jesse 1913-
McGEWB, SelBAAu, WhoAm 78, WhoBlA 77

The Man Who Outran Hitler
Kliatt - v14 - Winter '80 - p29
Co-author: Neimark, Paul

P

PAANANEN, Eloise K
see Engle, Eloise

PACE, Mildred Mastin 1907-
AuBYP SUP, ConAu 5NR,
SmATA 46

Wrapped For Eternity
BL - v70 - My 1 '74 - p1005
BL - v71 - Mr 15 '75 - p767
BL - v81 - Jl '85 - p1567
CCB-B - v28 - O '74 - p34
Choice - v12 - N '75 - p1133
GP - v16 - Mr '78 - p3271
JB - v42 - F '78 - p47
KR - v42 - Mr 15 '74 - p312
KR - v43 - Ja 1 '75 - p14
LJ - v99 - My 15 '74 - p1451
LJ - v99 - My 15 '74 - p1475
NYTBR - My 26 '74 - p8
NYTBR - N 3 '74 - p55
SB - v10 - My '74 - p58
SE - v39 - Mr '75 - p175
SLJ - v25 - S '78 - p43
Subject: Egypt; Mummies

PACKARD, Edward 1931-
ConAu 114, SmATA 47

The Cave Of Time
Analog - v100 - F '80 - p160
BW - v10 - Ja 20 '80 - p13
Hi Lo - v3 - Mr '82 - p4
SLJ - v26 - N '79 - p68
Subject: Adventure and adventurers—Fiction; Plot-your-own-stories; Space and time—Fiction

Deadwood City
NYTBR - v86 - Ja 25 '81 - p32
Sch Lib - v28 - Je '80 - p154
SLJ - v27 - Ja '81 - p64
TES - Jl 11 '80 - p28
VOYA - v4 - Ap '81 - p52
Subject: West (U.S.)—Fiction

Who Killed Harlowe Thrombey?
SLJ - v27 - My '81 - p85
Subject: Mystery and detective stories

Your Code Name Is Jonah
BW - v10 - Ja 20 '80 - p13
Hi Lo - v3 - Mr '82 - p4
SLJ - v27 - S '80 - p76
Time - v120 - Ag 23 '82 - p65
Subject: Adventure and adventurers—Fiction

PADEN, Betty Burns
WhoAmW 87

Truth Is Stranger Than Fiction
BL - v81 - Ja 15 '85 - p689
Subject: Curiosities and wonders

PAGE, N H

Bobby Orr-Number Four
BL - v79 - Ja 15 '83 - p669
VOYA - v5 - F '83 - p59
Subject: Hockey—Biography

PAIGE, David

A Day In The Life Of A Police Detective
BL - v77 - My 1 '81 - p1198
SLJ - v28 - N '81 - p96
Subject: Detectives; Occupations; Police

A Day In The Life Of A School Basketball Coach
BL - v77 - My 1 '81 - p1198
SLJ - v27 - My '81 - p87
Subject: Basketball; Occupations

PAINE, Roberta M 1925-
AuBYP SUP, ConAu 33R,
SmATA 13, WhoAmW 77

Looking At Sculpture
BS - v28 - N 1 '68 - p325
BW - v2 - N 3 '68 - p6
NYTBR - v73 - N 3 '68 - p54
PW - v194 - N 4 '68 - p50
SR - v51 - N 9 '68 - p68
Subject: Sculpture

PAISLEY, Tom 1932-
BioIn 11, ConAu 15NR, SmATA X

PAISLEY, Tom (continued)
Pseud./variant:
Bethancourt, T Ernesto

The Dog Days Of Arthur Cane
BB - v4 - N '76 - p3
BS - v36 - Mr '77 - p385
EJ - v67 - Ja '78 - p91
GP - v17 - Ja '79 - p3436
HB - v53 - Ap '77 - p157
Inst - v86 - N '76 - p146
JB - v43 - F '79 - p58
KR - v44 - Ag 1 '76 - p848
NYTBR - v0 - O 17 '76 - p41
PW - v210 - O 18 '76 - p64
Sch Lib - v27 - Je '79 - p164
SLJ - v23 - Ja '77 - p99
TES - v0 - N 24 '78 - p50
TLS - v0 - S 29 '78 - p1082
Subject: Dogs—Fiction

Doris Fein: Dead Heat At Long Beach
BL - v77 - Je 15 '81 - p1341
BS - v41 - Jl '81 - p157
CBRS - v9 - N '80 - p26
CCB-B - v34 - Jl '81 - p207
HB - v57 - F '81 - p56
Kliatt - v17 - Winter '83 - p4
KR - v49 - Jl 15 '81 - p875
LA - v58 - O '81 - p846
NYTBR - v87 - O 17 '82 - p45
PW - v217 - Ap 11 '80 - p78
SLJ - v26 - My '80 - p86
SLJ - v28 - S '81 - p132
VOYA - v4 - O '81 - p40
Subject: Adventure and adventurers—Fiction

Doris Fein: Deadly Aphrodite
BL - v77 - Je 15 '81 - p1341
BS - v41 - Jl '81 - p157
CBRS - v9 - N '80 - p26
CCB-B - v34 - Jl '81 - p207
HB - v57 - F '81 - p56
Kliatt - v17 - Winter '83 - p4
KR - v49 - Jl 15 '81 - p875
LA - v58 - O '81 - p846
NYTBR - v87 - O 17 '82 - p45
PW - v217 - Ap 11 '80 - p78
SLJ - v26 - My '80 - p86
SLJ - v28 - S '81 - p132
VOYA - v4 - O '81 - p40
Subject: Mystery and detective stories

Doris Fein: Murder Is No Joke
BL - v77 - Je 15 '81 - p1341
BS - v41 - Jl '81 - p157
CBRS - v9 - N '80 - p26
CCB-B - v34 - Jl '81 - p207
HB - v57 - F '81 - p56
Kliatt - v17 - Winter '83 - p4
KR - v49 - Jl 15 '81 - p875
LA - v58 - O '81 - p846
NYTBR - v87 - O 17 '82 - p45
PW - v217 - Ap 11 '80 - p78
SLJ - v26 - My '80 - p86
SLJ - v28 - S '81 - p132
VOYA - v4 - O '81 - p40
Subject: Crime and criminals—Fiction; Mystery and detective stories

Doris Fein: Phantom Of The Casino
BL - v77 - Je 15 '81 - p1341
BS - v41 - Jl '81 - p157
CBRS - v9 - N '80 - p26
CCB-B - v34 - Jl '81 - p207
HB - v57 - F '81 - p56
Kliatt - v17 - Winter '83 - p4
KR - v49 - Jl 15 '81 - p875
LA - v58 - O '81 - p846
NYTBR - v87 - O 17 '82 - p45
PW - v217 - Ap 11 '80 - p78
SLJ - v26 - My '80 - p86
SLJ - v28 - S '81 - p132
VOYA - v4 - O '81 - p40
Subject: Mystery and detective stories

Doris Fein: Quartz Boyar
BL - v77 - Je 15 '81 - p1341
BS - v41 - Jl '81 - p157
CBRS - v9 - N '80 - p26
CCB-B - v34 - Jl '81 - p207
HB - v57 - F '81 - p56
Kliatt - v17 - Winter '83 - p4
KR - v49 - Jl 15 '81 - p875
LA - v58 - O '81 - p846
NYTBR - v87 - O 17 '82 - p45
PW - v217 - Ap 11 '80 - p78
SLJ - v26 - My '80 - p86
SLJ - v28 - S '81 - p132
VOYA - v4 - O '81 - p40
Subject: Spies—Fiction

Doris Fein: Superspy
BL - v77 - Je 15 '81 - p1341
BS - v41 - Jl '81 - p157
CBRS - v9 - N '80 - p26
CCB-B - v34 - Jl '81 - p207
HB - v57 - F '81 - p56
Kliatt - v17 - Winter '83 - p4
KR - v49 - Jl 15 '81 - p875
LA - v58 - O '81 - p846
NYTBR - v87 - O 17 '82 - p45
PW - v217 - Ap 11 '80 - p78
SLJ - v26 - My '80 - p86
SLJ - v28 - S '81 - p132

PAISLEY, Tom (continued)
VOYA - v4 - O '81 - p40
Subject: New York (City)—Fiction; Spies—Fiction

see also Bethancourt, T Ernesto for additional titles

PALFREY, Sarah 1913?-
AuBYP SUP
Pseud./variant:
Cooke, Sarah Fabyan

Tennis For Anyone!
BL - v63 - Mr 15 '67 - p776
LJ - v92 - Ja 15 '67 - p352
PW - v190 - Ag 15 '66 - p65
Subject: Tennis

PALTROWITZ, Donna
see Paltrowitz, Stuart (co-author)

PALTROWITZ, Stuart 1946-
ConAu 118

Robotics
SLJ - v30 - Ap '84 - p117
Co-author: Paltrowitz, Donna
Subject: Robots

PANATI, Charles 1943-
ConAu 81

Links
BL - v74 - Je 1 '78 - p1538
KR - v46 - F 1 '78 - p130
LJ - v103 - Ap 15 '78 - p898
PW - v213 - F 6 '78 - p90

PARENTEAU, Shirley Laurolyn 1935-
ConAu 15NR, -85, SmATA 47, WhoAmW 77

The Talking Coffins Of Cryo-City
CBRS - v8 - Ja '80 - p48
KR - v48 - Mr 15 '80 - p366
SLJ - v26 - Ja '80 - p73

PARK, Anne

Tender Loving Care
BL - v80 - S 15 '83 - p160
SLJ - v30 - N '83 - p96
TES - D 23 '83 - p23
VOYA - v6 - F '84 - p336
Subject: Divorce—Fiction; Schools—Fiction

PARK, Barbara 1947-
ConAu 113, SmATA 40

Beanpole
BL - v80 - O 1 '83 - p300
B Rpt - v2 - Ja '84 - p37
CBRS - v12 - O '83 - p21
CCB-B - v37 - O '83 - p35
CSM - v75 - O 7 '83 - pB3
RT - v38 - O '84 - p72
SLJ - v30 - N '83 - p81
Subject: Size and shape—Fiction

Don't Make Me Smile
BL - v78 - S 1 '81 - p50
CBRS - v9 - Ag '81 - p129
CCB-B - v35 - N '81 - p53
HB - v58 - F '82 - p46
KR - v49 - D 15 '81 - p1520
SLJ - v28 - O '81 - p145
Subject: Divorce—Fiction

Skinnybones
BL - v79 - S 15 '82 - p118
CBRS - v10 - Ag '82 - p139
CLW - v54 - My '83 - p425
KR - v50 - Jl 15 '82 - p799
SLJ - v29 - D '82 - p86

PARKER, Richard 1915-
AuBYP, ConAu 73, OxChL, SmATA 14, TwCChW 83, WrDr 86

Quarter Boy
B&B - v22 - Je '77 - p74
BL - v73 - O 15 '76 - p325
CCB-B - v30 - Ap '77 - p131
CE - v54 - O '77 - p28
GP - v15 - My '76 - p2891
JB - v40 - O '76 - p283
KR - v44 - O 15 '76 - p1146
SLJ - v23 - S '76 - p136
TLS - Ap 2 '76 - p377
Subject: Artists—Fiction

PARKINSON, Ethelyn M 1906-
AuBYP SUP, ConAu 1NR, SmATA 11, WhoAm 86

Today I Am A Ham
BL - v64 - Jl 15 '68 - p1287
BS - v29 - Ja 1 '70 - p391
KR - v36 - Ap 1 '68 - p393
LJ - v93 - My 15 '68 - p2115

PASCAL, Francine 1938-
ConAu 115, FifBJA, SmATA 37

The Hand-Me-Down Kid
BL - v76 - Ap 15 '80 - p1206
CBRS - v8 - Spring '80 - p119

PASCAL, Francine (continued)
HB - v56 - Je '80 - p302
KR - v48 - Je 1 '80 - p714
RT - v35 - O '81 - p66
SLJ - v27 - S '80 - p76
Subject: Brothers and sisters—Fiction; Interpersonal relations—Fiction

Hangin' Out With Cici
Kliatt - v19 - Fall '85 - p16
Subject: Mothers and daughters—Fiction; Space and time—Fiction

My First Love And Other Disasters
BL - v75 - F 15 '79 - p936
CCB-B - v32 - Mr '79 - p123
KR - v47 - Jl 1 '79 - p745
NYTBR - Ap 29 '79 - p38
PW - v216 - Ja 8 '79 - p74
SLJ - v25 - Mr '79 - p149

PATENT, Dorothy Hinshaw 1940-
AuBYP SUP, ConAu 9NR, SmATA 22

Horses And Their Wild Relatives
BL - v78 - S 1 '81 - p50
BL - v83 - Ja 1 '87 - p715
HB - v57 - O '81 - p558
KR - v49 - Jl 15 '81 - p875
SB - v17 - N '81 - p96
SLJ - v28 - Ja '82 - p89
VOYA - v4 - O '81 - p50
Subject: Horses

Hunters And The Hunted: Surviving In The Animal World
ACSB - v15 - Winter '82 - p52
BL - v77 - My 15 '81 - p1255
HB - v57 - O '81 - p558
KR - v49 - Jl 1 '81 - p804
SB - v17 - My '82 - p271
SLJ - v28 - O '81 - p152
Subject: Animals

PATERSON, Katherine 1932-
ChlLR 7, ConAu 21R, ConLC 12, -30, DcLB 52, FifBJA, OxChL, SmATA 13, TwCChW 83, WhoAm 86, WrDr 86

Angels And Other Strangers
BB - v7 - D '79 - p4
HB - v55 - D '79 - p650
VOYA - v6 - O '83 - p188
Subject: Christmas—Fiction; Short stories

PATON WALSH, Gillian
see Walsh, Jill Paton

PATTEN, Lewis B 1915-1981
BioIn 12, ConAu 103, -21NR, -25R, EncFWF, WhAm 7, WhoAm 80, WhoWest 78

The Killings At Coyote Springs
BL - v73 - My 1 '77 - p1329
Kliatt - v12 - Spring '78 - p9

PATTERSON, Betty

I Reached For The Sky
LJ - v95 - O 15 '70 - p3635
Subject: Airlines—Hostesses

PATTERSON, Doris T 1917-

Your Family Goes Camping
BL - v56 - D 15 '59 - p237
Subject: Camping

PATTERSON, Gardner

Docker
BL - v77 - S 15 '80 - p118
CBRS - v9 - Winter '81 - p49
CCB-B - v34 - D '80 - p77
KR - v48 - N 1 '80 - p1399
NYTBR - v86 - F 15 '81 - p22
SLJ - v27 - O '80 - p157
Subject: Youth—Fiction

PATTERSON, Lillie
AuBYP, ConAu 73, InB&W 80, SmATA 14

Frederick Douglass
BL - v69 - My 1 '73 - p837
JNE - v38 - Fall '69 - p420
RR - v86 - Mr '69 - p172
Subject: Biography

Martin Luther King, Jr.
CCB-B - v23 - My '70 - p149
LJ - v95 - O 15 '70 - p3603
LJ - v95 - N 15 '70 - p4046
NYTBR, Pt. 2 - My 4 '69 - p44
RT - v32 - My '79 - p920
Subject: Biography

PATTERSON, Sarah 1959-

The Distant Summer
BL - v73 - S 15 '76 - p124
BS - v36 - S '76 - p186
EJ - v67 - Ja '78 - p91
KR - v44 - Ap 1 '76 - p420
LJ - v101 - Jl '76 - p1556
NYTBR - O 10 '76 - p36
PW - v209 - Ap 12 '76 - p59
PW - v211 - My 2 '77 - p68
SLJ - v22 - My '76 - p36

PATTERSON, Sarah (continued)
SLJ - v22 - My '76 - p83
TLS - Ap 23 '76 - p481

PATTON, A Rae 1908-
AmM&WS 86P, ConAu 5R

The Chemistry Of Life
BL - v67 - My 1 '71 - p749
HB - v47 - Ag '71 - p405
KR - v38 - O 1 '70 - p1114
LJ - v96 - Mr 15 '71 - p1129
SB - v6 - D '70 - p223
Subject: Biological chemistry

PAULSEN, Gary 1939-
ConAu 73, SmATA 22

Dogsong
EJ - v75 - F '86 - p105
J Read - v29 - Mr '86 - p565
LATBR - My 11 '86 - p7
RT - v39 - N '85 - p228
SLJ - v31 - Ap '85 - p98
VOYA - v8 - D '85 - p321
Subject: Eskimos—Fiction

The Foxman
BL - v73 - Je 15 '77 - p1576
BS - v37 - O '77 - p204
CCB-B - v31 - D '77 - p66
EJ - v67 - F '78 - p81
KR - v45 - Mr 15 '77 - p291
SLJ - v23 - Mr '77 - p153
Subject: Friendship—Fiction; Minnesota—Fiction

The Green Recruit
SLJ - v24 - My '78 - p88
Co-author: Peekner, Ray
Subject: Basketball—Fiction; Science fiction

Tiltawhirl John
KR - v46 - Ja 1 '78 - p8
SLJ - v24 - N '77 - p75
Subject: Amusement parks—Fiction; Runaways—Fiction

Winterkill
BL - v73 - Ap 15 '77 - p1268
BS - v37 - Ap '77 - p31
GP - v16 - S '77 - p3158
KR - v44 - S 15 '76 - p72
SLJ - v23 - N '76 - p72
TLS - v0 - Jl 15 '77 - p861
Subject: Police—Fiction

PAYNE, Donald Gordon
see Cameron, Ian

PAYNE, Elizabeth

The Pharaohs Of Ancient Egypt
BW - v11 - Je 14 '81 - p12
Subject: Egypt; Kings, queens, rulers, etc.

PEARCE, W E 1907-

Transistors And Circuits: Electronics For Young Experimenters
BL - v67 - Jl 1 '71 - p906
KR - v39 - F 15 '71 - p184
LJ - v96 - My 15 '71 - p1815
SA - v225 - D '71 - p114
SB - v7 - S '71 - p164
WLB - v46 - Mr '72 - p613
Co-author: Klein, Aaron
Subject: Electronics

PEASE, Howard 1894-1974
AuBYP, ConAu 5R, –106, JBA 51, SmATA 2, –25N, TwCChW 83, WhoAm 76

The Jinx Ship
BL - v24 - F '28 - p212
SR - v4 - Ja 28 '28 - p558

PEASE, Nick

The Case Of The Twisted Type
Hi Lo - v3 - F '82 - p2

PECK, Ira 1922-
ConAu 77

The Life And Words Of Martin Luther King, Jr.
B Rpt - v5 - My '86 - p35
NYTBR, Pt. 2 - My 4 '69 - p44
Subject: Biography

PECK, Richard 1934-
ConAu 19NR, ConLC 21, FifBJA, IntAu&W 82, OxChL, SmATA 18, –2AS, TwCChW 83, WhoAm 86, WrDr 86

Are You In The House Alone?
BL - v73 - O 15 '76 - p315
BL - v73 - O 15 '76 - p326
CCB-B - v30 - Mr '77 - p111
Comw - v104 - N 11 '77 - p731
EJ - v66 - S '77 - p84
EJ - v67 - Ja '78 - p91
EJ - v67 - My '78 - p90
HB - v53 - F '77 - p60
Kliatt - v12 - Winter '78 - p11
KR - v44 - S 1 '76 - p982
NYT - v126 - D 21 '76 - p31

PECK, Richard (continued)
NYTBR - N 14 '76 - p29
PW - v210 - S 13 '76 - p99
SLJ - v23 - D '76 - p69
SMQ - v8 - Fall '79 - p26
TES - Jl 11 '86 - p25
WCRB - v3 - S '77 - p58
Subject: Rape—Fiction

Don't Look And It Won't Hurt
BW - v6 - N 5 '72 - p8
Choice - v14 - N '77 - p1178
KR - v40 - Ag 15 '72 - p949
LJ - v97 - D 15 '72 - p4080
NYTBR - N 12 '72 - p8
PW - v202 - S 25 '72 - p60
Subject: Family life—Fiction

Dreamland Lake
BL - v70 - N 15 '73 - p335
BL - v70 - N 15 '73 - p342
CCB-B - v27 - Ja '74 - p83
KR - v41 - D 15 '73 - p1357
LJ - v98 - D 15 '73 - p3691
NYTBR - Ja 13 '74 - p10
NYTBR - F 23 '75 - p40
Teacher - v92 - Ap '75 - p110

Father Figure
BW - N 12 '78 - pE4
CCB-B - v32 - Ja '79 - p86
EJ - v68 - F '79 - p104
Emerg Lib - v11 - Ja '84 - p39
HB - v54 - D '78 - p647
Inst - v89 - Ja '80 - p112
NYTBR - S 30 '79 - p43
Par - v54 - Ja '79 - p20
PW - v216 - Jl 16 '79 - p68
TN - v37 - Fall '80 - p62
Subject: Brothers and sisters—Fiction; Fathers and sons—Fiction

Ghosts I Have Been
BL - v74 - O 1 '77 - p300
BL - v74 - Je 1 '78 - p1560
BW - D 11 '77 - pE4
CCB-B - v31 - Mr '78 - p117
CLW - v55 - S '83 - p80
EJ - v67 - S '78 - p90
HB - v54 - F '78 - p56
KR - v45 - S 15 '77 - p991
NYTBR - O 30 '77 - p34
NYTBR - N 13 '77 - p52
PW - v212 - Jl 11 '77 - p81
RT - v32 - O '78 - p43
SLJ - v24 - N '77 - p61
SLJ - v31 - N '84 - p27
Teacher - v95 - O '77 - p159
Subject: Supernatural—Fiction

Remembering The Good Times
B Rpt - v5 - N '86 - p37
CBRS - v13 - Ap '85 - p99
CCB-B - v38 - Je '85 - p192
EJ - v75 - D '86 - p60
HB - v61 - Jl '85 - p457
J Read - v29 - F '86 - p464
KR - v53 - My 15 '85 - pJ43
LATBR - Ag 10 '86 - p8
PW - v227 - My 17 '85 - p118
PW - v229 - Ap 25 '86 - p87
RT - v39 - Ja '86 - p464
SLJ - v31 - Ap '85 - p49
SLJ - v31 - Ap '85 - p99
SLJ - v32 - Ap '86 - p30
VOYA - v8 - Je '85 - p134
Subject: Friendship—Fiction

Sounds And Silences: Poetry For Now
Am - v123 - D 5 '70 - p499
BL - v67 - N 1 '70 - p224
BW - v4 - N 8 '70 - p5
CCB-B - v24 - D '70 - p64
CSM - v63 - Ja 23 '71 - p13
EJ - v60 - S '71 - p829
KR - v38 - Jl 15 '70 - p750
LJ - v95 - N 15 '70 - p4058
NYTBR, Pt. 2 - N 8 '70 - p54
PW - v198 - Jl 27 '70 - p74
SR - v53 - S 19 '70 - p35
TN - v27 - Ja '71 - p209
Subject: American poetry (Collections); English poetry

Through A Brief Darkness
BL - v73 - D 15 '76 - p615
BS - v33 - Ja 15 '74 - p472
CCB-B - v27 - Mr '74 - p116
GP - v14 - Ap '76 - p2844
JB - v40 - O '76 - p283
KR - v41 - D 1 '73 - p1314
LJ - v99 - F 15 '74 - p582
TES - S 22 '78 - p23
Subject: Mystery and detective stories

PECK, Robert Newton 1928-
AuBYP SUP, ConAu 81, ConLC 17, FifBJA, SmATA 21, -1AS, TwCChW 83, WrDr 86

Banjo
BL - v79 - D 15 '82 - p567
CBRS - v11 - N '82 - p30
CE - v59 - My '83 - p354
HB - v58 - D '82 - p653
LA - v60 - Mr '83 - p360
NYTBR - v88 - Ja 16 '83 - p22

PECK, Robert Newton (continued)
SLJ - v30 - N '83 - p81
Subject: Mountain life—Fiction; Schools—Fiction

Basket Case
WLB - v54 - Mr '80 - p456
Subject: Basketball—Fiction; Humorous stories; Schools—Fiction

A Day No Pigs Would Die
BL - v82 - Mr 1 '86 - p975
EJ - v69 - S '80 - p87
Emerg Lib - v9 - Ja '82 - p17
SLJ - v29 - Ag '83 - p27
Subject: Farm life—Fiction; Fathers and daughters—Fiction; Pigs—Fiction

Fawn
BL - v71 - Mr 15 '75 - p745
BS - v34 - F 15 '75 - p515
KR - v42 - D 1 '74 - p1271
KR - v42 - D 15 '74 - p1316
LJ - v100 - Mr 15 '75 - p603
NYTBR - F 2 '75 - p12
PW - v206 - D 9 '74 - p63
Subject: Ticonderoga, Battle of, 1758—Fiction

Millie's Boy
BW - v7 - N 11 '73 - p3C
JLH - v41 - S 15 '73 - p1044
LJ - v98 - O 15 '73 - p3158
PW - v204 - O 29 '73 - p36

Wild Cat
ACSB - v9 - Winter '76 - p34
BL - v72 - S 1 '75 - p44
CCB-B - v29 - N '79 - p52
Inst - v84 - My '75 - p106
KR - v43 - Ap 15 '75 - p457
NYTBR - v0 - My 4 '75 - p37
PW - v207 - Ap 7 '75 - p82
SLJ - v21 - My '75 - p58
Subject: Cats—Fiction

PEDERSEN, Elsa 1915-
AuBYP, ConAu 2NR

Cook Inlet Decision
NYTBR - My 12 '63 - p26

PEEKNER, Ray
see Paulsen, Gary (co-author)

PEET, Creighton 1899-1977
AuBYP, BioIn 11, ConAu 106, -69, SmATA 30

Man In Flight: How The Airlines Operate
BL - v69 - D 15 '72 - p406
CC - v89 - N 29 '72 - p1218
CCB-B - v26 - D '72 - p63
LJ - v98 - Ja 15 '73 - p269
Subject: Aeronautics

PEI, Mario
see Lambert, Eloise (co-author)

PELLETIER, Louis
see Snyder, Anne (co-author)

PELTIER, Leslie C 1900-1980
AmM&WS 76P, BioIn 1, -2, -7, -12, ConAu 17R, SmATA 13

Guideposts To The Stars: Exploring The Skies Throughout The Year
BL - v69 - Mr 15 '73 - p698
KR - v40 - D 1 '72 - p1363
LJ - v98 - My 15 '73 - p1684
SB - v9 - My '73 - p68
S & T - v46 - Jl '73 - p44
TLS - Ap 6 '73 - p401
Subject: Astronomy

PENRY-JONES, J

The Boys' Book Of Ships And Shipping
LJ - v91 - Ap 15 '66 - p2223
NYTBR - v71 - My 8 '66 - p25
SB - v2 - S '66 - p88
Subject: Ships

PEPE, Philip 1935-
ConAu 18NR, SmATA 20

Great Comebacks In Sport
BL - v71 - Je 15 '75 - p1077
LJ - v100 - Je 1 '75 - p1149
Subject: Athletes; Sports—Biography

PERL, Lila
AuBYP, ConAu 33R, SmATA 6

Don't Ask Miranda
Cur R - v19 - Je '80 - p216
J Read - v23 - D '79 - p279
Kliatt - v16 - Winter '82 - p14
Subject: Elections—Fiction; Schools—Fiction

PERL, Lila (continued)

Dumb Like Me, Olivia Potts
CCB-B - v30 - D '76 - p64
KR - v44 - S 1 '76 - p975
SLJ - v23 - D '76 - p68
Subject: Brothers and sisters—Fiction; Mystery and detective stories

Ghana And Ivory Coast: Spotlight On West Africa
BL - v71 - My 1 '75 - p916
HB - v51 - O '75 - p476
KR - v43 - Ap 1 '75 - p390
SLJ - v22 - S '75 - p124
Subject: Africa; Ivory Coast

Hey, Remember Fat Glenda?
BL - v78 - D 15 '81 - p552
CBRS - v10 - Ja '82 - p49
CCB-B - v35 - Ap '82 - p156
Inter BC - v13 - #4 '82 p25
Kliatt - v17 - Winter '83 - p13
KR - v50 - F 1 '82 - p136
SLJ - v28 - N '81 - p97
Subject: Weight control—Fiction

That Crazy April
Am - v131 - D 7 '74 - p373
B&B - v23 - Jl '78 - p58
BL - v70 - My 15 '74 - p1058
CE - v51 - N '74 - p92
Choice - v14 - N '77 - p1178
CLW - v46 - F '75 - p316
CLW - v47 - D '75 - p208
GP - v14 - My '75 - p2640
JB - v39 - Je '75 - p202
KR - v42 - Ap 1 '74 - p364
LJ - v99 - My 15 '74 - p1475
PW - v205 - Je 10 '74 - p41
TLS - Ap 4 '75 - p371
Subject: Family life—Fiction

PERRY, Jesse
see Kinnick, B J (co-author)

PERRY, Richard
ConAu 41R

The World Of The Giant Panda
BL - v66 - Mr 1 '70 - p813
Choice - v6 - F '70 - p1777
CSM - v62 - N 28 '69 - pB4
LJ - v94 - N 1 '69 - p4017
NH - v79 - Ap '70 - p77
NYTBR - Jl 1 '73 - p8
Obs - N 30 '69 - p35
PW - v196 - Ag 18 '69 - p73
SB - v6 - S '70 - p149
Subject: Animals

PERRY, Susan

How To Play Backgammon
SLJ - v28 - O '81 - p138
Subject: Games

How To Play Rummy Card Games
SLJ - v28 - O '81 - p138
Subject: Games

PERRY, Tyler

Girls, Answers To Your Questions About Guys
BL - v81 - Ja 15 '85 - p707
VOYA - v8 - Ap '85 - p66
Subject: Dating (Social customs); Etiquette; Sexual ethics

PETERS, Elizabeth (pseud.) 1927-
ConAu X, TwCCr&M 85, WrDr 86
Real Name:
Mertz, Barbara Gross

Summer Of The Dragon
BL - v75 - My 1 '79 - p1348
KR - v47 - F 15 '79 - p217
LJ - v104 - My 1 '79 - p1081
PW - v215 - Ap 2 '79 - p68

PETERSEN, P J 1941-
ConAu 112, IntAu&W 86, SmATA 43, -48

The Boll Weevil Express
BL - v79 - Je 1 '83 - p1269
BS - v43 - My '83 - p74
CBRS - v11 - Ap '83 - p95
CCB-B - v36 - My '83 - p175
Inter BC - v14 - #7 '83 p33
Kliatt - v19 - Spring '85 - p15
KR - v51 - Ap 1 '83 - p381
SLJ - v29 - Ap '83 - p126
VOYA - v6 - F '84 - p340
WLB - v57 - Ap '83 - p693
Subject: California—Fiction; Runaways—Fiction

Going For The Big One
BL - v83 - S 1 '86 - p66
B Rpt - v5 - S '86 - p35
CCB-B - v40 - S '86 - p16
SLJ - v33 - S '86 - p146
VOYA - v9 - Je '86 - p82
WLB - v60 - Ap '86 - p49
Subject: Brothers and sisters—Fiction; Survival—Fiction

PETERSON, Helen Stone 1910-
ConAu 37R, SmATA 8,
WhoAmW 77, WrDr 86

Susan B. Anthony
Comw - v95 - N 19 '71 - p189
LJ - v97 - Jl '72 - p2486
Subject: Biography

PETRY, Ann 1912?-
ChlLR 12, ConAu 4NR, ConLC 1,
-7, -18, ConNov 86, SmATA 5,
ThrBJA, TwCChW 83, WhoBlA 85,
WrDr 86

Harriet Tubman: Conductor On The Underground Railroad
BS - v30 - F 1 '71 - p482
CSM - v61 - My 1 '69 - pB7
Subject: Biography

Tituba Of Salem Village
Atl - v214 - D '64 - p163
BL - v69 - My 1 '73 - p839
CCB-B - v18 - Ja '65 - p78
CSM - F 25 '65 - p7
CSM - v57 - F 25 '65 - p7
CSM - v61 - My 1 '69 - pB7
HB - v41 - F '65 - p65
LJ - v89 - S 15 '64 - p3498
NYTBR, Pt. 2 - N 1 '64 - p8
SR - v47 - N 7 '64 - p55
Subject: Witchcraft

PETTERSSON, Allan Rune

Frankenstein's Aunt
BL - v78 - O 1 '81 - p238
Brit Bk N C - Spring '81 - p14
CBRS - v10 - Winter '82 - p59
CCB-B - v35 - D '81 - p75
JB - v45 - Ap '81 - p84
Kliatt - v17 - Winter '83 - p22
KR - v49 - D 15 '81 - p1520
Obs - N 30 '80 - p36
SLJ - v28 - S '81 - p140
TES - Ap 3 '81 - p28
TLS - N 21 '80 - p1330
Subject: Humorous stories;
Monsters—Fiction

PEVSNER, Stella
BioIn 12, ConAu 57, FifBJA,
SmATA 8

And You Give Me A Pain, Elaine
BL - v75 - S 15 '78 - p224
KR - v46 - O 15 '78 - p1139
Learning - v13 - Ap '85 - p28
PW - v214 - O 23 '78 - p61
SLJ - v25 - N '78 - p77
Subject: Brothers and sisters—
Fiction; Family life—Fiction

Call Me Heller, That's My Name
BL - v69 - Je 1 '73 - p950
BL - v76 - Je 15 '80 - p1545
CCB-B - v26 - Je '73 - p160
KR - v41 - Ap 1 '73 - p385
LJ - v98 - N 15 '73 - p3456
PW - v203 - Ap 16 '73 - p55
Subject: Family life—Fiction

Cute Is A Four-Letter Word
BL - v76 - Mr 1 '80 - p984
CBRS - v8 - Spring '80 - p119
CCB-B - v34 - S '80 - p18
CE - v57 - Mr '81 - p234
Emerg Lib - v9 - Mr '82 - p29
HB - v56 - Ag '80 - p410
KR - v48 - My 15 '80 - p646
RT - v35 - O '81 - p68
SLJ - v26 - Ag '80 - p78
Subject: Schools—Fiction

Keep Stompin' Till The Music Stops
BL - v73 - My 1 '77 - p1355
CCB-B - v31 - S '77 - p24
CLW - v49 - F '78 - p313
Inst - v87 - N '77 - p160
KR - v45 - My 1 '77 - p486
SE - v41 - O '77 - p532
SLJ - v24 - S '77 - p134
TN - v38 - Winter '82 - p115
WCRB - v4 - Mr '78 - p41
Subject: Family life—Fiction;
Learning disabilities—Fiction

A Smart Kid Like You
BB - v4 - Mr '76 - p4
BL - v71 - Jl 1 '75 - p1129
CCB-B - v29 - S '75 - p17
CLW - v47 - N '75 - p188
Comw - v102 - N 21 '75 - p569
J Read - v19 - F '76 - p421
KR - v43 - Ap 1 '75 - p375
NYTBR - N 16 '75 - p52
PW - v207 - Mr 31 '75 - p49
SLJ - v21 - My '75 - p58
Subject: Divorce—Fiction

PEYTON, K M 1929-
ChlLR 3, ConAu 69, IntAu&W 82X,
OxChL, SmATA 15, -X, ThrBJA,
TwCChW 78, -83, WrDr 86
Pseud./variant:
Peyton, Kathleen Wendy

The Beethoven Medal
BL - v69 - O 1 '72 - p140
BS - v32 - S 15 '72 - p284

PEYTON, K M (continued)
BW - v6 - N 5 '72 - p8
CCB-B - v26 - S '72 - p14
CE - v49 - F '73 - p258
EJ - v61 - N '72 - p1261
HB - v48 - O '72 - p475
KR - v40 - Jl 1 '72 - p728
Lis - v86 - N 11 '71 - p661
LJ - v97 - O 15 '72 - p3462
NO - v11 - N 18 '72 - p28
NS - v82 - N 12 '71 - p661
Obs - N 28 '71 - p35
PW - v202 - Jl 17 '72 - p122
Spec - v227 - N 13 '71 - p688
TLS - O 22 '71 - p1318
Subject: Social adjustment—Fiction

A Pattern Of Roses
B&B - v18 - N '72 - pR6
BL - v70 - S 15 '73 - p124
BL - v70 - Mr 15 '74 - p827
BS - v33 - O 15 '73 - p334
CCB-B - v27 - N '73 - p49
Choice - v12 - N '75 - p1133
CSM - v65 - N 7 '73 - pB4
CSM - v66 - D 5 '73 - pB12
GW - v107 - D 16 '72 - p24
HB - v49 - O '73 - p473
HB - v60 - Je '84 - p361
KR - v41 - Ag 1 '73 - p819
Lis - v88 - N 9 '72 - p644
LJ - v98 - S 15 '73 - p2667
LJ - v98 - D 15 '73 - p3691
NS - v84 - N 10 '72 - p692
Obs - N 26 '72 - p37
Obs - Je 8 '75 - p23
PW - v204 - S 17 '73 - p57
Spec - v229 - N 11 '72 - p750
Teacher - v91 - N '73 - p130
TES - D 10 '82 - p34
TES - Je 29 '84 - p32
TLS - N 3 '72 - p1324
TN - v30 - N '73 - p82
Subject: England—Fiction; Space and time—Fiction

Pennington's Last Term
A Lib - v3 - Ap '72 - p420
BL - v67 - Jl 1 '71 - p906
BL - v68 - Ap 1 '72 - p670
BS - v31 - Ag 15 '71 - p235
BW - v5 - My 9 '71 - p18
CCB-B - v25 - S '71 - p13
CE - v48 - N '71 - p100
CLW - v43 - Mr '72 - p430
EJ - v60 - N '71 - p1156
HB - v47 - Ag '71 - p390
KR - v39 - Ap 15 '71 - p443
LJ - v96 - Je 15 '71 - p2140
PW - v199 - My 31 '71 - p135
SR - v54 - S 18 '71 - p49
Subject: Schools—Fiction

PEYTON, Kathleen Wendy
see Peyton, K M

PFEFFER, Susan Beth 1948-
ChILR 11, ConAu 29R, SmATA 4, WhoAmW 77, WhoE 81, WrDr 86

About David
BS - v40 - N '80 - p303
CBRS - v8 - Ag '80 - p138
CCB-B - v34 - N '80 - p61
HB - v56 - D '80 - p649
Hi Lo - v2 - F '81 - p4
Kliatt - v16 - Spring '82 - p14
KR - v48 - O 1 '80 - p1303
LATBR - Jl 25 '82 - p9
NYTBR - v86 - F 1 '81 - p28
SLJ - v27 - N '80 - p87
TN - v42 - Summer '86 - p381
VOYA - v5 - Ag '82 - p50
WLB - v55 - D '80 - p292
Subject: Death—Fiction; Family problems—Fiction; Suicide—Fiction

The Beauty Queen
CCB-B - v28 - N '74 - p51
Hi Lo - v2 - F '81 - p4
Kliatt - v11 - Spring '77 - p7
KR - v42 - My 1 '74 - p489
LJ - v99 - S 15 '74 - p2296
PW - v205 - Je 10 '74 - p41
Subject: Beauty contests—Fiction; Family life—Fiction

Better Than All Right
EJ - v62 - Ja '73 - p147
KR - v40 - Jl 15 '72 - p808
LJ - v98 - Mr 15 '73 - p1015
NYTBR - N 12 '72 - p14
Subject: Loneliness—Fiction

Fantasy Summer
BL - v80 - Jl '84 - p1545
CBRS - v12 - Ag '84 - p153
CCB-B - v38 - O '84 - p33
EJ - v74 - D '85 - p55
RT - v39 - O '85 - p47
SLJ - v31 - N '84 - p136
VOYA - v7 - O '84 - p198
WCRB - v10 - N '84 - p46
Subject: Friendship—Fiction; New York (City)—Fiction; Self-perception—Fiction

Getting Even
B Rpt - v5 - N '86 - p31

PFEFFER, Susan Beth (continued)
SLJ - v33 - N '86 - p107
Subject: Family life—Fiction; Work—Fiction

Marly The Kid
Hi Lo - v2 - F '81 - p4
Subject: Family life—Fiction; Schools—Fiction

Prime Time
SLJ - v32 - O '85 - p186
Subject: Love—Fiction; Soap operas—Fiction

Starring Peter And Leigh
BL - v75 - Je 1 '79 - p1486
CCB-B - v32 - Jl '79 - p198
EJ - v69 - Mr '80 - p75
Emerg Lib - v9 - N '81 - p32
J Read - v23 - Ap '80 - p662
SLJ - v25 - My '79 - p66
TN - v37 - Fall '80 - p62
Subject: Actors and actresses—Fiction; Hemophilia—Fiction; Remarriage—Fiction

Take Two And...Rolling!
SLJ - v32 - N '85 - p100
Subject: Love—Fiction

Wanting It All
SLJ - v32 - Mr '86 - p178

What Do You Do When Your Mouth Won't Open?
BL - v77 - Jl 15 '81 - p1449
CBRS - v9 - Mr '81 - p69
CCB-B - v34 - Ap '81 - p159
CLW - v53 - D '81 - p231
Inter BC - v13 - #4 '82 p28
KR - v49 - S 1 '81 - p1084
RT - v36 - O '82 - p78
SLJ - v27 - My '81 - p68
VOYA - v4 - O '81 - p37
Subject: Public speaking—Fiction

Whatever Words You Want To Hear
BS - v34 - S 15 '74 - p286
KR - v42 - Ag 1 '74 - p811
LJ - v99 - D 15 '74 - p3273
PW - v206 - S 23 '74 - p155
Subject: Social adjustment—Fiction

PFLUG, Betsy

Egg-Speriment
KR - v41 - Ap 1 '73 - p392
LJ - v98 - O 15 '73 - p3140
Subject: Handicraft

PHELAN, Mary Kay 1914-
AuBYP SUP, ConAu 4NR, IntAu&W 82, SmATA 3, WhoAmW 81, WhoMW 76, WrDr 86

Four Days In Philadelphia, 1776
BL - v64 - Ja 1 '68 - p548
BW - v1 - N 5 '67 - p40
CE - v44 - Ap '68 - p502
KR - v35 - S 15 '67 - p1152
LJ - v92 - O 15 '67 - p3854
NYTBR, pt. 1 - v73 - F 25 '68 - p26
Subject: United States—History—Revolution, 1775-1783

PHILBROOK, Clem 1917-
AuBYP, ConAu 104, SmATA 24

Slope Dope
KR - v34 - Jl 1 '66 - p631
LJ - v91 - O 15 '66 - p5237
Subject: Skis and skiing—Fiction

PHILLIPS, Betty Lou
SmATA X
Pseud./variant:
Phillips, Elizabeth Louise

Brush Up On Hair Care
BL - v79 - Ja 15 '83 - p669
Hi Lo - v4 - Mr '83 - p3
SLJ - v29 - Ag '83 - p70
VOYA - v6 - Ap '83 - p51
Subject: Health

Earl Campbell, Houston Oiler Superstar
BL - v76 - Ja 1 '80 - p670
SLJ - v26 - Mr '80 - p135
Subject: Blacks—Biography; Football—Biography

Go! Fight! Win!
BL - v77 - Mr 1 '81 - p922
CCB-B - v34 - My '81 - p178
Hi Lo - v2 - Ap '81 - p3
SLJ - v27 - My '81 - p87
Subject: Cheerleading

PHILLIPS, Erin

Research For Romance
BL - v80 - Je 15 '84 - p1474
SLJ - v31 - S '84 - p137
VOYA - v7 - O '84 - p201
Subject: Love—Fiction

PHILLIPS, Maxine

Crime And The Law: A Look At The Criminal Justice System
BL - v79 - O 15 '82 - p299
Subject: Crime and criminals

Your Rights When You're Young
BL - v76 - D 15 '79 - p607
BL - v76 - Jl 15 '80 - p1662
CSM - v73 - D 1 '80 - pB11
CT - v9 - Ja '80 - p28
Hi Lo - v1 - D '79 - p5
SLJ - v27 - D '80 - p20
TN - v36 - Spring '80 - p329
Subject: Law and legislation

PHILP, Candace T

Rodeo Horses
BL - v80 - Ja 1 '84 - p678
SLJ - v30 - F '84 - p66

PHIPSON, Joan 1912-
AuBYP, ChlLR 5, ConAu X, IntAu&W 82X, OxAusL, SmATA 2, -3AS, ThrBJA, TwCChW 83, WrDr 86
Pseud./variant:
Fitzhardinge, Joan Margaret

The Family Conspiracy
Comw - v80 - My 22 '64 - p269
HB - v40 - Ap '64 - p179
LJ - v89 - Mr 15 '64 - p1452
NYTBR - Ap 5 '64 - p34
PW - v190 - Ag 1 '66 - p64
SR - v47 - Je 27 '64 - p45
TLS - N 23 '62 - p894
TLS - S 20 '74 - p1005

Hit And Run
BS - v46 - Jl '86 - p160
CBRS - v14 - My '86 - p114
CCB-B - v39 - N '85 - p54
EJ - v75 - O '86 - p85
EJ - v75 - D '86 - p60
HB - v62 - Ja '86 - p63
SLJ - v32 - O '85 - p186
VOYA - v9 - Ap '86 - p33
Subject: Australia—Fiction; Hit-and-run drivers—Fiction; Survival—Fiction

PICARD, Barbara Leonie 1917-
AuBYP, BioIn 11, ConAu 2NR, IntAu&W 86, OxChL, SmATA 2, ThrBJA, TwCChW 83, WrDr 86

One Is One
BL - v63 - Ja 15 '67 - p539
BS - v26 - D 1 '66 - p341
CCB-B - v20 - Ap '67 - p128
HB - v43 - F '67 - p73
HT - v15 - D '65 - p879
KR - v34 - Ag 15 '66 - p835
LA - v58 - Ap '81 - p453
LJ - v91 - D 15 '66 - p6204
NYTBR - v72 - Mr 26 '67 - p22
Obs - D 19 '65 - p23
Spec - N 12 '65 - p629
TLS - D 9 '65 - p1146

PICK, Christopher C

Oil Machines
ACSB - v13 - Spring '80 - p49
SB - v16 - S '80 - p34
Subject: Petroleum industry and trade

Undersea Machines
ACSB - v13 - Spring '80 - p49
SB - v16 - S '80 - p35
Subject: Diving (Submarine); Submarine boats

PIERCE, Travis
see Stewart, Jo (co-author)

PIERIK, Robert 1921-
ConAu 37R, SmATA 13

Archy's Dream World
KR - v40 - Ja 1 '72 - p4
LJ - v97 - My 15 '72 - p1930
Subject: Fathers and sons—Fiction

PIERSALL, James 1929-
WhoProB 73

Fear Strikes Out: The Jim Piersall Story
BL - v51 - Je 1 '55 - p406
HB - v31 - D '55 - p469
KR - v23 - Ap 15 '55 - p288
LJ - v80 - Ap 15 '55 - p872
Co-author: Hirshberg, Al
Subject: Baseball—Biography

see also Hirshberg, Al for additional titles

PIKE, Christopher

Slumber Party
Kliatt - v20 - Spring '86 - p12
SLJ - v33 - D '86 - p121
Subject: Horror stories; Mystery and detective stories

PIMLOTT, Douglas
see Rutter, Russell J (co-author)

PINE, Tillie S 1896-
AuBYP, BkP, ConAu 69, SmATA 13

Rocks And How We Use Them
LJ - v93 - Ja 15 '68 - p284
SB - v4 - My '68 - p29
Co-author: Levine, Joseph
Subject: Rocks

PINES, Nancy

Spotlight On Love
BL - v80 - F 1 '84 - p810
PW - v224 - O 14 '83 - p57
SLJ - v30 - Mr '84 - p174
VOYA - v7 - Ag '84 - p145
Subject: Actors and actresses—Fiction; Love—Fiction

PINIAT, John

Going For The Win
BL - v74 - My 15 '78 - p1487
Co-author: Werner, Herma
Subject: Basketball—Fiction

see also Werner, Herma for additional titles

PINKWATER, Daniel Manus 1941-
AuBYP SUP, BioIn 11, ChILR 4, ConAu 12NR, ConLC 35, FifBJA, SmATA 46, -8, -3AS, WhoAm 86

The Hoboken Chicken Emergency
BL - v73 - Ap 15 '77 - p1268
BW - Mr 20 '77 - pH4
CCB-B - v30 - Je '77 - p163
CE - v54 - O '77 - p28
CSM - v69 - My 4 '77 - pB8
HB - v53 - Je '77 - p316
KR - v45 - F 15 '77 - p166
New R - v177 - D 3 '77 - p28
NW - v90 - Jl 18 '77 - p92
NYTBR - Mr 27 '77 - p44
RT - v31 - Ap '78 - p841
SLJ - v24 - S '77 - p134
VLS - Mr '86 - p18
Subject: Chickens—Fiction; Humorous stories

Lizard Music
BL - v73 - S 1 '76 - p4126
BL - v73 - My 15 '77 - p1426
BW - F 13 '77 - pG10
CCB-B - v30 - Mr '77 - p112
Emerg Lib - v11 - Ja '84 - p22
HB - v53 - Ap '77 - p161
KR - v44 - Ag 1 '76 - p846
PW - v210 - O 18 '76 - p64
PW - v215 - Ap 23 '79 - p80
RT - v31 - O '77 - p19
SLJ - v23 - O '76 - p110
Teacher - v95 - O '77 - p158
VLS - Mr '86 - p18
Subject: Science fiction

The Snarkout Boys And The Avocado Of Death
VLS - Mr '86 - p18
Subject: Science fiction

Yobgorgle: Mystery Monster Of Lake Ontario
BL - v78 - F 15 '82 - p762
CBRS - v8 - Winter '80 - p68
SLJ - v26 - N '79 - p80
VLS - Mr '86 - p18
Subject: Sea monsters—Fiction

see also Pinkwater, Jill (co-author) for additional titles

PINKWATER, Jill

Superpuppy: How To Choose, Raise, And Train The Best Possible Dog For You
BL - v81 - Jl '85 - p1567
Kliatt - v16 - Fall '82 - p57
VOYA - v5 - O '82 - p67
Co-author: Pinkwater, Daniel Manus
Subject: Dogs

see also Pinkwater, Daniel Manus for additional titles

PIRMANTGEN, Patricia

The Beatles
SLJ - v22 - S '75 - p95
Subject: Musicians; Rock musicians

PLACE, Marian T 1910-
AuBYP, ConAu 20NR, SmATA 3

Frontiersman: The True Story Of Billy Dixon
LJ - v92 - N 15 '67 - p4257
NYTBR - v72 - Mr 26 '67 - p22
Subject: Biography

Juan's Eighteen-Wheeler Summer
BL - v79 - N 1 '82 - p373
CBRS - v11 - N '82 - p30
CCB-B - v36 - F '83 - p115
KR - v50 - Ag 1 '82 - p873
LA - v60 - O '83 - p906
SLJ - v29 - N '82 - p89

PLACE, Marian T (continued)
WCRB - v9 - Mr '83 - p55
Co-author: Preston, Charles G
Subject: California—Fiction; Mexican Americans—Fiction; Truck driving—Fiction

PLATT, Kin 1911-
AuBYP SUP, BioIn 8, -12, ConAu 11NR, ConLC 26, FifBJA, SmATA 21

The Ape Inside Me
BL - v76 - Ja 1 '80 - p662
B Rpt - v2 - S '83 - p25
B Rpt - v2 - N '83 - p37
BS - v39 - F '80 - p410
CBRS - v8 - N '79 - p29
CCB-B - v33 - My '80 - p180
Hi Lo - v1 - My '80 - p3
J Read - v24 - O '80 - p84
KR - v48 - F 1 '80 - p136
SLJ - v26 - N '79 - p92
Subject: Behavior—Fiction

The Blue Man
KR - v29 - Je 15 '61 - p501
LJ - v86 - N 15 '61 - p4040
NYTBR - S 24 '61 - p40

Boy Who Could Make Himself Disappear
BL - v65 - O 1 '68 - p190
BS - v28 - Jl 15 '68 - p173
BW - v2 - O 6 '68 - p20
CCB-B - v22 - S '68 - p14
KR - v36 - My 15 '68 - p556
LJ - v93 - O 15 '68 - p3986
SR - v51 - Ag 24 '68 - p43
Subject: Social adjustment—Fiction

Brogg's Brain
BL - v78 - O 15 '81 - p297
B Rpt - v2 - S '83 - p25
CBRS - v10 - S '81 - p9
CCB-B - v35 - O '81 - p35
CLW - v53 - Mr '82 - p356
Hi Lo - v3 - Mr '82 - p4
Inst - v91 - Ja '82 - p144
J Read - v25 - Ap '82 - p709
Kliatt - v17 - Spring '83 - p4
KR - v49 - N 1 '81 - p1349
SLJ - v28 - D '81 - p86
VOYA - v4 - D '81 - p34
Subject: Running—Fiction

Chloris And The Creeps
BS - v33 - Ag 15 '73 - p234
BW - v7 - N 11 '73 - p3C
CCB-B - v27 - Ja '74 - p84
KR - v41 - F 15 '73 - p188
LJ - v98 - Ap 15 '73 - p1389
PW - v203 - My 7 '73 - p66
Subject: Family life—Fiction

Chloris And The Freaks
BL - v72 - F 1 '76 - p762
BL - v72 - F 1 '76 - p788
CCB-B - v29 - Ap '76 - p131
Cur R - v16 - F '77 - p48
KR - v43 - D 15 '75 - p1379
NYTBR - N 16 '75 - p52
SLJ - v22 - D '75 - p32
SLJ - v22 - D '75 - p61
Subject: Astrology—Fiction; Divorce—Fiction; Family problems—Fiction

Crocker
B Rpt - v2 - Mr '84 - p39
BS - v43 - D '83 - p350
CBRS - v12 - N '83 - p32
CCB-B - v37 - Ja '84 - p95
SLJ - v30 - Ja '84 - p88
VOYA - v6 - F '84 - p340
Subject: Family life—Fiction

Dracula, Go Home!
BL - v75 - My 15 '79 - p1435
B Rpt - v2 - S '83 - p25
CBRS - v7 - My '79 - p99
CCB-B - v33 - S '79 - p16
Hi Lo - v1 - O '79 - p4
Kliatt - v15 - Spring '81 - p12
SLJ - v25 - My '79 - p82
Subject: Mystery and detective stories

Frank And Stein And Me
BL - v78 - Ag '82 - p1531
CBRS - v10 - Jl '82 - p129
Hi Lo - v4 - S '82 - p3
SLJ - v29 - Ja '83 - p87
Subject: Crime and criminals—Fiction; Monsters—Fiction

Headman
BL - v80 - O 15 '82 - p353
EJ - v66 - Ja '77 - p65
EJ - v67 - My '78 - p88
KR - v43 - Jl 15 '75 - p783
NYTBR - D 14 '75 - p8
SLJ - v22 - D '75 - p61
TN - v32 - Ap '76 - p285
Subject: Juvenile delinquency—Fiction

Hey, Dummy
BS - v31 - Ja 15 '72 - p471
CCB-B - v25 - Je '72 - p162
KR - v39 - N 15 '71 - p1213

PLATT, Kin (continued)
NYTBR - Mr 12 '72 - p8
NYTBR - My 6 '73 - p28
SMQ - v8 - Fall '79 - p27
TN - v36 - Winter '80 - p208
Subject: Friendship—Fiction; Mentally handicapped—Fiction

Mystery Of The Witch Who Wouldn't
BS - v29 - D 1 '69 - p354
KR - v37 - S 1 '69 - p939
LJ - v94 - D 15 '69 - p4618
Subject: Mystery and detective stories

Run For Your Life
BL - v74 - N 15 '77 - p545
CCB-B - v31 - Ja '78 - p85
Hi Lo - v1 - Mr '80 - p4
SLJ - v24 - D '77 - p65
Subject: Running—Fiction

Sinbad And Me
BS - v26 - O 1 '66 - p251
KR - v34 - Jl 1 '66 - p630
LJ - v91 - D 15 '66 - p6209
NYTBR, Pt. 2 - v73 - F 25 '68 - p18
SLJ - v24 - F '78 - p35
Teacher - v92 - O '74 - p108

PODOJIL, Catherine

Mother Teresa
BL - v79 - Ja 15 '83 - p660
Subject: Biography; Nuns

POGRUND, Phyllis
see Grebel, Rosemary (co-author)

POLLACK, Philip

Careers And Opportunities In Science
LJ - v93 - F 15 '68 - p885
SB - v3 - Mr '68 - p283
Co-author: Purcell, John
Subject: Science as a profession

POLLOCK, Bruce 1945-
SmATA 46

The Face Of Rock And Roll
Brit Bk N - N '86 - p624
LJ - v103 - D 15 '78 - p2532
SLJ - v25 - D '78 - p74
Co-author: Wagman, John
Subject: Rock music

It's Only Rock And Roll
BL - v76 - Je 15 '80 - p1523
BS - v40 - S '80 - p210
CBRS - v8 - Jl '80 - p129
CCB-B - v34 - S '80 - p19
J Read - v24 - Mr '81 - p549
KR - v48 - Jl 15 '80 - p914
SLJ - v26 - Ag '80 - p79
TN - v38 - Summer '82 - p364
Subject: Rock music—Fiction

Me, Minsky And Max
BL - v75 - D 1 '78 - p610
HB - v54 - D '78 - p647
KR - v46 - D 1 '78 - p1312
SLJ - v25 - Ja '79 - p62

POLLOCK, Rollene

Flying Wheels
BL - v75 - Jl 15 '79 - p1622
Hi Lo - v1 - O '79 - p4
Subject: Motorcycles—Fiction

POLLOWITZ, Melinda Kilborn 1944-
BioIn 13, ConAu 13NR, SmATA 26

Princess Amy
BL - v78 - N 1 '81 - p378
Hi Lo - v3 - Ja '82 - p3
VOYA - v4 - D '81 - p34
Subject: Adolescence—Fiction

POMEROY, Pete (pseud.) 1925-
AuBYP SUP, ConAu X, SmATA X
Real Name:
Roth, Arthur J

Wipeout!
LJ - v93 - My 15 '68 - p2130

see also Roth, Arthur J for additional titles

POOLE, A B

Cargo
BL - v79 - Ja 15 '83 - p660

POOLE, Gray
see Poole, Lynn (co-author)

POOLE, Josephine 1933-
ConAu 10NR, ConLC 17, IntAu&W 86X, SmATA 5, –2AS, TwCChW 83, WrDr 86
Pseud./variant:
Heylar, Jane Penelope Josephine

Touch And Go: A Story Of Suspense
BL - v73 - Mr 15 '77 - p1094
BS - v36 - Mr '77 - p387
CCB-B - v30 - D '76 - p15

POOLE, Josephine (continued)
Comw - v103 - N 19 '76 - p762
GP - v15 - N '76 - p2988
HB - v53 - F '77 - p60
JB - v41 - Ap '77 - p120
KR - v44 - Ag 1 '76 - p848
SLJ - v23 - D '76 - p69
TLS - D 10 '76 - p1548
Subject: Mystery and detective stories

POOLE, Lynn 1910-1969
AuBYP, -SUP, BioIn 8, ConAu 5R, CurBio 54, -69, MorJA, SmATA 1, WhAm 5

Men Who Dig Up History
BL - v64 - Jl 15 '68 - p1283
BS - v28 - My 1 '68 - p66
CCB-B - v21 - Jl '68 - p180
CSM - v60 - My 2 '68 - pB6
KR - v36 - F 1 '68 - p127
LJ - v93 - Mr 15 '68 - p1140
SB - v4 - S '68 - p116
SR - v51 - Je 15 '68 - p33
Co-author: Poole, Gray
Subject: Archaeology

PORCARI, Constance Kwolek
see Kwolek, Constance

POSELL, Elsa Z
AuBYP SUP, ConAu 20NR, SmATA 3

This Is An Orchestra
KR - v41 - D 15 '73 - p1368
LJ - v99 - Mr 15 '74 - p894
Subject: Music; Orchestra

POSEY, Jeanne K

The Horse Keeper's Handbook
LJ - v99 - N 1 '74 - p2868
RSR - v2 - O '74 - p157
Subject: Horses

POST, Elizabeth L 1920-
ConAu 49, WhoAm 86, WhoAmW 75

The Emily Post Book Of Etiquette For Young People
BS - v27 - Ja 1 '68 - p394
KR - v35 - N 15 '67 - p1376
LJ - v93 - Ja 15 '68 - p310
PW - v192 - N 6 '67 - p50
SR - v51 - My 18 '68 - p64
Subject: Etiquette

POTTER, Charles Francis 1885-1962
NatCAB 52, WhAm 4

More Tongue Tanglers And A Rigmarole
CSM - My 7 '64 - p3B
HB - v40 - Je '64 - p277
SR - v47 - Ag 15 '64 - p45
Subject: Fairy tales; Verses for children

POWERS, Bill 1931-
ConAu 77, SmATA 31

Flying High
BL - v74 - Mr 15 '78 - p1198
CCB-B - v31 - Ap '78 - p133
Inst - v87 - My '78 - p113
SLJ - v24 - My '78 - p88
Subject: Gymnastics—Fiction

A Test Of Love
BL - v75 - Jl 15 '79 - p1622
CBRS - v7 - Spring '79 - p119
CCB-B - v33 - S '79 - p16
Hi Lo - v1 - S '79 - p5
SLJ - v25 - My '79 - p75
Subject: Unwed mothers—Fiction

The Weekend
BB - v6 - N '78 - p3
BL - v74 - Ap 15 '78 - p1343
B Rpt - v2 - S '83 - p25
CCB-B - v31 - Je '78 - p165
CLW - v50 - N '78 - p182
Cur R - v17 - My '78 - p127
Hi Lo - v1 - S '79 - p2
Kliatt - v14 - Spring '80 - p8
NYTBR - Ap 30 '78 - p45
SLJ - v25 - S '78 - p163
Subject: Juvenile detention homes—Fiction

POWLEDGE, Fred 1935-
ConAu 9NR, SmATA 37, WrDr 86

You'll Survive!
BL - v83 - N 1 '86 - p413
CCB-B - v39 - Je '86 - p194
PW - v229 - My 30 '86 - p71
SLJ - v33 - N '86 - p107
VOYA - v9 - Ag '86 - p179
WLB - v61 - D '86 - p51
Subject: Adolescence

POWNALL, David 1938-
ConNov 86

The Bunch From Bananas
Brit Bk N C - Autumn '80 - p20
CBRS - v9 - Spring '81 - p109

POWNALL, David (continued)
TES - Jl 23 '82 - p24
Subject: Crime and criminals—Fiction; Humorous stories

POYNTER, Margaret 1927-
ConAu 16NR, SmATA 27

Crazy Minnie
Hi Lo - v1 - Mr '80 - p4
Subject: Grandmothers—Fiction; Orphans—Fiction

PRAGER, Arthur
ConAu 12NR, SmATA 44

World War II Resistance Stories
BL - v75 - Jl 15 '79 - p1622
CCB-B - v33 - S '79 - p16
CLW - v51 - Ap '80 - p415
SLJ - v26 - S '79 - p146
Co-author: Prager, Emily
Subject: World War, 1939-1945

PRAGER, Emily
see Prager, Arthur (co-author)

PRESBERG, Miriam Goldstein
see Gilbert, Miriam

PRESTON, Charles G
see Place, Marian T (co-author)

PRESTON, Edward (pseud.) 1925-
ConAu X
Real Name:
Guess, Edward Preston

Martin Luther King: Fighter For Freedom
LJ - v96 - Ap 15 '71 - p1432
Subject: Biography

PRICE, Willard 1887-1983
AuBYP, BioIn 2, ConAu 1NR, SmATA 48, TwCChW 83, Who 83, –85N, WrDr 84

Lion Adventure
KR - v35 - Ap 1 '67 - p415
PW - v191 - Je 5 '67 - p176
SLJ - v26 - Ag '80 - p79
TLS - My 25 '67 - p459

PRINCE, Alison 1931-
ConAu 29R, SmATA 28, WhoArt 84

The Turkey's Nest
BL - v76 - Mr 15 '80 - p1044
CBRS - v8 - Mr '80 - p79
CCB-B - v33 - Je '80 - p199
GP - v18 - N '79 - p3592
HB - v56 - Je '80 - p308
J Read - v24 - N '80 - p173
KR - v48 - Ap 1 '80 - p442
SLJ - v26 - My '80 - p79
TES - N 23 '79 - p31
TLS - D 14 '79 - p124
Subject: England—Fiction; Farm life—Fiction; Unwed mothers—Fiction

PRINGLE, Laurence 1935-
AuBYP SUP, ChlLR 4, ConAu 14NR, FourBJA, SmATA 4, WhoE 77

Dinosaurs And Their World
BL - v64 - My 15 '68 - p1096
KR - v36 - Mr 1 '68 - p267
LJ - v93 - Je 15 '68 - p2542
PW - v193 - Ap 15 '68 - p98
SB - v4 - S '68 - p114
Teacher - v94 - Ja '77 - p134
Subject: Dinosaurs

Radiation: Waves And Particles/benefits And Risks
ASBYP - v16 - Fall '83 - p53
BL - v79 - Ap 1 '83 - p1036
CCB-B - v36 - My '83 - p176
KR - v50 - D 15 '82 - p1339
SB - v19 - S '83 - p13
VOYA - v6 - Je '83 - p105
Subject: Science

PRONZINI, Bill 1943-
ConAu 14NR, TwCCr&M 85, WhoAm 86, WrDr 86

Midnight Specials
BL - v74 - N 15 '77 - p529
KR - v45 - Mr 15 '77 - p311
KR - v45 - Ap 15 '77 - p439
PW - v211 - Mr 28 '77 - p73
WLB - v52 - D '77 - p307
Subject: Mystery and detective stories; Railroads—Fiction

PROUDFIT, Isabel 1898-
AuBYP, MorJA

Riverboy: The Story Of Mark Twain
BL - v37 - N 15 '40 - p123
SR - v23 - N 16 '40 - p8
Subject: Biography; Clemens, Samuel Langhorne

PROVENSEN, Alice 1918-
ChILR 11, ConAu 5NR, IlsBYP, IlsCB 1957, -1967, SmATA 9, ThrBJA, WhoAm 86, WhoAmW 77, WhoChL

Leonardo Da Vinci: The Artist, Inventor, Scientist
NY - v60 - D 3 '84 - p188
SB - v21 - S '85 - p35
Sch Lib - v33 - Je '85 - p149
SE - v49 - Ap '85 - p326
SLJ - v31 - Ja '85 - p67
Spec - v253 - D 15 '84 - p30
TES - Je 7 '85 - p49
Time - v124 - D 17 '84 - p84
TLS - Ja 4 '85 - p18
USA T - v3 - D 7 '84 - p3D
Co-author: Provensen, Martin
Subject: Biography

PROVENSEN, Martin
see Provensen, Alice (co-author)

PURCELL, John
see Pollack, Philip (co-author)

PURDY, Susan 1939-
AuBYP, BioIn 8, ConAu 10NR, IlsCB 1957, SmATA 8, WhoAmW 77, WhoE 77

Books For You To Make
BL - v70 - Ja 1 '74 - p490
BW - v7 - N 11 '73 - p5C
KR - v41 - O 1 '73 - p1106
LJ - v99 - Ja 15 '74 - p211
Subject: Bookbinding

PYLE, Howard 1853-1911
ConAu 109, DcLB 42, IlrAm 1880, IlsBYP, JBA 34, OxAmL 83, OxChL, SmATA 16, TwCChW 83A, WhoChL

The Merry Adventures Of Robin Hood
B&B - v19 - O '73 - p137
BL - v43 - Ja 1 '47 - p140
Dr - Fall '73 - p75
LJ - v72 - Ja 1 '47 - p84
Obs - Ag 10 '69 - p26
TLS - D 3 '71 - p1509
Subject: Folklore

Q

QUIGLEY, Martin

The Original Colored House Of David
BS - v41 - N '81 - p320
CBRS - v10 - F '82 - p69
CCB-B - v35 - Ja '82 - p93
CLW - v53 - Mr '82 - p356
HB - v57 - D '81 - p670
NY - v57 - D 7 '81 - p238
NYTBR - v87 - F 28 '82 - p31
PW - v220 - N 6 '81 - p79
SLJ - v28 - D '81 - p72
VOYA - v5 - Je '82 - p36
Subject: Baseball—Fiction; Blacks—Fiction

QUIN-HARKIN, Janet 1941-
BioIn 12, ConAu 15NR, IntAu&W 82, SmATA 18

California Girl
BL - v78 - O 1 '81 - p189
Hi Lo - v3 - Ja '82 - p3
Hi Lo - v3 - Je '82 - p2
SLJ - v28 - N '81 - p110
VOYA - v4 - D '81 - p34
Subject: Love—Fiction

Daydreamer
BL - v79 - My 15 '83 - p1221
Kliatt - v17 - Spring '83 - p5
SLJ - v29 - My '83 - p84
VOYA - v6 - D '83 - p281
Subject: Love—Fiction

Exchange Of Hearts
BL - v0 - Je 15 '84 - p1474
SLJ - v31 - S '84 - p138
VOYA - v7 - O '84 - p202
Subject: Love—Fiction

Follow That Boy
SLJ - v32 - Ap '86 - p103
Subject: Love—Fiction

Ghost Of A Chance
BL - v80 - F 1 '84 - p810
SLJ - v30 - My '84 - p88
VOYA - v7 - Je '84 - p92
Subject: Love—Fiction

The Graduates
PW - v230 - Jl 25 '86 - p192
SLJ - v33 - S '86 - p148
VOYA - v9 - Ag '86 - p156
VOYA - v9 - D '86 - p231
Subject: Love—Fiction

The Great Boy Chase
SLJ - v32 - Ja '86 - p79
Subject: Dating (Social customs)—Fiction

Love Match
BL - v78 - Ja 15 '82 - p644
CCB-B - v35 - Mr '82 - p136
Hi Lo - v3 - Je '82 - p3
Kliatt - v16 - Spring '82 - p10
SLJ - v28 - Mr '82 - p160
Subject: Adolescence—Fiction; Sports—Fiction

Lovebirds
RT - v39 - O '85 - p48
Subject: Love—Fiction

Ten-Boy Summer
BL - v79 - S 1 '82 - p37
LATBR - v0 - Je 27 '82 - p13
SLJ - v29 - O '82 - p158
VOYA - v5 - D '82 - p35
Subject: Friendship—Fiction

The Trouble With Toni
B Rpt - v5 - N '86 - p36
SLJ - v33 - S '86 - p149
VOYA - v9 - D '86 - p231
Subject: Love—Fiction

The Two Of Us
SLJ - v31 - S '84 - p137
Subject: Love—Fiction

R

RABE, Berniece Louise 1928-
ConAu 1NR, FifBJA, IntAu&W 86, SmATA 7, WrDr 86

The Girl Who Had No Name
BL - v73 - Jl 1 '77 - p1654
CCB-B - v31 - Ja '78 - p85
HB - v53 - O '77 - p533
J Read - v22 - N '78 - p184
KR - v45 - Je 1 '77 - p581
LA - v55 - Ap '78 - p523
PW - v212 - Jl 4 '77 - p77
SLJ - v23 - My '77 - p71
Teacher - v95 - O '77 - p159
Subject: Country life—Fiction; Family life—Fiction

Naomi
BL - v71 - Je 1 '75 - p1016
BL - v73 - Mr 15 '77 - p1101
BS - v35 - S '75 - p169
CCB-B - v29 - D '75 - p69
Cur R - v16 - F '77 - p48
J Read - v20 - O '76 - p80
KR - v43 - Je 1 '75 - p612
NYTBR - Je 22 '75 - p8
PW - v207 - Je 30 '75 - p58
SLJ - v21 - Ap '75 - p69
Subject: Family life—Fiction; Farm life—Fiction

Rass
BL - v69 - My 15 '73 - p909
BW - v7 - My 13 '73 - p3
KR - v40 - D 15 '72 - p1432
LJ - v98 - My 15 '73 - p1692
NYTBR - Ag 12 '73 - p8
PW - v203 - Ap 16 '73 - p55
Subject: Farm life—Fiction; Fathers and sons—Fiction

Who's Afraid?
BL - v77 - S 15 '80 - p111
BS - v40 - S '80 - p210
CBRS - v8 - Ag '80 - p139
Hi Lo - v2 - S '80 - p3
KR - v48 - Jl 1 '80 - p841
SLJ - v27 - O '80 - p158
Subject: Mystery and detective stories

RABIN, Gil

False Start
BW - v3 - My 4 '69 - p28
CCB-B - v23 - F '70 - p105
CLW - v41 - Ap '70 - p534
KR - v37 - My 1 '69 - p515
LJ - v94 - O 15 '69 - p3835
LJ - v94 - D 15 '69 - p4582
LJ - v95 - F 15 '70 - p743
NYTBR - Ag 24 '69 - p20
Subject: Depression, 1929—Fiction; Family life—Fiction

RABINOWICH, Ellen 1946-
ConAu 106, SmATA 29

Rock Fever
BL - v76 - N 15 '79 - p297
BL - v76 - N 15 '79 - p497
Hi Lo - v1 - F '80 - p4
SLJ - v26 - F '80 - p60
Subject: Alcohol and youth—Fiction; Drug abuse—Fiction; Field hockey—Fiction

Toni's Crowd
BL - v75 - O 15 '78 - p370
CCB-B - v32 - F '79 - p104
CLW - v51 - O '79 - p142
Hi Lo - v1 - O '79 - p5
Kliatt - v14 - Spring '80 - p8
SLJ - v25 - N '78 - p78
Subject: Friendship—Fiction

Underneath I'm Different
BL - v79 - Ap 1 '83 - p1020
BS - v43 - My '83 - p74
CBRS - v11 - Ap '83 - p95
CCB-B - v36 - My '83 - p176
KR - v51 - Ja 15 '83 - p66
SLJ - v29 - Ap '83 - p127
VOYA - v6 - O '83 - p208
WCRB - v9 - Mr '83 - p55
Subject: Friendship—Fiction; Mental illness—Fiction; Weight control—Fiction

RADLAUER, Edward 1921-
AuBYP, ConAu 13NR, SmATA 15

Some Basics About Bicycles
BL - v75 - N 15 '78 - p552
J Read - v22 - My '79 - p773
SLJ - v25 - F '79 - p58
Subject: Bicyles and bicyling

Some Basics About Motorcycles
BL - v75 - N 15 '78 - p552
J Read - v22 - My '79 - p773
SLJ - v25 - F '79 - p58
Subject: Motorcycles

Some Basics About Skateboards
BL - v75 - N 15 '78 - p552
SLJ - v25 - F '79 - p58
Subject: Skateboarding

Some Basics About Vans
BL - v75 - N 15 '78 - p552
SLJ - v25 - F '79 - p58
Subject: Vans

RADLAUER, Ruth Shaw 1926-
BioIn 12, ConAu 13NR, -81, SmATA 15

Planets
SLJ - v31 - O '84 - p170
Co-author: Steinbridge, Charles H
Subject: Planets; Solar system

RAHN, Joan Elma 1929-
AmM&WS 86P, BioIn 13, ConAu 13NR, SmATA 27, WhoMW 84

Plants Up Close
ASBYP - v15 - Fall '82 - p42
BL - v78 - F 15 '82 - p758
Inst - v91 - Mr '82 - p22
KR - v50 - F 1 '82 - p138
SLJ - v28 - Ap '82 - p74
Subject: Botany

RAMSDELL, Sheldon
see Mergendahl, T E, Jr. (co-author)

RAND, Suzanne

The Boy She Left Behind
SLJ - v32 - S '85 - p152
Subject: Love—Fiction

The Girl Most Likely
SLJ - v32 - Ja '86 - p81
Subject: Love—Fiction

The Good Luck Girl
SLJ - v33 - S '86 - p150
VOYA - v9 - D '86 - p231
Subject: Love—Fiction

Green Eyes
Hi Lo - v3 - Ja '82 - p3
SLJ - v28 - F '82 - p86
Subject: Love—Fiction

Laurie's Song
BL - v78 - N 1 '81 - p379
Hi Lo - v3 - Ja '82 - p3
VOYA - v4 - F '82 - p37
Subject: Schools—Fiction

On Her Own
BL - v80 - Je 15 '84 - p1474
SLJ - v31 - S '84 - p138
VOYA - v7 - Ag '84 - p146
Subject: Love—Fiction

Too Much To Lose
BL - v80 - Ja 1 '84 - p677
Kliatt - v18 - Winter '84 - p16
SLJ - v30 - Mr '84 - p173
VOYA - v7 - Je '84 - p92
Subject: Love—Fiction

RANDALL, E T

Cosmic Kidnappers
SLJ - v32 - S '85 - p153
Subject: Plot-your-own-stories; Science fiction

Target: Earth
SLJ - v32 - S '85 - p153
Subject: Extraterrestrial beings; Plot-your-own-stories; Science fiction

Thieves From Space
SLJ - v32 - S '85 - p153
Subject: Extraterrestrial beings—Fiction; Plot-your-own-stories; Science fiction

Town In Terror
SLJ - v32 - S '85 - p153
Subject: Plot-your-own-stories; Science fiction

RANDALL, Florence Engel 1917-
AuBYP SUP, BlkAWP, ConAu 41R, IntAu&W 77, SmATA 5, WhoAmW 81, WrDr 86

The Almost Year
A Lib - v3 - Ap '72 - p420
Am - v125 - D 4 '71 - p490
BL - v67 - Jl 15 '71 - p953
BL - v68 - Ap 1 '72 - p670
BS - v31 - My 15 '71 - p100
CCB-B - v25 - N '71 - p50

RANDALL, Florence Engel (continued)
CE - v48 - Ja '72 - p208
CLW - v43 - N '71 - p174
Comw - v94 - My 21 '71 - p264
CSM - v63 - Je 5 '71 - p21
HB - v47 - Ag '71 - p392
KR - v39 - Mr 1 '71 - p243
LJ - v96 - My 15 '71 - p1782
LJ - v96 - My 15 '71 - p1816
LJ - v96 - D 15 '71 - p4159
NCW - v216 - Mr '73 - p92
NYTBR - Ap 11 '71 - p22
NYTBR, Pt. 2 - N 7 '71 - p28
PW - v199 - Ap 12 '71 - p83
TN - v28 - Ja '72 - p204
Subject: Family life—Fiction; Prejudices—Fiction

RANDALL, Lauren

To Love Is Not To Lose
SLJ - v28 - F '82 - p91

RANSOM, Candice F
SmATA 49

Nicole
BL - v83 - Ap 15 '87 - p1278
Subject: Girls—Fiction

RAPHAEL, Elaine
see Bolognese, Donald Alan (co-author)

RAPPOPORT, Ken 1935-
ConAu 20NR

Diamonds In The Rough
SLJ - v25 - My '79 - p83
WCRB - v5 - S '79 - p19
Subject: Baseball

RARDIN, Susan Lowry

Captives In A Foreign Land
BL - v81 - N 1 '84 - p374
CBRS - v13 - Winter '85 - p64
CCB-B - v38 - Ja '85 - p92
CSM - v77 - F 1 '85 - pB5
SE - v49 - Ap '85 - p328
SLJ - v31 - D '84 - p94
VOYA - v8 - Ap '85 - p50
Subject: Antinuclear movement—Fiction; Terrorism—Fiction

RASKIN, Edith Lefkowitz
see Raskin, Joseph (co-author)

RASKIN, Joseph 1897-1982
BioIn 12, ConAu 13NR, SmATA 12, –29N, WhAmArt 85, WhoAmJ 80, WhoWorJ 78

Spies And Traitors: Tales Of The Revolutionary And Civil Wars
B&B - v5 - My '77 - p2
BL - v72 - Jl 15 '76 - p1597
Comw - v103 - N 19 '76 - p758
KR - v44 - Ap 1 '76 - p400
LA - v54 - Ja '77 - p82
SLJ - v23 - O '76 - p110
Co-author: Raskin, Edith Lefkowitz
Subject: Spies

RAU, Margaret 1913-
BioIn 11, ChlLR 8, ConAu 8NR, IntAu&W 82, SmATA 9

The Minority Peoples Of China
BL - v79 - D 1 '82 - p502
BL - v81 - F 1 '85 - p792
CCB-B - v36 - N '82 - p52
Cur R - v22 - O '83 - p92
SLJ - v29 - D '82 - p68
Subject: China

RAUCHER, Herman 1928-
ConAu 29R, ConTFT 1, IntMPA 86, Novels, SmATA 8, WhoAm 86, WhoE 83, WrDr 86

Summer Of '42
Am - v124 - My 22 '71 - p549
B&B - v16 - S '71 - p51
BS - v30 - Mr 1 '71 - p527
KR - v39 - Ja 1 '71 - p23
LJ - v96 - My 1 '71 - p1638
LJ - v96 - My 15 '71 - p1831
LJ - v96 - D 15 '71 - p4161
NYTBR, pt. 1 - My 2 '71 - p36
PW - v199 - Ja 18 '71 - p46
TLS - Ag 20 '71 - p987
Subject: Social adjustment—Fiction

RAVIELLI, Anthony 1916-
AuBYP, ConAu 11NR, IlsCB 1957, –1967, SmATA 3, ThrBJA

What Is Tennis?
BL - v74 - Ap 1 '78 - p1264
HB - v54 - Ap '78 - p183
SLJ - v24 - Mr '78 - p132
Subject: Tennis

RAWLINGS, Marjorie 1896-1953
AmWomWr, ConAu 104, CurBio 42, -54, DcLB 9, -22, OxAmL 83, OxChL, ThrBJA, TwCChW 83, WhAm 3, YABC 1

The Yearling
Atl - Je '38 - p
BL - v34 - Ap 15 '38 - p300
BL - v81 - Ap 1 '85 - p1127
Comw - v28 - Ap 29 '38 - p24
CSM - Ap 27 '38 - p11
Nat - v146 - Ap 23 '38 - p483
New R - v94 - Ap 27 '38 - p370
NYTBR - Ap 3 '38 - p2
Par - v60 - Winter '85 - p164
Spec - v161 - N 11 '38 - p824
SR - v17 - Ap 2 '38 - p5
Time - v31 - Ap 4 '38 - p69
TLS - D 24 '38 - p813

RAWLS, Wilson 1919-
AuBYP SUP, AuNews 1, ConAu 1R, SmATA 22
Pseud./variant:
Rawls, Woodrow Wilson

Summer Of The Monkeys
BL - v72 - Jl 1 '76 - p1523
Subject: Animals—Fiction

Where The Red Fern Grows
BS - v34 - O 1 '74 - p311
NYTBR - S 8 '74 - p38
Par - v60 - Je '85 - p164
SLJ - v31 - S '84 - p48
Subject: Dogs—Fiction

RAWLS, Woodrow Wilson
see Rawls, Wilson

RAWSON, Ruth

Acting
BL - v67 - Ja 15 '71 - p394
EJ - v60 - N '71 - p1160
Subject: Actors and actresses

RAY, E Roy

What Does An Airline Crew Do?
BL - v65 - My 1 '69 - p1018
NYTBR - v73 - N 3 '68 - p58
SB - v5 - My '69 - p71
Subject: Aeronautics as a profession; Flight crews

RAY, N L

There Was This Man Running
BL - v78 - S 1 '81 - p50
CBRS - v9 - Je '81 - p99
CCB-B - v35 - N '81 - p55
SLJ - v27 - My '81 - p68
Subject: Extraterrestrial beings—Fiction; Kidnapping—Fiction; Science fiction

RAYMOND, Charles (joint pseud.)
ConAu X
Real Names:
Koch, Charlotte
Koch, Raymond

The Trouble With Gus
BW - v2 - My 5 '68 - p34
CCB-B - v22 - O '68 - p32
CSM - v60 - My 2 '68 - pB1
KR - v36 - Ja 15 '68 - p58
LJ - v93 - Ja 15 '68 - p294

RAZZELL, Arthur G 1925-
AuBYP SUP, SmATA 11, WrDr 84

Three And The Shape Of Three: Exploring Mathematics
BL - v66 - S 15 '69 - p139
LJ - v94 - N 15 '69 - p4300
SB - v5 - S '69 - p111
Co-author: Watts, K G O
Subject: Mathematics

READER, Dennis J

Coming Back Alive
BL - v77 - Mr 1 '81 - p923
CBRS - v9 - F '81 - p58
CCB-B - v35 - D '81 - p76
EJ - v72 - Ja '83 - p79
HB - v57 - Ag '81 - p436
Kliatt - v17 - Spring '83 - p12
KR - v49 - Mr 15 '81 - p361
SLJ - v27 - Ap '81 - p142
VOYA - v4 - O '81 - p37
Subject: California—Fiction; Friendship—Fiction; Survival—Fiction

READY, Anne Cooper

Her Father's Daughter
Kliatt - v16 - Winter '82 - p14
SLJ - v28 - Ap '82 - p84
VOYA - v5 - Je '82 - p36
Subject: Fathers—Fiction

REECE, Colleen

Long Way Home
Hi Lo - v3 - F '82 - p3

REECE, Colleen L

The Outsider
BL - v78 - Mr 15 '82 - p965
SLJ - v28 - Mr '82 - p158
Subject: Brothers and sisters—Fiction; Twins—Fiction

REED, Donald

Robert Redford
WCRB - v3 - My '77 - p24
Subject: Biography

REED, Fran

A Dream With Storms
BL - v76 - Ap 15 '80 - p1184
Hi Lo - v1 - D '79 - p3
Subject: Migrant labor—Fiction

REED, Kit 1932-
ConAu 16NR, DrmM 2, ScFSB, SmATA 34, TwCSFW 86, WhoAm 86, WrDr 86
Pseud./variant:
Hyde, Shelley

The Ballad Of T. Rantula
EJ - v71 - S '82 - p51
NYTBR - v86 - Mr 8 '81 - p35
Subject: Insects—Fiction

REEDER, Colonel Red 1902-
AuBYP, ConAu 1R, SmATA 4
Pseud./variant:
Reeder, Russell P, Jr.

West Point Plebe
CSM - N 10 '55 - p6B
KR - v23 - Je 1 '55 - p363
LJ - v80 - O 15 '55 - p2392
NYTBR - S 11 '55 - p28

REEDER, Russell P, Jr.
see Reeder, Colonel Red

REEMAN, Douglas 1924?-
ConAu 3NR, DcLEL 1940, IntAu&W 77, SmATA 28, WrDr 86

The Deep Silence
BL - v64 - Ap 15 '68 - p973
BS - v27 - F 15 '68 - p443
KR - v36 - Ja 1 '68 - p25
LJ - v93 - Ap 15 '68 - p1821
NYT - v117 - F 24 '68 - p27
NYTBR - v73 - Mr 3 '68 - p44
PW - v193 - Ja 15 '68 - p83
TN - v24 - Je '68 - p451

REES, David 1936-
ConAu 105, FifBJA, IntAu&W 86, OxChL, SmATA 36, TwCChW 83, WrDr 86

Risks
GP - v16 - Ap '78 - p3282
JB - v42 - Je '78 - p167
PW - v214 - O 9 '78 - p77
TLS - Ap 7 '78 - p383
Subject: Death—Fiction; Friendship—Fiction; Hitchhiking—Fiction

REES, E M

Thin Ice
SLJ - v32 - Ap '86 - p103
Subject: Ice skating—Fiction; Love—Fiction

REEVES, John R T 1947-

Questions And Answers About Acne
KR - v45 - Ap 15 '77 - p438
SLJ - v24 - S '77 - p149
Subject: Health

REEVES, Lawrence F 1926-
BioIn 13, ConAu 105, SmATA 29

Mopeds
B Rpt - v2 - Mr '84 - p40
VOYA - v6 - D '83 - p289
Subject: Mopeds

REIFF, Stephanie Ann 1948-
ConAu 93, ScF&FL 1, SmATA 47

Secrets Of Tut's Tomb And The Pyramids
Cur R - v217 - Ag '78 - p227
SLJ - v25 - S '78 - p43
SLJ - v25 - N '78 - p64
Subject: Egypt

Visions Of The Future: Magic Numbers And Cards
SLJ - v24 - My '78 - p64
Subject: Numerology; Tarot

REIFF, Tana

The Family From Vietnam
BL - v76 - Ap 15 '80 - p1184
CSM - v73 - D 1 '80 - pB11
Hi Lo - Je '80 - p3
Subject: Vietnamese Conflict, 1961-1975—Fiction

Juan And Lucy
BL - v76 - Ap 15 '80 - p1184

REIFF, Tana (continued)
Hi Lo - Je '80 - p3
Subject: Love—Fiction

Mollie's Year
BL - v76 - Ap 15 '80 - p1184
Hi Lo - Je '80 - p3
Subject: Self-reliance—Fiction; Widows—Fiction

A Place For Everyone
BL - v76 - Ap 15 '80 - p1184
Hi Lo - Je '80 - p3

The Shoplifting Game
BL - v76 - Ap 15 '80 - p1184
Hi Lo - Je '80 - p3

So Long, Snowman
BL - v76 - Ap 15 '80 - p1184
Hi Lo - Je '80 - p3

A Time To Choose
BL - v76 - Ap 15 '80 - p1184
Hi Lo - Je '80 - p3

REILLY, Pat

Kidnap In San Juan
BL - v80 - My 15 '84 - p1340
SLJ - v30 - My '84 - p102
VOYA - v7 - O '84 - p198
Subject: Kidnapping—Fiction

REINGOLD, Carmel Berman
AuBYP SUP

How To Cope: A New Guide To The Teen-Age Years
BS - v34 - Ap 15 '74 - p54
KR - v42 - F 15 '74 - p195
LJ - v99 - S 15 '74 - p2297
Subject: Adolescence

REISS, Bob

Franco Harris
BL - v74 - O 15 '77 - p381
SLJ - v24 - D '77 - p65
Subject: Football—Biography

REISS, Johanna 1932-
AuBYP SUP, BioIn 10, ConAu 85, FifBJA, HerW 84, SmATA 18, TwCChW 78B

The Upstairs Room
B&B - v19 - Ja '74 - p84
BL - v69 - O 15 '72 - p205
BW - v7 - Mr 11 '73 - p13
CCB-B - v26 - N '72 - p48
CE - v49 - F '73 - p258
Comw - v97 - N 17 '72 - p158
CSM - v64 - N 8 '72 - pB7
Econ - v249 - D 29 '73 - p61
EJ - v69 - O '80 - p15
Emerg Lib - v11 - N '83 - p20
HB - v49 - F '73 - p50
Inst - v82 - N '72 - p127
KR - v40 - Ag 15 '72 - p949
KR - v40 - D 15 '72 - p1420
LA - v58 - Ap '81 - p460
LJ - v97 - D 15 '72 - p4057
NS - v86 - N 9 '73 - p704
NYTBR - D 3 '72 - p82
NYTBR, Pt. 2 - N 5 '72 - p3
NYTBR, Pt. 2 - N 5 '72 - p29
PW - v202 - S 25 '72 - p59
Sch Lib - v33 - S '85 - p206
SLJ - v33 - N '86 - p30
SR - v1 - Ap 14 '73 - p87
Teacher - v90 - My '73 - p43
TLS - N 23 '73 - p1429
TN - v29 - Ap '73 - p254
Subject: Netherlands—German occupation, 1940-1945; World War, 1939-1945

REIT, Ann

The Bet
SLJ - v33 - O '86 - p192
Subject: Love—Fiction

The First Time
BL - v83 - O 1 '86 - p220
Kliatt - v20 - Fall '86 - p17
Subject: Love—Fiction

Phone Calls
BL - v80 - F 1 '84 - p810
SLJ - v30 - My '84 - p87
VOYA - v6 - O '83 - p211
VOYA - v7 - Je '84 - p93
Subject: Love—Fiction

Yours Truly, Love, Janie
Hi Lo - v3 - Ja '82 - p5
VOYA - v4 - F '82 - p37
Subject: Sports—Fiction

REIT, Seymour
AuBYP SUP, SmATA 21

Growing Up In The White House: The Story Of The Presidents' Children
KR - v36 - S 1 '68 - p983
LJ - v934 - N 15 '68 - p4422
PW - v194 - O 14 '68 - p66
Subject: Presidents

RENICK, Marion 1905-
AuBYP, ConAu 1R, MorJA, SmATA 1

Football Boys
BL - v64 - F 15 '68 - p702
KR - v35 - Ag 15 '67 - p960
LJ - v92 - D 15 '67 - p4632

REUBEN, Liz

Trading Secrets
BL - v79 - My 15 '83 - p1198
Hi Lo - v4 - Mr '83 - p4
Kliatt - v17 - Fall '83 - p10
VOYA - v6 - O '83 - p208
Subject: Schools—Fiction

REUBEN, Michael
see Hoard, Edison (co-author)

REVESZ, Therese Ruth

Witches
SLJ - v25 - N '78 - p55
Subject: Witchcraft

REVIS, Alesia
see Greenfield, Eloise (co-author)

REYNOLDS, Anne (pseud.) 1946-
IntAu&W 86X
Real Name:
Steinke, Ann E

Sailboat Summer
BL - v80 - S 1 '83 - p75
Kliatt - v17 - Fall '83 - p18
SLJ - v30 - N '83 - p96
VOYA - v6 - O '83 - p208
Subject: Love—Fiction; Sailing—Fiction

REYNOLDS, Marjorie 1903-
AuBYP, ConAu 5R

A Horse Called Mystery
Teacher - v90 - D '72 - p69

REYNOLDS, Pamela
ConAu 103, SmATA 34

Will The Real Monday Please Stand Up?
CCB-B - v29 - O '75 - p31
KR - v43 - Je 1 '75 - p612
PW - v207 - Je 9 '75 - p63
SLJ - v22 - O '75 - p81
Subject: Family problems—Fiction

RHODIN, Eric Nolan 1916-
ConAu 3NR

The Good Greenwood
BL - v68 - Ap 15 '72 - p718
BL - v68 - Ap 15 '72 - p725
BS - v33 - S 1 '73 - p259
HB - v48 - F '72 - p59
LJ - v96 - N 15 '71 - p3911
Subject: Death—Fiction; Friendship—Fiction

RHUE, Morton (pseud.)
ConAu X, SmATA X
Real Name:
Strasser, Todd

The Wave
GP - v21 - Mr '83 - p4027
JB - v46 - D '82 - p233
NS - v104 - D 3 '82 - p21
PW - v220 - N 27 '81 - p88
Sch Lib - v31 - Je '83 - p167
SE - v47 - Ap '83 - p289
TES - D 24 '82 - p25
VOYA - v4 - F '82 - p37
WCRB - v8 - Jl '82 - p47

see also Strasser, Todd for additional titles

RICE, Earle, Jr.

Death Angel
BL - v79 - Ap 15 '83 - p1078
Hi Lo - v3 - My '82 - p3
Subject: Drug abuse—Fiction; Mystery and detective stories

Fear On Ice
Hi Lo - v3 - Mr '82 - p2
SLJ - v28 - S '81 - p122
Subject: Sports—Fiction

Tiger, Lion, Hawk
BL - v74 - F 15 '78 - p997
BL - v75 - O 15 '78 - p357
Hi Lo - v1 - N '79 - p1
Hi Lo - v1 - Mr '80 - p2
Kliatt - v16 - Spring '82 - p6
TN - v36 - Winter '80 - p199
Subject: World War, 1939-1945—Fiction

RICH, Elizabeth 1935-
ConAu 29R

Flying Scared: Why We Are Being Skyjacked And How To Put A Stop To It
BS - v32 - Ag 1 '72 - p221
BW - v7 - Je 24 '73 - p13

RICH, Elizabeth (continued)
CSM - v64 - Jl 26 '72 - p9
KR - v40 - Je 1 '72 - p662
LJ - v97 - N 1 '72 - p3609
PW - v201 - My 29 '72 - p29
Subject: Hijacking of aircraft

RICH, Mark

Diesel Trucks, On The Move
SLJ - v25 - Mr '79 - p143
Subject: Trucks

RICHARD, Adrienne 1921-
AuBYP SUP, ConAu 29R, FifBJA, SmATA 5, WrDr 86

Into The Road
BL - v73 - Ja 1 '77 - p661
BL - v73 - Ja 1 '77 - p668
BS - v37 - Ap '77 - p31
CCB-B - v30 - Mr '77 - p113
GP - v16 - D '77 - p3219
HB - v53 - Ap '77 - p167
JB - v42 - F '78 - p48
Kliatt - v13 - Winter '79 - p15
KR - v44 - O 15 '76 - p1146
SLJ - v23 - D '76 - p62
TLS - O 28 '77 - p1274
Subject: Motorcycles—Fiction

Pistol
A Lib - v1 - Ap '70 - p386
A Lib - v5 - My '74 - p236
BL - v66 - N 1 '69 - p343
CCB-B - v23 - Mr '70 - p116
EJ - v59 - Ja '70 - p146
EJ - v63 - F '74 - p92
HB - v45 - D '69 - p679
KR - v37 - Ag 1 '69 - p784
LJ - v94 - O 15 '69 - p3841
NYTBR - N 30 '69 - p42
NYTBR, Pt. 2 - N 9 '69 - p60
PW - v196 - S 22 '69 - p85
SR - v53 - Ja 24 '70 - p75
TLS - Ap 28 '72 - p486
Subject: West (U.S.)—Fiction

RICHARDS, Norman 1932-
AuBYP SUP, ConAu 112, SmATA 48

The Story Of Old Ironsides
LJ - v92 - N 15 '67 - p4254
Subject: Constitution (Frigate); Ships

The Story Of The Alamo
CE - v47 - Ja '71 - p212
LJ - v96 - F 15 '71 - p744
Subject: Alamo—Siege, 1836

RICHMOND, Julius Benjamin
see Houser, Norman W (co-author)

RICHTER, Conrad 1890-1968
AuBYP SUP, ConAu 5R, -25R, CurBio 51, -68, DcLEL, McGEWB, SmATA 3, WhAm 5

The Light In The Forest
Atl - v192 - Jl '53 - p80
BL - v49 - Mr 1 '53 - p213
BL - v49 - Je 15 '53 - p341
BL - v63 - Ja 1 '67 - p493
BL - v69 - O 15 '72 - p178
CC - v83 - D 7 '66 - p1510
CSM - Je 4 '53 - p13
HB - v29 - D '53 - p469
HB - v43 - Ap '67 - p222
KR - v21 - Ap 1 '53 - p231
LJ - v78 - My 15 '53 - p917
LJ - v78 - Je 15 '53 - p1165
LJ - v91 - D 15 '66 - p6210
Nat - v176 - Je 6 '53 - p488
NY - v29 - My 16 '53 - p153
NYTBR - My 17 '53 - p5
NYTBR - v71 - N 6 '66 - p68
SR - v36 - My 16 '53 - p12

RICHTER, Elizabeth

Losing Someone You Love: When A Brother Or Sister Dies
BL - v82 - Ap 15 '86 - p1227
CBRS - v14 - My '86 - p114
KR - v54 - Mr 1 '86 - p394
NYTBR - v91 - Je 29 '86 - p30
SLJ - v32 - Ap '86 - p100
SLJ - v32 - Ag '86 - p88
VOYA - v9 - Ag '86 - p179
Subject: Death

RICHTER, Hans Peter 1925-
BioIn 9, ConAu 2NR, FourBJA, IntAu&W 86, OxChL, SmATA 6, TwCChW 83B, WhoWor 78

Friedrich
BL - v67 - Ap 1 '71 - p665
CCB-B - v24 - F '71 - p97
Child Lit - v9 - p203
EJ - v72 - Ja '83 - p26
Emerg Lib - v10 - S '82 - p29
HB - v47 - Ap '71 - p173
Inter BC - v13 - #6 '82 p19
KR - v38 - O 15 '70 - p1163
Lis - v86 - N 11 '71 - p661
LJ - v96 - My 15 '71 - p1806
NYTBR - Ja 10 '71 - p26
NYTBR, Pt. 2 - N 8 '70 - p34
PW - v199 - Ja 11 '71 - p63
Sch Lib - v33 - S '85 - p206

RICHTER, Hans Peter (continued)
TLS - D 3 '71 - p1512
Subject: Jews—Fiction

RIEGER, Shay 1929-
ConAu 29R

Animals In Clay
BL - v67 - Jl 15 '71 - p956
HB - v47 - Je '71 - p300
PW - v200 - Jl 5 '71 - p50
Subject: Animals; Art

RITCHIE-CALDER, Peter
see Calder, Ritchie

RIVERA, Geraldo 1943-
AuBYP SUP, BioIn 12, ConAu 108, CurBio 75, EncAJ, EncTwCJ, IntMPA 86, LesBEnT, SmATA 28, WhoAm 84

A Special Kind Of Courage: Profiles Of Young Americans
PW - v211 - Ap 4 '77 - p88
SLJ - v23 - Ja '77 - p108
Subject: Biography; Conduct of life; Courage

ROBB, Mary K 1908-
ConAu P-2

Making Teen Parties Click
P&R - v1 - Je '66 - p532
Subject: Entertaining; Games

ROBERTS, Charles G D 1860-1943
ConAu 105, CurBio 44, JBA 34, ObitOF 79, OxChL, SmATA 29, TwCChW 83, WebE&AL, WhAm 3

Red Fox
CSM - v64 - Ag 2 '72 - p11
CSM - v64 - D 4 '72 - p20
HB - v48 - Je '72 - p255
KR - v40 - My 1 '72 - p542
LJ - v97 - S 15 '72 - p2954
SB - v8 - S '72 - p157
SLJ - v27 - S '80 - p43
Time - v99 - Je 12 '72 - p90
Subject: Folklore

ROBERTS, Lawrence

Big Wheels
BL - v74 - N 15 '77 - p545
Cur R - v16 - D '77 - p361
Hi Lo - v2 - Mr '81 - p5

ROBERTS, Nancy 1924-
AuBYP SUP, ConAu 6NR, SmATA 28, WhoAmW 77

Appalachian Ghosts
BL - v75 - N 15 '78 - p549
Subject: Ghosts

ROBERTSON, Keith 1914-
AuBYP, ConAu 9R, MorBMP, MorJA, OxChL, SmATA 1, TwCChW 83, WrDr 86

Henry Reed's Big Show
BL - v67 - F 1 '71 - p452
CCB-B - v24 - Je '71 - p162
CE - v47 - Ap '71 - p377
HB - v47 - Ap '71 - p170
KR - v38 - N 1 '70 - p1193
LJ - v95 - D 15 '70 - p4355
LJ - v96 - Ja 15 '71 - p286
Subject: Theater—Fiction

The Year Of The Jeep
BL - v64 - Je 15 '68 - p1188
BW - v2 - Jl 28 '68 - p14
HB - v44 - Ag '68 - p432
KR - v36 - Ap 15 '68 - p461
LJ - v93 - Je 15 '68 - p2549
PW - v193 - My 6 '68 - p45
SE - v33 - My '69 - p556

ROBINS, Eleanor

The Bank Robber's Map
SLJ - v31 - Ap '85 - p92
Subject: Mystery and detective stories

The Hub Cap Mystery
SLJ - v31 - Ap '85 - p92
Subject: Mystery and detective stories

The Look Alike Mystery
SLJ - v31 - Ap '85 - p92
Subject: Mystery and detective stories

The Lost Dog Mystery
SLJ - v31 - Ap '85 - p92
Subject: Mystery and detective stories

Mystery Of The Old Book
SLJ - v31 - Ap '85 - p92
Subject: Mystery and detective stories

ROBINSON, Barbara Webb 1927-
AuBYP, BioIn 8, -11, ConAu 1R, FifBJA, SmATA 8

Temporary Times, Temporary Places
BL - v78 - Je 15 '82 - p1370
BS - v42 - Je '82 - p122
CBRS - v10 - My '82 - p99
EJ - v71 - D '82 - p67
Kliatt - v17 - Fall '83 - p18
KR - v50 - Ap 1 '82 - p423
LA - v59 - O '82 - p751
PW - v221 - Ja 22 '82 - p65
SLJ - v28 - Ap '82 - p84
Subject: Aunts—Fiction

ROBINSON, Louie
see Ashe, Arthur (co-author)

ROBISON, Nancy 1934-
ConAu 93, SmATA 32

Department Store Model
BL - v74 - O 15 '77 - p370
Cur R - v16 - D '77 - p361
Hi Lo - v2 - Mr '81 - p5
Subject: Models and modeling—Fiction

Hunters & Jumpers
BL - v80 - Ja 1 '84 - p678
SLJ - v30 - F '84 - p66
Subject: Horses

Janet Guthrie: Race Car Driver
SLJ - v25 - My '79 - p86
Subject: Automoblie racing drivers

Nancy Lopez: Wonder Woman Of Golf
BL - v75 - Jl 15 '79 - p1632
SLJ - v25 - My '79 - p86
Subject: Golfers; Mexican Americans

Plumber's Line
BL - v78 - F 15 '82 - p755
Hi Lo - v3 - F '82 - p2
Subject: Work—Fiction

The Ponies
BL - v80 - Ja 1 '84 - p678
SLJ - v30 - F '84 - p66
Subject: Ponies

Tracy Austin: Teen Tennis Champion
Hi Lo - v2 - Ap '81 - p4
JB - v44 - Je '80 - p146
SLJ - v27 - Ag '81 - p69
Subject: Tennis—Biography

U. And M.E.
BL - v78 - Mr 15 '82 - p965
SLJ - v28 - Mr '82 - p158
Subject: Schools—Fiction; Size and shape—Fiction; Track and field—Fiction

ROCKWELL, Jane

Cats And Kittens
BL - v70 - My 15 '74 - p1058
KR - v42 - F 15 '74 - p190
LJ - v99 - S 15 '74 - p2276
TES - O 20 '78 - p26
Subject: Cats

Dogs And Puppies
BL - v72 - Mr 1 '76 - p982
JB - v41 - Ap '77 - p99
KR - v44 - F 1 '76 - p137
SLJ - v22 - Ap '76 - p78
Subject: Dogs

RODERUS, Frank 1942-
ConAu 89, WrDr 86

Home To Texas
BL - v75 - N 1 '78 - p464

RODGERS, Mary 1931-
AuBYP SUP, ConAu 8NR, ConLC 12, FifBJA, NotNAT, SmATA 8, TwCChW 83, WhoAm 86, WhoThe 81, WrDr 86

Freaky Friday
BL - v68 - Je 15 '72 - p910
Brit Bk N C - Spring '81 - p14
BW - v6 - My 7 '72 - p5
CCB-B - v26 - S '72 - p15
Comw - v97 - N 17 '72 - p158
CSM - v64 - My 4 '72 - pB5
Emerg Lib - v11 - Ja '84 - p22
HB - v48 - Ag '72 - p378
KR - v40 - Mr 1 '72 - p267
LJ - v97 - Ap 15 '72 - p1608
NS - v86 - N 9 '73 - p700
NYTBR - Jl 16 '72 - p8
PW - v201 - F 14 '72 - p70
SLJ - v27 - Mr '81 - p109
Teacher - v90 - My '73 - p73
Teacher - v95 - O '77 - p80
TLS - N 23 '73 - p1433
VV - v19 - D 16 '74 - p51

RODMAN, Bella 1903-
AuBYP SUP, ConAu P-2

Lions In The Way
BL - v63 - O 1 '66 - p168
CCB-B - v20 - S '66 - p19

RODMAN, Bella (continued)
CE - v43 - F '67 - p355
CLW - v38 - Ja '67 - p341
Comw - v85 - N 11 '66 - p176
CSM - v58 - N 3 '66 - pB1
HB - v42 - O '66 - p576
KR - v34 - My 1 '66 - p483
LJ - v91 - Jl '66 - p3546
NYTBR - v71 - My 8 '66 - p14
NYTBR - v72 - N 5 '67 - p54
PW - v191 - Mr 27 '67 - p64
SR - v49 - N 12 '66 - p54
TCR - v68 - F '67 - p451
TN - v23 - Ja '67 - p195

RODOWSKY, Colby F 1932-
ConAu 69, SmATA 21

P.S. Write Soon
Emerg Lib - v9 - N '81 - p32
Inter BC - v10 - F 1 '79 - p26
JB - v43 - Ap '79 - p119
RT - v32 - D '78 - p364
Subject: Family life—Fiction; Pen pals—Fiction; Physically handicapped—Fiction

What About Me?
JB - v41 - D '77 - p366
J Read - v24 - Mr '81 - p522
PW - v215 - Ja 22 '79 - p371
TN - v36 - Winter '80 - p210
Subject: Death—Fiction; Down's syndrome—Fiction; Mentally handicapped—Fiction

ROE, Kathy Gibson

Goodbye, Secret Place
CBRS - v10 - Spring '82 - p119
CCB-B - v36 - O '82 - p36
KR - v50 - My 1 '82 - p559
SLJ - v28 - Mr '82 - p150
Subject: Friendship—Fiction

ROGER, Mae Durham
see Durham, Mae

ROGERS, James T 1921-
ConAu 45, WhoE 77

The Pantheon Story Of Mathematics For Young People
Am - v115 - N 5 '66 - p557
BL - v63 - F 1 '67 - p584
BS - v26 - N 1 '66 - p296
Comw - v85 - N 11 '66 - p180
CSM - v58 - N 3 '66 - pB10
KR - v34 - S 1 '66 - p916
LJ - v92 - Mr 15 '67 - p1330
NYT - v116 - F 2 '67 - p26
NYTBR - v71 - N 6 '66 - p34
PW - v190 - O 3 '66 - p85
SB - v3 - My '67 - p13
Subject: Mathematics

Story Of Mathematics
NS - v75 - My 24 '68 - p698
TLS - Je 6 '68 - p596
Subject: Mathematics

ROLLINS, Charlemae 1897-1979
AuBYP, BlkAWP, ConAu 9R, -104, InB&W 80, MorBMP, SelBAAf, SelBAAu, SmATA 3, -26N, WhoAm 76

Famous American Negro Poets
BL - v62 - S 15 '65 - p101
BS - v25 - Ap 15 '65 - p55
CCB-B - v19 - O '65 - p38
CLW - v37 - O '65 - p153
KR - v33 - Mr 1 '65 - p247
LJ - v90 - Ap 15 '65 - p2042
NYTBR - v70 - My 9 '65 - p10
Subject: Blacks—Poetry

Famous Negro Entertainers Of Stage, Screen And TV
BL - v63 - Je 15 '67 - p1102
BS - v27 - My 1 '67 - p66
CCB-B - v20 - Je '67 - p158
KR - v35 - Ap 1 '67 - p421
LJ - v92 - Je 15 '67 - p2454
Subject: Actors and actresses; Blacks—Biography

ROMEIKA, William L
see Cook, Joseph Jay (co-author)

RONAN, Eve
see Ronan, Margaret (co-author)

RONAN, Margaret

Curse Of The Vampires
Kliatt - v14 - Spring '80 - p58
SLJ - v28 - S '81 - p128
Co-author: Ronan, Eve

Superstars
Kliatt - v13 - Spring '79 - p33
Co-author: Ronan, Eve

ROSE, Karen

There Is A Season
BL - v64 - Mr 15 '68 - p870
CCB-B - v21 - F '68 - p100
CLW - v43 - F '72 - p331
KR - v35 - O 15 '67 - p1283

ROSE, Karen (continued)
LJ - v92 - S 15 '67 - p3203
LJ - v95 - F 15 '70 - p743
SR - v50 - D 16 '67 - p36

ROSE, Lew

Movie Kings: Hollywood's Famous Tough Guys And Monsters
BL - v77 - Je 15 '81 - p1342
Subject: Motion pictures

ROSE, Pete

Pete Rose: My Life In Baseball
CLW - v51 - Ap '80 - p415
SLJ - v26 - F '80 - p61
Subject: Baseball—Biography

ROSEN, Lillian

Just Like Everybody Else
BL - v78 - O 15 '81 - p297
CBRS - v10 - F '82 - p70
CE - v59 - S '82 - p58
SLJ - v28 - N '81 - p110
VOYA - v5 - Ap '82 - p37
Subject: Deaf—Fiction; Physically handicapped—Fiction

ROSEN, Winifred 1943-
ConAu 29R, SmATA 8

Cruisin For A Bruisin
CCB-B - v30 - F '77 - p97
TN - v37 - Fall '80 - p62
Subject: Adolescence—Fiction

ROSENBAUM, Eileen 1936-
AuBYP SUP, ConAu 21R

The Kidnapers Upstairs
CCB-B - v21 - Mr '68 - p115
KR - v36 - Ja 1 '68 - p6
LJ - v93 - Ap 15 '68 - p1803

ROSENBERG, Ethel Clifford 1915-
ConAu 16NR, SmATA 3, WhoAmW 77
Pseud./variant:
Clifford, Eth

The Year Of The Three-Legged Deer
BL - v69 - N 1 '72 - p246
CCB-B - v26 - Ja '73 - p73
CLW - v44 - O '72 - p193
KR - v40 - My 1 '72 - p536
LJ - v97 - N 15 '72 - p3804
NYTBR - Je 18 '72 - p8
Subject: Indians of North America—Fiction; Prejudices—Fiction

see also Clifford, Eth for additional titles

ROSENBERG, Sharon 1942-
ConAu 10NR, SmATA 8

The Illustrated Hassle-Free Make Your Own Clothes Book
Atl - v227 - Ap '71 - p104
B&B - v18 - Je '73 - p138
LJ - v96 - Je 15 '71 - p2149
LJ - v96 - D 15 '71 - p4161
TN - v28 - Ja '72 - p208
Co-author: Wiener, Joan
Subject: Dressmaking; Sewing

ROSENBERG, Sondra

Will There Never Be A Prince?
CCB-B - v24 - S '70 - p19
KR - v38 - F 15 '70 - p180
LJ - v95 - D 15 '70 - p4355
SR - v53 - My 9 '70 - p47
Subject: Weight control—Fiction

ROSENBLOOM, Joseph 1928-
ConAu 21NR, -57, DrAS 82H, SmATA 21, WhoWorJ 78, WrDr 86

Doctor Knock-Knock's Official Knock-Knock Dictionary
BL - v73 - Mr 15 '77 - p1094
NYTBR - v0 - My 1 '77 - p29
PW - v211 - Ja 10 '77 - p72
SLJ - v23 - Mr '77 - p147
Subject: Jokes

Maximilian You're The Greatest
BL - v75 - Jl 15 '79 - p1629
CBRS - v9 - F '81 - p58
Kliatt - v13 - Fall '79 - p26
SLJ - v25 - My '79 - p82
Subject: Mystery and detective stories

ROSS, Josephine

Alexander Fleming
BFYC - v20 - Autumn '85 - p26
SLJ - v31 - Ap '85 - p100
Subject: Biography

ROSS, Pat 1943-
SmATA 48

Young And Female: Turning Points In The Lives Of Eight American Women
BL - v69 - S 15 '72 - p102
BW - v6 - My 7 '72 - p13
CCB-B - v26 - O '72 - p30
CSM - v64 - My 4 '72 - pB5
EJ - v63 - Ap '74 - p90
KR - v40 - Je 1 '72 - p633
LJ - v97 - Je 15 '72 - p2244
NYTBR, Pt. 2 - My 7 '72 - p24
PW - v202 - Jl 31 '72 - p71
SE - v37 - D '73 - p788
Subject: Biography

ROTH, Arnold 1929-
AuBYP SUP, ConAu 21R, IlsBYP, SmATA 21, WhoE 77, WorECar

Pick A Peck Of Puzzles
BL - v63 - Mr 15 '67 - p797
CCB-B - v20 - F '67 - p97
HB - v43 - F '67 - p75
KR - v34 - S 1 '66 - p911
LJ - v91 - O 15 '66 - p5260
NYTBR - v71 - N 27 '66 - p42
SR - v49 - N 12 '66 - p48
Subject: Amusements

ROTH, Arthur J 1925-
AuBYP SUP, ConAu 7NR, SmATA 43
Pseud./variant:
Mara, Barney
Pomeroy, Pete

Avalanche
BL - v76 - Mr 15 '80 - p1045
Inst - v89 - Ja '80 - p102
Inst - v89 - Ja '80 - p114
Kliatt - v14 - Winter '80 - p14
Subject: Survival—Fiction

The Secret Lover Of Elmtree
BL - v73 - O 15 '76 - p315
BL - v73 - O 15 '76 - p326
BS - v36 - Mr '77 - p387
CCB-B - v30 - Ja '77 - p81
EJ - v67 - Ja '78 - p92
HB - v53 - F '77 - p61
Kliatt - v15 - Fall '81 - p14
KR - v44 - Ag 15 '76 - p910
NYTBR - N 28 '76 - p40
SLJ - v23 - N '76 - p72
Subject: Adoption—Fiction; Fathers and sons—Fiction

Two For Survival
BL - v73 - O 15 '76 - p326
CCB-B - v30 - N '76 - p47
CE - v53 - Ja '77 - p150
HB - v52 - D '76 - p630
KR - v44 - Ag 1 '76 - p849
RT - v31 - Ap '78 - p839
SLJ - v23 - O '76 - p111
Subject: Adventure and adventurers—Fiction; Survival—Fiction

see also Pomeroy, Pete for additional titles

ROTH, Charles E 1934-
ConAu 111, IntAu&W 86

Then There Were None
BL - v81 - D 1 '84 - p530
KR - v45 - S 15 '77 - p993
SB - v14 - S '78 - p115
SLJ - v25 - N '78 - p68
Subject: Animals; Indians of North America; Wildlife conservation

ROTH, David
ConAu 106, SmATA 36

The Winds Of Summer
BS - v32 - Jl 15 '72 - p199
CCB-B - v25 - Je '72 - p162
KR - v40 - Mr 15 '72 - p336
LJ - v97 - S 15 '72 - p2966
TLS - Ap 28 '72 - p481
Subject: Lobster fisheries—Fiction

ROTSLER, William 1926-
ScFSB, TwCSFW 86, WrDr 86

Star Trek II Short Stories
SLJ - v29 - Ag '83 - p79
Subject: Science fiction; Short stories

ROUECHE, Berton 1911-
BioIn 5, -13, ConAu 1NR, CurBio 59, DrAP&F 85, EncAJ, EncTwCJ, SmATA 28, WhoAm 86, WorAu 1975

Feral
Atl - v235 - Ja '75 - p91
BL - v71 - Ja 1 '75 - p444
BS - v34 - D 1 '74 - p404
EJ - v65 - Ja '76 - p96
KR - v42 - O 1 '74 - p1077
KR - v42 - O 15 '74 - p1117
LJ - v99 - D 1 '74 - p3150
NY - v50 - N 11 '74 - p215
NYTBR - D 29 '74 - p20

ROUECHE, Berton (continued)
PW - v206 - S 30 '74 - p53
PW - v208 - N 10 '75 - p57
SLJ - v21 - Ap '75 - p75
SLJ - v22 - D '75 - p33
TN - v32 - Ap '76 - p285
WLB - v49 - Ja '75 - p347

ROUNDS, Glen 1906-
AuBYP, BioIn 10, ConAu 7NR, IlsCB 1957, -1967, JBA 51, OxChL, SmATA 8, TwCChW 83, WhAmArt 85, WrDr 86

Blind Outlaw
BL - v77 - O 1 '80 - p257
CCB-B - v34 - Ja '81 - p100
CE - v57 - Mr '81 - p207
HB - v57 - F '81 - p52
KR - v49 - F 1 '81 - p142
LA - v58 - Ap '81 - p476
NYTBR - v86 - Ja 25 '81 - p27
PW - v218 - N 28 '80 - p51
RT - v34 - My '81 - p967
SLJ - v27 - D '80 - p62
Subject: Horses

Stolen Pony
KR - v37 - Ap 15 '69 - p443
LJ - v94 - S 15 '69 - p3208
Subject: Dogs—Fiction; Horses—Fiction

ROY, Ron 1940-
ConAu 114, SmATA 40

Avalanche!
BL - v78 - F 1 '82 - p708
CBRS - v10 - D '81 - p39
CCB-B - v35 - My '82 - p177
SLJ - v28 - F '82 - p79
VOYA - v4 - F '82 - p37
Subject: Avalanches—Fiction; Colorado—Fiction; Divorce—Fiction

I Am A Thief
BL - v78 - My 15 '82 - p1260
CBRS - v10 - Je '82 - p109
CCB-B - v36 - N '82 - p53
Hi Lo - v4 - Ja '83 - p1
RT - v37 - O '83 - p65
SLJ - v29 - S '82 - p127
Subject: Mothers and sons—Fiction; Shoplifting—Fiction

Nightmare Island
BL - v77 - Mr 1 '81 - p968
CBRS - v9 - Ap '81 - p79
HB - v57 - O '81 - p538
SLJ - v27 - Ag '81 - p70
Subject: Camping—Fiction; Fires—Fiction; Survival—Fiction

RUBENSTONE, Jessie 1912-
ConAu 69

Knitting For Beginners
BL - v70 - Ja 15 '74 - p545
CCB-B - v27 - Ja '74 - p85
CE - v50 - Mr '74 - p298
KR - v41 - O 1 '73 - p1106
LJ - v99 - F 15 '74 - p576
NYTBR - N 4 '73 - p62
Subject: Knitting

RUBIN, Arnold Perry 1946-
ConAu 69, WhoE 81

True Great Mysteries
Kliatt - v15 - Winter '81 - p57
SLJ - v27 - F '81 - p78

The Youngest Outlaws: Runaways In America
Cur R - v16 - F '77 - p30
TN - v34 - Fall '77 - p102
Subject: Runaways

RUBINSTEIN, Robert E

When Sirens Scream
BL - v77 - Jl 1 '81 - p1392
BL - v80 - Mr 15 '84 - p1071
CCB-B - v35 - O '81 - p36
J Read - v25 - F '82 - p487
SLJ - v27 - Ap '81 - p143
Subject: Atomic power plants—Fiction; Fathers and sons—Fiction

RUBLOWSKY, John 1928-
AuBYP SUP, ConAu 17R

Popular Music
BL - v64 - Ap 15 '68 - p965
Choice - v5 - Jl '68 - p634
LJ - v92 - S 15 '67 - p3214
LJ - v92 - N 1 '67 - p4002
Subject: Music

RUBY, Lois 1942-
ConAu 97, SmATA 35

Arriving At A Place You've Never Left
BL - v74 - O 1 '77 - p282
BL - v74 - O 1 '77 - p302
BS - v38 - Ap '78 - p13
CCB-B - v31 - D '77 - p68
Inst - v87 - My '78 - p123

RUBY, Lois (continued)
Kliatt - v14 - Spring '80 - p8
KR - v45 - D 1 '77 - p1271
WLB - v52 - D '77 - p337
Subject: Short stories

RUCKMAN, Ivy
ConAu 111, SmATA 37

Encounter
BL - v75 - O 15 '78 - p369
KR - v46 - N 1 '78 - p1194
SLJ - v25 - N '78 - p78
Subject: Unidentified flying objects

RUFF, Peter

Olivia Newton-John
Kliatt - v14 - Winter '80 - p63
SLJ - v26 - D '79 - p106
Subject: Singers

RUFFINS, Reynold
see Sarnoff, Jane (co-author)

RUIZ, Ramon E
see Atwater, James David (co-author)

RUMSEY, Marian 1928-
ConAu 21R, SmATA 16, Str&VC

Lion On The Run
BL - v69 - Je 1 '73 - p950
CSM - v65 - My 2 '73 - pB4
Inst - v83 - N '73 - p124
KR - v41 - Ja 1 '73 - p6
LJ - v98 - Jl '73 - p2197
Subject: Animals—Fiction

RUSCH, Richard B

Man's Marvelous Computer: The Next Quarter Century
BL - v67 - Ap 1 '71 - p665
KR - v38 - O 15 '70 - p1171
LJ - v96 - Mr 15 '71 - p1130
SB - v6 - Mr '71 - p294
Subject: Computers

RUSHING, Jane Gilmore 1925-
ConAu 49, WhoAm 86, WrDr 86

Mary Dove
Am - v130 - My 4 '74 - p348
BS - v34 - Ap 15 '74 - p49
BW - S 14 '75 - p4
EJ - v65 - Ja '76 - p98
KR - v42 - Ja 1 '74 - p23
LJ - v99 - Mr 15 '74 - p777
LJ - v99 - S 15 '74 - p2305
NYTBR - Mr 17 '74 - p38
PW - v205 - Ja 21 '74 - p78
Subject: Love—Fiction; West (U.S.)—Fiction

RUSSELL, Bill 1934-
CurBio 75, WebAB, WhoAm 86

Go Up For Glory
BL - v62 - Je 1 '66 - p940
BS - v26 - Ap 1 '66 - p19
KR - v34 - F 15 '66 - p212
KR - v34 - Mr 1 '66 - p255
LJ - v91 - Mr 15 '66 - p1440
NYTBR - v71 - Mr 20 '66 - p28
PW - v190 - O 17 '66 - p67
RR - v86 - Mr '69 - p171

RUSSELL, Kate

Billy Idol
B Rpt - v4 - Mr '86 - p35
SLJ - v32 - S '85 - p131
Subject: Musicians; Rock musicians

RUSSELL, Patrick (pseud.) 1942-
ConAu X, SmATA X
Real Name:
Sammis, John

The Tommy Davis Story
Comw - v93 - F 26 '71 - p523
KR - v37 - Mr 15 '69 - p311
LJ - v94 - My 15 '69 - p2125
PW - v195 - Ap 21 '69 - p66
SR - v52 - Je 28 '69 - p38
Subject: Baseball—Biography

RUTHERFORD, Douglas (pseud.) 1915-
ConAu X, SmATA X, TwCCr&M 85, WrDr 86
Real Name:
McConnell, James Douglas R

Killer On The Track
CCB-B - v28 - Ap '75 - p137
KR - v42 - N 15 '74 - p1206
Subject: Automobile racing—Fiction; Mystery and detective stories

RUTLAND, Jonathan

Ships
BL - v73 - Ja 15 '77 - p720
Inst - v91 - My '82 - p109
SLJ - v23 - My '77 - p64
Subject: Ships

RUTTER, Russell J

The World Of The Wolf
BL - v64 - My 1 '68 - p1014
CE - v45 - S '68 - p42
Choice - v20 - S '82 - p42
LJ - v93 - Ap 1 '68 - p1493
Co-author: Pimlott, Douglas
Subject: Wolves

RYAN, Elizabeth 1943-
ConAu 7NR, SmATA 30

Life Is A Lonely Place: Five Teenage Alcoholics
Kliatt - v15 - Winter '81 - p28
SLJ - v27 - Ja '81 - p72
Subject: Alcohol and youth

RYAN, Frank

Jumping For Joy
BL - v76 - Jl 1 '80 - p1614
CCB-B - v34 - O '80 - p40
SLJ - v27 - S '80 - p77
Subject: Jumping; Track and field

RYAN, Oneta

Love And Honors
BL - v80 - F 1 '84 - p810
SLJ - v30 - Ap '84 - p121
Subject: Love—Fiction

RYBOLT, Thomas R
see Mebane, Robert C (co-author)

RYLANT, Cynthia 1954-
SmATA 44

Every Living Thing
KR - v53 - O 1 '85 - p1090
PW - v228 - S 20 '85 - p108
Subject: Animals—Fiction; Pets—Fiction; Short stories

S

SAAL, Jocelyn

On Thin Ice
SLJ - v30 - Mr '84 - p170
VOYA - v6 - F '84 - p336
Subject: Ice skating—Fiction; Love—Fiction

Trusting Hearts
BL - v79 - Mr 15 '83 - p972
Subject: Hunting—Fiction; Love—Fiction; Veterinarians—Fiction

SABIN, Francene
ConAu 11NR, SmATA 27

Jimmy Connors: King Of The Courts
CE - v55 - Ja '79 - p171
KR - v46 - Mr 1 '78 - p251
SLJ - v24 - My '78 - p87
Subject: Tennis—Biography

Set Point
BL - v74 - O 1 '77 - p303
KR - v45 - Je 1 '77 - p580
SLJ - v24 - S '77 - p136
Subject: Evert, Chris; Tennis—Biography

SABIN, Louis 1930-
ConAu 11NR, SmATA 27
Pseud./variant:
Brandt, Keith

The Fabulous Dr. J
SLJ - v23 - Mr '77 - p148
Subject: Basketball—Biography; Irving, Julius

Johnny Bench: King Of Catchers
KR - v45 - Ap 1 '77 - p356
SLJ - v24 - S '77 - p136
Subject: Baseball—Biography

Pele: Soccer Superstar
CE - v53 - Mr '77 - p262
SLJ - v23 - Mr '77 - p148
Subject: Soccer—Biography

see also Brandt, Keith for additional titles

SACHS, Marilyn 1927-
ChILR 2, ConAu 13NR, ConLC 35, FourBJA, IntAu&W 86, OxChL, SmATA 3, -2AS, TwCChW 83, WrDr 86

Baby Sister
BL - v82 - F 15 '86 - p861
B Rpt - v5 - My '86 - p32
BS - v46 - Je '86 - p118
CBRS - v14 - Ap '86 - p103
CCB-B - v39 - Mr '86 - p136
KR - v54 - Ja 1 '86 - p54
SLJ - v32 - Ag '86 - p106
VOYA - v9 - Ag '86 - p150
Subject: Sisters—Fiction

Beach Towels
BL - v79 - N 15 '82 - p439
CBRS - v11 - D '82 - p37
CCB-B - v36 - Mr '83 - p133
Hi Lo - v4 - N '82 - p5
SLJ - v29 - F '83 - p92
Subject: Friendship—Fiction

Bus Ride
BL - v77 - S 15 '80 - p111
B Rpt - v2 - S '83 - p26
BS - v40 - S '80 - p210
CBRS - v8 - Ag '80 - p139
CCB-B - v33 - Jl '80 - p222
Hi Lo - v2 - S '80 - p3
J Read - v24 - Mr '81 - p548
KR - v48 - Jl 1 '80 - p841
PW - v217 - Je 6 '80 - p82
SLJ - v27 - S '80 - p77
WLB - v55 - S '80 - p57

Class Pictures
BL - v77 - O 15 '80 - p329
CBRS - v9 - O '80 - p19
CCB-B - v34 - F '81 - p118
HB - v56 - O '80 - p528
Kliatt - v17 - Winter '83 - p13
KR - v49 - F 15 '81 - p218
PW - v218 - N 7 '80 - p61
PW - v227 - Ja 25 '85 - p94
SLJ - v27 - N '80 - p79
Subject: Friendship—Fiction

Fourteen
BL - v79 - Mr 15 '83 - p972

SACHS, Marilyn (continued)
BL - v81 - Ag '85 - p1674
CBRS - v11 - My '83 - p104
CCB-B - v36 - Mr '83 - p133
HB - v59 - Ag '83 - p457
J Read - v27 - Mr '84 - p563
Kliatt - v19 - Spring '85 - p18
KR - v51 - My 1 '83 - p528
SLJ - v29 - Ap '83 - p117
Subject: Friendship—Fiction; Mothers and daughters—Fiction

Hello...Wrong Number
BL - v78 - F 15 '82 - p761
B Rpt - v2 - S '83 - p26
CBRS - v10 - Ja '82 - p50
CCB-B - v35 - F '82 - p115
Hi Lo - v3 - Mr '82 - p6
SLJ - v28 - F '82 - p92
VOYA - v4 - F '82 - p38
Subject: Friendship—Fiction; Telephone—Fiction

Peter And Veronica
BL - v65 - My 15 '69 - p1078
BW - v3 - My 4 '69 - p10
CCB-B - v23 - Ap '70 - p133
CLW - v43 - F '72 - p331
CSM - v61 - My 1 '69 - pB4
GW - v103 - D 19 '70 - p21
HB - v45 - Je '69 - p312
KR - v37 - Mr 15 '69 - p305
LJ - v94 - Ap 15 '69 - p1785
LJ - v95 - F 15 '70 - p743
NYTBR - My 25 '69 - p32
PW - v195 - Mr 17 '69 - p57
SR - v52 - My 10 '69 - p57
TLS - O 30 '70 - p1267
Subject: Friendship—Fiction; Prejudices—Fiction

A Summer's Lease
BL - v75 - Ap 1 '79 - p1220
HB - v55 - Je '79 - p311
Kliatt - v15 - Fall '81 - p14
KR - v47 - Je 15 '79 - p690
NYTBR - Ag 19 '79 - p20
PW - v215 - My 7 '79 - p84
SLJ - v25 - My '79 - p36
SLJ - v25 - My '79 - p75
Subject: Authorship—Fiction; Teachers—Fiction

Thunderbird
BL - v81 - Ap 15 '85 - p1179
BL - v82 - O 1 '85 - p213
B Rpt - v4 - Mr '86 - p33
CBRS - v13 - Jl '85 - p145
CCB-B - v39 - S '85 - p16
PW - v227 - Mr 29 '85 - p73
SLJ - v32 - O '85 - p187
Subject: Automobiles—Fiction; Friendship—Fiction

SACKETT, Samuel J 1928-
ConAu 1R, SmATA 12, WrDr 84

Cowboys And The Songs They Sang
ABC - v18 - Ja '68 - p34
BL - v64 - N 1 '67 - p337
CCB-B - v20 - Jl '67 - p175
HB - v43 - Ag '67 - p481
KR - v35 - Ap 15 '67 - p504
LJ - v92 - Jl '67 - p2656
NYTBR - v72 - N 5 '67 - p65
NYTBR, Pt. 2 - v72 - My 7 '67 - p41
PW - v191 - My 8 '67 - p62
SR - v50 - Je 17 '67 - p36
Subject: Cowboys

SAGARIN, Edward
see Aymar, Brandt (co-author)

SAHADI, Lou

Pro Football's Gamebreakers
BL - v74 - Ja 1 '78 - p743
LJ - v102 - S 15 '77 - p1865
PW - v212 - Ag 22 '77 - p58
WCRB - v4 - Ja '78 - p56
Subject: Football—Biography

ST. GEORGE, Judith 1931-
ConAu 14NR, SmATA 13, WrDr 86

Do You See What I See?
BL - v79 - Ja 15 '83 - p668
CBRS - v11 - D '82 - p38
CCB-B - v36 - Ja '83 - p96
Kliatt - v18 - Winter '84 - p18
KR - v50 - N 1 '82 - p1196
NYTBR - v88 - F 27 '83 - p37
SLJ - v29 - D '82 - p83
VOYA - v5 - D '82 - p35
Subject: Moving (Household)—Fiction; Mystery and detective stories

The Halo Wind
BL - v75 - D 1 '78 - p619
CCB-B - v32 - F '79 - p105
HB - v55 - F '79 - p66
SLJ - v25 - D '78 - p56
Subject: Indians of North America—Fiction; Overland journeys to the Pacific—Fiction

Shadow Of The Shaman
BL - v74 - F 15 '78 - p1012
KR - v46 - Ja 15 '78 - p47

ST. GEORGE, Judith (continued)
SLJ - v24 - My '78 - p85
Subject: Mystery and detective stories; Oregon—Fiction

SALWAY, Lance

A Nasty Piece Of Work
GP - v22 - Jl '83 - p4095
JB - v47 - Ag '83 - p174
Sch Lib - v31 - S '83 - p272
TES - Je 3 '83 - p43
Subject: Ghosts—Fiction; Short stories

SAMACHSON, Dorothy 1914-
AuBYP, ConAu 9R, SmATA 3

The First Artists
BL - v67 - O 1 '70 - p147
CCB-B - v24 - F '71 - p98
CSM - v62 - N 14 '70 - pB11
Inst - v130 - My '71 - p80
KR - v38 - S 15 '70 - p1056
LJ - v95 - N 15 '70 - p4059
LJ - v95 - D 15 '70 - p4326
SA - v223 - D '70 - p123
SB - v6 - D '70 - p195
Co-author: Samachson, Joseph
Subject: Art

SAMACHSON, Joseph
see Samachson, Dorothy (co-author)

SAMMIS, John
see Russell, Patrick

SAMPSON, Fay 1935-
ConAu 18NR, SmATA 42

The Watch On Patterick Fell
BL - v76 - F 1 '80 - p766
BS - v40 - Je '80 - p118
CBRS - v8 - Mr '80 - p79
CCB-B - v33 - Mr '80 - p140
GP - v17 - N '78 - p3410
HB - v56 - Je '80 - p309
JB - v43 - F '79 - p59
KR - v48 - Mr 1 '80 - p293
Obs - D 3 '78 - p36
SLJ - v26 - Mr '80 - p143
WLB - v54 - Ap '80 - p520
Subject: England—Fiction; Family problems—Fiction; Radioactive waste disposal—Fiction

SAMUELS, Gertrude
AuBYP, ConAu 6NR, NatPD 81, SmATA 17, WhoAmW 81, WhoWorJ 78

Adam's Daughter
BL - v74 - D 1 '77 - p609
CCB-B - v31 - F '78 - p101
KR - v45 - O 15 '77 - p1104
NYTBR - v0 - Ja 29 '78 - p26
PW - v212 - O 24 '77 - p77
SLJ - v24 - D '77 - p55
Subject: Fathers and daughters—Fiction; Parole—Fiction

Run, Shelley, Run!
Am - v130 - My 4 '74 - p350
BL - v70 - My 1 '74 - p996
BL - v71 - Mr 15 '75 - p748
BS - v34 - Ap 1 '74 - p7
CCB-B - v27 - Je '74 - p163
CSM - v66 - Ap 10 '74 - pF5
EJ - v64 - S '75 - p80
KR - v42 - Ja 15 '74 - p61
LJ - v99 - Ap 15 '74 - p1232
Ms - v3 - D '74 - p79
NY - v50 - D 2 '74 - p182
NYTBR - Ap 7 '74 - p8
PW - v205 - F 11 '74 - p65
Subject: Family problems—Fiction; Runaways—Fiction

SANDERLIN, Owenita 1916-
ConAu 7NR, IntAu&W 86, SmATA 11, WhoAmW 87, WrDr 86

Tennis Rebel
BL - v74 - My 15 '78 - p1487
Hi Lo - v1 - D '79 - p3
NYTBR - Ap 30 '78 - p45
SLJ - v24 - My '78 - p88
Subject: Divorce—Fiction; Tennis—Fiction

SANFORD, William R
see Green, Carl R (co-author)

SANT, Kathryn Storey

Desert Chase
BL - v76 - Mr 15 '80 - p1065
Subject: Crime and criminals—Fiction

SANTANA, Isabel

Love Song
SLJ - v28 - S '81 - p134
VOYA - v4 - D '81 - p34

SARASON, Martin

A Federal Case
BL - v74 - Mr 15 '78 - p1179
Subject: Crime and criminals—Fiction; Employment—Fiction

SARGENT, Shirley 1927-
AuBYP, ConAu 2NR, SmATA 11

Ranger In Skirts
CLW - v38 - Ja '67 - p342
LJ - v91 - N 15 '66 - p5765

SARNOFF, Jane 1937-
AuBYP SUP, ConAu 9NR, –53, FifBJA, SmATA 10

A Great Aquarium Book: The Putting-It-Together Guide For Beginners
BL - v74 - S 1 '77 - p44
CCB-B - v31 - Ja '78 - p86
CE - v54 - N '77 - p90
HB - v54 - F '78 - p70
NYTBR - Ag 14 '77 - p27
PW - v211 - Je 13 '77 - p107
SLJ - v24 - O '77 - p117
Teacher - v95 - O '77 - p165
Teacher - v95 - My '78 - p21
Co-author: Ruffins, Reynold
Subject: Aquarium fishes

SARNOFF, Paul 1918-
BioIn 12, ConAu 18NR

Ice Pilot: Bob Bartlett
KR - v34 - S 1 '66 - p911
LJ - v91 - D 15 '66 - p6205
Subject: Biography

SAROYAN, William 1908-1981
ConAu 103, ConLC 1, –8, –10, –29, CurBio 72, –81N, DcLB 7, –9, –Y81A, SmATA 23, –24N, WhoTwCL, WrDr 82

My Name Is Aram
EJ - v63 - Ja '74 - p43
Subject: Armenians in the United States—Fiction

SASEK, Miroslav 1916-1980
BkP, ChlLR 4, ConAu 101, –73, IlsCB 1957, –1967, SmATA 16, –23N, ThrBJA

This Is The United Nations
B&B - v13 - Jl '68 - p42
BL - v64 - Jl 15 '68 - p1288
BW - v2 - S 1 '68 - p12
CCB-B - v21 - Jl '68 - p181
HB - v44 - Ag '68 - p410
KR - v36 - My 15 '68 - p553
NYTBR - v73 - Je 23 '68 - p22
SE - v33 - My '69 - p563
SR - v51 - Je 15 '68 - p33
TLS - Je 6 '68 - p596
Subject: United Nations

SAUNDERS, F Wenderoth

Machines For You
Am - v117 - N 4 '67 - p520
HB - v44 - F '68 - p57
KR - v35 - S 1 '67 - p1052
LJ - v93 - My 15 '68 - p2116
SB - v3 - D '67 - p259
Subject: Machinery

SAVITT, Sam 1917-
AuBYP, ConAu 17NR, IntAu&W 77, SmATA 8, WhoAmA 84, WhoAmJ 80, WhoE 77, WrDr 80, –86

A Horse To Remember
BL - v80 - My 1 '84 - p1234
B Rpt - v3 - S '84 - p37
BS - v44 - Je '84 - p118
HB - v60 - Ag '84 - p478
SLJ - v30 - My '84 - p94
SLJ - v32 - Ag '86 - p37
Subject: Horse racing—Fiction; Horses—Fiction

Sam Savitt's True Horse Stories
LJ - v96 - Mr 15 '71 - p1119
PW - v198 - D 28 '70 - p61
Subject: Horses

SAVITZ, Harriet May 1933-
AuBYP SUP, ConAu 14NR, FifBJA, SmATA 5, WhoAmW 83, WhoE 85

If You Can't Be The Sun, Be A Star
BL - v78 - Ag '82 - p1528
SLJ - v29 - S '82 - p142
Subject: Adventure and adventurers—Fiction

The Lionhearted
EJ - v66 - Ja '77 - p65
Kliatt - v11 - Fall '77 - p8
Subject: Physically handicapped—Fiction

On The Move
RT - v31 - Ap '78 - p804
Subject: Physically handicapped—Fiction

SAVITZ, Harriet May (continued)

Run, Don't Walk
CBRS - v8 - N '79 - p29
Emerg Lib - v9 - N '81 - p32
Inter BC - v13 - Ap '82 - p16
SLJ - v26 - N '79 - p93
SLJ - v27 - My '81 - p27
Subject: Physically handicapped—Fiction

Wheelchair Champions
BL - v74 - Mr 15 '78 - p1176
KR - v46 - My 15 '78 - p550
SLJ - v24 - My '78 - p88
Subject: Physically handicapped; Sports—Biography

SAYERS, Gale
see Griese, Bob (co-author)

SCARIANO, Margaret

To Catch A Mugger
BL - v78 - Je 15 '82 - p1365
Subject: Crime and criminals—Fiction

Too Young To Know
CCB-B - v37 - Ja '84 - p96
SLJ - v30 - F '84 - p84
Subject: Love—Fiction

SCHAEFER, Jack 1907-
AuBYP, BioIn 5, –11, ConAu 15NR, IntMPA 78, SmATA 3, ThrBJA, TwCChW 78, WhoAm 86

Shane
KR - v17 - S 15 '49 - p521
LJ - v74 - O 1 '49 - p1461
SR - v32 - D 3 '49 - p58

SCHARFFENBERGER, Ann

The Mademoiselle Shape-Up Book
BL - v77 - Je 15 '81 - p1326
J Read - v25 - Ja '82 - p39
Kliatt - v15 - Fall '81 - p672
PW - v219 - Mr 20 '81 - p59
SLJ - v217 - Ag '81 - p84
Co-author: Weitz, Lawrence Joel
Subject: Exercise; Weight control

SCHATZ, Letta

Bola And The Oba's Drummers
BL - v64 - Mr 1 '68 - p787
CCB-B - v22 - S '68 - p16
Comw - v87 - N 10 '67 - p176
KR - v35 - Jl 15 '67 - p810
Subject: Africa—Fiction

SCHEER, George 1917-
AuBYP SUP, BioIn 10, –11, ConAu 13R

Yankee Doodle Boy
HB - v41 - F '65 - p65
LJ - v89 - D 15 '64 - p5019
NYTBR, Pt. 2 - N 1 '64 - p56
Subject: United States—History—Revolution, 1775-1783

SCHELL, Orville 1940-
AuBYP SUP, BioIn 12, –13, ConAu 25R, IntAu&W 86, SmATA 10, WhoAm 86, WrDr 86

Modern China: The Story Of A Revolution
BL - v69 - O 1 '72 - p140
BS - v32 - My 15 '72 - p99
CCB-B - v26 - O '72 - p31
HB - v48 - Je '72 - p279
KR - v40 - My 15 '72 - p593
Nat - v214 - Je 26 '72 - p829
NYTBR - My 14 '72 - p8
PW - v202 - Jl 31 '72 - p71
Co-author: Esherick, Joseph
Subject: China

SCHELLIE, Don 1932-
ConAu 101, SmATA 29

Kidnapping Mr. Tubbs
HB - v55 - O '78 - p527
KR - v46 - N 15 '78 - p1254
SLJ - v25 - O '78 - p159
Subject: Arizona—Fiction; Old age—Fiction

SCHIESEL, Jane
AuBYP SUP

The Otis Redding Story
BS - v33 - D 15 '73 - p430
KR - v41 - N 1 '73 - p1209
LJ - v98 - D 15 '73 - p3715
NYTBR - D 30 '73 - p10
PW - v204 - Jl 23 '73 - p70
Subject: Biography

SCHMITZ, Dorothy Childers

Dorothy Hamill: Skate To Victory
Cur R - v16 - D '77 - p363
SLJ - v24 - D '77 - p65
Subject: Biography; Ice skaters

Hang Gliding
SLJ - v25 - F '79 - p58
Subject: Hang gliding

SCHNEIDER, Alan J
see Laiken, Deirdre S (co-author)

SCHNEIDER, Meg

Romance!: Can You Survive It?
BL - v81 - O 15 '84 - p296
VOYA - v7 - F '85 - p349
Subject: Dating (Social customs)

SCHNEIDER, Tom

Walter Mondale: Serving All The People
BL - v81 - My 1 '85 - p1258
SLJ - v31 - Ag '85 - p69
Subject: Legislators; Vice-presidents

SCHODER, Judith

The Blood Suckers
Hi Lo - v3 - F '82 - p5
SLJ - v28 - Ap '82 - p69
VOYA - v5 - Ag '82 - p48
Subject: Vampires

Brotherhood Of Pirates
Hi Lo - v1 - Ja '80 - p4
SLJ - v26 - Ja '80 - p75
Subject: Pirates

see also Shebar, Sharon Sigmond (co-author) for additional titles

SCHOEN, Barbara 1924-
ConAu 21R, IntAu&W 86, SmATA 13, WrDr 86

Place And A Time
BL - v64 - S 1 '67 - p56
CCB-B - v20 - My '67 - p146
CSM - v59 - My 4 '67 - pB10
HB - v43 - Ap '67 - p214
KR - v35 - Ja 15 '67 - p68
LJ - v92 - My 15 '67 - p2033
NYTBR - v72 - Ap 16 '67 - p22
SR - v50 - Mr 18 '67 - p36

SCHOOR, Gene 1921-
AuBYP, ConAu 29R, SmATA 3

The Jim Thorpe Story: America's Greatest Athlete
KR - v19 - S 1 '51 - p490
LJ - v77 - Ja 1 '52 - p70
NYTBR - Ja 27 '52 - p28
Subject: Biography

The Story Of Ty Cobb: Baseball's Greatest Player
BL - v48 - My 15 '52 - p302
CSM - My 15 '52 - p11
KR - v20 - Ap 1 '52 - p229
LJ - v77 - My 1 '52 - p796
NYTBR - Ap 6 '52 - p32
PW - v192 - O 9 '67 - p62
SR - v35 - My 10 '52 - p59
Subject: Biography

SCHOTTER, Roni

A Matter Of Time
TN - v42 - Summer '86 - p382
Subject: Death—Fiction; Individuality—Fiction

SCHRAFF, Anne E 1939-
AuBYP SUP, ConAu 17NR, SmATA 27

The Day The World Went Away
KR - v41 - My 1 '73 - p522
LJ - v99 - S 15 '74 - p2297

SCHROEDER, Lynn
see Ostrander, Sheila (co-author)

SCHULMAN, L M 1934-
ConAu 12NR, SmATA 13

The Loners: Short Stories About The Young And Alienated
BL - v66 - My 1 '70 - p1094
CCB-B - v23 - Je '70 - p166
LJ - v95 - My 15 '70 - p1956
NYTBR - Mr 1 '70 - p34
PW - v197 - Ja 26 '70 - p278
SR - v53 - My 9 '70 - p70
Subject: Short stories

SCHULTZ, Marion

The Make-Believe Boyfriend
Kliatt - v19 - Fall '85 - p16
SLJ - v32 - S '85 - p152
Subject: Love—Fiction

SCHULZ, Charles M 1922-
ArtCS, AuBYP, ConAu 6NR, ConLC 12, EncTwCJ, LesBEnT, SmATA 10, ThrBJA, WhoAm 86, WrDr 86

Always Stick Up For The Underbird
SLJ - v24 - S '77 - p137
Subject: Cartoons and comics

Dr. Beagle And Mr. Hyde
SLJ - v28 - F '82 - p72
VOYA - v4 - F '82 - p44
Subject: Cartoons and comics

SCHULZ, Charles M (continued)

It's Chow Time, Snoopy
Kliatt - v17 - Ap '83 - p54
Subject: Comic books, strips, etc.

Nobody's Perfect, Charlie Brown
B&B - v14 - Ag '69 - p38
Subject: Comic books, strips, etc.; Wit and humor

Things I Learned After It Was Too Late (and Other Minor Truths)
SLJ - v28 - S '81 - p130
VOYA - v4 - O '81 - p51
Subject: Aphorisms and apothegms

You're The Greatest, Charlie Brown
BS - v30 - Mr 1 '71 - p532
SLJ - v26 - D '79 - p100
Subject: Comic books, strips, etc.; Decathlon—Fiction

SCHURFRANZ, Vivian 1925-
ConAu 61, SmATA 13

Roman Hostage
BB - v3 - O '75 - p4
BL - v71 - Ap 15 '75 - p868
CCB-B - v29 - N '75 - p53
NYTBR - Ag 24 '75 - p8
PW - v207 - Ap 28 '75 - p45
SLJ - v21 - Ap '75 - p70
Subject: Rome—History—Fiction

SCHURMAN, Dewey

Athletic Fitness
BL - v72 - N 1 '75 - p338
LJ - v100 - N 15 '75 - p2164
Subject: Exercise; Physical fitness

SCHWARTZ, Alvin 1927-
AuBYP SUP, ChlLR 3, ConAu 7NR, FifBJA, SmATA 4, WhoE 77

Cross Your Fingers, Spit In Your Hat
BL - v70 - Jl 15 '74 - p1255
CE - v51 - N '74 - p98
HB - v50 - Je '74 - p291
KR - v42 - My 1 '74 - p487
LA - v54 - S '77 - p697
LJ - v99 - S 15 '74 - p2277
NY - v50 - D 2 '74 - p199
NYTBR - v0 - My 5 '74 - p22
PW - v205 - Ap 1 '74 - p58
RT - v32 - Ja '79 - p446
RT - v33 - D '79 - p265
SR/W - v1 - My 4 '74 - p43
Teacher - v93 - Mr '76 - p18
Teacher - v96 - Mr '79 - p113
VV - v19 - D 16 '74 - p51
Subject: Superstition

More Scary Stories To Tell In The Dark
BL - v81 - Mr 1 '85 - p989
CAY - v6 - Spring '85 - p9
CCB-B - v38 - S '85 - p116
HB - v61 - Mr '85 - p183
RT - v38 - Ap '85 - p801
SLJ - v31 - F '85 - p79
VOYA - v8 - Ap '85 - p51
Subject: Folklore; Ghosts—Fiction; Horror stories

Tomfoolery
KR - v41 - D 15 '73 - p1354
NYTBR - D 2 '73 - p79
Subject: Riddles; Wit and humor

A Twister Of Twists, A Tangler Of Tongues
ANQ - v11 - Mr '73 - p110
BL - v69 - Ja 1 '73 - p451
BW - v6 - D 3 '72 - p20
CCB-B - v26 - Je '73 - p162
CE - v49 - F '73 - p258
HB - v49 - Ap '73 - p153
JAF - v86 - Ap '73 - p198
KR - v40 - O 1 '72 - p1149
LJ - v97 - D 1 '72 - p3911
LJ - v98 - My 15 '73 - p1685
NYT - v122 - D 13 '72 - p67
NYTBR - N 19 '72 - p8
NYTBR - D 3 '72 - p82
NYTBR, Pt. 2 - N 5 '72 - p29
PW - v202 - O 30 '72 - p56
RT - v32 - N '78 - p148
SR - v55 - D 9 '72 - p79
SR - v4 - My 28 '77 - p33
Teacher - v93 - Mr '76 - p18
Subject: Tongue twisters

Unriddling
BL - v80 - Ja 1 '84 - p685
CCB-B - v37 - Ap '84 - p154
CE - v60 - Mr '84 - p291
HB - v60 - F '84 - p77
NY - v59 - D 5 '83 - p207
SLJ - v30 - Mr '84 - p164
Subject: Folklore; Riddles

Witcracks: Jokes And Jests From American Folklore
BL - v70 - D 15 '73 - p446
CCB-B - v27 - Mr '74 - p117
HB - v50 - F '74 - p62
Inst - v83 - My '74 - p96
JAF - v87 - Jl '74 - p246
LJ - v98 - D 15 '73 - p3709
NYT - v123 - D 10 '73 - p35

SCHWARTZ, Alvin (continued)
SWR - v1 - D 4 '73 - p28
Subject: Jokes; Wit and humor

SCHWARTZ, Anita K

Eating Right
VOYA - v6 - Ag '83 - p156
Co-author: Guth, Deborah
Subject: Food; Nutrition

Keeping Fit
VOYA - v6 - Ag '83 - p156
Co-author: Guth, Deborah
Subject: Physical fitness

Looking Good
Cur R - v22 - My '83 - p181
VOYA - v6 - Ag '83 - p156
Co-author: Guth, Deborah
Subject: Physical fitness

SCHWEITZER, Byrd Baylor
see Baylor, Byrd

SCOGGIN, Margaret C 1905-1968
BioIn 1, -2, -3, -8, CurBio 52, -68, SmATA 47

Escapes And Rescues
BL - v56 - Jl 1 '60 - p663
HB - v36 - Ag '60 - p317
LJ - v85 - Jl '60 - p2684
Subject: Adventure and adventurers; Escapes

More Chucklebait: Funny Stories For Everyone
BL - v46 - N 1 '49 - p84
CSM - N 17 '49 - p10
HB - v25 - N '49 - p541
KR - v17 - S 1 '49 - p477
LJ - v74 - D 1 '49 - p1830
NYT - O 23 '49 - p50
Subject: Short stories

SCOPPETTONE, Sandra 1936-
AuBYP SUP, ConAu 5R, ConLC 26, FifBJA, NatPD, -81, SmATA 9, WhoAm 84

Happy Endings Are All Alike
CCB-B - v32 - Ja '79 - p86
CLW - v50 - O '78 - p117
SLJ - v25 - F '79 - p65
WLB - v53 - D '78 - p341
Subject: Lesbians—Fiction; Prejudices—Fiction; Rape—Fiction

The Late Great Me
BS - v36 - My '76 - p40
KR - v43 - N 15 '75 - p1304
KR - v43 - D 1 '75 - p1344
NYTBR - F 22 '76 - p38
PW - v208 - N 10 '75 - p47
SLJ - v22 - Ja '76 - p58
Subject: Alcohol and youth—Fiction

A Long Time Between Kisses
BL - v78 - Ap 1 '82 - p1014
BS - v42 - Je '82 - p123
CBRS - v10 - My '82 - p99
CCB-B - v35 - Jl '82 - p214
HB - v58 - Ag '82 - p417
KR - v50 - Ap 1 '82 - p424
NYTBR - v87 - Ap 25 '82 - p44
PW - v221 - My 7 '82 - p80
SLJ - v28 - Ap '82 - p85
VOYA - v5 - Ag '82 - p36
Subject: New York (City)—Fiction

SCOTT, Ann Herbert 1926-
AuBYP SUP, BkP, ConAu 21R, FourBJA, SmATA 29

Sam
BL - v64 - F 15 '68 - p702
BW - v2 - Ap 7 '68 - p14
CCB-B - v21 - F '68 - p100
Inst - v77 - F '68 - p190
LJ - v93 - F 15 '68 - p862
Par - v43 - Ag '68 - p76
Subject: Family life—Fiction

SCOTT, Carol J

Kentucky Daughter
BL - v81 - Je 15 '85 - p1461
BS - v45 - Je '85 - p119
CBRS - v13 - Jl '85 - p145
CCB-B - v38 - Je '85 - p194
CSM - v77 - Jl 5 '85 - pB5
PW - v227 - Mr 29 '85 - p73
SLJ - v31 - Ag '85 - p81
VOYA - v8 - O '85 - p260
Subject: Schools—Fiction

SCOTT, John 1912-1976
ConAu 6NR, IntAu&W 77, SmATA 14, WhAm 7

China: The Hungry Dragon
BL - v64 - Ja 15 '68 - p589
BS - v27 - Ja 1 '68 - p392
CCB-B - v21 - Je '68 - p165
KR - v35 - N 15 '67 - p1376
LJ - v93 - Ja 15 '68 - p310
NYTBR - v72 - N 5 '67 - p32
SR - v51 - My 11 '68 - p42

SCOTT, John (continued)
SS - v59 - N '68 - p281
Subject: China

SCOTT, John Anthony 1916-
AuBYP SUP, BioIn 6, ConAu 6NR, DrAS 82H, IntAu&W 86, SmATA 23, WrDr 86

Fanny Kemble's America
BL - v70 - S 1 '73 - p48
CCB-B - v27 - N '73 - p52
CE - v50 - N '73 - p102
Comw - v99 - N 23 '73 - p217
CSM - v65 - N 7 '73 - pB6
HB - v49 - D '73 - p599
KR - v41 - My 15 '73 - p572
LJ - v98 - My 15 '73 - p1656
LJ - v98 - My 15 '73 - p1692
LJ - v98 - D 15 '73 - p3691
NYTBR - Jl 15 '73 - p8
NYTBR - N 4 '73 - p52
Subject: Abolitionists; Biography

SCOTT, William R

Lonesome Traveler
BL - v67 - S 15 '70 - p83
BS - v30 - Je 15 '70 - p119
LJ - v95 - My 15 '70 - p1970
LJ - v95 - Je 1 '70 - p2180
LJ - v95 - D 15 '70 - p4328
PW - v197 - F 23 '70 - p150

SCUDDER, Mildred Lee
see Lee, Mildred

SEARIGHT, Mary Williams 1918-
ConAu 29R, SmATA 17, WhoAmW 77

Your Career In Nursing
BL - v67 - D 1 '70 - p305
BL - v74 - D 15 '77 - p678
BS - v30 - O 15 '70 - p299
KR - v45 - N 15 '77 - p1210
LJ - v95 - D 15 '70 - p4368
SB - v6 - D '70 - p248
SLJ - v24 - Mr '78 - p139
Subject: Nursing as a profession

SEAVER, Tom
see Drucker, Malka (co-author)

SEED, Suzanne 1940-
AuBYP SUP, WhoAmA 84, WhoAmW 81

Saturday's Child
AB - v52 - D 10 '73 - p2022
CCB-B - v26 - Jl '73 - p176
Comw - v99 - N 23 '73 - p218
CSM - v67 - Ja 22 '75 - p8
EJ - v63 - Ap '74 - p90
Inst - v83 - N '73 - p126
KR - v41 - Ap 15 '73 - p466
KR - v41 - D 15 '73 - p1361
LJ - v98 - My 15 '73 - p1692
NYTBR - Jl 15 '73 - p8
PW - v203 - Mr 12 '73 - p64
Subject: Occupations

SEEVERS, James A
see Ciupik, Larry A (co-author)

SEEWAGEN, George L

Tennis
BL - v65 - F 1 '69 - p596
KR - v36 - Ap 15 '68 - p474
LJ - v93 - My 15 '68 - p2128
Co-author: Sullivan, George Edward
Subject: Tennis

see also Sullivan, George Edward for additional titles

SEGAL, Erich 1937-
ASpks, ConAu 20NR, ConLC 3, -10, ConTFT 1, CurBio 71, HalFC 84, IntAu&W 82, NewYTBE 71, WhoAm 86, WrDr 86

Love Story
A Lib - v1 - Jl '70 - p715
Am - v122 - My 2 '70 - p478
Atl - v225 - Je '70 - p124
B&B - v16 - O '70 - p36
BL - v66 - Ap 15 '70 - p1022
BL - v67 - S 1 '70 - p54
BL - v67 - Ap 1 '71 - p654
BL - v67 - Jl 15 '71 - p934
BL - v68 - Jl 15 '72 - p980
BS - v29 - Mr 15 '70 - p474
CSM - v62 - Ap 30 '70 - p11
EJ - v62 - N '73 - p1189
HB - v46 - Ap '70 - p188
KR - v37 - D 1 '69 - p1287
Lis - v85 - Ap 1 '71 - p420
LJ - v95 - F 1 '70 - p514
LJ - v95 - My 15 '70 - p1971
LJ - v95 - D 15 '70 - p4328
NO - v9 - F 23 '70 - p19
NS - v80 - Ag 28 '70 - p249
NW - v75 - Mr 9 '70 - p94
NY - v46 - F 28 '70 - p116
NY - v46 - O 24 '70 - p170
NYT - v119 - F 13 '70 - p35
NYTBR - Mr 8 '70 - p31

SEGAL, Erich (continued)
Obs - Ag 23 '70 - p23
Obs - Ja 10 '71 - p23
PW - v196 - D 1 '69 - p39
PW - v198 - O 19 '70 - p55
Spec - v225 - Ag 29 '70 - p217
SR - v53 - D 26 '70 - p30
TLS - S 4 '70 - p965
TN - v27 - Ap '71 - p309
Subject: Love—Fiction

SEIDELMAN, James E 1926-
AuBYP, ConAu 25R, SmATA 6

Creating Mosaics
BL - v64 - Ap 1 '68 - p935
CC - v84 - D 13 '67 - p1602
KR - v35 - Ag 15 '67 - p963
LJ - v92 - D 15 '67 - p4618
Subject: Handicraft

Creating With Clay
KR - v35 - S 1 '67 - p1052
Co-author: Mintonye, Grace
Subject: Handicraft; Sculpture

Creating With Paint
LJ - v93 - Ja 15 '68 - p295
Co-author: Mintonye, Grace
Subject: Handicraft

Creating With Paper
KR - v35 - Ag 15 '67 - p963
LJ - v92 - D 15 '67 - p4618
SR - v51 - F 10 '68 - p70
TN - v77 - Ap '68 - p155
Co-author: Mintonye, Grace
Subject: Handicraft

SELDEN, George (pseud.) 1929-
AuBYP, ChlLR 8, ConAu X, –X, DcLB 52, FourBJA, MorBMP, OxChL, SmATA 4, TwCChW 83, WrDr 86
Real Name:
Thompson, George Selden

The Cricket In Times Square
BL - v57 - D 15 '60 - p250
Comw - v73 - N 18 '60 - p207
CSM - N 3 '60 - p1B
GW - D 1 '61 - p6
HB - v36 - O '60 - p407
LJ - v85 - D 15 '60 - p4570
NS - v62 - N 10 '61 - p704
NYTBR, Pt. 2 - N 13 '60 - p50
NYTBR, Pt. 2 - N 8 '70 - p6
PW - v198 - O 19 '70 - p56
Spec - N 10 '61 - p682
SR - v43 - N 12 '60 - p94
Subject: Animals—Fiction; Fantasy

Tucker's Countryside
BW - v3 - Jl 27 '69 - p12
CCB-B - v23 - D '69 - p64
Comw - v90 - My 23 '69 - p303
HB - v45 - Ag '69 - p412
KR - v37 - Ap 15 '69 - p443
LJ - v94 - Je 15 '69 - p2504
LJ - v94 - D 15 '69 - p4582
NO - v8 - Je 9 '69 - p23
NYTBR, Pt. 2 - My 4 '69 - p26
NYTBR, Pt. 2 - N 9 '69 - p62
PW - v195 - My 19 '69 - p70
SR - v52 - Je 28 '69 - p39
Subject: Animals—Fiction; Fantasy

SELDEN, Neil
IntAu&W 86

The Great Lakeside High Experiment
Hi Lo - v3 - Je '82 - p3
VOYA - v5 - O '82 - p46
Subject: Schools—Fiction

Night Driver
Hi Lo - v2 - F '81 - p5

SELF, Margaret Cabell 1902-
AuBYP, ConAu 3NR, IntAu&W 82, SmATA 24, WhoAm 82, WhoS&SW 76, WrDr 86

Sky Rocket: The Story Of A Little Bay Horse
Am - v123 - D 5 '70 - p497
BL - v67 - Mr 15 '71 - p621
BS - v30 - D 15 '70 - p415
LJ - v96 - Jl '71 - p2375
PW - v198 - S 28 '70 - p80
Subject: Horses—Fiction

SELLERS, Naomi
ConAu 1R, SmATA X
Pseud./variant:
Flack, Naomi John

Cross My Heart
BL - v50 - S 15 '53 - p38
HB - v29 - D '53 - p470
KR - v21 - Je 15 '53 - p360
LJ - v78 - O 1 '53 - p1702
NYT - Ag 16 '53 - p14

SELSAM, Millicent E 1912-
AuBYP, BkP, ChlLR 1, ConAu 5NR, IntAu&W 77, MorJA, SmATA 29

Milkweed
BL - v64 - D 1 '67 - p451
CCB-B - v21 - O '67 - p33
CSM - v60 - D 21 '67 - p11

SELSAM, Millicent E (continued)
HB - v43 - O '67 - p607
Inst - v77 - D '67 - p124
KR - v35 - Ag 15 '67 - p963
LJ - v92 - O 15 '67 - p3842
NY - v43 - D 16 '67 - p163
SA - v217 - D '67 - p145
SB - v3 - D '67 - p234
SR - v50 - Ag 19 '67 - p35
Subject: Milkweed

SENN, J A

The Wolf King And Other True Animal Stories
Hi Lo - v1 - Ap '80 - p3
Subject: Animals; Short stories

SETH, Marie (pseud.)
SmATA X
Real Name:
Lexau, Joan M

Dream Of The Dead
BL - v74 - D 15 '77 - p679
Subject: Ghosts—Fiction; Scotland—Fiction

SEULING, Barbara 1937-
ConAu 8NR, SmATA 10

The Last Cow On The White House Lawn
BL - v75 - S 1 '78 - p53
BW - S 10 '78 - pE6
KR - v46 - Jl 15 '78 - p752
PW - v213 - My 15 '78 - p104
SLJ - v25 - S '78 - p148
Subject: Presidents

SEYMOUR, William Kean 1887-
ConAu 9R, DcLEL

Happy Christmas
BS - v28 - O 15 '68 - p298
LJ - v93 - O 15 '68 - p3992
LJ - v93 - N 15 '68 - p4300
NYTBR - v73 - D 1 '68 - p76
TLS - O 3 '68 - p1108
Co-author: Smith, John
Subject: Christmas—Fiction

SHANKS, Ann Zane Kushner
BioIn 11, ConAu 53, SmATA 10, WhoAm 86, WhoAmW 77

Busted Lives: Dialogues With Kids In Jail
BS - v42 - O '82 - p287
CBRS - v10 - Jl '82 - p129
EJ - v72 - Ag '83 - p104
KR - v50 - Je 1 '82 - p638
SLJ - v28 - Ag '82 - p128
Subject: Juvenile delinquency

SHANNON, Jacqueline

Too Much T.J.
BL - v83 - O 15 '86 - p345
CBRS - v15 - S '86 - p10
PW - v230 - Ag 22 '86 - p100
Subject: Jealousy—Fiction; Remarriage—Fiction

SHAPIRO, Amy

Sun Signs: The Stars In Your Life
SLJ - v25 - S '78 - p128
Subject: Astrology; Horoscopes

SHAPIRO, Milton J 1926-
AuBYP, ConAu 81, SmATA 32

All-Stars Of The Outfield
BL - v67 - O 15 '70 - p196
BS - v30 - Je 1 '70 - p106
CCB-B - v24 - N '70 - p47
KR - v38 - Ap 15 '70 - p471
LJ - v95 - My 15 '70 - p1964
PW - v197 - Je 15 '70 - p65
SR - v53 - Je 27 '70 - p38
Subject: Baseball—Biography

Jackie Robinson Of The Brooklyn Dodgers
PW - v192 - Jl 24 '67 - p58
Subject: Baseball—Biography

Undersea Raiders: U.S. Submarines In World War II
SLJ - v26 - Mr '80 - p143
Subject: World War, 1939-1945

SHAPIRO, Neal

The World Of Horseback Riding
BL - v73 - Mr 15 '77 - p1095
LJ - v101 - D 15 '76 - p2594
SLJ - v23 - Mr '77 - p148
Co-author: Lehrman, Steve
Subject: Horses

SHARMAT, Marjorie Weinman 1928-
AuBYP SUP, BioIn 9, ConAu 12NR, FifBJA, IntAu&W 86, SmATA 33, TwCChW 83, WrDr 86

He Noticed I'm Alive...And Other Hopeful Signs
CBRS - v13 - O '84 - p21
Subject: Single-parent family—Fiction

SHARMAT, Marjorie Weinman (continued)

How To Have A Gorgeous Wedding
BL - v82 - N 15 '85 - p500
Kliatt - v19 - Fall '85 - p18
SLJ - v32 - S '85 - p150
Subject: Marriage—Fiction

How To Meet A Gorgeous Guy
BL - v80 - O 1 '83 - p300
B Rpt - v2 - Mr '84 - p36
BS - v43 - N '83 - p312
CBRS - v12 - O '83 - p22
CCB-B - v37 - Mr '84 - p135
KR - v51 - N 1 '83 - pJ208
SLJ - v30 - D '83 - p78
VOYA - v7 - Ap '84 - p27
Subject: Love—Fiction

I Saw Him First
BS - v43 - My '83 - p75
CBRS - v11 - My '83 - p104
CCB-B - v36 - Mr '83 - p134
KR - v51 - Ap 15 '83 - p462
SLJ - v29 - Ag '83 - p80
VOYA - v6 - Ag '83 - p146
Subject: Friendship—Fiction

SHAW, Arnold 1909-
AuBYP SUP, Baker 84, BioIn 3, ConAu 1NR, IntWWM 85, SmATA 4, WhoAm 86, WhoWor 78

The Rock Revolution: What's Happening In Today's Music
AB - v44 - S 15 '69 - p775
BL - v66 - S 15 '69 - p122
CCB-B - v23 - O '69 - p30
KR - v37 - Ap 1 '69 - p391
LJ - v94 - Ap 15 '69 - p1612
LJ - v94 - S 15 '69 - p3236
NY - v45 - D 13 '69 - p212
SN - v85 - Mr '70 - p36
SR - v52 - S 13 '69 - p37
Subject: Rock music

SHAW, Dale 1927-

Titans Of The American Stage
BL - v68 - Mr 1 '72 - p561
BL - v68 - Mr 1 '72 - p567
KR - v39 - O 15 '71 - p1136
LJ - v97 - Ja 15 '72 - p291
Subject: Actors and actresses

SHAW, Richard 1923-
ConAu 37R, SmATA 12, WrDr 86

Call Me Al Raft
BS - v72 - D 15 '75 - p581
BS - v35 - F '76 - p363
KR - v43 - Jl 15 '75 - p783
PW - v208 - D 1 '75 - p66
SLJ - v22 - S '75 - p126
Subject: California—Fiction; Fathers and sons—Fiction

Shape Up, Burke
BL - v72 - My 1 '76 - p1271
BS - v36 - Ja '77 - p324
CCB-B - v30 - O '76 - p32
J Read - v21 - O '77 - p86
KR - v44 - My 15 '76 - p601
PW - v210 - Jl 19 '76 - p132
SLJ - v22 - Ap '76 - p93
Subject: Fathers and sons—Fiction

SHAY, Lacey
see Shebar, Sharon Sigmond

SHEA, George
ConAu 108, SmATA 42

Big Bad Ernie
Hi Lo - v1 - Ja '80 - p4
Subject: Baseball—Fiction

I Died Here
Hi Lo - v1 - O '79 - p3
SLJ - v26 - D '79 - p82
Subject: Supernatural—Fiction

Nightmare Nina
Hi Lo - v1 - F '80 - p4
Subject: Dreams—Fiction; Kidnapping—Fiction; Mystery and detective stories

Strike Two
BL - v78 - O 15 '81 - p297
Hi Lo - v3 - F '82 - p1
SLJ - v28 - S '81 - p122
Subject: Baseball—Fiction

SHEBAR, Sharon Sigmond 1945-
ConAu 19NR, SmATA 36
Pseud./variant:
Shay, Lacey

The Bell Witch
BL - v79 - Je 15 '83 - p1334
B Rpt - v2 - N '83 - p37
Hi Lo - v4 - My '83 - p3
SLJ - v30 - O '83 - p162
VOYA - v6 - O '83 - p227
Co-author: Schoder, Judith
Subject: Ghosts

see also Schoder, Judith for additional titles

SHEFFER, H R

Airplanes
SLJ - v28 - Ag '82 - p122
Subject: Airplanes

Cycles
BL - v79 - Ag '83 - p1468
SLJ - v30 - S '83 - p128
Subject: Motorcycles

Great Cars
SLJ - v30 - S '83 - p128
Subject: Automobiles

The Last Meet
BL - v78 - S 15 '81 - p114
SLJ - v28 - O '81 - p147
Subject: Gymnastics—Fiction

Moto-Cross Monkey
BL - v78 - S 15 '81 - p114
SLJ - v28 - O '81 - p147
Subject: Motorcycle racing—Fiction

Paddlewheelers
SLJ - v28 - Ag '82 - p122
Subject: Paddle steamers

Partners On Wheels
BL - v17 - S 15 '81 - p114
SLJ - v28 - O '81 - p147
Subject: Roller skating—Fiction

Race Cars
SLJ - v28 - Ag '82 - p122
Subject: Automobile racing

R.V.'s
CCB-B - v37 - N '83 - p57
SLJ - v30 - S '83 - p128
Subject: Recreational vehicles

Sarah Sells Soccer
BL - v78 - S 15 '81 - p114
SLJ - v28 - O '81 - p147
Subject: Soccer—Fiction

Second String Nobody
BL - v78 - S 15 '81 - p114
SLJ - v28 - O '81 - p147
Subject: Football—Fiction

Street Hockey Lady
AHR - v78 - S 15 '81 - p114
SLJ - v28 - O '81 - p147
Subject: Field hockey—Fiction

Swim For Pride
BL - v78 - S 15 '81 - p114
SLJ - v28 - O '81 - p147
Subject: Swimming—Fiction

Tractors
BL - v79 - Ag '83 - p1468
SLJ - v30 - S '83 - p128
Subject: Tractors

Trains
SLJ - v28 - Ag '82 - p122
Subject: Railroads

Trucks
SLJ - v30 - S '83 - p128
Subject: Trucks

Two At The Net
BL - v78 - S 15 '81 - p114
SLJ - v28 - O '81 - p147
Subject: Tennis—Fiction

Vans
SLJ - v28 - Ag '82 - p122
Subject: Vans

Weekend In The Dunes
BL - v78 - S 15 '81 - p114
SLJ - v28 - O '81 - p147
Subject: Dune buggy racing—Fiction

Winner On The Court
BL - v78 - S 15 '81 - p114
SLJ - v28 - O '81 - p147
Subject: Basketball—Fiction

SHEFFIELD, Janet N 1926-
ConAu 65, SmATA 26

Not Just Sugar And Spice
CCB-B - v29 - Ap '76 - p133
KR - v43 - N 1 '75 - p1230
SLJ - v22 - Ja '76 - p50
Subject: Single-parent family—Fiction

SHELLEY, Mary 1797-1851
BioIn 12, -13, EncMys, HerW 84, IntDcWB, OxEng 85, ScFSB, SmATA 29, WhoHr&F, WhoSciF

Frankenstein
CF - v56 - D '76 - p64
Choice - v7 - Mr '70 - p80
Choice - v11 - Je '74 - p603
KR - v41 - Ag 1 '73 - p840
SEP - v246 - Ag '74 - p90
Teacher - v92 - F '75 - p38
TLS - O 16 '69 - p1215
VV - v19 - Jl 25 '74 - p25
Subject: Monsters—Fiction

SHELTON, William Roy 1919-
AuBYP SUP, AuNews 1, BioIn 2, ConAu 11NR, IntAu&W 86, SmATA 5, WhoS&SW 78

Flights Of The Astronauts
Am - v108 - Je 1 '63 - p807
Comw - v78 - My 24 '63 - p261
CSM - My 9 '63 - p7B
LJ - v88 - Ap 15 '63 - p1780
Subject: Project Mercury

SHEMIN, Margaretha 1928-
ConAu 13R, SmATA 4

The Empty Moat
BL - v66 - F 1 '70 - p672
CLW - v42 - O '70 - p138
HB - v45 - D '69 - p679
KR - v37 - N 15 '69 - p1203
LJ - v94 - D 15 '69 - p4614
PW - v197 - Je 1 '70 - p67
TN - v26 - Je '70 - p426
Subject: Netherlands—German occupation, 1940-1945—Fiction

The Little Riders
HB - v40 - F '64 - p59
LJ - v88 - D 15 '63 - p4858
NYTBR - Ja 19 '64 - p20
TLS - N 26 '64 - p1083

SHEPHERD, Elizabeth
AuBYP SUP, ConAu 33R, SmATA 4

The Discoveries Of Esteban The Black
CSM - v63 - Mr 20 '71 - p13
LJ - v95 - D 15 '70 - p4357
NYTBR - O 4 '70 - p30
Subject: Explorers

SHERBURNE, Zoa Morin 1912-
AuBYP, ConAu 1R, FourBJA, SmATA 3

The Girl In The Mirror
Am - v115 - N 5 '66 - p553
BL - v63 - N 1 '66 - p327
BS - v26 - N 1 '66 - p296
CCB-B - v20 - N '66 - p48
CSM - v58 - N 3 '66 - pB12
KR - v34 - Ag 1 '66 - p764
LJ - v91 - N 15 '66 - p5765
NYTBR - v71 - N 6 '66 - p20
SR - v49 - O 22 '66 - p61

The Girl Who Knew Tomorrow
Am - v123 - D 5 '70 - p498
BL - v66 - Je 15 '70 - p1274
BS - v30 - My 1 '70 - p63
J Read - v22 - N '78 - p128
KR - v38 - Mr 1 '70 - p250
LJ - v95 - D 15 '70 - p4368
Subject: Extrasensory perception—Fiction

Leslie
EJ - v62 - Mr '73 - p480
KR - v40 - O 1 '72 - p1154
LJ - v98 - Ja 15 '73 - p270
Subject: Drug abuse—Fiction

Too Bad About The Haines Girl
BL - v63 - Jl 1 '67 - p1141
BS - v26 - Mr 1 '67 - p443
CCB-B - v20 - My '67 - p146
CSM - v59 - My 4 '67 - pB10
EJ - v56 - N '67 - p1222
J Ho E - v61 - S '69 - p478
J Read - v22 - N '78 - p128
KR - v35 - Mr 15 '67 - p349
LJ - v92 - Ap 15 '67 - p1753
NYTBR - v72 - Mr 5 '67 - p30
NYTBR - v72 - N 5 '67 - p64
SR - v50 - Mr 18 '67 - p36
SR - v52 - Jl 19 '69 - p42
Subject: Pregnancy—Fiction

Why Have The Birds Stopped Singing?
BL - v70 - Jl 1 '74 - p1202
J Read - v22 - N '78 - p127
KR - v42 - Mr 15 '74 - p301
LJ - v99 - My 15 '74 - p1488
Subject: Epilepsy—Fiction; Space and time—Fiction

SHERMAN, D R 1934-
ConAu 8NR, SmATA 48

Brothers Of The Sea
BL - v63 - N 15 '66 - p364
BS - v26 - N 1 '66 - p285
KR - v34 - Jl 15 '66 - p712
LJ - v91 - O 15 '66 - p4977
NYTBR - v71 - S 25 '66 - p53
PW - v190 - Jl 18 '66 - p74
TLS - O 6 '66 - p922

SHEVELSON, Joseph

Roller Skating
Hi Lo - v1 - Ap '80 - p4
SLJ - v26 - S '79 - p147
Subject: Roller skating

SHIRER, William L 1904-
AuBYP, ConAu 7NR, CurBio 41, -62, DcLB 4, EncAJ, IntAu&W 86, SmATA 45, WebAB, -79, Who 85, WhoAm 86, WhoWor 78, WrDr 86

Rise And Fall Of Adolph Hitler
BL - v57 - Je 15 '61 - p641
CSM - My 11 '61 - p4B
HB - v37 - Ag '61 - p351
KR - v29 - F 1 '61 - p114
LJ - v86 - Ap 15 '61 - p1698
NYTBR, Pt. 2 - My 14 '61 - p12
Time - v78 - Ag 4 '61 - p73
Subject: Biography

SHORE, June Lewis
AuBYP SUP, AuNews 1, ConAu 105, SmATA 30

Summer Storm
BL - v74 - S 1 '77 - p44
CCB-B - v30 - Je '77 - p166
PW - v211 - F 14 '77 - p83
SLJ - v23 - My '77 - p71
Subject: Family life—Fiction; Kentucky—Fiction; Tornadoes—Fiction

SHOTWELL, Louisa R 1902-
AuBYP SUP, BioIn 3, ConAu 4NR, MorBMP, OxChL, SmATA 3, ThrBJA, TwCChW 78, -83, WrDr 86

Adam Bookout
BL - v64 - Ja 15 '68 - p595
BW - v1 - N 5 '67 - p22
CCB-B - v21 - F '68 - p100
CE - v44 - My '68 - p561
Comw - v87 - N 10 '67 - p177
Comw - v89 - F 21 '69 - p644
CSM - v60 - F 1 '68 - p11
HB - v44 - F '68 - p67
KR - v35 - O 15 '67 - p1272
LJ - v92 - N 15 '67 - p4255
NYTBR - v72 - N 5 '67 - p43
PW - v192 - S 18 '67 - p67
SR - v50 - O 21 '67 - p43
Subject: New York (City)—Fiction; Orphans—Fiction

SHREVE, Susan Richards 1939-
ConAu 5AS, ConLC 23, DrAP&F 85, SmATA 46, WhoAmW 87, WrDr 86

The Nightmares Of Geranium Street
BW - Ap 8 '79 - pL2
RT - v32 - F '79 - p607
Subject: Drug abuse—Fiction

The Revolution Of Mary Leary
BL - v79 - N 1 '82 - p364
BS - v42 - Ja '83 - p407
BW - v12 - O 10 '82 - p7
BW - v14 - S 9 '84 - p13
CBRS - v11 - D '82 - p37
CCB-B - v36 - N '82 - p55
HB - v58 - D '82 - p661
Inter BC - v15 - #3 '84 p17
Kliatt - v18 - Fall '84 - p20
KR - v50 - S 15 '82 - p1061
NYTBR - v87 - N 14 '82 - p63
SLJ - v29 - O '82 - p163
VOYA - v6 - Ap '83 - p41
WCRB - v8 - N '82 - p68
WLB - v57 - F '83 - p507
Subject: Baby sitters—Fiction; Mothers and daughters—Fiction; Runaways—Fiction

SHYNE, Kevin

The Man Who Dropped From The Sky
BL - v79 - Ja 15 '83 - p682
Hi Lo - v4 - Ja '83 - p4
Inter BC - v14 - #5 '83 p25
SLJ - v29 - F '83 - p83
VOYA - v6 - Je '83 - p105
Subject: Skydivers

SIEGAL, Mordecai

The Good Dog Book
BL - v74 - D 1 '77 - p609
Kliatt - v13 - Spring '79 - p57
KR - v45 - Ag 1 '77 - p844
PW - v211 - Je 20 '77 - p65
SR - v5 - N 26 '77 - p40
Subject: Dogs

SIEGEL, Alice
see **McLoone-Basta, Margo** (co-author)

SIEGEL, Bertram M
see Stone, A Harris (co-author)

SIEGEL, Dorothy Schainman 1932-
ConAu 9R

Winners: Eight Special Young People
BL - v74 - Ap 15 '78 - p1341
Subject: Physically handicapped

SIEGEL, Scott

Beat The Devil
BL - v80 - My 1 '84 - p1234

SIEGEL, Scott (continued)
SLJ - v31 - S '84 - p134
Subject: Devil—Fiction; Video games—Fiction

SIERRA, Patricia

One-Way Romance
BL - v82 - Ag '86 - p1683
Kliatt - v20 - Fall '86 - p18
PW - v230 - Jl 25 '86 - p193
Subject: Love—Fiction

SILSBEE, Peter

The Big Way Out
J Read - v29 - F '86 - p464
Subject: Family problems—Fiction; Fathers and sons—Fiction; Mental illness—Fiction

SILVERBERG, Robert 1935-
BioIn 12, -13, ConAu 20NR, -3AS, ConLC 7, ConSFA, DcLB 8, DrmM 1, ThrBJA, TwCSFW 86, WrDr 86

The Auk, The Dodo And The Oryx
BL - v63 - Jl 15 '67 - p1191
CCB-B - v20 - Jl '67 - p176
Inst - v130 - Ap '71 - p136
KR - v35 - Ap 1 '67 - p432
LJ - v92 - Je 15 '67 - p2464
NYTBR, Pt. 2 - v72 - My 7 '67 - p34
SB - v3 - S '67 - p135
SR - v50 - Je 17 '67 - p36
Subject: Animals

Planet Of Death
LJ - v92 - N 15 '67 - p4257
NYTBR - v72 - Mr 26 '67 - p22
NYTBR - v72 - N 5 '67 - p64

Three Survived
KR - v37 - Ap 15 '69 - p453
LJ - v94 - Ap 15 '69 - p1800
PW - v195 - Ap 7 '69 - p56
Subject: Science fiction

Vanishing Giants: The Story Of The Sequoias
BW - v3 - Jl 6 '69 - p10
CSM - v61 - My 15 '69 - p11
KR - v37 - Ap 1 '69 - p391
LJ - v94 - D 15 '69 - p4614
SB - v5 - S '69 - p150
Subject: Trees

World's Fair 1992
LJ - v95 - Je 15 '70 - p2316
NYTBR - S 20 '70 - p47
Subject: Science fiction

SILVERSTEIN, Alvin 1933-
AuBYP SUP, ConAu 2NR, ConLC 17, FifBJA, IntAu&W 82, SmATA 8

Alcoholism
ACSB - v9 - Spring '76 - p39
CLW - v47 - My '76 - p452
Cur R - v16 - Ag '77 - p175
KR - v43 - N 1 '75 - p1245
NYTBR - Ja 18 '76 - p12
SB - v12 - S '76 - p100
SLJ - v22 - F '76 - p49
Co-author: Silverstein, Virginia B
Subject: Alcohol and youth

Bionics
BL - v67 - F 1 '71 - p453
CE - v47 - My '71 - p438
KR - v38 - S 15 '70 - p1057
LJ - v96 - My 15 '71 - p1817
SB - v6 - Mr '71 - p327
Co-author: Silverstein, Virginia B
Subject: Bionics

The Chemicals We Eat And Drink
BL - v70 - N 1 '73 - p294
CCB-B - v27 - F '74 - p101
HB - v50 - Ap '74 - p171
KR - v41 - Ap 1 '73 - p393
KR - v41 - D 15 '73 - p1355
LJ - v99 - Mr 15 '74 - p894
SB - v10 - My '74 - p64
Co-author: Silverstein, Virginia B
Subject: Food

Heart Disease
BL - v73 - Ja 1 '77 - p669
CCB-B - v30 - My '77 - p150
SB - v13 - S '77 - p86
SLJ - v23 - Mr '77 - p148
Co-author: Silverstein, Virginia B
Subject: Heart

The Left-Hander's World
BL - v74 - Ja 1 '78 - p749
CCB-B - v31 - Je '78 - p166
HB - v54 - Je '78 - p308
SB - v14 - S '78 - p69
SLJ - v24 - Ap '78 - p88
Co-author: Silverstein, Virginia B
Subject: Left- and right-handedness

SILVERSTEIN, Virginia B
see Silverstein, Alvin (co-author)

SIMON, Hilda 1921-
AuBYP, ConAu 77, FourBJA, IlsCB 1957, -1967, SmATA 28

Chameleons And Other Quick-Change Artists
BL - v70 - F 15 '74 - p652
BL - v70 - F 15 '74 - p659
BS - v33 - D 1 '73 - p404
LJ - v99 - F 1 '74 - p374
SB - v10 - S '74 - p132
Subject: Animals

SIMON, R E
see Davis, Charles (co-author)

SIMON, Ruth 1918-
AuBYP

A Castle For Tess
KR - v35 - My 15 '67 - p602
LJ - v92 - N 15 '67 - p4270

SIMON, Seymour 1931-
AuBYP SUP, BioIn 9, ChlLR 9, ConAu 11NR, FifBJA, SmATA 4, WrDr 86

Creatures From Lost Worlds
SLJ - v26 - Ap '80 - p113
TLS - v0 - N 21 '80 - p1330
Subject: Monsters

Ghosts
BL - v72 - Ap 15 '76 - p1191
HB - v52 - Ag '76 - p421
KR - v44 - Ap 15 '76 - p479
RT - v31 - O '77 - p16
SLJ - v22 - My '76 - p64
SLJ - v25 - D '78 - p33
VOYA - v8 - Ap '85 - p77
Subject: Ghosts

SIMPSON, Janice C

Andrew Young: A Matter Of Choice
SLJ - v25 - N '78 - p64
Subject: Blacks—Biography; Statesmen

Kate Jackson: Special Kind Of Angel
SLJ - v26 - S '79 - p140
Subject: Actors and actresses

Ray Kroc: Big Mac Man
SLJ - v26 - S '79 - p140
Subject: Restauranteurs

Sylvester Stallone: Going The Distance
SLJ - v26 - S '79 - p140
Subject: Actors and actresses

SIMS, William

West Side Cop
LJ - v96 - Ap 15 '71 - p1514
Co-author: Skipper, G C
Subject: Occupations

SINGER, Isaac Bashevis 1904-
ChlLR 1, ConAu 1NR, ConLC 1, -3, -6, -9, -11, -15, -23, -38, DcLB 6, -28, -52, MorBMP, SmATA 27, ThrBJA, TwCChW 83, WrDr 86

Zlateh The Goat And Other Stories
Am - v115 - N 5 '66 - p554
Atl - v218 - D '66 - p150
BL - v63 - N 15 '66 - p378
BS - v26 - D 1 '66 - p342
CCB-B - v20 - Ja '67 - p79
CE - v44 - D '67 - p262
Comw - v85 - N 11 '66 - p174
CSM - v58 - N 3 '66 - pB10
HB - v42 - D '66 - p712
KR - v34 - O 1 '66 - p1045
LJ - v91 - D 15 '66 - p6197
NYRB - v7 - D 15 '66 - p29
NYTBR - v71 - O 9 '66 - p34
NYTBR - v71 - D 4 '66 - p66
PW - v190 - O 10 '66 - p74
SR - v49 - N 12 '66 - p49
TCR - v68 - D '66 - p275
TN - v23 - Ja '67 - p196
Subject: Folklore

SIROF, Harriet Toby 1930-
ConAu 20NR, DrAP&F 85, SmATA 37, WhoAmW 85, -87

The Real World
BL - v82 - F 1 '86 - p814
B Rpt - v5 - My '86 - p33
CBRS - v14 - Mr '86 - p93
CCB-B - v39 - F '86 - p117
SLJ - v32 - Ap '86 - p100
Subject: Feminism—Fiction; Mothers and daughters—Fiction

Save The Dam!
BL - v78 - Mr 15 '82 - p965
SLJ - v28 - Mr '82 - p158
Subject: Mystery and detective stories; Terrorism—Fiction

SKARMETA, Antonio

Chileno!
BL - v76 - D 1 '79 - p550
B Rpt - v2 - S '83 - p32
CCB-B - v33 - D '79 - p81
J Read - v23 - Ap '80 - p662
KR - v48 - F 15 '80 - p222

SKARMETA, Antonio (continued)
SLJ - v26 - N '79 - p94
TN - v38 - Fall '81 - p85
Subject: Exiles—Fiction

SKIDMORE, Hubert 1909?-1946
CurBio 46, WhAm 2

River Rising
BL - v36 - S '39 - p19
HB - v15 - S '39 - p302
LJ - v64 - S 1 '39 - p663
NYTBR - Ag 20 '39 - p10

SKIPPER, G C
see Sims, William (co-author)

SKIRROW, Desmond

The Case Of The Silver Egg
B&B - v12 - Mr '67 - p60
BL - v65 - Ja 1 '69 - p499
CSM - v58 - N 3 '66 - pB4
HB - v45 - Ap '69 - p173
KR - v36 - O 15 '68 - p1164
Obs - D 4 '66 - p28
PW - v194 - O 7 '68 - p54

SKULICZ, Matthew 1944-
ConAu 37R

Right On, Shane
KR - v39 - D 1 '71 - p1261
LJ - v97 - Ap 15 '72 - p1619
NYTBR - Je 18 '72 - p8
Subject: Conduct of life—Fiction

SKURZYNSKI, Gloria 1930-
BioIn 11, ConAu 13NR, -33R, FifBJA, SmATA 8

Manwolf
BL - v77 - Ap 15 '81 - p1156
BS - v41 - Ag '81 - p200
CBRS - v10 - Jl '81 - p119
CLW - v53 - S '81 - p93
HB - v57 - Ag '81 - p437
J Read - v25 - D '81 - p288
Rel St - v219 - My 8 '81 - p254
SLJ - v27 - My '81 - p77
VOYA - v4 - Ag '81 - p27
Subject: Poland—Fiction; Werewolves—Fiction

SLEPIAN, Jan 1921-
FifBJA, SmATA 45

The Alfred Summer
BL - v76 - Jl 15 '80 - p1677
BOT - v4 - F '81 - p79
CBRS - v8 - My '80 - p100
CCB-B - v34 - S '80 - p22
CE - v57 - Mr '81 - p208
CE - v57 - Mr '81 - p235
EJ - v70 - Ap '81 - p77
GP - v20 - Ja '82 - p4013
HB - v56 - Ag '80 - p411
JB - v46 - Je '82 - p109
J Read - v24 - D '80 - p270
KR - v48 - Ag 1 '80 - p985
LA - v57 - O '80 - p791
NYTBR - v85 - Ap 27 '80 - p52
NYTBR - v87 - S 12 '82 - p55
Obs - v0 - N 29 '81 - p27
Obs - v0 - Ap 11 '82 - p31
RT - v37 - F '84 - p507
Sch Lib - v30 - Je '82 - p137
SLJ - v26 - Ap '80 - p128
SLJ - v29 - Ag '83 - p27
SMQ - v9 - Fall '80 - p51
TES - v0 - N 20 '81 - p33
Subject: Courage—Fiction; Friendship—Fiction; Physically handicapped—Fiction

Lester's Turn
BL - v78 - S 1 '81 - p51
BS - v41 - O '81 - p279
CBRS - v9 - My '81 - p89
CCB-B - v34 - Jl '81 - p218
HB - v57 - Je '81 - p312
Inter BC - v13 - #4 '82 p10
KR - v49 - Jl 1 '81 - p806
NYTBR - v86 - My 17 '81 - p38
PW - v219 - Je 19 '81 - p100
RT - v37 - F '84 - p507
SLJ - v27 - My '81 - p78
VOYA - v4 - O '81 - p38
Subject: Cerebral palsy—Fiction; Friendship—Fiction

SLOANE, Eugene A 1926-
ConAu 65

The Complete Book Of Bicycling
A Lib - v4 - F '73 - p98
BL - v67 - F 15 '71 - p467
BW - v6 - Ja 2 '72 - p6
LJ - v95 - D 1 '70 - p4191
LJ - v96 - Ja 15 '71 - p294
LJ - v96 - Mr 1 '71 - p792
LJ - v97 - Ap 15 '72 - p1388
NYTBR - Je 4 '72 - p8
NYTBR - Je 2 '74 - p14
PW - v197 - Je 8 '70 - p156
Trav - v136 - Jl '71 - p77
WSJ - v176 - N 5 '70 - p14
WSJ - v176 - D 8 '70 - p22
Subject: Bicyles and bicyling

SLOTE, Alfred 1926-
AuBYP SUP, BioIn 13, ChlLR 4, FifBJA, SmATA 8

The Devil Rides With Me And Other Fantastic Stories
RT - v34 - Mr '81 - p736
SLJ - v26 - Mr '80 - p116
Subject: Science fiction; Short stories; Supernatural—Fiction

The Hotshot
BL - v73 - My 15 '77 - p1424
BW - Mr 11 '79 - pF2
CCB-B - v30 - Jl '77 - p180
Hi Lo - v1 - S '79 - p6
NYTBR - O 9 '77 - p28
RT - v31 - Ap '78 - p842
SLJ - v23 - My '77 - p80
Teacher - v96 - My '79 - p125
Subject: Hockey—Fiction

My Father, The Coach
CCB-B - v26 - N '72 - p49
KR - v40 - S 1 '72 - p1028
KR - v40 - D 15 '72 - p1414
LJ - v97 - D 15 '72 - p4088
Teacher - v91 - Ap '74 - p87
Teacher - v93 - S '75 - p57
Subject: Baseball—Fiction

My Trip To Alpha I
BL - v75 - O 15 '78 - p391
CCB-B - v32 - Ja '79 - p88
KR - v46 - N 15 '78 - p1249
SLJ - v25 - O '78 - p150
Subject: Science fiction

Stranger On The Ball Club
BL - v67 - Mr 15 '71 - p622
CCB-B - v24 - D '70 - p67
LJ - v95 - D 15 '70 - p4378
Spectr - v47 - Mr '71 - p46
SR - v54 - Jl 17 '71 - p36
Teacher - v93 - S '75 - p57
Subject: Baseball—Fiction; Friendship—Fiction

SMARIDGE, Norah Antoinette 1903-
AuBYP, ConAu 37R, SmATA 6

The Mysteries In The Commune
CBRS - v11 - Winter '83 - p61
CCB-B - v36 - D '82 - p78
SLJ - v29 - D '82 - p82
Subject: Mystery and detective stories

The Mystery Of Greystone Hall
Hi Lo - v1 - F '80 - p3
SLJ - v26 - D '79 - p99
Subject: England—Fiction; Mystery and detective stories

The Mystery In The Old Mansions
SLJ - v28 - D '81 - p83
Subject: Mystery and detective stories

The Teen-Ager's Guide To Collecting Practically Anything
BL - v69 - Mr 1 '73 - p645
Hob - v78 - Ap '73 - p157
KR - v40 - N 1 '72 - p1255
LJ - v98 - Mr 15 '73 - p1016
PW - v202 - D 18 '72 - p40
Co-author: Hunter, Hilda
Subject: Art

SMITH, April

James At 15
SLJ - v24 - Ja '78 - p98

SMITH, Beatrice Schillinger
ConAu 10NR, SmATA 12

The Road To Galveston
BL - v70 - F 15 '74 - p659
LJ - v99 - My 15 '74 - p1476
Subject: Fathers and sons—Fiction

SMITH, Betsy Covington 1937-
ConAu 111, SmATA 43

A Day In The Life Of A Firefighter
BL - v77 - My 1 '81 - p1198
SLJ - v28 - N '81 - p96
Subject: Firefighters; Occupations

SMITH, Bruce

The History Of Little Orphan Annie
BL - v78 - Ag '82 - p1497
LATBR - v0 - Jl 11 '82 - p7
LJ - v107 - Je 1 '82 - p1090
PW - v221 - Ap 23 '82 - p91
Subject: Comic books, strips, etc.

SMITH, Carole
see Hooker, Ruth (co-author)

SMITH, Dennis E 1938-
WrDr 86

Report From Engine Co. 82
AC - v87 - S '72 - p80
A Lib - v3 - Je '72 - p682
Am - v126 - My 20 '72 - p541
BL - v68 - Ap 15 '72 - p693
BS - v31 - F 1 '72 - p491
BS - v33 - Ag 1 '73 - p215

SMITH, Dennis E (continued)
BW - v6 - Mr 12 '72 - p8
BW - v7 - Ap 15 '73 - p13
Comw - v97 - F 2 '73 - p399
EJ - v62 - My '73 - p827
HB - v48 - O '72 - p495
JGE - v25 - Jl '73 - p155
LJ - v97 - F 1 '72 - p492
LJ - v97 - Jl '72 - p2496
LJ - v97 - D 15 '72 - p4059
NO - v11 - Mr 4 '72 - p23
NW - v79 - Ja 24 '72 - p72
NY - v47 - F 19 '72 - p116
NYT - v121 - F 1 '72 - p35
NYTBR - Ap 16 '72 - p20
PW - v202 - D 11 '72 - p37
SR - v55 - Ap 8 '72 - p68
SR - v55 - D 2 '72 - p89
Time - v99 - F 28 '72 - p82
TN - v29 - Ap '73 - p258
Subject: Firefighters; New York (City)

SMITH, Doris Buchanan 1934-
AuBYP SUP, ConAu 11NR, DcLB 52, FifBJA, SmATA 28, WrDr 86

Up And Over
BL - v72 - My 1 '76 - p1271
HB - v52 - Ag '76 - p408
KR - v44 - Mr 1 '76 - p262
SLJ - v23 - S '76 - p139

SMITH, Howard Everett, Jr. 1927-
BioIn 11, ConAu 21NR, -25R, IntAu&W 77, IntAu&W 86, SmATA 12, WrDr 86

Killer Weather: Stories Of Great Disasters
Choice - v20 - D '82 - p606
EJ - v72 - Mr '83 - p104
LJ - v107 - S 15 '82 - p1761
VOYA - v5 - F '83 - p54
Subject: Natural disasters; Storms; Weather

SMITH, Howard K 1914-
BioIn 6, -8, -10, -11, BioNews 74, ConAu 2NR, CurBio 76, EncAJ, IntAu&W 82, IntMPA 86, WrDr 86

Washington, D.C.: The Story Of Our Nation's Capital
BL - v64 - O 15 '67 - p275
BS - v27 - My 1 '67 - p67
HB - v43 - Ag '67 - p485
KR - v35 - Mr 15 '67 - p356
LJ - v92 - My 15 '67 - p2034
NYTBR - v72 - My 28 '67 - p20
PW - v191 - My 29 '67 - p64
SR - v50 - Je 17 '67 - p36

SMITH, James P

Pete Rose
BL - v73 - Je 15 '77 - p1572
SLJ - v23 - My '77 - p81
Subject: Baseball—Biography

SMITH, Jay H

Chris Evert
BL - v72 - O 15 '75 - p307
SLJ - v22 - D '75 - p69
Subject: Tennis—Biography

Olga Korbut
CCB-B - v29 - O '75 - p34
SLJ - v22 - S '75 - p96
Subject: Gymnasts

SMITH, John
see Seymour, William Kean (co-author)

SMITH, LeRoi Tex 1934-
AuBYP SUP, ConAu 29R

Fixing Up Motorcycles
BL - v70 - Ap 1 '74 - p844
KR - v41 - Jl 1 '73 - p744
LJ - v99 - Ap 1 '74 - p1048
LJ - v99 - Ap 15 '74 - p1239
Subject: Motorcycles

Make Your Own Hot Rod
BL - v68 - Ja 15 '72 - p407
BL - v68 - Ja 15 '72 - p431
LJ - v96 - O 1 '71 - p3150
LJ - v96 - N 15 '71 - p3919
Subject: Automobile racing

SMITH, Moyne
AuBYP

Seven Plays And How To Produce Them
BL - v64 - Jl 15 '68 - p1288
CCB-B - v22 - O '68 - p34
KR - v36 - Je 1 '68 - p611
LJ - v93 - Ap 15 '68 - p1816
SR - v51 - O 19 '68 - p37
Subject: Plays

SMITH, Nancy Covert 1935-
ConAu 10NR, SmATA 12

Josie's Handful Of Quietness
CLW - v47 - D '75 - p235

SMITH, Nancy Covert (continued)
SLJ - v22 - S '75 - p112
Subject: Friendship—Fiction; Migrant labor—Fiction

SMITH, Pauline Coggeshall 1908-
ConAu 29R, SmATA 27

Brush Fire!
BL - v75 - Je 15 '79 - p1533
Hi Lo - v1 - S '79 - p2
SLJ - v26 - S '79 - p148
Subject: Fires—Fiction; Gangs—Fiction

SMITH, Robert 1905-

Hit Hard! Throw Hard!: The Secrets Of Power Baseball
BL - v74 - O 1 '77 - p303
KR - v45 - Ag 15 '77 - p855
SLJ - v24 - D '77 - p63
Subject: Baseball

SMITH, Sally Liberman 1929-
BioIn 3, ConAu 11NR

Nobody Said It's Easy
BL - v61 - My 15 '65 - p915
CE - v42 - F '66 - p382
Choice - v2 - Jl '65 - p325
LJ - v90 - F 1 '65 - p657
Subject: Adolescence; Parent and child

SMITH, Susan Vernon
see Vernon, Rosemary

SMITH, Ward
see Goldsmith, Howard

SMITHERS, Chris
see Litterick, Ian (co-author)

SMITS, Teo 1905-
ConAu 77, WhoAm 78

Soccer For The American Boy
LJ - v95 - D 15 '70 - p4382
Teacher - v95 - My '78 - p109
Subject: Soccer

SNOW, Donald Clifford
see Fall, Thomas

SNOW, Edward Rowe 1902-1982
BioIn 1, -5, ConAu 6NR, -106, CurBio 58

Supernatural Mysteries And Other Tales
KR - v42 - O 1 '74 - p1095
PW - v206 - D 30 '74 - p97
Subject: Supernatural

Supernatural Mysteries: New England To The Bermuda Triangle
KR - v42 - O 1 '74 - p1095
PW - v206 - D 30 '74 - p97
Subject: Supernatural

SNYDER, Anne 1922-
ConAu 14NR, SmATA 4, WrDr 86

First Step
CCB-B - v29 - Je '76 - p165
Kliatt - v11 - Winter '77 - p8
SLJ - v22 - N '75 - p94
Subject: Alcohol and youth—Fiction

Goodbye, Paper Doll
BL - v77 - N 15 '80 - p455
EJ - v75 - Ja '86 - p86
Kliatt - v14 - Fall '80 - p66
SLJ - v27 - N '80 - p89
VOYA - v3 - F '81 - p34
WLB - v55 - F '81 - p454
Subject: Anorexia nervosa—Fiction

My Name Is Davy. I'm An Alcoholic
BS - v37 - Jl '77 - p127
CCB-B - v30 - Jl '77 - p180
EJ - v66 - S '77 - p77
Kliatt - v12 - Fall '78 - p14
KR - v45 - Ja 15 '77 - p49
NYTBR - My 1 '77 - p46
PW - v211 - Ja 17 '77 - p84
SLJ - v23 - F '77 - p74
WLB - v52 - My '78 - p721
Subject: Alcohol and youth—Fiction

Two Point Zero
Kliatt - v16 - Fall '82 - p16
NYTBR - v87 - Ap 25 '82 - p44
SLJ - v28 - My '82 - p88
Co-author: Pelletier, Louis

SNYDER, Gerald Seymour 1933-
ConAu 12NR, SmATA 48

The Right To Be Let Alone: Privacy In The United States
BL - v71 - Je 15 '75 - p1077
KR - v43 - Mr 15 '75 - p321

SNYDER, Gerald Seymour (continued)
SLJ - v22 - S '75 - p126
Subject: Privacy (Right of)

SNYDER, Zilpha Keatley 1927-
AuBYP, ConAu 9R, ConLC 17, MorBMP, OxChL, SmATA 28, –2AS, ThrBJA, TwCChW 83, WrDr 86

Black And Blue Magic
BL - v62 - My 1 '66 - p878
CCB-B - v20 - N '66 - p48
HB - v42 - Je '66 - p308
Inst - v75 - Je '66 - p139
KR - v34 - F 1 '66 - p108
LJ - v91 - Ap 15 '66 - p2214
NYTBR - v71 - Jl 24 '66 - p22

The Egypt Game
BL - v63 - My 15 '67 - p998
CCB-B - v20 - Je '67 - p160
HB - v43 - Ap '67 - p209
KR - v35 - F 15 '67 - p200
LJ - v92 - Ap 15 '67 - p1742
NYTBR - v72 - Jl 23 '67 - p22
NYTBR, Pt. 2 - N 5 '72 - p42
Par - v43 - Je '68 - p68
PW - v191 - Ap 24 '67 - p95
SR - v50 - My 13 '67 - p55

Eyes In The Fishbowl
BL - v64 - My 15 '68 - p1097
CCB-B - v21 - Jl '68 - p181
CSM - v60 - My 2 '68 - pB9
EJ - v58 - F '69 - p297
HB - v44 - Ap '68 - p182
KR - v36 - F 1 '68 - p124
LJ - v93 - Ap 15 '68 - p1804
NYTBR - v73 - My 26 '68 - p30
PW - v193 - Mr 11 '68 - p49
SR - v51 - My 11 '68 - p41
Subject: Department stores—Fiction; Fantasy

The Famous Stanley Kidnapping Case
BL - v76 - O 15 '79 - p358
BL - v79 - Ap 1 '83 - p1043
CBRS - v8 - D '79 - p40
CCB-B - v33 - D '79 - p82
CSM - v74 - O 8 '82 - p00B8
HB - v55 - D '79 - p666
Kliatt - v20 - Winter '86 - p116
KR - v47 - D 1 '79 - p1377
PW - v216 - D 3 '79 - p51
PW - v221 - My 7 '82 - p80
RT - v34 - O '80 - p103
SLJ - v26 - S '79 - p148
Subject: Italy—Fiction; Kidnapping—Fiction

SOBOL, Donald J 1924-
AuBYP, ChlLR 4, ConAu 18NR, FourBJA, SmATA 31, TwCChW 83, WhoAm 86, WrDr 86

Disaster
BL - v75 - Jl 15 '79 - p1630
PW - v215 - Ja 22 '79 - p370
SLJ - v27 - Ja '81 - p73
Subject: Disasters—Fiction

Encyclopedia Brown Gets His Man
BL - v64 - F 1 '68 - p643
CC - v84 - D 13 '67 - p1602
CSM - v59 - O 5 '67 - p10
KR - v35 - O 1 '67 - p1209
LJ - v92 - N 15 '67 - p4271
NYTBR - v72 - N 5 '67 - p44
PW - v193 - Ja 8 '68 - p67
Subject: Mystery and detective stories

Encyclopedia Brown's Book Of Wacky Crimes
BL - v79 - F 1 '83 - p727
SLJ - v28 - Ag '82 - p107
Subject: Crime and criminals—Fiction; Wit and humor

SOBOL, Ken 1938-
WrDr 86

The Clock Museum
CC - v84 - D 13 '67 - p1602
KR - v35 - O 1 '67 - p1214
LJ - v92 - D 15 '67 - p4618
SB - v3 - D '67 - p206
Subject: Clocks and watches

SOMMERS, Beverly

A Passing Game
BL - v80 - F 1 '84 - p810
SLJ - v30 - Ap '84 - p336
Subject: Football—Fiction; Love—Fiction

SORENSEN, Robert

Shadow Of The Past: True Life Sports Stories
Hi Lo - v1 - Mr '80 - p5
Subject: Athletes

SORENSEN, Virginia E 1912-
AuBYP, ConAu 13R, EncFWF, MorBMP, MorJA, OxChL, SmATA 2, TwCChW 83, WhoAm 86, WrDr 86

Miracles On Maple Hill
BL - v53 - S 1 '56 - p30

SORENSEN, Virginia E (continued)
Comw - v65 - N 16 '56 - p184
Inst - v82 - N '72 - p136
KR - v24 - Ag 1 '56 - p519
LJ - v81 - S 15 '56 - p2045
NS - v73 - My 26 '67 - p732
NYTBR - Ag 26 '56 - p28
TLS - My 25 '67 - p449

SORRELS, Roy

A New Life
BL - v79 - Ja 15 '83 - p661

SORRENTINO, Joseph N 1937-
BioIn 7, -11, ConAu 3NR, SmATA 6, WhoWest 78

Up From Never
BL - v68 - Ap 1 '72 - p665
BS - v31 - Ja 1 '72 - p448
KR - v39 - Jl 1 '71 - p731
KR - v39 - Jl 15 '71 - p752
LJ - v96 - S 1 '71 - p2630
NYTBR - Ap 9 '78 - p39
PW - v200 - Jl 5 '71 - p44
PW - v203 - Mr 19 '73 - p74
TN - v28 - Ap '72 - p313

SORTOR, June Elizabeth
see Sortor, Toni

SORTOR, Toni 1939-
ConAu X, SmATA X
Pseud./variant:
Sortor, June Elizabeth

Adventures Of B.J., The Amateur Detective
KR - v43 - Je 15 '75 - p661
SLJ - v21 - My '75 - p70
Subject: Mystery and detective stories

SOULE, Gardner 1913-
AuBYP SUP, ConAu 2NR, SmATA 14, WhoAm 86

UFO's And IFO's: A Factual Report On Flying Saucers
BL - v64 - Mr 1 '68 - p788
KR - v35 - D 1 '67 - p1430
LJ - v92 - D 15 '67 - p4628
Subject: Unidentified flying objects

SOUTH, Wesley W
see Drotning, Phillip T (co-author)

SPARGER, Rex

The Doll
BL - v79 - F 15 '83 - p772
SF&FBR - v0 - O '83 - p43
SLJ - v29 - My '83 - p188
WLB - v57 - My '83 - p773
Subject: Exorcism—Fiction

SPARKS, Beatrice 1918-
ConAu 97, SmATA 44
Pseud./variant:
Revealed as the author of *Go Ask Alice,* published anonymously

Go Ask Alice
CSM - N 11 '71 - pB6
LJ - v97 - Mr 15 '72 - p1174
Subject: Drug abuse—Fiction

Jay's Journal
Hi Lo - v2 - S '80 - p1
Subject: Witchcraft—Fiction

see also Anonymous

SPEARE, Elizabeth 1908-
AmWomWr, AuBYP, ChlLR 8, ConAu 1R, MorBMP, MorJA, OxChL, SmATA 5, TwCChW 83, WrDr 86

Sign Of The Beaver
BL - v79 - Ap 15 '83 - p1098
CBRS - v12 - O '83 - p22
CCB-B - v36 - Ap '83 - p159
CE - v62 - Ja '86 - p198
EJ - v72 - O '83 - p84
GP - v23 - Jl '84 - p4298
HB - v59 - Je '83 - p305
JB - v48 - Je '84 - p145
J Read - v27 - N '83 - p183
KR - v51 - My 15 '83 - p580
LA - v60 - N '83 - p1023
LA - v61 - Ap '84 - p423
NYT - v133 - D 1 '83 - p23
NYTBR - v88 - My 8 '83 - p37
RT - v37 - Mr '84 - p647
SLJ - v29 - Ap '83 - p118
SLJ - v29 - My '83 - p33
SLJ - v30 - Ag '84 - p39
SLJ - v31 - S '84 - p48
TLS - v0 - Mr 9 '84 - p253
Subject: Frontier and pioneer life—Fiction; Indians of North America—Fiction; Survival—Fiction

Witch Of Blackbird Pond
BL - v55 - D 15 '58 - p222

SPEARE, Elizabeth (continued)
CSM - D 18 '58 - p7
HB - v34 - D '58 - p472
KR - v26 - Ag 1 '58 - p548
LJ - v83 - D 15 '58 - p3579
NYTBR, Pt. 2 - N 2 '58 - p24
SE - v23 - D '59 - p406
SR - v41 - N 1 '58 - p62
Subject: Puritans—Fiction; Witchcraft—Fiction

SPECTOR, Debra

First Love
BL - v80 - S 1 '83 - p92
VOYA - v5 - F '83 - p14
VOYA - v6 - O '83 - p211
Subject: Love—Fiction

Night Of The Prom
BL - v78 - Mr 1 '82 - p855
Hi Lo - v3 - Je '82 - p3
SLJ - v28 - Ag '82 - p129
Subject: Schools—Fiction

Too Close For Comfort
BL - v79 - My 15 '83 - p1221
Kliatt - v17 - Spring '83 - p5
SLJ - v29 - My '83 - p84
VOYA - v6 - D '83 - p281
Subject: Love—Fiction

SPENCE, Martha

There Really Is Sound
Hi Lo - v2 - O '80 - p4

SPENCER, John Wallace

Limbo Of The Lost
PW - v204 - Jl 23 '73 - p72
Yacht - v132 - Jl '72 - p74
Subject: Disasters; Shipwrecks

SPENCER, Zane 1935-
ConAu 89, MichAu 80, SmATA 35

Branded Runaway
BL - v76 - Jl 15 '80 - p1673
Hi Lo - v2 - S '80 - p4
SLJ - v26 - Ag '80 - p71
Co-author: Leech, Jay
Subject: Survival—Fiction

SPIEGELMAN, Judith M
ConAu 21R, SmATA 5

With George Washington At Valley Forge
CCB-B - v21 - F '68 - p101
Subject: United States—History—Revolution, 1775-1783

SPIELBERG, Steven 1947-
BioIn 10, -11, -12, -13, ConLC 20, ConTFT 1, HalFC 84, IntMPA 86, NewYTBS 82, SmATA 32, WhoAm 86

Close Encounters Of The Third Kind
CLW - v50 - D '78 - p239
Kliatt - v12 - Fall '78 - p18
KR - v45 - N 1 '77 - p1162
KR - v45 - D 1 '77 - p1275
LJ - v102 - D 15 '77 - p2515
NAR - v263 - Fall '78 - p77
NYRB - v24 - Ja 26 '78 - p21
NYTBR - v0 - F 5 '78 - p22
SLJ - v24 - Mr '78 - p141
SLJ - v24 - My '78 - p37
TLS - v0 - Mr 17 '78 - p319
VOYA - v4 - Ap '81 - p41
Subject: Science fiction; Unidentified flying objects—Fiction

SPINNER, Stephanie
see Stoker, Bram (author of adapted works)

SPINO, Michael

Running Home
LJ - v103 - Ja 1 '78 - p102
Subject: Physical fitness

SPLAVER, Sarah 1921-
AuBYP SUP, ConAu 85, SmATA 28, WhoAmW 81, WhoE 81, WhoWorJ 78

Your Career If You're Not Going To College
BL - v68 - D 1 '71 - p329
PGJ - v51 - D '72 - p290
Subject: Vocational guidance

SPRAGUE, Gretchen 1926-
AuBYP, ConAu 13R, SmATA 27

A Question Of Harmony
BL - v62 - N 1 '65 - p269
BS - v25 - My 15 '65 - p101
CCB-B - v18 - Je '65 - p155
HB - v41 - Je '65 - p285
KR - v33 - F 1 '65 - p111
LJ - v90 - Ap 15 '65 - p2038
NYTBR - v70 - My 9 '65 - p26

SPRAGUE, Jane

That New Girl
WLB - v51 - F '77 - p491

SPRINGER, Marilyn Harris
see Harris, Marilyn

SPYKER, John Howland

Little Lives
BL - v75 - Ja 1 '79 - p738
BOT - v20 - F '79 - p57
LJ - v104 - F 15 '79 - p515
Time - v113 - Mr 12 '79 - p94
VV - v24 - F 12 '79 - p90
WCRB - v5 - Ja '79 - p26
Subject: New York (City)—Fiction

SPYRI, Johanna 1827?-1901
AuBYP, BioIn 1, -2, -3, -4, -12, JBA 34, -51, OxChL, OxGer, SmATA 19, WhoChL

Heidi
B&B - v14 - Ag '69 - p46
NYTBR - N 13 '55 - p42

STADELHOFEN, Marcie Miller

The Freedom Side
Hi Lo - v4 - Ja '83 - p1

STADTMAUER, Saul A

Visions Of The Future: Magic Boards
SLJ - v24 - My '78 - p64
Subject: Spiritualism

STAFFORD, Jean 1915-1979
AmWomWr, ConAu 3NR, ConLC 4, -7, -19, ConNov 76, DcLB 2, SmATA 22N, WhAm 7, WrDr 80

Elephi, The Cat With The High I.Q.
NYTBR - S 16 '61 - p38
PW - v190 - Ag 29 '66 - p351
Subject: Animals—Fiction

STAHEL, H R

Atlantis Illustrated
Kliatt - v16 - Fall '82 - p70
LATBR - Je 27 '82 - p7
Subject: Atlantis

STAMBLER, Irwin 1924-
AuBYP, ConAu 2NR, SmATA 5, WrDr 86

Weather Instruments: How They Work
KR - v36 - Mr 15 '68 - p349
LJ - v93 - O 15 '68 - p3974
SB - v4 - My '68 - p33
Subject: Weather

STAMPER, Judith Bauer

They Set World Records
BL - v80 - F 15 '84 - p853
SLJ - v30 - F '84 - p77
VOYA - v7 - Ap '84 - p50
Subject: Curiosities and wonders

STANEK, Lou Willett

Megan's Beat
BL - v79 - Je 15 '83 - p1342
CBRS - v12 - S '83 - p10
CCB-B - v36 - My '83 - p179
RT - v38 - O '84 - p74
SLJ - v30 - O '83 - p173
VOYA - v7 - Ap '84 - p36
Subject: Journalism—Fiction; Schools—Fiction

STANFORD, Don 1918-
BioIn 1, ConAu 53, WrDr 86

The Red Car
BL - v51 - D 15 '54 - p178
KR - v22 - Jl 15 '54 - p441
NYTBR, Pt. 2 - N 14 '54 - p8
SR - v37 - N 13 '54 - p94

STANGER, Margaret A

That Quail, Robert
BL - v63 - O 1 '66 - p146
BS - v26 - S 1 '66 - p200
BW - v2 - Mr 3 '68 - p18
HB - v43 - Ap '67 - p215
KR - v34 - Je 15 '66 - p609
LJ - v91 - Jl '66 - p3458
LJ - v91 - S 15 '66 - p4374
PW - v193 - Ja 15 '68 - p87
SB - v2 - Mr '67 - p297
TLS - N 2 '67 - p1046
Subject: Quails

STANLEY, Carol

I've Got A Crush On You
SLJ - v28 - S '81 - p141
VOYA - v4 - Ag '81 - p28

STEELE, William O 1917-1979
AuBYP, BioIn 12, -13, ConAu 2NR, MorJA, OxChL, SmATA 1, -27N, TwCChW 83, WrDr 80

The Old Wilderness Road
LJ - v94 - F 15 '69 - p888
NO - v8 - Ap 28 '69 - p19

STEELE, William O (continued)
NYTBR - v73 - N 3 '68 - p26
Subject: Kentucky—Biography

STEGEMAN, Janet Allais 1923-
SmATA 49

Last Seen On Hopper's Lane
BL - v79 - Ja 1 '83 - p620
CCB-B - v36 - Mr '83 - p135
HB - v58 - D '82 - p661
KR - v50 - N 15 '82 - p1241
NYTBR - v88 - F 27 '83 - p37
SLJ - v29 - D '82 - p83
Subject: Drug abuse—Fiction; Kidnapping—Fiction; Mystery and detective stories

STEIN, Cathi

Elton John
WLB - v51 - D '76 - p314
Subject: Biography

STEIN, R Conrad
ConAu 41R, SmATA 31

Hiroshima
BL - v79 - F 15 '83 - p780
BL - v80 - Mr 15 '84 - p1071
SLJ - v29 - Ap '83 - p119
SLJ - v31 - Ap '85 - p43
Subject: Atomic bomb; World War, 1939-1945

see also Hannahs, Herbert (co-author); Hardin, Gail (co-author) for additional titles

STEIN, Wendy

Becoming A Car Owner
Hi Lo - v2 - My '81 - p5
Subject: Automobiles

Taking The Wheel
Hi Lo - v2 - My '81 - p5
Subject: Automobiles

STEINBECK, John 1902-1968
AuBYP SUP, BioIn 13, ConAu 1NR, ConLC 1, -5, -9, -13, -21, DcLB 7, -9, -DS2, McGEWD 84, SmATA 9

The Pearl
Atl - v180 - D '47 - p138
BL - v44 - D 15 '47 - p152
Comw - v47 - Ja 23 '48 - p377
KR - v15 - O 1 '47 - p551
LJ - v72 - N 1 '47 - p1540
New R - v117 - D 22 '47 - p28
NY - v23 - D 27 '47 - p59
NYTBR - N 30 '47 - p4
SR - v30 - N 22 '47 - p14
Time - v50 - D 22 '47 - p90

Travels With Charley
Atl - v210 - Ag '62 - p138
BL - v58 - Jl 1 '62 - p748
BL - v58 - Jl 15 '62 - p784
CSM - Ag 2 '62 - p7
KR - v30 - Mr 1 '62 - p272
LJ - v87 - Je 15 '62 - p2378
NY - v38 - S 8 '62 - p152
NYTBR - Jl 29 '62 - p5
Spec - O 19 '62 - p604
SR - v45 - S 1 '62 - p31
Time - v80 - Ag 10 '62 - p70
TLS - N 2 '62 - p843
Subject: United States—Description and travel

STEINBRIDGE, Charles H
see Radlauer, Ruth Shaw (co-author)

STEINER, Barbara A 1934-
BioIn 11, ConAu 13NR, SmATA 13

Is There A Cure For Sophomore Year?
BL - v82 - Ja 15 '86 - p751
PW - v229 - Mr 21 '86 - p89
SLJ - v32 - Ap '86 - p104
VOYA - v9 - Ag '86 - p153
Subject: Schools—Fiction

See You In July
BL - v81 - F 1 '85 - p784
VOYA - v8 - Je '85 - p124
Subject: Love—Fiction

STEINER, Merrilee

Bareback
B Rpt - v4 - Mr '86 - p34
SLJ - v33 - S '86 - p151
VOYA - v9 - Ag '86 - p155
Subject: Horses—Fiction; Love—Fiction

STEINKE, Ann E
see Reynolds, Anne

STENEMAN, Shep

Garfield: The Complete Cat Book
CCB-B - v35 - F '82 - p118
EJ - v72 - F '83 - p100
SLJ - v28 - Ja '82 - p82
Subject: Cats; Comic books, strips, etc.

STEPHENSEN, A M (pseud.)
SmATA X

STEPHENSEN, A M (continued)
Real Name:
Manes, Stephen

Unbirthday
BL - v78 - F 15 '82 - p754
CCB-B - v35 - Mr '82 - p139
Kliatt - v16 - Spring '82 - p17
NYTBR - v87 - Ap 25 '82 - p44
SLJ - v28 - F '82 - p92
VOYA - v5 - Ag '82 - p37
Subject: Abortion—Fiction

see also Manes, Stephen for additional titles

STERLING, Philip 1907-
ConAu 49, SmATA 8

Four Took Freedom: The Lives Of Harriet Tubman, Frederick Douglas, Robert Small, And Blanche K. Bruce
NYTBR - v117 - Je 7 '68 - p37
Co-author: Logan, Rayford Wittingham
Subject: Blacks—Biography

Quiet Rebels: Four Puerto Rican Leaders
KR - v36 - S 1 '68 - p993
PW - v194 - Ag 5 '68 - p59
Subject: Puerto Ricans

Sea And Earth: The Life Of Rachel Carson
BL - v67 - D 1 '70 - p305
CCB-B - v24 - N '70 - p49
CE - v47 - Mr '71 - p316
Comw - v92 - My 22 '70 - p250
CSM - v62 - My 7 '70 - pB7
HB - v46 - Je '70 - p304
KR - v38 - My 15 '70 - p568
LJ - v95 - S 15 '70 - p3068
NYTBR - My 10 '70 - p26
PW - v197 - Je 1 '70 - p68
SB - v6 - S '70 - p133
SR - v53 - S 19 '70 - p35
Subject: Biography

STERNE, Emma 1894-1971
ConAu 5R, -5NR, MorJA, SmATA 6

The Long Black Schooner
Comw - v91 - F 27 '70 - p584
CSM - v60 - N 7 '68 - pB12
HB - v61 - Mr '85 - p213
NYTBR - v73 - My 5 '68 - p49
Subject: Amistad (Schooner); Ships

STEURER, Stephen J

Wheels Teacher's Guide
BL - v78 - O 15 '81 - p289
Subject: Teachers

Wheels Workbook
BL - v78 - O 15 '81 - p289
Hi Lo - v2 - My '81 - p5
LJ - v106 - O 1 '81 - p1890

STEVENS, Chris

Fastest Machines
ASBYP - v14 - Fall '81 - p29
SB - v17 - S '81 - p34
SLJ - v27 - F '81 - p53
Subject: Airplanes; Motorboats

STEVENS, Janice

Dream Summer
SLJ - v32 - S '85 - p150
Subject: Love—Fiction

Take Back The Moment
BL - v79 - Ap 1 '83 - p1038
Kliatt - v17 - Spring '83 - p13
RT - v38 - O '84 - p74
SLJ - v29 - Ag '83 - p80
VOYA - v6 - Je '83 - p98
Subject: Shoplifting—Fiction

STEVENSON, William 1925?-
BioIn 4, -12, ConAu 13R, TwCChW 78, WhoAm 86, WrDr 86

The Bushbabies
BL - v62 - N 15 '65 - p333
CLW - v37 - F '66 - p379
CSM - v57 - N 4 '65 - pB9
Emerg Lib - v12 - N '84 - p14
HB - v41 - D '65 - p613
Inst - v75 - F '66 - p160
KR - v33 - Ag 15 '65 - p821
LJ - v91 - Mr 15 '66 - p1710
NYTBR - v70 - D 26 '65 - p18
Punch - v250 - Ap 20 '66 - p594
RT - v34 - Mr '81 - p636
SR - v49 - Ja 22 '66 - p45
TLS - My 19 '66 - p437
Subject: Africa—Fiction

STEWART, Diana
see Hugo, Victor Marie (author of adapted works)

STEWART, Jo

Blues For Cassandra
Kliatt - v18 - Spring '84 - p144

STEWART, Jo (continued)

The Love Vote
Kliatt - v18 - Fall '84 - p14
SLJ - v31 - S '84 - p138
VOYA - v7 - D '84 - p259
Subject: Love—Fiction

The Promise Ring
BL - v75 - Je 15 '79 - p1533
Hi Lo - v1 - O '79 - p3
Subject: Friendship—Fiction

A Time To Choose
BL - v78 - F 15 '82 - p755
Hi Lo - v3 - F '82 - p2
Co-author: Pierce, Travis
Subject: Employment—Fiction; Youth—Fiction

STEWART, John Craig

The Last To Know
Kliatt - v16 - Spring '82 - p17
VOYA - v5 - Ag '82 - p37

STEWART, Marjabelle Young

The Teen Girl's Guide To Social Success
Kliatt - v17 - Winter '83 - p41
PW - v222 - N 26 '82 - p60
SLJ - v29 - Mr '83 - p198
Subject: Beauty (Personal)

STEWART, Mary Florence Elinor 1916-
BioIn 11, -12, ConAu 1NR, ConLC 7, -35, OxChL, SmATA 12, TwCCr&M 85, WhoAm 86, WrDr 86

Ludo And The Star Horse
BL - v71 - My 15 '75 - p967
GP - v15 - Mr '77 - p3077
KR - v43 - Ap 1 '75 - p376
PW - v207 - Ap 28 '75 - p45
SLJ - v22 - S '75 - p112
TLS - D 6 '74 - p1380
Subject: Astrology—Fiction; Fantasy

STEWART, Ramona 1922-
ASpks, BioIn 8, -9, -11, ConAu 6NR

Sixth Sense
KR - v47 - Ja 1 '79 - p32
PW - v215 - Ja 15 '79 - p115
Subject: Extrasensory perception—Fiction

STEWART, Winnie

Night On 'Gator Creek
BL - v81 - My 1 '85 - p1240
Subject: Boys—Fiction

STINE, H William

Best Friend
BL - v74 - Je 15 '78 - p1613
B Rpt - v2 - S '83 - p26
Cur R - v17 - My '78 - p87
Co-author: Stine, Megan
Subject: Friendship—Fiction

STINE, Megan
see Stine, H William (co-author)

STINE, R L

Blind Date
BL - v83 - S 15 '86 - p121
Kliatt - v20 - Fall '86 - p18
PW - v230 - Ag 22 '86 - p102
SLJ - v33 - N '86 - p108
Subject: Mystery and detective stories

STIRLING, Nora Bromley 1900-
AuBYP, BioIn 8, -9, ConAu 3NR, SmATA 3, WrDr 86

You Would If You Loved Me
CLW - v54 - O '82 - p117
Hi Lo - v4 - O '82 - p9

STOCKDALE, Bill
see Butterworth, Ben (co-author)

STODDARD, Hope 1900-
AuBYP, ConAu 49, SmATA 6

Famous American Women
BL - v67 - O 1 '70 - p141
BS - v30 - Jl 1 '70 - p147
CCB-B - v24 - O '70 - p34
KR - v38 - My 15 '70 - p569
LJ - v95 - S 15 '70 - p3068
PW - v197 - Je 1 '70 - p68
SR - v53 - Ag 22 '70 - p53
Subject: Biography

STOKER, Bram 1847-1912
BioIn 11, -12, -13, ConAu X, DcIrL, DcLB 36, SmATA X, TwCCr&M 80, WhoChL
Pseud./variant:
Stoker, Abraham

Dracula
Choice - v24 - D '86 - p599

STOKER, Bram (continued)
Kliatt - v18 - Spring '84 - p18
NYTBR - v89 - Mr 18 '84 - p34
TES - Ap 22 '83 - p27
VLS - N '85 - p27
Adapter: Spinner, Stephanie
Subject: Horror stories; Vampires—Fiction

STOLZ, Mary Slattery 1920-
AuBYP, ConAu 13NR, ConLC 12, MorBMP, MorJA, OxChL, SmATA 10, -3AS, TwCChW 83, WrDr 86

And Love Replied
BL - v55 - D 1 '58 - p188
HB - v34 - D '58 - p489
KR - v26 - Ag 15 '58 - p609
LJ - v83 - D 15 '58 - p3581
NYTBR - N 9 '58 - p48
SR - v41 - N 1 '58 - p62
Subject: Love—Fiction

By The Highway Home
BL - v68 - Ja 1 '72 - p395
BL - v68 - Ja 15 '72 - p431
BS - v31 - N 15 '71 - p387
CCB-B - v25 - Mr '72 - p115
CE - v49 - O '72 - p30
CLW - v43 - Ap '72 - p481
CSM - v63 - N 11 '71 - pB5
HB - v47 - O '71 - p486
KR - v39 - Ag 15 '71 - p883
LJ - v96 - O 15 '71 - p3480
NYTBR - Ag 24 '71 - p8
PW - v200 - S 20 '71 - p49
SR - v54 - N 13 '71 - p61
Teacher - v91 - N '73 - p131
Subject: Family life—Fiction

Cat In The Mirror
BB - v4 - F '76 - p4
BL - v72 - Ja 1 '76 - p628
CCB-B - v29 - D '75 - p70
HB - v51 - D '75 - p597
KR - v43 - S 1 '75 - p999
LA - v53 - My '76 - p522
PW - v208 - Ag 18 '75 - p68
SLJ - v22 - O '75 - p102
SLJ - v25 - S '78 - p43
Subject: Space and time—Fiction

The Edge Of Next Year
BL - v71 - S 15 '74 - p102
BS - v34 - Ja 15 '75 - p475
CCB-B - v28 - Mr '75 - p123
Choice - v12 - N '75 - p1134
Choice - v14 - N '77 - p1178
EJ - v64 - Ap '75 - p90
HB - v50 - O '74 - p144
Kliatt - v13 - Fall '79 - p14
KR - v42 - O 15 '74 - p1111
LJ - v99 - D 15 '74 - p3273
PT - v9 - Jl '75 - p95
PW - v206 - Ag 5 '74 - p58
SLJ - v28 - Ap '82 - p28
TN - v42 - Summer '86 - p382
Subject: Death—Fiction

Hospital Zone
BL - v53 - O 15 '56 - p97
HB - v32 - D '56 - p463
KR - v24 - Ag 15 '56 - p578
LJ - v81 - D 15 '56 - p3002
NYTBR, Pt. 2 - N 18 '56 - p10
SR - v39 - N 17 '56 - p70
Subject: Nursing—Fiction

In A Mirror
Atl - v192 - D '53 - p98
BL - v50 - O 1 '53 - p59
HB - v29 - O '53 - p360
HB - v29 - D '53 - p469
KR - v21 - Jl 15 '53 - p431
LJ - v78 - O 15 '53 - p1862
NYTBR, Pt. 2 - N 15 '53 - p10
SR - v36 - N 14 '53 - p68
Subject: Weight control—Fiction

Leap Before You Look
BS - v32 - Ja 15 '73 - p483
CCB-B - v26 - S '72 - p18
CE - v49 - D '72 - p146
J Read - v26 - F '83 - p411
KR - v40 - Ap 15 '72 - p486
LJ - v97 - S 15 '72 - p2967
NYTBR - S 3 '72 - p8
SR - v55 - Je 17 '72 - p75
Subject: Divorce—Fiction

The Sea Gulls Woke Me
BL - v48 - O 15 '51 - p69
CSM - S 13 '51 - p13
HB - v27 - S '51 - p335
KR - v19 - Jl 1 '51 - p322
LJ - v76 - D 1 '51 - p2017
NYTBR - S 16 '51 - p28
SR - v34 - O 20 '51 - p39
Subject: Love—Fiction

To Tell Your Love
BL - v47 - S 15 '50 - p45
BL - v47 - O 1 '50 - p63
HB - v26 - S '50 - p384
KR - v18 - Ag 1 '50 - p424
LJ - v75 - N 1 '50 - p1914
NYTBR - O 8 '50 - p34
SR - v33 - N 11 '50 - p50
Subject: Love—Fiction

STOLZ, Mary Slattery (continued)

A Wonderful, Terrible Time
BL - v64 - D 15 '67 - p504
BW - v1 - N 5 '67 - p22
CCB-B - v21 - F '68 - p102
CE - v46 - Ap '70 - p367
Comw - v87 - N 10 '67 - p176
Comw - v89 - F 21 '69 - p647
HB - v43 - D '67 - p754
Inst - v77 - Ap '68 - p155
KR - v35 - S 15 '67 - p1136
LJ - v92 - O 15 '67 - p3856
NYTBR - v72 - N 5 '67 - p43
PW - v192 - N 27 '67 - p43
Subject: Camping—Fiction

STONAKER, Frances Benson
AuBYP SUP

Famous Mathematicians
KR - v34 - Ja 15 '66 - p61
LJ - v91 - My 15 '66 - p2713
SB - v2 - D '66 - p175
Subject: Biography; Mathematics

STONE, A Harris
AuBYP SUP

Plants Are Like That
BL - v65 - S 15 '68 - p124
CE - v46 - S '69 - p38
CSM - v60 - My 2 '68 - pB8
KR - v36 - Mr 1 '68 - p267
LJ - v93 - Ap 15 '68 - p1804
SB - v5 - My '69 - p50
TLS - D 4 '69 - p1401
Co-author: Leskowitz, Irving
Subject: Botany

Rocks And Rills: A Look At Geology
BL - v64 - N 1 '67 - p339
CCB-B - v21 - O '67 - p34
CE - v45 - O '68 - p92
HB - v43 - O '67 - p611
KR - v35 - Je 15 '67 - p699
LJ - v92 - O 15 '67 - p3856
SA - v217 - D '67 - p142
SB - v3 - D '67 - p217
SR - v50 - Jl 22 '67 - p43
Co-author: Igmanson, Dale
Subject: Geology

Take A Balloon
KR - v35 - O 1 '67 - p1214
LJ - v93 - Ja 15 '68 - p296
PW - v192 - N 13 '67 - p80
SB - v3 - Mr '68 - p299
Co-author: Siegel, Bertram M
Subject: Physics; Science

STONE, Judith

Minutes To Live
SLJ - v27 - Ja '81 - p57
Subject: Survival

STONE, Nancy Y

Dune Shadow
BL - v77 - D 15 '80 - p576
CCB-B - v34 - Mr '81 - p140
SLJ - v27 - Ja '81 - p65
Subject: Sand dunes—Fiction; Survival—Fiction

STONE, Patti 1926-
ConAu 5R

Judy George: Student Nurse
BS - v26 - My 1 '66 - p59
CCB-B - v20 - Ja '67 - p81
KR - v34 - Ja 15 '66 - p64
LJ - v91 - My 15 '66 - p2713

STONE, William

Earth Moving Machines
ACSB - v13 - Spring '80 - p49
JB - v43 - D '79 - p330
SB - v16 - S '80 - p35
Subject: Machinery

STONE, Willie

I Was A Black Panther
BW - v4 - N 8 '70 - p12
Comw - v93 - N 20 '70 - p202
EJ - v60 - F '71 - p275
LJ - v96 - F 15 '71 - p736
Subject: Gangs—History

STONELEY, Jack

Scruffy
J Read - v23 - My '80 - p761
Subject: Dogs—Fiction

STORR, Catherine 1913-
AuBYP SUP, ConAu 13R, OxChL, SmATA 9, TwCChW 83, WrDr 86

Thursday
B&B - v20 - Ja '75 - p81
BL - v69 - N 15 '72 - p303
BS - v32 - O 15 '72 - p340
CE - v49 - Ap '73 - p376
HB - v49 - Ap '73 - p148
KR - v40 - Jl 1 '72 - p730
Lis - v86 - N 11 '71 - p661
LJ - v97 - O 15 '72 - p3465
NS - v82 - N 12 '71 - p661
NYTBR - O 1 '72 - p8

STORR, Catherine (continued)
NYTBR, Pt. 2 - N 5 '72 - p28
PW - v202 - Ag 14 '72 - p46
Spec - v227 - N 13 '71 - p696
TLS - O 22 '71 - p1318
Subject: Emotional problems—Fiction

STOUTENBURG, Adrien Pearl 1916-
AuBYP, ConAu 5R, ConPo 80, SmATA 3, ThrBJA, WhoAm 82, WrDr 86
Pseud./variant:
Kendall, Lace

American Tall Tale Animals
BL - v64 - Jl 1 '68 - p1237
LJ - v93 - O 15 '68 - p3974
NYTBR - v73 - My 5 '68 - p34
PW - v193 - Je 3 '68 - p129
Subject: Animals (Mythical); Folklore

American Tall Tales
BL - v63 - S 15 '66 - p123
HB - v42 - Ag '66 - p432
Inst - v76 - Ag '66 - p217
LJ - v91 - Jl '66 - p3554
NYTBR - v71 - My 8 '66 - p33
PW - v189 - My 9 '66 - p79
Subject: Folklore

see also Kendall, Lace for additional titles

STRANGER, Joyce (pseud.)
ConAu X, IntAu&W 86X, OxChL, SmATA X, TwCChW 83, WrDr 86
Real Name:
Wilson, Joyce Muriel

Rex
BL - v64 - Mr 1 '68 - p769
BS - v28 - My 15 '68 - p91
BW - v2 - Je 16 '68 - p6
HB - v44 - Je '68 - p342
KR - v36 - F 15 '68 - p208
LJ - v93 - My 1 '68 - p1920
LJ - v93 - My 15 '68 - p2133
NYTBR - v73 - Ap 21 '68 - p54
PW - v193 - F 12 '68 - p71
PW - v194 - Ag 12 '68 - p55
SR - v51 - N 9 '68 - p70

STRASSER, Todd 1950?-
BioIn 11, -13, ChlLR 11, ConAu 117, SmATA 45
Pseud./variant:
Rhue, Morton

Angel Dust Blues
CBRS - v8 - D '79 - p40
CCB-B - v33 - F '80 - p120
EJ - v69 - N '80 - p85
HB - v56 - Ap '80 - p178
Kliatt - v15 - Spring '81 - p14
NW - v94 - D 17 '79 - p96
SLJ - v26 - Ja '80 - p81
Subject: Drug abuse—Fiction

Ferris Bueller's Day Off
BL - v83 - S 1 '86 - p53
Kliatt - v20 - Fall '86 - p18
Subject: Schools—Fiction

Friends Till The End
BL - v77 - Ap 15 '81 - p1148
BS - v41 - Jl '81 - p159
CBRS - v9 - Ap '81 - p80
CCB-B - v34 - My '81 - p182
Emerg Lib - v14 - S '86 - p24
HB - v57 - Je '81 - p314
Inst - v90 - My '81 - p59
Inter BC - v14 - #1 '83 p34
J Read - v25 - D '81 - p287
KR - v49 - Ap 1 '81 - p437
SLJ - v27 - My '81 - p87
VOYA - v4 - Je '81 - p32
WLB - v55 - My '81 - p692
Subject: Death—Fiction; Leukemia—Fiction

Turn It Up!
BL - v80 - My 1 '84 - p1234
BS - v44 - Je '84 - p118
CBRS - v12 - Je '84 - p120
CCB-B - v37 - Ap '84 - p156
EJ - v74 - Ja '85 - p94
EJ - v74 - D '85 - p56
HB - v60 - Je '84 - p344
Kliatt - v20 - Winter '86 - p17
KR - v52 - My 1 '84 - pJ52
SLJ - v30 - Ag '84 - p87
VOYA - v7 - Je '84 - p98
Subject: Musicians—Fiction; Rock music—Fiction

A Very Touchy Subject
EJ - v75 - D '86 - p60
J Read - v29 - F '86 - p464
WLB - v59 - Mr '85 - p485
Subject: Friendship—Fiction

see also Rhue, Morton for additional titles

STREATFEILD, Noel 1895?-1986
BioIn 12, ConAu 120, –81, ConLC 21, JBA 51, OxChL, SmATA 20, –48N, TwCChW 83, WhoChL, WrDr 86

Thursday's Child
B&B - v16 - N '70 - p58
B&B - v18 - My '73 - p125
BL - v67 - Je 15 '71 - p873
BS - v31 - Ap 15 '71 - p47
BW - v5 - My 9 '71 - p17
Comw - v94 - My 21 '71 - p267
GW - v103 - D 19 '70 - p21
HB - v47 - Je '71 - p294
KR - v39 - Mr 1 '71 - p237
LJ - v96 - Je 15 '71 - p2142
NS - v80 - N 6 '70 - p611
PW - v199 - Mr 15 '71 - p73
Spec - v225 - D 5 '70 - pR8
TLS - O 30 '70 - p1263
Subject: England—Fiction; Orphans—Fiction

STREET, Nicki

The Joker
BL - v79 - Ap 15 '83 - p1078
Hi Lo - v3 - Ap '82 - p7
Co-author: Oreshnik, A F
Subject: Kidnapping—Fiction; Mystery and detective stories

see also Durish, Jack (co-author); Oreshnik, A F for additional titles

STRESHINSKY, Shirley
see Elder, Lauren (co-author)

STRETTON, Barbara 1936-
ConAu 116, SmATA 43

You Never Lose
BL - v78 - Ag '82 - p1519
B Rpt - v2 - My '83 - p39
BS - v42 - D '82 - p367
CBRS - v11 - D '82 - p39
CCB-B - v36 - Mr '83 - p136
J Read - v26 - F '83 - p468
SLJ - v29 - D '82 - p29
VOYA - v6 - Ap '83 - p42
Subject: Death—Fiction; Fathers and sons—Fiction; Football—Fiction

STRIEBER, Whitley

Wolf Of Shadows
BL - v82 - Ja 1 '86 - p687
CBRS - v14 - Winter '86 - p68
CCB-B - v39 - D '85 - p80
EJ - v75 - Mr '86 - p108
Fant R - v9 - Mr '86 - p24
KR - v53 - S 15 '85 - p992
New Age - v2 - D '85 - p68
NYTBR - v90 - D 1 '85 - p39
Obs - D 14 '86 - p21
PW - v228 - S 13 '85 - p131
SE - v50 - Ap '86 - p301
S Fict R - v15 - F '86 - p47
SLJ - v32 - O '85 - p188
VOYA - v9 - Ap '86 - p36
Subject: Nuclear warfare—Fiction; Survival—Fiction; Wolves—Fiction

STUART, Becky

Once In California
SLJ - v31 - S '84 - p139
VOYA - v7 - D '84 - p258
Subject: Love—Fiction; Twins—Fiction

STUART, Morna 1905-

Marassa And Midnight
CCB-B - v21 - Ap '68 - p134
HT - v16 - D '66 - p865
KR - v35 - Jl 15 '67 - p817
LJ - v92 - S 15 '67 - p3191
TLS - N 24 '66 - p1084
TN - v24 - Je '68 - p448

STUBENRAUCH, Bob
AuBYP SUP

Where Freedom Grew
BS - v30 - N 15 '70 - p358
BW - v4 - N 8 '70 - p20
LJ - v95 - D 15 '70 - p4357
NYTBR, Pt. 2 - N 8 '70 - p3
PW - v198 - N 9 '70 - p61
Subject: United States—History—Revolution, 1775-1783

STURTZEL, Howard A
see Annixter, Paul

STURTZEL, Jane Levington
see Annixter, Jane

SUHL, Yuri 1908-1986
AuBYP SUP, ChlLR 2, ConAu 2NR, –45, SmATA 8, –1AS, WhoWorJ 78

On The Other Side Of The Gate
BB - v3 - My '75 - p3
BL - v71 - Ap 15 '75 - p869
BL - v73 - Ap 1 '77 - p1178

SUHL, Yuri (continued)
BS - v35 - Jl '75 - p96
CCB-B - v29 - S '75 - p20
Cur R - v17 - O '78 - p343
EJ - v66 - Ja '77 - p65
HB - v51 - Je '75 - p271
Inst - v84 - My '75 - p106
JB - v42 - Ag '78 - p210
Kliatt - v11 - Winter '77 - p8
KR - v43 - F 1 '75 - p128
LA - v58 - Ap '81 - p460
NYTBR - D 28 '75 - p10
PW - v207 - Ap 21 '75 - p47
SLJ - v21 - Mr '75 - p110
Subject: Poland—Fiction; World War, 1939-1945—Fiction

Uncle Misha's Partisans
BL - v70 - N 1 '73 - p294
CCB-B - v27 - Ja '74 - p87
CE - v50 - F '74 - p230
CSM - v65 - N 7 '73 - pB4
Emerg Lib - v11 - N '83 - p21
GP - v14 - My '75 - p2632
HB - v50 - F '74 - p54
KR - v41 - Ag 15 '73 - p888
LJ - v98 - Jl '73 - p2197
Obs - Jl 20 '75 - p23
RT - v35 - Mr '82 - p721
TLS - Jl 11 '75 - p764
TN - v30 - Ap '74 - p309
Subject: Jews—Fiction; World War, 1939-1945—Fiction

SULLIVAN, George Edward 1927-
AuBYP, BioIn 12, ConAu 13R, SmATA 4, WhoAm 86, WrDr 86

The Art Of Base-Stealing
BL - v78 - Jl '82 - p1450
SLJ - v28 - My '82 - p89
VOYA - v5 - D '82 - p46
Subject: Baseball

Bert Jones: Born To Play Football
BL - v74 - Ja 1 '78 - p751
KR - v45 - N 15 '77 - p1209
SLJ - v24 - D '77 - p64
Subject: Football—Biography

Better Cross Country Running For Boys And Girls
BL - v80 - O 1 '83 - p303
B Rpt - v2 - Ja '84 - p58
CSM - v76 - Mr 2 '84 - pB6
Kliatt - v19 - Winter '85 - p75
SLJ - v30 - D '83 - p88
Subject: Running

Better Swimming And Diving For Boys And Girls
BL - v64 - Mr 1 '68 - p788
LJ - v92 - D 15 '67 - p4634
Subject: Diving; Swimming

The Complete Book Of Autograph Collecting
BL - v68 - F 1 '72 - p464
BL - v68 - F 1 '72 - p467
Comw - v95 - N 19 '71 - p191
Hob - v77 - Mr '72 - p158
Hob - v83 - S '78 - p106
LJ - v97 - Jl '72 - p2491
NYTBR - N 21 '71 - p8
Subject: Autographs

Mary Lou Retton
BL - v81 - Jl '85 - p1563
B Rpt - v5 - My '86 - p37
SLJ - v32 - S '85 - p140
Subject: Gymnasts

Modern Olympic Superstars
CCB-B - v33 - S '79 - p20
Hi Lo - v1 - O '79 - p5
SLJ - v25 - My '79 - p85
Subject: Athletes; Olympic Games

Mr. President: A Book Of U.S. Presidents
SLJ - v32 - F '86 - p90
Subject: Presidents

The Picture Story Of Catfish Hunter
BL - v73 - Jl 15 '77 - p1731
KR - v45 - Ap 15 '77 - p433
SLJ - v24 - S '77 - p138
Subject: Baseball—Biography

Pitchers And Pitching
BL - v69 - S 1 '72 - p43
CSM - v64 - My 4 '72 - pB6
KR - v40 - Mr 15 '72 - p340
LJ - v97 - My 15 '72 - p1930
Subject: Baseball

Pro Football's Greatest Upsets
LJ - v97 - My 15 '72 - p1931
SLJ - v28 - Ap '82 - p30
Subject: Football

Rise Of The Robots
BL - v67 - My 15 '71 - p800
BS - v31 - My 15 '71 - p100
CLW - v43 - D '71 - p224
LJ - v96 - My 15 '71 - p1817
SB - v7 - D '71 - p186
Subject: Robots

Strange But True Stories Of World War II
BL - v80 - S 15 '83 - p173

SULLIVAN, George Edward (continued)
SLJ - v30 - D '83 - p78
Subject: World War, 1939-1945

Superstars Of Women's Track
BL - v78 - Mr 15 '82 - p966
CLW - v53 - Ap '82 - p403
SLJ - v28 - D '81 - p87
Subject: Track and field

Supertanker
ACSB - v12 - Winter '79 - p38
BL - v74 - Jl 15 '78 - p1737
BS - v38 - S '79 - p181
KR - v46 - Jl 1 '78 - p698
Subject: Petroleum industry and trade; Ships; Tankers

Understanding Architecture
BL - v68 - S 1 '71 - p60
CCB-B - v25 - D '71 - p65
Subject: Architecture

Wilt Chamberlain
LJ - v96 - My 15 '71 - p1824
Subject: Basketball—Biography

see also Seewagen, George L (co-author) for additional titles

SULLIVAN, Mary Beth

Feeling Free
BL - v75 - Jl 15 '79 - p1631
CBRS - v7 - Ag '79 - p140
CCB-B - v33 - N '79 - p59
CE - v57 - Mr '81 - p208
Cur R - v19 - Je '80 - p223
Kliatt - v14 - Winter '80 - p34
KR - v47 - Ag 1 '79 - p859
SB - v15 - Mr '80 - p224
SLJ - v26 - O '79 - p156
Subject: Physically handicapped

SULLIVAN, Mary Wilson 1907-
ConAu 12NR, SmATA 13, WhoAmW 83

Bluegrass Iggy
BL - v72 - Ja 1 '76 - p629
KR - v43 - Ag 15 '75 - p919
SLJ - v22 - D '75 - p55
Subject: Bluegrass music—Fiction; Recycling (Waste)—Fiction

The Indestructible Old-Time String Band
KR - v43 - Jl 1 '75 - p714
NYTBR - S 7 '75 - p20
PW - v208 - Jl 14 '75 - p60
SLJ - v522 - S '75 - p113

What's This About Pete?
CCB-B - v30 - Ja '77 - p83
KR - v44 - Ap 15 '76 - p484
SLJ - v22 - Mr '76 - p118
Subject: Sex role—Fiction

SULLIVAN, Navin 1929-
ConAu 5R

Pioneer Astronomers
CSM - Jl 16 '64 - p5
HB - v40 - Ag '64 - p393
LJ - v89 - S 15 '64 - p3499
NH - v73 - N '64 - p6
SA - v211 - D '64 - p147
S & T - v29 - Ap '65 - p238
Subject: Astronomers

SULLIVAN, Wilson

Franklin Delano Roosevelt
BL - v67 - S 1 '70 - p59
BS - v30 - My 1 '70 - p63
Comw - v92 - My 22 '70 - p251
KR - v38 - My 15 '70 - p569
LJ - v95 - D 15 '70 - p4369
NYTBR - Ag 9 '70 - p22
NYTBR, Pt. 2 - N 8 '70 - p36
PW - v197 - Je 1 '70 - p68
SR - v53 - O 24 '70 - p67
Co-author: Freidel, Frank
Subject: Biography

SUMMERS, James Levingston 1910-
AuBYP, BioIn 13, ConAu 13R, MorJA, SmATA 28

The Iron Doors Between
BS - v28 - O 1 '68 - p279
BW - v2 - N 3 '68 - p18
HB - v44 - O '68 - p576
KR - v36 - Ag 1 '68 - p825
LJ - v93 - S 15 '68 - p3327

You Can't Make It By Bus
CCB-B - v23 - Ja '70 - p89
CSM - v61 - N 6 '69 - pB9
EJ - v63 - Ja '74 - p62
KR - v37 - N 15 '69 - p1204
LJ - v95 - Ja 15 '70 - p257
LJ - v96 - Ja 15 '71 - p282
NYTBR, Pt. 2 - N 9 '69 - p48
Subject: Mexican Americans—Fiction

SUNG, Betty Lee 1924-
AmM&WS 78S, ConAu 10NR, SmATA 26

The Chinese In America
BL - v69 - Ja 1 '73 - p451

SUNG, Betty Lee (continued)
BL - v69 - F 15 '73 - p553
CE - v49 - Mr '73 - p324
KR - v40 - Ag 15 '72 - p946
LJ - v98 - My 15 '73 - p1692
SE - v37 - D '73 - p789
TN - v41 - Fall '84 - p97
Subject: Chinese Americans

SUNSHINE, Tina

An X-Rated Romance
BL - v79 - S 1 '82 - p49
CCB-B - v36 - N '82 - p56
SLJ - v29 - Ja '83 - p88
VOYA - v5 - Ag '82 - p37
Subject: Mothers and daughters—Fiction; Schools—Fiction

SURGE, Frank 1931-
ConAu 69, SmATA 13

Famous Spies
CCB-B - v22 - Jl '69 - p182
LJ - v94 - O 15 '69 - p3824
Subject: Spies

Western Outlaws
LJ - v94 - D 15 '69 - p4609
Subject: West (U.S.)

SWARTHOUT, Glendon Fred 1918-
AuBYP, BioIn 11, ConAu 1NR, ConLC 35, ConNov 86, EncFWF, FourBJA, SmATA 26, WhoAm 86, WrDr 86

Bless The Beasts And Children
BL - v66 - Je 1 '70 - p1195
BL - v66 - Je 15 '70 - p1274
BL - v67 - Ap 1 '71 - p655
BL - v81 - Jl '85 - p1547
BS - v29 - Mr 1 '70 - p450
HM - v240 - Ap '70 - p107
KR - v38 - Ja 1 '70 - p24
KR - v38 - F 1 '70 - p119
LJ - v95 - Mr 1 '70 - p915
LJ - v95 - Ap 15 '70 - p1661
LJ - v95 - My 15 '70 - p1913
LJ - v95 - D 15 '70 - p4328
NO - v9 - Je 1 '70 - p17
NYTBR - Ap 5 '70 - p30
PW - v197 - Ja 19 '70 - p79
PW - v198 - O 5 '70 - p64
Spec - v225 - D 5 '70 - pR22
SR - v53 - My 2 '70 - p29
TN - v27 - Ap '71 - p309
Subject: Adolescence—Fiction; Camping—Fiction

Whichaway
BL - v63 - N 15 '66 - p378
BS - v26 - N 1 '66 - p296
CCB-B - v20 - Ap '67 - p130
KR - v34 - S 1 '66 - p915
LJ - v92 - Ja 15 '67 - p348
LJ - v98 - O 15 '73 - p3163
Nat R - v18 - D 13 '66 - p1285
NYTBR - v71 - N 6 '66 - p12
NYTBR - v71 - D 4 '66 - p66
Obs - D 3 '67 - p26
PW - v190 - O 10 '66 - p74
SR - v50 - Mr 18 '67 - p36
Co-author: Swarthout, Kathryn
Subject: Wilderness survival—Fiction

SWARTHOUT, Kathryn
see Swarthout, Glendon Fred (co-author)

SWEARINGEN, Martha

If Anything
BL - v76 - Mr 15 '80 - p1044
CBRS - v8 - F '80 - p60
KR - v47 - N 15 '79 - p1348
SLJ - v26 - Ap '80 - p128

SWEENEY, James Bartholemew 1910-
BioIn 12, ConAu 12NR, SmATA 21, WhoS&SW 75

A Combat Reporter's Report
BL - v77 - My 1 '81 - p1191
SLJ - v27 - My '81 - p78
Subject: Soldiers; War correspondents

True Spy Stories
BL - v78 - S 15 '81 - p99
SLJ - v28 - Mr '82 - p152
Subject: Spies; World War, 1939-1945

SWEENEY, Karen O'Connor 1938-
ConAu 89, SmATA X
Pseud./variant:
O'Connor, Karen

Entertaining
Inst - v87 - My '78 - p116
SLJ - v25 - S '78 - p149
Subject: Entertaining

see also O'Connor, Karen for additional titles

SWENSON, May 1919-
AmWomWr, AuBYP SUP, BioIn 10, -12, ConAu 5R, ConLC 4, ConPo 85, DcLB 5, SmATA 15, WhoAmW 87, WrDr 86

Poems To Solve
BL - v63 - Ap 1 '67 - p847
BS - v26 - D 1 '66 - p342
CLW - v38 - Ja '67 - p338
HB - v43 - F '67 - p77
Inst - v76 - F '67 - p186
KR - v34 - N 1 '66 - p1146
LJ - v92 - Ja 15 '67 - p348
PS - v42 - Spring '68 - p86
Subject: Fairy tales; Verses for children

SWIFT, Benjamin

Play-Off
BL - v78 - O 15 '81 - p297
Hi Lo - v3 - F '82 - p1
SLJ - v28 - S '81 - p122
Subject: Football—Fiction

SWIFT, Helen Miller 1914-
AuBYP, ConAu 1R

Head Over Heels
KR - v35 - D 15 '67 - p1477
LJ - v93 - Ja 15 '68 - p311

SWINBURNE, Irene
see Swinburne, Laurence (co-author)

SWINBURNE, Laurence 1924-
BioIn 11, ConAu 15NR, SmATA 9

The Deadly Diamonds
Cur R - v17 - Ag '78 - p228
SLJ - v25 - S '78 - p128
Co-author: Swinburne, Irene

T

TABRAH, Ruth M 1921-
ConAu 10NR, IntAu&W 82, SmATA 14, WhoAmW 75

Hawaii Nei
BL - v64 - Ja 15 '68 - p595
CCB-B - v21 - N '67 - p49
KR - v35 - S 1 '67 - p1065
LJ - v92 - N 15 '67 - p4265
SR - v50 - Ag 19 '67 - p35
TN - v24 - Je '68 - p448
Subject: Hawaii

TAMAR, Erika

Blues For Silk Garcia
EJ - v73 - D '84 - p65
VOYA - v6 - O '83 - p209
Subject: Fathers—Fiction; Musicians—Fiction

TATE, Joan 1922-
ConAu 1NR, IntAu&W 77, OxChL, SmATA 9, TwCChW 83, WrDr 86

Tina And David
BS - v33 - O 15 '73 - p334
CCB-B - v27 - My '74 - p151
KR - v41 - S 1 '73 - p973
LJ - v99 - Ja 15 '74 - p219
Subject: Friendship—Fiction

TAVES, Isabella 1915-
ConAu 8NR, SmATA 27, WhoAmW 75

Not Bad For A Girl
CCB-B - v26 - N '72 - p50
EJ - v61 - N '72 - p1262
Inst - v82 - N '72 - p126
KR - v40 - Je 1 '72 - p624
LJ - v97 - My 15 '72 - p1930
NYTBR, Pt. 2 - My 7 '72 - p24

TAYLOR, David
WrDr 86

Is There A Doctor In The Zoo?
BL - v74 - My 1 '78 - p1398
HB - v55 - O '78 - p547
Kliatt - v13 - Fall '79 - p33
KR - v46 - Ap 1 '78 - p426
KR - v46 - My 15 '78 - p556
LJ - v103 - My 1 '78 - p967
PW - v213 - Ap 3 '78 - p75
SB - v15 - My '79 - p37
SLJ - v25 - N '78 - p85
WLB - v53 - F '79 - p464
Subject: Veterinarians

TAYLOR, Dawson 1916-
ConAu 13R, MichAu 80

Aim For A Job In Automotive Service
BL - v65 - S 15 '68 - p111
LJ - v93 - S 15 '68 - p3327
Co-author: Bradley, James J
Subject: Automobiles

TAYLOR, Lester Barbour, Jr. 1932-
ConAu 11NR, SmATA 27

Rescue! True Stories Of Heroism
BL - v75 - O 15 '78 - p388
CBRS - v7 - Ja '79 - p50
CLW - v51 - N '79 - p181
Subject: Biography; Heroes

TAYLOR, Mildred D 1943-
ChlLR 9, ConAu 85, ConLC 21, DcLB 52, FifBJA, OxChL, SelBAAf, SmATA 15, TwCChW 83, WrDr 86

Roll Of Thunder, Hear My Cry
BL - v81 - D 15 '84 - p584
BW - Ap 23 '78 - pE2
CLW - v49 - D '77 - p212
CSM - v70 - O 23 '78 - pB9
CSM - v76 - O 5 '84 - pB7
EJ - v69 - S '80 - p87
GP - v16 - Ap '78 - p3283
JB - v42 - F '78 - p51
J Read - v25 - My '82 - p778
NYTBR - Mr 19 '78 - p51
Obs - D 11 '77 - p31
SE - v47 - Ap '83 - p289
TES - Jl 11 '80 - p28
TLS - D 2 '77 - p1415
TN - v38 - Winter '82 - p113
Subject: Blacks—Fiction; Race relations—Fiction

TAYLOR, Paula 1942-
ConAu 111, SmATA 48

Elton John
SLJ - v23 - S '76 - p114
Subject: Musicians

TAYLOR, Theodore Langhans 1921-
AuBYP SUP, ConAu 9NR, FourBJA, IntAu&W 86, OxChL, SmATA 5, –4AS, TwCChW 78, –83, WhoAm 86, WrDr 86

Air Raid: Pearl Harbor
BL - v68 - O 15 '71 - p206
CCB-B - v25 - O '71 - p35
CE - v48 - F '72 - p260
KR - v39 - Je 1 '71 - p598
LJ - v97 - Je 15 '72 - p2244
NYTBR - Jl 11 '71 - p8
NYTBR, Pt. 2 - N 7 '71 - p30
SR - v54 - Ag 21 '71 - p27
TN - v28 - Je '72 - p435
Subject: Pearl Harbor, Attack on, 1941

The Battle Off Midway Island
BL - v78 - D 1 '81 - p489
Emerg Lib - v9 - Ja '82 - p33
Kliatt - v16 - Winter '82 - p57
NYTBR - v0 - N 15 '81 - p54
SLJ - v28 - My '82 - p75
Subject: World War, 1939-1945

The Cay
A Lib - v1 - Ap '70 - p387
Am - v121 - D 13 '69 - p594
BL - v65 - Jl 15 '69 - p1277
BS - v30 - N 15 '70 - p363
BW - v3 - My 4 '69 - p36
CCB-B - v22 - Jl '69 - p183
CLW - v41 - F '70 - p383
GW - v103 - D 19 '70 - p21
HB - v45 - O '69 - p537
KR - v37 - My 15 '69 - p560
LA - v57 - Ja '80 - p91
Lis - v84 - N 12 '70 - p671
LJ - v94 - Je 15 '69 - p2505
LJ - v94 - D 15 '69 - p4583
NS - v80 - N 6 '70 - p610
NYTBR - Je 29 '69 - p26
NYTBR, Pt. 2 - N 9 '69 - p61
NYTBR, Pt. 2 - N 8 '70 - p6
Obs - D 6 '70 - p27
PW - v195 - Je 9 '69 - p63
SR - v52 - Je 28 '69 - p39
TES - Je 10 '83 - p22
TLS - O 30 '70 - p1258
TN - v26 - Ja '70 - p208
Subject: Friendship—Fiction; Shipwrecks—Fiction; Survival—Fiction

Sweet Friday Island
BL - v81 - O 1 '84 - p252
CCB-B - v38 - F '85 - p118
SLJ - v31 - N '84 - p139
VOYA - v7 - F '85 - p333

Teetoncey
BL - v71 - S 1 '74 - p47
CCB-B - v28 - N '74 - p56
HB - v50 - O '74 - p145
KR - v42 - Jl 15 '74 - p744
LJ - v99 - O 15 '74 - p2749
NYTBR - O 6 '74 - p8
PW - v206 - D 2 '74 - p62
Teacher - v93 - Ap '76 - p121
Subject: Outer Banks (N.C.)—Fiction

TCHUDI, Stephen N

The Burg-O-Rama Man
SE - v48 - My '84 - p377
VOYA - v6 - Ag '83 - p146
Subject: Advertising—Fiction; Schools—Fiction

Soda Poppery: The History Of Soft Drinks In America
BL - v82 - My 15 '86 - p1400
HB - v62 - Jl '86 - p469
NYTBR - v91 - Je 1 '86 - p48
SLJ - v33 - S '86 - p147
Subject: Soft drink industry—History

TEALL, Kaye M

TV Camera Three
BL - v74 - Ap 15 '78 - p1343
Hi Lo - v2 - F '81 - p5
Subject: Employment—Fiction

Witches Get Everything
Hi Lo - v1 - My '80 - p3
Subject: Crime and criminals—Fiction; Witchcraft—Fiction

TERASAKI, Gwen

Bridge To The Sun
BL - v54 - S 1 '57 - p8
CSM - S 25 '57 - p9
NYT - O 13 '57 - p6
SR - v40 - S 7 '57 - p20
Subject: World War, 1939-1945

TERHAAR, Jaap 1922-
ConAu 37R, FourBJA, SmATA 6

The World Of Ben Lighthart
BL - v74 - S 15 '77 - p193
BS - v37 - Ag '77 - p141
CCB-B - v30 - Jl '77 - p182
CLW - v49 - O '77 - p140
EJ - v66 - S '77 - p77
KR - v45 - Je 1 '77 - p582
LA - v54 - N '77 - p948
Subject: Blind—Fiction; Physically handicapped—Fiction

TERMAN, D

By Balloon To The Sahara
BW - v10 - Ja 20 '80 - p13
Hi Lo - v3 - Mr '82 - p4
SLJ - v26 - N '79 - p68
Subject: Balloon ascensions—Fiction; Hot air balloons—Fiction

TERRY, Luther L 1911-1985
BioIn 11, ConAu 115, –P-2, CurBio 61, –85N, NewYTBS 85, SmATA 11, –42N, WhAm 8, WhoWor 82

To Smoke Or Not To Smoke
BL - v66 - Ja 15 '70 - p622
BS - v29 - D 1 '69 - p355
KR - v37 - N 15 '69 - p1212
LJ - v95 - Mr 15 '70 - p1207
LJ - v96 - O 15 '71 - p3436
NYTBR - Ja 25 '70 - p26
Co-author: Horn, Daniel
Subject: Smoking

TERZIAN, James P 1915-
AuBYP SUP, ConAu 13R, SmATA 14

Mighty Hard Road: The Story Of Cesar Chavez
BL - v67 - Mr 1 '71 - p563
BL - v68 - Je 15 '72 - p895
BL - v70 - O 15 '73 - p226
BS - v31 - Mr 1 '72 - p547
CC - v87 - D 16 '70 - p1516
Inst - v82 - N '72 - p136
KR - v38 - N 15 '70 - p1258
LJ - v96 - Mr 15 '71 - p1130
NYTBR, Pt. 2 - N 8 '70 - p46
PW - v198 - N 9 '70 - p60
Co-author: Cramer, Kathryn
Subject: Biography

Pete Cass: Scrambler
PW - v194 - O 7 '68 - p55

THALER, Susan 1939-
ConAu 21R

Rosaria
Atl - v117 - N 4 '67 - p517
BS - v27 - O 1 '67 - p264
CCB-B - v21 - Ja '68 - p86
KR - v35 - Ag 1 '67 - p887
LJ - v92 - N 15 '67 - p4266

THOGER, Marie 1923-
ConAu 25R

Shanta
KR - v36 - Ja 1 '68 - p6
LJ - v93 - F 15 '68 - p874
NS - v73 - My 26 '67 - p732
TLS - N 24 '66 - p1084

THOMAS, Allison (pseud.)
SmATA X
Real Name:
Fleischer, Leonore

Sandy: The Autobiography Of A Dog
BL - v74 - My 1 '78 - p1404
KR - v46 - Mr 1 '78 - p291
PW - v213 - Ap 24 '78 - p75
SLJ - v25 - N '78 - p56
Co-author: Berloni, William
Subject: Dogs

THOMAS, Art 1952-
ConAu 105, SmATA 48

Bicycling Is For Me
BL - v76 - Ja 1 '80 - p670
SLJ - v26 - D '79 - p101
Subject: Bicyles and bicyling

THOMAS, Charles
see Hibbert, Christopher (co-author)

THOMAS, Dian 1945-
ConAu 65

Roughing It Easy
CSM - v68 - Ag 3 '76 - p21
RSR - v2 - O '74 - p35
Subject: Camping

THOMAS, Piri

Stories From El Barrio
Inter BC - v12 - #6 '81 p18
Inter BC - v14 - #1 '83 p15
Subject: Hispanic Americans—Fiction; Short stories

THOMPSON, Elizabeth Allen
see Allen, Elizabeth

THOMPSON, Estelle

Hunter In The Dark
BL - v75 - Ap 15 '79 - p1276
BW - F 18 '79 - pE7
TN - v36 - Summer '80 - p367
WLB - v53 - My '79 - p641

THOMPSON, George Selden
see Selden, George

THOMPSON, Jean 1933-

Brother Of The Wolves
BL - v75 - D 15 '78 - p691
CBRS - v7 - F '79 - p70
EJ - v68 - F '79 - p102
SE - v43 - Ap '79 - p301
SLJ - v25 - N '78 - p69
Subject: Dakota Indians—Fiction; Indians of North America—Fiction

THOMPSON, Paul

The Hitchhikers
Hi Lo - v2 - Mr '81 - p5
Kliatt - v15 - Spring '81 - p14
SLJ - v27 - S '80 - p88
Subject: Hitchhiking—Fiction; Runaways—Fiction

THOMPSON, Vivian Laubach 1911-
AuBYP, ConAu 1NR, IntAu&W 86, SmATA 3, WhoAmW 75, WrDr 86

Hawaiian Tales Of Heroes And Champions
BL - v68 - Mr 1 '72 - p567
CCB-B - v26 - O '72 - p32
CE - v49 - O '72 - p30
HB - v48 - F '72 - p46
KR - v39 - O 15 '71 - p1129
LJ - v97 - Ap 15 '72 - p1610
Subject: Folklore

THOMSON, Peter 1913-
AuBYP, ConAu 5R

Cougar
KR - v36 - Ja 1 '68 - p7

THORN, John 1947-
ConAu 17NR

Baseball's Ten Greatest Games
BL - v77 - Jl 1 '81 - p1392
CCB-B - v35 - N '81 - p60
J Read - v25 - Ap '82 - p709
LA - v59 - F '82 - p157
SLJ - v27 - My '81 - p78
Subject: Baseball

A Century Of Baseball Lore
KR - v42 - My 15 '74 - p575
LJ - v99 - Je 15 '74 - p1726
LJ - v99 - O 15 '74 - p2753
PW - v205 - Mr 25 '74 - p55
Subject: Baseball

Pro Football's Ten Greatest Games
J Read - v25 - Mr '82 - p613
SLJ - v28 - D '81 - p87
VOYA - v4 - F '82 - p45
Subject: Football

THORNE, Ian (pseud.)
ConAu X, SmATA X
Real Name:
May, Julian

Ancient Astronauts
Hi Lo - v4 - My '83 - p5
Subject: Civilization

Bermuda Triangle
Hi Lo - v4 - My '83 - p5
Subject: Bermuda triangle

Bigfoot
Hi Lo - v4 - My '83 - p5
Subject: Monsters

The Blob
SLJ - v29 - O '82 - p156
Subject: Science fiction

The Deadly Mantis
SLJ - v29 - O '82 - p156
Subject: Horror stories; Monsters—Fiction

Dracula
Cur R - v16 - D '77 - p354
SLJ - v24 - Ja '78 - p91
Subject: Monsters; Motion pictures

Frankenstein
Cur R - v16 - D '77 - p354
SLJ - v24 - Ja '78 - p91
Subject: Horror films; Monsters

Godzilla
Cur R - v16 - D '77 - p354
SLJ - v24 - Ja '78 - p91
Subject: Monsters; Motion pictures

It Came From Outer Space
SLJ - v29 - O '82 - p156
Subject: Extraterrestrial beings—Fiction; Science fiction

King Kong
Cur R - v16 - D '77 - p354

THORNE, Ian (continued)
SLJ - v24 - Ja '78 - p91
Subject: Monsters; Motion pictures

Loch Ness Monster
Hi Lo - v4 - My '83 - p5
Subject: Loch Ness monster; Monsters

Mad Scientists
Cur R - v16 - D '77 - p354
SLJ - v78 - Ja '78 - p91
Subject: Horror films

Monster Tales Of Native Americans
Cur R - v4 - My '83 - p5
Subject: Animals (Mythical); Indians of North America—Fiction; Monsters—Fiction

UFO's
Hi Lo - v4 - My '83 - p5
Subject: Unidentified flying objects

The Wolf Man
Cur R - v16 - D '77 - p354
SLJ - v24 - Ja '78 - p91
Subject: Monsters; Motion pictures

see also May, Julian for additional titles

THORNTON, Jane Foster

Breakaway
BL - v81 - F 1 '85 - p784
SLJ - v31 - Ja '85 - p90
VOYA - v8 - Ap '85 - p44
Subject: Love—Fiction

Close Harmony
BL - v81 - F 1 '85 - p784
SLJ - v31 - Ja '85 - p91
VOYA - v8 - Ap '85 - p44
Subject: Love—Fiction

THRASHER, Crystal Faye 1921-
ConAu 8NR, SmATA 27

The Dark Didn't Catch Me
BL - v71 - Ap 1 '75 - p820
CCB-B - v29 - D '75 - p71
CE - v52 - Ja '76 - p156
CLW - v47 - O '75 - p133
Comw - v102 - N 21 '75 - p569
CSM - v67 - My 7 '75 - pB2
HB - v51 - Je '75 - p272
Inst - v89 - Ja '80 - p112
J Read - v19 - Ja '76 - p331
KR - v43 - Mr 1 '75 - p240
NYT - v125 - D 20 '75 - p25
NYTBR - Mr 30 '75 - p8
NYTBR - Je 1 '75 - p28
NYTBR - N 16 '75 - p54
NYTBR - D 7 '75 - p66
PW - v207 - F 10 '75 - p56
SE - v47 - Ap '83 - p289
SLJ - v21 - Ap '75 - p60
Subject: Depression, 1929—Fiction

THYPIN, Marilyn

Checking And Balancing
BL - v76 - My 15 '80 - p1360
SLJ - v26 - Ag '80 - p79
Co-author: Glasner, Lynne
Subject: Consumer education; Finance (Personal)

Good Buy! Buying Home Furnishings
BL - v76 - Je 15 '80 - p1524
SLJ - v26 - Ag '80 - p79
Co-author: Glasner, Lynne
Subject: Consumer education; House furnishings

Health Care For The Wongs: Health Insurance, Choosing A Doctor
BL - v76 - Je 15 '80 - p1524
SLJ - v26 - Ag '80 - p79
Co-author: Glasner, Lynne
Subject: Consumer education

Leases And Landlords: Apartment Living
BL - v76 - My 15 '80 - p1360
SLJ - v26 - Ag '80 - p79
Co-author: Glasner, Lynne
Subject: Consumer education

More Food For Our Money: Food Planning And Buying
BL - v75 - Je 15 '79 - p1533
Co-author: Glasner, Lynne
Subject: Consumer education; Food; Nutrition

Put Your Money Down
BL - v75 - Je 15 '79 - p1533
Co-author: Glasner, Lynne
Subject: Consumer education

State Your Claim! Small Claims Court
BL - v76 - Je 15 '80 - p1525
SLJ - v26 - Ag '80 - p79
Co-author: Glasner, Lynne
Subject: Consumer education

Try It On: Buying Clothing
Hi Lo - v4 - My '83 - p7
SLJ - v26 - S '79 - p149

THYPIN, Marilyn (continued)
Co-author: Glasner, Lynne
Subject: Clothing and dress; Consumer education

Wheels And Deals: Buying A Car
BL - v75 - Jl 15 '79 - p1622
CSM - v73 - D 1 '80 - pB11
SLJ - v26 - S '79 - p149
Co-author: Glasner, Lynne
Subject: Automobiles; Consumer education

When Things Don't Work: Appliance Buying And Repairs
Hi Lo - v4 - My '83 - p7
SLJ - v26 - S '79 - p149
Co-author: Glasner, Lynne
Subject: Consumer education

TITLER, Dale Milton 1926-
AuBYP SUP, ConAu 81, SmATA 35

Haunted Treasures
KR - v44 - S 15 '76 - p1043
Subject: Buried treasure; Ghosts

Unnatural Resources: True Stories Of American Treasure
BL - v70 - D 1 '73 - p389
CLW - v45 - Mr '74 - p399
Inst - v83 - N '73 - p128
KR - v41 - Ag 15 '73 - p887
LJ - v99 - Ja 15 '74 - p213
Subject: Buried treasure

Wings Of Adventure
BL - v68 - My 15 '72 - p786
CSM - v64 - F 10 '72 - p11
LJ - v96 - D 15 '71 - p4094
PW - v200 - N 15 '71 - p68
Subject: Aeronautics; Air pilots

TOEPFER, Ray Grant 1923-
ConAu 21R

Liberty And Corporal Kincaid
BL - v64 - Je 15 '68 - p1189
BS - v27 - F 1 '68 - p431
KR - v35 - D 1 '67 - p1426
Subject: United States—History—Revolution, 1775-1783—Fiction

TOLAN, Stephanie S 1942-
ConAu 15NR, DrAP&F 85, SmATA 38

The Liberation Of Tansy Warner
BL - v76 - Jl 15 '80 - p1678
CBRS - v8 - Ag '80 - p139
CCB-B - v34 - S '80 - p23
J Read - v24 - Mr '81 - p549
KR - v48 - Jl 15 '80 - p914
SLJ - v27 - S '80 - p88
Subject: Fathers and daughters—Fiction; Identity—Fiction; Mothers and daughters—Fiction

TOMERLIN, John 1930-
AuBYP SUP

The Fledgling
BL - v65 - N 1 '68 - p316
BS - v28 - Ag 1 '68 - p195
CCB-B - v22 - F '69 - p102
CSM - v60 - N 7 '68 - pB11
KR - v36 - Jl 1 '68 - p699
LJ - v93 - S 15 '68 - p3327
SR - v51 - N 9 '68 - p69

The Nothing Special
BL - v65 - My 15 '69 - p1079
CSM - v61 - My 1 '69 - pB10
KR - v37 - F 15 '69 - p186
LJ - v94 - Ap 15 '69 - p1801
PW - v195 - Ap 21 '69 - p66
Subject: Automobile racing—Fiction

TOPPER, Frank

Mystery At The Bike Race
SLJ - v32 - S '85 - p153
Subject: Mystery and detective stories; Plot-your-own-stories

TOPPIN, Edgar Allan
see Dobler, Lavinia G (co-author); Drisko, Carol F (co-author)

TORCHIA, Joseph

The Kryptonite Kid
Esq - v95 - Mr '81 - p23
SLJ - v26 - N '79 - p98

TOWNSEND, John Rowe 1922-
AuBYP SUP, ChlLR 2, ConAu 37R, FourBJA, OxChL, PiP, SmATA 4, -2AS, TwCChW 83, WrDr 86

Good-Bye To The Jungle
BL - v64 - S 1 '67 - p67
BS - v27 - My 1 '67 - p67
HB - v43 - Je '67 - p355
Inst - v76 - Je '67 - p144
KR - v35 - F 15 '67 - p212
LJ - v92 - My 15 '67 - p2032
NY - v43 - D 16 '67 - p164
NYTBR - v72 - N 5 '67 - p64
NYTBR, Pt. 2 - v72 - My 7 '67 - p12
PW - v191 - Mr 20 '67 - p61

TOWNSEND, John Rowe (continued)
SR - v50 - Ap 22 '67 - p100
Subject: Family life—Fiction; Social adjustment—Fiction

Good Night, Prof, Dear
BL - v67 - Je 1 '71 - p832
BL - v68 - Ap 1 '72 - p665
BW - v5 - My 9 '71 - p18
CCB-B - v24 - Jl '71 - p179
CSM - v63 - My 6 '71 - pB6
EJ - v73 - Mr '84 - p89
HB - v47 - Je '71 - p294
KR - v39 - Ja 15 '71 - p57
LJ - v96 - Ap 15 '71 - p1520
NYTBR, Pt. 2 - My 2 '71 - p18
PW - v199 - Mr 22 '71 - p53
SR - v54 - My 15 '71 - p45
TN - v28 - Ap '72 - p314
Subject: Runaways—Fiction

Hell's Edge
BL - v65 - Jl 15 '69 - p1277
BS - v29 - Je 1 '69 - p103
CCB-B - v23 - S '69 - p19
KR - v37 - Ap 15 '69 - p454
NYTBR - Ag 31 '69 - p16
PW - v195 - My 12 '69 - p58
Subject: England—Fiction; Mystery and detective stories

Pirate's Island
B&B - v13 - My '68 - p46
BL - v64 - Ap 15 '68 - p999
BW - v2 - My 5 '68 - p24
CCB-B - v21 - Jl '68 - p182
CSM - v60 - My 2 '68 - pB10
HB - v44 - Ag '68 - p423
KR - v36 - Mr 1 '68 - p263
Lis - v79 - My 16 '68 - p643
LJ - v93 - Ap 15 '68 - p1805
NS - v75 - My 24 '68 - p695
NY - v44 - D 14 '68 - p208
NYTBR - v73 - My 26 '68 - p30
Obs - Ap 14 '68 - p27
PW - v193 - F 5 '68 - p66
SR - v51 - My 11 '68 - p40
TLS - Mr 14 '68 - p254
Subject: Family life—Fiction; Social adjustment—Fiction

The Summer People
BL - v69 - N 1 '72 - p241
BL - v69 - N 1 '72 - p247
BS - v32 - S 15 '72 - p285
CCB-B - v26 - D '72 - p67
Comw - v97 - N 17 '72 - p157
EJ - v73 - Mr '84 - p89
GW - v107 - D 16 '72 - p23
HB - v49 - Ap '73 - p129
KR - v40 - S 15 '72 - p1107
KR - v40 - D 15 '72 - p1422
LJ - v98 - Mr 15 '73 - p1016
NS - v84 - N 10 '72 - p692
NYTBR - N 19 '72 - p10
NYTBR, Pt. 2 - N 5 '72 - p28
Obs - N 26 '72 - p37
PW - v202 - O 16 '72 - p49
Spec - v229 - N 11 '72 - p750
SR - v55 - D 9 '72 - p79
TLS - N 3 '72 - p1324
TN - v29 - Je '73 - p358
Subject: England—Fiction

Trouble In The Jungle
A Lib - v1 - Ap '70 - p387
BL - v65 - My 1 '69 - p1019
BW - v3 - My 4 '69 - p28
CCB-B - v23 - F '70 - p106
CSM - v61 - My 1 '69 - pB7
HB - v45 - Ap '69 - p174
KR - v37 - Mr 1 '69 - p238
LJ - v94 - My 15 '69 - p2073
LJ - v94 - My 15 '69 - p2119
LJ - v94 - D 15 '69 - p4583
PW - v195 - Mr 17 '69 - p57
Subject: Crime and criminals—Fiction; Friendship—Fiction

TREADWAY, Rudy Peeples
AuBYP SUP

Go To It, You Dutchman! The Story Of Edward Bok
CCB-B - v23 - S '69 - p19
KR - v37 - Ap 1 '69 - p392
LJ - v94 - N 15 '69 - p4304
PW - v195 - Mr 10 '69 - p74
Subject: Biography

TREGASKIS, Richard 1916-1973
AuBYP, BioIn 7, -10, -12, -13, ConAu 2NR, CurBio 73, SmATA 26N, -3, WhAm 6

Guadalcanal Diary
SLJ - v29 - Ap '83 - p126
Subject: United States Marine Corps; World War, 1939-1945

John F. Kennedy And PT-109
BL - v67 - Ap 15 '62 - p580
CSM - My 10 '62 - p8B
LJ - v87 - Ap 15 '62 - p1697
NYTBR - F 25 '62 - p36
Subject: Biography

TREMAIN, Rose 1943-
ConAu 97, ConNov 86, WrDr 86

Sadler's Birthday
BL - v73 - Je 1 '77 - p1484
KR - v45 - Mr 15 '77 - p308
Lis - v95 - Ap 22 '76 - p518
LJ - v102 - Ap 15 '77 - p950
NY - v53 - Ag 1 '77 - p68
NYTBR - Jl 24 '77 - p14
Obs - Ap 25 '76 - p27
Obs - F 5 '84 - p52
PW - v211 - Mr 28 '77 - p73
TLS - Ap 30 '76 - p507

TRIPP, Jenny

The Man Who Was Left For Dead
SLJ - v27 - Ja '81 - p57
Subject: Bears; Wilderness survival

One Was Left Alive
SLJ - v27 - Ja '81 - p57
Subject: Aeronautics; Survival

TRUE, Dan

Flying Free
KR - v52 - Ag 1 '84 - p753
LJ - v109 - O 15 '84 - p1953
PW - v226 - S 14 '84 - p136
SLJ - v31 - Mr '85 - p188
Subject: Golden eagle; Wildlife rescue

TUCK, Jay Nelson

Heroes Of Puerto Rico
BL - v69 - Ja 15 '73 - p478
Co-author: Coolen, Norma
Subject: Puerto Ricans

TUNIS, Edwin 1897-1973
AuBYP, BioIn 13, ChlLR 2, ConAu 7NR, IlsCB 1946, -1957, -1967, MorJA, SmATA 28, WhoAmA 82N

Chipmunks On The Doorstep
A Lib - v3 - Ap '72 - p421
BL - v67 - Jl 15 '71 - p956
BL - v68 - Ap 1 '72 - p670
CCB-B - v25 - S '71 - p17
CE - v48 - N '71 - p106
CLW - v43 - Ap '72 - p480
HB - v47 - Ag '71 - p397
Inst - v81 - Je '72 - p66
KR - v39 - Ap 15 '71 - p441
LJ - v96 - Je 15 '71 - p2134
NYT - v121 - D 16 '71 - p67
NYTBR - My 16 '71 - p8
NYTBR, Pt. 2 - N 7 '71 - p30
PW - v199 - Je 21 '71 - p71
SA - v225 - D '71 - p108
SB - v7 - D '71 - p249
SR - v54 - Jl 17 '71 - p37
TN - v28 - Ja '72 - p204
Subject: Animals

TUNIS, John R 1889-1975
Au&ICB, AuBYP, BioIn 12, ConAu 61, ConLC 12, DcLB 22, MorJA, OxChL, SmATA 37, TwCChW 83

All-American
Atl - v170 - D '42 - p149
BL - v39 - O 1 '42 - p37
CC - v59 - S 30 '42 - p1187
Comw - v37 - N 20 '42 - p116
CSM - D 10 '42 - p16
HB - v18 - N '42 - p425
LJ - v67 - O 15 '42 - p897
LJ - v67 - N 1 '42 - p958
NY - v18 - D 12 '42 - p111
NYTBR - N 1 '42 - p9
SR - v25 - N 14 '42 - p26
SR - v25 - D 5 '42 - p60

Go, Team, Go
BL - v50 - Ap 1 '54 - p303
CSM - My 13 '54 - p12
HB - v30 - Ap '54 - p105
KR - v22 - Ja 1 '54 - p4
LJ - v79 - Ap 15 '54 - p791
NYTBR - F 28 '54 - p24
SR - v37 - Mr 20 '54 - p53
SR - v37 - Je 19 '54 - p40

His Enemy, His Friend
Am - v117 - N 4 '67 - p518
BL - v64 - Mr 1 '68 - p788
BS - v27 - N 1 '67 - p315
BW - v1 - N 19 '67 - p24
CCB-B - v21 - F '68 - p102
CLW - v39 - D '67 - p298
Comw - v87 - N 10 '67 - p181
CSM - v59 - N 2 '67 - pB13
EJ - v63 - F '74 - p91
HB - v44 - F '68 - p51
KR - v35 - S 15 '67 - p1147
LJ - v93 - F 15 '68 - p890
LJ - v95 - O 15 '70 - p3610
NYTBR - v72 - O 29 '67 - p44
NYTBR - v72 - N 5 '67 - p64
NYTBR, Pt. 2 - N 8 '70 - p30
NYTBR, Pt. 2 - F 13 '72 - p14
PW - v192 - O 23 '67 - p52
SR - v51 - Mr 16 '68 - p39
Subject: World War, 1939-1945—Fiction

TUNIS, John R (continued)

The Kid Comes Back
BL - v43 - S '46 - p20
HB - v22 - N '46 - p469
KR - v14 - S 1 '46 - p426
LJ - v71 - N 1 '46 - p1547
NYTBR - N 10 '46 - p5
NYTBR - S 11 '77 - p61
NYTBR - v91 - Ap 6 '86 - p20
SR - v29 - N 9 '46 - p54

World Series
BL - v38 - S '41 - p18
LJ - v66 - S 1 '41 - p737
NYTBR - O 19 '41 - p10
NYTBR - S 11 '77 - p61
NYTBR - v91 - Ap 6 '86 - p20

TURNER, Alice K 1940-
ConAu 53, IntAu&W 86, SmATA 10, WhoAm 86

Yoga For Beginners
KR - v41 - Ag 15 '73 - p891
LJ - v99 - Mr 15 '74 - p905
PW - v204 - Ag 13 '73 - p54
Subject: Yoga

TURNER, Ann W 1945-
ConAu 14NR, SmATA 14

Third Girl From The Left
BL - v82 - Je 1 '86 - p1455
BS - v46 - O '86 - p280
CBRS - v14 - Spring '86 - p137
CCB-B - v39 - Je '86 - p198
HB - v62 - S '86 - p600
KR - v54 - Je 1 '86 - p872
PW - v230 - Jl 25 '86 - p191
SLJ - v32 - Ag '86 - p108
VOYA - v9 - Ag '86 - p152
Subject: Montana—Fiction; Ranch life—Fiction

TURNER, William O 1914-
AuNews 1, ConAu 1R, IntAu&W 77, WrDr 80

The Treasure Of Fan-Tan Flat
NYTBR - Je 4 '61 - p18

TURNGREEN, Annette 1902?-1980
AuBYP, BioIn 12, ConAu 9R, –101, MorJA, SmATA 23N

Mystery Plays A Golden Flute
BS - v29 - Je 1 '69 - p103
KR - v37 - Ap 15 '69 - p454
LJ - v94 - My 15 '69 - p2124
PW - v195 - Ap 7 '69 - p56
Subject: Mystery and detective stories

Mystery Walks The Campus
CSM - N 15 '56 - p15
KR - v24 - Jl 15 '56 - p481
LJ - v82 - F 15 '57 - p596
Subject: Mystery and detective stories

TWYMAN, Gib

Born To Hit: The George Brett Story
B Rpt - v1 - Mr '83 - p54
Subject: Baseball—Biography

TYLER, Vicki

Senior Year
SLJ - v32 - Ap '86 - p104
Subject: Love—Fiction

U

UCHIDA, Yoshiko 1921-
AuBYP, ChlLR 6, ConAu 6NR, DrAP&F 85, MorJA, SmATA 1, -1AS, TwCChW 83, WrDr 86

Journey Home
BL - v75 - D 15 '78 - p691
CBRS - v7 - Ja '79 - p50
CCB-B - v32 - Ap '79 - p146
CE - v55 - Ap '79 - p298
KR - v47 - Ja 1 '79 - p6
LA - v56 - My '79 - p546
Par - v54 - Ap '79 - p24
SE - v43 - Ap '79 - p298
SE - v44 - O '80 - p481
SLJ - v25 - Ja '79 - p58
WCRB - v5 - Ja '79 - p54
Subject: Japanese Americans—Fiction; Prejudices—Fiction

Journey To Topaz
BL - v68 - Ja 1 '72 - p395
BW - v5 - N 7 '71 - p14
CCB-B - v25 - D '71 - p66
HB - v47 - D '71 - p615
Inst - v81 - N '71 - p133
Kliatt - v19 - Fall '85 - p18
LA - v58 - Ap '81 - p459
NYTBR - Mr 12 '72 - p8
PW - v200 - S 6 '71 - p51
SR - v54 - D 11 '71 - p46
Subject: Japanese Americans—Fiction

Samurai Of Gold Hill
BL - v69 - F 15 '73 - p553
BL - v69 - F 15 '73 - p575
CCB-B - v26 - My '73 - p147
HB - v49 - F '73 - p51
Kliatt - v19 - Fall '85 - p18
KR - v40 - N 1 '72 - p1241
SE - v37 - D '73 - p789
Subject: Japanese Americans—Fiction

UHLICH, R
see Lefkowitz, William (co-author)

UHLICH, Richard

Twenty Minutes To Live And Other Tales Of Suspense
Hi Lo - v1 - Ja '80 - p3
Subject: Short stories

see also Lefkowitz, William (co-author) for additional titles

ULYATT, Kenneth 1920-
ConAu 8NR, SmATA 14

Outlaws
BL - v74 - Jl 1 '78 - p1682
GP - v15 - Ap '77 - p3091
JB - v41 - Je '77 - p186
SLJ - v25 - S '78 - p165
Subject: West (U.S.)

UNKELBACH, Kurt 1913-
AuBYP SUP, ConAu 8NR, SmATA 4

The Dog Who Never Knew
KR - v35 - N 15 '67 - p1370
LJ - v93 - S 15 '68 - p3327
PW - v193 - My 27 '68 - p58

How To Bring Up Your Pet Dog
BL - v69 - N 15 '72 - p303
Subject: Dogs

UNTERMEYER, Louis 1885-1977
AuBYP, BioIn 11, ConAu 5R, -73, CurBio 78, -78N, DcLEL, OxAmL 83, SmATA 37, WhAm 7

The Firebringer And Other Great Stories
BL - v65 - Mr 1 '69 - p756
LJ - v94 - F 15 '69 - p889
NYTBR - v73 - N 3 '68 - p46
Subject: Folklore

URQUHART, David Inglis

The Internal Combustion Engine And How It Works
BL - v70 - Ja 15 '74 - p546
KR - v41 - O 15 '73 - p1169
LJ - v99 - F 15 '74 - p577
Subject: Engines

V

VAN DUYN, Janet 1910-
ConAu 69, SmATA 18

Builders On The Desert
KR - v42 - Ap 15 '74 - p431
LJ - v99 - O 15 '74 - p2743
SB - v10 - D '74 - p249
SE - v39 - Mr '75 - p175
SLJ - v25 - S '78 - p43
Subject: Egypt

VAN LAWICK-GOODALL, Jane
see Lawick-Goodall, Jane Van

VAN RYZIN, Lani

Cutting A Record In Nashville
BL - v76 - Je 15 '80 - p1525
Hi Lo - v2 - N '80 - p3
Subject: Music

Starting Your Own Band: Rock, Disco, Folk, Jazz, Country And Western
BL - v77 - O 1 '80 - p205
SLJ - v27 - Ag '81 - p79
Subject: Music; Vocational guidance

VAN STEENWYK, Elizabeth 1928-
AuBYP SUP, ConAu 18NR, SmATA 34

Dorothy Hamill: Olympic Champion
Hi Lo - v1 - S '79 - p4
Subject: Biography; Ice skaters

Harness Racing
SLJ - v30 - F '84 - p66
Subject: Horse racing

Mystery At Beach Bay
Hi Lo - v1 - Ja '80 - p4
Subject: Mystery and detective stories

Quarter Horse Winner
BL - v77 - D 15 '80 - p577
SLJ - v27 - Mr '81 - p52
Subject: Horses—Fiction

Rivals On Ice
CCB-B - v33 - D '79 - p83
SLJ - v26 - D '79 - p100
Subject: Friendship—Fiction; Ice skating—Fiction

VASS, George 1927-
ConAu 37R, SmATA 31

Reggie Jackson: From Superstar To Candy Bar
SLJ - v25 - My '79 - p86
Subject: Baseball—Biography; Blacks—Biography

Steve Garvey: The Bat Boy Who Became A Star
SLJ - v25 - My '79 - p86
Subject: Baseball—Biography

VEDRAL, Joyce

I Dare You
B Rpt - v2 - Mr '84 - p47
BS - v43 - N '83 - p312
CBRS - v12 - Ja '84 - p54
Cur R - v24 - S '84 - p29
SB - v20 - S '84 - p10
SLJ - v30 - N '83 - p98
VOYA - v6 - F '84 - p349
WLB - v58 - Ja '84 - p359
Subject: Psychology

VENTURO, Betty Lou Baker
see Baker, Betty Lou

VERDICK, Mary 1923-
ConAu 4NR

On The Ledge And Other Action Packed Stories
Hi Lo - v1 - Ap '80 - p4
Subject: Short stories

Write For The Job
Hi Lo - v2 - S '80 - p6
Subject: Employment

VERNON, Rosemary (pseud.)
ConAu X, SmATA X

VERNON, Rosemary (continued)
Real Name:
Smith, Susan Vernon

Love In The Fast Lane
SLJ - v31 - Ja '85 - p89
VOYA - v7 - O '84 - p202
Subject: Love—Fiction

The Popularity Plan
CBRS - v10 - Ja '82 - p46
EJ - v72 - Ja '83 - p79
Hi Lo - v3 - Je '82 - p2
SLJ - v28 - N '81 - p99
VOYA - v4 - O '81 - p39
Subject: Love—Fiction

The Problem With Love
Hi Lo - v3 - Je '82 - p3
SLJ - v28 - Ag '82 - p129
Subject: Love—Fiction

Question Of Love
SLJ - v32 - S '85 - p152
VOYA - v8 - O '85 - p264
Subject: Love—Fiction

VERRAL, Charles Spain 1904-
AuBYP, ConAu 16NR, -P-1, IntAu&W 77, SmATA 11, WhoE 85, WrDr 86

Babe Ruth: Sultan Of Swat
BL - v73 - D 15 '76 - p612
Comw - v103 - N 19 '76 - p764
SLJ - v23 - Ja '77 - p90
Subject: Baseball—Biography

VILOTT, Rhondi

Her Secret Self
BL - v79 - Ap 1 '83 - p1038
CCB-B - v36 - Ja '83 - p99
SLJ - v29 - F '83 - p93
Subject: Schools—Fiction

VINING, Elizabeth Gray
see Gray, Elizabeth Janet

VOIGT, Cynthia 1942-
BioIn 13, ConAu 18NR, ConLC 30, FifBJA, SmATA 33, WhoAm 84, WrDr 86

Building Blocks
BL - v80 - My 15 '84 - p1350
BW - v14 - Je 10 '84 - p6
CBRS - v12 - Spring '84 - p132
CCB-B - v37 - Ap '84 - p158
CLW - v56 - O '84 - p127
HB - v60 - Ag '84 - p470
J Read - v29 - F '86 - p464
KR - v52 - Mr 1 '84 - pJ24
LA - v61 - D '84 - p862
N Dir Wom - v15 - Mr '86 - p13
PW - v225 - Ap 27 '84 - p86
RT - v38 - O '84 - p92
SLJ - v30 - My '84 - p85
Subject: Fathers and sons—Fiction; Space and time—Fiction

VROMAN, Mary Elizabeth 1923-1967
BioIn 7, BlkAWP, ConAu 109, DcAfL, DcLB 33, InB&W 80, SelBAAf, SelBAAu

Harlem Summer
BL - v69 - My 1 '73 - p839
CCB-B - v20 - Jl '67 - p177
J Read - v24 - My '81 - p695
LJ - v92 - S 15 '67 - p3206
NYTBR, Pt. 2 - v72 - My 7 '67 - p16
NYTBR, Pt. 2 - My 4 '69 - p6
SR - v50 - My 13 '67 - p57
TN - v24 - N '67 - p100
Subject: New York (City)—Fiction; Vocations—Fiction

W

WAGMAN, John
see Pollock, Bruce (co-author)

WAGNER, Robin S
ConTFT 3, WhoAm 86

Mork And Mindy 2: The Incredible Shrinking Mork
SLJ - v27 - Ag '81 - p79

WALDEN, Amelia Elizabeth 1909-
AuBYP, BioIn 4, ConAu 2NR, IntAu&W 82, MorJA, SmATA 3, WhoAm 86, WhoAmW 87, WhoE 77, WrDr 84

Basketball Girl Of The Year
BS - v30 - Jl 1 '70 - p147
KR - v38 - F 1 '70 - p112
LJ - v95 - My 15 '70 - p1965
NYTBR - Ap 19 '70 - p26
Subject: Basketball—Fiction

Go, Philips, Go!
BL - v70 - Je 1 '74 - p1101
BL - v70 - Je 1 '74 - p1107
KR - v42 - Mr 15 '74 - p309
LJ - v99 - My 15 '74 - p1490
Subject: Basketball—Fiction

A Name For Himself
CCB-B - v21 - Ja '68 - p87
EJ - v56 - N '67 - p1222
KR - v35 - Mr 1 '67 - p280
LJ - v92 - Jl '67 - p2660

A Spy Case Built For Two
CCB-B - v22 - Je '69 - p166
KR - v37 - F 15 '69 - p187
LJ - v94 - My 15 '69 - p2124
PW - v195 - Ap 7 '69 - p56
Subject: Intelligence service—Fiction

The Spy Who Talked Too Much
BS - v28 - Je 1 '68 - p115
CSM - v60 - My 2 '68 - pB9
KR - v36 - Ja 15 '68 - p59
Subject: Intelligence service—Fiction

Valerie Valentine Is Missing
KR - v39 - S 1 '71 - p955
LJ - v96 - D 15 '71 - p4199
PW - v200 - S 20 '71 - p49
Subject: Mystery and detective stories

Walk In A Tall Shadow
BW - v2 - D 3 '68 - p18
CLW - v41 - F '70 - p390
KR - v36 - O 1 '68 - p1122
NYTBR - v73 - N 24 '68 - p42

When Love Speaks
NYTBR - F 4 '62 - p26

WALDORF, Mary

Thousand Camps
BL - v78 - Je 15 '82 - p1371
CBRS - v10 - Jl '82 - p130
PW - v221 - Je 11 '82 - p62
SLJ - v28 - Ap '82 - p77
Subject: California—Fiction; Indians of North America—Fiction; Space and time—Fiction

WALDRON, Ann 1924-
ConAu 7NR, SmATA 16, WhoAm 76

The Luckie Star
BL - v73 - Jl 1 '77 - p1656
CCB-B - v31 - O '77 - p39
CLW - v49 - F '78 - p313
KR - v45 - Ap 15 '77 - p428
SLJ - v24 - S '77 - p138
Subject: Buried treasure—Fiction

WALKER, Barbara J

The Picture Life Of Jimmy Carter
BL - v73 - My 15 '77 - p1423
SLJ - v23 - My '77 - p57
Subject: Biography; Presidents

WALKER, Nona

The Medicine Makers
BS - v26 - Jl 1 '66 - p143
SB - v2 - S '66 - p139
Subject: Drugs

WALKER, Robert
WhoAm 86

New York Inside Out
AB - v74 - O 29 '84 - p2997
BL - v81 - D 15 '84 - p551
Subject: Photography; New York (City)

WALKER, Sloan

The One And Only Crazy Car Book
KR - v41 - D 1 '73 - p1314
LJ - v99 - Ap 15 '74 - p1216
Subject: Automobiles

WALLACE, Barbara Brooks 1922-
BioIn 9, ConAu 11NR, IntAu&W 77, SmATA 4, WhoAmW 81, WrDr 86

Hawkins And The Soccer Solution
BL - v77 - My 15 '81 - p1258
CCB-B - v34 - Jl '81 - p221
SLJ - v27 - My '81 - p87
Subject: Soccer—Fiction

WALLACE, Bill
SmATA 47

A Dog Named Kitty
Kliatt - v18 - Spring '84 - p144
Subject: Dogs—Fiction

Trapped In Death Cave
BL - v80 - Je 15 '84 - p1488
CBRS - v12 - Ap '84 - p98
Kliatt - v19 - Fall '85 - p18
SLJ - v30 - My '84 - p102
Subject: Buried treasure—Fiction; Mystery and detective stories

WALLACE, Daisy
see Cuyler, Margery Stuyvesant

WALLACE, Lew 1827-1905
BioIn 7, –12, ConAu 120, DcAmDH, DcLEL, JBA 34, McGEWB, NotNAT B, WebAB, –79

Ben-Hur
BW - v6 - S 17 '72 - p15
BW - v6 - D 3 '72 - p20
CR - v221 - O '72 - p216
KR - v40 - Jl 1 '72 - p730

WALLACH, Theresa

Easy Motorcycle Riding
LJ - v96 - My 1 '71 - p294
LJ - v96 - My 15 '71 - p1825
Subject: Motorcycles

WALLENSTEIN, Barry

Roller Coaster Kid And Other Poems
BL - v78 - Je 1 '82 - p1305
CBRS - v10 - My '82 - p100
KR - v50 - Ap 1 '82 - p421
SLJ - v29 - S '82 - p130
VOYA - v5 - Ag '82 - p49
Subject: American poetry

WALLER, Leslie 1923-
AuBYP SUP, BioIn 6, ConAu 2NR, SmATA 20, WrDr 86

New Sound
BL - v65 - Jl 15 '69 - p1272
CCB-B - v22 - Jl '69 - p184
KR - v37 - Ap 15 '69 - p455
LJ - v94 - Mr 15 '69 - p1345
NS - v79 - F 13 '70 - p226
Obs - Mr 8 '70 - p30
SR - v52 - My 10 '69 - p60
TLS - Mr 12 '70 - p287

Overdrive
B&B - v14 - Ag '69 - p48
KR - v35 - O 15 '67 - p1284
LJ - v92 - N 15 '67 - p4257
NS - v77 - My 16 '69 - p699
NYTBR - v72 - N 5 '67 - p16

WALSH, Jill Paton 1937-
AuBYP SUP, ChlLR 2, ConAu X, ConLC 35, FourBJA, OxChL, SmATA 4, TwCChW 83
Pseud./variant:
Paton Walsh, Gillian

Fireweed
B&B - v15 - F '70 - p36
BL - v66 - Je 1 '70 - p1218
BL - v67 - Ap 1 '71 - p661
BW - v4 - My 17 '70 - p3
CCB-B - v24 - N '70 - p51
Comw - v92 - My 22 '70 - p248
CSM - v62 - My 7 '70 - pB6
Emerg Lib - v11 - N '83 - p20
HB - v46 - Je '70 - p283
KR - v38 - Mr 15 '70 - p330
LJ - v95 - My 15 '70 - p1912
LJ - v95 - My 15 '70 - p1957
NYTBR - Jl 5 '70 - p14
NYTBR, Pt. 2 - N 8 '70 - p34
PW - v197 - My 18 '70 - p38
Sch Lib - v32 - Je '84 - p107
SR - v53 - My 9 '70 - p69
Subject: London—Fiction

Unleaving
B&B - v21 - Je '76 - p48

WALSH, Jill Paton (continued)
BL - v72 - Je 1 '76 - p1401
BL - v72 - Je 1 '76 - p1410
BW - My 2 '76 - pL3
BW - D 12 '76 - pH4
CCB-B - v30 - D '76 - p67
Comw - v103 - N 19 '76 - p763
CSM - v68 - Jl 1 '76 - p23
Emerg Lib - v9 - Ja '82 - p19
GP - v15 - S '76 - p2938
GW - v114 - My 2 '76 - p23
HB - v52 - Ag '76 - p408
JB - v40 - O '76 - p292
Kliatt - v12 - Winter '78 - p11
KR - v44 - My 15 '76 - p601
NO - v15 - Ag 21 '76 - p17
NYTBR - Ag 8 '76 - p18
NYTBR - N 14 '76 - p52
PW - v209 - Ap 5 '76 - p102
SLJ - v22 - My '76 - p35
SLJ - v22 - My '76 - p74
TLS - Ap 2 '76 - p375
Subject: England—Fiction

WALTERS, Hugh (pseud.) 1910-
AuBYP, ConAu X, ConSFA, ScFSB, SmATA X, TwCSFW 86, WrDr 86
Real Name:
Hughes, Walter Llewellyn

The Mohole Menace
CLW - v41 - D '69 - p260
CSM - v61 - My 1 '69 - pB5
KR - v36 - Ag 15 '68 - p909
LJ - v94 - F 15 '69 - p889

WAMPLER, Jan

All Their Own: People And The Places They Build
BL - v73 - Jl 1 '77 - p1618
HE - v38 - Mr 4 '78 - p812
Kliatt - v12 - Fall '78 - p52
Nat - v224 - Ap 2 '77 - p408
SA - v236 - Je '77 - p136
TLS - D 23 '77 - p1494
WCRB - v4 - My '78 - p52
Subject: House construction

WARD, Don

New York Yankees
SLJ - v29 - Mr '83 - p170
Subject: Baseball

Super Bowl XVII
BL - v80 - Jl '84 - p1553
BL - v81 - Je 15 '85 - p1453
Subject: Football

WARD, Herman 1914-
ConAu 18NR, DrAS 82E

Poems For Pleasure
BS - v23 - Jl 15 '63 - p148
HB - v39 - O '63 - p522
LJ - v88 - S 15 '63 - p3371
NYTBR - Ag 4 '63 - p24
Subject: American poetry; English poetry

WARNER, Lucille Schulberg
ConAu 11NR, SmATA 30

From Slave To Abolitionist
BL - v73 - D 15 '76 - p612
BS - v37 - Ap '77 - p31
CCB-B - v30 - Ap '77 - p134
CE - v54 - Ja '78 - p142
HB - v53 - Ap '77 - p174
KR - v44 - S 15 '76 - p1049
LA - v54 - Ap '77 - p444
RT - v31 - Mr '78 - p709
SLJ - v23 - Ja '77 - p106
Subject: Blacks—History; Slavery

WARNER, Matt
see Fichter, George Siebert

WARREN, Fred
AuBYP SUP

The Music Of Africa
BL - v67 - Mr 1 '71 - p563
KR - v38 - D 1 '70 - p1299
LJ - v96 - F 15 '71 - p729
Subject: Music

WARREN, Mary Phraner 1929-

Walk In My Moccasins
CCB-B - v21 - D '67 - p68
LJ - v92 - Ja 15 '67 - p340

WARTSKI, Maureen Crane 1940-
SmATA 37
Pseud./variant:
Crane, M A

The Lake Is On Fire
CBRS - v10 - Winter '82 - p60
Inter BC - v13 - #4 '82 p10
Kliatt - v17 - Spring '83 - p13
PW - v220 - D 18 '81 - p71
SLJ - v28 - N '81 - p112
VOYA - v5 - Je '82 - p37
Subject: Blind—Fiction; Forests—Fiction

A Long Way From Home
CBRS - v9 - Winter '81 - p50

WARTSKI, Maureen Crane (continued)
CCB-B - v34 - My '81 - p183
Kliatt - v16 - Spring '82 - p18
Subject: Vietnamese Americans—Fiction

My Brother Is Special
CCB-B - v33 - N '79 - p62
CE - v57 - Mr '81 - p208
Inter BC - v13 - #4 '82 p11
Kliatt - v15 - Spring '81 - p16
Subject: Family life—Fiction; Mentally handicapped—Fiction; Special Olympics—Fiction

WARWICK, Dolores
ConAu X
Pseud./variant:
Frese, Dolores Warwick

Learn To Say Goodbye
BL - v68 - F 1 '72 - p464
Comw - v95 - N 19 '71 - p188
KR - v39 - S 15 '71 - p1023
LJ - v97 - F 15 '72 - p788
PW - v200 - S 20 '71 - p49
Subject: Orphans—Fiction

WATERS, John F 1930-
AuBYP SUP, ConAu 37R, IntAu&W 86, SmATA 4, WhoE 77, WrDr 86

What Does An Oceanographer Do?
BL - v66 - Je 1 '70 - p1218
CCB-B - v24 - N '70 - p51
KR - v38 - F 1 '70 - p109
SB - v6 - S '70 - p126
SR - v53 - Ap 18 '70 - p37
Subject: Occupations; Oceanography as a profession

WATKINS, William Jon 1942-
ConAu 41R, DrAP&F 85, ScFSB, TwCSFW 86, WrDr 86

A Fair Advantage
BL - v72 - F 15 '76 - p851
KR - v43 - D 15 '75 - p1384
SLJ - v22 - Ap '76 - p79
Subject: Wrestling—Fiction

WATSON, Sally 1924-
AuBYP SUP, BioIn 9, ConAu 3NR, FourBJA, IntAu&W 82, SmATA 3

Jade
BS - v28 - Mr 1 '69 - p491
BW - v3 - Jl 6 '69 - p10
CCB-B - v22 - Ap '69 - p135
CSM - v61 - My 1 '69 - pB6
HB - v45 - Ap '69 - p181
LJ - v94 - F 15 '69 - p889
SR - v52 - F 22 '69 - p47
Subject: Pirates—Fiction

WATTS, K G O
see Razzell, Arthur G (co-author)

WAYNE, Bennett

Adventure In Buckskin
Hi Lo - v1 - My '80 - p4
LJ - v98 - S 15 '73 - p2659
Subject: West (U.S.)

Big League Pitchers And Catchers
Hi Lo - Je '80 - p4
LJ - v99 - S 15 '74 - p2281
Subject: Baseball

The Founding Fathers
SLJ - v22 - N '75 - p68
Subject: Biography

Four Women Of Courage
Hi Lo - v1 - My '80 - p4
Subject: Biography

Indian Patriots Of The Eastern Woodlands
J Read - v20 - My '77 - p732
SLJ - v23 - N '76 - p64
Subject: Indians of North America—Biography

The Super Showmen
SLJ - v21 - Mr '75 - p102
Subject: Entertainers

Three Jazz Greats
BL - v74 - Ap 15 '78 - p1330
LJ - v98 - O 15 '73 - p3151
M Ed J - v60 - Ja '74 - p94
Subject: Musicians

Women Who Dared To Be Different
BL - v72 - My 1 '76 - p1247
LJ - v98 - S 15 '73 - p2659
Subject: Biography

Women With A Cause
BL - v72 - D 15 '75 - p583
SLJ - v22 - D '75 - p56
Subject: Biography

WEAVER, John L 1949-
ConAu 112, SmATA 42

Grizzly Bears
ASBYP - v16 - Spring '83 - p58
BL - v79 - Ja 1 '83 - p622
CCB-B - v36 - Mr '83 - p138
SB - v19 - Mr '84 - p218

WEAVER, John L (continued)
SLJ - v29 - F '83 - p85
Subject: Bears

WEAVER, Robert G 1920-
DrAP&F 85, DrAS 82E, IlsBYP

Nice Guy, Go Home
CCB-B - v22 - S '68 - p19
KR - v36 - F 1 '68 - p125
LJ - v93 - Ap 15 '68 - p1818
NYTBR - v73 - Ap 28 '68 - p30
Subject: Amish—Fiction

WEBER, Bruce 1942-
ConAu 21NR

All-Pro Basketball Stars
SLJ - v25 - My '79 - p84
Subject: Basketball—Biography

Magic Johnson/Larry Bird
BL - v82 - Ap 1 '86 - p1147
Kliatt - v20 - Spring '86 - p56
Subject: Basketball—Biography

WEBER, Judith Eichler

I Dedicate This Song To You
SLJ - v32 - Ag '86 - p108
Subject: Love—Fiction

WEBSTER, Joanne

Gypsy Gift
BS - v42 - N '82 - p328
CCB-B - v36 - N '82 - p58
PW - v221 - Je 18 '82 - p74
SLJ - v28 - Ap '82 - p86
Subject: Extrasensory perception—Fiction; Gypsies—Fiction

The Love Genie
BL - v77 - F 15 '81 - p813
CBRS - v9 - Mr '81 - p70
CCB-B - v34 - Ap '81 - p163
SLJ - v27 - F '81 - p78
TES - O 9 '81 - p29
Subject: Wishes—Fiction

WEEKS, Doug

Carlos: With My Own Hands
Hi Lo - v3 - S '81 - p5

Melanie: Proving Myself
CSM - v73 - D 1 '80 - pB11
Hi Lo - v3 - S '81 - p5

Paul: But What Suits Me?
Hi Lo - v3 - S '81 - p5

WEEKS, Morris, Jr.

Hello, Puerto Rico
BL - v69 - Ja 15 '73 - p479
Inter BC - v14 - #1 '83 p16
KR - v40 - Ap 1 '72 - p415
LJ - v97 - F 15 '72 - p781
LJ - v97 - Je 15 '72 - p2244
Subject: Puerto Rico

WEINBERG, Larry
SmATA X
Pseud./variant:
Weinberg, Lawrence

Dangerous Run
BL - v78 - My 15 '82 - p1237
Hi Lo - v3 - My '82 - p3
Kliatt - v16 - Spring '82 - p6
SLJ - v28 - My '82 - p76
VOYA - v5 - Ag '82 - p38
Subject: Fathers and sons—Fiction; Motor-truck drivers—Fiction

The Hooded Avengers
B Rpt - v2 - N '83 - p37
Kliatt - v17 - Spring '83 - p13
SLJ - v29 - My '83 - p94
VOYA - v6 - O '83 - p209

Shooting For The Stars
Hi Lo - v3 - My '82 - p3
Kliatt - v16 - Spring '82 - p6
SLJ - v29 - S '82 - p130
VOYA - v5 - Ag '82 - p38

WEINGARDEN, M

First Payday
Hi Lo - v2 - S '80 - p6

WEIR, LaVada
ConAu 9NR, SmATA 2, WrDr 86

Breaking Point
LJ - v99 - N 15 '74 - p3059
Subject: Schools—Fiction

Chaotic Kitchen
LJ - v99 - N 15 '74 - p3059
Subject: Cookery—Fiction

Edge Of Fear
LJ - v99 - N 15 '74 - p3059
Subject: Camping—Fiction

The Horse Flambeau
LJ - v99 - N 15 '74 - p3059
Subject: Horses—Fiction

Men!
CCB-B - v28 - F '75 - p100

WEIR, LaVada (continued)
LJ - v99 - N 15 '74 - p3059
Subject: Tennis—Fiction

The Roller Skating Book
Hi Lo - v1 - Ap '80 - p4
SLJ - v26 - Ag '80 - p72
Subject: Roller skating

Skateboards And Skateboarding
BL - v73 - Je 15 '77 - p1578
BW - Ap 10 '77 - pE10
EJ - v66 - N '77 - p81
KR - v45 - Ap 1 '77 - p357
PW - v211 - My 2 '77 - p70
SLJ - v24 - S '77 - p128
SR - v5 - N 26 '77 - p42
Teacher - v95 - O '77 - p167
Subject: Skateboarding

WEIS, Margaret
see Baldwin, Margaret

WEISS, Ann E 1943-
ConAu 11NR, SmATA 30

Save The Mustangs!
BL - v70 - Mr 15 '74 - p825
BL - v81 - Jl '85 - p1568
BW - My 19 '74 - p3
KR - v42 - F 15 '74 - p190
PW - v205 - My 20 '74 - p64
Subject: Mustang

WEISS, David
AuBYP SUP

The Great Fire Of London
BL - v65 - Ap 15 '69 - p951
BS - v28 - Ja 1 '69 - p423
CSM - v60 - N 7 '68 - pB12
LJ - v94 - F 15 '69 - p889
Subject: London

WEISS, Harvey 1922-
AuBYP, BioIn 5, ChILR 4, ConAu 6NR, IlsCB 1946, -1957, -1967, SmATA 27, ThrBJA, WhoAmA 84

Collage And Construction
BL - v66 - My 15 '70 - p1163
CCB-B - v24 - N '70 - p52
Comw - v92 - My 22 '70 - p253
HB - v46 - O '70 - p493
KR - v38 - Mr 1 '70 - p248
LJ - v95 - Je 15 '70 - p2310
NYTBR - Ag 23 '70 - p20
PW - v197 - Je 15 '70 - p66
SR - v53 - My 9 '70 - p46
Subject: Collage; Sculpture

Motors And Engines And How They Work
BL - v65 - Jl 15 '69 - p1277
CCB-B - v23 - Mr '70 - p122
CE - v46 - F '70 - p267
CSM - v61 - My 1 '69 - pB8
KR - v37 - My 15 '69 - p573
LJ - v94 - O 15 '69 - p3825
LJ - v94 - D 15 '69 - p4583
NYTBR - Jl 27 '69 - p18
SA - v221 - D '69 - p146
SB - v5 - My '69 - p68
TLS - Jl 5 '74 - p725
Subject: Engines; Power (Mechanical)

Sailing Small Boats
BL - v64 - F 15 '68 - p703
LJ - v93 - Ja 15 '68 - p311
NYTBR - v73 - Ap 7 '68 - p26
SB - v4 - My '68 - p59
Yacht - v123 - My '68 - p88
Subject: Sailing

WEITZ, Lawrence Joel
see Scharffenberger, Ann (co-author)

WELLS, H G 1866-1946
ConAu 110, DcLB 34, OxChL, OxEng 85, ScFSB, SmATA 20, SupFW, TwCSFW 86, WhoTwCL, WorAl

The Time Machine. The War Of The Worlds
Choice - v14 - Jl '77 - p686
WLB - v52 - D '77 - p307
Subject: Science fiction; Space and time—Fiction

WELLS, Robert 1913-
AuBYP, ScFSB

What Does A Test Pilot Do?
KR - v37 - D 1 '69 - p1274
SB - v5 - Mr '70 - p343
Subject: Aeronautics as a profession; Airplanes; Occupations

WELLS, Rosemary 1943-
ConAu 85, FourBJA, IlsBYP, IlsCB 1967, SmATA 18, -1AS, TwCChW 83, WrDr 86

None Of The Above
BL - v71 - S 15 '74 - p94
BS - v34 - F 15 '75 - p519
BW - N 10 '74 - p8
CCB-B - v28 - Ap '75 - p139
Comw - v101 - N 22 '74 - p194

WELLS, Rosemary (continued)
EJ - v65 - Ja '76 - p98
KR - v42 - O 1 '74 - p1067
KR - v43 - Ja 1 '75 - p12
LJ - v99 - N 15 '74 - p3059
LJ - v99 - D 15 '74 - p3248
NYTBR - N 24 '74 - p8
PW - v206 - Ag 5 '74 - p58
SLJ - v29 - N '82 - p34

WENZEL, Celeste Piano

The Crazy Custom Car Book
Hi Lo - v4 - N '82 - p4
Subject: Automobiles

WERNER, Herma 1926-
ConAu 15NR, SmATA 47
Pseud./variant:
Cowen, Eve

The Dragster
BL - v75 - Ap 15 '79 - p1290
Hi Lo - v1 - D '79 - p5
Subject: Automobile racing—Fiction

Rosina Torres, LPN
BL - v80 - Ja 15 '84 - p719
Co-author: Piniat, John
Subject: Nursing—Fiction

see also Cowen, Eve; Piniat, John for additional titles

WERSBA, Barbara 1932-
ChlLR 3, ConAu 16NR, ConLC 30, DcLB 52, OxChL, SmATA 1, -2AS, ThrBJA, TwCChW 83, WrDr 86

Crazy Vanilla
BL - v83 - N 1 '86 - p403
KR - v54 - N 1 '86 - p1652
PW - v230 - D 26 '86 - p57
SLJ - v33 - N '86 - p109
VOYA - v9 - D '86 - p223
Subject: Family problems—Fiction; Friendship—Fiction

The Dream Watcher
B&B - v14 - Ag '69 - p48
BL - v65 - N 1 '68 - p304
B Rpt - v1 - Mr '83 - p25
BW - v2 - N 3 '68 - p18
HB - v44 - O '68 - p567
KR - v36 - S 1 '68 - p988
LJ - v93 - S 15 '68 - p3328
LJ - v96 - Ja 15 '71 - p283
NS - v78 - O 31 '69 - p623
NYTBR - v73 - N 3 '68 - p2
NYTBR, Pt. 2 - N 5 '72 - p42
Obs - Ag 3 '69 - p25
RT - v34 - Ap '81 - p795
SR - v51 - N 9 '68 - p69
Teacher - v86 - Ap '69 - p184
TLS - Je 26 '69 - p686
Subject: Adolescence—Fiction

Run Softly, Go Fast
BL - v67 - Ap 1 '71 - p655
CCB-B - v24 - F '71 - p100
Comw - v93 - N 20 '70 - p202
EJ - v60 - Ap '71 - p530
EJ - v63 - My '74 - p90
HB - v46 - D '70 - p624
J Read - v22 - N '78 - p130
KR - v38 - O 15 '70 - p1164
LJ - v96 - F 15 '71 - p738
NYTBR - N 22 '70 - p38
SLJ - v29 - N '82 - p34
TN - v27 - Ap '71 - p309
Subject: Fathers and sons—Fiction; Youth—Fiction

WEST, Aille X

Trucks At The Track: And Seven More Exciting Stories Of Wheels And Cycles
BL - v77 - Je 15 '81 - p1342
Subject: Automobile racing

WEST, Nick

The Mystery Of The Coughing Dragon
LJ - v95 - D 15 '70 - p4374
Subject: Mystery and detective stories

The Mystery Of The Nervous Lion
LJ - v96 - D 15 '71 - p4198
Subject: Mystery and detective stories

WESTALL, Robert 1929-
BioIn 13, ConAu 18NR, ConLC 17, FifBJA, IntAu&W 82, OxChL, SmATA 23, -2AS, TwCChW 83, WrDr 86

The Scarecrows
Brit Bk N C - Autumn '81 - p27
Brit Bk N C - D '86 - p3
BS - v41 - Ja '82 - p404
CBRS - v10 - S '81 - p10
CCB-B - v35 - S '81 - p19
GP - v20 - My '81 - p3883
HB - v57 - O '81 - p546
JB - v45 - Ag '81 - p164
KR - v49 - S 15 '81 - p1166
NS - v102 - D 4 '81 - p20

WESTALL, Robert (continued)
NYTBR - v87 - My 16 '82 - p29
Obs - Mr 1 '81 - p33
Punch - v281 - Ag 5 '81 - p235
PW - v220 - S 18 '81 - p155
Sch Lib - v29 - Je '81 - p157
SLJ - v27 - Ag '81 - p80
TES - My 8 '81 - p27
TES - My 27 '83 - p29
TLS - Mr 27 '81 - p339
VOYA - v4 - D '81 - p34
Subject: Horror stories; Remarriage—Fiction; Stepfathers—Fiction

WESTMAN, Paul 1956-
ConAu 106, IntAu&W 86, SmATA 39

Andrew Young: Champion Of The Poor
SLJ - v30 - N '83 - p76
Subject: Biography; Civil rights; Legislators

Billy Graham: Reaching Out To The World
BL - v78 - Ap 15 '82 - p1099
Subject: Biography; Evangelists

Frank Borman: To The Moon And Back
BL - v78 - Ap 15 '82 - p1099
SLJ - v28 - Ap '82 - p77
Subject: Astronauts; Biography

Jacques Cousteau: Free Flight Undersea
BL - v77 - S 15 '80 - p125
SLJ - v27 - N '80 - p74
Subject: Biography; Oceanographers

Jesse Jackson: I Am Somebody
BL - v77 - Mr 15 '81 - p1035
Bl Bks B - v7 - #3 '81 p65
CCB-B - v34 - My '81 - p184
KR - v49 - Mr 1 '81 - p286
SLJ - v28 - N '81 - p99
Subject: Biography; Civil rights

John Glenn: Around The World In 90 Minutes
SLJ - v26 - Ja '80 - p69
Subject: Astronauts; Biography

John Young: Space Shuttle Commander
BL - v78 - Mr 1 '82 - p901
SLJ - v28 - Ap '82 - p77
Subject: Astronauts; Biography

Thor Heyerdahl: Across The Seas Of Time
BL - v79 - N 1 '82 - p374
Hi Lo - v4 - F '83 - p3
SLJ - v29 - Mr '83 - p185
SLJ - v30 - N '83 - p39
Subject: Biography; Explorers

WHEELER, W H

Counterfeit!
SLJ - v26 - D '79 - p98
Subject: Counterfeits and counterfeiting—Fiction

WHIPPLE, Dorothy Vermilya 1900-

Is The Grass Greener?: Answers To Questions About Drugs
BL - v68 - N 1 '71 - p243
BL - v68 - Ap 1 '72 - p665
KR - v39 - Ap 1 '71 - p384
LJ - v96 - Jl '71 - p2291
NYTBR, Pt. 2 - My 2 '71 - p32
SB - v7 - Mr '72 - p321
TN - v28 - Ap '72 - p314
Subject: Drug abuse

WHITE, E B 1899-1985
ChlLR 1, ConAu 116, –16NR, ConLC 10, –39, DcLB 11, –22, MorBMP, MorJA, PiP, SmATA 29, –44N, TwCChW 83, WhoChL
Pseud./variant:
White, Elwyn Brooks

The Trumpet Of The Swan
Am - v123 - D 5 '70 - p496
Atl - v226 - S '70 - p123
BL - v67 - S 1 '70 - p59
BW - v4 - My 17 '70 - p4
CCB-B - v24 - O '70 - p35
Comw - v93 - N 20 '70 - p201
CSM - v62 - Jl 25 '70 - p13
HB - v46 - Ag '70 - p391
Inst - v80 - Ag '70 - p173
KR - v38 - Ap 15 '70 - p455
LJ - v95 - Jl '70 - p2537
LJ - v95 - D 15 '70 - p4327
NO - v9 - Ag 10 '70 - p21
NS - v80 - N 6 '70 - p611
NY - v46 - D 5 '70 - p217
NYRB - v15 - D 17 '70 - p10
NYTBR - Je 28 '70 - p4
NYTBR - D 6 '70 - p58
NYTBR, Pt. 2 - N 8 '70 - p38
Par - v45 - O '70 - p20
PW - v197 - Ap 20 '70 - p62
Spec - v225 - D 5 '70 - pR19
SR - v53 - Je 27 '70 - p39

WHITE, E B (continued)
Teacher - v91 - My '74 - p81
Time - v96 - D 21 '70 - p68
TLS - D 11 '70 - p1458
WSJ - v176 - Jl 14 '70 - p16
Subject: Fantasy; Trumpeter swan—Fiction

WHITE, Florence Meiman 1910-
ConAu 41R, IntAu&W 77, SmATA 14

Cesar Chavez: Man Of Courage
LJ - v98 - N 15 '73 - p3460
Teacher - v91 - S '73 - p143
Subject: Biography; Mexican Americans

Escape! The Life Of Harry Houdini
CCB-B - v32 - Jl '79 - p204
Hi Lo - v1 - S '79 - p6
KR - v47 - My 1 '79 - p521
Subject: Biography; Magicians

Malcolm X: Black And Proud
SLJ - v22 - N '75 - p84
Subject: Biography; Little, Malcolm

WHITE, Robb 1909-
AuBYP, BioIn 3, ChlLR 3, ConAu 1NR, JBA 51, SmATA 1, -1AS, WhoAm 86

Deathwatch
BL - v68 - Jl 15 '72 - p1000
BS - v32 - Je 15 '72 - p152
EJ - v61 - N '72 - p1260
HB - v48 - O '72 - p475
KR - v40 - Mr 15 '72 - p336
LJ - v97 - Je 15 '72 - p2245
NYTBR - Je 4 '72 - p28
NYTBR, Pt. 2 - My 7 '72 - p4
NYTBR, Pt. 2 - N 5 '72 - p26
PW - v201 - My 15 '72 - p54
TN - v29 - Ap '73 - p258
Subject: Adventure and adventurers—Fiction; Deserts—Fiction

The Frogmen
BS - v33 - Je 15 '73 - p146
CE - v50 - N '73 - p98
KR - v41 - My 1 '73 - p522
LJ - v98 - N 15 '73 - p3471
NYTBR - S 16 '73 - p12
Subject: World War, 1939-1945—Fiction

The Long Way Down
B&B - v6 - Je '78 - p5
BL - v74 - O 15 '77 - p370
BS - v37 - Mr '78 - p400
CCB-B - v31 - My '78 - p150
KR - v45 - D 1 '77 - p1271
SLJ - v24 - N '77 - p77
Subject: Aerialists—Fiction; Circus—Fiction

No Man's Land
BS - v29 - D 1 '69 - p355
KR - v37 - O 15 '69 - p1124
LJ - v95 - Ja 15 '70 - p258
NY - v45 - D 13 '69 - p203
Subject: Adventure and adventurers—Fiction; Islands—Fiction

Up Periscope
Atl - v198 - D '56 - p104
BL - v53 - N 1 '56 - p122
HB - v32 - O '56 - p363
KR - v24 - Je 15 '56 - p406
LJ - v81 - O 15 '56 - p2473
NYTBR - S 23 '56 - p32
SR - v39 - N 17 '56 - p71
Subject: Submarines—Fiction

WHITE, Wallace 1930-

One Dark Night
BL - v76 - O 15 '79 - p347
B Rpt - v2 - S '83 - p26
CBRS - v8 - O '79 - p20
Hi Lo - v1 - F '80 - p5
SLJ - v26 - O '79 - p162
Subject: Alcohol and youth—Fiction; Uncles—Fiction

WHITEFORD, Andrew Hunter 1913-
AmM&WS 76P, ConAu 45, FifIDA, WhoAm 84

North American Indian Arts
BL - v68 - S 15 '71 - p101
CSM - v63 - Jl 10 '71 - p15
LJ - v96 - O 15 '71 - p3480
PW - v198 - D 7 '70 - p51
SA - v225 - D '71 - p109
WLB - v46 - S '71 - p83
Subject: Indians of North America

WHITEHEAD, Robert J
see Bamman, Henry A (co-author)

WHITELEY, Opal

Opal
BW - v15 - Je 16 '85 - p10
CSM - v68 - O 4 '76 - p23
Kliatt - v12 - Winter '78 - p25
KR - v44 - Ag 1 '76 - p900
LJ - v101 - O 15 '76 - p2168

WHITELEY, Opal (continued)
NYTBR - N 21 '76 - p61
PS - v59 - Fall '85 - p112
PW - v210 - Jl 12 '76 - p66

WHITNEY, David C 1921-
ConAu 5NR, SmATA 48, WhoAm 86, WhoWor 78

First Book Of Facts And How To Find Them
BL - v63 - Ja 1 '67 - p492
CCB-B - v20 - D '66 - p64
CE - v44 - N '67 - p190
CSM - v58 - N 3 '66 - pB8
LJ - v91 - O 15 '66 - p5242
NYTBR - v71 - N 6 '66 - p54
SR - v49 - N 12 '66 - p49
Subject: Reference books

WHITNEY, Phyllis A 1903-
AuBYP, AuNews 2, BioIn 12, ConAu 3NR, JBA 51, SmATA 30, TwCChW 83, TwCCr&M 85, WhoAm 86, WrDr 86

Hunter's Green
BL - v64 - Jl 1 '68 - p1221
BS - v28 - My 1 '68 - p61
KR - v36 - F 15 '68 - p213
KR - v36 - Mr 1 '68 - p279
LJ - v93 - Je 1 '68 - p2262
LJ - v93 - Jl '68 - p2740
PW - v193 - Ja 29 '68 - p92
TN - v25 - N '68 - p1

Mystery Of The Haunted Pool
BL - v57 - F 15 '61 - p368
CSM - N 23 '60 - p11
HB - v37 - F '61 - p52
KR - v28 - Jl 15 '60 - p560
LJ - v85 - S 15 '60 - p3227
NYTBR - F 19 '61 - p40
SR - v44 - Je 24 '61 - p20
Subject: Mystery and detective stories

Secret Of The Emerald Star
CCB-B - v18 - Mr '65 - p112
HB - v41 - F '65 - p54
Kliatt - v13 - Spring '79 - p15
Subject: Mystery and detective stories

Secret Of The Tiger's Eye
Inter BC - v15 - #7 '84 p20
Kliatt - v13 - Winter '79 - p17
Subject: Mystery and detective stories

Step To The Music
KR - v21 - O 15 '53 - p699
LJ - v78 - N 15 '53 - p2047
NYTBR - D 27 '53 - p14
SR - v36 - N 14 '53 - p70

WIBBERLEY, Leonard 1915-1983
AuBYP, BioIn 13, ChILR 3, ConAu 3NR, MorJA, OxChL, SmATA 45, TwCChW 83, TwCCr&M 85, TwCSFW 86, WrDr 86
Pseud./variant:
O'Connor, Patrick

Flint's Island
B&B - v19 - O '73 - p120
BL - v68 - Jl 1 '72 - p943
BW - v6 - My 7 '72 - p13
CCB-B - v26 - O '72 - p34
CSM - v64 - My 4 '72 - pB5
HB - v48 - O '72 - p471
KR - v40 - Mr 15 '72 - p336
LJ - v97 - My 15 '72 - p1918
NYTBR - N 26 '72 - p8
TLS - S 28 '73 - p1117
Subject: Buried treasure—Fiction; Pirates—Fiction

Meeting With A Great Beast
B&B - v18 - Mr '73 - p75
BL - v68 - D 15 '71 - p354
BL - v68 - Mr 1 '72 - p562
BS - v31 - N 15 '71 - p385
BW - v6 - Mr 12 '72 - p7
KR - v39 - S 1 '71 - p967
LJ - v96 - N 1 '71 - p3641
LJ - v96 - D 15 '71 - p4206
NYTBR - D 19 '71 - p20
PW - v200 - S 27 '71 - p64
TLS - O 10 '72 - p1375
Subject: Animals—Fiction

Perilous Gold
BL - v74 - Jl 15 '78 - p1729
KR - v46 - Ag 1 '78 - p812
PW - v213 - Je 19 '78 - p100
SLJ - v25 - S '78 - p166
Subject: Buried treasure—Fiction; Fathers and sons—Fiction; Submarines—Fiction

Sea Captain From Salem
BL - v57 - Jl 1 '61 - p674
CSM - My 11 '61 - p5B
HB - v37 - Ag '61 - p349
KR - v29 - F 1 '61 - p112
LJ - v86 - My 15 '61 - p1998

WIBBERLEY, Leonard (continued)
NYTBR, Pt. 2 - My 14 '61 - p18
Subject: United States—History—Revolution, 1775-1783—Fiction

see also O'Connor, Patrick for additional titles

WIDDER, Arthur 1928-
ConAu 5R

Adventures In Black
NYTBR - D 16 '62 - p25
Subject: Spies

WIENER, Joan
see Rosenberg, Sharon (co-author)

WIER, Ester 1910-
AuBYP, BioIn 6, ConAu 9R, DcLB 52, SmATA 3, ThrBJA, TwCChW 83, WrDr 86

The Loner
Am - v108 - Je 1 '63 - p806
Comw - v78 - My 24 '63 - p256
CSM - My 9 '63 - p4B
HB - v39 - Ag '63 - p392
HB - v60 - Ag '84 - p499
LJ - v88 - My 15 '63 - p2154
NYTBR, Pt. 2 - My 12 '63 - p2
Obs - Ap 10 '66 - p20
SR - v46 - Je 22 '63 - p47
TCR - v68 - F '67 - p451
TLS - My 19 '66 - p431

The Winners
CCB-B - v22 - O '68 - p36
KR - v36 - Ap 1 '68 - p404
LJ - v93 - Je 15 '68 - p2549

WIGHT, James Alfred
see Herriot, James

WILBUR, Richard 1921-
AuBYP SUP, ConAu 2BS, ConLC 3, -6, -9, IntAu&W 86, PlP&P, SmATA 9, WhoTwCL, WrDr 86

Opposites
BL - v70 - Mr 15 '74 - p828
BW - v7 - F 18 '73 - p15
BW - v7 - S 9 '73 - p8
CCB-B - v26 - Jl '73 - p180
Choice - v12 - N '75 - p1134
CSM - v66 - D 5 '73 - pB12
HB - v49 - Ag '73 - p388
HR - v26 - Fall '73 - p588
NY - v49 - D 3 '73 - p214
NYTBR - Jl 1 '73 - p8
NYTBR - N 4 '73 - p57
PW - v203 - Je 25 '73 - p73
SLJ - v25 - N '78 - p31
Teacher - v91 - D '73 - p73
TN - v30 - Ja '74 - p206

WILCOX, Collin 1924-
ConAu 21R, ScF&FL 1, WhoAm 86, WrDr 86

The Watcher
BL - v74 - Ap 15 '78 - p1327
KR - v46 - Ja 1 '78 - p21
LJ - v103 - Mr 1 '78 - p589
New R - v179 - N 4 '78 - p53
PW - v213 - Ja 2 '78 - p62
Subject: Adventure and adventurers—Fiction

WILCOX, Tamara
ConAu 19NR

Bats, Cats, And Sacred Cows
SLJ - v24 - My '78 - p63
Subject: Animals

Mysterious Detectives: Psychics
SLJ - v25 - S '78 - p128
Subject: Crime and criminals; Parapsychology

WILDER, Edna

Once Upon An Eskimo Time
Kliatt - v21 - Spring '87 - p40
Subject: Eskimos

WILDER, Laura Ingalls 1867-1957
AmWomWr, AuBYP, ChlLR 2, ConAu 111, DcLB 22, JBA 51, OxChL, SmATA 29, TwCChW 83, WhoChL

The First Four Years
B&B - v19 - O '73 - p137
BL - v67 - Ap 15 '71 - p705
CCB-B - v24 - My '71 - p147
CE - v48 - O '71 - p34
CSM - v63 - My 6 '71 - pB2
HB - v47 - Je '71 - p289
Inst - v130 - Je '71 - p74
Inst - v82 - N '72 - p136
KR - v39 - Ja 15 '71 - p58
Life - v71 - Jl 2 '71 - p12
LJ - v96 - My 15 '71 - p1818
NO - v10 - Mr 15 '71 - p19
NYRB - v18 - Ap 20 '72 - p13
NYTBR - Mr 28 '71 - p28
PW - v199 - Mr 22 '71 - p53
SR - v54 - Mr 20 '71 - p31
Teacher - v90 - Ja '73 - p90
Time - v97 - Mr 15 '71 - p92

WILDER, Laura Ingalls (continued)
TLS - S 28 '73 - p1116
Subject: Frontier and pioneer life—Fiction; South Dakota—Fiction

The Little House Books
NYRB - v18 - Ap 20 '72 - p13
NYTBR, Pt. 2 - F 13 '72 - p12
Subject: Family life—Fiction; Frontier and pioneer life—Fiction

Little House In The Big Woods
LJ - v98 - O 15 '73 - p3163
SE - v50 - Ap '86 - p263
WCRB - v10 - Ja '84 - p19
Subject: Family life—Fiction; Frontier and pioneer life—Fiction

WILFORD, John Noble 1933-
AuBYP SUP, ConAu 15NR, IntAu&W 86, WhoAm 86, WhoE 85

We Reach The Moon
B&B - v15 - O '69 - p62
BL - v66 - Mr 15 '70 - p874
BL - v66 - Mr 15 '70 - p930
BL - v70 - S 15 '73 - p127
BS - v29 - Ja 1 '70 - p391
BW - v3 - Ag 10 '69 - p13
CCB-B - v24 - Jl '70 - p187
LJ - v95 - Ja 15 '70 - p170
LJ - v95 - Ap 15 '70 - p1649
LJ - v98 - S 15 '73 - p2669
NYTBR - v74 - D 21 '69 - p12
SB - v6 - My '70 - p67
SR - v52 - O 25 '69 - p33
SR - v53 - My 9 '70 - p47
S & T - v39 - Mr '70 - p184
S & T - v39 - Ap '70 - p248
TN - v28 - Ap '72 - p292
TN - v28 - Ap '72 - p302
Subject: Project Apollo; Space flight

WILKINSON, Frederick

Arms And Armor
BL - v81 - Ja 1 '85 - p640
BL - v82 - Je 15 '86 - p1537
SLJ - v31 - My '85 - p97
Subject: Arms and armor

WILLETT, John

The Singer In The Stone
BL - v77 - Je 15 '81 - p1348
CBRS - v9 - Je '81 - p100
CCB-B - v35 - S '81 - p19
KR - v49 - My 15 '81 - p636
SLJ - v28 - S '81 - p132
Subject: Fantasy; Space and time—Fiction

WILLIAM, Kate

Double Love
BL - v80 - O 15 '83 - p351
CCB-B - v37 - Ja '84 - p99
SLJ - v30 - Ja '84 - p90
Subject: Love—Fiction

WILLIAMS, Brian

Aircraft
BB - v5 - Ap '77 - p3
BL - v78 - Ap 15 '82 - p1091
SB - v19 - S '83 - p35
SLJ - v29 - N '82 - p92
Subject: Aeronautics

WILLIAMS, Gurney, III 1941-
ConAu 69

Ghosts And Poltergeists
BL - v76 - O 1 '79 - p282
Subject: Ghosts; Poltergeists

WILLIAMS, Jay 1914-1978
ChILR 8, ConAu 2NR, CurBio 78, -78N, FourBJA, SmATA 41, TwCChW 83, TwCCr&M 85

The Horn Of Roland
KR - v36 - O 1 '68 - p1120
NYTBR - v73 - N 3 '68 - p46

Life In The Middle Ages
Am - v115 - N 5 '66 - p556
B&B - v13 - D '67 - p44
BL - v63 - Ja 1 '67 - p492
BS - v26 - O 1 '66 - p252
CC - v83 - D 7 '66 - p1509
CCB-B - v21 - N '67 - p51
CLW - v38 - Ja '67 - p339
Comw - v85 - N 11 '66 - p178
CSM - v58 - N 3 '66 - pB9
HB - v43 - F '67 - p86
KR - v34 - S 15 '66 - p988
LJ - v91 - O 15 '66 - p5257
NS - v74 - N 3 '67 - p604
NY - v42 - D 17 '66 - p240
NYTBR - v71 - N 6 '66 - p39
Obs - D 3 '67 - p26
PW - v190 - O 17 '66 - p63
TCR - v68 - N '66 - p184
TLS - N 30 '67 - p1159
Subject: Middle ages

WILLIAMSON, Amy

Star Light Star Bright
BL - v79 - N 15 '82 - p438
Subject: Schools—Fiction

WILSON, Holly
AuBYP, MichAu 80

Snowbound In Hidden Valley
NYTBR - My 26 '57 - p26

WILSON, Joyce Muriel
see Stranger, Joyce

WILSON, Lionel 1924-
ConAu 105, SmATA 33

Attack Of The Killer Grizzly
SLJ - v27 - Ja '81 - p57
Subject: Bears

WILSON, Mitchell A 1913-1973
BioIn 5, -6, -9, ConAu 3NR, DcLEL 1940, IntAu&W 77, NewYTBE 73, OxAmL 83

Seesaws To Cosmic Rays: A First View Of Physics
BL - v64 - O 15 '67 - p276
CCB-B - v20 - Jl '67 - p178
CLW - v39 - Ja '68 - p375
Inst - v77 - O '67 - p175
KR - v35 - My 15 '67 - p613
LJ - v92 - Jl '67 - p2661
NYTBR, Pt. 2 - v72 - My 7 '67 - p43
PW - v191 - Je 5 '67 - p177
SB - v3 - S '67 - p108
SR - v50 - My 13 '67 - p58
Subject: Physics

WILSON, Pat

Young Sportsman's Guide To Water Safety
LJ - v92 - Ja 15 '67 - p352
Subject: Sports

WILSON, Tom 1931-
ConAu 106, SmATA 33, WhoAm 86

Encore! Encore!
Kliatt - v14 - Winter '80 - p73
Subject: Wit and humor

This Book Is For The Birds
Kliatt - v14 - Spring '80 - p59
Subject: Wit and humor

WINDSOR, Patricia 1938-
ConAu 19NR, FifBJA, SmATA 30, WhoAmW 83, WrDr 86
Pseud./variant:
Daniel, Colin

Killing Time
BL - v77 - O 1 '80 - p206
CBRS - v9 - N '80 - p30
CCB-B - v34 - Ja '81 - p103
KR - v48 - D 15 '80 - p1575
PW - v218 - N 21 '80 - p59
SLJ - v27 - D '80 - p74
VOYA - v4 - Je '81 - p53
VOYA - v6 - Ag '83 - p158
VOYA - v6 - O '83 - p234
Subject: City and town life—Fiction

The Summer Before
BL - v69 - Jl 1 '73 - p1019
BS - v33 - Je 15 '73 - p147
CCB-B - v27 - S '73 - p20
Comw - v99 - N 23 '73 - p216
EJ - v64 - Ja '75 - p112
KR - v41 - My 15 '73 - p569
PW - v203 - Je 18 '73 - p70
TLS - D 5 '75 - p1455
Subject: Death—Fiction; Emotional problems—Fiction

see also Daniel, Colin for additional titles

WINN, Janet
see Boehm, Bruce (co-author)

WINSLOW, Joan

Romance Is A Riot
B Rpt - v2 - Mr '84 - p38
BS - v43 - Ja '84 - p391
CCB-B - v37 - Ap '84 - p158
Kliatt - v19 - Fall '85 - p20
SLJ - v30 - Ja '84 - p90
VOYA - v6 - F '84 - p341
Subject: Family problems—Fiction

WINTHROP, Elizabeth 1948-
ConAu X, DrAP&F 85, FifBJA, SmATA 8
Pseud./variant:
Mahony, Elizabeth Winthrop

A Little Demonstration Of Affection
BB - v3 - Ag '75 - p4
BL - v71 - Ap 15 '75 - p869
BS - v35 - Jl '75 - p95
BW - Jl 13 '75 - p4
CCB-B - v28 - Jl '75 - p188
Kliatt - v11 - Spring '77 - p9
KR - v43 - Ap 1 '75 - p387
NYTBR - My 4 '75 - p30
PW - v207 - Je 16 '75 - p82

WINTHROP, Elizabeth (continued)
SLJ - v22 - S '75 - p128
SLJ - v22 - D '75 - p32
Subject: Brothers and sisters—Fiction

Marathon Miranda
EJ - v69 - F '80 - p69
LA - v57 - Ja '80 - p84
SLJ - v27 - My '81 - p27
Subject: Adoption—Fiction; Physically handicapped—Fiction; Running—Fiction

Miranda In The Middle
BL - v77 - S 15 '80 - p124
CBRS - v9 - S '80 - p10
CCB-B - v34 - Ja '81 - p103
HB - v56 - D '80 - p644
Kliatt - v17 - Winter '83 - p15
KR - v49 - Ja 15 '81 - p76
SLJ - v27 - N '80 - p81
Subject: Friendship—Fiction

WIRTHS, Claudine G

I Hate School: How To Hang In And When To Drop Out
KR - v54 - S 1 '86 - p1379
Co-author: Bowman-Kruhm, Mary
Subject: High school dropouts; Study (Method of)

WISE, Robert

Mystery Of Totem Pole Inlet
SLJ - v21 - My '75 - p69
Subject: Mystery and detective stories

WISEMAN, Ann Sayre 1926-
ConAu 9NR, SmATA 31
Pseud./variant:
Denzer, Ann Wiseman

Cuts Of Cloth
Kliatt - v13 - Spring '79 - p63
PW - v214 - O 30 '78 - p51
SLJ - v25 - F '79 - p60
Subject: Clothing and dress; Dressmaking; Sewing

WISEMAN, David 1916-
ConAu 109, FifBJA, IntAu&W 86, SmATA 43

Jeremy Visick
BL - v77 - Jl 1 '81 - p1397
BL - v81 - Je 1 '85 - p1408
CBRS - v10 - Jl '81 - p120
CCB-B - v35 - S '81 - p20
CE - v58 - Ja '82 - p182
CLW - v53 - S '81 - p94
Emerg Lib - v11 - Ja '84 - p22
HB - v57 - Ap '81 - p193
J Read - v25 - N '81 - p181
KR - v49 - Je 15 '81 - p741
PW - v219 - Mr 6 '81 - p95
SLJ - v27 - Ap '81 - p134
Subject: Cornwall—Fiction; Miners—Fiction; Space and time—Fiction

Thimbles
BL - v78 - Mr 15 '82 - p965
CCB-B - v35 - Jl '82 - p219
CLW - v54 - D '82 - p226
EJ - v71 - S '82 - p88
JB - v47 - O '83 - p215
KR - v50 - My 1 '82 - p556
LA - v60 - Mr '83 - p364
PW - v221 - Ja 22 '82 - p65
SLJ - v28 - Mr '82 - p153
TES - My 17 '85 - p25
Subject: England—Fiction; Space and time—Fiction

WISLER, G Clifton 1950-
SmATA 46, WrDr 86

Winter Of The Wolf
BL - v77 - D 1 '80 - p518
CBRS - v9 - F '81 - p59
HB - v57 - Ap '81 - p193
J Read - v25 - O '81 - p88
RT - v35 - O '81 - p113
SLJ - v27 - Ja '81 - p66
VOYA - v4 - D '81 - p35
Subject: Comanche Indians—Fiction; Frontier and pioneer life—Fiction; Wolves—Fiction

WITHERIDGE, Elizabeth
AuBYP SUP, ConAu 97, IntAu&W 82

And What Of You, Josephine Charlotte?
BW - v3 - S 7 '69 - p16
CLW - v41 - D '69 - p261
Comw - v90 - My 23 '69 - p298
KR - v37 - Mr 15 '69 - p317
NYTBR - Ap 6 '69 - p18
PW - v195 - My 5 '69 - p52
RR - v28 - Jl '69 - p700
Subject: Slavery

WITHERS, Carl A 1900-1970
AuBYP, ConAu 73, SmATA 14

The American Riddle Book
NYTBR - S 19 '54 - p26
Subject: Riddles

WITTY, Ken

A Day In The Life Of An Illustrator
BL - v77 - My 1 '81 - p1198
SLJ - v28 - N '81 - p96
Subject: Artists; Illustrators; Occupations

see also Witty, Margot (co-author) for additional titles

WITTY, Margot

A Day In The Life Of A Meteorologist
BL - v77 - My 1 '81 - p1198
SLJ - v28 - N '81 - p96
Co-author: Witty, Ken
Subject: Occupations; Weather

see also Witty, Ken for additional titles

WOHL, Gary
see Chodes, John (co-author); Edwards, Audrey Marie (co-author)

WOJCIECHOWSKA, Maia 1927-
ChlLR 1, ConAu 4NR, ConLC 26, MorBMP, OxChL, PiP, SmATA 28, -1AS, TwCChW 83, WrDr 86

Don't Play Dead Before You Have To
CCB-B - v24 - Ja '71 - p83
CE - v47 - D '70 - p160
EJ - v60 - F '71 - p277
KR - v38 - My 15 '70 - p560
LJ - v95 - Je 15 '70 - p2316
NYTBR - Ag 16 '70 - p22
SR - v53 - N 14 '70 - p77
Subject: Youth—Fiction

A Kingdom In A Horse
Am - v113 - N 20 '65 - p640
BS - v25 - D 1 '65 - p360
CCB-B - v19 - Ap '66 - p140
CLW - v37 - Mr '66 - p478
CSM - v57 - N 4 '65 - pB11
Inst - v75 - F '66 - p160
Inst - v82 - N '72 - p136
KR - v33 - O 1 '65 - p1046
LJ - v90 - D 15 '65 - p5533
NYTBR - v70 - N 7 '65 - p20
Teacher - v90 - Ap '73 - p90

Shadow Of A Bull
HB - v40 - Je '64 - p293
LJ - v89 - Mr 15 '64 - p1470
NW - v65 - Mr 15 '65 - p102
NY - v40 - D 5 '64 - p224
NYTBR - Mr 22 '64 - p22
NYTBR, Pt. 2 - N 5 '72 - p42
Par - v40 - N '65 - p153
SLJ - v31 - Ag '85 - p28
SR - v47 - Ap 25 '64 - p40
SR - v48 - Mr 27 '65 - p32
TCR - v68 - O '66 - p90

A Single Light
BL - v64 - Jl 1 '68 - p1236
BW - v2 - My 5 '68 - p22
CCB-B - v21 - Jl '68 - p183
HB - v44 - Je '68 - p331
Inst - v78 - O '68 - p158
Inter BC - v11 - Ja 10 '80 - p22
KR - v36 - Mr 15 '68 - p344
LJ - v93 - Jl '68 - p2738
NYTBR - v73 - My 5 '68 - p3
NYTBR, Pt. 2 - F 13 '72 - p14
PW - v193 - Mr 25 '68 - p49
PW - v199 - Je 7 '71 - p58
SR - v51 - My 11 '68 - p42

Tuned Out
BS - v28 - N 1 '68 - p326
CCB-B - v22 - F '69 - p104
CSM - v60 - N 7 '68 - pB12
EJ - v58 - My '69 - p779
J Read - v22 - N '78 - p127
KR - v36 - O 1 '68 - p1123
LJ - v94 - Ja 15 '69 - p316
NYTBR - v73 - N 24 '68 - p42
NYTBR, Pt. 2 - F 15 '70 - p22
PW - v196 - Jl 28 '69 - p59
SR - v51 - N 9 '68 - p70
SR - v52 - Jl 19 '69 - p42
Subject: Drug abuse—Fiction

WOLFF, Craig Thomas

Wayne Gretzky: Portrait Of A Hockey Player
BL - v79 - Jl '83 - p1405
Kliatt - v17 - Spring '83 - p51
SLJ - v29 - My '83 - p96
Subject: Hockey—Biography

WOLFSON, Victor 1910-
BioIn 1, ConAu 33R, NotNAT, WhoWorJ 78

The Man Who Cared: A Life Of Harry S. Truman
BS - v26 - Je 1 '66 - p103
KR - v34 - Ja 15 '66 - p61

WOLFSON, Victor (continued)
LJ - v92 - F 15 '67 - p900
NYTBR - v71 - My 8 '66 - p22
Subject: Biography

WOLITZER, Hilma 1930-
BioIn 11, ConAu 18NR, ConLC 17, DrAP&F 85, FifBJA, SmATA 31, WhoAm 86, WrDr 86

Out Of Love
BW - v10 - Mr 2 '80 - p13
J Read - v25 - My '82 - p778
Kliatt - v14 - Winter '80 - p15
PW - v215 - Je 18 '79 - p94
Subject: Divorce—Fiction

WOLKOFF, Judie
see Murphy, Barbara Beasley (co-author)

WOOD, Dorothy
see Wood, Frances (co-author)

WOOD, Frances
ConAu 107, SmATA 34

Forests Are For People: The Heritage Of Our National Forests
BL - v67 - Ap 15 '71 - p699
BS - v31 - Ap 15 '71 - p47
KR - v38 - Ja '71 - p64
SB - v7 - My '71 - p82
Co-author: Wood, Dorothy
Subject: Forests

WOOD, James Playsted 1905-
AuBYP, ConAu 3NR, FourBJA, IntAu&W 82, SmATA 1, WhAm 8, WhoAm 82, WrDr 84

This Is Advertising
BS - v28 - N 1 '68 - p326
Subject: Advertising

WOOD, Nancy 1936-
ConAu 9NR, MacBEP, SmATA 6

Hollering Sun
BL - v68 - Jl 1 '72 - p943
BL - v69 - O 15 '72 - p178
BS - v32 - N 15 '72 - p396
CCB-B - v26 - Ja '73 - p84
CE - v49 - N '72 - p88
KR - v40 - Ap 1 '72 - p415
KR - v40 - D 15 '72 - p1426
LJ - v97 - S 15 '72 - p2957
LJ - v97 - D 15 '72 - p4058
NYTBR - Ag 13 '72 - p8
PW - v202 - Jl 31 '72 - p70
SE - v37 - D '73 - p789
Subject: Taos Indians

WOOD, Paul W 1922-
ConAu 61

Stained Glass Crafting
BL - v64 - Je 15 '68 - p1166
B Rpt - v2 - Ja '84 - p40
Kliatt - v18 - Winter '84 - p75
LJ - v93 - F 15 '68 - p892
Subject: Glass painting and staining

WOOD, Phyllis Anderson 1923-
AuBYP SUP, ConAu 14NR, IntAu&W 77, SmATA 33, WrDr 86

Andy
CCB-B - v25 - O '71 - p36
KR - v39 - Ja 15 '71 - p58
LJ - v96 - F 15 '71 - p738
PW - v199 - Mr 15 '71 - p73
Subject: Youth—Fiction

A Five-Color Buick And A Blue-Eyed Cat
CLW - v47 - D '75 - p235
Kliatt - v11 - Fall '77 - p9
KR - v43 - Ap 15 '75 - p467
SLJ - v21 - Ja '75 - p58
Subject: Pets—Fiction

Get A Little Lost, Tia
BL - v75 - S 15 '78 - p181
CBRS - v7 - F '79 - p70
Hi Lo - v1 - S '79 - p5
SLJ - v25 - Ja '79 - p63
Subject: Brothers and sisters—Fiction

I Think This Is Where We Came In
BL - v72 - Je 1 '76 - p1410
Cur R - v16 - D '77 - p360
Kliatt - v12 - Winter '78 - p12
KR - v44 - Ap 1 '76 - p407
SLJ - v22 - Mr '76 - p119
Subject: Camping—Fiction; Dogs—Fiction; Friendship—Fiction

Meet Me In The Park, Angie
CBRS - v12 - Ap '84 - p99
SLJ - v30 - Mr '84 - p177
VOYA - v7 - Je '84 - p100
Subject: Marriage—Fiction

Pass Me A Pine Cone
BL - v78 - Ag '82 - p1520
B Rpt - v1 - Mr '83 - p40
Hi Lo - v4 - Ja '83 - p2

WOOD, Phyllis Anderson (continued)
SLJ - v29 - N '82 - p104
Subject: Moving (Household)—Fiction; Schools—Fiction; Sierra Nevada Mountains—Fiction

Song Of The Shaggy Canary
BL - v70 - My 15 '74 - p1060
CCB-B - v28 - Ja '75 - p88
CLW - v47 - N '75 - p166
KR - v42 - Mr 15 '74 - p310
LJ - v99 - Ap 15 '74 - p1234

This Time Count Me In
BL - v77 - O 15 '80 - p323
CCB-B - v34 - Ap '81 - p164
Hi Lo - v2 - Mr '81 - p4
SLJ - v27 - F '81 - p79
VOYA - v5 - Ap '82 - p58
Subject: Friendship—Fiction; Schools—Fiction

Win Me And You Lose
Hi Lo - v2 - N '80 - p6
Subject: Crime and criminals—Fiction; Divorce—Fiction; Fathers and sons—Fiction

WOODFORD, Peggy 1937-
ConAu 104, SmATA 25, WrDr 86

Please Don't Go
A Lib - v5 - O '74 - p493
BL - v69 - Je 1 '73 - p951
BW - v7 - My 13 '73 - p5
HB - v49 - Je '73 - p277
KR - v41 - F 15 '73 - p196
Obs - N 26 '72 - p37
Spec - v229 - N 11 '72 - p748
TES - Je 6 '86 - p53
TLS - D 8 '72 - p1497
Subject: France—Fiction

WOODRUFF, Marian

Forbidden Love
SLJ - v30 - N '83 - p88
VOYA - v6 - O '83 - p211
Subject: Love—Fiction

It Must Be Magic
BL - v79 - Ap 1 '83 - p1039
SLJ - v29 - F '83 - p93
VOYA - v6 - Ap '83 - p43
Subject: Schools—Fiction

Kiss Me, Creep
RT - v39 - O '85 - p48
SLJ - v31 - Ja '85 - p89
Subject: Love—Fiction

WOODS, Geraldine
see Woods, Harold (co-author)

WOODS, Harold 1945-
ConAu 97, SmATA 42

Bill Cosby: Making America Laugh And Learn
BL - v80 - N 1 '83 - p422
SLJ - v30 - N '83 - p76
Co-author: Woods, Geraldine
Subject: Blacks—Biography; Comedians

The Book Of The Unknown
ASBYP - v16 - Spring '83 - p58
Cur R - v23 - F '84 - p60
SB - v18 - Mr '83 - p207
SLJ - v29 - Mr '83 - p186
Co-author: Woods, Geraldine
Subject: Curiosities and wonders

WOOLFOLK, Dorothy

Abbey Is Missing
BL - v80 - Mr 1 '84 - p965
SLJ - v30 - F '84 - p86
Subject: Mystery and detective stories

WORMSER, Richard 1908-
ConSFA, IntMPA 78

The Black Mustanger
A Lib - v3 - Ap '72 - p421
Am - v125 - D 4 '71 - p490
BL - v67 - Jl 15 '71 - p956
BL - v68 - Ap 1 '72 - p670
CCB-B - v25 - D '71 - p68
KR - v39 - Ap 1 '71 - p369
LJ - v96 - Je 15 '71 - p2134
PW - v199 - Ap 26 '71 - p60
TN - v28 - Ja '72 - p205
Subject: Horses—Fiction; West (U.S.)—Fiction

WORTHLEY, Jean Reese 1925-
ConAu 77

The Complete Family Nature Guide
CSM - v68 - Je 21 '76 - p18
LJ - v101 - Ap 15 '76 - p1035
SB - v13 - My '77 - p40
Subject: Natural history

WORTIS, Avi
see Avi

WOSMEK, Frances 1917-
ConAu 11NR, SmATA 29, WrDr 84

Never Mind Murder
BL - v74 - N 1 '77 - p471
KR - v45 - D 1 '77 - p1272
SLJ - v24 - D '77 - p62
Subject: Mystery and detective stories

WRIGHT, Bob

The Falling Star Mystery
SLJ - v30 - N '83 - p86
Subject: Mystery and detective stories

The Gold Coin Robbery
SLJ - v30 - N '83 - p86
Subject: Mystery and detective stories

The Mummy's Crown
SLJ - v30 - N '83 - p86
Subject: Mystery and detective stories

The Red Hot Rod
SLJ - v30 - N '83 - p86
Subject: Mystery and detective stories

The Secret Staircase
SLJ - v30 - N '83 - p86
Subject: Mystery and detective stories

The Siamese Turtle Mystery
SLJ - v30 - N '83 - p86
Subject: Mystery and detective stories

The Silver Buckle Mystery
SLJ - v30 - N '83 - p86
Subject: Mystery and detective stories

The Tree House Mystery
SLJ - v30 - N '83 - p86
Subject: Mystery and detective stories

The Video Game Spy
SLJ - v30 - N '83 - p86
Subject: Mystery and detective stories

WRIGHT, Elinor Bruce
see Lyon, Elinor

WRIGHT, Enid Meadowcroft
see Meadowcroft, Enid LaMonte

WRIGHTSON, Patricia 1921-
AuBYP, ChlLR 4, ConAu 19NR, FourBJA, OxChL, SmATA 8, -4AS, TwCChW 83, WrDr 86

A Racecourse For Andy
BL - v64 - My 1 '68 - p1049
BL - v65 - Ap 1 '69 - p902
BW - v2 - My 5 '68 - p2
BW - v2 - My 5 '68 - p3
CCB-B - v21 - Je '68 - p167
HB - v44 - Je '68 - p326
HB - v56 - Ap '80 - p196
KR - v36 - F 15 '68 - p184
LJ - v93 - Ap 15 '68 - p1806
SMQ - v8 - Fall '79 - p27
SR - v51 - My 11 '68 - p40
TN - v25 - Ja '69 - p206
Subject: Australia—Fiction; Mentally handicapped—Fiction

WULFFSON, Don L 1943-
ConAu 19NR, SmATA 32

Incredible True Adventures
BL - v82 - My 15 '86 - p1389
CCB-B - v40 - N '86 - p60
SLJ - v33 - O '86 - p184
Subject: Adventure and adventurers

WUNSCH, Josephine Mclean 1914-
AuBYP, BioIn 8, ConAu 1R, MichAu 80, WhoMW 84, WrDr 86

Free As A Bird
BL - v80 - Je 15 '84 - p1474
VOYA - v7 - O '84 - p201
Subject: Love—Fiction

Girl In The Rough
B&B - My '83 - p31
Hi Lo - v3 - Ja '82 - p4
SLJ - v28 - Mr '82 - p154
VOYA - v4 - F '82 - p39

WUORIO, Eva-Lis 1918-
AuBYP SUP, ConAu 77, SmATA 34, ThrBJA

Save Alice!
BL - v65 - Ja 15 '69 - p548
CCB-B - v22 - F '69 - p104
CSM - v60 - N 7 '68 - pB14
KR - v36 - N 1 '68 - p1228
LJ - v94 - F 15 '69 - p890
PW - v194 - O 14 '68 - p65

WYKEHAM, Nicholas

Farm Machines
ACSB - v13 - Spring '80 - p49

WYKEHAM, Nicholas (continued)
SB - v16 - S '80 - p34
Subject: Agriculture; Machinery

WYLER, Rose 1909-
AuBYP, BkP, ConAu 93, SmATA 18, ThrBJA
Pseud./variant:
Ames, Rose Wyler

The First Book Of Science Experiments
BL - v67 - My 1 '71 - p752
SB - v7 - My '71 - p16
Subject: Science

WYNDHAM, Lee (pseud.) 1912-1978
AuBYP, ConAu X, IntAu&W 82, MorJA, SmATA X, TwCChW 78, WrDr 76
Real Name:
Hyndman, Jane Andrews Lee

Candy Stripers
BL - v55 - Ja 1 '59 - p244
KR - v26 - Ag 15 '58 - p610
LJ - v83 - D 15 '58 - p3581
Subject: Hospitals—Fiction; Volunteer workers—Fiction

WYSS, Johann David 1743-1818
AuBYP SUP, BioIn 1, -3, OxChL, OxGer, SmATA 29, Str&VC, WhoChL

The Swiss Family Robinson
BS - v31 - F 15 '72 - p524
NYTBR - D 21 '13 - p756
TES - D 2 '83 - p25
TLS - D 11 '70 - p1446

Y

YADIN, Yigael 1917-
ConAu 9R, CurBio 66, WhoWor 78

The Story Of Masada
AJA - v71 - Jl '67 - p324
Atl - v219 - Ja '67 - p121
BL - v63 - D 1 '66 - p407
BS - v26 - N 1 '66 - p292
BS - v29 - My 1 '69 - p59
BW - v3 - Jl 13 '69 - p16
Choice - v4 - Ap '67 - p205
Econ - v221 - D 3 '66 - p1037
HT - v17 - Ja '67 - p64
KR - v37 - Ap 1 '69 - p384
Lis - v77 - Ja 12 '67 - p66
LJ - v91 - D 1 '66 - p5965
LJ - v92 - Ja 15 '67 - p361
NS - v72 - D 2 '66 - p832
NYTBR - v71 - D 4 '66 - p56
NYTBR - Jl 13 '69 - p26
Obs - S 11 '66 - p27
PW - v190 - S 19 '66 - p71
PW - v195 - Mr 24 '69 - p55
SR - v49 - N 26 '66 - p39
Time - v88 - D 9 '66 - p120
TLS - D 8 '66 - p1154
WSJ - v47 - Ja 27 '67 - p6
Subject: Archaeology

YATES, Brock
see Garlits, Don (co-author)

YATES, Elizabeth 1905-
Au&ICB, AuBYP, ConAu 21NR, JBA 51, MorBMP, OxChL, SmATA 4, TwCChW 83, WrDr 86

Skeezer: Dog With A Mission
CCB-B - v27 - Ja '74 - p88
PW - v205 - Ja 28 '74 - p301
Subject: Child psychotherapy; Dogs

YEP, Laurence Michael 1948-
ChlLR 3, ConAu 1NR, ConLC 35, DcLB 52, FifBJA, SmATA 7, TwCChW 83, TwCSFW 86, WhoAm 86, WrDr 86

Child Of The Owl
BB - v5 - S '77 - p4
BL - v73 - Ap 1 '77 - p1173
BL - v81 - F 1 '85 - p793
BS - v37 - Jl '77 - p128
BW - My 1 '77 - pE1
BW - D 11 '77 - pE4
CCB-B - v30 - Ap '77 - p135
CE - v54 - O '77 - p30
CLW - v49 - N '77 - p189
Comw - v104 - N 11 '77 - p731
CSM - v69 - My 4 '77 - pB2
Cur R - v16 - Ag '77 - p206
EJ - v67 - F '78 - p100
HB - v53 - Ag '77 - p447
Inst - v86 - My '77 - p119
KR - v45 - F 1 '77 - p99
LA - v54 - O '77 - p809
Ms - v9 - Ag '80 - p92
New R - v177 - D 3 '77 - p28
NYTBR - My 22 '77 - p29
NYTBR - N 13 '77 - p50
PW - v211 - F 28 '77 - p123
SE - v41 - O '77 - p531
SLJ - v23 - Ap '77 - p73
SLJ - v23 - My '77 - p36
TN - v38 - Winter '82 - p116
Subject: Chinese Americans—Fiction; Grandmothers—Fiction

Dragon Of The Lost Sea
BL - v79 - O 1 '82 - p250
BS - v42 - D '82 - p368
BW - v13 - Ja 9 '83 - p11
CCB-B - v36 - N '82 - p59
CE - v59 - My '83 - p356
J Read - v26 - Mr '83 - p565
KR - v50 - O 1 '82 - p1107
LA - v60 - My '83 - p650
SLJ - v29 - N '82 - p93
VOYA - v5 - F '83 - p47
Subject: Fantasy

Kind Hearts And Gentle Monsters
BL - v78 - Mr 1 '82 - p855
BS - v42 - Ag '82 - p207
CBRS - v10 - My '82 - p100
CCB-B - v35 - My '82 - p180
HB - v58 - Je '82 - p302
J Read - v26 - N '82 - p185
KR - v50 - Mr 1 '82 - p279
NYTBR - v87 - My 23 '82 - p37
RT - v37 - O '83 - p66

YEP, Laurence Michael (continued)
SLJ - v28 - Ap '82 - p86
VOYA - v5 - O '82 - p48
Subject: Friendship—Fiction

Liar, Liar
Emerg Lib - v13 - S '85 - p46
PW - v224 - S 16 '83 - p126
SLJ - v30 - N '83 - p99
VOYA - v7 - Ap '84 - p37
Subject: Crime and criminals—Fiction

The Mark Twain Murders
BL - v79 - S 1 '82 - p50
CBRS - v10 - Jl '82 - p130
CCB-B - v35 - Jl '82 - p220
CE - v59 - N '82 - p136
J Read - v26 - D '82 - p277
KR - v50 - Ap 15 '82 - p497
LA - v60 - Mr '83 - p361
PW - v221 - My 21 '82 - p76
SLJ - v28 - My '82 - p85
VOYA - v5 - O '82 - p46
Subject: California—Fiction; Mystery and detective stories

YERKOW, Charles 1912-
AuBYP SUP

Automobiles: How They Work
LJ - v92 - My 15 '67 - p2024
SB - v2 - D '66 - p225
Subject: Automobiles

YOLEN, Jane H 1939-
AuBYP, ChlLR 4, ConAu 11NR, DcLB 52, FourBJA, SmATA 40, -1AS, TwCChW 83, WhoAm 86, WrDr 86

Friend: The Story Of George Fox And The Quakers
BL - v68 - Ap 1 '72 - p663
BL - v68 - Ap 1 '72 - p680
BS - v32 - Ap 15 '72 - p47
CCB-B - v26 - O '72 - p35
CLW - v43 - My '72 - p535
CSM - v64 - My 4 '72 - pB5
KR - v40 - Ja 15 '72 - p77
LJ - v97 - Je 15 '72 - p2245
LJ - v97 - D 15 '72 - p4058
NYTBR - S 10 '72 - p8
Subject: Biography; Friends, Society of

The Gift Of Sarah Barker
BL - v77 - My 15 '81 - p1250
CBRS - v9 - Je '81 - p100
CCB-B - v35 - D '81 - p80
HB - v57 - Ag '81 - p439
J Read - v25 - D '81 - p287
KR - v49 - S 15 '81 - p1166
SLJ - v28 - O '81 - p154
Subject: Shakers—Fiction

YORK, Carol Beach 1928-
AuBYP SUP, ConAu 6NR, FifBJA, SmATA 6

Remember Me When I Am Dead
BL - v77 - S 15 '80 - p124
CBRS - v8 - Jl '80 - p130
CCB-B - v34 - O '80 - p43
Cur R - v21 - F '82 - p34
KR - v48 - Ag 1 '80 - p980
PW - v217 - Mr 21 '80 - p69
SLJ - v27 - O '80 - p165
Subject: Death—Fiction; Remarriage—Fiction; Sisters—Fiction

Revenge Of The Dolls
CLW - v51 - Ap '80 - p415
J Read - v23 - Ap '80 - p662
LA - v57 - Ja '80 - p84
SLJ - v27 - N '80 - p47
Subject: Mystery and detective stories

Takers And Returners: A Novel Of Suspense
CCB-B - v27 - N '73 - p55
KR - v41 - Ja 1 '73 - p9
LJ - v98 - Ap 15 '73 - p1392
Subject: Juvenile delinquency—Fiction

When Midnight Comes....
BL - v76 - N 15 '79 - p510
BS - v39 - Mr '80 - p467
CCB-B - v33 - Mr '80 - p144
KR - v48 - F 15 '80 - p217
SLJ - v26 - D '79 - p99
Subject: Cousins—Fiction; Supernatural—Fiction

YOUD, Samuel
see Christopher, John

YOUNG, Al 1939-
BlkAWP, ConAu 29R, ConNov 86, SelBAAu, WhoAm 78, WrDr 86

Snakes
B&B - v16 - Ag '71 - p34
BL - v67 - N 1 '70 - p215
BL - v67 - N 15 '70 - p265
BL - v67 - Ap 1 '71 - p655
Bl S - v12 - Mr '81 - p83
BW - v4 - My 17 '70 - p6
KR - v38 - F 15 '70 - p204

YOUNG, Al (continued)
KR - v38 - Mr 15 '70 - p335
LJ - v95 - Ap 15 '70 - p1505
NY - v46 - Jl 11 '70 - p77
NYTBR - My 17 '70 - p38
PW - v197 - F 9 '70 - p76
SR - v53 - Ag 22 '70 - p55
Time - v95 - Je 29 '70 - p76
TLS - Jl 30 '71 - p881
TN - v27 - Ap '71 - p309
Subject: Bands (Music)—Fiction; Drug abuse—Fiction

YOUNG, Jean

Woodstock Craftsman's Manual
BS - v32 - Jl 15 '72 - p191
CCB-B - v26 - O '72 - p36
Cr H - v32 - O '72 - p8
CSM - v64 - N 8 '72 - p8
Hob - v77 - O '72 - p158
Inst - v82 - Ag '72 - p176
LJ - v97 - Ag '72 - p2571
LJ - v97 - N 15 '72 - p3823
LJ - v97 - D 15 '72 - p4059
NYTBR - Jl 2 '72 - p8
PW - v201 - Je 12 '72 - p65
Subject: Handicraft

YOUNG, Mary

Singing Windows
NYTBR - Ap 22 '62 - p20
Subject: Glass painting and staining

YOUNG, Percy M 1912-
AuBYP, Baker 84, ConAu 13R, OxMus, SmATA 31

World Conductors
BL - v62 - Jl 15 '66 - p1085
HB - v42 - Je '66 - p326
KR - v34 - Ja 1 '66 - p14
LJ - v91 - My 15 '66 - p2715
Subject: Conductors (Music)

YOUNGBLOOD, Marilyn

Send In The Clowns
BL - v80 - F 1 '84 - p810
SLJ - v30 - Ap '84 - p129
VOYA - v7 - Je '84 - p92
Subject: Circus—Fiction; Love—Fiction

Snap Judgment
SLJ - v31 - S '84 - p138
Subject: Love—Fiction

Z

ZACH, Cheryl

Waiting For Amanda
SLJ - v31 - Ap '85 - p102
VOYA - v8 - Je '85 - p124

ZAGOREN, Ruby 1922-1974
AuBYP, ConAu P-1

Venture For Freedom: The True Story Of An African Yankee
BL - v65 - Jl 1 '69 - p1229
BW - v3 - Ag 3 '69 - p13
LJ - v95 - Jl '70 - p2537
NYTBR, Pt. 2 - My 4 '69 - p20
PW - v195 - My 19 '69 - p71
Subject: Slavery

ZANGER, Jack 1926?-1970
BioIn 8

Great Catchers Of The Major Leagues
CSM - v62 - My 7 '70 - p00B7
LJ - v95 - My 15 '70 - p1964
SR - v53 - Je 27 '70 - p38

ZARING, Jane 1936-
ConAu 108, SmATA 40

Sharkes In The North Woods: Or Nish Na Bosh Na Is Nicer Now
BL - v79 - Ja 15 '83 - p681
SLJ - v29 - S '82 - p131
Subject: Camping—Fiction; Crime and criminals—Fiction; Kidnapping—Fiction

ZIEMIAN, Joseph 1922-1971
ConAu 65

The Cigarette Sellers Of Three Crosses Square
BL - v72 - S 15 '75 - p170
CCB-B - v29 - Mr '76 - p120
EJ - v72 - Ja '83 - p26
Kliatt - v11 - Spring '77 - p22
LA - v54 - Ja '77 - p83
Obs - Je 21 '70 - p31
PW - v211 - My 2 '77 - p70
SLJ - v22 - N '75 - p95
Subject: World War, 1939-1945

ZIM, Herbert S 1909-
AuBYP, BkP, ChILR 2, ConAu 17NR, CurBio 56, JBA 51, SmATA 30, –2AS, WhoAm 86, WrDr 84

Life And Death
BL - v66 - Jl 1 '70 - p1343
BW - v4 - My 17 '70 - p30
CCB-B - v24 - O '70 - p36
CSM - v62 - My 7 '70 - pB1
KR - v38 - Ap 1 '70 - p388
LJ - v95 - S 15 '70 - p3056
NYTBR - Ap 26 '70 - p30
NYTBR, Pt. 2 - N 8 '70 - p38
PW - v197 - Ap 27 '70 - p79
SB - v6 - S '70 - p137
SR - v53 - Je 27 '70 - p39
Co-author: Zim, Sonia Bleeker
Subject: Death

Your Brain And How It Works
CCB-B - v26 - O '72 - p36
CLW - v44 - N '72 - p248
KR - v40 - Mr 15 '72 - p333
LJ - v97 - S 15 '72 - p2957
TLS - Je 15 '73 - p689
Subject: Brain

ZIM, Sonia Bleeker
see Zim, Herbert S (co-author)

ZINDEL, Paul 1936-
ChILR 3, ConAu 73, ConLC 6, –26, DcLB 7, –52, OxChL, SmATA 16, TwCChW 83, WhoAm 86

Confessions Of A Teenage Baboon
BS - v37 - F '78 - p368
BW - D 11 '77 - pE4
CCB-B - v31 - My '78 - p151
EJ - v67 - S '78 - p90
EJ - v68 - O '79 - p103
JB - v42 - Ag '78 - p214
J Read - v22 - F '79 - p477
Kliatt - v13 - Winter '79 - p17
KR - v45 - S 15 '77 - p996
PW - v212 - S 19 '77 - p146
SLJ - v24 - N '77 - p78
TES - Ag 4 '78 - p18

ZINDEL, Paul (continued)
TLS - Ap 7 '78 - p383
Subject: Social adjustment—Fiction

I Never Loved Your Mind
BS - v30 - Jl 1 '70 - p147
BS - v31 - Mr 1 '72 - p547
EJ - v59 - D '70 - p1305
KR - v38 - My 15 '70 - p560
LJ - v95 - Je 15 '70 - p2317
LJ - v96 - Ja 15 '71 - p283
NY - v46 - D 5 '70 - p218
NYRB - v15 - D 17 '70 - p10
NYTBR, Pt. 2 - My 24 '70 - p14
NYTBR, Pt. 2 - N 8 '70 - p34
Obs - Ap 4 '71 - p36
PW - v197 - Ap 13 '70 - p85
TLS - Ap 2 '71 - p385
TN - v30 - Ja '74 - p197
Subject: Dropouts—Fiction; Youth—Fiction

My Darling, My Hamburger
BS - v29 - D 1 '69 - p356
CCB-B - v24 - S '70 - p20
Comw - v91 - N 21 '69 - p257
EJ - v59 - D '70 - p1305
HB - v46 - Ap '70 - p171
KR - v37 - N 15 '69 - p1204
LJ - v94 - N 15 '69 - p4303
NYTBR - D 7 '69 - p68
NYTBR, Pt. 2 - N 9 '69 - p2
NYTBR, Pt. 2 - N 9 '69 - p60
NYTBR, Pt. 2 - N 7 '71 - p47
Obs - Ap 19 '70 - p29
PW - v196 - S 22 '69 - p85
PW - v199 - Je 7 '71 - p58
Sch Lib - v32 - S '84 - p208
SR - v54 - O 23 '71 - p87
TES - Jl 7 '78 - p30
TLS - Ap 16 '70 - p416
TN - v37 - Fall '80 - p65
Subject: Youth—Fiction

Pardon Me, You're Stepping On My Eyeball
BL - v73 - O 1 '76 - p246
BL - v73 - O 1 '76 - p258
BS - v36 - Mr '77 - p389
CCB-B - v30 - Ap '77 - p136
CLW - v50 - O '78 - p104
Comw - v103 - N 19 '76 - p763
CSM - v68 - N 3 '76 - p20
EJ - v66 - S '77 - p84
GP - v15 - Ja '77 - p3041
HB - v52 - O '76 - p505
JB - v41 - Je '77 - p188
KR - v446 - Ag 1 '76 - p849
NYT - v126 - D 21 '76 - p31
NYTBR - N 14 '76 - p29
NYTBR - N 14 '76 - p52
NYTBR - O 23 '77 - p51
Obs - N 28 '76 - p31
PW - v210 - Ag 9 '76 - p78
SLJ - v23 - O '76 - p121
TLS - D 10 '76 - p1549
Subject: Family life—Fiction

The Pigman
BL - v65 - Ja 1 '69 - p493
BS - v28 - N 1 '68 - p327
CCB-B - v22 - Ap '69 - p136
EJ - v61 - N '72 - p1163
EJ - v73 - Ja '84 - p85
HB - v45 - F '69 - p61
J Read - v22 - N '78 - p129
KR - v36 - O 1 '68 - p1123
LJ - v93 - N 15 '68 - p4425
NS - v77 - My 16 '69 - p698
NYTBR - v73 - N 3 '68 - p2
NYTBR, Pt. 2 - N 8 '70 - p30
NYTBR, Pt. 2 - F 13 '72 - p14
Obs - Jl 4 '76 - p19
PW - v194 - S 30 '68 - p61
SLJ - v28 - Ap '82 - p28
Spec - v222 - My 16 '69 - p657
SR - v52 - Ja 18 '69 - p41
TLS - Ap 3 '69 - p354
Subject: Elderly—Fiction; Social adjustment—Fiction

The Pigman's Legacy
BOT - v4 - F '81 - p79
BS - v40 - Ja '81 - p354
CCB-B - v34 - O '80 - p44
EJ - v70 - Ap '81 - p79
HB - v56 - O '80 - p531
JB - v45 - F '81 - p36
J Read - v24 - Ap '81 - p647
KR - v48 - S 15 '80 - p1237
NYTBR - v86 - Ja 25 '81 - p27
PW - v218 - O 10 '80 - p74
PW - v220 - O 30 '81 - p66
SLJ - v27 - O '80 - p160
TES - N 21 '80 - p32

The Undertaker's Gone Bananas
BL - v75 - S 1 '78 - p42
BW - v10 - F 24 '80 - p13
CCB-B - v32 - O '78 - p40
CLW - v55 - S '83 - p80
EJ - v69 - F '80 - p70
KR - v46 - S 15 '78 - p1022
PW - v213 - Je 26 '78 - p117
SLJ - v25 - O '78 - p160
SLJ - v27 - N '80 - p47

ZINDEL, Paul (continued)
WCRB - v4 - N '78 - p81
Subject: Crime and criminals—Fiction; Mystery and detective stories

see also Dragonwagon, Crescent (co-author) for additional titles

ZISTEL, Era
ConAu 19NR

Hi Fella
CLW - v49 - My '78 - p455
KR - v45 - Ag 15 '77 - p853
SLJ - v24 - S '77 - p139
Subject: Dogs—Fiction

ZIZMOR, Jonathan

Doctor Zizmor's Guide To Clearer Skin
CCB-B - v34 - Mr '81 - p143
KR - v48 - D 1 '80 - p1522
Co-author: English, Diane
Subject: Health

ZOLNA, Ed

Mastering Softball
BL - v77 - Jl 1 '81 - p1383
Kliatt - v15 - Fall '81 - p72
Co-author: Conklin, Mike
Subject: Baseball

TITLE INDEX

Title Index

Bigfoot - Thorne, Ian
Bigfoot: America's Number One Monster - Cohen, Daniel
Bigfoot: Man, Monster, Or Myth - Carmichael, Carrie
Biggest Machines - Kiley, Denise
Biggest Tongue Twister Book In The World - Brandreth, Gyles
Bike Tripping - Cuthbertson, Tom
Bikes: A How-To-Do-It Guide To Selection, Care, Repair, Maintenance, Decoration, Etc. - Henkel, Stephen C
Bill Cosby: Making America Laugh And Learn - Woods, Harold
Billy Graham: Reaching Out To The World - Westman, Paul
Billy Idol - Russell, Kate
The Biological Revolution: A Background Book On Making A New World - Jacker, Corinne
Bionics - Silverstein, Alvin
Birds Of North America - Fichter, George Siebert
The Birthday Murderer: A Mystery - Bennett, Jay
Bittersweet Sixteen - Bush, Nancy
Bizarre Crimes - Berger, Gilda
Bizarre Murders - Berger, Gilda
Black And Blue Magic - Snyder, Zilpha Keatley
Black Beach - Hiller, Doris
Black Cats And Other Superstitions - Blumenthal, Shirley
Black Cop: A Biography Of Tilmon O'Bryant - Friedman, Ina Rosen
Black Friday - Green, Carl R
Black Gold - Butterworth, W E
Black Heroes Of The American Revolution - Davis, Burke
The Black Is Beautiful Beauty Book - Miller, Melba
Black Magic At Brillstone - Heide, Florence Parry
The Black Mustanger - Wormser, Richard
Black Pearl - O'Dell, Scott
Black Pilgrimage - Feelings, Thomas
Black Pioneers Of Science And Invention - Haber, Louis
Black Soldier - Clarke, John
The Black Stallion - Farley, Walter
The Black Stone Knife - Marriott, Alice
Black Suits From Outer Space - DeWeese, Gene
The Black Tiger - O'Connor, Patrick
Black Tiger At Lemans - O'Connor, Patrick
Blacksmith At Blueridge - Bunting, Eve
Bless The Beasts And Children - Swarthout, Glendon Fred
Blimp - Cavallaro, Ann
Blind Date - Stine, R L
The Blind Guards Of Easter Island - Meyer, Miriam Weiss
Blind Outlaw - Rounds, Glen
Blind Sunday - Evans, Jessica
Blinded By The Light - Brancato, Robin Fidler
Blink Of The Mind - Francis, Dorothy Brenner
Blissful Joy And The SATs: A Multiple-Choice Romance - Greenwald, Sheila
The Blob - Thorne, Ian
The Blood Suckers - Schoder, Judith
The Bloody Country - Collier, James Lincoln
Blowfish Live In The Sea - Fox, Paula
Blubber - Blume, Judy
The Blue Man - Platt, Kin
Blue Willow - Gates, Doris
Bluegrass Iggy - Sullivan, Mary Wilson
Blues For Cassandra - Stewart, Jo
Blues For Silk Garcia - Tamar, Erika
Bobby Clarke - Dolan, Edward Francis, Jr.
Bobby Orr: Lightning On Ice - Liss, Howard
Bobby Orr-Number Four - Page, N H
The Bobby Orr Story - Devaney, John
Body In The Brillstone Garage - Heide, Florence Parry
Bodyworks: The Kids' Guide To Food And Physical Fitness - Bershad, Carol
Bola And The Oba's Drummers - Schatz, Letta
The Boll Weevil Express - Petersen, P J

Book Of Air Force Airplanes And Helicopters - Davis, Clive E

The Book Of Expert Driving - Fales, E D, Jr.

The Book Of Negro Humor - Hughes, Langston

A Book Of Stars For You - Branley, Franklyn M

The Book Of The Unknown - Woods, Harold

A Book Of Witches - Manning-Sanders, Ruth

Books For You To Make - Purdy, Susan

Born To Hit: The George Brett Story - Twyman, Gib

Bow Island - Carpelan, Bo

The Boxcar At The Center Of The Universe - Kennedy, Richard

The Boy Drummer Of Vincennes - Carmer, Carl

The Boy She Left Behind - Rand, Suzanne

Boy Who Could Make Himself Disappear - Platt, Kin

The Boy Who Drank Too Much - Greene, Shep

The Boy Who Sailed Around The World Alone - Graham, Robin Lee

Boyd's Book Of Odd Facts - Boyd, L M

The Boyhood Of Grace Jones - Langton, Jane

The Boys And Girls Book About Stepfamilies - Gardner, Richard Alan

The Boys' Book Of Ships And Shipping - Penry-Jones, J

The Boys' Sherlock Holmes - Doyle, Arthur Conan

The Boys Who Saved The Children - Baldwin, Margaret

Brady - Fritz, Jean

Brainstorm - Myers, Walter Dean

Branded Runaway - Spencer, Zane

Brashki: A Gypsy Fantasy - Housh, Barbara

The Brave Balloonists: America's First Airmen - Douty, Esther Morris

Break A Leg, Betsy Maybe! - Kingman, Lee

Break Dancing - Marlow, Curtis

Break-In - Eisenberg, Lisa

Breakaway - Hallman, Ruth

Breakaway - Thornton, Jane Foster

Breaking Camp - Kroll, Steven

Breaking Point - Weir, LaVada

Breaking Up - Klein, Norma

Breaking Up Is Hard To Do - Hart, Bruce

A Breath Of Air And A Breath Of Smoke - Marr, John S

Brian Piccolo: A Short Season - Morris, Jeannie

Brian's Song - Blinn, William

The Bridge At Selma - Miller, Marilyn

Bridge To The Sun - Terasaki, Gwen

Bridges And How They Are Built - Goldwater, Daniel

The Bridges At Toko-Ri - Michener, James A

Bring Me All Of Your Dreams - Larrick, Nancy

Brogg's Brain - Platt, Kin

Brother Of The Wolves - Thompson, Jean

Brotherhood Of Pirates - Schoder, Judith

Brothers And Sisters: Modern Stories By Black Americans - Adoff, Arnold

Brothers Of The Sea - Sherman, D R

Brown Rabbit: Her Story - Morse, Evangeline

Brown! The Sports Career Of James Brown - Hahn, James

Bruce Jenner - Chodes, John

Brush Fire! - Smith, Pauline Coggeshall

Brush Up On Hair Care - Phillips, Betty Lou

Buck - Larimer, Tamela

Buckaroo - McKimmey, James

The Bucket Of Thunderbolts - Olsen, Gene

Bugs In Your Ears - Bates, Betty

Builders On The Desert - Van Duyn, Janet

Building Blocks - Voigt, Cynthia

A Building Goes Up - Kahn, Ely Jacques

Bull Pen Hero - Etter, Lester Frederick

The Bunch From Bananas - Pownall, David

The Burg-O-Rama Man - Tchudi, Stephen N

Burn Out - Kropp, Paul

The Burning Glass - Johnson, Annabel

The Burning Thorn: An Anthology Of Poetry - Greaves, Griselda

Bus Ride - Sachs, Marilyn

The Bushbabies - Stevenson, William

Busted Lives: Dialogues With Kids In Jail - Shanks, Ann Zane Kushner

But I'm Ready To Go - Albert, Louise

By Balloon To The Sahara - Terman, D

By Crumbs, It's Mine - Beatty, Patricia Robbins

By Secret Railway - Meadowcroft, Enid LaMonte

By The Highway Home - Stolz, Mary Slattery

C. C. Poindexter - Meyer, Carolyn

The Cage - Brown, Roy Frederick

Calamity Kate - Deary, Terry

Calendar - Adler, Irving

California Girl - Quin-Harkin, Janet

Call Me Al Raft - Shaw, Richard

Call Me Beautiful - Blair, Shannon

Call Me Heller, That's My Name - Pevsner, Stella

Call Me Moose - Cone, Molly Lamken

Call Of The Wild - Lewis, Carrie

The Call Of The Wild - London, Jack

Calling Earth - Land, Charles

Cameras And Courage: Margaret Bourke-White - Noble, Iris

Campfire Nights - Cowan, Dale

Campus Mystery - Brisco, Patty

Can You Give First Aid? - Bontrager, Frances M

Can You Sue Your Parents For Malpractice? - Danziger, Paula

The Canada Goose - Ahlstrom, Mark E

Canalboat To Freedom - Fall, Thomas

Canary Red - McKay, Robert W

A Candle, A Feather, A Wooden Spoon - Jacobs, Linda C

A Candle In Her Room - Arthur, Ruth M

Candle In The Mist - Means, Florence Crannell

Candy Stripers - Wyndham, Lee

Can't Catch Me, I'm The Gingerbread Man - Gilson, Jamie Marie

Canyon Winter - Morey, Walter Nelson

A Cap For Mary Ellis - Newell, Hope

Captain - Hall, Lynn

Captain Morgana Mason - Francis, Dorothy Brenner

The Captains - Clary, Jack

Captive Thunder - Butler, Beverly

Captives In A Foreign Land - Rardin, Susan Lowry

A Car Called Camellia - O'Connor, Patrick

Career Prep: Electronics Servicing - Abrams, Kathleen S

Career Prep: Working In A Hospital - Miner, Jane Claypool

Careers And Opportunities In Science - Pollack, Philip

Careers For Dog Lovers - Hall, Lynn

Careers In Sports - McGonagle, Bob

Cargo - Poole, A B

Caring For Your Car - Grebel, Rosemary

Carlos: With My Own Hands - Weeks, Doug

Carlotta's House - Malin, Amita

Carnival Of Speed: True Adventures In Motor Racing - Nolan, William Francis

Carol Johnston: The One-Armed Gymnast - Donovan, Pete

Carrie Loves Superman - Miklowitz, Gloria D

Cars - Clark, James I

The Cartoonist - Byars, Betsy

The Case Of The Ancient Astronauts - Gallagher, I J

The Case Of The Blackmail Boys - Dicks, Terrance

The Case Of The Cinema Swindle - Dicks, Terrance

The Case Of The Cop Catchers - Dicks, Terrance

Title Index

Checking And Balancing - Thypin, Marilyn
Checkmate Julie - Jacobs, Linda C
The Cheerleader - Klein, Norma
The Chemicals We Eat And Drink - Silverstein, Alvin
The Chemistry Of Life - Patton, A Rae
Chief - Bonham, Frank
Child Of Fire - O'Dell, Scott
Child Of The Owl - Yep, Laurence Michael
Child Of Tomorrow - Bartholomew, Barbara
Children Of The Incas - Mangurian, David
Children Of The Wild - Burger, John Robert
Chileno! - Skarmeta, Antonio
China - Clayton, Robert
China And The Chinese - Harrington, Lyn
China: The Hungry Dragon - Scott, John
The Chinese In America - Sung, Betty Lee
Chip Mitchell: The Case Of The Stolen Computer Brains - D'Ignazio, Fred
Chipmunks On The Doorstep - Tunis, Edwin
Chloris And The Creeps - Platt, Kin
Chloris And The Freaks - Platt, Kin
Choices - Miner, Jane Claypool
Chris Evert - Smith, Jay H
Chris! The Sports Career Of Chris Evert Lloyd - Hahn, James
Christmas Date - Harper, Elaine
Christy's Love - Johnson, Maud
Chuck Foreman - DeRosier, John
The Cigarette Sellers Of Three Crosses Square - Ziemian, Joseph
The Cincinnati Bengals - May, Julian
Circus Days Under The Big Top - Glendinning, Richard
City Cop - Cook, Fred J
Clarence Darrow: Defender Of The People - Faber, Doris
Class Dismissed II - Glenn, Mel
Class Pictures - Sachs, Marilyn
Classics Of The Silent Screen - Franklin, Joe
Claudia, Where Are You? - Colman, Hila
The Cliffs Of Cairo - Marston, Elsa
The Climbing Rope - Kester, Ellen Skinner
Climbing To The Sun - Carroll, Jeffrey
The Clock Museum - Sobol, Ken
Close But Not Quite - Deegan, Paul Joseph
Close Encounters Of The Third Kind - Spielberg, Steven
Close Harmony - Thornton, Jane Foster
Close To The Edge - Miklowitz, Gloria D
A Closer Look At Apes - Cook, David
The Clue Of The Black Cat - Berna, Paul
A Clutch Of Vampires - McNally, Raymond T
Clyde's Clam Farm - Harmon, Lyn
The Coach Nobody Liked - Carson, John F
Cobra In The Tub: And Eight More Stories Of Mystery And Suspense - Mueser, Annie
Cockle Stew And Other Rhymes - Massie, Diane Redfield
Codes, Ciphers, And Secret Writing - Gardner, Martin
Coins You Can Collect - Hobson, Burton Harold
Collage And Construction - Weiss, Harvey
Collision Course - Hinton, Nigel
Colonizing Space - Bergaust, Erik
Color It Love - Lawrence, Amy
The Color Of Man - Cohen, Robert C
A Combat Reporter's Report - Sweeney, James Bartholemew
Come Alive At 505 - Brancato, Robin Fidler
The Comeback Guy - Frick, Constance H
Comet! - Bromley, Dudley
Comets And Meteors - Couper, Heather
Coming Back Alive - Reader, Dennis J
Coming On Strong - Columbu, Franco

Commander Of The Flying Tigers: Claire Lee Chennault - Archibald, Joe

Communication - Adler, Irving

Communication: From Stone Age To Space Age - Neal, Harry Edward

Communications Machines - Howard, Sam

Compacts, Subs And Minis - Abodaher, David J

The Complete Book Of Autograph Collecting - Sullivan, George Edward

The Complete Book Of Bicycling - Sloane, Eugene A

The Complete Family Nature Guide - Worthley, Jean Reese

Computer - Jones, Weyman B

Computer Talk - Berger, Melvin

Computers And You - Litterick, Ian

Computers: Tools For Today - DeRossi, Claude J

Confessions Of A Teenage Baboon - Zindel, Paul

Confessions Of A Teenage TV Addict - Leroe, Ellen

Confessions Of A Toe-Hanger - Harris, Christie

Connecticut Low - Boehm, Bruce

Conqueror Of The Clouds - Hallstead, William Finn, III

Constance: A Story Of Early Plymouth - Clapp, Patricia

The Contender - Lipsyte, Robert

Cook Inlet Decision - Pedersen, Elsa

Cool Cat - Bonham, Frank

The Corduroy Road - Clyne, Patricia Edwards

Corvette: America's Supercar - Hoffman, Jeffrey

Cosmic Kidnappers - Randall, E T

Cougar - Thomson, Peter

Count Me Gone - Johnson, Annabel

Counterfeit! - Wheeler, W H

Cover Girl - Greene, Yvonne

Cowboys And The Songs They Sang - Sackett, Samuel J

Cowboys Don't Cry - Halvorson, Marilyn

Crash Dive - Frederick, Lee

Crash In The Wilderness - Black, Susan Adams

The Crazy Custom Car Book - Wenzel, Celeste Piano

Crazy Eights - Dana, Barbara

Crazy Minnie - Poynter, Margaret

Crazy To Race - Butterworth, W E

Crazy Vanilla - Wersba, Barbara

Creating Mosaics - Seidelman, James E

Creating With Clay - Seidelman, James E

Creating With Paint - Seidelman, James E

Creating With Paper - Seidelman, James E

Creatures From Lost Worlds - Simon, Seymour

Creatures From UFO's - Cohen, Daniel

Creatures Of Mystery - Fortman, Jan

The Creep - Dodson, Susan

The Cricket In Times Square - Selden, George

Crime And The Law: A Look At The Criminal Justice System - Phillips, Maxine

Crocker - Platt, Kin

Cross-Country Caper - Kinter, Judith

Cross My Heart - Sellers, Naomi

Cross Your Fingers, Spit In Your Hat - Schwartz, Alvin

The Crossbreed - Eckert, Allan W

Cruisin For A Bruisin - Rosen, Winifred

Crush - Futcher, Jane

The Crystal Image: A Poetry Anthology - Janeczko, Paul

The Crystal Nights - Murray, Michele

Curious Facts - May, John

Curse Not The Darkness - Hoard, Edison

The Curse Of King Tut And Other Mystery Stories - Hogan, Elizabeth

Curse Of The Sunken Treasure - Austin, R G

Curse Of The Vampires - Ronan, Margaret

The Curse Of The Viking Grave - Mowat, Farley

The Custard Kid - Deary, Terry

Dear Bill, Remember Me? - Mazer, Norma Fox

Dear Diary - Betancourt, Jeanne

Dear Lola: Or How To Build Your Own Family - Angell, Judie

Death Angel - Rice, Earle, Jr.

Death Be Not Proud - Gunther, John

Death: Everyone's Heritage - Landau, Elaine

Death Run - Murphy, Jim

Death Sentence - Kelley, Leo P

The Death Ticket - Bennett, Jay

Deathman, Do Not Follow Me - Bennett, Jay

Deathwatch - White, Robb

Decathlon Men: Greatest Athletes In The World - Finlayson, Ann

Deenie - Blume, Judy

Deep-Sea World: The Story Of Oceanography - Coombs, Charles Ira

The Deep Search - Koob, Theodora

The Deep Silence - Reeman, Douglas

Deepwater Family - Duncan, Fred B

Deer Jackers - Evers, Alf

Deer Valley Girl - Lenski, Lois

Delpha Green And Company - Cleaver, Vera

The Demeter Star - Oreshnik, A F

Demon Tree - Daniel, Colin

Denison's Daughter - Hall, Lynn

Department Store Model - Robison, Nancy

The Desert Chase - Butterworth, Ben

Desert Chase - Sant, Kathryn Storey

Desert Road Racer - Ogan, Margaret E Nettles

Desperate Search - East, Ben

Destination Unknown - Fife, Dale

The Devil Rides With Me And Other Fantastic Stories - Slote, Alfred

Devil Wind - Bridges, Laurie

Devilhorn - Bonham, Frank

Devil's Race - Avi

The Devil's Shadow - Alderman, Clifford Lindsey

Dial Leroi Rupert, DJ - Gilson, Jamie Marie

The Diamond Smugglers - Butterworth, Ben

Diamonds Are Trouble - Corbett, Scott

Diamonds In The Dirt - Campbell, Archie

Diamonds In The Rough - Rappoport, Ken

Diana: Alone Against The Sea - McLenighan, Valjean

Diana: The People's Princess - Darling, David J

Diane's New Love - Headley, Elizabeth Cavanna

The Diary Of Trilby Frost - Glaser, Dianne

Did You Hear What Happened To Andrea? - Miklowitz, Gloria D

Diesel Trucks, On The Move - Rich, Mark

Digging Up The Bible Lands - Harker, Ronald

Dinky Hocker Shoots Smack - Kerr, M E

Dinosaur Riddles - Heck, Joseph

Dinosaurs And Their World - Pringle, Laurence

Dirt Bike - Kropp, Paul

Dirt Bike Adventure - Miller, W Wesley

Dirt Track Summer - Gault, William Campbell

The Disappearance - Guy, Rosa

Disaster - Sobol, Donald J

The Disco Kid - Gathje, Curtis

The Discoveries Of Esteban The Black - Shepherd, Elizabeth

Discovering Insects - Blough, Glenn O

The Distant Summer - Patterson, Sarah

Dive For The Sun - Love, Sandra

Dive From The Sky! - Halacy, Daniel Stephen, Jr.

The Divorce Express - Danziger, Paula

Do Bananas Chew Gum? - Gilson, Jamie Marie

Do You Really Love Me? - Lenz, Jeanne R

Do You See My Love For You Growing? - Coombs, Orde M

Do You See What I See? - St. George, Judith

Docker - Patterson, Gardner

Doctor Knock-Knock's Official Knock-Knock Dictionary - Rosenbloom, Joseph

Doctor Zizmor's Guide To Clearer Skin - Zizmor, Jonathan

The Dog Days Of Arthur Cane - Paisley, Tom

A Dog Named Kitty - Wallace, Bill

A Dog Named Wolf - Munsterhjelm, Erik

The Dog Who Never Knew - Unkelbach, Kurt

Dogs And More Dogs - Bradbury, Bianca

Dogs And Puppies - Rockwell, Jane

Dogsbody - Jones, Diana Wynne

Dogsong - Paulsen, Gary

The Doll - Sparger, Rex

Dolphin Island - Clarke, Arthur C

The Donkey Planet - Corbett, Scott

Don't Ask Miranda - Perl, Lila

Don't Blame The Music - Cooney, Caroline B

Don't Cry For Me - Jarunkova, Klara

Don't Fence Me In - Cole, Brenda

Don't Look And It Won't Hurt - Peck, Richard

Don't Make Me Smile - Park, Barbara

Don't Play Dead Before You Have To - Wojciechowska, Maia

Don't Say Good-Bye - Goudge, Eileen

Don't Shoot - Chadwick, Roxane

Don't Take Teddy - Friis-Baastad, Babbis

Don't Tell Me That You Love Me - Colman, Hila

The Dope Book: All About Drugs - Lieberman, Mark

Dope Deal - Kropp, Paul

Doris Fein: Dead Heat At Long Beach - Paisley, Tom

Doris Fein: Deadly Aphrodite - Paisley, Tom

Doris Fein: Legacy Of Terror - Bethancourt, T Ernesto

Doris Fein: Murder Is No Joke - Paisley, Tom

Doris Fein: Phantom Of The Casino - Paisley, Tom

Doris Fein: Quartz Boyar - Paisley, Tom

Doris Fein: Superspy - Paisley, Tom

Dorothy Hamill: Olympic Champion - Van Steenwyk, Elizabeth

Dorothy Hamill: Skate To Victory - Schmitz, Dorothy Childers

Dorp Dead - Cunningham, Julia Woolfolk

Double Feature - DuJardin, Rosamond

Double Love - William, Kate

Dove - Graham, Robin Lee

Down By The River - Adler, C S

Down To The Sea In Subs: My Life In The U.S. Navy - Lockwood, Charles A

Dr. Beagle And Mr. Hyde - Schulz, Charles M

Dr. Doom: Superstar - Bethancourt, T Ernesto

Dr. Elizabeth - Clapp, Patricia

Dr. J - Gutman, Bill

Dr. J: A Biography Of Julius Erving - Haskins, James

Dr. Martin Luther King, Jr. - Miklowitz, Gloria D

Dracula - Stoker, Bram

Dracula - Thorne, Ian

Dracula, Go Home! - Platt, Kin

Dracula's Daughter - Green, Carl R

Draft Horses - Nentl, Jerolyn Ann

Drag Racing - Coombs, Charles Ira

Drag Racing For Beginners - Edmonds, Ivy Gordon

Drag Strip - Gault, William Campbell

Dragon Of The Lost Sea - Yep, Laurence Michael

The Dragster - Werner, Herma

Draw 50 Airplanes, Aircraft And Spacecraft - Ames, Lee Judah

Draw 50 Famous Cartoons - Ames, Lee Judah

Draw 50 Famous Faces - Ames, Lee Judah

Drawing Fashions: Figures, Faces And Techniques - Bolognese, Donald Alan

Dream Dancer - Bolton, Evelyn

Title Index

Emmy, Beware! - Abels, Harriette Sheffer

The Empty Moat - Shemin, Margaretha

An Empty Spoon - Decker, Sunny

An Empty World - Christopher, John

Enchantress From The Stars - Engdahl, Sylvia Louise

Encore! Encore! - Wilson, Tom

Encounter - Ruckman, Ivy

Encyclopedia Brown Gets His Man - Sobol, Donald J

Encyclopedia Brown's Book Of Wacky Crimes - Sobol, Donald J

End Of Summer - Grohskopf, Bernice

The Endless Steppe: Growing Up In Siberia - Hautzig, Esther

Endless Summer - Bayner, Rose

Energy Machines - Ackins, Ralph

Enrico Fermi: Atomic Pioneer - Faber, Doris

Enter Laughing - Leroe, Ellen

Entertaining - Sweeney, Karen O'Connor

Eric Heiden: Winner In Gold - Aaseng, Nathan

Escape From Nowhere - Eyerly, Jeannette

Escape From Splatterbang - Fisk, Nicholas

Escape From The Tower Of London - Nagel, Shirley

Escape Into Daylight - Household, Geoffrey

Escape To Witch Mountain - Key, Alexander

Escape! - Bova, Ben

Escape! The Life Of Harry Houdini - White, Florence Meiman

Escapes And Rescues - Scoggin, Margaret C

Especially Humphrey - Lewiton, Mina

Every Living Thing - Rylant, Cynthia

Everybody's Dancing In Socks And On Skates - Bednar, Jane

Everyday Inventions - Hooper, Meredith

Everyone's Watching Tammy - Jacobs, Linda C

Everything But Tuesdays And Sundays Filichia, Peter

The Evolution Of The Machine - Calder, Ritchie

Exchange Of Hearts - Quin-Harkin, Janet

The Executioner: A Story Of Revenge - Bennett, Jay

Exiles Of The Stars - Norton, Andre

Exploring Earth And Space - Hyde, Margaret Oldroyd

Exploring The Universe - Gallant, Roy A

An Eye On Israel - Bouma, Hans

Eye Spy - Anderson, Doug

Eyes In The Fishbowl - Snyder, Zilpha Keatley

The Fabulous Dr. J - Sabin, Louis

Face At The Brillstone Window - Heide, Florence Parry

Face At The Edge Of The World - Bunting, Eve

The Face Of Prayer - Menashe, Abraham

The Face Of Rock And Roll - Pollock, Bruce

The Face That Stopped Time - Cebulash, Mel

Facts About Sex For Today's Youth - Gordon, Sol

Facts About VD For Today's Youth - Gordon, Sol

A Fair Advantage - Watkins, William Jon

Fair Day, And Another Step Begun - Lyle, Katie Letcher

Fair Game - Brown, Jackum

Fair Game - O'Hanlon, Jacklyn

Fair Play - Kropp, Paul

Falling In Love Is No Snap - Foley, June

Falling Star - Eisenberg, Lisa

The Falling Star Mystery - Wright, Bob

False Start - Rabin, Gil

Family - Donovan, John

The Family Conspiracy - Phipson, Joan

A Family Failing - Arundel, Honor

The Family From Vietnam - Reiff, Tana

The Family Howl - Dinneen, Betty

Famous American Indians - Heuman, William

The Firebug Mystery - Christian, Mary Blount

The Firefighters - James, Stuart

Firestorm - Gee, Maurine H

Fireweed - Walsh, Jill Paton

The First Artists - Samachson, Dorothy

The First Book Of Automobiles - Bendick, Jeanne

First Book Of Facts And How To Find Them - Whitney, David C

First Book Of How To Write A Report - Brandt, Sue Reading

The First Book Of India - Bothwell, Jean

The First Book Of Puppets - Jagendorf, Moritz

The First Book Of Science Experiments - Wyler, Rose

The First Four Years - Wilder, Laura Ingalls

First Impression - Abels, Harriette Sheffer

First, Last, And Always - Conklin, Barbara

First Love - Spector, Debra

First Love Farewell - Emery, Anne

First Orchid For Pat - Emery, Anne

First Payday - Weingarden, M

First Person, Singular - Demas, Vida

First Ride - Kaplan, Janice

First Step - Snyder, Anne

The First Time - Reit, Ann

Fisk Of Fenway Park: New England's Favorite Catcher - Jackson, Robert Blake

Five Against The Odds - Frick, Constance H

A Five-Color Buick And A Blue-Eyed Cat - Wood, Phyllis Anderson

Five Dog Night And Other Tales - Keller, Roseanne

Five From Me, Five From You - Macdonald, Shelagh

Fixing Up Motorcycles - Smith, LeRoi Tex

Flag For The Fort - Carmer, Carl

The Fledgling - Tomerlin, John

Flight To Fear - Belina, Tom

Flight To The South Pole - Bamman, Henry A

Flight Today And Tomorrow - Hyde, Margaret Oldroyd

Flights Of The Astronauts - Shelton, William Roy

The Flint Hills Foal - Francis, Dorothy Brenner

Flint's Island - Wibberley, Leonard

Flood At Reedsmere - Burton, Hester

Flowers For Lisa - Ladd, Veronica

Flowers Of Anger - Hall, Lynn

Fly Away Paul - Davies, Peter

Fly Free - Adler, C S

The Flying Cow - Collins, Ruth Philpott

Flying Free - True, Dan

Flying High - Powers, Bill

Flying-Model Airplanes - Berliner, Don

Flying Scared: Why We Are Being Skyjacked And How To Put A Stop To It - Rich, Elizabeth

Flying Wheels - Pollock, Rollene

Foal Creek - Cohen, Peter Zachary

Fog - Lee, Mildred

Follow That Boy - Quin-Harkin, Janet

The Followers - Bunting, Eve

Football Boys - Renick, Marion

Football Talk For Beginners - Liss, Howard

Football's Crushing Blockers - Aaseng, Nathan

Football's Cunning Coaches - Aaseng, Nathan

For Always - Bunting, Eve

Forbidden Kisses - Goudge, Eileen

Forbidden Love - Woodruff, Marian

The Forbidden Towers - Gaskin, Carol

Forests Are For People: The Heritage Of Our National Forests - Wood, Frances

Forever - Blume, Judy

The Forever Formula - Bonham, Frank

Forever Free - Adamson, Joy

Forgotten World - Abels, Harriette Sheffer

The Fortune Cake - Jordan, Hope Dahle

Fortune Telling - Baldwin, Margaret

Forty Days Lost - East, Ben

Gardine Vs. Hanover - Oppenheimer, Joan Letson

Garfield: The Complete Cat Book - Steneman, Shep

Genealogy: How To Find Your Roots - Gilfond, Henry

Genesis Two - Davies, L P

Genius With A Scalpel: Harvey Cushing - Denzel, Justin F

Gentle Ben - Morey, Walter Nelson

Gentlehands - Kerr, M E

The George Foster Story - Drucker, Malka

George Washington Carver: Negro Scientist - Epstein, Sam

Geraldine Ferraro - Lawson, Donald Elmer

Get A Little Lost, Tia - Wood, Phyllis Anderson

Get Me Out Of Here!: Real Life Stories Of Teenage Heroism - Carlson, Gordon

Get What You Pay For - Huffman, Suanne

Get Where You're Going - Gillis, Ruby

Getting Even - Pfeffer, Susan Beth

Getting In - Lowell, Anne Hunter

Getting Into Pro Baseball - Dyer, Mike

Getting Into Pro Basketball - Lyttle, Richard Bard

Getting Into Pro Football - McCallum, John Dennis

Getting Into Pro Soccer - Fischler, Stanley I

Getting It All Together - Capizzi, Michael

Getting Nowhere - Greene, Constance C

Getting Ready For The World Of Work - Armstrong, Fiona

Getting Ready To Work - McHugh, John

Getting Started In Tennis - Ashe, Arthur

Ghana And Ivory Coast: Spotlight On West Africa - Perl, Lila

Ghost Behind Me - Bunting, Eve

The Ghost In The Noonday Sun - Fleischman, Sid

Ghost Of A Chance - Quin-Harkin, Janet

The Ghost Of Ballyhooly - Cavanna, Betty

Ghost Of Frankenstein - Green, Carl R

The Ghost Of Spirit River - Dixon, Jeanne

Ghostly Terrors - Cohen, Daniel

Ghosts - Simon, Seymour

Ghosts And Poltergeists - Williams, Gurney, III

Ghosts I Have Been - Peck, Richard

The Ghosts Of Departure Point - Bunting, Eve

The Ghosts Of Now - Nixon, Joan Lowery

Giana - Machol, Libby

The Giant Squid - Bunting, Eve

Gideon - Aaron, Chester

A Gift Of Magic - Duncan, Lois S

The Gift Of Sarah Barker - Yolen, Jane H

Gimme Something, Mister! - Hallman, Ruth

The Girl - Branscum, Robbie

Girl - Green, Gerald

A Girl Called Boy - Hurmence, Belinda

The Girl From Puerto Rico - Colman, Hila

Girl From Two Miles High - Molloy, Anne S

A Girl Grows Up - Fedder, Ruth

The Girl In The Mirror - Sherburne, Zoa Morin

The Girl In The Painting - Bunting, Eve

Girl In The Rough - Wunsch, Josephine Mclean

The Girl Inside - Baer, Judy

The Girl Inside - Eyerly, Jeannette

A Girl Like Me - Eyerly, Jeannette

A Girl Like Tracy - Crane, Caroline

Girl Meets Boy - Colman, Hila

The Girl Most Likely - Rand, Suzanne

Girl Sports - Jacobs, Karen Folger

The Girl Who Had No Name - Rabe, Berniece Louise

The Girl Who Knew Tomorrow - Sherburne, Zoa Morin

Hank Aaron Clinches The Pennant - May, Julian

Hannah Herself - Franchere, Ruth

The Happenings At North End School - Colman, Hila

Happy Christmas - Seymour, William Kean

Happy Endings Are All Alike - Scoppettone, Sandra

Hard Luck Horse - Brown, Fern G

Harlem - Halliburton, Warren J

Harlem Summer - Vroman, Mary Elizabeth

Harness Racing - Van Steenwyk, Elizabeth

Harnessing The Sun: The Story Of Solar Energy - Knight, David C

Harriet Tubman: Conductor On The Underground Railroad - Petry, Ann

Harriet Tubman: Guide To Freedom - Epstein, Sam

Harry Houdini - Kraske, Robert

The Haunted Motorcycle Shop - Abels, Harriette Sheffer

Haunted Summer - Jordan, Hope Dahle

Haunted Treasures - Titler, Dale Milton

The Haunting Of Kildoran Abbey - Bunting, Eve

The Haunting Of Safekeep - Bunting, Eve

Have A Heart - Leroe, Ellen

Have We Lived Before? - Atkinson, Linda

Hawaii Nei - Tabrah, Ruth M

Hawaiian Tales Of Heroes And Champions - Thompson, Vivian Laubach

Hawkins And The Soccer Solution - Wallace, Barbara Brooks

He Noticed I'm Alive...And Other Hopeful Signs - Sharmat, Marjorie Weinman

A Head On Her Shoulders - Bond, Gladys Baker

Head Over Heels - Swift, Helen Miller

Head Over Wheels - Kingman, Lee

The Headless Roommate And Other Tales Of Terror - Cohen, Daniel

Headman - Platt, Kin

Heads You Win, Tails I Lose - Holland, Isabelle

Health Care For The Wongs: Health Insurance, Choosing A Doctor - Thypin, Marilyn

Hearing Ear Dogs - Emert, Phyllis R

Heart Disease - Silverstein, Alvin

Hearts Don't Lie - Fields, Terri

Heavens To Bitsy - Harrell, Janice

The Heavyweight Champions - Durant, John

Heidi - Spyri, Johanna

Helicopter Pilot - Butterworth, W E

Helicopters - Berliner, Don

Hello, Puerto Rico - Weeks, Morris, Jr.

Hello...Wrong Number - Sachs, Marilyn

Hell's Edge - Townsend, John Rowe

Helmet For My Pillow - Leckie, Robert

Help Yourself To Health - Day, Nancy Raines

Helter-Skelter - Moyes, Patricia

Henry Aaron: Quiet Superstar - Hirshberg, Al

Henry Reed's Big Show - Robertson, Keith

Henry Winkler: Born Actor - Jacobs, Linda C

Henry! The Sports Career Of Henry Aaron - Hahn, James

Her Father's Daughter - Ready, Anne Cooper

Her Secret Self - Vilott, Rhondi

Here By The Sea - Baker, Laura Nelson

Here Comes Bobby Orr - Jackson, Robert Blake

Here I Am! - Baron, Virginia Olsen

Here To Stay - Kennedy, M L

A Hero Ain't Nothin' But A Sandwich - Childress, Alice

Heroes - Carabatsos, James

Heroes, Gods And Monsters Of The Greek Myths - Evslin, Bernard

Heroes Of Puerto Rico - Tuck, Jay Nelson

Hey, Big Spender! - Bonham, Frank

Hey, Dollface - Hautzig, Deborah

Hey, Dummy - Platt, Kin

Hey, Remember Fat Glenda? - Perl, Lila

Hot Rodding For Beginners - Edmonds, Ivy Gordon

Hot Skateboarding - Dixon, Pahl

Hot Wire - Butterworth, W E

The Hotel Mystery - Butterworth, W E

The Hotshot - Slote, Alfred

Houdini And Other Masters Of Magic - Fortman, Jan

Houdini: Master Of Escape - Kendall, Lace

The Hound Of The Baskervilles - Doyle, Arthur Conan

The Hour Of The Oxrun Dead - Grant, C L

The House At 12 Rose Street - Brodsky, Mimi

A House For Jonnie O - Elfman, Blossom

The House Of Dies Drear - Hamilton, Virginia

House Of Laughs - Eisenberg, Lisa

How Automobiles Are Made - Cooke, David C

How Did We Find Out About Antarctica? - Asimov, Isaac

How Did We Find Out About Atoms? - Asimov, Isaac

How Did We Find Out About Comets? - Asimov, Isaac

How Did We Find Out About Dinosaurs? - Asimov, Isaac

How Did We Find Out About Earthquakes? - Asimov, Isaac

How Did We Find Out About Energy? - Asimov, Isaac

How Did We Find Out About Germs? - Asimov, Isaac

How Did We Find Out About Life In The Deep Sea? - Asimov, Isaac

How Did We Find Out About Our Human Roots? - Asimov, Isaac

How Did We Find Out About Outer Space? - Asimov, Isaac

How Did We Find Out About Solar Power? - Asimov, Isaac

How Did We Find Out About Volcanoes? - Asimov, Isaac

How Do They Get Rid Of It? - Hilton, Suzanne

How Does It Feel When Your Parents Get Divorced? - Berger, Terry

How It Feels To Be Adopted - Krementz, Jill

How It Feels When A Parent Dies - Krementz, Jill

How Many Miles To Babylon? - Fox, Paula

How To Be A Successful Teenager - Menninger, William C

How To Be A Super Camp Counselor - Mangan, Doreen

How To Be A Winner - Fanburg, Walter H

The How-To Book Of International Dolls: A Comprehensive Guide To Making, Costuming And Collecting Dolls - Holz, Loretta

How To Bring Up Your Pet Dog - Unkelbach, Kurt

How To Buy A Car - Cohen, Daniel

How To Cope: A New Guide To The Teen-Age Years - Reingold, Carmel Berman

How To Draw Comics The Marvel Way - Lee, Stan

How To Draw Monsters - Evans, Larry

How To Get A Good Job - Claypool, Jane

How To Get In Shape For Sports - Englebardt, Stanley L

How To Have A Gorgeous Wedding - Sharmat, Marjorie Weinman

How To Live With A Single Parent - Gilbert, Sara Dulaney

How To Meet A Gorgeous Guy - Sharmat, Marjorie Weinman

How To Play Backgammon - Perry, Susan

How To Play Rummy Card Games - Perry, Susan

How To Star In Basketball - Masin, Herman L

How To Star In Football - Masin, Herman L

How To Test Your ESP - Cohen, Daniel

How To Understand Auto Racing - Olney, Ross Robert

How To Watch Wildlife - Burness, Gordon

How To Write A Term Paper - James, Elizabeth

The Hub Cap Mystery - Robins, Eleanor

The Human Body: The Heart - Elgin, Kathleen

Humands - Mariotti, Mario

Hunchback Of Notre Dame - Hugo, Victor Marie

Hunger For Racing - Douglas, James M

Hunter In The Dark - Hughes, Monica

Hunter In The Dark - Thompson, Estelle

Hunters & Jumpers - Robison, Nancy

Hunters And The Hunted: Surviving In The Animal World - Patent, Dorothy Hinshaw

Hunter's Green - Whitney, Phyllis A

Hurry Home, Candy - DeJong, Meindert

Hut School And The Wartime Home-Front Heroes - Burch, Robert J

Hyperspace!: Facts And Fun From All Over The Universe - Adler, David A

I Am A Dancer - Haney, Lynn

I Am A Thief - Roy, Ron

I Am The Darker Brother - Adoff, Arnold

I Am The Greatest: And Other True Stories Of Sports Greats - Koller, William D

I Can't Forget You - Fisher, Lois I

I Dare You - Vedral, Joyce

I Dedicate This Song To You - Weber, Judith Eichler

I Died Here - Shea, George

I Don't Belong Here - French, Dorothy Kayser

I Don't Want To Be Your Shadow - Aydt, Deborah

I, Dwayne Kleber - Connor, James, III

I Gotta Be Free - Hallman, Ruth

I Hate School: How To Hang In And When To Drop Out - Wirths, Claudine G

I Heard The Owl Call My Name - Craven, Margaret

I Know What You Did Last Summer - Duncan, Lois S

I Never Loved Your Mind - Zindel, Paul

I Reached For The Sky - Patterson, Betty

I Saw Him First - Sharmat, Marjorie Weinman

I Think I'm Having A Baby - Hansen, Caryl

I Think This Is Where We Came In - Wood, Phyllis Anderson

I Wanna Go Home! - Ketcham, Hank

I Was A Black Panther - Stone, Willie

I Will Go Barefoot All Summer For You - Lyle, Katie Letcher

I Would Rather Be A Turnip - Cleaver, Vera

The Ice Ghosts Mystery - Curry, Jane Louise

Ice Hawk - Godfrey, Martyn

Ice Pilot: Bob Bartlett - Sarnoff, Paul

If Anything - Swearingen, Martha

If Beale Street Could Talk - Baldwin, James

If I Asked You, Would You Stay? - Bunting, Eve

If I Love You, Am I Trapped Forever? - Kerr, M E

If I Loved You Wednesday - Eyerly, Jeannette

If The Earth Falls In - Clark, Mavis Thorpe

If Winter Comes - Hall, Lynn

If You Believe In Me - Kaplan, Janice

If You Can't Be The Sun, Be A Star - Savitz, Harriet May

I'll Always Get Up - Brown, Larry

I'll Get There. It Better Be Worth The Trip - Donovan, John

I'll Love You When You're More Like Me - Kerr, M E

I'll Take Manhattan - Barlette, Danielle

The Illustrated Bird - Oster, Maggie

The Illustrated Hassle-Free Make Your Own Clothes Book - Rosenberg, Sharon

I'm Deborah Sampson: A Soldier In The War Of The Revolution - Clapp, Patricia

I'm Really Dragged, But Nothing Gets Me Down - Hentoff, Nat

It's An Aardvark-Eat-Turtle World - Danziger, Paula

It's An Odd World - Hagerman, Paul Stirling

It's Chow Time, Snoopy - Schulz, Charles M

It's Good To Be Alive - Campanella, Roy

It's Just Too Much - Okimoto, Jean Davies

It's Like This, Cat - Neville, Emily Cheney

It's Not The End Of The World - Blume, Judy

It's Not What You Expect - Klein, Norma

It's Only Rock And Roll - Pollock, Bruce

It's Our Government: Congress, The President, And The Courts - Lefkowitz, William

I've Got A Crush On You - Stanley, Carol

Jack London: The Pursuit Of A Dream - Franchere, Ruth

Jackie Robinson: Baseball's Gallant Fighter - Epstein, Sam

Jackie Robinson Of The Brooklyn Dodgers - Shapiro, Milton J

Jackson Five - Morse, Charles

Jacques Cousteau: Free Flight Undersea - Westman, Paul

Jade - Watson, Sally

James At 15 - Smith, April

James Weldon Johnson - Felton, Harold W

Jane-Emily - Clapp, Patricia

Jane Fonda: Something To Fight For - Fox, Mary Virginia

Jane Frederick: Pentathlon Champion - Emert, Phyllis R

Jane Goodall: Living Chimp Style - Fox, Mary Virginia

Jane Pauley: A Heartland Style - Jacobs, Linda C

Janet Guthrie: First Woman At Indy - Olney, Ross Robert

Janet Guthrie: First Woman Driver At Indianapolis - Dolan, Edward Francis, Jr.

Janet Guthrie: Foot To The Floor - Fox, Mary Virginia

Janet Guthrie: Race Car Driver - Robison, Nancy

The Japanese Helped Build America - Dowdell, Dorothy Karns

Jasmine Finds Love - Claypool, Jane

Jay's Journal - Sparks, Beatrice

Jazz Country - Hentoff, Nat

Jeanne D'Arc - Fisher, Aileen

Jed And Jessie - Connell, Abby

Jeff White: Young Trapper - Dietz, Lew

Jeff White: Young Woodsman - Dietz, Lew

The Jell-O Syndrome - Morris, Winifred

Jennie Kissed Me - Holland, Isabelle

Jenny Kimura - Cavanna, Betty

Jeremy - Minahan, John

Jeremy Visick - Wiseman, David

Jesse Jackson: I Am Somebody - Westman, Paul

Jesse James - Ernst, John

Jet And Rocket Engines - Edmonds, Ivy Gordon

Jim And The Dolphin - Butterworth, Ben

Jim And The Sun Goddess - Butterworth, Ben

Jim Hart: Underrated Quarterback - Lipman, David

Jim In Training - Butterworth, Ben

Jim Palmer: Great Comeback Competitor - Cohen, Joel H

The Jim Thorpe Story: America's Greatest Athlete - Schoor, Gene

Jimmy Connors: King Of The Courts - Sabin, Francene

Jimmy Young: Heavyweight Challenger - Dolan, Edward Francis, Jr.

The Jinx Ship - Pease, Howard

Jody - Hulse, Jerry

Joe Louis: The Brown Bomber - Libby, Bill

John F. Kennedy - Graves, Charles P

John F. Kennedy And PT-109 - Tregaskis, Richard

John Glenn: Around The World In 90 Minutes - Westman, Paul

John Travolta - Munshower, Suzanne

John Young: Space Shuttle Commander - Westman, Paul

Johnny Bench: King Of Catchers - Sabin, Louis
Johnny Lee - Honig, Donald
Johnny Tall Dog - Kelley, Leo P
Johnny Tremain - Forbes, Esther
Johnny's Song: Poetry Of A Vietnam Veteran - Mason, Steve
The Joker - Street, Nicki
Jokes, Puns, And Riddles - Clark, David Allen
Jokes To Read In The Dark - Corbett, Scott
Josie's Handful Of Quietness - Smith, Nancy Covert
Journey For Tobiyah - Morgan, Barbara Ellen
Journey Home - Uchida, Yoshiko
Journey Into Jazz - Hentoff, Nat
Journey To Topaz - Uchida, Yoshiko
The Journey With Jonah - L'Engle, Madeleine
The Joy Of Camping - Langer, Richard W
Juan And Lucy - Reiff, Tana
Juan's Eighteen-Wheeler Summer - Place, Marian T
Judy George: Student Nurse - Stone, Patti
Julie Of The Wolves - George, Jean Craighead
Jumbo Jets - Jacobs, Lou, Jr.
Jump Ship To Freedom - Collier, James Lincoln
Jumping For Joy - Ryan, Frank
The Junior Illustrated Encyclopedia Of Sports - Kamm, Herbert
Just A Little Inconvenience - Brooke, Joshua
Just Dial A Number - Maxwell, Edith
Just Friends - Knudsen, James
Just Gin - Kendal, Wallis
Just Like Everybody Else - Rosen, Lillian
Just Like Everyone Else - Bunting, Eve
Just Like Sisters - Gaeddert, Lou Ann
Just My Luck - Moore, Emily
Just Once - Christian, Mary Blount
Just One Friend - Hall, Lynn
Just The Right Age - Chatterton, Louise
Just The Two Of Us - Colman, Hila
Just Too Cool - Callan, Jamie
Just You And Me - Martin, Ann M
Justice Sandra Day O'Connor - Fox, Mary Virginia
Karen - Killilea, Marie
Kate - Little, Jean
Kate Herself - Erskine, Helen
Kate Jackson: Special Kind Of Angel - Simpson, Janice C
Kathleen, Please Come Home - O'Dell, Scott
Katia - Almedingen, E M
Keep Stompin' Till The Music Stops - Pevsner, Stella
The Keeper - Naylor, Phyllis Reynolds
Keeping And Changing Jobs - McHugh, John
Keeping Fit - Schwartz, Anita K
Kentucky Daughter - Scott, Carol J
Keoni, My Brother - Nielsen, Virginia
The Key Word And Other Mysteries - Asimov, Isaac
Kicking The Football Soccer Style - Gogolak, Peter
The Kid - Axthelm, Pete
Kid Brother - Mulligan, Kevin
The Kid Comes Back - Tunis, John R
Kidnap In San Juan - Reilly, Pat
The Kidnapers Upstairs - Rosenbaum, Eileen
Kidnapped - Eisenberg, Lisa
Kidnapping Mr. Tubbs - Schellie, Don
The Kidnapping Of Anna - Hooker, Ruth
The Kidnapping Of Christina Lattimore - Nixon, Joan Lowery
The Kids' Book Of Disco - Bruning, Nancy P
The Kids' Book Of Lists - McLoone-Basta, Margo
The Kid's Complete Guide To Money - Kyte, Kathy S
The Kid's Guide To Home Video - Cohen, Daniel
Kids On The Run - Berry, James R
Kildee House - Montgomery, Rutherford George

Lawrence Of Arabia - Knightley, Phillip
Laws And Trials That Created History - Aymar, Brandt
Lead On Love - Hart, Nicole
Leap Before You Look - Stolz, Mary Slattery
Leap Into Danger - Hamre, Leif
Learn To Say Goodbye - Warwick, Dolores
Leases And Landlords: Apartment Living - Thypin, Marilyn
The Leaving - Hall, Lynn
The Left-Hander's World - Silverstein, Alvin
The Legend Of Tarik - Myers, Walter Dean
Leif Garrett - Berman, Connie
The Lemon Meringue Dog - Morey, Walter Nelson
Leonardo Da Vinci: The Artist, Inventor, Scientist - Provensen, Alice
The Leopard's Tooth - Kotzwinkle, William
Leroy And The Old Man - Butterworth, W E
Leslie - Sherburne, Zoa Morin
Lester's Turn - Slepian, Jan
Let The Hurricane Roar - Lane, Rose Wilder
Let X Be Excitement - Harris, Christie
Let's Face It: The Guide To Good Grooming For Girls Of Color - Archer, Elsie
Letter Perfect - Crawford, Charles P
The Lever And The Pulley - Hellman, Harold
Liar, Liar - Yep, Laurence Michael
The Liberation Of Tansy Warner - Tolan, Stephanie S
Liberty And Corporal Kincaid - Toepfer, Ray Grant
Lies - Hopper, Nancy J
Life And Death - Zim, Herbert S
The Life And Death Of Martin Luther King, Jr. - Haskins, James
The Life And Legend Of George McJunkin - Folsom, Franklin Brewster
The Life And Words Of Martin Luther King, Jr. - Peck, Ira
Life In The Middle Ages - Williams, Jay
Life Is A Lonely Place: Five Teenage Alcoholics - Ryan, Elizabeth
Life. Is. Not. Fair. - Bargar, Gary W
Life On A Lost Continent: A Natural History Of New Zealand - Day, Beth
Lift Line: Stories Of Downhill And Cross-Country Skiing - Fenner, Phyllis Reid
Light A Single Candle - Butler, Beverly
The Light In The Forest - Richter, Conrad
Lights, Camera, Love - Maravel, Gailanne
The Lilies Of The Field - Barrett, William E
Limbo Of The Lost - Spencer, John Wallace
Linda Goodman's Sun Signs - Goodman, Linda
Links - Panati, Charles
Lion Adventure - Price, Willard
Lion Gate And Labyrinth - Baumann, Hans
The Lion Of Judah: Haile Selassie I, Emperor Of Ethiopia - Gorham, Charles
Lion On The Run - Rumsey, Marian
The Lionhearted - Savitz, Harriet May
Lions In The Way - Rodman, Bella
Lisa And Lottie - Kastner, Erich
Lisa, Bright And Dark - Neufeld, John
Listen For Rachel - Kassem, Lou
Listen For The Fig Tree - Mathis, Sharon Bell
Listen To Me, I'm Angry - Laiken, Deirdre S
Listening In - Kevles, Bettyann
Little Big Top - Heller, Doris
Little Big Top - Hiller, Doris
A Little Demonstration Of Affection - Winthrop, Elizabeth
Little Giants Of Pro Sports - Aaseng, Nathan
The Little House Books - Wilder, Laura Ingalls

The Man Who Outran Hitler - Owens, Jesse

The Man Who Was Left For Dead - Tripp, Jenny

The Man Without A Face - Holland, Isabelle

Managing Your Money - Miller, Nancy Gridley

Manana Is Now: The Spanish-Speaking In The United States - Eiseman, Alberta

Mandy - Andrews, Julie

Manhattan Is Missing - Hildick, E W

Manners Made Easy - Beery, Mary

Man's Marvelous Computer: The Next Quarter Century - Rusch, Richard B

A Man's Pride: Losing A Father - Miner, Jane Claypool

Man's Reach For The Stars - Gallant, Roy A

Manwolf - Skurzynski, Gloria

Many Waters Cannot Quench Love - Bibby, Violet

Marassa And Midnight - Stuart, Morna

Marathon Miranda - Winthrop, Elizabeth

The Marathon Race Mystery - McNear, Robert

Marathon: The World Of The Long-Distance Athlete - Campbell, Gail

Marcia, Private Secretary - MacDonald, Zillah

Marcus Allen - Leder, Jane M

Marcus Garvey - Davis, Daniel Sheldon

Marian Anderson: Lady From Philadelphia - Newman, Shirlee P

Marie Curie - Keller, Mollie

The Marina Mystery - Leonard, Constance

Mark Fidrych - Gutman, Bill

The Mark Of Conte - Levitin, Sonia

The Mark Twain Murders - Yep, Laurence Michael

Marly The Kid - Pfeffer, Susan Beth

Marooned On Mars - DelRey, Lester

Martha Berry - Blackburn, Joyce Knight

Martin De Porres, Hero - Bishop, Claire Huchet

Martin Luther King: Fighter For Freedom - Preston, Edward

Martin Luther King, Jr. - Patterson, Lillie

Martin Luther King: The Peaceful Warrior - Clayton, Ed

Martina Navratilova - Dolan, Edward Francis, Jr.

Martina Navratilova - Leder, Jane M

The Marvelous Misadventures Of Sebastian - Alexander, Lloyd

Marvin And Tige - Glass, Frankcina

Mary Dove - Rushing, Jane Gilmore

Mary Ellen And Ida: Portraits Of Two Women - Beal, Stephen

Mary Lou Retton - Sullivan, George Edward

Mary Lou Retton: Gold Medal Gymnast - Lundgren, Hal

Mary Mcleod Bethune - Anderson, Lavere

The Mask - Bunting, Eve

Mask For My Heart - Dryden, Pamela

Masks And Mask Makers - Hunt, Kari

Master Entrick: An Adventure, 1754-1756 - Mott, Michael

Master Magicians: Their Lives And Most Famous Tricks - Gibson, Walter B

Master Mike And The Miracle Maid - Hill, Elizabeth Starr

The Master Of Jethart - Dwyer-Joyce, Alice

Master Of Mazes - Gaskin, Carol

Mastering Softball - Zolna, Ed

Masterpieces Of Horror - Morris, Rosamund

Masterpieces Of Mystery And Detection - Morris, Rosamund

Masterpieces Of Suspense - Morris, Rosamund

Masters Of Magic - Kendall, Lace

Math Menagerie - Kadesch, Robert R

Mathematics: Exploring The World Of Numbers And Space - Adler, Irving

A Matter Of Finding The Right Girl - Filichia, Peter

A Matter Of Miracles - Fenton, Edward B

A Matter Of Time - Schotter, Roni

Max In Love - Kaye, Marilyn
Max On Earth - Kaye, Marilyn
Maximilian You're The Greatest - Rosenbloom, Joseph
Max's Wonderful Delicatessen - Madison, Winifred
Maybe Next Year.... - Hest, Amy
Mayday! Mayday! - Milton, Hilary
Me And Mr. Stenner - Hunter, Evan
Me And You And A Dog Named Blue - Corcoran, Barbara
Me, Cassie - Feagles, Anita MacRae
The Me Inside Of Me - Bethancourt, T Ernesto
Me, Minsky And Max - Pollock, Bruce
The Meat In The Sandwich - Bach, Alice
Medic - Engle, Eloise
Medical Emergency - Abels, Harriette Sheffer
The Medicine Makers - Walker, Nona
Meet Me In The Park, Angie - Wood, Phyllis Anderson
Meet The Vampire - McHargue, Georgess
Meet The Werewolf - McHargue, Georgess
Meeting With A Great Beast - Wibberley, Leonard
Megan's Beat - Stanek, Lou Willett
Melanie: Proving Myself - Weeks, Doug
Melissa's Medley - Love, Sandra
Memorable World Series Moments - Aaseng, Nathan
The Men From P.I.G. And R.O.B.O.T. - Harrison, Harry Max
Men In The Sea - Briggs, Peter
Men Who Dig Up History - Poole, Lynn
Men! - Weir, LaVada
Menfreya In The Morning - Holt, Victoria
The Merry Adventures Of Robin Hood - Pyle, Howard
The Merrymaid - Hardwick, Mollie
Meteor From The Moon - Abels, Harriette Sheffer
Mexican Road Race - O'Connor, Patrick
Mexican Whirlwind - Crary, Margaret
Micro Man - Kropp, Paul
Microcomputers - Christian, Mary Blount
Middl'un - Burleson, Elizabeth
Midnight Specials - Pronzini, Bill
Midnight Wheels - Hallman, Ruth
Mighty Hard Road: The Story Of Cesar Chavez - Terzian, James P
Migrant Girl - Laklan, Carli
Mike Schmidt: Baseball's King Of Swing - Hochman, Stan
The Miler - Nelson, Cordner
Military Dogs - Emert, Phyllis R
Milkweed - Selsam, Millicent E
Millie's Boy - Peck, Robert Newton
The Mimosa Tree - Cleaver, Vera
Mind Your Manners - Allen, Betty
The Minority Peoples Of China - Rau, Margaret
Minutes To Live - Stone, Judith
Miracle At Midway - Mercer, Charles Edward
Miracle Of Time: Adopting A Sister - Miner, Jane Claypool
Miracles On Maple Hill - Sorensen, Virginia E
Miracles: Poems By Children Of The English-Speaking World - Lewis, Richard
Miranda In The Middle - Winthrop, Elizabeth
The Mirror Planet - Bunting, Eve
Mischievous Ghosts - Kettelkamp, Larry Dale
The Missing Aircraft - Butterworth, Ben
The Missing Persons League - Bonham, Frank
The Missing Rock Star Caper - McVey, R Parker
Missing Since Monday - Martin, Ann M
The Missing Sunrise - Oppenheimer, Joan Letson
Missing! Stories Of Strange Disappearances - Cohen, Daniel
Mistaken Journey - East, Ben
Mixed-Marriage Daughter - Colman, Hila
Moby Dick - Melville, Herman
The Mock Revolt - Cleaver, Vera

Model Behavior - McNamara, John

Model Cars - Knudson, Richard L

Modern American Career Women - Clymer, Eleanor

Modern American Career Women - Erlich, Lillian

Modern Auto Racing Superstars - Olney, Ross Robert

Modern Baseball Superstars - Gutman, Bill

Modern China: The Story Of A Revolution - Schell, Orville

Modern Drag Racing Superstars - Olney, Ross Robert

Modern Fencing: Foil Epee, Sabre From Initiation To Competition - Alaux, Michel

Modern Football Superstars - Gutman, Bill

Modern Hockey Superstars - Gutman, Bill

Modern Motorcycle Superstars - Olney, Ross Robert

Modern Olympic Superstars - Sullivan, George Edward

Modern Soccer Superstars - Gutman, Bill

Modern Speed Record Superstars - Olney, Ross Robert

Modern Women Superstars - Gutman, Bill

The Mohole Menace - Walters, Hugh

The Mole People - Green, Carl R

Mollie Make-Believe - Bach, Alice

Mollie's Year - Reiff, Tana

Mom, The Wolf Man And Me - Klein, Norma

Monster At Loch Ness - Berke, Sally

Monster Hunting Today - Cohen, Daniel

Monster Tales Of Native Americans - Thorne, Ian

The Monster That Wouldn't Die And Other Strange But True Stories - Otfinoski, Steven

Monsters From The Movies - Aylesworth, Thomas G

Monsters, Ghoulies And Creepy Creatures: Fantastic Stories And Poems - Hopkins, Lee Bennett

The Monsters Of Star Trek - Cohen, Daniel

Monsters You Never Heard Of - Cohen, Daniel

Moose, The Thing, And Me - Butterworth, W E

Mopeds - Reeves, Lawrence F

More Chucklebait: Funny Stories For Everyone - Scoggin, Margaret C

More Food For Our Money: Food Planning And Buying - Thypin, Marilyn

More Incredible! - McFarland, Kevin

More Jokes, Jokes, Jokes - Hoke, Helen L

More Modern Baseball Superstars - Gutman, Bill

More Modern Women Superstars - Gutman, Bill

More Scary Stories To Tell In The Dark - Schwartz, Alvin

More Strange But True Baseball Stories - Liss, Howard

More Than Just Pets: Why People Study Animals - Caputo, Robert

More Tongue Tanglers And A Rigmarole - Potter, Charles Francis

More Words Of Science - Asimov, Isaac

Mork And Mindy 2: The Incredible Shrinking Mork - Wagner, Robin S

Moses Malone - Leder, Jane M

Mother Teresa - Podojil, Catherine

Mother Teresa: Caring For All God's Children - Lee, Betsy

Moto-Cross Monkey - Sheffer, H R

Motorcycle - Jaspersohn, William

Motorcycle Racer - Covington, John P

Motorcycle Racing For Beginners - Edmonds, Ivy Gordon

Motorcycle Road Racer - Kaatz, Evelyn

Motors And Engines And How They Work - Weiss, Harvey

Motown And Didi - Myers, Walter Dean

Mountain Fear: When A Brother Dies - Miner, Jane Claypool

Mountain Rescue - Baker, A A

Movie Kings: Hollywood's Famous Tough Guys And Monsters - Rose, Lew

The New Life - La Vida Neuva: The Mexican-Americans Today - Dobrin, Arnold
New Sound - Waller, Leslie
The New World Of Computers - Lewis, Alfred
The New World Of Helicopters - Delear, Frank J
New York - Bliven, Bruce, Jr.
New York City Too Far From Tampa Blues - Bethancourt, T Ernesto
New York Inside Out - Walker, Robert
The New York Jets - May, Julian
New York Yankees - Ward, Don
Nice Guy, Go Home - Weaver, Robert G
Nicole - Ransom, Candice F
Night After Night - Goudge, Eileen
The Night Creature - Laymon, Richard
Night Driver - Selden, Neil
Night Fall - Aiken, Joan
Night Kites - Kerr, M E
Night Of Fire And Blood - Kelley, Leo P
Night Of The Prom - Spector, Debra
Night On 'Gator Creek - Stewart, Winnie
Night Spell - Newman, Robert Howard
A Night To Remember - Lord, Walter
The Night Walkers - Coontz, Otto
Nightmare Island - Roy, Ron
Nightmare Nina - Shea, George
Nightmares From Space - DeWeese, Gene
The Nightmares Of Geranium Street - Shreve, Susan Richards
Nightshade - Osburn, Jesse
Nikki 108 - Blue, Rose
Nilda - Mohr, Nicholasa
Nine Black American Doctors - Hayden, Robert Carter
The Nitty Gritty - Bonham, Frank
No Easy Circle - Naylor, Phyllis Reynolds
No Man For Murder - Ellis, Melvin Richard
No Man's Land - White, Robb
No Moon On Graveyard Head - Dorian, Edith
No Pain, No Gain - Allman, Paul
No Place To Go - Miner, Jane Claypool
No Place To Hide - Fries, Chloe
No Place To Run - Murphy, Barbara Beasley
No Promises In The Wind - Hunt, Irene
No Rent To Pay - Jackson, Anita
The No-Return Trail - Levitin, Sonia
No Talent Letterman - Jackson, Caary Paul
No Way - Kropp, Paul
Nobody Has To Be A Kid Forever - Colman, Hila
Nobody Knows But Me - Bunting, Eve
Nobody Promised Me - Mack, John
Nobody Said It's Easy - Smith, Sally Liberman
Nobody Told Me What I Need To Know - Colman, Hila
Nobody Wants Annie - Altman, Linda Jacobs
Nobody Waved Good-Bye - Haggard, Elizabeth
Nobody's Baby Now - Benjamin, Carol Lea
Nobody's Perfect, Charlie Brown - Schulz, Charles M
Nolle Smith: Cowboy, Engineer, Statesman - Gugliotta, Bobette
None Of The Above - Wells, Rosemary
The Nonsense Book Of Riddles, Rhymes, Tongue Twisters, Puzzles And Jokes From American Folklore - Emrich, Duncan
Noodles, Nitwits, And Numskulls - Leach, Maria
North American Indian Arts - Whiteford, Andrew Hunter
North Of Danger - Fife, Dale
North To Freedom - Holm, Anne S
North Town - Graham, Lorenz Bell
Northlight, Lovelight - Folch-Ribas, Jacques
Not Bad For A Girl - Taves, Isabella
Not Just Sugar And Spice - Sheffield, Janet N
Notes From A Naturalist's Sketchbook - Leslie, Clare Walker
The Nothing Special - Tomerlin, John

Now Or Never - Halacy, Daniel Stephen, Jr.

Nurse In Training - Laklan, Carli

Nurses And What They Do - Kay, Eleanor

Nursing As A Career - Chandler, Caroline A

O Captain: The Death Of Abraham Lincoln - Hayman, LeRoy

The Ocean World - Kovalik, Vladimir

Of Course You Can Sew! - Corrigan, Barbara

Offensive Football - Griese, Bob

Oh, Rick! - Bunting, Eve

Oil And Natural Gas - Kraft, Betsy Harvey

Oil Machines - Pick, Christopher C

The Old Wilderness Road - Steele, William O

Old Yeller - Gipson, Frederick B

Olga Korbut - Smith, Jay H

Olivia Newton-John - Ruff, Peter

On Astrology - Livingston, Peter

On City Streets - Larrick, Nancy

On ESP - Curtis, Robert H

On Her Own - Rand, Suzanne

On My Own - Davis, Charles

On Stage: Flip Wilson - Braun, Thomas

On The Air: Radio Broadcasting - Hawkins, Robert

On The Ledge And Other Action Packed Stories - Verdick, Mary

On The Move - Savitz, Harriet May

On The Other Side Of The Gate - Suhl, Yuri

On The Red World - Kelley, Leo P

On The Run - Eisenberg, Lisa

On The Run - Montgomery, Herb

On The Way Up: What It's Like To Be In The Minor Leagues - Klein, Dave

On Thin Ice - Saal, Jocelyn

On Your Own - Owen, Evan

The Once In Awhile Hero - Adler, C S

Once In California - Stuart, Becky

Once Upon An Eskimo Time - Wilder, Edna

Once Upon The Little Big Horn - Lampman, Evelyn Sibley

The One And Only Crazy Car Book - Walker, Sloan

One Boy Too Many - Caudell, Marian

One Cool Sister And Other Modern Stories - Mooney, Thomas J

One Dark Night - White, Wallace

One Day For Peace - Crosby, Alexander L

One Fat Summer - Lipsyte, Robert

One For The Road - Hansen, Caryl

One Is One - Picard, Barbara Leonie

One More Flight - Bunting, Eve

One Of The Guys - Makris, Kathryn

One Order To Go - Glenn, Mel

One Punch Away - Greenya, John

One Special Summer - Harrell, Janice

One Summer - Galan, Fernando Javier

One Summer In Between - Mather, Melissa

One Was Left Alive - Tripp, Jenny

One-Way Romance - Sierra, Patricia

One-Way To Ansonia - Angell, Judie

Onion Journey - Cunningham, Julia Woolfolk

Only A Dream Away - Makris, Kathryn

Opal - Whiteley, Opal

The Opal-Eyed Fan - Norton, Andre

Opposites - Wilbur, Richard

Orders To Vietnam - Butterworth, W E

The Original Colored House Of David - Quigley, Martin

Orphans Of The Wind - Haugaard, Erik Christian

The Other Side Of Dark - Nixon, Joan Lowery

The Other Side Of Yellow - Hull, Jessie Redding

The Otis Redding Story - Schiesel, Jane

Our Career In Civil Service - Liston, Robert A

Our Eddie - Ish-Kishor, Sulamith

Our Fragile Earth - Helfman, Elizabeth S

Our John Willie - Cookson, Catherine McMullen

Title Index

Planet Of Ice - Abels, Harriette Sheffer
The Planet Of Junior Brown - Hamilton, Virginia
Planets - Radlauer, Ruth Shaw
The Plant People - Carlson, Dale Bick
Plants Are Like That - Stone, A Harris
Plants Up Close - Rahn, Joan Elma
"Play Ball! - Mays, Willie
Play-Off - Swift, Benjamin
Playing Games - Hehl, Eileen
Please Don't Go - Woodford, Peggy
Please Don't Kiss Me Now - Gerber, Merrill Joan
Please Let Me In - Beckman, Patti
Please Remember Me - Brady, Mari
Please Say Yes - Crawford, Alice Owen
Pleasure Horses - Nentl, Jerolyn Ann
Plumber's Line - Robison, Nancy
Pocket Billiards - Balukas, Jean
A Pocketful Of Stars - Knight, Damon
Poems For Pleasure - Ward, Herman
Poems To Solve - Swenson, May
Point Spread - Dygard, Thomas J
Police Lab - Berger, Melvin
Pollution: The Noise We Hear - Jones, Claire
Poltergeists - Knight, David C
The Ponies - Robison, Nancy
Pope John Paul II: Bringing Love To A Troubled World - Di Franco, Anthony
Popular Music - Rublowsky, John
The Popularity Plan - Vernon, Rosemary
Popularity Plus - Alexander, Marsha
Portrait Of Ivan - Fox, Paula
Portrait Of Love - Nobile, Jeanette
Portrait Of Margarita - Arthur, Ruth M
Power Hockey - Awrey, Don
Practical Macrame - Andes, Eugene
Prank - Lasky, Kathryn
Pregnant Too Soon - Lindsay, Jeanne Warren
Prehistoric Man - Bailey, John
Prepare To Dive: The Story Of Man Undersea - Coggins, Jack
Presenting Superhunk - Goudge, Eileen
Pretty Girl: A Guide To Looking Good, Naturally - McGrath, Judith
Prime Time - Pfeffer, Susan Beth
Prince - Matthews, Gordon
Prince Charles: England's Future King - Nugent, Jean
The Princes Of Earth - Kurland, Michael
Princess Amy - Pollowitz, Melinda Kilborn
Prison Satellite - Kelley, Leo P
Prisoner Of Pedro Cay - Butterworth, Ben
Prisoners In The Snow - Catherall, Arthur
The Pro Basketball Reading Kit - Allison, Jon
Pro Basketball's Big Men - Klein, Dave
Pro Football's Gamebreakers - Sahadi, Lou
Pro Football's Greatest Upsets - Sullivan, George Edward
Pro Football's Ten Greatest Games - Thorn, John
The Problem With Love - Vernon, Rosemary
Project: Scoop - Hayes, William D
The Promise Ring - Stewart, Jo
A Proud Taste For Scarlet And Miniver - Konigsburg, E L
The Proving Trail - L'Amour, Louis
P.S. I Love You - Conklin, Barbara
P.S. Write Soon - Rodowsky, Colby F
Psychiatry - Klagsbrun, Francine Lifton
Psychic Experiences: E.S.P. Investigated - Ostrander, Sheila
Psychic Stories Strange But True - Atkinson, Linda
Public Enemy: And Other True Stories From The Files Of The Fbi - Martinelli, Pat
The Puma - Filson, Brent
Puniddles - McMillan, Bruce
The Punishment Of The Stingy And Other Indian Stories - Grinnell, George Bird
Put Your Money Down - Thypin, Marilyn
Putting On An Act - Killien, Christi

Quarter Boy - Parker, Richard
Quarter Horse Winner - Van Steenwyk, Elizabeth
Quarterback Gamble - Gault, William Campbell
Quarterback Walk-On - Dygard, Thomas J
Quarterback's Aim - Lord, Beman
Queenie Peavy - Burch, Robert J
The Questing Heart - Lawrence, Mildred
A Question Of Harmony - Sprague, Gretchen
Question Of Love - Vernon, Rosemary
Questions And Answers About Acne - Reeves, John R T
Questions And Answers About Alcoholism - Curtis, Robert H
A Quiet Place - Burchard, Peter Duncan
Quiet Rebels: Four Puerto Rican Leaders - Sterling, Philip
A Quilt For Bermuda - Cutting, Edith
Rabbit Ears - Montgomery, Robert
Raccoons Are The Brightest People - North, Sterling
Race Cars - Sheffer, H R
Race To Win - Cowen, Eve
A Racecourse For Andy - Wrightson, Patricia
The Racing Bugs - Olney, Ross Robert
Racing In Her Blood - Altman, Millys N
Radiation: Waves And Particles/benefits And Risks - Pringle, Laurence
Radigan Cares - Eyerly, Jeannette
Raging Rapids - Brisco, Patty
Rainbow Jordan - Childress, Alice
The Rains Of Eridan - Hoover, H M
Raising Daisy Rothschild - Leslie-Melville, Betty
Rallying - Knudson, Richard L
Ralph Bunche: Champion Of Peace - Cornell, Jean Gay
Ralph J. Bunche: Fighter For Peace - Kugelmass, J Alvin
Ramona The Pest - Cleary, Beverly
Ranger In Skirts - Sargent, Shirley
Ransom - Duncan, Lois S
Rascal: A Memoir Of A Better Era - North, Sterling
Rasmus And The Vagabond - Lindgren, Astrid
Rass - Rabe, Berniece Louise
The Rattlesnake - Green, Carl R
Rattlesnake Run - Lazarus, Keo Felker
The Raven - Green, Carl R
Ray Kroc: Big Mac Man - Simpson, Janice C
Read For The Job - Hermann, Charles F
Reading, Writing, Chattering Chimps - Amon, Aline
Ready, Set, Go: How To Find A Career That's Right For You - Gilbert, Sara Dulaney
Real Ghosts - Cohen, Daniel
Real Magic - Cohen, Daniel
The Real World - Sirof, Harriet Toby
Rebound Caper - Dygard, Thomas J
The Red Car - Stanford, Don
Red Fox - Roberts, Charles G D
The Red Hot Rod - Wright, Bob
Red Sky At Morning - Bradford, Richard Roark
Red Sky At Night - Bradbury, Bianca
Redcoat In Boston - Finlayson, Ann
Reflections On A Gift Of Watermelon Pickle And Other Modern Verse - Dunning, Stephen
Reggie Jackson: From Superstar To Candy Bar - Vass, George
The Reggie Jackson Story - Libby, Bill
Reggie Jackson: The Three Million Dollar Man - Allen, Maury
Remember Me When I Am Dead - York, Carol Beach
Remembering The Good Times - Peck, Richard
Remove Protective Coating A Little At A Time - Donovan, John
Report From Engine Co. 82 - Smith, Dennis E
Report On Planet Three And Other Speculations - Clarke, Arthur C
Reptiles And Amphibians Of North America - Fichter, George Siebert
Rescue Chopper - Hallman, Ruth
Rescue! True Stories Of Heroism - Taylor, Lester Barbour, Jr.

Research For Romance - Phillips, Erin
The Restless Dead: Ghostly Tales From Around The World - Cohen, Daniel
Restoring Yesterday's Cars - Knudson, Richard L
Return Of Silver Chief - O'Brien, Jack
The Return Of The Headless Horseman - Christopher, Matt
Return To Earth - Hoover, H M
Revenge In The Silent Tomb - Fortune, J J
Revenge Of The Dolls - York, Carol Beach
The Revolution Of Mary Leary - Shreve, Susan Richards
Rex - Stranger, Joyce
Rhythm Of Love - Foster, Stephanie
Rich And Famous: The Further Adventures Of George Stable - Collier, James Lincoln
Rick Barry: Basketball Ace - O'Connor, Dick
Rick Springfield - Gillianti, Simone
Rico's Cat - Brookins, Dana
Ride When You're Ready - Bolton, Evelyn
Rider's Rock - Lyon, Elinor
Right On, Shane - Skulicz, Matthew
The Right To Be Let Alone: Privacy In The United States - Snyder, Gerald Seymour
Ring The Judas Bell - Forman, James Douglas
Rise And Fall Of Adolph Hitler - Shirer, William L
Rise Of The Robots - Sullivan, George Edward
Rising Damp - Corcoran, Barbara
The Rising Of The Lark - Moray, Ann
Risks - Rees, David
Rivals - Hopper, Nancy J
Rivals On Ice - Van Steenwyk, Elizabeth
River Of The Wolves - Meader, Stephen W
River Rats, Inc. - George, Jean Craighead
River Rising - Skidmore, Hubert
Riverboy: The Story Of Mark Twain - Proudfit, Isabel
The Road From West Virginia - Hardin, Gail
Road Race Round The World: New York To Paris, 1908 - Jackson, Robert Blake
Road Racing In America - Engel, Lyle Kenyon
The Road To Galveston - Smith, Beatrice Schillinger
Roads: From Footpaths To Thruways - Doherty, C H
Roadside Valentine - Adler, C S
The Robber Ghost - Anckarsvard, Karin
Robert Frost: America's Poet - Faber, Doris
Robert Redford - Reed, Donald
Roberta Flack - Morse, Charles
The Robot People - Bunting, Eve
Robotics - Paltrowitz, Stuart
Robots - Kleiner, Art
Rock Fever - Rabinowich, Ellen
Rock 'n' Roll Romance - Lantz, Francess Lin
The Rock Revolution: What's Happening In Today's Music - Shaw, Arnold
Rocket Pioneer - Coombs, Charles Ira
Rocket Ship Galileo - Heinlein, Robert A
Rocketship: An Incredible Journey Through Science Fiction And Science Fact - Malone, Robert
Rocks And How We Use Them - Pine, Tillie S
Rocks And Minerals - Fichter, George Siebert
Rocks And Rills: A Look At Geology - Stone, A Harris
Rocky - Libby, Bill
Rod Carew - Batson, Larry
Rodeo Horses - Philp, Candace T
Rodeo Riders - Munn, Vella
Rodeo Summer - Gulley, Judie
Roger Williams, Defender Of Freedom - Edwards, Cecile Pepin
Roll Of Thunder, Hear My Cry - Taylor, Mildred D
Roller Coaster Kid And Other Poems - Wallenstein, Barry
Roller Hockey - Hollander, Zander

Roller Skating - Shevelson, Joseph
The Roller Skating Book - Weir, LaVada
The Roman Empire - Asimov, Isaac
Roman Hostage - Schurfranz, Vivian
The Roman Republic - Asimov, Isaac
Romance Is A Riot - Winslow, Joan
Romance On Trial - Cavanna, Betty
Romance!: Can You Survive It? - Schneider, Meg
Ron Guidry: Louisiana Lightning - Allen, Maury
Ronnie And Rosey - Angell, Judie
Rookie In The Backcourt - Cox, William R
A Room Made Of Windows - Cameron, Eleanor
The Roper Brothers And Their Magnificent Steam Automobile - Butterworth, W E
Rosalinda - Leach, Christopher
Rosaria - Thaler, Susan
Roses - Cohen, Barbara
Rosina Torres, LPN - Werner, Herma
Rough Ice - Lord, Beman
Rough Rider - Naden, C J
The Rough Road - MacPherson, Margaret
Roughing It Easy - Thomas, Dian
Rounds With A Country Vet - McPhee, Richard B
Rowan Farm - Benary-Isbert, Margot
Royal Blood - Channing, Alissa
Ruffian - Callahan, Dorothy M
Ruffles And Drums - Cavanna, Betty
Rumble Fish - Hinton, S E
Run, Don't Walk - Savitz, Harriet May
Run For Your Life - Ellis, Jim
Run For Your Life - Platt, Kin
Run, Shelley, Run! - Samuels, Gertrude
Run Softly, Go Fast - Wersba, Barbara
Runaway - Kropp, Paul
Runaway Voyage - Cavanna, Betty
The Runaway's Diary - Harris, Marilyn
Runner-Up - Neigoff, Mike
The Running Back - McKay, Robert W
Running Home - Spino, Michael
Running In Circles - Broger, Achim
Running Is For Me - Neff, Fred
Running Scared - Morton, Jane
The Russian Ballet School - Harris, Leon A, Jr.
Ruth Marini: World Series Star - Cebulash, Mel
R.V.'s - Sheffer, H R
Rx For Love - Graham, Leslie
Sad Song Of The Coyote - Ellis, Melvin Richard
Saddle Up: The Farm Journal Book Of Western Horsemanship - Ball, Charles Elihue
Sadler's Birthday - Tremain, Rose
Sailboat Racing - Jones, Claire
Sailboat Summer - Reynolds, Anne
Sailing Small Boats - Weiss, Harvey
Sally Ride: America's First Woman In Space - Blacknall, Carolyn
Sally Ride And The New Astronauts: Scientists In Space - O'Connor, Karen
Sally Ride, Astronaut - Behrens, June
Sam - Corcoran, Barbara
Sam - Scott, Ann Herbert
Sam Savitt's True Horse Stories - Savitt, Sam
The Samurai And The Long-Nosed Devils - Namioka, Lensey
Samurai Of Gold Hill - Uchida, Yoshiko
The Sanctuary Tree - Johnston, Norma
The Sand Ponies - Murphy, Shirley Rousseau
Sandy And The Rock Star - Morey, Walter Nelson
Sandy: The Autobiography Of A Dog - Thomas, Allison
Sarah Bishop - O'Dell, Scott
Sarah Sells Soccer - Sheffer, H R
Sarang: The Story Of The Bengal Tiger And Of Two Children In Search Of A Miracle - Caras, Roger A
Satellites: Servants Of Man - Carlisle, Norman V
Saturday Night - Holmes, Marjorie Rose
Saturday's Child - Seed, Suzanne

Savage Sam - Gipson, Frederick B
Savage Spirit - Cameron, Meg
Save Alice! - Wuorio, Eva-Lis
Save Queen Of Sheba - Moeri, Louise
Save The Dam! - Sirof, Harriet Toby
Save The Mustangs! - Weiss, Ann E
Saving The Big-Deal Baby - Armstrong, Louise
Say Hello To The Hit Man - Bennett, Jay
Sayers! The Sports Career Of Gale Sayers - Hahn, James
Scarab For Luck - Meadowcroft, Enid LaMonte
The Scarecrows - Westall, Robert
Scarface Joe - Edwards, Page, Jr.
Science Experiments You Can Eat - Cobb, Vicki
Science Fiction's Greatest Monsters - Cohen, Daniel
Science Ship - Briggs, Peter
Score!: A Baker's Dozen Sports Stories - MacKellar, William
Scott May: Basketball Champion - Dolan, Edward Francis, Jr.
Scrub Dog Of Alaska - Morey, Walter Nelson
Scruffy - Stoneley, Jack
Sea And Earth: The Life Of Rachel Carson - Sterling, Philip
The Sea Around Us - Carson, Rachel
Sea Captain From Salem - Wibberley, Leonard
The Sea Gulls Woke Me - Stolz, Mary Slattery
Sea Machines - Fenner, Sal
Search And Rescue - Mullin, Penn
Search And Rescue Dogs - Emert, Phyllis R
The Search For Charlie - Dixon, Paige
The Search For King Arthur - Hibbert, Christopher
The Searching Heart - Aks, Patricia
Season Of Love - Clay, Catherine Lee
Season Of Mist - Malek, Doreen Owens
The Seasons Of Time: Tanka Poetry Of Ancient Japan - Baron, Virginia Olsen
Second Chance - Green, Iris
Second Chances - Levinson, Nancy Smiler
The Second Mrs. Giaconda - Konigsburg, E L
Second Star To The Right - Hautzig, Deborah
Second String Nobody - Sheffer, H R
The Secret Cross Of Lorraine - Brow, Thea
The Secret Everyone Knows - Brooks, Cathleen
The Secret Garden - Burnett, Frances Hodgson
Secret Identity - Campbell, Joanna
The Secret Lover Of Elmtree - Roth, Arthur J
The Secret Of Bitter Creek - Leiser, Harry W
The Secret Of Stonehouse - Hall, Lynn
The Secret Of The Crooked Cat - Arden, William
Secret Of The Emerald Star - Whitney, Phyllis A
The Secret Of The Haunted Mirror - Carey, Mary Virginia
The Secret Of The Old Brownstone - Knott, Bill
Secret Of The Tiger's Eye - Whitney, Phyllis A
Secret Selves - Angell, Judie
The Secret Ship - Kluger, Ruth
Secret Spy - Martin, Albert
The Secret Staircase - Wright, Bob
Secrets - Enderle, Judith
Secrets - Lorimer, L T
Secrets In The Garden - Harrell, Janice
Secrets Of A Silent Stranger - Hallman, Ruth
Secrets Of The Great Magicians - Carmichael, Carrie
Secrets Of The Super Athletes: Basketball - Fremon, David
Secrets Of The Supernatural - Mason, Herbert Molloy, Jr.
Secrets Of Tut's Tomb And The Pyramids - Reiff, Stephanie Ann
See You In July - Steiner, Barbara A
Seeing Is Not Believing - Brandreth, Gyles

Some Basics About Motorcycles - Radlauer, Edward
Some Basics About Skateboards - Radlauer, Edward
Some Basics About Vans - Radlauer, Edward
Some Friend! - Carrick, Carol
Some Things Fierce And Fatal - Kahn, Joan
Someone Is Hiding On Alcatraz Island - Bunting, Eve
Something Left To Lose - Brancato, Robin Fidler
Something Out There - Davis, Leslie
Something To Count On - Moore, Emily
Something To Shout About - Beatty, Patricia Robbins
Sometimes I Don't Love My Mother - Colman, Hila
Sometimes I Think I Hear My Name - Avi
Sometimes Nightmares Are Real - Conway, Caron A
Song Of The Shaggy Canary - Wood, Phyllis Anderson
Sonora Beautiful - Clifton, Lucille
Sophia Scarlotti And Ceecee - Feagles, Anita MacRae
Sophia Scrooby Preserved - Bacon, Martha
Sorority Girl - Emery, Anne
Sorrow's Song - Callen, Larry
The Soul Brothers And Sister Lou - Hunter, Kristin Eggleston
Soulscript - Jordan, June
Sounder - Armstrong, William Howard
Sounds And Silences: Poetry For Now - Peck, Richard
South Of The Border - Kingsbury, Dawn
Southern Fried Rat And Other Gruesome Tales - Cohen, Daniel
Southpaw Speed - Archibald, Joe
Space And Beyond - Montgomery, Raymond A
Space Hostages - Fisk, Nicholas
Space Machines - Ciupik, Larry A
The Space People - Bunting, Eve
Space Wars: And Six More Stories Of Time And Space - Coleman, Joseph
The Spanish Letters - Hunter, Mollie
The Spanish Smile - O'Dell, Scott
A Special Kind Of Courage: Profiles Of Young Americans - Rivera, Geraldo
Speedway Challenge - Gault, William Campbell
The Spider, The Cave And The Pottery Bowl - Clymer, Eleanor
Spider Webb Mysteries - Gohman, Fred
Spies And More Spies - Arthur, Robert
Spies And Traitors: Tales Of The Revolutionary And Civil Wars - Raskin, Joseph
Spin Out - Godfrey, Martyn
The Spirit Of Jem - Newby, P H
Spirit On The Wall - Garcia, Ann O'neal
Spirits And Spells - Coville, Bruce
Splinter Of The Mind's Eye - Foster, Alan Dean
Split Decision: Facing Divorce - Miner, Jane Claypool
Split Second: The World Of High Speed Photography - Dalton, Stephen
Sport - Fitzhugh, Louise
A Sporting Proposition - Aldridge, James
Sports Cars - Jackson, Robert Blake
Sports Hero: Brooks Robinson - Burchard, Marshall
Sports Hero: Joe Morgan - Burchard, Marshall
Sports Hero: Johnny Bench - Burchard, Marshall
Sports Hero: Kareem Abdul Jabbar - Burchard, Marshall
Sports Heroes Who Wouldn't Quit - Butler, Hal
Sports Star: Brad Park - Burchard, Sue H
Sports Star: Dorothy Hammill - Burchard, Sue H
Sports Star: Elvin Hayes - Burchard, Sue H
Sports Star: Fernando Valenzuela - Burchard, Sue H
Sports Star: Herschel Walker - Burchard, Sue H
Sports Star: John McEnroe - Burchard, Sue H

Sports Star: Larry Bird - Burchard, Sue H
Sports Star: Nadia Comaneci - Burchard, Sue H
Sports Star: Reggie Jackson - Burchard, Sue H
Sports Star: Tommy John - Burchard, Sue H
Sports Star: Tony Dorsett - Burchard, Sue H
Sports Star: Wayne Gretzky - Burchard, Sue H
Spotlight On Literature - Goodman, Burton
Spotlight On Love - Pines, Nancy
The Spring Street Boys Go All Out - Cebulash, Mel
The Spring Street Boys Settle A Score - Cebulash, Mel
The Spring Street Boys Teamup - Cebulash, Mel
Sprints And Distances: Sports In Poetry - Morrison, Lillian
The Spuddy - Beckwith, Lillian
A Spy Case Built For Two - Walden, Amelia Elizabeth
The Spy Who Never Was And Other True Spy Stories - Knight, David C
The Spy Who Talked Too Much - Walden, Amelia Elizabeth
Squib - Bawden, Nina
Stable Of Fear - Bolton, Evelyn
Stages In Adult Life - Charuhas, Mary
Stained Glass Crafting - Wood, Paul W
The Stainless Steel Rat Saves The World - Harrison, Harry Max
Stamp Twice For Murder - Cavanna, Betty
Stanley's Secret Trip - Hull, Jessie Redding
Star Gold - Kelley, Leo P
Star Light Star Bright - Williamson, Amy
Star Of Danger - Levin, Jane Whitbread
Star Struck! - Blair, Shannon
Star Trek II Short Stories - Rotsler, William
Starring Peter And Leigh - Pfeffer, Susan Beth
Starstruck - Gioffre, Marisa
Starting A New Job - McHugh, John
Starting Out: The Guide I Wish I'd Had When I Left Home - Krakowski, Lili
Starting Your Own Band: Rock, Disco, Folk, Jazz, Country And Western - Van Ryzin, Lani
State Your Claim! Small Claims Court - Thypin, Marilyn
Stay On Your Toes, Maggie Adams! - Dean, Karen Strickler
Steffie Can't Come Out To Play - Arrick, Fran
Steinmetz: Wizard Of Light - Guy, Anne Welsh
Step On A Crack - Anderson, Mary
Step To The Music - Whitney, Phyllis A
Stepchild - Berger, Terry
Steve Bellamy - Butterworth, W E
Steve Cauthen - Miklowitz, Gloria D
Steve Garvey: Storybook Star - Cohen, Joel H
Steve Garvey: The Bat Boy Who Became A Star - Vass, George
Steven Spielberg: Creator Of E.T. - Collins, Tom
Stevie Wonder - Hasegawa, Sam
Sticks And Stones - Hall, Lynn
Stock Car Racing: Grand National Competition - Jackson, Robert Blake
The Stolen Lake - Aiken, Joan
Stolen Pony - Rounds, Glen
The Stone Carnation - Hintze, Naomi A
Stop And Search - Butterworth, W E
Stop, Thief! - Butterworth, W E
Stories From El Barrio - Thomas, Piri
Stories From Shakespeare - Chute, Marchette
Stories Of Famous Explorers By Land - Knight, Frank
The Storm - Nye, Peter
Storm In Her Heart - Cavanna, Betty
Storm Warning: The Story Of Hurricanes And Tornadoes - Buehr, Walter
The Story Of A Young Gymnast Tracee Talavera - Jacobs, Karen Folger

Sunday Father - Neufeld, John

Sunny Side Up - Grimes, Frances Hurley

Sunshine - Klein, Norma

Sunworld - Kelley, Leo P

Super Bowl Superstars: The Most Valuable Players In The NFL's Championship Game - Alfano, Pete

Super Bowl XVII - Ward, Don

Super Champions Of Auto Racing - Olney, Ross Robert

Super Champions Of Ice Hockey - Olney, Ross Robert

The Super Showmen - Wayne, Bennett

Superanimals And Their Unusual Careers - Clemens, Virginia Phelps

Supermex: The Lee Trevino Story - Jackson, Robert Blake

Supermonsters - Cohen, Daniel

The Supernatural - Berger, Melvin

Supernatural Mysteries And Other Tales - Snow, Edward Rowe

Supernatural Mysteries: New England To The Bermuda Triangle - Snow, Edward Rowe

Superpuppy: How To Choose, Raise, And Train The Best Possible Dog For You - Pinkwater, Jill

A Superstar Called Sweetpea - Davidson, Mary S

Superstars - Ronan, Margaret

Superstars Of Women's Track - Sullivan, George Edward

Superstars Stopped Short - Aaseng, Nathan

Supertanker - Sullivan, George Edward

The Surfer And The City Girl - Cavanna, Betty

Surf's Up For Laney - Caldwell, Claire

Surf's Up!: An Anthology Of Surfing - Klein, H Arthur

Survival Camp! - Bunting, Eve

Susan B. Anthony - Peterson, Helen Stone

Susannah And The Blue House Mystery - Elmore, Patricia

Susie King Taylor, Civil War Nurse - Booker, Simeon

Suspect - Giff, Patricia Reilly

Suzy Who? - Madison, Winifred

S.W.A.K.: Sealed With A Kiss - Enderle, Judith

Swan Lake - Diamond, Donna

Sweet Bells Jangled Out Of Tune - Brancato, Robin Fidler

The Sweet Dreams Love Book - Laiken, Deirdre S

Sweet Friday Island - Taylor, Theodore Langhans

Sweet Talk - Goudge, Eileen

Swiftwater - Annixter, Paul

Swim For Pride - Sheffer, H R

The Swiss Family Robinson - Wyss, Johann David

Sycamore Year - Lee, Mildred

Sylvester Stallone: Going The Distance - Simpson, Janice C

Take A Balloon - Stone, A Harris

Take A Number - O'Neill, Mary

Take Back The Moment - Stevens, Janice

Take Care Of Millie - Hull, Jessie Redding

Take Off - Kropp, Paul

Take Two And...Rolling! - Pfeffer, Susan Beth

Takers And Returners: A Novel Of Suspense - York, Carol Beach

Taking Care - Howe, Fanny

Taking Sides - Klein, Norma

Taking Terri Mueller - Mazer, Norma Fox

Taking The Wheel - Stein, Wendy

Tales Of A Dead King - Myers, Walter Dean

Tales Of Terror - Chittum, Ida

Tales Of The Elders: A Memory Book Of Men And Women Who Came To America As Immigrants, 1900-1930 - Bales, Carol Ann

The Talking Coffins Of Cryo-City - Parenteau, Shirley Laurolyn

Talking With The Animals - Cohen, Daniel

Tall Tales: American Myths - Lisker, Tom

A Tangle Of Roots - Girion, Barbara

Tangled Butterfly - Bauer, Marion Dane

Things I Learned After It Was Too Late (and Other Minor Truths) - Schulz, Charles M

Third And Goal - Cox, William R

Third Girl From The Left - Turner, Ann W

The Thirteenth Year - Blue, Rose

This Book Is For The Birds - Wilson, Tom

This Day Is Mine: Living With Leukemia - Miner, Jane Claypool

This House Is Haunted! - Hoffman, Elizabeth P

This Is Advertising - Wood, James Playsted

This Is An Orchestra - Posell, Elsa Z

This Is Espie Sanchez - Dunnahoo, Terry

This Is The United Nations - Sasek, Miroslav

This Place Has No Atmosphere - Danziger, Paula

This School Is Driving Me Crazy - Hentoff, Nat

This Side Of Victory - Koob, Theodora

This Slender Reed: A Life Of James K. Polk - Lomask, Milton Nachman

This Strange New Feeling - Lester, Julius

This Time Count Me In - Wood, Phyllis Anderson

This Time Of Darkness - Hoover, H M

Thor Heyerdahl: Across The Seas Of Time - Westman, Paul

Thor Heyerdahl: Viking Scientist - Blassingame, Wyatt

The Thoroughbred - Campbell, Joanna

Thoroughbreds - Callahan, Dorothy M

Thorpe! The Sports Career Of James Thorpe - Hahn, James

Those Who Dared: Adventure Stories From The Bible - McGraw, Barbara

Thousand Camps - Waldorf, Mary

Three And The Shape Of Three: Exploring Mathematics - Razzell, Arthur G

Three Jazz Greats - Wayne, Bennett

Three-Legged Race - Crawford, Charles P

Three Mile House - McAuliffe, Jim

Three Survived - Silverberg, Robert

The Throme Of The Erril Of Sherill - McKillip, Patricia A

Through A Brief Darkness - Peck, Richard

The Throwing Season - French, Michael

Thunder Road - Gault, William Campbell

Thunderbird - Sachs, Marilyn

Thurgood Marshall: Fighter For Justice - Fenderson, Lewis H

Thursday - Storr, Catherine

Thursday's Child - Streatfeild, Noel

Tiger Eyes - Blume, Judy

Tiger, Lion, Hawk - Rice, Earle, Jr.

Tiger Rose - Eisenberg, Lisa

Tight Spot - Birch, Claire

Tiltawhirl John - Paulsen, Gary

Time And Again - Finney, Jack

Time Bomb At Brillstone - Heide, Florence Parry

Time Cat: The Remarkable Journeys Of Jason And Gareth - Alexander, Lloyd

A Time For Tenderness - Cavanna, Betty

The Time Keeper - Bartholomew, Barbara

The Time Machine. The War Of The Worlds - Wells, H G

The Time Of The Witch - Hahn, Mary Downing

Time Of Trial - Burton, Hester

A Time To Choose - Reiff, Tana

A Time To Choose - Stewart, Jo

Time To Take Sides - Gold, Sharlya

Tina And David - Tate, Joan

Tina Gogo - Angell, Judie

Tiny: The Story Of Nate Archibald - Devaney, John

Tit For Tat And Other Latvian Folk Tales - Durham, Mae

Titans Of The American Stage - Shaw, Dale

Tituba Of Salem Village - Petry, Ann

To Be A Slave - Lester, Julius

To Catch A Mugger - Scariano, Margaret

To Love Is Not To Lose - Randall, Lauren

To My Son, The Teen-Age Driver - Felsen, Henry Gregor
To Sir, With Love - Braithwaite, Edward
To Smoke Or Not To Smoke - Terry, Luther L
To Take A Dare - Dragonwagon, Crescent
To Tell Your Love - Stolz, Mary Slattery
To The Bright And Shining Sun - Burke, James Lee
Toby Alone - Branscum, Robbie
Today I Am A Ham - Parkinson, Ethelyn M
Together In America: The Story Of Two Races And One Nation - Johnston, Johanna
Tom Seaver: Portrait Of A Pitcher - Drucker, Malka
Tom Sullivan's Adventures In Darkness - Gill, Derek L T
Tomfoolery - Schwartz, Alvin
The Tommy Davis Story - Russell, Patrick
Tomorrow's Children - Asimov, Isaac
Toni's Crowd - Rabinowich, Ellen
Tony Dorsett: From Heisman To Superbowl In One Year - Conrad, Dick
The Tony Dorsett Story - Musick, Phil
Too Bad About The Haines Girl - Sherburne, Zoa Morin
Too Close For Comfort - Spector, Debra
Too Hot To Handle - Goudge, Eileen
Too Much T.J. - Shannon, Jacqueline
Too Much To Lose - Rand, Suzanne
Too Much Too Soon - Goudge, Eileen
Too Young For Love - Maravel, Gailanne
Too Young To Know - Ogilvie, Elisabeth
Too Young To Know - Scariano, Margaret
Toothpick - Ethridge, Kenneth E
The Top-Flight Fully-Automated Junior High School Girl Detective - Hildick, E W
Top Hand - Kroll, Francis Lynde
Top Recording Artist And TV Star! Shaun Cassidy - Berman, Connie
Tornado! - Milton, Hilary
Totems And Tribes - Lyon, Nancy
Touch And Go: A Story Of Suspense - Poole, Josephine
Touch Blue - Morrison, Lillian
A Touch Of Ginger - Goudge, Eileen
Touch Of Magic - Cavanna, Betty
Touchdown! - Hollander, Phyllis
Touching - Neufeld, John
Tough Choices - Mendonca, Susan
The Tough Guy: Black In A White World - Miner, Jane Claypool
Tough Is Not Enough - Hallman, Ruth
The Tournaments - Deegan, Paul Joseph
Toward Infinity - Knight, Damon
Town In Terror - Randall, E T
The Town Is On Fire - Healey, Larry
Track Is For Me - Dickmeyer, Lowell
Track's Magnificent Milers - Aaseng, Nathan
Tractors - Sheffer, H R
Tracy Austin: Teen Tennis Champion - Robison, Nancy
Trading Secrets - Reuben, Liz
Trail Bikes - Jefferis, David
Trains - Sheffer, H R
The Traitors - Forman, James Douglas
Transistors And Circuits: Electronics For Young Experimenters - Pearce, W E
Transport 7-41-R - Degens, T
Trapped - Jeffries, Roderic Graeme
Trapped In Death Cave - Wallace, Bill
Trapped In Devil's Hole - East, Ben
Trapped In The U.S.S.R. - Fortune, J J
The Travels Of Colin O'Dae - Franchere, Ruth
Travels With Charley - Steinbeck, John
Treasure In Devil's Bay - Brown, Alexis
The Treasure Of Alpheus Winterborn - Bellairs, John
The Treasure Of Fan-Tan Flat - Turner, William O
The Treasure Of The Turkish Pasha - Biber, Yehoash
Treat Me Right - Goudge, Eileen
Tree Boy - Nagel, Shirley
The Tree House Mystery - Wright, Bob

SUBJECT INDEX

Subject Index

ADOLESCENT PARENTS

Lindsay, Jeanne Warren - *Teens Parenting*

ADOPTION

Krementz, Jill - *How It Feels To Be Adopted*
Lindsay, Jeanne Warren - *Pregnant Too Soon*

ADOPTION—Fiction

Aks, Patricia - *The Searching Heart*
Bates, Betty - *Bugs In Your Ears*
Bates, Betty - *It Must've Been The Fish Sticks*
Lowry, Lois - *Find A Stranger, Say Goodbye*
Neufeld, John - *Edgar Allan*
Roth, Arthur J - *The Secret Lover Of Elmtree*
Winthrop, Elizabeth - *Marathon Miranda*

ADULTERY—Fiction

Lorimer, L T - *Secrets*

ADVENTURE AND ADVENTURERS

Bosworth, J Allan - *A Darkness Of Giants*
Gardner, Sandra - *Six Who Dared*
Gunning, Thomas G - *Amazing Escapes*
Scoggin, Margaret C - *Escapes And Rescues*
Wulffson, Don L - *Incredible True Adventures*

ADVENTURE AND ADVENTURERS—Fiction

Aiken, Joan - *The Stolen Lake*
Blue, Zachary - *The Petrova Twist*
Breckler, Rosemary - *Where Are The Twins?*
Crayder, Dorothy - *She, The Adventuress*
Deane, Shirley - *Vendetta*
Frost, Betty - *Voyage Of The Vagabond*
Healey, Larry - *The Hoard Of The Himalayas*
Jeffries, Roderic Graeme - *Trapped*
Myers, Walter Dean - *Adventure In Granada*
Myers, Walter Dean - *The Hidden Shrine*
Myers, Walter Dean - *The Legend Of Tarik*
Newby, P H - *The Spirit Of Jem*
Packard, Edward - *The Cave Of Time*
Packard, Edward - *Your Code Name Is Jonah*
Paisley, Tom - *Doris Fein: Dead Heat At Long Beach*
Roth, Arthur J - *Two For Survival*
Savitz, Harriet May - *If You Can't Be The Sun, Be A Star*
White, Robb - *Deathwatch*
White, Robb - *No Man's Land*
Wilcox, Collin - *The Watcher*

ADVERTISING

Wood, James Playsted - *This Is Advertising*

ADVERTISING—Fiction

Kidd, Ronald - *Dunker*
Tchudi, Stephen N - *The Burg-O-Rama Man*

AERIALISTS—Fiction

White, Robb - *The Long Way Down*

AERODYNAMICS

Corbett, Scott - *What Makes A Plane Fly?*
Freeman, Mae Blacker - *When Air Moves*

AERONAUTICS

Douty, Esther Morris - *The Brave Balloonists: America's First Airmen*
Elder, Lauren - *And I Alone Survived*
Fuller, Elizabeth - *My Search For The Ghost Of Flight 401*
Hyde, Margaret Oldroyd - *Flight Today And Tomorrow*
Madison, Arnold - *Great Unsolved Cases*
McFarland, Kenton Dean - *Airplanes: How They Work*
Olney, Ross Robert - *Out To Launch*
Peet, Creighton - *Man In Flight: How The Airlines Operate*
Titler, Dale Milton - *Wings Of Adventure*
Tripp, Jenny - *One Was Left Alive*
Williams, Brian - *Aircraft*

AERONAUTICS AS A PROFESSION

Ray, E Roy - *What Does An Airline Crew Do?*

ALCOHOL AND YOUTH—Fiction (continued)

White, Wallace - *One Dark Night*

ALLEGORIES

Macaulay, David Alexander - *Baaa*

ALLIED HEALTH PERSONNEL—Fiction

Miklowitz, Gloria D - *Paramedic Emergency!*

ALLIGATORS

Adrian, Mary - *The American Alligator*

AMATEUR MOTION PICTURES

Bendick, Jeanne - *Filming Works Like This*

AMERICAN FICTION—Black authors

Adoff, Arnold - *Brothers And Sisters: Modern Stories By Black Americans*
James, Charles L - *From The Roots: Short Stories By Black Americans*

AMERICAN FIELD SERVICE

Machol, Libby - *Giana*

AMERICAN POETRY

Brewton, Sara Westbrook - *America Forever New*
Dunning, Stephen - *Reflections On A Gift Of Watermelon Pickle And Other Modern Verse*
Froman, Robert Winslow - *Seeing Things*
Glenn, Mel - *Class Dismissed II*
Livingston, Myra Cohn - *The Malibu And Other Poems*
McDonald, Gerald - *A Way Of Knowing: A Collection Of Poems For Boys*
Merriam, Eve - *Out Loud*
Morrison, Lillian - *The Sidewalk Racer And Other Poems Of Sports And Motion*
Wallenstein, Barry - *Roller Coaster Kid And Other Poems*
Ward, Herman - *Poems For Pleasure*

AMERICAN POETRY (COLLECTIONS)

Adoff, Arnold - *Celebrations: A New Anthology Of Black American Poetry*
Janeczko, Paul - *The Crystal Image: A Poetry Anthology*
Peck, Richard - *Sounds And Silences: Poetry For Now*

AMERICAN POETRY—Black authors

Adoff, Arnold - *Celebrations: A New Anthology Of Black American Poetry*
Adoff, Arnold - *I Am The Darker Brother*
Adoff, Arnold - *It Is The Poem Singing Into Your Eyes*
Adoff, Arnold - *My Black Me*
Jordan, June - *Soulscript*

AMERICAN POETRY—Translations

Brandon, William - *The Magic World*

AMISH—Fiction

Weaver, Robert G - *Nice Guy, Go Home*

AMISTAD (SCHOONER)

Sterne, Emma - *The Long Black Schooner*

AMNESIA—Fiction

Holland, Isabelle - *Perdita*

AMPHIBIANS

Fichter, George Siebert - *Reptiles And Amphibians Of North America*

AMPUTEES—Biography

McGravie, Anne V - *All The Way Back*

AMUSEMENT PARKS—Fiction

Paulsen, Gary - *Tiltawhirl John*

AMUSEMENT RIDES

Hahn, Christine - *Amusement Park Machines*

AMUSEMENTS

Roth, Arnold - *Pick A Peck Of Puzzles*

ANGER

Laiken, Deirdre S - *Listen To Me, I'm Angry*

ANIMALS

Adamson, Joy - *Pippa, The Cheetah, And Her Cubs*
Buchenholz, Bruce - *A Way With Animals*
Buck, Margaret Waring - *Where They Go In Winter*
Caputo, Robert - *More Than Just Pets: Why People Study Animals*
Clemens, Virginia Phelps - *Superanimals And Their Unusual Careers*
Cohen, Daniel - *Talking With The Animals*
Dugdale, Vera - *Album Of North American Animals*
Fortman, Jan - *Creatures Of Mystery*
Gutman, Bill - *Women Who Work With Animals*
Holden, Raymond P - *Wildlife Mysteries*
Meyers, James - *Incredible Animals*
Meyers, Susan - *Pearson: A Harbor Seal Pup*
Patent, Dorothy Hinshaw - *Hunters And The Hunted: Surviving In The Animal World*
Perry, Richard - *The World Of The Giant Panda*
Rieger, Shay - *Animals In Clay*
Roth, Charles E - *Then There Were None*
Senn, J A - *The Wolf King And Other True Animal Stories*
Silverberg, Robert - *The Auk, The Dodo And The Oryx*
Simon, Hilda - *Chameleons And Other Quick-Change Artists*
Tunis, Edwin - *Chipmunks On The Doorstep*
Wilcox, Tamara - *Bats, Cats, And Sacred Cows*

ANIMALS (MYTHICAL)

Cohen, Daniel - *Monster Hunting Today*
Cohen, Daniel - *Monsters You Never Heard Of*
Evans, Larry - *How To Draw Monsters*
Stoutenburg, Adrien Pearl - *American Tall Tale Animals*
Thorne, Ian - *Monster Tales Of Native Americans*

ANIMALS—Fiction

Bunting, Eve - *The Followers*
Burnford, Sheila - *The Incredible Journey*
DeJong, Meindert - *Hurry Home, Candy*
Kjelgaard, Jim - *Outlaw Red*
Leslie-Melville, Betty - *Raising Daisy Rothschild*
Montgomery, Rutherford George - *Kildee House*
Rawls, Wilson - *Summer Of The Monkeys*
Rumsey, Marian - *Lion On The Run*
Rylant, Cynthia - *Every Living Thing*
Selden, George - *The Cricket In Times Square*
Selden, George - *Tucker's Countryside*
Stafford, Jean - *Elephi, The Cat With The High I.Q.*
Wibberley, Leonard - *Meeting With A Great Beast*

ANOREXIA NERVOSA—Fiction

Hautzig, Deborah - *Second Star To The Right*
Snyder, Anne - *Goodbye, Paper Doll*

ANTARCTIC REGIONS

Asimov, Isaac - *How Did We Find Out About Antarctica?*

ANTINUCLEAR MOVEMENT—Fiction

Rardin, Susan Lowry - *Captives In A Foreign Land*

ANTS

Lisker, Tom - *Terror In The Tropics: The Army Ants*

APARTMENTS

James, Elizabeth - *A Place Of Your Own*

APES

Berger, Gilda - *Apes In Fact And Fiction*
Cook, David - *A Closer Look At Apes*

APES—Fiction

Donovan, John - *Family*

APHORISMS AND APOTHEGMS

Schulz, Charles M - *Things I Learned After It Was Too Late (and Other Minor Truths)*

APPALACHIAN MOUNTAINS—Fiction

Lawrence, Mildred - *Walk A Rocky Road*

APPLICATIONS FOR POSITIONS

Armstrong, Fiona - *Getting Ready For The World Of Work*
McHugh, John - *Filling Out Job Application Forms*

AQUARIUM FISHES

Fletcher, Alan Mark - *Unusual Aquarium Fishes*
Sarnoff, Jane - *A Great Aquarium Book: The Putting-It-Together Guide For Beginners*

ARABS—Fiction

Kennedy, Richard - *The Boxcar At The Center Of The Universe*

ARCHAEOLOGY

Freeman, Mae Blacker - *Finding Out About The Past*
Glubok, Shirley - *Art And Archaeology*
Gorenstein, Shirley - *Introduction To Archaeology*
Harker, Ronald - *Digging Up The Bible Lands*
James, T G H - *The Archaeology Of Ancient Egypt*
Magnusson, Magnus - *Introducing Archaeology*
Poole, Lynn - *Men Who Dig Up History*
Yadin, Yigael - *The Story Of Masada*

ARCHAEOLOGY—Fiction

DuPrau, Jeanne - *Golden God*
Myers, Walter Dean - *Tales Of A Dead King*

ARCHITECTURE

Kahn, Ely Jacques - *A Building Goes Up*
Sullivan, George Edward - *Understanding Architecture*

ARCTIC REGIONS—Fiction

Houston, James - *Frozen Fire: A Tale Of Courage*

ARIZONA—Fiction

Schellie, Don - *Kidnapping Mr. Tubbs*

ARKANSAS—Fiction

Branscum, Robbie - *Toby Alone*
Hall, Lynn - *The Solitary*

ARMENIANS IN THE UNITED STATES—Fiction

Saroyan, William - *My Name Is Aram*

ARMS AND ARMOR

Nickel, Helmut - *Warriors And Worthies: Arms And Armours Through The Ages*
Wilkinson, Frederick - *Arms And Armor*

ARSON—Fiction

Christian, Mary Blount - *The Firebug Mystery*
Kropp, Paul - *Burn Out*
Murphy, Barbara Beasley - *Ace Hits Rock Bottom*

ART

Glubok, Shirley - *The Art Of Ancient Peru*
Glubok, Shirley - *The Art Of Colonial America*
Glubok, Shirley - *The Art Of The New American Nation*
Glubok, Shirley - *The Art Of The Spanish In The United States And Puerto Rico*
Marshall, Anthony D - *Africa's Living Arts*
Oster, Maggie - *The Illustrated Bird*
Rieger, Shay - *Animals In Clay*
Samachson, Dorothy - *The First Artists*
Smaridge, Norah Antoinette - *The Teen-Ager's Guide To Collecting Practically Anything*

ARTIFICIAL SATELLITES

Carlisle, Norman V - *Satellites: Servants Of Man*

ARTISTS

DeArmond, Dale - *Dale DeArmond: A First Book Collection Of Her Prints*
Feelings, Thomas - *Black Pilgrimage*
Witty, Ken - *A Day In The Life Of An Illustrator*

ARTISTS—Fiction

Goffstein, M B - *Daisy Summerfield's Style*

ARTISTS—Fiction (continued)

Levoy, Myron - *A Shadow Like A Leopard*
Parker, Richard - *Quarter Boy*

ASSISTANCE IN EMERGENCIES

Chan, Janis Fisher - *Where To Go For Help*

ASTROLOGY

Goodman, Linda - *Linda Goodman's Sun Signs*
Jones, McClure - *Lucky Sun Signs For Teens*
Livingston, Peter - *On Astrology*
Shapiro, Amy - *Sun Signs: The Stars In Your Life*

ASTROLOGY—Fiction

Platt, Kin - *Chloris And The Freaks*
Stewart, Mary Florence Elinor - *Ludo And The Star Horse*

ASTRONAUTICS

Ciupik, Larry A - *Space Machines*
Clarke, Arthur C - *Report On Planet Three And Other Speculations*
Coombs, Charles Ira - *Skylab*
Gallant, Roy A - *Man's Reach For The Stars*
Goodwin, Harold L - *All About Rockets And Space Flight*
Hoyt, Mary Finch - *American Women Of The Space Age*
Malone, Robert - *Rocketship: An Incredible Journey Through Science Fiction And Science Fact*

ASTRONAUTS

Behrens, June - *Sally Ride, Astronaut*
Blacknall, Carolyn - *Sally Ride: America's First Woman In Space*
O'Connor, Karen - *Sally Ride And The New Astronauts: Scientists In Space*
Oliver, Carl R - *Plane Talk: Aviators' And Astronauts' Own Stories*
Westman, Paul - *Frank Borman: To The Moon And Back*
Westman, Paul - *John Glenn: Around The World In 90 Minutes*
Westman, Paul - *John Young: Space Shuttle Commander*

ASTRONOMERS

Sullivan, Navin - *Pioneer Astronomers*

ASTRONOMY

Adler, David A - *Hyperspace!: Facts And Fun From All Over The Universe*
Gallant, Roy A - *Exploring The Universe*
Lauber, Patricia - *Look-It-Up Book Of Stars And Planets*
Moore, Patrick - *Seeing Stars*
Peltier, Leslie C - *Guideposts To The Stars: Exploring The Skies Throughout The Year*

ATHLETES

Aaseng, Nathan - *Little Giants Of Pro Sports*
Aaseng, Nathan - *Superstars Stopped Short*
Aaseng, Nathan - *Winners Never Quit: Athletes Who Beat The Odds*
Bontemps, Arna Wendell - *Famous Negro Athletes*
Butler, Hal - *Sports Heroes Who Wouldn't Quit*
Campbell, Gail - *Marathon: The World Of The Long-Distance Athlete*
Chodes, John - *Bruce Jenner*
Clary, Jack - *The Captains*
Gelman, Steve - *Young Olympic Champions*
Gutman, Bill - *Modern Women Superstars*
Gutman, Bill - *More Modern Women Superstars*
Hahn, James - *Thorpe! The Sports Career Of James Thorpe*
Hahn, James - *Zaharias! The Sports Career Of Mildred Zaharias*
Hollander, Phyllis - *American Women In Sports*
Hollander, Phyllis - *Winners Under 21*
Izenberg, Jerry - *Great Latin Sports Figures: Proud People*
Litsky, Frank - *The Winter Olympics*
Olney, Ross Robert - *Modern Speed Record Superstars*
Pepe, Philip - *Great Comebacks In Sport*
Sorensen, Robert - *Shadow Of The Past: True Life Sports Stories*
Sullivan, George Edward - *Modern Olympic Superstars*

ATLANTIS

McMullen, David - *Atlantis: The Missing Continent*
Stahel, H R - *Atlantis Illustrated*

ATLANTIS—Fiction

Ellerby, Leona - *King Tut's Game Board*

ATOMIC BOMB

Stein, R Conrad - *Hiroshima*

ATOMIC BOMB—Fiction

Miklowitz, Gloria D - *After The Bomb*

ATOMIC POWER PLANTS—Fiction

DelRey, Lester - *Nerves*
Rubinstein, Robert E - *When Sirens Scream*

ATOMS

Asimov, Isaac - *How Did We Find Out About Atoms?*

AUNTS—Fiction

Branscum, Robbie - *The Murder Of Hound Dog Bates*
Degens, T - *The Visit*
Robinson, Barbara Webb - *Temporary Times, Temporary Places*

AUSTRALIA—Fiction

Clark, Mavis Thorpe - *If The Earth Falls In*
Eisenberg, Lisa - *Fast Food King*
Phipson, Joan - *Hit And Run*
Wrightson, Patricia - *A Racecourse For Andy*

AUTHORSHIP—Fiction

Sachs, Marilyn - *A Summer's Lease*

AUTOGRAPHS

Morrison, Lillian - *Best Wishes, Amen*
Sullivan, George Edward - *The Complete Book Of Autograph Collecting*

AUTOMOBILES

Abodaher, David J - *Compacts, Subs And Minis*
Bendick, Jeanne - *The First Book Of Automobiles*
Clark, James I - *Cars*
Cohen, Daniel - *How To Buy A Car*
Cooke, David C - *How Automobiles Are Made*
Fales, E D, Jr. - *The Book Of Expert Driving*
Felsen, Henry Gregor - *To My Son, The Teen-Age Driver*
Grebel, Rosemary - *Caring For Your Car*
Harris, Leon A, Jr. - *Behind The Scenes In A Car Factory*
Hoffman, Jeffrey - *Corvette: America's Supercar*
Jackson, Robert Blake - *Sports Cars*
Joyce, Donald P - *Studying For A Driver's License*
Knudson, Richard L - *Model Cars*
Knudson, Richard L - *Rallying*
Knudson, Richard L - *Restoring Yesterday's Cars*
Lent, Henry B - *The Look Of Cars: Yesterday, Today, Tomorrow*
Lord, Beman - *Look At Cars*
Marshall, Ray - *Watch It Work! The Car*
Oates, Jean - *Maintaining Your Car*
Sheffer, H R - *Great Cars*
Stein, Wendy - *Becoming A Car Owner*
Stein, Wendy - *Taking The Wheel*
Taylor, Dawson - *Aim For A Job In Automotive Service*
Thypin, Marilyn - *Wheels And Deals: Buying A Car*
Walker, Sloan - *The One And Only Crazy Car Book*
Wenzel, Celeste Piano - *The Crazy Custom Car Book*
Yerkow, Charles - *Automobiles: How They Work*

AUTOMOBILES—Fiction

Biro, Val - *Gumdrop*
Butterworth, W E - *Dave White And The Electric Wonder Car*
Butterworth, W E - *The Roper Brothers And Their Magnificent Steam Automobile*
Carlson, Nola - *A New Face In The Mirror*
Felsen, Henry Gregor - *Hot Rod*
Felsen, Henry Gregor - *Street Rod*
Hallman, Ruth - *Midnight Wheels*
Sachs, Marilyn - *Thunderbird*

AUTOMOBILE RACING

Ashford, Jeffrey - *Grand Prix Monaco*
Coombs, Charles Ira - *Auto Racing*
Denan, Jay - *The Glory Ride*
Edmonds, Ivy Gordon - *Hot Rodding For Beginners*
Engel, Lyle Kenyon - *Road Racing In America*
Gerber, Dan - *Indy*

AUTOMOBILE RACING (continued)

Jackson, Robert Blake - *Grand Prix At The Glen*
Jackson, Robert Blake - *Road Race Round The World: New York To Paris, 1908*
Jackson, Robert Blake - *Stock Car Racing: Grand National Competition*
Knudson, Richard L - *Land Speed Record Breakers*
Leder, Jane M - *Champ Cars*
Nolan, William Francis - *Carnival Of Speed: True Adventures In Motor Racing*
Olney, Ross Robert - *How To Understand Auto Racing*
Olney, Ross Robert - *The Racing Bugs*
Sheffer, H R - *Race Cars*
Smith, LeRoi Tex - *Make Your Own Hot Rod*
West, Aille X - *Trucks At The Track: And Seven More Exciting Stories Of Wheels And Cycles*

AUTOMOBILE RACING—Fiction

Altman, Millys N - *Racing In Her Blood*
Butterworth, W E - *Crazy To Race*
Butterworth, W E - *Grand Prix Driver*
Butterworth, W E - *Team Racer*
Gault, William Campbell - *The Checkered Flag*
Gault, William Campbell - *Dirt Track Summer*
Gault, William Campbell - *Drag Strip*
Gault, William Campbell - *Speedway Challenge*
Gault, William Campbell - *Thunder Road*
McCrackin, Mark - *A Winning Position*
O'Connor, Patrick - *A Car Called Camellia*
Ogan, Margaret E Nettles - *Desert Road Racer*
Ogan, Margaret E Nettles - *Grand National Racer*
Ogan, Margaret E Nettles - *Green Thirteen*
Rutherford, Douglas - *Killer On The Track*
Tomerlin, John - *The Nothing Special*
Werner, Herma - *The Dragster*

AUTOMOBLIE RACING DRIVERS

Dolan, Edward Francis, Jr. - *Janet Guthrie: First Woman Driver At Indianapolis*
Fox, Mary Virginia - *Janet Guthrie: Foot To The Floor*
Jackson, Robert Blake - *Behind The Wheel*
Olney, Ross Robert - *A. J. Foyt: The Only Four Time Winner*
Olney, Ross Robert - *Auto Racing's Young Lions*
Olney, Ross Robert - *Janet Guthrie: First Woman At Indy*
Olney, Ross Robert - *Modern Auto Racing Superstars*
Olney, Ross Robert - *Modern Drag Racing Superstars*
Olney, Ross Robert - *Super Champions Of Auto Racing*
Robison, Nancy - *Janet Guthrie: Race Car Driver*

AVALANCHES—Fiction

Catherall, Arthur - *Prisoners In The Snow*
Roy, Ron - *Avalanche!*

AVAVARE INDIANS—Fiction

Baker, Betty Lou - *Walk The World's Rim*

BABY SITTERS—Fiction

Beckman, Delores - *My Own Private Sky*
Shreve, Susan Richards - *The Revolution Of Mary Leary*

BACKPACKING

Colwell, Robert - *Introduction To Backpacking*
Larson, Randy - *Backpacking*

BAKER, JOHN

Buchanan, William - *A Shining Season*

BAKERS AND BAKERIES—Fiction

Newton, Suzanne - *M. V. Sexton Speaking*

BAKING—Fiction

Gilson, Jamie Marie - *Can't Catch Me, I'm The Gingerbread Man*

BALLET DANCING

Allan, Mabel Esther - *The Ballet Family*
Haney, Lynn - *I Am A Dancer*

BALLET DANCING (continued)

Harris, Leon A, Jr. - *The Russian Ballet School*

BALLET DANCING—Fiction

Dean, Karen Strickler - *Between Dances: Maggie Adams' Eighteenth Summer*
Dean, Karen Strickler - *Maggie Adams, Dancer*
Dean, Karen Strickler - *Stay On Your Toes, Maggie Adams!*
Hest, Amy - *Maybe Next Year....*

BALLETS—Stories, plots, etc.

Diamond, Donna - *Swan Lake*

BALLOON ASCENSIONS

Douty, Esther Morris - *The Brave Balloonists: America's First Airmen*
McMullen, David - *Mystery In Peru: The Lines Of Nazca*
Mohn, Peter B - *Hot Air Ballooning*

BALLOON ASCENSIONS—Fiction

Terman, D - *By Balloon To The Sahara*

BALLS (SPORTING GOODS)

Morrison, Susan Dudley - *Balls*

BANDS (MUSIC)

Chiefari, Janet - *Introducing The Drum And Bugle Corps*
Martin, Susan - *Duran Duran*

BANDS (MUSIC)—Fiction

Young, Al - *Snakes*

BANKS, GRAHAM

Brady, Mari - *Please Remember Me*

BAR MITZVAH—Fiction

Blue, Rose - *The Thirteenth Year*

BASEBALL

Aaseng, Nathan - *Baseball: You Are The Manager*
Aaseng, Nathan - *Memorable World Series Moments*
Bethel, Dell - *Inside Baseball*
Cebulash, Mel - *Big League Baseball Reading Kit*
Durso, Joseph - *Amazing: The Miracle Of The Mets*
Dyer, Mike - *Getting Into Pro Baseball*
Fenten, D X - *Behind The Sports Scene*
Gergen, Joe - *World Series Heroes And Goats: The Men Who Made History In America's October Classic*
Gutman, Bill - *Great Baseball Stories*
Hinz, Bob - *Philadelphia Phillies*
Hollander, Zander - *The Baseball Book*
Klein, Dave - *On The Way Up: What It's Like To Be In The Minor Leagues*
Liss, Howard - *More Strange But True Baseball Stories*
Mantle, Mickey - *The Education Of A Baseball Player*
Martin, Mollie - *Atlanta Braves*
Mays, Willie - *"Play Ball!"*
Morgan, Joe - *Baseball My Way*
Rappoport, Ken - *Diamonds In The Rough*
Smith, Robert - *Hit Hard! Throw Hard!: The Secrets Of Power Baseball*
Sullivan, George Edward - *The Art Of Base-Stealing*
Sullivan, George Edward - *Pitchers And Pitching*
Thorn, John - *Baseball's Ten Greatest Games*
Thorn, John - *A Century Of Baseball Lore*
Ward, Don - *New York Yankees*
Wayne, Bennett - *Big League Pitchers And Catchers*
Zolna, Ed - *Mastering Softball*

BASEBALL—Biography

Aaseng, Nathan - *Pete Rose: Baseball's Charlie Hustle*
Allen, Maury - *Reggie Jackson: The Three Million Dollar Man*
Allen, Maury - *Ron Guidry: Louisiana Lightning*
Baldwin, Stan - *Bad Henry: An Authorized Hank Aaron Story*
Batson, Larry - *Rod Carew*
Brandt, Keith - *Pete Rose: "Mr. 300"*
Buck, Ray - *Pete Rose: "Charlie Hustle"*
Burchard, Marshall - *Sports Hero: Brooks Robinson*
Burchard, Marshall - *Sports Hero: Joe Morgan*
Burchard, Marshall - *Sports Hero: Johnny Bench*
Burchard, Sue H - *Sports Star: Fernando Valenzuela*
Burchard, Sue H - *Sports Star: Reggie Jackson*

BASEBALL—Fiction (continued)

Slote, Alfred - *Stranger On The Ball Club*

BASKETBALL

Allison, Jon - *The Pro Basketball Reading Kit*
Bishop, Curtis Kent - *Fast Break*
Cebulash, Mel - *The Champion's Jacket*
Fremon, David - *Secrets Of The Super Athletes: Basketball*
Hoffman, Anne Byrne - *Echoes From The Schoolyard*
Lineham, Don - *Soft Touch: A Sport That Lets You Touch Life*
Lyttle, Richard Bard - *Getting Into Pro Basketball*
Masin, Herman L - *How To Star In Basketball*
Paige, David - *A Day In The Life Of A School Basketball Coach*

BASKETBALL—Biography

Batson, Larry - *Walt "Clyde" Frazier*
Burchard, Marshall - *Sports Hero: Kareem Abdul Jabbar*
Burchard, Sue H - *Sports Star: Elvin Hayes*
Burchard, Sue H - *Sports Star: Larry Bird*
Corn, Frederick Lynn - *Basketball's Magnificent Bird: The Larry Bird Story*
Devaney, John - *Tiny: The Story Of Nate Archibald*
Dolan, Edward Francis, Jr. - *Scott May: Basketball Champion*
Gutman, Bill - *Dr. J*
Hahn, James - *Wilt! The Sports Career Of Wilton Chamberlain*
Haskins, James - *Dr. J: A Biography Of Julius Erving*
Haskins, James - *From Lew Alcindor To Kareem Abdul-Jabbar*
Jackson, Robert Blake - *Earl The Pearl: The Story Of Baltimore's Earl Monroe*
Klein, Dave - *Pro Basketball's Big Men*
Leder, Jane M - *Moses Malone*
O'Connor, Dick - *Rick Barry: Basketball Ace*
Sabin, Louis - *The Fabulous Dr. J*
Sullivan, George Edward - *Wilt Chamberlain*
Weber, Bruce - *All-Pro Basketball Stars*
Weber, Bruce - *Magic Johnson/larry Bird*

BASKETBALL—Fiction

Boatright, Lori - *Out Of Bounds*
Cox, William R - *Rookie In The Backcourt*
Crary, Margaret - *Mexican Whirlwind*
Crawford, Alice Owen - *Please Say Yes*
Deegan, Paul Joseph - *Almost A Champion*
Deegan, Paul Joseph - *Close But Not Quite*
Deegan, Paul Joseph - *Dan Moves Up*
Deegan, Paul Joseph - *The Important Decision*
Deegan, Paul Joseph - *The Team Manager*
Deegan, Paul Joseph - *The Tournaments*
Dygard, Thomas J - *Outside Shooter*
Dygard, Thomas J - *Rebound Caper*
Kidd, Ronald - *Dunker*
Lee, H Alton - *Seven Feet Four And Growing*
Madden, Betsy - *The All-America Coeds*
Myers, Walter Dean - *Hoops*
Myers, Walter Dean - *The Outside Shot*
Paulsen, Gary - *The Green Recruit*
Peck, Robert Newton - *Basket Case*
Piniat, John - *Going For The Win*
Sheffer, H R - *Winner On The Court*
Walden, Amelia Elizabeth - *Basketball Girl Of The Year*
Walden, Amelia Elizabeth - *Go, Philips, Go!*

BAYEUX TAPESTRY

Denny, Norman George - *The Bayeux Tapestry: The Story Of The Norman Conquest, 1066*

BEACHES—Fiction

Byars, Betsy - *The Animal, The Vegetable And John D Jones*

BEARS

Geringer, Laura - *Seven True Bear Stories*
Tripp, Jenny - *The Man Who Was Left For Dead*
Weaver, John L - *Grizzly Bears*
Wilson, Lionel - *Attack Of The Killer Grizzly*

BEARS—Fiction

East, Ben - *Grizzly!*
Morey, Walter Nelson - *Gentle Ben*

BEAUTY CONTESTS—Fiction

Pfeffer, Susan Beth - *The Beauty Queen*

BEAUTY (PERSONAL)

Archer, Elsie - *Let's Face It: The Guide To Good Grooming For Girls Of Color*
Lawson, Donna - *Beauty Is No Big Deal: The Common Sense Beauty Book*
McGrath, Judith - *Pretty Girl: A Guide To Looking Good, Naturally*
Miller, Melba - *The Black Is Beautiful Beauty Book*
Stewart, Marjabelle Young - *The Teen Girl's Guide To Social Success*

BEAUTY (PERSONAL)—Fiction

Clifton, Lucille - *Sonora Beautiful*

BEAVERS

Annixter, Jane - *Ahmeek*
Nentl, Jerolyn Ann - *The Beaver*

BEES—Fiction

Cavanagh, Helen - *Honey*

BEHAVIOR

Buchenholz, Bruce - *A Way With Animals*
Buck, Margaret Waring - *Where They Go In Winter*

BEHAVIOR—Fiction

Brown, Roy Frederick - *The Cage*
Cuyler, Margery Stuyvesant - *The Trouble With Soap*
Greenwald, Sheila - *The Atrocious Two*
Manes, Stephen - *Be A Perfect Person In Just Three Days!*
Platt, Kin - *The Ape Inside Me*

BERMUDA TRIANGLE

Collins, Jim - *The Bermuda Triangle*
Dolan, Edward Francis, Jr. - *The Bermuda Triangle And Other Mysteries Of Nature*
Thorne, Ian - *Bermuda Triangle*

BIBLE

Gaines, M C - *Picture Stories From The Bible: The New Testament In Full-Color Comic-Strip Form*
McGraw, Barbara - *Those Who Dared: Adventure Stories From The Bible*

BICYLES AND BICYLING

Cuthbertson, Tom - *Anybody's Bike Book*
Cuthbertson, Tom - *Bike Tripping*
Dahnsen, Alan - *Bicycles*
Henkel, Stephen C - *Bikes: A How-To-Do-It Guide To Selection, Care, Repair, Maintenance, Decoration, Etc.*
Leete, Harley M - *The Best Of Bicycling*
Lindblom, Steven - *The Fantastic Bicycles Book*
Mohn, Peter B - *Bicycle Touring*
Radlauer, Edward - *Some Basics About Bicycles*
Sloane, Eugene A - *The Complete Book Of Bicycling*
Thomas, Art - *Bicycling Is For Me*

BICYLES AND BICYLING—Fiction

Gemme, Leila Boyle - *Ten-Speed Taylor*

BIOGRAPHY

Alderman, Clifford Lindsey - *Annie Oakley And The World Of Her Time*
Anderson, Lavere - *Allan Pinkerton: First Private Eye*
Anderson, Lavere - *Mary Mcleod Bethune*
Apsler, Alfred - *Fighter For Independence: Jawaharlal Nehru*
Archibald, Joe - *Commander Of The Flying Tigers: Claire Lee Chennault*
Atwater, James David - *Out From Under: Benito Juarez And Mexico's Struggle For Independence*
Axthelm, Pete - *The Kid*
Bacon, Margaret Hope - *Lamb's Warrior: The Life Of Isaac T. Hopper*
Bales, Carol Ann - *Tales Of The Elders: A Memory Book Of Men And Women Who Came To America As Immigrants, 1900-1930*
Behrens, June - *Sally Ride, Astronaut*
Berman, Connie - *Leif Garrett*
Berman, Connie - *The Shaun Cassidy Scrapbook*
Berman, Connie - *Top Recording Artist And TV Star! Shaun Cassidy*
Biemiller, Ruth - *Dance: The Story Of Katherine Dunham*
Bishop, Claire Huchet - *Martin De Porres, Hero*
Blackburn, Joyce Knight - *Martha Berry*

BIOGRAPHY (continued)

Blacknall, Carolyn - *Sally Ride: America's First Woman In Space*
Blassingame, Wyatt - *Thor Heyerdahl: Viking Scientist*
Booker, Simeon - *Susie King Taylor, Civil War Nurse*
Bragdon, Lillian - *Luther Burbank, Nature's Helper*
Brown, Marion Marsh - *The Silent Storm*
Burchard, Sue H - *Sports Star: Dorothy Hammill*
Burchard, Sue H - *Sports Star: Nadia Comaneci*
Carruth, Ella Kaiser - *She Wanted To Read: Story Of Mary McLeod Bethune*
Clapp, Patricia - *Dr. Elizabeth*
Clark, James L - *In The Steps Of The Great American Museum Collector, Carl Ethan Akeley*
Clayton, Ed - *Martin Luther King: The Peaceful Warrior*
Clements, Bruce - *From Ice Set Free*
Clymer, Eleanor - *Modern American Career Women*
Collins, Jim - *The Strange Story Of Uri Geller*
Collins, Tom - *Steven Spielberg: Creator Of E.T.*
Crocker, Chris - *Cyndi Lauper*
Darling, David J - *Diana: The People's Princess*
Davidson, Margaret - *The Golda Meir Story*
Denzel, Justin F - *Genius With A Scalpel: Harvey Cushing*
Di Franco, Anthony - *Pope John Paul II: Bringing Love To A Troubled World*
Donovan, Pete - *Carol Johnston: The One-Armed Gymnast*
Drimmer, Frederick - *The Elephant Man*
Edwards, Cecile Pepin - *Roger Williams, Defender Of Freedom*
Eimerl, Sarel Henry - *Hitler Over Europe*
Epstein, Sam - *George Washington Carver: Negro Scientist*
Epstein, Sam - *Winston Churchill*
Epstein, Sam - *Young Paul Revere's Boston*
Erlich, Lillian - *Modern American Career Women*
Ernst, John - *Jesse James*
Faber, Doris - *Clarence Darrow: Defender Of The People*
Faber, Doris - *Enrico Fermi: Atomic Pioneer*
Faber, Doris - *Horace Greeley: The People's Editor*
Faber, Doris - *Lucretia Mott*
Faber, Doris - *Robert Frost: America's Poet*
Fecher, Constance - *The Last Elizabethan: A Portrait Of Sir Walter Raleigh*
Felton, Harold W - *Mumbet: The Story Of Elizabeth Freeman*
Fenderson, Lewis H - *Thurgood Marshall: Fighter For Justice*
Ferrigno, Lou - *The Incredible Lou Ferrigno*
Fisher, Aileen - *Jeanne D'Arc*
Fortunato, Pat - *When We Were Young: An Album Of Stars*
Fox, Mary Virginia - *Jane Fonda: Something To Fight For*
Fox, Mary Virginia - *Jane Goodall: Living Chimp Style*
Fox, Mary Virginia - *Janet Guthrie: Foot To The Floor*
Fox, Mary Virginia - *Justice Sandra Day O'Connor*
Fox, Mary Virginia - *Lady For The Defense: A Biography Of Belva Lockwood*
Franchere, Ruth - *Cesar Chavez*
Franchere, Ruth - *Jack London: The Pursuit Of A Dream*
Fritz, Jean - *What's The Big Idea, Ben Franklin?*
Fritz, Jean - *Why Don't You Get A Horse, Sam Adams?*
Garraty, John A - *Theodore Roosevelt: The Strenuous Life*
Gilbert, Miriam - *Shy Girl: The Story Of Eleanor Roosevelt*
Gill, Derek L T - *Tom Sullivan's Adventures In Darkness*
Gorham, Charles - *The Lion Of Judah: Haile Selassie I, Emperor Of Ethiopia*
Graham, Shirley Lola - *The Story Of Phillis Wheatley, Poetess Of The American Revolution*
Graves, Charles P - *John F. Kennedy*
Greenfeld, Howard - *Pablo Picasso*
Grey, Elizabeth - *Friend Within The Gates: The Story Of Nurse Edith Cavell*
Guy, Anne Welsh - *Steinmetz: Wizard Of Light*
Hayman, LeRoy - *O Captain: The Death Of Abraham Lincoln*

BIOGRAPHY (continued)
Hoyt, Edwin P - *Andrew Johnson*
Hulse, Jerry - *Jody*
Jackson, Jesse - *Make A Joyful Noise Unto The Lord!: The Life Of Mahalia Jackson*
Jacobs, David - *Beethoven*
Jacobs, Linda C - *Jane Pauley: A Heartland Style*
Johnson, Gerald W - *Franklin D. Roosevelt: Portrait Of A Great Man*
Johnston, Johanna - *Paul Cuffee: America's First Black Captain*
Kahn, Albert E - *Days With Ulanova: An Intimate Portrait Of The Legendary Russian Ballerina*
Katz, Susan - *Kristy And Jimmy*
Keller, Mollie - *Marie Curie*
Kendall, Lace - *Houdini: Master Of Escape*
Killilea, Marie - *Karen*
Komroff, Manuel - *Napoleon*
Kraske, Robert - *Harry Houdini*
Kugelmass, J Alvin - *Ralph J. Bunche: Fighter For Peace*
Kyle, Elisabeth - *Girl With A Pen, Charlotte Bronte*
Lawson, Donald Elmer - *Geraldine Ferraro*
Lee, Betsy - *Mother Teresa: Caring For All God's Children*
Levinger, Elma Ehrlich - *Albert Einstein*
Lewis, Claude Aubrey - *Benjamin Banneker: The Man Who Saved Washington*
Libby, Bill - *Rocky*
Lomask, Milton Nachman - *This Slender Reed: A Life Of James K. Polk*
McCague, James - *Tecumseh*
Meigs, Cornelia - *Invincible Louisa: The Story Of The Author Of Little Women*
Meltzer, Milton - *Langston Hughes*
Montgomery, Elizabeth Rider - *Duke Ellington*
Montgomery, Elizabeth Rider - *Walt Disney*
Montgomery, Elizabeth Rider - *Will Rogers: Cowboy Philosopher*
Morin, Relman - *Dwight D. Eisenhower: A Gauge Of Greatness*
Morris, Terry - *Shalom, Golda*
Muesner, Anne Marie - *The Picture Story Of Steve Cauthen*
Munshower, Suzanne - *John Travolta*
Newman, Shirlee P - *Marian Anderson: Lady From Philadelphia*
Noble, Iris - *Cameras And Courage: Margaret Bourke-White*
O'Regan, Susan K - *Neil Diamond*
Patterson, Lillie - *Frederick Douglass*
Patterson, Lillie - *Martin Luther King, Jr.*
Peck, Ira - *The Life And Words Of Martin Luther King, Jr.*
Peterson, Helen Stone - *Susan B. Anthony*
Petry, Ann - *Harriet Tubman: Conductor On The Underground Railroad*
Place, Marian T - *Frontiersman: The True Story Of Billy Dixon*
Podojil, Catherine - *Mother Teresa*
Preston, Edward - *Martin Luther King: Fighter For Freedom*
Proudfit, Isabel - *Riverboy: The Story Of Mark Twain*
Provensen, Alice - *Leonardo Da Vinci: The Artist, Inventor, Scientist*
Reed, Donald - *Robert Redford*
Rivera, Geraldo - *A Special Kind Of Courage: Profiles Of Young Americans*
Ross, Josephine - *Alexander Fleming*
Ross, Pat - *Young And Female: Turning Points In The Lives Of Eight American Women*
Sarnoff, Paul - *Ice Pilot: Bob Bartlett*
Schiesel, Jane - *The Otis Redding Story*
Schmitz, Dorothy Childers - *Dorothy Hamill: Skate To Victory*
Schoor, Gene - *The Jim Thorpe Story: America's Greatest Athlete*
Schoor, Gene - *The Story Of Ty Cobb: Baseball's Greatest Player*
Scott, John Anthony - *Fanny Kemble's America*
Shirer, William L - *Rise And Fall Of Adolph Hitler*
Stein, Cathi - *Elton John*
Sterling, Philip - *Sea And Earth: The Life Of Rachel Carson*
Stoddard, Hope - *Famous American Women*
Stonaker, Frances Benson - *Famous Mathematicians*
Sullivan, Wilson - *Franklin Delano Roosevelt*
Taylor, Lester Barbour, Jr. - *Rescue! True Stories Of Heroism*
Terzian, James P - *Mighty Hard Road: The Story Of Cesar Chavez*
Treadway, Rudy Peeples - *Go To It, You Dutchman! The Story Of Edward Bok*

BIOGRAPHY (continued)

Tregaskis, Richard - *John F. Kennedy And PT-109*
Van Steenwyk, Elizabeth - *Dorothy Hamill: Olympic Champion*
Walker, Barbara J - *The Picture Life Of Jimmy Carter*
Wayne, Bennett - *The Founding Fathers*
Wayne, Bennett - *Four Women Of Courage*
Wayne, Bennett - *Women Who Dared To Be Different*
Wayne, Bennett - *Women With A Cause*
Westman, Paul - *Andrew Young: Champion Of The Poor*
Westman, Paul - *Billy Graham: Reaching Out To The World*
Westman, Paul - *Frank Borman: To The Moon And Back*
Westman, Paul - *Jacques Cousteau: Free Flight Undersea*
Westman, Paul - *Jesse Jackson: I Am Somebody*
Westman, Paul - *John Glenn: Around The World In 90 Minutes*
Westman, Paul - *John Young: Space Shuttle Commander*
Westman, Paul - *Thor Heyerdahl: Across The Seas Of Time*
White, Florence Meiman - *Cesar Chavez: Man Of Courage*
White, Florence Meiman - *Escape! The Life Of Harry Houdini*
White, Florence Meiman - *Malcolm X: Black And Proud*
Wolfson, Victor - *The Man Who Cared: A Life Of Harry S. Truman*
Yolen, Jane H - *Friend: The Story Of George Fox And The Quakers*

BIOLOGICAL CHEMISTRY

Patton, A Rae - *The Chemistry Of Life*

BIOLOGY

Jacker, Corinne - *The Biological Revolution: A Background Book On Making A New World*

BIONICS

Silverstein, Alvin - *Bionics*

BIRDS

Adler, C S - *Fly Free*
Dugdale, Vera - *Album Of North American Birds*
Fichter, George Siebert - *Birds Of North America*
Oster, Maggie - *The Illustrated Bird*

BIRDS—Fiction

Bunting, Eve - *One More Flight*

BIRTHDAYS—Fiction

Letchworth, Beverly J - *Pax And The Mutt*

BLACKS—Addresses, essays, lectures

Coombs, Orde M - *Do You See My Love For You Growing?*

BLACKS—Biography

Adoff, Arnold - *Malcolm X*
Alexander, Rae Pace - *Young And Black In America*
Allen, Maury - *Reggie Jackson: The Three Million Dollar Man*
Anderson, Lavere - *Mary Mcleod Bethune*
Bishop, Claire Huchet - *Martin De Porres, Hero*
Bontemps, Arna Wendell - *Famous Negro Athletes*
Bontemps, Arna Wendell - *Free At Last: The Life Of Frederick Douglas*
Braun, Thomas - *On Stage: Flip Wilson*
Brownmiller, Susan - *Shirley Chisholm*
Burchard, Marshall - *Sports Hero: Joe Morgan*
Burchard, Sue H - *Sports Star: Elvin Hayes*
Burchard, Sue H - *Sports Star: Herschel Walker*
Burchard, Sue H - *Sports Star: Reggie Jackson*
Clayton, Ed - *Martin Luther King: The Peaceful Warrior*
Conrad, Dick - *Walter Payton: The Running Machine*
Cornell, Jean Gay - *Louis Armstrong: Ambassador Satchmo*
Cornell, Jean Gay - *Mahalia Jackson: Queen Of Gospel Song*
Cornell, Jean Gay - *Ralph Bunche: Champion Of Peace*
David, Jay - *Growing Up Black*
Davis, Burke - *Black Heroes Of The American Revolution*
Davis, Daniel Sheldon - *Marcus Garvey*
Dobler, Lavinia G - *Pioneers And Patriots: The Lives Of Six Negroes Of The Revolutionary Era*

BLACKS—Biography (continued)

Dolan, Edward Francis, Jr. - *Jimmy Young: Heavyweight Challenger*
Drotning, Phillip T - *Up From The Ghetto*
Drucker, Malka - *The George Foster Story*
Durham, Philip - *The Adventures Of The Negro Cowboys*
Eaton, Jeanette - *Trumpeter's Tale: The Story Of Young Louis Armstrong*
Edwards, Audrey Marie - *Muhammad Ali, The People's Champ*
Edwards, Audrey Marie - *The Picture Life Of Muhammad Ali*
Edwards, Audrey Marie - *The Picture Life Of Stevie Wonder*
Epstein, Sam - *George Washington Carver: Negro Scientist*
Epstein, Sam - *Harriet Tubman: Guide To Freedom*
Feelings, Thomas - *Black Pilgrimage*
Felton, Harold W - *James Weldon Johnson*
Felton, Harold W - *Nat Love, Negro Cowboy*
Flynn, James J - *Negroes Of Achievement In Modern America*
Folsom, Franklin Brewster - *The Life And Legend Of George McJunkin*
Freedman, Florence B - *Two Tickets To Freedom*
Friedman, Ina Rosen - *Black Cop: A Biography Of Tilmon O'Bryant*
Gloeckner, Carolyn - *Sugar Ray Leonard*
Gordy, Berry, Sr. - *Movin' Up: Pop Gordy Tells His Story*
Gugliotta, Bobette - *Nolle Smith: Cowboy, Engineer, Statesman*
Haber, Louis - *Black Pioneers Of Science And Invention*
Hahn, James - *Ali! The Sports Career Of Muhammad Ali*
Hahn, James - *Brown! The Sports Career Of James Brown*
Hahn, James - *Henry! The Sports Career Of Henry Aaron*
Hahn, James - *Sayers! The Sports Career Of Gale Sayers*
Hahn, James - *Wilt! The Sports Career Of Wilton Chamberlain*
Hasegawa, Sam - *Stevie Wonder*
Haskins, James - *Always Movin' On*
Haskins, James - *Barbara Jordan: Speaking Out*
Haskins, James - *The Life And Death Of Martin Luther King, Jr.*
Haskins, James - *The Story Of Stevie Wonder*
Hayden, Robert Carter - *Eight Black American Inventors*
Hayden, Robert Carter - *Nine Black American Doctors*
Hayden, Robert Carter - *Seven Black American Scientists*
Hoard, Edison - *Curse Not The Darkness*
Jacobs, Linda C - *Barbara Jordan: Keeping Faith*
Jones, Hettie - *Big Star Fallin' Mama: Five Black Women In Music*
Leder, Jane M - *Marcus Allen*
Leder, Jane M - *Walter Payton*
Libby, Bill - *Joe Louis: The Brown Bomber*
Libby, Bill - *The Reggie Jackson Story*
Liss, Howard - *Picture Story Of Dave Winfield*
Miklowitz, Gloria D - *Dr. Martin Luther King, Jr.*
Morse, Charles - *Jackson Five*
Morse, Charles - *Roberta Flack*
Newman, Matthew - *Dwight Gooden*
Ortiz, Victoria - *Sojourner Truth, A Self-Made Woman*
Phillips, Betty Lou - *Earl Campbell, Houston Oiler Superstar*
Rollins, Charlemae - *Famous Negro Entertainers Of Stage, Screen And TV*
Simpson, Janice C - *Andrew Young: A Matter Of Choice*
Sterling, Philip - *Four Took Freedom: The Lives Of Harriet Tubman, Frederick Douglas, Robert Small, And Blanche K. Bruce*
Vass, George - *Reggie Jackson: From Superstar To Candy Bar*
Woods, Harold - *Bill Cosby: Making America Laugh And Learn*

BLACKS—Civil rights

Harris, Janet - *The Long Freedom Road: The Civil Rights Story*
Haskins, James - *The Life And Death Of Martin Luther King, Jr.*
Mack, John - *Nobody Promised Me*
Miller, Marilyn - *The Bridge At Selma*

BLACKS—Collected works

David, Jay - *Growing Up Black*

BLACKS—Education

Decker, Sunny - *An Empty Spoon*

BLACKS—Fiction

Armstrong, William Howard - *Sounder*
Baldwin, James - *If Beale Street Could Talk*
Bunting, Eve - *Face At The Edge Of The World*
Capizzi, Michael - *Getting It All Together*
Collier, James Lincoln - *Jump Ship To Freedom*
Greenya, John - *One Punch Away*
Guy, Rosa - *New Guys Around The Block*
Lester, Julius - *Long Journey Home*
Mathis, Sharon Bell - *Teacup Full Of Roses*
Myers, Walter Dean - *Motown And Didi*
Myers, Walter Dean - *The Outside Shot*
Quigley, Martin - *The Original Colored House Of David*
Taylor, Mildred D - *Roll Of Thunder, Hear My Cry*

BLACKS—History

Drisko, Carol F - *The Unfinished March: The History Of The Negro In The United States, Reconstruction To World War I*
Johnston, Johanna - *Together In America: The Story Of Two Races And One Nation*
Katz, William Loren - *A History Of Black Americans*
Warner, Lucille Schulberg - *From Slave To Abolitionist*

BLACKS—Poetry

Abdul, Raoul - *The Magic Of Black Poetry*
Adoff, Arnold - *My Black Me*
Bontemps, Arna Wendell - *Golden Slippers: An Anthology Of Negro Poetry For Young Readers*
Rollins, Charlemae - *Famous American Negro Poets*

BLACKS—Social conditions—Fiction

Childress, Alice - *A Hero Ain't Nothin' But A Sandwich*
Guy, Rosa - *Edith Jackson*
Hunter, Kristin Eggleston - *Guests In The Promised Land*
Hunter, Kristin Eggleston - *The Soul Brothers And Sister Lou*
Mathis, Sharon Bell - *Listen For The Fig Tree*

BLACKWELL, ELIZABETH

Clapp, Patricia - *Dr. Elizabeth*

BLESSING AND CURSING

Cohen, Daniel - *Famous Curses*

BLIND

Gill, Derek L T - *Tom Sullivan's Adventures In Darkness*

BLIND—Fiction

Butler, Beverly - *Light A Single Candle*
Conklin, Barbara - *Summer Dreams*
Kent, Deborah - *Belonging*
Mathis, Sharon Bell - *Listen For The Fig Tree*
TerHaar, Jaap - *The World Of Ben Lighthart*
Wartski, Maureen Crane - *The Lake Is On Fire*

BLUE RIDGE MOUNTAINS—Fiction

Lyle, Katie Letcher - *Finders Weepers*

BLUEGRASS MUSIC—Fiction

Sullivan, Mary Wilson - *Bluegrass Iggy*

BOATS AND BOATING—Fiction

Heuman, William - *Horace Higby, Coxswain Of The Crew*

BOOKBINDING

Purdy, Susan - *Books For You To Make*

BOOKS AND READING—Fiction

Haynes, Mary - *Wordchanger*

BOSTON—Social life and customs

Epstein, Sam - *Young Paul Revere's Boston*

BOTANY

Rahn, Joan Elma - *Plants Up Close*
Stone, A Harris - *Plants Are Like That*

BOXING—Biography

Dolan, Edward Francis, Jr. - *Jimmy Young: Heavyweight Challenger*
Durant, John - *The Heavyweight Champions*
Edwards, Audrey Marie - *Muhammad Ali, The People's Champ*

BOXING—Biography (continued)

Edwards, Audrey Marie - *The Picture Life Of Muhammad Ali*
Gloeckner, Carolyn - *Sugar Ray Leonard*
Hahn, James - *Ali! The Sports Career Of Muhammad Ali*
Hano, Arnold - *Muhammad Ali: The Champion*
Libby, Bill - *Joe Louis: The Brown Bomber*
Libby, Bill - *Rocky*

BOXING—Fiction

Greenya, John - *One Punch Away*
Lipsyte, Robert - *The Contender*

BOYS—Fiction

Stewart, Winnie - *Night On 'Gator Creek*

BRAIDS (HAIRDRESSING)

Coen, Patricia - *Beautiful Braids*

BRAIN

Zim, Herbert S - *Your Brain And How It Works*

BRAZILIAN HONEYBEE

Blau, Melinda - *Killer Bees*

BRIBERY—Fiction

French, Michael - *The Throwing Season*

BRIDGES

Goldwater, Daniel - *Bridges And How They Are Built*

BROTHERS AND SISTERS—Fiction

Ames, Mildred - *The Dancing Madness*
Asher, Sandy - *Things Are Seldom What They Seem*
Bradbury, Bianca - *Where's Jim Now?*
Butterworth, W E - *The Roper Brothers And Their Magnificent Steam Automobile*
Cleaver, Vera - *Where The Lilies Bloom*
Cookson, Catherine McMullen - *Our John Willie*
Corcoran, Barbara - *Making It*
Fries, Chloe - *No Place To Hide*
Greene, Constance C - *Beat The Turtle Drum*
Greene, Yvonne - *Little Sister*
Hinton, S E - *Rumble Fish*
Hinton, S E - *Tex*
Kerr, M E - *Night Kites*
Lasky, Kathryn - *Prank*
Miner, Jane Claypool - *Miracle Of Time: Adopting A Sister*
Miner, Jane Claypool - *Mountain Fear: When A Brother Dies*
Mulligan, Kevin - *Kid Brother*
Oppenheimer, Joan Letson - *Gardine Vs. Hanover*
Pascal, Francine - *The Hand-Me-Down Kid*
Peck, Richard - *Father Figure*
Perl, Lila - *Dumb Like Me, Olivia Potts*
Petersen, P J - *Going For The Big One*
Pevsner, Stella - *And You Give Me A Pain, Elaine*
Reece, Colleen L - *The Outsider*
Winthrop, Elizabeth - *A Little Demonstration Of Affection*
Wood, Phyllis Anderson - *Get A Little Lost, Tia*

BROWN, LARRY

Brown, Larry - *I'll Always Get Up*

BULLIES—Fiction

Adler, C S - *The Once In Awhile Hero*

BURIED TREASURE

Madison, Arnold - *Lost Treasures Of America*
Titler, Dale Milton - *Haunted Treasures*
Titler, Dale Milton - *Unnatural Resources: True Stories Of American Treasure*

BURIED TREASURE—Fiction

Austin, R G - *Curse Of The Sunken Treasure*
Bellairs, John - *The Treasure Of Alpheus Winterborn*
Hiller, Doris - *Black Beach*
Love, Sandra - *Dive For The Sun*
Lyle, Katie Letcher - *Finders Weepers*
Oreshnik, A F - *The Demeter Star*
Waldron, Ann - *The Luckie Star*
Wallace, Bill - *Trapped In Death Cave*
Wibberley, Leonard - *Flint's Island*
Wibberley, Leonard - *Perilous Gold*

CALENDAR

Adler, Irving - *Calendar*

CALIFORNIA—Fiction

Filson, Brent - *Smoke Jumpers*
Petersen, P J - *The Boll Weevil Express*
Place, Marian T - *Juan's Eighteen-Wheeler Summer*
Reader, Dennis J - *Coming Back Alive*
Shaw, Richard - *Call Me Al Raft*
Waldorf, Mary - *Thousand Camps*
Yep, Laurence Michael - *The Mark Twain Murders*

CAMP COUNSELORS

Mangan, Doreen - *How To Be A Super Camp Counselor*

CAMPING

Kenealy, James P - *Better Camping For Boys*
Langer, Richard W - *The Joy Of Camping*
Larson, Randy - *Backpacking*
Lawrence, Amy - *Color It Love*
Patterson, Doris T - *Your Family Goes Camping*
Thomas, Dian - *Roughing It Easy*

CAMPING—Fiction

Angell, Judie - *In Summertime It's Tuffy*
Bunting, Eve - *Survival Camp!*
Conford, Ellen - *Hail, Hail Camp Timberwood*
Cowan, Dale - *Campfire Nights*
Danziger, Paula - *There's A Bat In Bunk Five*
Hallman, Ruth - *Tough Is Not Enough*
Kester, Ellen Skinner - *The Climbing Rope*
Kherdian, David - *It Started With Old Man Bean*
Knudson, R R - *You Are The Rain*
Kroll, Steven - *Breaking Camp*
Norris, Gunilla B - *The Good Morrow*
Roy, Ron - *Nightmare Island*
Stolz, Mary Slattery - *A Wonderful, Terrible Time*
Swarthout, Glendon Fred - *Bless The Beasts And Children*
Weir, LaVada - *Edge Of Fear*
Wood, Phyllis Anderson - *I Think This Is Where We Came In*
Zaring, Jane - *Sharkes In The North Woods: Or Nish Na Bosh Na Is Nicer Now*

CANCER—Biography

Brady, Mari - *Please Remember Me*
Buchanan, William - *A Shining Season*

CANCER—Fiction

Bach, Alice - *Waiting For Johnny Miracle*
Graham, Leslie - *Rx For Love*
Klein, Norma - *Sunshine*

CARTOONING

Ames, Lee Judah - *Draw 50 Famous Cartoons*
Kresse, Bill - *An Introduction To Cartooning*

CARTOONS AND COMICS

Schulz, Charles M - *Always Stick Up For The Underbird*
Schulz, Charles M - *Dr. Beagle And Mr. Hyde*

CATHER, WILLA SIBERT—Fiction

Franchere, Ruth - *Willa: The Story Of Willa Cather's Growing Up*

CATS

Besser, Marianne - *The Cat Book*
Burger, Carl - *All About Cats*
Jacobson, Ethel - *The Cats Of Sea-Cliff Castle*
Millard, Adele - *Cats In Fact And Legend*
Rockwell, Jane - *Cats And Kittens*
Steneman, Shep - *Garfield: The Complete Cat Book*

CATS—Fiction

Aaron, Chester - *Catch Calico!*
Adler, C S - *The Cat That Was Left Behind*
Alexander, Lloyd - *Time Cat: The Remarkable Journeys Of Jason And Gareth*
Brookins, Dana - *Rico's Cat*
Hildick, E W - *Manhattan Is Missing*
Millard, Adele - *Cats In Fact And Legend*
Peck, Robert Newton - *Wild Cat*

CAUTHEN, STEVE

Axthelm, Pete - *The Kid*

CAVE DWELLERS—Fiction

Garcia, Ann O'neal - *Spirit On The Wall*

CAVES—Fiction

Liberatore, Karen - *The Horror Of Montauk Cave*
Littke, Lael J - *Cave-In!*

CEREBRAL PALSY

Killilea, Marie - *Karen*

CEREBRAL PALSY—Fiction

Slepian, Jan - *Lester's Turn*

CHARITIES—Fiction

Bonham, Frank - *Hey, Big Spender!*

CHARLESTON (S.C.)—Fiction

Davidson, Mary S - *A Superstar Called Sweetpea*

CHEERLEADING

Phillips, Betty Lou - *Go! Fight! Win!*

CHEERLEADING—Fiction

Klein, Norma - *The Cheerleader*

CHEMISTS

Keller, Mollie - *Marie Curie*

CHESS—Fiction

Jacobs, Linda C - *Checkmate Julie*

CHEYENNE INDIANS—Wars, 1964—Fiction

Henry, Will - *Maheo's Children*

CHICKENS—Fiction

Pinkwater, Daniel Manus - *The Hoboken Chicken Emergency*

CHILD ABUSE—Fiction

Adler, C S - *Fly Free*
Armstrong, Louise - *Saving The Big-Deal Baby*
Hunt, Irene - *The Lottery Rose*
Kropp, Paul - *Runaway*
Kropp, Paul - *Take Off*
Levinson, Nancy Smiler - *Silent Fear*

CHILD MOLESTING—Fiction

Asher, Sandy - *Things Are Seldom What They Seem*
Dodson, Susan - *The Creep*

CHILD PSYCHOTHERAPY

MacCracken, Mary - *Lovey: A Very Special Child*
Yates, Elizabeth - *Skeezer: Dog With A Mission*

CHIMPANZEES

Amon, Aline - *Reading, Writing, Chattering Chimps*
Fox, Mary Virginia - *Jane Goodall: Living Chimp Style*
Lawick-Goodall, Jane Van - *In The Shadow Of Man*

CHINA

Christesen, Barbara - *Myths Of The Orient*
Clayton, Robert - *China*
Harrington, Lyn - *China And The Chinese*
Rau, Margaret - *The Minority Peoples Of China*
Schell, Orville - *Modern China: The Story Of A Revolution*
Scott, John - *China: The Hungry Dragon*

CHINESE AMERICANS

Sung, Betty Lee - *The Chinese In America*

CHINESE AMERICANS—Fiction

Claypool, Jane - *Jasmine Finds Love*
Yep, Laurence Michael - *Child Of The Owl*

CHRISTIAN LIFE—Fiction

Kester, Ellen Skinner - *The Climbing Rope*

CHRISTMAS—Fiction

Paterson, Katherine - *Angels And Other Strangers*
Seymour, William Kean - *Happy Christmas*

CINEMATOGRAPHY

Bendick, Jeanne - *Filming Works Like This*

CIPHERS

Brandreth, Gyles - *Writing Secret Codes And Sending Hidden Messages*
Gardner, Martin - *Codes, Ciphers, And Secret Writing*

CIRCUS

Fenten, D X - *Behind The Circus Scene*
Glendinning, Richard - *Circus Days Under The Big Top*

CIRCUS—Fiction

Hiller, Doris - *Little Big Top*
White, Robb - *The Long Way Down*
Youngblood, Marilyn - *Send In The Clowns*

CITY AND TOWN LIFE—Fiction

Bonham, Frank - *Cool Cat*
Bonham, Frank - *The Golden Bees Of Tulami*
Brodsky, Mimi - *The House At 12 Rose Street*
Cleaver, Vera - *The Mimosa Tree*
Connor, James, III - *I, Dwayne Kleber*
Hinton, S E - *Rumble Fish*
Howe, Fanny - *Yeah, But*
Murphy, Barbara Beasley - *No Place To Run*
Windsor, Patricia - *Killing Time*

CIVIL RIGHTS

Gaines, Ernest J - *The Autobiography Of Miss Jane Pitman*
Jordan, June - *Dry Victories*
Miklowitz, Gloria D - *Dr. Martin Luther King, Jr.*
Miller, Marilyn - *The Bridge At Selma*
Westman, Paul - *Andrew Young: Champion Of The Poor*
Westman, Paul - *Jesse Jackson: I Am Somebody*

CIVILIZATION

Baumann, Hans - *Lion Gate And Labyrinth*
Gallagher, I J - *The Case Of The Ancient Astronauts*
Hogben, Lancelot - *The Wonderful World Of Mathematics*
Thorne, Ian - *Ancient Astronauts*

CIVILIZATION—Fiction

Macaulay, David Alexander - *Baaa*

CLAIRVOYANCE

Cohen, Daniel - *The Magic Art Of Foreseeing The Future*

CLEMENS, SAMUEL LANGHORNE

Proudfit, Isabel - *Riverboy: The Story Of Mark Twain*

CLIMATOLOGY

Bova, Ben - *Man Changes The Weather*

CLOCKS AND WATCHES

Neal, Harry Edward - *The Mystery Of Time*
Sobol, Ken - *The Clock Museum*

CLOTHING AND DRESS

Thypin, Marilyn - *Try It On: Buying Clothing*
Wiseman, Ann Sayre - *Cuts Of Cloth*

COLLAGE

Weiss, Harvey - *Collage And Construction*

COLOR OF MAN

Cohen, Robert C - *The Color Of Man*

COLORADO—Fiction

Roy, Ron - *Avalanche!*

COMANCHE INDIANS—Fiction

Beatty, Patricia Robbins - *Wait For Me, Watch For Me, Eula Bee*
Wisler, G Clifton - *Winter Of The Wolf*

COMEDIANS

Braun, Thomas - *On Stage: Flip Wilson*
Woods, Harold - *Bill Cosby: Making America Laugh And Learn*

COMEDIANS—Fiction

Conford, Ellen - *Strictly For Laughs*

COMETS

Asimov, Isaac - *How Did We Find Out About Comets?*
Couper, Heather - *Comets And Meteors*

COMIC BOOKS, STRIPS, ETC.

Lee, Stan - *How To Draw Comics The Marvel Way*
Schulz, Charles M - *It's Chow Time, Snoopy*
Schulz, Charles M - *Nobody's Perfect, Charlie Brown*
Schulz, Charles M - *You're The Greatest, Charlie Brown*
Smith, Bruce - *The History Of Little Orphan Annie*
Steneman, Shep - *Garfield: The Complete Cat Book*

COMMUNICATION

Adler, Irving - *Communication*
Amon, Aline - *Reading, Writing, Chattering Chimps*
Cohen, Daniel - *Talking With The Animals*
Howard, Sam - *Communications Machines*
Neal, Harry Edward - *Communication: From Stone Age To Space Age*

COMPUTERS

Berger, Melvin - *Computer Talk*
Christian, Mary Blount - *Microcomputers*
DeRossi, Claude J - *Computers: Tools For Today*
Jones, Weyman B - *Computer*
Lewis, Alfred - *The New World Of Computers*
Litterick, Ian - *Computers And You*
Rusch, Richard B - *Man's Marvelous Computer: The Next Quarter Century*

COMPUTERS—Fiction

Bethancourt, T Ernesto - *The Great Computer Dating Caper*
D'Ignazio, Fred - *Chip Mitchell: The Case Of The Stolen Computer Brains*
Goudge, Eileen - *Gone With The Wish*
Harris, Lavinia - *The Great Rip-Off*
Kropp, Paul - *Micro Man*

CONDUCT OF LIFE

Charuhas, Mary - *Stages In Adult Life*
Rivera, Geraldo - *A Special Kind Of Courage: Profiles Of Young Americans*

CONDUCT OF LIFE—Fiction

Dygard, Thomas J - *Halfback Tough*
Hall, Lynn - *If Winter Comes*
Miklowitz, Gloria D - *Close To The Edge*
Skulicz, Matthew - *Right On, Shane*

CONDUCTORS (MUSIC)

Ewen, David - *Famous Conductors*
Young, Percy M - *World Conductors*

CONSTITUTION (FRIGATE)

Richards, Norman - *The Story Of Old Ironsides*

CONSUMER EDUCATION

Cohen, Daniel - *How To Buy A Car*
Kyte, Kathy S - *The Kid's Complete Guide To Money*
Thypin, Marilyn - *Checking And Balancing*
Thypin, Marilyn - *Good Buy! Buying Home Furnishings*
Thypin, Marilyn - *Health Care For The Wongs: Health Insurance, Choosing A Doctor*
Thypin, Marilyn - *Leases And Landlords: Apartment Living*
Thypin, Marilyn - *More Food For Our Money: Food Planning And Buying*
Thypin, Marilyn - *Put Your Money Down*
Thypin, Marilyn - *State Your Claim! Small Claims Court*
Thypin, Marilyn - *Try It On: Buying Clothing*
Thypin, Marilyn - *Wheels And Deals: Buying A Car*
Thypin, Marilyn - *When Things Don't Work: Appliance Buying And Repairs*

CONTINENTAL DRIFT

Anderson, Alan H, Jr. - *The Drifting Continents*

CONTINENTAL SHELF

Carlisle, Norman V - *The New American Continent*

COOKERY

Adams, Charlotte - *The Teen-Ager's Menu Cookbook*
Blue, Betty A - *Authentic Mexican Cooking*
Cobb, Vicki - *Science Experiments You Can Eat*

COOKERY—Fiction

Weir, LaVada - *Chaotic Kitchen*

CORNWALL—Fiction

Wiseman, David - *Jeremy Visick*

CORSICA—Fiction

Deane, Shirley - *Vendetta*

COSTUME

Dines, Glen - *Sun, Sand, And Steel: Costumes And Equipment Of The Spanish-Mexican Southwest*

COUNTERFEITS AND COUNTERFEITING—Fiction

Wheeler, W H - *Counterfeit!*

COUNTRY LIFE—Fiction

Burch, Robert J - *Queenie Peavy*
Lenski, Lois - *Deer Valley Girl*
Rabe, Berniece Louise - *The Girl Who Had No Name*

COUNTRY MUSICIANS

Hemphill, Paul - *The Nashville Sound*

COURAGE

Carlson, Gordon - *Get Me Out Of Here!: Real Life Stories Of Teenage Heroism*
Rivera, Geraldo - *A Special Kind Of Courage: Profiles Of Young Americans*

COURAGE—Fiction

Butterworth, W E - *Hot Wire*
Slepian, Jan - *The Alfred Summer*

COUSINS—Fiction

Brooks, Jerome - *The Big Dipper Marathon*
Gaeddert, Lou Ann - *Just Like Sisters*
Hopper, Nancy J - *Rivals*
York, Carol Beach - *When Midnight Comes....*

COWBOYS

Durham, Philip - *The Adventures Of The Negro Cowboys*
Felton, Harold W - *Nat Love, Negro Cowboy*
Folsom, Franklin Brewster - *The Life And Legend Of George McJunkin*
Munn, Vella - *Rodeo Riders*
Sackett, Samuel J - *Cowboys And The Songs They Sang*

CREDIT CARDS—Fiction

Hildick, E W - *The Top-Flight Fully-Automated Junior High School Girl Detective*

CRIME AND CRIMINALS

Atkinson, Linda - *Incredible Crimes*
Berger, Gilda - *Bizarre Crimes*
Berger, Gilda - *Bizarre Murders*
Berger, Melvin - *Police Lab*
Ernst, John - *Jesse James*
Larranaga, Robert O - *Famous Crimefighters*
Madison, Arnold - *Great Unsolved Cases*
Martinelli, Pat - *Public Enemy: And Other True Stories From The Files Of The Fbi*
Phillips, Maxine - *Crime And The Law: A Look At The Criminal Justice System*
Wilcox, Tamara - *Mysterious Detectives: Psychics*

CRIME AND CRIMINALS—Fiction

Baird, Thomas P - *Finding Fever*
Bennett, Jay - *Say Hello To The Hit Man*
Bennett, Jay - *Slowly, Slowly I Raise The Gun*
Borisoff, Norman - *Easy Money*
Bunting, Eve - *The Big Find*
Butterworth, W E - *Leroy And The Old Man*
Dodson, Susan - *The Creep*
Giff, Patricia Reilly - *Suspect*
Hassler, Jon Francis - *Four Miles To Pinecone*
Kropp, Paul - *Hot Cars*
Milton, Hilary - *Shutterbugs And Car Thieves*
Morey, Walter Nelson - *The Lemon Meringue Dog*
Murphy, Barbara Beasley - *No Place To Run*
Nixon, Joan Lowery - *Days Of Fear*
Paisley, Tom - *Doris Fein: Murder Is No Joke*
Platt, Kin - *Frank And Stein And Me*
Pownall, David - *The Bunch From Bananas*

DEAF

Ferrigno, Lou - *The Incredible Lou Ferrigno*
Ireland, Karin - *Kitty O'Neil: Daredevil Woman*

DEAF—Fiction

Corcoran, Barbara - *A Dance To Still Music*
Hallman, Ruth - *Breakaway*
Rosen, Lillian - *Just Like Everybody Else*

DEATH

Gunther, John - *Death Be Not Proud*
Krementz, Jill - *How It Feels When A Parent Dies*
Landau, Elaine - *Death: Everyone's Heritage*
Richter, Elizabeth - *Losing Someone You Love: When A Brother Or Sister Dies*
Zim, Herbert S - *Life And Death*

DEATH—Fiction

Angell, Judie - *Ronnie And Rosey*
Beckman, Gunnel - *Admission To The Feast*
Blume, Judy - *Tiger Eyes*
Branscum, Robbie - *Toby Alone*
Cleaver, Vera - *Grover*
Colman, Hila - *Sometimes I Don't Love My Mother*
Donovan, John - *I'll Get There. It Better Be Worth The Trip*
Girion, Barbara - *A Tangle Of Roots*
Glaser, Dianne - *The Diary Of Trilby Frost*
Greene, Constance C - *Beat The Turtle Drum*
Haddad, Carolyn - *The Last Ride*
Hall, Lynn - *Shadows*
Halvorson, Marilyn - *Cowboys Don't Cry*
Mann, Peggy - *There Are Two Kinds Of Terrible*
Mazer, Harry - *When The Phone Rang*
Miner, Jane Claypool - *Mountain Fear: When A Brother Dies*
Murphy, Jim - *Death Run*
Pfeffer, Susan Beth - *About David*
Rees, David - *Risks*
Rhodin, Eric Nolan - *The Good Greenwood*
Rodowsky, Colby F - *What About Me?*
Schotter, Roni - *A Matter Of Time*
Stolz, Mary Slattery - *The Edge Of Next Year*
Strasser, Todd - *Friends Till The End*
Stretton, Barbara - *You Never Lose*
Windsor, Patricia - *The Summer Before*
York, Carol Beach - *Remember Me When I Am Dead*

DECATHLON

Chodes, John - *Bruce Jenner*
Finlayson, Ann - *Decathlon Men: Greatest Athletes In The World*

DECATHLON—Fiction

Schulz, Charles M - *You're The Greatest, Charlie Brown*

DEPARTMENT STORES

Harris, Leon A, Jr. - *Behind The Scenes In A Department Store*

DEPARTMENT STORES—Fiction

Abels, Harriette Sheffer - *Emmy, Beware!*
Snyder, Zilpha Keatley - *Eyes In The Fishbowl*

DEPRESSION, 1929—Fiction

Colman, Hila - *Ellie's Inheritance*
Hunt, Irene - *No Promises In The Wind*
Rabin, Gil - *False Start*
Thrasher, Crystal Faye - *The Dark Didn't Catch Me*

DESERTS—Fiction

Luger, H C - *The Elephant Tree*
Miller, W Wesley - *Dirt Bike Adventure*
White, Robb - *Deathwatch*

DESIGN (DECORATIVE)—Iran

Dowlatshahi, Ali - *Persian Designs And Motifs For Artists And Craftsmen*

DETECTIVES

Anderson, Lavere - *Allan Pinkerton: First Private Eye*
Paige, David - *A Day In The Life Of A Police Detective*

DEVIL—Fiction

Avi - *Devil's Race*
Siegel, Scott - *Beat The Devil*

DINOSAURS

Asimov, Isaac - *How Did We Find Out About Dinosaurs?*
Pringle, Laurence - *Dinosaurs And Their World*

DIPTHERIA—Fiction

Anderson, Lavere - *Balto*

DISASTERS

Oleksy, Walter - *Nature Gone Wild!*
Spencer, John Wallace - *Limbo Of The Lost*

DISASTERS—Fiction

Sobol, Donald J - *Disaster*

DISC JOCKEYS—Fiction

Brancato, Robin Fidler - *Come Alive At 505*
Gilson, Jamie Marie - *Dial Leroi Rupert, DJ*

DISCO DANCING

Bednar, Jane - *Everybody's Dancing In Socks And On Skates*

DISCO DANCING—Fiction

Gathje, Curtis - *The Disco Kid*

DISCRIMINATION—Fiction

Colman, Hila - *Mixed-Marriage Daughter*

DISEASES—Fiction

Abels, Harriette Sheffer - *Medical Emergency*

DIVINATION

Cohen, Daniel - *The Magic Art Of Foreseeing The Future*
Hoffman, Elizabeth P - *Visions Of The Future: Palm Reading*

DIVING

Horner, Dave - *Better Scuba Diving For Boys*
Sullivan, George Edward - *Better Swimming And Diving For Boys And Girls*

DIVING (SUBMARINE)

Coggins, Jack - *Prepare To Dive: The Story Of Man Undersea*
Marx, Robert F - *They Dared The Deep: A History Of Diving*
Pick, Christopher C - *Undersea Machines*

DIVORCE

Berger, Terry - *How Does It Feel When Your Parents Get Divorced?*
Bradley, Buff - *Where Do I Belong?: A Kids' Guide To Stepfamilies*

DIVORCE—Fiction

Blume, Judy - *It's Not The End Of The World*
Bunting, Eve - *A Part Of The Dream*
Colman, Hila - *After The Wedding*
Conrad, Pam - *Holding Me Here*
Corcoran, Barbara - *Hey, That's My Soul You're Stomping On*
Danziger, Paula - *The Divorce Express*
Danziger, Paula - *It's An Aardvark-Eat-Turtle World*
Fitzhugh, Louise - *Sport*
Gaeddert, Lou Ann - *Just Like Sisters*
Gerber, Merrill Joan - *Please Don't Kiss Me Now*
Goldman, Katie - *In The Wings*
Hamilton, Dorothy - *Amanda Fair*
Hunter, Evan - *Me And Mr. Stenner*
Jones, Cordelia - *A Cat Called Camouflage*
Klein, Norma - *Breaking Up*
Klein, Norma - *Taking Sides*
Levine, Betty - *The Great Burgerland Disaster*
Mazer, Harry - *Guy Lenny*
Mazer, Norma Fox - *Taking Terri Mueller*
Mendonca, Susan - *Tough Choices*
Miner, Jane Claypool - *Split Decision: Facing Divorce*
Moore, Emily - *Something To Count On*
Neufeld, John - *Sunday Father*
Okimoto, Jean Davies - *My Mother Is Not Married To My Father*
Park, Anne - *Tender Loving Care*
Park, Barbara - *Don't Make Me Smile*
Pevsner, Stella - *A Smart Kid Like You*
Platt, Kin - *Chloris And The Freaks*
Roy, Ron - *Avalanche!*
Sanderlin, Owenita - *Tennis Rebel*
Stolz, Mary Slattery - *Leap Before You Look*
Wolitzer, Hilma - *Out Of Love*

DIVORCE—Fiction (continued)

Wood, Phyllis Anderson - *Win Me And You Lose*

DOGS

Borland, Hal - *Penny: The Story Of A Free-Soul Basset Hound*
Bradbury, Bianca - *Dogs And More Dogs*
Emert, Phyllis R - *Guide Dogs*
Emert, Phyllis R - *Hearing Ear Dogs*
Emert, Phyllis R - *Law Enforcement Dogs*
Emert, Phyllis R - *Military Dogs*
Emert, Phyllis R - *Search And Rescue Dogs*
Emert, Phyllis R - *Sled Dogs*
Henry, Marguerite - *Album Of Dogs*
Leder, Jane M - *Stunt Dogs*
Newman, Matthew - *Watch/Guard Dogs*
Pinkwater, Jill - *Superpuppy: How To Choose, Raise, And Train The Best Possible Dog For You*
Rockwell, Jane - *Dogs And Puppies*
Siegal, Mordecai - *The Good Dog Book*
Thomas, Allison - *Sandy: The Autobiography Of A Dog*
Unkelbach, Kurt - *How To Bring Up Your Pet Dog*
Yates, Elizabeth - *Skeezer: Dog With A Mission*

DOGS—Fiction

Adler, C S - *Shelter On Blue Barns Road*
Baird, Thomas P - *Finding Fever*
Bartos-Hoeppner, Barbara - *Avalanche Dog*
Green, Gerald - *Girl*
Hall, Lynn - *Danger Dog*
Hall, Lynn - *Shadows*
Hall, Lynn - *Stray*
Kantor, MacKinlay - *The Daughter Of Bugle Ann*
Kantor, MacKinlay - *The Voice Of Bugle Ann*
Kjelgaard, Jim - *Big Red*
Kjelgaard, Jim - *Dave And His Dog, Mulligan*
Knight, Eric - *Lassie Come-Home*
Letchworth, Beverly J - *Pax And The Mutt*
Lewiton, Mina - *Especially Humphrey*
London, Jack - *The Call Of The Wild*
Munsterhjelm, Erik - *A Dog Named Wolf*
O'Brien, Jack - *Return Of Silver Chief*
Paisley, Tom - *The Dog Days Of Arthur Cane*
Rawls, Wilson - *Where The Red Fern Grows*
Rounds, Glen - *Stolen Pony*
Stoneley, Jack - *Scruffy*
Wallace, Bill - *A Dog Named Kitty*
Wood, Phyllis Anderson - *I Think This Is Where We Came In*
Zistel, Era - *Hi Fella*

DOLLMAKING

Holz, Loretta - *The How-To Book Of International Dolls: A Comprehensive Guide To Making, Costuming And Collecting Dolls*

DONKEYS—Fiction

Corbett, Scott - *The Donkey Planet*

DOWN'S SYNDROME—Fiction

Rodowsky, Colby F - *What About Me?*

DRAG RACING

Coombs, Charles Ira - *Drag Racing*
Edmonds, Ivy Gordon - *Drag Racing For Beginners*
Garlits, Don - *King Of The Dragsters: The Story Of Big Daddy Garlits*
Olney, Ross Robert - *Modern Drag Racing Superstars*

DRAWING—Technique

Ames, Lee Judah - *Draw 50 Airplanes, Aircraft And Spacecraft*
Ames, Lee Judah - *Draw 50 Famous Faces*
Ellison, Elsie C - *Fun With Lines And Curves*
Evans, Larry - *How To Draw Monsters*
Lee, Stan - *How To Draw Comics The Marvel Way*

DREAMS—Fiction

Shea, George - *Nightmare Nina*

DREAMS—Poetry

Larrick, Nancy - *Bring Me All Of Your Dreams*

DRESSMAKING

Corrigan, Barbara - *Of Course You Can Sew!*

DRESSMAKING (continued)

Rosenberg, Sharon - *The Illustrated Hassle-Free Make Your Own Clothes Book*
Wiseman, Ann Sayre - *Cuts Of Cloth*

DROPOUTS—Fiction

Clarke, John - *High School Drop Out*
Zindel, Paul - *I Never Loved Your Mind*

DRUG ABUSE

Gorodetzky, Charles W - *What You Should Know About Drugs*
Houser, Norman W - *Drugs: Facts On Their Use And Abuse*
Lieberman, Mark - *The Dope Book: All About Drugs*
Whipple, Dorothy Vermilya - *Is The Grass Greener?: Answers To Questions About Drugs*

DRUG ABUSE—Fiction

Adler, C S - *Shadows On Little Reef Bay*
Anonymous - *Go Ask Alice*
Blue, Rose - *Nikki 108*
Butterworth, W E - *The Narc*
Childress, Alice - *A Hero Ain't Nothin' But A Sandwich*
Coles, Robert Martin - *The Grass Pipe*
Cunningham, Chet - *Narc One Going Down*
Eyerly, Jeannette - *Escape From Nowhere*
Garden, Nancy - *The Loners*
Kinter, Judith - *Cross-Country Caper*
Kropp, Paul - *Dope Deal*
Rabinowich, Ellen - *Rock Fever*
Rice, Earle, Jr. - *Death Angel*
Sherburne, Zoa Morin - *Leslie*
Shreve, Susan Richards - *The Nightmares Of Geranium Street*
Sparks, Beatrice - *Go Ask Alice*
Stegeman, Janet Allais - *Last Seen On Hopper's Lane*
Strasser, Todd - *Angel Dust Blues*
Wojciechowska, Maia - *Tuned Out*
Young, Al - *Snakes*

DRUGS

Walker, Nona - *The Medicine Makers*

DUNE BUGGY RACING—Fiction

Sheffer, H R - *Weekend In The Dunes*

DWELLINGS

Anema, Durlynn - *Sharing An Apartment*

EARRINGS

Holmes, Anita - *Pierced And Pretty: The Complete Guide To Ear Piercing, Pierced Earrings, And How To Create Your Own*

EARTHQUAKES

Asimov, Isaac - *How Did We Find Out About Earthquakes?*

EARTHQUAKES—Fiction

Fries, Chloe - *No Place To Hide*

ECOLOGY

Hirsch, S Carl - *The Living Community: A Venture Into Ecology*

ECOLOGY—Fiction

George, Jean Craighead - *Who Really Killed Cock Robin?*
Luger, H C - *Chasing Trouble*

EGYPT

Holmes, Burnham - *Nefertiti: The Mystery Queen*
James, T G H - *The Archaeology Of Ancient Egypt*
Knapp, Ron - *Tutankhamun And The Mysteries Of Ancient Egypt*
Pace, Mildred Mastin - *Wrapped For Eternity*
Payne, Elizabeth - *The Pharaohs Of Ancient Egypt*
Reiff, Stephanie Ann - *Secrets Of Tut's Tomb And The Pyramids*
Van Duyn, Janet - *Builders On The Desert*

EGYPT—Fiction

Ellerby, Leona - *King Tut's Game Board*
Marston, Elsa - *The Cliffs Of Cairo*
Myers, Walter Dean - *Tales Of A Dead King*

ELDERLY—Fiction

Zindel, Paul - *The Pigman*

ELEANOR OF AQUITAINE—Fiction

Konigsburg, E L - *A Proud Taste For Scarlet And Miniver*

ELECTIONS—Fiction

Ibbitson, John - *The Wimp*
Perl, Lila - *Don't Ask Miranda*

ELECTRONICS

Abrams, Kathleen S - *Career Prep: Electronics Servicing*
Bendick, Jeanne - *Electronics For Young People*
Pearce, W E - *Transistors And Circuits: Electronics For Young Experimenters*

EMIGRATION AND IMMIGRATION—Fiction

Angell, Judie - *One-Way To Ansonia*

EMOTIONAL PROBLEMS—Fiction

Avi - *Sometimes I Think I Hear My Name*
Bunting, Eve - *One More Flight*
Delton, Jina - *Two Blocks Down*
Hautzig, Deborah - *Second Star To The Right*
Holland, Isabelle - *Amanda's Choice*
Lee, Mildred - *The Skating Rink*
Storr, Catherine - *Thursday*
Windsor, Patricia - *The Summer Before*

EMOTIONS

Daniels, Kim - *Your Changing Emotions*
Hyde, Margaret Oldroyd - *Know Your Feelings*

EMPLOYMENT

Cole, Sheila R - *Working Kids On Working*
Lembeck, Ruth - *Teenage Jobs*
McHugh, John - *Interviewing For Jobs*
Verdick, Mary - *Write For The Job*

EMPLOYMENT—Fiction

Bonham, Frank - *The Nitty Gritty*
Borisoff, Norman - *The Goof-Up*
Cunningham, Chet - *Apprentice To A Rip-Off*
Sarason, Martin - *A Federal Case*
Stewart, Jo - *A Time To Choose*
Teall, Kaye M - *TV Camera Three*

ENERGY CONSERVATION

Branley, Franklyn M - *Feast Or Famine?: The Energy Future*

ENGINES

Corbett, Scott - *What About The Wankel Engine?*
Urquhart, David Inglis - *The Internal Combustion Engine And How It Works*
Weiss, Harvey - *Motors And Engines And How They Work*

ENGLAND—Fiction

Gardam, Jane - *The Summer After The Funeral*
Green, Janet - *Us: Inside A Teenage Gang*
Jeffries, Roderic Graeme - *Trapped*
Leach, Christopher - *Rosalinda*
Maddock, Reginald - *The Pit*
Nagel, Shirley - *Escape From The Tower Of London*
Peyton, K M - *A Pattern Of Roses*
Prince, Alison - *The Turkey's Nest*
Sampson, Fay - *The Watch On Patterick Fell*
Smaridge, Norah Antoinette - *The Mystery Of Greystone Hall*
Streatfeild, Noel - *Thursday's Child*
Townsend, John Rowe - *Hell's Edge*
Townsend, John Rowe - *The Summer People*
Walsh, Jill Paton - *Unleaving*
Wiseman, David - *Thimbles*

ENGLISH LANGUAGE

Asimov, Isaac - *More Words Of Science*
Garrison, Webb B - *What's In A Word?*
Garrison, Webb B - *Why You Say It*
Nurnberg, Maxwell - *Wonders In Words*

ENGLISH POETRY

Lewis, Richard - *Miracles: Poems By Children Of The English-Speaking World*
Lewis, Richard - *Out Of The Earth I Sing: Poetry And Songs Of Primitive Peoples Of The World*
McDonald, Gerald - *A Way Of Knowing: A Collection Of Poems For Boys*
Peck, Richard - *Sounds And Silences: Poetry For Now*
Ward, Herman - *Poems For Pleasure*

ENTERTAINERS

Alderman, Clifford Lindsey - *Annie Oakley And The World Of Her Time*
Berman, Connie - *Leif Garrett*
Katz, Susan - *Kristy And Jimmy*
Wayne, Bennett - *The Super Showmen*

ENTERTAINING

Robb, Mary K - *Making Teen Parties Click*
Sweeney, Karen O'Connor - *Entertaining*

EPILEPSY—Fiction

Sherburne, Zoa Morin - *Why Have The Birds Stopped Singing?*

ESCAPES

Alter, Robert Edmond - *Who Goes Next?*
Baldwin, Margaret - *Kisses Of Death: A World War II Escape Story*
Gunning, Thomas G - *Amazing Escapes*
Scoggin, Margaret C - *Escapes And Rescues*

ESKIMOS

Wilder, Edna - *Once Upon An Eskimo Time*

ESKIMOS—Fiction

Chadwick, Roxane - *Don't Shoot*
George, Jean Craighead - *Julie Of The Wolves*
Paulsen, Gary - *Dogsong*

ETHICS—Fiction

Allman, Paul - *No Pain, No Gain*

ETIQUETTE

Allen, Betty - *Mind Your Manners*
Archer, Elsie - *Let's Face It: The Guide To Good Grooming For Girls Of Color*
Beery, Mary - *Manners Made Easy*
Beery, Mary - *Young Teens Away From Home*
Perry, Tyler - *Girls, Answers To Your Questions About Guys*
Post, Elizabeth L - *The Emily Post Book Of Etiquette For Young People*

EUROPEAN WAR, 1914-1918

Jackson, Robert Blake - *Fighter Pilots Of World War I*
Knightley, Phillip - *Lawrence Of Arabia*

EVANGELISTS

Westman, Paul - *Billy Graham: Reaching Out To The World*

EVERT, CHRIS

Sabin, Francene - *Set Point*

EXERCISE

Englebardt, Stanley L - *How To Get In Shape For Sports*
Scharffenberger, Ann - *The Mademoiselle Shape-Up Book*
Schurman, Dewey - *Athletic Fitness*

EXILES—Fiction

Skarmeta, Antonio - *Chileno!*

EXORCISM—Fiction

Logan, Les - *The Game*
Sparger, Rex - *The Doll*

EXPLORERS

Blassingame, Wyatt - *Thor Heyerdahl: Viking Scientist*
Knight, Frank - *Stories Of Famous Explorers By Land*
Shepherd, Elizabeth - *The Discoveries Of Esteban The Black*
Westman, Paul - *Thor Heyerdahl: Across The Seas Of Time*

EXTRASENSORY PERCEPTION

Atkinson, Linda - *Psychic Stories Strange But True*
Cohen, Daniel - *How To Test Your ESP*
Curtis, Robert H - *On ESP*

EXTRASENSORY PERCEPTION—Fiction

Asimov, Isaac - *Earth Invaded*
Bunting, Eve - *The Mask*
Duncan, Lois S - *A Gift Of Magic*
Sherburne, Zoa Morin - *The Girl Who Knew Tomorrow*
Stewart, Ramona - *Sixth Sense*
Webster, Joanne - *Gypsy Gift*

EXTRATERRESTRIAL BEINGS

Randall, E T - *Target: Earth*

EXTRATERRESTRIAL BEINGS—Fiction

DeWeese, Gene - *Black Suits From Outer Space*
Randall, E T - *Thieves From Space*
Ray, N L - *There Was This Man Running*
Thorne, Ian - *It Came From Outer Space*

FAIRY TALES

Aiken, Conrad - *Cats And Bats And Things With Wings: Poems*
Diamond, Donna - *Swan Lake*
Massie, Diane Redfield - *Cockle Stew And Other Rhymes*
O'Neill, Mary - *Take A Number*
Potter, Charles Francis - *More Tongue Tanglers And A Rigmarole*
Swenson, May - *Poems To Solve*

FAMILY LIFE—Fiction

Anderson, Mary - *Step On A Crack*
Arthur, Ruth M - *The Whistling Boy*
Arundel, Honor - *A Family Failing*
Bach, Alice - *The Meat In The Sandwich*
Bates, Betty - *The Ups And Downs Of Jorie Jenkins*
Bradbury, Bianca - *The Loner*
Butterworth, W E - *Steve Bellamy*
Byars, Betsy - *The Cartoonist*
Cameron, Eleanor - *A Room Made Of Windows*
Carlson, Dale Bick - *A Wild Heart*
Carlson, Natalie Savage - *The Half Sisters*
Cavanna, Betty - *Accent On April*
Claypool, Jane - *A Love For Violet*
Clifton, Lucille - *Sonora Beautiful*
Colman, Hila - *Claudia, Where Are You?*
Colman, Hila - *Daughter Of Discontent*
Colman, Hila - *Nobody Has To Be A Kid Forever*
Colman, Hila - *Nobody Told Me What I Need To Know*
Cone, Molly Lamken - *Call Me Moose*
Danziger, Paula - *Can You Sue Your Parents For Malpractice?*
Danziger, Paula - *It's An Aardvark-Eat-Turtle World*
Danziger, Paula - *The Pistachio Prescription*
Donovan, John - *Remove Protective Coating A Little At A Time*
Gilson, Jamie Marie - *Can't Catch Me, I'm The Gingerbread Man*
Greene, Constance C - *Getting Nowhere*
Holland, Isabelle - *Amanda's Choice*
Hunt, Irene - *No Promises In The Wind*
Ish-Kishor, Sulamith - *Our Eddie*
Johnston, Norma - *The Sanctuary Tree*
Jordan, June - *His Own Where*
Kastner, Erich - *Lisa And Lottie*
Klein, Norma - *It's Not What You Expect*
Konigsburg, E L - *About The B'nai Bagels*
Koob, Theodora - *The Deep Search*
Kropp, Paul - *Dead On*
Littke, Lael J - *Tell Me When I Can Go*
Little, Jean - *Look Through My Window*
Mathis, Sharon Bell - *Teacup Full Of Roses*
Mazer, Norma Fox - *Up In Seth's Room*
McFall, Karen - *Pat King's Family*
McKay, Robert W - *Dave's Song*
Meyer, Carolyn - *C. C. Poindexter*
Miklowitz, Gloria D - *Close To The Edge*
Morey, Walter Nelson - *Year Of The Black Pony*
Okimoto, Jean Davies - *It's Just Too Much*
Oppenheimer, Joan Letson - *Gardine Vs. Hanover*
Peck, Richard - *Don't Look And It Won't Hurt*
Perl, Lila - *That Crazy April*
Pevsner, Stella - *And You Give Me A Pain, Elaine*
Pevsner, Stella - *Call Me Heller, That's My Name*
Pevsner, Stella - *Keep Stompin' Till The Music Stops*
Pfeffer, Susan Beth - *The Beauty Queen*
Pfeffer, Susan Beth - *Getting Even*
Pfeffer, Susan Beth - *Marly The Kid*
Platt, Kin - *Chloris And The Creeps*
Platt, Kin - *Crocker*
Rabe, Berniece Louise - *The Girl Who Had No Name*
Rabe, Berniece Louise - *Naomi*
Rabin, Gil - *False Start*
Randall, Florence Engel - *The Almost Year*
Rodowsky, Colby F - *P.S. Write Soon*
Scott, Ann Herbert - *Sam*
Shore, June Lewis - *Summer Storm*

FAMILY LIFE—Fiction (continued)

Stolz, Mary Slattery - *By The Highway Home*
Townsend, John Rowe - *Good-Bye To The Jungle*
Townsend, John Rowe - *Pirate's Island*
Wartski, Maureen Crane - *My Brother Is Special*
Wilder, Laura Ingalls - *The Little House Books*
Wilder, Laura Ingalls - *Little House In The Big Woods*
Zindel, Paul - *Pardon Me, You're Stepping On My Eyeball*

FAMILY PROBLEMS

Gilbert, Sara Dulaney - *Trouble At Home*

FAMILY PROBLEMS—Fiction

Adler, C S - *Shelter On Blue Barns Road*
Anderson, Mary - *Catch Me, I'm Falling In Love*
Bolton, Carole - *The Good-Bye Year*
Colman, Hila - *What's The Matter With The Dobsons?*
Conrad, Pam - *Holding Me Here*
Cooney, Caroline B - *Don't Blame The Music*
Corcoran, Barbara - *Hey, That's My Soul You're Stomping On*
Daly, Maureen - *Acts Of Love*
Degens, T - *Friends*
Guy, Rosa - *Edith Jackson*
Hahn, Mary Downing - *The Time Of The Witch*
Hall, Lynn - *The Leaving*
Hall, Lynn - *The Solitary*
Holland, Isabelle - *Heads You Win, Tails I Lose*
Holland, Isabelle - *The Man Without A Face*
Hunt, Irene - *William*
Kerr, M E - *Night Kites*
Kingman, Lee - *Head Over Wheels*
Kropp, Paul - *No Way*
Kropp, Paul - *Take Off*
Mathis, Sharon Bell - *Listen For The Fig Tree*
Mazer, Harry - *When The Phone Rang*
Meriwether, Louise - *Daddy Was A Number Runner*
Miklowitz, Gloria D - *The Day The Senior Class Got Married*
Miner, Jane Claypool - *A Day At A Time: Dealing With An Alcoholic*
Miner, Jane Claypool - *Miracle Of Time: Adopting A Sister*
O'Hanlon, Jacklyn - *Fair Game*
Pfeffer, Susan Beth - *About David*
Platt, Kin - *Chloris And The Freaks*
Reynolds, Pamela - *Will The Real Monday Please Stand Up?*
Sampson, Fay - *The Watch On Patterick Fell*
Samuels, Gertrude - *Run, Shelley, Run!*
Silsbee, Peter - *The Big Way Out*
Wersba, Barbara - *Crazy Vanilla*
Winslow, Joan - *Romance Is A Riot*

FANTASY

Aiken, Joan - *The Whispering Mountain*
Asimov, Isaac - *Tomorrow's Children*
Austin, R G - *The Castle Of No Return*
Austin, R G - *Lost In A Strange Land*
Cunningham, Julia Woolfolk - *Macaroon*
Dahl, Roald - *Charlie And The Great Glass Elevator*
Gaskin, Carol - *The Forbidden Towers*
Gaskin, Carol - *The Magician's Ring*
Gaskin, Carol - *Master Of Mazes*
Gaskin, Carol - *The War Of The Wizards*
Jones, Diana Wynne - *Dogsbody*
Kennedy, Richard - *The Boxcar At The Center Of The Universe*
Key, Alexander - *Escape To Witch Mountain*
Lynn, Elizabeth A - *The Silver Horse*
McKillip, Patricia A - *The Throme Of The Erril Of Sherill*
Murphy, Shirley Rousseau - *Caves Of Fire And Ice*
Nichols, Ruth - *A Walk Out Of The World*
Norton, Andre - *Fur Magic*
Selden, George - *The Cricket In Times Square*
Selden, George - *Tucker's Countryside*
Snyder, Zilpha Keatley - *Eyes In The Fishbowl*
Stewart, Mary Florence Elinor - *Ludo And The Star Horse*
White, E B - *The Trumpet Of The Swan*
Willett, John - *The Singer In The Stone*
Yep, Laurence Michael - *Dragon Of The Lost Sea*

FARM LIFE—Fiction

Hall, Lynn - *The Leaving*
Heck, Bessie Holland - *Golden Arrow*
Peck, Robert Newton - *A Day No Pigs Would Die*

FARM LIFE—Fiction (continued)

Prince, Alison - *The Turkey's Nest*
Rabe, Berniece Louise - *Naomi*
Rabe, Berniece Louise - *Rass*

FASHION DRAWING

Bolognese, Donald Alan - *Drawing Fashions: Figures, Faces And Techniques*

FATHERS AND DAUGHTERS—Fiction

Colman, Hila - *Don't Tell Me That You Love Me*
Colman, Hila - *Just The Two Of Us*
Colman, Hila - *What's The Matter With The Dobsons?*
Corcoran, Barbara - *Me And You And A Dog Named Blue*
Feagles, Anita MacRae - *The Year The Dreams Came Back*
Girion, Barbara - *A Tangle Of Roots*
Hall, Lynn - *Denison's Daughter*
Holland, Isabelle - *Hitchhike*
Lorimer, L T - *Secrets*
O'Dell, Scott - *The Spanish Smile*
Peck, Robert Newton - *A Day No Pigs Would Die*
Samuels, Gertrude - *Adam's Daughter*
Tolan, Stephanie S - *The Liberation Of Tansy Warner*

FATHERS AND SONS—Fiction

Avi - *Wolf Rider: A Tale Of Terror*
Bennett, Jay - *Slowly, Slowly I Raise The Gun*
Boehm, Bruce - *Connecticut Low*
Brancato, Robin Fidler - *Uneasy Money*
Carter, Alden R - *Wart, Son Of Toad*
Filson, Brent - *The Puma*
Fox, Paula - *Blowfish Live In The Sea*
Fox, Paula - *Portrait Of Ivan*
Fries, Chloe - *The Full Of The Moon*
Glenn, Mel - *One Order To Go*
Halvorson, Marilyn - *Cowboys Don't Cry*
Hentoff, Nat - *This School Is Driving Me Crazy*
Lyle, Katie Letcher - *Dark But Full Of Diamonds*
Mann, Peggy - *There Are Two Kinds Of Terrible*
Mazer, Harry - *The War On Villa Street*
Peck, Richard - *Father Figure*
Pierik, Robert - *Archy's Dream World*
Rabe, Berniece Louise - *Rass*
Roth, Arthur J - *The Secret Lover Of Elmtree*
Rubinstein, Robert E - *When Sirens Scream*
Shaw, Richard - *Call Me Al Raft*
Shaw, Richard - *Shape Up, Burke*
Silsbee, Peter - *The Big Way Out*
Smith, Beatrice Schillinger - *The Road To Galveston*
Stretton, Barbara - *You Never Lose*
Voigt, Cynthia - *Building Blocks*
Weinberg, Larry - *Dangerous Run*
Wersba, Barbara - *Run Softly, Go Fast*
Wibberley, Leonard - *Perilous Gold*
Wood, Phyllis Anderson - *Win Me And You Lose*

FATHERS—Fiction

Naylor, Phyllis Reynolds - *The Keeper*
Ready, Anne Cooper - *Her Father's Daughter*
Tamar, Erika - *Blues For Silk Garcia*

FEAR—Fiction

Bolton, Evelyn - *Stable Of Fear*
Mullin, Penn - *Search And Rescue*

FEMINISM—Fiction

Colman, Hila - *Girl Meets Boy*
Sirof, Harriet Toby - *The Real World*

FENCING

Alaux, Michel - *Modern Fencing: Foil Epee, Sabre From Initiation To Competition*

FERAL CHILDREN

Burger, John Robert - *Children Of The Wild*

FERAL CHILDREN—Fiction

George, Jean Craighead - *River Rats, Inc.*

FERNS

Guilcher, Jean Michel - *A Fern Is Born*

FIELD HOCKEY—Fiction

Rabinowich, Ellen - *Rock Fever*
Sheffer, H R - *Street Hockey Lady*

FOOD (continued)

Thypin, Marilyn - *More Food For Our Money: Food Planning And Buying*

FOOTBALL

Aaseng, Nathan - *Football's Crushing Blockers*
Aaseng, Nathan - *Football's Cunning Coaches*
Alfano, Pete - *Super Bowl Superstars: The Most Valuable Players In The NFL's Championship Game*
Berger, Melvin - *The Photo Dictionary Of Football*
Berger, Phil - *Championship Teams Of The NFL*
Gogolak, Peter - *Kicking The Football Soccer Style*
Griese, Bob - *Offensive Football*
Hollander, Phyllis - *Touchdown!*
Hollander, Zander - *Strange But True Football Stories*
Liss, Howard - *Football Talk For Beginners*
Liss, Howard - *The Front 4: Let's Meet At The Quarterback*
Masin, Herman L - *How To Star In Football*
May, Julian - *The Cincinnati Bengals*
May, Julian - *The New York Jets*
McCallum, John Dennis - *Getting Into Pro Football*
Sullivan, George Edward - *Pro Football's Greatest Upsets*
Thorn, John - *Pro Football's Ten Greatest Games*
Ward, Don - *Super Bowl XVII*

FOOTBALL—Biography

Brown, Larry - *I'll Always Get Up*
Burchard, Sue H - *Sports Star: Herschel Walker*
Burchard, Sue H - *Sports Star: Tony Dorsett*
Conrad, Dick - *Tony Dorsett: From Heisman To Superbowl In One Year*
Conrad, Dick - *Walter Payton: The Running Machine*
DeRosier, John - *Chuck Foreman*
Dolan, Edward Francis, Jr. - *Archie Griffin*
Gutman, Bill - *Modern Football Superstars*
Hahn, James - *Brown! The Sports Career Of James Brown*
Hahn, James - *Sayers! The Sports Career Of Gale Sayers*
Hahn, James - *Tark! The Sports Career Of Francis Tarkenton*
Jameson, Jon - *The Picture Life Of O. J. Simpson*
Leder, Jane M - *Marcus Allen*
Leder, Jane M - *Walter Payton*
Lipman, David - *Jim Hart: Underrated Quarterback*
Morris, Jeannie - *Brian Piccolo: A Short Season*
Musick, Phil - *The Tony Dorsett Story*
Phillips, Betty Lou - *Earl Campbell, Houston Oiler Superstar*
Reiss, Bob - *Franco Harris*
Sahadi, Lou - *Pro Football's Gamebreakers*
Sullivan, George Edward - *Bert Jones: Born To Play Football*

FOOTBALL—Fiction

Allman, Paul - *No Pain, No Gain*
Archibald, Joe - *Phantom Blitz*
Bunting, Eve - *The Waiting Game*
Cox, William R - *Third And Goal*
Dygard, Thomas J - *Halfback Tough*
Dygard, Thomas J - *Point Spread*
Dygard, Thomas J - *Quarterback Walk-On*
Dygard, Thomas J - *Winning Kicker*
Gault, William Campbell - *Quarterback Gamble*
Heuman, William - *Gridiron Stranger*
Knudson, R R - *Zanballer*
Lord, Beman - *Quarterback's Aim*
McKay, Robert W - *The Running Back*
Miner, Jane Claypool - *New Beginning: An Athlete Is Paralyzed*
Sheffer, H R - *Second String Nobody*
Sommers, Beverly - *A Passing Game*
Stretton, Barbara - *You Never Lose*
Swift, Benjamin - *Play-Off*

FORCE AND ENERGY

Asimov, Isaac - *How Did We Find Out About Energy?*

FORESTS

Nagel, Shirley - *Tree Boy*
Wood, Frances - *Forests Are For People: The Heritage Of Our National Forests*

FORESTS—Fiction

Wartski, Maureen Crane - *The Lake Is On Fire*

FORTUNE TELLING

Baldwin, Margaret - *Fortune Telling*

FOSSILS

Asimov, Isaac - *How Did We Find Out About Dinosaurs?*
Asimov, Isaac - *How Did We Find Out About Our Human Roots?*

FOSTER HOME CARE—Fiction

Adler, C S - *The Cat That Was Left Behind*
Angell, Judie - *Tina Gogo*
Bauer, Marion Dane - *Foster Child*
Byars, Betsy - *The Pinballs*
Childress, Alice - *Rainbow Jordan*
Guy, Rosa - *The Disappearance*
Levinson, Nancy Smiler - *Silent Fear*
Myers, Walter Dean - *Won't Know Till I Get There*
Oppenheimer, Joan Letson - *Which Mother Is Mine?*

FOXES

Ahlstrom, Mark E - *The Foxes*

FRANCE—History

Jablonski, Edward - *Warriors With Wings: The Story Of The Lafayette Escadrille*

FRANCE—Fiction

Berna, Paul - *The Mule On The Expressway*
Brow, Thea - *The Secret Cross Of Lorraine*
Cavanna, Betty - *Stamp Twice For Murder*
Hugo, Victor Marie - *Hunchback Of Notre Dame*
Woodford, Peggy - *Please Don't Go*

FRAUD

Cohen, Daniel - *Frauds, Hoaxes, And Swindles*

FRIENDS, SOCIETY OF

Yolen, Jane H - *Friend: The Story Of George Fox And The Quakers*

FRIENDSHIP—Fiction

Angell, Judie - *Ronnie And Rosey*
Angell, Judie - *Tina Gogo*
Asher, Sandy - *Summer Begins*
Avi - *Sometimes I Think I Hear My Name*
Bach, Alice - *The Meat In The Sandwich*
Bargar, Gary W - *Life. Is. Not. Fair.*
Barrett, William E - *The Lilies Of The Field*
Betancourt, Jeanne - *Between Us*
Boehm, Bruce - *Connecticut Low*
Brancato, Robin Fidler - *Something Left To Lose*
Branscum, Robbie - *The Girl*
Bunting, Eve - *The Big Find*
Bunting, Eve - *The Waiting Game*
Butterworth, W E - *Under The Influence*
Byars, Betsy - *The Pinballs*
Carpelan, Bo - *Bow Island*
Carrick, Carol - *Some Friend!*
Cavanna, Betty - *Almost Like Sisters*
Cebulash, Mel - *The Champion's Jacket*
Cleaver, Vera - *The Mock Revolt*
Colman, Hila - *Accident*
Conklin, Barbara - *The Summer Jenny Fell In Love*
Corcoran, Barbara - *Me And You And A Dog Named Blue*
Corcoran, Barbara - *Rising Damp*
Crawford, Charles P - *Letter Perfect*
Crawford, Charles P - *Three-Legged Race*
Cuyler, Margery Stuyvesant - *The Trouble With Soap*
Degens, T - *Friends*
Delton, Jina - *Two Blocks Down*
Donovan, John - *Remove Protective Coating A Little At A Time*
Ethridge, Kenneth E - *Toothpick*
Garrigue, Sheila - *Between Friends*
Gauch, Patricia Lee - *Fridays*
Gerson, Corinne - *Passing Through*
Gonzalez, Gloria - *The Glad Man*
Goudge, Eileen - *Don't Say Good-Bye*
Greenwald, Sheila - *Blissful Joy And The SATs: A Multiple-Choice Romance*
Grohskopf, Bernice - *End Of Summer*
Hall, Lynn - *Flowers Of Anger*
Hall, Lynn - *Just One Friend*
Hall, Lynn - *The Siege Of Silent Henry*
Hall, Lynn - *Stray*
Hassler, Jon Francis - *Four Miles To Pinecone*
Hautzig, Deborah - *Hey, Dollface*
Heide, Florence Parry - *When The Sad One Comes To Stay*
Hinton, S E - *That Was Then, This Is Now*
Holland, Isabelle - *The Man Without A Face*

FRIENDSHIP—Fiction (continued)

Howe, Fanny - *Yeah, But*
Jacobs, Linda C - *Everyone's Watching Tammy*
Jacobs, Linda C - *Will The Real Jeannie Murphy Please Stand Up*
Knudsen, James - *Just Friends*
Kropp, Paul - *Amy's Wish*
Lee, Mildred - *Sycamore Year*
LeGuin, Ursula Kroeber - *Very Far Away From Anywhere Else*
Levoy, Myron - *A Shadow Like A Leopard*
Little, Jean - *Kate*
Little, Jean - *Look Through My Window*
Mazer, Norma Fox - *Mrs. Fish, Ape, And Me, The Dump Queen*
Miles, Betty - *All It Takes Is Practice*
Moore, Emily - *Just My Luck*
Norris, Gunilla B - *The Good Morrow*
Okimoto, Jean Davies - *Who Did It, Jenny Lake?*
Oppenheimer, Joan Letson - *The Missing Sunrise*
Paulsen, Gary - *The Foxman*
Peck, Richard - *Remembering The Good Times*
Pfeffer, Susan Beth - *Fantasy Summer*
Platt, Kin - *Hey, Dummy*
Quin-Harkin, Janet - *Ten-Boy Summer*
Rabinowich, Ellen - *Toni's Crowd*
Rabinowich, Ellen - *Underneath I'm Different*
Reader, Dennis J - *Coming Back Alive*
Rees, David - *Risks*
Rhodin, Eric Nolan - *The Good Greenwood*
Roe, Kathy Gibson - *Goodbye, Secret Place*
Sachs, Marilyn - *Beach Towels*
Sachs, Marilyn - *Class Pictures*
Sachs, Marilyn - *Fourteen*
Sachs, Marilyn - *Hello... Wrong Number*
Sachs, Marilyn - *Peter And Veronica*
Sachs, Marilyn - *Thunderbird*
Sharmat, Marjorie Weinman - *I Saw Him First*
Slepian, Jan - *The Alfred Summer*
Slepian, Jan - *Lester's Turn*
Slote, Alfred - *Stranger On The Ball Club*
Smith, Nancy Covert - *Josie's Handful Of Quietness*
Stewart, Jo - *The Promise Ring*
Stine, H William - *Best Friend*
Strasser, Todd - *A Very Touchy Subject*
Tate, Joan - *Tina And David*
Taylor, Theodore Langhans - *The Cay*
Townsend, John Rowe - *Trouble In The Jungle*
Van Steenwyk, Elizabeth - *Rivals On Ice*
Wersba, Barbara - *Crazy Vanilla*
Winthrop, Elizabeth - *Miranda In The Middle*
Wood, Phyllis Anderson - *I Think This Is Where We Came In*
Wood, Phyllis Anderson - *This Time Count Me In*
Yep, Laurence Michael - *Kind Hearts And Gentle Monsters*

FRONTIER AND PIONEER LIFE—Fiction

Beatty, Patricia Robbins - *Something To Shout About*
Collier, James Lincoln - *The Bloody Country*
Morey, Walter Nelson - *Year Of The Black Pony*
Speare, Elizabeth - *Sign Of The Beaver*
Wilder, Laura Ingalls - *The First Four Years*
Wilder, Laura Ingalls - *The Little House Books*
Wilder, Laura Ingalls - *Little House In The Big Woods*
Wisler, G Clifton - *Winter Of The Wolf*

GAMBLING—Fiction

Carlson, Dale Bick - *Baby Needs Shoes*
Dygard, Thomas J - *Point Spread*

GAMES

Clark, James I - *Video Games*
Leder, Jane M - *Video Games*
Longman, Harold S - *Would You Put Your Money In A Sand Bank?: Fun With Words*
Mariotti, Mario - *Hanimals*
Mariotti, Mario - *Humands*
Olney, Ross Robert - *The Amazing Yo-Yo*
Perry, Susan - *How To Play Backgammon*
Perry, Susan - *How To Play Rummy Card Games*
Robb, Mary K - *Making Teen Parties Click*

GANGS—Fiction

Bonham, Frank - *Cool Cat*
Bunting, Eve - *Someone Is Hiding On Alcatraz Island*

GHOULS AND OGRES—Fiction

Hopkins, Lee Bennett - *Monsters, Ghoulies And Creepy Creatures: Fantastic Stories And Poems*

GIACOMIN, EDDIE

Delano, Hugh - *Eddie*

GILBRETH, FRANK BUNKER

Gilbreth, Frank B, Jr. - *Cheaper By The Dozen*

GILBRETH, LILLIAN EVELYN

Gilbreth, Frank B, Jr. - *Cheaper By The Dozen*

GIRLS—Fiction

Cohen, Barbara - *Roses*
Miller, Sandy - *Smart Girl*
Mooney, Thomas J - *One Cool Sister And Other Modern Stories*
Morris, Winifred - *The Jell-O Syndrome*
Ransom, Candice F - *Nicole*

GLACIER NATIONAL PARK—Fiction

Dixon, Paige - *Summer Of The White Goat*

GLASS PAINTING AND STAINING

Wood, Paul W - *Stained Glass Crafting*
Young, Mary - *Singing Windows*

GOATS—Fiction

Bonham, Frank - *Devilhorn*

GODDARD, ROBERT HUTCHINGS—Fiction

Coombs, Charles Ira - *Rocket Pioneer*

GOLDEN EAGLE

True, Dan - *Flying Free*

GOLDFISH

Oneal, Zibby - *The Language Of Goldfish*

GOLFERS

Hahn, James - *Zaharias! The Sports Career Of Mildred Zaharias*
Jackson, Robert Blake - *Supermex: The Lee Trevino Story*
Robison, Nancy - *Nancy Lopez: Wonder Woman Of Golf*

GOPHERS—Fiction

Luger, H C - *Chasing Trouble*

GRANDFATHERS—Fiction

Aaron, Chester - *Catch Calico!*
Brisco, Patty - *Raging Rapids*
Butterworth, W E - *Leroy And The Old Man*
Clifford, Eth - *The Strange Reincarnations Of Hendrik Verloom*
Francis, Dorothy Brenner - *Captain Morgana Mason*
Harris, Mark Jonathan - *The Last Run*
Kerr, M E - *Gentlehands*
Mazer, Norma Fox - *A Figure Of Speech*

GRANDMOTHERS—Biography

Beal, Stephen - *Mary Ellen And Ida: Portraits Of Two Women*

GRANDMOTHERS—Fiction

Benjamin, Carol Lea - *Nobody's Baby Now*
Brancato, Robin Fidler - *Sweet Bells Jangled Out Of Tune*
Cavanna, Betty - *The Surfer And The City Girl*
Corcoran, Barbara - *The Faraway Island*
French, Dorothy Kayser - *I Don't Belong Here*
Garcia, Ann O'neal - *Spirit On The Wall*
Lyle, Katie Letcher - *Finders Weepers*
Poynter, Margaret - *Crazy Minnie*
Yep, Laurence Michael - *Child Of The Owl*

GREAT BRITAIN—History

Hibbert, Christopher - *The Search For King Arthur*
Konigsburg, E L - *A Proud Taste For Scarlet And Miniver*

GREAT BRITAIN—History—Fiction

Bibby, Violet - *Many Waters Cannot Quench Love*
Burton, Hester - *In Spite Of All Terror*
Hunter, Mollie - *The Spanish Letters*

GREAT LAKES REGION—History

Ault, Phil - *These Are The Great Lakes*

GREAT SMOKEY MOUNTAINS—Fiction

Cleaver, Vera - *Where The Lilies Bloom*

GREECE—Fiction

Leonard, Constance - *Strange Waters*

GREEK LETTER SOCIETIES—Fiction

Lowell, Anne Hunter - *Getting In*

GUNTHER, JOHN

Gunther, John - *Death Be Not Proud*

GYMNASTICS

Claus, Marshall - *Better Gymnastics For Boys*

GYMNASTICS—Fiction

Powers, Bill - *Flying High*
Sheffer, H R - *The Last Meet*

GYMNASTS

Burchard, Sue H - *Sports Star: Nadia Comaneci*
Donovan, Pete - *Carol Johnston: The One-Armed Gymnast*
Jacobs, Karen Folger - *The Story Of A Young Gymnast Tracee Talavera*
Litsky, Frank - *Winners In Gymnastics*
Lundgren, Hal - *Mary Lou Retton: Gold Medal Gymnast*
Moran, Lyn - *The Young Gymnasts*
Smith, Jay H - *Olga Korbut*
Sullivan, George Edward - *Mary Lou Retton*

GYPSIES—Fiction

Webster, Joanne - *Gypsy Gift*

HANDICRAFT

Barkin, Carol - *Slapdash Decorating*
D'Amato, Janet Potter - *Who's A Horn? What's An Antler?: Crafts Of Bone And Horn*
Ellison, Elsie C - *Fun With Lines And Curves*
Kinney, Jean - *21 Kinds Of American Folk Art And How To Make Each One*
Pflug, Betsy - *Egg-Speriment*
Seidelman, James E - *Creating Mosaics*
Seidelman, James E - *Creating With Clay*
Seidelman, James E - *Creating With Paint*
Seidelman, James E - *Creating With Paper*
Young, Jean - *Woodstock Craftsman's Manual*

HANG GLIDING

Schmitz, Dorothy Childers - *Hang Gliding*

HAWAII

Tabrah, Ruth M - *Hawaii Nei*

HAWAII—Fiction

Claypool, Jane - *Jasmine Finds Love*
Corcoran, Barbara - *Make No Sound*
Corcoran, Barbara - *The Shadowed Path*
Hiller, Doris - *Black Beach*
Okimoto, Jean Davies - *Who Did It, Jenny Lake?*

HEALTH

Bershad, Carol - *Bodyworks: The Kids' Guide To Food And Physical Fitness*
Betancourt, Jeanne - *Smile!: How To Cope With Braces*
Day, Nancy Raines - *Help Yourself To Health*
Gersh, Marvin J - *The Handbook Of Adolescence*
Gilbert, Sara Dulaney - *Feeling Good: A Book About You And Your Body*
Lappin, Myra A - *Need A Doctor?*
Lubowe, Irwin Irville - *A Teen-Age Guide To Healthy Skin And Hair*
McGrath, Judith - *Pretty Girl: A Guide To Looking Good, Naturally*
Miller, Melba - *The Black Is Beautiful Beauty Book*
Phillips, Betty Lou - *Brush Up On Hair Care*
Reeves, John R T - *Questions And Answers About Acne*
Zizmor, Jonathan - *Doctor Zizmor's Guide To Clearer Skin*

HEART

Elgin, Kathleen - *The Human Body: The Heart*
Silverstein, Alvin - *Heart Disease*

HELICOPTERS

Berliner, Don - *Helicopters*
Delear, Frank J - *The New World Of Helicopters*

HEMOPHILIA—Fiction

Pfeffer, Susan Beth - *Starring Peter And Leigh*

HERCULES—Fiction

Newman, Robert Howard - *The Twelve Labors Of Hercules*

HEROES

Taylor, Lester Barbour, Jr. - *Rescue! True Stories Of Heroism*

HIGH SCHOOL DROPOUTS

Wirths, Claudine G - *I Hate School: How To Hang In And When To Drop Out*

HIGH SCHOOL DROPOUTS—Fiction

Mann, Peggy - *The Drop-In*

HIGH SCHOOLS—Poetry

Glenn, Mel - *Class Dismissed II*

HIJACKING OF AIRCRAFT

Rich, Elizabeth - *Flying Scared: Why We Are Being Skyjacked And How To Put A Stop To It*

HIJACKING OF AIRCRAFT—Fiction

Belina, Tom - *Flight To Fear*

HIMALAYA MOUNTAINS

Hillary, Louise - *A Yak For Christmas*

HIPPIES—Fiction

Kingman, Lee - *The Peter Pan Bag*
Kwolek, Constance - *Loner*

HISPANIC AMERICANS—Fiction

Thomas, Piri - *Stories From El Barrio*

HISTORY—Errors, inventions, etc.

Cohen, Daniel - *Great Mistakes*

HIT-AND-RUN DRIVERS—Fiction

Atkinson, Linda - *Hit And Run*
Hinton, Nigel - *Collision Course*
Phipson, Joan - *Hit And Run*

HITCHHIKING—Fiction

Hallman, Ruth - *I Gotta Be Free*
Holland, Isabelle - *Hitchhike*
Rees, David - *Risks*
Thompson, Paul - *The Hitchhikers*

HOCKEY

Aaseng, Nathan - *Hockey: You Are The Coach*
Awrey, Don - *Power Hockey*
Etter, Lester Frederick - *The Game Of Hockey*
Olney, Ross Robert - *Super Champions Of Ice Hockey*
Orr, Frank - *The Story Of Hockey*

HOCKEY—Biography

Burchard, Sue H - *Sports Star: Brad Park*
Burchard, Sue H - *Sports Star: Wayne Gretzky*
Delano, Hugh - *Eddie*
Devaney, John - *The Bobby Orr Story*
Dolan, Edward Francis, Jr. - *Bobby Clarke*
Etter, Lester Frederick - *Hockey's Masked Men: Three Great Goalies*
Gutman, Bill - *Modern Hockey Superstars*
Jackson, Robert Blake - *Here Comes Bobby Orr*
Leder, Jane M - *Wayne Gretzky*
Liss, Howard - *Bobby Orr: Lightning On Ice*
Liss, Howard - *Hockey's Greatest All-Stars*
Page, N H - *Bobby Orr-Number Four*
Wolff, Craig Thomas - *Wayne Gretzky: Portrait Of A Hockey Player*

HOCKEY—Fiction

Gault, William Campbell - *The Big Stick*
Gault, William Campbell - *Thin Ice*
Godfrey, Martyn - *Ice Hawk*
Honig, Donald - *Fury On Skates*
Ilowite, Sheldon A - *Fury On Ice: A Canadian-American Hockey Story*
Slote, Alfred - *The Hotshot*

HOLOCAUST, JEWISH (1939-1945)

Baldwin, Margaret - *The Boys Who Saved The Children*
Lyttle, Richard Bard - *Nazi Hunting*

HOLOCAUST, JEWISH (1939-1945)—Fiction

Aaron, Chester - *Gideon*

HOMOSEXUALITY—Fiction

Bargar, Gary W - *What Happened To Mr. Forster?*

HONESTY—Fiction

Christian, Mary Blount - *Deadline For Danger*

HONG KONG—Fiction

Myers, Walter Dean - *The Hidden Shrine*

HOROSCOPES

Goodman, Linda - *Linda Goodman's Sun Signs*
Jones, McClure - *Lucky Sun Signs For Teens*
Shapiro, Amy - *Sun Signs: The Stars In Your Life*

HORROR FILMS

Aylesworth, Thomas G - *Movie Monsters*
Cohen, Daniel - *Horror In The Movies*
Edelson, Edward - *Great Monsters Of The Movies*
Thorne, Ian - *Frankenstein*
Thorne, Ian - *Mad Scientists*

HORROR STORIES

Cohen, Daniel - *The Headless Roommate And Other Tales Of Terror*
Cohen, Daniel - *Southern Fried Rat And Other Gruesome Tales*
Coontz, Otto - *The Night Walkers*
Coville, Bruce - *Spirits And Spells*
Green, Carl R - *Black Friday*
Green, Carl R - *Dracula's Daughter*
Green, Carl R - *Ghost Of Frankenstein*
Green, Carl R - *The Mole People*
Green, Carl R - *The Raven*
Green, Carl R - *Tarantula*
Green, Carl R - *Werewolf Of London*
Liberatore, Karen - *The Horror Of Montauk Cave*
Morris, Rosamund - *Masterpieces Of Horror*
Pike, Christopher - *Slumber Party*
Schwartz, Alvin - *More Scary Stories To Tell In The Dark*
Stoker, Bram - *Dracula*
Thorne, Ian - *The Deadly Mantis*
Westall, Robert - *The Scarecrows*

HORSE RACING

Callahan, Dorothy M - *Thoroughbreds*
Van Steenwyk, Elizabeth - *Harness Racing*

HORSE RACING—Fiction

Savitt, Sam - *A Horse To Remember*

HORSES

Ball, Charles Elihue - *Saddle Up: The Farm Journal Book Of Western Horsemanship*
Callahan, Dorothy M - *Ruffian*
Clay, Patrice - *We Work With Horses*
Davidson, Margaret - *Seven True Horse Stories*
Francis, Dorothy Brenner - *The Flint Hills Foal*
Johnson, Pat - *Horse Talk*
Nentl, Jerolyn Ann - *Draft Horses*
Nentl, Jerolyn Ann - *Pleasure Horses*
Patent, Dorothy Hinshaw - *Horses And Their Wild Relatives*
Posey, Jeanne K - *The Horse Keeper's Handbook*
Robison, Nancy - *Hunters & Jumpers*
Rounds, Glen - *Blind Outlaw*
Savitt, Sam - *Sam Savitt's True Horse Stories*
Shapiro, Neal - *The World Of Horseback Riding*

HORSES—Fiction

Aldridge, James - *A Sporting Proposition*
Bolton, Evelyn - *Dream Dancer*
Bolton, Evelyn - *Goodbye Charlie*
Bolton, Evelyn - *Lady's Girl*
Bolton, Evelyn - *Ride When You're Ready*
Bolton, Evelyn - *Stable Of Fear*
Brown, Fern G - *Hard Luck Horse*
Calhoun, Mary Huiskamp - *The Horse Comes First*
Campbell, Joanna - *The Thoroughbred*
Cohen, Peter Zachary - *Bee*
Cook, Olive Rambo - *Serilda's Star*

HORSES—Fiction (continued)

Ellis, Melvin Richard - *The Wild Horse Killers*
Farley, Walter - *The Black Stallion*
Gulley, Judie - *Rodeo Summer*
Hall, Lynn - *Flowers Of Anger*
Hall, Lynn - *The Horse Trader*
Harris, Mark Jonathan - *The Last Run*
Heck, Bessie Holland - *Golden Arrow*
Holland, Isabelle - *Perdita*
Kropp, Paul - *Wild One*
Lawson, Robert - *Mr. Revere And I*
Morey, Walter Nelson - *Year Of The Black Pony*
Rounds, Glen - *Stolen Pony*
Savitt, Sam - *A Horse To Remember*
Self, Margaret Cabell - *Sky Rocket: The Story Of A Little Bay Horse*
Steiner, Merrilee - *Bareback*
Van Steenwyk, Elizabeth - *Quarter Horse Winner*
Weir, LaVada - *The Horse Flambeau*
Wormser, Richard - *The Black Mustanger*

HOSPITALS

Beame, Rona - *Emergency!*
Feagles, Anita MacRae - *Emergency Room*

HOSPITALS—Fiction

Jones, Rebecca C - *Angie And Me*
Miner, Jane Claypool - *This Day Is Mine: Living With Leukemia*
Wyndham, Lee - *Candy Stripers*

HOT AIR BALLOONS

Mohn, Peter B - *Hot Air Ballooning*

HOT AIR BALLOONS—Fiction

Terman, D - *By Balloon To The Sahara*

HOUSE CONSTRUCTION

Wampler, Jan - *All Their Own: People And The Places They Build*

HOUSE FURNISHINGS

Thypin, Marilyn - *Good Buy! Buying Home Furnishings*

HOUSE PLANTS

Elbert, Virginie Fowler - *Grow A Plant Pet*

HUGHES, LANGSTON

Haskins, James - *Always Movin' On*

HUMOROUS STORIES

Beatty, Patricia Robbins - *By Crumbs, It's Mine*
Butterworth, W E - *Moose, The Thing, And Me*
DeWeese, Gene - *Major Corby And The Unidentified Flapping Object*
Higdon, Hal - *The Electronic Olympics*
Manes, Stephen - *Be A Perfect Person In Just Three Days!*
Peck, Robert Newton - *Basket Case*
Pettersson, Allan Rune - *Frankenstein's Aunt*
Pinkwater, Daniel Manus - *The Hoboken Chicken Emergency*
Pownall, David - *The Bunch From Bananas*

HUNTING—Fiction

Hughes, Monica - *Hunter In The Dark*
Morey, Walter Nelson - *Sandy And The Rock Star*
Saal, Jocelyn - *Trusting Hearts*

HURRICANES

Buehr, Walter - *Storm Warning: The Story Of Hurricanes And Tornadoes*

HURRICANES—Fiction

Christian, Mary Blount - *The Mystery Of The Double Double Cross*

ICE SKATERS

Aaseng, Nathan - *Eric Heiden: Winner In Gold*
Burchard, Sue H - *Sports Star: Dorothy Hammill*
Schmitz, Dorothy Childers - *Dorothy Hamill: Skate To Victory*
Van Steenwyk, Elizabeth - *Dorothy Hamill: Olympic Champion*

ICE SKATING

Kalb, Jonah - *The Easy Ice Skating Book*

ICE SKATING—Fiction

Rees, E M - *Thin Ice*
Saal, Jocelyn - *On Thin Ice*
Van Steenwyk, Elizabeth - *Rivals On Ice*

IDENTITY—Fiction

Dana, Barbara - *Crazy Eights*
Feagles, Anita MacRae - *Sophia Scarlotti And Ceecee*
Miles, Betty - *Looking On*
Newton, Suzanne - *M. V. Sexton Speaking*
Oppenheimer, Joan Letson - *Working On It*
Tolan, Stephanie S - *The Liberation Of Tansy Warner*

ILLEGITIMACY—Fiction

Klein, Norma - *Mom, The Wolf Man And Me*

ILLUSTRATORS

Witty, Ken - *A Day In The Life Of An Illustrator*

IMPOSTERS AND IMPOSTURE—Fiction

Clifford, Eth - *The Strange Reincarnations Of Hendrik Verloom*

INDIA

Bothwell, Jean - *The First Book Of India*
Galbraith, Catherine Atwater - *India: Now And Through Time*

INDIAN POETRY

Belting, Natalia Maree - *Whirlwind Is A Ghost Dancing*
Brandon, William - *The Magic World*

INDIAN WARFARE

Hofsinde, Robert - *Indian Warriors And Their Weapons*

INDIANS OF NORTH AMERICA

Baylor, Byrd - *They Put On Masks*
Erdoes, Richard - *The Sun Dance People: The Plains Indians, Their Past And Present*
Lyon, Nancy - *Totems And Tribes*
Roth, Charles E - *Then There Were None*
Whiteford, Andrew Hunter - *North American Indian Arts*

INDIANS OF NORTH AMERICA—Biography

Brown, Marion Marsh - *Homeward The Arrow's Flight*
Hahn, James - *Thorpe! The Sports Career Of James Thorpe*
Heuman, William - *Famous American Indians*
McCague, James - *Tecumseh*
Wayne, Bennett - *Indian Patriots Of The Eastern Woodlands*

INDIANS OF NORTH AMERICA—Fiction

Bauer, Marion Dane - *Tangled Butterfly*
Beatty, Patricia Robbins - *Wait For Me, Watch For Me, Eula Bee*
Bonham, Frank - *Chief*
Carroll, Jeffrey - *Climbing To The Sun*
Clymer, Eleanor - *The Spider, The Cave And The Pottery Bowl*
Coates, Belle - *Mak*
Compton, Margaret - *American Indian Fairy Tales*
Curtis, Edward S - *The Girl Who Married A Ghost: And Other Tales From The North American Indian*
French, Michael - *The Throwing Season*
Grinnell, George Bird - *The Punishment Of The Stingy And Other Indian Stories*
Knudson, R R - *Fox Running*
Lampman, Evelyn Sibley - *The Year Of Small Shadow*
Marriott, Alice - *The Black Stone Knife*
Miner, Jane Claypool - *Navajo Victory: Being A Native American*
Norton, Andre - *Fur Magic*
O'Dell, Scott - *Zia*
Rosenberg, Ethel Clifford - *The Year Of The Three-Legged Deer*
St. George, Judith - *The Halo Wind*
Speare, Elizabeth - *Sign Of The Beaver*
Thompson, Jean - *Brother Of The Wolves*
Thorne, Ian - *Monster Tales Of Native Americans*
Waldorf, Mary - *Thousand Camps*

INDIANS OF SOUTH AMERICA

Glubok, Shirley - *The Art Of Ancient Peru*
Mangurian, David - *Children Of The Incas*
McMullen, David - *Mystery In Peru: The Lines Of Nazca*

INDIVIDUALITY—Fiction

Bunting, Eve - *Just Like Everyone Else*
Cone, Molly Lamken - *Call Me Moose*
Danziger, Paula - *Can You Sue Your Parents For Malpractice?*
Kent, Deborah - *Belonging*
Schotter, Roni - *A Matter Of Time*

INHERITANCE AND SUCCESSION—Fiction

Bennett, Jay - *Slowly, Slowly I Raise The Gun*
Elmore, Patricia - *Susannah And The Blue House Mystery*

INSECTIVOROUS PLANTS

Fortman, Jan - *Creatures Of Mystery*
Lerner, Carol - *Pitcher Plants*

INSECTS

Blough, Glenn O - *Discovering Insects*

INSECTS—Fiction

Reed, Kit - *The Ballad Of T. Rantula*

INTELLIGENCE SERVICE—Fiction

Walden, Amelia Elizabeth - *A Spy Case Built For Two*
Walden, Amelia Elizabeth - *The Spy Who Talked Too Much*

INTERIOR DECORATION

Barkin, Carol - *Slapdash Decorating*
James, Elizabeth - *A Place Of Your Own*

INTERPERSONAL RELATIONS—Fiction

Asher, Sandy - *Things Are Seldom What They Seem*
Baird, Thomas P - *Finding Fever*
Byars, Betsy - *The Animal, The Vegetable And John D Jones*
Conford, Ellen - *Why Me?*
Daly, Maureen - *Acts Of Love*
Hall, Lynn - *If Winter Comes*
Howe, Fanny - *Yeah, But*
Killien, Christi - *Putting On An Act*
McNamara, John - *Model Behavior*
Pascal, Francine - *The Hand-Me-Down Kid*

INTERPLANATARY VOYAGES

Clarke, Arthur C - *Report On Planet Three And Other Speculations*
Gallagher, I J - *The Case Of The Ancient Astronauts*

INVENTIONS

Hooper, Meredith - *Everyday Inventions*

INVENTIONS—Fiction

Bethancourt, T Ernesto - *The Great Computer Dating Caper*

IRELAND—Fiction

Bunting, Eve - *The Haunting Of Kildoran Abbey*
Cavanna, Betty - *The Ghost Of Ballyhooly*
Corcoran, Barbara - *Rising Damp*
Cordell, Alexander - *Witches' Sabbath*
Fisher, Leonard Everett - *Across The Sea From Galway*

IRISH AMERICANS—Fiction

Fisher, Leonard Everett - *Across The Sea From Galway*
Marzollo, Jean - *Halfway Down Paddy Lane*

IRVING, JULIUS

Gutman, Bill - *Dr. J*
Sabin, Louis - *The Fabulous Dr. J*

ISLANDS—Fiction

Morey, Walter Nelson - *Sandy And The Rock Star*
O'Dell, Scott - *The Spanish Smile*
White, Robb - *No Man's Land*

ISRAEL—Fiction

Forman, James Douglas - *My Enemy, My Brother*
Goldreich, Gloria - *Lori*
Lampel, Rusia - *That Summer With Ora*

ISRAEL—Poetry

Bouma, Hans - *An Eye On Israel*

ITALIAN AMERICANS

LaGumina, Salvatore J - *An Album Of The Italian-American*

ITALY—Fiction

Snyder, Zilpha Keatley - *The Famous Stanley Kidnapping Case*

IVORY COAST

Bernheim, Marc - *African Success Story: The Ivory Coast*
Perl, Lila - *Ghana And Ivory Coast: Spotlight On West Africa*

JACKALS

Dinneen, Betty - *The Family Howl*

JAPAN

Goldston, Robert C - *Pearl Harbor*

JAPAN—Fiction

Namioka, Lensey - *The Samurai And The Long-Nosed Devils*

JAPANESE AMERICANS

Dowdell, Dorothy Karns - *The Japanese Helped Build America*

JAPANESE AMERICANS—Fiction

Cavanna, Betty - *Jenny Kimura*
Miklowitz, Gloria D - *The War Between The Classes*
Uchida, Yoshiko - *Journey Home*
Uchida, Yoshiko - *Journey To Topaz*
Uchida, Yoshiko - *Samurai Of Gold Hill*

JAZZ MUSIC—Fiction

Hentoff, Nat - *Jazz Country*
Hentoff, Nat - *Journey Into Jazz*

JEALOUSY—Fiction

Shannon, Jacqueline - *Too Much T.J.*

JEFFERSON, THOMAS—Fiction

Monjo, F N - *Grand Papa And Ellen Aroon*

JEWS—Biography

Bull, Angela - *Anne Frank*

JEWS—Fiction

Angell, Judie - *One-Way To Ansonia*
Blue, Rose - *The Thirteenth Year*
Colman, Hila - *Ellie's Inheritance*
Colman, Hila - *Mixed-Marriage Daughter*
Herman, Charlotte - *What Happened To Heather Hopkowitz?*
Ish-Kishor, Sulamith - *Our Eddie*
Jacobs, Linda C - *A Candle, A Feather, A Wooden Spoon*
Konigsburg, E L - *About The B'nai Bagels*
Little, Jean - *Kate*
Mazer, Harry - *The Last Mission*
Orgel, Doris - *A Certain Magic*
Richter, Hans Peter - *Friedrich*
Suhl, Yuri - *Uncle Misha's Partisans*

JOB HUNTING

Claypool, Jane - *How To Get A Good Job*
McHugh, John - *Getting Ready To Work*

JOB SECURITY

McHugh, John - *Keeping And Changing Jobs*

JOCKEYS

Axthelm, Pete - *The Kid*
Miklowitz, Gloria D - *Steve Cauthen*
Muesner, Anne Marie - *The Picture Story Of Steve Cauthen*

JOKES

Berger, Melvin - *The Funny Side Of Science*
Corbett, Scott - *Jokes To Read In The Dark*
Doty, Roy - *Pinocchio Was Nosey*
Heck, Joseph - *Dinosaur Riddles*
Rosenbloom, Joseph - *Doctor Knock-Knock's Official Knock-Knock Dictionary*
Schwartz, Alvin - *Witcracks: Jokes And Jests From American Folklore*

JOURNALISM—Fiction

Christian, Mary Blount - *Deadline For Danger*
Conford, Ellen - *We Interrupt This Semester For An Important Bulletin*
Stanek, Lou Willett - *Megan's Beat*

JUBILEE SINGERS—Fiction

Bontemps, Arna Wendell - *Chariot In The Sky*

JUMPING

Ryan, Frank - *Jumping For Joy*

JUVENILE DELINQUENCY

Shanks, Ann Zane Kushner - *Busted Lives: Dialogues With Kids In Jail*

JUVENILE DELINQUENCY—Fiction

Bonham, Frank - *Durango Street*
Bonham, Frank - *Viva Chicano*
Brown, Jackum - *Fair Game*
Fleischman, H Samuel - *Gang Girl*
Hinton, S E - *The Outsiders*
Morton, Jane - *Running Scared*
Platt, Kin - *Headman*
York, Carol Beach - *Takers And Returners: A Novel Of Suspense*

JUVENILE DETENTION HOMES—Fiction

Powers, Bill - *The Weekend*

KELLER, HELEN

Brown, Marion Marsh - *The Silent Storm*

KENTUCKY—Biography

Steele, William O - *The Old Wilderness Road*

KENTUCKY—Fiction

Shore, June Lewis - *Summer Storm*

KIDNAPPING—Fiction

Christian, Mary Blount - *The Mystery Of The Double Double Cross*
Clark, Mary Higgins - *A Stranger Is Watching*
Dixon, Paige - *The Search For Charlie*
Hooker, Ruth - *The Kidnapping Of Anna*
Household, Geoffrey - *Escape Into Daylight*
Martin, Ann M - *Missing Since Monday*
Mazer, Norma Fox - *The Solid Gold Kid*
Mazer, Norma Fox - *Taking Terri Mueller*
McVey, R Parker - *Mystery At The Ball Game*
Nixon, Joan Lowery - *The Kidnapping Of Christina Lattimore*
Ray, N L - *There Was This Man Running*
Reilly, Pat - *Kidnap In San Juan*
Shea, George - *Nightmare Nina*
Snyder, Zilpha Keatley - *The Famous Stanley Kidnapping Case*
Stegeman, Janet Allais - *Last Seen On Hopper's Lane*
Street, Nicki - *The Joker*
Zaring, Jane - *Sharkes In The North Woods: Or Nish Na Bosh Na Is Nicer Now*

KIEP, OTTO

Clements, Bruce - *From Ice Set Free*

KINGS, QUEENS, RULERS, ETC.

Holmes, Burnham - *Nefertiti: The Mystery Queen*
Johnston, Johanna - *Kings, Lovers & Fools*
Knapp, Ron - *Tutankhamun And The Mysteries Of Ancient Egypt*
Payne, Elizabeth - *The Pharaohs Of Ancient Egypt*

KNITTING

Rubenstone, Jessie - *Knitting For Beginners*

KON-TIKI

Hesselberg, Erik - *Kon-Tiki And I*
Heyerdahl, Thor - *Kon-Tiki*

KOREAN WAR, 1950—Fiction

Michener, James A - *The Bridges At Toko-Ri*

LABOR UNIONS

Fisher, Leonard Everett - *The Unions*

LABORATORY ANIMALS—Fiction

Donovan, John - *Family*

LANDLORD AND TENANT—Fiction

Myers, Walter Dean - *The Young Landlords*

LANGUAGE AND LANGUAGES

Adler, Irving - *Language And Man*
Gallant, Roy A - *Man Must Speak: The Story Of Language And How We Use It*

LATIN AMERICANS—Fiction

Bonham, Frank - *Viva Chicano*

LAW AND LEGISLATION

Atkinson, Linda - *Your Legal Rights*

LAW AND LEGISLATION (continued)

Phillips, Maxine - *Your Rights When You're Young*

LEARNING DISABILITIES—Fiction

Hall, Lynn - *Just One Friend*
Pevsner, Stella - *Keep Stompin' Till The Music Stops*

LEFT- AND RIGHT-HANDEDNESS

DeKay, James T - *The Natural Superiority Of The Left-Hander*
Silverstein, Alvin - *The Left-Hander's World*

LEGISLATORS

Brownmiller, Susan - *Shirley Chisholm*
Haskins, James - *Barbara Jordan: Speaking Out*
Jacobs, Linda C - *Barbara Jordan: Keeping Faith*
Lawson, Donald Elmer - *Geraldine Ferraro*
Schneider, Tom - *Walter Mondale: Serving All The People*
Westman, Paul - *Andrew Young: Champion Of The Poor*

LEONARDO DA VINCI—Fiction

Konigsburg, E L - *The Second Mrs. Giaconda*

LESBIANS—Fiction

Klein, Norma - *Breaking Up*
Scoppettone, Sandra - *Happy Endings Are All Alike*

LEUKEMIA—Fiction

Beckman, Gunnel - *Admission To The Feast*
Hughes, Monica - *Hunter In The Dark*
Kropp, Paul - *Amy's Wish*
Miner, Jane Claypool - *This Day Is Mine: Living With Leukemia*
Strasser, Todd - *Friends Till The End*

LEVERS

Hellman, Harold - *The Lever And The Pulley*

LIBRARY SCIENCE AS A PROFESSION

Mack, John - *Nobody Promised Me*

LIFE ON OTHER PLANETS—Fiction

Hull, Jessie Redding - *Stanley's Secret Trip*

LIFE SAVING—England

Hodges, C Walter - *The Overland Launch*

LIONS—Legends and stories

Adamson, Joy - *Elsa And Her Cubs*
Adamson, Joy - *Forever Free*

LITTLE BIG HORN, BATTLE OF THE, 1876

Lampman, Evelyn Sibley - *Once Upon The Little Big Horn*

LITTLE, MALCOLM

Adoff, Arnold - *Malcolm X*
White, Florence Meiman - *Malcolm X: Black And Proud*

LOBSTER FISHERIES—Fiction

Roth, David - *The Winds Of Summer*

LOCH NESS MONSTER

Berke, Sally - *Monster At Loch Ness*
Thorne, Ian - *Loch Ness Monster*

LONDON

Weiss, David - *The Great Fire Of London*

LONDON—Fiction

Brown, Roy Frederick - *The White Sparrow*
Burnett, Frances Hodgson - *A Little Princess*
Garfield, Leon - *Smith*
Lingard, Joan - *Into Exile*
Nagel, Shirley - *Escape From The Tower Of London*
Walsh, Jill Paton - *Fireweed*

LONELINESS—Fiction

Glass, Frankcina - *Marvin And Tige*
Pfeffer, Susan Beth - *Better Than All Right*

LONGEVITY

Hirsch, S Carl - *Four Score...And More: The Life Span Of Man*

LOST AND FOUND POSSESSIONS—Fiction

Lynn, Elizabeth A - *The Silver Horse*

LOST CHILDREN—Fiction

Mullin, Penn - *Search And Rescue*

LOVE—Fiction

Abels, Harriette Sheffer - *First Impression*
Aks, Patricia - *Change Of Heart*
Alexander, Bea - *In The Long Run*
Alexander, Marsha - *Popularity Plus*
Arundel, Honor - *Emma In Love*
Aydt, Deborah - *I Don't Want To Be Your Shadow*
Baer, Judy - *The Girl Inside*
Barlette, Danielle - *I'll Take Manhattan*
Barlette, Danielle - *Lovebound*
Bayner, Rose - *Endless Summer*
Blair, Shannon - *Call Me Beautiful*
Blair, Shannon - *Star Struck!*
Blair, Shannon - *Wrong Kind Of Boy*
Blake, Susan - *Summer Breezes*
Bradbury, Bianca - *The Loving Year*
Bush, Nancy - *Bittersweet Sixteen*
Byron, Amanda - *The Warning*
Caldwell, Claire - *Surf's Up For Laney*
Campbell, Joanna - *Loving*
Carlson, Nola - *A New Face In The Mirror*
Casey, Sara - *Cassie And Chris*
Caudell, Marian - *One Boy Too Many*
Cavanna, Betty - *Mystery At Love's Creek*
Cavanna, Betty - *Passport To Romance*
Cavanna, Betty - *Romance On Trial*
Cavanna, Betty - *A Time For Tenderness*
Chatterton, Louise - *Just The Right Age*
Cohen, Barbara - *Lovers' Games*
Cole, Brenda - *Don't Fence Me In*
Colman, Hila - *Girl Meets Boy*
Colman, Hila - *Triangle Of Love*
Conklin, Barbara - *First, Last, And Always*
Conklin, Barbara - *Summer Dreams*
Conklin, Barbara - *The Summer Jenny Fell In Love*
Connell, Abby - *Jed And Jessie*
Cooney, Caroline B - *An April Love Story*
Cooney, Caroline B - *Holly In Love*
Corcoran, Barbara - *When Darkness Falls*
Cowan, Dale - *Campfire Nights*
Crawford, Alice Owen - *Please Say Yes*
Daly, Maureen - *Seventeenth Summer*
Davis, Leslie - *Something Out There*
Dean, Karen Strickler - *Stay On Your Toes, Maggie Adams!*
Ellis, Carol - *A Kiss For Good Luck*
Emerson, Mark - *Looking At You*
Emery, Anne - *A Dream To Touch*
Emery, Anne - *First Love Farewell*
Emery, Anne - *First Orchid For Pat*
Enderle, Judith - *Secrets*
Enderle, Judith - *S.W.A.K.: Sealed With A Kiss*
Eyerly, Jeannette - *If I Loved You Wednesday*
Fields, Terri - *Hearts Don't Lie*
Filichia, Peter - *A Matter Of Finding The Right Girl*
Flynn, Charlotte - *Dangerous Beat*
Foster, Stephanie - *Love Times Two*
Foster, Stephanie - *Rhythm Of Love*
Francis, Dorothy Brenner - *Kiss Me, Kit!*
Francis, Dorothy Brenner - *The Magic Circle*
Girion, Barbara - *In The Middle Of A Rainbow*
Glass, Frankcina - *Marvin And Tige*
Goudge, Eileen - *Afraid To Love*
Goudge, Eileen - *Before It's Too Late*
Goudge, Eileen - *Forbidden Kisses*
Goudge, Eileen - *Gone With The Wish*
Goudge, Eileen - *Hands Off, He's Mine*
Goudge, Eileen - *Kiss And Make Up*
Goudge, Eileen - *Looking For Love*
Goudge, Eileen - *Night After Night*
Goudge, Eileen - *Presenting Superhunk*
Goudge, Eileen - *Smart Enough To Know*
Goudge, Eileen - *Sweet Talk*
Goudge, Eileen - *Too Hot To Handle*
Goudge, Eileen - *Too Much Too Soon*
Goudge, Eileen - *Treat Me Right*
Goudge, Eileen - *Winner All The Way*
Graham, Leslie - *Rx For Love*
Green, Iris - *Second Chance*
Greene, Bette - *The Summer Of My German Soldier*
Gregory, Diana - *Two's A Crowd*
Grimes, Frances Hurley - *Sunny Side Up*
Hansen, Caryl - *One For The Road*
Harper, Elaine - *Christmas Date*
Harper, Elaine - *Short Stop For Romance*
Harper, Elaine - *Turkey Trot*
Harrell, Janice - *Heavens To Bitsy*
Harrell, Janice - *Killebrew's Daughter*
Harrell, Janice - *One Special Summer*
Hart, Nicole - *Lead On Love*

LOVE—Fiction (continued)

LOVE—Fiction (continued)

Youngblood, Marilyn - *Snap Judgment*

MACHINERY

Ackins, Ralph - *Energy Machines*
Calder, Ritchie - *The Evolution Of The Machine*
Kiley, Denise - *Biggest Machines*
Marston, Hope Irvin - *Machines On The Farm*
Saunders, F Wenderoth - *Machines For You*
Stone, William - *Earth Moving Machines*
Wykeham, Nicholas - *Farm Machines*

MACRAME

Andes, Eugene - *Practical Macrame*

MACY, ANNE

Brown, Marion Marsh - *The Silent Storm*

MAGIC

Carmichael, Carrie - *Secrets Of The Great Magicians*
Cohen, Daniel - *Real Magic*

MAGIC—Fiction

Gaskin, Carol - *The War Of The Wizards*
McIlwraith, Maureen Mollie Hunter McVeigh - *The Walking Stones: A Story Of Suspense*
Nixon, Joan Lowery - *A Deadly Game Of Magic*

MAGICIANS

Cohen, Daniel - *Magicians, Wizards, And Sorcerers*
Fortman, Jan - *Houdini And Other Masters Of Magic*
Gibson, Walter B - *Master Magicians: Their Lives And Most Famous Tricks*
Kendall, Lace - *Masters Of Magic*
Kraske, Robert - *Harry Houdini*
White, Florence Meiman - *Escape! The Life Of Harry Houdini*

MAINE—Fiction

Molloy, Anne S - *Girl From Two Miles High*

MAMMALS

Lauber, Patricia - *Look-It-Up Book Of Mammals*

MAN (PREHISTORIC)

Asimov, Isaac - *How Did We Find Out About Our Human Roots?*
Bailey, John - *Prehistoric Man*
Gallagher, I J - *The Case Of The Ancient Astronauts*
Meyer, Miriam Weiss - *The Blind Guards Of Easter Island*

MAN (PRIMITIVE)

Nance, John - *Lobo Of The Tasaday*

MAN—Origin

Clymer, Eleanor - *The Case Of The Missing Link*

MANUAL LABOR

Hardin, Gail - *The Road From West Virginia*

MARATHON RUNNING—Fiction

Alexander, Bea - *In The Long Run*

MARINE BIOLOGY

Asimov, Isaac - *How Did We Find Out About Life In The Deep Sea?*

MARINE FAUNA

Cromie, William J - *Living World Of The Sea*

MARINE RESOURCES

Kovalik, Vladimir - *The Ocean World*

MARRIAGE—Fiction

Colman, Hila - *After The Wedding*
Colman, Hila - *Don't Tell Me That You Love Me*
Cone, Molly Lamken - *Paul David Silverman Is A Father*
Dean, Karen Strickler - *Between Dances: Maggie Adams' Eighteenth Summer*
Head, Ann - *Mr. And Mrs. Bo Jo Jones*
Miklowitz, Gloria D - *The Day The Senior Class Got Married*
Sharmat, Marjorie Weinman - *How To Have A Gorgeous Wedding*

MARRIAGE—Fiction (continued)

Wood, Phyllis Anderson - *Meet Me In The Park, Angie*

MASKS

Hunt, Kari - *Masks And Mask Makers*

MATHEMATICS

Adler, Irving - *Mathematics: Exploring The World Of Numbers And Space*
Diggins, Julia E - *String, Straightedge, And Shadow: The Story Of Geometry*
Hogben, Lancelot - *The Wonderful World Of Mathematics*
Kadesch, Robert R - *Math Menagerie*
Meyer, Jerome Sydney - *Fun With The New Math*
Razzell, Arthur G - *Three And The Shape Of Three: Exploring Mathematics*
Rogers, James T - *The Pantheon Story Of Mathematics For Young People*
Rogers, James T - *Story Of Mathematics*
Stonaker, Frances Benson - *Famous Mathematicians*

MEDICAL EMERGENCIES

Feagles, Anita MacRae - *Emergency Room*

MEDICINE

Engle, Eloise - *Medic*
Lappin, Myra A - *Need A Doctor?*

MENTAL ILLNESS—Fiction

Neufeld, John - *Lisa, Bright And Dark*
Rabinowich, Ellen - *Underneath I'm Different*
Silsbee, Peter - *The Big Way Out*

MENTALLY HANDICAPPED—Fiction

Bates, Betty - *Love Is Like Peanuts*
Byars, Betsy - *The Summer Of The Swans*
Koob, Theodora - *The Deep Search*
Long, Judy - *Volunteer Spring*
Miner, Jane Claypool - *She's My Sister: Having A Retarded Sister*
Platt, Kin - *Hey, Dummy*
Rodowsky, Colby F - *What About Me?*
Wartski, Maureen Crane - *My Brother Is Special*
Wrightson, Patricia - *A Racecourse For Andy*

MENTALLY ILL

MacCracken, Mary - *Lovey: A Very Special Child*

MENTALLY ILL—Fiction

Albert, Louise - *But I'm Ready To Go*
Bauer, Marion Dane - *Tangled Butterfly*
Naylor, Phyllis Reynolds - *The Keeper*

METEORS

Couper, Heather - *Comets And Meteors*

MEXICAN AMERICANS

Dobrin, Arnold - *The New Life - La Vida Neuva: The Mexican-Americans Today*
Newlon, Clarke - *Famous Mexican-Americans*
Robison, Nancy - *Nancy Lopez: Wonder Woman Of Golf*
White, Florence Meiman - *Cesar Chavez: Man Of Courage*

MEXICAN AMERICANS—Fiction

Bethancourt, T Ernesto - *The Me Inside Of Me*
Dunnahoo, Terry - *This Is Espie Sanchez*
Dunnahoo, Terry - *Who Cares About Espie Sanchez?*
Dunnahoo, Terry - *Who Needs Espie Sanchez?*
O'Dell, Scott - *Child Of Fire*
Place, Marian T - *Juan's Eighteen-Wheeler Summer*
Summers, James Levingston - *You Can't Make It By Bus*

MEXICO—Fiction

Baker, Betty Lou - *Dunderhead War*
Bunting, Eve - *A Part Of The Dream*

MEXICO—History

Atwater, James David - *Out From Under: Benito Juarez And Mexico's Struggle For Independence*

MICHIGAN, LAKE

East, Ben - *Frozen Terror*

MICROBIOLOGY

Asimov, Isaac - *How Did We Find Out About Germs?*

MICROSCOPE AND MICROSCOPY

Grillone, Lisa - *Small Worlds Close Up*

MIDDLE AGES

Williams, Jay - *Life In The Middle Ages*

MIDLANDS—Fiction

Allan, Mabel Esther - *The Horns Of Danger*

MIGRANT LABOR—Fiction

Gates, Doris - *Blue Willow*
Laklan, Carli - *Migrant Girl*
Reed, Fran - *A Dream With Storms*
Smith, Nancy Covert - *Josie's Handful Of Quietness*

MILITARY EDUCATION

Holmes, Burnham - *Basic Training*

MILKWEED

Selsam, Millicent E - *Milkweed*

MINEROLOGY

Fichter, George Siebert - *Rocks And Minerals*

MINERS—Fiction

Wiseman, David - *Jeremy Visick*

MINES AND MINERAL RESOURCES—Fiction

Edwards, Page, Jr. - *Scarface Joe*

MINNESOTA—Fiction

Paulsen, Gary - *The Foxman*

MISSING PERSONS

Cohen, Daniel - *Missing! Stories Of Strange Disappearances*

MODELS AND MODELING—Fiction

Greene, Yvonne - *Cover Girl*
McNamara, John - *Model Behavior*
Robison, Nancy - *Department Store Model*

MOHAWK INDIANS—Fiction

Ishmole, Jack - *Walk In The Sky*

MONEY—Fiction

Austin, R G - *Famous And Rich*

MONSTERS

Aylesworth, Thomas G - *Monsters From The Movies*
Aylesworth, Thomas G - *Movie Monsters*
Cohen, Daniel - *The Greatest Monsters In The World*
Cohen, Daniel - *Monster Hunting Today*
Cohen, Daniel - *The Monsters Of Star Trek*
Cohen, Daniel - *Monsters You Never Heard Of*
Cohen, Daniel - *Science Fiction's Greatest Monsters*
Cohen, Daniel - *Supermonsters*
Evans, Larry - *How To Draw Monsters*
McNally, Raymond T - *A Clutch Of Vampires*
Simon, Seymour - *Creatures From Lost Worlds*
Thorne, Ian - *Bigfoot*
Thorne, Ian - *Dracula*
Thorne, Ian - *Frankenstein*
Thorne, Ian - *Godzilla*
Thorne, Ian - *King Kong*
Thorne, Ian - *Loch Ness Monster*
Thorne, Ian - *The Wolf Man*

MONSTERS—Fiction

Austin, R G - *Vampires, Spies And Alien Beings*
Godfrey, Martyn - *The Beast*
Green, Carl R - *Black Friday*
Green, Carl R - *The Mole People*
Hopkins, Lee Bennett - *Monsters, Ghoulies And Creepy Creatures: Fantastic Stories And Poems*
Otfinoski, Steven - *Village Of Vampires*
Pettersson, Allan Rune - *Frankenstein's Aunt*
Platt, Kin - *Frank And Stein And Me*
Shelley, Mary - *Frankenstein*
Thorne, Ian - *The Deadly Mantis*
Thorne, Ian - *Monster Tales Of Native Americans*

MONTANA—Fiction

Beatty, Patricia Robbins - *Something To Shout About*

MONTANA—Fiction (continued)

Corcoran, Barbara - *Sam*
Dixon, Paige - *The Search For Charlie*
Turner, Ann W - *Third Girl From The Left*

MOON—Fiction

Danziger, Paula - *This Place Has No Atmosphere*

MOON IN ART

Komaroff, Katherine - *Sky Gods: The Sun And Moon In Art And Myth*

MOPEDS

Reeves, Lawrence F - *Mopeds*

MOTHERS AND DAUGHTERS—Fiction

Ames, Mildred - *The Dancing Madness*
Asher, Sandy - *Summer Begins*
Bates, Betty - *My Mom, The Money Nut*
Bunting, Eve - *The Haunting Of Safekeep*
Bunting, Eve - *A Part Of The Dream*
Colman, Hila - *Sometimes I Don't Love My Mother*
Gerber, Merrill Joan - *Please Don't Kiss Me Now*
Gioffre, Marisa - *Starstruck*
Klass, Sheila Solomon - *The Bennington Stitch*
Lowry, Lois - *Find A Stranger, Say Goodbye*
Miklowitz, Gloria D - *Love Story, Take Three*
Pascal, Francine - *Hangin' Out With Cici*
Sachs, Marilyn - *Fourteen*
Shreve, Susan Richards - *The Revolution Of Mary Leary*
Sirof, Harriet Toby - *The Real World*
Sunshine, Tina - *An X-Rated Romance*
Tolan, Stephanie S - *The Liberation Of Tansy Warner*

MOTHERS AND SONS—Fiction

Bates, Betty - *It Must've Been The Fish Sticks*
Kidd, Ronald - *Who Is Felix The Great?*
Mann, Peggy - *There Are Two Kinds Of Terrible*
Roy, Ron - *I Am A Thief*

MOTION PICTURES

Aylesworth, Thomas G - *Monsters From The Movies*
Collins, Tom - *Steven Spielberg: Creator Of E.T.*
Franklin, Joe - *Classics Of The Silent Screen*
Montgomery, Elizabeth Rider - *Walt Disney*
Rose, Lew - *Movie Kings: Hollywood's Famous Tough Guys And Monsters*
Thorne, Ian - *Dracula*
Thorne, Ian - *Godzilla*
Thorne, Ian - *King Kong*
Thorne, Ian - *The Wolf Man*

MOTION PICTURES—Fiction

Meyer, Carolyn - *The Luck Of Texas McCoy*

MOTOR-TRUCK DRIVERS

Faust, S R - *Loaded And Rollin'*

MOTOR-TRUCK DRIVERS—Fiction

Weinberg, Larry - *Dangerous Run*

MOTORBOATS

Stevens, Chris - *Fastest Machines*

MOTORCYCLE RACING

Edmonds, Ivy Gordon - *Motorcycle Racing For Beginners*
Jefferis, David - *Trail Bikes*
Naden, C J - *Rough Rider*
Olney, Ross Robert - *Modern Motorcycle Superstars*

MOTORCYCLE RACING—Fiction

Campbell, Archie - *Diamonds In The Dirt*
Covington, John P - *Motorcycle Racer*
Kaatz, Evelyn - *Motorcycle Road Racer*
Kropp, Paul - *Dirt Bike*
Miller, W Wesley - *Dirt Bike Adventure*
Nussbaum, Albert F - *Gypsy*
Ogan, Margaret E Nettles - *Acuna Brutes*
Sheffer, H R - *Moto-Cross Monkey*

MOTORCYCLES

Jaspersohn, William - *Motorcycle*
Naden, C J - *High Gear*
Radlauer, Edward - *Some Basics About Motorcycles*

MOTORCYCLES (continued)

Sheffer, H R - *Cycles*
Smith, LeRoi Tex - *Fixing Up Motorcycles*
Wallach, Theresa - *Easy Motorcycle Riding*

MOTORCYCLES—Fiction

Heck, Bessie Holland - *Golden Arrow*
Pollock, Rollene - *Flying Wheels*
Richard, Adrienne - *Into The Road*

MOUNTAIN LIFE—Fiction

Branscum, Robbie - *The Murder Of Hound Dog Bates*
Branscum, Robbie - *Toby Alone*
Carroll, Jeffrey - *Climbing To The Sun*
Hallman, Ruth - *Tough Is Not Enough*
Kassem, Lou - *Listen For Rachel*
Peck, Robert Newton - *Banjo*

MOUNTAINEERING—Fiction

Healey, Larry - *The Hoard Of The Himalayas*

MOVING (HOUSEHOLD)—Fiction

Bolton, Carole - *The Good-Bye Year*
Conford, Ellen - *Anything For A Friend*
Danziger, Paula - *This Place Has No Atmosphere*
Garrigue, Sheila - *Between Friends*
Halvorson, Marilyn - *Cowboys Don't Cry*
St. George, Judith - *Do You See What I See?*
Wood, Phyllis Anderson - *Pass Me A Pine Cone*

MUMMIES

McHargue, Georgess - *Mummies*
Pace, Mildred Mastin - *Wrapped For Eternity*

MUNOZ MARIN, LUIS

Norris, Marianna - *Father And Son For Freedom*

MUNOZ RIVERA, LUIS

Norris, Marianna - *Father And Son For Freedom*

MUSEUMS—Fiction

Carey, Mary Virginia - *The Mystery Of The Wandering Cave Man*

MUSIC

Chapin, Victor - *The Violin And Its Masters*
Myrus, Donald - *Ballads, Blues, And The Big Beat*
Posell, Elsa Z - *This Is An Orchestra*
Rublowsky, John - *Popular Music*
Van Ryzin, Lani - *Cutting A Record In Nashville*
Van Ryzin, Lani - *Starting Your Own Band: Rock, Disco, Folk, Jazz, Country And Western*
Warren, Fred - *The Music Of Africa*

MUSICIANS

Bain, Geri - *The Picture Life Of Bruce Springsteen*
Cornell, Jean Gay - *Louis Armstrong: Ambassador Satchmo*
Crofut, William - *Troubadour: A Different Battlefield*
Eaton, Jeanette - *Trumpeter's Tale: The Story Of Young Louis Armstrong*
Edwards, Audrey Marie - *The Picture Life Of Stevie Wonder*
Gelfand, M Howard - *Paul Mccartney*
Gill, Derek L T - *Tom Sullivan's Adventures In Darkness*
Gillianti, Simone - *Rick Springfield*
Hasegawa, Sam - *Stevie Wonder*
Haskins, James - *The Story Of Stevie Wonder*
Jones, Hettie - *Big Star Fallin' Mama: Five Black Women In Music*
Kaye, Annene - *Van Halen*
Martin, Susan - *Duran Duran*
Matthews, Gordon - *Prince*
Montgomery, Elizabeth Rider - *Duke Ellington*
Morse, Charles - *Jackson Five*
O'Regan, Susan K - *Neil Diamond*
Pirmantgen, Patricia - *The Beatles*
Russell, Kate - *Billy Idol*
Taylor, Paula - *Elton John*
Wayne, Bennett - *Three Jazz Greats*

MUSICIANS—Fiction

Alexander, Lloyd - *The Marvelous Misadventures Of Sebastian*
Gilson, Jamie Marie - *Dial Leroi Rupert, DJ*
Miller, Sandy - *Two Loves For Jenny*
Strasser, Todd - *Turn It Up!*
Tamar, Erika - *Blues For Silk Garcia*

MUSTANG

Henry, Marguerite - *Mustang, Wild Spirit Of The West*
Weiss, Ann E - *Save The Mustangs!*

MUSTANG—Fiction

Ellis, Melvin Richard - *The Wild Horse Killers*
Harris, Mark Jonathan - *The Last Run*

MYSTERY AND DETECTIVE STORIES

Abels, Harriette Sheffer - *Emmy, Beware!*
Adorjan, Carol - *The Cat Sitter Mystery*
Aiken, Joan - *Night Fall*
Ainsworth, Norma Ruedi - *Mystery Of The Crying Child*
Allan, Mabel Esther - *The Horns Of Danger*
Allan, Mabel Esther - *Mystery Began In Madeira*
Arden, William - *Alfred Hitchcock And The Three Investigators In The Mystery Of The Dancing Devil*
Arden, William - *The Mystery Of The Purple Pirate*
Arden, William - *The Secret Of The Crooked Cat*
Arthur, Robert - *Alfred Hitchcock And The Three Investigators In The Mystery Of The Green Ghost*
Arthur, Robert - *Alfred Hitchcock And The Three Investigators In The Mystery Of The Talking Skull*
Arthur, Robert - *Alfred Hitchcock And The Three Investigators In The Mystery Of The Vanishing Treasure*
Asimov, Isaac - *The Best Mysteries Of Isaac Asimov: The Master's Choice Of His Own Favorites*
Asimov, Isaac - *The Key Word And Other Mysteries*
Avi - *Wolf Rider: A Tale Of Terror*
Bennett, Jay - *The Birthday Murderer: A Mystery*
Bennett, Jay - *The Dangling Witness*
Bennett, Jay - *The Death Ticket*
Bennett, Jay - *Deathman, Do Not Follow Me*
Bennett, Jay - *The Executioner: A Story Of Revenge*
Bennett, Jay - *The Long Black Coat*
Bennett, Jay - *The Pigeon*
Bennett, Jay - *The Skeleton Man*
Berna, Paul - *The Mystery Of Saint-Salgue*
Bethancourt, T Ernesto - *Doris Fein: Legacy Of Terror*
Bethancourt, T Ernesto - *Dr. Doom: Superstar*
Birch, Claire - *Tight Spot*
Bonham, Frank - *Mystery Of The Fat Cat*
Bonham, Frank - *The Mystery Of The Red Tide*
Branscum, Robbie - *The Murder Of Hound Dog Bates*
Brisco, Patty - *Campus Mystery*
Bromley, Dudley - *Bad Moon*
Brookins, Dana - *Alone In Wolf Hollow*
Brow, Thea - *The Secret Cross Of Lorraine*
Campbell, Archie - *Diamonds In The Dirt*
Carey, Mary Virginia - *The Mystery Of Death Trap Mine*
Carey, Mary Virginia - *The Mystery Of The Blazing Cliffs*
Carey, Mary Virginia - *The Mystery Of The Invisible Dog*
Carey, Mary Virginia - *The Mystery Of The Magic Circle*
Carey, Mary Virginia - *The Mystery Of The Singing Serpent*
Carey, Mary Virginia - *The Mystery Of The Wandering Cave Man*
Carey, Mary Virginia - *The Secret Of The Haunted Mirror*
Carr, Harriett H - *The Mystery Of The Aztec Idol*
Catherall, Arthur - *Sicilian Mystery*
Catherall, Arthur - *Ten Fathoms Deep*
Cavanna, Betty - *The Ghost Of Ballyhooly*
Cavanna, Betty - *Mystery At Love's Creek*
Cavanna, Betty - *Mystery In Marrakech*
Cavanna, Betty - *The Mystery Of The Emerald Buddha*
Cavanna, Betty - *Stamp Twice For Murder*
Cebulash, Mel - *The Face That Stopped Time*
Christian, Mary Blount - *The Firebug Mystery*
Christian, Mary Blount - *The Mystery Of The Double Double Cross*
Christopher, Matt - *The Return Of The Headless Horseman*
Cooney, Linda A - *Deadly Design*
Coontz, Otto - *Mystery Madness*
Corbett, Scott - *Diamonds Are Trouble*
Corcoran, Barbara - *When Darkness Falls*

Subject Index

MYSTERY AND DETECTIVE STORIES (continued)

Cunningham, Chet - *Locked Storeroom Mystery*
Curry, Jane Louise - *The Ice Ghosts Mystery*
Davis, Leslie - *Something Out There*
Deary, Terry - *Calamity Kate*
Dee, M M - *The Mystery Of Room 105*
Dee, M M - *The Mystery Of The Frightened Aunt*
Dee, M M - *Mystery On The Night Shift*
Dicks, Terrance - *The Case Of The Blackmail Boys*
Dicks, Terrance - *The Case Of The Cinema Swindle*
Dicks, Terrance - *The Case Of The Cop Catchers*
Dicks, Terrance - *The Case Of The Crooked Kids*
Dicks, Terrance - *The Case Of The Ghost Grabbers*
Dicks, Terrance - *The Case Of The Missing Masterpiece*
D'Ignazio, Fred - *Chip Mitchell: The Case Of The Stolen Computer Brains*
Doyle, Arthur Conan - *The Adventures Of Sherlock Holmes*
Doyle, Arthur Conan - *The Boys' Sherlock Holmes*
Doyle, Arthur Conan - *The Hound Of The Baskervilles*
Duncan, Lois S - *I Know What You Did Last Summer*
Duncan, Lois S - *Killing Mr. Griffin*
Duncan, Lois S - *Locked In Time*
Durish, Jack - *Dream Pirate*
Eisenberg, Lisa - *Falling Star*
Eisenberg, Lisa - *Fast Food King*
Eisenberg, Lisa - *Golden Idol*
Eisenberg, Lisa - *House Of Laughs*
Eisenberg, Lisa - *Killer Music*
Eisenberg, Lisa - *Man In The Cage*
Eisenberg, Lisa - *Tiger Rose*
Ellis, Melvin Richard - *No Man For Murder*
Elmore, Patricia - *Susannah And The Blue House Mystery*
Evarts, Hal G, Jr. - *The Pegleg Mystery*
Fiore, Evelyn L - *Mystery At Lane's End*
Flynn, Charlotte - *Dangerous Beat*
Forshay-Lunsford, Cin - *Walk Through Cold Fire*
French, Dorothy Kayser - *Pioneer Saddle Mystery*
Gilman, Dorothy - *The Elusive Mrs. Polifax*
Gohman, Fred - *Spider Webb Mysteries*
Greenwald, Sheila - *The Atrocious Two*
Guy, Rosa - *The Disappearance*
Guy, Rosa - *New Guys Around The Block*
Hallman, Ruth - *Midnight Wheels*
Hastings, Beverly - *Watcher In The Dark*
Healey, Larry - *The Hoard Of The Himalayas*
Healey, Larry - *The Town Is On Fire*
Heide, Florence Parry - *Black Magic At Brillstone*
Heide, Florence Parry - *Body In The Brillstone Garage*
Heide, Florence Parry - *Face At The Brillstone Window*
Heide, Florence Parry - *Mystery Of The Forgotten Island*
Heide, Florence Parry - *Mystery Of The Midnight Message*
Heide, Florence Parry - *Time Bomb At Brillstone*
Hildick, E W - *Manhattan Is Missing*
Hildick, E W - *The Top-Flight Fully-Automated Junior High School Girl Detective*
Hogan, Elizabeth - *The Curse Of King Tut And Other Mystery Stories*
Holland, Isabelle - *Perdita*
Hooker, Ruth - *The Kidnapping Of Anna*
Howe, Janet Rogers - *The Mystery Of The Marmalade Cat*
Jane, Mary C - *Mystery On Nine-Mile Marsh*
Johnson, Martha P - *Mystery At Winter Lodge*
Jordan, Hope Dahle - *The Fortune Cake*
Kahn, Joan - *Some Things Fierce And Fatal*
Kidd, Ronald - *Sizzle And Splat*
Knott, Bill - *The Secret Of The Old Brownstone*
Kropp, Paul - *Burn Out*
Kropp, Paul - *Micro Man*
Leonard, Constance - *Stowaway*
Leonard, Constance - *Strange Waters*
Levy, Elizabeth - *The Case Of The Counterfeit Racehorse*
Levy, Elizabeth - *The Case Of The Frightened Rock Star*
Levy, Elizabeth - *The Case Of The Wild River Ride*
Levy, Elizabeth - *The Dani Trap*
Lynds, Dennis - *The Mystery Of The Dead Man's Riddle*

MYSTERY AND DETECTIVE STORIES (continued)

Lynds, Dennis - *The Mystery Of The Deadly Double*
Marston, Elsa - *The Cliffs Of Cairo*
McAuliffe, Jim - *Three Mile House*
McNear, Robert - *The Marathon Race Mystery*
McVey, R Parker - *The Missing Rock Star Caper*
McVey, R Parker - *Mystery At The Ball Game*
Morris, Rosamund - *Masterpieces Of Mystery And Detection*
Morris, Rosamund - *Masterpieces Of Suspense*
Mueser, Annie - *Cobra In The Tub: And Eight More Stories Of Mystery And Suspense*
Murphy, Jim - *Death Run*
Myers, Walter Dean - *Adventure In Granada*
Myers, Walter Dean - *The Hidden Shrine*
Myers, Walter Dean - *Tales Of A Dead King*
Nelson, Marg - *Mystery At Land's End*
Nixon, Joan Lowery - *A Deadly Game Of Magic*
Nixon, Joan Lowery - *The Ghosts Of Now*
Nixon, Joan Lowery - *The Kidnapping Of Christina Lattimore*
Nixon, Joan Lowery - *The Other Side Of Dark*
Okimoto, Jean Davies - *Who Did It, Jenny Lake?*
Packard, Edward - *Who Killed Harlowe Thrombey?*
Paisley, Tom - *Doris Fein: Deadly Aphrodite*
Paisley, Tom - *Doris Fein: Murder Is No Joke*
Paisley, Tom - *Doris Fein: Phantom Of The Casino*
Peck, Richard - *Through A Brief Darkness*
Perl, Lila - *Dumb Like Me, Olivia Potts*
Pike, Christopher - *Slumber Party*
Platt, Kin - *Dracula, Go Home!*
Platt, Kin - *Mystery Of The Witch Who Wouldn't*
Poole, Josephine - *Touch And Go: A Story Of Suspense*
Pronzini, Bill - *Midnight Specials*
Rabe, Berniece Louise - *Who's Afraid?*
Rice, Earle, Jr. - *Death Angel*
Robins, Eleanor - *The Bank Robber's Map*
Robins, Eleanor - *The Hub Cap Mystery*
Robins, Eleanor - *The Look Alike Mystery*
Robins, Eleanor - *The Lost Dog Mystery*
Robins, Eleanor - *Mystery Of The Old Book*
Rosenbloom, Joseph - *Maximilian You're The Greatest*
Rutherford, Douglas - *Killer On The Track*
St. George, Judith - *Do You See What I See?*
St. George, Judith - *Shadow Of The Shaman*
Shea, George - *Nightmare Nina*
Sirof, Harriet Toby - *Save The Dam!*
Smaridge, Norah Antoinette - *The Mysteries In The Commune*
Smaridge, Norah Antoinette - *The Mystery In The Old Mansions*
Smaridge, Norah Antoinette - *The Mystery Of Greystone Hall*
Sobol, Donald J - *Encyclopedia Brown Gets His Man*
Sortor, Toni - *Adventures Of B.J., The Amateur Detective*
Stegeman, Janet Allais - *Last Seen On Hopper's Lane*
Stine, R L - *Blind Date*
Street, Nicki - *The Joker*
Topper, Frank - *Mystery At The Bike Race*
Townsend, John Rowe - *Hell's Edge*
Turngren, Annette - *Mystery Plays A Golden Flute*
Turngren, Annette - *Mystery Walks The Campus*
Van Steenwyk, Elizabeth - *Mystery At Beach Bay*
Walden, Amelia Elizabeth - *Valerie Valentine Is Missing*
Wallace, Bill - *Trapped In Death Cave*
West, Nick - *The Mystery Of The Coughing Dragon*
West, Nick - *The Mystery Of The Nervous Lion*
Whitney, Phyllis A - *Mystery Of The Haunted Pool*
Whitney, Phyllis A - *Secret Of The Emerald Star*
Whitney, Phyllis A - *Secret Of The Tiger's Eye*
Wise, Robert - *Mystery Of Totem Pole Inlet*
Woolfolk, Dorothy - *Abbey Is Missing*
Wosmek, Frances - *Never Mind Murder*
Wright, Bob - *The Falling Star Mystery*

MYSTERY AND DETECTIVE STORIES (continued)

Wright, Bob - *The Gold Coin Robbery*
Wright, Bob - *The Mummy's Crown*
Wright, Bob - *The Red Hot Rod*
Wright, Bob - *The Secret Staircase*
Wright, Bob - *The Siamese Turtle Mystery*
Wright, Bob - *The Silver Buckle Mystery*
Wright, Bob - *The Tree House Mystery*
Wright, Bob - *The Video Game Spy*
Yep, Laurence Michael - *The Mark Twain Murders*
York, Carol Beach - *Revenge Of The Dolls*
Zindel, Paul - *The Undertaker's Gone Bananas*

MYTHOLOGY (GREEK)

Evslin, Bernard - *Heroes, Gods And Monsters Of The Greek Myths*

NAMES (PERSONAL)

Lambert, Eloise - *Our Names: Where They Came From And What They Mean*

NANTUCKET (MASS.)—Fiction

Corcoran, Barbara - *The Faraway Island*

NATURAL DISASTERS

Oleksy, Walter - *Nature Gone Wild!*
Smith, Howard Everett, Jr. - *Killer Weather: Stories Of Great Disasters*

NATURAL HISTORY

Day, Beth - *Life On A Lost Continent: A Natural History Of New Zealand*
Leslie, Clare Walker - *Notes From A Naturalist's Sketchbook*
Worthley, Jean Reese - *The Complete Family Nature Guide*

NAVAJO INDIANS—Fiction

O'Dell, Scott - *Sing Down The Moon*

NETHERLANDS—German occupation, 1940-1945

Frank, Anne - *Anne Frank: Diary Of A Young Girl*
Reiss, Johanna - *The Upstairs Room*

NETHERLANDS—German occupation, 1940-1945—Fiction

Shemin, Margaretha - *The Empty Moat*

NEW MEXICO—Fiction

Duncan, Lois S - *Summer Of Fear*

NEW ORLEANS—Fiction

Hallman, Ruth - *Gimme Something, Mister!*

NEW YORK (CITY)

Beame, Rona - *Emergency!*
Bliven, Bruce, Jr. - *New York*
Cook, Fred J - *City Cop*
Durso, Joseph - *Amazing: The Miracle Of The Mets*
Halliburton, Warren J - *Harlem*
Mayerson, Charlotte Leon - *Two Blocks Apart: Juan Gonzales And Peter Quinn*
Smith, Dennis E - *Report From Engine Co. 82*
Walker, Robert - *New York Inside Out*

NEW YORK (CITY)—Fiction

Bennett, Jay - *The Pigeon*
Collier, James Lincoln - *Rich And Famous: The Further Adventures Of George Stable*
Colman, Hila - *Ellie's Inheritance*
Colman, Hila - *The Girl From Puerto Rico*
Fitzhugh, Louise - *Sport*
Foley, June - *Falling In Love Is No Snap*
Hansen, Joyce - *Home Boy*
Kaplow, Robert - *Two In The City*
Levoy, Myron - *The Witch Of Fourth Street And Other Stories*
McCannon, Dindga - *Peaches*
Mohr, Nicholasa - *El Bronx Remembered*
Murphy, Barbara Beasley - *Ace Hits The Big Time*
Myers, Walter Dean - *Motown And Didi*
Myers, Walter Dean - *The Young Landlords*
Paisley, Tom - *Doris Fein: Superspy*
Pfeffer, Susan Beth - *Fantasy Summer*
Scoppettone, Sandra - *A Long Time Between Kisses*
Shotwell, Louisa R - *Adam Bookout*
Spyker, John Howland - *Little Lives*
Vroman, Mary Elizabeth - *Harlem Summer*

NEW ZEALAND

Day, Beth - *Life On A Lost Continent: A Natural History Of New Zealand*

NEWSPAPERS

Fenten, D X - *Behind The Newspaper Scene*

NEZ PERCE INDIANS—Wars, 1877—Fiction

Forman, James Douglas - *People Of The Dream*

NOISE POLLUTION

Jones, Claire - *Pollution: The Noise We Hear*

NORSEMEN—Fiction

Haugaard, Erik Christian - *A Slave's Tale*

NUCLEAR EXPLOSIONS

Baxter, John - *The Fire Came By*

NUCLEAR WARFARE—Fiction

Hall, Lynn - *If Winter Comes*
Strieber, Whitley - *Wolf Of Shadows*

NUMEROLOGY

Reiff, Stephanie Ann - *Visions Of The Future: Magic Numbers And Cards*

NUMISMATICS

Hobson, Burton Harold - *Coins You Can Collect*

NUNS

Lee, Betsy - *Mother Teresa: Caring For All God's Children*
Podojil, Catherine - *Mother Teresa*

NUNS—Fiction

Barrett, William E - *The Lilies Of The Field*

NURSING AS A PROFESSION

Chandler, Caroline A - *Nursing As A Career*
Kay, Eleanor - *Nurses And What They Do*
Searight, Mary Williams - *Your Career In Nursing*

NURSING—Fiction

Laklan, Carli - *Nurse In Training*
McDonnell, Virginia B - *Trouble At Mercy Hospital*
Newell, Hope - *A Cap For Mary Ellis*
Stolz, Mary Slattery - *Hospital Zone*
Werner, Herma - *Rosina Torres, LPN*

NUTRITION

Bershad, Carol - *Bodyworks: The Kids' Guide To Food And Physical Fitness*
Schwartz, Anita K - *Eating Right*
Thypin, Marilyn - *More Food For Our Money: Food Planning And Buying*

NYAD, DIANA

McLenighan, Valjean - *Diana: Alone Against The Sea*

OCCULT SCIENCES

Berger, Melvin - *The Supernatural*
Cohen, Daniel - *Real Magic*

OCCULT SCIENCES—Fiction

Bridges, Laurie - *Devil Wind*
Byron, Amanda - *The Warning*

OCCUPATIONS

Clay, Patrice - *We Work With Horses*
Ellis, Jim - *Run For Your Life*
Gutman, Bill - *Women Who Work With Animals*
Hannahs, Herbert - *People Are My Profession*
Liston, Robert A - *Our Career In Civil Service*
Mergendahl, T E, Jr. - *What Does A Photographer Do?*
Paige, David - *A Day In The Life Of A Police Detective*
Paige, David - *A Day In The Life Of A School Basketball Coach*
Seed, Suzanne - *Saturday's Child*
Sims, William - *West Side Cop*
Smith, Betsy Covington - *A Day In The Life Of A Firefighter*
Waters, John F - *What Does An Oceanographer Do?*
Wells, Robert - *What Does A Test Pilot Do?*
Witty, Ken - *A Day In The Life Of An Illustrator*
Witty, Margot - *A Day In The Life Of A Meteorologist*

OCCUPATIONS—Fiction

Gilbert, Miriam - *Glory Be! The Career Of A Young Hair Stylist*
Gioffre, Marisa - *Starstruck*
Harris, Christie - *Let X Be Excitement*

OCEAN

Carson, Rachel - *The Sea Around Us*
Kovalik, Vladimir - *The Ocean World*

OCEAN BOTTLES

Kraske, Robert - *The Twelve Million Dollar Note*

OCEANOGRAPHERS

Westman, Paul - *Jacques Cousteau: Free Flight Undersea*

OCEANOGRAPHY

Asimov, Isaac - *How Did We Find Out About Life In The Deep Sea?*
Briggs, Peter - *Men In The Sea*
Briggs, Peter - *Science Ship*
Coombs, Charles Ira - *Deep-Sea World: The Story Of Oceanography*

OCEANOGRAPHY AS A PROFESSION

Kovalik, Vladimir - *The Ocean World*
Waters, John F - *What Does An Oceanographer Do?*

OKEFENOKEE SWAMP—Fiction

Cline, Linda - *Weakfoot*

OKLAHOMA—Fiction

Bauer, Marion Dane - *Shelter From The Wind*

OLD AGE—Fiction

Brancato, Robin Fidler - *Sweet Bells Jangled Out Of Tune*
Colman, Hila - *The Amazing Miss Laura*
Corcoran, Barbara - *Hey, That's My Soul You're Stomping On*
French, Dorothy Kayser - *I Don't Belong Here*
Kelley, Leo P - *Earth Two*
Mazer, Norma Fox - *A Figure Of Speech*
Myers, Walter Dean - *Won't Know Till I Get There*
Schellie, Don - *Kidnapping Mr. Tubbs*

OLYMPIC GAMES

Aaseng, Nathan - *Eric Heiden: Winner In Gold*
Arnold, Caroline - *The Summer Olympics*
Gelman, Steve - *Young Olympic Champions*
Litsky, Frank - *The Winter Olympics*
Sullivan, George Edward - *Modern Olympic Superstars*

OPTICAL ILLUSIONS

Brandreth, Gyles - *Seeing Is Not Believing*

ORCHESTRA

Posell, Elsa Z - *This Is An Orchestra*

ORCHESTRA—Fiction

Kidd, Ronald - *Sizzle And Splat*

OREGON—Fiction

Bonham, Frank - *Devilhorn*
St. George, Judith - *Shadow Of The Shaman*

ORPHANS—Fiction

Andrews, Julie - *Mandy*
Angell, Judie - *Dear Lola: Or How To Build Your Own Family*
Brookins, Dana - *Alone In Wolf Hollow*
Burnett, Frances Hodgson - *The Secret Garden*
Coates, Belle - *Mak*
Cookson, Catherine McMullen - *Our John Willie*
Cunningham, Julia Woolfolk - *Dorp Dead*
Miner, Jane Claypool - *Miracle Of Time: Adopting A Sister*
Newton, Suzanne - *M. V. Sexton Speaking*
Poynter, Margaret - *Crazy Minnie*
Shotwell, Louisa R - *Adam Bookout*
Streatfeild, Noel - *Thursday's Child*
Warwick, Dolores - *Learn To Say Goodbye*

ORTHODONTICS

Betancourt, Jeanne - *Smile!: How To Cope With Braces*

OUTER BANKS (N.C.)—Fiction

Taylor, Theodore Langhans - *Teetoncey*

OUTER SPACE—Exploration

Asimov, Isaac - *How Did We Find Out About Outer Space?*
Clarke, Arthur C - *Report On Planet Three And Other Speculations*
Gallant, Roy A - *Man's Reach For The Stars*

OUTER SPACE—Fiction

Kelley, Leo P - *Good-Bye To Earth*

OVERLAND JOURNEYS TO THE PACIFIC

Berry, Erick - *When Wagon Trains Rolled To Santa Fe*

OVERLAND JOURNEYS TO THE PACIFIC—Fiction

Levitin, Sonia - *The No-Return Trail*
St. George, Judith - *The Halo Wind*

OZARK MOUNTAINS—Fiction

Cleaver, Vera - *The Whys And Wherefores Of Littabelle Lee*

PADDLE STEAMERS

Sheffer, H R - *Paddlewheelers*

PALEONTOLOGY

Matthews, William H, III - *Wonders Of Fossils*

PALMISTRY

Hoffman, Elizabeth P - *Visions Of The Future: Palm Reading*

PAPER AIRPLANES

Botermans, Jack - *Paper Flight: 48 Models Ready For Take-Off*

PARACHUTING

Mohn, Peter B - *The Golden Knights*

PARAPSYCHOLOGY

Wilcox, Tamara - *Mysterious Detectives: Psychics*

PARAPSYCHOLOGY—Fiction

Newman, Robert Howard - *Night Spell*

PARENT AND CHILD

Krementz, Jill - *How It Feels When A Parent Dies*
Smith, Sally Liberman - *Nobody Said It's Easy*

PARENT AND CHILD—Fiction

Armstrong, Louise - *Saving The Big-Deal Baby*
Avi - *Sometimes I Think I Hear My Name*
Colman, Hila - *Tell Me No Lies*
Danziger, Paula - *The Divorce Express*
Foley, June - *Falling In Love Is No Snap*
Greene, Constance C - *Getting Nowhere*
Kerr, M E - *I'll Love You When You're More Like Me*
Oppenheimer, Joan Letson - *Which Mother Is Mine?*

PAROLE—Fiction

Samuels, Gertrude - *Adam's Daughter*

PEARL DIVING AND DIVERS—Fiction

O'Dell, Scott - *Black Pearl*

PEARL HARBOR, ATTACK ON, 1941

Goldston, Robert C - *Pearl Harbor*
Taylor, Theodore Langhans - *Air Raid: Pearl Harbor*

PEN PALS—Fiction

Kingsbury, Dawn - *South Of The Border*
Rodowsky, Colby F - *P.S. Write Soon*

PENNSYLVANIA—Fiction

Collier, James Lincoln - *The Bloody Country*
Healey, Larry - *The Town Is On Fire*

PETROLEUM

Kraft, Betsy Harvey - *Oil And Natural Gas*

PETROLEUM INDUSTRY AND TRADE

Butterworth, W E - *Black Gold*
Pick, Christopher C - *Oil Machines*
Sullivan, George Edward - *Supertanker*

PETROLOGY

Fichter, George Siebert - *Rocks And Minerals*

PETS—Fiction

Rylant, Cynthia - *Every Living Thing*
Wood, Phyllis Anderson - *A Five-Color Buick And A Blue-Eyed Cat*

PHILIPPINES—Native races

Nance, John - *Lobo Of The Tasaday*

PHONO TAPES

Leder, Jane M - *Cassettes & Records*

PHOTOGRAPHERS

Hoobler, Dorothy - *Photographing History: The Career Of Matthew Brady*
Noble, Iris - *Cameras And Courage: Margaret Bourke-White*

PHOTOGRAPHY

Dalton, Stephen - *Split Second: The World Of High Speed Photography*
Mergendahl, T E, Jr. - *What Does A Photographer Do?*
Walker, Robert - *New York Inside Out*

PHYSICAL FITNESS

Bershad, Carol - *Bodyworks: The Kids' Guide To Food And Physical Fitness*
Englebardt, Stanley L - *How To Get In Shape For Sports*
Schurman, Dewey - *Athletic Fitness*
Schwartz, Anita K - *Keeping Fit*
Schwartz, Anita K - *Looking Good*
Spino, Michael - *Running Home*

PHYSICALLY HANDICAPPED

Aaseng, Nathan - *Winners Never Quit: Athletes Who Beat The Odds*
Donovan, Pete - *Carol Johnston: The One-Armed Gymnast*
Drimmer, Frederick - *The Elephant Man*
Greenfield, Eloise - *Alesia*
Harries, Joan - *They Triumphed Over Their Handicaps*
Ireland, Karin - *Kitty O'Neil: Daredevil Woman*
Jones, Ron - *The Acorn People*
McGravie, Anne V - *All The Way Back*
Savitz, Harriet May - *Wheelchair Champions*
Siegel, Dorothy Schainman - *Winners: Eight Special Young People*
Sullivan, Mary Beth - *Feeling Free*

PHYSICALLY HANDICAPPED—Fiction

Beckman, Delores - *My Own Private Sky*
Brancato, Robin Fidler - *Winning*
Brooks, Jerome - *The Big Dipper Marathon*
Burnett, Frances Hodgson - *The Secret Garden*
Callen, Larry - *Sorrow's Song*
Colman, Hila - *Accident*
Dyer, T A - *A Way Of His Own*
French, Dorothy Kayser - *Pioneer Saddle Mystery*
Garcia, Ann O'neal - *Spirit On The Wall*
Gerson, Corinne - *Passing Through*
Hallman, Ruth - *Breakaway*
Jones, Rebecca C - *Angie And Me*
Kent, Deborah - *Belonging*
Kingman, Lee - *Head Over Wheels*
Levinson, Nancy Smiler - *World Of Her Own*
Luis, Earlene W - *Wheels For Ginny's Chariot*
Miner, Jane Claypool - *New Beginning: An Athlete Is Paralyzed*
Rodowsky, Colby F - *P.S. Write Soon*
Rosen, Lillian - *Just Like Everybody Else*
Savitz, Harriet May - *The Lionhearted*
Savitz, Harriet May - *On The Move*
Savitz, Harriet May - *Run, Don't Walk*
Slepian, Jan - *The Alfred Summer*
TerHaar, Jaap - *The World Of Ben Lighthart*
Winthrop, Elizabeth - *Marathon Miranda*

PHYSICIANS

Brown, Marion Marsh - *Homeward The Arrow's Flight*
Clapp, Patricia - *Dr. Elizabeth*
Denzel, Justin F - *Genius With A Scalpel: Harvey Cushing*
Hayden, Robert Carter - *Nine Black American Doctors*
Lappin, Myra A - *Need A Doctor?*
Latham, Jean Lee - *Elizabeth Blackwell: Pioneer Woman Doctor*

PHYSICS

Stone, A Harris - *Take A Balloon*
Wilson, Mitchell A - *Seesaws To Cosmic Rays: A First View Of Physics*

PHYSICS—Fiction

Haynes, Mary - *Wordchanger*

PIANO—Construction

Anderson, David - *The Piano Makers*

PICCOLO, BRIAN—Drama

Blinn, William - *Brian's Song*

PIGS—Fiction

Peck, Robert Newton - *A Day No Pigs Would Die*

PILGRIM FATHERS—Fiction

Clapp, Patricia - *Constance: A Story Of Early Plymouth*

PILOTS AND PILOTAGE—Fiction

Miller, Sandy - *Chase The Sun*

PINATAS

Brock, Virginia - *Pinatas*

PIRATES

Larranaga, Robert O - *Pirates And Buccaneers*
Schoder, Judith - *Brotherhood Of Pirates*

PIRATES—Fiction

Arden, William - *The Mystery Of The Purple Pirate*
Oleksy, Walter - *The Pirates Of Deadman's Cay*
Watson, Sally - *Jade*
Wibberley, Leonard - *Flint's Island*

PLANETS

Radlauer, Ruth Shaw - *Planets*

PLAYS

Aiken, Joan - *Winterthing*
Chute, Marchette - *Stories From Shakespeare*
L'Engle, Madeleine - *The Journey With Jonah*
Smith, Moyne - *Seven Plays And How To Produce Them*

PLOT-YOUR-OWN-STORIES

Gaskin, Carol - *The Forbidden Towers*
Gaskin, Carol - *The Magician's Ring*
Gaskin, Carol - *Master Of Mazes*
Gaskin, Carol - *The War Of The Wizards*
McNear, Robert - *The Marathon Race Mystery*
McVey, R Parker - *The Missing Rock Star Caper*
McVey, R Parker - *Mystery At The Ball Game*
Packard, Edward - *The Cave Of Time*
Randall, E T - *Cosmic Kidnappers*
Randall, E T - *Target: Earth*
Randall, E T - *Thieves From Space*
Randall, E T - *Town In Terror*
Topper, Frank - *Mystery At The Bike Race*

POETRY

Baron, Virginia Olsen - *Here I Am!*
Baron, Virginia Olsen - *The Seasons Of Time: Tanka Poetry Of Ancient Japan*
Belting, Natalia Maree - *Whirlwind Is A Ghost Dancing*
Brewton, Sara Westbrook - *America Forever New*
Brewton, Sara Westbrook - *Shrieks At Midnight*
Greaves, Griselda - *The Burning Thorn: An Anthology Of Poetry*
Larrick, Nancy - *Bring Me All Of Your Dreams*
Larrick, Nancy - *On City Streets*
Lewis, Richard - *Out Of The Earth I Sing: Poetry And Songs Of Primitive Peoples Of The World*
Mason, Steve - *Johnny's Song: Poetry Of A Vietnam Veteran*
Morrison, Lillian - *Best Wishes, Amen*
Morrison, Lillian - *The Sidewalk Racer And Other Poems Of Sports And Motion*
Morrison, Lillian - *Sprints And Distances: Sports In Poetry*
Ness, Evaline - *Amelia Mixed The Mustard And Other Poems*

POLAND—Fiction

Skurzynski, Gloria - *Manwolf*
Suhl, Yuri - *On The Other Side Of The Gate*

POLICE

Cook, Fred J - *City Cop*
Friedman, Ina Rosen - *Black Cop: A Biography Of Tilmon O'Bryant*
Paige, David - *A Day In The Life Of A Police Detective*

POLICE DOGS—Fiction

Morey, Walter Nelson - *The Lemon Meringue Dog*

POLICE—Fiction

Butterworth, W E - *The Narc*
Dunnahoo, Terry - *This Is Espie Sanchez*
Dunnahoo, Terry - *Who Cares About Espie Sanchez?*
Levy, Elizabeth - *The Dani Trap*
Murphy, Jim - *Death Run*
Paulsen, Gary - *Winterkill*

POLITICS—Fiction

Colman, Hila - *Daughter Of Discontent*
Eyerly, Jeannette - *Radigan Cares*

POLLUTION

Halacy, Daniel Stephen, Jr. - *Now Or Never*
Hilton, Suzanne - *How Do They Get Rid Of It?*
Milgrom, Harry - *ABC Of Ecology*

POLTERGEISTS

Kettelkamp, Larry Dale - *Mischievous Ghosts*
Knight, David C - *Poltergeists*
Williams, Gurney, III - *Ghosts And Poltergeists*

PONIES

Robison, Nancy - *The Ponies*

PONIES—Fiction

Doty, Jean Slaughter - *Winter Pony*
Hall, Lynn - *Captain*

POPES

Di Franco, Anthony - *Pope John Paul II: Bringing Love To A Troubled World*

POULTRY BREEDING—Fiction

McKay, Robert W - *Dave's Song*

POVERTY—Fiction

Armstrong, William Howard - *Sounder*
Letchworth, Beverly J - *Pax And The Mutt*

POWER (MECHANICAL)

Weiss, Harvey - *Motors And Engines And How They Work*

POWER RESOURCES

Ackins, Ralph - *Energy Machines*
Asimov, Isaac - *How Did We Find Out About Solar Power?*
Branley, Franklyn M - *Feast Or Famine?: The Energy Future*

PRAYER

Menashe, Abraham - *The Face Of Prayer*

PREGNANCY

Ewy, Donna - *Teen Pregnancy: The Challenges We Faced, The Choices We Made*
Lindsay, Jeanne Warren - *Pregnant Too Soon*

PREGNANCY—Fiction

Cone, Molly Lamken - *Paul David Silverman Is A Father*
Kropp, Paul - *Baby, Baby*
Lyle, Katie Letcher - *Fair Day, And Another Step Begun*
Sherburne, Zoa Morin - *Too Bad About The Haines Girl*

PREJUDICES—Fiction

Bargar, Gary W - *Life. Is. Not. Fair.*
Butler, Beverly - *Captive Thunder*
Cleaver, Vera - *I Would Rather Be A Turnip*
Cox, William R - *Third And Goal*
Hall, Lynn - *Sticks And Stones*
Honig, Donald - *Johnny Lee*
Kropp, Paul - *Fair Play*
Lampman, Evelyn Sibley - *The Year Of Small Shadow*
Miklowitz, Gloria D - *The War Between The Classes*
Miner, Jane Claypool - *Navajo Victory: Being A Native American*
Randall, Florence Engel - *The Almost Year*
Rosenberg, Ethel Clifford - *The Year Of The Three-Legged Deer*

PREJUDICES—Fiction (continued)

Sachs, Marilyn - *Peter And Veronica*
Scoppettone, Sandra - *Happy Endings Are All Alike*
Uchida, Yoshiko - *Journey Home*

PRESIDENTS

Reit, Seymour - *Growing Up In The White House: The Story Of The Presidents' Children*
Seuling, Barbara - *The Last Cow On The White House Lawn*
Sullivan, George Edward - *Mr. President: A Book Of U.S. Presidents*
Walker, Barbara J - *The Picture Life Of Jimmy Carter*

PRINCES

Nugent, Jean - *Prince Charles: England's Future King*

PRINCESSES

Darling, David J - *Diana: The People's Princess*

PRISONERS—Personal narratives

Barness, Richard - *Graystone College*

PRISONERS—Fiction

Corcoran, Barbara - *The Woman In Your Life*
Godfrey, Martyn - *Spin Out*
Mazer, Harry - *The Last Mission*

PRIVACY (RIGHT OF)

Snyder, Gerald Seymour - *The Right To Be Let Alone: Privacy In The United States*

PROFESSIONS—Fiction

Hentoff, Nat - *Jazz Country*

PROJECT APOLLO

Wilford, John Noble - *We Reach The Moon*

PROJECT MERCURY

Shelton, William Roy - *Flights Of The Astronauts*

PROSTITUTION—Fiction

Arrick, Fran - *Steffie Can't Come Out To Play*

PSYCHIATRY

Klagsbrun, Francine Lifton - *Psychiatry*

PSYCHICAL RESEARCH

Atkinson, Linda - *Psychic Stories Strange But True*
Berger, Melvin - *The Supernatural*
Collins, Jim - *The Strange Story Of Uri Geller*
Lawless, Joann A - *Mysteries Of The Mind*
Ostrander, Sheila - *Psychic Experiences: E.S.P. Investigated*

PSYCHOLOGY

Laiken, Deirdre S - *Listen To Me, I'm Angry*
Vedral, Joyce - *I Dare You*

PUBERTY

Betancourt, Jeanne - *Am I Normal?*
Betancourt, Jeanne - *Dear Diary*

PUBLIC RELATIONS AS A PROFESSION

Davis, Charles - *On My Own*

PUBLIC SPEAKING—Fiction

Pfeffer, Susan Beth - *What Do You Do When Your Mouth Won't Open?*

PUERTO RICANS

Cooper, Paulette - *Growing Up Puerto Rican*
Gruber, Ruth - *Felisa Rincon De Gautier: The Mayor Of San Juan*
Mann, Peggy - *Luis Munoz Marin: The Man Who Remade Puerto Rico*
Norris, Marianna - *Father And Son For Freedom*
Sterling, Philip - *Quiet Rebels: Four Puerto Rican Leaders*
Tuck, Jay Nelson - *Heroes Of Puerto Rico*

PUERTO RICANS—Fiction

Colman, Hila - *The Girl From Puerto Rico*
Mohr, Nicholasa - *El Bronx Remembered*
Mohr, Nicholasa - *Nilda*

PUERTO RICO

Bowen, J David - *The Island Of Puerto Rico*
Brau, Maria M - *Island In The Crossroads: The History Of Puerto Rico*
Weeks, Morris, Jr. - *Hello, Puerto Rico*

PULLEYS

Hellman, Harold - *The Lever And The Pulley*

PUPPETS AND PUPPET PLAYS

Jagendorf, Moritz - *The First Book Of Puppets*

PURITANS—Fiction

Speare, Elizabeth - *Witch Of Blackbird Pond*

PUZZLES

Anderson, Doug - *Eye Spy*

QUAILS

Stanger, Margaret A - *That Quail, Robert*

RABIES—Fiction

Aaron, Chester - *Catch Calico!*

RACCOONS—Fiction

Cunningham, Julia Woolfolk - *Macaroon*
North, Sterling - *Raccoons Are The Brightest People*
North, Sterling - *Rascal: A Memoir Of A Better Era*

RACE RELATIONS—Fiction

Bargar, Gary W - *Life. Is. Not. Fair.*
Brodsky, Mimi - *The House At 12 Rose Street*
Engel, Beth Bland - *Big Words*
Graham, Lorenz Bell - *North Town*
Graham, Lorenz Bell - *Whose Town?*
Kropp, Paul - *Fair Play*
Miles, Betty - *All It Takes Is Practice*
Miner, Jane Claypool - *The Tough Guy: Black In A White World*
Murphy, Barbara Beasley - *Home Free*
Taylor, Mildred D - *Roll Of Thunder, Hear My Cry*

RADIO BROADCASTING

Fenten, D X - *Behind The Radio Scene*
Hawkins, Robert - *On The Air: Radio Broadcasting*

RADIO BROADCASTING—Fiction

Conford, Ellen - *Strictly For Laughs*

RADIOACTIVE WASTE DISPOSAL—Fiction

Sampson, Fay - *The Watch On Patterick Fell*

RAILROADS

Sheffer, H R - *Trains*

RAILROADS—Fiction

Pronzini, Bill - *Midnight Specials*

RANCH LIFE—Fiction

Aaron, Chester - *Duchess*
Meyer, Carolyn - *The Luck Of Texas McCoy*
Turner, Ann W - *Third Girl From The Left*

RAPE—Fiction

Miklowitz, Gloria D - *Did You Hear What Happened To Andrea?*
Peck, Richard - *Are You In The House Alone?*
Scoppettone, Sandra - *Happy Endings Are All Alike*

RATTLESNAKES

Green, Carl R - *The Rattlesnake*

READING DISABILITY—Fiction

Gilson, Jamie Marie - *Do Bananas Chew Gum?*

REBUSES

McMillan, Bruce - *Puniddles*

RECREATIONAL VEHICLES

Sheffer, H R - *R.V.'s*

RECYCLING (WASTE)—Fiction

Sullivan, Mary Wilson - *Bluegrass Iggy*

REFERENCE BOOKS

Whitney, David C - *First Book Of Facts And How To Find Them*

REFORMATORIES—Fiction

Dana, Barbara - *Crazy Eights*

REFUGEES—Fiction

Degens, T - *Transport 7-41-R*
Hamori, Laszlo - *Dangerous Journey*

REINCARNATION

Atkinson, Linda - *Have We Lived Before?*

RELIGIONS

Clarke, Thomas J - *People And Their Religions*

RELIGIONS—Fiction

Kerr, M E - *What I Really Think Of You*

REMARRIAGE

Berger, Terry - *Stepchild*
Bradley, Buff - *Where Do I Belong?: A Kids' Guide To Stepfamilies*

REMARRIAGE—Fiction

Bates, Betty - *Bugs In Your Ears*
Betancourt, Jeanne - *Between Us*
Fitzhugh, Louise - *Sport*
Greene, Constance C - *Getting Nowhere*
Hunter, Evan - *Me And Mr. Stenner*
Klein, Norma - *Breaking Up*
Lyle, Katie Letcher - *Dark But Full Of Diamonds*
Okimoto, Jean Davies - *It's Just Too Much*
Oppenheimer, Joan Letson - *Gardine Vs. Hanover*
Pfeffer, Susan Beth - *Starring Peter And Leigh*
Shannon, Jacqueline - *Too Much T.J.*
Westall, Robert - *The Scarecrows*
York, Carol Beach - *Remember Me When I Am Dead*

REPORT WRITING

Brandt, Sue Reading - *First Book Of How To Write A Report*
James, Elizabeth - *How To Write A Term Paper*

REPORTERS AND REPORTING—Fiction

Conford, Ellen - *We Interrupt This Semester For An Important Bulletin*

REPTILES

Fichter, George Siebert - *Reptiles And Amphibians Of North America*

RESCUE WORK

East, Ben - *Desperate Search*

RESCUE WORK—Fiction

Hallman, Ruth - *Rescue Chopper*
Littke, Lael J - *Cave-In!*
Mullin, Penn - *Search And Rescue*

RESEARCH

James, Elizabeth - *How To Write A Term Paper*

RESPONSIBILITY—Fiction

Hall, Lynn - *Danger Dog*

RESTAURANTEURS

Simpson, Janice C - *Ray Kroc: Big Mac Man*

REVERE, PAUL—Fiction

Lawson, Robert - *Mr. Revere And I*

RHEUMATOID ARTHRITIS—Fiction

Jones, Rebecca C - *Angie And Me*

RIDDLES

Corbett, Scott - *Jokes To Read In The Dark*
Doty, Roy - *Pinocchio Was Nosey*
Emrich, Duncan - *The Nonsense Book Of Riddles, Rhymes, Tongue Twisters, Puzzles And Jokes From American Folklore*
Heck, Joseph - *Dinosaur Riddles*
Schwartz, Alvin - *Tomfoolery*
Schwartz, Alvin - *Unriddling*
Withers, Carl A - *The American Riddle Book*

RIOTS

Miller, Marilyn - *The Bridge At Selma*

RIVERS—Fiction

Adler, C S - *Down By The River*

ROADS—History

Doherty, C H - *Roads: From Footpaths To Thruways*

ROBBERS AND OUTLAWS—Fiction

Deary, Terry - *The Custard Kid*
Eisenberg, Lisa - *Man In The Cage*
Hallman, Ruth - *Gimme Something, Mister!*

ROBOTS

Kleiner, Art - *Robots*
Paltrowitz, Stuart - *Robotics*
Sullivan, George Edward - *Rise Of The Robots*

ROBOTS—Fiction

Bunting, Eve - *The Robot People*

ROCK MUSIC

Pollock, Bruce - *The Face Of Rock And Roll*
Shaw, Arnold - *The Rock Revolution: What's Happening In Today's Music*

ROCK MUSIC—Fiction

Bethancourt, T Ernesto - *New York City Too Far From Tampa Blues*
Foster, Stephanie - *Rhythm Of Love*
Kaye, Marilyn - *Max In Love*
Lantz, Francess Lin - *Good Rockin' Tonight*
Lantz, Francess Lin - *Rock 'n' Roll Romance*
Pollock, Bruce - *It's Only Rock And Roll*
Strasser, Todd - *Turn It Up!*

ROCK MUSICIANS

Bain, Geri - *The Picture Life Of Bruce Springsteen*
Crocker, Chris - *Cyndi Lauper*
Gelfand, M Howard - *Paul Mccartney*
Kaye, Annene - *Van Halen*
Martin, Susan - *Duran Duran*
Matthews, Gordon - *Prince*
Pirmantgen, Patricia - *The Beatles*
Russell, Kate - *Billy Idol*

ROCKET ENGINES

Edmonds, Ivy Gordon - *Jet And Rocket Engines*

ROCKS

Pine, Tillie S - *Rocks And How We Use Them*

ROCKY MOUNTAINS—Fiction

Morey, Walter Nelson - *Canyon Winter*

RODEOS

Munn, Vella - *Rodeo Riders*

RODEOS—Fiction

Gulley, Judie - *Rodeo Summer*
Kaplan, Janice - *First Ride*

ROLLER DISCO

Bednar, Jane - *Everybody's Dancing In Socks And On Skates*

ROLLER SKATING

Shevelson, Joseph - *Roller Skating*
Weir, LaVada - *The Roller Skating Book*

ROLLER SKATING—Fiction

Hopkins, Lee Bennett - *Wonder Wheels*
Lee, Mildred - *The Skating Rink*
Sheffer, H R - *Partners On Wheels*

ROLLER-SKATE HOCKEY

Hollander, Zander - *Roller Hockey*

ROME—History

Asimov, Isaac - *The Roman Empire*
Asimov, Isaac - *The Roman Republic*
Brooks, Polly Schoyer - *When The World Was Rome*

ROME—History—Fiction

Schurfranz, Vivian - *Roman Hostage*

RUBBER INDUSTRY AND TRADE

McMillan, Bruce - *Making Sneakers*

RUNAWAYS

Berry, James R - *Kids On The Run*
Hyde, Margaret Oldroyd - *My Friend Wants To Run Away*
Rubin, Arnold Perry - *The Youngest Outlaws: Runaways In America*

RUNAWAYS—Fiction

Angell, Judie - *Dear Lola: Or How To Build Your Own Family*
Arrick, Fran - *Steffie Can't Come Out To Play*
Bauer, Marion Dane - *Shelter From The Wind*
Brisco, Patty - *Raging Rapids*
Broger, Achim - *Running In Circles*
Davies, Peter - *Fly Away Paul*
Haggard, Elizabeth - *Nobody Waved Good-Bye*
Hallman, Ruth - *Breakaway*
Hallman, Ruth - *I Gotta Be Free*
Harris, Marilyn - *The Runaway's Diary*
Kropp, Paul - *Runaway*
Kropp, Paul - *Take Off*
Leach, Christopher - *Free, Alone And Going*
Major, Kevin - *Hold Fast*
O'Dell, Scott - *Kathleen, Please Come Home*
Paulsen, Gary - *Tiltawhirl John*
Petersen, P J - *The Boll Weevil Express*
Samuels, Gertrude - *Run, Shelley, Run!*
Shreve, Susan Richards - *The Revolution Of Mary Leary*
Thompson, Paul - *The Hitchhikers*
Townsend, John Rowe - *Good Night, Prof, Dear*

RUNNERS (SPORTS)

Aaseng, Nathan - *Track's Magnificent Milers*
Buchanan, William - *A Shining Season*

RUNNING

Neff, Fred - *Running Is For Me*
Sullivan, George Edward - *Better Cross Country Running For Boys And Girls*

RUNNING—Fiction

Cowen, Eve - *Catch The Sun*
Kinter, Judith - *Cross-Country Caper*
Knudson, R R - *Fox Running*
Mazer, Harry - *The War On Villa Street*
Platt, Kin - *Brogg's Brain*
Platt, Kin - *Run For Your Life*
Winthrop, Elizabeth - *Marathon Miranda*

RUSSIA—Fiction

Almedingen, E M - *Katia*
Jones, Adrienne - *Another Place, Another Spring*

RUSSIAN AMERICANS—Fiction

Angell, Judie - *One-Way To Ansonia*

SAFETY

Bendick, Jeanne - *The Emergency Book*

SAILING

Jones, Claire - *Sailboat Racing*
Weiss, Harvey - *Sailing Small Boats*

SAILING—Fiction

Blake, Susan - *Summer Breezes*
Dengler, Marianna - *Catch The Passing Breeze*
Leonard, Constance - *The Marina Mystery*
Reynolds, Anne - *Sailboat Summer*

SALEM (MASS.)—History—Fiction

Fritz, Jean - *Early Thunder*

SAMURAI—Fiction

Namioka, Lensey - *The Samurai And The Long-Nosed Devils*

SAND DUNES—Fiction

Stone, Nancy Y - *Dune Shadow*

SANTA FE TRAIL

Berry, Erick - *When Wagon Trains Rolled To Santa Fe*

SASQUATCH

Carmichael, Carrie - *Bigfoot: Man, Monster, Or Myth*
Cohen, Daniel - *Bigfoot: America's Number One Monster*

SAYERS, GALE—Drama

Blinn, William - *Brian's Song*

SCHOOLS—Fiction

Adler, C S - *The Once In Awhile Hero*
Altman, Linda Jacobs - *Nobody Wants Annie*
Asher, Sandy - *Summer Begins*
Bach, Alice - *They'll Never Make A Movie Starring Me*
Bates, Betty - *My Mom, The Money Nut*
Blume, Judy - *Blubber*
Bunting, Eve - *The Girl In The Painting*
Bunting, Eve - *Nobody Knows But Me*
Bunting, Eve - *Two Different Girls*

SCHOOLS—Fiction (continued)

Burch, Robert J - *Hut School And The Wartime Home-Front Heroes*
Burch, Robert J - *Queenie Peavy*
Burnett, Frances Hodgson - *A Little Princess*
Butterworth, W E - *Moose, The Thing, And Me*
Carter, Alden R - *Wart, Son Of Toad*
Cavanna, Betty - *Accent On April*
Cavanna, Betty - *Storm In Her Heart*
Cebulash, Mel - *Go All Out*
Cebulash, Mel - *Hit The Road*
Cebulash, Mel - *Settle A Score*
Cebulash, Mel - *The Spring Street Boys Go All Out*
Cebulash, Mel - *The Spring Street Boys Settle A Score*
Cebulash, Mel - *The Spring Street Boys Teamup*
Cebulash, Mel - *Team Up*
Claypool, Jane - *A Love For Violet*
Coles, Robert Martin - *Dead End School*
Conford, Ellen - *Anything For A Friend*
Conford, Ellen - *Seven Days To A Brand-New Me*
Cooney, Caroline B - *Don't Blame The Music*
Corcoran, Barbara - *Sam*
Crawford, Charles P - *Letter Perfect*
Cutting, Edith - *A Quilt For Bermuda*
Cuyler, Margery Stuyvesant - *The Trouble With Soap*
Danziger, Paula - *The Cat Ate My Gymsuit*
Danziger, Paula - *The Pistachio Prescription*
Dengler, Marianna - *A Certain Kind Of Courage*
Dygard, Thomas J - *Halfback Tough*
Dygard, Thomas J - *Rebound Caper*
Ellen, Jaye - *The Trouble With Charlie*
Emery, Anne - *Sorority Girl*
Enderle, Judith - *S.W.A.K.: Sealed With A Kiss*
Ethridge, Kenneth E - *Toothpick*
First, Julia - *Amy*
Foley, June - *Love By Any Other Name*
Frick, Constance H - *The Comeback Guy*
Futcher, Jane - *Crush*
Godfrey, Martyn - *Ice Hawk*
Gold, Sharlya - *Time To Take Sides*
Goldman, Katie - *In The Wings*
Hentoff, Nat - *This School Is Driving Me Crazy*
Hopper, Nancy J - *Lies*
Ibbitson, John - *The Wimp*
Jackson, Jesse - *Tessie*
Johns, Janetta - *The Truth About Me And Bobby V.*
Kaufman, Bel - *Up The Down Staircase*
Kingman, Lee - *Break A Leg, Betsy Maybe!*
Klein, Norma - *The Cheerleader*
Kropp, Paul - *Micro Man*
Leroe, Ellen - *Have A Heart*
Levitin, Sonia - *The Mark Of Conte*
Mazer, Norma Fox - *Mrs. Fish, Ape, And Me, The Dump Queen*
Miklowitz, Gloria D - *The Day The Senior Class Got Married*
Miner, Jane Claypool - *No Place To Go*
Miner, Jane Claypool - *The Tough Guy: Black In A White World*
Moore, Emily - *Something To Count On*
Oppenheimer, Joan Letson - *Working On It*
Owen, Evan - *On Your Own*
Park, Anne - *Tender Loving Care*
Peck, Robert Newton - *Banjo*
Peck, Robert Newton - *Basket Case*
Perl, Lila - *Don't Ask Miranda*
Pevsner, Stella - *Cute Is A Four-Letter Word*
Peyton, K M - *Pennington's Last Term*
Pfeffer, Susan Beth - *Marly The Kid*
Rand, Suzanne - *Laurie's Song*
Reuben, Liz - *Trading Secrets*
Robison, Nancy - *U. And M.E.*
Scott, Carol J - *Kentucky Daughter*
Selden, Neil - *The Great Lakeside High Experiment*
Spector, Debra - *Night Of The Prom*
Stanek, Lou Willett - *Megan's Beat*
Steiner, Barbara A - *Is There A Cure For Sophomore Year?*
Strasser, Todd - *Ferris Bueller's Day Off*
Sunshine, Tina - *An X-Rated Romance*
Tchudi, Stephen N - *The Burg-O-Rama Man*
Vilott, Rhondi - *Her Secret Self*
Weir, LaVada - *Breaking Point*
Williamson, Amy - *Star Light Star Bright*
Wood, Phyllis Anderson - *Pass Me A Pine Cone*
Wood, Phyllis Anderson - *This Time Count Me In*
Woodruff, Marian - *It Must Be Magic*

SCIENCE

Asimov, Isaac - *More Words Of Science*
Berger, Melvin - *The Funny Side Of Science*

SCIENCE (continued)

Cobb, Vicki - *Science Experiments You Can Eat*
Mebane, Robert C - *Adventures With Atoms And Molecules*
Meyer, Jerome Sydney - *Great Accidents In Science That Changed The World*
Pringle, Laurence - *Radiation: Waves And Particles/benefits And Risks*
Stone, A Harris - *Take A Balloon*
Wyler, Rose - *The First Book Of Science Experiments*

SCIENCE AS A PROFESSION

Pollack, Philip - *Careers And Opportunities In Science*

SCIENCE FICTION

Abels, Harriette Sheffer - *Forgotten World*
Abels, Harriette Sheffer - *Green Invasion*
Abels, Harriette Sheffer - *Medical Emergency*
Abels, Harriette Sheffer - *Meteor From The Moon*
Abels, Harriette Sheffer - *Mystery On Mars*
Abels, Harriette Sheffer - *Planet Of Ice*
Abels, Harriette Sheffer - *Silent Invaders*
Abels, Harriette Sheffer - *Strangers On NMA-6*
Abels, Harriette Sheffer - *Unwanted Visitors*
Asimov, Isaac - *Earth Invaded*
Asimov, Isaac - *Tomorrow's Children*
Bonham, Frank - *The Forever Formula*
Bonham, Frank - *The Missing Persons League*
Bova, Ben - *Out Of The Sun*
Bradbury, Ray - *Dandelion Wine*
Bromley, Dudley - *Bedford Fever*
Bromley, Dudley - *Comet!*
Bromley, Dudley - *Final Warning*
Bromley, Dudley - *Fireball*
Bromley, Dudley - *Lost Valley*
Bromley, Dudley - *The Seep*
Bunting, Eve - *Day Of The Earthlings*
Bunting, Eve - *The Island Of One*
Bunting, Eve - *The Mirror Planet*
Bunting, Eve - *The Space People*
Bunting, Eve - *The Undersea People*
Carlson, Dale Bick - *The Frog People*
Carlson, Dale Bick - *The Plant People*
Christopher, John - *An Empty World*
Christopher, John - *The Lotus Caves*
Christopher, John - *White Mountains*
Christopher, John - *Wild Jack*
Clarke, Arthur C - *Dolphin Island*
Cohen, Daniel - *Science Fiction's Greatest Monsters*
Coleman, Joseph - *Space Wars: And Six More Stories Of Time And Space*
Coppard, Audrey - *Who Has Poisoned The Sea?*
Corbett, Scott - *The Donkey Planet*
Danziger, Paula - *This Place Has No Atmosphere*
DelRey, Lester - *Marooned On Mars*
DelRey, Lester - *Nerves*
DeWeese, Gene - *Black Suits From Outer Space*
DeWeese, Gene - *Nightmares From Space*
Dunbar, Robert Everett - *Into Jupiter's World*
Engdahl, Sylvia Louise - *Enchantress From The Stars*
Fisk, Nicholas - *Escape From Splatterbang*
Fisk, Nicholas - *Space Hostages*
Foster, Alan Dean - *Splinter Of The Mind's Eye*
Francis, Dorothy Brenner - *Blink Of The Mind*
Goldberger, Judith M - *The Looking Glass Factor*
Goldsmith, Howard - *Invasion: 2200 A.D.*
Harrison, Harry Max - *The Men From P.I.G. And R.O.B.O.T.*
Herbert, Frank - *Under Pressure*
Hill, Douglas Arthur - *Galactic Warlord*
Hoover, H M - *The Bell Tree*
Hoover, H M - *The Lost Star*
Hoover, H M - *The Rains Of Eridan*
Hoover, H M - *Return To Earth*
Hoover, H M - *This Time Of Darkness*
Jackson, Anita - *ZB-4*
Kaye, Marilyn - *Max On Earth*
Kelley, Leo P - *Backward In Time*
Kelley, Leo P - *Dead Moon*
Kelley, Leo P - *Death Sentence*
Kelley, Leo P - *Earth Two*
Kelley, Leo P - *King Of The Stars*
Kelley, Leo P - *On The Red World*
Kelley, Leo P - *Prison Satellite*
Kelley, Leo P - *Star Gold*
Kelley, Leo P - *Sunworld*
Kelley, Leo P - *Vacation In Space*
Kelley, Leo P - *Where No Sun Shines*
Kelley, Leo P - *Worlds Apart*
Key, Alexander - *The Golden Enemy*
Knight, Damon - *A Pocketful Of Stars*
Knight, Damon - *Toward Infinity*

SCIENCE FICTION (continued)

Kurland, Michael - *The Princes Of Earth*
Land, Charles - *Calling Earth*
Lazarus, Keo Felker - *The Gismo*
Lee, Robert C - *Summer Of The Green Star*
L'Engle, Madeleine - *A Wind In The Door*
Myers, Walter Dean - *Brainstorm*
Nelson, O Terry - *Girl Who Owned A City*
Norton, Andre - *Exiles Of The Stars*
Paulsen, Gary - *The Green Recruit*
Pinkwater, Daniel Manus - *Lizard Music*
Pinkwater, Daniel Manus - *The Snarkout Boys And The Avocado Of Death*
Randall, E T - *Cosmic Kidnappers*
Randall, E T - *Target: Earth*
Randall, E T - *Thieves From Space*
Randall, E T - *Town In Terror*
Ray, N L - *There Was This Man Running*
Rotsler, William - *Star Trek II Short Stories*
Silverberg, Robert - *Three Survived*
Silverberg, Robert - *World's Fair 1992*
Slote, Alfred - *The Devil Rides With Me And Other Fantastic Stories*
Slote, Alfred - *My Trip To Alpha I*
Spielberg, Steven - *Close Encounters Of The Third Kind*
Thorne, Ian - *The Blob*
Thorne, Ian - *It Came From Outer Space*
Wells, H G - *The Time Machine. The War Of The Worlds*

SCIENTIFIC EXPEDITIONS

Holden, Raymond P - *All About Famous Scientific Expeditions*

SCOLIOSIS—Fiction

Blume, Judy - *Deenie*

SCOTLAND—Fiction

MacPherson, Margaret - *The Rough Road*
McIlwraith, Maureen Mollie Hunter McVeigh - *The Walking Stones: A Story Of Suspense*
Ogilvie, Elisabeth - *Too Young To Know*
Seth, Marie - *Dream Of The Dead*

SCULPTORS—Fiction

Madison, Winifred - *Max's Wonderful Delicatessen*

SCULPTURE

Paine, Roberta M - *Looking At Sculpture*
Seidelman, James E - *Creating With Clay*
Weiss, Harvey - *Collage And Construction*

SEA MONSTERS—Fiction

Pinkwater, Daniel Manus - *Yobgorgle: Mystery Monster Of Lake Ontario*

SEA STORIES

Catherall, Arthur - *Ten Fathoms Deep*
Fife, Dale - *Destination Unknown*
London, Jack - *The Call Of The Wild*
Melville, Herman - *Moby Dick*

SEAFARING LIFE

Duncan, Fred B - *Deepwater Family*

SEASHORE—Fiction

Avi - *A Place Called Ugly*

SELF-ACCEPTANCE—Fiction

Bolton, Evelyn - *Ride When You're Ready*
Brooks, Jerome - *The Big Dipper Marathon*

SELF-ASSERTION—Fiction

Miklowitz, Gloria D - *Love Story, Take Three*

SELF-CONFIDENCE—Fiction

Hallman, Ruth - *Panic Five*

SELF-PERCEPTION—Fiction

Angell, Judie - *Secret Selves*
Pfeffer, Susan Beth - *Fantasy Summer*

SELF-RELIANCE—Fiction

Hall, Lynn - *The Solitary*
Hinton, S E - *Tex*
Hughes, Monica - *Hunter In The Dark*
Reiff, Tana - *Mollie's Year*

SEWING

Corrigan, Barbara - *Of Course You Can Sew!*
Rosenberg, Sharon - *The Illustrated Hassle-Free Make Your Own Clothes Book*
Wiseman, Ann Sayre - *Cuts Of Cloth*

SEX INSTRUCTION FOR YOUTH

Betancourt, Jeanne - *Am I Normal?*
Betancourt, Jeanne - *Dear Diary*
Gordon, Sol - *Facts About Sex For Today's Youth*
Guttmacher, Alan F - *Understanding Sex*
Johnson, Corinne Benson - *Love And Sex And Growing Up*
Johnson, Eric Warner - *Love And Sex In Plain Language*
Johnson, Eric Warner - *Sex: Telling It Straight*

SEX ROLE—Fiction

Blume, Judy - *Forever*
Bunting, Eve - *Maggie The Freak*
Chetin, Helen - *Frances Ann Speaks Out: My Father Raped Me*
Godfrey, Martyn - *Fire! Fire!*
Hallman, Ruth - *Midnight Wheels*
Klein, Norma - *The Cheerleader*
Sullivan, Mary Wilson - *What's This About Pete?*

SEXUAL ETHICS

Perry, Tyler - *Girls, Answers To Your Questions About Guys*

SEXUAL ETHICS—Fiction

Hansen, Caryl - *I Think I'm Having A Baby*

SEXUAL HARASSMENT—Fiction

O'Hanlon, Jacklyn - *Fair Game*

SHAKERS—Fiction

Howard, Elizabeth - *Out Of Step With The Dancers*
Yolen, Jane H - *The Gift Of Sarah Barker*

SHARKS

Bunting, Eve - *The Great White Shark*

SHEEP—Fiction

Macaulay, David Alexander - *Baaa*

SHIPS

Fenner, Sal - *Sea Machines*
Halacy, Daniel Stephen, Jr. - *The Shipbuilders: From Clipper Ships To Submarines To Hovercraft*
Knight, Frank - *Ships: From Noah's Ark To Nuclear Submarine*
Lord, Walter - *A Night To Remember*
Penry-Jones, J - *The Boys' Book Of Ships And Shipping*
Richards, Norman - *The Story Of Old Ironsides*
Rutland, Jonathan - *Ships*
Sterne, Emma - *The Long Black Schooner*
Sullivan, George Edward - *Supertanker*

SHIPWRECKS

Spencer, John Wallace - *Limbo Of The Lost*

SHIPWRECKS—Fiction

Love, Sandra - *Dive For The Sun*
Taylor, Theodore Langhans - *The Cay*

SHOES

McMillan, Bruce - *Making Sneakers*
Morrison, Susan Dudley - *Shoes For Sport*

SHOPLIFTING—Fiction

Hamilton, Dorothy - *Amanda Fair*
Kropp, Paul - *No Way*
Roy, Ron - *I Am A Thief*
Stevens, Janice - *Take Back The Moment*

SHORT STORIES

Adoff, Arnold - *Brothers And Sisters: Modern Stories By Black Americans*
Alden, Raymond MacDonald - *Why The Chimes Rang, And Other Stories*
Anderson, Joy - *The Pai-Pai Pig*
Asimov, Isaac - *Earth Invaded*
Carlson, Diane - *You Can't Tell Me What To Do!*
Carlson, Gordon - *Get Me Out Of Here!: Real Life Stories Of Teenage Heroism*
Chittum, Ida - *Tales Of Terror*

SHORT STORIES (continued)

Cohen, Daniel - *The Restless Dead: Ghostly Tales From Around The World*
Dahl, Roald - *The Wonderful Story Of Henry Sugar And Six More*
Doyle, Arthur Conan - *The Boys' Sherlock Holmes*
Fenner, Phyllis Reid - *Lift Line: Stories Of Downhill And Cross-Country Skiing*
Gallo, Donald R - *Sixteen: Short Stories By Outstanding Young Adult Writers*
Gutman, Bill - *"My Father, The Coach" And Other Sports Stories*
Hogan, Elizabeth - *The Curse Of King Tut And Other Mystery Stories*
Hopkins, Lee Bennett - *A-Haunting We Will Go*
Hopkins, Lee Bennett - *Monsters, Ghoulies And Creepy Creatures: Fantastic Stories And Poems*
Keller, Roseanne - *Five Dog Night And Other Tales*
Keller, Roseanne - *Two For The Road*
Lester, Julius - *This Strange New Feeling*
Levoy, Myron - *The Witch Of Fourth Street And Other Stories*
Mazer, Norma Fox - *Dear Bill, Remember Me?*
McCarthy, Pat - *True Ghost Stories: Tales Of The Supernatural Based On Actual Reports*
McHargue, Georgess - *Little Victories, Big Defeats: War As The Ultimate Pollution*
Mooney, Thomas J - *One Cool Sister And Other Modern Stories*
Olsen, Tillie - *Tell Me A Riddle*
Otfinoski, Steven - *Sky Ride And Other Exciting Stories*
Otfinoski, Steven - *The Zombie Maker: Stories Of Amazing Adventures*
Paterson, Katherine - *Angels And Other Strangers*
Rotsler, William - *Star Trek II Short Stories*
Ruby, Lois - *Arriving At A Place You've Never Left*
Rylant, Cynthia - *Every Living Thing*
Salway, Lance - *A Nasty Piece Of Work*
Schulman, L M - *The Loners: Short Stories About The Young And Alienated*
Scoggin, Margaret C - *More Chucklebait: Funny Stories For Everyone*
Senn, J A - *The Wolf King And Other True Animal Stories*
Slote, Alfred - *The Devil Rides With Me And Other Fantastic Stories*
Thomas, Piri - *Stories From El Barrio*
Uhlich, Richard - *Twenty Minutes To Live And Other Tales Of Suspense*
Verdick, Mary - *On The Ledge And Other Action Packed Stories*

SIBERIA—Description and travel

Hautzig, Esther - *The Endless Steppe: Growing Up In Siberia*

SICK—Fiction

Miner, Jane Claypool - *This Day Is Mine: Living With Leukemia*

SIERRA NEVADA MOUNTAINS—Fiction

Bosworth, J Allan - *Among Lions*
Wood, Phyllis Anderson - *Pass Me A Pine Cone*

SINGERS

Berman, Connie - *The Shaun Cassidy Scrapbook*
Berman, Connie - *Top Recording Artist And TV Star! Shaun Cassidy*
Cornell, Jean Gay - *Mahalia Jackson: Queen Of Gospel Song*
Crocker, Chris - *Cyndi Lauper*
Jackson, Jesse - *Make A Joyful Noise Unto The Lord!: The Life Of Mahalia Jackson*
Morse, Charles - *Roberta Flack*
Ruff, Peter - *Olivia Newton-John*

SINGLE-PARENT FAMILY

Gilbert, Sara Dulaney - *How To Live With A Single Parent*

SINGLE-PARENT FAMILY—Fiction

Bach, Alice - *A Father Every Few Years*
Beckman, Delores - *My Own Private Sky*
Foley, June - *Falling In Love Is No Snap*
Gerber, Merrill Joan - *Please Don't Kiss Me Now*
Kidd, Ronald - *Who Is Felix The Great?*
Miner, Jane Claypool - *A Man's Pride: Losing A Father*

SINGLE-PARENT FAMILY—Fiction (continued)

Sharmat, Marjorie Weinman - *He Noticed I'm Alive...And Other Hopeful Signs*
Sheffield, Janet N - *Not Just Sugar And Spice*

SISTERS—Fiction

Cooney, Caroline B - *Don't Blame The Music*
Guest, Elissa Haden - *Over The Moon*
Hamilton, Dorothy - *Amanda Fair*
Miner, Jane Claypool - *She's My Sister: Having A Retarded Sister*
Sachs, Marilyn - *Baby Sister*
York, Carol Beach - *Remember Me When I Am Dead*

SIZE AND SHAPE—Fiction

Park, Barbara - *Beanpole*
Robison, Nancy - *U. And M.E.*

SKATEBOARDING

Cuthbertson, Tom - *Anybody's Skateboard Book*
Dixon, Pahl - *Hot Skateboarding*
Radlauer, Edward - *Some Basics About Skateboards*
Weir, LaVada - *Skateboards And Skateboarding*

SKATEBOARDING—Fiction

Bunting, Eve - *For Always*

SKIN DIVING—Fiction

Oreshnik, A F - *The Demeter Star*

SKIS AND SKIING

Evans, Harold - *We Learned To Ski*

SKIS AND SKIING—Biography

Hahn, James - *Killy! The Sports Career Of Jean-Claude Killy*

SKIS AND SKIING—Fiction

Cavanna, Betty - *Angel On Skis*
Cowen, Eve - *High Escape*
Fenner, Phyllis Reid - *Lift Line: Stories Of Downhill And Cross-Country Skiing*
Laklan, Carli - *Ski Bum*
Neigoff, Mike - *Ski Run*
Philbrook, Clem - *Slope Dope*

SKUNKS—Fiction

Mannix, Daniel - *The Outcasts*

SKYDIVERS

Shyne, Kevin - *The Man Who Dropped From The Sky*

SKYDIVING

Mohn, Peter B - *The Golden Knights*

SLAVE TRADE—Fiction

Fox, Paula - *The Slave Dancer*

SLAVERY

Bacon, Margaret Hope - *Lamb's Warrior: The Life Of Isaac T. Hopper*
Lester, Julius - *To Be A Slave*
Warner, Lucille Schulberg - *From Slave To Abolitionist*
Witheridge, Elizabeth - *And What Of You, Josephine Charlotte?*
Zagoren, Ruby - *Venture For Freedom: The True Story Of An African Yankee*

SLAVERY—Fiction

Collier, James Lincoln - *Jump Ship To Freedom*
Gaines, Ernest J - *The Autobiography Of Miss Jane Pitman*
Hurmence, Belinda - *A Girl Called Boy*
Lester, Julius - *This Strange New Feeling*
Meltzer, Milton - *Underground Man*

SLED DOGS-FICTION

Anderson, Lavere - *Balto*

SMOKING

Marr, John S - *A Breath Of Air And A Breath Of Smoke*
Terry, Luther L - *To Smoke Or Not To Smoke*

SMUGGLING—Fiction

Adler, C S - *Shadows On Little Reef Bay*
Bennett, Jay - *The Killing Tree*

SNAKES

Eckert, Allan W - *The King Snake*
Leen, Nina - *Snakes*

SNAKES—Fiction

Miller, W Wesley - *Dirt Bike Adventure*

SOAP OPERAS—Fiction

Leroe, Ellen - *Confessions Of A Teenage TV Addict*
Maravel, Gailanne - *Lights, Camera, Love*
Pfeffer, Susan Beth - *Prime Time*

SOCCER

Considine, Tim - *The Photographic Dictionary Of Soccer*
Coombs, Charles Ira - *Be A Winner In Soccer*
Fischler, Stanley I - *Getting Into Pro Soccer*
Gogolak, Peter - *Kicking The Football Soccer Style*
Smits, Teo - *Soccer For The American Boy*

SOCCER—Biography

Dolan, Edward Francis, Jr. - *Kyle Rote, Jr., American-Born Soccer Star*
Gault, Clare - *Pele: The King Of Soccer*
Gutman, Bill - *Modern Soccer Superstars*
Hahn, James - *Pele! The Sports Career Of Edson Do Nascimento*
Sabin, Louis - *Pele: Soccer Superstar*

SOCCER—Fiction

Dygard, Thomas J - *Soccer Duel*
Lord, Beman - *Shrimp's Soccer Goal*
Sheffer, H R - *Sarah Sells Soccer*
Wallace, Barbara Brooks - *Hawkins And The Soccer Solution*

SOCIAL ADJUSTMENT—Fiction

Bach, Alice - *Mollie Make-Believe*
Blue, Rose - *Nikki 108*
Bradford, Richard Roark - *Red Sky At Morning*
Burch, Robert J - *The Whitman Kick*
Carlson, Dale Bick - *A Wild Heart*
Christian, Mary Blount - *Felina*
Cleaver, Vera - *Delpha Green And Company*
Cleaver, Vera - *The Mimosa Tree*
Demas, Vida - *First Person, Singular*
Donovan, John - *I'll Get There. It Better Be Worth The Trip*
Jordan, June - *His Own Where*
Kendal, Wallis - *Just Gin*
Lee, Mildred - *Fog*
Mazer, Norma Fox - *Up In Seth's Room*
Meyer, Carolyn - *C. C. Poindexter*
Morton, Jane - *Running Scared*
Peyton, K M - *The Beethoven Medal*
Pfeffer, Susan Beth - *Whatever Words You Want To Hear*
Platt, Kin - *Boy Who Could Make Himself Disappear*
Raucher, Herman - *Summer Of '42*
Townsend, John Rowe - *Good-Bye To The Jungle*
Townsend, John Rowe - *Pirate's Island*
Zindel, Paul - *Confessions Of A Teenage Baboon*
Zindel, Paul - *The Pigman*

SOCIAL PROBLEMS—Fiction

Hinton, S E - *Rumble Fish*
Hinton, S E - *That Was Then, This Is Now*

SOCIAL WORK AS A PROFESSION

Ellis, Jim - *Run For Your Life*
Hannahs, Herbert - *People Are My Profession*

SOFT DRINK INDUSTRY—History

Tchudi, Stephen N - *Soda Poppery: The History Of Soft Drinks In America*

SOIL CONSERVATION

Helfman, Elizabeth S - *Our Fragile Earth*

SOLAR ENERGY

Asimov, Isaac - *How Did We Find Out About Solar Power?*
Knight, David C - *Harnessing The Sun: The Story Of Solar Energy*

SOLAR SYSTEM

Radlauer, Ruth Shaw - *Planets*

SOLDIERS

Knightley, Phillip - *Lawrence Of Arabia*
Sweeney, James Bartholemew - *A Combat Reporter's Report*

SOUTH DAKOTA—Fiction

Wilder, Laura Ingalls - *The First Four Years*

SPACE AND TIME—Fiction

Bethancourt, T Ernesto - *Tune In Yesterday*
Fortune, J J - *Revenge In The Silent Tomb*
Hurmence, Belinda - *A Girl Called Boy*
Jones, Diana Wynne - *The Homeward Bounders*
Kelley, Leo P - *Backward In Time*
Kelley, Leo P - *Worlds Apart*
Love, Sandra - *Dive For The Sun*
Marzollo, Jean - *Halfway Down Paddy Lane*
Packard, Edward - *The Cave Of Time*
Pascal, Francine - *Hangin' Out With Cici*
Peyton, K M - *A Pattern Of Roses*
Sherburne, Zoa Morin - *Why Have The Birds Stopped Singing?*
Stolz, Mary Slattery - *Cat In The Mirror*
Voigt, Cynthia - *Building Blocks*
Waldorf, Mary - *Thousand Camps*
Wells, H G - *The Time Machine. The War Of The Worlds*
Willett, John - *The Singer In The Stone*
Wiseman, David - *Jeremy Visick*
Wiseman, David - *Thimbles*

SPACE COLONIES

Bergaust, Erik - *Colonizing Space*

SPACE FLIGHT

Goodwin, Harold L - *All About Rockets And Space Flight*
O'Connor, Karen - *Sally Ride And The New Astronauts: Scientists In Space*
Wilford, John Noble - *We Reach The Moon*

SPACE FLIGHT—Fiction

Hull, Jessie Redding - *Stanley's Secret Trip*

SPACE STATIONS

Coombs, Charles Ira - *Skylab*

SPACE VEHICLES

Ames, Lee Judah - *Draw 50 Airplanes, Aircraft And Spacecraft*
Baxter, John - *The Fire Came By*
Ciupik, Larry A - *Space Machines*

SPAIN—Fiction

Myers, Walter Dean - *Adventure In Granada*

SPANISH AMERICANS

Eiseman, Alberta - *Manana Is Now: The Spanish-Speaking In The United States*

SPECIAL OLYMPICS—Fiction

Wartski, Maureen Crane - *My Brother Is Special*

SPIES

Knight, David C - *The Spy Who Never Was And Other True Spy Stories*
Komroff, Manuel - *True Adventures Of Spies*
Raskin, Joseph - *Spies And Traitors: Tales Of The Revolutionary And Civil Wars*
Surge, Frank - *Famous Spies*
Sweeney, James Bartholemew - *True Spy Stories*
Widder, Arthur - *Adventures In Black*

SPIES—Fiction

Arthur, Robert - *Spies And More Spies*
Hitchcock, Alfred - *Alfred Hitchcock's Sinister Spies*
Martin, Albert - *Secret Spy*
Paisley, Tom - *Doris Fein: Quartz Boyar*
Paisley, Tom - *Doris Fein: Superspy*

SPIRITUALISM

Fuller, Elizabeth - *My Search For The Ghost Of Flight 401*
Stadtmauer, Saul A - *Visions Of The Future: Magic Boards*

SPIRITUALISM—Fiction

Hoppe, Joanne - *April Spell*

SPORTS

Bishop, Curtis Kent - *Sideline Pass*
Dickmeyer, Lowell - *Teamwork*
Englebardt, Stanley L - *How To Get In Shape For Sports*
Kamm, Herbert - *The Junior Illustrated Encyclopedia Of Sports*
McGonagle, Bob - *Careers In Sports*
Wilson, Pat - *Young Sportsman's Guide To Water Safety*

SPORTS—Biography

Jacobs, Karen Folger - *Girl Sports*

SPORTS—Biography (continued)

Koller, William D - *I Am The Greatest: And Other True Stories Of Sports Greats*
Pepe, Philip - *Great Comebacks In Sport*
Savitz, Harriet May - *Wheelchair Champions*

SPORTS—Fiction

Aks, Patricia - *Change Of Heart*
Bach, Alice - *The Meat In The Sandwich*
Bunting, Eve - *Maggie The Freak*
Cebulash, Mel - *Go All Out*
Cebulash, Mel - *Hit The Road*
Cebulash, Mel - *Settle A Score*
Cebulash, Mel - *The Spring Street Boys Go All Out*
Cebulash, Mel - *The Spring Street Boys Settle A Score*
Cebulash, Mel - *The Spring Street Boys Teamup*
Cebulash, Mel - *Team Up*
Cowen, Eve - *Race To Win*
Gutman, Bill - *"My Father, The Coach" And Other Sports Stories*
Higdon, Hal - *The Electronic Olympics*
MacKellar, William - *Score!: A Baker's Dozen Sports Stories*
Miller, Christopher Ransom - *Stroke Of Luck*
O'Connor, Dick - *Foul Play*
Quin-Harkin, Janet - *Love Match*
Reit, Ann - *Yours Truly, Love, Janie*
Rice, Earle, Jr. - *Fear On Ice*

STARS

Branley, Franklyn M - *A Book Of Stars For You*
Moore, Patrick - *Seeing Stars*

STATESMEN

Davidson, Margaret - *The Golda Meir Story*
Fritz, Jean - *What's The Big Idea, Ben Franklin?*
Gugliotta, Bobette - *Nolle Smith: Cowboy, Engineer, Statesman*
Simpson, Janice C - *Andrew Young: A Matter Of Choice*

STEPFATHERS—Fiction

Hunter, Evan - *Me And Mr. Stenner*
Westall, Robert - *The Scarecrows*

STEPPARENTS

Berger, Terry - *Stepchild*
Bradley, Buff - *Where Do I Belong?: A Kids' Guide To Stepfamilies*
Gardner, Richard Alan - *The Boys And Girls Book About Stepfamilies*

STONEHENGE

Lyon, Nancy - *The Mystery Of Stonehenge*

STORMS

Buehr, Walter - *Storm Warning: The Story Of Hurricanes And Tornadoes*
East, Ben - *Danger In The Air*
Smith, Howard Everett, Jr. - *Killer Weather: Stories Of Great Disasters*

STORMS—Fiction

Abels, Harriette Sheffer - *September Storm*

STRIKES AND LOCKOUTS—Fiction

Corcoran, Barbara - *Strike!*
Gold, Sharlya - *Time To Take Sides*
McKay, Robert W - *The Troublemaker*

STUDENT (FOREIGN)—Fiction

Crary, Margaret - *Mexican Whirlwind*

STUDY (METHOD OF)

Wirths, Claudine G - *I Hate School: How To Hang In And When To Drop Out*

STUNT MEN AND WOMEN

Emmens, Carol Ann - *Stunt Work And Stunt People*
Gardner, Sandra - *Six Who Dared*
Ireland, Karin - *Kitty O'Neil: Daredevil Woman*

SUBMARINE BOATS

Coggins, Jack - *Prepare To Dive: The Story Of Man Undersea*
Pick, Christopher C - *Undersea Machines*

SUBMARINES—Fiction

White, Robb - *Up Periscope*
Wibberley, Leonard - *Perilous Gold*

SUBWAYS—Fiction

Holman, Felice - *Slake's Limbo*

SUICIDE—Fiction

Arrick, Fran - *Tunnel Vision*
Bunting, Eve - *Face At The Edge Of The World*
Gerson, Corinne - *Passing Through*
Pfeffer, Susan Beth - *About David*

SUMMER EMPLOYMENT—Fiction

Lipsyte, Robert - *The Summerboy*

SUMMER RESORTS—Fiction

Gelman, Jan - *Summer In The Sun*

SUN LORE

Komaroff, Katherine - *Sky Gods: The Sun And Moon In Art And Myth*

SUPERNATURAL

Mason, Herbert Molloy, Jr. - *Secrets Of The Supernatural*
Otfinoski, Steven - *The Monster That Wouldn't Die And Other Strange But True Stories*
Snow, Edward Rowe - *Supernatural Mysteries And Other Tales*
Snow, Edward Rowe - *Supernatural Mysteries: New England To The Bermuda Triangle*

SUPERNATURAL—Fiction

Brunn, Robert - *The Initiation*
Chittum, Ida - *Tales Of Terror*
Coville, Bruce - *Spirits And Spells*
Daniel, Colin - *Demon Tree*
Hoppe, Joanne - *April Spell*
Kotzwinkle, William - *The Leopard's Tooth*
Kropp, Paul - *Dead On*
Otfinoski, Steven - *The Zombie Maker: Stories Of Amazing Adventures*
Peck, Richard - *Ghosts I Have Been*
Shea, George - *I Died Here*
Slote, Alfred - *The Devil Rides With Me And Other Fantastic Stories*
York, Carol Beach - *When Midnight Comes....*

SUPERSTITION

Blumenthal, Shirley - *Black Cats And Other Superstitions*
Schwartz, Alvin - *Cross Your Fingers, Spit In Your Hat*

SUPERSTITION—Fiction

Katz, Bobbi - *Volleyball Jinx*

SURFING

Cook, Joseph Jay - *Better Surfing For Boys*
Edwards, Phil - *You Should Have Been Here An Hour Ago*
Klein, H Arthur - *Surf's Up!: An Anthology Of Surfing*

SURFING—Fiction

Bowen, Robert Sydney - *Wipeout*
Caldwell, Claire - *Surf's Up For Laney*

SURVIVAL

Black, Susan Adams - *Crash In The Wilderness*
Elder, Lauren - *And I Alone Survived*
Gunning, Thomas G - *Amazing Escapes*
Stone, Judith - *Minutes To Live*
Tripp, Jenny - *One Was Left Alive*

SURVIVAL—Fiction

Brown, Roy Frederick - *The White Sparrow*
Bunting, Eve - *Survival Camp!*
Christopher, John - *An Empty World*
Clark, Mavis Thorpe - *If The Earth Falls In*
Dyer, T A - *A Way Of His Own*
George, Jean Craighead - *Julie Of The Wolves*
George, Jean Craighead - *River Rats, Inc.*
Hallman, Ruth - *Panic Five*
Houston, James - *Frozen Fire: A Tale Of Courage*
Knudson, R R - *You Are The Rain*
Kropp, Paul - *Snow Ghost*
Luger, H C - *The Elephant Tree*
Mazer, Harry - *Snow Bound*
Miklowitz, Gloria D - *After The Bomb*
Milton, Hilary - *Mayday! Mayday!*
Moeri, Louise - *Save Queen Of Sheba*
Nelson, O Terry - *Girl Who Owned A City*
O'Dell, Scott - *Sarah Bishop*
Petersen, P J - *Going For The Big One*
Phipson, Joan - *Hit And Run*
Reader, Dennis J - *Coming Back Alive*
Roth, Arthur J - *Avalanche*
Roth, Arthur J - *Two For Survival*

SURVIVAL—Fiction (continued)

Roy, Ron - *Nightmare Island*
Speare, Elizabeth - *Sign Of The Beaver*
Spencer, Zane - *Branded Runaway*
Stone, Nancy Y - *Dune Shadow*
Strieber, Whitley - *Wolf Of Shadows*
Taylor, Theodore Langhans - *The Cay*

SWEDEN—Fiction

Anckarsvard, Karin - *The Robber Ghost*

SWIMMERS

McLenighan, Valjean - *Diana: Alone Against The Sea*

SWIMMING

Honig, Donald - *Going The Distance*
Sullivan, George Edward - *Better Swimming And Diving For Boys And Girls*

SWIMMING—Fiction

Love, Sandra - *Melissa's Medley*
Sheffer, H R - *Swim For Pride*

SWINDLERS AND SWINDLING

Cohen, Daniel - *Frauds, Hoaxes, And Swindles*

TANKERS

Sullivan, George Edward - *Supertanker*

TAOS INDIANS

Wood, Nancy - *Hollering Sun*

TAROT

Reiff, Stephanie Ann - *Visions Of The Future: Magic Numbers And Cards*

TEACHERS

Decker, Sunny - *An Empty Spoon*
Steurer, Stephen J - *Wheels Teacher's Guide*

TEACHERS—Fiction

Braithwaite, Edward - *To Sir, With Love*
Colman, Hila - *The Happenings At North End School*
Crawford, Charles P - *Letter Perfect*
Danziger, Paula - *The Cat Ate My Gymsuit*
Elfman, Blossom - *The Girls Of Huntington House*
Sachs, Marilyn - *A Summer's Lease*

TELEPHONE—Fiction

Sachs, Marilyn - *Hello... Wrong Number*

TELEVISION

Cohen, Daniel - *The Kid's Guide To Home Video*
Fenten, D X - *Behind The Television Scene*
Jacobs, Linda C - *Jane Pauley: A Heartland Style*

TELEVISION—Fiction

Leroe, Ellen - *Confessions Of A Teenage TV Addict*

TELEVISION PROGRAMS

Harris, Leon A, Jr. - *Behind The Scenes Of Television Programs*

TENNESSEE—Fiction

Kassem, Lou - *Listen For Rachel*

TENNIS

Ashe, Arthur - *Getting Started In Tennis*
Cook, Joseph Jay - *Famous Firsts In Tennis*
Hopman, Harry - *Better Tennis For Boys And Girls*
Palfrey, Sarah - *Tennis For Anyone!*
Ravielli, Anthony - *What Is Tennis?*
Seewagen, George L - *Tennis*

TENNIS—Biography

Aaseng, Nathan - *Winning Men Of Tennis*
Aaseng, Nathan - *Winning Women Of Tennis*
Burchard, Sue H - *Sports Star: John McEnroe*
Dolan, Edward Francis, Jr. - *Martina Navratilova*
Glickman, William G - *Winners On The Tennis Court*
Hahn, James - *Chris! The Sports Career Of Chris Evert Lloyd*
Hahn, James - *King! The Sports Career Of Billie Jean King*
Leder, Jane M - *Martina Navratilova*
Robison, Nancy - *Tracy Austin: Teen Tennis Champion*

TENNIS—Biography (continued)

Sabin, Francene - *Jimmy Connors: King Of The Courts*
Sabin, Francene - *Set Point*
Smith, Jay H - *Chris Evert*

TENNIS—Fiction

Sanderlin, Owenita - *Tennis Rebel*
Sheffer, H R - *Two At The Net*
Weir, LaVada - *Men!*

TERMINALLY ILL—Fiction

Ethridge, Kenneth E - *Toothpick*

TERRORISM—Fiction

Bennett, Jay - *The Pigeon*
Rardin, Susan Lowry - *Captives In A Foreign Land*
Sirof, Harriet Toby - *Save The Dam!*

TEXAS—Fiction

Andrews, Wendy - *Are We There Yet?*

THAILAND—Fiction

Cavanna, Betty - *The Mystery Of The Emerald Buddha*

THANKSGIVING DAY

Barth, Edna - *Turkeys, Pilgrims, And Indian Corn*

THEATER—Fiction

Goldman, Katie - *In The Wings*
Kennedy, Kim - *In-Between Love*
Kingman, Lee - *Break A Leg, Betsy Maybe!*
Robertson, Keith - *Henry Reed's Big Show*

TICONDEROGA, BATTLE OF, 1758—Fiction

Peck, Robert Newton - *Fawn*

TIME

Neal, Harry Edward - *The Mystery Of Time*

TITANIC (STEAMSHIP)

Lord, Walter - *A Night To Remember*

TONGUE TWISTERS

Brandreth, Gyles - *Biggest Tongue Twister Book In The World*
Schwartz, Alvin - *A Twister Of Twists, A Tangler Of Tongues*

TORNADOES

Buehr, Walter - *Storm Warning: The Story Of Hurricanes And Tornadoes*

TORNADOES—Fiction

Milton, Hilary - *Tornado!*
Shore, June Lewis - *Summer Storm*

TOYS—Fiction

Lynn, Elizabeth A - *The Silver Horse*

TRACK AND FIELD

Aaseng, Nathan - *Track's Magnificent Milers*
Coombs, Charles Ira - *Be A Winner In Track And Field*
Dickmeyer, Lowell - *Track Is For Me*
Emert, Phyllis R - *Jane Frederick: Pentathlon Champion*
Ryan, Frank - *Jumping For Joy*
Sullivan, George Edward - *Superstars Of Women's Track*

TRACK AND FIELD—Fiction

French, Michael - *The Throwing Season*
Lord, Beman - *Shot-Put Challenge*
Neigoff, Mike - *Runner-Up*
Nelson, Cordner - *The Miler*
Owen, Evan - *On Your Own*
Robison, Nancy - *U. And M.E.*

TRACTOR TRAILERS

Nentl, Jerolyn Ann - *Big Rigs*

TRACTORS

Sheffer, H R - *Tractors*

TRAFALGAR (CAPE), BATTLE OF, 1805—Fiction

Burton, Hester - *Castors Away*

TRAFFIC ACCIDENTS—Fiction

Atkinson, Linda - *Hit And Run*
Bunting, Eve - *The Ghosts Of Departure Point*
Butterworth, W E - *Hot Wire*
Haddad, Carolyn - *The Last Ride*

TRAFFIC ACCIDENTS—Fiction (continued)

Huntsberry, William E - *The Big Hang-Up*
Jordan, Hope Dahle - *Haunted Summer*

TRAMPS—Fiction

Kennedy, Richard - *The Boxcar At The Center Of The Universe*

TREES

Nagel, Shirley - *Tree Boy*
Silverberg, Robert - *Vanishing Giants: The Story Of The Sequoias*

TRIALS

Aymar, Brandt - *Laws And Trials That Created History*

TRIALS (MURDER)

David, Andrew - *Famous Criminal Trials*

TRUCK DRIVING—Fiction

Place, Marian T - *Juan's Eighteen-Wheeler Summer*

TRUCKS

Barrett, N S - *Trucks*
Rich, Mark - *Diesel Trucks, On The Move*
Sheffer, H R - *Trucks*

TRUCKS—Fiction

Butterworth, W E - *Hot Wire*

TRUMPETER SWAN

Hutchins, Ross E - *The Last Trumpeters*

TRUMPETER SWAN—Fiction

White, E B - *The Trumpet Of The Swan*

TURKEY—Social life and customs—Fiction

Chetin, Helen - *Perihan's Promise, Turkish Relatives, And The Dirty Old Imam*

TWINS

Abbe, Kathryn M - *Twins On Twins*

TWINS—Fiction

Bach, Alice - *Waiting For Johnny Miracle*
Foster, Stephanie - *Love Times Two*
Kingman, Lee - *Head Over Wheels*
Miner, Jane Claypool - *Mountain Fear: When A Brother Dies*
Reece, Colleen L - *The Outsider*
Stuart, Becky - *Once In California*

UNCLES—Fiction

Mazer, Norma Fox - *Mrs. Fish, Ape, And Me, The Dump Queen*
White, Wallace - *One Dark Night*

UNDERGROUND RAILROAD—Fiction

Fritz, Jean - *Brady*
Meadowcroft, Enid LaMonte - *By Secret Railway*
Meltzer, Milton - *Underground Man*

UNDERWATER EXPLORATION

Briggs, Peter - *Men In The Sea*
Coggins, Jack - *Prepare To Dive: The Story Of Man Undersea*

UNIDENTIFIED FLYING OBJECTS

Cohen, Daniel - *Creatures From UFO's*
Cohen, Daniel - *The World Of UFOs*
Collins, Jim - *Unidentified Flying Objects*
Dolan, Edward Francis, Jr. - *The Bermuda Triangle And Other Mysteries Of Nature*
Mayer, Ann M - *Who's Out There? UFO Encounters*
Oleksy, Walter - *UFO: Teen Sightings*
Ruckman, Ivy - *Encounter*
Soule, Gardner - *UFO's And IFO's: A Factual Report On Flying Saucers*
Thorne, Ian - *UFO's*

UNIDENTIFIED FLYING OBJECTS—Fiction

DeWeese, Gene - *Major Corby And The Unidentified Flapping Object*
Spielberg, Steven - *Close Encounters Of The Third Kind*

UNITED NATIONS

Sasek, Miroslav - *This Is The United Nations*

UNITED STATES—Social life and customs—Fiction

Clarke, Mary Stetson - *The Iron Peacock*
Cohen, Barbara - *Benny*
Marzollo, Jean - *Halfway Down Paddy Lane*

UNITED STATES—Supreme Court

Fox, Mary Virginia - *Justice Sandra Day O'Connor*
Latham, Frank B - *FDR And The Supreme Court Fight 1937: A President Tries To Reorganize The Federal Judiciary*

UNIVERSITIES AND COLLEGES—Fiction

Myers, Walter Dean - *The Outside Shot*

UNWED MOTHERS—Fiction

Dizenzo, Patricia - *Phoebe*
Elfman, Blossom - *The Girls Of Huntington House*
Elfman, Blossom - *A House For Jonnie O*
Eyerly, Jeannette - *A Girl Like Me*
Klein, Norma - *Mom, The Wolf Man And Me*
Kropp, Paul - *Baby, Baby*
Lee, Mildred - *Sycamore Year*
Luger, H C - *Lauren*
Powers, Bill - *A Test Of Love*
Prince, Alison - *The Turkey's Nest*

URBAN RENEWEL—Fiction

Knott, Bill - *The Secret Of The Old Brownstone*

VACATIONS—Fiction

Andrews, Wendy - *Vacation Fever!*
Avi - *A Place Called Ugly*
Burchard, Peter Duncan - *A Quiet Place*

VALENTINE'S DAY—Fiction

Adler, C S - *Roadside Valentine*

VAMPIRES

Garden, Nancy - *Vampires*
McHargue, Georgess - *Meet The Vampire*
Schoder, Judith - *The Blood Suckers*

VAMPIRES—Fiction

Brunn, Robert - *The Initiation*
Green, Carl R - *Dracula's Daughter*
Stoker, Bram - *Dracula*

VANDALISM—Fiction

Lasky, Kathryn - *Prank*

VANS

Dexler, Paul R - *Vans: The Personality Vehicles*
Radlauer, Edward - *Some Basics About Vans*
Sheffer, H R - *Vans*

VENEREAL DISEASES

Busch, Phyllis S - *What About VD?*
Gordon, Sol - *Facts About VD For Today's Youth*
Hyde, Margaret Oldroyd - *VD: The Silent Epidemic*

VENEREAL DISEASES—Fiction

Blume, Judy - *Forever*

VERMONT—Fiction

Lenski, Lois - *Deer Valley Girl*

VERSES FOR CHILDREN

Aiken, Conrad - *Cats And Bats And Things With Wings: Poems*
Massie, Diane Redfield - *Cockle Stew And Other Rhymes*
O'Neill, Mary - *Take A Number*
Potter, Charles Francis - *More Tongue Tanglers And A Rigmarole*
Swenson, May - *Poems To Solve*

VETERANS (DISABLED)—U.S.—Biography

McGravie, Anne V - *All The Way Back*

VETERINARIANS

Herriot, James - *All Creatures Great And Small*
Lloyd-Jones, Buster - *Animals Came In One By One*
McPhee, Richard B - *Rounds With A Country Vet*
Taylor, David - *Is There A Doctor In The Zoo?*

VETERINARIANS—Fiction

Bradbury, Bianca - *In Her Father's Footsteps*
Lee, H Alton - *Seven Feet Four And Growing*
Saal, Jocelyn - *Trusting Hearts*

VICE-PRESIDENTIAL CANDIDATES

Lawson, Donald Elmer - *Geraldine Ferraro*

VICE-PRESIDENTS

Schneider, Tom - *Walter Mondale: Serving All The People*

VIDEO GAMES

Clark, James I - *Video Games*
Leder, Jane M - *Video Games*

VIDEO GAMES—Fiction

Siegel, Scott - *Beat The Devil*

VIETNAMESE AMERICANS—Fiction

Wartski, Maureen Crane - *A Long Way From Home*

VIETNAMESE CONFLICT, 1961-1975—Fiction

Butterworth, W E - *Orders To Vietnam*
Butterworth, W E - *Stop And Search*
Crosby, Alexander L - *One Day For Peace*
Haldeman, Joe - *War Year*
Reiff, Tana - *The Family From Vietnam*

VISUAL PERCEPTION

Anderson, Doug - *Eye Spy*

VOCATIONAL GUIDANCE

Abrams, Kathleen S - *Career Prep: Electronics Servicing*
Alexander, Sue - *Finding Your First Job*
Armstrong, Fiona - *Getting Ready For The World Of Work*
Armstrong, Fiona - *You And The World Of Work*
Claypool, Jane - *How To Get A Good Job*
Dyer, Mike - *Getting Into Pro Baseball*
Fischler, Stanley I - *Getting Into Pro Soccer*
Gilbert, Sara Dulaney - *Ready, Set, Go: How To Find A Career That's Right For You*
Hall, Lynn - *Careers For Dog Lovers*
Hawkins, Robert - *On The Air: Radio Broadcasting*
Keefe, John E - *Aim For A Job In Appliance Service*
Liebers, Arthur - *You Can Be A Carpenter*
Liebers, Arthur - *You Can Be A Mechanic*
Liebers, Arthur - *You Can Be A Plumber*
Liebers, Arthur - *You Can Be A Professional Driver*
Liston, Robert A - *Your Career In Civil Service*
Lyttle, Richard Bard - *Getting Into Pro Basketball*
Mangan, Doreen - *How To Be A Super Camp Counselor*
McCall, Virginia Nielsen - *Your Career In Parks And Recreation*
McCallum, John Dennis - *Getting Into Pro Football*
McGonagle, Bob - *Careers In Sports*
McHugh, John - *Finding A Job*
McHugh, John - *Getting Ready To Work*
McHugh, John - *Starting A New Job*
Miner, Jane Claypool - *Career Prep: Working In A Hospital*
Splaver, Sarah - *Your Career If You're Not Going To College*
Van Ryzin, Lani - *Starting Your Own Band: Rock, Disco, Folk, Jazz, Country And Western*

VOCATIONS—Fiction

Vroman, Mary Elizabeth - *Harlem Summer*

VOLCANOES

Asimov, Isaac - *How Did We Find Out About Volcanoes?*
Buehr, Walter - *Volcano*

VOLCANOES—Fiction

Healey, Larry - *Angry Mountain*

VOLLEYBALL—Fiction

Katz, Bobbi - *Volleyball Jinx*

VOLUNTEER WORKERS—Fiction

Wyndham, Lee - *Candy Stripers*

WEREWOLVES—Fiction

Green, Carl R - *Werewolf Of London*
Skurzynski, Gloria - *Manwolf*

WEST (U.S.)

Surge, Frank - *Western Outlaws*
Ulyatt, Kenneth - *Outlaws*
Wayne, Bennett - *Adventure In Buckskin*

WEST (U.S.)—Fiction

Balmes, Pat - *Danger At The Flying Y*
Beatty, Patricia Robbins - *By Crumbs, It's Mine*
Beatty, Patricia Robbins - *Wait For Me, Watch For Me, Eula Bee*
Deary, Terry - *The Custard Kid*
Johnson, Annabel - *The Burning Glass*
Leiser, Harry W - *The Secret Of Bitter Creek*
Moeri, Louise - *Save Queen Of Sheba*
Packard, Edward - *Deadwood City*
Richard, Adrienne - *Pistol*
Rushing, Jane Gilmore - *Mary Dove*
Wormser, Richard - *The Black Mustanger*

WESTERN FILMS—Fiction

Meyer, Carolyn - *The Luck Of Texas McCoy*

WHALING

Meadowcroft, Enid LaMonte - *When Nantucket Men Went Whaling*

WHALING—Fiction

Melville, Herman - *Moby Dick*

WHOOPING CRANES—Fiction

Callen, Larry - *Sorrow's Song*

WIDOWS—Fiction

Reiff, Tana - *Mollie's Year*

WIFE ABUSE—Fiction

Conrad, Pam - *Holding Me Here*

WILDERNESS SURVIVAL

East, Ben - *Danger In The Air*
East, Ben - *Desperate Search*
East, Ben - *Forty Days Lost*
East, Ben - *Found Alive*
East, Ben - *Frozen Terror*
East, Ben - *Mistaken Journey*
East, Ben - *Trapped In Devil's Hole*
Tripp, Jenny - *The Man Who Was Left For Dead*

WILDERNESS SURVIVAL—Fiction

Swarthout, Glendon Fred - *Whichaway*

WILDFLOWERS

Fichter, George Siebert - *Wildflowers Of North America*

WILDLIFE CONSERVATION

O'Donoghue, Bryan - *Wild Animal Rescue!*
Roth, Charles E - *Then There Were None*

WILDLIFE CONSERVATION—Fiction

Chadwick, Roxane - *Don't Shoot*

WILDLIFE RESCUE

True, Dan - *Flying Free*

WILDLIFE WATCHING

Burness, Gordon - *How To Watch Wildlife*

WINTER

Nestor, William P - *Into Winter: Discovering A Season*

WISHES—Fiction

Hahn, Mary Downing - *The Time Of The Witch*
Webster, Joanne - *The Love Genie*

WIT AND HUMOR

Brewton, Sara Westbrook - *Shrieks At Midnight*
Clark, David Allen - *Jokes, Puns, And Riddles*
DeKay, James T - *The Natural Superiority Of The Left-Hander*
Hoke, Helen L - *More Jokes, Jokes, Jokes*
Hughes, Langston - *The Book Of Negro Humor*
Leach, Maria - *Noodles, Nitwits, And Numskulls*
Schulz, Charles M - *Nobody's Perfect, Charlie Brown*
Schwartz, Alvin - *Tomfoolery*

WIT AND HUMOR (continued)

Schwartz, Alvin - *Witcracks: Jokes And Jests From American Folklore*
Sobol, Donald J - *Encyclopedia Brown's Book Of Wacky Crimes*
Wilson, Tom - *Encore! Encore!*
Wilson, Tom - *This Book Is For The Birds*

WITCHCRAFT

Alderman, Clifford Lindsey - *A Cauldron Of Witches*
Alderman, Clifford Lindsey - *The Devil's Shadow*
Alderman, Clifford Lindsey - *Witchcraft In America*
Blue, Rose - *We've Got The Power: Witches Among Us*
Blumberg, Rhoda - *Witches*
Jackson, Shirley - *The Witchcraft Of Salem Village*
Petry, Ann - *Tituba Of Salem Village*
Revesz, Therese Ruth - *Witches*

WITCHCRAFT—Fiction

Borisoff, Norman - *Bewitched And Bewildered: A Spooky Love Story*
Calhoun, Mary Huiskamp - *White Witch Of Kynance*
Carey, Mary Virginia - *The Mystery Of The Magic Circle*
Carey, Mary Virginia - *The Mystery Of The Singing Serpent*
Clapp, Patricia - *Witches' Children: A Story Of Salem*
Duncan, Lois S - *Summer Of Fear*
Hahn, Mary Downing - *The Time Of The Witch*
Hildick, E W - *The Active-Enzyme Lemon-Freshened Junior High School Witch*
Kelley, Leo P - *Night Of Fire And Blood*
Manning-Sanders, Ruth - *A Book Of Witches*
Sparks, Beatrice - *Jay's Journal*
Speare, Elizabeth - *Witch Of Blackbird Pond*
Teall, Kaye M - *Witches Get Everything*

WOLVES

Clarkson, Ewan - *Wolves*
Rutter, Russell J - *The World Of The Wolf*

WOLVES—Fiction

Caras, Roger A - *The Custer Wolf: Biography Of An American Renegade*
George, Jean Craighead - *Julie Of The Wolves*
Strieber, Whitley - *Wolf Of Shadows*
Wisler, G Clifton - *Winter Of The Wolf*

WORK

McHugh, John - *Keeping And Changing Jobs*
McHugh, John - *Starting A New Job*

WORK—Fiction

Miner, Jane Claypool - *A Man's Pride: Losing A Father*
Pfeffer, Susan Beth - *Getting Even*
Robison, Nancy - *Plumber's Line*

WORLD WAR, 1939-1945

Baldwin, Margaret - *Kisses Of Death: A World War II Escape Story*
Bull, Angela - *Anne Frank*
Eimerl, Sarel Henry - *Hitler Over Europe*
Forester, C S - *Last Nine Days Of The Bismarck*
Frank, Anne - *Anne Frank: Diary Of A Young Girl*
Graff, Stewart - *The Story Of World War II*
Jackson, Robert Blake - *Fighter Pilots Of World War II*
Kluger, Ruth - *The Secret Ship*
Leckie, Robert - *Helmet For My Pillow*
Levin, Jane Whitbread - *Star Of Danger*
McKown, Robin - *Patriot Of The Underground*
Mercer, Charles Edward - *Miracle At Midway*
Prager, Arthur - *World War II Resistance Stories*
Reiss, Johanna - *The Upstairs Room*
Shapiro, Milton J - *Undersea Raiders: U.S. Submarines In World War II*
Stein, R Conrad - *Hiroshima*
Sullivan, George Edward - *Strange But True Stories Of World War II*
Sweeney, James Bartholemew - *True Spy Stories*
Taylor, Theodore Langhans - *The Battle Off Midway Island*
Terasaki, Gwen - *Bridge To The Sun*
Tregaskis, Richard - *Guadalcanal Diary*
Ziemian, Joseph - *The Cigarette Sellers Of Three Crosses Square*

WORLD WAR, 1939-1945—Fiction

Aaron, Chester - *Gideon*
Bonnell, Dorothy Haworth - *Passport To Freedom*
Burch, Robert J - *Hut School And The Wartime Home-Front Heroes*
Burton, Hester - *In Spite Of All Terror*
Clarke, John - *Black Soldier*
Degens, T - *Transport 7-41-R*
Degens, T - *The Visit*
Fife, Dale - *North Of Danger*
Frederick, Lee - *Crash Dive*
Greene, Bette - *The Summer Of My German Soldier*
Hallman, Ruth - *Secrets Of A Silent Stranger*
Mazer, Harry - *The Last Mission*
Rice, Earle, Jr. - *Tiger, Lion, Hawk*
Suhl, Yuri - *On The Other Side Of The Gate*
Suhl, Yuri - *Uncle Misha's Partisans*
Tunis, John R - *His Enemy, His Friend*
White, Robb - *The Frogmen*

WRESTLING—Fiction

Filson, Brent - *The Puma*
Watkins, William Jon - *A Fair Advantage*

YELLOW FEVER—Fiction

Fleischman, Paul - *Path Of The Pale Horse*

YETI

Antonopulos, Barbara - *The Abominable Snowman*

YOGA

Landau, Elaine - *Yoga For You*
Turner, Alice K - *Yoga For Beginners*

YOUTH

Anastos, Ernie - *'Twixt: Teens Yesterday And Today*
Boone, Pat - *'Twixt Twelve And Twenty*

YOUTH—Fiction

Klein, Norma - *It's Not What You Expect*
Kwolek, Constance - *Loner*
Luger, H C - *Chasing Trouble*
Mills, Donia Whiteley - *A Long Way Home From Troy*
Patterson, Gardner - *Docker*
Stewart, Jo - *A Time To Choose*
Wersba, Barbara - *Run Softly, Go Fast*
Wojciechowska, Maia - *Don't Play Dead Before You Have To*
Wood, Phyllis Anderson - *Andy*
Zindel, Paul - *I Never Loved Your Mind*
Zindel, Paul - *My Darling, My Hamburger*

ZOOLOGISTS

Clark, James L - *In The Steps Of The Great American Museum Collector, Carl Ethan Akeley*
Fox, Mary Virginia - *Jane Goodall: Living Chimp Style*

ZOOLOGY

Caputo, Robert - *More Than Just Pets: Why People Study Animals*
Dinneen, Betty - *The Family Howl*
Holden, Raymond P - *Wildlife Mysteries*